# HANDBOOK OF
# CIVIL ENGINEERING
# CALCULATIONS

# ABOUT THE AUTHOR

**Tyler G. Hicks, P.E.**, is editor *of Standard Handbook of Engineering Calculations, Standard Handbook of Mechanical Engineering Calculations, McGraw-Hill's Interactive Chemical Engineer's Solutions Suite, McGraw-Hill's Interactive Civil Engineer's Solutions Suite,* and other bestselling titles. He is also a consulting engineer with International Engineering Associates. A graduate mechanical engineer, he has taught at several universities and lectured throughout the world.

# HANDBOOK OF CIVIL ENGINEERING CALCULATIONS

**Tyler G. Hicks, P.E.,** Editor

*International Engineering Associates*
*Member: American Society of Mechanical Engineers*
*United States Naval Institute*

**S. David Hicks,** Coordinating Editor

**Second Edition**

New York   Chicago   San Francisco   Lisbon   London   Madrid
Mexico City   Milan   New Delhi   San Juan   Seoul
Singapore   Sydney   Toronto

**The McGraw·Hill Companies**

**Library of Congress Cataloging-in-Publication Data**

Hicks, Tyler Gregory, 1921-
   Handbook of civil engineering calculations / Tyler G. Hicks.—2nd ed.
      p.      cm.
   Includes bibliographical references and index.
   ISBN 0-07-147293-2 (alk. paper)
   1. Engineering mathematics—Handbooks, manuals, etc.   2. Civil
engineering—Mathematics—Handbooks, manuals, etc.   I. Title.

   TA332.H53   2007
   624.01'51—dc22

                                                    2007012838

**Handbook of Civil Engineering Calculations, Second Edition**

ISBN-13: 978-0-07-147293-7
ISBN-10:      0-07-147293-2

**Sponsoring Editor**
Larry Hager

**Editorial Supervisor**
Jody McKenzie

**Project Manager**
Vastavikta Sharma, International
Typesetting and Composition

**Acquisitions Coordinator**
Laura Hahn

**Copy Editor**
Anju Panthari

**Proofreader**
Julie Searls

**Indexer**
Tyler Hicks

**Production Supervisor**
George Anderson

**Composition**
International Typesetting and Composition

**Illustration**
International Typesetting and Composition

*To civil engineers—everywhere: The results of your design and construction skills are with all civilized humanity every day of their lives. There is little anyone can do without enjoying the result of your labors. May this handbook help your work be more widely recognized and appreciated—worldwide.*

# CONTENTS

# PREFACE

This handbook presents a comprehensive collection of civil engineering calculation procedures useful to practicing civil engineers, surveyors, structural designers, drafters, candidates for professional engineering licenses, and students. Engineers in other disciplines—mechanical, electrical, chemical, environmental, etc.—will also find this handbook useful for making occasional calculations outside their normal field of specialty.

Each calculation procedure presented in this handbook gives numbered steps for performing the calculation, along with a numerical example illustrating the important concepts in the procedure. Many procedures include "Related Calculations" comments, which expand the application of the computation method presented. All calculation procedures in this handbook use both the USCS (United States Customary System) and the SI (System International) for numerical units. Hence, the calculation procedures presented are useful to engineers throughout the world.

Major calculation procedures presented in this handbook include stress and strain, flexural analysis, deflection of beams, statically indeterminate structures, steel beams and columns, riveted and welded connections, composite members, plate girders, load and resistance factor design method (LRFD) for structural steel design, plastic design of steel structures, reinforced and prestressed concrete engineering and design, surveying, route design, highway bridges, timber engineering, soil mechanics, fluid mechanics, pumps, piping, water supply and water treatment, wastewater treatment and disposal, hydro power, and engineering economics.

Each section of this handbook is designed to furnish comprehensive coverage of the topics in it. Where there are major subtopics within a section, the section is divided into parts to permit in-depth coverage of each subtopic.

Civil engineers design buildings, bridges, highways, airports, water supply, sewage treatment, and a variety of other key structures and facilities throughout the world. Because of the importance of such structures and facilities to the civilized world, civil engineers have long needed a handbook that would simplify and speed their daily design calculations. This handbook provides an answer to that need.

Since the first edition of this handbook was published in 2000, there have been major changes in the field of civil engineering. These changes include:

- **Anti-terrorism construction** features to protect large buildings structurally against catastrophes such as occurred at New York's World Trade Center on 9/11/01.

- **Increased security features** are now included for all major buildings to which the public has access. The increased security is to prevent internal sabotage and terrorism that might endanger occupants and the structure.

- **Building Code changes can be expected** as a result of the terror attacks in New York and in other cities around the world. These changes will alter design procedures civil engineers have been following for many years.

- **Structural designs to thwart terrorism attempts are being studied** by the American Society of Civil Engineers, National Institute of Standards and Technology, American Concrete Institute International, American Institute of Steel Construction, American Society of Plumbing Engineers, American Welding Society, Concrete Reinforcing

Steel Institute, National Fire Sprinkler Association, National Precast Concrete Association, Portland Cement Association, Precast/Prestressed Concrete Institute, along with other organizations.

- **"Green" building design and construction** to reduce energy costs in new, existing, and rehabilitated buildings.
- **Major steps to improve indoor air quality (IAQ)** for all buildings well beyond elimination of occupant smoking of cigarettes, cigars, or pipes. IAQ is of major concern in office buildings, schools, hotels, factories, and other buildings having even modest tenant occupancy numbers.
- **Better hurricane and tornado design** of buildings and bridges is being implemented for new structures, following the damages caused by Hurricane Katrina and similar storms. Designers want to make new structures as hurricane- and tornado-proof as possible. This is an excellent goal, remembering the number of lives lost in hurricanes and tornados.
- **Improved construction of, and wave resistance for, buildings** in the tsunami areas of the world is a new goal for civil engineers worldwide. The enormous tsunami of December 26, 2004, that struck 12 Indian Ocean nations, killing more than 226,000 people, has civil engineers searching for better ways to design structures to resist the enormous forces of nature while protecting occupants. Civil engineers in Indonesia, Sri Lanka, India, and Thailand are actively working on structures having greater wind and water resistance. Also under study are: (a) early-warning systems to alert people to the onset of a tsunami and, (b) better escape routes for people fleeing affected areas. Achieving these important design goals will, hopefully, reduce the death and injury toll in future tsunami incidents.
- **New approaches to levee and flood wall design,** especially in the New Orleans and similar areas where devastation was caused by high water brought on by hurricanes. In New Orleans alone, some 35+ miles of flood walls are being redesigned and rebuilt. The T-wall type of structure, covered in this handbook, is currently favored over the I-wall. The latter type was of little use during Hurricane Katrina because soil around it was eroded by the water when the wall collapsed backwards. All these changes will be the work of civil engineers, with the assistance of other specialized professionals.

With so many changes "on the drawing board," engineers and designers are seeking ways to include the changes in their current and future designs of buildings, bridges, and other structures. This second edition includes many of the proposed changes so that designers can include them in their thinking and calculations.

Several new calculation procedures for prestressed concrete members are presented in Section 5. These calculation procedures will be especially helpful to engineers designing for the future. And this leads us to consideration of the use of computer programs for civil engineering design work of all types.

While there are computer programs that help the civil engineer with a variety of engineering calculations, such programs are highly specialized and do not have the breadth of coverage this handbook provides. Further, such computer programs are usually expensive. Because of their high cost, these computer programs can be justified only when a civil engineer makes a number of repetitive calculations on almost a daily basis. In contrast, this handbook can be used in the office, field, drafting room, or laboratory. It provides industry-wide coverage in a convenient and affordable package. As such, this handbook fills a long-existing need felt by civil engineers worldwide.

In contrast, civil engineers using civil-engineering computer programs often find data-entry time requirements are excessive for quick one-off-type calculations. When one-off-type calculations are needed, most civil engineers today turn to their electronic calculator, desktop, or laptop computer and perform the necessary steps to obtain the solution desired. But where repetitive calculations are required, a purchased computer program will save time and energy in the usual medium-size or large civil-engineering design office. Small civil-engineering offices generally resort to manual calculation for even repetitive procedures because the investment for one or more major calculation programs is difficult to justify in economic terms.

Even when purchased computer programs are extensively used, careful civil engineers still insist on manually checking results on a random basis to be certain the program is accurate. This checking can be speeded by any of the calculation procedures given in this handbook. Many civil engineers remark to the author that they feel safer, knowing they have manually verified the computer results on a spot-check basis. With liability for civil-engineering designs extending beyond the lifetime of the designer, every civil engineer seeks the "security blanket" provided by manual verification of the results furnished by a computer program run on a desktop, laptop, or workstation computer. This handbook gives the tools needed for manual verification of some 2,000 civil-engineering calculation procedures.

Each section in this handbook is written by one or more experienced professional engineers who is a specialist in the field covered. The contributors draw on their wide experience in their field to give each calculation procedure an in-depth coverage of its topic. So the person using the procedure gets step-by-step instructions for making the calculation plus background information on the subject that is the topic of the procedure.

And because the handbook is designed for worldwide use, both earlier, and more modern, topics are covered. For example, the handbook includes concise coverage of riveted girders, columns, and connections. While today's civil engineer may say that riveted construction is a method long past its prime, there are millions of existing structures worldwide that were built using rivets. So when a civil engineer is called on to expand, rehabilitate, or tear down such a structure, he or she must be able to analyze the riveted portions of the structure. This handbook provides that capability in a convenient and concise form.

In the realm of modern design techniques, the load and resistance factor method (LRFD) is covered with more than ten calculation procedures showing its use in various design situations. The LRFD method is ultimately expected to replace the well-known and widely used allowable stress design (ASD) method for structural steel building frameworks. In today's design world many civil engineers are learning the advantages of the LRFD method and growing to prefer it over the ASD method.

Also included in this handbook is a comprehensive section titled "How to Use This Handbook." It details the variety of ways a civil engineer can use this handbook in his or her daily engineering work. Included as part of this section are steps showing the civil engineer how to construct a private list of SI conversion factors for the specific work the engineer specializes in.

The step-by-step *practical* and *applied* calculation procedures in this handbook are arranged so they can be followed by anyone with an engineering or scientific background. Each worked-out procedure presents *fully explained and illustrated steps* for solving similar problems in civil-engineering design, research, field, academic, or license-examination situations. For any applied problem, all the civil engineer need do is place his or her calculation sheets alongside this handbook and follow the step-by-step procedure line for line to obtain the desired solution for the actual real-life problem. By following the calculation procedures in this handbook, the civil engineer, scientist, or technician will obtain accurate results in minimum time with least effort. And the approaches and solutions presented are modern throughout.

The editor hopes this handbook is helpful to civil engineers worldwide. If the handbook user finds procedures that belong in the book but have been left out, the editor urges the engineer to send the title of the procedure to him, in care of the publisher. If the procedure is useful, the editor will ask for the entire text. And if the text is publishable, the editor will include the calculation procedure in the next edition of the handbook. Full credit will be given to the person sending the procedure to the editor. And if users find any errors in the handbook, the editor will be grateful for having these called to his attention. Such errors will be corrected in the next printing of the handbook. In closing, the editor hopes that civil engineers worldwide find this handbook helpful in their daily work.

TYLER G. HICKS, P.E.

# HOW TO USE THIS HANDBOOK

There are two ways to enter this handbook to obtain the maximum benefit from the time invested. The first entry is through the index; the second is through the table of contents of the section covering the discipline, or related discipline, concerned. Each method is discussed in detail below.

**Index.** Great care and considerable time were expended on preparation of the index of this handbook so that it would be of maximum use to every reader. As a general guide, enter the index using the generic term for the type of calculation procedure being considered. Thus, for the design of a beam, enter at *beam(s)*. From here, progress to the specific type of beam being considered—such as *continuous, of steel*. Once the page number or numbers of the appropriate calculation procedure are determined, turn to them to find the step-by-step instructions and worked-out example that can be followed to solve the problem quickly and accurately.

**Contents.** The contents at the beginning of each section lists the titles of the calculation procedures contained in that section. Where extensive use of any section is contemplated, the editor suggests that the reader might benefit from an occasional glance at the table of contents of that section. Such a glance will give the user of this handbook an understanding of the breadth and coverage of a given section, or a series of sections. Then, when he or she turns to this handbook for assistance, the reader will be able more rapidly to find the calculation procedure he or she seeks.

**Calculation Procedures.** Each calculation procedure is a unit in itself. However, any given calculation procedure will contain subprocedures that might be useful to the reader. Thus, a calculation procedure on pump selection will contain subprocedures on pipe friction loss, pump static and dynamic heads, etc. Should the reader of this handbook wish to make a computation using any of such subprocedures, he or she will find the worked-out steps that are presented both useful and precise. Hence, the handbook contains numerous valuable procedures that are useful in solving a variety of applied civil engineering problems.

One other important point that should be noted about the calculation procedures presented in this handbook is that many of the calculation procedures are equally applicable in a variety of disciplines. Thus, a beam-selection procedure can be used for civil-, chemical-, mechanical-, electrical-, and nuclear-engineering activities, as well as some others. Hence, the reader might consider a temporary neutrality for his or her particular specialty when using the handbook because the calculation procedures are designed for universal use.

Any of the calculation procedures presented can be programmed on a computer. Such programming permits rapid solution of a variety of design problems. With the growing use of low-cost time sharing, more engineering design problems are being solved using a remote terminal in the engineering office. The editor hopes that engineers throughout the world will make greater use of work stations and portable computers in solving applied engineering problems. This modern equipment promises greater speed and accuracy for nearly all the complex design problems that must be solved in today's world of engineering.

To make the calculation procedures more amenable to computer solution (while maintaining ease of solution with a handheld calculator), a number of the algorithms in the handbook have been revised to permit faster programming in a computer environment. This enhances ease of solution for any method used—work station, portable computer, or calculator.

**SI Usage.** The technical and scientific community throughout the world accepts the SI (System International) for use in both applied and theoretical calculations. With such widespread acceptance of SI, every engineer must become proficient in the use of this system of units if he or she is to remain up-to-date. For this reason, every calculation procedure in this handbook is given in both the United States Customary System (USCS) and SI. This will help all engineers become proficient in using both systems of units. In this handbook the USCS unit is generally given first, followed by the SI value in parentheses or brackets. Thus, if the USCS unit is 10 ft, it will be expressed as 10 ft (3 m).

Engineers accustomed to working in USCS are often timid about using SI. There really aren't any sound reasons for these fears. SI is a logical, easily understood, and readily manipulated group of units. Most engineers grow to prefer SI, once they become familiar with it and overcome their fears. This handbook should do much to "convert" USCS-user engineers to SI because it presents all calculation procedures in both the known and unknown units.

Overseas engineers who must work in USCS because they have a job requiring its usage will find the dual-unit presentation of calculation procedures most helpful. Knowing SI, they can easily convert to USCS because all procedures, tables, and illustrations are presented in dual units.

**Learning SI.** An efficient way for the USCS-conversant engineer to learn SI follows these steps:

1. List the units of measurement commonly used in your daily work.

2. Insert, opposite each USCS unit, the usual SI unit used; Table 1 shows a variety of commonly used quantities and the corresponding SI units.

3. Find, from a table of conversion factors, such as Table 2, the value to use to convert the USCS unit to SI, and insert it in your list. (Most engineers prefer a conversion factor that can be used as a multiplier of the USCS unit to give the SI unit.)

4. Apply the conversion factors whenever you have an opportunity. Think in terms of SI when you encounter a USCS unit.

5. Recognize—here and now—that the most difficult aspect of SI is becoming comfortable with the names and magnitude of the units. Numerical conversion is simple, once you've set up *your own* conversion table. So think pascal whenever you encounter pounds per square inch pressure, newton whenever you deal with a force in pounds, etc.

**SI Table for a Civil Engineer.** Let's say you're a civil engineer and you wish to construct a conversion table and SI literacy document for yourself. List the units you commonly meet in your daily work; Table 1 is the list compiled by one civil engineer. Next, list the SI unit equivalent for the USCS unit. Obtain the equivalent from Table 2. Then, using Table 2 again, insert the conversion multiplier in Table 1.

Keep Table 1 handy at your desk and add new units to it as you encounter them in your work. Over a period of time you will build a personal conversion table that will be valuable to you whenever you must use SI units. Further, since *you* compiled the table, it will have a familiar and nonfrightening look, which will give you greater confidence in using SI.

**TABLE 1.** Commonly Used USCS and SI Units*

| USCS unit | SI unit | SI symbol | Conversion factor—multiply USCS unit by this factor to obtain the SI unit |
|---|---|---|---|
| square feet | square meters | $m^2$ | 0.0929 |
| cubic feet | cubic meters | $m^3$ | 0.2831 |
| pounds per square inch | kilopascal | kPa | 6.894 |
| pound force | newton | N | 4.448 |
| foot pound torque | newton-meter | Nm | 1.356 |
| kip-feet | kilo-newton | kNm | 1.355 |
| gallons per minute | liters per second | L/s | 0.06309 |
| kips per square inch | megapascal | MPa | 6.89 |
| inch | millimeter | mm | 25.4 |
| feet | millimeter | mm | 304.8 |
| | meter | m | 0.3048 |
| square inch | square millimeter | $mm^2$ | 0.0006452 |
| cubic inch | cubic millimeter | $mm^3$ | 0.00001638 |
| $inch^4$ | $millimeter^4$ | $mm^4$ | 0.000000416 |
| pound per cubic foot | kilogram per cubic meter | $kg/m^3$ | 16.0 |
| pound per foot | kilogram per meter | kg/m | 1.49 |
| pound per foot force | Newton per meter | N/m | 14.59 |
| pound per inch force | Newton per meter | N/m | 175.1 |
| pound per foot density | kilogram per meter | kg/m | 1.488 |
| pound per inch density | kilogram per meter | kg/m | 17.86 |
| pound per square inch load concentration | kilogram per square meter | $kg/m^2$ | 703.0 |
| pound per square foot load concentration | kilogram per square meter | $kg/m^2$ | 4.88 |
| pound per square foot pressure | Pascal | Pa | 47.88 |
| inch-pound torque | Newton-meter | N-m | 0.1129 |
| chain | meter | m | 20.117 |
| fathom | meter | m | 1.8288 |
| cubic foot per second | cubic meter per second | $m^3/s$ | 0.02831 |
| $foot^4$ (area moment of inertia) | $meter^4$ | $m^4$ | 0.0086309 |
| mile | meter | m | 0.0000254 |
| square mile | square meter | $m^2$ | 2589998.0 |
| pound per gallon (UK liquid) | kilogram per cubic meter | $kg/m^3$ | 99.77 |
| pound per gallon (U.S. liquid) | kilogram per cubic meter | $kg/m^3$ | 119.83 |
| poundal | Newton | N | 0.11382 |
| square (100 square feet) | square meter | $m^2$ | 9.29 |
| ton (long 2,240 lb) | kilogram | kg | 1016.04 |
| ton (short 2,000 lb) | kilogram | kg | 907.18 |
| ton, short, per cubic yard | kilogram per cubic meter | $kg/m^3$ | 1186.55 |
| ton, long, per cubic yard | kilogram per cubic meter | $kg/m^3$ | 1328.93 |
| ton force (2,000 lbf) | Newton | N | 8896.44 |
| yard, length | meter | m | 0.0914 |

(*continued*)

**TABLE 1.** Commonly Used USCS and SI Units* (*Continued*)

| USCS unit | SI unit | SI symbol | Conversion factor—multiply USCS unit by this factor to obtain the SI unit |
|---|---|---|---|
| square yard | square meter | $m^2$ | 0.08361 |
| cubic yard | cubic meter | $m^3$ | 0.076455 |
| acre feet | cubic meter | $m^3$ | 1233.49 |
| acre | square meter | $m^2$ | 4046.87 |
| cubic foot per minute | cubic meter per second | $m^3/s$ | 0.0004719 |

*Because of space limitations this table is abbreviated. For a typical engineering practice an actual table would be many times this length.

**TABLE 2.** Typical Conversion Table*

| To convert from | To | Multiply by | |
|---|---|---|---|
| square feet | square meters | 9.290304 | E – 02 |
| foot per second squared | meter per second squared | 3.048 | E – 01 |
| cubic feet | cubic meters | 2.831685 | E – 02 |
| pound per cubic inch | kilogram per cubic meter | 2.767990 | E + 04 |
| gallon per minute | liters per second | 6.309 | E – 02 |
| pound per square inch | kilopascal | 6.894757 | |
| pound force | Newton | 4.448222 | |
| kip per square foot | Pascal | 4.788026 | E + 04 |
| acre-foot per day | cubic meter per second | 1.427641 | E – 02 |
| acre | square meter | 4.046873 | E + 03 |
| cubic foot per second | cubic meter per second | 2.831685 | E – 02 |

*Note*: The E indicates an exponent, as in scientific notation, followed by a positive or negative number, representing the power of 10 by which the given conversion factor is to be multiplied before use. Thus, for the square feet conversion factor, $9.290304 \times 1/100 = 0.09290304$, the factor to be used to convert square feet to square meters. For a positive exponent, as in converting acres to square meters, multiply by $4.046873 \times 1000 = 4046.8$.

Where a conversion factor cannot be found, simply use the dimensional substitution. Thus, to convert pounds per cubic inch to kilograms per cubic meter, find 1 lb = 0.4535924 kg, and 1 $in^3$ = 0.00001638706 $m^3$. Then, 1 $lb/in^3$ = 0.4535924 kg/0.00001638706 $m^3$ 27,680.01, or 2.768 E + 4.

*This table contains only selected values. See the U.S. Department of the Interior *Metric Manual*, or National Bureau of Standards, *The International System of Units* (SI), both available from the U.S. Government Printing Office (GPO), for far more comprehensive listings of conversion factors.

**Units Used.** In preparing the calculation procedures in this handbook, the editors and contributors used standard SI units throughout. In a few cases, however, certain units are still in a state of development. For example, the unit *tonne* is used in certain industries, such as waste treatment. This unit is therefore used in the waste treatment section of this handbook because it represents current practice. However, only a few SI units are still under development. Hence, users of this handbook face little difficulty from this situation.

**Computer-aided Calculations.** Widespread availability of programmable pocket calculators and low-cost laptop computers allows engineers and designers to save thousands of hours of calculation time. Yet each calculation procedure must be programmed, unless the engineer is willing to use off-the-shelf software. The editor—observing thousands of engineers over the years—detects reluctance among technical personnel to use untested and unproven software programs in their daily calculations. Hence, the tested and proven procedures in this handbook form excellent programming input for programmable pocket calculators, laptop computers, minicomputers, and mainframes.

A variety of software application programs can be used to put the procedures in this handbook on a computer. Typical of these are MathSoft, Algor, and similar programs.

There are a number of advantages for the engineer who programs his or her own calculation procedures, namely: (1) The engineer knows, understands, and approves *every* step in the procedure; (2) there are *no* questionable, unknown, or legally worrisome steps in the procedure; (3) the engineer has complete faith in the result because he or she knows every component of it; and (4) if a variation of the procedure is desired, it is relatively easy for the engineer to make the needed changes in the program, using this handbook as the source of the steps and equations to apply.

Modern computer equipment provides greater speed and accuracy for almost all complex design calculations. The editor hopes that engineers throughout the world will make greater use of available computing equipment in solving applied engineering problems. Becoming computer literate is a necessity for every engineer, no matter which field he or she chooses as a specialty. The procedures in this handbook simplify every engineer's task of becoming computer literate because the steps given comprise—to a great extent—the steps in the computer program that can be written.

# SECTION 1

# STRUCTURAL STEEL ENGINEERING AND DESIGN

**MAX KURTZ, P.E.**
*Consulting Engineer*

METRICATED BY

**GERALD M. EISENBERG**
*Project Engineering Administrator*
*American Society of Mechanical Engineers*

## Part 2: Structural Steel Design

# PART 1

# STATICS, STRESS AND STRAIN, AND FLEXURAL ANALYSIS

## Principles of Statics; Geometric Properties of Areas

If a body remains in equilibrium under a system of forces, the following conditions obtain:

1. The algebraic sum of the components of the forces in any given direction is zero.

2. The algebraic sum of the moments of the forces with respect to any given axis is zero.

The above statements are verbal expressions of the equations of equilibrium. In the absence of any notes to the contrary, a clockwise moment is considered positive; a counterclockwise moment, negative.

## GRAPHICAL ANALYSIS OF A
## FORCE SYSTEM

The body in Fig. 1a is acted on by forces A, B, and C, as shown. Draw the vector representing the equilibrant of this system.

### Calculation Procedure:

#### 1. *Construct the system force line*
In Fig. 1b, draw the vector chain A-B-C, which is termed the *force line*. The vector extending from the initial point to the terminal point of the force line represents the resultant R. In any force system, the resultant R is equal to and collinear with the equilibrant E, but acts in the opposite direction. The equilibrant of a force system is a single force that will balance the system.

#### 2. *Construct the system rays*
Selecting an arbitrary point O as the pole, draw the rays from O to the ends of the vectors and label them as shown in Fig. 1b.

#### 3. *Construct the string polygon*
In Fig. 1a, construct the string polygon as follows: At an arbitrary point a on the action line of force A, draw strings parallel to rays ar and ab. At the point where the string ab intersects the action line of force B, draw a string parallel to ray bc. At the point where string bc intersects the action line of force C, draw a string parallel to cr. The intersection point Q of ar and cr lies on the action line of R.

#### 4. *Draw the vector for the resultant and equilibrant*
In Fig. 1a, draw the vector representing R. Establish the magnitude and direction of this vector from the force polygon. The action line of R passes through Q.

Last, draw a vector equal to and collinear with that representing R but opposite in direction. This vector represents the equilibrant E.

**Related Calculations.** Use this general method for any force system acting in a single plane. With a large number of forces, the resultant of a smaller number of forces can be combined with the remaining forces to simplify the construction.

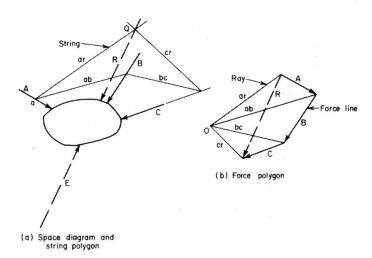

(a) Space diagram and
string polygon

(b) Force polygon

**FIGURE 1.** Equilibrant of force system.

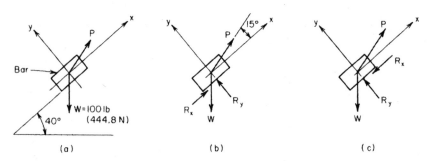

**FIGURE 2.** Equilibrant of force system.

## ANALYSIS OF STATIC FRICTION

The bar in Fig. 2a weighs 100 lb (444.8 N) and is acted on by a force $P$ that makes an angle of 55° with the horizontal. The coefficient of friction between the bar and the inclined plane is 0.20. Compute the minimum value of $P$ required (a) to prevent the bar from sliding down the plane; (b) to cause the bar to move upward along the plane.

### Calculation Procedure:

### 1. Select coordinate axes
Establish coordinate axes $x$ and $y$ through the center of the bar, parallel and perpendicular to the plane, respectively.

### 2. Draw a free-body diagram of the system
In Fig. 2b, draw a free-body diagram of the bar. The bar is acted on by its weight $W$, the force $P$, and the reaction $R$ of the plane on the bar. Show $R$ resolved into its $x$ and $y$ components, the former being directed upward.

### 3. Resolve the forces into their components
The forces $W$ and $P$ are the important ones in this step, and they must be resolved into their $x$ and $y$ components. Thus

$$W_x = -100 \sin 40° = -64.3 \text{ lb } (-286.0 \text{ N})$$
$$W_y = -100 \cos 40° = -76.6 \text{ lb } (-340.7 \text{ N})$$
$$P_x = P \cos 15° = 0.966P$$
$$P_y = P \sin 15° = 0.259P$$

### 4. Apply the equations of equilibrium
Consider that the bar remains at rest and apply the equations of equilibrium. Thus

$$\Sigma F_x = R_x + 0.966P - 64.3 = 0 \qquad R_x = 64.3 - 0.966P$$
$$\Sigma F_y = R_y + 0.259P - 76.6 = 0 \qquad R_y = 76.6 - 0.259P$$

### 5. Assume maximum friction exists and solve for the applied force
Assume that $R_x$, which represents the frictional resistance to motion, has its maximum potential value. Apply $R_x = \mu R_y$, where $\mu$ = coefficient of friction. Then $R_x = 0.20R_y =$

$0.20(76.6 - 0.259P) = 15.32 - 0.052P$. Substituting for $R_x$ from step 4 yields $64.3 - 0.966P = 15.32 - 0.052P$; so $P = 53.6$ lb (238.4 N).

### 6. Draw a second free-body diagram
In Fig. 2c, draw a free-body diagram of the bar, with $R_x$ being directed downward.

### 7. Solve as in steps 1 through 5
As before, $R_y = 76.6 - 0.259P$. Also the absolute value of $R_x = 0.966P - 64.3$. But $R_x = 0.20R_y = 15.32 \times 0.052P$. Then $0.966P - 64.3 = 15.32 - 0.052P$; so $P = 78.2$ lb (347.6N).

## ANALYSIS OF A STRUCTURAL FRAME

The frame in Fig. 3a consists of two inclined members and a tie rod. What is the tension in the rod when a load of 1000 lb (4448.0 N) is applied at the hinged apex? Neglect the weight of the frame and consider the supports to be smooth.

**Calculation Procedure:**

### 1. Draw a free-body diagram of the frame
Since friction is absent in this frame, the reactions at the supports are vertical. Draw a free-body diagram as in Fig. 3b.

With the free-body diagram shown, compute the distances $x_1$ and $x_2$. Since the frame forms a 3-4-5 right triangle, $x_1 = 16(4/5) = 12.8$ ft (3.9 m) and $x_2 = 12(3/5) = 7.2$ ft (2.2 m).

### 2. Determine the reactions on the frame
Take moments with respect to $A$ and $B$ to obtain the reactions:

$\Sigma M_B = 20R_L - 1000(7.2) = 0$

$\Sigma M_A = 1000(12.8) - 20R_R = 0$

$R_L = 360$ lb (1601.2 N)

$R_R = 640$ lb (2646.7 N)

### 3. Determine the distance y in Fig. 3c
Draw a free-body diagram of member $AC$ in Fig. 3c. Compute $y = 13(3/5) = 7.8$ ft (2.4 m).

### 4. Compute the tension in the tie rod
Take moments with respect to $C$ to find the tension $T$ in the tie rod:

$\Sigma M_C = 360(12.8) - 7.8T = 0$

$T = 591$ lb (2628.8 N)

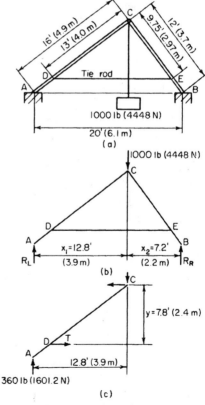

**FIGURE 3**

**5. *Verify the computed result***
Draw a free-body diagram of member *BC,* and take moments with respect to *C.* The result verifies that computed above.

## GRAPHICAL ANALYSIS OF A PLANE TRUSS

Apply a graphical analysis to the cantilever truss in Fig. 4*a* to evaluate the forces induced in the truss members.

### Calculation Procedure:

**1. *Label the truss for analysis***
Divide the space around the truss into regions bounded by the action lines of the external and internal forces. Assign an uppercase letter to each region (Fig. 4).

**2. *Determine the reaction force***
Take moments with respect to joint 8 (Fig. 4) to determine the horizontal component of the reaction force $R_U$. Then compute $R_U$. Thus $\Sigma M_8 = 12R_{UH} - 3(8 + 16 + 24) - 5(6 + 12 + 18) = 0$, so $R_{UH} = 27$ kips (120.1 kN) to the right.

Since $R_U$ is collinear with the force *DE,* $R_{UV}/R_{UH} = {}^{12}/{}_{24}$, so $R_{UV} = 13.5$ kips (60.0 kN) upward, and $R_U = 30.2$ kips (134.3 kN).

**3. *Apply the equations of equilibrium***
Use the equations of equilibrium to find $R_L$. Thus $R_{LH} = 27$ kips (120.1 kN) to the left, $R_{LV} = 10.5$ kips (46.7 kN) upward, and $R_L = 29.0$ kips (129.0 kN).

**4. *Construct the force polygon***
Draw the force polygon in Fig. 4*b* by using a suitable scale and drawing vector **fg** to represent force *FG.* Next, draw vector **gh** to represent force *GH,* and so forth. Omit the arrowheads on the vectors.

**5. *Determine the forces in the truss members***
Starting at joint 1, Fig. 4*b,* draw a line through *a* in the force polygon parallel to member *AJ* in the truss, and one through *h* parallel to member *HJ.* Designate the point of intersection of these lines as *j.* Now, vector **aj** represents the force in *AJ,* and vector **hj** represents the force in *HJ.*

**6. *Analyze the next joint in the truss***
Proceed to joint 2, where there are now only two unknown forces—*BK* and *JK.* Draw a line through *b* in the force polygon parallel to *BK* and one through *j* parallel to *JK.* Designate the point of intersection as *k.* The forces *BK* and *JK* are thus determined.

**7. *Analyze the remaining joints***
Proceed to joints 3, 4, 5, and 6, in that order, and complete the force polygon by continuing the process. If the construction is accurately performed, the vector **pe** will parallel the member *PE* in the truss.

**8. *Determine the magnitude of the internal forces***
Scale the vector lengths to obtain the magnitude of the internal forces. Tabulate the results as in Table 1.

**9. *Establish the character of the internal forces***
To determine whether an internal force is one of tension or compression, proceed in this way: Select a particular joint and proceed around the joint in a clockwise direction, listing

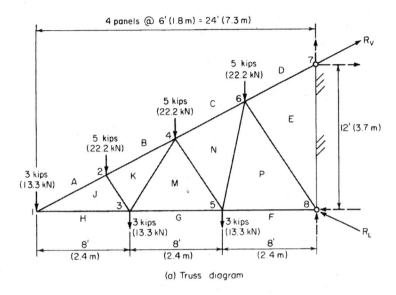

(a) Truss diagram

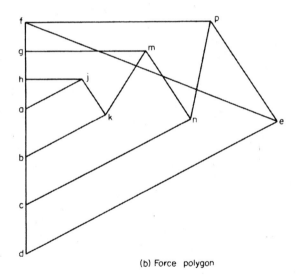

(b) Force polygon

**FIGURE 4**

the letters in the order in which they appear. Then refer to the force polygon pertaining to that joint, and proceed along the polygon in the same order. This procedure shows the direction in which the force is acting at that joint.

For instance, by proceeding around joint 4, *CNMKB* is obtained. By tracing a path along the force polygon in the order in which the letters appear, force *CN* is found to act

**TABLE 1.** Forces in Truss Members (Fig. 4)

| Member | Force | |
|--------|------|------|
| | kips | kN |
| AJ | +6.7 | +29.8 |
| BK | +9.5 | +42.2 |
| CN | +19.8 | +88.0 |
| DE | +30.2 | −134.2 |
| HJ | −6.0 | −26.7 |
| GM | −13.0 | −57.8 |
| FP | −20.0 | −88.9 |
| JK | −4.5 | 20.0 |
| KM | +8.1 | +36.0 |
| MN | −8.6 | −38.2 |
| NP | +10.4 | +46.2 |
| PE | −12.6 | 56.0 |

upward to the right; *NM* acts upward to the left; *MK* and *KB* act downward to the left. Therefore, *CN, MK,* and *KB* are directed away from the joint (Fig. 4); this condition discloses that they are tensile forces. Force *NM* is directed toward the joint; therefore, it is compressive.

The validity of this procedure lies in the drawing of the vectors representing external forces while proceeding around the truss in a clockwise direction. Tensile forces are shown with a positive sign in Table 1; compressive forces are shown with a negative sign.

**Related Calculations.** Use this general method for any type of truss.

## TRUSS ANALYSIS BY THE METHOD OF JOINTS

Applying the method of joints, determine the forces in the truss in Fig. 5a. The load at joint 4 has a horizontal component of 4 kips (17.8 kN) and a vertical component of 3 kips (13.3 kN).

**Calculation Procedure:**

### 1. Compute the reactions at the supports
Using the usual analysis techniques, we find $R_{LV} = 19$ kips (84.5 kN); $R_{LH} = 4$ kips (17.8 kN); $R_R = 21$ kips (93.4 kN).

### 2. List each truss member and its slope
Table 2 shows each truss member and its slope.

### 3. Determine the forces at a principal joint
Draw a free-body diagram, Fig. 5b, of the pin at joint 1. For the free-body diagram, assume that the unknown internal forces *AJ* and *HJ* are tensile. Apply the equations of equilibrium to evaluate these forces, using the subscripts *H* and *V*, respectively, to identify the

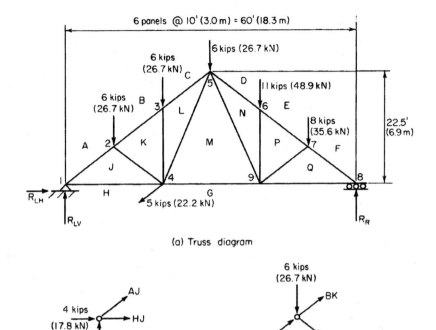

(a) Truss diagram

(b) Free-body diagram
of joint 1

(c) Free-body diagram
of joint 2

**FIGURE 5**

horizontal and vertical components. Thus $\Sigma F_H = 4.0 + AJ_H + HJ = 0$ and $\Sigma F_V = 19.0 + AJ_V = 0$; $\therefore AJ_V = -19.0$ kips ($-84.5$ kN); $AJ_H = -19.0/0.75 = -25.3$ kips ($-112.5$ kN). Substituting in the first equation gives $HJ = 21.3$ kips (94.7 kN).

The algebraic signs disclose that $AJ$ is compressive and $HJ$ is tensile. Record these results in Table 2, showing the tensile forces as positive and compressive forces as negative.

### 4. Determine the forces at another joint

Draw a free-body diagram of the pin at joint 2 (Fig. 5c). Show the known force $AJ$ as compressive, and assume that the unknown forces $BK$ and $JK$ are tensile. Apply the equations of equilibrium, expressing the vertical components of $BK$ and $JK$ in terms of their horizontal components. Thus $\Sigma F_H = 25.3 + BK_H + JK_H = 0$; $\Sigma F_V = -6.0 + 19.0 + 0.75BK_H - 0.75JK_H = 0$.

Solve these simultaneous equations, to obtain $BK_H = -21.3$ kips ($-94.7$ kN); $JK_H = -4.0$ kips ($-17.8$ kN); $BK_V = -16.0$ kips ($-71.2$ kN); $JK_V = -3.0$ kips ($-13.3$ kN). Record these results in Table 2.

### 5. Continue the analysis at the next joint

Proceed to joint 3. Since there are no external horizontal forces at this joint, $CL_H = BK_H = 21.3$ kips (94.7 kN) of compression. Also, $KL = 6$ kips (26.7 kN) of compression.

**TABLE 2.** Forces in Truss Members (Fig. 5)

| Member | Slope | Horizontal component | Vertical component | Force kips | Force kN |
|--------|-------|----------------------|--------------------|------------|----------|
| AJ | 0.75 | 25.3 | 19.0 | −31.7 | −141.0 |
| BK | 0.75 | 21.3 | 16.0 | −26.7 | −118.8 |
| CL | 0.75 | 21.3 | 16.0 | −26.7 | −118.8 |
| DN | 0.75 | 22.7 | 17.0 | −28.3 | −125.9 |
| EP | 0.75 | 22.7 | 17.0 | −28.3 | −125.9 |
| FQ | 0.75 | 28.0 | 21.0 | −35.0 | −155.7 |
| HJ | 0.0 | 21.3 | 0.0 | +21.3 | +94.7 |
| GM | 0.0 | 16.0 | 0.0 | +16.0 | +71.2 |
| GQ | 0.0 | 28.0 | 0.0 | +28.0 | +124.5 |
| JK | 0.75 | 4.0 | 3.0 | −5.0 | −22.2 |
| KL | ∞ | 0.0 | 6.0 | −6.0 | −26.7 |
| LM | 2.25 | 5.3 | 12.0 | + 13.1 | +58.3 |
| MN | 2.25 | 6.7 | 15.0 | + 16.4 | +72.9 |
| NP | ∞ | 0.0 | 11.0 | −11.0 | −48.9 |
| PQ | 0.75 | 5.3 | 4.0 | −6.7 | −29.8 |

### 6. Proceed to the remaining joints in their numbered order

Thus, for *joint 4*: $\Sigma F_H = -4.0 - 21.3 + 4.0 + LM_H + GM = 0$; $\Sigma F_V = -3.0 - 3.0 - 6.0 + LM_V = 0$; $LM_V = 12.0$ kips (53.4 kN); $LM_H = 12.0/2.25 = 5.3$ kips (23.6 kN). Substituting in the first equation gives $GM = 16.0$ kips (71.2 kN).

*Joint 5:* $\Sigma F_H = 21.3 - 53 + DN_H + MN_H = 0$; $\Sigma F_V = -6.0 + 16.0 - 12.0 - 0.750DN_H - 2.25MN_H = 0$; $DN_H = -22.7$ kips ($-101.0$ kN); $MN_H = 6.7$ kips (29.8 kN); $DN_V = -17.0$ kips ($-75.6$ kN); $MN_V = 15.0$ kips (66.7 kN).

*Joint 6:* $EP_H = DN_H = 22.7$ kips (101.0 kN) of compression; $NP = 11.0$ kips (48.9 kN) of compression.

*Joint 7:* $\Sigma F_H = 22.7 - PQ_H + FQ_H = 0$; $\Sigma F_V = -8.0 - 17.0 - 0.75PQ_H - 0.75FQ_H = 0$; $PQ_H = -5.3$ kips ($-23.6$ kN); $FQ_H = -28.0$ kips ($-124.5$ kN); $PQ_V = -4.0$ kips ($-17.8$ kN); $FQ_V = -21.0$ kips ($-93.4$ kN).

*Joint 8:* $\Sigma F_H = 28.0 - GQ = 0$; $GQ = 28.0$ kips (124.5 kN); $\Sigma F_V = 21.0 - 21.0 = 0$.

*Joint 9:* $\Sigma F_H = -16.0 - 6.7 - 5.3 + 28.0 = 0$; $\Sigma F_V \ 15.0 - 11.0 - 4.0 = 0$.

### 7. Complete the computation

Compute the values in the last column of Table 2 and enter them as shown.

## TRUSS ANALYSIS BY THE METHOD OF SECTIONS

Using the method of sections, determine the forces in members *BK* and *LM* in Fig. 6*a*.

### Calculation Procedure:

### 1. Draw a free-body diagram of one portion of the truss

Cut the truss at the plane *aa* (Fig. 6*a*), and draw a free-body diagram of the left part of the truss. Assume that *BK* is tensile.

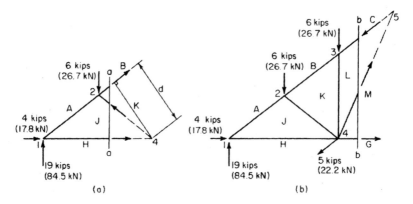

**FIGURE 6**

### 2. Determine the magnitude and character of the first force

Take moments with respect to joint 4. Since each halt of the truss forms a 3-4-5 right triangle, $d = 20(3/5) = 12$ ft (3.7 m), $\Sigma M_4 = 19(20) - 6(10) + 12BK = 0$, and $BK = -26.7$ kips ($-118.8$ kN).

The negative result signifies that the assumed direction of $BK$ is incorrect; the force is, therefore, compressive.

### 3. Use an alternative solution

Alternatively, resolve $BK$ (again assumed tensile) into its horizontal and vertical components at joint 1. Take moments with respect to joint 4. (A force may be resolved into its components at any point on its action line.) Then, $\Sigma M_4 = 19(20) + 20BK_V = -16.0$ kips ($-71.2$ kN); $BK = -16.0(5/3) = -26.7$ kips ($-118.8$ kN).

### 4. Draw a second free-body diagram of the truss

Cut the truss at plane $bb$ (Fig. 6b), and draw a free-body diagram of the left part. Assume $LM$ is tensile.

### 5. Determine the magnitude and character of the second force

Resolve $LM$ into its horizontal and vertical components at joint 4. Take moments with respect to joint 1: $\Sigma M_1 = 6(10 + 20) + 3(20) - 20LM_V = 0$; $LM_V = 12.0$ kips (53.4 kN); $LM_H = 12.0/2.25 = 3.3$ kips (23.6 kN); $LM = 13.1$ kips (58.3 kN).

## REACTIONS OF A THREE-HINGED ARCH

The parabolic arch in Fig. 7 is hinged at $A$, $B$, and $C$. Determine the magnitude and direction of the reactions at the supports.

### Calculation Procedure:

### 1. Consider the entire arch as a free body and take moments

Since a moment cannot be transmitted across a hinge, the bending moments at $A$, $B$, and $C$ are zero. Resolve the reactions $R_A$ and $R_C$ (Fig. 7) into their horizontal and vertical components.

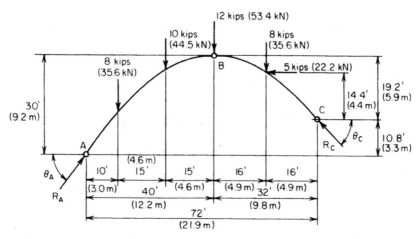

**FIGURE 7**

Considering the entire arch $ABC$ as a free body, take moments with respect to $A$ and $C$. Thus $\Sigma M_A = 8(10) + 10(25) + 12(40) + 8(56) - 5(25.2) - 72R_{CV} - 10.8R_{CH} = 0$, or $72R_{CV} + 10.8R_{CH} = 1132$, Eq. $a$. Also, $\Sigma M_C = 72R_{AV} - 10.8R_{AH} - 8(62) - 10(47) - 12(32) - 8(16) - 5(14.4) = 0$, or $72R_{AV} - 10.8R_{AH} = 1550$, Eq. $b$.

## 2. Consider a segment of the arch and take moments
Considering the segment $BC$ as a free body, take moments with respect to $B$. Then $\Sigma M_B = 8(16) + 5(4.8) - 32R_{CV} + 19.2R_{CH} = 0$, or $32R_{CV} - 19.2R_{CH} = 152$, Eq. $c$.

## 3. Consider another segment and take moments
Considering segment $AB$ as a free body, take moments with respect to $B$: $\Sigma M_B = 40R_{AV} - 30R_{AH} - 8(30) - 10(15) = 0$, or $40R_{AV} - 30R_{AH} = 300$, Eq. $d$.

## 4. Solve the simultaneous moment equations
Solve Eqs. $b$ and $d$ to determine $R_A$; solve Eqs. $a$ and $c$ to determine $R_C$. Thus $R_{AV} = 24.4$ kips (108.5 kN); $R_{AH} = 19.6$ kips (87.2 kN); $R_{CV} = 13.6$ kips (60.5 kN); $R_{CH} = 14.6$ kips (64.9 kN). Then $R_A = [(24.4)^2 + (19.6)^2]^{0.5} = 31.3$ kips (139.2 kN). Also $R_C = [(13.6)^2 + (14.6)^2]^{0.5} = 20.0$ kips (8.90 kN). And $\theta_A = \arctan(24.4/19.6) = 51°14'$; $\theta_C = \arctan(13.6/14.6) = 42°58'$.

# LENGTH OF CABLE CARRYING KNOWN LOADS

A cable is supported at points $P$ and $Q$ (Fig. 8a) and carries two vertical loads, as shown. If the tension in the cable is restricted to 1800 lb (8006 N), determine the minimum length of cable required to carry the loads.

## Calculation Procedure:

### 1. Sketch the loaded cable
Assume a position of the cable, such as $PRSQ$ (Fig. 8a). In Fig. 8b, locate points $P'$ and $Q'$, corresponding to $P$ and $Q$, respectively, in Fig. 8a.

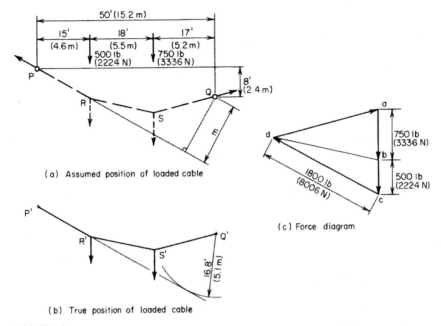

(a) Assumed position of loaded cable

(b) True position of loaded cable

(c) Force diagram

**FIGURE 8**

## 2. Take moments with respect to an assumed point
Assume that the maximum tension of 1800 lb (8006 N) occurs in segment *PR* (Fig. 8). The reaction at *P*, which is collinear with *PR*, is therefore 1800 lb (8006 N). Compute the true perpendicular distance *m* from *Q* to *PR* by taking moments with respect to *Q*. Or $\Sigma M_Q = 1800m - 500(35) - 750(17) = 0$; $m = 16.8$ ft (5.1 m). This dimension establishes the true position of *PR*.

## 3. Start the graphical solution of the problem
In Fig. 8*b*, draw a circular arc having *Q'* as center and a radius of 16.8 ft (5.1 m). Draw a line through *P'* tangent to this arc. Locate *R'* on this tangent at a horizontal distance of 15 ft (4.6 m) from *P'*.

## 4. Draw the force vectors
In Fig. 8*c*, draw vectors **ab, bc,** and **cd** to represent the 750-lb (3336-N) load, the 500-lb (2224-N) load, and the 1800-lb (8006-N) reaction at *P*, respectively. Complete the triangle by drawing vector **da,** which represents the reaction at *Q*.

## 5. Check the tension assumption
Scale *da* to ascertain whether it is less than 1800 lb (8006 N). This is found to be so, and the assumption that the maximum tension exists in *PR* is validated.

## 6. Continue the construction
Draw a line through *Q'* in Fig. 8*b* parallel to *da* in Fig. 8*c*. Locate *S'* on this line at a horizontal distance of 17 ft (5.2 m) from *Q*.

## 7. Complete the construction
Draw *R'S'* and *db*. Test the accuracy of the construction by determining whether these lines are parallel.

### 8. Determine the required length of the cable

Obtain the required length of the cable by scaling the lengths of the segments to Fig. 8*b*.
Thus $P'R' = 17.1$ ft (5.2 m); $R'S' = 18.4$ ft (5.6 m); $S'Q' = 17.6$ ft (5.4 m); and length of
cable $= 53.1$ ft (16.2 m).

## PARABOLIC CABLE TENSION AND LENGTH

A suspension bridge has a span of 960 ft (292.61 m) and a sag of 50 ft (15.2 m). Each
cable carries a load of 1.2 kips per linear foot (kips/lin ft) (17,512.68 N/m) uniformly
distributed along the horizontal. Compute the tension in the cable at midspan and at the
supports, and determine the length of the cable.

### Calculation Procedure:

### 1. Compute the tension at midspan

A cable carrying a load uniformly distributed along the horizontal assumes the form of a
parabolic arc. In Fig. 9, which shows such a cable having supports at the same level, the
tension at midspan is $H = wL^2/(8d)$, where $H =$ midspan tension, kips (kN); $w =$ load on
a unit horizontal distance, kips/lin ft (kN/m); $L =$ span, ft (m); $d =$ sag, ft (m). Substituting yields $H = 1.2(960)^2/[8(50)] = 2765$ kips (12,229 kN).

### 2. Compute the tension at the supports

Use the relation $T = [H^2 + (wL/2)^2]^{0.5}$, where $T =$ tension at supports, kips (kN), and the
other symbols are as before. Thus, $T = [(2765^2) + (1.2 \times 480^2]^{0.5} = 2824$ kips (12,561
kN).

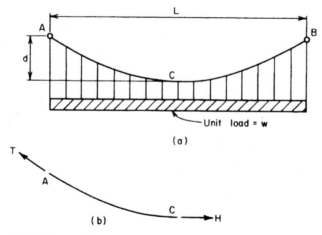

**FIGURE 9.** Cable supporting load uniformly distributed along horizontal.

### 3. *Compute the length of the cable*
When $d/L$ is 1/20 or less, the cable length can be approximated from $S = L + 8d^2/(3L)$, where $S$ = cable length, ft (m). Thus, $S = 960 + 8(50)^2/[3(960)] = 966.94$ ft (294.72 m).

## CATENARY CABLE SAG AND DISTANCE BETWEEN SUPPORTS

A cable 500 ft (152.4 m) long and weighing 3 pounds per linear foot (lb/lin ft) (43.8 N/m) is supported at two points lying in the same horizontal plane. If the tension at the supports is 1800 lb (8006 N), find the sag of the cable and the distance between the supports.

### Calculation Procedure:

### 1. *Compute the catenary parameter*
A cable of uniform cross section carrying only its own weight assumes the form of a catenary. Using the notation of the previous procedure, we find the catenary parameter $c$ from $d + c = T/w = 1800/3 = 600$ ft (182.9 m). Then $c = [(d + c)^2 - (S/2)^2]^{0.5} = [(600)^2]^{0.5} - (250)^2]^{0.5} = 545.4$ ft (166.2 m).

### 2. *Compute the cable sag*
Since $d + c = 600$ ft (182.9 m) and $c = 545.4$ ft (166.2 m), we know $d = 600 - 545.4 = 54.6$ ft (l6.6 m).

### 3. *Compute the span length*
Use the relation $L = 2c \ln (d + c + 0.5S)/c$, or $L = 2(545.5) \ln (600 + 250) 545.4 = 484.3$ ft (147.6 m).

## STABILITY OF A RETAINING WALL

Determine the factor of safety (FS) against sliding and overturning of the concrete retaining wall in Fig. 10. The concrete weighs 150 lb/ft³ (23.56 kN/m³), the earth weighs 100 lb/ft³ (15.71 kN/m³), the coefficient of friction is 0.6, and the coefficient of active earth pressure is 0.333.

### Calculation Procedure:

### 1. *Compute the vertical loads on the wall*
Select a 1-ft (304.8-mm) length of wall as typical of the entire structure. The horizontal pressure of the confined soil varies linearly with the depth and is represented by the triangle $BGF$ in Fig. 10

Resolve the wall into the elements $AECD$ and $AEB$; pass the vertical plane $BF$ through the soil. Calculate the vertical loads, and locate their resultants with respect to the toe $C$. Thus $W_1 = 15(1)(150) = 2250$ lb (10,008 N); $W_2 = 0.5(15)(5)(150) = 5625$; $W_3 = 0.5(15)(5)(100) = 3750$. Then $\Sigma W = 11,625$ lb (51,708 N). Also, $x_1 = 0.5$ ft; $x_2 = 1 + 0333(5) = 2.67$ ft (0.81 m); $x_3 = 1 + 0.667(5) = 433$ ft (1.32 m).

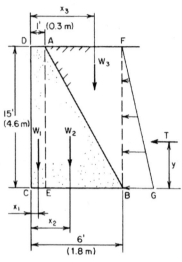

**FIGURE 10**

### 2. Compute the resultant horizontal soil thrust

Compute the resultant horizontal thrust $T$ lb of the soil by applying the coefficient of active earth pressure. Determine the location of $T$. Thus $BG = 0.333(15)(100) = 500$ lb/lin ft (7295 N/m); $T = 0.5(15)(500) = 3750$ lb (16,680 N); $y = 0.333(15) = 5$ ft (1.5 m).

### 3. Compute the maximum frictional force preventing sliding

The maximum frictional force $F_m = \mu(\Sigma W)$, where $\mu$ = coefficient of friction. Or $F_m = 0.6(11,625) = 6975$ lb (31,024.8 N).

### 4. Determine the factor of safety against sliding

The factor of safety against sliding is FSS = $F_m/T = 6975/3750 = 1.86$.

### 5. Compute the moment of the overturning and stabilizing forces

Taking moments with respect to $C$, we find the overturning moment = $3750(5) = 18,750$ lb·ft (25,406.3 N·m). Likewise, the stabilizing moment = $2250(0.5) + 5625(2.67) + 3750(4.33) = 32,375$ lb·ft (43,868.1 N·m).

### 6. Compute the factor of safety against overturning

The factor of safety against overturning is FSO = stabilizing moment, lb·ft (N·m)/overturning moment, lb·ft (N·m) = $32,375/18,750 = 1.73$.

## ANALYSIS OF A SIMPLE SPACE TRUSS

In the space truss shown in Fig. 11a, $A$ lies in the $xy$ plane, $B$ and $C$ lie on the $z$ axis, and $D$ lies on the $x$ axis. A horizontal load of 4000 lb (17,792 N) lying in the $xy$ plane is applied at $A$. Determine the force induced in each member by applying the method of joints, and verify the results by taking moments with respect to convenient axes.

### Calculation Procedure:

### 1. Determine the projected length of members

Let $d_x$, $d_y$, and $d_z$ denote the length of a member as projected on the $x$, $y$, and $x$ axes, respectively. Record in Table 3 the projected lengths of each member. Record the remaining values as they are obtained.

### 2. Compute the true length of each member

Use the equation $d = (d_x^2 + d_y^2 + d_z^2)^{0.5}$, where $d$ = the true length of a member.

### 3. Compute the ratio of the projected length to the true length

For each member, compute the ratios of the three projected lengths to the true length. For example, for member $AC$, $d_z/d = 6/12.04 = 0.498$.

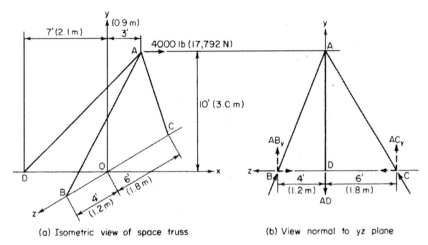

(a) Isometric view of space truss    (b) View normal to yz plane

**FIGURE 11**

These ratios are termed *direction cosines* because each represents the cosine of the angle between the member and the designated axis, or an axis parallel thereto.

Since the axial force in each member has the same direction as the member itself, a direction cosine also represents the ratio of the component of a force along the designated axis to the total force in the member. For instance, let $AC$ denote the force in member $AC$, and let $AC_x$ denote its component along the $x$ axis. Then $AC_x/AC = d_x/d = 0.249$.

### 4. Determine the component forces

Consider joint $A$ as a free body, and assume that the forces in the three truss members are tensile. Equate the sum of the forces along each axis to zero. For instance, if the truss members are in tension, the $x$ components of these forces are directed to the left, and $\Sigma F_x = 4000 - AB_x - AC_x - AD_x = 0$.

Express each component in terms of the total force to obtain $\Sigma F_x = 4000 - 0.268AB - 0.249AC - 0.707AD = 0$; $\Sigma F_y = -0.894AB - 0.831AC - 0.707AD = 0$; $\Sigma F_z = 0.358AB - 0.498AC = 0$.

**TABLE 3.** Data for Space Truss (Fig. 11)

| Member | AB | | AC | | AD | |
|---|---|---|---|---|---|---|
| $d_x$, ft (m) | 3 | (0.91) | 3 | (0.91) | 10 | (3.03) |
| $d_y$, ft (m) | 10 | (3.0) | 10 | (3.0) | 10 | (3.0) |
| $d_z$, ft (m) | 4 | (1.2) | 6 | (1.8) | 0 | (0) |
| $d$, ft (m) | 11.18 | (3.4) | 12.04 | (3.7) | 14.14 | (4.3) |
| $d_x/d$ | 0.268 | | 0.249 | | 0.707 | |
| $d_y/d$ | 0.894 | | 0.831 | | 0.707 | |
| $d_z/d$ | 0.358 | | 0.498 | | 0 | |
| Force, lb (N) | $-3830$ | $(-17,036)$ | $-2750$ | $(-12,232)$ | $+8080$ | $(+35,940)$ |

**5. Solve the simultaneous equations in step 4 to evaluate the forces in the truss members**
A positive result in the solution signifies tension; a negative result, compression. Thus, $AB$ = 3830-lb (17,036-N) compression; $AC$ = 2750-lb (12,232-N) compression; and $AD$ = 8080-lb (35,940-N) tension. To verify these results, it is necessary to select moment axes yielding equations independent of those previously developed.

**6. Resolve the reactions into their components**
In Fig. 11*b*, show the reactions at the supports $B$, $C$, and $D$, each reaction being numerically equal to and collinear with the force in the member at that support. Resolve these reactions into their components.

**7. Take moments about a selected axis**
Take moments with respect to the axis through $C$ parallel to the $x$ axis. (Since the $x$ components of the forces are parallel to this axis, their moments are zero.) Then $\Sigma M_{Cx} = 10AB_y - 6AD_y = 10(0.894)(3830) - 6(0.707)(8080) = 0$.

**8. Take moments about another axis**
Take moments with respect to the axis through $D$ parallel to the $x$ axis. So $\Sigma M_{Dx} = 4AB_y - 6AC_y = 4(0.894)(3830) - 6(0.831)(2750) = 0$.
The computed results are thus substantiated.

## ANALYSIS OF A COMPOUND SPACE TRUSS

The compound space truss in Fig. 12*a* has the dimensions shown in the orthographic projections, Fig. 12*b* and *c*. A load of 5000 lb (22,240 N), which lies in the *xy* plane and makes an angle of 30° with the vertical, is applied at $A$. Determine the force induced in each member, and verify the results.

**Calculation Procedure:**

**1. Compute the true length of each truss member**
Since the truss and load system are symmetric with respect to the *xy* plane, the internal forces are also symmetric. As one component of an internal force becomes known, it will be convenient to calculate the other components at once, as well as the total force.
    Record in Table 4 the length of each member as projected on the coordinate axes. Calculate the true length of each member, using geometric relations.

**2. Resolve the applied load into its x and y components**
Use only the absolute values of the forces. Thus $P_x$ = 5000 sin 30° = 2500 lb (11,120 N); $P_y$ = 5000 cos 30° = 4330 lb (19,260 N).

**3. Compute the horizontal reactions**
Compute the horizontal reactions at $D$ and at line $CC'$ (Fig. 12*b*). Thus $\Sigma M_{CC'} = 4330(12) - 2500(7) - 10H_1 = 0$; $H_1$ = 3446 lb (15,328 N); $H_2$ = 3446 - 2500 = 946 lb (4208 N).

**4. Compute the vertical reactions**
Consider the equilibrium of joint $D$ and the entire truss when you are computing the vertical reactions. In all instances, assume that an unknown internal force is tensile. Thus, at

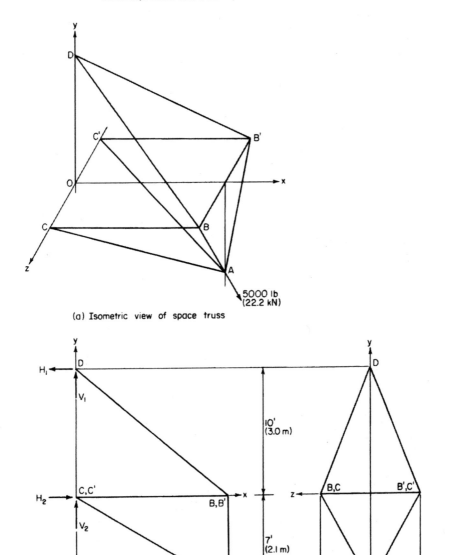

(a) Isometric view of space truss

(b) View normal to xy plane

(c) View normal to yz plane

**FIGURE 12**

**TABLE 4.**   Data for Space Truss (Fig. 12)

| Member | AB | AC | BC | BD | BB' |
|---|---|---|---|---|---|
| $d_x$, ft (m) | 0 (0) | 12 (3.7) | 12 (3.7) | 12 (3.7) | 0 (0) |
| $d_y$, ft (m) | 7 (2.1) | 7 (2.1) | 0 (0) | 10 (3.0) | 0 (0) |
| $d_z$, ft (m) | 4 (1.2) | 4 (1.2) | 0 (0) | 4 (1.2) | 8 (2.4) |
| $d$, ft (m) | 8.06 (2.5) | 14.46 (4.4) | 12.00 (3.7) | 16.12 (4.9) | 8 (2.4) |
| $F_x$, lb (N) | 0 (0) | 1,250 (5,560) | 1,723 (7,664) | 1,723 (7,664) | 0 (0) |
| $F_y$, lb (N) | 1,436 (6,367) | 729 (3,243) | 0 (0) | 1,436 (6,367) | 0 (0) |
| $F_z$, lb (N) | 821 (3,652) | 417 (1,655) | 0 (0) | 574 (2,553) | 1,395 (6,205) |
| $F$, lb (N) | +1,653 (+7,353) | +1,506 (+6,699) | −1,723 | (−7,664) +2,315(+10,297) | −1,395 (−6,205) |

joint $D$: $\Sigma F_x = -H_1 + 2BD_x = 0$; $BD_x = 1723$-lb (7664-N) tension; $BD_y = 1723(10/12)$ $= 1436$ lb (6387 N); likewise, $\Sigma F_y = V_1 - 2BD_y = V_1 - 2(1436) = 0$; $V_1 = 2872$ lb (12,275 N).

For the entire truss, $\Sigma F_y = V_1 + V_2 - 4330 = 0$; $V_2 = 1458$ lb (6485 N).

The $z$ components of the reactions are not required in this solution. Thus, the remaining calculations for $BD$ are $BD_z = 1723(4/12) = 574$ lb (2553 N); $BD = 1723(16.12/12)$ $= 2315$ lb (10,297 N).

**5. Compute the unknown forces by using the equilibrium of a joint**
Calculate the forces $AC$ and $BC$ by considering the equilibrium of joint $C$. Thus $\Sigma F_x = 0.5H_2 + AC_x + BC = 0$, Eq. $a$; $\Sigma F_y = 0.5V_2 - AC_y = 0$, Eq. $b$. From Eq. $b$, $AC_y = 729$-lb (3243-N) tension. Then $AC_x = 729(12/7) = 1250$ lb (5660 N). From Eq. $a$, $BC = 1723$-lb (7664-N) compression. Then $AC_z = 729(4/7) = 417$ lb (1855 N); $AC = 729(14.46/7) = 1506$ lb (6699 N).

**6. Compute another set of forces by considering joint equilibrium**
Calculate the forces $AB$ and $BB'$ by considering the equilibrium of joint $B$. Thus $\Sigma F_y = BD_y - AB_y = 0$; $AB_y = 1436$-lb (6387-N) tension; $AB_z = 1436(4/7) = 821$ lb (3652 N); $AB = 1436 (8.06/7) = 1653$ lb (7353 N); $\Sigma F_z = -AB_z - BD_z - BB' = 0$; $BB' = 1395$-lb (6205-N) compression.

All the internal forces are now determined. Show in Table 4 the tensile forces as positive, and the compressive forces as negative.

**7. Check the equilibrium of the first joint considered**
The first joint considered was $A$. Thus $\Sigma F_x = -2AC_x + 2500 = -2(1250) + 2500 = 0$, and $\Sigma F_y = 2AB_y + 2AC_y - 4330 = 2(1436) + 2(729) - 4330 = 0$. Since the summation of forces for both axes is zero, the joint is in equilibrium.

**8. Check the equilibrium of the second joint**
Check the equilibrium of joint $B$ by taking moments of the forces acting on this joint with respect to the axis through $A$ parallel to the $x$ axis (Fig. 12c). Thus $\Sigma M_{Ax} = -7BB' + 7BD_z + 4BD_y = -7(1395) + 7(574) + 4(1436) = 0$.

**9. Check the equilibrium of the right-hand part of the structure**
Cut the truss along a plane parallel to the $yz$ plane. Check the equilibrium of the right-hand part of the structure. Now $\Sigma F_x = -2BD_x + 2BC - 2AC_x + 2500 = -2(1723) + 2(1723) - 2(1250) + 2500 = 0$, and $\Sigma F_y = 2BD_y + 2AC_y - 4330 = 2(1436) + 2(729) - 4330 = 0$. The calculated results are thus substantiated in these equations.

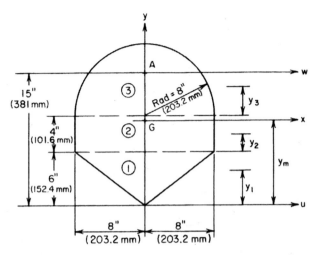

**FIGURE 13**

## GEOMETRIC PROPERTIES OF AN AREA

Calculate the polar moment of inertia of the area in Fig. 13: (*a*) with respect to its centroid, and (*b*) with respect to point *A*.

### Calculation Procedure:

#### 1. Establish the area axes
Set up the horizontal and vertical coordinate axes $u$ and $y$, respectively.

#### 2. Divide the area into suitable elements
Using the American Institute of Steel Construction (AISC) *Manual,* obtain the properties of elements 1, 2, and 3 (Fig. 13) after locating the horizontal centroidal axis of each element. Thus $y_1 = \frac{2}{3}(6) = 4$ in. (101.6 mm); $y_2 = 2$ in. (50.8 mm); $y_3 = 0.424(8) = 3.4$ in. (86.4 mm).

#### 3. Locate the horizontal centroidal axis of the entire area
Let $x$ denote the horizontal centroidal axis of the entire area. Locate this axis by computing the statical moment of the area with respect to the $u$ axis. Thus

| Element | Area, sq.in. (cm²) | | × | Arm, in. (cm) | = | Moment, in³ (cm³) |
|---------|-----------|---------|---|---------------|---|---------|
| 1 | $0.5(6)(16) = 48$ | (309.7) | | 4 (10.2) | = | 192 (3,158.9) |
| 2 | $4(16) = 64$ | (412.9) | | 8 (20.3) | = | 512 (8,381.9) |
| 3 | $1.57(8)^2 = 100.5$ | (648.4) | | 13.4 (34.9) | = | 1,347 (22,045.6) |
| Total | 212.5 | (1,351.0) | | | | 2,051 (33,586.4) |

Then $y_m = 2051/212.5 = 9.7$ in. (246.4 mm). Since the area is symmetric with respect to the $y$ axis, this is also a centroidal axis. The intersection point $G$ of the $x$ and $y$ axes is, therefore, the centroid of the area.

### 4. Compute the distance between the centroidal axis and the reference axis

Compute $k$, the distance between the horizontal centroidal axis of each element and the $x$ axis. Only absolute values are required. Thus $k_1 = 9.7 - 4.0 = 5.7$ in. (1448 mm); $k_2 = 9.7 - 8.0 = 1.7$ in. (43.2 mm); $k_3 = 13.4 - 9.7 = 3.7$ in. (94.0 mm).

### 5. Compute the moment of inertia of the entire area—x axis

Let $I_0$ denote the moment of inertia of an element with respect to its horizontal centroidal axis and $A$ its area. Compute the moment of inertia $I_x$ of the entire area with respect to the $x$ axis by applying the transfer equation $I_x \Sigma I_0 + \Sigma A K^2$. Thus

| Element | $I_0$, in$^4$ (dm$^4$) | $Ak^2$, in$^4$ (dm$^4$) |
|---------|------------------------|-------------------------|
| 1 | $\frac{1}{36}(16)(6)^3 = 96\ (0.40)$ | $48(5.7)^2 = 1560\ (6.49)$ |
| 2 | $\frac{1}{12}(16)(4)^3 = 85\ (0.35)$ | $64(1.7)^2 = 185\ (0.77)$ |
| 3 | $0.110(8)^4 = 451\ (1.88)$ | $100.5(3.7)^2 = 1376\ (5.73)$ |
| Total | $632\ (2.63)$ | $3121\ (12.99)$ |

Then, $I_x = 632 + 3121 = 3753$ in$^4$ (15.62 dm$^4$).

### 6. Determine the moment of inertia of the entire area—y axis

For this computation, subdivide element 1 into two triangles having the $y$ axis as a base. Thus

| Element | $I$ about $y$ axis, in$^4$ (dm$^4$) |
|---------|-------------------------------------|
| 1 | $2(\frac{1}{12})(6)(8)^3 = 0512\ (2.13)$ |
| 2 | $\frac{1}{12}(4)(16)^3 = 1365\ (5.68)$ |
| 3 | $\frac{1}{2}(0.785)(8)^4 = 1607\ (6.89)$ |
|   | $I_y = 3484\ (14.5)$ |

### 7. Compute the polar moment of inertia of the area

Apply the equation for the polar moment of inertia $J_G$ with respect to $G$: $J_G = I_x + I_y = 3753 + 3484 = 7237$ in$^4$ (30.12 dm$^4$).

### 8. Determine the moment of inertia of the entire area—w axis

Apply the equation in step 5 to determine the moment of inertia $I_w$ of the entire area with respect to the horizontal axis $w$ through $A$. Thus $k = 15.0 - 9.7 = 5.3$ in. (134.6 mm); $I_w = I_x + Ak^2 = 3753 + 212.5(5.3)^2 = 9722$ in$^4$ (40.46 dm$^4$).

### 9. Compute the polar moment of inertia

Compute the polar moment of inertia of the entire area with respect to $A$. Then $J_A = I_w + I_y = 9722 \pm 3484 = 13,206$ in$^4$ (54.97 dm$^4$).

## PRODUCT OF INERTIA OF AN AREA

Calculate the product of inertia of the isosceles trapezoid in Fig. 14 with respect to the rectangular axes $u$ and $v$.

### Calculation Procedure:

#### 1. Locate the centroid of the trapezoid
Using the AISC *Manual* or another suitable reference, we find $h$ = centroid distance from the axis (Fig. 14) $= (9/3)[(2 \times 5 + 10)/(5 + 10)] = 4$ in. (101.6 mm).

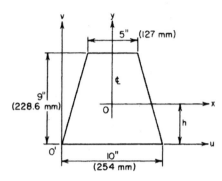

**FIGURE 14**

#### 2. Compute the area and product of inertia $P_{xy}$
The area of the trapezoid is $A = \frac{1}{2}(9)(5 + 10) = 67.5$ sq.in. (435.5 cm²). Since the area is symmetrically disposed with respect to the $y$ axis, the product of inertia with respect to the $x$ and $y$ axes is $P_{xy} = 0$.

#### 3. Compute the product of inertia by applying the transfer equation
The transfer equation for the product of inertia is $P_{uv} = P_{xy} + Ax_m y_m$, where $x_m$ and $y_m$ are the coordinates of $O'$ with respect to the centroidal $x$ and $y$ axes, respectively. Thus $P_{uv} = 0 + 67.5(-5)(-4) = 1350$ in⁴ (5.6 dm⁴).

## PROPERTIES OF AN AREA WITH RESPECT TO ROTATED AXES

In Fig. 15, $x$ and $y$ are rectangular axes through the centroid of the isosceles triangle; $x'$ and $y'$ are axes parallel to $x$ and $y$, respectively; $x''$ and $y''$ are axes making an angle of 30° with $x'$ and $y'$, respectively. Compute the moments of inertia and the product of inertia of the triangle with respect to the $x''$ and $y''$ axes.

### Calculation Procedure:

#### 1. Compute the area of the figure
The area of this triangle = 0.5(base)(altitude) = 0.5(8)(9) = 36 sq.in. (232.3 cm²).

#### 2. Compute the properties of the area with respect to the x and y axes
Using conventional moment-of-inertia relations, we find $I_x = bd^3/36 = 8(9)3/36 = 16^2$ in⁴ (0.67 dm⁴); $I_y = b^3d/48 = (8)3(9)/48 = 96$ in⁴ (0.39 dm⁴). By symmetry, the product of inertia with respect to the $x$ and $y$ axes is $P_{xy} = 0$.

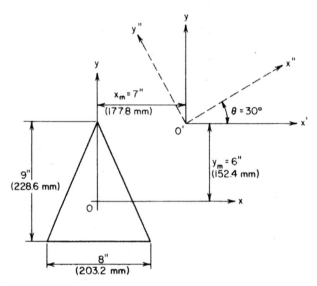

**FIGURE 15**

### 3. Compute the properties of the area with respect to the x' and y' axes

Using the usual moment-of-inertia relations, we find $I_{x'} = I_x + Ay_m^2 = 162 + 36(6)2 = 1458$ in⁴ (6.06 dm⁴); $I_{y'} = I_y + Ax_m^2 = 96 + 36(7)^2 = 1660$ in⁴ (7.74 dm⁴); $P_{x'y'} = P_{xy} + Ax_my_m = 0 + 36(7)(6) = 1512$ in⁴ (6.29 dm⁴).

### 4. Compute the properties of the area with respect to the x" and y" axes

For the x" axis, $I_{x''} = I_{x'} \cos^2\theta + I_{y'} \sin^2\theta - P_{x'y'} \sin 2\theta = 1458(0.75) + 1860(0.25) - 1512(0.866) = 249$ in⁴ (1.03 dm⁴).

For the y" axis, $I_{y''} = I_{x'} \sin^2\theta + I_{y'} \cos^2\theta + P_{x'y'} \sin 2\theta = 1458(0.25) + 1860(0.75) + 1512(0.866) = 3069$ in⁴ (12.77 dm⁴).

The product of inertia is $P_{x''y''} = P_{x'y'} \cos 2\theta + [(I_{x'} - I_{y'})/2] \sin 2\theta = 1512(0.5) + 1(1458 - 1860)/2]0.866 = 582$ in⁴ (2.42 dm⁴).

## Analysis of Stress and Strain

The notational system for axial stress and strain used in this section is as follows: $A$ = cross-sectional area of a member; $L$ = original length of the member; $\Delta l$ = increase in length; $P$ = axial force; $s$ = axial stress; $\epsilon$ = axial strain = $\Delta l/L$; $E$ = modulus of elasticity of material = $s/\epsilon$. The units used for each of these factors are given in the calculation procedure. In all instances, it is assumed that the induced stress is below the proportional limit. The basic stress and elongation equations used are $s = P/A$; $\Delta l = sL/E = PL/(AE)$. For steel, $E = 30 \times 10^6$ lb/sq.in. (206 GPa).

## STRESS CAUSED BY AN AXIAL LOAD

A concentric load of 20,000 lb (88,960 N) is applied to a hanger having a cross-sectional area of 1.6 sq.in. (1032.3 mm$^2$). What is the axial stress in the hanger?

### Calculation Procedure:

### 1. Compute the axial stress
Use the general stress relation $s = P/A = 20,000/1.6 = 12,500$ lb/sq.in. (86,187.5 kPa).

**Related Calculations.** Use this general stress relation for a member of any cross-sectional shape, provided the area of the member can be computed and the member is made of only one material.

## DEFORMATION CAUSED BY AN AXIAL LOAD

A member having a length of 16 ft (4.9 m) and a cross-sectional area of 2.4 sq.in. (1548.4 mm$^2$) is subjected to a tensile force of 30,000 lb (133.4 kN). If $E = 15 \times 10^6$ lb/sq.in. (103 GPa), how much does this member elongate?

### Calculation Procedure:

### 1. Apply the general deformation equation
The general deformation equation is $\Delta l = PL/(AE) = 30,000(16)(12)/[2.4(15 \times 10^6)]1 = 0.16$ in. (4.06 mm).

**Related Calculations.** Use this general deformation equation for any material whose modulus of elasticity is known. For composite materials, this equation must be altered before it can be used.

## DEFORMATION OF A BUILT-UP MEMBER

A member is built up of three bars placed end to end, the bars having the lengths and cross-sectional areas shown in Fig. 16. The member is placed between two rigid surfaces and axial loads of 30 kips (133 kN) and 10 kips (44 kN) are applied at $A$ and $B$, respectively. If $E = 2000$ kips/sq.in. (13,788 MPa), determine the horizontal displacement of $A$ and $B$.

### Calculation Procedure:

### 1. Express the axial force in terms of one reaction
Let $R_L$ and $R_R$ denote the reactions at the left and right ends, respectively. Assume that both reactions are directed to the left. Consider a tensile force as positive and a compressive force as negative. Consider a deformation positive if the body elongates and negative if the body contracts.

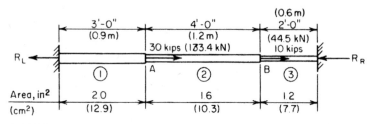

**FIGURE 16**

Express the axial force $P$ in each bar in terms of $R_L$ because both reactions are assumed to be directed toward the left. Use subscripts corresponding to the bar numbers (Fig. 16). Thus, $P_1 = R_L$ $P_2 = -30$; $P_3 = R_L - 40$.

## 2. Express the deformation of each bar in terms of the reaction and modulus of elasticity

Thus, $\Delta l_1 = R_L(36)/(2.0E) = 18RL/E$; $\Delta l_2 = (R_L - 30)(48)/(1.6E) = (30RL - 900)/E$; $\Delta l_3 = (R_L - 40)24/(1.2E) = (20R_L - 800)/E$.

## 3. Solve for the reaction

Since the ends of the member are stationary, equate the total deformation to zero, and solve for $R_L$. Thus $\Delta l_t = (68R_L - 1700)/E = 0$; $R_L = 25$ kips (111 kN). The positive result confirms the assumption that $R_L$ is directed to the left.

## 4. Compute the displacement of the points

Substitute the computed value of $R_L$ in the first two equations of step 2 and solve for the displacement of the points $A$ and $B$. Thus $\Delta l_1 = 18(25)/2000 = 0.225$ in. (5.715 mm); $\Delta l_2 = [30(25) - 900]/2000 = -0.075$ in ($-1.905$ mm).

Combining these results, we find the displacement of $A = 0.225$ in. (5.715 mm) to the right; the displacement of $B = 0.225 - 0.075 = 0.150$ in. (3.81 mm) to the right.

## 5. Verify the computed results

To verify this result, compute $R_R$ and determine the deformation of bar 3. Thus $\Sigma F_H = -R_L + 30 + 10 - R_R = 0$; $R_R = 15$ kips (67 kN). Since bar 3 is in compression, $\Delta l_3 = -15(24)/[1.2(2000)] = -0.150$ in ($-3.81$ mm). Therefore, $B$ is displaced 0.150 in. (3.81 mm) to the right. This verifies the result obtained in step 4.

## REACTIONS AT ELASTIC SUPPORTS

The rigid bar in Fig. 17a is subjected to a load of 20,000 lb (88,960 N) applied at $D$. It is supported by three steel rods, 1, 2, and 3 (Fig. 17a). These rods have the following relative cross-sectional areas: $A_1 = 1.25$, $A_2 = 1.20$, $A_3 = 1.00$. Determine the tension in each rod caused by this load, and locate the center of rotation of the bar.

## Calculation Procedure:

### 1. Draw a free-body diagram; apply the equations of equilibrium

Draw the free-body diagram (Fig. 17b) of the bar. Apply the equations of equilibrium: $\Sigma F_V P_1 + P_2 + P_3 - 20,000 = 0$, or $P_1 + P_2 + P_3 = 20,000$, Eq. $a$; also, $\Sigma M_C = 16P_1 + 10P_2 - 20,000(12) = 0$, or $16P_1 + 10P_2 = 240,000$, Eq. $b$.

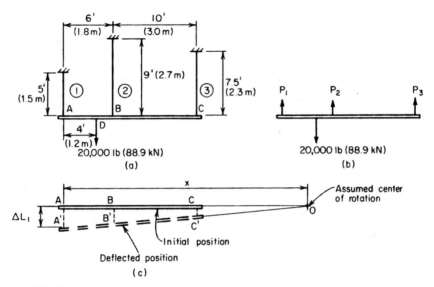

**FIGURE 17**

## 2. Establish the relations between the deformations

Selecting an arbitrary center of rotation $O$, show the bar in its deflected position (Fig. 17c). Establish the relationships among the three deformations. Thus, by similar triangles, $(\Delta l_1 - \Delta l_2)/(\Delta l_2 - \Delta l_3) = 6/10$, or $10\Delta l_1 - 16\Delta l_2 + 6\Delta l_3 = 0$, Eq. c.

## 3. Transform the deformation equation to an axial-force equation

By substituting axial-force relations in Eq. c, the following equation is obtained: $10P_1(5)/(1.25E) - 16P_2(9)/(1.20E) + 6P_3(7.5)/E = 0$, or $40P_1 - 120P_2 + 45P_3 = 0$, Eq. c'.

## 4. Solve the simultaneous equations developed

Solve the simultaneous equations a, b, and c' to obtain $P_1 = 11,810$ lb (52,530 N); $P_2 = 5100$ lb (22,684 N); $P_3 = 3090$ lb (13,744 N).

## 5. Locate the center of rotation

To locate the center of rotation, compute the relative deformation of rods 1 and 2. Thus $\Delta l_1 = 11,810(5)/(1.25E) = 47,240/E$; $\Delta l_2 = 5100(9)/(1.20E) = 38,250/E$.

In Fig. 17c, by similar triangles, $x/(x - 6) = \Delta l_1/\Delta l_2 = 1.235$; $x = 31.5$ ft (9.6 m).

## 6. Verify the computed values of the tensile forces

Calculate the moment with respect to $A$ of the applied and resisting forces. Thus $M_{Aa} = 20,000(4) = 80,000$ lb·ft (108,400 N·m); $M_{Ar} = 5100(6) + 3090(16) = 80,000$ lb·ft (108,400 N·m). Since the moments are equal, the results are verified.

## ANALYSIS OF CABLE SUPPORTING A CONCENTRATED LOAD

A cold-drawn steel wire $\frac{1}{4}$ in. (6.35 mm) in diameter is stretched tightly between two points lying on the same horizontal plane 80 ft (24.4 m) apart. The stress in the wire is 50,000 lb/sq.in. (344,700 kPa). A load of 200 lb (889.6 N) is suspended at the center of

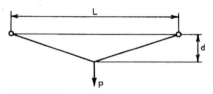

**FIGURE 18**

the cable. Determine the sag of the cable and the final stress in the cable. Verify that the results obtained are compatible.

**Calculation Procedure:**

**1. Derive the stress and strain relations for the cable**
With reference to Fig. 18, $L$ = distance between supports, ft (m); $P$ = load applied at center of cable span, lb (N); $d$ = deflection of cable center, ft (m); $\epsilon$ = strain of cable caused by $P$; $s_1$ and $s_2$ = initial and final tensile stress in cable, respectively, lb/sq.in. (kPa).

Refer to the geometry of the deflection diagram. Taking into account that $d/L$ is extremely small, derive the following approximations: $s_2 = PL/(4Ad)$, Eq. $a$; $\epsilon = 2(d/L)^2$, Eq. $b$.

**2. Relate stress and strain**
Express the increase in stress caused by $P$ in terms of $\epsilon$, and apply the above two equations to derive $2E(d/L)^3 + s_1(d/L) = P/(4A)$, Eq. $c$.

**3. Compute the deflection at the center of the cable**
Using Eq. $c$, we get $2(30)(10)^6(d/L)^3 + 50,000d/L = 200/[4(0.049)]$, so $d/L = 0.0157$ and $\therefore d = 0.0157(80) = 1.256$ ft (0.382 m).

**4. Compute the final tensile stress**
Write Eq. $a$ as $s_2 = [P/(4A)]/(d/L) = 1020/0.0157 = 65,000$ lb/sq.in. (448,110 kPa).

**5. Verify the results computed**
To demonstrate that the results are compatible, accept the computed value of $d/L$ as correct. Then apply Eq. $b$ to find the strain, and compute the corresponding stress. Thus $\epsilon = 2(0.0157)2 = 4.93 \times 10^{-4}$; $s_2 = s_1 + E\epsilon = 50,000 + 30 \times 10^6 \times 4.93 \times 10^{-4} = 64,800$ lb/sq.in. (446,731 kPa). This agrees closely with the previously calculated stress of 65,000 lb/sq.in. (448,110 kPa).

## DISPLACEMENT OF TRUSS JOINT

In Fig. 19a, the steel members $AC$ and $BC$ both have a cross-sectional area of 1.2 sq.in. (7.7 cm²). If a load of 20 kips (89.0 kN) is suspended at $C$, how much is joint $C$ displaced?

**Calculation Procedure:**

**1. Compute the length of each member and the tensile forces**
Consider joint $C$ as a free body to find the tensile force in each member. Thus $L_{AC} = 192$ in. (487.7 cm); $L_{BC} = 169.7$ in. (431.0 cm); $P_{AC} = 14,640$ lb (65,118.7 N); $P_{BC} = 17,930$ lb (79,752.6 N).

**2. Determine the elongation of each member**
Use the relation $\Delta l = PL/(AE)$. Thus $\Delta l_{AC} = 14,640(192)/[1.2(30 \times 10^6)] = 0.0781$ in. (1.983 mm); $\Delta l_{BC} = 17,930(169.7)/[1.2(30 \times 10^6)] = 0.0845$ in. (2.146 mm).

**3. Construct the Williott displacement diagram**
Selecting a suitable scale, construct the Williott displacement diagram as follows: Draw (Fig. 19b) line $Ca$ parallel to member $AC$, with $Ca = 0.0781$ in. (1.98 mm). Similarly, draw $Cb$ parallel to member $BC$, with $Cb = 0.0845$ in. (2.146 mm).

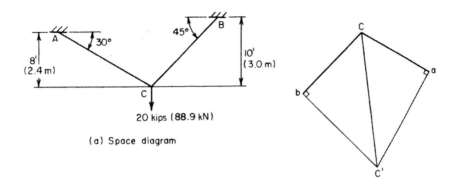

(a) Space diagram

(b) Displacement diagram

**FIGURE 19**

## 4. Determine the displacement

Erect perpendiculars to $Ca$ and $Cb$ at $a$ and $b$, respectively. Designate the intersection point of these perpendiculars as $C'$.

Line $CC'$ represents, in both magnitude and direction, the approximate displacement of joint $C$ under the applied load. Scaling distance $CC'$ to obtain the displacement shows that the displacement of $C = 0.134$ in. (3.4036 mm).

## AXIAL STRESS CAUSED BY IMPACT LOAD

A body weighing 18 lb (80.1 N) falls 3 ft (0.9 m) before contacting the end of a vertical steel rod. The rod is 5 ft (1.5 m) long and has a cross-sectional area of 1.2 sq.in. (7.74 cm²). If the entire kinetic energy of the falling body is absorbed by the rod, determine the stress induced in the rod.

### Calculation Procedure:

### 1. State the equation for the induced stress

Equate the energy imparted to the rod to the potential energy lost by the falling body:
$s = (P/A)\{1 + [1 + 2Eh/(LP/A)]^{0.5}\}$, where $h$ = vertical displacement of body, ft (m).

### 2. Substitute the numerical values

Thus, $P/A = 18/1.2 = 15$ lb/sq.in. (103 kPa); $h = 3$ ft (0.9 m); $L = 5$ ft (1.5 m); $[2Eh/(LP/A)] = 2(30) \times (10^6)(3)]/[5(15)] = 2,400,000$. Then $s = 23,250$ lb/sq.in. (160,285.5 kPa).

**Related Calculations.** Where the deformation of the supporting member is negligible in relation to the distance $h$, as it is in the present instance, the following approximation is used: $s = [2PEh/(AL)]^{0.5}$.

## STRESSES ON AN OBLIQUE PLANE

A prism *ABCD* in Fig. 20*a* has the principal stresses of 6300- and 2400-lb/sq.in. (43,438.5- and 16,548.0-kPa) tension. Applying both the analytical and graphical methods, determine the normal and shearing stress on plane *AE*.

### Calculation Procedure:

### 1. *Compute the stresses, using the analytical method*
A principal stress is a normal stress not accompanied by a shearing stress. The plane on which the principal stress exists is termed a *principal plane.* For a condition of plane stress, there are two principal planes through every point in a stressed body and these planes are mutually perpendicular. Moreover, one principal stress is the maximum normal stress existing at that point; the other is the minimum normal stress.

Let $s_x$ and $s_y$ = the principal stress in the $x$ and $y$ direction, respectively; $s_n$ = normal stress on the plane making an angle $\theta$ with the $y$ axis; $s_s$ = shearing stress on this plane. All stresses are expressed in pounds per square inch (kilopascals) and all angles in degrees. Tensile stresses are positive; compressive stresses are negative.

Applying the usual stress equations yields $s_n = s_y + (s_x - s_y) \cos^2 \theta$; $s_s = \frac{1}{2}(s_x - s_y)$ $\sin 2\theta$. Substituting gives $s_n = 2400 + (6300 - 2400)0.766^2 = 4690$-lb/sq.in. (32,337.6-kPa) tension, and $s_s = \frac{1}{2}(6300 - 2400)0.985 = 1920$ lb/sq.in. (13,238.4 kPa).

### 2. *Apply the graphical method of solution*
Construct, in Fig. 20*b*, Mohr's circle of stress thus: Using a suitable scale, draw $OA = s_y$, and $OB = s_x$. Draw a circle having *AB* as its diameter. Draw the radius *CD* making an angle of $2\theta = 80°$ with *AB*. Through *D*, drop a perpendicular *DE* to *AB*. Then $OE = s_n$ and $ED = s_s$. Scale *OE* and *ED* to obtain the normal and shearing stresses on plane *AE*.

*Related Calculations.* The normal stress may also be computed from $s_n = (s_x + s_y)0.5 + (s_x - s_y)0.5 \cos 2\theta$.

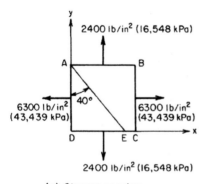

2400 lb/in² (16,548 kPa)

6300 lb/in² (43,439 kPa)

6300 lb/in² (43,439 kPa)

40°

2400 lb/in² (16,548 kPa)

(a) Stresses on prism

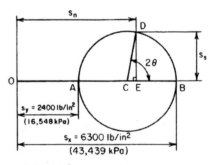

$s_y$ = 2400 lb/in² (16,548 kPa)

$s_x$ = 6300 lb/in² (43,439 kPa)

(b) Mohr's circle of stress

**FIGURE 20**

## EVALUATION OF PRINCIPAL STRESSES

The prism $ABCD$ in Fig. 21$a$ is subjected to the normal and shearing stresses shown. Construct Mohr's circle to determine the principal stresses at $A$, and locate the principal planes.

### Calculation Procedure:

### 1. Draw the lines representing the normal stresses (Fig. 21b)
Through the origin $O$, draw a horizontal base line. Locate points $E$ and $F$ such that $OE = 8400$ lb/sq.in. (57,918.0 kPa) and $OF = 2000$ lb/sq.in. (13,790.0 kPa). Since both normal stresses are tensile, $E$ and $F$ lie to the right of $O$. Note that the construction required here is the converse of that required in the previous calculation procedure.

### 2. Draw the lines representing the shearing stresses
Construct the vertical lines $EG$ and $FH$ such that $EG = 3600$ lb/sq.in. (24,822.0 kPa), and $FH = -3600$ lb/sq.in. ($-24,822.0$ kPa).

### 3. Continue the construction
Draw line $GH$ to intersect the base line at $C$.

### 4. Construct Mohr's circle
Draw a circle having $GH$ as diameter, intersecting the base line at $A$ and $B$. Then lines $OA$ and $OB$ represent the principal stresses.

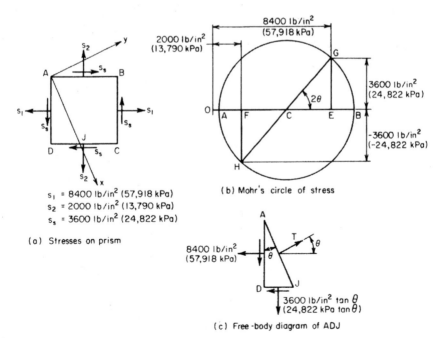

$s_1 = 8400$ lb/in² (57,918 kPa)
$s_2 = 2000$ lb/in² (13,790 kPa)
$s_s = 3600$ lb/in² (24,822 kPa)

(a) Stresses on prism

(b) Mohr's circle of stress

(c) Free-body diagram of ADJ

**FIGURE 21**

### 5. Scale the diagram
Scale $OA$ and $OB$ to obtain $f_{max} = 10,020$ lb/sq.in. (69,087.9 kPa); $f_{min} = 380$ lb/sq.in. (2620.1 kPa). Both stresses are tension.

### 6. Determine the stress angle
Scale angle $BCG$ and measure it as 48°22′. The angle between the $x$ axis, on which the maximum stress exists, and the side $AD$ of the prism is one-half of $BCG$.

### 7. Construct the x and y axes
In Fig. 21$a$, draw the $x$ axis, making a counterclockwise angle of 24°11′ with $AD$. Draw the $y$ axis perpendicular thereto.

### 8. Verify the locations of the principal planes
Consider $ADJ$ as a free body. Set the length $AD$ equal to unity. In Fig. 21$c$, since there is no shearing stress on $AJ$, $\Sigma F_H = T \cos \theta - 8400 - 3600 \tan \theta = 0$; $T \cos \theta = 8400 + 3600(0.45) = 10,020$ lb/sq.in. (69,087.9 kPa). The stress on $AJ = T/AJ = T \cos \theta = 10,020$ lb/sq.in. (69,087.9 kPa).


## HOOP STRESS IN THIN-WALLED CYLINDER UNDER PRESSURE

A steel pipe 5 ft (1.5 m) in diameter and $^3/_8$ in. (9.53 mm) thick sustains a fluid pressure of 180 lb/sq.in. (1241.1 kPa). Determine the hoop stress, the longitudinal stress, and the increase in diameter of this pipe. Use 0.25 for Poisson's ratio.


### Calculation Procedure:

### 1. Compute the hoop stress
Use the relation $s = pD/(2t)$, where $s$ = hoop or tangential stress, lb/sq.in. (kPa); $p$ = radial pressure, lb/sq.in. (kPa); $D$ = internal diameter of cylinder, in. (mm); $t$ = cylinder wall thickness, in. (mm). Thus, for this cylinder, $s = 180(60)/[2(^3/_8)] = 14,400$ lb/sq.in. (99,288.0 kPa).

### 2. Compute the longitudinal stress
Use the relation $s' = pD/(4t)$, where $s'$ = longitudinal stress, i.e., the stress parallel to the longitudinal axis of the cylinder, lb/sq.in. (kPa), with other symbols as before. Substituting yields $s' = 7200$ lb/sq.in. (49,644.0 kPa).

### 3. Compute the increase in the cylinder diameter
Use the relation $\Delta D = (D/E)(s - vs')$, where $v$ = Poisson's ratio. Thus $\Delta D = 60(14,400 - 0.25 \times 7200)/(30 \times 10^6) = 0.0252$ in. (0.6401 mm).


## STRESSES IN PRESTRESSED CYLINDER

A steel ring having an internal diameter of 8.99 in. (228.346 mm) and a thickness of $^1/_4$ in. (6.35 mm) is heated and allowed to shrink over an aluminum cylinder having an external diameter of 9.00 in. (228.6 mm) and a thickness of $^1/_2$ in. (12.7 mm). After the steel cools, the cylinder is subjected to an internal pressure of 800 lb/sq.in. (5516 kPa). Find the stresses in the two materials. For aluminum, $E = 10 \times 10^6$ lb/sq.in. (6.895 × 10$^7$ kPa).

## Calculation Procedure:

### 1. Compute the radial pressure caused by prestressing

Use the relation $p = 2\Delta D/\{D^2[1/(t_aE_a) + 1/(t_sE_s)]\}$, where $p$ = radial pressure resulting from prestressing, lb/sq.in. (kPa), with other symbols the same as in the previous calculation procedure and the subscripts $a$ and $s$ referring to aluminum and steel, respectively. Thus, $p = 2(0.01)/\{9^2[1/(0.5 \times 10 \times 10^6) + 1/(0.25 \times 30 \times 10^6)]\} = 741$ lb/sq.in. (5109.2 kPa).

### 2. Compute the corresponding prestresses

Using the subscripts 1 and 2 to denote the stresses caused by prestressing and internal pressure, respectively, we find $s_{a1} = pD/(2t_a)$, where the symbols are the same as in the previous calculation procedure. Thus, $s_{a1} = 741(9)/[2(0.5)] = 6670$-lb/sq.in. (45,989.7-kPa) compression. Likewise, $s_{s1} = 741(9)/[2(0.25)] = 13,340$-lb/sq.in. (91,979-kPa) tension.

### 3. Compute the stresses caused by internal pressure

Use the relation $s_{s2}/s_{a2} = E_s/E_a$ or, for this cylinder, $s_{s2}/s_{a2} = (30 \times 10^6)/(10 \times 10^6) = 3$. Next, compute $s_{a2}$ from $t_a s_{a2} \, t_s s_{s2} = pD/2$, or $s_{a2} = 800(9)/[2(0.5 + 0.25 \times 3)] = 2880$-lb/sq.in. (19,857.6-kPa) tension. Also, $s_{s2} = 3(2880) = 8640$-lb/sq.in. (59,572.8-kPa) tension.

### 4. Compute the final stresses

Sum the results in steps 2 and 3 to obtain the final stresses: $s_{a3} = 6670 - 2880 = 3790$-lb/sq.in. (26,132.1-kPa) compression; $s_{s3} = 13,340 + 8640 = 21,980$-lb/sq.in. (151,552.1-kPa) tension.

### 5. Check the accuracy of the results

Ascertain whether the final diameters of the steel ring and aluminum cylinder are equal. Thus, setting $s' = 0$ in. $\Delta D = (D/E)(s - vs')$, we find $\Delta D_a = -3790(9)/(10 \times 10^6) = -0.0034$ in. (−0.0864 mm), $D_a = 9.0000 - 0.0034 = 8.9966$ in. (228.51 mm). Likewise, $\Delta D_s = 21,980(9)/(30 \times 10^6) = 0.0066$ in. (0.1676 mm), $D_s = 8.99 + 0.0066 = 8.9966$ in. (228.51 mm). Since the computed diameters are equal, the results are valid.


## HOOP STRESS IN THICK-WALLED CYLINDER

A cylinder having an internal diameter of 20 in. (508 mm) and an external diameter of 36 in. (914 mm) is subjected to an internal pressure of 10,000 lb/sq.in. (68,950 kPa) and an external pressure of 2000 lb/sq.in. (13,790 kPa) as shown in Fig. 22. Determine the hoop stress at the inner and outer surfaces of the cylinder.


## Calculation Procedure:

### 1. Compute the hoop stress at the inner surface of the cylinder

Use the relation $s_i = [p_1(r_1^2 + r_2^2) - 2p_2r_2^2]/(r_2^2 - r_1^2)$, where $s_i$ = hoop stress at inner surface, lb/sq.in. (kPa); $p_1$ = internal pressure, lb/sq.in. (kPa); $r_1$ = internal radius, in. (mm); $r_2$ = external radius, in. (mm); $p_2$ = external pressure, lb/sq.in. (kPa). Substituting gives $s_i = [10,000(100 + 324) - 2(2000)(324)]/(324 - 100) = 13,100$-lb/sq.in. (90,324.5-kPa) tension.

### 2. Compute the hoop stress at the outer cylinder surface

Use the relation $s_0 = [2p_1r_1^2 - p_2(r_1^2 + r_2^2)]/(r_2^2 - r_1^2)$, where the symbols are as before. Substituting gives $s_0 = [2(10,000)(100) - 2000(100 + 324)]/(324 - 100) = 5100$-lb/sq.in. (35,164.5-kPa) tension.

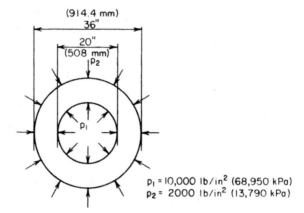

$p_1 = 10,000$ lb/in² (68,950 kPa)
$p_2 = 2000$ lb/in² (13,790 kPa)

**FIGURE 22.** Thick-walled cylinder under internal and external pressure.

### 3. Check the accuracy of the results

Use the relation $s_1r_1 - s_0r_2 = [(r_2 - r_1)/(r_2 + r_1)](p_1r_1 + p_2r_2)$. Substituting the known values verifies the earlier calculations.

## THERMAL STRESS RESULTING FROM HEATING A MEMBER

A steel member 18 ft (5.5 m) long is set snugly between two walls and heated 80°F (44.4°C). If each wall yields 0.015 in. (0.381 mm), what is the compressive stress in the member? Use a coefficient of thermal expansion of $6.5 \times 10^{-6}$/°F ($1.17 \times 10^{-5}$/°C) for steel.

### Calculation Procedure:

### 1. Compute the thermal expansion of the member without restraint

Replace the true condition of partial restraint with the following equivalent conditions: The member is first allowed to expand freely under the temperature rise and is then compressed to its true final length.

To compute the thermal expansion without restraint, use the relation $AL = cL\Delta T$, where $c$ = coefficient of thermal expansion, /°F (/°C); $\Delta T$ = increase in temperature, °F (°C); $L$ = original length of member, in. (mm); $\Delta L$ = increase in length of the member, in. (mm). Substituting gives $\Delta L = 6.5(10^{-6})(18)(12)(80) = 0.1123$ in. (2.852 mm).

### 2. Compute the linear restraint exerted by the walls

The walls yield $2(0.015) = 0.030$ in. (0.762 mm). Thus, the restraint exerted by the walls is $\Delta L_w = 0.1123 - 0.030 = 0.0823$ in. (2.090 mm).

### 3. Determine the compressive stress

Use the relation $s = E\Delta L/L$, where the symbols are as given earlier. Thus, $s = 30(10^6)(0.0823)/[18(12)]$ 11,430 lb/sq.in. (78,809.9 kPa).

## THERMAL EFFECTS IN COMPOSITE MEMBER HAVING ELEMENTS IN PARALLEL

A $1/2$-in. (12.7-mm) diameter Copperweld bar consists of a steel core $3/8$ in. (9.53 mm) in diameter and a copper skin $1/16$ in. (1.6 mm) thick. What is the elongation of a 1-ft (0.3-m) length of this bar, and what is the internal force between the steel and copper arising from a temperature rise of 80°F (44.4°C)? Use the following values for thermal expansion coefficients: $c_s = 6.5 \times 10^{-6}$ and $c_c = 9.0 \times 10^{-6}$, where the subscripts $s$ and $c$ refer to steel and copper, respectively. Also, $E_c = 15 \times 10^6$ lb/sq.in. (1.03 $\times 10^8$ kPa).

### Calculation Procedure:

### 1. Determine the cross-sectional areas of the metals

The total area $A = 0.1963$ sq.in. (1.266 cm²). The area of the steel $A_s = 0.1105$ sq.in. (0.712 cm²). By difference, the area of the copper $A_c = 0.0858$ sq.in. (0.553 cm²).

### 2. Determine the coefficient of expansion of the composite member

Weight the coefficients of expansion of the two members according to their respective AE values. Thus

| | |
|---|---|
| $A_s E_s$ (relative) = 0.1105 × 30 × 10⁶ = 3315 | |
| $A_c E_c$ (relative) = 0.0858 × 15 × 10⁶ = 1287 | |
| Total | 4602 |

Then the coefficient of thermal expansion of the composite member is $c = (3315c_s + 1287c_c)/4602 = 7.2 \times 10^{-6}/°F$ (1.30 $\times 10^{-5}/°C$).

### 3. Determine the thermal expansion of the 1-ft (0.3-m) section

Using the relation $\Delta L = cL\Delta T$, we get $\Delta L = 7.2(10^6)(12)(80) = 0.00691$ in. (0.17551 mm).

### 4. Determine the expansion of the first material without restraint

Using the same relation as in step 3 for copper *without* restraint yields $\Delta L_c = 9.0(10^{-6}) \times (12)(80) = 0.00864$ in. (0.219456 mm).

### 5. Compute the restraint of the first material

The copper is restrained to the amount computed in step 3. Thus, the restraint exerted by the steel is $\Delta L_{cs} = 0.00864 - 0.00691 = 0.00173$ in. (0.043942 mm).

### 6. Compute the restraining force exerted by the second material

Use the relation $P = (A_c E_c \Delta L_{cs})/L$, where the symbols are as given before: $P = [1,287,000(0.00173)]/12 = 185$ lb (822.9 N).

### 7. Verify the results obtained

Repeat steps 4, 5, and 6 with the two materials interchanged. So $\Delta L_s = 6.5(10^{-6})(12)(80) = 0.00624$ in. (0.15849 mm); $\Delta L_{sc} = 0.00691 - 0.00624 = 0.00067$ in. (0.01701 mm). Then $P = 3,315,000(0.00067)/12 = 185$ lb (822.9 N), as before.

## THERMAL EFFECTS IN COMPOSITE
## MEMBER HAVING ELEMENTS IN SERIES

The aluminum and steel bars in Fig. 23 have cross-sectional areas of 1.2 and 1.0 sq.in. (7.7 and 6.5 cm²), respectively. The member is restrained against lateral deflection. A temperature rise of 100°F (55°C) causes the length of the member to increase to 42.016 in. (106.720 cm). Determine the stress and deformation of each bar. For aluminum, $E = 10 \times 10^6$ $c = 13.0 \times 10^{-6}$; for steel, $c = 6.5 \times 10^{-6}$.

### Calculation Procedure:

#### 1. Express the deformation of each bar resulting from the temperature change and the compressive force

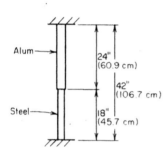

**FIGURE 23**

The temperature rise causes the bar to expand, whereas the compressive force resists this expansion. Thus, the net expansion is the difference between these two changes, or $\Delta L_a = cL\Delta T - PL/(AE)$, where the subscript $a$ refers to the aluminum bar; the other symbols are the same as given earlier. Substituting gives $\Delta L_a = 13.0 \times 10^{-6}(24)(100) - P(24)/[1.2(10 \times 10^6)] = (31,200 - 2P)10^{-6}$, Eq. a. Likewise, for steel: $\Delta L_s = 6.5 \times 10^{-6}(18)(100) - P(18)/[1.0(30 \times 10^6)] = (11,700 - 0.6P)10^{-6}$, Eq. b.

#### 2. Sum the results in step 1 to obtain the total deformation of the member

Set the result equal to 0.016 in. (0.4064 mm); solve for P. Or, $\Delta L = (42,900 - 2.6P)10^{-6} = 0.016$ in. (0.4064 mm); $P = (42,900 - 16,000)/2.6 = 10,350$ lb (46,037 N).

#### 3. Determine the stresses and deformation

Substitute the computed value of $P$ in the stress equation $s = P/A$. For aluminum $s_a = 10,350/1.2 = 8630$ lb/sq.in. (59,503.9 kPa). Then $\Delta L_a = (31,200 - 2 \times 10,350)10^{-6} = 0.0105$ in. (0.2667 mm). Likewise, for steel $s_s = 10,350/1.0 = 10,350$ lb/sq.in. (71,363.3 kPa); and $\Delta L_s = (11,700 - 0.6 \times 10,350)10^{-6} = 0.0055$ in. (0.1397 mm).

## SHRINK-FIT STRESS AND RADIAL
## PRESSURE

An open steel cylinder having an internal diameter of 4 ft (1.2 m) and a wall thickness of 5/16 in. (7.9 mm) is to be heated to fit over an iron casting. The internal diameter of the cylinder before heating is 1/32 in. (0.8 mm) less than that of the casting. How much must the temperature of the cylinder be increased to provide a clearance of 1/32 in. (0.8 mm) all around between the cylinder and casting? If the casting is considered rigid, what stress will exist in the cylinder after it cools, and what radial pressure will it then exert on the casting?

**Calculation Procedure:**

**1. Compute the temperature rise required**
Use the relation $\Delta T = \Delta D/(cD)$, where $\Delta T$ = temperature rise required, °F (°C); $\Delta D$ = change in cylinder diameter, in. (mm); $c$ = coefficient of expansion of the cylinder = $6.5 \times 10^{-6}$/°F ($1.17 \times 10^{-5}$/°C); $D$ = cylinder internal diameter before heating, in. (mm). Thus $\Delta T = (3/32)/[6.5 \times 10^{-6}(48)] = 300$°F (167°C).

**2. Compute the hoop stress in the cylinder**
Upon cooling, the cylinder has a diameter $1/32$ in. (0.8 mm) larger than originally. Compute the hoop stress from $s = E\Delta D/D = 30 \times 10^6(1/32)/48 = 19,500$ lb/sq.in. (134,452.5 kPa).

**3. Compute the associated radial pressure**
Use the relation $p = 2ts/D$, where $p$ = radial pressure, lb/sq.in. (kPa), with the other symbols as given earlier. Thus $p = 2(5/16)(19,500)/48 = 254$ lb/sq.in. (1751.3 kPa).

## TORSION OF A CYLINDRICAL SHAFT

A torque of 8000 lb·ft (10,840 N·m) is applied at the ends of a 14-ft (4.3-m) long cylindrical shaft having an external diameter of 5 in. (127 mm) and an internal diameter of 3 in. (76.2 mm). What are the maximum shearing stress and the angle of twist of the shaft if the modulus of rigidity of the shaft is $6 \times 10^6$ lb/sq.in. ($4.1 \times 10^4$ MPa)?

**Calculation Procedure:**

**1. Compute the polar moment of inertia of the shaft**
For a hollow circular shaft, $J = (\pi/32)(D^4 - d^4)$, where $J$ = polar moment of inertia of a transverse section of the shaft with respect to the longitudinal axis, in$^4$ (cm$^4$); $D$ = external diameter of shaft, in. (mm); $d$ = internal diameter of shaft, in. (mm). Substituting gives $J = (\pi/32)(5^4 - 3^4) = 53.4$ in$^4$ (2222.6 cm$^4$).

**2. Compute the shearing stress in the shaft**
Use the relation $s_s = TR/J$, where $s_s$ = shearing stress, lb/sq.in. (MPa); $T$ = applied torque, lb·in. (N·m); $H$ = radius of shaft, in. (mm). Thus $s_s = [(8000)(12)(2.5)]/53.4 = 4500$ lb/sq.in. (31,027.5 kPa).

**3. Compute the angle of twist of the shaft**
Use the relation $\theta = TL/JG$, where $\theta$ = angle of twist, rad; $L$ = shaft length, in. (mm); $G$ = modulus of rigidity, lb/sq.in. (GPa). Thus $\theta = (8000)(12)(14)(12)/[53.4(6,000,000)] = 0.050$ rad, or 2.9°.

## ANALYSIS OF A COMPOUND SHAFT

The compound shaft in Fig. 24 was formed by rigidly joining two solid segments. What torque may be applied at $B$ if the shearing stress is not to exceed 15,000 lb/sq.in. (103.4 MPa) in the steel and 10,000 lb/sq.in. (69.0 MPa) in the bronze? Here $G_s = 12 \times 10^6$ lb/sq.in. (82.7 GPa); $G_b = 6 \times 10^6$ lb/sq.in. (41.4 GPa).

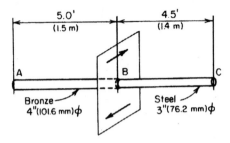

**FIGURE 24.** Compound shaft.

## Calculation Procedure:

### 1. Determine the relationship between the torque in the shaft segments

Since segments $AB$ and $BC$ (Fig. 24) are twisted through the same angle, the torque applied at the junction of these segments is distributed in proportion to their relative rigidities. Using the subscripts $s$ and $b$ to denote steel and bronze, respectively, we see that $\theta = T_s L_s/(J_s G_s) = T_b L_b/(J_b G_b)$, where the symbols are as given in the previous calculation procedure. Solving yields $T_s = (5/4.5)(34/44)(12/6)T_b = 0.703\, T_b$.

### 2. Establish the relationship between the shearing stresses

For steel, $s_{ss} = 16T_s/(\pi D^3)$, where the symbols are as given earlier. Thus $s_{ss} = 16(0.703T_b)/(\pi 3^3)$. Likewise, for bronze, $s_{sb} = 16T_b/(\pi 4^3)$, $\therefore s_{ss} = 0.703(4^3/3^3)s_{sb} = 1.67s_{sb}$.

### 3. Compute the allowable torque

Ascertain which material limits the capacity of the member, and compute the allowable torque by solving the shearing-stress equation for $T$.

If the bronze were stressed to 10,000 lb/sq.in. (69.0 MPa), inspection of the above relations shows that the steel would be stressed to 16,700 lb/sq.in. (115.1 MPa), which exceeds the allowed 15,000 lb/sq.in. (103.4 MPa). Hence, the steel limits the capacity. Substituting the allowed shearing stress of 15,000 lb/sq.in. (103.4 MPa) gives $T_s = 15,000\pi(3^3)/[16(12) = 6630$ lb·ft (8984.0 N·m); also, $T_b = 6630/0.703 = 9430$ lb·ft (12,777.6 N·m). Then $T = 6630 + 9430 = 16,060$ lb·ft (21,761.3 N·m).

# Stresses in Flexural Members

In the analysis of beam action, the general assumption is that the beam is in a horizontal position and carries vertical loads lying in an axis of symmetry of the transverse section of the beam.

The vertical shear $V$ at a given section of the beam is the algebraic sum of all vertical forces to the left of the section, with an upward force being considered positive.

The bending moment $M$ at a given section of the beam is the algebraic sum of the moments of all forces to the left of the section with respect to that section, a clockwise moment being considered positive.

If the proportional limit of the beam material is not exceeded, the bending stress (also called the flexural, or fiber, stress) at a section varies linearly across the depth of the section, being zero at the neutral axis. A positive bending moment induces compressive stresses in the fibers above the neutral axis and tensile stresses in the fibers below. Consequently, the elastic curve of the beam is concave upward where the bending moment is positive.

## SHEAR AND BENDING MOMENT IN A BEAM

Construct the shear and bending-moment diagrams for the beam in Fig. 25. Indicate the value of the shear and bending moment at all significant sections.

### Calculation Procedure:

### 1. Replace the distributed load on each interval with its equivalent concentrated load

Where the load is uniformly distributed, this equivalent load acts at the center of the interval of the beam. Thus $W_{AB} = 2(4) = 8$ kips (35.6 kN); $W_{BC} = 2(6) = 12$ kips (53.3 kN); $W_{AC} = 8 + 12 = 20$ kips (89.0 kN); $W_{CD} = 3(15) = 45$ kips (200.1 kN); $W_{DE} = 1.4(5) = 7$ kips (31.1 kN).

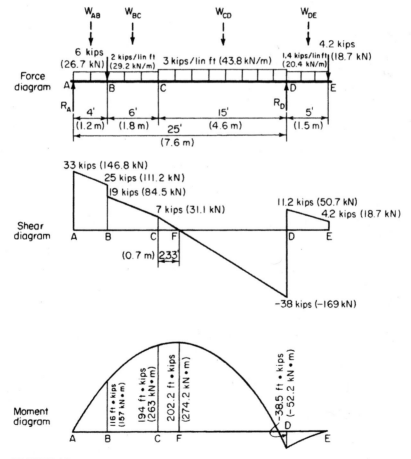

**FIGURE 25**

### 2. Determine the reaction at each support

Take moments with respect to the other support. Thus $\Sigma M_D = 25R_A - 6(21) - 20(20) - 45(7.5) + 7(2.5) + 4.2(5) = 0$; $\Sigma M_A = 6(4) + 20(5) + 45(17.5) + 7(27.5) + 4.2(30) - 25R_D = 0$. Solving gives $R_A = 33$ kips (146.8 kN); $R_D = 49.2$ kips (218.84 kN).

### 3. Verify the computed results and determine the shears

Ascertain that the algebraic sum of the vertical forces is zero. If this is so, the computed results are correct.

Starting at $A$, determine the shear at every significant section, or directly to the left or right of that section if a concentrated load is present. Thus $V_A$ at right $= 33$ kips (146.8 kN); $V_B$ at left $= 33 - 8 = 25$ kips (111.2 kN); $V_B$ at right $= 25 - 6 = 19$ kips (84.5 kN); $V_C = 19 - 12 = 7$ kips (31.1 kN); $V_D$ at left $= 7 - 45 = -38$ kips (−169.0 kN); $V_D$ at right $= -38 + 49.2 = 11.2$ kips (49.8 kN); $V_E$ at left $= 11.2 - 7 = 4.2$ kips (18.7 kN); $V_E$ at right $= 4.2 - 4.2 = 0$.

### 4. Plot the shear diagram

Plot the points representing the forces in the previous step in the shear diagram. Since the loading between the significant sections is uniform, connect these points with straight lines. In general, the slope of the shear diagram is given by $dV/dx = -w$, where $w =$ unit load at the given section and $x =$ distance from left end to the given section.

### 5. Determine the bending moment at every significant section

Starting at $A$, determine the bending moment at every significant section. Thus $M_A = 0$; $M_B = 33(4) - 8(2) = 116$ ft·kips (157 kN·m); $M_C = 33(10) - 8(8) - 6(6) - 12(3) = 194$ ft·kips (263 kN·m). Similarly, $M_D = -38.5$ ft·kips (−52.2 kN·m); $M_E = 0$.

### 6. Plot the bending-moment diagram

Plot the points representing the values in step 5 in the bending-moment diagram (Fig. 25). Complete the diagram by applying the slope equation $dM/dx = V$. where $V$ denotes the shear at the given section. Since this shear varies linearly between significant sections, the bending-moment diagram comprises a series of parabolic arcs.

### 7. Alternatively, apply a moment theorem

Use this theorem: If there are no externally applied moments in an interval 1-2 of the span, the difference between the bending moments is $M_2 - = M_1 = \int_1^2 V\, dx =$ the area under the shear diagram across the interval.

Calculate the areas under the shear diagram to obtain the following results: $M_A = 0$; $M_B = M_A + \frac{1}{2}(4)(33 + 25) = 116$ ft·kips (157.3 kN·m); $M_C = 116 + \frac{1}{2}(6)(19 + 7) = 194$ ft·kips (263 kN·m); $M_D = 194 + \frac{1}{2}(15)(7 - 38) = -38.5$ ft·kips (−52.2 kN·m); $M_E = -38.5 + \frac{1}{2}(5)(11.2 + 4.2) = 0$.

### 8. Locate the section at which the bending moment is maximum

As a corollary of the equation in step 6, the maximum moment occurs where the shear is zero or passes through zero under a concentrated load. Therefore, $CF = 7/3 = 2.33$ ft (0.710 m).

### 9. Compute the maximum moment

Using the computed value for $CF$, we find $M_F = 194 + \frac{1}{2}(2.33)(7) = 202.2$ ft·kips (274.18 kN·m).

## BEAM BENDING STRESSES

A beam having the trapezoidal cross section shown in Fig. 26a carries the loads indicated in Fig. 26b. What is the maximum bending stress at the top and at the bottom of this beam?

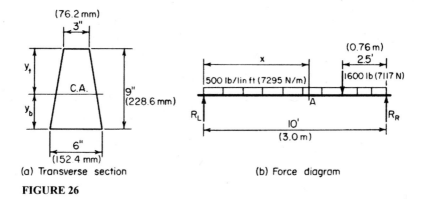

(a) Transverse section          (b) Force diagram

**FIGURE 26**

## Calculation Procedure:

### 1. Compute the left reaction and the section at which the shear is zero

The left reaction $R_L = \frac{1}{2}(10)(500) + 1600(2.5/10) = 2900$ lb (12,899.2 N). The section $A$ at which the shear is zero is $x = 2900/500 = 5.8$ ft (1.77 m).

### 2. Compute the maximum moment

Use the relation $M_A = \frac{1}{2}(2900)(5.8) = 8410$ lb·ft (11,395.6 N·m) = 100,900 lb·in. (11,399.682 N·m).

### 3. Locate the centroidal axis of the section

Use the AISC *Manual* for properties of the trapezoid. Or $y_t = (9/3)[(2 \times 6 + 3)1(6 + 3)] = 5$ in. (127 mm); $y_b = 4$ in. (101.6 mm).

### 4. Compute the moment of inertia of the section

Using the AISC *Manual*, $I = (9^3/36)[(6^2 + 4 \times 6 \times 3 + 3^2)/(6 + 3)] = 263.3$ in⁴ (10,959.36 cm⁴).

### 5. Compute the stresses in the beam

Use the relation $f = My/I$, where $f$ = bending stress in a given fiber, lb/sq.in. (kPa); $y$ = distance from neutral axis to given fiber, in. Thus $f_{top} = 100,900(5)/263.3 = 1916$-lb/sq.in. (13,210.8-kPa) compression, $f_{bottom} = 100,900(4)/263.3 = 1533$-lb/sq.in. (10,570.0-kPa) tension.

In general, the maximum bending stress at a section where the moment is $M$ is given by $f = M_C/I$, where $c$ = distance from the neutral axis to the outermost fiber, in. (mm). For a section that is symmetric about its centroidal axis, it is convenient to use the section modulus $S$ of the section, this being defined as $S = I/c$. Then $f = M/S$.

## ANALYSIS OF A BEAM ON MOVABLE SUPPORTS

The beam in Fig. 27a rests on two movable supports. It carries a uniform live load of $w$ lb/lin ft and a uniform dead load of $0.2w$ lb/lin ft. If the allowable bending stresses in tension and compression are identical, determine the optimal location of the supports.

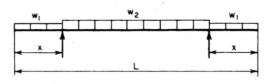

(a) Loads carried by overhanging beam

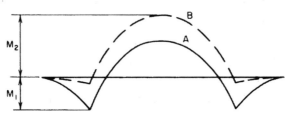

Diagram A. Full load on entire span
Diagram B. Dead load on overhangs; full load
between supports

(b) Bending-moment diagrams

**FIGURE 27**

## Calculation Procedure:

### 1. Place full load on the overhangs, and compute the negative moment

Refer to the moment diagrams. For every position of the supports, there is a corresponding maximum bending stress. The position for which this stress has the smallest value must be identified.

As the supports are moved toward the interior of the beam, the bending moments between the supports diminish in algebraic value. The optimal position of the supports is that for which the maximum potential negative moment $M_1$ is numerically equal to the maximum potential positive moment $M_2$. Thus, $M_1 = -1.2w(x^2/2) = -0.6wx^2$.

### 2. Place only the dead load on the overhangs and the full load between the supports. Compute the positive moment.

Sum the areas under the shear diagram to compute $M_2$. Thus, $M_2 = \frac{1}{2}[1.2w(L/2 - x)^2 - 0.2wx^2] = w(0.15L^2 - 0.6Lx + 0.5x^2)$.

### 3. Equate the absolute values of $M_1$ and $M_2$ and solve for x

Substituting gives $0.6x^2 = 0.15L^2 - 0.6Lx + 0.5x^2$; $x = L\overline{10.5^{0.5}} - 3) = 0.240L$.

## FLEXURAL CAPACITY OF A COMPOUND BEAM

A W16 × 45 steel beam in an existing structure was reinforced by welding a WT6 × 20 to the bottom flange, as in Fig. 28. If the allowable bending stress is 20,000 lb/sq.in. (137,900 kPa), determine the flexural capacity of the built-up member.

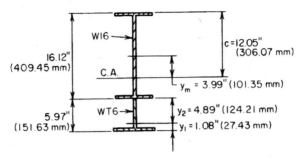

**FIGURE 28.** Compound beam.

## Calculation Procedure:

### 1. Obtain the properties of the elements

Using the AISC *Manual*, determine the following properties. For the W16 × 45, $d = 16.12$ in. (409.45 mm); $A = 13.24$ sq.in. (85.424 cm²); $I = 583$ in⁴ (24,266 cm⁴). For the WT6 × 20, $d = 5.97$ in. (151.63 mm); $A = 5.89$ sq.in. (38.002 cm²); $I = 14$ in⁴ (582.7 cm⁴); $y_1 = 1.08$ in. (27.43 mm); $y_2 = 5.97 - 1.08 = 4.89$ in. (124.21 mm).

### 2. Locate the centroidal axis of the section

Locate the centroidal axis of the section with respect to the centerline of the W16 × 45, and compute the distance $c$ from the centroidal axis to the outermost fiber. Thus, $y_m = 5.89[(8.06 + 4.89)]/(5.89 + 13.24) = 3.99$ in. (101.346 mm). Then $c = 8.06 + 3.99 = 12.05$ in. (306.07 mm).

### 3. Find the moment of inertia of the section with respect to its centroidal axis

Use the relation $I_0 + Ak^2$ for each member, and take the sum for the two members to find $I$ for the built-up beam. Thus, for the W16 × 45: $k = 3.99$ in. (101.346 mm); $I_0 + Ak^2$ $583 + 13.24(3.99)^2 = 793$ in⁴ (33,007.1 cm⁴). For the WT6 × 20: $k = 8.06 - 3.99 + 4.89 = 8.96$ in. (227.584 mm); $I_0 + Ak^2 = 14 + 5.89(8.96)^2 = 487$ in⁴ (20,270.4 cm⁴). Then $I = 793 + 487 = 1280$ in⁴ (53,277.5 cm⁴).

### 4. Apply the moment equation to find the flexural capacity

Use the relation $M = fI/c = 20,000(1280)/[12.05(12)] = 177,000$ lb·ft (240,012 N·m).

## ANALYSIS OF A COMPOSITE BEAM

An 8 × 12 in. (203.2 × 304.8 mm) timber beam (exact size) is reinforced by the addition of a 7 × ¹/₂ in. (177.8 × 12.7 mm) steel plate at the top and a 7-in. (177.8-mm) 9.8-lb (43.59-N) steel channel at the bottom, as shown in Fig. 29a. The allowable bending stresses are 22,000 lb/sq.in. (151,690 kPa) for steel and 1200 lb/sq.in. (8274 kPa) for timber. The modulus of elasticity of the timber is $1.2 × 10^6$ lb/sq.in. ($8.274 × 10^6$ kPa). How does the flexural strength of the reinforced beam compare with that of the original timber beam?

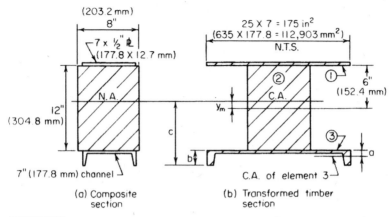

**FIGURE 29**

## Calculation Procedure:

### 1. Compute the rigidity of the steel compared with that of the timber

Let $n$ = the relative rigidity of the steel and timber. Then $n = E_s/E_t = (30 \times 10^6)/(1.2 \times 10^6) = 25$.

### 2. Transform the composite beam to an equivalent homogeneous beam

To accomplish this transformation, replace the steel with timber. Sketch the cross section of the transformed beam as in Fig. 29*b*. Determine the sizes of the hypothetical elements by retaining the dimensions normal to the axis of bending but multiplying the dimensions parallel to this axis by $n$.

### 3. Record the properties of each element of the transformed section

Element 1: $A = 25(7)(\frac{1}{2}) = 87.5$ sq.in. (564.55 cm²); $I_0$ is negligible.
Element 2: $A = 8(12) = 96$ sq.in. (619.4 cm²); $I_0 = \frac{1}{2}(8)12^3 = 1152$ in⁴ (4.795 dm⁴).
Element 3: Refer to the AISC *Manual* for the data; $A = 25(2.85) = 71.25$ sq.in. (459.71 cm²); $I_0 = 25(0.98) = 25$ in⁴ (1040.6 cm⁴); $a = 0.55$ in. (13.97 mm); $b = 2.09$ in. (53.09 mm).

### 4. Locate the centroidal axis of the transformed section

Take static moments of the areas with respect to the centerline of the 8 × 12 in. (203.2 × 304.8 mm) rectangle. Then $y_m = [87.5(6.25) - 71.25(6.55)]/(87.5 + 96 + 71.25) = 0.31$ in. (7.87 mm). The neutral axis of the composite section is at the same location as the centroidal axis of the transformed section.

### 5. Compute the moment of inertia of the transformed section

Apply the relation in step 3 of the previous calculation procedure. Then compute the distance $c$ to the outermost fiber. Thus, $I = 1152 + 25 + 87.5(6.25 - 0.31)^2 + 96(0.31)^2 + 71.25(6.55 + 0.31)^2 = 7626$ in⁴ (31.74 dm⁴). Also, $c = 0.31 + 6 + 2.09 = 8.40$ in. (213.36 mm).

### 6. Determine which material limits the beam capacity

Assume that the steel is stressed to capacity, and compute the corresponding stress in the transformed beam. Thus, $f = 22,000/25 = 880$ lb/sq.in. (6067.6 kPa) < 1200 lb/sq.in. (8274 kPa).

In the actual beam, the maximum timber stress, which occurs at the back of the channel, is even less than 880 lb/sq.in. (6067.6 kPa). Therefore, the strength of the member is controlled by the allowable stress in the steel.

### 7. Compare the capacity of the original and reinforced beams

Let subscripts 1 and 2 denote the original and reinforced beams, respectively. Compute the capacity of these members, and compare the results. Thus $M_1 = fI/c = 1200(1152)/6 = 230,000$ lb·in. (25,985.4 N·m); $M_2 = 880(7626)/8.40 = 799,000$ lb·in. (90,271.02 N·m); $M_2/M_1 = 799,000/230,000 = 3.47$. Thus, the reinforced beam is nearly $3\frac{1}{2}$ times as strong as the original beam, before reinforcing.

# BEAM SHEAR FLOW AND SHEARING STRESS

A timber beam is formed by securely bolting a $3 \times 6$ in. (76.2 × 152.4 mm) member to a $6 \times 8$ in. (152.4 × 203.2 mm) member (exact size), as shown in Fig. 30. If the beam carries a uniform load of 600 lb/lin ft (8.756 kN/m) on a simple span of 13 ft (3.9 m), determine the longitudinal shear flow and the shearing stress at the juncture of the two elements at a section 3 ft (0.91 m) from the support.

### Calculation Procedure:

### 1. Compute the vertical shear at the given section

Shear flow is the shearing force acting on a unit distance. In this instance, the shearing force on an area having the same width as the beam and a length of 1 in. (25.4 mm) measured along the beam span is required.

Using dimensions and data from Fig. 30, we find $R = \frac{1}{2}(600)(13) = 3900$ lb (17,347.2 N); $V = 3900 - 3(600) = 2100$ lb (9340.8 N).

### 2. Compute the moment of inertia of the cross section

$$I = (\tfrac{1}{12})(bd^3) = (\tfrac{1}{12})(6)(11)^3 = 666 \text{ in}^4 \ (2.772 \text{ dm}^4)$$

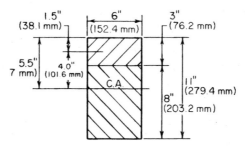

**FIGURE 30**

### 3. Determine the static moment of the cross-sectional area
Calculate the static moment $Q$ of the cross-sectional area above the plane under consideration with respect to the centroidal axis of the section. Thus, $Q = Ay = 3(6)(4) = 72 \text{ in}^3$ (1180.1 cm³).

### 4. Compute the shear flow
Compute the shear flow $q$, using $q = VQ/I = 2100(72)/666 = 227$ lb/lin in. (39.75 kN/m).

### 5. Compute the shearing stress
Use the relation $v = q/t = VQ/(It)$, where $t$ = width of the cross section at the given plane. Then $v = 227/6 = 38$ lb/sq.in. (262.0 kPa).

   Note that $v$ represents both the longitudinal and the transverse shearing stress at a particular point. This is based on the principle that the shearing stresses at a given point in two mutually perpendicular directions are equal.


## LOCATING THE SHEAR CENTER OF A SECTION

A cantilever beam carries the load shown in Fig. 31a and has the transverse section shown in Fig. 31b. Locate the shear center of the section.


## Calculation Procedure:

### 1. Construct a free-body diagram of a portion of the beam
Consider that the transverse section of a beam is symmetric solely about its horizontal centroidal axis. If bending of the beam is not to be accompanied by torsion, the vertical

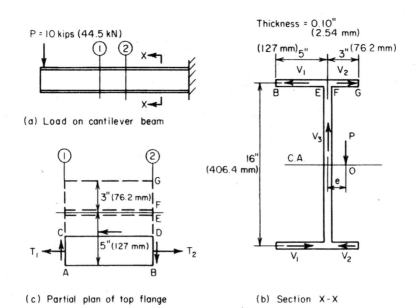

(a) Load on cantilever beam

(c) Partial plan of top flange

(b) Section X-X

**FIGURE 31**

shearing force at any section must pass through a particular point on the centroidal axis designated as the *shear*, or *flexural*, center.

Cut the beam at section 2, and consider the left portion of the beam as a free body. In Fig. 31$b$, indicate the resisting shearing forces $V_1$, $V_2$, and $V_3$ that the right-hand portion of the beam exerts on the left-hand portion at section 2. Obtain the directions of $V_1$ and $V_2$ this way: Isolate the segment of the beam contained between sections 1 and 2; then isolate a segment $ABDC$ of the top flange, as shown in Fig. 31$c$. Since the bending stresses at section 2 exceed those at section 1, the resultant tensile force $T_2$ exceeds $T_1$. The resisting force on $CD$ is therefore directed to the left. From the equation of equilibrium $\Sigma M = 0$ it follows that the resisting shears on $AC$ and $BD$ have the indicated direction to constitute a clockwise couple.

This analysis also reveals that the shearing stress varies linearly from zero at the edge of the flange to a maximum value at the juncture with the web.

## 2. Compute the shear flow
Determine the shear flow at $E$ and $F$ (Fig. 31) by setting $Q$ in $q = VQ/I$ equal to the static moment of the overhanging portion of the flange. (For convenience, use the dimensions to the centerline of the web and flange.) Thus $I = \frac{1}{12}(0.10)(16)^3 + 2(8)(0.10)(8)^2 = 137$ in$^4$ (5702.3 cm$^4$); $Q_{BE} = 5(0.10)(8) = 4.0$ in$^3$ (65.56 cm$^3$); $Q_{FG} = 3(0.10)(8) = 2.4$ in$^3$ (39.34 cm$^3$); $q_E = VQ_{BE}/I = 10,000(4.0)/137 = 292$ lb/lin in (51,137.0 N/m); $q_F = 10,000(2.4)/137 = 175$ lb/lin in (30,647.2 N/m).

## 3. Compute the shearing forces on the transverse section
Since the shearing stress varies linearly across the flange, $V_1 = \frac{1}{2}(292)(5) = 730$ lb (3247.0 N); $V_2 = \frac{1}{2}(175)(3) = 263$ lb (1169.8 N); $V_3 = P = 10,000$ lb (44,480 N).

## 4. Locate the shear center
Take moments of all forces acting on the left-hand portion of the beam with respect to a longitudinal axis through the shear center $O$. Thus $V_3e + 16(V_2 - V_1) = 0$, or $10,000e + 16(263 - 730) = 0$; $e = 0.747$ in. (18.9738 mm).

## 5. Verify the computed values
Check the computed values of $q_E$ and $q_F$ by considering the bending stresses directly. Apply the equation $\Delta f = Vy/I$, where $\Delta f =$ increase in bending stress per unit distance along the span at distance $y$ from the neutral axis. Then $\Delta f = 10,000(8)/137 = 584$ lb/(sq.in.·in) (158.52 MPa/m).

In Fig. 31$c$, set $AB = 1$ in. (25.4 mm). Then $q_E = 584(5)(0.10) = 292$ lb/lin in (51,137.0 N/m); $q_F = 584(3)(0.10) = 175$ lb/lin in (30,647.1 N/m).

Although a particular type of beam (cantilever) was selected here for illustrative purposes and a numeric value was assigned to the vertical shear, note that the value of $e$ is independent of the type of beam, form of loading, or magnitude of the vertical shear. The location of the shear center is a geometric characteristic of the transverse section.

# BENDING OF A CIRCULAR FLAT PLATE

A circular steel plate 2 ft (0.61 m) in diameter and $\frac{1}{2}$ in. (12.7 mm) thick, simply supported along its periphery, carries a uniform load of 20 lb/sq.in. (137.9 kPa) distributed over the entire area. Determine the maximum bending stress and deflection of this plate, using 0.25 for Poisson's ratio.

## Calculation Procedure:

### 1. Compute the maximum stress in the plate

If the maximum deflection of the plate is less than about one-half the thickness, the effects of diaphragm behavior may be disregarded.

Compute the maximum stress, using the relation $f = (^3/_8)(3 + v)w(R/t)^2$, where $R$ = plate radius, in. (mm); $t$ = plate thickness, in. (mm); $v$ = Poisson's ratio. Thus, $f = (^3/_8)(3.25)(20)(12/0.5)^2 = 14,000$ lb/sq.in. (96,530.0 kPa).

### 2. Compute the maximum deflection of the plate

Use the relation $y = (1 - v)(5 + v)fR^2/[2(3 + v)Et] = 0.75(5.25)(14,000)(12)^2/[2(3.25)(30 \times 10^6)(0.5)] = 0.081$ in. (2.0574 mm). Since the deflection is less than one-half the thickness, the foregoing equations are valid in this case.

## BENDING OF A RECTANGULAR FLAT PLATE

A $2 \times 3$ ft ($61.0 \times 91.4$ cm) rectangular plate, simply supported along its periphery, is to carry a uniform load of 8 lb/sq.in. (55.2 kPa) distributed over the entire area. If the allowable bending stress is 15,000 lb/sq.in. (103.4 MPa), what thickness of plate is required?

## Calculation Procedure:

### 1. Select an equation for the stress in the plate

Use the approximation $f = a^2b^2w/[2(a^2 + b^2)t^2]$, where $a$ and $b$ denote the length of the plate sides, in. (mm).

### 2. Compute the required plate thickness

Solve the equation in step 1 for $t$. Thus $t^2 = a^2b^2w/[2(a^2 + b^2)f] = 2^2(3)^2(144)(8)/[2(2^2 + 3^2)(15,000)] = 0.106$; $t = 0.33$ in. (8.382 mm).

## COMBINED BENDING AND AXIAL LOAD ANALYSIS

A post having the cross section shown in Fig. 32 carries a concentrated load of 100 kips (444.8 kN) applied at $R$. Determine the stress induced at each corner.

## Calculation Procedure:

### 1. Replace the eccentric load with an equivalent system

Use a concentric load of 100 kips (444.8 kN) and two couples producing the following moments with respect to the coordinate axes:

$$M_x = 100,000(2) = 200,000 \text{ lb·in. (25,960 N·m)}$$

$$M_y = 100,000(1) = 100,000 \text{ lb·in. (12,980 N·m)}$$

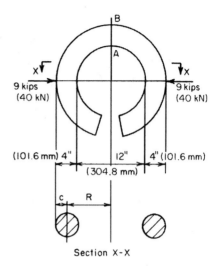

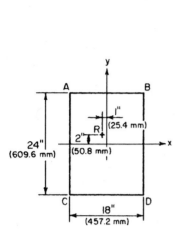

FIGURE 32. Transverse section of a post.

FIGURE 33. Curved member in bending.

## 2. Compute the section modulus

Determine the section modulus of the rectangular cross section with respect to each axis. Thus $S_x = (\frac{1}{6})bd^2 = (\frac{1}{6})(18)(24)^2 = 1728$ in³ (28,321.9 cm³); $S_y = (\frac{1}{6})(24)(18)^2 = 1296$ in³ (21,241 cm³).

## 3. Compute the stresses produced

Compute the uniform stress caused by the concentric load and the stresses at the edges caused by the bending moments. Thus $f_1 = P/A = 100,000/[18(24)] = 231$ lb/sq.in. (1592.7 kPa); $f_x = M_x/S_x = 200,000/1728 = 116$ lb/sq.in. (799.8 kPa); $f_y = M_y/S_y = 100,000/1296 = 77$ lb/sq.in. (530.9 kPa).

## 4. Determine the stress at each corner

Combine the results obtained in step 3 to obtain the stress at each corner. Thus $f_A = 231 + 116 + 77 = 424$ lb/sq.in. (2923.4 kPa); $f_B = 231 + 116 - 77 = 270$ lb/sq.in. (1861.5 kPa); $f_C = 231 - 116 + 77 = 192$ lb/sq.in. (1323.8 kPa); $f_D = 231 - 116 - 77 = 38$ lb/sq.in. (262.0 kPa). These stresses are all compressive because a positive stress is considered compressive, whereas a tensile stress is negative.

## 5. Check the computed corner stresses

Use the following equation that applies to the special case of a rectangular cross section: $f = (P/A)(1 \pm 6e_x/d_x + 6e_y/d_y)$, where $e_x$ and $e_y$ = eccentricity of load with respect to the $x$ and $y$ axes, respectively; $d_x$ and $d_y$ = side of rectangle, in. (mm), normal to $x$ and $y$ axes, respectively. Solving for the quantities within the brackets gives $6e_x/d_x = 6(2)/24 = 0.5$; $6e_y/d_y = 6(1)/18 = 0.33$. Then $f_A = 231(1 + 0.5 + 0.33) = 424$ lb/sq.in. (2923.4 kPa); $f_B = 231(1 + 0.5 - 0.33) = 270$ lb/sq.in. (1861.5 kPa); $f_C = 231(1 - 0.5 + 0.33) = 192$ lb/sq.in. (1323.8 kPa); $f_D = 231(1 - 0.5 - 0.33) = 38$ lb/sq.in. (262.0 kPa). These results verify those computed in step 4.

## FLEXURAL STRESS IN A CURVED MEMBER

The ring in Fig. 33 has an internal diameter of 12 in. (304.8 mm) and a circular cross section of 4-in (101.6-mm) diameter. Determine the normal stress at $A$ and at $B$ (Fig. 33).

### Calculation Procedure:

### 1. Determine the geometrical properties of the cross section

The area of the cross section is $A = 0.7854(4)^2 = 12.56$ sq.in. (81.037 cm²); the section modulus is $S = 0.7854(2)^3 = 6.28$ in³ (102.92 cm³). With $c = 2$ in. (50.8 mm), the radius of curvature to the centroidal axis of this section is $R = 6 + 2 = 8$ in. (203.2 mm).

### 2. Compute the R/c ratio and determine the correction factors

Refer to a table of correction factors for curved flexural members, such as Roark—*Formulas for Stress and Strain*, and extract the correction factors at the inner and outer surface associated with the $R/c$ ratio. Thus $R/c = 8/2 = 4$; $k_i = 1.23$; $k_o = 0.84$.

### 3. Determine the normal stress

Find the normal stress at $A$ and $B$ caused by an equivalent axial load and moment. Thus $f_A = P/A + k_i(M/S) = 9000/12.56 + 1.23(9000 \times 8)/6.28 = 14,820$-lb/sq.in. (102,183.9-kPa) compression; $f_B = 9000/12.56 - 0.84(9000 \times 8)/6.28 = 8930$-lb/sq.in. (61,572.3-kPa) tension.

## SOIL PRESSURE UNDER DAM

A concrete gravity dam has the profile shown in Fig. 34. Determine the soil pressure at the toe and heel of the dam when the water surface is level with the top.

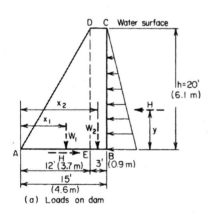

(a) Loads on dam

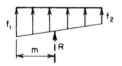

(b) Soil pressure under dam

**FIGURE 34**

### Calculation Procedure:

### 1. Resolve the dam into suitable elements

The soil prism underlying the dam may be regarded as a structural member subjected to simultaneous axial load and bending, the cross section of the member being identical with the bearing surface of the dam. Select a 1-ft (0.3-m) length of dam as representing the entire structure. The weight of the concrete is 150 lb/ft³ (23.56 kN/m³).

Resolve the dam into the elements *AED* and *EBCD*. Compute the weight of each element, and locate the resultant of the weight with respect to the toe. Thus $W_1 = \frac{1}{2}(12)(20)(150) = 18,000$ lb (80.06 kN); $W_2 = 3(20)(150) = 9000$ lb

(40.03 kN); $\Sigma W = 18{,}000 + 9000 = 27{,}000$ lb (120.10 kN). Then $x_1 = (^2/_3)(12) = 8.0$ ft (2.44 m); $x^2 = 12 + 1.5 = 13.5$ ft (4.11 m).

### 2. Find the magnitude and location of the resultant of the hydrostatic pressure

Calling the resultant $H = ^1/_2wh^2 = ^1/_2(62.4)(20)^2 = 12{,}480$ lb (55.51 kN), where $w$ = weight of water, lb/ft$^3$ (N/m$^3$), and $h$ = water height, ft (m), then $y = (^1/_3)(20) = 6.67$ ft (2.03 m).

### 3. Compute the moment of the loads with respect to the base centerline

Thus, $M = 18{,}000(8 - 7.5) + 9000(13.5 - 7.5) - 12{,}480(6.67) = 20{,}200$ lb·ft (27,391 N·m) counterclockwise.

### 4. Compute the section modulus of the base

Use the relation $S = (^1/_6)bd^2 = (^1/_6)(1)(15)^2 = 37.5$ ft$^3$ (1.06 m$^3$).

### 5. Determine the soil pressure at the dam toe and heel

Compute the soil pressure caused by the combined axial load and bending. Thus $f_1 = \Sigma W/A + M/S = 27{,}000/15 + 20{,}200/37.5 = 2339$ lb/sq.ft. (111.99 kPa); $f_2 = 1800 - 539 = 1261$ lb/sq.ft. (60.37 kPa).

### 6. Verify the computed results

Locate the resultant $R$ of the trapezoidal pressure prism, and take its moment with respect to the centerline of the base. Thus $R = 27{,}000$ lb (120.10 kN); $m = (15/3)[(2 \times 1261 + 2339)/(1261 + 2339)] = 6.75$ ft (2.05 m); $M_R = 27{,}000(7.50 - 6.75) = 20{,}200$ lb·ft (27,391 N·m). Since the applied and resisting moments are numerically equal, the computed results are correct.

## LOAD DISTRIBUTION IN PILE GROUP

A continuous wall is founded on three rows of piles spaced 3 ft (0.91 m) apart. The longitudinal pile spacing is 4 ft (1.21 m) in the front and center rows and 6 ft (1.82 m) in the rear row. The resultant of vertical loads on the wall is 20,000 lb/lin ft (291.87 kN/m) and lies 3 ft 3 in. (99.06 cm) from the front row. Determine the pile load in each row.

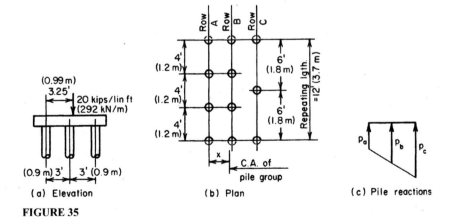

(a) Elevation  (b) Plan  (c) Pile reactions

**FIGURE 35**

### Calculation Procedure:

### 1. Identify the "repeating group" of piles

The concrete footing (Fig. 35a) binds the piles, causing the surface along the top of the piles to remain a plane as bending occurs. Therefore, the pile group may be regarded as a structural member subjected to axial load and bending, the cross section of the member being the aggregate of the cross sections of the piles.

Indicate the "repeating group" as shown in Fig. 35b.

### 2. Determine the area of the pile group and the moment of inertia

Calculate the area of the pile group, locate its centroidal axis, and find the moment of inertia. Since all the piles have the same area, set the area of a single pile equal to unity. Then $A = 3 + 3 + 2 = 8$.

Take moments with respect to row $A$. Thus $8x = 3(0) + 3(3) + 2(6)$; $x = 2.625$ ft (66.675 mm). Then $I = 3(2.625)^2 + 3(0.375)^2 + 2(3.375)^2 = 43.9$.

### 3. Compute the axial load and bending moment on the pile group

The axial load $P = 20,000(12) = 240,000$ lb (1067.5 kN); then $M = 240,000(3.25 - 2.625) = 150,000$ lb·ft (203.4 kN·m).

### 4. Determine the pile load in each row

Find the pile load in each row resulting from the combined axial load and moment. Thus, $P/A = 240,000/8 = 30,000$ lb (133.4 kN) per pile; then $M/I = 150,000/43.9 = 3420$. Also, $p_a = 30,000 - 3420(2.625) = 21,020$ lb (93.50 kN) per pile; $p_b = 30,000 + 3420(0.375) = 31,280$ lb (139.13 kN) per pile; $p_c = 30,000 + 3420(3.375) = 41,540$ lb (184.76 kN) per pile.

### 5. Verify the above results

Compute the total pile reaction, the moment of the applied load, and the pile reaction with respect to row $A$. Thus, $R = 3(21,020) + 3(31,280) + 2(41,540) = 239,980$ lb (1067.43 kN); then $M_a = 240,000(3.25) = 780,000$ lb·ft (1057.68 kN·m), and $M_r = 3(31,280)(3) + 2(41,540)(6) = 780,000$ lb·ft (1057.68 kN·m). Since $M_a = M_r$, the computed results are verified.

# Deflection of Beams

In this handbook the slope of the elastic curve at a given section of a beam is denoted by $\theta$, and the deflection, in inches, by $y$. The slope is considered positive if the section rotates in a clockwise direction under the bending loads. A downward deflection is considered positive. In all instances, the beam is understood to be prismatic, if nothing is stated to the contrary.

## DOUBLE-INTEGRATION METHOD OF DETERMINING BEAM DEFLECTION

The simply supported beam in Fig. 36 is subjected to a counterclockwise moment $N$ applied at the right-hand support. Determine the slope of the elastic curve at each support and the maximum deflection of the beam.

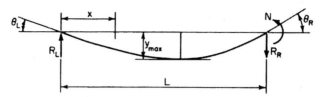

**FIGURE 36.** Deflection of simple beam under end moment.

## Calculation Procedure:

### 1. Evaluate the bending moment at a given section
Make this evaluation in terms of the distance $x$ from the left-hand support to this section. Thus $R_L = N/L$; $M = Nx/L$.

### 2. Write the differential equation of the elastic curve; integrate twice
Thus $EI\ d^2y/dx^2 = -M = -Nx/L$; $EI\ dy/dx = EI\theta = -Nx^2/(2L) + c_1$; $EIy = -Nx^3/(6L) + c_1x + c_2$.

### 3. Evaluate the constants of integration
Apply the following boundary conditions: When $x = 0$, $y = 0$; $\therefore c_2 = 0$; when $x = L$, $y = 0$; $\therefore c_1 = NL/6$.

### 4. Write the slope and deflection equations
Substitute the constant values found in step 3 in the equations developed in step 2. Thus $\theta = [N/(6EIL)](L^2 - 3x^2)$; $y = [Nx/(6EIL)](L^2 - x^2)$.

### 5. Find the slope at the supports
Substitute the values $x = 0$, $x = L$ in the slope equation to determine the slope at the supports. Thus $\theta_L = NL/(6EI)$; $\theta_R = -NL/(3EI)$.

### 6. Solve for the section of maximum deflection
Set $\theta = 0$ and solve for $x$ to locate the section of maximum deflection. Thus $L^2 - 3x^2 = 0$; $x = L/3^{0.5}$. Substituting in the deflection equation gives $y_{max} = NL^2/(9EI3^{0.5})$.


## MOMENT-AREA METHOD OF DETERMINING BEAM DEFLECTION

Use the moment-area method to determine the slope of the elastic curve at each support and the maximum deflection of the beam shown in Fig. 37.


## Calculation Procedure:

### 1. Sketch the elastic curve of the member and draw the M/(EI) diagram
Let $A$ and $B$ denote two points on the elastic curve of a beam. The moment-area method is based on the following theorems:

The difference between the slope at $A$ and that at $B$ is numerically equal to the area of the $M/(EI)$ diagram within the interval $AB$.

The deviation of $A$ from a tangent to the elastic curve through $B$ is numerically equal to the static moment of the area of the $M/(EI)$ diagram within the interval $AB$ with respect to $A$. This tangential deviation is measured normal to the unstrained position of the beam.

Draw the elastic curve and the $M/(EI)$ diagram as shown in Fig. 37.

### 2. Calculate the deviation $t_1$ of B from the tangent through A

Thus, $t_1$ = moment of $\Delta ABC$ about $BC = [NL/(2EI)](L/3) = NL^2/(6EI)$. Also, $\theta_L = t_1/L = NL/(6EI)$.

### 3. Determine the right-hand slope in an analogous manner

### 4. Compute the distance to the section where the slope is zero

Area $\Delta AED$ = area $\Delta ABC(x/L)^2 = Nx^2/(2EIL)$; $\theta_E = \theta_L$ − area $\Delta AED = NL/(6EI)$ − $Nx^2/(2EIL) = 0$; $x = L/3^{0.5}$.

### 5. Evaluate the maximum deflection

Evaluate $y_{max}$ by calculating the deviation $t_2$ of $A$ from the tangent through $E'$ (Fig. 37). Thus area $\Delta AED = \theta_L = NL/(6EI)$; $y_{max} = t_2 = NL/(6EI)](2x/3) = [NL/(6EI)][(2L/(3 \times 3^{0.5})] = NL^2/(9EI3^{0.5})$, as before.


## CONJUGATE-BEAM METHOD OF DETERMINING BEAM DEFLECTION

The overhanging beam in Fig. 38 is loaded in the manner shown. Compute the deflection at $C$.


### Calculation Procedure:

### 1. Assign supports to the conjugate beam

If a conjugate beam of identical span as the given beam is loaded with the $M/(EI)$ diagram of the latter, the shear $V'$ and bending moment $M'$ of the conjugate beam are equal,

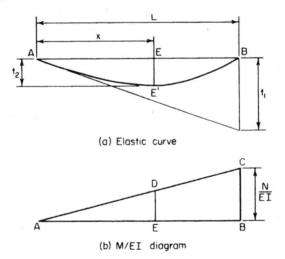

(a) Elastic curve

(b) M/EI diagram

**FIGURE 37**

respectively, to the slope $\theta$ and deflection $y$ at the corresponding section of the given beam.

Assign supports to the conjugate beam that are compatible with the end conditions of the given beam. At $A$, the given beam has a specific slope but zero deflection. Correspondingly, the conjugate beam has a specific shear but zero moment; i.e., it is simply supported at $A$.

At $C$, the given beam has a specific slope and a specific deflection. Correspondingly, the conjugate beam has both a shear and a bending moment; i.e., it has a fixed support at $C$.

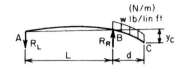

(a) Force diagram of given beam

### 2. Construct the M/(EI) diagram of the given beam

Load the conjugate beam with this area. The moment at $B$ is $-wd^2/2$; the moment varies linearly from $A$ to $B$ and parabolically from $C$ to $B$.

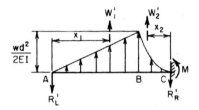

(b) Force diagram of conjugate beam

**FIGURE 38.** Deflection of overhanging beam.

### 3. Compute the resultant of the load in selected intervals

Compute the resultant $W_1'$ of the load in interval $AB$ and the resultant $W_2'$ of the load in the interval $BC$. Locate these resultants. (Refer to the AISC *Manual* for properties of the complement of a half parabola.) Then $W_1' = (L/2)[wd^2/(2EI)] = wd^2L/(4EI)$; $x_1 = {}^2/_3L$; $W_2' = (d/3)[wd^2/(2EI)] = wd^3/(6EI)$; $x_2 = {}^3/_4d$.

### 4. Evaluate the conjugate-beam reaction

Since the given beam has zero deflection at $B$, the conjugate beam has zero moment at this section. Evaluate the reaction $R_L'$ accordingly. Thus $M_B' = -R_L'L + W_1'L/3 = 0$; $R_L' = W_1'/3 = wd^2L/(12EI)$.

### 5. Determine the deflection

Determine the deflection at $C$ by computing $M_c'$. Thus $y_c = M_c' = -R_L'(L + d) + W_1'(d + L/3) + W_2'(3d/4) = wd^3(4L + 3d)/(24EI)$.

## UNIT-LOAD METHOD OF COMPUTING BEAM DEFLECTION

The cantilever beam in Fig. 39$a$ carries a load that varies uniformly from $w$ lb/lin ft at the free end to zero at the fixed end. Determine the slope and deflection of the elastic curve at the free end.

### Calculation Procedure:

### 1. Apply a unit moment to the beam

Apply a counterclockwise unit moment at $A$ (Fig. 39$b$). (This direction is selected because it is known that the end section rotates in this manner.) Let $x =$ distance from $A$ to given

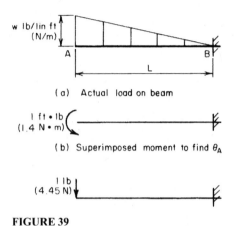

(a)   Actual load on beam

1 ft • lb
(1.4 N • m)

(b)  Superimposed moment to find $\theta_A$

1 lb
(4.45 N)

**FIGURE 39**

section; $w_x$ = load intensity at the given section; $M$ and $m$ = bending moment at the given section induced by the actual load and by the unit moment, respectively.

### 2. Evaluate the moments in step 1

Evaluate $M$ and $m$. By proportion, $w_x = w(L - x)/L$; $M = -(x^2/6)(2w + w_x) = -(wx^2/6)[2 + (L - x)/L] = -wx^2(3L - x)/(6L)$; $m = -1$.

### 3. Apply a suitable slope equation

Use the equation $\theta_A = \int_0^L [Mm/(EI)]\, dx$. Then $EI\theta_A = \int_0^L [wx^2 3L - x)/(6L)]\, dx = [w/(6L)] \times \int_0^L (3Lx^2 - x^3)\, dx = [w/(6L)](3Lx^3/3 - x^4/4)]_0^L = [w/(6L)](L^4 - L^4/4)$; thus, $\theta_A - \frac{1}{8}wL^3/(EI)$ counterclockwise. This is the slope at $A$.

### 4. Apply a unit load to the beam

Apply a unit downward load at $A$ as shown in Fig. 39c. Let $m'$ denote the bending moment at a given section induced by the unit load.

### 5. Evaluate the bending moment induced by the unit load; find the deflection

Apply $y_A = \int_0^L [Mm'/(EI)]\, dx$. Then $m' = -x$; $EIy_A = \int_0^L [wx^3(3L - x)/(6L)]\, dx = [w/(6L)] \times \int_0^L x^3(3L - x)\, dx$; $y_A = (11/120)wL^4/(EI)$.

The first equation in step 3 is a statement of the work performed by the unit moment at $A$ as the beam deflects under the applied load. The left-hand side of this equation expresses the external work, and the right-hand side expresses the internal work. These work equations constitute a simple proof of Maxwell's theorem of reciprocal deflections, which is presented in a later calculation procedure.

## DEFLECTION OF A CANTILEVER FRAME

The prismatic rigid frame $ABCD$ (Fig. 40a) carries a vertical load $P$ at the free end. Determine the horizontal displacement of $A$ by means of both the unit-load method and the moment-area method.

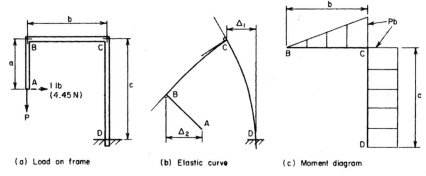

(a) Load on frame        (b) Elastic curve        (c) Moment diagram

**FIGURE 40**

### Calculation Procedure:

### 1. Apply a unit horizontal load
Apply the unit horizontal load at $A$, directed to the right.

### 2. Evaluate the bending moments in each member
Let $M$ and $m$ denote the bending moment at a given section caused by the load $P$ and by the unit load, respectively. Evaluate these moments in each member, considering a moment positive if it induces tension in the outer fibers of the frame. Thus:

*Member AB:* Let $x$ denote the vertical distance from $A$ to a given section. Then $M = 0$; $m = x$.

*Member BC:* Let $x$ denote the horizontal distance from $B$ to a given section. Then $M = Px$; $m = a$.

*Member CD:* Let $x$ denote the vertical distance from $C$ to a given section. Then $M = Pb$; $m = a - x$.

### 3. Evaluate the required deflection
Calling the required deflection $\Delta$, we apply $\Delta = \int [Mm/(EI)]\, dx$; $EI\Delta = \int_0^b Pax\, dx + \int_0^c Pb(a - x)\, dx = Pax^2/2]_0^b + Pb(ax - x^2/2)]_0^c = Pab^2/2 + Pabc - Pbc^2/2$; $\Delta = [Pb/(2EI)](ab + 2ac - c^2)$.

If this value is positive, $A$ is displaced in the direction of the unit load, i.e., to the right. Draw the elastic curve in hyperbolic fashion (Fig. 40b). The above three steps constitute the unit-load method of solving this problem.

### 4. Construct the bending-moment diagram
Draw the diagram as shown in Fig. 40c.

### 5. Compute the rotation and horizontal displacement by the moment-area method
Determine the rotation and horizontal displacement of $C$. (Consider only absolute values.) Since there is no rotation at $D$, $EI\theta_C = Pbc$; $EI\Delta_1 = Pbc^2/2$.

### 6. Compute the rotation of one point relative to another and the total rotation
Thus $EI\theta_{BC} = Pb^2/2$; $EI\theta_B = Pbc + Pb^2/2 = Pb(c + b/2)$. The horizontal displacement of $B$ relative to $C$ is infinitesimal.

**7. Compute the horizontal displacement of one point relative to another**

Thus, $EI\Delta_2 = EI\theta_B a = Pb(ac + ab/2)$.

**8. Combine the computed displacements to obtain the absolute displacement**

Thus $EI\Delta = EI(\Delta_2 - EI\Delta_1) = Pb(ac + ab/2 - c^2/2)$; $\Delta = [Pb/(2EI)](2ac + ab - c^2)$.

# Statically Indeterminate Structures

A structure is said to be *statically determinate* if its reactions and internal forces may be evaluated by applying solely the equations of equilibrium and *statically indeterminate* if such is not the case. The analysis of an indeterminate structure is performed by combining the equations of equilibrium with the known characteristics of the deformation of the structure.

## SHEAR AND BENDING MOMENT OF A BEAM ON A YIELDING SUPPORT

The beam in Fig. 41a has an $EI$ value of $35 \times 10^9$ lb·sq.in. (100,429 kN·m²) and bears on a spring at $B$ that has a constant of 100 kips/in (175,126.8 kN/m); i.e., a force of 100 kips (444.8 kN) will compress the spring 1 in. (25.4 mm). Neglecting the weight of the member, construct the shear and bending-moment diagrams.

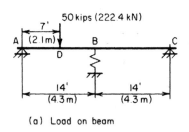

(a) Load on beam

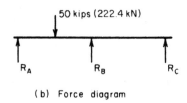

(b) Force diagram

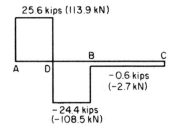

(c) Shear diagram

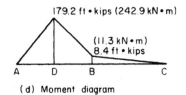

(d) Moment diagram

**FIGURE 41**

**Calculation Procedure:**

**1. Draw the free-body diagram of the beam**

Draw the diagram in Fig. 41b. Consider this as a simply supported member carrying a 50-kip (222.4-kN) load at $D$ and an upward load $R_B$ at its center.

**2. Evaluate the deflection**

Evaluate the deflection at $B$ by applying the equations presented for cases 7 and 8 in the AISC *Manual*. With respect to the 50-kip (222.4-kN) load, $b = 7$ ft (2.1 m) and $x = 14$ ft (4.3 m). If $y$ is in inches and $R_B$ is in pounds, $y = 50,000(7)(14)(28^2 - 7^2 - 14^2)1728/[6(35)(10)^9 28] - R_B(28)^3 1728/[48(35)(10)^9] = 0.776 - (2.26/10^5)R_B$.

**3. Express the deflection in terms of the spring constant**

The deflection at $B$ is, by proportion, $y/1 = R_B/100,000$; $y = R_B/100,000$.

**4. Equate the two deflection expressions, and solve for the upward load**

Thus $R_B/10^5 = 0.776 - (2.26/10^5)R_B$; $R_B = 0.776(10)^5/3.26 = 23,800$ lb (105,862.4 N).

**5. Calculate the reactions $R_A$ and $R_C$ by taking moments**

We have $\Sigma M_C = 28R_A - 50,000(21) + 23,800(14) = 0$; $R_A = 25,600$ lb (113,868.8 N); $\Sigma M_A = 50,000(7) - 23,800(14) - 28R_C = 0$; $R_C = 600$ lb (2668.8 N).

**6. Construct the shear and moment diagrams**

Construct these diagrams as shown in Fig. 41. Then $M_D = 7(25,600) = 179,200$ lb·ft (242,960 N·m); $M_B = 179,200 - 7(24,400) = 8400$ lb·ft (11,390.4 N·m).

## MAXIMUM BENDING STRESS IN BEAMS JOINTLY SUPPORTING A LOAD

In Fig. 42a, a W16 × 40 beam and a W12 × 31 beam cross each other at the vertical line $V$, the bottom of the 16-in. (406.4-mm) beam being 3/8 in. (9.53 mm) above the top of the 12-in. (304.8-mm) beam before the load is applied. Both members are simply supported.

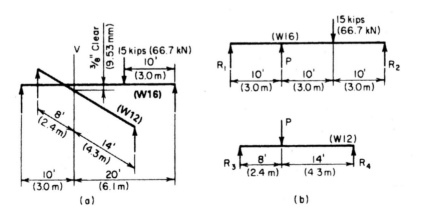

**FIGURE 42.** Load carried by two beams.

A column bearing on the 16-in. (406.4-mm) beam transmits a load of 15 kips (66.72 kN) at the indicated location. Compute the maximum bending stress in the 12-in. (304.8-mm) beam.

## Calculation Procedure:

### 1. Determine whether the upper beam engages the lower beam
To ascertain whether the upper beam engages the lower one as it deflects under the 15-kip (66.72-kN) load, compute the deflection of the 16-in. (406.4-mm) beam at $V$ if the 12-in. (304.8-mm) beam were absent. This distance is 0.74 in. (18.80 mm). Consequently, the gap between the members is closed, and the two beams share the load.

### 2. Draw a free-body diagram of each member
Let $P$ denote the load transmitted to the 12-in. (304.8-mm) beam by the 16-in. (406.4-mm) beam [or the reaction of the 12-in. (304.8-mm) beam on the 16-in. (406.4-mm) beam]. Draw, in Fig. 42b, a free-body diagram of each member.

### 3. Evaluate the deflection of the beams
Evaluate, in terms of $P$, the deflections $y_{12}$ and $y_{16}$ of the 12-in. (304.8-mm) and 16-in. (406.4-mm) beams, respectively, at line $V$.

### 4. Express the relationship between the two deflections
Thus, $y_{12} = y_{16} - 0.375$.

### 5. Replace the deflections in step 4 with their values as obtained in step 3
After substituting these deflections, solve for $P$.

### 6. Compute the reactions of the lower beam
Once the reactions of the lower beam are computed, obtain the maximum bending moment. Then compute the corresponding flexural stress.

## THEOREM OF THREE MOMENTS

For the two-span beam in Fig. 43 and 44, compute the reactions at the supports. Apply the theorem of three moments to arrive at the results.

## Calculation Procedure:

### 1. Using the bending-moment equation, determine $M_B$
Figure 43 represents a general case. For a prismatic beam, the bending moments at the three successive supports are related by $M_1L_1 + 2M_2(L_1 + L_2) + M_3L_2 - \frac{1}{4}w_1L_1^3 - \frac{1}{4}w_2L_2^3 - P_1L_1^2(k_1 - k_1^3) - P_2L_2^2(k_2 - k_2^3)$. Substituting in this equation gives $M_1 = M_3 = 0$; $L_1 = 10$ ft (3.0 m); $L_2 = 15$ ft (4.6 m); $w_1 = 2$ kips/lin ft (29.2 kN/m); $w_2 = 3$ kips/lin ft (43.8 kN/m); $P_1 = 6$ kips (26.7 kN); $P_2 = 10$ kips (44.5 kN); $k_1 = 0.5$; $k_2 = 0.4$; $2M_B(10 + 15) = \frac{1}{4}(2)(10)^3 - \frac{1}{4}(3)(15)^3 - 6(10)^2(0.5 - 0.125) - 10(15)^2(0.4 - 0.064)$; $M_B = -80.2$ ft·kips (−108.8 kN·m).

### 2. Draw a free-body diagram of each span
Figure 43 shows the free-body diagrams.

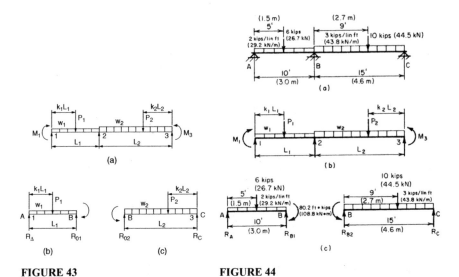

**FIGURE 43**                    **FIGURE 44**

## 3. Take moments with respect to each support to find the reactions

*Span AB*: $\Sigma M_A = 6(5) + 2(10)(5) + 80.2 - 10R_{B1} = 0$; $R_{B1} = 21.02$ kips (93.496 kN); $\Sigma M_B = 10R_A - 6(5) - 2(10)(5) + 80.2 = 0$; $R_A = 4.98$ kips (22.151 kN).

*Span BC*: $\Sigma M_B = -80.2 + 10(9) + 3(15)(7.5) - 15R_C = 0$; $R_C = 23.15$ kips (102.971 kN); $\Sigma M_C = 15R_{B2} - 80.2 - 10(6) - 3(15)(7.5) = 0$; $R_{B2} = 31.85$ kips (144.668 kN); $R_B = 21.02 + 31.85 = 52.87$ kips (235.165 kN).

# THEOREM OF THREE MOMENTS: BEAM WITH OVERHANG AND FIXED END

Determine the reactions at the supports of the continuous beam in Fig. 44a. Use the theorem of three moments.

## Calculation Procedure:

### 1. Transform the given beam to one amenable to analysis by the theorem of three moments

Perform the following operations to transform the beam:

a. Remove the span $AB$, and introduce the shear $V_B$ and moment $M_B$ that the load on $AB$ induces at $B$, as shown in Fig. 44b.

b. Remove the fixed support at $D$ and add the span $DE$ of zero length, with a hinged support at $E$.

For the interval $BD$, the transformed beam is then identical in every respect with the actual beam.

## 2. Apply the equation for the theorem of three moments

Consider span $BC$ as span 1 and $CD$ as span 2. For the 5-kip (22.2-kN) load, $k_2 = 12/16 = 0.75$; for the 10-kip (44.5-kN) load, $k_2 = 8/16 = 0.5$. Then $-12(10) + 2M_C(10 + 16) + 16M_D = \frac{1}{4}(4)(10)^3 - 5(16)^2(0.75 - 0.422) - 10(16)^2(0.5 - 0.125)$. Simplifying gives $13M_C + 4M_D = -565.0$, Eq. $a$.

## 3. Apply the moment equation again

Considering $CD$ as span 1 and $DE$ as span 2, apply the moment equation again. Or, for the 5-kip (22.2-kN) load, $k_1 = 0.25$; for the 10-kip (44.5-kN) load, $k_1 = 0.5$. Then $16M_C + 2M_D(16 + 0) = -5(16)^2(0.25 - 0.016) - 10(16)^2(0.50 - 0.125)$. Simplifying yields $M_C + 2M_D = -78.7$, Eq. $b$.

## 4. Solve the moment equations

Solving Eqs. $a$ and $b$ gives $M_C = -37.1$ ft·kips ($-50.30$ kN·m); $M_D = -20.8$ ft·kips ($-28.20$ kN·m).

## 5. Determine the reactions by using a free-body diagram

Find the reactions by drawing a free-body diagram of each span and taking moments with respect to each support. Thus $R_B = 20.5$ kips (91.18 kN); $R_C = 32.3$ kips (143.67 kN); $R_D = 5.2$ kips (23.12 kN).

# BENDING-MOMENT DETERMINATION BY MOMENT DISTRIBUTION

Using moment distribution, determine the bending moments at the supports of the member in Fig. 45. The beams are rigidly joined at the supports and are composed of the same material.

## Calculation Procedure:

## 1. Calculate the flexural stiffness of each span

Using $K$ to denote the flexural stiffness, we see that $K = I/L$ if the far end remains fixed during moment distribution; $K = 0.75I/L$ if the far end remains hinged during moment distribution. Then $K_{AB} = 270/18 = 15$; $K_{BC} = 192/12 = 16$; $K_{CD} = 0.75(240/20) = 9$. Record all the values on the drawing as they are obtained.

## 2. For each span, calculate the required fixed-end moments at those supports that will be considered fixed

These are the external moments with respect to the span; a clockwise moment is considered positive. (For additional data, refer to cases 14 and 15 in the AISC *Manual.*) Then $M_{AB} = -wL^2/12 = -2(18)^2/12 = -54.0$ ft·kips ($-73.2$ kN·m); $M_{BA} = +54.0$ ft·kips (73.22 kN·m). Similarly, $M_{BC} = -48.0$ ft·kips ($-65.1$ kN·m); $M_{CB} = +48.0$ ft·kips (65.1 kN·m); $M_{CD} = -24(15)(5)(15 + 20)/[2(20)^2] = -78.8$ ft·kips ($-106.85$ kN·m).

## 3. Calculate the unbalanced moments

Computing the unbalanced moments at $B$ and $C$ yields the following: At $B$, $+54.0 - 48.0 = +6.0$ ft·kips (8.14 kN·m); at $C$, $+48.0 - 78.8 = -30.8$ ft·kips ($-41.76$ kN·m).

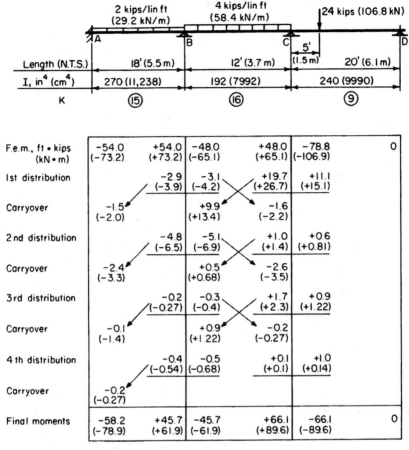

**FIGURE 45.** Moment distribution.

### 4. Apply balancing moments; distribute them in proportion to the stiffness of the adjoining spans

Apply the balancing moments at $B$ and $C$, and distribute them to the two adjoining spans in proportion to their stiffness. Thus $M_{BA} = -6.0(15/31) = -2.9$ ft·kips ($-3.93$ kN·m); $M_{BC} = -6.0(16/31) = -3.1$ ft·kips ($-4.20$ kN·m); $M_{CB} = +30.8(16/25) = +19.7$ ft·kips ($26.71$ kN·m); $M_{CD} = +30.8(9/25) = +11.1$ ft·kips ($15.05$ kN·m).

### 5. Perform the "carry-over" operation for each span

To do this, take one-half the distributed moment applied at one end of the span, and add this to the moment at the far end if that end is considered to be fixed during moment distribution.

**6. Perform the second cycle of moment balancing and distribution**
Thus $M_{BA} = -9.9(15/31) = -4.8$; $M_{BC} = -9.9(16/31) = -5.1$; $M_{CB} = +1.6(16/25) = +1.0$; $M_{CD} = +1.6(9/25) = +0.6$.

**7. Continue the foregoing procedure until the carry-over moments become negligible**
Total the results to obtain the following bending moments: $M_A = -58.2$ ft·kips $(-78.91$ kN m$)$; $M_B = -45.7$ ft·kips $(-61.96$ kN·m$)$; $M_C = -66.1$ ft·kips $(-89.63$ kN·m$)$.

## ANALYSIS OF A STATICALLY INDETERMINATE TRUSS

Determine the internal forces of the truss in Fig. 46a. The cross-sectional areas of the members are given in Table 5.

### Calculation Procedure:

### 1. Test the structure for static determinateness
Apply the following criterion. Let $j$ = number of joints; $m$ = number of members; $r$ = number of reactions. Then if $2j = m + r$, the truss is statically determinate; if $2j < m + r$, the truss is statically indeterminate and the deficiency represents the degree of indeterminateness.

In this truss, $j = 6$, $m = 10$, $r = 3$, consisting of a vertical reaction at $A$ and $D$ and a horizontal reaction at $D$. Thus $2j = 12$; $m + r = 13$. The truss is therefore statically indeterminate to the first degree; i.e., there is one redundant member.

The method of analysis comprises the following steps: Assume a value for the internal force in a particular member, and calculate the relative displacement $\Delta_i$, of the two ends of that member caused solely by this force. Now remove this member to secure a determinate truss, and calculate the relative displacement $\Delta_a$ caused solely by the applied loads. The true internal force is of such magnitude that $\Delta_i = -\Delta_a$.

### 2. Assume a unit force for one member
Assume for convenience that the force in $BF$ is 1-kip (4.45-kN) tension. Remove this member, and replace it with the assumed 1-kip (4.45-kN) force that it exerts at joints $B$ and $F$, as shown in Fig. 46b.

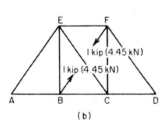

FIGURE 46. Statically indeterminate truss.

**TABLE 5.**  Forces in Truss Members (Fig. 46)

| Member | $A$, sq.in. ($cm^2$) | $L$, in. (mm) | $U$, kips (kN) | $S$, kips (kN) | $U^2L/A$ | $SUL/A$ | $S'$, kips (kN) |
|---|---|---|---|---|---|---|---|
| AB | 5 | 108 | 0 | +15.25 | 0 | 0 | +15.25 |
|  | (32.2) | (2,743.2) | (0) | (+67.832) | (0) | (0) | (+67.832) |
| BC | 5 | 108 | −0.60 | +15.25 | +7.8 | −197.6 | +14.07 |
|  | (32.2) | (2,743.2) | (−2.668) | (+67.832) | (+615.54) | (−15,417.78) | (+62.588) |
| CD | 5 | 108 | 0 | +13.63 | 0 | 0 | +13.63 |
|  | (32.2) | (2,743.2) | (0) | (+60.626) | (0) | (0) | (+60.626) |
| EF | 4 | 108 | −0.60 | −13.63 | +9.7 | +220.8 | −14.81 |
|  | (25.8) | (2,743.2) | (−2.688) | (−60.626) | (+756.84) | (+17,198.18) | (−65.874) |
| BE | 4 | 144 | −0.80 | +4.50 | +23.0 | −129.6 | +2.92 |
|  | (25.8) | (3,657.6) | (−3.558) | (+20.016) | (+1,794.68) | (−10,096.24) | (+12.988) |
| CF | 4 | 144 | −0.80 | +2.17 | +23.0 | −62.5 | +0.59 |
|  | (25.8) | (3,657.6) | (−3.558) | (+9.952) | (+1.794.68) | (−4,868.55) | (+2.624) |
| AE | 6 | 180 | 0 | −25.42 | 0 | 0 | −25.42 |
|  | (38.7) | (4,572.0) | (0) | (−113.068) | (0) | (0) | (−113.068) |
| BF | 5 | 180 | +1.00 | 0 | +36.0 | 0 | +1.97 |
|  | (32.2) | (4,572.0) | (+4.448) | (0) | (+2,809.18) | (0) | (+8.762) |
| CE | 5 | 180 | +1.00 | −2.71 | +36.0 | −97.6 | −0.74 |
|  | (32.2) | (4,572.0) | (+4.448) | (−9.652) | (+2,809.18) | (−6,095.82) | (−3.291) |
| DF | 6 | 180 | 0 | −32.71 | 0 | 0 | −32.71 |
|  | (38.7) | (4,572.0) | (0) | (−145.494) | (0) | (0) | (−145.494) |
| Total |  |  |  |  | + 135.5 | −266.5 |  |
|  |  |  |  |  | (+10,580.1) | (−19,280.2) |  |

### 3. Calculate the force induced in each member solely by the unit force

Calling the induced force $U$, produced solely by the unit tension in $BF$, record the results in Table 5, considering tensile forces as positive and compressive forces as negative.

### 4. Calculate the force induced in each member solely by the applied loads

With $BF$ eliminated, calculate the force $S$ induced in each member solely by the applied loads.

### 5. Evaluate the true force in the selected member

Use the relation $BF = -[\Sigma SUL/(AE)]/[\Sigma U^2L/(AE)]$. The numerator represents $\Delta_a$; the denominator represents $\Delta_i$ for a 1-kip (4.45-kN) tensile force in $BF$. Since $E$ is constant, it cancels. Substituting the values in Table 5 gives $BF = -(-266.5/135.5) = 1.97$ kips (8.76 kN). The positive result confirms the assumption that $BF$ is tensile.

### 6. Evaluate the true force in each member

Use the relation $S' = S + 1.97\ U$, where $S' =$ true force. The results are shown in Table 5.

# Moving Loads and Influence Lines

## ANALYSIS OF BEAM CARRYING MOVING CONCENTRATED LOADS

The loads shown in Fig. 47*a* traverse a beam of 40-ft (12.2-m) simple span while their spacing remains constant. Determine the maximum bending moment and maximum shear induced in the beam during transit of these loads. Disregard the weight of the beam.

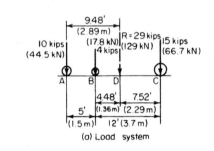

(a) Load system

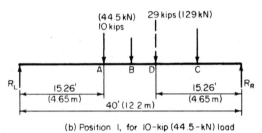

(b) Position 1, for 10-kip (44.5-kN) load

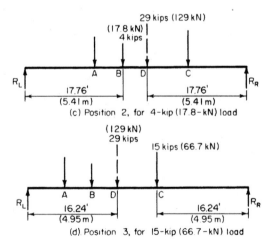

(c) Position 2, for 4-kip (17.8-kN) load

(d) Position 3, for 15-kip (66.7-kN) load

**FIGURE 47**

## Calculation Procedure:

### 1. Determine the magnitude of the resultant and its location

Since the member carries only concentrated loads, the maximum moment at any instant occurs under one of these loads. Thus, the problem is to determine the position of the load system that causes the *absolute* maximum moment.

The magnitude of the resultant $R$ is $R = 10 + 4 + 15 = 29$ kips (129.0 kN). To determine the location of $R$, take moments with respect to $A$ (Fig. 47). Thus $\Sigma M_A = 29AD = 4(5) + 15(17)$, or $AD = 9.48$ ft (2.890 m).

### 2. Assume several trial load positions

Assume that the maximum moment occurs under the 10-kip (44.5-kN) load. Place the system in the position shown in Fig. 47b, with the 10-kip (44.5-kN) load as far from the adjacent support as the resultant is from the other support. Repeat this procedure for the two remaining loads.

### 3. Determine the support reactions for the trial load positions

For these three trial positions, calculate the reaction at the support adjacent to the load under consideration. Determine whether the vertical shear is zero or changes sign at this load. Thus, for position 1: $R_L = 29(15.26)/40 = 11.06$ kips (49.194 kN). Since the shear does not change sign at the 10-kip (44.5-kN) load, this position lacks significance.

Position 2: $R_L = 29(17.76)/40 = 12.88$ kips (57.290 kN). The shear changes sign at the 4-kip (17.8-kN) load.

Position 3: $R_R = 29(16.24)/40 = 11.77$ kips (52.352 kN). The shear changes sign at the 15-kip (66.7-kN) load.

### 4. Compute the maximum bending moment associated with positions having a change in the shear sign

This applies to positions 2 and 3. The absolute maximum moment is the larger of these values. Thus, for position 2: $M = 12.88(17.76) - 10(5) = 178.7$ ft·kips (242.32 kN·m). Position 3: $M = 11.77(16.24) = 191.1$ ft·kips (259.13 kN·m). Thus, $M_{max} = 191.1$ ft·kips (259.13 kN·m).

### 5. Determine the absolute maximum shear

For absolute maximum shear, place the 15-kip (66.7-kN) load an infinitesimal distance to the left of the right-hand support. Then $V_{max} = 29(40 - 7.52)/40 = 23.5$ kips (104.53 kN).

When the load spacing is large in relation to the beam span, the absolute maximum moment may occur when only part of the load system is on the span. This possibility requires careful investigation.

## INFLUENCE LINE FOR SHEAR IN A BRIDGE TRUSS

The Pratt truss in Fig. 48a supports a bridge at its bottom chord. Draw the influence line for shear in panel *cd* caused by a moving load traversing the bridge floor..

## Calculation Procedure:

### 1. Compute the shear in the panel being considered with a unit load to the right of the panel

Cut the truss at section *YY*. The algebraic sum of vertical forces acting on the truss at panel points to the left of *YY* is termed the shear in panel *cd*.

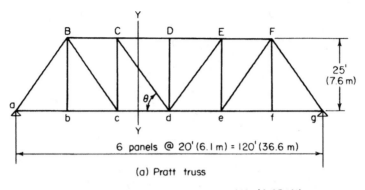

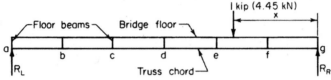

(a) Pratt truss

(b) Transmission of load through floor beams

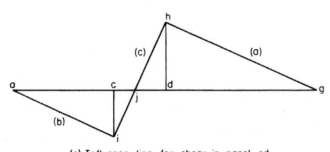

(c) Influence line for shear in panel cd

**FIGURE 48**

Consider that a moving load traverses the bridge floor from right to left and that the portion of the load carried by the given truss is 1 kip (4.45 kN). This unit load is transmitted to the truss as concentrated loads at two adjacent bottom-chord panel points, the latter being components of the unit load. Let $x$ denote the instantaneous distance from the right-hand support to the moving load.

Place the unit load to the right of $d$, as shown in Fig. 48b, and compute the shear $V_{cd}$ in panel $cd$. The truss reactions may be obtained by considering the unit load itself rather than its panel-point components. Thus: $R_L = x/120$; $V_{cd} = R_L = x/120$, Eq. $a$.

**2. Compute the panel shear with the unit load to the left of the panel considered**

Placing the unit load to the left of $c$ yields $V_{cd} = R_L - 1 = x/120 - 1$, Eq. $b$.

**3. Determine the panel shear with the unit load within the panel**

Place the unit load within panel $cd$. Determine the panel-point load $P_c$ at $c$, and compute $V_{cd}$. Thus $P_c = (x - 60)/20 = x/20 - 3$; $V_{cd} = R_L - P_c = x/120 - (x/20 - 3) = -x/24 + 3$, Eq. $c$.

### 4. Construct a diagram representing the shear associated with every position of the unit load

Apply the foregoing equations to represent the value of $V_{cd}$ associated with every position of the unit load. This diagram, Fig. 48c, is termed an *influence line*. The point $j$ at which this line intersects the base is referred to as the *neutral point*.

### 5. Compute the slope of each segment of the influence line

Line $a$, $dV_{cd}/dx = 1/120$; line $b$, $dV_{cd}/dx = 1/120$; line $c$, $dV_{cd}/dx = -1/24$. Lines $a$ and $b$ are therefore parallel because they have the same slope.

## FORCE IN TRUSS DIAGONAL CAUSED BY A MOVING UNIFORM LOAD

The bridge floor in Fig. 48a carries a moving uniformly distributed load. The portion of the load transmitted to the given truss is 2.3 kips/lin ft (33.57 kN/m). Determine the limiting values of the force induced in member $Cd$ by this load.

### Calculation Procedure:

### 1. Locate the neutral point, and compute dh

The force in $Cd$ is a function of $V_{cd}$. Locate the neutral point $j$ in Fig. 48c and compute *dh*. From Eq. $c$ of the previous calculation procedure, $V_{cd} = -jg/24 + S = 0$; $jg = 72$ ft (21.9 m). From Eq. $a$ of the previous procedure, $dh = 60/120 = 0.5$.

### 2. Determine the maximum shear

To secure the maximum value of $V_{cd}$, apply uniform load continuously in the interval $jg$. Compute $V_{cd}$ by multiplying the area under the influence line by the intensity of the applied load. Thus, $V_{cd} = \frac{1}{2}(72)(0.5)(2.3) = 41.4$ kips (184.15 kN).

### 3. Determine the maximum force in the member

Use the relation $Cd_{max} = V_{cd}(\csc \theta)$, where $\csc \theta = [(20^2 + 25^2)/25^2]^{0.5} = 1.28$. Then $Cd_{max} = 41.4(1.28) = 53.0$-kip (235.74-kN) tension.

### 4. Determine the minimum force in the member

To secure the minimum value of $V_{cd}$, apply uniform load continuously in the interval $aj$. Perform the final calculation by proportion. Thus, $Cd_{min}/Cd_{max} = $ area $aij$/area $jhg = -(2/3)^2 = 9$. Then $Cd_{min} = -(4/9)(53.0) = 23.6$-kip (104.97-kN) compression.

## FORCE IN TRUSS DIAGONAL CAUSED BY MOVING CONCENTRATED LOADS

The truss in Fig. 49a supports a bridge that transmits the moving-load system shown in Fig. 49b to its bottom chord. Determine the maximum tensile force in $De$.

### Calculation Procedure:

### 1. Locate the resultant of the load system

The force in $De$ (Fig. 49) is a function of the shear in panel $de$. This shear is calculated without recourse to a set rule in order to show the principles involved in designing for moving loads.

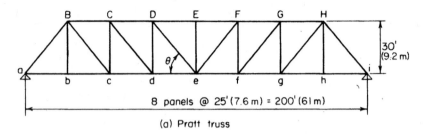

(a) Pratt truss

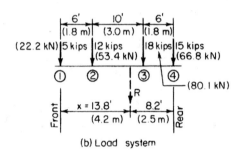

(b) Load system

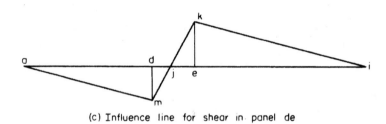

(c) Influence line for shear in panel de

**FIGURE 49**

To locate the resultant of the load system, take moments with respect to load 1. Thus, $R$ = 50 kips (222.4 kN). Then $\Sigma M_1 = 12(6) + 18(16) + 15(22) = 50x$; $x = 13.8$ ft (4.21 m).

### 2. Construct the influence line for $V_{de}$

In Fig. 49c, draw the influence line for $V_{de}$. Assume right-to-left locomotion, and express the slope of each segment of the influence line. Thus slope of $ik$ = slope of $ma$ = 1/200; slope of $km = -7/200$.

### 3. Assume a load position, and determine whether $V_{de}$ increases or decreases

Consider that load 1 lies within panel $de$ and the remaining loads lie to the right of this panel. From the slope of the influence line, ascertain whether $V_{de}$ increases or decreases as the system is displaced to the left. Thus $dV_{de}/dx = 5(-7/200) + 45(1/200) > 0$; $\therefore V_{de}$ increases.

### 4. Repeat the foregoing calculation with other assumed load positions

Consider that loads 1 and 2 lie within the panel $de$ and the remaining loads lie to the right of this panel. Repeat the foregoing calculation. Thus $dV_{de}/dx = 17(-7/200) + 33(1/200)$ < 0; $\therefore V_{de}$ decreases.

From these results it is concluded that as the system moves from right to left, $V_{de}$ is maximum at the instant that load 2 is at $e$.

### 5. Place the system in the position thus established, and compute $V_{de}$

Thus, $R_L = 50(100 + 6 - 13.8)/200 = 23.1$ kips (102.75 kN). The load at panel point $d$ is $P_d = 5(6)/25$ 1.2 kips (5.34 kN); $V_{de} = 23.1 - 1.2 = 21.9$ kips (97.41 kN).

### 6. Assume left-to-right locomotion; proceed as in step 3

Consider that load 4 is within panel $de$ and the remaining loads are to the right of this panel. Proceeding as in step 3, we find $dV_{de}/dx = 15(7/200) + 35(-1/200) > 0$.

So, as the system moves from left to right, $V_{de}$ is maximum at the instant that load 4 is at $e$.

### 7. Place the system in the position thus established, and compute $V_{de}$

Thus $V_{de} = R_L = [50(100 - 8.2)1/200 = 23.0$ kips (102.30 kN); $\therefore V_{de,\,max} = 23.0$ kips (102.30 kN).

### 8. Compute the maximum tensile force in De

Using the same relation as in step 3 of the previous calculation procedure, we find csc $\theta = [(25^2 + 30^2)/30^2]^{0.5} = 1.30$; then $De = 23.0(1.30) = 29.9$-kip (133.00-kN) tension.

## INFLUENCE LINE FOR BENDING MOMENT IN BRIDGE TRUSS

The Warren truss in Fig. 50$a$ supports a bridge at its top chord. Draw the influence line for the bending moment at $b$ caused by a moving load traversing the bridge floor.

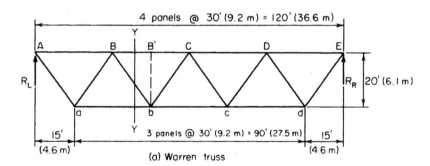

(a) Warren truss

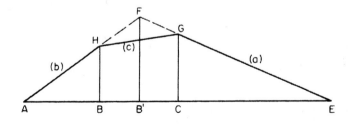

(b) Influence line for bending moment at b

**FIGURE 50**

## Calculation Procedure:

### 1. Place the unit load in position, and compute the bending moment

The moment of all forces acting on the truss at panel points to the left of $b$ with respect to $b$ is termed the bending moment at that point. Assume that the load transmitted to the given truss is 1 kip (4.45 kN), and let $x$ denote the instantaneous distance from the right-hand support to the moving load.

Place the unit load to the right of $C$, and compute the bending moment $M_b$. Thus $R_L = x/120$; $M_b = 45R_L = 3x/8$, Eq. a.

### 2. Place the unit load on the other side and compute the bending moment

Placing the unit load to the left of $B$ and computing $M_b$, $M_b = 45R_L - (x - 75) = -5x/8 + 75$, Eq. b.

### 3. Place the unit load within the panel; compute the panel-point load and bending moment

Place the unit load within panel $BC$. Determine the panel-point load $P_B$ and compute $M_b$. Thus $= P_B(x - 60)/30 = x/30 - 2$; $M_b = 45R_L - 15P_B = 3x/8 - 15(x/30 - 2) = -x/8 + 30$, Eq. c.

### 4. Applying the foregoing equations, draw the influence line

Figure 50b shows the influence line for $M_b$. Computing the significant values yields $CG = (3/8)(60) = 22.50$ ft·kips (30.51 kN·m); $BH = -(5/8)(90) + 75 = 18.75$ ft·kips (25.425 kN·m).

### 5. Compute the slope of each segment of the influence line

This computation is made for subsequent reference. Thus, line $a$, $dM_b/dx = 3/8$; line $b$, $dM_b/dx = -5/8$; line $c$, $dM_b/dx = -1/8$.

## FORCE IN TRUSS CHORD CAUSED BY MOVING CONCENTRATED LOADS

The truss in Fig. 50a carries the moving-load system shown in Fig. 51. Determine the maximum force induced in member $BC$ during transit of the loads.

### Calculation Procedure:

### 1. Assume that locomotion proceeds from right to left, and compute the bending moment

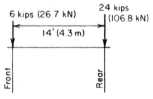

6 kips (26 7 kN)    24 kips (106.8 kN)
14' (4.3 m)
Front    Rear

**FIGURE 51**

The force in $BC$ is a function of the bending moment $M_b$ at $b$. Refer to the previous calculation procedure for the slope of each segment of the influence line. Study of these slopes shows that $M_b$ increases as the load system moves until the rear load is at $C$, the front load being 14 ft (4.3 m) to the left of $C$. Calculate the value of $M_b$ corresponding to this load disposition by applying the computed properties of the influence line. Thus, $M_b = 22.50(24) + (22.50 - 1/8 \times 14)(6) = 664.5$ ft·kips (901.06 kN·m).

### 2. Assume that locomotion proceeds from left to right, and compute the bending moment

Study shows that $M_b$ increases as the system moves until the rear load is at $C$, the front load being 14 ft (4.3 m) to the right of $C$. Calculate the corresponding value of $M_b$. Thus, $M_b = 22.50(24) + (22.50 - 3/8 \times 14)(6) = 6435$ ft·kips (872.59 kN·m). $\therefore M_{b,\max} = 664.5$ ft·kips (901.06 kN·m).

### 3. Determine the maximum force in the member

Cut the truss at plane $YY$. Determine the maximum force in $BC$ by considering the equilibrium of the left part of the structure. Thus, $\Sigma M_b = M_b - 20BC = 0$; $BC = 664.5/20 = 33.2$-kips (147.67-kN) compression.

## INFLUENCE LINE FOR BENDING MOMENT IN THREE-HINGED ARCH

The arch in Fig. 52$a$ is hinged at $A$, $B$, and $C$. Draw the influence line for bending moment at $D$, and locate the neutral point.

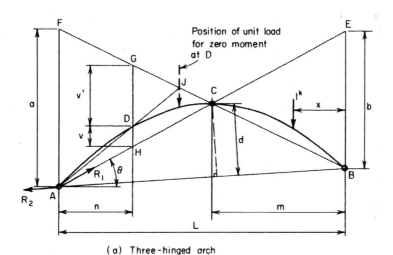

(a) Three-hinged arch

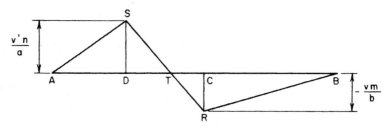

(b) Influence line for bending moment at D

**FIGURE 52**

## Calculation Procedure:

### 1. Start the graphical construction

Draw a line through $A$ and $C$, intersecting the vertical line through $B$ at $E$. Draw a line through $B$ and $C$, intersecting the vertical line through $A$ and $F$. Draw the vertical line $GH$ through $D$.

Let $\theta$ denote the angle between $AE$ and the horizontal. Lines through $B$ and $D$ perpendicular to $AE$ (omitted for clarity) make an angle $\theta$ with the vertical.

### 2. Resolve the reaction into components

Resolve the reaction at $A$ into the components $R_1$ and $R_2$ acting along $AE$ and $AB$, respectively (Fig. 52).

### 3. Determine the value of the first reaction

Let $x$ denote the horizontal distance from the right-hand support to the unit load, where $x$ has any value between 0 and $L$. Evaluate $R_1$ by equating the bending moment at $B$ to zero. Thus $M_B = R_1 b \cos \theta - x = 0$; or $= R_1 = x/(b \cos \theta)$.

### 4. Evaluate the second reaction

Place the unit load within the interval $CB$. Evaluate $R_2$ by equating the bending moment at $C$ to zero. Thus $M_C = R_2 d = 0$; $\therefore R_2 = 0$.

### 5. Calculate the bending moment at D when the unit load lies within the interval CB

Thus, $M_D = -R_1 v \cos \theta = -[(v \cos \theta)/(b \cos \theta)]x$, or $M_D = -vx/b$, Eq. $a$. When $x = m$, $M_D = -vm/b$.

### 6. Place the unit load in a new position, and determine the bending moment

Place the unit load within the interval $AD$. Working from the right-hand support, proceed in an analogous manner to arrive at the following result: $M_D = v'(L - x)/a$, Eq. $b$. When $x = L - n$, $M_D = v'n/a$.

### 7. Place the unit load within another interval, and evaluate the second reaction

Place the unit load within the interval $DC$, and evaluate $R_2$. Thus $M_C = R_2 d - (x - m) = 0$, or $R_2 = (x - m)/d$.

Since both $R_1$ and $R_2$ vary linearly with respect to $x$, it follows that $M_D$ is also a linear function of $x$.

### 8. Complete the influence line

In Fig. 52b, draw lines $BR$ and $AS$ to represent Eqs. $a$ and $b$, respectively. Draw the straight line $SR$, thus completing the influence line. The point $T$ at which this line intersects the base is termed the neutral point.

### 9. Locate the neutral point

To locate $T$, draw a line through $A$ and $D$ in Fig. 52a intersecting $BF$ at $J$. The neutral point in the influence line lies vertically below $J$; that is, $M_D$ is zero when the action line of the unit load passes through $J$.

The proof is as follows: Since $M_D = 0$ and there are no applied loads in the interval $AD$, it follows that the total reaction at $A$ is directed along $AD$. Similarly, since $M_C = 0$ and there are no applied loads in the interval $CB$, it follows that the total reaction at $B$ is directed along $BC$. Because the unit load and the two reactions constitute a balanced system of forces, they are collinear. Therefore, $J$ lies on the action line of the unit load.

Alternatively, the location of the neutral point may be established by applying the geometric properties of the influence line.

## DEFLECTION OF A BEAM UNDER MOVING LOADS

The moving-load system in Fig. 53a traverses a beam on a simple span of 40 ft (12.2 m). What disposition of the system will cause the maximum deflection at midspan?

### Calculation Procedure:

### 1. Develop the equations for the midspan deflection under a unit load

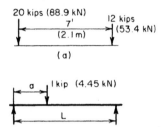

The maximum deflection will manifestly occur when the two loads lie on opposite sides of the centerline of the span. In calculating the deflection at midspan caused by a load applied at any point on the span, it is advantageous to apply Maxwell's theorem of reciprocal deflections, which states the following: *The deflection at A caused by a load at B equals the deflection at B caused by this load at A.*

**FIGURE 53**

In Fig. 53b, consider the beam on a simple span $L$ to carry a unit load applied at a distance $a$ from the left-hand support. By referring to case 7 of the AISC *Manual* and applying the principle of reciprocal deflections, derive the following equations for the midspan deflection under the unit load: When $a < L/2$, $y = (3L^2a - 4a^3)/(48EI)$. When $a < L/2$, $y = [3L^2(L - a) - 4(L - a)^3]/(48EI)$.

### 2. Position the system for purposes of analysis

Position the system in such a manner that the 20-kip (89.0-kN) load lies to the left of center and the 12-kip (53.4-kN) load lies to the right of center. For the 20-kip (89.0-kN) load, set $a = x$. For the 12-kip (53.4-kN) load, $a = x + 7$; $L - a = 40 - (x + 7) = 33 - x$.

### 3. Express the total midspan deflection in terms of x

Substitute in the preceding equations. Combining all constants into a single term $k$, we find $ky = 20(3) \times 40^2x - 4x^3) + 12[3 \times 40^2(33 - x) - 4(33 - x)^3]$.

### 4. Solve for the unknown distance

Set $dy/dx = 0$ and solve for $x$. Thus, $x = 17.46$ ft (5.321 m).

For maximum deflection, position the load system with the 20-kip (89.0-kN) load 17.46 ft (5.321 m) from the left-hand support.

# Riveted and Welded Connections

In the design of riveted and welded connections in this handbook, the American Institute of Steel Construction *Specification for the Design, Fabrication and Erection of Structural Steel for Buildings* is applied. This is presented in Part 5 of the *Manual of Steel Construction.*

The structural members considered here are made of ASTM A36 steel having a yield-point stress of 36,000 lb/sq.in. (248,220 kPa). (The yield-point stress is denoted by $F_y$ in the *Specification.*) All connections considered here are made with A141 hot-driven rivets or fillet welds of A233 class E60 series electrodes.

From the *Specification,* the allowable stresses are as follows: Tensile stress in connected member, 22,000 lb/sq.in. (151,690.0 kPa); shearing stress in rivet, 15,000 lb/sq.in. (103,425.0 kPa); bearing stress on projected area of rivet, 48,500 lb/sq.in. (334,408.0 kPa); stress on throat of fillet weld, 13,600 lb/sq.in. (93,772.0 kPa).

Let $n$ denote the number of sixteenths included in the size of a fillet weld. For example, for a $3/8$-in. (9.53-mm) weld, $n = 6$. Then weld size $= n/16$. And throat area per linear inch of weld $= 0.707n/16 = 0.0442n$ sq.in.. Also, capacity of weld $= 13,600(0.0442n) = 600n$ lb/lin in (108.0$n$ N/mm).

As shown in Fig. 54, a rivet is said to be in single shear if the opposing forces tend to shear the shank along one plane and in *double shear* if they tend to shear it along two planes. The symbols $R_{ss}$, $R_{ds}$, and $R_b$ are used here to designate the shearing capacity of a rivet in single shear, the shearing capacity of a rivet in double shear, and the bearing capacity of a rivet, respectively, expressed in pounds (newtons).

## CAPACITY OF A RIVET

Determine the values of $R_{ss}$, $R_{ds}$, and $R_b$ for a $3/4$-in. (19.05-mm) and $7/8$-in. (22.23-mm) rivet.

### Calculation Procedure:

#### 1. Compute the cross-sectional area of the rivet
For the $3/4$-in. (19.05-mm) rivet, area $= A = 0.785(0.75)^2 = 0.4418$ sq.in. (2.8505 cm²). Likewise, for the $7/8$-in. (22.23-mm) rivet, $A = 0.785(0.875)^2 = 0.6013$ sq.in. (3.8796 cm²).

#### 2. Compute the single and double shearing capacity of the rivet
Let $t$ denote the thickness, in inches (millimeters) of the connected member, as shown in Fig. 54. Multiply the stressed area by the allowable stress to determine the shearing capacity of the rivet. Thus, for the 34-in. (19.05-mm) rivet, $R_{ss} = 0.4418(15,000) = 6630$ lb (29,490.2 N); $R_{ds} = 2(0.4418)(15,000) = 13,250$ lb (58,936.0 N). Note that the factor of 2 is used for a rivet in double shear.

Likewise, for the $7/8$-in. (22.23-mm) rivet, $R_{ss} = 0.6013(15,000) = 9020$ lb (40,121.0 N); $R_{ds} = 2(0.6013)(15,000) = 18,040$ lb (80,242.0 N).

#### 3. Compute the rivet bearing capacity
The effective bearing area of a rivet of diameter $d$ in. (mm) $= dt$. Thus, for the $3/4$-in. (19.05-mm) rivet, $R_b = 0.75t(48,500) = 36,380t$ lb (161,709$t$ N). For the $7/8$-in. (22.23-mm) rivet, $R_b = 0.875t(48,500) = 42,440t$ lb (188,733$t$ N). By substituting the value of $t$ in either relation, the numerical value of the bearing capacity could be obtained.

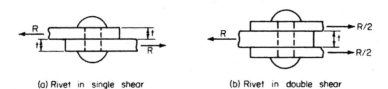

(a) Rivet in single shear          (b) Rivet in double shear

**FIGURE 54**

## *INVESTIGATION OF A LAP SPLICE*

The hanger in Fig. 55a is spliced with nine 3/4-in. (19.05-mm) rivets in the manner shown. Compute the load $P$ that may be transmitted across the joint.

### Calculation Procedure:

### 1. *Compute the capacity of the joint in shear and bearing*
There are three criteria to be considered: the shearing strength of the connection, the bearing strength of the connection, and the tensile strength of the net section of the plate at each row of rivets.

Since the load is concentric, assume that the load transmitted through each rivet is $^1/_9 P$. As plate $A$ (Fig. 55) deflects, it bears against the upper half of each rivet. Consequently, the reaction of the rivet on plate $A$ is exerted *above* the horizontal diametral plane of the rivet.

Computing the capacity of the joint in shear and in bearing yields $P_{SS} = 9(6630) = 59,700$ lb (265,545.6 N); $P_b = 9(36,380)(0.375) = 122,800$ lb (546,214.4 N).

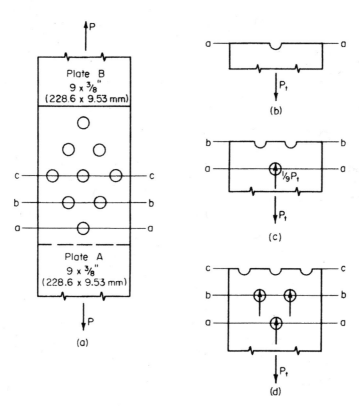

**FIGURE 55**

### 2. Compute the tensile capacity of the plate

The tensile capacity $P_t$ lb (N) of plate $A$ (Fig. 55) is required. In structural fabrication, rivet holes are usually punched $1/16$ in. (1.59 mm) larger than the rivet diameter. However, to allow for damage to the adjacent metal caused by punching, the *effective* diameter of the hole is considered to be $1/8$ in. (3.18 mm) larger than the rivet diameter.

Refer to Fig. 55b, c, and d. Equate the tensile stress at each row of rivets to 22,000 lb/sq.in. (151,690.0 kPa) to obtain $P_t$. Thus, at $aa$, residual tension = $P_t$, net area = $(9 - 0.875)(0.375) = 3.05$ sq.in. (19.679 cm²). The stress $s = P_t/3.05 = 22,000$ lb/sq.in. (151,690.0 kPa); $P_t = 67,100$ lb (298,460.0 N).

At $bb$, residual tension = $8/9 P_t$, net area = $(9 - 1.75)(0.375) = 2.72$ sq.in. (17.549 cm²); $s = 8/9 P_t/2.72 = 22,000$; $P_t = 67,300$ lb (299,350.0 N).

At $cc$, residual tension = $2/3 P_t$, net area = $(9 - 2.625)(0.375) = 2.39$ sq.in. (15.420 cm²); $s = 2/3 P_t/2.39 = 22,000$; $P_t = 78,900$ lb (350,947.0 N).

### 3. Select the lowest of the five computed values as the allowable load

Thus, $P = 59,700$ lb (265,545.6 N).

## DESIGN OF A BUTT SPLICE

A tension member in the form of a $10 \times 1/2$ in. (254.0 × 12.7 mm) steel plate is to be spliced with $7/8$-in. (22.23-mm) rivets. Design a butt splice for the maximum load the member may carry.

### Calculation Procedure:

### 1. Establish the design load

In a butt splice, the load is transmitted from one member to another through two auxiliary plates called *cover*, *strap*, or *splice* plates. The rivets are therefore in double shear.

Establish the design load, $P$ lb (N), by computing the allowable load at a cross section having one rivet hole. Thus net area = $(10 - 1)(0.5) = 4.5$ sq.in. (29.03 cm²). Then $P = 4.5(22,000) = 99,000$ lb (440,352.0 N).

### 2. Determine the number of rivets required

Applying the values of rivet capacity found in an earlier calculation procedure in this section of the handbook, determine the number of rivets required. Thus, since the rivets are in double shear, $R_{ds} = 18,040$ lb (80,241.9 N); $R_b = 42,440(0.5) = 21,220$ lb (94,386.6 N). Then $99,000/18,040 = 5.5$ rivets; use the next largest whole number, or 6 rivets.

### 3. Select a trial pattern for the rivets; investigate the tensile stress

Conduct this investigation of the tensile stress in the main plate at each row of rivets.

The trial pattern is shown in Fig. 56. The rivet spacing satisfies the requirements of the AISC *Specification*. Record the calculations as shown:

| Section | Residual tension in main plate, lb (N) | ÷ | Net area, sq.in. (cm²) | = | Stress, lb/in² (kPa) |
|---------|----------------------------------------|---|------------------------|---|----------------------|
| $aa$    | 99,000 (440,352.0)                     |   | 4.5 (29.03)            |   | 22,000 (151,690.0)   |
| $bb$    | 82,500 (366,960.0)                     |   | 4.0 (25.81)            |   | 20,600 (142,037.0)   |
| $cc$    | 49,500 (220,176.0)                     |   | 3.5 (22.58)            |   | 14,100 (97,219.5)    |

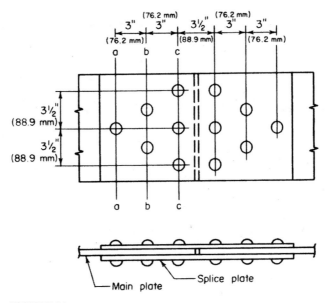

**FIGURE 56**

Study of the above computations shows that the rivet pattern is satisfactory.

### 4. Design the splice plates

To the left of the centerline, each splice plate bears against the *left* half of the rivet. Therefore, the entire load has been transmitted to the splice plates at *cc*, which is the critical section. Thus the tension in splice plate = $\frac{1}{2}(99,000)$ = 49,500 lb (220,176.0 N); plate thickness required = $49,500/[22,000(7)]$ = 0.321 in. (8.153 mm). Make the splice plates 10 × $\frac{3}{8}$ in. (254.0 × 9.53 mm).


## DESIGN OF A PIPE JOINT

A steel pipe 5 ft 6 in. (1676.4 mm) in diameter must withstand a fluid pressure of 225 lb/sq.in. (1551.4 kPa). Design the pipe and the longitudinal lap splice, using $\frac{3}{4}$-in. (19.05-mm) rivets.


### Calculation Procedure:

### 1. Evaluate the hoop tension in the pipe

Let *L* denote the length (Fig. 57) of the repeating group of rivets. In this case, this equals the rivet pitch. In Fig. 57, let *T* denote the hoop tension, in pounds (newtons), in the distance *L*. Evaluate the tension, using $T = pDL/2$, where $p$ = internal pressure, lb/sq.in. (kPa); $D$ = inside diameter of pipe, in. (mm); $L$ = length considered, in. (mm). Thus, $T = 225(66)L/2 = 7425L$.

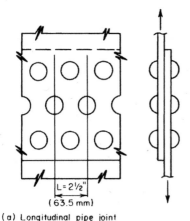

(a) Longitudinal pipe joint

(b) Free-body diagram of upper half
of pipe and contents

**FIGURE 57**

### 2. Determine the required number of rows of rivets

Adopt, tentatively, the minimum allowable pitch, which is 2 in. (50.8 mm) for $^3/_4$-in. (19.05-mm) rivets. Then establish a feasible rivet pitch. From an earlier calculation procedure in this section, $R_{ss} = 6630$ lb (29,490.0 N). Then $T = 7425(2) = 6630n$; $n = 2.24$. Use the next largest whole number of rows, or three rows of rivets. Also, $L_{max} = 3(6630)/7425 = 2.68$ in. (68.072 mm). Use a $2^1/_2$-in. (63.5-mm) pitch, as shown in Fig. 57a.

### 3. Determine the plate thickness

Establish the thickness $t$ in (mm) of the steel plates by equating the stress on the net section to its allowable value. Since the holes will be drilled, take $^{13}/_{16}$ in. (20.64 mm) as their diameter. Then $T = 22,000t(2.5 - 0.81) = 7425(2.5)$; $t = 0.50$ in. (12.7 mm); use $^1/_2$-in. (12.7-mm) plates. Also, $R_b = 36,380(0.5) > 6630$ lb (29,490.2 N). The rivet capacity is therefore limited by shear, as assumed.

## MOMENT ON RIVETED CONNECTION

The channel in Fig. 58a is connected to its supporting column with $^3/_4$-in. (19.05-mm) rivets and resists the couple indicated. Compute the shearing stress in each rivet.

### Calculation Procedure:

### 1. Compute the polar moment of inertia of the rivet group

The moment causes the channel (Fig. 58) to rotate about the centroid of the rivet group and thereby exert a tangential thrust on each rivet. This thrust is directly proportional to the radial distance to the center of the rivet.

Establish coordinate axes through the centroid of the rivet group. Compute the polar moment of inertia of the group with respect to an axis through its centroid, taking the cross-sectional area of a rivet as unity. Thus, $J = \Sigma(x^2 + y^2) = 8(2.5)^2 + 4(1.5)^2 + 4(4.5)^2 = 140$ sq.in. (903.3 cm$^2$).

### 2. Compute the radial distance to each rivet

Using the right-angle relationship, we see that $r_1 = r_4 = (2.5^2 + 4.5^2)^{0.5} = 5.15$ in. (130.810 mm); $r_2 = r_3 = (2.5^2 + 1.5^2)^{0.5} = 2.92$ in. (74.168 mm).

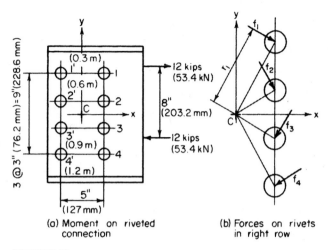

(a) Moment on riveted connection

(b) Forces on rivets in right row

**FIGURE 58**

### 3. Compute the tangential thrust on each rivet

Use the relation $f = Mr/J$. Since $M = 12,000(8) = 96,000$ lb·in. (10,846.1 N·m), $f_1 = f_4 = 96,000(5.15)/140 = 3530$ lb (15,701.4 N); and $f_2 = f_3 = 96,000(2.92)/140 = 2000$ lb (8896.0 N). The directions are shown in Fig. 58b.

### 4. Compute the shearing stress

Using $s = P/A$, we find $s_1 = s_4 = 3530/0.442 = 7990$ lb/sq.in. (55,090 kPa); also, $s_2 = s_3 = 2000/0.442 = 4520$ lb/sq.in. (29,300 kPa).

### 5. Check the rivet forces

Check the rivet forces by summing their moments with respect to an axis through the centroid. Thus $M_1 = M_4 = 3530(5.15) = 18,180$ in·lb (2054.0 N·m); $M_2 = M_3 = 2000(2.92) = 5840$ in·lb (659.8 N·m). Then EM = $4(18,180) + 4(5840) = 96,080$ in·lb (10,855.1 N·m).

## ECCENTRIC LOAD ON RIVETED CONNECTION

Calculate the maximum force exerted on a rivet in the connection shown in Fig. 59a.

### Calculation Procedure:

#### 1. Compute the effective eccentricity

To account implicitly for secondary effects associated with an eccentrically loaded connection, the AISC *Manual* recommends replacing the true eccentricity with an *effective* eccentricity.

To compute the effective eccentricity, use $e_e = e_a - (1 + n)/2$, where $e_e$ = effective eccentricity, in. (mm); $e_a$ = actual eccentricity of the load, in. (mm); $n$ = number of rivets in a vertical row. Substituting gives $e_e = 8 - (1 + 3)/2 = 6$ in. (152.4 mm).

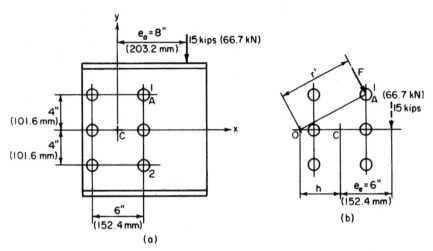

**FIGURE 59**

### 2. Replace the eccentric load with an equivalent system

The equivalent system is comprised of a concentric load $P$ lb (N) and a clockwise moment $M$ in·lb (N·m). Thus, $P = 15,000$ lb (66,720.0 N), $M = 15,000(6) = 90,000$ in·lb (10,168.2 N·m).

### 3. Compute the polar moment of inertia of the rivet group

Compute the polar moment of inertia of the rivet group with respect to an axis through its centroid. Thus, $J = \Sigma(x^2 + y^2) = 6(3)^2 + 4(4)^2 = 118$ sq.in. (761.3 cm²).

### 4. Resolve the tangential thrust on each rivet into its horizontal and vertical components

Resolve the tangential thrust $f$ lb (N) on each rivet caused by the moment into its horizontal and vertical components, $f_x$ and $f_y$, respectively. These forces are as follows: $f_x = My/J$ and $f_y = Mx/J$. Computing these forces for rivets 1 and 2 (Fig. 59) yields $f_x = 90,000(4)7118 = 3050$ lb (13,566.4 N); $f_y = 90,000(3)7118 = 2290$ lb (10,185.9 N).

### 5. Compute the thrust on each rivet caused by the concentric load

This thrust is $f_y' = 15,000/6 = 2500$ lb (11,120.0 N).

### 6. Combine the foregoing results to obtain the total force on the rivets being considered

The total force $F$ lb (N) on rivets 1 and 2 is desired. Thus, $F_x = f_x = 3050$ lb (13,566.4 N); $F_y = f_y + f_y' = 2290 + 2500 = 4790$ lb (21,305.9 N). Then $F = [(3050)^2 + (4790)^2]^{0.5} = 5680$ lb (25,264.6 N).

The above six steps comprise method 1. A second way of solving this problem, method 2, is presented below.

The total force on each rivet may also be found by locating the instantaneous center of rotation associated with this eccentric load and treating the connection as if it were subjected solely to a moment (Fig. 59b).

### 7. Locate the instantaneous center of rotation

To locate this center, apply the relation $h = J/(e_eN)$, where $N = $ total number of rivets and the other relations are as given earlier. Then $h = 118/[6(6)] = 3.28$ in. (83.31 m).

**8. Compute the force on the rivets**
Considering rivets 1 and 2, use the equation $F = Mr'/J$, where $r' =$ distance from the instantaneous center of rotation $O$ to the center of the given rivet, in. For rivets 1 and 2, $r' = 7.45$ in. (189.230 mm). Then $F = 90,000(7.45)/118 = 5680$ lb (25,264.6 N). The force on rivet 1 has an action line normal to the radius $OA$.

## DESIGN OF A WELDED LAP JOINT

The 5-in. (127.0-mm) leg of a $5 \times 3 \times 3/8$ in. ($127.0 \times 76.2 \times 9.53$ mm) angle is to be welded to a gusset plate, as shown in Fig. 60. The member will be subjected to repeated variation in stress. Design a suitable joint.

**Calculation Procedure:**

**1. Determine the properties of the angle**
In accordance with the AISC *Specification*, arrange the weld to have its centroidal axis coincide with that of the member. Refer to the AISC *Manual* to obtain the properties of the angle. Thus $A = 2.86$ sq.in. (18.453 cm²); $y_1 = 1.70$ in. (43.2 mm); $y_2 = 5.00 - 1.70 = 3.30$ in. (83.820 mm).

**2. Compute the design load and required weld length**
The design load $P$ lb (N) $= As = 2.86(22,000) = 62,920$ lb (279,868.2 N). The AISC *Specification* restricts the weld size to $5/16$ in. (7.94 mm). Hence, the weld capacity $= 5(600)$ 3000 lb/lin in (525,380.4 N/m); $L =$ weld length, in. (mm) $= P$/capacity, lb/lin in $= 62,920/3000 = 20.97$ in. (532.638 mm).

**3. Compute the joint dimensions**
In Fig. 60, set $c = 5$ in. (127.0 mm), and compute $a$ and $b$ by applying the following equations: $a = Ly_2/w - c/2$; $b = Ly_1/w - c/2$. Thus, $a = (20.97 \times 3.30)/5 - 5/2 = 11.34$ in. (288.036 mm); $b = (20.97 \times 1.70)/5 - 5/2 = 4.63$ in. (117.602 mm). Make $a = 11.5$ in. (292.10 mm) and $b = 5$ in. (127.0 mm).

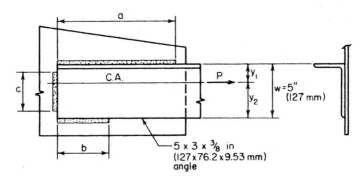

**FIGURE 60**

## ECCENTRIC LOAD ON A WELDED CONNECTION

The bracket in Fig. 61 is connected to its support with a $1/4$-in. (6.35-mm) fillet weld. Determine the maximum stress in the weld.

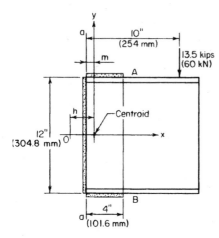

FIGURE 61

### Calculation Procedure:

#### 1. Locate the centroid of the weld group

Refer to the previous eccentric-load calculation procedure. This situation is analogous to that. Determine the stress by locating the instantaneous center of rotation. The maximum stress occurs at $A$ and $B$ (Fig. 61).

Considering the weld as concentrated along the edge of the supported member, locate the centroid of the weld group by taking moments with respect to line $aa$. Thus $m = 2(4)(2)/(12 + 2 \times 4) = 0.8$ in. (20.32 mm).

#### 2. Replace the eccentric load with an equivalent concentric load and moment

Thus $P = 13,500$ lb (60,048.0 N); $M = 124,200$ in·lb (14,032.1 N·m).

#### 3. Compute the polar moment of inertia of the weld group

This moment should be computed with respect to an axis through the centroid of the weld group. Thus $I_x = (1/12)(12)^3 + 2(4)(6)^2 = 432$ in$^3$ (7080.5 cm$^3$); $I_y = 12(0.8)^2 + 2(1/12)(4)^3 + 2(4)(2 - 0.8)^2 = 29.9$ in$^3$ (490.06 cm$^3$). Then $J = I_x + I_y = 461.9$ in$^3$ (7570.54 cm$^3$).

#### 4. Locate the instantaneous center of rotation O

This center is associated with this eccentric load by applying the equation $h = J/(eL)$, where $e$ = eccentricity of load, in. (mm), and $L$ = total length of weld, in. (mm). Thus, $e = 10 - 0.8 = 9.2$ in. (233.68 mm); $L = 12 + 2(4) = 20$ in. (508.0 mm); then $h = 461.9/[9.2(20)] = 2.51$ in. (63.754 mm).

#### 5. Compute the force on the weld

Use the equation $F = Mr'/J$, lb/lin in (N/m), where $r'$ = distance from the instantaneous center of rotation to the given point, in. (mm). At $A$ and $B$, $r' = 8.28$ in. (210.312 mm); then $F = [124,200(8.28)]/461.9 = 2230$ lb/lin in (390,532.8 N/m).

#### 6. Calculate the corresponding stress on the throat

Thus, $s = P/A = 2230/[0.707(0.25)] = 12,600$ lb/sq.in.86,877.0 kPa), where the value 0.707 is the sine of $45°$, the throat angle.

# PART 2

# STRUCTURAL STEEL DESIGN

## Structural Steel Beams and Plate Girders

In the following calculation procedures, the design of steel members is executed in accordance with the *Specification for the Design, Fabrication and Erection of Structural Steel for Buildings* of the American Institute of Steel Construction. This specification is presented in the AISC *Manual of Steel Construction.*

Most allowable stresses are functions of the yield-point stress, denoted as $F_y$ in the *Manual.* The appendix of the *Specification* presents the allowable stresses associated with each grade of structural steel together with tables intended to expedite the design. The *Commentary* in the *Specification* explains the structural theory underlying the *Specification.*

Unless otherwise noted, the structural members considered here are understood to be made of ASTM A36 steel, having a yield-point stress of 36,000 lb/sq.in. (248,220.0 kPa).

The notational system used conforms with that adopted earlier, but it is augmented to include the following: $A_f$ = area of flange, sq.in. (cm$^2$); $A_w$ = area of web, sq.in. (cm$^2$); $b_f$ = width of flange, in. (mm); $d$ = depth of section, in. (mm); $d_w$ = depth of web, in. (mm); $t_f$ = thickness of flange, in. (mm); $t_w$ = thickness of web, in. (mm); $L'$ = unbraced length of compression flange, in. (mm); $f_y$ = yield-point stress, lb/sq.in. (kPa).

## MOST ECONOMIC SECTION FOR A BEAM WITH A CONTINUOUS LATERAL SUPPORT UNDER A UNIFORM LOAD

A beam on a simple span of 30 ft (9.2 m) carries a uniform superimposed load of 1650 lb/lin ft (24,079.9 N/m). The compression flange is laterally supported along its entire length. Select the most economic section.

### Calculation Procedure:

### 1. Compute the maximum bending moment and the required section modulus

Assume that the beam weighs 50 lb/lin ft (729.7 N/m) and satisfies the requirements of a compact section as set forth in the *Specification.*

The maximum bending moment is $M = (1/8)wL^2 = (1/8)(1700)(30)^2(12) = 2,295,000$ in·lb (259,289.1 N·m).

Referring to the *Specification* shows that the allowable bending stress is 24,000 lb/sq.in. (165,480.0 kPa). Then $S = M/f = 2,295,000/24,000 = 95.6$ in$^3$ (1566.88 cm$^3$).

### 2. Select the most economic section
Refer to the AISC *Manual*, and select the most economic section. Use W18 × 55 = 98.2 in³ (1609.50 cm³); section compact. The disparity between the assumed and actual beam weight is negligible.

A second method for making this selection is shown below.

### 3. Calculate the total load on the member
Thus, the total load = $W$ = 30(1700) = 51,000 lb (226,848.0 N).

### 4. Select the most economic section
Refer to the tables of allowable uniform loads in the *Manual*, and select the most economic section. Thus use W18 × 55; $W_{allow}$ = 52,000 lb (231,296.0 N). The capacity of the beam is therefore slightly greater than required.

## MOST ECONOMIC SECTION FOR A BEAM WITH INTERMITTENT LATERAL SUPPORT UNDER UNIFORM LOAD

A beam on a simple span of 25 ft (7.6 m) carries a uniformly distributed load, including the estimated weight of the beam, of 45 kips (200.2 kN). The member is laterally supported at 5-ft (1.5-m) intervals. Select the most economic member (*a*) using A36 steel; (*b*) using A242 steel, having a yield-point stress of 50,000 lb/sq.in. (344,750.0 kPa) when the thickness of the metal is ³⁄₄ in. (19.05 mm) or less.

### Calculation Procedure:

### 1. Using the AISC allowable-load tables, select the most economic member made of A36 steel
After a trial section has been selected, it is necessary to compare the unbraced length $L'$ of the compression flange with the properties $L_c$ and $L_u$ of that section in order to establish the allowable bending stress. The variables are defined thus: $L_c$ = maximum unbraced length of the compression flange if the allowable bending stress = $0.66f_y$, measured in ft (m); $L_u$ = maximum unbraced length of the compression flange, ft (m), if the allowable bending stress is to equal $0.60f_y$.

The values of $L_c$ and $L_u$ associated with each rolled section made of the indicated grade of steel are recorded in the allowable-uniform-load tables of the AISC *Manual*. The $L_c$ value is established by applying the definition of a *laterally supported* member as presented in the *Specification*. The value of $L_u$ is established by applying a formula given in the *Specification*.

There are four conditions relating to the allowable stress:

| Condition | Allowable stress |
|---|---|
| Compact section: $L' \leq L_c$ | $0.66f_y$ |
| Compact section: $L_c < L' \leq L_u$ | $0.60f_y$ |
| Noncompact section: $L' \leq L_u$ | $0.60f_y$ |
| $L' > L_u$ | Apply the *Specification* formula—use the larger value obtained when the two formulas given are applied. |

The values of allowable uniform load given in the AISC *Manual* apply to beams of A36 steel satisfying the first or third condition above, depending on whether the section is compact or noncompact.

Referring to the table in the *Manual*, we see that the most economic section made of A36 steel is W16 × 45; $W_{allow}$ = 46 kips (204.6 kN), where $W_{allow}$ = allowable load on the beam, kips (kN). Also, $L_c$ = 7.6 > 5. Hence, the beam is acceptable.

### 2. Compute the equivalent load for a member of A242 steel

To apply the AISC *Manual* tables to choose a member of A242 steel, assume that the shape selected will be compact. Transform the actual load to an equivalent load by applying the conversion factor 1.38, that is, the ratio of the allowable stresses. The conversion factors are recorded in the *Manual* tables. Thus, equivalent load = 45/1.38 = 32.6 kips (145.0 N).

### 3. Determine the highest satisfactory section

Enter the *Manual* allowable-load table with the load value computed in step 2, and select the lightest section that appears to be satisfactory. Try W16 × 36; $W_{allow}$ = 36 kips (160.1 N). However, this section is noncompact in A242 steel, and the equivalent load of 32.6 kips (145.0 N) is not valid for this section.

### 4. Revise the equivalent load

To determine whether the W16 × 36 will suffice, revise the equivalent load. Check the $L_u$ value of this section in A242 steel. Then equivalent load = 45/1.25 = 36 kips (160.1 N), $L_u$ = 6.3 ft (1.92 m) > 5 ft (1.5 m); use W16 × 36.

### 5. Verify the second part of the design

To verify the second part of the design, calculate the bending stress in the W16 × 36, using $S$ = 56.3 in$^3$ (922.76 cm$^3$) from the *Manual*. Thus $M$ = $(1/8)WL$ = $(1/8)(45,000)(25)(12)$ = 1,688,000 in·lb (190,710.2 N·m); $f = M/S$ = 1,688,000/56.3 = 30,000 lb/sq.in. (206,850.0 kPa). This stress is acceptable.

## DESIGN OF A BEAM WITH REDUCED ALLOWABLE STRESS

The compression flange of the beam in Fig. 1a will be braced only at points $A$, $B$, $C$, $D$, and $E$. Using AISC data, a designer has selected W21 × 55 section for the beam. Verify the design.

### Calculation Procedure:

### 1. Calculate the reactions; construct the shear and bending-moment diagrams

The results of this step are shown in Fig. 1.

### 2. Record the properties of the selected section

Using the AISC *Manual*, record the following properties of the 21WF55 section: $S$ = 109.7 in$^3$ (1797.98 cm$^3$); $I_y$ = 44.0 in$^4$ (1831.41 cm$^4$); $b_f$ = 8.215 in. (208.661 mm); $t_f$ = 0.522 in. (13.258 mm); $d$ = 20.80 in. (528.32 mm); $t_w$ = 0.375 in. (9.525 mm); $d/A_f$ = 4.85/in. (0.1909/mm); $L_c$ = 8.9 ft (2.71 m); $L_u$ = 9.4 ft (2.87 m).

Since $L' > L_u$, the allowable stress must be reduced in the manner prescribed in the *Manual*.

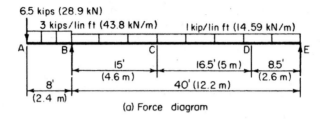

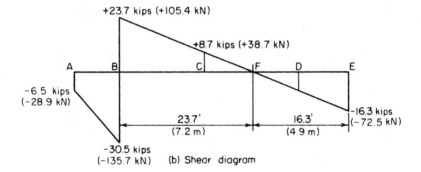

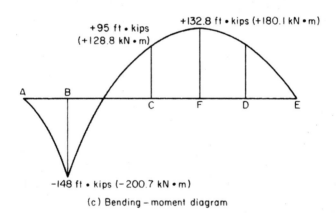

**FIGURE 1**

### 3. *Calculate the radius of gyration*

Calculate the radius of gyration with respect to the $y$ axis of a T section comprising the compression flange and one-sixth the web, neglecting the area of the fillets. Referring to Fig. 2, we see $A_f = 8.215(0.522) = 4.29$ sq.in. $(27.679 \text{ cm}^2)$; $(1/6)A_w = (1/6)(19.76)(0.375) = 1.24$; $A_T = 5.53$ sq.in. $(35.680 \text{ cm}^2)$; $I_T = 0.5I_y$ of the section $= 22.0$ in$^4$ $(915.70 \text{ cm}^4)$; $r = (22.0/5.53)^{0.5} = 1.99$ in. $(50.546 \text{ mm})$.

### 4. Calculate the allowable stress in each interval between lateral supports

By applying the provisions of the *Manual*, calculate the allowable stress in each interval between lateral supports, and compare this with the actual stress. For A36 steel, the *Manual* formula (4) reduces to $f_1 = 22,000 - 0.679(L'/r)^2/C_b$ lb/sq.in. (kPa). By *Manual* formula (5), $f_2 = 12,000,000/(L'd/A_f)$ lb/sq.in. (kPa). Set the allowable stress equal to the greater of these values.

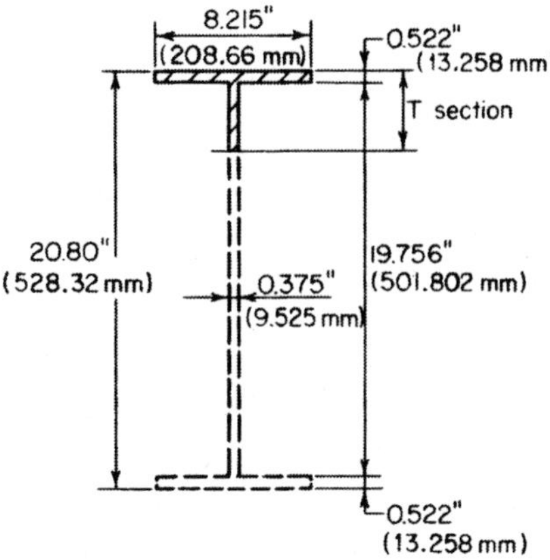

**FIGURE 2.** Dimensions of W21 × 55.

For interval *AB*: $L' = 8$ ft (2.4 m) $< L_c$; ∴ $f_{allow} = 24,000$ lb/sq.in. (165,480.0 kPa); $f_{max} = 148,000(12)/109.7 = 16,200$ lb/sq.in. (111,699.0 kPa)—this is acceptable.

For interval *BC*: $L'/r = 15(12)/1.99 = 90.5$; $M_1/M_2 = 95/(-148) = -0.642$; $C_b = 1.75 - 1.05(-0.642) + 0.3(-0.642)^2 = 2.55$; ∴ set $C_b = 2.3$; $f_1 = 22,000 - 0.679(90.5)^2/2.3 = 19,600$ lb/sq.in. (135,142.0 kPa); $f_2 = 12,000,000/[15(12)(4.85)] = 13,700$ lb/sq.in. (94,461.5 kPa); $f_{max} = 16,200 < 19,600$ lb/sq.in. (135,142.0 kPa). This is acceptable.

Interval *CD*: Since the maximum moment occurs within the interval rather than at a boundary section, $C_b = 1$; $L'/r = 16.5(12)/1.99 = 99.5$; $f_1 = 22,000 - 0.679(99.5)^2 = 15,300$ lb/sq.in. (105,493.5 kPa); $f_2 = 12,000,000/[16.5(12)(4.85)] = 12,500$ lb/sq.in. (86,187.5 kPa); $f_{max} = 132,800(12)/109.7 = 14,500 < 15,300$ lb/sq.in. (105,493.5 kPa). This stress is acceptable.

Interval *DE*: The allowable stress is 24,000 lb/sq.in. (165,480.0 kPa), and the actual stress is considerably below this value. The W21 × 55 is therefore satisfactory. Where deflection is the criterion, the member should be checked by using the *Specification*.

## DESIGN OF A COVER-PLATED BEAM

Following the fabrication of a W18 × 60 beam, a revision was made in the architectural plans, and the member must now be designed to support the loads shown in Fig. 3a. Cover plates are to be welded to both flanges to develop the required strength. Design these plates and their connection to the W shape, using fillet welds of A233 class E60 series electrodes. The member has continuous lateral support.

### Calculation Procedure:

### 1. Construct the shear and bending-moment diagrams

These are shown in Fig. 3. Also, $M_E = 340.3$ ft·kips (461.44 kN·m).

### 2. Calculate the required section modulus, assuming the built-up section will be compact

The section modulus $S = M/f = 340.3(12)/24 = 170.2$ in³ (2789.58 cm³).

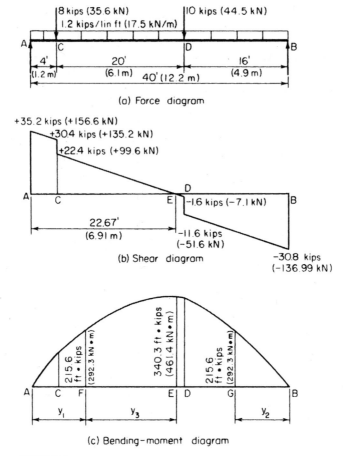

(a) Force diagram

(b) Shear diagram

(c) Bending-moment diagram

**FIGURE 3**

### 3. *Record the properties of the beam section*

Refer to the AISC *Manual*, and record the following properties for the W18 × 60; $d =$ 18.25 in. (463.550 mm); $b_f =$ 7.56 in. (192.024 mm); $t_f =$ 0.695 in. (17.653 mm); $I =$ 984 in$^4$ (40.957 cm$^4$); $S =$ 107.8 in$^3$ (1766.84 cm$^3$).

### 4. *Select a trial section*

Apply the approximation $A = 1.05(S - S_{WF})/d_{WF}$, where $A$ = area of one cover plate, sq.in. (cm$^2$); $S$ = section modulus required, in$^3$ (cm$^3$); $S_{WF}$ = section modulus of wide-flange shape, in$^3$ (cm$^3$); $d_{WF}$ = depth of wide-flange shape, in. (mm). Then $A = [1.05(170.2 - 107.8)]/18.25 = 3.59$ sq.in. (23.163 cm$^2$).

Try 10 × ³⁄₈ in. (254.0 × 9.5 mm) plates with $A = 3.75$ sq.in. (24.195 cm$^2$). Since the beam flange is 7.5 in. (190.50 mm) wide, ample space is available to accommodate the welds.

### 5. *Ascertain whether the assumed size of the cover plates satisfies the AISC* Specification

Using the appropriate AISC *Manual* section, we find $7.56/0.375 = 20.2 < 32$, which is acceptable; $1/2(10 - 7.56)/0.375 = 3.25 < 16$, which is acceptable.

### 6. *Test the adequacy of the trial section*

Calculate the section modulus of the trial section. Referring to Fig. 4a, we see $I = 984 + 2(3.75)(9.31)^2 - 1634$ in⁴ (68,012.1 cm⁴); $S = I/c = 1634/9.5 = 172.0$ in³ (2819.08 cm³). The reinforced section is therefore satisfactory.

### 7. *Locate the points at which the cover plates are not needed*

To locate the points at which the cover plates may theoretically be dispensed with, calculate the moment capacity of the wide-flange shape alone. Thus, $M = fS = 24(107.8)/12 = 215.6$ ft·kips (292.3 kN·m).

### 8. *Locate the points at which the computed moment occurs*

These points are $F$ and $G$ (Fig. 3). Thus, $M_F = 35.2y_2 - 8(y_1 - 4) - 1/2(1.2y_2{}^2) = 215.6$; $y_2 = 8.25$ ft (2.515 m); $M_G = 30.8y_2 - 1/2(1.2y_2^2) = 215.6$; $y_2 = 8.36$ ft (2.548 m).

Alternatively, locate $F$ by considering the area under the shear diagram between $E$ and $F$. Thus $M_F = 340.3 - 1/2(1.2y_3^2) = 215.6$; $y_3 = 14.42$ ft (4.395 m); $y_1 = 22.67 - 14.42 = 8.25$ ft (2.515 m).

For symmetry, center the cover plates about midspan, placing the theoretical cutoff points at 8 ft 3 in. (2.51 m) from each support.

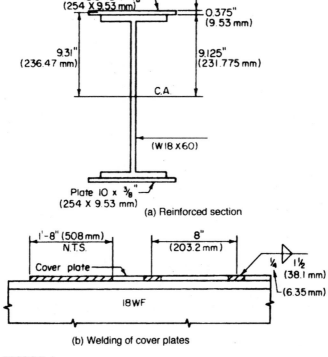

(a) Reinforced section

(b) Welding of cover plates

**FIGURE 4**

### 9. Calculate the axial force in the cover plate

Calculate the axial force $P$ lb (N) in the cover plate at its end by computing the mean bending stress. Determine the length of fillet weld required to transmit this force to the W shape. Thus $f_{mean} = My/I = 215,600(12)(9.31)/1634 = 14,740$ lb/sq.in. (101,632.3 kPa). Then $P = Af_{mean} = 3.75(14,740) = 55,280$ lb (245,885.4 N). Use a $1/4$-in. (6.35-mm) fillet weld, which satisfies the requirements of the *Specification*. The capacity of the weld = $4(600) = 2400$ lb/lin in. (420,304.3 N/m). Then the length $L$ required for this weld is $L = 55,280/2400 = 23.0$ in. (584.20 mm).

### 10. Extend the cover plates

In accordance with the *Specification*, extend the cover plates 20 in. (508.0 mm) beyond the theoretical cutoff point at each end, and supply a continuous $1/4$-in. fillet weld along both edges in this extension. This requirement yields 40 in. (1016.0 mm) of weld as compared with the 23 in. (584.2 mm) needed to develop the plate.

### 11. Calculate the horizontal shear flow at the inner surface of the cover plate

Choose $F$ or $G$, whichever is larger. Design the intermittent fillet weld to resist this shear flow. Thus $V_F = 35.2 - 8 - 1.2(8.25) = 17.3$ kips (76.95 kN); $V_G = -30.8 + 1.2(8.36) = -20.8$ kips (−92.51 kN). Then $q = VQ/I = 20,800(3.75)(9.31)/1634 = 444$ lb/lin in. (77,756.3 N/m).

The *Specification* calls for a minimum weld length of 1.5 in. (38.10 mm). Let $s$ denote the center-to-center spacing as governed by shear. Then $s = 2(1.5)(2400)/444 = 16.2$ in. (411.48 mm). However, the *Specification* imposes additional restrictions on the weld spacing. To preclude the possibility of error in fabrication, provide an identical spacing at the top and bottom. Thus, $s_{max} = 21(0.375) = 7.9$ in. (200.66 mm). Therefore, use a $1/4$-in. (6.35-mm) fillet weld, 1.5 in. (38.10 mm) long, 8 in. (203.2 mm) on centers, as shown in Fig. 4a.

## DESIGN OF A CONTINUOUS BEAM

The beam in Fig. 5a is continuous from $A$ to $D$ and is laterally supported at 5-ft (1.5-m) intervals. Design the member.

### Calculation Procedure:

### 1. Find the bending moments at the interior supports; calculate the reactions and construct shear and bending-moment diagrams

The maximum moments are +101.7 ft·kips (137.9 kN·m) and −130.2 ft·kips (176.55 kN·m).

### 2. Calculate the modified maximum moments

Calculate these moments in the manner prescribed in the AISC *Specification*. The clause covering this calculation is based on the postelastic behavior of a continuous beam. (Refer to a later calculation procedure for an analysis of this behavior.)

Modified maximum moments: $+101.7 + 0.1(0.5)(115.9 + 130.2) = +114.0$ ft·kips (154.58 kN·m); $0.9(-130.2) = -117.2$ ft·kips (−158.92 kN·m); design moment = 117.2 ft·kips (158.92 kN·m).

### 3. Select the beam size

Thus, $S = M/f = 117.2(12)/24 = 58.6$ in³ (960.45 cm³). Use W16 × 40 with $S = 64.4$ in³ (1055.52 cm³); $L_c = 7.6$ ft (2.32 m).

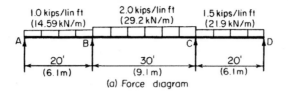

(a) Force diagram

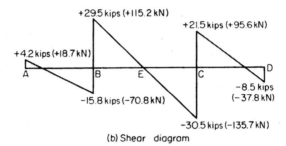

(b) Shear diagram

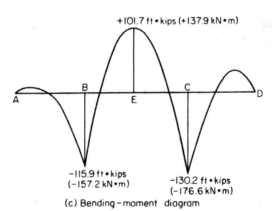

(c) Bending-moment diagram

**FIGURE 5**

## SHEARING STRESS IN A BEAM— EXACT METHOD

Calculate the maximum shearing stress in a W18 × 55 beam at a section where the vertical shear is 70 kips (311.4 kN).

### Calculation Procedure:

#### 1. Record the relevant properties of the member

The shearing stress is a maximum at the centroidal axis and is given by $v = VQ/(It)$. The static moment of the area above this axis is found by applying the properties of the

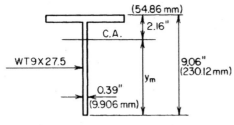

**FIGURE 6**

WT9 × 27.5, which are presented in the AISC *Manual*. Note that the T section considered is one-half the wide-flange section being used. See Fig. 6.

The properties of these sections are $I_w$ = 890 in⁴ (37,044.6 cm⁴); $A_T$ = 8.10 sq.in. (52.261 cm²); $t_w$ = 0.39 in. (9.906 mm); $y_m$ = 9.06 – 2.16 = 6.90 in. (175.26 mm).

**2. Calculate the shearing stress at the centroidal axis**
Substituting gives $Q$ = 8.10(6.90) = 55.9 in³ (916.20 cm³); then $v$ = 70,000(55.9)/[890(0.39)] = 11,270 lb/sq.in. (77,706.7 kPa).

## SHEARING STRESS IN A BEAM— APPROXIMATE METHOD

Solve the previous calculation procedure, using the approximate method of determining the shearing stress in a beam.

**Calculation Procedure:**

**1. Assume that the vertical shear is resisted solely by the web**
Consider the web as extending the full depth of the section and the shearing stress as uniform across the web. Compare the results obtained by the exact and the approximate methods.

**2. Compute the shear stress**
Take the depth of the web as 18.12 in. (460.248 mm), $v$ = 70,000/[18.12(0.39)] = 9910 lb/sq.in. (68,329.45 kPa). Thus, the ratio of the computed stresses is 11,270/9910 = 1.14.

Since the error inherent in the approximate method is not unduly large, this method is applied in assessing the shear capacity of a beam. The allowable shear $V$ for each rolled section is recorded in the allowable-uniform-load tables of the AISC *Manual*.

The design of a rolled section is governed by the shearing stress only in those instances where the ratio of maximum shear to maximum moment is extraordinarily large. This condition exists in a heavily loaded short-span beam and a beam that carries a large concentrated load near its support.

## MOMENT CAPACITY OF A WELDED PLATE GIRDER

A welded plate girder is composed of a 66 × ³⁄₈ in. (1676.4 × 9.53 mm) web plate and two 20 × ³⁄₄ in. (508.0 × 19.05 mm) flange plates. The unbraced length of the compression flange is 18 ft (5.5 m). If $C_b$ = 1, what bending moment can this member resist?

## Calculation Procedure:

### 1. Compute the properties of the section
The tables in the AISC *Manual* are helpful in calculating the moment of inertia. Thus $A_f$ = 15 sq.in. (96.8 cm²); $A_w$ = 24.75 sq.in. (159.687 cm²); $I$ = 42,400 in⁴ (176.481 dm⁴); $S$ = 1256 in³ (20,585.8 cm³).

For the *T* section comprising the flange and one-sixth the web, $A$ = 15 + 4.13 = 19.13 sq.in. (123.427 cm²); then $I$ = (1/12)(0.75)(20)³ = 500 in⁴ (2081.1 dm⁴); $r$ = (500/19.13)⁰·⁵ = 5.11 in. (129.794 mm); $L'/r$ = 18(12)/5.11 = 42.3.

### 2. Ascertain if the member satisfies the AISC Specification
Let $h$ denote the clear distance between flanges, in. (cm). Then: flange, ¹/₂(20)/0.75 = 13.3 < 16—this is acceptable; web, $h/t_w$ = 66/0.375 = 176 < 320—this is acceptable.

### 3. Compute the allowable bending stress
Use $f_1$ = 22,000 − 0.679(L'/r)²/C_b, or $f_1$ = 22,000 − 0.679(42.3)² = 20,800 lb/sq.in. (143,416.0 kPa); $f_2$ = 12,000,000/(L'd/A_f) = 12,000,000(15)/[18(12)(67.5)] = 12,300 lb/sq.in. (84,808.5 kPa). Therefore, use 20,800 lb/sq.in. (143,416.0 kPa) because it is the larger of the two stresses.

### 4. Reduce the allowable bending stress In accordance with the AISC Specification
Using the equation given in the *Manual* yields $f_3$ = 20,800{1 − 0.005(24.75/15)[176 − 24,000/(20,800)⁰·⁵]} = 20,600 lb/sq.in. (142,037.0 kPa).

### 5. Determine the allowable bending moment
Use $M = f_3 S$ = 20.6(1256)/12 = 2156 ft·kips (2923.5 kN·m).

## ANALYSIS OF A RIVETED PLATE GIRDER

A plate girder is composed of one web plate 48 × ³/₈ in. (1219.2 × 9.53 mm); four flange angles 6 × 4 × ³/₄ in. (152.4 × 101.6 × 19.05 mm); two cover plates 14 × ¹/₂ in. (355.6 × 12.7 mm). The flange angles are set 48.5 in. (1231.90 mm) back to back with their 6-in. (152.4-mm) legs outstanding; they are connected to the web plate by ⁷/₈-in. (22.2-mm) rivets. If the member has continuous lateral support, what bending moment may be applied? What spacing of flange-to-web rivets is required in a panel where the vertical shear is 180 kips (800.6 kN)?

## Calculation Procedure:

### 1. Obtain the properties of the angles from the AISC Manual
Record the angle dimensions as shown in Fig. 7.

### 2. Check the cover plates for compliance with the AISC Specification
The cover plates are found to comply with the pertinent sections of the *Specification*.

### 3. Compute the gross flange area and rivet-hole area
Ascertain whether the *Specification* requires a reduction in the flange area. Therefore gross flange area = 2(6.94) + 7.0 = 20.88 sq.in. (134.718 cm²); area of rivet holes = 2(¹/₂)(1)4(³/₄)(1) = 4.00 sq.in. (25.808 cm²); allowable area of holes = 0.15(20.88) = 3.13.

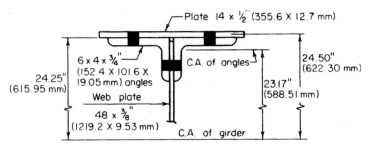

**FIGURE 7**

The excess area = hole area − allowable area = 4.00 − 3.13 = 0.87 sq.in. (5.613 cm²). Consider that this excess area is removed from the outstanding legs of the angles, at both the top and the bottom.

### 4. Compute the moment of inertia of the net section

|                                              | in⁴    | dm⁴      |
|----------------------------------------------|--------|----------|
| One web plate, $I_0$                         | 3,456  | 14.384   |
| Four flange angles, $I_0$                    | 35     | 0.1456   |
| $Ay^2 = 4(6.94)(23.17)^2$                    | 14,900 | 62.0184  |
| Two cover plates:                            |        |          |
| $Ay^2 = 2(7.0)(24.50)^2$                     | 8,400  | 34.9634  |
| $I$ of gross section                         | 26,791 | 111.5123 |
| Deduct $2(0.87)(23.88)^2$ for excess area    | 991    | 4.12485  |
| $I$ of net section                           | 25,800 | 107.387  |

### 5. Establish the allowable bending stress

Use the *Specification*. Thus $h/t_w$ = (48.5 − 8)/0.375 < 24,000/(22,000)$^{0.5}$; ∴ 22,000 lb/sq.in. (151,690.0 kPa). Also, $M$ = $fI/c$ = 22(25,800)/[24.75(12)] = 1911 ft·kips (2591.3 kN·m).

### 6. Calculate the horizontal shear flow to be resisted

Here $Q$ of flange = 13.88(23.17) + 7.0(24.50) − 0.87(23.88) = 472 in³ (7736.1 cm³); $q$ = $VQ/I$ = 180,000(472)/25,800 = 3290 lb/lin in. (576,167.2 N/m).

From a previous calculation procedure, $R_{ds}$ = 18,040 lb (80,241.9 N); $R_b$ = 42,440(0.375) = 15,900 lb (70,723.2 N); $s$ = 15,900/3290 = 4.8 in. (121.92 mm), where $s$ = allowable rivet spacing, in. (mm). Therefore, use a 4³/₄-in. (120.65-mm) rivet pitch. This satisfies the requirements of the *Specification*.

*Note:* To determine the allowable rivet spacing, divide the horizontal shear flow into the rivet capacity.

## DESIGN OF A WELDED PLATE GIRDER

A plate girder of welded construction is to support the loads shown in Fig. 8a. The distributed load will be applied to the top flange, thereby offering continuous lateral support.

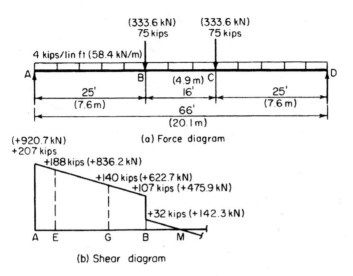

(a) Force diagram

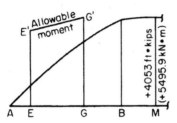

(b) Shear diagram

(c) Bending-moment diagram

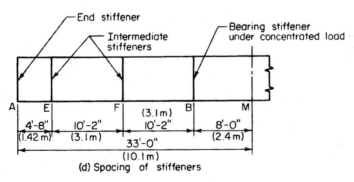

(d) Spacing of stiffeners

**FIGURE 8**

At its ends, the girder will bear on masonry buttresses. The total depth of the girder is restricted to approximately 70 in. (1778.0 mm). Select the cross section, establish the spacing of the transverse stiffeners, and design both the intermediate stiffeners and the bearing stiffeners at the supports.

## Calculation Procedure:

### 1. Construct the shear and bending-moment diagrams
These diagrams are shown in Fig. 8.

### 2. Choose the web-plate dimensions
Since the total depth is limited to about 70 in. (1778.0 mm), use a 68-in. (1727.2-mm) deep web plate. Determine the plate thickness, using the *Specification* limits, which are a slenderness ratio $h/t_w$ of 320. However, if an allowable bending stress of 22,000 lb/sq.in. (151,690.0 kPa) is to be maintained, the *Specification* imposes an upper limit of $(22,000)^{0.5} = 162$. Then $t_w = h/162 = 68/162 = 0.42$ in. (10.668 mm); use a $7/16$-in. (11.112-mm) plate. Hence, the area of the web $A_w = 29.75$ sq.in. (191.947 cm²).

### 3. Select the flange plates
Apply the approximation $A_f = Mc/(2fy^2) - A_w/6$, where $y =$ distance from the neutral axis to the centroidal axis of the flange, in. (mm).

Assume 1-in. (25.4-mm) flange plates. Then $A_f = 4053(12)(35)/[2(22)(34.5)^2] - 29.75/6 = 27.54$ sq.in. (177.688 cm²). Try $22 \times 1^{1}/4$ in. (558.8 × 31.75 mm) plates with $A_f = 27.5$ sq.in. (177.43 cm²). The width-thickness ratio of projection $= 11/1.25 = 8.8 < 16$. This is acceptable.

Thus, the trial section will be one web plate $68 \times 7/16$ in. (1727 × 11.11 mm); two flange plates $22 \times 1^{1}/4$ in. (558.8 × 31.75 mm).

### 4. Test the adequacy of the trial section
For this test, compute the maximum flexural and shearing stresses. Thus, $I = (1/12)(0.438)(68)^3 + 2(27.5)(34.63)^2 = 77,440$ in³ (1,269,241.6 cm³); $f = Mc/I = 4053(12)(35.25)/77,440 = 22.1$ kips/sq.in. (152.38 MPa). This is acceptable. Also, $v = 207/29.75 = 6.96 < 14.5$ kips/sq.in. (99.98 MPa). This is acceptable. Hence, the trial section is satisfactory.

### 5. Determine the distance of the stiffeners from the girder ends
Refer to Fig. 8d for the spacing of the intermediate stiffeners. Establish the length of the end panel AE. The *Specification* stipulates that the smaller dimension of the end panel shall not exceed $11,000(0.438)/(6960)^{0.5} = 57.8 < 68$ in. (1727.2 mm). Therefore, provide stiffeners at 56 in. (1422.4 mm) from the ends.

### 6. Ascertain whether additional intermediate stiffeners are required
See whether stiffeners are required in the interval EB by applying the *Specification* criteria.

Stiffeners are not required when $h/t_w < 260$ and the shearing stress within the panel is below the value given by either of two equations in the *Specification*, whichever equation applies. Thus $EB = 396 - (56 + 96) = 244$ in. (6197.6 mm); $h/t_w = 68/0.438 = 155 < 260$; this is acceptable. Also, $a/h = 244/68 = 3.59$.

In lieu of solving either of the equations given in the *Specification*, enter the table of $a/h$, $h/t_w$ values given in the AISC *Manual* to obtain the allowable shear stress. Thus, with $a/h > 3$ and $h/t_w = 155$, $v_{allow} = 3.45$ kips/sq.in. (23.787 MPa) from the table.

At $E$, $V = 207 - 4.67(4) = 188$ kips (836.2 kN); $v = 188/29.75 = 6.32$ kips/sq.in. (43.576 MPa) > 3.45 kips/sq.in. (23.787 MPa); therefore, intermediate stiffeners are required in $EB$.

### 7. Provide stiffeners, and investigate the suitability of their tentative spacing

Provide stiffeners at $F$, the center of $EB$. See whether this spacing satisfies the *Specification*. Thus $[260/(h/t_w)]^2 = (260/155)^2 = 2.81$; $a/h = 122/68 = 1.79 < 2.81$. This is acceptable.

Entering the table referred to in step 6 with $a/h = 1.79$ and $h/t_w = 155$ shows $v_{\text{allow}} = 7.85 > 6.32$. This is acceptable.

Before we conclude that the stiffener spacing is satisfactory, it is necessary to investigate the combined shearing and bending stress and the bearing stress in interval $EB$.

### 8. Analyze the combination of shearing and bending stress

This analysis should be made throughout $EB$ in the light of the *Specification* requirements. The net effect is to reduce the allowable bending moment whenever $V > 0.6V_{\text{allow}}$. Thus, $V_{\text{allow}} = 7.85(29.75) = 234$ kips (1040.8 kN); and $0.6(234) = 140$ kips (622.7 kN).

In Fig. 8*b*, locate the boundary section $G$ where $V = 140$ kips (622.7 kN). The allowable moment must be reduced to the left of $G$. Thus, $AG = (207 - 140)/4 = 16.75$ ft (5.105 m); $M_G = 2906$ ft·kips (3940.5 kN·m); $M_E = 922$ ft·kips (1250.2 kN·m). At $G$, $M_{\text{allow}} = 4053$ ft·kips (5495.8 kN·m). At $E$, $f_{\text{allow}} = [0.825 - 0.375(188/234)](36) = 18.9$ kips/sq.in. (130.31 MPa); $M_{\text{allow}} = 18.9(77,440)/[35.25(12)] = 3460$ ft·kips (4691.8 kN·m).

In Fig. 8*c*, plot points E' and G' to represent the allowable moments and connect these points with a straight line. In all instances, $M < M_{\text{allow}}$.

### 9. Use an alternative procedure, if desired

As an alternative procedure in step 8, establish the interval within which $M > 0.75M_{\text{allow}}$ and reduce the allowable shear in accordance with the equation given in the *Specification*.

### 10. Compare the bearing stress under the uniform load with the allowable stress

The allowable stress given in the *Specification* $f_{b,\text{allow}} = [5.5 + 4/(a/h)^2]10,000/(h/t_w)^2$ kips/sq.in. (MPa), or, for this girder, $f_{b,\text{allow}} = (5.5 + 4/1.79^2)10,000/155^2 = 2.81$ kips/sq.in. (19.374 MPa). Then $f_b = 4/[12(0.438)] = 0.76$ kips/sq.in. (5.240 MPa). This is acceptable. The stiffener spacing in interval $EB$ is therefore satisfactory in all respects.

### 11. Investigate the need for transverse stiffeners in the center interval

Considering the interval $BC$, $V = 32$ kips (142.3 kN); $v = 1.08$ kips/sq.in. (7.447 MPa); $a/h = 192/68 = 2.82 \simeq [260/(h/t_w)]^2$.

The *Manual* table used in step 6 shows that $v_{\text{allow}} > 1.08$ kips/sq.in. (7.447 MPa); $f_{b,\text{allow}} = (5.5 + 4/2.82^2)10,000/155^2 = 2.49$ kips/sq.in. (17.169 MPa) > 0.76 kips/sq.in. (5.240 MPa). This is acceptable. Since all requirements are satisfied, stiffeners are not needed in interval $BC$.

### 12. Design the intermediate stiffeners in accordance with the Specification

For the interval $EB$, the preceding calculations yield these values: $v = 6.32$ kips/sq.in. (43.576 MPa); $v_{\text{allow}} = 7.85$ kips/sq.in. (54.125 MPa). Enter the table mentioned in step 6 with $a/h = 1.79$ and $h/t_w = 155$ to obtain the percentage of web area, shown in italics in the table. Thus, $A_{st}$ required $= 0.0745(29.75)(6.32/7.85) = 1.78$ sq.in. (11.485 cm²). Try two $4 \times \frac{1}{4}$ in. (101.6 $\times$ 6.35 mm) plates; $A_{st} = 2.0$ sq.in. (12.90 cm²); width-thickness ratio $= 4/0.25 = 16$. This is acceptable. Also, $(h/50)^4 = (68/50)^4 = 3.42$ in⁴ (142.351 cm⁴);

$I = (1/12)(0.25)(8.44)^3 = 12.52$ in$^4$ (521.121 cm$^4$) > 3.42 in$^4$ (142.351 cm$^4$). This is acceptable.

The stiffeners must be in intimate contact with the compression flange, but they may terminate 1$^3$/$_4$ in. (44.45 mm) from the tension flange. The connection of the stiffeners to the web must transmit the vertical shear specified in the *Specification*.

### 13. Design the bearing stiffeners at the supports

Use the directions given in the *Specification*. The stiffeners are considered to act in conjunction with the tributary portion of the web to form a column section, as shown in Fig. 9. Thus, area of web = 5.25(0.438) = 2.30 sq.in. (14.839 cm$^2$). Assume an allowable stress of 20 kips/sq.in. (137.9 MPa). Then, plate area required = 207/20 − 2.30 = 8.05 sq.in. (51.938 cm$^2$).

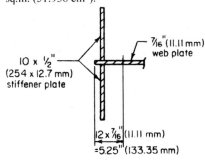

**FIGURE 9.** Effective column section.

Try two plates 10 × $^1$/$_2$ in. (254.0 × 12.7 mm), and compute the column capacity of the section. Thus, $A$ = 2(10)(0.5) + 2.30 = 12.30 sq.in. (79.359 cm$^2$); $I$ = (1/12)(0.5)(20.44)$^3$ = 356 in$^4$ (1.4818 dm$^4$); $r$ = (356/12.30)$^{0.5}$ = 5.38 in. (136.652 mm); $L/r$ = 0.75(68)/5.38 = 9.5.

Enter the table of slenderness ratio and allowable stress in the *Manual* with the slenderness ratio of 9.5, and obtain an allowable stress of 21.2 kips/sq.in. (146.17 MPa). Then $f$ = 207/12.30 = 16.8 kips/sq.in. (115.84 MPa) < 21.2 kips/sq.in. (146.17 MPa). This is acceptable.

Compute the bearing stress in the stiffeners. In computing the bearing area, assume that each stiffener will be clipped 1 in. (25.4 mm) to clear the flange-to-web welding. Then $f$ = 207/[2(9)(0.5)] = 23 kips/sq.in. (158.6 MPa). The *Specification* provides an allowable stress of 33 kips/sq.in. (227.5 MPa).

The 10 × $^1$/$_2$ in. (254.0)(12.7 mm) stiffeners at the supports are therefore satisfactory with respect to both column action and bearing.

# Steel Columns and Tension Members

The general remarks appearing at the opening of the previous part apply to this part as well.

A column is a compression member having a length that is very large in relation to its lateral dimensions. The *effective* length of a column is the distance between adjacent points of contraflexure in the buckled column or in the imaginary extension of the buckled column, as shown in Fig. 10. The column length is denoted by $L$, and the effective length by $KL$. Recommended design values of $K$ are given in the AISC *Manual*.

The capacity of a column is a function of its effective length and the properties of its cross section. It therefore becomes necessary to formulate certain principles pertaining to the properties of an area.

Consider that the moment of inertia $I$ of an area is evaluated with respect to a group of concurrent axes. There is a distinct value of $I$ associated with each axis, as given by earlier equations in this section. The *major* axis is the one for which $I$ is maximum; the *minor* axis is the one for which $I$ is minimum. The major and minor axes are referred to collectively as the *principal* axes.

With reference to the equation given earlier, namely, $I_{x''} = I_{x'} \cos^2 \theta + I_{y'} \sin^2 \theta - P_{x'y'} \sin 2\theta$, the orientation of the principal axes relative to the given $x'$ and $y'$ axes is found by differentiating $I_{x''}$ with respect to $\theta$, equating this derivative to zero, and solving for $\theta$ to obtain $\tan 2\theta = 2P_{x'y'}/(I_{y'} - I_{x'})$, Fig. 15.

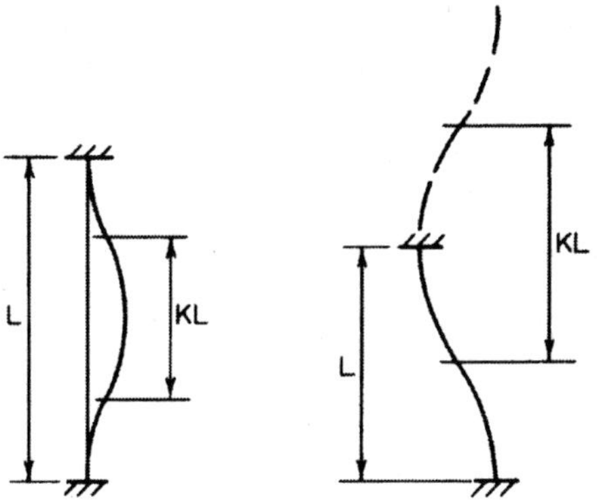

**FIGURE 10.** Effective column lengths.

The following statements are corollaries of this equation:

1. The principal axes through a given point are mutually perpendicular, since the two values of $\theta$ that satisfy this equation differ by 90°.
2. The product of inertia of an area with respect to its principal axes is zero.
3. Conversely, if the product of inertia of an area with respect to two mutually perpendicular axes is zero, these are principal axes.
4. An axis of symmetry is a principal axis, for the product of inertia of the area with respect to this axis and one perpendicular thereto is zero.

Let $A_1$ and $A_2$ denote two areas, both of which have a radius of gyration $r$ with respect to a given axis. The radius of gyration of their composite area is found in this manner: $I_c = I_1 + I_2 = A_1r^2 + A_2r^2 = (A_1 + A_2)r^2$. But $A_1 + A_2 = A_c$. Substituting gives $I_c = A_wr^2$; therefore, $r_c = r$.

This result illustrates the following principle: If the radii of gyration of several areas with respect to a given axis are all equal, the radius of gyration of their composite area equals that of the individual areas.

The equation $I_x = \Sigma I_0 + \Sigma Ak^2$, when applied to a single area, becomes $I_x = I_0 + Ak^2$. Then $Ar_x^2 = Ar_0^2 + Ak^2$, or $r_x = (r_0^2 + k^2)^{0.5}$. If the radius of gyration with respect to a centroidal axis is known, the radius of gyration with respect to an axis parallel thereto may be readily evaluated by applying this relationship.

The Euler equation for the strength of a slender column reveals that the member tends to buckle about the minor centroidal axis of its cross section. Consequently, all column design equations, both those for slender members and those for intermediate-length members, relate the capacity of the column to its minimum radius of gyration. The first step in the investigation of a column, therefore, consists in identifying the minor centroidal axis and evaluating the corresponding radius of gyration.

## CAPACITY OF A BUILT-UP COLUMN

A compression member consists of two C15 × 40 channels laced together and spaced 10 in. (254.0 mm) back to back with flanges outstanding, as shown in Fig. 11. What axial load may this member carry if its effective length is 22 ft (6.7 m)?

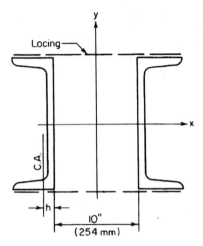

**FIGURE 11.** Built-up column.

## Calculation Procedure:

### 1. *Record the properties of the individual channel*

Since $x$ and $y$ are axes of symmetry, they are the principal centroidal axes. However, it is not readily apparent which of these is the minor axis, and so it is necessary to calculate both $r_x$ and $r_y$. The symbol $r$, without a subscript, is used to denote the *minimum* radius of gyration, in inches (centimeters).

Using the AISC *Manual*, we see that the channel properties are $A = 11.70$ sq.in. (75.488 cm²); $h = 0.78$ in. (19.812 mm); $r_1 = 5.44$ in. (138.176 mm); $r_2 = 0.89$ in. (22.606 mm).

### 2. *Evaluate the minimum radius of gyration of the built-up section; determine the slenderness ratio*

Thus, $r_x = 5.44$ in. (138.176 mm); $r_y = (r_2^2 + 5.78^2)^{0.5} > 5.78$ in. (146.812 mm); therefore, $r = 5.44$ in. (138.176 mm); $KL/r = 22(12)/5.44 = 48.5$.

### 3. *Determine the allowable stress in the column*

Enter the *Manual* slenderness-ratio allowable-stress table with a slenderness ratio of 48.5 to obtain the allowable stress $f = 18.48$ kips/sq.in. (127.420 MPa). Then, the column capacity $= P = Af = 2(11.70)(18.48) = 432$ kips (1921.5 kN).

## CAPACITY OF A DOUBLE-ANGLE STAR STRUT

A star strut is composed of two 5 × 5 × ³⁄₈ in. (127.0 × 127.0 × 9.53 mm) angles intermittently connected by ³⁄₈-in. (9.53-mm) batten plates in both directions. Determine the capacity of the member for an effective length of 12 ft (3.7 m).

## Calculation Procedure:

### 1. *Identify the minor axis*

Refer to Fig. 12a. Since $p$ and $q$ are axes of symmetry, they are the principal axes; $p$ is manifestly the minor axis because the area lies closer to $p$ than $q$.

### 2. *Determine $r_v^2$*

Refer to Fig. 12b, where $v$ is the major and $z$ the minor axis of the angle section. Apply $I_{x''} = I_{x'} \cos^2 \theta + I_{y'} \sin^2 \theta - P_{x'y'} \sin 2\theta$, and set $P_{vz} = 0$ to get $r_y^2 = r_v^2 \cos^2 \theta + r_x^2 \sin^2 \theta$; therefore, $r_v^2 \sec^2 \theta - r_x^2 \tan^2 \theta$. For an equal-leg angle, $\theta = 45°$, and this equation reduces to $r_v^2 = 2r_y^2 - r_z^2$.

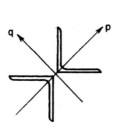

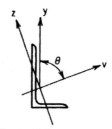

(b) Centroidal axes
of angle section

(a) Star strut

**FIGURE 12**

### 3. Record the member area and compute $r_v$

From the *Manual*, $A = 3.61$ sq.in. (23.291 cm²); $r_y = 1.56$ in. (39.624 mm); $r_z = 0.99$ in. (25.146 mm); $r_v = (2 \times 1.56^2 - 0.99^2)^{0.5} = 1.97$ in. (50.038 mm).

### 4. Determine the minimum radius of gyration of the built-up section; compute the strut capacity

Thus, $r = r_p = 1.97$ in. (50.038 mm); $KL/r = 12(12)/1.97 = 73$. From the *Manual*, $f = 16.12$ kips/sq.in. (766.361 MPa). Then $P = Af = 2(3.61)(16.12) = 116$ kips (515.97 kN).

## SECTION SELECTION FOR A COLUMN WITH TWO EFFECTIVE LENGTHS

A 30-ft (9.2-m) long column is to carry a 200-kip (889.6-kN) load. The column will be braced about both principal axes at top and bottom and braced about its minor axis at mid-height. Architectural details restrict the member to a nominal depth of 8 in. (203.2 mm). Select a section of A242 steel by consulting the allowable-load tables in the AISC *Manual* and then verify the design.

### Calculation Procedure:

### 1. Select a column section

Refer to Fig. 13. The effective length with respect to the minor axis may be taken as 15 ft (4.6 m). Then $K_xL = 30$ ft (9.2 m) and $K_yL = 15$ ft (4.6 m).

The allowable column loads recorded in the *Manual* tables are calculated on the premise that the column tends to buckle about the minor axis. In the present instance, however, this premise is not necessarily valid. It is expedient for design purposes to conceive of a uniform-strength column, i.e., one for which $K_x$ and $K_y$ bear the same ratio as $r_x$ and $r_y$, thereby endowing the column with an identical slenderness ratio with respect to the two principal axes.

Select a column section on the basis of the $K_yL$ value; record the value of $r_x/r_y$ of this section. Using linear interpolation in the *Manual* Table shows that a W8 × 40 column has a capacity of 200 kips (889.6 kN) when $K_yL = 15.3$ ft (4.66 m); at the bottom of the table it is found that $r_x/r_y = 1.73$.

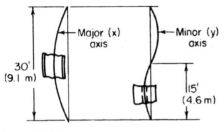

**FIGURE 13**

### 2. Compute the value of $K_xL$ associated with a uniform-strength column, and compare this with the actual value

Thus, $K_xL = 1.73(15.3) = 26.5$ ft (8.1 m) < 30 ft (9.2 m). The section is therefore inadequate.

### 3. Try a specific column section of larger size

Trying W8 × 48, the capacity = 200 kips (889.6 kN) when $K_yL$ 17.7 ft (5.39 m). For uniform strength, $K_xL = 1.74(17.7) = 30.8 > 30$ ft (9.39 m > 9.2 m). The W8 × 48 therefore appears to be satisfactory.

### 4. Verify the design

To verify the design, record the properties of this section and compute the slenderness ratios. For this grade of steel and thickness of member, the yield-point stress is 50 kips/sq.in. (344.8 MPa), as given in the *Manual*. Thus, $A = 14.11$ sq.in. (91038 cm²); $r_x = 3.61$ in. (91.694 mm); $r_y = 2.08$ in. (52.832 mm). Then $K_xL/r_x = 30(12)/3.61 = 100$; $K_yL/r_y = 15(12)/2.08 = 87$.

### 5. Determine the allowable stress and member capacity

From the *Manual*, $f = 14.71$ kips/sq.in. (101.425 MPa) with a slenderness ratio of 100. Then $P = 14.11(14.71) = 208$ kips (925.2 kN). Therefore, use W8 × 48 because the capacity of the column exceeds the intended load.

## STRESS IN COLUMN WITH PARTIAL RESTRAINT AGAINST ROTATION

The beams shown in Fig. 14*a* are rigidly connected to a W14 × 95 column of 28-ft (8.5-m) height that is pinned at its foundation. The column is held at its upper end by cross bracing lying in a plane normal to the web. Compute the allowable axial stress in the column in the absence of bending stress.

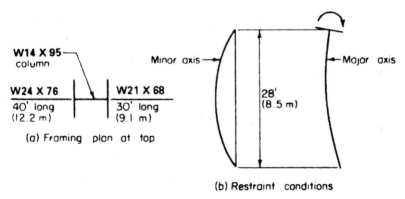

(b) Restraint conditions

**FIGURE 14**

### Calculation Procedure:

### 1. *Draw schematic diagrams to indicate the restraint conditions*
Show these conditions in Fig. 14*b*. The cross bracing prevents sidesway at the top solely with respect to the minor axis, and the rigid beam-to-column connections afford partial fixity with respect to the major axis.

### 2. *Record the $I_x$ values of the column and beams*

|         |        | $I_x$  |
|---------|--------|--------|
| Section | in⁴    | cm⁴    |
| W14 × 95 | 1064  | 44,287 |
| W24 × 76 | 2096  | 87,242 |
| W21 × 68 | 1478  | 61,519 |

### 3. *Calculate the rigidity of the column relative to that of the restraining members at top and bottom*
Thus, $I_c/L_c$ = 1064/28 = 38. At the top, $\Sigma(I_g/L_g)$ = 2096/40 + 1478/30 = 101.7. At the top, the rigidity $G_t$ = 38/101.7 = 0.37.

In accordance with the instructions in the *Manual*, set the rigidity at the bottom $G_b$ = 10.

### 4. *Determine the value of $K_x$*
Using the *Manual* alignment chart, determine that $K_x$ = 1.77.

### 5. *Compute the slenderness ratio with respect to both principal axes, and find the allowable stress*
Thus, $K_x L/r_x$ = 1.77(28)(12)/6.17 = 96.4; $K_y L/r_y$ = 28(12)/3.71 = 90.6.

Using the larger value of the slenderness ratio, find from the *Manual* the allowable axial stress in the absence of bending $= f$ = 13.43 kips/sq.in. (92.600 MPa).

## LACING OF BUILT-UP COLUMN

Design the lacing bars and end tie plates of the member in Fig. 15. The lacing bars will be connected to the channel flanges with ¹/₂-in. (12.7-mm) rivets.

### Calculation Procedure:

### 1. *Establish the dimensions of the lacing system to conform to the AISC* Specification
The function of the lacing bars and tie plates is to preserve the integrity of the column and to prevent local failure.

Refer to Fig. 15. The standard gage in 15-in. (381.0-mm) channel = 2 in. (50.8 mm), from the AISC *Manual*. Then *h* = 14 < 15 in. (381.0 mm); therefore, use single lacing.

Try $\theta$ = 60°; then, $v$ = 2(14) cos 60° = 16.16 in. (410.5 mm). Set $v$ = 16 in. (406.4 mm); therefore, *d* = 16.1 in. (408.94 mm). For the built-up section, $KL/r$ = 48.5; for the single channel, $KL/r$ = 16/0.89 < 48.5. This is acceptable. The spacing of the bars is therefore satisfactory.

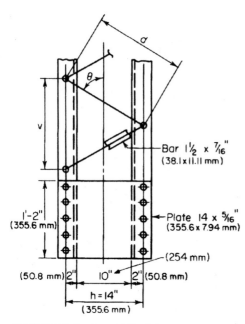

**FIGURE 15.** Lacing and tie plates.

### 2. Design the lacing bars

The lacing system must be capable of transmitting an assumed transverse shear equal to 2 percent of the axial load; this shear is carried by two bars, one on each side. A lacing bar is classified as a secondary member. To compute the transverse shear, assume that the column will be loaded to its capacity of 432 kips (1921.5 N).

Then force per bar = $\frac{1}{2}(0.02)(432)$ × (16.1/14) = 5.0 kips (22.24 N). Also, $L/r \leq 140$; therefore, $r = 16.1/140 = 0.115$ in. (2.9210 mm).

For a rectangular section of thickness $t$, $r = 0.289t$. Then $t = 0.115/0.289 = 0.40$ in. (10.160 mm). Set $t = \frac{7}{16}$ in. (11.11 mm); $r = 0.127$ in. (3.226 mm); $L/r = 16.1/0.127 = 127; f = 9.59$ kips/sq.in.(66. 123 MPa); $A = 5.0/9.59 = 0.52$ sq.in. (3.355 cm²). From the *Manual*, the minimum width required for $\frac{1}{2}$-in. (12.7 mm) rivets = $1\frac{1}{2}$ in. (38.1 mm). Therefore, use a flat bar $1\frac{1}{2} \times \frac{7}{16}$ in. (38.1 × 11.11 mm); $A = 0.66$ sq.in. (4.258 cm²).

### 3. Design the end tie plates in accordance with the Specification

The minimum length = 14 in. (355.6 mm); $t = 14/50 = 0.28$. Therefore, use plates 14 × $\frac{5}{16}$ in. (355.6 × 7.94 mm). The rivet pitch is limited to six diameters, or 3 in. (76.2 mm).

## SELECTION OF A COLUMN WITH A LOAD AT AN INTERMEDIATE LEVEL

A column of 30-ft (9.2-m) length carries a load of 130 kips (578.2 kN) applied at the top and a load of 56 kips (249.1 kN) applied to the web at midheight. Select an 8-in. (203.2-mm) column of A242 steel, using $K_xL = 30$ ft (9.2 m) and $K_yL = 15$ ft (4.6 m).

### Calculation Procedure:

### 1. Compute the effective length of the column with respect to the major axis

The following procedure affords a rational method of designing a column subjected to a load applied at the top and another load applied approximately at the center. Let $m$ = load at intermediate level, kips per total load, kips (kilonewtons). Replace the factor $K$ with a factor $K'$ defined by $K' = K(1 - m/2)^{0.5}$. Thus, for this column, $m = 56/186 = 0.30$. And $K'_xL = 30(1 - 0.15)^{0.5} = 27.6$ ft (8.41 m).

### 2. Select a trial section on the basis of the $K_yL$ value

From the AISC *Manual* for a W8 × 40, capacity = 186 kips (827.3 kN) when $K_yL = 16.2$ ft (4.94 m) and $r_x/r_y = 1.73$.

### 3. Determine whether the selected section is acceptable
Compute the value of $K_xL$ associated with a uniform-strength column, and compare this with the actual effective length. Thus, $K_xL = 1.73(16.2) = 28.0 > 27.6$ ft (8.41 m). Therefore, the W8 × 40 is acceptable.

## DESIGN OF AN AXIAL MEMBER FOR FATIGUE

A web member in a welded truss will sustain precipitous fluctuations of stress caused by moving loads. The structure will carry three load systems having the following characteristics:

| System | Force induced in member, kips (kN) | | No. of times applied |
|--------|------------------------------------|----------------|---------------------|
|        | Maximum compression | Maximum tension |                     |
| A      | 46 (204.6)          | 18 (80.1)       | 60,000              |
| B      | 40 (177.9)          | 9 (40.0)        | 1,000,000           |
| C      | 32 (142.3)          | 8 (35.6)        | 2,500,000           |

The effective length of the member is 11 ft (3.4 m). Design a double-angle member.

### Calculation Procedure:

### 1. Calculate for each system the design load, and indicate the yield-point stress on which the allowable stress is based
The design of members subjected to a repeated variation of stress is regulated by the AISC *Specification*. For each system, calculate the design load and indicate the yield-point stress on which the allowable stress is based. Where the allowable stress is less than that normally permitted, increase the design load proportionally to compensate for this reduction. Let + denote tension and − denote compression. Then

| System | Design load, kips (kN) | Yield-point stress, kips/sq.in. (MPa) |
|--------|------------------------|----------------------------------------|
| A      | $-46 - 2/3(18) = -58 (-257.9)$ | 36 (248.2) |
| B      | $-40 - 2/3(9) = -46 (-204.6)$  | 33 (227.5) |
| C      | $1.5(-32 - 3/4 \times 8) = -57 (-253.5)$ | 33 (227.5) |

### 2. Select a member for system A and determine if it is adequate for system C
From the AISC *Manual*, try two angles 4 × 3½ × ⅜ in. (101.6 × 88.90 × 9.53 mm), with long legs back to back; the capacity is 65 kips (289.1 kN). Then $A = 5.34$ sq.in. (34.453 cm²); $r = r_x = 1.25$ in. (31.750 mm); $KL/r = 11(12)/1.25 = 105.6$.

From the *Manual*, for a yield-point stress of 33 kips/sq.in. (227.5 MPa), $f = 11.76$ kips/sq.in. (81.085 MPa). Then the capacity $P = 5.34(11.76) = 62.8$ kips (279.3 kN) > 57 kips (253.5 kN). This is acceptable. Therefore, use two angles 4 × 3½ × ⅜ in. (101.6 × 88.90 × 9.53 mm), long legs back to back.

## INVESTIGATION OF A BEAM COLUMN

A W12 × 53 column with an effective length of 20 ft (6.1 m) is to carry an axial load of 160 kips (711.7 kN) and the end moments indicated in Fig. 16. The member will be secured against sidesway in both directions. Is the section adequate?

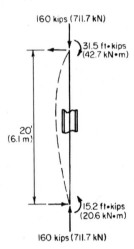

160 kips (711.7 kN)

31.5 ft•kips
(42.7 kN•m)

20'
(6.1 m)

15.2 ft•kips
(20.6 kN•m)

160 kips (711.7 kN)

**FIGURE 16.** Beam column.

### Calculation Procedure:

**1. Record the properties of the section**
The simultaneous set of values of axial stress and bending stress must satisfy the inequalities set forth in the AISC *Specification*.

The properties of the section are $A$ = 15.59 sq.in. (100.586 cm²); $S_x$ = 70.7 in³ (1158.77 cm³); $r_x$ = 5.23 in. (132.842 mm); $r_y$ = 2.48 in. (62.992 mm). Also, from the *Manual*, $L_c$ = 10.8 ft (3.29 m); $L_u$ = 21.7 ft (6.61 m).

**2. Determine the stresses listed below**
The stresses that must be determined are the axial stress $f_a$; the bending stress $f_b$; the axial stress $F_a$, which would be permitted in the absence of bending; and the bending stress $F_b$, which would be permitted in the absence of axial load. Thus, $f_a$ = 160/15.59 = 10.26 kips/sq.in. (70.742 MPa); $f_b$ = 31.5(12)/70.7 = 5.35 kips/sq.in. (36.888 MPa); $KL/r$ = 240/2.48 = 96.8; therefore, $F_a$ = 13.38 kips/sq.in. (92.255 MPa); $L_u <$ $KL < L_c$; therefore, $F_b$ = 22 kips/sq.in. (151.7 MPa). (Although this consideration is irrelevant in the present instance, note that the *Specification* establishes two maximum $d/t$ ratios for a compact section. One applies to a beam, the other to a beam column.)

**3. Calculate the moment coefficient $C_m$**
Since the algebraic sign of the bending moment remains unchanged, $M_1/M_2$ is positive. Thus, $C_m$ = 0.6 + 0.4(15.2/31.5) = 0.793.

**4. Apply the appropriate criteria to test the adequacy of the section**
Thus, $f_a/F_a$ = 10.26/13.38 = 0.767 > 0.15. The following requirements therefore apply: $f_a/F_a + [C_m/(1 - f_a/F'_e)](f_b/F_b) \leq 1$; $f_a/(0.6f_y) + f_b/F_b \leq 1$ where $F'_e$ = 149,000/$(KL/r)^2$ kips/sq.in. and $KL$ and $r$ are evaluated with respect to the plane of bending.

Evaluating gives $F'_e$ = 149,000(5.23)²/240² = 70.76 kips/sq.in. (487.890 MPa); $f_a/F'_e$ = 10.26/70.76 = 0145. Substituting in the first requirements equation yields 0.767 + (0.793/0.855)(5.35/22) = 0.993. This is acceptable. Substituting in the second requirements equation, we find 10.26/22 + 5.35/22 = 0.709. This section is therefore satisfactory.

## APPLICATION OF BEAM-COLUMN FACTORS

For the previous calculation procedure, investigate the adequacy of the W12 × 53 section by applying the values of the beam-column factors $B$ and $a$ given in the AISC *Manual*.

## Calculation Procedure:

### 1. *Record the basic values of the previous calculation procedure*

The beam-column factors were devised in an effort to reduce the labor entailed in analyzing a given member as a beam column when $f_a/F_a > 0.15$. They are defined by $B = A/S$ per inch (decimeter); $a = 0.149 \times 10^6 I$ in$^4$ (6201.9$I$ dm$^4$).

Let $P$ denote the applied axial load and $P_{allow}$ the axial load that would be permitted in the absence of bending. The equations given in the previous procedure may be transformed to $P + BMC_m(F_a/F_b)a/[a - P(KL)^2] \leq P_{allow}$, and $PF_a/(0.6f_y) + BMF_a/F_b \leq P_{allow}$, where $KL$, $B$, and $a$ are evaluated with respect to the plane of bending.

The basic values of the previous procedure are $P = 160$ kips (711.7 kN); $M = 31.5$ ft·kips (42.71 kN·m); $F_b = 22$ kips/sq.in. (151.7 MPa); $C_m = 0.793$.

### 2. *Obtain the properties of the section*

From the *Manual* for a W12 × 53, $A = 15.59$ sq.in. (100.587 cm$^2$); $B_x = 0.221$ per inch (8.70 per meter); $a_x = 63.5 \times 10^6$ in$^4$ (264.31 × 10$^3$ dm$^4$). Then when $KL = 20$ ft (6.1 m), $P_{allow} = 209$ kips (929.6 kN).

### 3. *Substitute in the first transformed equation*

Thus, $F_a = P_{allow}/A = 209/15.59 = 13.41$ kips/sq.in. (92.461 MPa), $P(KL)^2 = 160(240)^2 = 9.22 \times 10^6$ kip·sq.in. (2.648 × 10$^4$ kN·m$^2$), and $a_x/[a_x - P(KL)^2] = 63.5/(63.5 - 9.22) = 1.17$; then $160 + 0.221(31.5)(12)(0.793)(13.41/22)(1.17) = 207 < 209$ kips (929.6 kN). This is acceptable.

### 4. *Substitute in the second transformed equation*

Thus, $160(13.41/22) + 0.221(31.5)(12)(13.41/22) = 148 < 209$ kips (929.6 kN). This is acceptable. The W12 × 53 section is therefore satisfactory.

## NET SECTION OF A TENSION MEMBER

The 7 × ¼ in. (177.8 × 6.35 mm) plate in Fig. 17 carries a tensile force of 18,000 lb (80,064.0 N) and is connected to its support with three ³/₄-in. (19.05-mm) rivets in the manner shown. Compute the maximum tensile stress in the member.

## Calculation Procedure:

### 1. *Compute the net width of the member at each section of potential rupture*

The AISC *Specification* prescribes the manner of calculating the net section of a tension member. The effective diameter of the holes is considered to be ¹/₈ in. (3.18 mm) greater than that of the rivets.

After computing the net width of each section, select the minimum value as the effective width. The *Specification* imposes an upper limit of 85 percent of the gross width.

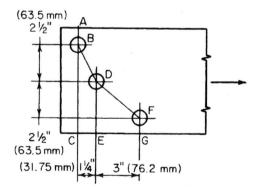

**FIGURE 17**

Refer to Fig. 17. From $B$ to $D$, $s = 1.25$ in. (31.750 mm), $g = 2.5$ in. (63.50 mm); from $D$ to $F$, $s = 3$ in. (76.2 mm), $g = 2.5$ in. (63.50 mm); $w_{AC} = 7 - 0.875 = 6.12$ in. (155.45 mm); $w_{ABDE} = 7 - 2(0.875) + 1.25^2/[4(2.5)] = 5.41$ in. (137.414 mm); $w_{ABDFG} = 7 - 3(0.875) + 1.25^2/(4 \times 2.5) + 3^2/(4 \times 2.5) = 5.43$ in. (137.922 mm); $w_{max} = 0.85(7) = 5.95$ in. (151.13 mm). Selecting the lowest value gives $w_{eff} = 5.41$ in. (137.414 mm).

**2. Compute the tensile stress on the effective net section**
Thus, $f = 18,000/[5.41(0.25)] = 13,300$ lb/sq.in. (91,703.5 kPa).

## DESIGN OF A DOUBLE-ANGLE TENSION MEMBER

The bottom chord of a roof truss sustains a tensile force of 141 kps (627.2 kN). The member will be spliced with 3/4-in. (19.05-mm) rivets as shown in Fig. 18a. Design a double-angle member and specify the minimum rivet pitch.

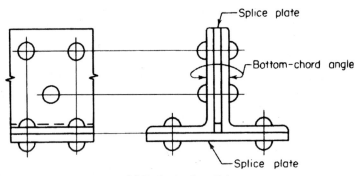

(a) Method of splicing

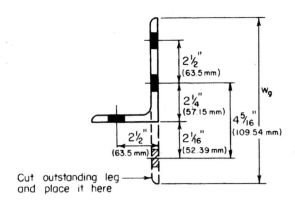

(b) Development of angle for net section

**FIGURE 18**

## Calculation Procedure:

### 1. Show one angle in its developed form
Cut the outstanding leg, and position it to be coplanar with the other one, as in Fig. 18$b$. The gross width of the angle $w_g$ is the width of the equivalent plate thus formed; it equals the sum of the legs of the angle less the thickness.

### 2. Determine the gross width in terms of the thickness
Assume tentatively that 2.5 rivet holes will be deducted to arrive at the net width. Express $w_g$ in terms of the thickness $t$ of each angle. Then net area required = $141/22$ = 6.40 sq.in. (41.292 cm$^2$); also, $2t(w_g - 2.5 \times 0.875)$ = 6.40; $w_g$ = $3.20/t + 2.19$.

### 3. Assign trial thickness values, and determine the gross width
Construct a tabulation of the computed values. Then select the most economical size of member. Thus

| $t$, in. (mm) | $w_g$, in. (mm) | $w_g + t$, in. (mm) | Available size, in. (mm) | Area, sq.in. (cm$^2$) (cm$^2$) |
|---|---|---|---|---|
| $^1/_2$(12.7) | 8.59 (218.186) | 9.09 (230.886) | $6 \times 3^1/_2 \times {}^1/_2$ (152.4 × 88.9 × 12.7) | 4.50 (29.034) |
| $^7/_{16}$ (11.11) | 9.50 (241.300) | 9.94 (252.476) | $6 \times 4 \times {}^7/_{16}$ (152.4 × 101.6 × 11.11) | 4.18 (26.969) |
| $^3/_8$ (9.53) | 10.72 (272.228) | 11.10 (281.940) | None | |

The most economical member is the one with the least area. Therefore, use two angles $6 \times 4 \times {}^7/_{16}$ in. (152.4 × 101.6 × 11.11 mm).

### 4. Record the standard gages
Refer to the *Manual* for the standard gages, and record the values shown in Fig. 18$b$.

### 5. Establish the rivet pitch
Find the minimum value of $s$ to establish the rivet pitch. Thus, net width required = $^1/_2[6.40/(7/16)]$ = 7.31 in. (185.674 mm); gross width = $6 + 4 - 0.44$ = 9.56 in. (242.824 mm). Then $9.56 - 3(0.875) + s^2/(4 \times 2.5) + s^2/(4 \times 4.31)$ = 7.31; $s$ = 1.55 in. (39.370 mm).

For convenience, use the standard pitch of 3 in. (76.2 mm). This results in a net width of 7.29 in. (185.166 mm); the deficiency is negligible.


# Plastic Design of Steel Structures

Consider that a structure is subjected to a gradually increasing load until it collapses. When the yield-point stress first appears, the structure is said to be in a state of *initial yielding*. The load that exists when failure impends is termed the *ultimate load*.

In elastic design, a structure has been loaded to capacity when it attains initial yielding, on the theory that plastic deformation would annul the utility of the structure. In plastic design, on the other hand, it is recognized that a structure may be loaded beyond initial yielding if:

1. The tendency of the fiber at the yield-point stress toward plastic deformation is resisted by the adjacent fibers.
2. Those parts of the structure that remain in the elastic-stress range are capable of supporting this incremental load.

The ultimate load is reached when these conditions cease to exist and thus the structure collapses.

Thus, elastic design is concerned with an allowable *stress*, which equals the yield-point stress divided by an appropriate factor of safety. In contrast, plastic design is concerned with an allowable *load*, which equals the ultimate load divided by an appropriate factor called the *load factor*. In reality, however, the distinction between elastic and plastic design has become rather blurred because specifications that ostensibly pertain to elastic design make covert concessions to plastic behavior. Several of these are underscored in the calculation procedures that follow.

In the plastic analysis of flexural members, the following simplifying assumptions are made:

1. As the applied load is gradually increased, a state is eventually reached at which all fibers at the section of maximum moment are stressed to the yield-point stress, in either tension or compression. The section is then said to be in a state of *plastification*.
2. While plastification is proceeding at one section, the adjacent sections retain their linear-stress distribution.

Although the foregoing assumptions are fallacious, they introduce no appreciable error.

When plastification is achieved at a given section, no additional bending stress may be induced in any of its fibers, and the section is thus rendered impotent to resist any incremental bending moment. As loading continues, the beam behaves as if it had been constructed with a hinge at the given section. Consequently, the beam is said to have developed a *plastic hinge* (in contradistinction to a true hinge) at the plastified section.

The *yield moment* $M_y$ of a beam section is the bending moment associated with initial yielding. The plastic moment $M_p$ is the bending moment associated with plastification.

The *plastic modulus* $Z$ of a beam section, which is analogous to the section modulus used in elastic design, is defined by $Z = M_p/f_y$, where $f_y$ denotes the yield-point stress. The *shape factor* SF is the ratio of $M_p$ to $M_y$, being so named because its value depends on the shape of the section. Then SF $= M_p/M_y = f_y Z/(f_y S) = Z/S$.

In the following calculation procedures, it is understood that the members are made of A36 steel.

## ALLOWABLE LOAD ON BAR SUPPORTED BY RODS

A load is applied to a rigid bar that is symmetrically supported by three steel rods as shown in Fig. 19. The cross-sectional areas of the rods are: rods $A$ and $C$, 1.2 sq.in. (7.74 cm$^2$); rod $B$, 1.0 sq.in. (6.45 cm$^2$). Determine the maximum load that may be applied, (*a*) using elastic design with an allowable stress of 22,000 lb/sq.in. (151,690.0 kPa); (*b*) using plastic design with a load factor of 1.85.

**Calculation Procedure:**

### 1. Express the relationships among the tensile stresses in the rods

The symmetric disposition causes the bar to deflect vertically without rotating, thereby elongating the three rods by the same amount. As the first method of solving this problem, assume that the load is gradually increased from zero to its allowable value.

Expressing the relationships among the tensile stresses, we have $\Delta L = s_A L_A/E = s_B L_B/E = s_C L_C/E$; therefore, $s_A = s_C$, and $s_A = s_B L_B/L_A = 0.75 s_B$ for this arrangement of rods. Since $s_B$ is the maximum stress, the allowable stress first appears in rod $B$.

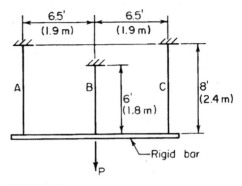

**FIGURE 19**

### 2. Evaluate the stresses at the instant the load attains its allowable value

Calculate the load carried by each rod, and sum these loads to find $P_{\text{allow}}$. Thus $s_B = 22,000$ lb/sq.in. (151,690.0 kPa); $s_B = 0.75(22,000) = 16,500$ lb/sq.in. (113,767.5 kPa); $P_A = P_C = 16,500(1.2) = 19,800$ lb (88,070.4 N); $P_B = 22,000(1.0) = 22,000$ lb (97,856.0 N); $P_{\text{allow}} = 2(19,800) + 22,000 = 61,600$ lb (273,996.8 N).

Next, consider that the load is gradually increased from zero to its ultimate value. When rod $B$ attains its yield-point stress, its tendency to deform plastically is inhibited by rods $A$ and $C$ because the rigidity of the bar constrains the three rods to elongate uniformly. The structure therefore remains stable as the load is increased beyond the elastic range until rods $A$ and $C$ also attain their yield-point stress.

### 3. Find the ultimate load

To find the ultimate load $P_u$, equate the stress in each rod to $f_y$, calculate the load carried by each rod, and sum these loads to find the ultimate load $P_u$. Thus, $P_A = P_C = 36,000(1.2) = 43,200$ lb (192,153.6 N); $P_B = 36,000(1.0) = 36,000$ lb (160,128.0 N); $P_u = 2(43,200) + 36,000 = 122,400$ lb (544,435.2 N).

### 4. Apply the load factor to establish the allowable load

Thus, $P_{\text{allow}} = P_u/\text{LF} = 122,400/1.85 = 66,200$ lb (294,457.6 N).

## DETERMINATION OF SECTION SHAPE FACTORS

Without applying the equations and numerical values of the plastic modulus given in the AISC *Manual*, determine the shape factor associated with a rectangle, a circle, and a W16 × 40. Explain why the circle has the highest and the W section the lowest factor of the three.

### Calculation Procedure:

### 1. Calculate $M_y$ for each section

Use the equation $M_y = Sf_y$ for each section. Thus, for a rectangle, $M_y = bd^2 f_y/6$. For a circle, using the properties of a circle as given in the *Manual*, we find $M_y = \pi d^3 f_y/32$. For a W16 × 40, $A = 11.77$ sq.in. (75.940 cm²), $S = 64.4$ in³ (1055.52 cm³), and $M_y = 64.4 f_y$.

### 2. Compute the resultant forces associated with plastification

In Fig. 20, the resultant forces are $C$ and $T$. Once these forces are known, their action lines and $M_p$ should be computed.

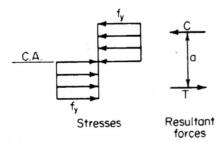

C.A.

Stresses          Resultant forces

**FIGURE 20.** Conditions at section of plastification.

Thus, for a rectangle, $C = bdf_y/2$, $a = d/2$, and $M_p = aC = bd^2 f_y/4$. For a circle, $C = \pi d^2 f_y/8$, $a = 4d(3\pi)$, and $M_p = aC = d^3 f_y/6$. For a W16 × 40, $C = \frac{1}{2}(11.77 \text{ sq.in.}) = 5.885 f_y$.

To locate the action lines, refer to the *Manual* and note the position of the centroidal axis of the WT8 × 20 section, i.e., a section half the size of that being considered. Thus; $a = 2(8.00 - 1.82) = 12.36$ in. (313.944 mm); $M_p = aC = 12.36(5.885 f_y) = 72.7 f_y$.

### 3. Divide $M_p$ by $M_y$ to obtain the shape factor

For a rectangle, SF $= (bd^2/4)/(bd^2/6) = 1.50$.
For a circle, SF $= (d^3/6)/(\pi d^3/32) = 1.70$.
For a WT16 × 40, SF $= 72.7/64.4 = 1.13$.

### 4. Explain the relative values of the shape factor

To explain the relative values of the shape factor, express the resisting moment contributed by a given fiber at plastification and at initial yielding, and compare the results. Let $dA$ denote the area of the given fiber and $y$ its distance from the neutral axis. At plastification, $dM_p = f_y y dA$. At initial yielding, $f = f_y y/c$; $dM_y = f_y y^2 dA/c$; $dM_p/dM_y = c/y$.

By comparing a circle and a hypothetical W section having the same area and depth, the circle is found to have a larger shape factor because of its relatively low values of $y$.

As this analysis demonstrates, the process of plastification mitigates the detriment that accrues from placing any area near the neutral axis, since the stress at plastification is independent of the position of the fiber. Consequently, a section that is relatively inefficient with respect to flexure has a relatively high shape factor. The AISC *Specification* for elastic design implicitly recognizes the value of the shape factor by assigning an allowable bending stress of $0.75 f_y$ to rectangular bearing plates and $0.90 f_y$ to pins.

## DETERMINATION OF ULTIMATE LOAD BY THE STATIC METHOD

The W18 × 45 beam in Fig. 21*a* is simply supported at *A* and fixed at *C*. Disregarding the beam weight, calculate the ultimate load that may be applied at *B* (*a*) by analyzing the behavior of the beam during its two phases; (*b*) by analyzing the bending moments that exist at impending collapse. (The first part of the solution illustrates the postelastic behavior of the member.)

### Calculation Procedure:

### 1. Calculate the ultimate-moment capacity of the member

*Part a*: As the load is gradually increased from zero to its ultimate value, the beam passes through two phases. During phase 1, the *elastic phase*, the member is restrained against rotation at *C*. This phase terminates when a plastic hinge forms at that end. During phase 2-the *postelastic*, or *plastic, phase*—the member functions as a simply supported beam. This phase terminates when a plastic hinge forms at *B*, since the member then becomes unstable.

Using data from the AISC *Manual,* we have $Z = 89.6$ in³ (1468.54 cm³). Then $M_p = f_yZ = 36(89.6)/12 = 268.8$ ft·kips (364.49 kN·m).

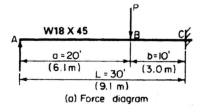

(a) Force diagram

### 2. Calculate the moment BD

Let $P_1$ denote the applied load at completion of phase 1. In Fig. 21*b*, construct the bending-moment diagram *ADEC* corresponding to this load. Evaluate $P_1$ by applying the equations for case 14 in the AISC *Manual.* Calculate the moment *BD*. Thus, $CE = -ab(a + L)P_1/(2L^2) = -20(10)(50)P_1/[2(900)] = -268.8$; $P_1 = 48.38$ kips (215.194 kN); $BD = ab^2(a + 2L)P_1/(2L^3) = 20(100)(80)(48.38)/[2(27,000)] = 143.3$ ft·kips (194.31 kN·m).

### 3. Determine the incremental load at completion of phase 2

Let $P_2$ denote the incremental applied load at completion of phase 2, i.e., the actual load on the beam minus $P_1$. In Fig. 21*b*, construct the bending-moment diagram *AFEC* that exists when phase 2 terminates. Evaluate $P_2$

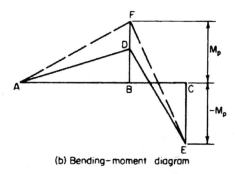

(b) Bending-moment diagram

**FIGURE 21**

by considering the beam as simply supported. Thus, $BF = 268.8$ ft·kips (364.49 kN·m); $DF = 268.8 - 143.3 = 125.5$ ft·kips (170.18 kN·m); but $DF = abP_2/L = 20(10)P_2/30 = 125.5$; $P_2 = 18.82$ kips (83.711 kN).

### 4. Sum the results to obtain the ultimate load

Thus, $P_u = 48.38 + 18.82 = 67.20$ kips (298.906 kN).

### 5. Construct the force and bending-moment diagrams for the ultimate load

*Part b:* The following considerations are crucial: The bending-moment diagram always has vertices at *B* and *C*, and formation of two plastic hinges will cause failure of the beam. Therefore, the plastic moment occurs at *B* and *C* at impending failure. *The sequence in which the plastic hinges are formed at these sections is immaterial.*

These diagrams are shown in Fig. 22. Express $M_p$ in terms of $P_u$, and evaluate $P_u$. Thus, $BF = 20R_A = 268.8$; therefore, $R_A = 13.44$ kips (59.781 kN). Also, $CE = 30R_A - 10P_u = 30 \times 13.44 - 10P_u = -268.8$; $P_u = 67.20$ kips (298.906 kN).

Here is an alternative method: $BF = (abP_u/L) - aM_p/L = M_p$, or $20(10)P_u/30 = 50M_p/30$; $P_u = 67.20$ kips (298.906 kN).

This solution method used in part *b* is termed the static, or equilibrium, method. As this solution demonstrates, it is unnecessary to trace the stress history of the member as it passes through its successive phases, as was done in part *a*; the analysis can be confined to the conditions that exist at impending failure. This procedure also illustrates the following important characteristics of plastic design:

1. Plastic design is far simpler than elastic design.
2. Plastic design yields results that are much more reliable than those secured through elastic design. For example, assume that the support at *C* does not completely

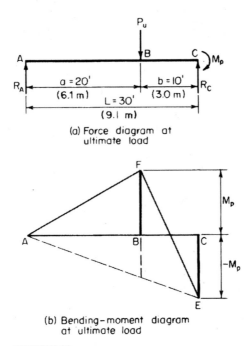

(a) Force diagram at
ultimate load

(b) Bending-moment diagram
at ultimate load

**FIGURE 22**

inhibit rotation at that end. This departure from design conditions will invalidate the elastic analysis but will in no way affect the plastic analysis.

## DETERMINING THE ULTIMATE LOAD BY THE MECHANISM METHOD

Use the mechanism method to solve the problem given in the previous calculation procedure.

### Calculation Procedure:

#### 1. Indicate, in hyperbolic manner, the virtual displacement of the member from its initial to a subsequent position

To the two phases of beam behavior previously considered, it is possible to add a third. Consider that when the ultimate load is reached, the member is subjected to an incremental deflection. This will result in collapse, but the behavior of the member can be analyzed during an infinitesimally small deflection from its stable position. This is termed a virtual deflection, or displacement.

Since the member is incapable of supporting any load beyond that existing at completion of phase 2, this virtual deflection is not characterized by any change in bending stress. Rotation therefore occurs solely at the real and plastic hinges. Thus, during phase

3, the member behaves as a mechanism (i.e., a constrained chain of pin-connected rigid bodies, or links).

In Fig. 23, indicate, in hyperbolic manner, the virtual displacement of the member from its initial position $ABC$ to a subsequent position $AB'C$. Use dots to represent plastic hinges. (The initial position may be represented by a straight line for simplicity because the analysis is concerned solely with the deformation that occurs *during* phase 3.)

### 2. Express the linear displacement under the load and the angular displacement at every plastic hinge

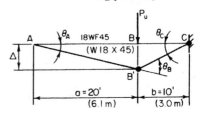

**FIGURE 23**

Use a convenient unit to express these displacements. Thus, $\Delta = a\theta_A = b\theta_C$; therefore, $\theta_C = a\theta_A/b = 2\theta_A$; $\theta_B = \theta_A + \theta_C = 3\theta_A$.

### 3. Evaluate the external and internal work associated with the virtual displacement

The work performed by a constant force equals the product of the force and its displacement parallel to its action line. Also, the work performed by a constant moment equals the product of the moment and its angular displacement. Work is a positive quantity when the displacement occurs in the direction of the force or moment. Thus, the external work $W_E = P_u\Delta = P_u a\theta_A = 20P_u\theta_A$. And the internal work $W_I = M_p(\theta_B + \theta_C) = 5M_p\theta_A$.

### 4. Equate the external and internal work to evaluate the ultimate load

Thus, $20P_u\theta_A = 5M_p\theta_A$; $P_u = (5/20)(268.8) = 67.20$ kips (298.906 kN).

The solution method used here is also termed the *virtual-work*, or *kinematic*, method.

## ANALYSIS OF A FIXED-END BEAM UNDER CONCENTRATED LOAD

If the beam in the two previous calculation procedures is fixed at $A$ as well as at $C$, what is the ultimate load that may be applied at $B$?

### Calculation Procedure:

### 1. Determine when failure impends

When hinges form at $A$, $B$, and $C$, failure impends. Repeat steps 3 and 4 of the previous calculation procedure, modifying the calculations to reflect the revised conditions. Thus $W_E = 20P_u\theta_A$; $W_I = M_P(\theta_a + \theta_B + \theta_C) = 6M_p\theta_A$; $20P_u\theta_A = 6M_p\theta_A$; $P_u = (6/20)(268.8) = 80.64$ kips (358.687 kN).

### 2. Analyze the phases through which the member passes

This member passes through three phases until the ultimate load is reached. Initially, it behaves as a beam fixed at both ends, then as a beam fixed at the left end only, and finally as a simply supported beam. However, as already discussed, these considerations are extraneous in plastic design.

## ANALYSIS OF A TWO-SPAN BEAM WITH CONCENTRATED LOADS

The continuous W18 × 45 beam in Fig. 24 carries two equal concentrated loads having the locations indicated. Disregarding the weight of the beam, compute the ultimate value of these loads, using both the static and the mechanism method.

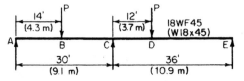

**FIGURE 24**

### Calculation Procedure:

### 1. Construct the force and bending-moment diagrams

The continuous beam becomes unstable when a plastic hinge forms at $C$ and at another section. The bending-moment diagram has vertices at $B$ and $D$, but it is not readily apparent at which of these sections the second hinge will form. The answer is found by assuming a plastic hinge at $B$ and at $D$, in turn, computing the corresponding value of $P_u$, and selecting the lesser value as the correct result. Part $a$ will use the static method; part $b$, the mechanism method.

Assume, for part $a$, a plastic hinge at $B$ and at $C$. In Fig. 25, construct the force diagram and bending-moment diagram for span $AC$. The moment diagram may be drawn in the manner shown in Fig. 25$b$ or $c$, whichever is preferred. In Fig. 25$c$, $ACH$ represents the moments that would exist in the absence of restraint at $C$, and $ACJ$ represents, in absolute value, the moments induced by this restraint. Compute the load $P_u$ associated with the assumed hinge location. From previous calculation procedures, $M_p = 268.8$ ft·kips (364.49 kN·m); then $M_B = 14 \times 16P_u/30 - 14M_p/30 = M_p$; $P_u = 44(268.8)/224 = 52.8$ kips (234.85 kN).

### 2. Assume another hinge location and compute the ultimate load associated with this location

Now assume a plastic hinge at $C$ and $D$. In Fig. 25, construct the force diagram and bending-moment diagram for $CE$. Computing the load $P_u$ associated with this assumed location, we find $M_D = 12 \times 24P_u/36 - 24M_p/36 = M_p$; $P_u = 60(268.8)/288 = 56.0$ kips (249.09 kN).

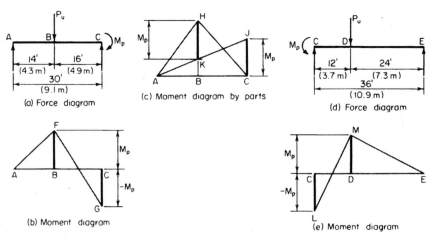

**FIGURE 25**

### 3. Select the lesser value of the ultimate load

The correct result is the lesser of these alternative values, or $P_u = 52.8$ kips (234.85 kN). At this load, plastic hinges exist at $B$ and $C$ but not at $D$.

### 4. For the mechanism method, assume a plastic-hinge location

It will be assumed that plastic hinges are located at $B$ and $C$ (Fig. 26). Evaluate $P_u$. Thus,

$\theta_C = 14\theta_A/16$; $\theta_B = 30\theta_A/16$; $\Delta = 14\theta_A$; $W_E = P_u\Delta = 14P_u\theta_A$; $W_I = M_p(\theta_B + \theta_C) = 2.75M_p\theta_A$; $14P_u\theta_A = 2.75M_p\theta_A$; $P_u = 52.8$ kips (234.85 kN).

### 5. Assume a plastic hinge at another location

Select $C$ and $D$ for the new location. Repeat the above procedure. The result will be identical with that in step 2.

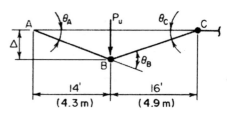

**FIGURE 26**

## SELECTION OF SIZES FOR A CONTINUOUS BEAM

Using a load factor of 1.70, design the member to carry the working loads (with beam weight included) shown in Fig. 27a. The maximum length that can be transported is 60 ft (18.3 m).

### Calculation Procedure:

### 1. Determine the ultimate loads to be supported

Since the member must be spliced, it will be economical to adopt the following design:

a. Use the particular beam size required for each portion, considering that the two portions will fail simultaneously at ultimate load. Therefore, three plastic hinges will exist at failure—one at the interior support and one in the interior of each span.

b. Extend one beam beyond the interior support, splicing the member at the point of contraflexure in the adjacent span. Since the maximum simple-span moment is greater for $AB$ than for $BC$, it is logical to assume that for economy the left beam rather than the right one should overhang the support.

Multiply the working loads by the load factor to obtain the ultimate loads to be supported. Thus, $w = 1.2$ kips/lin ft (17.51 kN/m); $w_u = 1.70(1.2) = 2.04$ kips/lin ft (29.77 kN/m); $P = 10$ kips (44.5 kN); $P_u = 1.70(10) = 17$ kips (75.6 kN).

### 2. Construct the ultimate-load and corresponding bending-moment diagram for each span

Set the maximum positive moment $M_D$ in span $AB$ and the negative moment at $B$ equal to each other in absolute value.

### 3. Evaluate the maximum positive moment in the left span

Thus, $R_A = 45.9 - M_B/40$; $x = R_A/2.04$; $M_D = \frac{1}{2}R_Ax = R_A^2/4.08 = M_B$. Substitute the value of $R_A$ and solve. Thus, $M_D = 342$ ft·kips (463.8 kN·m).

An indirect but less cumbersome method consists of assigning a series of trial values to $M_B$ and calculating the corresponding value of $M_D$, continuing the process until the required equality is obtained.

### 4. Select a section to resist the plastic moment

Thus, $Z = M_p/f_y = 342(12)136 = 114$ in³ (1868.5 cm³). Referring to the AISC *Manual*, use a W21 × 55 with $Z = 125.4$ in³ (2055.31 cm³).

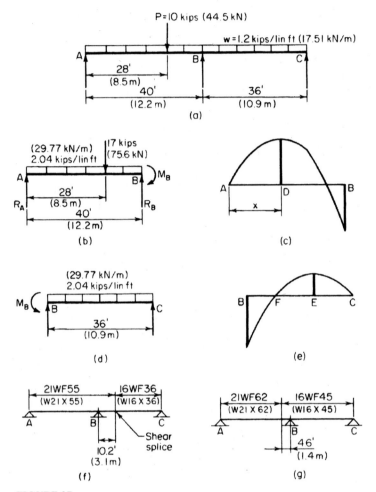

**FIGURE 27**

## 5. Evaluate the maximum positive moment in the right span

Equate $M_B$ to the true plastic-moment capacity of the W21 × 55. Evaluate the maximum positive moment $M_E$ in span $BC$, and locate the point of contraflexure. Therefore, $M_B = -36(125.4)/12 = -376.2$ ft·kips (−510.13 kN·m); $M_E = 169.1$ ft·kips (229.30 kN·m); $BF = 10.2$ ft (3.11 m).

## 6. Select a section to resist the plastic moment

The moment to be resisted is $M_E$. Thus, $Z = 169.1(12)/36 = 56.4$ in³ (924.40 cm³). Use W16 × 36 with $Z = 63.9$ in³ (1047.32 cm³).

The design is summarized in Fig. 27f. By inserting a hinge at $F$, the continuity of the member is destroyed and its behavior is thereby modified under gradually increasing load. However, the ultimate-load conditions, which constitute the only valid design criteria, are not affected.

### 7. Alternatively, design the member with the right-hand beam overhanging the support

Compare the two designs for economy. The latter design is summarized in Fig. 27g. The total beam weight associated with each scheme is as shown in the following table.

| Design 1 | Design 2 |
|---|---|
| 55(50.2) = 2,761 lb (12,280.9 N) | 62(35.4) = 2,195 lb (9,763.4 N) |
| 36(25.8) =   929 lb (4,132.2 N) | 45(40.6) = 1,827 lb (8,126.5 N) |
| Total  3,690 lb (16,413.1 N) | 4,022 lb (17,889.9 N) |

For completeness, the column sizes associated with the two schemes should also be compared.

## MECHANISM-METHOD ANALYSIS OF A RECTANGULAR PORTAL FRAME

Calculate the plastic moment and the reactions at the supports at ultimate load of the prismatic frame in Fig. 28a. Use a load factor of 1.85, and apply the mechanism method.

### Calculation Procedure:

### 1. Compute the ultimate loads to be resisted

There are three potential modes of failure to consider:

a. Failure of the beam $BD$ through the formation of plastic hinges at $B$, $C$, and $D$ (Fig. 28b)
b. Failure by sidesway through the formation of plastic hinges at $B$ and $D$ (Fig. 28c)
c. A composite of the foregoing modes of failure, characterized by the formation of plastic hinges at $C$ and $D$

Since the true mode of failure is not readily discernible, it is necessary to analyze each of the foregoing. The true mode of failure is the one that yields the highest value of $M_p$.

Although the work quantities are positive, it is advantageous to supply each angular displacement with an algebraic sign. A rotation is considered positive if the angle on the interior side of the frame increases. The algebraic sum of the angular displacements must equal zero.

Computing the ultimate loads to be resisted yields $P_u = 1.85(40) = 74$ kips (329.2 kN); $Q_u = 1.85(12) = 22.2$ kips (98.75 kN).

### 2. Assume the mode of failure in Fig. 28b and compute $M_p$

Thus, $\Delta_1 = 10\theta$; $W_E = 74(10\theta) = 740\theta$. Then indicate in a tabulation, such as that shown here, where the plastic moment occurs. Include all significant sections for completeness.

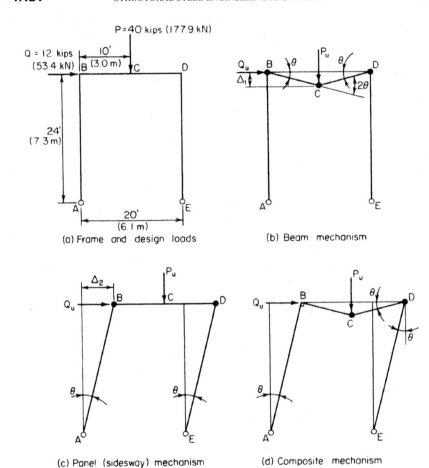

(a) Frame and design loads

(b) Beam mechanism

(c) Panel (sidesway) mechanism

(d) Composite mechanism

**FIGURE 28**

| Section | Angular displacement | Moment | $W_1$ |
|---|---|---|---|
| A | | | |
| B | $-\theta$ | $M_p$ | $M_p\theta$ |
| C | $+2\theta$ | $M_p$ | $2M_p\theta$ |
| D | $-\theta$ | $M_p$ | $M_p\theta$ |
| E | . . | . . | . . |
| Total | | | $4M_p\theta$ |

Then $4M_p\theta = 740\theta$; $M_p = 185$ ft·kips (250.9 kN·m).

## 3. Repeat the foregoing procedure for failure by sidesway

Thus, $\Delta_2 = 24\theta$; $W_E = 22.2(24\theta) = 532.8\theta$.

| Section | Angular displacement | Moment | $W_1$ |
|---------|---------------------|--------|-------|
| A | $-\theta$ | | |
| B | $+\theta$ | $M_p$ | $M_p\theta$ |
| C | | | |
| D | $-\theta$ | $M_p$ | $M_p\theta$ |
| E | $+\theta$ | | |
| Total | | | $2M_p\theta$ |

Then $2M_p\theta = 532.8\theta$; $M_p = 266.4$ ft·kips (361.24 kN·m).

### 4. Assume the composite mode of failure and compute $M_p$

Since this results from superposition of the two preceding modes, the angular displacements and the external work may be obtained by adding the algebraic values previously found. Thus, $W_E = 740\theta + 532.8\theta = 1272.8\theta$. Then the tabulation is as shown:

| Section | Angular displacement | Moment | $W_1$ |
|---------|---------------------|--------|-------|
| A | $-\theta$ | | |
| B | | | |
| C | $+2\theta$ | $M_p$ | $2M_p\theta$ |
| D | $-2\theta$ | $M_p$ | $2M_p\theta$ |
| E | $+\theta$ | | |
| Total | | | $4M_p\theta$ |

Then $4M_p\theta = 1272.8\theta$; $M_p = 318.2$ ft·kips (431.48 kN·m).

### 5. Select the highest value of $M_p$ as the correct result

Thus, $M_p = 318.2$ ft·kips (431.48 kN·m). The structure fails through the formation of plastic hinges at $C$ and $D$. That a hinge should appear at $D$ rather than at $B$ is plausible when it is considered that the bending moments induced by the two loads are of like sign at $D$ but of opposite sign at $B$.

### 6. Compute the reactions at the supports

Draw a free-body diagram of the frame at ultimate load (Fig. 29). Compute the reactions at the supports by applying the computed values of $M_C$ and $M_D$. Thus, $\Sigma M_E = 20V_A + 22.2(24) - 74(10) = 0$; $V_A = 10.36$ kips (46.081 kN); $V_E = 74 - 10.36 = 63.64$ kips (283.071 kN); $M_C = 10V_A + 24H_A = 103.6 + 24H_A = 318.2$; $H_A = 8.94$ kips (39.765 kN); $H_E = 22.2 - 8.94 = 13.26$ kips (58.980 kN); $M_D = -24H_E = -24(13.26) = -318.2$ ft·kips ($-431.48$ kN·m). Thus, the results are verified.

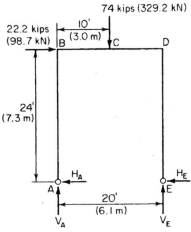

**FIGURE 29**

## ANALYSIS OF A RECTANGULAR PORTAL FRAME BY THE STATIC METHOD

Compute the plastic moment of the frame in Fig. 28a by using the static method.

### Calculation Procedure:

### 1. Determine the relative values of the bending moments

Consider a bending moment as positive if the fibers on the interior side of the neutral plane are in tension. Consequently, as the mechanisms in Fig. 28 reveal, the algebraic sign of the plastic moment at a given section agrees with that of its angular displacement during collapse.

Determine the relative values of the bending moments at $B$, $C$, and $D$. Refer to Fig. 29. As previously found by statics, $V_A = 10.36$ kips (46.081 kN), $M_B = 24H_A$, $M_C = 24H_A + 10V_A$; therefore, $M_C = M_B + 103.6$, Eq. a. Also, $M_D = 24H_A + 20V_A - 74(10)$; $M_D = M_B - 532.8$, Eq. b; or $M_D = M_C - 636.4$, Eq. c.

### 2. Assume the mode the failure in Fig. 28b

This requires that $M_B = M_D = -M_p$. This relationship is incompatible with Eq. b, and the assumed mode of failure is therefore incorrect.

### 3. Assume the mode of failure in Fig. 28c

This requires that $M_B = M_p$, and $M_C < M_p$; therefore, $M_C < M_B$. This relationship is incompatible with Eq. a, and the assumed mode of failure is therefore incorrect.

By a process of elimination, it has been ascertained that the frame will fail in the manner shown in Fig. 28d.

### 4. Compute the value of $M_p$ for the composite mode of failure

Thus, $M_C = M_p$, and $M_D = -M_p$. Substitute these values in Eq. c. Or, $-M_p = M_p - 636.4$; $M_p = 318.2$ ft·kips (431.48 kN·m).

## THEOREM OF COMPOSITE MECHANISMS

By analyzing the calculations in the calculation procedure before the last one, establish a criterion to determine when a composite mechanism is significant (i.e., under what conditions it may yield an $M_p$ value greater than that associated with the basic mechanisms).

### Calculation Procedure:

### 1. Express the external and internal work associated with a given mechanism

Thus, $W_E = e\theta$, and $W_I = iM_p\theta$, where the coefficients $e$ and $i$ are obtained by applying the mechanism method. Then $M_p = e/i$.

### 2. Determine the significance of mechanism sign

Let the subscripts 1 and 2 refer to the basic mechanisms and the subscript 3 to their composite mechanism. Then $M_{p1} = e_1/i_1$; $M_{p2} = e_2/i_2$.

When the basic mechanisms are superposed, the values of $W_E$ are additive. If the two mechanisms do not produce rotations of opposite sign at any section, the values of $W_I$ are also additive, and $M_{p3} = e_3/i_3 = (e_1 + e_2)/(i_1 + i_2)$. This value is intermediate between $M_{p1}$

and $M_{p2}$, and the composite mechanism therefore lacks significance. But if the basic mechanisms produce rotations of opposite sign at any section whatsoever, $M_{p3}$ *may* exceed both $M_{p1}$ and $M_{p2}$.

In summary, a composite mechanism is significant only if the two basic mechanisms of which it is composed produce rotations of opposite sign at any section. This theorem, which establishes a necessary but not sufficient condition, simplifies the analysis of a complex frame by enabling the engineer to discard the nonsignificant composite mechanisms at the outset.

## ANALYSIS OF AN UNSYMMETRIC RECTANGULAR PORTAL FRAME

The frame in Fig. 30a sustains the ultimate loads shown. Compute the plastic moment and ultimate-load reactions.

### Calculation Procedure:

#### 1. Determine the solution method to use
Apply the mechanism method. In Fig. 30b, indicate the basic mechanisms.

#### 2. Identify the significant composite mechanisms
Apply the theorem of the previous calculation procedure. Using this theorem, identify the significant composite mechanisms. For mechanisms 1 and 2, the rotations at B are of opposite sign; their composite therefore warrants investigation.

For mechanisms 1 and 3, there are no rotations of opposite sign; their composite therefore fails the test. For mechanisms 2 and 3, the rotations at B are of opposite sign; their composite therefore warrants investigation.

#### 3. Evaluate the external work associated with each mechanism

| Mechanism | $W_E$ |
|-----------|-------|
| 1 | $80\Delta_1 = 80(10\theta) = 800\theta$ |
| 2 | $2\Delta_2 = 20(15\theta) = 300\theta$ |
| 3 | $300\theta$ |
| 4 | $1100\theta$ |
| 5 | $600\theta$ |

#### 4. List the sections at which plastic hinges form; record the angular displacement associated with each mechanism
Use a list such as the following:

| Mechanism | Section | | | |
|-----------|---------|---------|---------|---------|
| | *B* | *C* | *D* | *F* |
| 1 | $-\theta$ | $+2\theta$ | $-\theta$ | |
| 2 | $+\theta$ | . . | $-1.2\theta$ | |
| 3 | $-1.5\theta$ | . . | . . . | $+2.5\theta$ |
| 4 | . . | $+2\theta$ | $-2.25\theta$ | |
| 5 | $-0.5\theta$ | . . | $-1.25\theta$ | $+2.5\theta$ |

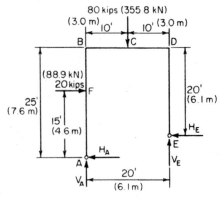

(a) Frame and ultimate loads

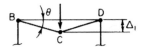

Mechanism I

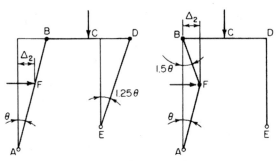

Mechanism 2                    Mechanism 3
(b) Basic mechanisms

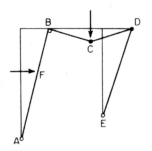

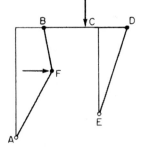

Mechanism 4                    Mechanism 5
Composite of I and 2          Composite of 2 and 3
(c) Composite mechanisms

**FIGURE 30**

### 5. Evaluate the internal work associated with each mechanism

Equate the external and internal work to find $M_p$. Thus, $M_{p1} = 800/4 = 200$; $M_{p2} = 300/2.25 = 133.3$; $M_{p3} = 300/4 = 75$; $M_{p4} = 1100/4.25 = 258.8$; $M_{p5} = 600/4.25 = 141.2$. Equate the external and internal work to find $M_p$.

### 6. Select the highest value as the correct result

Thus, $M_p = 258.8$ ft·kips (350.93 kN·m). The frame fails through the formation of plastic hinges at $C$ and $D$.

### 7. Determine the reactions at ultimate load

To verify the foregoing solution, ascertain that the bending moment does not exceed $M_p$ in absolute value anywhere in the frame. Refer to Fig. 30a.

Thus, $M_D = -20H_E = -258.8$; therefore, $H_E = 12.94$ kips (57.557 kN); $M_C = M_D + 10V_E = 258.8$; therefore, $V_E = 51.76$ kips (230.23 kN); then $H_A = 7.06$ kips (31.403 kN); $V_A = 28.24$ kips (125.612 kN).

Check the moments. Thus $\Sigma M_E = 20V_A + 5H_A + 20(10) - 80(10) = 0$; this is correct. Also, $M_F = 15H_A = 105.9$ ft·kips (143.60 kN·m) $< M_p$. This is correct. Last, $M_B = 25H_A - 20(10) = -23.5$ ft·kips (−31.87 kN·m) $> -M_p$. This is correct.

## ANALYSIS OF GABLE FRAME BY STATIC METHOD

The prismatic frame in Fig. 31a carries the ultimate loads shown. Determine the plastic moment by applying the static method.

### Calculation Procedure:

### 1. Compute the vertical shear $V_A$ and the bending moment at every significant section, assuming $H_A = 0$

Thus, $V_A = 41$ kips (182.4 kN). Then $M_B = 0$; $M_C = 386$; $M_D = 432$; $M_E = 276$; $M_F = -100$.

Note that failure of the frame will result from the formation of two plastic hinges. It is helpful, therefore, to construct a "projected" bending-moment diagram as an aid in locating these hinges. The computed bending moments are used in plotting the projected bending-moment diagram.

### 2. Construct a projected bending-moment diagram

To construct this diagram, consider the rafter $BD$ to be projected onto the plane of column $AB$ and the rafter $FD$ to be projected onto the plane of column $GF$. Juxtapose the two halves, as shown in Fig. 31b. Plot the values calculated in step 1 to obtain the bending-moment diagram corresponding to the assumed condition of $H_A = 0$.

The bending moments caused solely by a specific value of $H_A$ are represented by an isosceles triangle with its vertex at $D'$. The true bending moments are obtained by superposition. It is evident by inspection of the diagram that plastic hinges form at $D$ and $F$ and that $H_A$ is directed to the right.

### 3. Evaluate the plastic moment

Apply the true moments at $D$ and $F$. Thus, $M_D = M_p$ and $M_F = -M_p$; therefore, $432 - 37H_A = -(-100 - 25H_A)$; $H_A = 5.35$ kips (23.797 kN) and $M_p = 234$ ft·kips (317 kN·m).

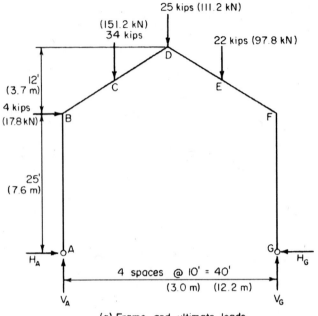

(a) Frame and ultimate loads

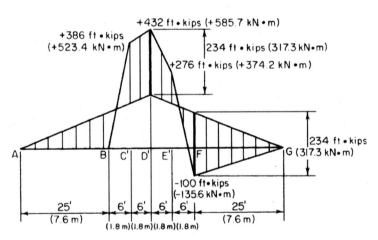

(b) Projected bending–moment diagram

**FIGURE 31**

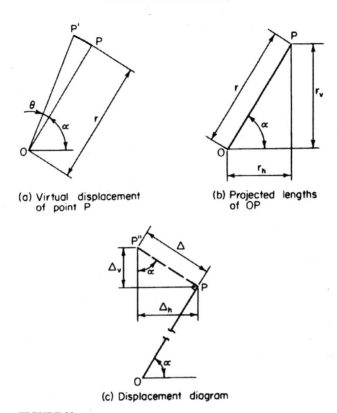

(a) Virtual displacement
of point P

(b) Projected lengths
of OP

(c) Displacement diagram

**FIGURE 32**

## THEOREM OF VIRTUAL DISPLACEMENTS

In Fig. 32a, point $P$ is displaced along a virtual (infinitesimally small) circular arc $PP'$ centered at $O$ and having a central angle $\theta$. Derive expressions for the horizontal and vertical displacement of $P$ in terms of the given data. (These expressions are applied later in analyzing a gable frame by the mechanism method.)

**Calculation Procedure:**

### 1. Construct the displacement diagram
In Fig. 32b, let $r_h$ = length of horizontal projection of $OP$; $r_v$ = length of vertical projection of $OP$; $\Delta_h$ = horizontal displacement of $P$; $\Delta_v$ = vertical displacement of $P$.

In Fig. 32c, construct the displacement diagram. Since $PP'$ is infinitesimally small, replace this circular arc with the straight line $PP''$ that is tangent to the arc at $P$ and therefore normal to radius $OP$.

### 2. Evaluate $\Delta_h$ and $\Delta_v$, considering only absolute values
Since $\theta$ is infinitesimally small, set $PP'' = r\theta$; $\Delta_h = PP'' \sin \alpha = r\theta \sin \alpha$; $\Delta_v = PP'' \cos \alpha = r\theta \cos \alpha$. But $r \sin \alpha = r_v$ and $r \cos \alpha = r_h$; therefore, $\Delta_h = r_v\theta$ and $\Delta_v = r_h\theta$.

These results may be combined and expressed verbally thus: If a point is displaced along a virtual circular arc, its displacement as projected on the $u$ axis equals the displacement angle times the length of the radius as projected on an axis normal to $u$.

## GABLE-FRAME ANALYSIS BY USING THE MECHANISM METHOD

For the frame in Fig. 31$a$, assume that plastic hinges form at $D$ and $F$. Calculate the plastic moment associated with this assumed mode of failure by applying the mechanism method.

### Calculation Procedure:

#### 1. Indicate the frame configuration following a virtual displacement
During collapse, the frame consists of three rigid bodies: $ABD$, $DF$, and $GF$. To evaluate the external and internal work performed during a virtual displacement, it is necessary to locate the instantaneous center of rotation of each body.

In Fig. 33 indicate by dash lines the configuration of the frame following a virtual displacement. In Fig. 33, $D$ is displaced to $D'$ and $F$ to $F'$. Draw a straight line through $A$ and $D$ intersecting the prolongation of $GF$ at $H$.

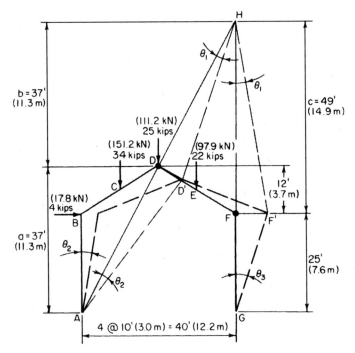

**FIGURE 33.** Virtual displacement of frame.

Since $A$ is the center of rotation of $ABD$, $DD'$ is normal to $AD$ and $HD$; since $G$ is the center of rotation of $GF$, $FF'$ is normal to $GF$ and $HF$. Therefore, $H$ is the instantaneous center of rotation of $DF$.

### 2. Record the pertinent dimensions and rotations
Record the dimensions $a$, $b$, and $c$ in Fig. 33, and express $\theta_2$ and $\theta_3$ in terms of $\theta_1$. Thus, $\theta_2/\theta_1 = HD/AD$; $\therefore \theta_2 = \theta_1$. Also, $\theta_3/\theta_1 = HF/GF = 49/25$; $\therefore \theta_3 = 1.96\theta_1$.

### 3. Determine the angular displacement, and evaluate the internal work
Determine the angular displacement (in absolute value) at $D$ and $F$, and evaluate the internal work in terms of $\theta_1$. Thus, $\theta_D = \theta_1 + \theta_2 = 2\theta_1$; $\theta_F = \theta_1 + \theta_3 = 2.96\theta_1$. Then $W_I = M_p(\theta_D + \theta_F) = 4.96M_p\theta_1$.

### 4. Apply the theorem of virtual displacements to determine the displacement of each applied load
Determine the displacement of each applied load in the direction of the load. Multiply the displacement by the load to obtain the external work. Record the results as shown:

| Section | Load kips | kN | Displacement in direction of load ft | m | External work ft·kips | kN·m |
|---------|------|-------|----------------------------------|-----|---------|----------|
| B | 4 | 17.8 | $\Delta_h = 25\theta_2 = 25\theta_1$ | $7.6\theta_1$ | $100\theta_1$ | $135.6\theta_1$ |
| C | 34 | 151.2 | $\Delta_v = 10\theta_2 = 10\theta_1$ | $3.0\theta_1$ | $340\theta_1$ | $461.0\theta_1$ |
| D | 25 | 111.2 | $\Delta_v = 20\theta_1$ | $6.1\theta_1$ | $500\theta_1$ | $678.0\theta_1$ |
| E | 22 | 97.9 | $\Delta_v = 10\theta_1$ | $3.0\theta_1$ | $220\theta_1$ | $298.3\theta_1$ |
| Total | | | | | $1160\theta_1$ | $1572.9\theta_1$ |

### 5. Equate the external and internal work to find $M_p$
Thus, $4.96M_p\theta_1 = 1160\theta_1$; $M_p = 234$ ft·kips (317.3 kN·m).

Other modes of failure may be assumed and the corresponding value of $M_p$ computed in the same manner. The failure mechanism analyzed in this procedure (plastic hinges at $D$ and $F$) yields the highest value of $M_p$ and is therefore the true mechanism.

# REDUCTION IN PLASTIC-MOMENT CAPACITY CAUSED BY AXIAL FORCE

A W10 × 45 beam-column is subjected to an axial force of 84 kips (373.6 kN) at ultimate load. (a) Applying the exact method, calculate the plastic moment this section can develop with respect to the major axis. (b) Construct the interaction diagram for this section, and then calculate the plastic moment by assuming a linear interaction relationship that approximates the true relationship.

## Calculation Procedure:

### 1. Record the relevant properties of the member
Let $P$ = applied axial force, kips (kN); $P_y$ = axial force that would induce plastification if acting alone, kips (kN) = $Af_y$; $M_p'$ = plastic-moment capacity of the section in combination with $P$, ft·kips (kN·m).

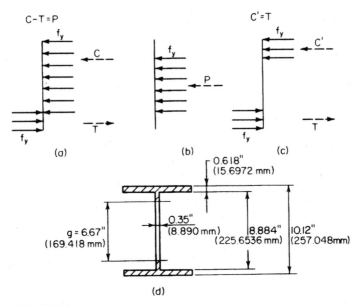

**FIGURE 34**

A typical stress diagram for a beam-column at plastification is shown in Fig. 34a. To simplify the calculations, resolve this diagram into the two parts shown at the right. This procedure is tantamount to assuming that the axial load is resisted by a central core and the moment by the outer segments of the section, although in reality they are jointly resisted by the integral action of the entire section.

From the AISC *Manual*, for a W10 × 45: $A = 13.24$ sq.in. (85.424 cm²); $d = 10.12$ in. (257.048 mm); $t_f = 0.618$ in. (15.6972 mm); $t_w = 0.350$ in. (8.890 mm); $d_w = 10.12 - 2(0.618) = 8.884$ in. (225.6536 mm); $Z = 55.0$ in³ (901.45 cm³).

### 2. Assume that the central core that resists the 84-kip (373.6-kN) load is encompassed within the web; determine the core depth

Calling the depth of the core $g$, refer to Fig. 34d. Then $g = 84/[0.35(36)] = 6.67 < 8.884$ in. (225.6536 mm).

### 3. Compute the plastic modulus of the core, the plastic modulus of the remaining section, and the value of $M'_p$

Using data from the *Manual* for the plastic modulus of a rectangle, we find $Z_c = \frac{1}{4} t_w g^2 = \frac{1}{4}(0.35)(6.67)^2 = 3.9$ in³ (63.92 cm³); $Z_r = 55.0 - 3.9 = 51.1$ in³ (837.53 cm³); $M'_p = 51.1(36)/12 = 153.3$ ft·kips (207.87 kN·m). This constitutes the solution of part *a*. The solution of part *b* is given in steps 4 through 6.

### 4. Assign a series of values to the parameter $g$, and compute the corresponding sets of values of P and $M'_p$

Apply the results to plot the interaction diagram in Fig. 35. This comprises the parabolic curves *CB* and *BA*, where the points *A*, *B*, and *C* correspond to the conditions $g = 0$, $g = d_w$, and $g = d$, respectively.

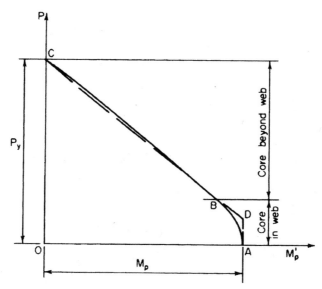

**FIGURE 35.** Interaction diagram for axial force and moment.

The interaction diagram is readily analyzed by applying the following relationships: $dP/dg = f_y t$; $dM_p'/dg = -\frac{1}{2}f_y tg$; $\therefore dP/dM_p' = -2/g$. This result discloses that the change in slope along $CB$ is very small, and the curvature of this arc is negligible.

### 5. *Replace the true interaction diagram with a linear one*
Draw a vertical line $AD = 0.15P_y$, and then draw the straight line $CD$ (Fig. 35). Establish the equation of $CD$. Thus, slope of $CD = -0.85P_y/M_p$; $P = -0.85P_y M_p'/M_p$, or $M_p' = 1.18(1 - P/P_y)M_p$.

The provisions of one section of the AISC *Specification* are based on the linear interaction diagram.

### 6. *Ascertain whether the data are represented by a point on AD or CD; calculate $M_p'$, accordingly*
Thus, $P_y = Af_y = 13.24(36) = 476.6$ kips (2119.92 kN); $P/P_y = 84/476.6 = 0.176$; therefore, apply the last equation given in step 5. Thus, $M_p = 55.0(36)/12 = 165$ ft·kips (223.7 kN·m); $M_p' = 1.18(1 - 0.176)(165) = 160.4$ ft·kips (217.50 kN·m). This result differs from that in part *a* by 4.6 percent.

# Load and Resistance Factor Method

Abraham J. Rokach, MSCE, Associate Director of Education, American Institute of Steel Construction, Inc., writing in *Theory and Problems of Structural Steel Design*, McGraw-Hill, states "In 1986 a new method of structural steel design was introduced in the United

States with the publication of the *Load and Resistance Factor Design Specification for Structural Steel Buildings.* Load and resistance factor design, or LRFD, has joined the old allowable stress design (ASD) method as a recognized means for the design of structural steel frameworks for buildings.

"Although ASD has enjoyed a long history of successful usage and is familiar to engineers and architects, the author and most experts prefer LRFD because it is a truer representation of the actual behavior of structural steel and unlike ASD, it can provide equivalent margins of safety for all structures under all loading conditions. . . . For these reasons it is anticipated that LRFD will replace ASD as the standard method of structural steel design."

The following selected procedures in this handbook cover structural steel design for buildings using the *load and resistance factor design* (LRFD) method drawn from the excellent Rokach book listed above. And competent authorities on the LRFD method, listed below, are cited frequently in the Rokach book, and in this handbook, usually in abbreviated form:

AISC: American Institute of Steel Construction, Inc., Chicago, IL.

AISC *LRFD Specification*: *Load and Resistance Factor Design Specification for Structural Steel Buildings,* published by AISC.

AISC *LRFD Manual*: *Load and Resistance Factor Design Manual of Steel Construction,* also published by AISC.

Equations in the following calculation procedures in this handbook are numbered as follows. Those equations appearing in the AISC *LRFD Specification* are accompanied by their AISC numbers in parentheses, thus ( ); other equations are numbered in brackets, thus [ ].

It is recommended that the designer have copies of both the AISC *LRFD Specification* and the AISC *Manual* on his or her desk when preparing any structural steel design using the LRFD method. Both are available from the AISC at 1 E Wacker Dr, Suite 3100, Chicago IL 60601.

Abraham J. Rokach writes, further, in his book cited above, "The ASD method is characterized by the use of one judgemental factor of safety. A limiting stress (usually $F_y$) is divided by a factor of safety (FS, determined by the authors of the *Specification*) to arrive at an allowable stress

$$\text{Allowable stress} = F_y/FS$$

Actual stresses in a steel member are calculated by dividing forces or moments by the appropriate section property (e.g. area or section modulus). The actual stresses are then compared with the allowable stresses to ascertain that

$$\text{Actual stress} = \text{allowable stress}$$

No distinction is made among the various kinds of loads. Because of the greater variability and uncertainty of the live load and other loads in comparison with the dead load, a uniform reliability for all structures is not possible.

". . . Briefly, LRFD uses a different factor for each type of load and another factor for the strength or resistance. Each factor is the result of a statistical study of the variability of the subject quantity. Because the different factors reflect the degrees of uncertainty in the various loads and the resistance, a uniform reliability is possible."

# DETERMINING IF A GIVEN BEAM IS COMPACT OR NON-COMPACT

A designer plans to use a W6 × 15 and a W12 × 65 beam in (a) A6 steel [$F_y$ = 36 ksi (248 MPa)], and (b) with $F_y$ = 50 ksi 344.5 MPa and wishes to determine if the beams are compact or non-compact.

## Calculation Procedure:

### For the W6 × 15 beam

### 1. Analyze the W6 × 15 beam
Referring to the AISC *Manual* table, namely "Limiting Width-Thickness Ratios for Beams" and its illustration "Definition of widths (b and h) and thickness," the flanges of a W shape are given by

$$\lambda_p = \frac{65}{\sqrt{F_y}}$$

where $\lambda_p$ = limiting width-thickness ratio for compact section.
Substituting for each of the two beams, we have

$$\lambda_p = \frac{65}{\sqrt{F_y}} = \begin{cases} \dfrac{65}{\sqrt{36}} = 10.8 & \text{if} \quad F_y = 36 \text{ ksi (248 MPa)} \\[2ex] \dfrac{65}{\sqrt{50}} = 9.2 & \text{if} \quad F_y = 50 \text{ ksi (344.5 MPa)} \end{cases}$$

### 2. Compute the data for the web of a W shape
Using the same equation as in Step 1, for the web of a W shape

$$\lambda_p = \frac{640}{\sqrt{F_y}} = \begin{cases} \dfrac{640}{\sqrt{36}} = 106.7 & \text{if} \quad F_y = 36 \text{ ksi (248 MPa)} \\[2ex] \dfrac{640}{\sqrt{50}} = 90.5 & \text{if} \quad F_y = 50 \text{ ksi (344.5 MPa)} \end{cases}$$

### 3. Determine if the beam is compact
From the Properties Tables for W Shapes, in Part 1 of the AISC *LRFD Manual* (Compact Section Criteria): for a W6 × 15

$$\text{flange } \frac{b}{t} = \frac{b_f}{2t_f} = 11.5$$

$$\text{web } \frac{h_c}{t_w} = 21.6$$

Since flange ($b/t$ = 11.5) > ($\lambda_p$ = 10.8), the W × 15 beam is noncompact in A36 steel. Likewise, it is noncompact if $F_y$ = 50 ksi (344.4 Mpa).

### For the W12 × 65 beam

### 4. Compute the properties of the beam shape
From the AISC *Manual* "Properties Tables for W Shapes," for a W12 × 65

$$\text{flange } \frac{b}{t} = \frac{b_f}{2t_f} = 9.9$$

$$\text{web } \frac{h_c}{t_w} = 24.9$$

(a) In A36 steel

$$\text{flange } \lambda_p = 10.8$$

See W6 × 15

$$\text{web } \lambda_p = 24.9$$

Since flange ($b/t = 9.9$) < ($\lambda_p = 10.8$), and web ($h_c/t_w = 24.9$) < ($\lambda_p = 106.7$), a W12 × 65 beam is compact in A36 steel.

(b) However, if $F_y = 50$ ksi (344.5 MPa)

$$\text{flange } \lambda_p = 9.2$$

See W6 × 15

$$\text{web } \lambda_p = 90.5$$

Because flange ($b/t = 9.9$) > ($\lambda_p = 9.2$), a W12 × 65 beam is noncompact if $F_y = 50$ ksi (344.5 MPa)

**Related Calculations:** The concept of compactness, states Abraham J. Rokach, MSCE, AISC, relates to local buckling. Cross-sections of structural members are classified as compact, noncompact, or slender-element sections. A section is compact if the flanges are continuously connected to the web, and the width-thickness ratios of all its compression elements are equal to, or less than, $\lambda_p$.

Structural steel members with compact sections can develop their full strength without local instability. In design, the limit state of local buckling need not be considered for compact members.

This procedure is the work of Abraham J. Rokach, MSCE, AISC, Associate Director of Education, American Institute of Steel Construction. SI values were prepared by the handbook editor.

## DETERMINING COLUMN AXIAL SHORTENING WITH A SPECIFIED LOAD

A W10 × 49 column, 10 ft (3 m) long, carries a service load of 250 kips (113.5 Mg). What axial shortening will occur in this column with this load?

### Calculation Procedure:

### 1. Choose a suitable axial displacement equation for this column
The LRFD equation for axial shortening of a loaded column is

$$\text{Shortening, } \Delta = \frac{Pl}{EA_g}$$

where $\Delta$ = axial shortening, in. (cm); $P$ = unfactored axial force in member, kips (kg); $l$ = length of member, in. (cm); $E$ = modulus of elasticity of steel = 29,000 ksi (199.8 MPa); $A_g$ = cross sectional area of member, sq.in. (sq cm).

## 2. Compute the column axial shortening
Substituting,

$$\text{Shortening, } \Delta = \frac{Pl}{EA_g} = \frac{250 \text{ kips} \times (10.0 \text{ ft} \times 12 \text{ in./ft})}{29,000 \text{ kips/sq.in.} \times 14.4 \text{ sq.in.}}$$

$$= 0.072 \text{ in. } (0.183 \text{ cm}).$$

**Related Calculations:** Use this equation to compute axial shortening of any steel column in LRFD work. This procedure is the work of Abraham J. Rokach, MSCE, American Institute of Steel Construction.


# DETERMINING THE COMPRESSIVE STRENGTH OF A WELDED SECTION

The structural section in Fig. 36a is used as a 40-ft (12.2-m) column. Its effective length factor $K_x = K_y = 1.0$. Determine the design compressive strength if the steel is A36.


## Calculation Procedure:

### 1. Choose a design compressive strength
The design compressive strength is given by:

$$\phi_c P_n = \phi_c F_{cr} A_g$$

The values of $\phi_c F_{cr}$ can be obtained from the Table, "Design Stress for Compression Members of 36 ksi Specified Yield-Stress Steel, $\phi = 0.85$" in the AISC *Manual*, if $Kl/r$ is known. With $Kl$ = 1.0 × 40.0 ft × 12 in/ft = 480 in. (1219 cm), then

$$r = \sqrt{\frac{I}{A}}$$

$$A = (18 \text{ in.})^2 - (17 \text{ in.})^2 = 35.0 \text{ sq.in.}$$

$$I_x = I_y = I = \frac{(18 \text{ in.})^2 - (17 \text{ in.})^4}{12} = 1788 \text{ in}^4 \text{ } (0.00074 \text{ m}^4)$$

### 2. Find the Kl/r ratio for this section
With the data we have,

$$r = \sqrt{\frac{1788 \text{ in}^4}{35.0 \text{ in}^4}} = 7.15 \text{ in.}$$

$$\frac{Kl}{r} = \frac{480 \text{ in.}}{7.15 \text{ in.}} = 67.2$$

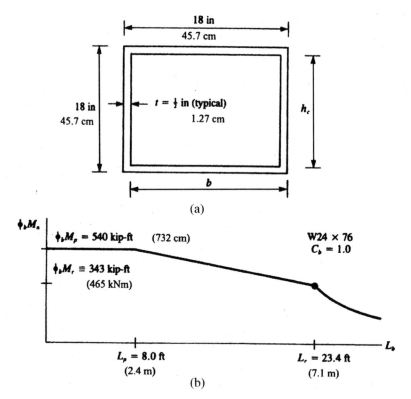

**FIGURE 36**

## 3. Determine the design compressive strength of this section

Using the suitable AISC *Manual* table, namely "Design Stress for Compression Members of 36 ksi Specified Yield-Stress Steel, $\phi_c = 0.85$," and interpolating, for $Kl/r = 67.2$, $\phi_c F_{cr} = 24.13$ ksi (166.3 Mpa) the design compressive strength $\phi_c P_n = 24.13$kips/sq.in. $\times$ 35.0 sq.in. = 845 kips (3759 kN).

**Related Calculations.** This procedure is the work of Abraham J. Rokach, MSCE, Associate Director of Education, American Institute of Steel Construction. SI values were prepared by the handbook editor.

## DETERMINING BEAM FLEXURAL DESIGN STRENGTH FOR MINOR- AND MAJOR-AXIS BENDING

For a simply supported W24 × 76 beam, laterally braced only at the supports, determine the flexural design strength for (a) minor-axis bending and (b) major-axis bending.

Use the "Load Factor Design Selection Table for Beams" in Part 3 of the AISC *LRFD Manual.*

## Calculation Procedure:

### 1. Determine if the beam is a compact section
The W24 × 76 is a compact section. This can be verified by noting that in the Properties Tables in Part 1 of the AISC *LRFD Manual*, both $b_f/2t_f$ and $h_c/t_w$ for a W24 × 76 beam are less than the respective flange and web values of $\lambda_p$ for $F_y = 36$ ksi (248 MPa).

### 2. Find the flexural design strength for minor-axis bending
For minor- (or $y$-) axis bending, $M_{ny} = M_{py} Z_y F_y$ regardless of unbraced length (Eq. [56]). The flexural design strength for minor-axis bending of a W24 × 76 is always equal to $\phi_b M_{ny} = \phi_b Z_y F_y = 0.90 \times 28.6$ in$^3$ × 36 ksi = 927 kip-in. = 77kip-ft (104 kNm).

### 3. Compute the flexural design strength for major-axis bending
The flexural design strength for major-axis bending depends on $C_b$ and $L_b$. For a simply supported member, the end moments $M_1 = M_2 = 0$; $C_b = 1.0$.

### 4. Plot the results
For $0 < L_b < (L_p = 8.0\text{ft})$, $\phi_p M_n = \phi_b M_p = 540$ kip-ft (732 kNm).

At $L_b = L_r = 23.4$ ft, $\phi_p M_{nx} = \phi_b M_r = 343$ kip-ft (465 kNm). Linear interpolation is required for $L_p < L_b < L_r$. For $L_b > L_r$, refer to the beam graphs in Part 3 of the AISC *LRFD Manual.*

Figure 36*b* shows the data plotted for this beam, after using data from the AISC table referred to above.

**Related Calculations.** This procedure is the work of Abraham J. Rokach, MSCE, Associate Director of Education, American Institute of Steel Construction. SI values were prepared by the handbook editor.

# DESIGNING WEB STIFFENERS
# FOR WELDED BEAMS

The welded beam in Fig. 37*a* (selected from the table of Built-Up Wide-Flange Sections in Part 3 of the AISC *LRFD Manual*) frames into the column in Fig. 37*b*. Design web stiffeners to double the shear strength of the web at the end panel.

## Calculation Procedure:

### 1. Determine the nominal shear strength for a stiffened web
At the end panels there is no tension field action. The nominal shear strength for a stiffened web is, using the AISC *LRFD Manual* equation, $V_n = 0.64 A_w F_y C_v$. Assuming

$$\frac{h}{t_w} > 234 \sqrt{\frac{k}{F_y}}, \qquad C_v = \frac{44{,}000}{(h/t_w)^2 F_y}$$

Substituting, we obtain

$$V_n = 0.6 A_w F_y \times \frac{44{,}000}{(h/t_w)^2 F_y} = A_w \frac{26{,}400\ k}{(h/t_w)^2}$$

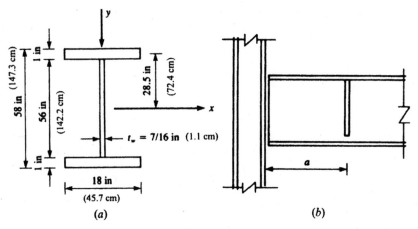

**FIGURE 37**

The case of no-stiffeners corresponds to $k = 5$.

## 2. Check the original assumptions for doubling the shear strength

To double the shear strength, I $k = 2 \times 5 = 10$. Then in AISC Eq. *A-G3-4*,

$$k = 5 + \frac{5}{(a/h)^2} = 10$$

This implies $a/h = 1.0$ or $a = k$; thus, the clear distance between transverse web stiffeners $a = h = 56$ in. (142.2 cm). Checking the original assumption we obtain

$$\left(\frac{h}{t_w} = \frac{56 \text{ in.}}{0.44 \text{ in.}} = 128.9\right) > \left(234\sqrt{\frac{k}{F_y}} = 234\sqrt{\frac{10}{36}} = 123.3\right) \qquad \text{o.k.}$$

## 3. Design the stiffener, trying a pair of stiffener plates

Stiffener design can be performed thusly. Because tension field action is not utilized, the equation $I_{st} \geq at_w^3 j$ must be satisfied, where

$$j = \frac{2.5}{(a/h)^2} - 2 \geq 0.5$$

$$j = \frac{2.5}{1^2} - 2 = 0.5$$

$$I_{st} \geq 56 \text{ in.} \times (0.44 \text{ in.})^3 \times 0.5 = 2.34 \text{ in}^4 \ (97.4 \text{ cm}^4)$$

Try a pair of stiffener plates, 2.5 in. $\times$ 0.25 in. (6.35 $\times$ 0.635 cm), as in Fig. 38. The moment of inertia of the stiffener pair about the web centerline

$$I_{st} = \frac{0.25 \text{ in.} \times (5.44 \text{ in.})^3}{12} = 3.35 \text{ in.}^4 > 2.34 \text{ in.}^4 \quad \text{o.k.} \quad (139.4 \text{ cm}^4 > 97.4 \text{ cm}^4) \quad \text{o.k.}$$

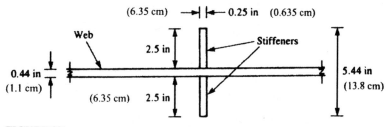

**FIGURE 38**

### 4. Try a single stiffener plate
Using the plate in Fig. 39, which is 3.5 × 0.25 in. (8.89 × 0.635 cm), the moment of inertia of the stiffener about the face of the web is

$$I_{st} = \frac{0.25 \text{ in.} \times (3.5 \text{ in.})^3}{3} = 3.57 \text{ in.}^4 > 2.34 \text{ in.}^4 \quad \text{o.k.} \quad (148.6 \text{ cm}^4 > 97.4 \text{ cm}^4) \quad \text{o.k.}$$

**Related Calculations.** This procedure is the work of Abraham J. Rokach, MSCE, Associate Director of Education, American Institute of Steel Construction. SI values were prepared by the handbook editor.

---

## DETERMINING THE DESIGN MOMENT AND SHEAR STRENGTH OF A BUILT-UP WIDE-FLANGE WELDED BEAM SECTION

For the welded section in Fig. 37a (selected from the table of Built-Up Wide-Flange Sections in Part 3 of the AISC *LRFD Manual*), determine the design moment and shear strengths. Bending is about the major axis; $C_b = 1.0$. The (upper) compression flange is continuously braced by the floor deck. Steel is A36.

### Calculation Procedure:

### 1. Check the beam compactness and flange local buckling

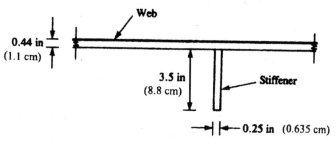

**FIGURE 39**

Working with the "Flexural Strength Parameters" table in the Appendix of the AISC *LRFD Specification*, the compactness of the beam (for a doubly symmetric I shape bending about its major axis) should first be checked:

**Flange**

$$\lambda = \frac{b}{t} = \frac{b_f}{2t_f} = \frac{18 \text{ in.}}{2 \times 1 \text{ in.}} = 9.0$$

For the definition of $b$ for a welded I shape, see the AISC *LRFD Manual*.

**Flange**

$$\lambda_p = \frac{65}{\sqrt{F_y}} = \frac{65}{\sqrt{36}} = 10.833$$

For the flange, $\lambda < \lambda_p$. Therefore, the flange is compact, and $M_{nx} = M_{px}$ for the limit state of flange local buckling (FLB).

**Web**

$$\lambda = \frac{h_c}{t_w} = \frac{56 \text{ in.}}{\sqrt{\frac{7}{16} \text{in}}} = 128.0$$

**Web**

$$\lambda_p = \frac{640}{\sqrt{F_y}} = \frac{640}{\sqrt{36}} = 106.7$$

**Web**

$$\lambda_r = \frac{970}{\sqrt{F_y}} = \frac{970}{\sqrt{36}} = 161.7$$

For the web, $(\lambda_p = 106.7) < (\lambda = 128.0) < (\lambda_r = 161.7)$. The web is noncompact: $M_{rx} < M_{nx} < M_{px}$; for the limit state of web local buckling (WLB); $M_{nx}$ is determined from AISC *LRFD Manual* Eq. (*A-F1-3*).

**2. Analyze the lateral bracing relating to the limit state of lateral-torsional buckling (LTB)**
For this continuously braced member $L_b = 0$; $M_{nx} = M_{px}$ for LTB. Summarizing:

| Limit State | $M_{nx}$ |
|---|---|
| LTB | $M_{px}$ |
| FLB | $M_{px}$ |
| WLB | $M_{rx} < M_{nx} < M_{px}$ |

The limit state of WLB (with minimum $M_{nx}$) governs. To determine $M_{px}$, $M_{rx}$, and $M_{nx}$ for a doubly symmetric I-shaped member bending about the major axis, refer again to the AISC *LRFD Manual* table. There $M_{px} = F_y Z_x$, $M_{rx} = F_y S_x$ for WLB and from Eq. (*A-F1-3*) (for WLB):

$$M_{nx} = M_{px} - (M_{px} - M_{rx})\left(\frac{\lambda - \lambda_p}{\lambda_r - \lambda_p}\right)$$

The properties $S_x$ and $Z_x$ of the cross section in Fig. 40 must now be calculated.

$$S_x = \frac{I_x}{C}, \quad \text{where} \quad c = \frac{d}{2} = \frac{58 \text{ in.}}{2} = 29 \text{ in. (73.7 cm)}$$

The contributions of the two flanges and the web to the moment of inertia $I_x$ are

| Elements | $\frac{BT^3}{12} + AD^2$ | |
|---|---|---|
| 2 Flanges | $\left[\frac{18 \text{ in.} \times (1 \text{ in.})^3}{12} + (18 \text{ in.} \times 1 \text{ in.})(28.5 \text{ in.})^2\right]2$ <br> $(1,217,227 \text{ cm}^4)$ | $= 29,244 \text{ in}^4$ |
| Web | $\frac{0.44 \text{ in.} \times (56 \text{ in.})^3}{12} + 0$ | $= 6,403 \text{ in}^4 \ (266,513 \text{ cm}^4)$ |
| $I_x$ | $S_x = \frac{35,647 \text{ in.}^4}{29 \text{ in.}}$ | $1230 \text{ in.}^3 \ (20,156 \text{ cm}^3)$ |

To determine $Z_x$, we calculate $\Sigma AD$, where $A$ is the cross-sectional area of each element and $D$ represents its distance from the centroidal $x$ axis.

In calculating $Z_x$, the upper and lower halves of the web are taken separately.

| Elements | $AD$ |
|---|---|
| Flanges | $[(18 \text{ in.} \times 1 \text{ in.}) \times 28.5 \text{ in.}]2 = 1026 \text{ in.}^3 \ (16,813 \text{ cm}^3)$ |
| $2\frac{1}{2}$ Webs | $[(28 \text{ in.} \times 0.44 \text{ in.}) \times 14 \text{ in.}]2 = 343 \text{ in.}^3 \ (5,620 \text{ cm}^3)$ |
| $Z_x$ | $1369 \text{ in.}^3 \ (22,433 \text{ cm}^3)$ |
|  | $Z_x = 1369 \text{ in.}^3 \ (22,433 \text{ cm}^3)$ |

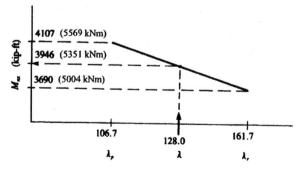

**FIGURE 40**

### 3. Determine the welded section flexural strength

Determining flexural strengths, we obtain

$$M_{px} = F_y Z_x = \frac{36 \text{ kips/sq.in.} \times 1369 \text{ in.}^3}{12 \text{ in./ft}} = 4107 \text{ kip-ft (5569 kNm)}$$

$$M_{rx} = F_y S_x = \frac{36 \text{ kips/sq.in.} \times 1230 \text{ in.}^3}{12 \text{ in./ft}} = 3690 \text{ kip-ft (5004 kNm)}$$

The value of $M_n$ can be obtained by linear interpolation using Fig. 40 or AISC Eq. (A-F1-3): $M_{nx} = 3946$ kip-ft (5351 kNm).

The design flexural strength $\phi_b M_{nx} = 0.90 \times 3946$ kip-ft $= 3551$ kip-ft (4815 kNm).

Shear strength for an unstiffened web is governed by one of the equations below, depending on $h/t_w$.

$$\text{For } \frac{h}{t_w} \leq \frac{418}{\sqrt{F_y}} \qquad\qquad V_n = 0.6 F_y A_w \qquad\qquad [1]$$

$$\text{For } \frac{418}{\sqrt{F_y}} < \frac{h}{t_w} \leq \frac{523}{\sqrt{F_y}} \qquad V_n = 0.6 F_y A_w \frac{418/\sqrt{F_y}}{h/t_w} \qquad [2]$$

$$\text{For } \frac{h}{t_w} < \frac{523}{\sqrt{F_y}} \qquad\qquad V_n = A_w \frac{132,000}{(h/t_w)^2} \qquad\qquad [3]$$

where   $V_n$ = nominal shear strength, kips (kN)
$A_w$ = area of the web, sq.in. = $d t_w$
$d$ = overall depth, in. (cm)
$t_w$ = thickness of web, in. (cm)
$h$ = the following web dimensions, in: clear distance between fillets, for rolled shapes; clear distance between flanges for welded sections

Here, $h/t_w = 56$ in./0.44 in. = 128.0.

$$128 > \frac{523}{\sqrt{F_y}} = \frac{523}{\sqrt{36}}$$

Equation (3) governs:

$$V_n = A_w \frac{132,000}{(h/t_w)^2} = \frac{(58 \text{ in.} \times 0.44 \text{ in.}) \times 132,000}{(128.0)^2}$$

$$= 204.4 \text{ kips (909.2 kN)}$$

The design shear strength $\phi_v V_n = 0.90 \times 204.4$ kips = 184.0 kips (818.4 kN)

**Related Calculations.** This procedure is the work of Abraham J. Rokach, MSCE, Associate Director of Education, American Institute of Steel Construction. SI values were prepared by the handbook editor.

## *FINDING THE LIGHTEST SECTION*
## *TO SUPPORT A SPECIFIED LOAD*

Find the lightest W8 in A36 steel to support a factored load of 100 kips (444.8 kN) in tension with an eccentricity of 6 in. (15.2 cm). The member is 6 ft (1.8 m) long and is laterally braced only at the supports; $C_b = 1.0$. Try the orientations (a) to (c) shown in Fig. 41.

### Calculation Procedure:

### 1. *Try the first orientation, (a), Fig. 41*
Given

$$P_u = 100 \text{ kips (44.8 kN)}; \quad M_u = P_u e = \frac{100 \text{ kips} \times 6 \text{ in.}}{12 \text{ in./ft}} = 50 \text{ kip-ft (67.8 kNm)}$$

For orientation (a) in Fig. 41

$$P_u = 100 \text{ kips}, \qquad M_{ux} = 50 \text{ kip-ft}, \qquad M_{uy} = 0$$

Try a W8 × 28: the design tensile strength (for a cross section with no holes)

$$\phi_t P_n = \phi_t F_y A_g = 0.90 \times 36 \text{ ksi} \times 8.25 \text{ sq.in.} = 267 \text{ kips (1188 kN)}$$

For $(L_b = 6.0 \text{ ft}) < (L_p = 6.8 \text{ ft})$, the design flexural strength for x-axis bending

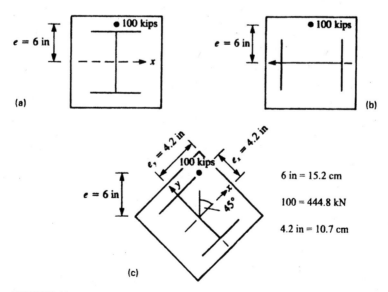

(a)

(b)

$$e = 6 \text{ in}$$

6 in = 15.2 cm

100 = 444.8 kN

4.2 in = 10.7 cm

(c)

**FIGURE 41**

$$\phi_b M_{nx} = \phi_b M_p = \phi_b Z_x F_y = \frac{0.90 \times 27.2 \text{ in.}^3 \times 36 \text{ ksi}}{12 \text{ in./ft}} = 73.4 \text{ kip-ft (99.5 kNm)}$$

which is also the tabulated value for $\phi_b M_p$ for a W8 × 28 in the Beam Selection Table in Part 3 of the AISC *LRFD Manual*.

Since

$$\frac{P_u}{\phi_t P_n} = \frac{100 \text{ kips}}{267 \text{ kips}} = 0.37 > 0.2$$

the first of two interaction formulas applies.

$$\frac{P_u}{\phi_t P_n} = \frac{8}{9}\left(\frac{M_{ux}}{\phi_b M_{nx}} + \frac{M_{uy}}{\phi_b M_{ny}}\right) \leq 1.0$$

$$0.37 + \frac{8}{9}\left(\frac{50 \text{ kip-ft}}{73.4 \text{ kip-ft}} + 0\right) = 0.37 + 0.61 = 0.98 < 1.0 \quad \text{o.k.}$$

### 2. Analyze the second orientation being considered

For orientation (*b*) in Fig. 41

$$P_u = 100 \text{ kips (444.8 kN)}, \qquad M_{ux} = 0, \qquad M_{uy} = 50 \text{ kip-ft (67.8 kNm)}$$

Again, try a W8 × 28. For all $L_b$. the design flexural strength for *y*-axis bending

$$\phi_b M_{ny} = \phi_b M_p = \phi_b Z_y F_y$$

$$= \frac{0.90 \times 10.1 \text{ in.}^3 \times 36 \text{ ksi}}{12 \text{ in./ft}} = 27.2 \text{ kip-ft (36.9 kNm)}$$

Because $M_{uy} = 50$ kip-ft $> \phi_b M_{ny} = 27.2$ kip-ft, a W8 × 28 is inadequate. Try a W8 × 48: $A_g = 14.1$ sq.in. (90.0 cm²), $Z_y = 22.9$ in.³ (375.3 cm³)

$$\phi_b M_{ny} = \frac{0.90 \times 22.9 \text{ in.}^3 \times 36 \text{ ksi}}{12 \text{ in./ft}} = 61.8 \text{ kip-ft (83.8 kNm)}$$

$$\phi_t P_n = \phi_t F_y A_g = 0.90 \times 36 \frac{\text{kips}}{\text{sq.in.}} \times 14.1 \text{ sq.in.} = 457 \text{ kips (2032.7 kN)}$$

Because $(P_u/\phi_t P_n) = (100 \text{ kips}/457 \text{ kips}) = 0.22 > 0.2$, interaction formula (*H1-1a*) again applies.

$$\frac{P_u}{\phi_t P_n} + \frac{8}{9}\left(\frac{M_{ux}}{\phi_b M_{nx}} + \frac{M_{uy}}{\phi_b M_{ny}}\right) \leq 1.0$$

$$0.22 + \frac{8}{9}\left(0 + \frac{50 \text{ kip-ft}}{61.8 \text{ kip-ft}}\right) = 0.22 + 0.72 = 0.94 < 1.0 \quad \text{o.k.}$$

### 3. Find the section for a load eccentric with respect to both principal axes

For orientation (*c*) in Fig. 41, assume that the load is eccentric with respect to both principal axes. Referring to Fig. 41*c*

$$e_x = e \cos 45° = 6 \text{ in.} \times 0.707 = 4.2 \text{ in. (10.7 cm)}$$
$$e_y = e \sin 45° = 6 \text{ in.} \times 0.707 = 4.2 \text{ in. (10.7 cm)}$$

$$M_{ux} = P_u e_x = \frac{100 \text{ kips} \times 4.2 \text{ in.}}{12 \text{ in.ft}} = 35.4 \text{ kip-ft (48 kNm)}$$

$$M_{uy} = P_u e_y = \frac{100 \text{ kips} \times 4.2 \text{ in.}}{12 \text{ in.ft}} = 35.4 \text{ kip-ft (48 kNm)}$$

Again, try a W8 × 48. As above

$$\frac{P_u}{\phi_t P_n} + \frac{100 \text{ kips}}{457} = 0.22 > 0.2$$

$$\phi_t M_{ny} = 61.8 \text{ kip-ft (83.8 kNm)}$$

Although the W8 × 48 is not listed in the Beam Selection Table in the AISC *LRFD Manual*, $L_p$ and $\phi_b M_{nx}$ can be calculated. From Eq. (*Fl-4*) (Chap. 5):

$$L_p = \frac{300 r_y}{\sqrt{F_y}} = \frac{300 r_y}{\sqrt{36}} = 50 r_y$$

$$= 50 \times 2.08 \text{ in.} = 104 \text{ in.} = 8.7 \text{ ft (2.65 m)}$$

Since $(L_b = 6.0 \text{ ft}) < (L_p = 8.7 \text{ ft})$

$$\phi_b M_{nx} = \phi_b M_p = \phi_b Z_x F_y$$

$$= \frac{0.90 \times 49.0 \text{ in.}^3 \times 36 \text{ ksi}}{12 \text{ in.ft}} = 132 \text{ kip-ft (178.9 kNm)}$$

In Interaction Formula (*H1-1a*)

$$0.22 + \frac{8}{9}\left(\frac{35.4 \text{ kip-ft}}{132 \text{ kip-ft}} + \frac{35.4 \text{ kip-ft}}{61.8 \text{ kip-ft}}\right) \leq 1.0$$

$$0.22 + {}^8/_9(0.27 + 0.57)$$

$$0.22 + 0.75 = 0.97 < 1.0 \quad \text{o.k.}$$

The most efficient configuration is orientation (*a*), strong axis bending, which requires a W8 × 28 as opposed to a W8 × 48 for the other two cases.

**Related Calculations.** This procedure is the work of Abraham J. Rokach, MSCE, Associate Director of Education, American Institute of Steel Construction. SI values were prepared by the handbook editor.

## COMBINED FLEXURE AND COMPRESSION IN BEAM-COLUMNS IN A BRACED FRAME

Select, in A36 steel, a W14 section for a beam-column in a braced frame with the following combination of factored loads: $P_u = 800$ kips (3558 kN); first-order moments

$M_x = 200$ kip-ft (271 kNm); $M_y = 0$; single-curvature bending (i.e. equal and opposite end moments); and no transverse loads along the member. The floor-to-floor height is 15 ft (4.57 m).

## Calculation Procedure:

### 1. Find the effective axial load for the beam-column
This procedure considers singly and doubly symmetric beam-columns: members subjected combined axial compression and bending about one or both principal axes. The combination of compression with flexure may result from (either)

(a)  A compressive force that is eccentric with respect to the centroidal axis of the column, as in Fig. 42a
(b)  A column subjected to lateral force or moment, as in Fig. 42b
(c)  A beam transmitting wind or other axial forces, as in Fig. 42c

**Interaction Formulas:**
The cross sections of beam-columns must comply with formula (*H1-1a*) or (*H1-1b*), whichever is applicable.
   For $(P_u/\phi_c P_n) \geq 0.2$

$$\frac{P_u}{\phi_c P_n} + \frac{8}{9}\left( \frac{M_{ux}}{\phi_b M_{nx}} + \frac{M_{uy}}{\phi_b M_{ny}} \right) \leq 1.0 \qquad (H1\text{-}1a)$$

   For $(P_u/\phi_c P_n) < 0.2$

$$\frac{P_u}{2\phi_c P_n} + \left( \frac{M_{ux}}{\phi_b M_{nx}} + \frac{M_{uy}}{\phi_b M_{ny}} \right) \leq 1.0 \qquad (H1\text{-}1b)$$

   For beam-columns:

   $M_{ux}, M_{uy} =$ required flexural strengths (based on the factored loads) including second-order effects, kip-in or kip-ft

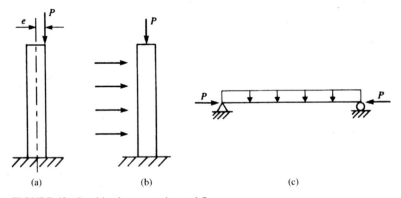

(a)                    (b)                    (c)

**FIGURE 42.** Combined compression and flexure.

$P_u$ = required compressive strength (based on the factored loads), kips
$\phi_c P_n$ = design compressive strength, kips (kN)
$\phi_b M_{nx}, \phi_b M_{ny}$ = design flexural strengths, kip-ft (kNm)
$\phi_c$ = resistance factor for compression = 0.85
$\phi_b$ = resistance factor for flexure = 0.90

The subscript $x$ refers to bending about the major principal centroidal (or $x$) axis; $y$ refers to the minor principal centroidal (or $y$) axis.

### Simplified Second-Order Analysis

*Second-order moments* in beam-columns are the additional moments caused by the axial compressive forces acting on a displaced structure. Normally, structural analysis is first-order; that is, the everyday methods used in practice (whether done manually or by one of the popular computer programs) assume the forces as acting on the original undeflected structure. Second-order effects are neglected. To satisfy the AISC *LRFD Specification,* second-order moments in beam-columns must be considered in their design.

Instead of rigorous second-order analysis, the AISC *LRFD Specification* presents a simplified alternative method. The components of the total factored moment determined from a first-order elastic analysis (neglecting secondary effects) are divided into two groups, $M_{nt}$ and $M_{lt}$.

1. $M_{nt}$—the required flexural strength in a member assuming there is no lateral transla-tion of the structure. It includes the first-order moments resulting from the gravity loads (i.e., dead and live loads), calculated manually or by computer.
2. $N_{lt}$—the required flexural strength in a member due to lateral frame translation. In a braced frame, $M_{lt} = 0$. In an unbraced frame, $M_{lt}$ includes the moments from the later-al loads. If both the frame and its vertical loads are symmetric, $M_{lt}$ from the vertical loads is zero. However, if either the vertical loads (i.e., dead and live loads) or the frame geometry is asymmetric and the frame is not braced, lateral translation occurs and $M_{lt} \neq 0$. To determine $M_{lt}$ (*a*) apply fictitious horizontal reactions at each floor level to prevent lateral translation and (*b*) use the reverse of these reactions as "sway forces" to obtain $M_{lt}$. This procedure is illustrated in Fig. 43. As is indicated there, $M_{lt}$ for an un-braced frame is the sum of the moments due to the lateral loads and the "sway forces."

Once $M_{nt}$ and $M_{lt}$ have been obtained, they are multiplied by their respective magnifi-cation factors, $B_1$ and $B_2$, and added to approximate the actual second-order factored mo-ment $M_u$.

$$M_u = B_1 M_{nt} + B_2 M_{lt} \qquad (H1\text{-}2)$$

As shown in Fig. 44, $B_1$ accounts for the secondary $P - \delta$ effect in all frames (includ-ing sway-inhibited), and $B_2$ covers the $P - \Delta$ effect in unbraced frames. The analytical ex-pressions for $B_1$ and $B_2$ follow.

$$B_1 = \frac{C_m}{(1 - P_u/P_e)} \geq 1.0 \qquad (H1\text{-}3)$$

where $P_u$ is the factored axial compressive force in the member, kips

$$P_e = \frac{\pi^2 EI}{(Kl)^2} \qquad [8.1]$$

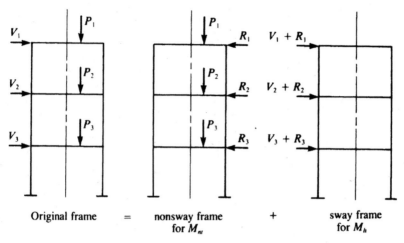

Original frame   =   nonsway frame        +        sway frame
                      for $M_{nt}$                    for $M_{lt}$

**FIGURE 43.** Frame models for $M_{nt}$ and $M_{lt}$.

where $K = 1.0$, $I$ is the moment of inertia (in.⁴) (cm⁴) and $l$ is the unbraced length (in.) (cm). (Both $I$ and $l$ are taken in the plane of bending only.)

The coefficient $C_m$ is determined as follows.

(1) For restrained beam-columns not subjected to transverse loads between their supports in the plane of bending

$$C_m = 0.6 - 0.4 \, \frac{M_1}{M_2} \qquad (H1\text{-}4)$$

where $M_1/M_2$ is the ratio of the smaller to larger moment at the ends of the portion of the member unbraced in the plane of bending under consideration. If the rotations

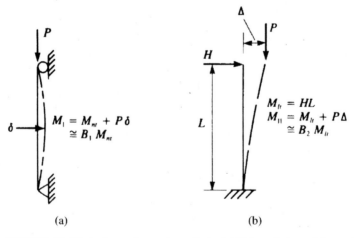

(a)                              (b)

**FIGURE 44.** Illustrations of secondary effects. (*a*) Column in braced frame; (*b*) Column in unbraced frame.

due to end moments $M_1$ and $M_2$ are in opposite directions, then $M_1/M_2$ is negative; otherwise $M_1/M_2$ is positive.
(2) For beam-columns subjected to transverse loads between supports, if the ends are restrained against rotation, $C_m = 0.85$; if the ends are *unrestrained* against rotation, $C_m = 1.0$.

Two equations are given for $B_2$ in the AISC *LRFD Specification*:

$$B_1 = \frac{1}{1 - \Sigma P_u\left(\dfrac{\Delta_{oh}}{\Sigma\,HL}\right)} \qquad\qquad (H1\text{-}5)$$

or

$$B_2 = \frac{1}{1 - \dfrac{\Sigma\,P_u}{\Sigma\,P_e}} \qquad\qquad (H1\text{-}6)$$

where $\Sigma P_u$ = required axial strength of all columns in a story (i.e., the total factored gravity load above that level), kips
$\Sigma_{ch}$ = translational deflection of the story under consideration, in.
$\Sigma H$ = sum of all horizontal forces producing $\Delta_{oh}$, kips
$L$ = story height, in.
$\Sigma P_e$ = summation of $P_e$ for all columns in a story.

Values of $P_e$ are obtained from Eq. [8.1], considering the actual $K$ and $l$ of each column in its plane of bending. Equation (H1-5) is generally the more convenient of the two formulas for evaluating $B_2$. The quantity $\Delta_{oh}/L$ is the *story drift index*. Often, especially for tall buildings, the maximum drift index is a design criterion. Using it in Eq. (H1-5) facilitates the determination of $B_2$.

For columns with biaxial bending in frames unbraced in both directions, two values of $B_1$ ($B_{1x}$ and $B_{1y}$) are needed for each column and two values of $B_2$ for each story, one for each major direction. Once the appropriate $B_1$ and $B_2$ have been evaluated, Eq. (H1-2) can be used to determine $M_{ux}$ and $M_{uy}$ for the applicable interaction formula.

### Preliminary Design
The selection of a trial W shape for beam-column design can be facilitated by means of an approximate interaction equation given in the AISC *LRFD Manual*. Bending moments are convened to equivalent axial loads as follows.

$$P_{u,\text{eff}} = P_u + M_{ux}m + M_{uy}mU \qquad\qquad [8.2]$$

where $P_{u,\text{eff}}$ is the effective axial load to be checked against the Column Load Table in Part 2 of the AISC *LRFD Manual*; $P_u$, $M_{ux}$, and $M_{uy}$ are as defined in interaction formulas (H1-1a) and (H1-1b) ($P_u$, kips; $M_{ux}$, $M_{uy}$, kip-ft); and $m$ and $U$ are factors adapted from the AISC *LRFD Manual*.

Once a satisfactory trial section has been selected (i.e., $P_{u,\text{eff}}$ the tabulated $\phi_c P_n$), it should be verified with formula (H1-1a) or (H1-1b).

For a braced frame, $K = 1.0$ for design; $K_x L_x = K_y L_y = 1.0 \times 15$ ft. Select a trial W14 shape using Eq. [8.2].

$$P_{u,\text{eff}} = P_u + M_{ux}m + M_{uy}mU$$

For a W14 with $KL = 15$ ft $m = 1.0$ and $U = 1.5$. Substituting in Eq. [8.2], we obtain

$$P_{u,\text{eff}} = 800 + 200 \times 2.0 + 0 = 1200 \text{ kips (5338 kN)}$$

In the AISC Column Load Tables (p. 2-19 of the *LRFD Manual*) if $F_y = 36$ ksi (248 mPa) and $KL = 15$ ft (4.57 m), $\phi_c P_n = 1280$ kips ($>P_{u,\text{eff}} = 1200$ kips) for a Wl4 $\times$ 159.

## 2. *Analyze the braced frame*

Try a W14 $\times$ 159. To determine $M_{ux}$ (the second-order moment), use Eq. (H1-2).

$$M_u = B_1 M_{nt} + B_2 M_{lt}$$

Because the frame is braced, $M_{lt} = 0$.

$$M_u = B_1 M_{nt} \quad \text{or} \quad M_{ux} = B_1 \times 200 \text{ kip-ft}$$

According to Eq. (H1-3)

$$B_1 = \frac{C_m}{(1 - P_u/P_e)} \geq 1.0$$

where $C_m = 0.6 - 0.4(M_1/M_2)$ for beam-columns not subjected to lateral loads between supports.

For $M_1 = M_2 = 200$ kip-ft (271 kNm) in single curvature bending (i.e., end moments in opposite directions)

$$\frac{M_1}{M_2} = -\frac{200}{200} = -1.0$$

$$C_m = 0.6 - 0.4(-1.0) = 1.0$$

For a W14 $\times$ 159, $I_x = 1900$ in.$^4$ (79,084 cm$^4$)

$$P_l = \frac{\pi^2 E I_x}{(Kl)^2} = \frac{\pi^2 \times 29,000 \text{ kips/sq.in.} \times 1900 \text{ in.}^4}{(1.0 \times 15 \text{ ft} \times 12 \text{ in./ft})^2} = 16,784 \text{ kips (74,655 kN)}$$

In Eq. (H1-3)

$$B_1 = \frac{1.0}{1 - 800 \text{ kips}/16,784 \text{ kips}} = 1.05$$

Here, $M_{ux} = 1.05 \times 200$ kip-ft $= 210$ kip-ft (284.6 kNm) the second-order required flexural strength. (Substituting $M_{ux} = 210$ kip-ft in preliminary design, Eq. [8.2] still leads to a W14 $\times$ 159 as the trial section.)

Selecting the appropriate beam-column interaction formula, (H1-1a) or (H1-1b), we have

$$\frac{P_u}{\phi_c P_n} = \frac{800 \text{ kips}}{1280 \text{ kips}} = 0.63 > 0.2$$

Use formula (H1-1a), which, for $M_{uy} = 0$, reduces to

$$\frac{P_u}{\phi_c P_n} + \frac{8}{9} \frac{M_{ux}}{\phi_b M_{nx}} \leq 1.0$$

## 3. Determine the design flexural strength

To determine $\phi_b M_{nx}$ (the design flexural strength), refer to the Load Factor Design Selection Table for Beams in the AISC *LRFD Manual*. Since the W14 × 159 is not tabulated therein, the basic equations are used instead.

$$C_b = 1.75 + 1.05 \frac{M_1}{M_2} + 0.3\left(\frac{M_1}{M_2}\right)^2 \le 2.3$$

Again, $M_1/M_2 = -1.0$.

$$C_b = 1.75 + 1.05(-1.0) + 0.3(-1.0)^2 = 1.0$$

If $C_b = 1.0$, $M_n = M_p Z_x F_y$ for bending about the x axis if $L_b \le L_p$; $L_p = (300 r_y/F_y)$ for W shapes bent about the x axis [Eq. *(F1-4)*]. For a W14 × 159, $r_y = 4.0$ in. (10.2 cm) and

$$L_p = \frac{(300 \times 4.0 \text{ in.})/(12 \text{ in./ft})}{\sqrt{36}} = 16.7 \text{ ft (5.1 m)}$$

Because $(L_b = 15.0 \text{ ft}) < (L_p = 16.7 \text{ ft})$,

$$M_{nx} = Z_x F_y = \frac{287 \text{ in.}^3 \times 36 \text{ kips/sq.in.}}{12 \text{ in./ft}} = 861 \text{ kip-ft (1167 kNm)}$$

and $\phi_b M_{nx} = 0.90 \times 861$ kip-ft $= 775$ kip-ft (1050 kNm).
Substituting the interaction formula, we obtain

$$0.65 + \frac{8}{9} \times \frac{210 \text{ kip-ft}}{775 \text{ kip-ft}}$$

$$= 0.63 + 0.24 = 0.87 < 1.0 \quad \text{o.k.}$$

By a similar solution of interaction formula *(H1-1a)*, it can be shown that a W14 × 145 is also adequate.

**Related Calculations.** This procedure is the work of Abraham J. Rokach, MSCE, Associate Director of Education, American Institute of Steel Construction. SI values were prepared by the handbook editor.

## SELECTION OF CONCRETE-FILLED STEEL COLUMN

Select a 6-in. (15.2-cm) concrete-filled steel-pipe column for a required axial compressive strength of 200 kips (889.6 kN), where $KL = 10.0$ ft (3.05 m), $F_y = 36$ ksi (248 MPa), $f_c' = 3.5$ ksi (24.1 MPa), using normal-weight concrete $= 145$ lb/cu ft (2320 kg/cu m).

## Calculation Procedure:

### 1. Try a standard-weight concrete-filled pipe
### 2. Analyze the selected column

Check minimum wall thickness of pipe, Fig. 45:

$$t \geq D \sqrt{\frac{F_y}{8E}} = 6.625 \text{ in.} \sqrt{\frac{36 \text{ ksi}}{8 \times 29,000 \text{ ksi}}} = 0.083 \text{ in. } (0.21 \text{ cm})$$

$t = 0.280 \text{ in.} > 0.083 \text{ in.}$   o.k.

Check minimum cross-sectional area of steel pipe:

$$A_s = \pi(R^2 - R_i^2) \; \frac{\pi}{4}(D^2 - D_i^2)$$

$$= \frac{\pi}{4}[(6.625 \text{ in.})^2 - (6.065 \text{ in.})^2] = 5.6 \text{ sq.in. } (36.1 \text{ cm}^2)$$

$$A_c = \pi R_i^2 = \frac{\pi}{4}D_i^2 = \frac{\pi}{4} \times (6.065 \text{ in.})^2 = 28.9 \text{ sq.in. } (186.5 \text{ cm}^2)$$

$$\frac{A_s}{A_s + A_c} = \frac{5.6 \text{ sq.in}}{5.6 \text{ sq.in} + 28.9 \text{ sq.in}} = 0.16 > 4\% \quad \text{o.k.}$$

### 3. *Analyze the selected column*
In the absence of reinforcing bars:

$$F_{my} = F_y + c_2 f_c' \frac{A_c}{A_s}$$

$$E_m = E + c_3 E_c \frac{A_c}{A_s}$$

where $E_c = w^{1.5} \sqrt{f_c'}$, $c_2 = 0.85$, $c_3 = 0.4$.
   The modulus of elasticity of the concrete

$$E_c = 145^{1.5} \sqrt{3.5} = 3267 \text{ ksi}$$

The modified yield stress for composite design is

$$F_{my} = 36 \text{ ksi} + 0.85 \times 3.5 \text{ ksi} \times \frac{28.9 \text{ sq.in.}}{5.6 \text{ sq.in.}}$$

$$= 51.4 \text{ ksi } (354.1 \text{ MPa})$$

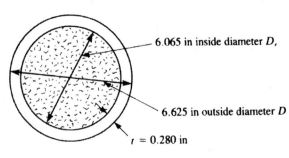

6.065 in inside diameter $D$,

6.625 in outside diameter $D$

$t = 0.280$ in

**FIGURE 45**

The modified modulus of elasticity for composite design is

$$E_m = 29{,}000 \text{ ksi} + 0.4 \times 3267 \text{ ksi} \times \frac{28.9 \text{ sq.in.}}{5.6 \text{ sq.in.}}$$

$$= 35{,}744 \text{ ksi } (246{,}276 \text{ MPa})$$

The radius of gyration of a hollow circular shape

$$r = \frac{\sqrt{D^2 + D_i^2}}{4} \qquad \text{(See AISC } LRFD \text{ Manual, p. 7-21.)}$$

$$= \frac{\sqrt{(6.625 \text{ in.})^2 + (6.065 \text{ in.})^2}}{4} = 2.25 \text{ in. } (5.72 \text{ cm})$$

for the bare steel pipe.
The modified radius of gyration for composite design

$$r_m = r \geq 0.3D \text{ (the overall dimension)}$$

$$= 2.25 \text{ in.} \geq (0.3 \times 6.625 \text{ in.} = 1.99 \text{ in.})$$

$$= 2.25 \text{ in. } (5.72 \text{ cm})$$

The slenderness parameter

$$\lambda_c = \frac{Kl}{r_m \pi} \sqrt{\frac{F_{my}}{E_m}}$$

$$= \frac{10.0 \text{ ft} \times 12 \text{ in./ft}}{2.25 \text{ in.} \times \pi} \sqrt{\frac{51.4 \text{ ksi}}{35{,}744 \text{ ksi}}} = 0.64$$

Because $\lambda_c < 1.5$

$$F_{cr} = (0.658^{\lambda_c^2}) F_{my}$$

$$= 0.658^{(0.64)^2} \times 51.4 \text{ ksi} = 43.2 \text{ ksi } (297.6 \text{ MMPa})$$

The design compressive strength

$$\phi_c P_n = \phi_c A_s F_{cr}$$

$$= 0.85 \times 5.6 \text{ sq.in.} \times 43.2 \text{ kips/sq.in.}$$

$$= 205 \text{ kips} > 200 \text{ kips required}$$

$\phi_c P_n = 205$ kips (911.8 kN) for this case is also tabulated on p. 4-100 of the AISC *LRFD Manual*.

The 6-in. (15.2 cm) standard-weight concrete-filled pipe-column is satisfactory.

**Related Calculations.** This procedure is the work of Abraham J. Rokach, MSCE, Associate Director of Education, American Institute of Steel Construction. SI values were prepared by the handbook editor.

## DETERMINING DESIGN COMPRESSIVE STRENGTH OF COMPOSITE COLUMNS

Determine the design compressive strength of a W8 × 40 (A36 steel) encased in a 16 × 16 in. (40.6 × 40.6 cm) ($f_c'$ = 3.5 ksi) (24.1 MPa) normal-weight concrete column in Fig. 46. Reinforcement is four No. 7 (Grade 60) bars longitudinally, and No. 3 ties at 10 in. (25.4 cm) horizontally.

### Calculation Procedure:

### 1. Check the minimum requirements for the column
Checking minimum requirements

(*a*) For a W8 × 40, $A_s$ = 11.7 sq.in., total area = 16 in. × 16 in. = 256 sq.in. (1652 cm²)

$$\frac{11.7 \text{ sq.in.}}{256 \text{ sq.in.}} = 4.6\% > 4\% \text{ minimum} \qquad \text{o.k.}$$

(*b*) Lateral tie spacing = 10 in. (25.4 cm)

$$< {}^2/_3 \times 16 \text{ in. outer dimension} = 10.7 \text{ in. (27.2 cm)} \qquad \text{o.k.}$$

Minimum clear cover = 1.5 in. (3.8 cm)    o.k.
Horizontal No.3 bars: $A_r$ = 0.11 sq.in. per bar

$$> 0.007 \text{ sq.in.} \times 10 \text{ in. spacing} = 0.07 \text{ sq.in. (0.45 cm}^2) \qquad \text{o.k.}$$

Vertical No.7 bars: $A_r$ = 0.60 sq.in. per bar

$$> 0.007 \text{ sq.in.} \times 11.4 \text{ in. spacing} = 0.08 \text{ sq.in. (0.52 cm}^2) \qquad \text{o.k.}$$

(*c*) 3.0 ksi < ($f_c'$ = 3.5 ksi) < 8.0 ksi for normal weight concrete    o.k.
(*d*) Use $F_{yr}$ = 55 ksi (378.9 MPa) for reinforcement in calculations, even though actual $F_{yr}$ = 60 ksi (413.4 MPa) for Grade 60 bars.

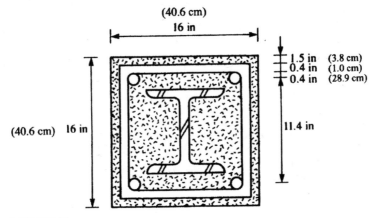

**(40.6 cm)**
**16 in**

1.5 in    (3.8 cm)
0.4 in    (1.0 cm)
0.4 in    (28.9 cm)

(40.6 cm)    16 in

11.4 in

**FIGURE 46**

## 2. *Determine the modified yield stress and modulus of elasticity*

Determine $F_{my}$ and $E_m$:

$$F_{my} = F_y + c_1 F_{yr} \frac{A_r}{A_s} + c_2 f_c' \frac{A_c}{A_s}$$

where $A_r$ = the cross-sectional area of four No. 7 longitudinal bars = $4 \times 0.6$ sq.in. = 2 4 sq.in.    (15.5 cm²)

$A_s$ = cross-sectional area of W8 × 40 = 11.7 sq.in. (75.5 cm²)

$A_c$ = 16 in. × 16 in. – (11.7 sq.in. + 2.4 sq.in.) = 242 sq.in. (1561 cm²)

For concrete-encased shapes, $c_1 = 0.7$ and $c_2 = 0.6$.

$$F_{my} = 36 \text{ ksi} + 0.7 \times 55 \text{ ksi} \times \frac{2.4 \text{ sq.in.}}{11.7 \text{ sq.in.}} + 0.6 \times 3.5 \text{ ksi} \times \frac{242 \text{ sq.in.}}{11.7 \text{ sq.in.}}$$

$$= 87.3 \text{ ksi (601.5 MPa)}$$

$$E_m = E + c_e E_c \frac{A_c}{A_s}$$

where $c_3 = 0.2$ for concrete-encased shapes

$E_c = w^{1.5} \sqrt{f_c'} = 145^{1.5} \sqrt{3.5} = 3267$ ksi (24,577 MPa) for 3.5-ksi normal-weight (145 lb/ft³) (2320 kg/cu m) concrete

$E_m = 29{,}000$ ksi $+ 0.2 \times 3267$ ksi $\times 242$ sq.in./11.7 sq.in. $= 42{,}513$ ksi (292,915 MPa)

The modified radius of gyration

$$r_m = r_y(\text{W8} \times 40) \geq 0.3 \times 16 \text{ in. (overall dimension)}$$

$$= 2.04 \text{ in.} \geq 4.80 \text{ in. (12.2 cm)}$$

$$= 4.80 \text{ in. (12.2 cm)}$$

The slenderness parameter

$$\lambda_c = \frac{kl}{R_m \pi} \sqrt{\frac{E_{my}}{E_m}}$$

$$= \frac{15.0 \text{ ft} \times 12 \text{ in.ft}}{4.80 \text{ in.} \times \pi} \sqrt{\frac{87.3 \text{ ksi}}{42{,}513 \text{ ksi}}} = 0.54$$

The critical stress

$$F_{cr} = (0.658^{\lambda_c^2}) F_{my}$$

$$= 0.658^{(0.54)^2} \times 87.3 \text{ ksi} = 77.2 \text{ ksi (531.9 MPa)}$$

## 3. *Compute the design compressive strength*

The design compressive strength

$$\phi_c P_n = \phi_c A_s F_{cr}$$

$$= 0.85 \times 11.7 \text{ sq.in.} \times 77.2 \text{ kips/sq.in. (531.9 MPa)}$$

$$= 768 \text{ kips (5292 MPa)}$$

($\phi_c P_n = 768$ kips for this case is also tabulated on p. 4-73 of the AISC *LRFD Manual*.)
The 768-kip design strength is considerably more than the 238-kip (1640 Mpa) design
strength of a noncomposite W8 × 40 column under the same conditions.

**Related Calculations.** This procedure is the work of Abraham J. Rokach, MSCE, Associate Director of Education, American Institute of Steel Construction. SI values were
prepared by the handbook editor.

## ANALYZING A CONCRETE SLAB
## FOR COMPOSITE ACTION

A W18 × 40 interior beam is shown in Fig. 47. Steel is A36, beam span is 30 ft 0 in. (9.14
m), and beam spacing 10 ft 0 in. (3.04 m). The beams are to act compositely with a 5-in.
(12.7-cm) normal-weight concrete slab; $f_c' = 5.0$ ksi (41.3 kN). Determine: (*a*) The effective width of concrete slab for composite action; (*b*) $V_h$ (the total horizontal shear force to
be transferred) for full composite action; (*c*) The number of 0.75-in. (1.9-cm) diameter
shear studs required if $F_u = 60$ ksi (413.4 kN).

### Calculation Procedure:

### 1. Find the effective width of concrete slab for composite action
For an interior beam, the effective slab width on either side of the beam centerline is the
minimum of

$$\frac{L}{8} = \frac{30.0 \text{ ft}}{8} = 3.75 \text{ ft} = 45 \text{ in. (114.3 cm)}$$

$$\frac{s}{2} = \frac{10.0 \text{ ft}}{2} = 5.00 \text{ ft (1.52 m)}$$

The effective slab width is 2 × 45 in. = 90 in. (228.6 cm).

### 2. Determine the total horizontal shear force for full composite action
In positive moment regions, $V_h$ for full composite action is the smaller of

$$0.85 f_c' A_c = 0.85 \times 5 \text{ ksi} \times (90 \text{ in.} \times 5 \text{ in.})$$

$$= 1913 \text{ kips (8509 kN)}$$

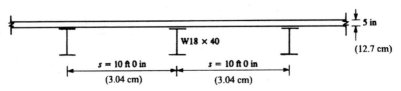

**FIGURE 47**

$$A_s F_y = 11.8 \text{ sq.in.} \times 36 \text{ ksi} = 425 \text{ kips (1890 kN)}$$

$$V_h = 425 \text{ kips (1890 kN)}$$

### 3. *Find the number of shear studs required*

The nominal strength of a single shear stud [from Eq. *(15-1)*] is

$$Q_n = 0.5 A_{sc} \sqrt{f_c' E_c} \le A_{sc} F_u$$

For a $3/4$-in.-diameter stud,

$$A_{sc} = \pi \left( \frac{0.75 \text{ in.}}{2} \right)^2 = 0.44 \text{ sq.in. (2.84 cm}^2)$$

$$E_c = w^{1.5} \sqrt{f_c'} = 145^{1.5} \sqrt{5.0} = 3904 \text{ ksi (26,899 kNm)}$$

$$F_u = 60 \text{ ksi (413 kNm)}$$

$$Q_n = 0.5 \times 0.44 \text{ sq.in. } \sqrt{5.0 \text{ ksi}} \times \overline{3904 \text{ ksi}} \le 0.44 \text{ sq.in.} \times 60 \text{ ksi (413 kNm)}$$

$$= 30.9 \text{ kips} \le 26.4 \text{ kips (117.4 kN)}$$

$$= 26.4 \text{ kips per stud (117.4 kN per stud)}$$

The number of shear connectors between the points of zero and maximum moments is

$$n = \frac{V_h}{Q_n} = \frac{425 \text{ kips}}{26.4} \text{ kips/stud}$$

$$= 16.1 \text{ or 17 studs}$$

For the beam shown in Fig. 48, the required number of shear studs is $2n = 2 \times 17 = 34$.
  Assuming a single line of shear studs (over the beam web), stud spacing $= 30.0 \text{ ft}/34$ $= 0.88 \text{ ft} = 10.6 \text{ in. (26.9 cm)}$. This is greater than the six-stud diameter [or $6 \times 3/4 \text{ in.} = 4.5 \text{ in. (11.4 cm)}$] minimum spacing, and less than the eight slab thickness [or $8 \times 5 \text{ in.} = 40 \text{ in. (101.6 cm)}$] maximum spacing, which is satisfactory.

*Related Calculations.* This procedure is the work of Abraham J. Rokach, MSCE, Associate Director of Education, American Institute of Steel Construction. SI values were prepared by the handbook editor.

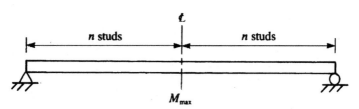

**FIGURE 48**

## DETERMINING THE DESIGN SHEAR STRENGTH OF A BEAM WEB

The end of a W12 × 86 beam (A36 steel) has been prepared as shown in Fig. 49 for connection to a supporting member. The three holes are $^{15}/_{16}$ in. (2.38 cm) in diameter for $^{7}/_{8}$-in. (2.22-cm)-diameter bolts. Determine the design shear strength of the beam web.

### Calculation Procedure:

### 1. Find the applicable limit states

The applicable limit states are shear yielding, shear fracture, and block shear rupture. For shear yielding [of gross section (1) in Fig. 49 ]

$$\phi R_n = 0.90 \times 0.6 A_{vg} F_y \qquad (J5\text{-}3)$$

$$A_{vg} = (d\text{-cope})t = (12.53 \text{ in.} - 2 \text{ in.}) \times 0.515 \text{ in.} = 5.42 \text{ sq.in. } (34.96 \text{ cm}^2)$$

$$\phi R_n = 0.9 \times 0.6 \times 5.42 \text{ sq.in.} \times 36 \text{ ksi} = 105 \text{ kips } (467 \text{ kN})$$

For shear fracture [of net section (1) in Fig. 11-9]

$$\phi R_n = 0.75 \times 0.6 A_{ns} F_u \qquad (J4\text{-}1)$$

$$A_{ns} = (d\text{-cope-}3d_h)t = (12.53 \text{ in.} - 2 \text{ in.} - 3 \times {}^{15}/_{16} \text{ in.}) \times 0.515 \text{ in.} = 3.97 \text{ sq.in. } (25.6 \text{ cm}^2)$$

$$\phi R_n = 0.75 \times 0.6 \times 3.97 \text{ sq.in.} \times 58 \text{ ksi} = 104 \text{ kips } (462.6 \text{ kN})$$

For block shear rupture [of section (2) in Fig. 49] $\phi = 0.75$ and $R_n =$ the greater value of

$$0.6 A_{vg} F_y + A_n F_u \qquad (C\text{-}J4\text{-}1)$$

$$0.6 A_{ns} F_u + A_g F_y \qquad (C\text{-}J4\text{-}2)$$

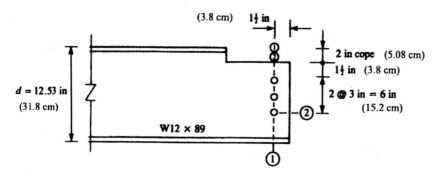

**FIGURE 49**

where $A_{vg}$ = gross area of the vertical part of (2)
 $\quad A_{ns}$ = net area of the vertical part of (2)
 $\quad A_g$ = gross area of the horizontal part of (2)
 $\quad A_n$ = net area of the horizontal part of (2)

$$A_{vg} = (1\tfrac{1}{2} \text{ sq.in.} \times 3 \text{ in.}) \times 0.515 \text{ in.} = 3.86 \text{ sq.in. } (24.9 \text{ cm}^2)$$

$$A_{ns} = (1\tfrac{1}{2} \text{ in.} + 2 \times 3 \text{ in.} \times 2\tfrac{1}{2} \times \tfrac{15}{16}) \times 0.515 \text{ in.} = 2.66 \text{ sq.in. } (17.2 \text{ cm}^2)$$

$$A_g = 1\tfrac{1}{2} \text{ in.} \times 0.515 \text{ in.} = 0.77 \text{ sq.in. } (4.96 \text{ cm}^2)$$

$$A_n = (1\tfrac{1}{2} \text{ in.} - \tfrac{1}{2} \times \tfrac{15}{16} \text{ in.}) \times 0.515 \text{ in.} = 0.53 \text{ sq.in. } (3.42 \text{ cm}^2)$$

### 2. Determine the design shear strength
$R_n$ is the greater of

$$0.6 \times 3.86 \text{ sq.in.} \times 36 \frac{\text{kips}}{\text{sq.in.}} + 0.53 \text{ sq.in.} \times 56 \frac{\text{kips}}{\text{sq.in.}} = 114 \text{ kips } (507 \text{ kN})$$

$$0.6 \times 2.66 \text{ sq.in.} \times 58 \frac{\text{kips}}{\text{sq.in.}} + 0.77 \text{ sq.in.} \times 36 \frac{\text{kips}}{\text{sq.in.}} = 120 \text{ kips } (533.8 \text{ kN})$$

$$R_n = 120 \text{ kips } (533.8 \text{ kN})$$

$$\phi R_n = 0.75 \times 120 \text{ kips} = 90 \text{ kips } (400.3 \text{ kN})$$

The design shear strength is 90 kips (400.3 kN), based on the governing limit state of block shear rupture.

**Related Calculations.** This procedure is the work of Abraham J. Rokach, MSCE, Associate Director of Education, American Institute of Steel Construction. SI values were prepared by the handbook editor.

## DESIGNING A BEARING PLATE FOR A BEAM AND ITS END REACTION

The unstiffened end of a W21 × 62 beam in A36 steel rests on a concrete support ($f'_c = 3$ ksi) [20.7 MPa], Fig. 50. Design a bearing plate for the beam and its (factored) end reaction of 100 kips (444.8 kN). Assume the area of concrete support $A_2 = 6 \times A_1$ (the area of the bearing plate).

### Calculation Procedure:

### 1. Find the bearing length
For the concentrated compressive reaction of 100 kips (444.8 kN) acting on the bottom flange, the applicable limit states are (1) local web yielding and (2) web crippling. (It is assumed that the beam is welded to the base plate and both are anchor-bolted to the concrete support. This should provide adequate lateral bracing to prevent sidesway web buckling.)

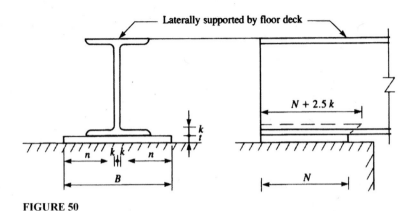

**FIGURE 50**

Corresponding to the applicable limit states are Eqs. (K1-3) and (K1-5), each of which has N, the length of bearing, as a parameter.

Solving for N, we obtain

$$R_u \leq = \phi R_n = \phi(2.5k + N)F_t t_w$$

$$100 \text{ kips} \leq 1.0(2.5 \times 1^3/_8 \text{ in.} + N) \times 36 \text{ kips/sq.in.} \times 0.40 \text{ in. } (1.01 \text{ cm}) \quad (K1\text{-}3)$$

$$N \geq 3.5 \text{ in. } (8.89 \text{ cm})$$

$$R_u \leq \phi R_n = \phi 68 t_w^2 \left[ 1 + 3 \left( \frac{N}{d} \right) \left( \frac{t_w}{t_f} \right)^{1.5} \right] \sqrt{\frac{F_y t_f}{t_w}} \qquad (K1\text{-}5)$$

$$N \geq 8.6 \text{ in. } (21.8 \text{ cm})$$

The minimum length of bearing is N = 8.6 in. (21.8 cm). Rounding up to the next full inch, let N = 9 in. (22.9 cm)

## 2. Compute the area of the bearing plate

The area of the bearing plate is determined by the bearing strength of the concrete support. Using the following equation, the design bearing strength is

$$\phi_c P_p = \phi_c \times 0.85 f_c' A_1 \sqrt{\frac{A_2}{A_1}}$$

where $\sqrt{A_2/A_1} \leq 2$.

Substituting in Eq. [11.6], we obtain

$$100 \text{ kips} = 0.60 \times 0.85 \times 3 \ \frac{\text{kips}}{\text{sq.in.}} \times A_1 \times 2$$

The area of the bearing plate $A_1 = 32.7$ sq.in. (210.9 cm²).

Because the bearing plate dimensions are

$$BN \geq A_1: \qquad B \geq \frac{A_1}{N} = \frac{32.7 \text{ sq.in.}}{9 \text{ in.}} = 3.6 \text{ in. } (9.14 \text{ cm})$$

However, $B$ cannot be less than the flange width of the W21 $\times$ 62 beam, $b_f = 8.24$. Rounding up, let $B = 9$ in. (22.9 cm). A formula for bearing plate thickness is given on page 3.50 of the AISC *LRFD Manual*:

$$t = \sqrt{\frac{2.22Rn^2}{A_1F_y}}$$

where $R = 100$ kips (444.8 kN)

$$n = \frac{B - 2k}{2} = \frac{9 \text{ in.} - 2 \times 1\frac{3}{8} \text{ in.}}{2} = 3.13 \text{ in. (7.95 cm)}$$

$A_1 = BN = 9$ in. $\times$ 9 in. $= 81$ sq.in. (522.6 cm²)

$F_y = 36$ ksi (248 MPa)

### 3. Select the bearing-plate dimensions

$$t = \sqrt{\frac{2.22 \times 100 \text{ kips} \times (3.13 \text{ in.})^2}{81 \text{ sq.in.} \times 36 \text{ ksi}}} = 0.86 \text{ in. (2.18 cm)}$$

Use a bearing plate 1 in. $\times$ 9 in. $\times$ 9 in. (2.54 $\times$ 22.9 $\times$ 22.9 cm).

**Related Calculations.** This procedure is the work of Abraham J. Rokach, MSCE, Associate Director of Education, American Institute of Steel Construction. SI values were prepared by the handbook editor.

# DETERMINING BEAM LENGTH TO ELIMINATE BEARING PLATE

Determine if the bearing plate chosen in the preceeding procedure can be eliminated by altering the design.

## Calculation Procedure:

### 1. Compute the needed thickness of the bottom flange

For the W21 $\times$ 62 beam to bear directly on the concrete support, its bottom flange must be sufficiently thick to act as a bearing plate. Let

$$t = \sqrt{\frac{2.22Rn^2}{A_1F_y}} = 0.615 \text{ in. (1.56 cm)}$$

the flange thickness of the W21 $\times$ 62 beam. Because $B = b_f = 8.24$ in. (20.9 cm)

$$n = \frac{B - 2k}{2} = \frac{8.24 \text{ in.} - 2 \times 1\frac{3}{8} \text{ in.}}{2} = 2.75 \text{ in. (6.99 cm)}$$

$$t = \sqrt{\frac{2.22 \times 100 \text{ kips} \times (2.75 \text{ in.})^2}{A_1 \times 36 \text{ kips.in.}^2}} = 0.615 \text{ in. (1.56 cm)}$$

## 2. Find the required length of bearing of the beam

$A_1 = 123$ sq.in. (>32.7 sq.in. required for bearing on concrete)

$$N = \frac{A_1}{B} = \frac{A_1}{b_f} = \frac{123 \text{ sq.in.}}{8.24 \text{ in.}} = 15.0 \text{ in. (38.1 cm)}$$

By increasing the length of bearing of the beam to 15 in. (38.1 cm), the bearing plate can be eliminated.

**Related Calculations.** This procedure is the work of Abraham J. Rokach, MSCE, Associate Director of Education, American Institute of Steel Construction. SI values were prepared by the handbook editor.

---

## PART 3

# HANGERS, CONNECTORS, AND WIND-STRESS ANALYSIS

---

In the following Calculation Procedures, structural steel members are designed in accordance with the *Specification for the Design, Fabrication and Erection of Structural Steel for Buildings* of the American Institute of Steel Construction. In the absence of any statement to the contrary, it is to be understood that the structural-steel members are made of ASTM A36 steel, which has a yield-point stress of 36,000 lb/sq.in. (248.2 MPa).

Reinforced-concrete members are designed in accordance with the specification *Building Code Requirements for Reinforced Concrete* of the American Concrete Institute.

## DESIGN OF AN EYEBAR

A hanger is to carry a load of 175 kips (778.4 kN). Design an eyebar of A440 steel.

## Calculation Procedure:

### 1. Record the yield-point stresses of the steel

Refer to Fig. 1 for the notational system. Let subscripts 1 and 2 refer to cross sections through the body of the bar and through the center of the pin hole, respectively.

Eyebars are generally flame-cut from plates of high-strength steel. The design provisions of the AISC *Specification* reflect the results of extensive testing of such members. A section of the *Specification* permits a tensile stress of $0.60f_y$ at 1 and $0.45f_y$ at 2, where $f_y$ denotes the yield-point stress.

From the AISC *Manual* for A440 steel:

If $t \leq 0.75$ in. (19.1 mm), $f_y = 50$ kips/sq.in. (344.7 MPa).
If $0.75 < t \leq 1.5$ in. (38 mm), $f_y = 46$ kips/sq.in. (317.1 MPa).
If $1.5 < t \leq 4$ in. (102 mm), $f_y = 42$ kips/sq.in. (289.5 MPa).

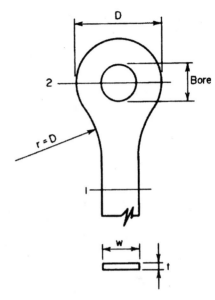

FIGURE 1. Eyebar hanger.

## 2. Design the body of the member, using a trial thickness
The *Specification* restricts the ratio $w/t$ to a value of 8. Compute the capacity $P$ of a $^3/_4$-in. (19.1-mm) eyebar of maximum width. Thus $w = 8(^3/_4) = 6$ in. (152 mm); $f = 0.6(50) = 30$ kips/sq.in. (206.8 MPa); $P = 6(0.75)30 = 135$ kips (600.5 kN). This is not acceptable because the desired capacity is 175 kips (778.4 kN). Hence, the required thickness exceeds the trial value of $^3/_4$ in. (19.1 mm). With $t$ greater than $^3/_4$ in. (19.1 mm), the allowable stress at 1 is $0.60f_y$, or $0.60(46$ kips/sq.in.$) = 27.6$ kips/sq.in. (190.3 MPa); say 27.5 kips/sq.in. (189.6 MPa) for design use. At 2 the allowable stress is $0.45(46) = 20.7$ kips/sq.in. (142.7 MPa), say 20.5 kips/sq.in. (141.3 MPa) for design purposes.

To determine the required area at 1, use the relation $A_1 = P/f$, where $f =$ allowable stress as computed above. Thus, $A_1 = 175/27.5 = 6.36$ sq.in. (4103 mm²). Use a plate $6^1/_2 \times 1$ in. (165 × 25.4 mm) in which $A_1 = 6.5$ sq.in. (4192 mm²).

## 3. Design the section through the pin hole
The AISC *Specification* limits the pin diameter to a minimum value of $7w/8$. Select a pin diameter of 6 in. (152 mm). The bore will then be $6^1/_{32}$ in. (153 mm) diameter. The net width required will be $P/(ft) = 175/[20.5(1.0)] = 8.54$ in. (217 mm); $D_{min} = 6.03 + 8.54 = 14.57$ in. (370 mm). Set $D = 14^3/_4$ in. (375 mm), $A_2 = 1.0(14.75 - 6.03) = 8.72$ sq.in. (5626 mm²); $A_2/A_1 = 1.34$. This result is satisfactory, because the ratio of $A_2/A_1$ must lie between 1.33 and 1.50.

## 4. Determine the transition radius r
In accordance with the *Specification*, set $r = D = 14^3/_4$ in. (374.7 mm).

## ANALYSIS OF A STEEL HANGER

A $12 \times ^1/_2$ in. (305 × 12.7 mm) steel plate is to support a tensile load applied 2.2 in. (55.9 mm) from its center. Determine the ultimate load.

## Calculation Procedure:

### 1. Determine the distance x
The plastic analysis of steel structures is developed in Sec. 1 of this handbook. Figure 2a is the load diagram, and Fig. 2b is the stress diagram at plastification. The latter may be replaced for convenience with the stress diagram in Fig. 2c, where $T_1 = C$; $P_u =$ ultimate

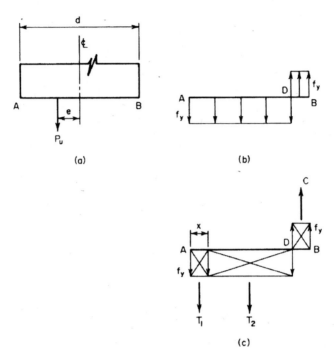

**FIGURE 2**

load; $e$ = eccentricity; $M_u$ = ultimate moment = $P_u e$; $f_y$ = yield-point stress; $d$ = depth of section; $t$ = thickness of section.

By using Fig. 2c,

$$P_u = T_2 = f_y t(d - 2x) \tag{1}$$

Also, $T_1 = f_y t x$, and $M_u = P_u e = T_1(d - x)$, so

$$x = \frac{d}{2} + e - \left[ \left( \frac{d}{2} + e \right)^2 - ed \right]^{0.5} \tag{2}$$

Or, $x = 6 + 2.2 - [(6 + 2.2)^2 - 2.2 \times 12]^{0.5} = 1.81$ in. (45.9 mm).

**2. Find $P_u$**
By Eq. 1, $P_u = 36,000(0.50)(12 - 3.62) = 151,000$ lb (671.6 kN).


## ANALYSIS OF A GUSSET PLATE

The gusset plate in Fig. 3 is ¹/₂ in. (12.7 mm) thick and connects three web members to the bottom chord of a truss. The plate is subjected to the indicated ultimate forces, and transfer of these forces from the web members to the plate is completed at section *a-a*. Investigate the adequacy of this plate. Use 18,000 lb/sq.in. (124.1 MPa) as the yield-point

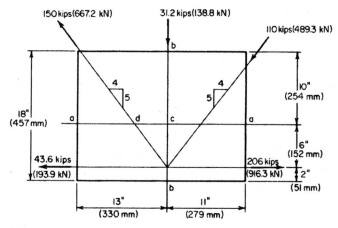

**FIGURE 3.** Gusset plate.

stress in shear, and disregard interaction of direct stress and shearing stress in computing the ultimate-load and ultimate-moment capacity.

## Calculation Procedure:

### 1. Resolve the diagonal forces into their horizontal and vertical components

Let $H_u$ and $V_u$ denote the ultimate shearing force on a horizontal and vertical plane, respectively. Resolving the diagonal forces into their horizontal and vertical components gives $(4^2 + 5^2)^{0.5} = 6.40$. Horizontal components: $150(4/6.40) = 93.7$ kips (416.8 kN); $110(4/6.40) = 68.7$ kips (305.6 kN). Vertical components: $150(5/6.40) = 117.1$ kips (520.9 kN); $110(5/6.40) = 85.9$ kips (382.1 kN).

### 2. Check the force system for equilibrium

Thus, $\Sigma F_H = 206.0 - 43.6 - 93.7 - 68.7 = 0$; this is satisfactory, as is $\Sigma F_V = 117.1 - 85.9 - 31.2 = 0$.

### 3. Compare the ultimate shear at section a-a with the allowable value

Thus, $H_u = 206.0 - 43.6 = 162.4$ kips (722.4 kN). To compute $H_{u,\text{allow}}$ assume that the shearing stress is equal to the yield-point stress across the entire section. Then $H_{u,\text{allow}} = 24(0.5)(18) = 216$ kips (960.8 kN). This is satisfactory.

### 4. Compare the ultimate shear at section b-b with the allowable value

Thus, $V_u = 117.1$ kips (520.9 kN); $V_{u,\text{allow}} = 18(0.5)(18) = 162$ kips (720.6 kN). This is satisfactory.

### 5. Compare the ultimate moment at section a-a with the plastic moment

Thus, $cd = 4(6)/5 = 4.8$ in. (122 mm); $M_u = 4.8(117.1 + 85.9) = 974$ in.·kips (110.1 kN·m). Or, $M_u = 6(206 - 43.6) = 974$ in.·kips (110.1 kN·m). To find the plastic moment $M_p$, use the relation $M_u = f_y bd^2/4$, or $M_p = 36(0.5)(24)^2/4 = 2592$ in.·kips (292.9 kN·m). This is satisfactory.

### 6. Compare the ultimate direct force at section b-b with the allowable value

Thus, $P_u = 93.7 + 43.6 = 137.3$ kips (610.7 kN); or $P_u = 206.0 - 68.7 = 137.3$ kips (610.7 kN); $e = 9 - 2 = 7$ in. (177.8 mm). By Eq. 2, $x = 9 + 7 - [(9 + 7)^2 - 7 \times 18]^{0.5} = 4.6$ in. (116.8 mm). By Eq. 1, $P_{u,allow} = 36,000(0.5)(18 - 9.2) = 158.4$ kips (704.6 kN). This is satisfactory.

On horizontal sections above $a$-$a$, the forces in the web members have not been completely transferred to the gusset plate, but the eccentricities are greater than those at $a$-$a$. Therefore, the calculations in step 5 should be repeated with reference to one or two sections above $a$-$a$ before any conclusion concerning the adequacy of the plate is drawn.

## DESIGN OF A SEMIRIGID CONNECTION

A W14 × 38 beam is to be connected to the flange of a column by a semirigid connection that transmits a shear of 25 kips (111.2 kN) and a moment of 315 in.·kips (35.6 kN·m). Design the connection for the moment, using A141 shop rivets and A325 field bolts of $^7/_8$-in. (22.2-mm) diameter.

### Calculation Procedure:

### 1. Record the relevant properties of the W14 × 38

A semirigid connection is one that offers only partial restraint against rotation. For a relatively small moment, a connection of the type shown in Fig. 4a will be adequate. In designing this type of connection, it is assumed for simplicity that the moment is resisted entirely by the flanges; and the force in each flange is found by dividing the moment by the beam depth.

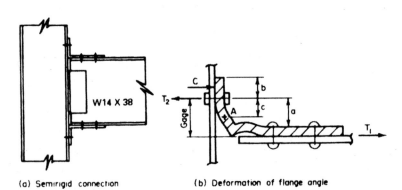

(a) Semirigid connection          (b) Deformation of flange angle

**FIGURE 4.** (a) Semirigid connection; (b) deformation of flange angle.

Figure 4b indicates the assumed deformation of the upper angle, $A$ being the point of contraflexure in the vertical leg. Since the true stress distribution cannot be readily ascertained, it is necessary to make simplifying assumptions. The following equations evolve from a conservative analysis of the member: $c = 0.6a$; $T_2 = T_1(1 + 3a/4b)$.

Study shows that use of an angle having two rows of bolts in the vertical leg would be unsatisfactory because the bolts in the outer row would remain inactive until those in the inner row yielded. If the two rows of bolts are required, the flange should be connected by means of a tee rather than an angle.

The following notational system will be used with reference to the beam dimensions: $b$ = flange width; $d$ = beam depth; $t_f$ = flange thickness; $t_w$ = web thickness.

Record the relevant properties of the W14 × 38; $d$ = 14.12 in. (359 mm); $t_f$ = 0.513 in. (13 mm). (Obtain these properties from a table of structural-shape data.)

## 2. Establish the capacity of the shop rivets and field bolts used in transmitting the moment

From the AISC *Specification*, the rivet capacity in single shear = 0.6013(15) = 9.02 kips (40.1 kN); rivet capacity in bearing 0.875(0.513)(48.5) = 21.77 kips (96.8 kN); bolt capacity in tension = 0.6013(40) = 24.05 kips (106.9 kN).

## 3. Determine the number of rivets required in each beam flange

Thus, $T_1$ = moment/$d$ = 315/14.12 = 22.31 kips (99.7 kN); number of rivets = $T_1$/rivet capacity in single shear = 22.31/9.02 = 2.5; use four rivets, the next highest even number.

## 4. Assuming tentatively that one row of field bolts will suffice, design the flange angle

Try an angle 8 × 4 × ³/₄ in. (203 × 102 × 19 mm), 8 in. (203 mm) long, having a standard gage of 2¹/₂ in. (63.5 mm) in the vertical leg. Compute the maximum bending moment $M$ in this leg. Thus, $c = 0.6(2.5 - 0.75) = 1.05$ in. (26.7 mm); $M = T_1c = 23.43$ in.·kips (2.65 kN·m). Then apply the relation $f = M/S$ to find the flexural stress. Or, $f = 23.43/[(¹/₆)(8)(0.75)^2] = 31.24$ kips/sq.in. (215.4 MPa).

Since the cross section is rectangular, the allowable stress is 27 kips/sq.in. (186.1 MPa), as given by the AISC *Specification*. (The justification for allowing a higher flexural stress in a member of rectangular cross section as compared with a wide-flange member is presented in Sec. 1.)

Try a ⁷/₈-in. (22-mm) angle, with $c = 0.975$ in. (24.8 mm); $M = 21.75$ in.·kips (2.46 kN·m); $f = 21.75/(¹/₆)(8)(0.875)^2 = 21.3$ kips/sq.in. (146.8 MPa). This is an acceptable stress.

## 5. Check the adequacy of the two field bolts in each angle

Thus, $T_2 = 22.31[1 + 3 × 1.625/(4 × 1.5)] = 40.44$ kips (179.9 kN); the capacity of two bolts = 2(24.05) = 48.10 kips (213.9 kN). Hence the bolts are acceptable because their capacity exceeds the load.

## 6. Summarize the design

Use angles 8 × 4 × ⁷/₈ in. (203 × 102 × 19 mm), 8 in. (203 mm) long. In each angle, use four rivets for the beam connection and two bolts for the column connection. For transmitting the shear, the standard web connection for a 14-in. (356-mm) beam shown in the AISC *Manual* is satisfactory.

## RIVETED MOMENT CONNECTION

A W18 × 60 beam frames to the flange of a column and transmits a shear of 40 kips (177.9 kN) and a moment of 2500 in.·kips (282.5 kN·m). Design the connection, using ⁷/₈-in. (22-mm) diameter rivets of A141 steel for both the shop and field connections.

## Calculation Procedure:

### 1. *Record the relevant properties of the W18 × 60*

The connection is shown in Fig. 5a. Referring to the row of rivets in Fig. 5b, consider that there are $n$ rivets having a uniform spacing $p$. The moment of inertia and section modulus of this rivet group with respect to its horizontal centroidal axis are

$$I = p^2 n \times \frac{n^2 - 1}{12} \qquad S = \frac{pn(n + 1)}{6} \tag{3}$$

Record the properties of the W18 × 60: $d = 18.25$ in. (463.6 mm); $b = 7.558$ in. (192 mm); $k = 1.18$ in. (30.0 mm); $t_f = 0.695$ in. (17.7 mm); $t_w = 0.416$ in. (10.6 mm).

### 2. *Establish the capacity of a rivet*

Thus: single shear, 9.02 kips (40.1 kN); double shear, 18.04 kips (80.2 kN); bearing on beam web, 0.875(0.416)(48.5) = 17.65 kips (78.5 kN).

### 3. *Determine the number of rivets required on line 1 as governed by the rivet capacity*

Try 15 rivets having the indicated disposition. Apply Eq. 3 with $n = 17$; then make the necessary correction. Thus, $I = 9(17)(17^2 - 1)/12 - 2(9)^2 = 3510$ sq.in. (22,645 cm$^2$); $S = 3510/24 = 146.3$ in. (3716 mm).

Let $F$ denote the force on a rivet, and let the subscripts $x$ and $y$ denote the horizontal and vertical components, respectively. Thus, $F_x = M/S = 2500/146.3 = 17.09$ kips

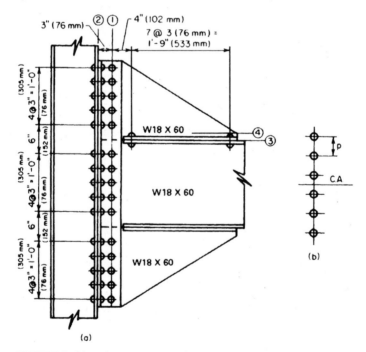

(a)

**FIGURE 5.** Riveted moment connection.

(76.0 kN); $F_y = 40/15 = 2.67$ kips (11.9 kN); $F = (17.09^2 + 2.67^2)^{0.5} = 17.30 < 17.65$. Therefore, this is acceptable.

### 4. Compute the stresses in the web plate at line 1

The plate is considered continuous; the rivet holes are assumed to be 1 in. (25.4 mm) in diameter for the reasons explained earlier.

The total depth of the plate is 51 in. (1295.4 mm), the area and moment of inertia of the net section are $A_n = 0.416(51 - 15 \times 1) = 14.98$ sq.in. (96.6 cm²) and $I_n = (1/12)(0.416)(51)^3 - 1.0(0.416)(3510) = 3138$ in⁴ (130,603.6 cm⁴).

Apply the general shear equation. Since the section is rectangular, the maximum shearing stress is $v = 1.5V/A_n = 1.5(40)/14.98 = 4.0$ kips/sq.in. (27.6 MPa). The AISC *Specification* gives an allowable stress of 14.5 kips/sq.in. (99.9 MPa).

The maximum flexural stress is $f = Mc/I_n = 2500(25.5)13138 = 20.3 < 27$ kips/sq.in. (186.1 MPa). This is acceptable. The use of 15 rivets is therefore satisfactory.

### 5. Compute the stresses in the rivets on line 2

The center of rotation of the angles cannot be readily located because it depends on the amount of initial tension to which the rivets are subjected. For a conservative approximation, assume that the center of rotation of the angles coincides with the horizontal centroidal axis of the rivet group. The forces are $F_x = 2500/[2(146.3)] = 8.54$ kips (37.9 kN); $F_y = 40/30 = 1.33$ kips (5.9 kN). The corresponding stresses in tension and shear are $s_t = F_x/A = 8.54/0.6013 = 14.20$ kips/sq.in. (97.9 MPa); $s_s = F_y/A = 1.33/0.6013 = 2.21$ kips/sq.in. (15.2 MPa). The *Specification* gives $s_{t,\text{allow}} = 28 - 1.6(2.21) > 20$ kips/sq.in. (137.9 kPa). This is acceptable.

### 6. Select the size of the connection angles

The angles are designed by assuming a uniform bending stress across a distance equal to the spacing $p$ of the rivets; the maximum stress is found by applying the tensile force on the extreme rivet.

Try $4 \times 4 \times {}^3/_4$ in. (102 × 102 × 19 mm) angles, with a standard gage of $2^1/_2$ in. (63.5 mm) in the outstanding legs. Assuming the point of contraflexure to have the location specified in the previous calculation procedure, we get $c = 0.6(2.5 - 0.75) = 1.05$ in. (26.7 mm); $M = 8.54(1.05) = 8.97$ in.·kips (1.0 kN·m); $f = 8.97/[({}^1/_6)(3)(0.75)^2] = 31.9 > 27$ kips/sq.in. (186.1 MPa). Use $5 \times 5 \times {}^7/_8$ in. (127 × 127 × 22 mm) angles, with a $2^1/_2$-in. (63.5-mm) gage in the outstanding legs.

### 7. Determine the number of rivets required on line 3

The forces in the rivets above this line are shown in Fig. 6a. The resultant forces are $H = 64.11$ kips (285.2 kN); $V = 13.35$ kips (59.4 kN). Let $M_3$ denote the moment of $H$

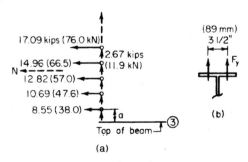

(a)

(b)

**FIGURE 6**

with respect to line 3. Then $a = \frac{1}{2}(24 - 18.25) = 2.88$ in. (73.2 mm); $M_3 = 633.3$ in.·kips (71.6 kN·m).

With reference to Fig. 6b, the tensile force $F_y$ in the rivet is usually limited by the bending capacity of beam flange. As shown in the AISC *Manual*, the standard gage in the W18 × 60 is $3\frac{1}{2}$ in. (88.9 mm). Assume that the point of contraflexure in the beam flange lies midway between the center of the rivet and the face of the web. Referring to Fig. 4b, we have $c = \frac{1}{2}(1.75 - 0.416/2) = 0.771$ in. (19.6 mm); $M_{allow} = fS = 27(\frac{1}{6})(3)(0.695)^2 = 0.52$ in.·kips (0.74 kN·m). If the compressive force $C$ is disregarded, $F_{y,allow} = 6.52/0.771 = 8.46$ kips (37.6 kN).

Try 16 rivets. The moment on the rivet group is $M = 633.3 - 13.35(14.5) = 440$ in.·kips (49.7 kN·m). By Eq. 3, $S = 2(3)(8)(9)/6 = 72$ in. (1829 mm). Also, $F_y = 440/72 + 13.35/16 = 6.94 < 8.46$ kips (37.6 kN). This is acceptable. (The value of $F_y$ corresponding to 14 rivets is excessive.)

The rivet stresses are $s_t = 6.94/0.6013 = 11.54$ kips/sq.in. (79.6 MPa); $s_s = 64.11/[16(0.6013)] = 6.67$ kips/sq.in. (45.9 MPa). From the *Specification*, $s_{t,allow} = 28 - 1.6(6.67) = 17.33$ kips/sq.in. (119.5 MPa). This is acceptable. The use of 16 rivets is therefore satisfactory.

### 8. Compute the stresses in the bracket at the toe of the fillet (line 4)

Since these stresses are seldom critical, take the length of the bracket as 24 in. (609.6 mm) and disregard the eccentricity of $V$. Then $M = 633.3 - 64.11(1.18) = 558$ in.·kips (63.1 kN·m); $f = 558/[(\frac{1}{6})(0.416)(24)^2] + 13.35/[0.416(24)] = 15.31$ kips/sq.in. (105.5 MPa). This is acceptable. Also, $v = 1.5(64.11)/[0.416(24)] = 9.63$ kips/sq.in. (66.4 MPa) This is also acceptable.

# DESIGN OF A WELDED FLEXIBLE BEAM CONNECTION

A W18 × 64 beam is to be connected to the flange of its supporting column by means of a welded framed connection, using E60 electrodes. Design a connection to transmit a reaction of 40 kips (177.9 kN). The AISC table of welded connections may be applied in selecting the connection, but the design must be verified by computing the stresses.

## Calculation Procedure:

### 1. Record the pertinent properties of the beam

It is necessary to investigate both the stresses in the weld and the shearing stress in the beam induced by the connection. The framing angles must fit between the fillets of the beam. Record the properties: $T = 15\frac{3}{8}$ in. (390.5 mm); $t_w = 0.403$ in. (10.2 mm).

### 2. Select the most economical connection from the AISC Manual

The most economical connection is: angles $3 \times 3 \times \frac{5}{16}$ in. (76 × 76 × 7.9 mm), 12 in. (305 mm) long; weld size $> \frac{3}{16}$ in. (4.8 mm) for connection to beam web, $\frac{1}{4}$ in. (6.4 mm) for connection to the supporting member.

According to the AISC table, weld $A$ has a capacity of 40.3 kips (179.3 kN), and weld $B$ has a capacity of 42.8 kips (190.4 kN). The minimum web thickness required is 0.25 in. (6.4 mm). The connection is shown in Fig. 7a.

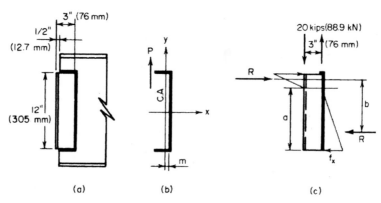

**FIGURE 7.** Welded flexible beam connection.

### 3. Compute the unit force in the shop weld
The shop weld connects the angles to the beam web. Refer to Sec. 1 for two calculation procedures for analyzing welded connections.

The weld for one angle is shown in Fig. 7b. The allowable force, as given in Sec. 1, is $m = 2(2.5)(1.25)/[2(2.5) + 12] = 0.37$ in. (9.4 mm); $P = 20,000$ lb (88.9 kN); $M = 20,000(3 - 0.37) = 52,600$ in.·lb (5942.7 N·m); $I_x = (^1/_{12})(12)^3 + 2(2.5)(6)^2 = 324$ in$^3$ (5309.4 cm$^3$); $I_y = 12(0.37)^2 + 2(^1/_{12})(2.5)^3 + 2(2.5)(0.88)^2 = 8$ in$^3$ (131.1 cm$^3$); $J = 324 + 8 = 332$ in$^3$ (5440.5 cm$^3$); $f_x = My/J = 52,600(6)/332 = 951$ lb/lin in. (166.5 N/mm); $f_y = Mx/J = 52,600(2.5)(0.37)/332 = 337$ lb/lin in. (59.0 N/mm); $f_y = 20,000/(2 \times 2.5 + 12) = 1176$ lb/lin in. (205.9 N/mm); $F_x = 951$ lb/lin in. (166.5 N/mm); $F_y = 337 + 1176 = 1513$ lb/lin in. (265.0 N/mm); $F = (951^2 + 1513^2)^{0.5} = 1787 < 1800$, which is acceptable.

### 4. Compute the shearing stress in the web
The allowable stress given in the AISC *Manual* is 14,500 lb/sq.in. (99.9 MPa). The two angles transmit a unit shearing force of 3574 lb/lin in. (0.64 kN/mm) to the web. The shearing stress is $v = 3574/0.403 = 8870$ lb/sq.in. (61.1 MPa), which is acceptable.

### 5. Compute the unit force in the field weld
The field weld connects the angles to the supporting member. As a result of the 3-in. (76.2-mm) eccentricity on the outstanding legs, the angles tend to rotate about a neutral axis located near the top, bearing against the beam web above this axis and pulling away from the web below this axis. Assume that the distance from the top of the angle to the neutral axis is one-sixth of the length of the angle. The resultant forces are shown in Fig. 7c. Then $a = (^5/_6)12 = 10$ in. (254 mm); $b = (^2/_3)12 = 8$ in. (203 mm); $B = 20,000(3)/8 = 7500$ lb (33.4 kN); $f_x = 2R/a = 1500$ lb/lin in. (262.7 N/mm); $f_y = 20,000/12 = 1667$ lb/lin in. (291.9 N/mm); $F (1500^2 + 1667^2)^{0.5} = 2240 < 2400$ lb/lin in. (420.3 N/mm), which is acceptable. The weld is returned a distance of $^1/_2$ in. (12.7 mm) across the top of the angle, as shown in the AISC *Manual*.

## DESIGN OF A WELDED SEATED BEAM CONNECTION

A W27 × 94 beam with a reaction of 77 kips (342.5 kN) is to be supported on a seat. Design a welded connection, using E60 electrodes.

## Calculation Procedure:

### 1. Record the relevant properties of the beam

Refer to the AISC *Manual*. The connection will consist of a horizontal seat plate and a stiffener plate below the seat, as shown in Fig. 8a. Record the relevant properties of the W27 × 94: $k = 1.44$ in. (36.6 mm); $b = 9.99$ in. (253.7 mm); $t_f = 0.747$ in. (19.0 mm); $t_w = 0.490$ in. (12.4 mm).

### 2. Compute the effective length of bearing

Equate the compressive stress at the toe of the fillet to its allowable value of 27 kips/sq.in. (186.1 MPa) as given in the AISC *Manual*. Assume that the reaction distributes itself through the web at an angle of 45°. Refer to Fig. 8b. Then $N = P/27t_w - k$, or $N = 77/27(0.490) - 1.44 = 4.38$ in. (111.3 mm).

### 3. Design the seat plate

As shown in the AISC *Manual*, the beam is set back about $1/2$ in. (12.7 mm) from the face of the support. Make $W = 5$ in. (127.0 mm). The minimum allowable distance from the edge of the seat plate to the edge of the flange equals the weld size plus $5/16$ in. (7.8 mm). Make the seat plate 12 in. (304.8 mm) long; its thickness will be made the same as that of the stiffener.

### 4. Design the weld connecting the stiffener plate to the support

The stresses in this weld are not amenable to precise analysis. The stiffener rotates about a neutral axis, bearing against the support below this axis and pulling away from the support above this axis. Assume for simplicity that the neutral axis coincides with the centroidal axis of the weld group; the maximum weld stress occurs at the top. A weld length of 0.2L is supplied under the seat plate on each side of the stiffener. Refer to Fig. 8c.

Compute the distance $e$ from the face of the support to the center of the bearing, measuring $N$ from the edge of the seat. Thus, $e = W - N/2 = 5 - 4.38/2 = 2.81$ in. (71.4 mm); $P = 77$ kips (342.5 kN); $M = 77(2.81) = 216.4$ in.·kips (24.5 kN·m); $m = 0.417L$; $I_x = 0.25L^3 f_1 = Mc/I_x = 216.4(0.417L)/0.25L^3 = 361.0/L^2$ kips/lin in.; $f_2 = P/A = 77/2.4L = 32.08/L$

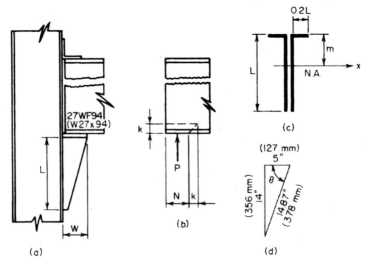

**FIGURE 8.** Welded seated beam connection.

kips/lin in. Use a $5/16$-in. (7.9-mm) weld, which has a capacity of 3 kips/lin in. (525.4 N/mm). Then $F^2 = f_1^2 + f_2^2 = 130,300/L^4 + 1029/L^2 \le 3^2$. This equation is satisfied by $L = 14$ in. (355.6 mm).

### 5. Determine the thickness of the stiffener plate

Assume this plate is triangular (Fig. 8d). The critical section for bending is assumed to coincide with the throat of the plate, and the maximum bending stress may be obtained by applying $f = (P/tW \sin^2 \theta)(1 + 6e'/W)$, where $e' =$ distance from center of seat to center of bearing.

Using an allowable stress of 22,000 lb/sq.in. (151.7 MPa), we have $e' = e - 2.5 = 0.31$ in. (7.9 mm), $t = \{77/[22 \times 5(14/14,87)^2]\}(1 + 6 \times 0.31/5) = 1.08$ in. (27.4 mm).

Use a $1^1/8$-in. (28.6-mm) stiffener plate. The shearing stress in the plate caused by the weld is $v = 2(3000)/1.125 = 5330 < 14,500$ lb/sq.in. (99.9 MPa), which is acceptable.

## DESIGN OF A WELDED MOMENT CONNECTION

A W16 × 40 beam frames to the flange of a W12 × 72 column and transmits a shear of 42 kips (186.8 kN) and a moment of 1520 in.·kips (171.1 kN·m). Design a welded connection, using E60 electrodes.

### Calculation Procedure:

### 1. Record the relevant properties of the two sections

In designing a welded moment connection, it is assumed for simplicity that the beam flanges alone resist the bending moment. Consequently, the beam transmits three forces to the column: the tensile force in the top flange, the compressive force in the bottom flange, and the vertical load. Although the connection is designed ostensibly on an elastic design basis, it is necessary to consider its behavior at ultimate load, since a plastic hinge would form at this joint. The connection is shown in Fig. 9.

Record the relevant properties of the sections: for the W16 × 40, $d = 16.00$ in. (406.4 mm); $b = 7.00$ in. (177.8 mm); $t_f = 0.503$ in. (12.8 mm); $t_w = 0.307$ in. (7.8 mm); $A_f = 7.00(0.503) = 3.52$ sq.in. (22.7 cm²). For the W12 × 72, $k = 1.25$ in. (31.8 mm); $t_f = 0.671$ in. (17.04 mm); $t_w = 0.403$ in. (10.2 mm).

### 2. Investigate the need for column stiffeners: design the stiffeners if they are needed

The forces in the beam flanges introduce two potential modes of failure: crippling of the column web caused by the compressive force, and fracture of the weld transmitting the tensile force as a result of the bending of the column flange.

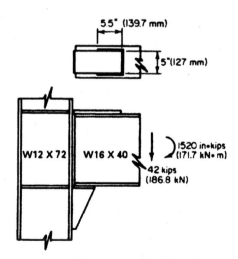

**FIGURE 9.** Welded moment connection.

The AISC *Specification* establishes the criteria for ascertaining whether column stiffeners are required. The first criterion is obtained by equating the compressive stress in the column web at the toe of the fillet to the yield-point stress $f_y$; the second criterion was obtained empirically. At the ultimate load, the capacity of the unreinforced web = $(0.503 + 5 \times 1.25)0.430f_y = 2.904f_y$; capacity of beam flange = $3.52f_y$; $0.4(A_f)^{0.5} = 0.4(3.52)^{0.5} = 0.750 > 0.671$ in. (17.04 mm).

Stiffeners are therefore required opposite both flanges of the beam. The required area is $A_{st} = 3.52 - 2.904 = 0.616$ sq.in. (3.97 cm²). Make the stiffener plates 3½ in. (88.9 mm) wide to match the beam flange. From the AISC, $t_{min} = 3.5/8.5 = 0.41$ in. (10.4 mm). Use two 3½ × ½ in. (88.9 × 12.7 mm) stiffener plates opposite both beam flanges.

### 3. Design the connection plate for the top flange

Compute the flange force by applying the total depth of the beam. Thus, $F = 1520/16.00 = 95$ kips (422.6 kN); $A = 95/22 = 4.32$ sq.in. (27.87 cm²).

Since the beam flange is 7 in. (177.8 mm) wide, use a plate 5 in. (127 mm) wide and $7/8$ in. (22.2 mm) thick, for which $A = 4.38$ sq.in. (28.26 cm²). This plate is butt-welded to the column flange and fillet-welded to the beam flange. In accordance with the AISC *Specification*, the minimum weld size is $5/16$ in. (7.94 mm) and the maximum size is $13/16$ in. (20.6 mm). Use a $5/8$-in. (15.9-mm) weld, which has a capacity of 6000 lb/lin in. (1051 N/mm). Then, length of weld = $95/6 = 15.8$ in. (401.3 mm), say 16 in. (406.4 mm). To ensure that yielding of the joint at ultimate load will occur in the plate rather than in the weld, the top plate is left unwelded for a distance approximately equal to its width, as shown in Fig. 9.

### 4. Design the seat

The connection plate for the bottom flange requires the same area and length of weld as does the plate for the top flange The stiffener plate and its connecting weld are designed in the same manner as in the previous calculation procedure.

## RECTANGULAR KNEE OF RIGID BENT

Figure 10*a* is the elevation of the knee of a rigid bent. Design the knee to transmit an ultimate moment of 8100 in.·kips (914.5 kN·m).

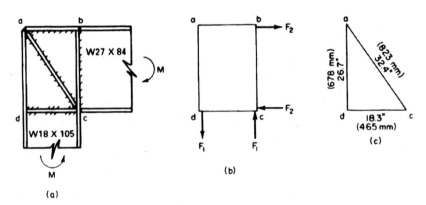

**FIGURE 10.** Rectangular knee.

**Calculation Procedure:**

### 1. Record the relevant properties of the two sections

Refer to the AISC *Specification* and *Manual*. It is assumed that the moment in each member is resisted entirely by the flanges and that the distance between the resultant flange forces is 0.95 times the depth of the member.

Record the properties of the members: for the W18 × 105, $d = 18.32$ in. (465.3 mm); $b_f = 11.79$ in. (299.5 mm); $t_f = 0.911$ in. (23.1 mm); $t_w = 0.554$ in. (14.1 mm); $k = 1.625$ in. (41.3 mm). For the W27 × 84, $d = 26.69$ in. (677.9 mm); $b_f = 9.96$ in. (253 mm); $t_f = 0.636$ in. (16.2 mm); $t_w = 0.463$ in. (11.8 mm).

### 2. Compute $F_1$

Thus, $F_1 = M_u/(0.95d) = 8100/[0.95(18.32)] = 465$ kips (2068.3 kN).

### 3. Determine whether web stiffeners are needed to transmit $F_1$

The shearing stress is assumed to vary linearly from zero at $a$ to its maximum value at $d$. The allowable average shearing stress is taken as $f_y/(3)^{0.5}$, where $f_y$ denotes the yield-point stress. The capacity of the web $= 0.554(26.69)(36/3^{0.5}) = 307$ kips (1365.5 kN). Therefore, use diagonal web stiffeners.

### 4. Design the web stiffeners

Referring to Fig. 10c, we see that $ac = (18.3^2 + 26.7^2)^{0.5} = 32.4$ in. (823 mm). The force in the stiffeners $= (465 - 307)32.4/26.7 = 192$ kips (854.0 kN). (The same result is obtained by computing $F_2$ and considering the capacity of the web across $ab$.) Then, $A_{st} = 192/36 = 5.33$ sq.in. (34.39 cm²). Use two plates 4 × 3/4 in. (101.6 × 19.1 mm).

### 5. Design the welds, using E60 electrodes

The AISC *Specification* stipulates that the weld capacity at ultimate load is 1.67 times the capacity at the working load. Consequently, the ultimate-load capacity is 1000 lb/lin in. (175 N/mm) times the number of sixteenths in the weld size. The welds are generally designed to develop the full moment capacity of each member. Refer to the AISC *Specification*.

*Weld at ab.* This weld transmits the force in the flange of the 27-in. (685.8-mm) member to the web of the 18-in. (457.2-mm) member. Then $F = 9.96(0.636)(36) = 228$ kips (1014.1 kN), weld force $= 228/[2(d - 2t_f)] = 228/[2(18.32 - 1.82)] = 6.91$ kips/lin in. (1210.1 N/mm). Use a 7/16-in. (11.1-mm) weld.

*Weld at bc.* Use a full-penetration butt weld.

*Weld at ac.* Use the minimum size of 1/4 in. (6.4 mm). The required total length of weld is $L = 192/4 = 48$ in. (1219.2 mm).

*Weld at dc.* Let $F_3$ denote that part of $F_2$ that is transmitted to the web of the 18-in. (457.2-mm) member through bearing, and let $F_4$ denote the remainder of $F_2$. Force $F_3$ distributes itself through the 18-in. (457.2-mm) member at 45° angles, and the maximum compressive stress occurs at the toe of the fillet. Find $F_3$ by equating this stress to 36 kips/sq.in. (248.2 MPa); or $F_3 = 36(0.554)(0.636 + 2 \times 1.625) = 78$ kips (346.9 kN). To evaluate $F_4$, apply the moment capacity of the 27-in. (685.8-mm) member. Or $F_4 = 228 - 78 = 150$ kips (667.2 kN).

The minimum weld size of 1/4 in. (6.4 mm) is inadequate. Use a 5/16-in. (7.9-mm) weld. The required total length is $L = 150/5 = 30$ in. (762.0 mm).

## CURVED KNEE OF RIGID BENT

In Fig. 11 the rafter and column are both W21 × 82, and the ultimate moment at the two sections of tangency—$p$ and $q$—is 6600 in.·kips (745.7 kN·m). The section of contraflexure in

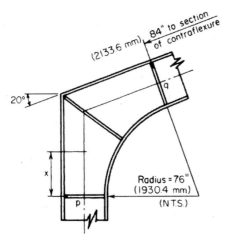

**FIGURE 11.** Curved knee.

each member lies 84 in. (2133.6 mm) from the section of tangency. Design the knee.

**Calculation Procedure:**

**1. Record the relevant properties of the members**

Refer to the Commentary in the AISC *Manual*. The notational system is the same as that used in the *Manual*, plus $a$ = distance from section of contraflexure to section of tangency; $b$ = member flange width; $x$ = distance from section of tangency to given section; $M$ = ultimate moment at given section; $M_p$ = plastic-moment capacity of knee at the given section.

Assume that the moment gradient $dM/dx$ remains constant across the knee. The web thickness of the knee is made equal to that of the main material. The flange thickness of the knee, however, must exceed that of the main material, for this reason: As $x$ increases, both $M$ and $M_p$ increase, but the former increases at a faster rate when $x$ is small. The critical section occurs where $dM/dx = dM_p/dx$.

An exact solution to this problem is possible, but the resulting equation is rather cumbersome. An approximate solution is given in the AISC *Manual*.

Record the relevant properties of the the W21 × 82: $d$ = 20.86 in. (529.8 mm); $b$ = 8.96 in. (227.6 mm); $t_f$ = 0.795 in. (20.2 mm); $t_w$ = 0.499 in. (12.7 mm).

**2. Design the cross section of the knee, assuming tentatively that flexure is the sole criterion**

Use a trial thickness of $1/2$ in. (12.7 mm) for the web plate and a 9-in. (228.6-mm) width for the flange plate. Then $a$ = 84 in. (2133.6 mm); $n$ = $a/d$ = 84/20.86 = 4.03. From the AISC *Manual*, $m$ = 0.14 ± $t'$ = $t(1 + m)$ = 0.795(1.14) = 0.906 in. (23.0 mm). Make the flange plate 1 in. (25.4 mm) thick.

**3. Design the stiffeners; investigate the knee for compliance with the AISC Commentary**

From the Commentary, *item 5*: Provide stiffener plates at the sections of tangency and at the center of the knee. Make the stiffener plates 4 × $7/8$ in. (102 × 22 mm), one on each side of the web.

*Item 3*: Thus, $\phi$ = $1/2(90° - 20°)$ = 35°; $\phi$ = 35/57.3 = 0.611 rad; $L$ = $R\phi$ = 76(0.611) = 46.4 in. (1178.6 mm); or $L$ = $\pi R(70°/360°)$ = 46.4 in. (1178.6 mm); $L_{cr}$ = 6$b$ = 6(9) = 54 in. (1373 mm), which is acceptable.

*Item 4*: Thus, $b/t'$ = 9; 2$R/b$ = 152/9 = 16.9, which is acceptable.

## BASE PLATE FOR STEEL COLUMN CARRYING AXIAL LOAD

A W14 × 53 column carries a load of 240 kips (1067.5 kN) and is supported by a footing made of 3000-lb/sq.in. (20,682-kPa) concrete. Design the column base plate.

**Calculation Procedure:**

### 1. Compute the required area of the base plate; establish the plate dimensions

Refer to the base-plate diagram in the AISC *Manual*. The column load is assumed to be uniformly distributed within the indicated rectangle, and the footing reaction is assumed to be uniformly distributed across the base plate. The required thickness of the plate is established by computing the bending moment at the circumference of the indicated rectangle. Let $f$ = maximum bending stress in plate; $p$ = bearing stress; $t$ = thickness of plate.

The ACI *Code* permits a bearing stress of 750 lb/sq.in. (5170.5 kPa) if the entire concrete area is loaded and 1125 lb/sq.in. (7755.8 kPa) if one-third of this area is loaded. Applying the 750-lb/sq.in. (5170.5-kPa) value, we get plate area = load, lb/750 = 240,000/750 = 320 sq.in. (2064.5 cm$^2$).

The dimensions of the W14 $\times$ 53 are $d$ = 13.94 in. (354.3 mm); $b$ = 8.06 in. (204.7 mm); $0.95d$ = 13.24 in. (335.3 mm); $0.80b$ = 6.45 in. (163.8 mm). For economy, the projections $m$ and $n$ should be approximately equal. Set $B$ = 15 in. (381 mm) and $C$ = 22 in. (558.8 mm); then, area = 15(22) = 330 sq.in. (2129 cm$^2$); $p$ = 240,000/330 = 727 lb/sq.in. (5011.9 kPa).

### 2. Compute the required thickness of the base plate

Thus, $m = \frac{1}{2}(22 - 13.24)$ = 4.38 in. (111.3 mm), which governs. Also, $n = \frac{1}{2}(15 - 6.45)$ = 4.28 in. (108.7 mm).

The AISC *Specification* permits a bending stress of 27,000 lb/sq.in. (186.1 MPa) in a rectangular plate. The maximum bending stress is $f = M/S = 3pm^2/t^2$; $t = m(3p/f)^{0.5}$ = $4.38(3 \times 727/27,000)^{0.5}$ = 1.24 in. (31.5 mm).

### 3. Summarize the design

Thus, $B$ = 15 in. (381 mm); $C$ = 22 in. (558.8 mm); $t = 1\frac{1}{4}$ in. (31.8 mm).

## BASE FOR STEEL COLUMN WITH END MOMENT

A steel column of 14-in. (355.6-mm.) depth transmits to its footing an axial load of 30 kips (133.4 kN) and a moment of 1100 in.·kips (124.3 kN·m) in the plane of its web. Design the base, using A307 anchor bolts and 3000-lb/sq.in. (20.7-MPa) concrete.

**Calculation Procedure:**

### 1. Record the allowable stresses and modular ratio

Refer to Fig. 12. If the moment is sufficiently large, it causes uplift at one end of the plate and thereby induces tension in the anchor bolt at that end. A rigorous analysis of the stresses in a column base transmitting a moment is not possible. For simplicity, compute the stresses across a horizontal plane through the base plate by treating this as the cross section of a reinforced-concrete beam, the anchor bolt on the tension side acting as the reinforcing steel. The effects of initial tension in the bolts are disregarded.

The anchor bolts are usually placed $2\frac{1}{2}$ (63.5 mm) or 3 in. (76.2 mm) from the column flange. Using a plate of 26-in. (660-mm) depth as shown in Fig. 12a, let $A_s$ = anchor-bolt cross-sectional area; $B$ = base-plate width; $C$ = resultant compressive force on base plate; $T$ = tensile force in anchor bolt; $f_s$ = stress in anchor bolt; $p$ = maximum bearing stress; $p'$ = bearing stress at column face; $t$ = base-plate thickness.

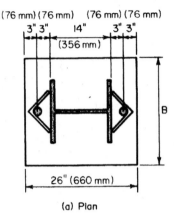

(a) Plan

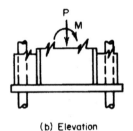

(b) Elevation

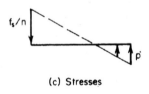

(c) Stresses

**FIGURE 12.** Anchor-bolt details. (*a*) Plan; (*b*) elevation; (*c*) stresses.

Recording the allowable stresses and modular ratio by using the ACI *Code*, we get $p = 750$ lb/sq.in. (5170 kPa) and $n = 9$. From the AISC *Specification*, $f_s = 14,000$ lb/sq.in. (96.5 MPa); the allowable bending stress in the plate is 27,000 lb/sq.in. (186.1 MPa).

### 2. Construct the stress and force diagrams

These are shown in Fig. 13. Then $f_s/n = 14/9 = 1.555$ kips/sq.in. (10.7 MPa); $kd = 23(0.750/2.305) = 7.48$ in. (190.0 mm); $jd = 23 - 7.48/3 = 20.51$ in. (521.0 mm).

### 3. Design the base plate

Thus, $C = {}^1\!/_2(7.48)(0.750B) = 2.805B$. Take moments with respect to the anchor bolt, or $\Sigma M = 30(10) + 1100 - 2.805B(20.51) = 0$; $B = 24.3$ in. (617.2 mm).

Assume that the critical bending stress in the base plate occurs at the face of the column. Compute the bending moment at the face for a 1-in. (25.4-mm) width of plate. Referring to Fig. 13c, we have $p' = 0.750(1.48/7.48) = 0.148$ kips/sq.in. (1020.3 kPa); $M = (6^2/6)(0.148 + 2 \times 0.750) = 9.89$ in.·kips (1.12 kN·m); $t^2 - 6M/27 = 2.20$ sq.in. (14.19 cm$^2$); $t = 1.48$ in. (37.6 mm). Make the base plate 25 in. (635 mm) wide and $1^1\!/_2$ in. (38.1 mm) thick.

### 4. Design the anchor bolts

From the calculation in step 3, $C = 2.805B = 2.805(24.3) = 68.2$ kips (303.4 kN); $T = 68.2 - 30 = 38.2$ kips (169.9 kN); $A_s = 38.2/14 = 2.73$ sq.in. (17.61 cm$^2$). Refer to the AISC *Manual*. Use $2^1\!/_4$-in. (57.2-mm) anchor bolts, one on each side of the flange. Then $A_s = 3.02$ sq.in. (19.48 cm$^2$).

### 5. Design the anchorage for the bolts

The bolts are held by angles welded to the column flange, as shown in Fig. 12 and in the AISC *Manual*. Use $^1\!/_2$-in. (12.7-mm) angles 12 in. (304.8 mm) long. Each line of weld resists a force of $^1\!/_2 T$. Refer to Fig. 13d and compute the unit force $F$ at the extremity of the weld. Thus, $M = 19.1(3) = 57.3$ in.·kips (6.47 kN·m); $S_x = (^1\!/_6)(12)^2$ 24 sq.in. (154.8 cm$^2$); $F_x = 57.3/24 = 2.39$ kips/lin in. (0.43 kN/mm); $F_y = 19.1/12 = 1.59$ kips/lin in (0.29 kN/mm); $F = (2.39^2 + 1.59^2)^{0.5} = 2.87$ kips/lin in. (0.52 kN/mm). Use a $^5\!/_{16}$-in. (4.8-mm) fillet weld of E60 electrodes, which has a capacity of 3 kips/lin in. (0.54 kN/mm).

## GRILLAGE SUPPORT FOR COLUMN

A steel column in the form of a W14 × 320 reinforced with two 20 × $1^1\!/_2$ in. (508 × 38.1 mm) cover plates carries a load of 2790 kips (12,410 kN). Design the grillage under this column, using an allowable bearing stress of 750 lb/sq.in. (5170.5 kPa) on the concrete. The space between the beams will be filled with concrete.

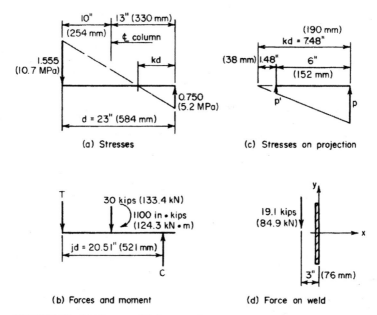

**FIGURE 13.** (*a*) Stresses; (*b*) forces and moment; (*c*) stresses on projection; (*d*) force on weld.

## Calculation Procedure:

### 1. Establish the dimensions of the grillage

Refer to Fig. 14. A load of this magnitude cannot be transmitted from the column to its footing through the medium of a base plate alone. It is therefore necessary to interpose steel beams between the base plate and the footing; these may be arranged in one tier or in two orthogonal tiers. Integrity of each tier is achieved by tying the beams together by pipe separators. This type of column support is termed a *grillage*. In designing the grillage, it is assumed that bearing pressures are uniform across each surface under consideration.

The area of grillage required = load, kips/allowable stress, kips/sq.in. = 2790/0.750 = 3720 sq.in. (23,994 cm²). Set $A$ = 60 in. (1524 mm) and $B$ = 62 in. (1574.8 mm), giving an area of 3720 sq.in. (23,994 cm²), as required.

### 2. Design the upper-tier beams

There are three criteria: bending stress, shearing stress, and compressive stress in the web at the toe of the fillet. The concrete between the beams supplies lateral restraint, and the allowable bending stress is therefore 24 kips/sq.in. (165.5 MPa).

Since the web stresses are important criteria, a grillage is generally constructed of S shapes rather than wide-flange beams to take advantage of the thick webs of S shapes. The design of the beams requires the concurrent determination of the length $a$ of the base plate. Let $f$ = bending stress; $f_b$, = compressive stress in web at fillet toe; $v$ = shearing stress; $P$ = load carried by single beam; $S$ = section modulus of single beam; $k$ = distance from outer surface of beam to toe of fillet; $t_w$ = web thickness of beam; $a_1$ = length of plate as governed by flexure; $a_2$ = length of plate as governed by compressive stress in web.

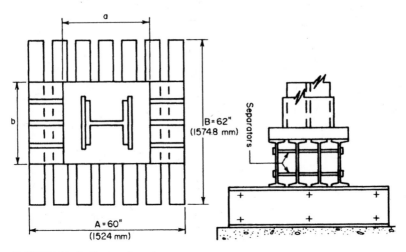

**FIGURE 14.** Grillage under column.

Select a beam size on the basis of stresses $f$ and $f_b$, and then investigate $v$. The maximum bending moment occurs at the center of the span; its value is $M = P(A - a)/8 = fS$; therefore, $a_1 = A - 8fS/P$.

At the toe of the fillet, the load $P$ is distributed across a distance $a + 2k$. Then $f_b = P/(a + 2k)t_w$; therefore, $a_2 = P/f_b t_w - 2k$. Try four beams; then $P = 2790/4 = 697.5$ kips (3102.5 kN); $f = 24$ kips/sq.in. (165.5 MPa); $f_b = 27$ kips/sq.in. (186.1 MPa). Upon substitution, the foregoing equations reduce to $a_1 = 60 - 0.2755$; $a_2 = 25.8/t_w - 2k$.

Select the trial beam sizes shown in the accompanying table, and calculate the corresponding values of $a_1$ and $a_2$.

| Size | $S$, in³ (cm³) | $t_w$, in. (mm) | $k$, in. (mm) | $a_1$, in. (mm) | $a_2$, in. (mm) |
|------|------|------|------|------|------|
| S18 × 54.7 | 88.4 (1448.6) | 0.460 (11.68) | 1.375 (34.93) | 35.7 (906.8) | 53.3 (1353.8) |
| S18 × 70 | 101.9 (1669.8) | 0.711 (18.06) | 1.375 (34.93) | 32.0 (812.8) | 33.6 (853.4) |
| S20 × 65.4 | 116.9 (1915.7) | 0.500 (12.7) | 1.563 (39.70) | 27.9 (708.7) | 48.5 (1231.9) |
| S20 × 75 | 126.3 (2069.7) | 0.641 (16.28) | 1.563 (39.70) | 25.3 (642.6) | 37.1 (942.3) |

Try S18 × 70, with $a = 34$ in. (863.6 mm). The flange width is 6.25 in. (158.8 mm). The maximum vertical shear occurs at the edge of the plate; its magnitude is $V = P(A - a)(2A) = 697.5(60 - 34)/[2(60)] = 151.1$ kips (672.1 kN); $v = 151.1/[18(0.711)] = 11.8 < 14.5$ kips/sq.in. (99.9 MPa), which is acceptable.

### 3. Design the base plate
Refer to the second previous calculation procedure. To permit the deposition of concrete, allow a minimum space of 2 in. (50.8 mm) between the beam flanges. The minimum value of $b$ is therefore $b = 4(6.25) + 3(2) = 31$ in. (787.4 mm).

The dimensions of the effective bearing area under the column are $0.95(16.81 + 2 \times 15) = 18.82$ in. (478.0 mm); $0.80(20) = 16$ in. (406.4 mm). The projections of the plate are $(34 - 18.82)/2 = 7.59$ in. (192.8 mm); $(31 - 16)/2 = 7.5$ in. (190.5 mm).

Therefore, keep $b = 31$ in. (787 mm), because this results in a well-proportioned plate. The pressure under the plate $= 2790/[34(31)] = 2.65$ kips/sq.in. (18.3 MPa). For a 1-in. (25.4-mm) width of plate, $M = \frac{1}{2}(2.65)/(7.59)^2 = 76.33$ in.·kips (8.6 kN·m); $S = M/f = 76.33/27 = 2.827$ in.$^3$ (46.33 cm$^3$); $t = (6S)^{0.5} = 4.12$ in. (104.6 mm).

Plate thicknesses within this range vary by $\frac{1}{8}$-in. (3.2-mm) increments, as stated in the AISC *Manual.* However, a section of the AISC *Specification* requires that plates over 4 in. (102 mm) thick be planed at all bearing surfaces. Set $t = 4\frac{1}{2}$ in. (114.3 mm) to allow for the planing.

### 4. Design the beams at the lower tier

Try seven beams. Thus, $P = 2790/7 = 398.6$ kips (1772.9 kN); $M = 398.6(62 - 31)/8 = 1545$ in.·kips (174.6 kN·m); $S_3 = 1545/24 = 64.4$ in$^3$ (1055.3 cm$^3$).

Try S15 × 50. Then $S = 64.2$ in$^3$ (1052.1 cm$^3$); $t_w = 0.550$ in. (14.0 mm); $k = 1.25$ in. (31.8 mm); $b = 5.64$ in. (143.3 mm). The space between flanges is $[60 - 7 \times 5.641]/6 = 3.42$ in. (86.9 mm). This result is satisfactory. Then $f_b = 398.6/[0.550(31 + 2 \times 1.25)] = 21.6 < 27$ kips/sq.in. (186.1 MPa), which is satisfactory; $V = 398.6(62 - 31)/[2(62)] = 99.7$ kips (443.5 kN); $v = 99.7/[15(0.550)] = 12.1 < 14.5$, which is satisfactory.

### 5. Summarize the design

Thus: $A = 60$ in. (1524 mm); $B = 62$ in. (1574.8 mm); base plate is 31 × 34 × 4½ in. (787.4 × 863.6 × 114.3 mm), upper-tier steel, four beams S18 × 70; lower-tier steel, seven beams 15150.0.

## WIND-STRESS ANALYSIS
## BY PORTAL METHOD

The bent in Fig. 15 resists the indicated wind loads. Applying the portal method of analysis, calculate all shears, end moments, and axial forces.

### Calculation Procedure:

### 1. Compute the shear factor for each column

The portal method is an approximate and relatively simple method of wind-stress analysis that is frequently applied to regular bents of moderate height. It considers the bent to be composed of a group of individual portals and makes the following assumptions. (1) The wind load is distributed among the aisles of the bent in direct proportion to their relative widths. (2) The point of contraflexure in each member lies at its center.

Because of the first assumption, the shear in a given column is directly proportional to the average width of the adjacent aisles. (An alternative form of the portal method assumes that the wind load is distributed uniformly among the aisles, irrespective of their relative widths.)

In this analysis, we consider the *end moments* of a member, i.e., the moments exerted at the ends of the member by the joints. The sign conventions used are as follows. An end moment is positive if it is clockwise. The shear is positive if the lateral forces exerted on the member by the joints constitute a couple having a counterclockwise moment. An axial force is positive if it is tensile.

Figure 16a and b represents a beam and column, respectively, having positive end moments and positive shear. By applying the second assumption, $M_a = M_b = M$, Eq. a; $V = 2M/L$, or $M = VL/2$, Eq. b; $H = 2M/L$, or $M = HL/2$, Eq. c. In Fig. 15, the calculated data for each member are recorded in the order indicated.

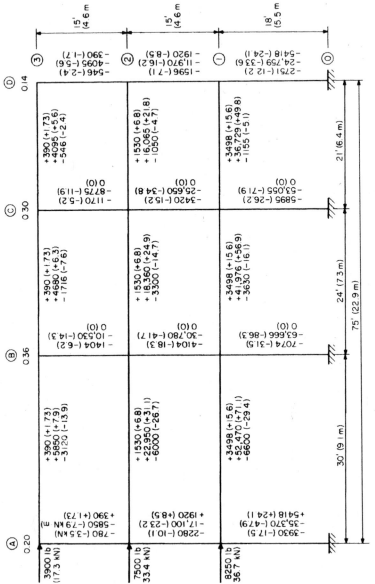

**FIGURE 15.** Wind-stress analysis by portal method.

Note: Data recorded in following order: shear, end moments, axial force.

**1.186**

The shear factor equals the ratio of the average width of the adjacent aisles to the total width. Or, line $A$, $15/75 = 0.20$; line $B$, $(15 + 12)/75 = 0.36$; line $C$, $(12 + 10.5)/75 = 0.30$; line $D$, $10.5/75 = 0.14$. For convenience, record these values in Fig. 15.

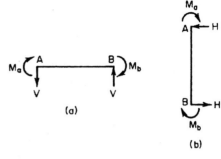

### 2. Compute the shear in each column

For instance, column $A$-2-3, $H = -3900(0.20) = -780$ lb (−3.5 kN); column $C$-1-2, $H = -(3900 + 7500)0.30 = -3420$ lb (−15.2 kN).

**FIGURE 16**

### 3. Compute the end moments of each column

Apply Eq. $c$. For instance, column $A$-2-3, $M = \frac{1}{2}(-780)15 = -5850$ ft·lb (−7932.6 N·m); column $D$-0-1, $M = \frac{1}{2}(-2751)18 = -24{,}759$ ft·lb (−33,573.2 N·m).

### 4. Compute the end moments of each beam

Do this by equating the algebraic sum of end moments at each joint to zero. For instance, at line 3: $M_{AB} = 5850$ ft·lb (7932.6 N·m); $M_{BC} = -5850 + 10{,}530 = 4680$ ft·lb (6346.1 N·m); $M_{CD} = -4680 + 8775 = 4095$ ft·lb (5552.8 N·m). At line 2: $M_{AB} = 5850 + 17{,}100 = 22{,}950$ ft·lb (31,120.2 N·m); $M_{BC} = -22{,}950 + 30{,}780 + 10{,}530 = 18{,}360$ ft·lb (24,896.0 N·m).

### 5. Compute the shear in each beam

Do this by applying Eq. $b$. For instance, beam $B$-2-$C$, $V = 2(18{,}360)724 = 1530$ lb (6.8 kN).

### 6. Compute the axial force in each member

Do this by drawing free-body diagrams of the joints and applying the equations of equilibrium. It is found that the axial forces in the interior columns are zero. This condition stems from the first assumption underlying the portal method and the fact that each interior column functions as both the leeward column of one portal and the windward column of the adjacent portal.

The absence of axial forces in the interior columns in turn results in the equality of the shear in the beams at each tier. Thus, the calculations associated with the portal method of analysis are completely self-checking.

## WIND-STRESS ANALYSIS BY CANTILEVER METHOD

For the bent in Fig. 17, calculate all shears, end moments, and axial forces induced by the wind loads by applying the cantilever method of wind-stress analysis. For this purpose, assume that the columns have equal cross-sectional areas.

### Calculation Procedure:

### 1. Compute the shear and moment on the bent at midheight of each horizontal row of columns

The cantilever method, which is somewhat more rational than the portal method, considers that the bent behaves as a vertical cantilever. Consequently, the direct stress in a

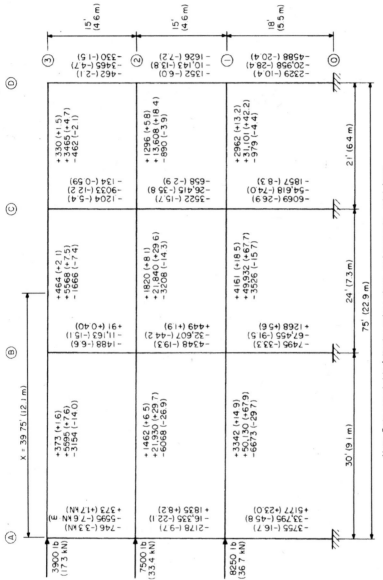

**FIGURE 17.** Wind-stress analysis by cantilever method.

Note: Data recorded in following order: shear, end moments, axial force.

column is directly proportional to the distance from the column to the centroid of the combined column area. As in the portal method, the assumption is made that the point of contraflexure in each member lies at its center. Refer to the previous calculation procedure for the sign convention.

Computing the shear and moment on the bent at midheight, we have the following. Upper row: $H = 3900$ lb (17.3 kN); $M = 3900(7.5) = 29,250$ ft·lb (39,663.0 N·m). Center row: $H = 3900 + 7500 = 11,400$ lb (50.7 kN); $M = 3900(22.5) + 7500(7.5) = 144,000$ ft·lb (195.3 kN·m). Lower row: $H = 11,400 + 8250 = 19,650$ lb (87.5 kN); $M = 3900(39) + 7500(24) + 8250(9) = 406,400$ ft·lb (551.1 kN·m), or $M = 144,000 + 11,400(16.5) + 8250(9) = 406,400$ ft·lb (551.1 kN·m), as before.

## 2. Locate the centroidal axis of the combined column area, and compute the moment of inertia of the area with respect to this axis

Take the area of one column as a unit. Then $x = (30 + 54 + 75)/4 = 39.75$ ft (12.12 m); $I = 39.75^2 + 9.75^2 + 14.25^2 + 35.25^2 = 3121$ sq.ft. (289.95 m²).

## 3. Compute the axial force in each column

Use the equation $f = My/I$. The $y/I$ values are

|     | A | B | C | D |
|-----|-------|-------|--------|---------|
| y   | 39.75 | 9.75 | -14.25 | -35.25 |
| y/I | 0.01274 | 0.00312 | -0.00457 | -0.01129 |

Then column A-2-3, $P = 29,250(0.01274) = 373$ kips (1659 kN); column B-0-1, $P = 406,400(0.00312) = 1268$ kips (5640 kN).

## 4. Compute the shear in each beam by analyzing each joint as a free body

Thus, beam A-3-B, $V = 373$ lb (1659 N); beam B-3-C, $V = 373 + 91 = 464$ lb (2.1 kN); beam C-3-D, $V = 464 - 134 = 330$ lb (1468 N); beam A-2-B, $V = 1835 - 373 = 1462$ lb (6.5 kN); beam B-2-C, $V = 1462 + 449 - 91 = 1820$ lb (8.1 kN).

## 5. Compute the end moments of each beam

Apply Eq. b of the previous calculation procedure. Or for beam A-3-B, $M = \frac{1}{2}(373)(30) = 5595$ ft·lb (7586.8 N·m).

## 6. Compute the end moments of each column

Do this by equating the algebraic sum of the end moments at each joint to zero.

## 7. Compute the shear in each column

Apply Eq. c of the previous calculation procedure. The sum of the shears in each horizontal row of columns should equal the wind load above that plane. For instance, for the center row, $\Sigma H = -(2178 + 4348 + 3522 + 1352) = -11,400$ lb (-50.7 kN), which is correct.

## 8. Compute the axial force in each beam by analyzing each joint as a free body

Thus, beam A-3-B, $P = -3900 + 746 = -3154$ lb (-14.0 kN); beam B-3-C, $P = -3154 + 1488 = -1666$ lb (-7.4 kN).

# WIND-STRESS ANALYSIS BY SLOPE-DEFLECTION METHOD

Analyze the bent in Fig. 18a by the slope-deflection method. The moment of inertia of each member is shown in the drawing.

### Calculation Procedure:

#### 1. Compute the end rotations caused by the applied moments and forces; superpose the rotation caused by the transverse displacement

This method of analysis has not been applied extensively in the past because the arithmetic calculations involved become voluminous where the bent contains many joints. However, the increasing use of computers in structural design is overcoming this obstacle and stimulating a renewed interest in the method.

Figure 19 is the elastic curve of a member subjected to moments and transverse forces applied solely at its ends. The sign convention is as follows: an end moment is positive if

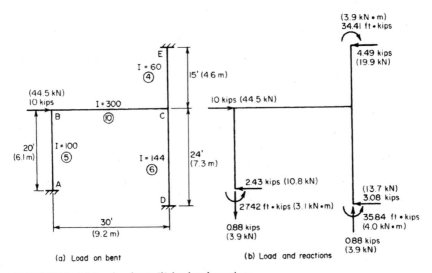

(a) Load on bent          (b) Load and reactions

**FIGURE 18.** (a) Load on bent; (b) load and reactions.

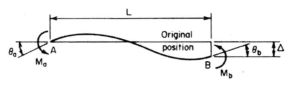

**FIGURE 19.** Elastic curve of beam.

it is clockwise; an angular displacement is positive if the rotation is clockwise; the transverse displacement $\Delta$ is positive if it rotates the member in a clockwise direction.

Computing the end rotations gives $\theta_a = (L/6EI)(2M_a - M_b) + \Delta/L$; $\theta_b = (L/6EI)(-M_a + 2M_b) + \Delta/L$. These results may be obtained by applying the moment-area method or unit-load method given in Sec. 1.

## 2. Solve the foregoing equations for the end moments

Thus,

$$M_a = \left(\frac{2EI}{L}\right)\left(2\theta_a + \theta_b - \frac{3\Delta}{L}\right) \qquad M_b = \left(\frac{2EI}{L}\right)\left(\theta_a + 2\theta_b - \frac{3\Delta}{L}\right) \qquad (4)$$

These are the basic slope-deflection equations.

## 3. Compute the value of I/L for each member of the bent

Let $K$ denote this value, which represents the relative stiffness of the member. Thus $K_{ab} = 100/20 = 5$; $K_{cd} = 144/24 = 6$; $K_{be} = 300/30 = 10$; $K_{ce} = 60/15 = 4$. These values are recorded in circles in Fig. 18.

## 4. Apply Eq. 4 to each joint in turn

When the wind load is applied, the bent will deform until the horizontal reactions at the supports total 10 kips (44.5 kN). It is evident, therefore, that the end moments of a member are functions of the *relative* rather than the absolute stiffness of that member. Therefore, in writing the moment equations, the coefficient $2EI/L$ may be replaced with $I/L$; to view this in another manner, $E = \frac{1}{2}$.

Disregard the deformation associated with axial forces in the members, and assume that joints $B$ and $C$ remain in a horizontal line. The symbol $M_{ab}$ denotes the moment exerted on member $AB$ at joint $A$. Thus $M_{ab} = 5(\theta_b - 3\Delta/20) = 5\theta_b - 0.75\Delta$; $M_{dc} = 6(\theta_c - 3\Delta/24) = 6\theta_c - 0.75\Delta$; $M_{ec} = 4(\theta_c + 3\Delta/15) = 4\theta_c + 0.80\Delta$; $M_{ba} = 5(2\theta_b - 3\Delta/20) = 10\theta_b - 0.75\Delta$; $M_{cd} = 6(2\theta_c - 3\Delta/24) = 12\theta_c - 0.75\Delta$; $M_{ce} = 4(2\theta_c + 3\Delta/15) = 8\theta_c + 0.80\Delta$; $M_{cd} = 10(2\theta_b + \theta_c) = 20\theta_b + 10\theta_c$; $M_{cb} = 10(\theta_b + 2\theta_c) = 10\theta_b + 20\theta_c$.

## 5. Write the equations of equilibrium for the joints and for the bent

Thus, joint $B$, $M_{ba} + M_{bc} = 0$, Eq. a; joint $C$, $M_{cb} + M_{cd} + M_{ce} = 0$, Eq. b. Let $H$ denote the horizontal reaction at a given support. Consider a horizontal force positive if directed toward the right. Then $H_a + H_d + H_e + 10 = 0$, Eq. c.

## 6. Express the horizontal reactions in terms of the end moments

Rewrite Eq. c. Or, $(M_{ab} + M_{ba})/20 + (M_{dc} + M_{cd})/24 - (M_{ec} + M_{ce})/15 + 10 = 0$, or $6M_{ab} + 6M_{ba} + 5M_{dc} + 5M_{cd} - 8M_{ec} - 8M_{ce} = -1200$, Eq. c'.

## 7. Rewrite Eqs. a, b, and c' by replacing the end moments with the expressions obtained in step 4

Thus, $30\theta_b + 10\theta_c - 0.75\Delta = 0$, Eq. A; $10\theta_b + 40\theta_c + 0.05\Delta = 0$, Eq. B; $90\theta_b - 6\theta_c - 29.30\Delta = -1200$, Eq. C.

## 8. Solve the simultaneous equations in step 7 to obtain the relative values of $\theta_b$, $\theta_c$, and $\Delta$

Thus $\theta_b = 1.244$; $\theta_c = -0.367$; $\Delta = 44.85$.

## 9. Apply the results in step 8 to evaluate the end moments

The values, in foot-kips, are: $M_{ab} = -27.42$ ($-37.18$ kN·m); $M_{dc} = -35.84$ ($-48.6$ kN·m); $M_{ec} = 34.41$ (46.66 kN·m); $M_{ba} = -21.20$ ($-28.75$ kN·m); $M_{cd} = -38.04$ ($-51.58$ kN·m); $M_{ce} = 32.94$ (44.67 kN·m); $M_{bc} = 21.21$ (28.76 kN·m); $M_{cb} = 5.10$ (6.92 kN·m).

### 10. Compute the shear in each member by analyzing the member as a free body

The shear is positive if the transverse forces exert a counterclockwise moment. Thus $H_{ab}$ = $(M_{ab} + M_{ba})/20$ = −2.43 kips (−10.8 kN); $H_{cd}$ = −3.08 kips (−13.7 kN); $H_{ce}$ = 4.49 kips (19.9 kN); $V_{bc}$ = 0.88 kip (3.9 kN).

### 11. Compute the axial force in AB and BC

Thus $P_{ab}$ = 0.88 kip (3.91 kN); $P_{bc}$ = −7.57 kips (−33.7 kN). The axial forces in $EC$ and $CD$ are found by equating the elongation of one to the contraction of the other.

### 12. Check the bent for equilibrium

The forces and moments acting on the structure are shown in Fig. 18$b$. The three equations of equilibrium are satisfied.


## WIND DRIFT OF A BUILDING

Figure 20$a$ is the partial elevation of the steel framing of a skyscraper. The wind shear directly above line 11 is 40 kips (177.9 kN), and the wind force applied at lines 11 and 12 is 4 kips (17.8 kN) each. The members represented by solid lines have the moments of inertia shown in Table 1, and the structure is to be analyzed for wind stress by the portal method. Compute the wind drift for the bent bounded by lines 11 and 12; that is, find the horizontal displacement of the joints on line 11 relative to those on line 12 as a result of wind.

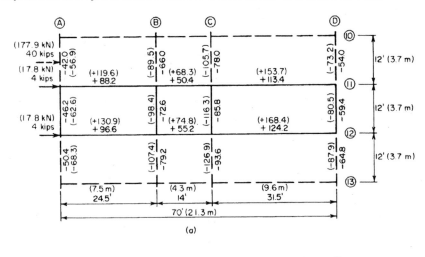

(a)

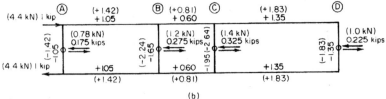

(b)

**FIGURE 20**

**TABLE 1.** Calculation of Wind Drift

| Member | $I$, in$^4$ (cm$^4$) | $L$, ft (in.) | $M_e$, ft-kips (kN·m) | $m_e$, ft-kips (kN·m) | $M_e m_e L/I$ |
|---|---|---|---|---|---|
| A-11-12 | 1,500 (62,430) | 12 (3.66) | 46.2 (62.6) | 1.05 (1.42) | 0.39 |
| B-11-12 | 1,460 (60,765) | 12 (3.66) | 72.6 (98.5) | 1.65 (2.24) | 0.98 |
| C-11-12 | 1,800 (74,916) | 12 (3.66) | 85.8 (116.3) | 1.95 (2.64) | 1.12 |
| D-11-12 | 2,000 (83,240) | 12 (3.66) | 59.4 (80.6) | 1.35 (1.83) | 0.48 |
| A-12-B | 660 (27,469) | 24.5 (7.47) | 88.2 (119.6) | 1.05 (1.42) | 3.44 |
| B-12-C | 300 (12,486) | 14 (4.27) | 50.4 (68.3) | 0.60 (0.81) | 1.41 |
| C-12-D | 1,400 (58,268) | 31.5 (9.60) | 113.4 (153.8) | 1.35 (1.83) | 3.44 |
| A-12-B | 750 (31,213) | 24.5 (7.47) | 96.6 (130.9) | 1.05 (1.42) | 3.31 |
| B-12-C | 400 (16,648) | 14 (4.27) | 55.2 (74.9) | 0.60 (0.81) | 1.16 |
| C-12-D | 1,500 (62,430) | 31.5 (9.60) | 124.2 (168.4) | 1.35 (1.83) | 3.52 |
| Total | | | | | 19.25 |

## Calculation Procedure:

### 1. Using the portal method of wind-stress analysis, compute the shear in each column caused by the unit loads

Apply the unit-load method presented in Sec. 1. For this purpose, consider that unit horizontal loads are applied to the structure in the manner shown in Fig. 20*b*.

The results obtained in steps 1, 2, and 3 below are recorded in Fig. 20*b*. To apply the portal method of wind-stress analysis, see the fourteenth calculation procedure in this section.

### 2. Compute the end moments of each column caused by the unit loads

### 3. Equate the algebraic sum of end moments at each joint to zero; from this find the end moments of the beams caused by the unit loads

### 4. Find the end moments of each column

Multiply the results obtained in step 2 by the wind shear in each panel to find the end moments of each column in Fig. 20*a*. For instance, the end moments of column C-11-12 are −1.95(44) = −85.8 ft·kips (−116.3 kN·m). Record the result in Fig. 20*a*.

### 5. Find the end moments of the beams caused by the true loads

Equate the algebraic sum of end moments at each joint to zero to find the end moments of the beams caused by the true loads.

### 6. State the equation for wind drift

In Fig. 21, $M_e$ and $m_e$ denote the end moments caused by the true load and unit load, respectively. Then the

$$\text{Wind drift } \Delta = \frac{\Sigma M_e m_e L}{3EI} \tag{5}$$

### 7. Compute the wind drift by completing Table 1

In recording end moments, algebraic signs may be disregarded because the product $M_e m_e$ is always positive. Taking the total of the last column in Table 1, we find

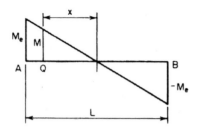 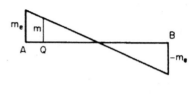

**FIGURE 21.** Bending-moment diagrams.

$\Delta = 19.25(12)^2/[3(29)(10)^3] = 0.382$ in. (9.7 mm). For dimensional homogeneity, the left side of Eq. 5 must be multiplied by 1 kip (4.45 kN). The product represents the external work performed by the unit loads.

## REDUCTION IN WIND DRIFT BY USING DIAGONAL BRACING

With reference to the previous calculation procedure, assume that the wind drift of the bent is to be restricted to 0.20 in. (5.1 mm) by introducing diagonal bracing between lines $B$ and $C$. Design the bracing, using the gross area of the member.

### Calculation Procedure:

### 1. State the change in length of the brace

The bent will be reinforced against lateral deflection by a pair of diagonal cross braces, each brace being assumed to act solely as a tension member. Select the lightest single-angle member that will satisfy the stiffness requirements; then compute the wind drift of the reinforced bent.

Assume that the bent in Fig. 22 is deformed in such a manner that $B$ is displaced a horizontal distance $A$ relative to $D$. Let $A$ = cross-sectional area of member $CB$; $P$ = axial force in $CB$; $P_h$ = horizontal component of $P$; $\delta L$ = change in length of $CB$. From the geometry of Fig. 22, $\delta L = \Delta \cos \theta = a\Delta/L$ approximately.

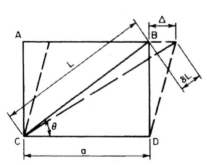

**FIGURE 22**

### 2. Express $P_h$ in terms of $\Delta$
Thus, $P = aAE\Delta/L^2$; $P_h = P \cos \theta = Pa/L$; then

$$P_h = \frac{a^2 AE\Delta}{L^3} \qquad (6)$$

### 3. Select a trial size for the diagonal bracing; compute the tensile capacity
A section of the AISC *Specification* limits the slenderness ratio for bracing members in tension to 300, and another section provides

an allowable stress of 22 kips/sq.in. (151.7 MPa). Thus, $L^2 = 14^2 + 12^2 = 340$ sq.ft. (31.6 sq.in.); $L = 18.4$ ft (5.61 m); $r_{min} = (18.4 \times 12)/300 = 0.74$ in. (18.8 mm).

Try a $4 \times 4 \times \frac{1}{4}$ in. (101.6 $\times$ 101.6 $\times$ 6.35 mm) angle; $r = 0.79$ in. (20.1 mm); $A = 1.94$ sq.in. (12.52 cm²); $P_{max} = 1.94(22) = 42.7$ kips (189.9 kN).

**4. Compute the wind drift if the assumed size of bracing is used**

By Eq. 6, $P_h = \{196/[(340)(18.4)(12)]\} \, 1.94(29)(10)^3 \Delta = 147\Delta$ kips (653.9$\Delta$ N). The wind shear resisted by the columns of the bent is reduced by $P_h$, and the wind drift is reduced proportionately.

From the previous calculation procedure, the following values are obtained: without diagonal bracing, $\Delta = 0.382$ in. (9.7 mm); with diagonal bracing, $\Delta = 0.382/(44 - P_h)/44 = 0.382 - 1.28\Delta$. Solving gives $\Delta = 0.168 < 0.20$ in. (5.1 mm), which is acceptable.

**5. Check the axial force in the brace**

Thus, $P_h = 147(0.168) = 24.7$ kips (109.9 kN); $P = P_h L/a = 24.7(18.4)/14 = 32.5 < 42.7$ kips (189.9 kN), which is satisfactory. Therefore, the assumed size of the member is satisfactory.

## LIGHT-GAGE STEEL BEAM WITH UNSTIFFENED FLANGE

A beam of light-gage cold-formed steel consists of two $7 \times 1\frac{1}{2}$ in. (177.8 $\times$ 38.1 mm) by no. 12 gage channels connected back to back to form an I section. The beam is simply supported on a 16-ft (4.88-m) span, has continuous lateral support, and carries a total dead load of 50 lb/lin ft (730 N/m). The live-load deflection is restricted to 1/360 of the span. If the yield-point stress $f_y$ is 33,000 lb/sq.in. (227.5 MPa), compute the allowable unit live load for this member.

### Calculation Procedure:

**1. Record the relevant properties of the section**

Apply the AISC *Specification for the Design of Light Gage Cold-Formed Steel Structural Members*. This is given in the AISC publication *Light Gage Cold-Formed Steel Design Manual*. Use the same notational system, except denote the flat width of an element by $g$ rather than $w$.

The publication mentioned above provides a basic design stress of 20,000 lb/sq.in. (137.9 MPa) for this grade of steel. However, since the compression flange of the given member is unstiffened in accordance with the definition in one section of the publication, it may be necessary to reduce the allowable compressive stress. A table in the *Manual* gives the dimensions, design properties, and allowable stress of each section, but the allowable stress will be computed independently in this calculation procedure.

Let $V$ = maximum vertical shear; $M$ = maximum bending moment; $w$ = unit load; $f_b$ = basic design stress; $f_c$ = allowable bending stress in compression; $v$ = shearing stress; $\Delta$ = maximum deflection.

Record the relevant properties of the section as shown in Fig. 23: $I_x = 12.4$ in⁴ (516.1 cm⁴); $S_x = 3.54$ in³ (58.0 cm³); $R = \frac{3}{16}$ in. (4.8 mm).

**2. Compute $f_c$**

Thus, $g = B/2 - t - R = 1.1935$ in. (30.3 mm); $g/t = 1.1935/0.105 = 11.4$. From the *Manual*, the allowable stress corresponding to this ratio is $f_c = 1.667f_b - 8640 - 1(f_b - 12,950)g/t]/15 = 1.667(20,000) - 8640 - (20,000 - 12,950)11.4/15 = 19,340$ lb/sq.in. (133.3 MPa).

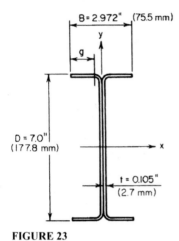

B = 2.972" (75.5 mm)

D = 7.0"
(177.8 mm)

t = 0.105"
(2.7 mm)

**FIGURE 23**

### 3. Compute the allowable unit live load if flexure is the sole criterion

Thus $M = f_c S_x = 19,340(3.54)/12 = 5700$ ft·lb (7729.2 N·m); $w = 8M/L^2 = 8(5700)/16^2 = 178$ lb/lin ft (2.6 kN/m); $w_{LL} = 178 - 50 = 128$ lb/lin ft (1.87 kN/m).

### 4. Investigate the deflection under the computed live load

Using $E = 29,500,000$ lb/sq.in. (203,373 MPa) as given in the AISC *Manual*, we have $\Delta_{LL} = 5w_{LL}L^4/(384EI_x) = 5(128)(16)^4(12)^3/[384(29.5)(10)^6 12.4] = 0.516$ in. (13.1 mm); $\Delta_{LL,allow} = 16(12)/360 = 0.533$ in. (13.5 mm), which is satisfactory.

### 5. Investigate the shearing stress under the computed total load

Refer to the AISC *Specification*. For the individual channel, $h = D - 2t = 6.79$ in. (172.5 mm); $h/t = 64.7$; $64,000,000/64.7^2 > 2/3f_b$; therefore, $v_{allow} = 13,330$ lb/sq.in. (91.9 MPa); the web area $= 0.105(6.79) = 0.713$ sq.in. (4.6 cm²); $V = 1/4(178)16 = 712$ lb (3.2 kN); $v = 712/0.713 < v_{allow}$, which is satisfactory. The allowable unit live load is therefore 128 lb/lin ft (1.87 kN/m).

## LIGHT-GAGE STEEL BEAM WITH STIFFENED COMPRESSION FLANGE

A beam of light-gage cold-formed steel has a hat cross section 8 × 12 in. (203.2 × 304.8 mm) of no. 12 gage, as shown in Fig. 24. The beam is simply supported on a span of 13 ft

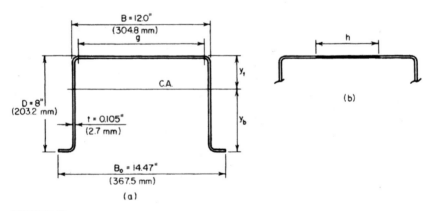

**FIGURE 24**

(3.96 m). If the yield-point stress is 33,000 lb/sq.in. (227.5 MPa), compute the allowable unit load for this member and the corresponding deflection.

## Calculation Procedure:

### 1. *Record the relevant properties of the entire cross-sectional area*

Refer to the AISC *Specification* and *Manual*. The allowable load is considered to be the ultimate load that the member will carry divided by a load factor of 1.65. At ultimate load, the bending stress varies considerably across the compression flange. To surmount the difficulty that this condition introduces, the AISC *Specification* permits the designer to assume that the stress is uniform across an *effective flange width* to be established in the prescribed manner. The investigation is complicated by the fact that the effective flange width and the bending stress in compression are interdependent quantities, for the following reason. The effective width depends on the compressive stress; the compressive stress, which is less than the basic design stress, depends on the location of the neutral axis; the location of the neutral axis, in turn, depends on the effective width.

The beam deflection is also calculated by establishing an effective flange width. However, since the beam capacity is governed by stresses at the ultimate load and the beam deflection is governed by stresses at working load, the effective widths associated with these two quantities are unequal.

A table in the AISC *Manual* contains two design values that afford a direct solution to this problem. However, the values are computed independently here to demonstrate how they are obtained. The notational system presented in the previous calculation procedure is used, as well as $A'$ = area of cross section exclusive of compression flange; $H$ = static moment of cross-sectional area with respect to top of section; $y_b$ and $y_t$ = distance from centroidal axis of cross section to bottom and top of section, respectively.

We use the AISC *Manual* to determine the relevant properties of the entire cross-sectional area, as shown in Fig. 24: $A$ = 3.13 sq.in. (20.2 cm²); $y_b$ = 5.23 in. (132.8 mm); $I_x$ = 26.8 in⁴ (1115.5 cm⁴); $R$ = ³/₁₆ in. (4.8 mm).

### 2. *Establish the value of $f_c$ for load determination*

Use the relation $(8040t^2/f_c^{0.5})\{1 - 2010/[(f_c^{0.5}g)/t]\} = (H/D)(f_c + f_b)/f_c - A'$. Substituting gives $g = B - 2(t + R) = 12.0 - 2(0.105 + 0.1875) = 11.415$ in. (289.9 mm); $g/t$ = 108.7; $gt$ = 1.20 sq.in. (7.74 cm²); $A$ = 3.13 − 1.20 = 1.93 sq.in. (12.45 cm²); $y_t$ = 8.0 − 5.23 = 2.77 in. (70.36 cm); $H$ = 3.13(2.77) = 8.670 in³ (142.1 cm³). The foregoing equation then reduces to $(88.64/f_c^{0.5})(1 - 18.49/f_c^{0.5}) = 1.084(f_c + 20,000)/f_c - 1.93$. By successive approximations, $f_c$ = 14,800 lb/sq.in. (102.0 MPa).

### 3. *Compute the corresponding effective flange width for load determination in accordance with the AISC* Manual

Thus, $b = (8040t/f_c^{0.5})1 - 2010/[(f_c^{0.5}g)/t] = (8040 \times 0.105/14,800^{0.5})[1 - 2010/(14,800^{0.5} \times 108.7)] = 5.885$ in. (149.5 mm).

### 4. *Locate the centroidal axis of the cross section having this effective width; check the value of $f_c$*

Refer to Fig. 24b. Thus $h = g - b = 11.415 - 5.885 = 5.530$ in. (140.5 mm); $ht$ = 0.581 sq.in. (3.75 cm²); $A$ = 3.13 − 0.581 = 2.549 sq.in. (16.45 cm²); $H$ = 8.670 in³ (142.1 cm³); $y_t$ = 8.670/2.549 = 3.40 in. (86.4 mm); $y_b$ = 4.60 in. (116.8 mm); $f_c = y_t/y_b$ = 3.40(20,000)/4.60 = 14,800 lb/sq.in. (102.0 MPa), which is satisfactory.

### 5. *Compute the allowable load*

The moment of inertia of the net section may be found by applying the value of the gross section and making the necessary corrections. Applying $S_x = I_x/y_b$, we get $I_x$ = 26.8 +

$3.13(3.40 - 2.77)^2 - 0.581(3.40 - 0.053)^2 = 21.53$ in$^4$ (896.15 cm$^4$). Then $S_x = 21.53/4.60 = 4.68$ in$^3$ (76.69 cm$^3$). This value agrees with that recorded in the AISC *Manual*.

Then $M = f_b S_x = 20,000(4.68)/12 = 7800$ ft·lb (10,576 N·m); $w = 8M/L^2 = 8(7800)/13^2 = 369$ lb/lin ft (5.39 kN/m).

### 6. Establish the value of $f_y$ for deflection determination

Apply $(10,320t^2/f_c^{0.5})[1 - 2580/(f_c^{0.5}g/t)] = (H/D)(f_c + f_b)/f_c - A'$, or $(113.8/f_c^{0.5}) \times (1 - 23.74/f_c^{0.5}) = 1.084(f_c + 20,000)/f_c - 1.93$. By successive approximation, $f_c = 13,300$ lb/sq.in. (91.7 MPa).

### 7. Compute the corresponding effective flange width for deflection determination

Thus, $b = (10,320t/f_c^{0.5})[1 - 2580/(f_c^{0.5}g/t)] = (10,320 \times 0.105/13,300^{0.5})[1 - 2580/(13,300^{0.5} \times 108.7)] = 7.462$ in. (189.5 mm).

### 8. Locate the centroidal axis of the cross section having this effective width; check the value of $f_c$

Thus $h = 11.415 - 7.462 = 3.953$ in. (100.4 mm); $ht = 0.415$ sq.in. (2.68 cm$^2$); $A = 313 - 0.415 = 2.715$ sq.in. (17.52 cm$^2$); $H = 8.670$ in$^3$ (142.1 cm$^3$); $y_t = 8.670/2.715 = 3.19$ in. (81.0 mm); $y_b = 4.81$ in. (122.2 mm); $f_c = (3.19/4.81)20,000 = 13,300$ lb/sq.in. (91.7 MPa), which is satisfactory.

### 9. Compute the deflection

For the net section, $I_x = 26.8 + 3.13(3.19 - 2.77)^2 - 0.415(3.19 - 0.053)^2 = 23.3$ in$^4$ (969.8 cm$^4$). This value agrees with that tabulated in the AISC *Manual*. The deflection is $\Delta = 5wL^4/(384EI_x) = 5(369)(13)^4(12)^3/[384(29.5)(10)^6 23.3] = 0.345$ in. (8.8 mm).

**Related Calculations.**    New stadiums for football and baseball teams feature unique civil engineering design approaches to steel beams, columns, and surface areas. Thus, the Arizona Cardinals' new football stadium in Glendale, Arizona, will have two Brunel trusses supporting the roof of the stadium.

The Brunel trusses also support two transparent retractable panels that permit open-air games in good weather. In inclement weather, the two panels can be moved together to enclose the roof of the stadium. When the roof panels are closed the entire stadium can be climate-controlled using the facilities' air-conditioning system.

To further simulate outdoor conditions for the playing field, the entire 100-yard-long (100 m) natural-grass field can be rolled outdoors. Then the natural grass can receive both sunlight and rain to help the grass grow in a normal way. The field weighs some 9500 tons. It is moved outdoors on 542 wheels and has built-in drainage and watering piping. Some 76 motor-driven steel wheels power the movement of the field into, and out of, the stadium.

When the playing field is moved out of the stadium, other uses that do not require grass turf can be made of the facility. Thus, concerts, circus performances, industry shows, conventions, and the like, can be held in the stadium while the turf field is outdoors.

This structure is one example of the advancing use of civil engineering to meet the requirements of today's growing population. A sports stadium is leading the way to innovative design concepts aimed at making people's lives safer and more enjoyable.

# SECTION 2
# REINFORCED AND PRESTRESSED CONCRETE ENGINEERING AND DESIGN

## MAX KURTZ, P.E.
*Consulting Engineer*

## TYLER G. HICKS, P.E.
*International Engineering Associates*

## PART 1

# REINFORCED CONCRETE

The design of reinforced-concrete members in this handbook is executed in accordance with the specification titled *Building Code Requirements for Reinforced Concrete* of the American Concrete Institute (ACI). The ACI *Reinforced Concrete Design Handbook* contains many useful tables that expedite design work. The designer should become thoroughly familiar with this handbook and use the tables it contains whenever possible.

The spacing of steel reinforcing bars in a concrete member is subject to the restrictions imposed by the ACI *Code*. With reference to the beam and slab shown in Fig. 1, the reinforcing steel is assumed, for simplicity, to be concentrated at its centroidal axis, and the effective depth of the flexural member is taken as the distance from the extreme compression fiber to this axis. (The term *depth* hereafter refers to the *effective* rather than the overall depth of the beam.) For design purposes, it is usually assumed that the distance from the exterior surface to the center of the first row of steel bars is $2^1/2$ in. (63.5 mm) in a beam with web stirrups, 2 in. (50.8 mm) in a beam without stirrups, and 1 in. (25.4 mm) in a slab. Where two rows of steel bars are provided, it is usually assumed that the distance from the exterior surface to the centroidal axis of the reinforcement is $3^1/2$ in. (88.9 mm). The ACI *Handbook* gives the minimum beam widths needed to accommodate various combinations of bars in one row.

In a well-proportioned beam, the width-depth ratio lies between 0.5 and 0.75. The width and overall depth are usually an even number of inches.

The basic notational system pertaining to reinforced concrete beams is as follows: $f_c'$ = ultimate compressive strength of concrete, lb/sq.in. (kPa); $f_c$ = maximum compressive stress in concrete, lb/sq.in. (kPa); $f_s$ = tensile stress in steel, lb/sq.in. (kPa); $f_y$ = yield-point stress in steel, lb/sq.in. (kPa); $\epsilon_c$ = strain of extreme compression fiber; $\epsilon_s$ = strain of steel; $b$ = beam width, in. (mm); $d$ = beam depth, in. (mm); $A_s$ = area of tension reinforcement, sq.in. (cm²); $p$ = tension-reinforcement ratio, $A_s/(bd)$; $q$ = tension-reinforcement index, $pf_y/f_c'$; $n$ = ratio of modulus of elasticity of steel to that of concrete, $E_s/E_c$; $C$ = resultant compressive force on transverse section, lb (N); $T$ = resultant tensile force on transverse section, lb (N).

Where the subscript $b$ is appended to a symbol, it signifies that the given quantity is evaluated at balanced-design conditions.

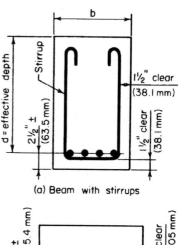

(a) Beam with stirrups

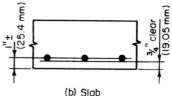

(b) Slab

**FIGURE 1.** Spacing of reinforcing bars.

# Design of Flexural Members by Ultimate-Strength Method

In the ultimate-strength design of a reinforced-concrete structure, as in the plastic design of a steel structure, the capacity of the structure is found by determining the load that will cause failure and dividing this result by the prescribed load factor. The load at impending failure is termed the *ultimate load*, and the maximum bending moment associated with this load is called the *ultimate moment*.

Since the tensile strength of concrete is relatively small, it is generally disregarded entirely in analyzing a beam. Consequently, the effective beam section is considered to comprise the reinforcing steel and the concrete on the compression side of the neutral axis, the concrete between these component areas serving merely as the ligature of the member.

The following notational system is applied in ultimate-strength design: $a$ = depth of compression block, in. (mm); $c$ = distance from extreme compression fiber to neutral axis, in. (mm); $\phi$ = capacity-reduction factor.

Where the subscript $u$ is appended to a symbol, it signifies that the given quantity is evaluated at ultimate load.

For simplicity (Fig. 2), designers assume that when the ultimate moment is attained at a given section, there is a uniform stress in the concrete extending across a depth $a$, and that $f_c = 0.85f_c'$, and $a = k_1c$, where $k_1$ has the value stipulated in the ACI *Code*.

A reinforced-concrete beam has three potential modes of failure: crushing of the concrete, which is assumed to occur when $\epsilon_c$ reaches the value of 0.003; yielding of the steel, which begins when $f_s$ reaches the value $f_y$; and the simultaneous crushing of the concrete and yielding of the steel. A beam that tends to fail by the third mode is said to be in *balanced design*. If the value of $p$ exceeds that corresponding to balanced design (i.e., if there is an excess of reinforcement), the beam tends to fail by crushing of the concrete. But if the value of $p$ is less than that corresponding to balanced design, the beam tends to fail by yielding of the steel.

Failure of the beam by the first mode would occur precipitously and without warning, whereas failure by the second mode would occur gradually, offering visible evidence of progressive failure. Therefore, to ensure that yielding of the steel would occur prior to failure of the concrete, the ACI *Code* imposes an upper limit of $0.75p_b$ on $p$.

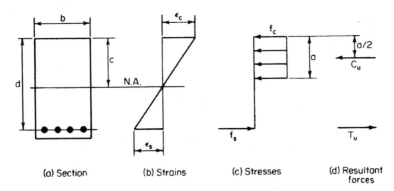

(a) Section     (b) Strains     (c) Stresses     (d) Resultant forces

**FIGURE 2.** Conditions at ultimate moment.

To allow for material imperfections, defects in workmanship, etc., the *Code* introduces the capacity-reduction factor $\phi$. A section of the *Code* sets $\phi = 0.90$ with respect to flexure and $\phi = 0.85$ with respect to diagonal tension, bond, and anchorage.

The basic equations for the ultimate-strength design of a rectangular beam reinforced solely in tension are

$$C_u = 0.85abf_c' \qquad T_u = A_s f_y \tag{1}$$

$$q = \frac{[A_s/(bd)]f_y}{f_c'} \tag{2}$$

$$a = 1.18qd \qquad c = \frac{1.18qd}{k_1} \tag{3}$$

$$M_u = \phi A_s f_y \left( d - \frac{a}{2} \right) \tag{4}$$

$$M_u = \phi A_s f_y d (1 - 0.59q) \tag{5}$$

$$M_u = \phi b d^2 f_c' q (1 - 0.59q) \tag{6}$$

$$A_s = \frac{bdf_c - [(bdf_c)^2 - 2bf_c M_u/\phi]^{0.5}}{f_y} \tag{7}$$

$$p_b = \frac{0.85k_1 f_c'}{f_y} \frac{87,000}{87,000 + f_y} \tag{8}$$

$$q_b = 0.85k_1 \left( \frac{87,000}{87,000 + f_y} \right) \tag{9}$$

In accordance with the *Code*,

$$q_{max} = 0.75q_b = 0.6375k_1 \left( \frac{87,000}{87,000 + f_y} \right) \tag{10}$$

Figure 3 shows the relationship between $M_u$ and $A_s$ for a beam of given size. As $A_s$ increases, the internal forces $C_u$ and $T_u$ increase proportionately, but $M_u$ increases by a smaller proportion because the action line of $C_u$ is depressed. The $M_u$-$A_s$ diagram is parabolic, but its curvature is small. By comparing the coordinates of two points $P_a$ and $P_b$, the following result is obtained, in which the subscripts correspond to that of the given point:

$$\frac{M_{ua}}{A_{sa}} > \frac{M_{ub}}{A_{sb}} \tag{11}$$

where $A_{sa} < A_{sb}$

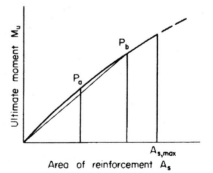

**FIGURE 3**

## CAPACITY OF A RECTANGULAR BEAM

A rectangular beam having a width of 12 in. (304.8 mm) and an effective depth of 19.5 in. (495.3 mm) is reinforced with steel bars having an area of 5.37 sq.in. (34.647 cm$^2$). The beam is made of 2500-lb/sq.in. (17,237.5-kPa) concrete, and the steel has a yield-point stress of 40,000 lb/sq.in. (275,800 kPa). Compute the ultimate moment this beam may resist (*a*) without referring to any design tables and without applying the basic equations of ultimate-strength design except those that are readily apparent; (*b*) by applying the basic equations.

### Calculation Procedure:

#### 1. Compute the area of reinforcement for balanced design
Use the relation $\epsilon_s = f_y/E_s = 40,000/29,000,000 = 0.00138$. For balanced design, $c/d = \epsilon_c/(\epsilon_c + \epsilon_s) = 0.003/(0.003 + 0.00138) = 0.685$. Solving for $c$ by using the relation for $c/d$, we find $c = 13.36$ in. (339.344 mm). Also, $a = k_1 c = 0.85(13.36) = 11.36$ in. (288.544 mm). Then $T_u = C_u = ab(0.85)f'_c = 11.36(12)(0.85)(2500) = 290,000$ lb (1,289,920 N); $A_s = T_u/f_y = 290,000/40,000 = 7.25$ sq.in. (46,777 cm$^2$); and $0.75A_s = 5.44$ sq.in. (35.097 cm$^2$). In the present instance, $A_s = 5.37$ sq.in. (34.647 cm$^2$). This is acceptable.

#### 2. Compute the ultimate-moment capacity of this member
Thus $T_u = A_s f_y = 5.37(40,000) = 215,000$ lb (956,320 N); $C_u = ab(0.85)f'_c = 25,500a = 215,000$ lb (956,320 N); $a = 8.43$ in. (214.122 mm); $M_u = \phi T_u(d - a/2) = 0.90(215,000)(19.5 - 8.43/2) = 2,960,000$ in.·lb (334,421 N·m). These two steps comprise the solution to part *a*. The next two steps comprise the solution of part *b*.

#### 3. Apply Eq. 10; ascertain whether the member satisfies the Code
Thus, $q_{max} = 0.6375k_1(87,000)/(87,000 + f_y) = 0.6375(0.85)(87/127) = 0.371$; $q = [A_s/(bd)]f'_c = [5.37/(12 \times 19.5)]40/2.5 = 0.367$. This is acceptable.

#### 4. Compute the ultimate-moment capacity
Applying Eq. 5 yields $M_u = \phi A_s f_y d(1 - 0.59q) = 0.90(5.37)(40,000)(19.5)(1 - 0.59 \times 0.367) = 2,960,000$ in.·lb (334,421 N·m). This agrees exactly with the result computed in step 2.

## DESIGN OF A RECTANGULAR BEAM

A beam on a simple span of 20 ft (6.1 m) is to carry a uniformly distributed live load of 1670 lb/lin ft (24,372 N/m) and a dead load of 470 lb/lin ft (6859 N/m), which includes the estimated weight of the beam. Architectural details restrict the beam width to 12 in. (304.8 mm) and require that the depth be made as small as possible. Design the section, using $f'_c = 3000$ lb/sq.in. (20,685 kPa) and $f_y = 40,000$ lb/sq.in. (275,800 kPa).

### Calculation Procedure:

#### 1. Compute the ultimate load for which the member is to be designed
The beam depth is minimized by providing the maximum amount of reinforcement permitted by the *Code*. From the previous calculation procedure, $q_{max} = 0.371$.

Use the load factors given in the *Code*: $w_{DL} = 470$ lb/lin ft (6859 N/m); $w_{LL} = 1670$ lb/lin ft (24,372 N/m); $L = 20$ ft (6.1 m). Then $w_u = 1.5(470) + 1.8(1670) = 3710$ lb/lin ft (54,143 N/m); $M_u = \frac{1}{8}(3710)(20)^2 12 = 2,230,000$ in.·lb (251,945.4 N·m).

## 2. Establish the beam size

Solve Eq. 6 for $d$. Thus, $d^2 = M_u/\phi bf_c'q(1 - 0.59q)] = 2,230,000/[0.90(12)(3000) \times (0.371)(0.781)]$; $d = 15.4$ in. (391.16 mm).

Set $d = 15.5$ in. (393.70 mm). Then the corresponding reduction in the value of $q$ is negligible.

## 3. Select the reinforcing bars

Using Eq. 2, we find $A_s = qbdf_c'/f_y = 0.371(12)(15.5)(3/40) = 5.18$ sq.in. (33.421 cm²). Use four no. 9 and two no. 7 bars, for which $A_s = 5.20$ sq.in. (33.550 cm²). This group of bars cannot be accommodated in the 12-in. (304.8-mm) width and must therefore be placed in two rows. The overall beam depth will therefore be 19 in. (482.6 mm).

## 4. Summarize the design

Thus, the beam size is $12 \times 19$ in. (304.8 × 482.6 mm); reinforcement, four no. 9 and two no. 7 bars.

# DESIGN OF THE REINFORCEMENT IN A RECTANGULAR BEAM OF GIVEN SIZE

A rectangular beam 9 in. (228.6 mm) wide with a 13.5-in. (342.9-mm) effective depth is to sustain an ultimate moment of 95 ft·kips (128.8 kN·m). Compute the area of reinforcement, using $f_c' = 3000$ lb/sq.in. (20,685 kPa) and $f_y = 40,000$ lb/sq.in. (275,800 kPa).

## Calculation Procedure:

### 1. Investigate the adequacy of the beam size

From previous calculation procedures, $q_{max} = 0.371$. By Eq. 6, $M_{u,max} = 0.90 \times (9)(13.5)^2(3)(0.371)(0.781) = 1280$ in·kips (144.6 kN·m); $M_u = 95(12) = 1140$ in.·kips (128.8 kN·m). This is acceptable.

### 2. Apply Eq. 7 to evaluate $A_s$

Thus, $f_c = 0.85(3) = 2.55$ kips/sq.in. (17.582 MPa); $bdf_c = 9(13.5)(2.55) = 309.8$ kips (1377.99 kN); $A_s = [309.8 - (309.8^2 - 58,140)^{0.5}]/40 = 2.88$ sq.in. (18.582 cm²).

# CAPACITY OF A T BEAM

Determine the ultimate moment that may be resisted by the T beam in Fig. 4a if $f_c' = 3000$ lb/sq.in. (20,685 kPa) and $f_y = 40,000$ lb/sq.in. (275,800 kPa).

## Calculation Procedure:

### 1. Compute $T_u$ and the resultant force that may be developed in the flange

Thus, $T_u = 8.20(40,000) = 328,000$ lb (1,458,944 N); $f_c = 0.85(3000) = 2550$ lb/sq.in. (17,582.3 kPa); $C_{uf} = 18(6)(2550) = 275,400$ lb (1,224,979 N). Since $C_{uf} < T_u$, the deficiency must be supplied by the web.

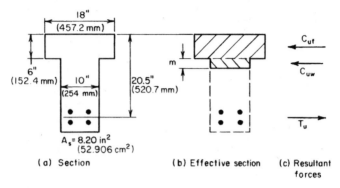

(a) Section          (b) Effective section     (c) Resultant forces

**FIGURE 4**

### 2. Compute the resultant force developed in the web and the depth of the stress block in the web

Thus, $C_{uw} = 328,000 - 275,400 = 52,600$ lb (233,964.8 N); $m$ = depth of the stress block $= 52,600/[2550(10)] = 2.06$ in. (52.324 mm).

### 3. Evaluate the ultimate-moment capacity

Thus, $M_u = 0.90[275,400(20.5 - 3) + 52,600(20.5 - 6 - 1.03)] = 4,975,000$ in.·lb (562,075.5 N·m).

### 4. Determine if the reinforcement complies with the Code

Let $b'$ = width of web, in. (mm); $A_{s1}$ = area of reinforcement needed to resist the compressive force in the overhanging portion of the flange, sq.in. (cm²); $A_{s2}$ = area of reinforcement needed to resist the compressive force in the remainder of the section, sq.in. (cm²). Then $p_2 = A_{s2}/(b'd)$; $A_{s1} = 2550(6)(18 - 10)740,000 = 3.06$ sq.in. (19.743 cm²); $A_{s2} = 8.20 - 3.06 = 5.14$ sq.in. (33.163 cm²). Then $p_2 = 5.14/[10(20.5)] = 0.025$.

A section of the ACI *Code* subjects the reinforcement ratio $p_2$ to the same restriction as that in a rectangular beam. By Eq. 8, $p_{2,\max} = 0.75p_b = 0.75(0.85)(0.85)(3/40)(87/127) = 0.0278 > 0.025$. This is acceptable.

## CAPACITY OF A T BEAM OF GIVEN SIZE

The T beam in Fig. 5 is made of 3000-lb/sq.in. (20,685-kPa) concrete, and $f_y = 40,000$ lb/sq.in. (275,800 kPa). Determine the ultimate-moment capacity of this member if it is reinforced in tension only.

### Calculation Procedure:

### 1. Compute $C_{u1}$, $C_{u2,\max}$, and $s_{max}$

Let the subscript 1 refer to the overhanging portion of the flange and the subscript 2 refer to the remainder of the compression zone. Then $f_c = 0.85(3000) = 2550$ lb/sq.in. (17,582.3 kPa); $C_{u1} = 2550(5)(16 - 10) = 76,500$ lb (340,272 N). From the previous calculation procedure, $p_{2,\max} = 0.0278$. Then $A_{s2,\max} = 0.0278(10)(19.5) = 5.42$ sq.in. (34.970 cm²);

$C_{u2,max} = 5.42(40,000) = 216,800$ lb
$(964,326.4$ N$)$; $s_{max} = 216,800/[10(2550)]$
$= 8.50$ in. $(215.9$ mm$)$.

**2. Compute the ultimate-moment capacity**
Thus, $M_{u,max} = 0.90[(76,500(19.5 - 5/2)$
$+ 216,800(19.5 - 8.50/2)] = 4,145,000$
in.·lb $(468,300$ N·m$)$.

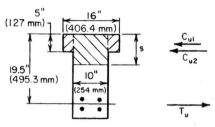

**FIGURE 5**

# DESIGN OF REINFORCEMENT IN A T BEAM OF GIVEN SIZE

The T beam in Fig. 5 is to resist an ultimate moment of 3,960,000 in.·lb (447,400.8 N·m). Determine the required area of reinforcement, using $f_c' = 3000$ lb/sq.in. (20,685 kPa) and $f_y = 40,000$ lb/sq.in. (275,800 kPa).

## Calculation Procedure:

### 1. Obtain a moment not subject to reduction
From the previous calculation procedure, the ultimate-moment capacity of this member is 4,145,000 in.·lb (468,300 N·m). To facilitate the design, divide the given ultimate moment $M_u$ by the capacity-reduction factor to obtain a moment $M_u'$ that is not subject to reduction. Thus $M_u' = 3,960,000/0.9 = 4,400,000$ in.·lb (497,112 N·m).

### 2. Compute the value of s associated with the given moment
From step 2 in the previous calculation procedure, $M_{u1}' = 1,300,000$ in.·lb (146,874 N·m). Then $M_{u2}' = 4,400,000 - 1,300,000 = 3,100,000$ in.·lb (350,238 N·m). But $M_{u2}' = 2550(10s)(19.5 - s/2)$, so $s = 7.79$ in. (197.866 mm).

### 3. Compute the area of reinforcement
Thus, $C_{u2} = M_{u2}'/(d - 1/2s) = (19.5 - 3.90) = 198,700$ lb (883,817.6 N). From step 1 of the previous calculation procedure, $C_{u1} = 76,500$ lb (340,272 N); $T_u = 76,500 + 198,700 = 275,200$ lb (1,224,089.6 N); $A_s = 275,200/40,000 = 6.88$ sq.in. (174.752 mm).

### 4. Verify the solution
To verify the solution, compute the ultimate-moment capacity of the member. Use the notational system given in earlier calculation procedures. Thus, $C_{uf} = 16(5)(2550) = 204,000$ lb (907,392 N); $C_{uw} = 275,200 - 204,000 = 71,200$ lb (316,697.6 N); $m = 71,200/[2550(10)] = 2.79$ in. (70.866 mm); $M_u = 0.90 [204,000(19.5 - 2.5) + 71,200(19.5 - 5 - 1.40)] = 3,960,000$ in.·lb (447,400.8 N·m). Thus, the result is verified because the computed moment equals the given moment.

# REINFORCEMENT AREA FOR A DOUBLY REINFORCED RECTANGULAR BEAM

A beam that is to resist an ultimate moment of 690 ft·kips (935.6 kN·m) is restricted to a 14-in. (355.6-mm) width and 24-in. (609.6-mm) total depth. Using $f_c' = 5000$ lb/sq.in. and $f_y = 50,000$ lb/sq.in. (344,750 kPa), determine the area of reinforcement.

**Calculation Procedure:**

### 1. *Compute the values of $q_b$, $q_{max}$, and $p_{max}$ for a singly reinforced beam*

As the following calculations will show, it is necessary to reinforce the beam both in tension and in compression. In Fig. 6, let $A_s$ = area of tension reinforcement, sq.in. (cm²); $A'_s$ = area of compression reinforcement, sq.in. (cm²); $d'$ = distance from compression face of concrete to centroid of compression reinforcement, in. (mm); $f_s$ = stress in tension steel, lb/sq.in. (kPa); $f'_s$ = stress in compression steel, lb/sq.in. (kPa); $\epsilon'_s$ = strain in compression steel; $p = A_s/(bd)$; $p' = A'_s/(bd)$; $q = pf_y/f'_c$; $M_u$ = ultimate moment to be resisted by member, in.·lb (N·m); $M_{u1}$ = ultimate-moment capacity of member if reinforced solely in tension; $M_{u2}$ = increase in ultimate-moment capacity resulting from use of compression reinforcement; $C_{u1}$ = resultant force in concrete, lb (N); $C_{u2}$ = resultant force in compression steel, lb (N).

If $f' = f_y$, the tension reinforcement may be resolved into two parts having areas of $A_s - A'_s$ and $A'_s$. The first part, acting in combination with the concrete, develops the moment $M_{u1}$. The second part, acting in combination with the compression reinforcement, develops the moment $M_{s2}$.

To ensure that failure will result from yielding of the tension steel rather than crushing of the concrete, the ACI *Code* limits $p - p'$ to a maximum value of $0.75p_b$, where $p_b$ has the same significance as for a singly reinforced beam. Thus the *Code*, in effect, permits setting $f'_s = f_y$ if inception of yielding in the compression steel will precede or coincide with failure of the concrete at balanced-design ultimate moment. This, however, introduces an inconsistency, for the limit imposed on $p - p'$ precludes balanced design.

By Eq. 9, $q_b = 0.85(0.80)(87/137) = 0.432$; $q_{max} = 0.75(0.432) = 0.324$; $p_{max} = 0.324(5/50) = 0.0324$.

### 2. *Compute $M_{u1}$, $M_{u2}$, and $C_{u2}$*

Thus, $M_u = 690,000(12) = 8,280,000$ in.·lb (935,474.4 N·m). Since two rows of tension bars are probably required, $d = 24 - 3.5 = 20.5$ in. (520.7 mm). By Eq. 6, $M_{u1} = 0.90(14)(20.5)^2(5000) \times (0.324)(0.809) = 6,940,000$ in.·lb (784,081.2 N·m); $M_{u2} = 8,280,000 - 6,940,000 = 1,340,000$ in.·lb (151,393.2 N·m); $C_{u2} = M_{u2}/(d - d') = 1,340,000/(20.5 - 2.5) = 74,400$ lb (330,931.2 N).

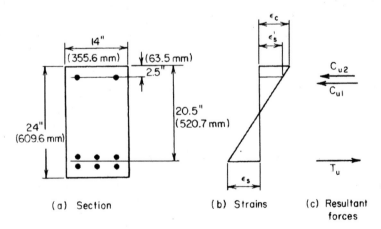

(a) Section          (b) Strains          (c) Resultant forces

**FIGURE 6.** Doubly reinforced rectangular beam.

### 3. Compute the value of $\epsilon_s'$ under the balanced-design ultimate moment

Compare this value with the strain at incipient yielding. By Eq. 3, $c_b = 1.18q_bd/k_1 = 1.18(0.432)(20.5)/0.80 = 13.1$ in. (332.74 mm); $\epsilon_s'/\epsilon_c = (13.1 - 2.5)/13.1 = 0.809$; $\epsilon_s' = 0.809(0.003) = 0.00243$; $\epsilon_y = 50/29,000 = 0.0017 < \epsilon_s'$. The compression reinforcement will therefore yield before the concrete fails, and $f_s' = f_y$ may be used.

### 4. Alternatively, test the compression steel for yielding

Apply

$$p - p' \geq \frac{0.85k_1 f_c' d'(87,000)}{f_y d(87,000 - f_y)} \tag{12}$$

If this relation obtains, the compression steel will yield. The value of the right-hand member is $0.85(0.80)(5/50)(2.5/20.5)(87/37) = 0.0195$. From the preceding calculations, $p - p' = 0.0324 > 0.0195$. This is acceptable.

### 5. Determine the areas of reinforcement

By Eq. 2, $A_s = A_s' = q_{max}bdf_c'/f_y = 0.324(14)(20.5)(5/50) = 9.30$ sq.in. (60.00 cm²); $A_s' = C_{u2}/(\phi f_y) = 74,400/[0.90(50,000)] = 1.65$ sq.in. (10.646 cm²); $A_s = 9.30 + 1.65 = 10.95$ sq.in. (70.649 cm²).

### 6. Verify the solution

Apply the following equations for the ultimate-moment capacity:

$$a = \frac{(A_s - A_s')f_y}{0.85f_c'b} \tag{13}$$

So $a = 9.30(50,000)/[0.85(5000)(14)] = 7.82$ in. (198.628 mm). Also,

$$M_u = \phi f_y \left[ (A_s - A_s')\left(d - \frac{a}{2}\right) + A_s'(d - d') \right] \tag{14}$$

So $M_u = 0.90(50,000)(9.30 \times (16.59 + 1.65 \times 18) = 8,280,000$ in.·lb (935,474.4 N·m), as before. Therefore, the solution has been verified.

## DESIGN OF WEB REINFORCEMENT

A 15-in. (381-mm) wide 22.5-in. (571.5-mm) effective-depth beam carries a uniform ultimate load of 10.2 kips/lin ft (148.86 kN/m). The beam is simply supported, and the clear distance between supports is 18 ft (5.5 m). Using $f_c' = 3000$ lb/sq.in. (20,685 kPa) and $f_y = 40,000$ lb/sq.in. (275,800 kPa), design web reinforcement in the form of vertical U stirrups for this beam.

### Calculation Procedure:

### 1. Construct the shearing-stress diagram for half-span

The ACI *Code* provides two alternative methods for computing the allowable shearing stress on an unreinforced web. The more precise method recognizes the contribution of both the shearing stress and flexural stress on a cross section in producing diagonal

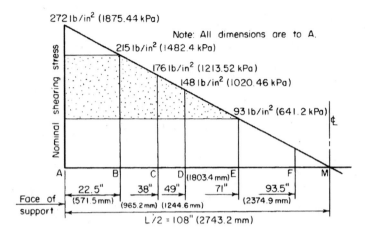

**FIGURE 7.** Shearing stress diagram.

tension. The less precise and more conservative method restricts the shearing stress to a stipulated value that is independent of the flexural stress.

For simplicity, the latter method is adopted here. A section of the *Code* sets $\phi = 0.85$ with respect to the design of web reinforcement. Let $v_u$ = nominal ultimate shearing stress, lb/sq.in. (kPa); $v_c$ = shearing stress resisted by concrete, lb/sq.in. (kPa); $v_u'$ = shearing stress resisted by the web reinforcement, lb/sq.in. (kPa); $A_v$ = total cross-sectional area of stirrup, sq.in. (cm$^2$); $V_u$ = ultimate vertical shear at section, lb (N); $s$ = center-to-center spacing of stirrups, in. (mm).

The shearing-stress diagram for half-span is shown in Fig. 7. Establish the region $AF$ within which web reinforcement is required. The *Code* sets the allowable shearing stress in the concrete at

$$v_c = 2\phi(f_c')^{0.5} \tag{15}$$

The equation for nominal ultimate shearing stress is

$$v_u = \frac{V_u}{bd} \tag{16}$$

Then, $v_c = 2(0.85)(3000)^{0.5} = 93$ lb/sq.in. (641.2 kPa).

At the face of the support, $V_u = 9(10,200) = 91,800$ lb (408,326.4 N); $v_u = 91,800/[15(22.5)] = 272$ lb/sq.in. (1875.44 kPa). The slope of the shearing-stress diagram $= -272/108 = -2.52$ lb/(in$^2$·in.) ($-0.684$ kPa/mm). At distance $d$ from the face of the support, $v_u = 272 - 22.5(2.52) = 215$ lb/sq.in. (1482.4 kPa); $v_u' = 215 - 93 = 122$ lb/sq.in. (841.2 kPa).

Let $E$ denote the section at which $v_u = v_c$. Then, $AE = (272 - 93)/2.52 = 71$ in. (1803.4 mm). A section of the *Code* requires that web reinforcement be continued for a distance $d$ beyond the section where $v_u = v_c$; $AF = 71 + 22.5 = 93.5$ in. (2374.9 mm).

### 2. Check the beam size for Code compliance
Thus, $v_{u,\max} = 10\phi(f_c')^{0.5} = 466 > 215$ lb/sq.in. (1482.4 kPa). This is acceptable.

### 3. Select the stirrup size
Equate the spacing near the support to the minimum practical value, which is generally considered to be 4 in. (101.6 mm). The equation for stirrup spacing is

$$s = \frac{\phi A_v f_y}{v_c' b} \tag{17}$$

Then $A_v = s v_u' b/(\phi f_y) = 4(122)(15)/[0.85(40,000)] = 0.215$ sq.in. (1.3871 cm²). Since each stirrup is bent into the form of a U, the total cross-sectional area is twice that of a straight bar. Use no. 3 stirrups for which $A_v = 2(0.11) = 0.22$ sq.in. (1.419 cm²).

### 4. Establish the maximum allowable stirrup spacing
Apply the criteria of the Code, or $s_{max} = d/4$ if $v > 6\phi(f_c')^{0.5}$. The right-hand member of this inequality has the value 279 lb/sq.in. (1923.70 kPa), and this limit therefore does not apply. Then $s_{max} = d/2 = 11.25$ in. (285.75 mm), or $s_{max} = A_v/(0.0015b) = 0.22/[0.0015(15)] = 9.8$ in. (248.92 mm). The latter limit applies, and the stirrup spacing will therefore be restricted to 9 in. (228.6 mm).

### 5. Locate the beam sections at which the required stirrup spacing is 6 in. (152.4 mm) and 9 in. (228.6 mm)
Use Eq. 17. Then $\phi A_v f_y/b = 0.85(0.22)(40,000)/15 = 499$ lb/in. (87.38 kN/m). At $C$: $v_u' = 499/6 = 83$ lb/sq.in. (572.3 kPa); $v_u = 83 + 93 = 176$ lb/sq.in. (1213.52 kPa); $AC = (272 - 176)/2.52 = 38$ in. (965.2 mm). At $D$: $v_u' = 499/9 = 55$ lb/sq.in. (379.2 kPa); $v_u = 55 + 93 = 148$ lb/sq.in. (1020.46 kPa); $AD = (272 - 148)/2.52 = 49$ in. (1244.6 mm).

### 6. Devise a stirrup spacing conforming to the computed results
The following spacing, which requires 17 stirrups for each half of the span, is satisfactory and conforms with the foregoing results:

| Quantity | Spacing, in. (mm) | Total, in. (mm) | Distance from last stirrup to face of support, in. (mm) |
|---|---|---|---|
| 1 | 2  (50.8) | 2  (50.8) | 2  (50.8) |
| 9 | 4 (101.6) | 36  (914.4) | 38  (965.2) |
| 2 | 6 (152.4) | 12  (304.8) | 50 (1270) |
| 5 | 9 (228.6) | 45 (1143) | 95 (2413) |

---

## DETERMINATION OF BOND STRESS

---

A beam of 4000-lb/sq.in. (27,580-kPa) concrete has an effective depth of 15 in. (381 mm) and is reinforced with four no. 7 bars. Determine the ultimate bond stress at a section where the ultimate shear is 72 kips (320.3 kN). Compare this with the allowable stress.

### Calculation Procedure:

### 1. Determine the ultimate shear flow $h_u$
The adhesion of the concrete and steel must be sufficiently strong to resist the horizontal shear flow. Let $u_u$ = ultimate bond stress, lb/sq.in. (kPa); $V_u$ = ultimate vertical shear, lb (N);

$\Sigma o$ = sum of perimeters of reinforcing bars, in. (mm). Then the ultimate shear flow at any plane between the neutral axis and the reinforcing steel is $h_u = V_u/(d - a/2)$.

In conformity with the notational system of the working-stress method, the distance $d - a/2$ is designated as $jd$. Dividing the shear flow by the area of contact in a unit length and introducing the capacity-reduction factor yield

$$u_u = \frac{V_u}{\phi \Sigma ojd} \tag{18}$$

A section of the ACI *Code* sets $\phi = 0.85$ with respect to bond, and $j$ is usually assigned the approximate value of 0.875 when this equation is used.

**2. Calculate the bond stress**
Thus, $\Sigma o = 11.0$ in. (279.4 mm), from the ACI *Handbook*. Then $u_u$ = 72,000/[0.85(11.0) (0.875) × (15)] = 587 lb/sq.in. (4047.4 kPa).

The allowable stress is given in the *Code* as

$$u_{u,\text{allow}} = \frac{9.5(f_c')^{0.5}}{D} \tag{19}$$

but not above 800 lb/sq.in. (5516 kPa). Thus, $u_{u,\text{allow}}$ = 9.5(4,000)$^{0.5}$/0.875 = 687 lb/sq.in. (4736.9 kPa).

# DESIGN OF INTERIOR SPAN OF A ONE-WAY SLAB

A floor slab that is continuous over several spans carries a live load of 120 lb/sq.ft. (5745 N/m²) and a dead load of 40 lb/sq.ft. (1915 N/m²), exclusive of its own weight. The clear spans are 16 ft (4.9 m). Design the interior span, using $f_c'$ = 3000 lb/sq.in. (20,685 kPa) and $f_y$ = 50,000 lb/sq.in. (344,750 kPa).

**Calculation Procedure:**

**1. Find the minimum thickness of the slab as governed by the Code**
Refer to Fig. 8. The maximum potential positive or negative moment may be found by applying the type of loading that will induce the critical moment and then evaluating this moment. However, such an analysis is time-consuming. Hence, it is wise to apply the moment equations recommended in the ACI *Code* whenever the span and loading conditions satisfy the requirements given there. The slab is designed by considering a 12-in. (304.8-mm) strip as an individual beam, making $b$ = 12 in. (304.8 mm).

Assuming that $L$ = 17 ft (5.2 m), we know the minimum thickness of the slab is $t_{\text{min}} = L/35 = 17(12)/35 = 5.8$ in. (147.32 mm).

**2. Assuming a slab thickness, compute the ultimate load on the member**
Tentatively assume $t$ = 6 in. (152.4 mm). Then the beam weight = (6/12)(150 lb/ft³ = 75 lb/lin ft (1094.5 N/m). Also, $w_u$ = 1.5(40 + 75) + 1.8(120) = 390 lb/lin ft (5691.6 N/m).

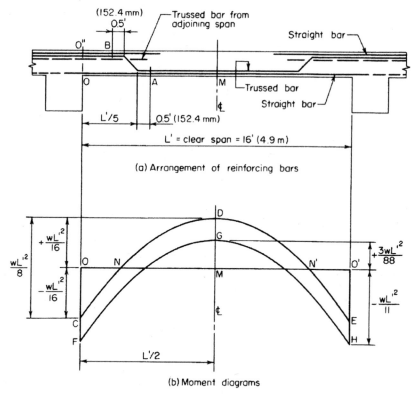

(a) Arrangement of reinforcing bars

(b) Moment diagrams

**FIGURE 8**

### 3. Compute the shearing stress associated with the assumed beam size

From the *Code* for an interior span, $V_u = \frac{1}{2}w_uL' = \frac{1}{2}(390)(16) = 3120$ lb (13,877.8 N); $d = 6 - 1 = 5$ in. (127 mm); $v_u = 3120/[12(5)] = 52$ lb/sq.in. (358.54 kPa); $v_c = 93$ lb/sq.in. (641.2 kPa). This is acceptable.

### 4. Compute the two critical moments

Apply the appropriate moment equations. Compare the computed moments with the moment capacity of the assumed beam size to ascertain whether the size is adequate. Thus, $M_{u,neg} = (\frac{1}{11}/w_uL'^2) = (\frac{1}{11})(390)(16)^2(12) = 108,900$ in.·lb (12,305.5 N·m), where the value 12 converts the dimension to inches. Then $M_{u,pos} = \frac{1}{16}w_uL'^2 = 74,900$ in.·lb (8462.2 N·m). By Eq. 10, $q_{max} = 0.6375(0.85)(87/137) = 0.344$. By Eq. 6, $M_{u,allow} = 0.90(12)(5)^2(3000)(0.344)(0.797) = 222,000$ in.·lb (25,081.5 N·m). This is acceptable. The slab thickness will therefore be made 6 in. (152.4 mm).

### 5. Compute the area of reinforcement associated with each critical moment

By Eq. 7, $bdf_c = 12(5)(2.55) = 153.0$ kips (680.54 kN); then $2bf_cM_{u,neg}/\phi = 2(12)(2.55)(108.9)/0.90 = 7405$ kips$^2$ (146,505.7 kN$^2$); $A_{s,neg} = [153.0 - (153.0^2 - 7405)^{0.5}]/50 = 0.530$ sq.in. (3.4196 cm$^2$). Similarly, $A_{s,pos} = 0.353$ sq.in. (2.278 cm$^2$).

## 6. *Select the reinforcing bars, and locate the bend points*

For positive reinforcement, use no. 4 trussed bars 13 in. (330.2 mm) on centers, alternating with no. 4 straight bars 13 in. (330.2 mm) on centers, thus obtaining $A_s = 0.362$ sq.in. (2.336 cm²).

For negative reinforcement, supplement the trussed bars over the support with no. 4 straight bars 13 in. (330.2 mm) on centers, thus obtaining $A_s = 0.543$ sq.in. (3.502 cm²).

The trussed bars are usually bent upward at the fifth points, as shown in Fig. 8a. The reinforcement satisfies a section of the ACI *Code* which requires that "at least . . . one-fourth the positive moment reinforcement in continuous beams shall extend along the same face of the beam into the support at least 6 in. (152.4 mm)."

## 7. *Investigate the adequacy of the reinforcement beyond the bend points*

In accordance with the *Code*, $A_{min} = A_t = 0.0020bt = 0.0020(12)(6) = 0.144$ sq.in. (0.929 cm²).

A section of the *Code* requires that reinforcing bars be extended beyond the point at which they become superfluous with respect to flexure a distance equal to the effective depth or 12 bar diameters, whichever is greater. In the present instance, extension $= 12(0.5) = 6$ in. (152.4 mm). Therefore, the trussed bars in effect terminate as positive reinforcement at section $A$ (Fig. 8). Then $L'/5 = 3.2$ ft (0.98 m); $AM = 8 - 3.2 - 0.5 = 4.3$ ft (1.31 m).

The conditions immediately to the left of $A$ are $M_u = M_{u.pos} - \frac{1}{2}w_u(AM)^2 = 74,900 - \frac{1}{2}(390)(4.3)^2(12) = 31,630$ in.·lb (3573.56 N·m); $A_{s.pos} = 0.181$ sq.in. (1.168 cm²); $q = 0.181(50)/[12(5)(3)] = 0.0503$. By Eq. 5, $M_{u.allow} = 0.90(0.181)(50,000)(5)(0.970) = 39,500$ in.·lb (4462.7 N·m). This is acceptable.

Alternatively, Eq. 11 may be applied to obtain the following conservative approximation: $M_{u.allow} = 74,900(0.181)/0.353 = 38,400$ in.·lb (4338.43 N·m).

The trussed bars in effect terminate as negative reinforcement at $B$, where $O''B = 3.2 - 0.33 - 0.5 = 2.37$ ft (72.23 m). The conditions immediately to the right of $B$ are $|M_u| = M_{u.neg} - 12(3120 \times 2.37 - \frac{1}{2} \times 390 \times 2.37^2) = 33,300$ in.·lb (3762.23 N·m). Then $A_{s.neg} = 0.362$ sq.in. (2.336 cm²). As a conservative approximation, $M_{u.allow} = 108,900(0.362)/0.530 = 74,400$ in.·lb (8405.71 N·m). This is acceptable.

## 8. *Locate the point at which the straight bars at the top may be discontinued*

## 9. *Investigate the bond stresses*

In accordance with Eq. 19, $U_{u.allow} = 800$ lb/sq.in. (5516 kPa).

If $CDE$ in Fig. 8b represents the true moment diagram, the bottom bars are subjected to bending stress in the interval $NN'$. Manifestly, the maximum bond stress along the bottom occurs at these boundary points (points of contraflexure), where the shear is relatively high and the straight bars alone are present. Thus $MN = 0.354L'$; $V_u$ at $N/V_u$ at support $= 0.354L'/(0.5L') = 0.71$; $V_u$ at $N = 0.71(3120) = 2215$ lb (9852.3 N). By Eq. 18, $u_u = V_u/(\phi\Sigma ojd) = 2215/[0.85(1.45)(0.875)(5)] = 411$ lb/sq.in. (2833.8 kPa). This is acceptable. It is apparent that the maximum bond stress in the top bars has a smaller value.

## ANALYSIS OF A TWO-WAY SLAB BY THE YIELD-LINE THEORY

The slab in Fig. 9a is simply supported along all four edges and is isotropically reinforced. It supports a uniformly distributed ultimate load of $w_u$ lb/sq.ft. (kPa). Calculate the ultimate unit moment $m_u$ for which the slab must be designed.

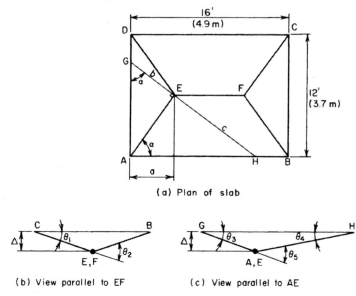

(a) Plan of slab

(b) View parallel to EF      (c) View parallel to AE

**FIGURE 9.** Analysis of two-way slab by mechanism method.

## Calculation Procedure:

### 1. Draw line GH perpendicular to AE at E; express distances b and c in terms of a

Consider a slab to be reinforced in orthogonal directions. If the reinforcement in one direction is identical with that in the other direction, the slab is said to be *isotropically reinforced*; if the reinforcements differ, the slab is described as *orthogonally anisotropic*. In the former case, the capacity of the slab is identical in all directions; in the latter case, the capacity has a unique value in every direction. In this instance, assume that the slab size is excessive with respect to balanced design, the result being that the failure of the slab will be characterized by yielding of the steel.

In a steel beam, a plastic hinge forms at a *section*; in a slab, a plastic hinge is assumed to form along a straight line, termed a yield line. It is plausible to assume that by virtue of symmetry of loading and support conditions the slab in Fig. 9a will fail by the formation of a central yield line $EF$ and diagonal yield lines such as $AE$, the ultimate moment at these lines being positive. The ultimate *unit* moment $m_u$ is the moment acting on a unit length.

Although it is possible to derive equations that give the location of the yield lines, this procedure is not feasible because the resulting equations would be unduly cumbersome. The procedure followed in practice is to assign a group of values to the distance $a$ and to determine the corresponding values of $m_u$. The true value of $m_u$ is the highest one obtained. Either the static or mechanism method of analysis may be applied; the latter will be applied here.

Expressing the distances $b$ and $c$ in terms of $a$ gives $\tan a = 6/a = AE/b = c/(AE)$; $b = aAE/6$; $c = 6AE/a$.

### 2. Find the rotation of the plastic hinges

Allow line $EF$ to undergo a virtual displacement $\Delta$ after the collapse load is reached. During the virtual displacement, the portions of the slab bounded by the yield lines and the supports rotate as planes. Refer to Fig. 9b and c: $\theta_1 = \Delta/6$; $\theta_2 = 2\theta_1 = \Delta/3 = 0.333\Delta$; $\theta_3 = \Delta/b$; $\theta_4 = \Delta/c$; $\theta_5 = \Delta(1/b + 1/c) = [\Delta/(AE)](6/a + a/6)$.

### 3. Select a trial value of a, and evaluate the distances and angles

Using $a = 4.5$ ft (1.37 m) as the trial value, we find $AE = (a^2 + 6^2)^{0.5} = 7.5$ ft (2.28 m); $b = 5.63$ ft (1.716 m); $c = 10$ ft (3.0 m); $\theta_5 = (\Delta/7.5)(6/4.5 + 4.5/6) = 0.278\Delta$.

### 4. Develop an equation for the external work $W_E$ performed by the uniform load on a surface that rotates about a horizontal axis

In Fig. 10, consider that the surface $ABC$ rotates about axis $AB$ through an angle $\theta$ while carrying a uniform load of $w$ lb/sq.ft. (kPa). For the elemental area $dA_s$, the deflection, total load, and external work are $\delta = x\theta$; $dW = w\,dA$; $dW_E = \delta\,dW = x\theta w\,dA$. The total work for the surface is $W_E = w\theta \int x \times dA$, or

$$W_E = w\theta Q \tag{20}$$

where $Q$ = static moment of total area, with respect to the axis of rotation.

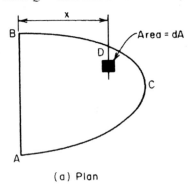

(a) Plan

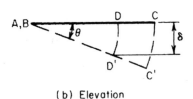

(b) Elevation

**FIGURE 10**

### 5. Evaluate the external and internal work for the slab

Using the assumed value, we see $a = 4.5$ ft (1.37 m), $EF = 16 - 9 = 7$ ft (2.1 m). The external work for the two triangles is $2w_u(\Delta/4.5)(1/6)(12)(4.5)^2 = 18w_u\Delta$. The external work for the two trapezoids is $2w_u(\Delta/6)(1/6)(16 + 2 \times 7)(6)^2 = 60w_u\Delta$. Then $W_E = w_u\Delta(18 + 60) = 78w_u\Delta$; $W_I = m_u(7\theta_2 + 4 \times 7.5\theta_5) = 10.67m_u\Delta$.

### 6. Find the value of $m_u$ corresponding to the assumed value of a

Equate the external and internal work to find this value of $m_u$. Thus, $10.67m_u\Delta = 78w_u\Delta$; $m_u = 7.31w_u$.

### 7. Determine the highest value of $m_u$

Assign other trial values to $a$, and find the corresponding values of $m_u$. Continue this procedure until the highest value of $m_u$ is obtained. This is the true value of the ultimate unit moment.

# Design of Flexural Members by the Working-Stress Method

As demonstrated earlier, the analysis or design of a composite beam by the working-stress method is most readily performed by transforming the given beam to an equivalent homogeneous beam. In the case of a reinforced-concrete member, the transformation is made by replacing the reinforcing steel with a strip of concrete having an area $nA_s$ and located at the same distance from the neutral axis as the steel. This substitute concrete is assumed capable of sustaining tensile stresses.

The following symbols, shown in Fig. 11, are to be added to the notational system given earlier: $kd$ = distance from extreme compression fiber to neutral axis, in. (mm); $jd$ = distance between action lines of $C$ and $T$, in. (mm); $z$ = distance from extreme compression fiber to action line of $C$, in. (mm).

The basic equations for the working-stress design of a rectangular beam reinforced solely in tension are

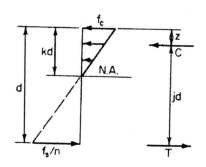

**FIGURE 11.** Stress and resultant forces.

$$k = \frac{f_c}{f_c + f_s/n} \qquad (21)$$

$$j = 1 - \frac{k}{3} \qquad (22)$$

$$M = Cjd = \tfrac{1}{2}f_c kjbd^2 \qquad (23)$$

$$M = \tfrac{1}{6}f_c k(3 - k)bd^2 \qquad (24)$$

$$M = Tjd = f_s A_s jd \qquad (25)$$

$$M = f_s pjbd^2 \qquad (26)$$

$$M = \frac{f_s k^2(3 - k)bd^2}{6n(1 - k)} \qquad (27)$$

$$p = \frac{f_c k}{2f_s} \qquad (28)$$

$$p = \frac{k^2}{2n(1) -} \qquad (29)$$

$$k = [2pn + (pn)^2]^{0.5} - pn \qquad (30)$$

For a given set of values of $f_c$, $f_s$, and $n$, $M$ is directly proportional to the beam property $bd^2$. Let $K$ denote the constant of proportionality. Then

$$M = Kbd^2 \qquad (31)$$

where

$$K = \tfrac{1}{2}f_c kj = f_s pj \qquad (32)$$

The allowable flexural stress in the concrete and the value of $n$, which are functions of the ultimate strength $f_c'$, are given in the ACI *Code*, as is the allowable flexural stress in the steel. In all instances in the following procedures, the assumption is that the reinforcement is intermediate-grade steel having an allowable stress of 20,000 lb/sq.in. (137,900 kPa).

Consider that the load on a beam is gradually increased until a limiting stress is induced. A beam that is so proportioned that the steel and concrete simultaneously attain their limiting

**TABLE 1.**   Values of Design Parameters at Balanced Design

| $f_c'$ and $n$ | $f_c$ | $f_s$ | $K$ | $k$ | $j$ | $p$ |
|---|---|---|---|---|---|---|
| 2500 | 1125 | 20,000 | 178 | 0.360 | 0.880 | 0.0101 |
| 10 | | | | | | |
| 3000 | 1350 | 20,000 | 223 | 0.378 | 0.874 | 0.0128 |
| 9 | | | | | | |
| 4000 | 1800 | 20,000 | 324 | 0.419 | 0.853 | 0.0188 |
| 8 | | | | | | |
| 5000 | 2250 | 20,000 | 423 | 0.441 | 0.853 | 0.0248 |
| 7 | | | | | | |

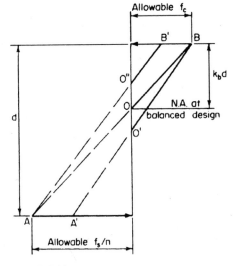

**FIGURE 12**

stress is said to be in *balanced design*. For each set of values of $f_c'$ and $f_s$, there is a corresponding set of values of $K, k, j,$ and $p$ associated with balanced design. These values are recorded in Table 1.

In Fig. 12, $AB$ represents the stress line of the transformed section for a beam in balanced design. If the area of reinforcement is increased while the width and depth remain constant, the neutral axis is depressed to $O'$, and $A'O'B$ represents the stress line under the allowable load. But if the width is increased while the depth and area of reinforcement remain constant, the neutral axis is elevated to $O''$, and $AO''B'$ represents the stress line under the allowable load. This analysis leads to these conclusions: If the reinforcement is in excess of that needed for balanced design, the concrete is the first material to reach its limiting stress under a gradually increasing load. If the beam size is in excess of that needed for balanced design, the steel is the first material to reach its limiting stress.

## STRESSES IN A RECTANGULAR BEAM

A beam of 2500-lb/sq.in (17,237.5-kPa) concrete has a width of 12 in. (304.8 mm) and an effective depth of 19.5 in. (495.3 mm). It is reinforced with one no. 9 and two no. 7 bars. Determine the flexural stresses caused by a bending moment of 62 ft·kips (84.1 kN·m) (*a*) without applying the basic equations of reinforced-concrete beam design; (*b*) by applying the basic equations.

## Calculation Procedure:

### 1. Record the pertinent beam data

Thus $f'_c = 2500$ lb/sq.in. (17,237.5 kPa); $\therefore n = 10$; $A_s = 2.20$ sq.in. (14.194 cm$^2$); $nA_s = 22.0$ sq.in. (141.94 cm$^2$). Then $M = 62,000(12) = 744,000$ in.·lb (84,057.1 N·m).

### 2. Transform the given section to an equivalent homogeneous section, as in Fig. 13b

### 3. Locate the neutral axis of the member

The neutral axis coincides with the centroidal axis of the transformed section. To locate the neutral axis, set the static moment of the transformed area with respect to its centroidal axis equal to zero: $12(kd)^2/2 - 22.0(19.5 - kd) = 0$; $kd = 6.82$; $d - kd = 12.68$ in. (322.072 mm).

### 4. Calculate the moment of inertia of the transformed section

Then evaluate the flexural stresses by applying the stress equation: $I = (1/3)(12)(6.82)^3 + 22.0(12.68)^2 = 4806$ in$^4$ (200,040.6 cm$^4$); $f_c = Mkd/I = 744,000(6.82)/4806 = 1060$ lb/sq.in. (7308.7 kPa); $f_s = 10(744,000)(12.68)/4806 = 19,600$ lb/sq.in.

### 5. Alternatively, evaluate the stresses by computing the resultant forces C and T

Thus $jd = 19.5 - 6.82/3 = 17.23$ in. (437.642 mm); $C = T = M/jd = 744,000/17.23 = 43,200$ lb (192,153.6 N). But $C = 1/2f_c(6.82)12$; $\therefore f_c = 1060$ lb/sq.in. (7308.7 kPa); and $T = 2.20f_s$; $\therefore f_s = 19,600$ lb/sq.in. (135,142 kPa). This concludes part $a$ of the solution. The next step constitutes the solution to part $b$.

### 6. Compute pn and then apply the basic equations in the proper sequence

Thus $p = A_s/(bd) = 2.20/[12(19.5)] = 0.00940$; $pn = 0.0940$. Then by Eq. 30, $k = [0.188 + (0.094)^2]^{0.5} - 0.094 = 0.350$. By Eq. 22, $j = 1 - 0.350/3 = 0.883$. By Eq. 23, $f_c = 2M/(kjbd^2) = 2(744,000)/[0.350(0.883)(12)(19.5)^2] = 1060$ lb/sq.in. (7308.7 kPa). By Eq. 25, $f_s = M/(A_s jd) = 744,000/[2.20(0.883)(19.5)] = 19,600$ lb/sq.in. (135,142 kPa).

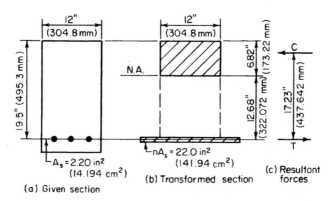

(a) Given section
(b) Transformed section
(c) Resultant forces

**FIGURE 13**

## CAPACITY OF A RECTANGULAR BEAM

The beam in Fig. 14a is made of 2500-lb/sq.in. (17,237.5-kPa) concrete. Determine the flexural capacity of the member (a) without applying the basic equations of reinforced-concrete beam design; (b) by applying the basic equations.

### Calculation Procedure:

### 1. Record the pertinent beam data
Thus, $f_c' = 2500$ lb/sq.in. (17,237.5 kPa); $\therefore f_{c,\text{allow}} = 1125$ lb/sq.in. (7756.9 kPa); $n = 10$; $A_s = 3.95$ sq.in. (25.485 cm²); $nA_s = 39.5$ sq.in. (254.85 cm²).

### 2. Locate the centroidal axis of the transformed section
Thus, $16(kd)^2/2 - 39.5(23.5 - kd) = 0$; $kd = 8.58$ in. (217.93 mm); $d - kd = 14.92$ in. (378.968 mm).

### 3. Ascertain which of the two allowable stresses governs the capacity of the member
For this purpose, assume that $f_c = 1125$ lb/sq.in. (7756.9 kPa). By proportion, $f_s = 10(1125)(14.92/8.58) = 19,560$ lb/sq.in. (134,866 kPa) < 20,000 lb/sq.in. (137,900 kPa). Therefore, concrete stress governs.

### 4. Calculate the allowable bending moment
Thus, $jd = 23.5 - 8.58/3 = 20.64$ in. (524.256 mm); $M = Cjd = \frac{1}{2}(1125)(16)(8.58)(20.64) = 1,594,000$ in.·lb (180,090.1 N·m); or $M = Tjd = 3.95(19,560)(20.64) = 1,594,000$ in.·lb (180,090.1 N·m). This concludes part a of the solution. The next step comprises part b.

### 5. Compute p and compare with $p_b$ to identify the controlling stress
Thus, from Table 1, $p_b = 0.0101$; then $p = A_s/(bd) = 3.95/[16(23.5)] = 0.0105 > p_b$. Therefore, concrete stress governs.

Applying the basic equations in the proper sequence yields $pn = 0.1050$; by Eq. 30, $k = [0.210 + 0.105^2]^{0.5} - 0.105 = 0.365$; by Eq. 24, $M = (\frac{1}{6})(1125)(0.365)(2.635)(16)(23.5)^2 = 1,593,000$ in.·lb (179,977.1 N·m). This agrees closely with the previously computed value of M.

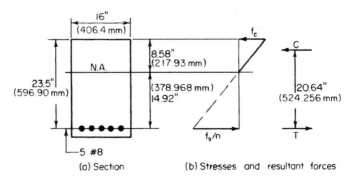

(a) Section          (b) Stresses and resultant forces

**FIGURE 14**

## DESIGN OF REINFORCEMENT IN A
## RECTANGULAR BEAM OF GIVEN SIZE

A rectangular beam of 4000-lb/sq.in. (27,580-kPa) concrete has a width of 14 in. (355.6 mm) and an effective depth of 23.5 in. (596.9 mm). Determine the area of reinforcement if the beam is to resist a bending moment of (a) 220 ft·kips (298.3 kN·m); (b) 200 ft·kips (271.2 kN·m).

### Calculation Procedure:

### 1. Calculate the moment capacity of this member at balanced design

Record the following values: $f_{c,\text{allow}} = 1800$ lb/sq.in. (12,411 kPa); $n = 8$. From Table 1, $j_b = 0.860$; $K_b = 324$ lb/sq.in. (2234.0 kPa); $M_b = K_b\,b\,d^2 = 324(14)(23.5)^2 = 2,505,000$ in.·lb (283,014.9 N·m).

### 2. Determine which material will be stressed to capacity under the stipulated moment

For part a, $M = 220,000(12) = 2,640,000$ in.·lb (3,579,840 N·m) $> M_b$. This result signifies that the beam size is deficient with respect to balanced design, and the concrete will therefore be stressed to capacity.

### 3. Apply the basic equations in proper sequence to obtain $A_s$

By Eq. 24, $k(3 - k) = 6M/(f_c bd^2) = 6(2,640,000)/[1800(14)(23.5)^2] = 1.138$; $k = 0.446$. By Eq. 29, $p = k^2/[2n(1 - k)] = 0.446^2/[16(0.554)] = 0.0224$; $A_s = pbd = 0.0224(14)(23.5) = 7.37$ sq.in. (47.551 cm²).

### 4. Verify the result by evaluating the flexural capacity of the member

For part b, compute $A_s$ by the exact method and then describe the approximate method used in practice.

### 5. Determine which material will be stressed to capacity under the stipulated moment

Here $M = 200,000(12) = 2,400,000$ in.·lb (3,254,400 N·m) $< M_b$. This result signifies that the beam size is excessive with respect to balanced design, and the steel will therefore be stressed to capacity.

### 6. Apply the basic equations in proper sequence to obtain $A_s$

By using Eq. 27, $k^2(3 - k)/(1 - k) = 6nM/(f_s bd^2) = 6(8)(2,400,000)/[20,000(14)(23.5)^2] = 0.7448$; $k = 0.411$. By Eq. 22, $j = 1 - 0.411/3 = 0.863$. By Eq. 25, $A_s = M/(f_s jd) = 2,400,000/[20,000(0.863)(23.5)] = 5.92$ sq.in. (38.196 cm²).

### 7. Verify the result by evaluating the flexural capacity of this member

The value of $j$ obtained in step 6 differs negligibly from the value $j_b = 0.860$. Consequently, in those instances where the beam size is only moderately excessive with respect to balanced design, the practice is to consider that $j = j_b$ and to solve Eq. 25 directly on this basis. This practice is conservative, and it obviates the need for solving a cubic equation, thus saving time.

## DESIGN OF A RECTANGULAR BEAM

A beam on a simple span of 13 ft (3.9 m) is to carry a uniformly distributed load, exclusive of its own weight, of 3600 lb/lin ft (52,538.0 N/m) and a concentrated load of 17,000 lb (75,616 N) applied at midspan. Design the section, using $f'_c$ = 3000 lb/sq.in. (20,685 kPa).

### Calculation Procedure:

### 1. Record the basic values associated with balanced design

There are two methods of allowing for the beam weight: (*a*) to determine the bending moment with an estimated beam weight included; (*b*) to determine the beam size required to resist the external loads alone and then increase the size slightly. The latter method is used here.

From Table 1, $K_b$ = 223 lb/sq.in. (1537.6 kPa); $p_b$ = 0.0128; $j_b$ = 0.874.

### 2. Calculate the maximum moment caused by the external loads

Thus, the maximum moment $M_e = \frac{1}{4}PL + \frac{1}{8}wL^2 = \frac{1}{4}(17,000)(13)(12) + \frac{1}{8}(3600)$ $(13)^2(12)$ = 1,576,000 in.·lb (178,056.4 N·m).

### 3. Establish a trial beam size

Thus, $bd^2 = M/K_b$ = 1,576,000/223 = 7067 in$^3$ (115,828.1 cm$^3$). Setting $b = (\frac{2}{3})d$, we find $b$ − 14.7 in. (373.38 mm), $d$ = 22.0 in. (558.8 mm). Try $b$ = 15 in. (381 mm) and $d$ = 22.5 in. (571.5 mm), producing an overall depth of 25 in. (635 mm) if the reinforcing bars may be placed in one row.

### 4. Calculate the maximum bending moment with the beam weight included; determine whether the trial section is adequate

Thus, beam weight = 15(25)(150)/144 = 391 lb/lin ft (5706.2 N/m); $M_w = (\frac{1}{8})(391)$ $(13)^2(12)$ = 99,000 in.·lb (11,185.0 N·m); $M$ = 1,576,000 + 99,000 = 1,675,000 in.·lb (189,241.5 N·m); $M_b = K_b bd^2$ = 223(15)(22.5)$^2$ = 1,693,000 in.·lb (191,275.1 N·m). The trial section is therefore satisfactory because it has adequate capacity.

### 5. Design the reinforcement

Since the beam size is slightly excessive with respect to balanced design, the steel will be stressed to capacity under the design load. Equation 25 is therefore suitable for this calculation. Thus, $A_s = M/(f_s jd)$ = 1,675,000/[20,000(0.874)(22.5)] = 4.26 sq.in. (27.485 cm$^2$).

An alternative method of calculating $A_s$ is to apply the value of $p_b$, while setting the beam width equal to the dimension actually required to produce balanced design. Thus, $A_s$ = 0.0128(15)(1675)(22.5)/1693 = 4.27 sq.in. (27.550 cm$^2$).

Use one no. 10 and three no. 9 bars, for which $A_s$ = 4.27 sq.in. (27.550 cm$^2$) and $b_{min}$ = 12.0 in. (304.8 mm).

### 6. Summarize the design

Thus, beam size is 15 × 25 in. (381 × 635 mm); reinforcement is with one no. 10 and three no. 9 bars.

## DESIGN OF WEB REINFORCEMENT

A beam 14 in. (355.6 mm) wide with an 18.5-in. (469.9-mm) effective depth carries a uniform load of 3.8 kips/lin ft (55.46 N/m) and a concentrated midspan load of 2 kips (8.896 kN). The beam is simply supported, and the clear distance between supports is 13 ft (3.9 m).

Using $f'_c$ = 3000 lb/sq.in. (20,685 kPa) and an allowable stress $f_v$ in the stirrups of 20,000 lb/sq.in. (137,900 kPa), design web reinforcement in the form of vertical U stirrups.

### Calculation Procedure:

### 1. *Construct the shearing-stress diagram for half-span*
The design of web reinforcement by the working-stress method parallels the design by the ultimate-strength method, given earlier. Let $v$ = nominal shearing stress, lb/sq.in. (kPa); $v'_c$ = shearing stress resisted by concrete; $v'$ = shearing stress resisted by web reinforcement.

The ACI *Code* provides two alternative methods of computing the shearing stress that may be resisted by the concrete. The simpler method is used here. This sets

$$v_c = 1.1(f'_c)^{0.5} \tag{33}$$

The equation for nominal shearing stress is

$$v = \frac{V}{bd} \tag{34}$$

The shearing-stress diagram for a half-span is shown in Fig. 15. Establish the region $AD$ within which web reinforcement is required. Thus, $v_c = 1.1(3000)^{0.5}$ = 60 lb/sq.in. (413.7 kPa). At the face of the support, $V$ = 6.5(3800) + 1000 = 25,700 lb (114,313.6 N); $v$ = 25,700/[14(18.5)] = 99 lb/sq.in. (682.6 kPa).

At midspan, $V$ = 1000 lb (4448 N); $v$ = 4 lb/sq.in. (27.6 kPa); slope of diagram = $-(99 - 4)/78$ = $-1.22$ lb/(in²·in.) ($-0.331$ kPa/mm). At distance $d$ from the face of the support, $v$ = 99 $-$ 18.5(1.22) = 76 lb/sq.in. (524.02 kPa); $v'$ = 76 $-$ 60 = 16 lb/sq.in. (110.3 kPa); $AC$ = (99 $-$ 60)/1.22 = 32 in. (812.8 mm); $AD$ = $AC$ + $d$ = 32 + 18.5 = 50.5 in. (1282.7 mm).

### 2. *Check the beam size for compliance with the* Code
Thus, $v_{max}$ = 5$(f'_c)^{0.5}$ $-$ 274 lb/sq.in. (1889.23 kPa) > 76 lb/sq.in. (524.02 kPa). This is acceptable.

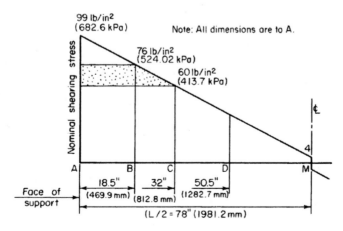

**FIGURE 15.** Shearing-stress diagram.

### 3. *Select the stirrup size*
Use the method given earlier in the ultimate-strength calculation procedure to select the stirrup size, establish the maximum allowable spacing, and devise a satisfactory spacing.

## CAPACITY OF A T BEAM

Determine the flexural capacity of the T beam in Fig. 16*a*, using $f'_c = 3000$ lb/sq.in. (20,685 kPa).

### Calculation Procedure:

### 1. *Record the pertinent beam values*
The neutral axis of a T beam often falls within the web. However, to simplify the analysis, the resisting moment developed by the concrete lying between the neutral axis and the flange is usually disregarded. Let $A_f$ denote the flange area. The pertinent beam values are $f_{c,allow} = 1350$ lb/sq.in. (9308.3 kPa); $n = 9$; $k_b = 0.378$; $nA_s = 9(4.00) = 36.0$ sq.in. (232.3 cm²).

### 2. *Tentatively assume that the neutral axis lies in the web*
Locate this axis by taking static moments with respect to the top line. Thus $A_f = 5(16) = 80$ sq.in. (516.2 cm²); $kd = [80(2.5) + 36.0(21.5)]/(80 + 36.0) = 8.40$ in. (213.36 mm).

### 3. *Identify the controlling stress*
Thus $k = 8.40/21.5 = 0.391 > k_b$; therefore, concrete stress governs.

### 4. *Calculate the allowable bending moment*
Using Fig. 16*c*, we see $f_{c1} = 1350(3.40)/8.40 = 546$ lb/sq.in. (3764.7 kPa); $C = \frac{1}{2}(80)(1350 + 546) = 75,800$ lb (337,158.4 N). The action line of this resultant force lies at the centroidal axis of the stress trapezoid. Thus, $z = (\frac{5}{3})(1350 + 2 \times 546)/(1350 + 546) = 2.15$ in. (54.61 mm); or $z = (\frac{5}{3}) (8.40 + 2 \times 3.40)/(8.40 + 3.40) = 2.15$ in. (54.61 mm); $M = Cjd = 75,800(19.35) = 1,467,000$ in.·lb (165,741 N·m).

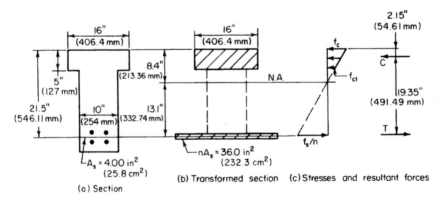

**FIGURE 16**

**5. *Alternatively, calculate the allowable bending moment by assuming that the flange extends to the neutral axis***

Then apply the necessary correction. Let $C_1$ = resultant compressive force if the flange extended to the neutral axis, lb (N); $C_2$ = resultant compressive force in the imaginary extension of the flange, lb (N). Then $C_1$ = $^1/2(1350)(16)(8.40)$ = 90,720 lb (403,522.6 N); $C_2$ = $90,720(3.40/8.40)^2$ = 14,860 lb (66,097.3 N); $M$ = 90,720(21.5 − 8.40/3) − 14,860(21.5 − 5 − 3.40/3) = 1,468,000 in.·lb (165,854.7 N·m).

## DESIGN OF A T BEAM HAVING CONCRETE STRESSED TO CAPACITY

A concrete girder of 2500-lb/sq.in. (17,237.5-kPa) concrete has a simple span of 22 ft (6.7 m) and is built integrally with a 5-in. (127-mm) slab. The girders are spaced 8 ft (2.4 m) on centers; the overall depth is restricted to 20 in. (508 mm) by headroom requirements. The member carries a load of 4200 lb/lin ft (61,294.4 N/m), exclusive of the weight of its web. Design the section, using tension reinforcement only.

### Calculation Procedure:

**1. *Establish a tentative width of web***

Since the girder is built integrally with the slab that it supports, the girder and slab constitute a structural entity in the form of a T beam. The effective flange width is established by applying the criteria given in the ACI *Code*, and the bending stress in the flange is assumed to be uniform across a line parallel to the neutral axis. Let $A_f$ = area of flange sq.in. (cm²); $b$ = width of flange, in. (mm); $b'$ = width of web, in. (mm); $t$ = thickness of flange, in. (mm); $s$ = center-to-center spacing of girders.

To establish a tentative width of web, try $b'$ = 14 in. (355.6 mm). Then the weight of web = 14(15)(150)/144 = 219, say 220 lb/lin ft (3210.7 N/m); $w$ = 4200 + 220 = 4420 lb/lin ft (64,505.0 N/m).

Since two rows of bars are probably required, $d$ = 20 − 3.5 = 16.5 in. (419.1 mm). The critical shear value is $V$ = $w(0.5L - d)$ = 4420(11 − 1.4) = 42,430 lb (188,728.7 N); $v$ = $V/b'd$ = 42,430/[14(16.5)] = 184 lb/sq.in. (1268.7 kPa). From the *Code*, $v_{max}$ − $5(f_c')^{0.5}$ = 250 lb/sq.in. (1723.8 kPa). This is acceptable.

Upon designing the reinforcement, consider whether it is possible to reduce the width of the web.

**2. *Establish the effective width of the flange according to the* Code**

Thus, $^1/4L$ = $^1/4(22)(12)$ = 66 in. (1676.4 mm); 16t + b' = 16(5) + 14 = 94 in. (2387.6 mm); $s$ = 8(12) = 96 in. (2438.4 mm); therefore $b$ = 66 in. (1676.4 mm).

**3. *Compute the moment capacity of the member at balanced design***

Compare the result with the moment in the present instance to identify the controlling stress. With Fig. 16 as a guide, $k_b d$ = 0.360(16.5) = 5.94 in. (150.876 mm); $A_f$ = 5(66) = 330 sq.in. (2129.2 cm²); $f_{c1}$ = 1125(0.94)/5.94 = 178 lb/sq.in. (1227.3 kPa); $C_b$ = $T_b$ = $^1/2(330)$ (1125 + 178) = 215,000 lb (956,320 N); $z_b$ = $(^5/3)(5.94 + 2 \times 0.94)/(5.94 + 0.94)$ = 1.89 in. (48.0 mm); $jd$ = 14.61 in. (371.094 mm); $M_b$ = 215,000(14.61) = 3,141,000 in.·lb (354,870.2 N·m); $M$ = $(^1/8)(4420)(22)^2(12)$ = 3,209,000 in.·lb (362,552.8 N·m).

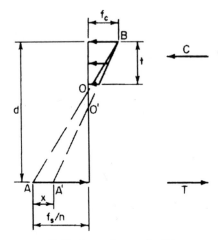

**FIGURE 17.** Stress diagram for T beam.

The beam size is slightly deficient with respect to balanced design, and the concrete will therefore be stressed to capacity under the stipulated load. In Fig. 17, let $AOB$ represent the stress line associated with balanced design and $A'O'B$ represent the stress line in the present instance. (The magnitude of $AA'$ is exaggerated for clarity.)

### 4. Develop suitable equations for the beam

Refer to Fig. 17:

$$T = T_b + \frac{bt^2x}{2d} \tag{35}$$

where $T$ and $T_b$ = tensile force in present instance and at balanced design, respectively. And

$$M = M_b + \frac{bt^2(3d - 2t)x}{6d} \tag{36}$$

### 5. Apply the equations from step 4

Thus, $M - M_b = 68,000$ in.·lb (7682.6 N·m). By Eq. 36, $x = 68,000(6)(16.5)/[66(25)(49.5 - 10)] = 103$ lb/sq.in. (710.2 kPa); $f_s = 20,000 - 10(103) = 18,970$ lb/sq.in. (130,798.2 kPa). By Eq. 35, $T = 215,000 + 66(25)(103)/33 = 220,200$ lb (979,449.6 N).

### 6. Design the reinforcement; establish the web width

Thus $A_s = 220,200/18,970 = 11.61$ sq.in. (74.908 cm²). Use five no. 11 and three no. 10 bars, placed in two rows. Then $A_s = 11.61$ sq.in. (74.908 cm²); $b'_{min} = 14.0$ in. (355.6 mm). It is therefore necessary to maintain the 14-in. (355.6-mm) width.

### 7. Summarize the design

Width of web: 14 in. (355.6 mm); reinforcement: five no. 11 and three no. 10 bars.

### 8. Verify the design by computing the capacity of the member

Thus $nA_s = 116.1$ sq.in. (749.08 cm²); $kd = [330(2.5) + 116.1(16.5)]/(330 + 116.1) = 6.14$ in. (155.956 mm); $k = 6.14/16.5 = 0.372 > k_b$; therefore, concrete is stressed to capacity. Then $f_s = 10(1125)(10.36)/6.14 = 18,980$ lb/sq.in. (130,867.1 kPa); $z = (5/3)(6.14 + 2 \times 1.14)/(6.14 + 1.14) = 1.93$ in. (49.022 mm); $jd = 14.57$ in. (370.078 mm); $M_{allow} = 11.61(18,980)(14.57) = 3,210,000$ in.·lb (362,665.8 N·m). This is acceptable.

## DESIGN OF A T BEAM HAVING STEEL STRESSED TO CAPACITY

Assume that the girder in the previous calculation procedure carries a total load, including the weight of the web, of 4100 lb/lin ft (59,835.0 N/m). Compute the area of reinforcement.

## Calculation Procedure:

### 1. Identify the controlling stress

Thus, $M = (1/8)(4100)(22)^2(12) = 2,977,000$ in.·lb (336,341.5 N·m). From the previous calculation procedure, $M_b = 3,141,000$ in.·lb (354,870.2 N·m). Since $M_b > M$, the beam size is slightly excessive with respect to balanced design, and the steel will therefore be stressed to capacity under the stipulated load.

### 2. Compute the area of reinforcement

As an approximation, this area may be found by applying the value of $jd$ associated with balanced design, although it is actually slightly larger. From the previous calculation procedure, $jd = 14.61$ in. (371.094 mm). Then $A_s = 2,977,000/[20,000(14.61)] = 10.19$ sq.in. (65.746 cm$^2$).

### 3. Verify the design by computing the member capacity

Thus, $nA_s = 101.9$ sq.in. (657.46 cm$^2$); $kd = (330 \times 2.5 + 101.9 \times 16.5)/(330 + 101.9) = 5.80$ in. (147.32 mm); $z = (5/3)(5.80 + 2 \times 0.80)/(5.80 + 0.80) = 1.87$ in. (47.498 mm); $jd = 14.63$ in. (371.602 mm); $M_{\text{allow}} = 10.19(20,000)(14.63) = 2,982,000$ in.·lb (336,906.4 N·m). This is acceptable.

## REINFORCEMENT FOR DOUBLY REINFORCED RECTANGULAR BEAM

A beam of 4000-lb/sq.in. (27,580-kPa) concrete that will carry a bending moment of 230 ft·kips (311.9 kN·m) is restricted to a 15-in. (381-mm) width and a 24-in. (609.6-mm) total depth. Design the reinforcement.

## Calculation Procedure:

### 1. Record the pertinent beam data

In Fig. 18, where the imposed moment is substantially in excess of that corresponding to balanced design, it is necessary to reinforce the member in compression as well as tension. The loss in concrete area caused by the presence of the compression reinforcement may be disregarded.

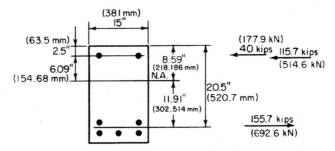

**FIGURE 18.** Doubly reinforced beam.

Since plastic flow generates a transfer of compressive stress from the concrete to the steel, the ACI *Code* provides that "in doubly reinforced beams and slabs, an effective modular ratio of $2n$ shall be used to transform the compression reinforcement and compute its stress, which shall not be taken as greater than the allowable tensile stress." This procedure is tantamount to considering that the true stress in the compression reinforcement is twice the value obtained by assuming a linear stress distribution.

Let $A_s$ = area of tension reinforcement, sq.in. (cm²); $A'_s$ = area of compression reinforcement, sq.in. (cm²); $f_s$ = stress in tension reinforcement, lb/sq.in. (kPa); $f'_s$ = stress in compression reinforcement, lb/sq.in. (kPa); $C'$ = resultant force in compression reinforcement, lb (N); $M_1$ = moment capacity of member if reinforced solely in tension to produce balanced design; $M_2$ = incremental moment capacity resulting from use of compression reinforcement.

The data recorded for the beam are $f_c$ = 1800 lb/sq.in. (12.411 kPa); $n$ = 8; $K_b$ = 324 lb/sq.in. (2234.0 kPa); $k_b$ = 0.419; $j_b$ = 0.860; $M$ = 230,000(12) = 2,760,000 in.·lb (311,824.8 N·m).

### 2. *Ascertain whether one row of tension bars will suffice*
Assume tentatively that the presence of the compression reinforcement does not appreciably alter the value of $j$. Then $jd$ = 0.860(21.5) = 18.49 in. (469.646 mm); $A_s$ = $M/(f_s jd)$ = 2,760,000/[20,000(18.49)] = 7.46 sq.in. (48.132 cm²). This area of steel cannot be accommodated in the 15-in. (381-mm) beam width, and two rows of bars are therefore required.

### 3. *Evaluate the moments $M_1$ and $M_2$*
Thus, $d$ = 24 − 3.5 = 20.5 in. (520.7 mm); $M_1$ = $K_b bd^2$ = 324(15)(20.5)² = 2,040,000 in.·lb (230,479.2 N·m); $M_2$ = 2,760,000 − 2,040,000 = 720,000 in.·lb (81,345.6 N·m).

### 4. *Compute the forces in the reinforcing steel*
For convenience, assume that the neutral axis occupies the same position as it would in the absence of compression reinforcement. For $M_1$, arm = $j_b d$ = 0.860(20.5) = 17.63 in. (447.802 mm); for $M_2$, arm = 20.5 − 2.5 = 18.0 in. (457.2 mm); $T$ = 2,040,000/17.63 + 720,000/18.0 = 155,700 lb (692,553.6 N); $C'$ = 40,000 lb (177,920 N).

### 5. *Compute the areas of reinforcement and select the bars*
Thus $A_s$ = $T/f_s$ = 155,700/20,000 = 7.79 sq.in. (50.261 cm²); $kd$ = 0.419(20.5) = 8.59 in. (218.186 mm); $d - kd$ = 11.91 in. (302.514 mm). By proportion, $f'_s$ = 2(20,000) (6.09)/11.91 = 20,500 lb/sq.in. (141,347.5 kPa); therefore, set $f'_s$ = 20,000 lb/sq.in. (137,900 kPa). Then, $A'_s$ = $C'/f'_s$ = 40,000/20,000 = 2.00 sq.in. (12.904 cm²). Thus tension steel: five no. 11 bars, $A_s$ = 7.80 sq.in. (50.326 cm²); compression steel: two no. 9 bars, $A_s$ = 2.00 sq.in. (12.904 cm²).

## DEFLECTION OF A CONTINUOUS BEAM

The continuous beam in Fig. 19a and b carries a total load of 3.3 kips/lin ft (48.16 kN/m). When it is considered as a T beam, the member has an effective flange width of 68 in. (1727.2 mm). Determine the deflection of the beam upon application of full live load, using $f'_c$ = 2500 lb/sq.in. (17,237.5 kPa) and $f_y$ = 40,000 lb/sq.in. (275,800 kPa).

### Calculation Procedure:

### 1. *Record the areas of reinforcement*
At support: $A_s$ = 4.43 sq.in. (28.582 cm²) (top); $A'_s$ = 1.58 sq.in. (10.194 cm²) (bottom). At center: $A_s$ = 3.16 sq.in. (20.388 cm²) (bottom).

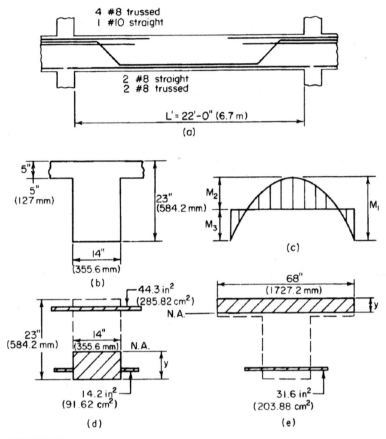

**FIGURE 19**

### 2. Construct the bending-moment diagram

Apply the ACI equation for maximum midspan moment. Refer to Fig. 19c: $M_1 = (\frac{1}{8})wL'^2 = (\frac{1}{8})3.3(22)^2 - 200$ ft·kips (271.2 kN·m); $M_2 = (\frac{1}{16})WL'^2 = 100$ ft·kips (135.6 kN·m); $M_3 = 100$ ft·kips (135.6 kN·m).

### 3. Determine upon what area the moment of inertia should be based

Apply the criterion set forth in the ACI *Code* to determine whether the moment of inertia is to be based on the transformed gross section or the transformed cracked section. At the support $pf_y = 4.43(40,000)/[14(20.5)] = 617 > 500$. Therefore, use the cracked section.

### 4. Determine the moment of inertia of the transformed cracked section at the support

Refer to Fig. 19d: $nA_s = 10(4.43) = 44.3$ sq.in. (285.82 cm²); $(n - 1)A_s = 9(1.58) = 14.2$ sq.in. (91.62 cm²). The static moment with respect to the neutral axis is $Q = -\frac{1}{2}(14y^2) + 44.3(20.5 - y) - 14.2(y - 2.5) = 0$; $y = 8.16$ in. (207.264 mm). The moment of inertia with respect to the neutral axis is $I_1 = (\frac{1}{3})14(8.16)^3 + 14.2(8.16 - 2.5)^2 + 44.3(20.5 - 8.16)^2 = 9737$ in⁴ (40.53 dm⁴).

### 5. Calculate the moment of inertia of the transformed cracked section at the center

Referring to Fig. 19e and assuming tentatively that the neutral axis falls within the flange, we see $nA_s = 10(3.16) = 31.6$ sq.in. (203.88 cm²). The static moment with respect to the neutral axis is $Q = \frac{1}{2}(68y^2) - 31.6(20.5 - y) = 0$; $y = 3.92$ in. (99.568 mm). The neutral axis therefore falls within the flange, as assumed. The moment of inertia with respect to the neutral axis is $I_2 = (\frac{1}{3})68(3.92)3 + 31.6(20.5 - 3.92)^2 = 10,052$ in⁴ (41.840 dm⁴).

### 6. Calculate the deflection at midspan

Use the equation

$$\Delta = \frac{L'^2}{EI} \left( \frac{5M_1}{48} - \frac{M_3}{8} \right) \tag{37}$$

where $I$ = average moment of inertia, in⁴ (dm⁴). Thus, $I = \frac{1}{2}(9737 + 10,052) = 9895$ in⁴ (41.186 dm⁴); $E = 145^{1.5} \times 33f_c')^{0.5} = 57,600(2500)^{0.5} = 2,880,000$ lb/sq.in. (19,857.6 MPa). Then $\Delta = [22^2 \times 1728/(2880 \times 9895)](5 \times 200/48 - 100/8) = 0.244$ in. (6.198 mm).

Where the deflection under sustained loading is to be evaluated, it is necessary to apply the factors recorded in the ACI *Code*.

# Design of Compression Members by Ultimate-Strength Method

The notational system is $P_u$ = ultimate axial compressive load on member, lb (N); $P_b$ = ultimate axial compressive load at balanced design, lb (N); $P_0$ = allowable ultimate axial compressive load in absence of bending moment, lb (N); $M_u$ = ultimate bending moment in member, lb.·in (N·m); $M_b$ = ultimate bending moment at balanced design; $d'$ = distance from exterior surface to centroidal axis of adjacent row of steel bars, in. (mm); $t$ = overall depth of rectangular section or diameter of circular section, in. (mm).

A compression member is said to be *spirally reinforced* if the longitudinal reinforcement is held in position by spiral hooping and *tied* if this reinforcement is held by means of intermittent lateral ties.

The presence of a bending moment in a compression member reduces the ultimate axial load that the member may carry. In compliance with the ACI *Code*, it is necessary to design for a minimum bending moment equal to that caused by an eccentricity of $0.05t$ for spirally reinforced members and $0.10t$ for tied members. Thus, every compression member that is designed by the ultimate-strength method must be treated as a beam column. This type of member is considered to be in balanced design if failure would be characterized by the simultaneous crushing of the concrete, which is assumed to occur when $\epsilon_c = 0.003$, and incipient yielding of the tension steel, which occurs when $f_s = f_y$. The ACI *Code* set $\phi = 0.75$ for spirally reinforced members and $\phi = 0.70$ for tied members.

## ANALYSIS OF A RECTANGULAR MEMBER BY INTERACTION DIAGRAM

A short tied member having the cross section shown in Fig. 20a is to resist an axial load and a bending moment that induces compression at $A$ and tension at $B$. The member is made of 3000-lb/sq.in. (20,685-kPa) concrete, and the steel has a yield point of 40,000 lb/sq.in.

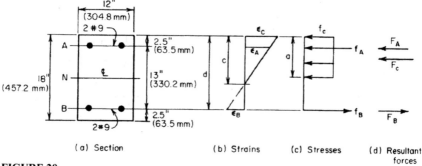

**FIGURE 20**

(a) Section   (b) Strains   (c) Stresses   (d) Resultant forces

(275,800 kPa). By starting with $c = 8$ in. (203.2 mm) and assigning progressively higher values to $c$, construct the interaction diagram for this member.

## Calculation Procedure:

### 1. Compute the value of c associated with balanced design

An interaction diagram, as the term is used here, is one in which every point on the curve represents a set of simultaneous values of the ultimate moment and allowable ultimate axial load. Let $\epsilon_A$ and $\epsilon_B$ = strain of reinforcement at A and B, respectively; $\epsilon_c$ = strain of extreme fiber of concrete; $F_A$ and $F_B$ = stress in reinforcement at A and B, respectively, lb/sq.in. (kPa); $F_A$ and $F_B$ = resultant force in reinforcement at A and B, respectively; $F_c$ = resultant force in concrete, lb (N).

Compression will be considered positive and tension negative. For simplicity, disregard the slight reduction in concrete area caused by the steel at A.

Referring to Fig. 20b, compute the value of $c$ associated with balanced design. Computing $P_b$ and $M_b$ yields $c_b/d = 0.003/(0.003 + f_y/E_s) = 87,000/(87,000 + f_y)$; $c_b = 10.62$ in. (269.748 mm). Then $\epsilon_A/\epsilon_B = (10.62 - 2.5)/(15.5 - 10.62) > 1$; therefore, $f_A = f_y$; $a_b = 0.85(10.62) = 9.03$ in. (229.362 mm); $F_c = 0.85(3000)(12a_b) = 276,300$ lb (1,228,982.4 N); $F_A = 40,000(2.00) = 80,000$ lb (355,840 N); $F_B = -80,000$ lb ($-355,840$ N); $P_b = 0.70(276,300) = 193,400$ lb (860,243.2 N). Also,

$$M_b = 0.70 \left[ \frac{F_c(t - a)}{2} + \frac{(F_A - F_B)(t - 2d')}{2} \right]$$

(38)

Thus, $M_b = 0.70[276,300(18 - 9.03)/2 + 160,000(6.5)] = 1,596,000$ in.·lb (180,316.1 N·m).

When $c > c_b$, the member fails by crushing of the concrete; when $c < c_b$, it fails by yielding of the reinforcement at line B.

### 2. Compute the value of c associated with incipient yielding of the compression steel

Compute the corresponding values of $P_u$ and $M_u$. Since $\epsilon_A$ and $\epsilon_B$ are numerically equal, the neutral axis lies at N. Thus, $c = 9$ in. (228.6 mm); $a = 0.85(9) = 7.65$ in. (194.31 mm); $F_c = 30,600(7.65) = 234,100$ lb (1,041,276.8 N); $F_A = 80,000$ lb (355,840 N); $F_B = -80,000$ lb ($-355,840$ N); $P_u = 0.70 (234,100) = 163,900$ lb (729,027.2 N); $M_u = 0.70(234,100 \times 5.18 + 160,000 \times 6.5) = 1,577,000$ in.·lb (178,169.5 N·m).

### 3. *Compute the minimum value of c at which the entire concrete area is stressed to 085f'c*

Compute the corresponding values of $P_u$ and $M_u$. Thus, $a = t = 18$ in. (457.2 mm); $c = 18/0.85 = 21.8$ in. (537.972 mm); $f_B = \epsilon_c E_s(c - d)/c = 87,000(21.18 - 15.5)/21.18 = 23,300$ lb/sq.in. (160,653.5 kPa); $F_c = 30,600(18) = 550,800$ lb (2,449,958.4 N); $F_A = 80,000$ lb (355,840 N); $F_B = 46,600$ lb (207,276.8 N); $P_u = 0.70(550,800 + 80,000 + 46,600) = 474,200$ lb (2,109,241.6 N); $M_u = 0.70(80,000 - 46,600)6.5 = 152,000$ in.·lb (17,192.9 N·m).

### 4. *Compute the value of c at which $M_u$ = 0; compute $P_0$*

The bending moment vanishes when $F_B$ reaches 80,000 lb (355,840 N). From the calculation in step 3, $f_b = 87,000(c - d)/c = 40,000$ lb/sq.in. (275,800 kPa); therefore, $c = 28.7$ in. (728.98 mm); $P_o = 0.70(550,800 + 160,000) = 497,600$ lb (2,213,324.8 N).

### 5. *Assign other values to c, and compute $P_u$ and $M_u$*

By assigning values to c ranging from 8 to 28.7 in. (203.2 to 728.98 mm), typical calculations are: when $c = 8$ in. (203.2 mm), $f_B = -40,000$ lb/sq.in. (−275,800 kPa); $f_A = 40,000(5.5/7.5) = 29,300$ lb/sq.in. (202,023.5 kPa); $a = 6.8$ in. (172.72 mm); $F_c = 30,600(6.8) = 208,100$ lb (925,628.8 N); $P_u = 0.70(208,100 + 58,600 - 80,000) = 130,700$ lb (581,353.6 N); $M_u = 0.70$ (208,100 × 5.6 + 138,600 × 6.5) = 1,446,000 in.·lb (163,369.1 N·m).

When $c = 10$ in. (254 mm), $f_A = 40,000$ lb/sq.in. (275,800 kPa); $f_B = -40,000$ lb/sq.in. (−275,800 kPa); $a = 8.5$ in. (215.9 mm); $F_c = 30,600(8.5) = 260,100$ lb (1,156,924.8 N); $P_u = 0.70(260,100) = 182,100$ lb (809,980 N); $M_u = 0.70(260,100 × 4.75 + 160,000 × 6.5) = 1,593,000$ in.·lb (179,997.1 N·m).

When $c = 14$ in. (355.6 mm), $f_B = 87,000(14 - 15.5)/14 = -9320$ lb/sq.in. (−64,261.4 kPa); $a = 11.9$ in. (302.26 mm); $F_c = 30,600(11.9) = 364,100$ lb (1,619,516.8 N); $P_u = 0.70(364,100 + 80,000 - 18,600) = 297,900$ lb (1,325,059.2 N); $M_u = 0.70(364,100 × 3.05 + 98,600 × 6.5) = 1,226,000$ in.·lb (138,513.5 N·m).

### 6. *Plot the points representing computed values of $P_u$ and $M_u$ in the interaction diagram*

Figure 21 shows these points. Pass a smooth curve through these points. Note that when $P_u < P_b$, a reduction in $M_u$ is accompanied by a reduction in the allowable load $P_u$.

## AXIAL-LOAD CAPACITY OF RECTANGULAR MEMBER

The member analyzed in the previous calculation procedure is to carry an eccentric longitudinal load. Determine the allowable ultimate load if the eccentricity as measured from N is (a) 9.2 in. (233.68 mm); (b) 6 in. (152.4 mm).

### Calculation Procedure:

### 1. *Evaluate the eccentricity associated with balanced design*

Let e denote the eccentricity of the load and $e_b$ the eccentricity associated with balanced design. Then $M_u = P_u e$. In Fig. 21, draw an arbitrary radius vector OD; then tan $\theta = ED/OE =$ eccentricity corresponding to point D.

Proceeding along the interaction diagram from A to C, we see that the value of c increases and the value of e decreases. Thus, c and e vary in the reverse manner. To evaluate the allowable loads, it is necessary to identify the portion of the interaction diagram to which each eccentricity applies.

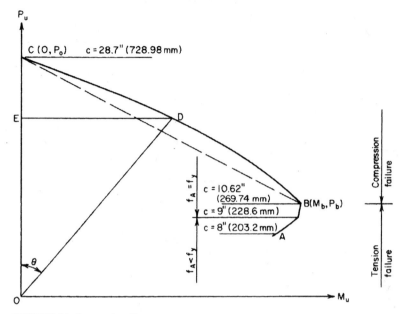

**FIGURE 21.** Interaction diagram.

From the computations of the previous calculation procedure, $e_b = M_b/P_b = 1,596,000/193,400 = 8.25$ in. (209.55 mm). This result discloses that an eccentricity of 9.2 in. (233.68 mm) corresponds to a point on $AB$ and an eccentricity of 6 in. (152.4 mm) corresponds to a point on $BC$.

### 2. Evaluate $P_u$ when e = 9.2 in. (233.68 mm)

It was found that $c = 9$ in. (228.6 mm) is a significant value. The corresponding value of $e$ is $1,577,000/163,900 = 9.62$ in. (244.348 mm). This result discloses that in the present instance $c > 9$ in. (228.6 mm) and consequently $f_A = f_y$; $F_A = 80,000$ lb (355,840 N); $F_B = -80,000$ lb $(-355,840$ N); $F_c = 30,600a$; $P_u/0.70 = 30,600a$; $M_u/0.70 = 30,600a(18 - a)/2 + 160,000(6.5)$; $e = M_u/P_u = 9.2$ in. (233.68 mm). Solving gives $a = 8.05$ in. (204.47 mm), $P_u = 172,400$ lb (766,835.2 N).

### 3. Evaluate $P_u$ when e = 6 in. (152.4 mm)

To simplify this calculation, the ACI *Code* permits replacement of curve $BC$ in the interaction diagram with a straight line through $B$ and $C$. The equation of this line is

$$P_u = P_o - (P_o - B_b) \frac{M_u}{M_b} \tag{39}$$

By replacing $M_u$ with $P_u e$, the following relation is obtained:

$$P_u = \frac{P_o}{1 + (P_o - P_b)e/M_b} \tag{39a}$$

In the present instance, $P_o = 497,600$ lb (2,213,324.8 N); $p_b = 193,400$ lb (860,243.2 N); $M_b = 1,596,000$ in.·lb (180,316.1 N·m). Thus $P_u = 232,100$ lb (1,032,380 N).

## ALLOWABLE ECCENTRICITY OF A MEMBER

The member analyzed in the previous two calculation procedures is to carry an ultimate longitudinal load of 150 kips (667.2 kN) that is eccentric with respect to axis $N$. Determine the maximum eccentricity with which the load may be applied.

### Calculation Procedure:

#### 1. *Express $P_u$ in terms of c, and solve for c*

From the preceding calculation procedures, it is seen that the value of $c$ corresponding to the maximum eccentricity lies between 8 and 9 in. (203.2 and 228.6 mm), and therefore $f_A$ $< f_y$. Thus $f_B = -40,000$ lb/sq.in. ($-275,800$ kPa); $f_A = 40,000(c - 2.5)/(15.5 - c)$; $F_c = 30,600(0.85c) = 26,000c$; $150,000 = 0.70\{26,000c + 80,000[(c - 2.5)/(15.5 - c) - 1]\}$; $c = 8.60$ in. (218.44 mm).

#### 2. *Compute $M_u$ and evaluate the eccentricity*

Thus, $a = 7.31$ in. (185.674 mm); $F_c = 223,700$ lb (995,017.6 N); $f_A = 35,360$ lb/sq.in. (243,807.2 kPa); $M_u = 0.70(223,700 \times 5.35 + 150,700 \times 6.5) = 1,523,000$ in.·lb (172,068.5 N·m); $e = M_u/P_u = 10.15$ in. (257.81 mm).

# Design of Compression Members by Working-Stress Method

The notational system is as follows: $A_g$ = gross area of section, sq.in. (cm²); $A_s$ = area of tension reinforcement, sq.in. (cm²); $A_{st}$ = total area of longitudinal reinforcement, sq.in. (cm²); $D$ = diameter of circular section, in. (mm); $p_g = A_{st}/A_g$; $P$ = axial load on member, lb (N); $f_s$ = allowable stress in longitudinal reinforcement, lb/sq.in. (kPa); $m = f_y/(0.85f_c')$.

The working-stress method of designing a compression member is essentially an adaptation of the ultimate-strength method. The allowable ultimate loads and bending moments are reduced by applying an appropriate factor of safety, and certain simplifications in computing the ultimate values are introduced.

The allowable concentric load on a short spirally reinforced column is $P = A_g(0.25f_c' + f_s p_g)$, or

$$P = 0.25f_c'A_g + f_sA_{st} \tag{40}$$

where $f_s = 0.40f_y$, but not to exceed 30,000 lb/sq.in. (206,850 kPa).

The allowable concentric load on a short tied column is $P = 0.85A_g(0.25f_c' + f_s p_g)$, or

$$P = 0.2125f_c'A_g + 0.85f_sA_{st} \tag{41}$$

A section of the ACI *Code* provides that $P_g$ may range from 0.01 to 0.08. However, in the case of a circular column in which the bars are to be placed in a single circular row, the upper limit of $P_g$ is often governed by clearance. This section of the *Code* also stipulates that the minimum bar size to be used is no. 5 and requires a minimum of six bars for a spirally reinforced column and four bars for a tied column.

## DESIGN OF A SPIRALLY REINFORCED COLUMN

A short circular column, spirally reinforced, is to support a concentric load of 420 kips (1868.16 kN). Design the member, using $f'_c = 4000$ lb/sq.in. (27,580 kPa) and $f_y = 50,000$ lb/sq.in. (344,750 kPa).

### Calculation Procedure:

#### 1. Assume $p_g = 0.025$ and compute the diameter of the section
Thus, $0.25f'_c = 1000$ lb/sq.in. (6895 kPa); $f_s = 20,000$ lb/sq.in. (137,900 kPa). By Eq. 40, $A_g = 420/(1 + 20 \times 0.025) = 280$ sq.in. (1806.6 cm$^2$). Then $D = (A_g/0.785)^{0.5} = 18.9$ in. (130.32 mm). Set $D = 19$ in. (131.01 mm), making $A_g = 283$ sq.in. (1825.9 cm$^2$).

#### 2. Select the reinforcing bars
The load carried by the concrete $= 283$ kips (1258.8 kN). The load carried by the steel $= 420 - 283 = 137$ kips (609.4 kN). Then the area of the steel is $A_{st}, = 137/20 = 6.85$ sq.in. (44.196 cm$^2$). Use seven no. 9 bars, each having an area of 1 sq.in. (6.452 cm$^2$). Then $A_{st}, = 7.00$ sq.in. (45.164 cm$^2$). The *Reinforced Concrete Handbook* shows that a 19-in. (482.6-mm) column can accommodate 11 no. 9 bars in a single row.

#### 3. Design the spiral reinforcement
The portion of the column section bounded by the outer circumference of the spiral is termed the *core* of the section. Let $A_c$ = core area, sq.in. (cm$^2$); $D_c$ = core diameter, in. (mm); $a$ = cross-sectional area of spiral wire, sq.in. (cm$^2$); $g$ = pitch of spiral, in. (mm); $p_s$ = ratio of volume of spiral reinforcement to volume of core.

The ACI *Code* requires 1.5-in. (38.1-mm) insulation for the spiral, with $g$ restricted to a maximum of $D_c/6$. Then $D_c = 19 - 3 = 16$ in. (406.4 mm); $A_c = 201$ sq.in. (1296.9 cm$^2$); $D_c/6 = 2.67$ in. (67.818 mm). Use a 2.5-in. (63.5-mm) spiral pitch. Taking a 1-in. (25.4-mm) length of column,

$$p_s = \frac{\text{volume of spiral}}{\text{volume of core}} = \frac{a_s \pi D_c/g}{\pi D_c^2/4}$$

or

$$a_s = \frac{g D_c p_s}{4} \tag{42}$$

The required value of $p_s$, as given by the ACI *Code* is

$$p_s = \frac{0.45(A_g/A_c - 1)f'_c}{f_y} \tag{43}$$

or $p_s = 0.45(283/201 - 1)4/50 = 0.0147$; $a_s = 2.5(16)(0.0147)/4 = 0.147$ sq.in. (0.9484 cm$^2$). Use $^1/_2$-in. (12.7-mm) diameter wire with $a_s = 0.196$ sq.in. (1.2646 cm$^2$).

#### 4. Summarize the design
Thus: column size: 19-in. (482.6-mm) diameter; longitudinal reinforcement: seven no. 9 bars; spiral reinforcement: $^1/_2$-in. (12.7-mm) diameter wire, 2.5-in. (63.5-mm) pitch.

## ANALYSIS OF A RECTANGULAR MEMBER BY INTERACTION DIAGRAM

A short tied member having the cross section shown in Fig. 22 is to resist an axial load and a bending moment that induces rotation about axis $N$. The member is made of 4000-lb/sq.in. (27,580-kPa) concrete, and the steel has a yield point of 50,000 lb/sq.in. (344,750 kPa). Construct the interaction diagram for this member.

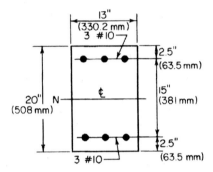

**FIGURE 22**

### Calculation Procedure:

### 1. *Compute a and M*

Consider a composite member of two materials having equal strength in tension and compression, the member being subjected to an axial load $P$ and bending moment $M$ that induce the allowable stress in one or both materials. Let $P_a$ = allowable axial load in absence of bending moment, as computed by dividing the allowable ultimate load by a factor of safety; $M_f$ = allowable bending moment in absence of axial load, as computed by dividing the allowable ultimate moment by a factor of safety.

Find the simultaneous allowable values of $P$ and $M$ by applying the interaction equation

$$\frac{P}{P_a} + \frac{M}{M_f} = 1 \tag{44}$$

Alternative forms of this equation are

$$M = M_f\left(1 - \frac{P}{P_a}\right) \qquad P = P_a\left(1 - \frac{M}{M_f}\right) \tag{44a}$$

$$P = \frac{P_a M_f}{M_f + PP_a Ml} \tag{44b}$$

Equation 44 is represented by line $AB$ in Fig. 23; it is also valid with respect to a reinforced-concrete member for a certain range of values of $P$ and $M$. This equation is not applicable in the following instances: (*a*) If $M$ is relatively small, Eq. 44 yields a value of $P$ in excess of that given by Eq. 41. Therefore, the interaction diagram must contain line $CD$, which represents the maximum value of $P$.

(*b*) If $M$ is relatively large, the section will crack, and the equal-strength assumption underlying Eq. 44 becomes untenable.

Let point $E$ represent the set of values of $P$ and $M$ that will cause cracking in the extreme concrete fiber. And let $P_b$ = axial load represented by point $E$; $M_b$ = bending moment represented by point $E$; $M_o$ = allowable bending moment in reinforced-concrete member in absence of axial load, as computed by dividing the allowable ultimate moment by a factor of safety. ($M_o$ differs from $M_f$ in that the former is based on a cracked section

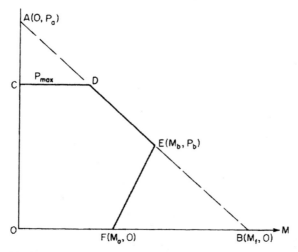

**FIGURE 23.** Interaction diagram.

and the latter on an uncracked section. The subscript $b$ as used by the ACI *Code* in the present instance does *not* refer to balanced design. However, its use illustrates the analogy with ultimate-strength analysis.) Let $F$ denote the point representing $M_o$.

For simplicity, the interaction diagram is assumed to be linear between $E$ and $F$. The interaction equation for a cracked section may therefore be expressed in any of the following forms:

$$M = M_o + \left(\frac{P}{P_b}\right)(M_b - M_o) \qquad P = P_b \left(\frac{M - M_o}{M_b - M_o}\right) \tag{45a}$$

$$P = \frac{P_b M_o}{M_o - M_b + P_b M/P} \tag{45b}$$

The ACI *Code* gives the following approximations: For spiral columns:

$$M_o = 0.12 A_{st} f_y D_s \tag{46a}$$

where $D_s$ = diameter of circle through center of longitudinal reinforcement. For symmetric tied columns:

$$M_o = 0.40 A_s f_y (d - d') \tag{46b}$$

For unsymmetric tied columns:

$$M_o = 0.40 A_s f_y \, jd \tag{46c}$$

For symmetric spiral columns:

$$\frac{M_b}{P_b} = 0.43 p_g m D_s + 0.14t \tag{47a}$$

For symmetric tied columns:

$$\frac{M_b}{P_b} = d(0.67 p_g m + 0.17) \tag{47b}$$

For unsymmetric tied columns:

$$\frac{M_b}{P_b} = \frac{p'm(d - d') + 0.1d}{(p' - p)m + 0.6} \tag{47c}$$

where $p'$ = ratio of area of compression reinforcement to effective area of concrete. The value of $P_a$ is taken as

$$P_a = 0.34 f_c' A_g (1 + p_g m) \tag{48}$$

The value of $M_f$ is found by applying the section modulus of the transformed un-cracked section, using a modular ratio of $2n$ to account for stress transfer between steel and concrete engendered by plastic flow. (If the steel area is multiplied by $2n - 1$, allowance is made for the reduction of the concrete area.)

Computing $P_a$ and $M_f$ yields $A_g$ = 260 sq.in. (1677.5 cm²); $A_{st}$ = 7.62 sq.in. (49.164 cm²); $p_g$ = 7.62/260 = 0.0293; $m$ = 50/[0.85(4)] = 14.7; $p_g m$ = 0.431; $n$ = 8; $P_a$ = 0.34(4)(260)(1.431) = 506 kips (2250.7 kN).

The section modulus to be applied in evaluating $M_f$ is found thus: $I = (^1/_{12})(13)(20)^3 + 7.62(15)(7.5)^2$ = 15,100 in⁴ (62.85 dm⁴); $S = I/c$ = 15,100/10 = 1510 in³ (24,748.9 cm³); $M_f = Sf_c$ = 1510(1.8) = 2720 in.·kips (307.3 kN·m).

## 2. Compute $P_b$ and $M_b$

By Eq. 47b, $M_b/P_b$ = 17.5(0.67 × 0.431 + 0.17) = 8.03 in. (203.962 mm). By Eq. 44b, $P_b = P_a M_f/(M_f + 8.03 P_a)$ = 506 × 2720/(2720 + 8.03 × 506) = 203 kips (902.9 kN); $M_b$ = 8.03(203) = 1630 in.·kips (184.2 kN·m).

## 3. Compute $M_o$

By Eq. 46b, $M_o$ = 0.40(3.81)(50)(15) = 1140 in.·kips (128.8 kN·m).

## 4. Compute the limiting value of P

As established by Eq. 41, $P_{max}$ = 0.2125(4)(260) + 0.85(20)(7.62) = 351 kips (1561.2 kN).

## 5. Construct the interaction diagram

The complete diagram is shown in Fig. 23.

# AXIAL-LOAD CAPACITY OF A RECTANGULAR MEMBER

The member analyzed in the previous calculation procedure is to carry an eccentric longitudinal load. Determine the allowable load if the eccentricity as measured from $N$ is (a) 10 in. (254 mm); (b) 6 in. (152.4 mm).

### Calculation Procedure:

**1. Evaluate P when e = 10 in. (254 mm)**
As the preceding calculations show, the eccentricity corresponding to point $E$ in the interaction diagram is 8.03 in. (203.962 mm). Consequently, an eccentricity of 10 in. (254 mm) corresponds to a point on $EF$, and an eccentricity of 6 in. (152.4 mm) corresponds to a point on $ED$.

By Eq. 45b, $P = 203(1140)7(1140 - 1630 + 203 \times 10) = 150$ kips (667.2 kN).

**2. Evaluate P when e = 6 in. (152.4 mm)**
By Eq. 44b, $P = 506(2720)/(2720 + 506 \times 6) = 239$ kips (1063.1 kN).

# Design of Column Footings

A reinforced-concrete footing supporting a single column differs from the usual type of flexural member in the following respects: It is subjected to bending in all directions, the ratio of maximum vertical shear to maximum bending moment is very high, and it carries a heavy load concentrated within a small area. The consequences are as follows: The footing requires two-way reinforcement, its depth is determined by shearing rather than bending stress, the punching-shear stress below the column is usually more critical than the shearing stress that results from ordinary beam action, and the design of the reinforcement is controlled by the bond stress as well as the bending stress.

Since the footing weight and soil pressure are collinear, the former does not contribute to the vertical shear or bending moment. It is convenient to visualize the footing as being subjected to an upward load transmitted by the underlying soil and a downward reaction supplied by the column, this being, of course, an inversion of the true form of loading. The footing thus functions as an overhanging beam. The effective depth of footing is taken as the distance from the top surface to the center of the upper row of bars, the two rows being made identical to avoid confusion.

Refer to Fig. 24, which shows a square footing supporting a square, symmetrically located concrete column. Let $P$ = column load, kips (kN); $p$ = net soil pressure (that caused by the column load alone), lb/sq.ft. (kPa); $A$ = area of footing, sq/ft. (m²); $L$ = side of footing,

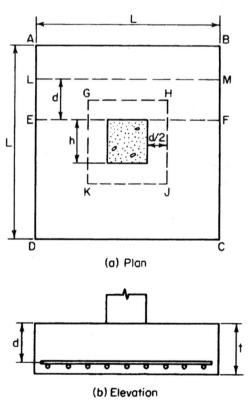

(a) Plan

(b) Elevation

**FIGURE 24**

ft (m); $h$ = side of column, in (mm); $d$ = effective depth of footing, ft (m); $t$ = thickness of footing, ft (m); $f_b$ = bearing stress at interface of column, lb/sq.in. (kPa); $v_1$ = nominal shearing stress under column, lb/sq.in. (kPa); $v_2$ = nominal shearing stress caused by beam action, lb/sq.in. (kPa); $b_o$ = width of critical section for $v_1$, ft (m); $V_1$ and $V_2$ = vertical shear at critical section for stresses $v_1$ and $v_2$, respectively.

In accordance with the ACI *Code*, the critical section for $v_1$ is the surface *GHJK*, the sides of which lie at a distance $d/2$ from the column faces. The critical section for $v_2$ is plane *LM*, located at a distance $d$ from the face of the column. The critical section for bending stress and bond stress is plane *EF* through the face of the column. In calculating $v_2$, $f$, and $u$, no allowance is made for the effects of the orthogonal reinforcement.

## DESIGN OF AN ISOLATED SQUARE FOOTING

A 20-in (508-mm) square tied column reinforced with eight no. 9 bars carries a concentric load of 380 kips (1690.2 kN). Design a square footing by the working-stress method using these values: the allowable soil pressure is 7000 lb/sq.ft. (335.2 kPa); $f'_c$ = 3000 lb/sq.in. (20,685 kPa); and $f_s$ = 20,000 lb/sq.in. (137,900 kPa).

### Calculation Procedure:

**1.  Record the allowable shear, bond, and bearing stresses**
From the ACI *Code* table, $v_1$ = 110 lb/sq.in. (758.5 kPa); $v_2$ = 60 lb/sq.in. (413.7 kPa); $f_b$ = 1125 lb/sq.in. (7756.9 kPa); $u$ = 4.8$(f'_c)^{0.5}$/bar diameter = 264/bar diameter.

**2.  Check the bearing pressure on the footing**
Thus, $f_b$, = 380/[20(20)] = 0.95 kips/sq.in. (7.258 MPa) < 1.125 kips/sq.in. (7.7568 MPa). This is acceptable.

**3.  Establish the length of footing**
For this purpose, assume the footing weight is 6 percent of the column load. Then $A$ = 1.06(380)/7 = 57.5 sq.ft. (5.34 sq.in.). Make $L$ = 7 ft 8 in. = 7.67 ft (2.338 m); $A$ = 58.8 sq.ft. (5.46 m²).

**4.  Determine the effective depth as controlled by $v_1$**
Apply

$$(4v_1 + p)d^2 + h(4v_1 + 2p)d = p(A - h^2) \qquad (49)$$

Verify the result after applying this equation. Thus $p$ = 380/58.8 = 6.46 kips/sq.ft. (0.309 MPa) = 0.11(144) = 15.84 kips/sq.ft. (0.758 MPa); 69.8$d^2$ + 127.1$d$ = 361.8; $d$ = 1.54 ft (0.469 m). Checking in Fig. 24, we see $GH$ = 1.67 + 1.54 = 3.21 ft (0.978 m); $V_1$ = 6.46(58.8 − 3.21²) = 313 kips (1392.2 kN); $v_1$ = $V_1/(b_od)$ = 313/[4(3.21)(1.54)] = 15.83 kips/sq.in. (0.758 MPa). This is acceptable.

**5.  Establish the thickness and true depth of footing**
Compare the weight of the footing with the assumed weight. Allowing 3 in. (76.2 mm) for insulation and assuming the use of no. 8 bars, we see that $t$ = $d$ + 4.5 in. (114.3 mm). Then $t$ = 1.54(12) + 4.5 = 23.0 in. (584.2 mm). Make $t$ = 24 in. (609.6 mm); $d$ = 19.5 in. = 1.63 ft (0.496 m). The footing weight = 58.8(2)(0.150) = 17.64 kips (1384.082 kN). The assumed weight = 0.06(380) = 22.8 kips (101.41 kN). This is acceptable.

**6.  Check $v_2$**
In Fig. 24, $AL$ = (7.67 − 1.67)/2 − 1.63 = 1.37 ft (0.417 m); $V_2$ = 380(1.37/7.67) = 67.9 kips (302.02 kN); $v_2$ = $V_2/(Ld)$ = 67,900/[92(19.5)] = 38 lb/sq.in. (262.0 kPa) < 60 lb/sq.in. (413.7 kPa). This is acceptable.

### 7. Design the reinforcement

In Fig. 24, $EA = 3.00$ ft (0.914 m); $V_{EF} = 380(3.00/7.67) = 148.6$ kips (666.97 kN); $M_{EF} = 148.6(^{1}/_{2})(3.00)(12) = 2675$ in.·kips (302.22 kN·m); $A_s = 2675/[20(0.874)(19.5)] = 7.85$ sq.in. (50.648 cm²). Try 10 no. 8 bars each way. Then $A_s = 7.90$ sq.in. (50.971 cm²); $\Sigma o = 31.4$ in. (797.56 mm); $u = V_{EF}/\Sigma ojd = 148,600/[31.4(0.874)(19.5)] = 278$ lb/sq.in. (1916.81 kPa); $u_{\text{allow}} = 264/1 = 264$ lb/sq.in. (1820.3 kPa).

The bond stress at $EF$ is slightly excessive. However, the ACI *Code*, in sections based on ultimate-strength considerations, permits disregarding the local bond stress if the average bond stress across the length of embedment is less than 80 percent of the allowable stress. Let $L_e$ denote this length. Then $L_e = EA - 3 = 33$ in. (838.2 mm); $0.80u_{\text{allow}} = 211$ lb/sq.in. (1454.8 kPa); $u_{av} = A_s f_s/(L_e \Sigma o) = 0.79(20,000)/[33(3.1)] = 154$ lb/sq.in. (1061.8 kPa). This is acceptable.

### 8. Design the dowels to comply with the Code

The function of the dowels is to transfer the compressive force in the column reinforcing bars to the footing. Since this is a tied column, assume the stress in the bars is $0.85(20,000) = 17,000$ lb/sq.in. (117,215.0 kPa). Try eight no. 9 dowels with $f_y = 40,000$ lb/sq.in. (275,800.0 kPa). Then $u = 264/(9/8) = 235$ lb/sq.in. (1620.3 kPa); $L_e = 1.00(17,000)/[235(3.5)] = 20.7$ in. (525.78 mm). Since the footing can provide a 21-in. (533.4-mm) embedment length, the dowel selection is satisfactory. Also, the length of lap $= 20(9/8) = 22.5$ in. (571.5 mm); length of dowels $= 20.7 + 22.5 = 43.2$, say 44 in. (1117.6 mm). The footing is shown in Fig. 25.

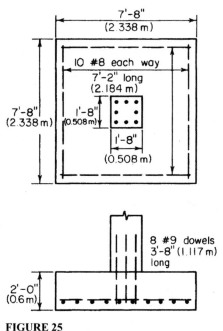

**FIGURE 25**

## COMBINED FOOTING DESIGN

An 18-in. (457.2-mm) square exterior column and a 20-in. (508.0-mm) square interior column carry loads of 250 kips (1112 kN) and 370 kips (1645.8 kN), respectively. The column centers are 16 ft (4.9 m) apart, and the footing cannot project beyond the face of the exterior column. Design a combined rectangular footing by the working-stress method, using $f_c' = 3000$ lb/sq.in. (20,685.0 kPa), $f_s = 20,000$ lb/sq.in. (137,900.0 kPa), and an allowable soil pressure of 5000 lb/sq.in. (239.4 kPa).

### Calculation Procedure:

### 1. Establish the length of footing, applying the criterion of uniform soil pressure under total live and dead loads

In many instances, the exterior column of a building cannot be individually supported because the required footing would project beyond the property limits. It then becomes necessary to use a combined footing that supports the exterior column and the adjacent

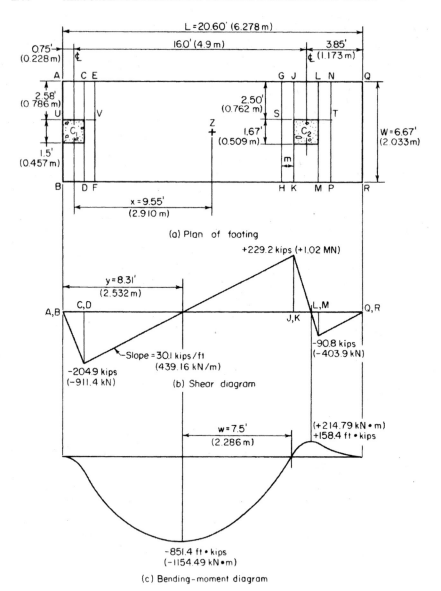

(a) Plan of footing

(b) Shear diagram

(c) Bending-moment diagram

**FIGURE 26**

interior column, the footing being so proportioned that the soil pressure is approximately uniform.

The footing dimensions are shown in Fig. 26a, and the reinforcement is seen in Fig. 27. It is convenient to visualize the combined footing as being subjected to an upward load transmitted by the underlying soil and reactions supplied by the columns. The member

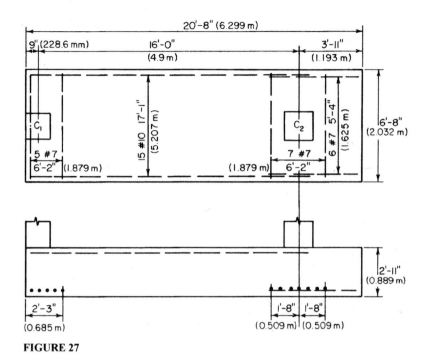

**FIGURE 27**

thus functions as a beam that overhangs one support. However, since the footing is considerably wider than the columns, there is a transverse bending as well as longitudinal bending in the vicinity of the columns. For simplicity, assume that the transverse bending is confined to the regions bounded by planes $AB$ and $EF$ and by planes $GH$ and $NP$, the distance $m$ being $h/2$ or $d/2$, whichever is smaller.

In Fig. 26$a$, let $Z$ denote the location of the resultant of the column loads. Then $x = 370(16)/(250 + 370) = 9.55$ ft (2.910 m). Since $Z$ is to be the centroid of the footing, $L = 2(0.75 + 9.55) = 20.60$ ft (6.278 m). Set $L = 20$ ft 8 in. (6.299 m), but use the value 20.60 ft (6.278 m) in the stress calculations.

## 2. Construct the shear and bending-moment diagrams
The net soil pressure per foot of length $= 620/20.60 = 30.1$ kips/lin ft (439.28 kN/m). Construct the diagrams as shown in Fig. 26.

## 3. Establish the footing thickness
Use

$$(Pv_2 + 0.17VL + Pp')d - 0.17Pd^2 - VLp' \qquad (50)$$

where $P$ = aggregate column load, kips (kN); $V$ = maximum vertical shear at a column face, kips (kN); $p'$ = gross soil pressure, kips/sq.ft. (MPa).

Assume that the longitudinal steel is centered $3\frac{1}{2}$ in. (88.9 mm) from the face of the footing. Then $P = 620$ kips (2757.8 kN); $V = 229.2$ kips (1019.48 kN); $v_2 = 0.06(144) = 8.64$ kips/sq.ft. (0.414 MPa); $9260d - 105.4d^2 = 23,608$; $d = 2.63$ ft (0.801 m); $t = 2.63 + 0.29 = 2.92$ ft. Set $t = 2$ ft 11 in. (0.889 m); $d = 2$ ft $7\frac{1}{2}$ in. (0.800 m).

### 4. Compute the vertical shear at distance d from the column face

Establish the width of the footing. Thus $V = 229.2 - 2.63(30.1) = 150.0$ kips (667.2 kN); $v = V/(Wd)$, or $W = V/(vd) = 150/[8.64(2.63)] = 6.60$ ft (2.012 m). Set $W = 6$ ft 8 in.(2.032 m).

### 5. Check the soil pressure

The footing weight $= 20.67(6.67)(2.92)(0.150) = 60.4$ kips (268.66 kN); $p' = (620 + 60.4)/[(20.67)(6.67)] = 4.94$ kips/sq.ft. (0.236 MPa) $< 5$ kips/sq.ft. (0.239 MPa). This is acceptable.

### 6. Check the punching shear

Thus, $p = 4.94 - 2.92(0.150) = 4.50$ kips/sq.ft. (0.215 MPa). At C1: $b_o = 18 + 31.5 + 2 (18 + 15.8) = 117$ in. (2971.8 mm); $V = 250 - 4.50(49.5)(33.8)/144 = 198$ kips (880.7 kN); $v_1 = 198,000/[117(31.5)] = 54$ lb/sq.in. (372.3 kPa) $< 110$ lb/sq.in. (758.5 kPa); this is acceptable.

At C2: $b_o = 4(20 + 31.5) = 206$ in. (5232.4 mm); $V = 370 - 4.50(51.5)^2/144 = 287$ kips (1276.6 kN); $v_1 = 287,000/[206(31.5)] = 44$ lb/sq.in. (303.4 kPa). This is acceptable.

### 7. Design the longitudinal reinforcement for negative moment

Thus, $M = 851,400$ ft·lb $= 10,217,000$ in.·lb (1,154,316.6 N·m); $M_b = 223(80)(31.5)^2 = 17,700,000$ in.·lb (1,999,746.0 N·m). Therefore, the steel is stressed to capacity, and $A_s = 10,217,000/[20,000(0.874)(31.5)] = 18.6$ sq.in. (120.01 cm²). Try 15 no. 10 bars with $A_s = 19.1$ sq.in. (123.2 cm²); $\Sigma o = 59.9$ in. (1521.46 mm).

The bond stress is maximum at the point of contraflexure, where $V = 15.81(30.1) - 250 = 225.9$ kips (1004.80 kN); $u = 225,900/[59.9(0.874)(31.5)] = 137$ lb/sq.in. (944.6 kPa); $u_{allow} = 3.4(3000)^{0.5}/1.25 = 149$ lb/sq.in. (1027.4 kPa). This is acceptable.

### 8. Design the longitudinal reinforcement for positive moment

For simplicity, design for the maximum moment rather than the moment at the face of the column. Then $A_s = 158,400(12)/[20,000(0.874)(31.5)] = 3.45$ sq.in. (22.259 cm²). Try six no. 7 bars with $A_s = 3.60$ sq.in. (23.227 cm²); $\Sigma o = 16.5$ in. (419.10 mm). Take $LM$ as the critical section for bond, and $u = 90,800/[16.5(0.874)(31.5)] = 200$ lb/sq.in. (1379.0 kPa); $u_{allow} = 4.8(3000)^{0.5}/0.875 = 302$ lb/sq.in. (2082.3 kPa). This is acceptable.

### 9. Design the transverse reinforcement under the interior column

For this purpose, consider member $GNPH$ as an independent isolated footing. Then $V_{ST} = 370(2.50/6.67) = 138.8$ kips (617.38 kN); $M_{ST} = {}^1/_2(138.8)(2.50)(12) = 2082$ in.·kips (235.22 kN·m). Assume $d = 35 - 4.5 = 30.5$ in. (774.7 mm); $A_s = 2,082,000/[20,000(0.874)(30.5)] = 3.91$ sq.in. (25.227 cm²). Try seven no. 7 bars; $A_s = 4.20$ sq.in. (270.098 cm²); $\Sigma o = 19.2$ in. (487.68 mm); $u = 138,800/[19.2(0.874)(30.5)] = 271$ lb/sq.in. (1868.5 kPa); $u_{allow} = 302$ lb/sq.in. (2082.3 kPa). This is acceptable.

Since the critical section for shear falls outside the footing, shearing stress is not a criterion in this design.

### 10. Design the transverse reinforcement under the exterior column; disregard eccentricity

Thus, $V_{UV} = 250(2.58/6.67) = 96.8$ kips (430.57 kN); $M_{UV} = {}^1/_2(96.8)(2.58)(12) = 1498$ in.·kips (169.3 kN·m); $A_s = 2.72$ sq.in. (17.549 cm²). Try five no. 7 bars; $A_s = 3.00$ sq.in. (19.356 cm²); $\Sigma o - 13.7$ in. (347.98 mm); $u = 96,800/[13.7(0.874)(31.5)] = 257$ lb/sq.in. (1772.0 kPa). This is acceptable.

# Cantilever Retaining Walls

Retaining walls having a height ranging from 10 to 20 ft (3.0 to 6.1 m) are generally built as reinforced-concrete cantilever members. As shown in Fig. 28, a cantilever wall comprises a vertical stem to retain the soil, a horizontal base to support the stem, and in many instances a key that projects into the underlying soil to augment the resistance to sliding. Adequate drainage is an essential requirement, because the accumulation of water or ice behind the wall would greatly increase the horizontal thrust.

The calculation of earth thrust in this section is based on Rankine's theory, which is developed in a later calculation procedure. When a live load, termed a *surcharge*, is applied to the retained soil, it is convenient to replace this load with a hypothetical equivalent prism of earth. Referring to Fig. 28, consider a portion $QR$ of the wall, $R$ being at distance $y$ below the top. Take the length of wall normal to the plane of the drawing as 1 ft (0.3 m). Let $T$ = resultant earth thrust on $QR$; $M$ = moment of this thrust with respect to $R$; $h$ = height of equivalent earth prism that replaces surcharge; $w$ = unit weight of earth; $C_a$ = coefficient of active earth pressure; $C_p$ = coefficient of passive earth pressure. Then

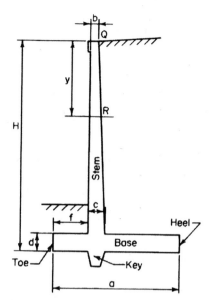

**FIGURE 28.** Cantilever retaining wall.

$$T = \tfrac{1}{2}C_a wy(y + 2h) \tag{51}$$

$$M = (\tfrac{1}{6})C_a wy^2(y + 3h) \tag{52}$$

## DESIGN OF A CANTILEVER RETAINING WALL

Applying the working-stress method, design a reinforced-concrete wall to retain an earth bank 14 ft (4.3 m) high. The top surface is horizontal and supports a surcharge of 500 lb/sq.ft. (23.9 kPa). The soil weighs 130 lb/ft³ (20.42 kN/m³), and its angle of internal friction is 35°; the coefficient of friction of soil and concrete is 0.5. The allowable soil pressure is 4000 lb/sq.ft. (191.5 kPa); $f_c' = 3000$ lb/sq.in. (20,685 kPa) and $f_y = 40,000$ lb/sq.in. (275,800 kPa). The base of the structure must be set 4 ft (1.2 m) below ground level to clear the frost line.

### Calculation Procedure:

#### 1. Secure a trial section of the wall
Apply these relations: $a = 0.60H$; $b \le 8$ in. (203.2 mm); $c = d = b + 0.045h$; $f = a/3 - c/2$.

The trial section is shown in Fig. 29a, and the reinforcement is shown in Fig. 30. As the calculation will show, it is necessary to provide a key to develop the required resistance to sliding. The sides of the key are sloped to ensure that the surrounding soil will remain undisturbed during excavation.

## 2. Analyze the trial section for stability

The requirements are that there be a factor of safety (FS) against sliding and overturning of at least 1.5 and that the soil pressure have a value lying between 0 and 4000 lb/sq.ft. (0 and 191.5 kPa). Using the equation developed later in this handbook gives $h$ = surcharge/soil weight = 500/130 = 3.85 ft (1.173 m); sin 35° = 0.574; tan 35° = 0.700; $C_a$ = 0.271; $C_p$ = 3.69; $C_a w$ = 35.2 lb/ft$^3$ (5.53 kN/m$^3$); $C_p w$ = 480 lb/ft$^3$ (75.40 kN/m$^3$); $T_{AB}$ = $1/2$(35.2)18(18 + 2 × 3.85) = 8140 lb (36,206.7 N); $M_{AB}$ = ($1/6$)35.2(18)$^2$(18 + 3 × 3.85) = 56,200 ft·lb (76,207.2 N·m).

The critical condition with respect to stability is that in which the surcharge extends to G. The moments of the stabilizing forces with respect to the toe are computed in Table 2. In Fig. 29c, $x$ = 81,030/21,180 = 3.83 ft (1.167 m); $e$ = 5.50 − 3.83 = 1.67 ft (0.509 m). The fact that the resultant strikes the base within the middle third attests to the absence of uplift. By $f$ = $(P/A)(1 ± 6e_x/d_x ± 6e_y/d_y)$, $p_a$ = (21,180/11)(1 + 6 × 1.67/11) = 3680 lb/sq.ft. (176.2 kPa); $p_b$ = (21,180/11)(1 − 6 × 1.67/11) = 171 lb/sq.ft. (8.2 kPa). Check: $x$ = (11/3)(3680 + 2 × 171)/(3680 + 171) = 3.83 ft (1.167 m), as before. Also, $p_c$ = 2723 lb/sq.ft. (130.4 kPa); $p_d$ = 2244 lb/sq.ft. (107.4 kPa); FS against overturning = 137,230/56,200 = 2.44. This is acceptable.

Lateral displacement of the wall produces sliding of earth on earth to the left of C and of concrete on earth to the right of C. In calculating the passive pressure, the layer of earth lying above the base is disregarded, since its effectiveness is unknown. The resistance to sliding is as follows: friction, A to C (Fig. 29): $1/2$(3680 + 2723)(3)(0.700) = 6720 lb (29,890.6 N); friction, C to B: $1/2$(2723 + 171)(8)(0.5) = 5790 lb (25,753.9 N); passive earth pressure: $1/2$(480)(2.75)$^2$ = 1820 lb (8095.4 N). The total resistance to sliding is the sum of these three items, or 14,330 lb (63,739.8 N). Thus, the FS against sliding is 14,330/8140 = 1.76. This is acceptable because it exceeds 1.5. Hence the trial section is adequate with respect to stability.

## 3. Calculate the soil pressures when the surcharge extends to H

Thus $W_s$ = 500(6.5) = 3250 lb (14,456 N); $\Sigma W$ = 21,180 + 3250 = 24,430 lb (108,664.6 N); $M_a$ = 81,030 + 3250(7.75) = 106,220 ft·lb (144,034.3 N·m); $x$ = 106,220/24,430 = 4.35 ft (1.326 m); $e$ = 1.15 ft (0.351 m); $p_a$ = 3613 lb/sq.ft. (173 kPa); $p_b$ = 828 lb/sq.ft. (39.6 kPa); $p_c$ = 2853 lb/sq.ft. (136.6 kPa); $p_d$ = 2474 lb/sq.ft. (118.5 kPa).

**TABLE 2.**  Stability of Retaining Wall

| Force, lb (N) | | Arm, ft (m) | Moment, ft·lb (N·m) |
|---|---|---|---|
| $W_1$ 1.5(11)(150) | = 2,480 (11,031.0) | 5.50 (1.676) | 13,640 (18,495.8) |
| $W_2$ 0.67(16.5)(150) | = 1,650 (7,339.2) | 3.33 (1.015) | 5,500 (7,458.0) |
| $W_3$ 0.5(0.83)(16.5)(150) | = 1,030 (4,581.4) | 3.95 (1.204) | 4,070 (5,518.9) |
| $W_4$ 1.25(1.13)(150) | = 210 (934.1) | 3.75 (1.143) | 790 (1,071.2) |
| $W_5$ 0.5(0.83)(16.5)(130) | = 890 (3,958.7) | 4.23 (1.289) | 3,760 (5,098.6) |
| $W_6$ 6.5(16.5)(130) | = 13,940 (62,005.1) | 7.75 (2.362) | 108,000 (146,448.0) |
| $W_7$ 2.5(3)(130) | = 980 (4,359.1) | 1.50 (0.457) | 1,470 (1993.3) |
| Total | 21,180 (94,208.6) | | 137,230 (186,083.8) |
| Overturning moment | | | 56,200 (76,207.2) |
| Net moment about A | | | 81,030 (109,876.6) |

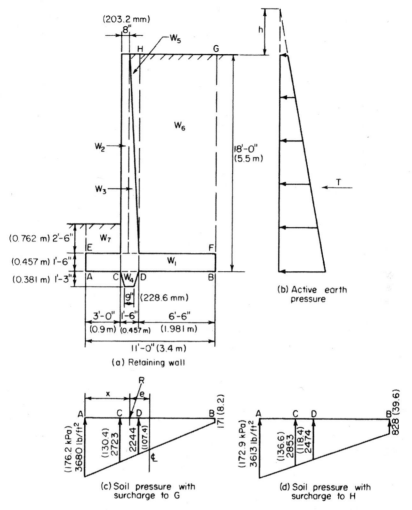

**FIGURE 29**

### 4. Design the stem

At the base of the stem, $y = 16.5$ ft (5.03 m) and $d = 18 - 3.5 = 14.5$ in. (368.30 mm); $T_{EF} = 7030$ lb (31,269.4 N); $M_{EF} = 538,000$ in.·lb (60,783.24 N·m). The allowable shear at a distance $d$ above the base is $V_{\text{allow}} = vbd = 60(12)(14.5) = 10,440$ lb (46,437.1 N). This is acceptable. Also, $M_b = 223(12)(14.5)^2 = 563,000$ in.·lb (63,607.74 N·m); therefore, the steel is stressed to capacity, and $A_s = 538,000/[20,000(0.874)(14.5)] = 2.12$ sq.in. (13.678 cm²). Use no. 9 bars 5½ in. (139.70 mm) on centers. Thus, $A_s = 2.18$ sq.in. (14.065 cm²); $\Sigma o = 7.7$ in. (195.58/mm); $u = 7030/[7.7(0.874)(14.5)] = 72$ lb/sq.in. (496.5 kPa); $u_{\text{allow}} = 235$ lb/sq.in. (1620.3 kPa). This is acceptable.

Alternate bars will be discontinued at the point where they become superfluous. As the following calculations demonstrate, the theoretical cutoff point lies at $y = 11$ ft 7 in.

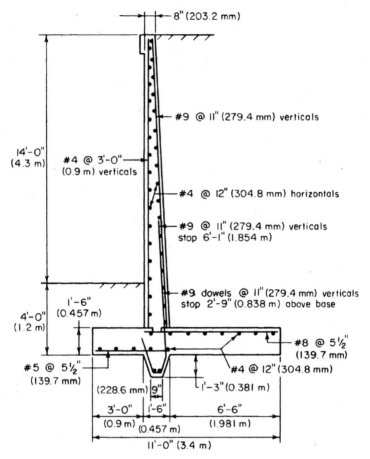

**FIGURE 30**

(3.531 m), where $M = 218,400$ in.·lb (24,674.8 N·m); $d = 4.5 + 10(11.58/16.5) = 11.52$ in. (292.608 mm); $A_s = 218,400/[20,000\ (0.874)(11.52)] = 1.08$ sq.in. (6.968 cm²). This is acceptable. Also, $T = 3930$ lb (17,480.6 N); $u = 101$ lb/sq.in. (696.4 kPa). This is acceptable. From the ACI *Code*, anchorage $= 12(9/8) = 13.5$ in. (342.9 mm).

The alternate bars will therefore be terminated at 6 ft 1 in. (1.854 m) above the top of the base. The *Code* requires that special precautions be taken where more than half the bars are spliced at a point of maximum stress. To circumvent this requirement, the short bars can be extended into the footing; therefore only the long bars require splicing. For the dowels, $u_{allow} = 0.75(235) = 176$ lb/sq.in. (1213.5 kPa); length of lap $= 1.00$ (20,000)/[176(3.5)] $= 33$ in. (838.2 mm).

### 5. *Design the heel*

Let $V$ and $M$ denote the shear and bending moment, respectively, at section $D$. Case 1: surcharge extending to $G$—downward pressure $p = 16.5(130) + 1.5(150) = 2370$ lb/sq.ft.(113.5 kPa); $V = 6.5[2370 - 1/2(2244 + 171)] = 7560$ lb (33,626.9 N); $M = 12(6.5)^2 [1/2 \times 2370 - 1/6(2244 + 2 \times 171)] = 383,000$ in.·lb (43,271.3 N·m).

Case 2: surcharge extending to $H-p = 2370 + 500 = 2870$ lb/sq.ft.(137.4 kPa); $V = 6.5[2870 - \frac{1}{2}(2474 + 828)] = 7920$ lb (35,228.1 N) $< V_{allow}$; $M = 12(6.5)^2 [\frac{1}{2} \times 2870 - \frac{1}{6}(2474 + 2 \times 828)] = 379,000$ in.·lb (42,819.4 N·m); $A_s = 2.12(383/538) = 1.51$ sq.in. (9.742 cm$^2$).

To maintain uniform bar spacing throughout the member, use no. 8 bars $5\frac{1}{2}$ in. (139.7 mm) on centers. In the heel, tension occurs at the top of the slab, and $A_s = 1.72$ sq.in. (11.097 cm$^2$); $\Sigma o = 6.9$ in. (175.26 mm); $u = 91$ lb/sq.in. (627.4 kPa); $u_{allow} = 186$ lb/sq.in. (1282.5 kPa). This is acceptable.

### 6. Design the toe
For this purpose, assume the absence of backfill on the toe, but disregard the minor modification in the soil pressure that results. Let $V$ and $M$ denote the shear and bending moment, respectively, at section $C$ (Fig. 29). The downward pressure $p = 1.5(150) = 225$ lb/sq.ft.(10.8 kPa).

Case 1: surcharge extending to $G$ (Fig. 29)—$V = 3[\frac{1}{2}(3680 + 2723) - 225] = 8930$ lb (39,720.6 N); $M = 12(3)^2[(\frac{1}{6})(2723 + 2 \times 3680) - \frac{1}{2}(225)] = 169,300$ in.·lb (19,127.5 N·m).

Case 2: surcharge extending to $H$ (Fig. 29)—$V = 9020$ lb (40,121.0 N) $< V_{allow}$; $M = 169,300$ in.·lb (19,127.5 N·m); $A_s = 2.12(169,300/538,000) = 0.67$ sq.in. (4.323 cm$^2$). Use no. 5 bars $5\frac{1}{2}$ in. (139.7 mm) on centers. Then $A_s = 0.68$ sq.in. (4.387 cm$^2$); $\Sigma o = 4.3$ in. (109.22 mm); $u = 166$ lb/sq.in. (1144.4 kPa); $u_{allow} = 422$ lb/sq.in. (2909.7 kPa). This is acceptable.

The stresses in the key are not amenable to precise evaluation. Reinforcement is achieved by extending the dowels and short bars into the key and bending them.

In addition to the foregoing reinforcement, no. 4 bars are supplied to act as temperature reinforcement and spacers for the main bars, as shown in Fig. 30.

---

## PART 2

# PRESTRESSED CONCRETE

---

Prestressed-concrete construction is designed to enhance the suitability of concrete as a structural material by inducing prestresses opposite in character to the stresses resulting from gravity loads. These prestresses are created by the use of steel wires or strands, called tendons, that are incorporated in the member and subjected to externally applied tensile forces. This prestressing of the steel may be performed either before or after pouring of the concrete. Thus, two methods of prestressing a concrete beam are available: pretensioning and posttensioning.

In pretensioning, the tendons are prestressed to the required amount by means of hydraulic jacks, their ends are tied to fixed abutments, and the concrete is poured around the tendons. When hardening of the concrete has advanced to the required state, the tendons are released. The tendons now tend to contract longitudinally to their original length and to expand laterally to their original diameter, both these tendencies being opposed by the surrounding concrete. As a result of the longitudinal restraint, the concrete exerts a tensile force on the steel and the steel exerts a compressive force on the concrete. As a result of the lateral restraint, the tendons are deformed to a wedge shape across a relatively short distance at each end of the member. It is within this distance, termed the *transmission length*, that the steel becomes bonded to the concrete and the two materials exert their prestressing forces on each other. However, unless greater precision is warranted, it is assumed for simplicity that the prestressing forces act at the end sections.

The tendons may be placed either in a straight line or in a series of straight-line segments, being deflected at designated points by means of holding devices. In the latter case, prestressing forces between steel and concrete occur both at the ends and at these deflection points.

In posttensioning, the procedure usually consists of encasing the tendons in metal or rubber hoses, placing these in the forms, and then pouring the concrete. When the concrete has hardened, the tendons are tensioned and anchored to the ends of the concrete beam by means of devices called *end anchorages*. If the hoses are to remain in the member, the void within the hose is filled with grout. Posttensioning has two important advantages compared with pretensioning: It may be performed at the job site, and it permits the use of parabolic tendons.

The term at transfer refers to the instant at which the prestressing forces between steel and concrete are developed. (In posttensioning, where the tendons are anchored to the concrete one at a time, in reality these forces are developed in steps.) Assume for simplicity that the tendons are straight and that the resultant prestressing force in these tendons lies below the centroidal axis of the concrete section. At transfer, the member cambers (deflects upward), remaining in contact with the casting bed only at the ends. Thus, the concrete beam is compelled to resist the prestressing force and to support its own weight simultaneously.

At transfer, the prestressing force in the steel diminishes because the concrete contracts under the imposed load. The prestressing force continues to diminish as time elapses as a result of the relaxation of the steel and the shrinkage and plastic flow of the concrete subsequent to transfer. To be effective, prestressed-concrete construction therefore requires the use of high-tensile steel in order that the reduction in prestressing force may be small in relation to the initial force. In all instances, we assume that the ratio of final to initial prestressing force is 0.85. Moreover, to simplify the stress calculations, we also assume that the full initial prestressing force exists at transfer and that the entire reduction in this force occurs during some finite interval following transfer.

Therefore, two loading states must be considered in the design: the initial state, in which the concrete sustains the initial prestressing force and the beam weight; and the final state, in which the concrete sustains the final prestressing force, the beam weight, and all superimposed loads. Consequently, the design of a prestressed-concrete beam differs from that of a conventional type in that designers must consider two stresses at each point, the initial stress and the final stress, and these must fall between the allowable compressive and tensile stresses. A beam is said to be in *balanced design* if the critical initial and final stresses coincide precisely with the allowable stresses.

The term *prestress* designates the stress induced by the *initial* prestressing force. The terms *prestress shear* and *prestress moment* refer to the vertical shear and bending moment, respectively, that the initial prestressing force induces in the concrete at a given section.

The *eccentricity* of the prestressing force is the distance from the action line of this resultant force to the centroidal axis of the section. Assume that the tendons are subjected to a uniform prestress. The locus of the centroid of the steel area is termed the *trajectory* of the steel or of the prestressing force.

The sign convention is as follows: The eccentricity is positive if the action line of the prestressing force lies below the centroidal axis. The trajectory has a positive slope if it inclines downward to the right. A load is positive if it acts downward. The vertical shear at a given section is positive if the portion of the beam to the left of this section exerts an upward force on the concrete. A bending moment is positive if it induces compression above the centroidal axis and tension below it. A compressive stress is positive; a tensile stress, negative.

The notational system is as follows. Cross-sectional properties: $A$ = gross area of section, sq.in. (cm$^2$); $A_s$ = area of prestressing steel, sq.in. (cm$^2$); $d$ = effective depth of section at ultimate strength, in. (mm); $h$ = total depth of section, in. (mm); $I$ = moment of inertia of gross area, in$^4$ (cm$^4$); $y_b$ = distance from centroidal axis to bottom fiber, in. (mm); $S_b$ = section modulus with respect to bottom fiber = $I/y_b$, in$^3$ (cm$^3$); $k_b$ = distance from centroidal axis to lower kern point, in. (mm); $k_t$ = distance from centroidal axis to upper kern point, in. (mm). *Forces and moments*: $F_i$ = initial prestressing force, lb (N); $F_f$ = final prestressing force, lb (N); $\eta = F_f/F_i$; $e$ = eccentricity of prestressing force, in. (mm); $e_{con}$ = eccentricity of prestressing force having concordant trajectory; $\theta$ = angle between trajectory (or tangent to trajectory) and horizontal line; $m$ = slope of trajectory; $w$ = vertical load exerted by curved tendons on concrete in unit distance; $w_w$ = unit beam weight; $w_s$ = unit superimposed load; $w_{DL}$ = unit dead load; $w_{LL}$ = unit live load; $w_u$ = unit ultimate load; $V_p$ = prestress shear; $M_p$ = prestress moment; $M_w$ = bending moment due to beam weight; $M_s$ = bending moment due to superimposed load; $C_u$ = resultant compressive force at ultimate load; $T_u$ = resultant tensile force at ultimate load. *Stresses*: $f_c'$ = ultimate compressive strength of concrete, lb/sq.in. (kPa); $f_{ci}'$ compressive strength of concrete at transfer; $f_s'$ = ultimate strength of prestressing steel; $f_{su}$ = stress in prestressing steel at ultimate load; $f_{bp}$ = stress in bottom fiber due to initial prestressing force; $f_{bw}$ = bending stress in bottom fiber due to beam weight; $f_{bs}$ = bending stress in bottom fiber due to superimposed loads; $f_{bi}$ = stress in bottom fiber at initial state = $f_{bp}$ + $f_{bw}$; $f_{bf}$ = stress in bottom fiber at final state = $\eta f_{bp} + f_{bw} + f_{bs}$; $f_{cai}$ = initial stress at centroidal axis. *Camber*: $\Delta_p$ = camber due to initial prestressing force, in. (mm); $\Delta_w$ = camber due to beam weight; $\Delta_i$ = camber at initial state; $\Delta_f$ = camber at final state.

The symbols that refer to the bottom fiber are transformed to their counterparts for the top fiber by replacing the subscript $b$ with $t$. For example, $f_{ti}$ denotes the stress in the top fiber at the initial state.

## DETERMINATION OF PRESTRESS SHEAR AND MOMENT

The beam in Fig. 31*a* is simply supported at its ends and prestressed with an initial force of 300 kips (1334.4 kN). At section $C$, the eccentricity of this force is 8 in. (203.2 mm), and the slope of the trajectory is 0.014. (In the drawing, vertical distances are exaggerated in relation to horizontal distances.) Find the prestress shear and prestress moment at $C$.

### Calculation Procedure:

#### 1. Analyze the prestressing forces

If the composite concrete-and-steel member is regarded as a unit, the prestressing forces that the steel exerts on the concrete are purely internal. Therefore, if a beam is simply supported, the prestressing force alone does not induce any reactions at the supports.

Refer to Fig. 31*b*, and consider the forces acting on the beam segment $GB$ solely as a result of $F_i$. The left portion of the beam exerts a tensile force $F_i$ on the tendons. Since $GB$

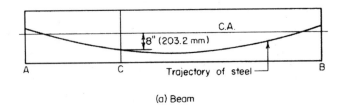

(a) Beam

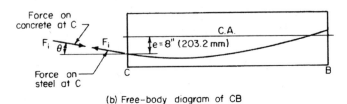

(b) Free-body diagram of CB

**FIGURE 31**

is in equilibrium, the left portion also induces compressive stresses on the concrete at $C$, these stresses having a resultant that is numerically equal to and collinear with $F_i$.

### 2. *Express the prestress shear and moment in terms of $F_i$*

Using the sign convention described, express the prestress shear and moment in terms of $F_i$ and $\theta$. (The latter is positive if the slope of the trajectory is positive.) Thus $V_p = -F_i \sin \theta$; $M_p = -F_i e \cos \theta$.

### 3. *Compute the prestress shear and moment*

Since $\theta$ is minuscule, apply these approximations: $\sin \theta = \tan \theta$, and $\cos \theta = 1$. Then

$$V_p = -F_i \tan \theta \tag{53}$$

Or, $V_p = -300{,}000(0.014) = -4200$ lb $(-18{,}681.6$ N$)$.
   Also,

$$M_p = -F_i e \tag{54}$$

Or, $M_p = -300{,}000(8) = -2{,}400{,}000$ in.·lb $(-271{,}152$ N·m$)$.

## STRESSES IN A BEAM WITH STRAIGHT TENDONS

A $12 \times 18$ in. $(304.8 \times 457.2$ mm$)$ rectangular beam is subjected to an initial prestressing force of 230 kips $(1023.0$ kN$)$ applied 3.3 in. $(83.82$ mm$)$ below the center. The beam is on a simple span of 30 ft $(9.1$ m$)$ and carries a superimposed load of 840 lb/lin ft $(12{,}258.9$ N/m$)$. Determine the initial and final stresses at the supports and at midspan. Construct diagrams to represent the initial and final stresses along the span.

## Calculation Procedures:

### 1. Compute the beam properties
Thus, $A = 12(18) = 216$ sq.in. (1393.6 cm$^2$); $S_b = S_t = (\frac{1}{6})(12)(18)^2 = 648$ in$^3$ (10,620.7 cm$^3$); $w_w = (216/144)(150) = 225$ lb/lin ft (3,283.6 N/m).

### 2. Calculate the prestress in the top and bottom fibers
Since the section is rectangular, apply $f_{bp} = (F_i/A)(1 + 6e/h) = (230,000/216)(1 + 6 \times 3.3/18) = +2236$ lb/sq.in. (+15,417.2 kPa); $f_{tp} = (F_i/A)(1 - 6e/h) = -106$ lb/sq.in. (−730.9 kPa).

For convenience, record the stresses in Table 1 as they are obtained.

### 3. Determine the stresses at midspan due to gravity loads
Thus $M_s = (\frac{1}{8})(840)(30)^2(12) = 1,134,000$ in.·lb (128,119.32 N·m); $f_{bs} = -1,134,000/648 = -1750$ lb/sq.in. (−12,066.3 kPa); $f_{ts} = +1750$ lb/sq.in. (12,066.3 kPa). By proportion, $f_{bw} = -1750(225/840) = -469$; $f_{tw} = +469$ lb/sq.in. (+3233.8 kPa).

### 4. Compute the initial and final stresses at the supports
Thus, $f_{bi} = +2236$ lb/sq.in. (+15,417.2 kPa); $f_{ti} = -106$ lb/sq.in. (−730.9 kPa); $f_{bf} = 0.85(2236) = +1901$ lb/sq.in. (+13,107.4 kPa); $f_{tf} = 0.85(-106) = -90$ lb/sq.in. (−620.6 kPa).

### 5. Determine the initial and final stresses at midspan
Thus $f_{bi} = +2236 - 469 = +1767$ lb/sq.in. (+12,183.5 kPa); $f_{ti} = -106 + 469 = +363$ lb/sq.in. (+2502.9 kPa); $f_{bf} = +1901 - 469 - 1750 = -318$ lb/sq.in. (−2192.6 kPa); $f_{tf} = -90 + 469 + 1750 = +2129$ lb/sq.in. (+14,679.5 kPa).

### 6. Construct the initial-stress diagram
In Fig. 32a, construct the initial-stress diagram $A_rA_bBC$ at the support and the initial-stress diagram $M_tM_bDE$ at midspan. Draw the parabolic arcs $BD$ and $CE$. The stress diagram at an intermediate section $Q$ is obtained by passing a plane normal to the longitudinal axis.

**TABLE 3.** Stresses in Prestressed-Concrete Beam

|  | At support | | At midspan | |
|---|---|---|---|---|
|  | Bottom fiber | Top fiber | Bottom fiber | Top fiber |
| (a) Initial prestress, lb/sq.in. (kPa) | +2,236 (+15,417.2) | −106 (−730.9) | +2,236 (+15,417.2) | −106 (−730.9) |
| (b) Final prestress, lb/sq.in. (kPa) | +1,901 (+13,107.4) | −90 (−620.6) | +1,901 (+13,107.4) | −90 (−620.6) |
| (c) Stress due to beam weight, lb/sq.in. (kPa) | . . . . . | . . . . . | −469 (−3,233.8) | +469 (3,233.8) |
| (d) Stress due to superimposed load, lb/sq.in. (kPa) | . . . . . | . . . . . | −1,750 (−12,066.3) | +1,750(+12,066.3) |
| Initial stress: (a) + (c) | +2,236 (+15,417.2) | −106 (−730.9) | +1,767 (+12,183.5) | +363 (+2,502.9) |
| Final stress: (b) + (c) + (d) | +1,901 (+13,107.4) | −90 (−620.6) | −318 (−2,192.6) | +2,129(+14,679.5) |

The offset from a reference line through $B$ to the arc $BD$ represents the value of $f_{bw}$ at that section.

### 7. Construct the final-stress diagram

Construct Fig. 32b in an analogous manner. The offset from a reference line through $B'$ to the arc $B'D'$ represents the value of $f_{bw} + f_{bs}$ at the given section.

### 8. Alternatively, construct composite stress diagrams for the top and bottom fibers

The diagram pertaining to the bottom fiber is shown in Fig. 33. The difference between the ordinates to $DE$ and $AB$ represents $f_{bi}$ and the difference between the ordinates to $FG$ and $AC$ represents $f_{bf}$.

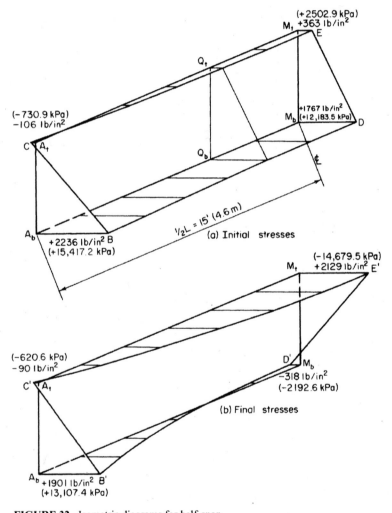

**FIGURE 32.** Isometric diagrams for half-span.

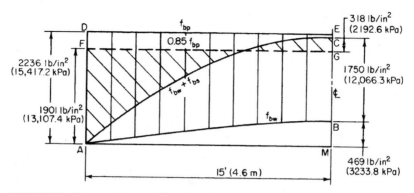

**FIGURE 33.** Stresses in bottom fiber along half-span.

This procedure illustrates the following principles relevant to a beam with straight tendons carrying a uniform load: At transfer, the critical stresses occur at the supports; under full design load, the critical stresses occur at midspan if the allowable final stresses exceed $\eta$ times the allowable initial stresses in absolute value.

The primary objective in prestressed-concrete design is to maximize the capacity of a given beam by maximizing the absolute values of the prestresses at the section having the greatest superimposed-load stresses. The three procedures that follow, when taken as a unit, illustrate the manner in which the allowable prestresses may be increased numerically by taking advantage of the beam-weight stresses, which are opposite in character to the prestresses. The next procedure will also demonstrate that when a beam is not in balanced design, there is a range of values of $F_i$ that will enable the member to carry this maximum allowable load. In summary, the objective is to maximize the capacity of a given beam and to provide the minimum prestressing force associated with this capacity.

## DETERMINATION OF CAPACITY AND PRESTRESSING FORCE FOR A BEAM WITH STRAIGHT TENDONS

An 8 × 10 in. (203.2 × 254 mm) rectangular beam, simply supported on a 20-ft (6.1-m) span, is to be prestressed by means of straight tendons. The allowable stresses are: *initial*, + 2400 and − 190 lb/sq.in. (+16,548 and −1310.1 kPa); *final*, + 2250 and −425 lb/sq.in. (+15,513.8 and −2930.3 kPa). Evaluate the allowable unit superimposed load, the maximum and minimum prestressing force associated with this load, and the corresponding eccentricities.

### Calculation Procedure:

#### 1. Compute the beam properties
Here $A = 80$ sq.in. (516.16 cm²); $S = 133$ cu in (2179.9 cu cm); $w_w = 83$ lb/lin ft (1211.3 N/m).

## 2. Compute the stresses at midspan due to the beam weight

Thus, $M_w = (\frac{1}{8})(83)(20)^2(12) = 49,800$ in.·lb (5626.4 N·m); $f_{bw} = -49,800/133 = -374$ lb/sq.in. $(-2578.7$ kPa); $f_{tw} = +374$ lb/sq.in. (2578.7 kPa).

## 3. Set the critical stresses equal to their allowable values to secure the allowable unit superimposed load

Use Fig. 32 or 33 as a guide. At support: $f_{bi} = +2400$ lb/sq.in. $(+16,548$ kPa); $f_{ti} = -190$ lb/sq.in. $(-1310.1$ kPa); at midspan, $f_{bf} = 0.85(2400) - 374 + f_{bs} = -425$ lb/sq.in. $(-2930.4$ kPa); $f_{tf} = 0.85(-190) + 374 + f_{ts} = +2250$ lb/sq.in. $(+15,513.8$ kPa). Also, $f_{bs} = -2091$ lb/sq.in. $(-14,417.4$ kPa); $f_{ts} = +2038$ lb/sq.in. $(+14,052$ kPa).

Since the superimposed-load stresses at top and bottom will be numerically equal, the latter value governs the beam capacity. Or $w_s = w_w, f_{ts}/f_{tw} = 83(2038/374) = 452$ lb/lin ft (6596.4 N/m).

## 4. Find $F_{i,max}$ and its eccentricity

The value of $w_s$ was found by setting the critical value of $f_{ti}$ and of $f_{tf}$ equal to their respective allowable values. However, since $S_b$ is excessive for the load $w_s$, there is flexibility with respect to the stresses at the bottom. The designer may set the critical value of either $f_{bi}$ or $f_{bf}$ equal to its allowable value or produce some intermediate condition. As shown by the calculations in step 3, $f_{bf}$ may vary within a range of $2091 - 2038 = 53$ lb/sq.in. (365.4 kPa). Refer to Fig. 34, where the lines represent the stresses indicated.

Points $B$ and $F$ are fixed, but points $A$ and $E$ may be placed anywhere within the 53-lb/sq.in. (365.4-kPa) range. To maximize $F_i$, place $A$ at its limiting position to the right; that is, set the critical value of $f_{bi}$ rather than that of $f_{bf}$ equal to the allowable value. Then $f_{cai} = F_{i,max}/A = \frac{1}{2}(2400 - 190) = +1105$ lb/sq.in. $(+7619.0$ kPa); $F_{i,max} = 1105(80) = 88,400$ lb (393,203.2 N); $f_{hp} = 1105 + 88,400e/133 = +2400$; $e = 1.95$ in. (49.53 mm).

## 5. Find $F_{i,min}$ and its eccentricity

For this purpose, place $A$ at its limiting position to the left. Then $f_{hp} = 2,400 - (53/0.85) = +2338$ lb/sq.in. $(+16,120.5$ kPa); $f_{cai} = +1074$ lb/sq.in. $(+7405.2$ kPa); $F_{i,min} = 85,920$ lb (382,172.2 N); $e = 1.96$ in. (49.78 mm).

## 6. Verify the value of $F_{i,max}$ by checking the critical stresses

At support: $f_{bi} = +2400$ lb/sq.in. $(+16,548.0$ kPa); $f_{ti} = -190$ lb/sq.in. $(-1310.1$ kPa). At midspan: $f_{bf} = +2040 - 374 - 2038 = -372$ lb/sq.in. $(-2564.9$ kPa); $f_{tf} = -162 + 374 + 2038 = +2250$ lb/sq.in. $(+15,513.8$ kPa).

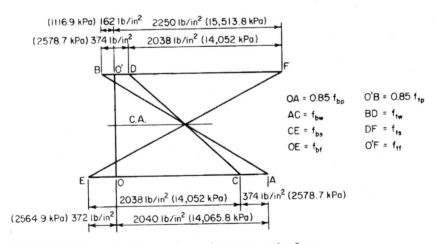

**FIGURE 34.** Stresses at midspan under maximum prestressing force.

## 7. Verify the value of $F_{i,min}$ by checking the critical stresses

At support: $f_{bi} = +2338$ lb/sq.in. (16,120.5 kPa); $f_{ti} = -190$ lb/sq.in. ($-1310.1$ kPa). At midspan: $f_{bf} = 0.85(2338) - 374 - 2038 = -425$ lb/sq.in. ($-2930.4$ kPa); $f_{tf} = +2250$ lb/sq.in. ($+15,513.8$ kPa).

## BEAM WITH DEFLECTED TENDONS

The beam in the previous calculation procedure is to be prestressed by means of tendons that are deflected at the quarter points of the span, as shown in Fig. 35a. Evaluate the allowable unit superimposed load, the magnitude of the prestressing force, the eccentricity $e_1$ in the center interval, and the maximum and minimum allowable values of the eccentricity $e_2$ at the supports. What increase in capacity has been obtained by deflecting the tendons?

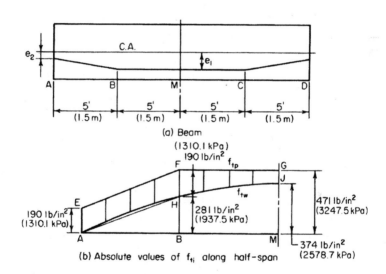

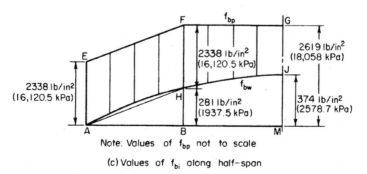

**FIGURE 35**

## Calculation Procedure:

### 1. Compute the beam-weight stresses at B

In the composite stress diagram, Fig. 35b, the difference between an ordinate to $EFG$ and the corresponding ordinate to $AHJ$ represents the value of $f_{ti}$ at the given section. It is apparent that if $AE$ does not exceed $HF$, then $f_{ti}$ does not exceed $HE$ in absolute value anywhere along the span. Therefore, for the center interval $BC$, the critical stresses at transfer occur at the boundary sections $B$ and $C$. Analogous observations apply to Fig. 35c.

Computing the beam-weight stresses at $B$ yields $f_{bw} = (^3/_4)(-374) = -281$ lb/sq.in. $(-1937.5$ kPa); $f_{tw} = +281$ lb/sq.in. $(+1937.5$ kPa).

### 2. Tentatively set the critical stresses equal to their allowable values to secure the allowable unit superimposed load

Thus, at $B$: $f_{bi} = f_{bp} - 281 = +2400$; $f_{ti} = f_{tp} + 281 = -190$; $f_{bp} = +2681$ lb/sq.in. $(+18,485.5$ kPa); $f_{tp} = -471$ lb/sq.in. $(-3247.5$ kPa).

At $M$: $f_{bf} = 0.85(2681) - 374 + f_{bs} = -425$; $f_{tf} = 0.85(-471) + 374 + f_{ts} = +2250$; $f_{bs} = -2330$ lb/sq.in. $(-16,065.4$ kPa); $f_{ts} = +2277$ lb/sq.in. $(+15,699.9$ kPa). The latter value controls.

Also, $w_s = 83(2277/374) = 505$ lb/lin ft $(7369.9$ N/m); $505/452 = 1.12$. The capacity is increased 12 percent.

When the foregoing calculations are compared with those in the previous calculation procedure, the effect of deflecting the tendons is to permit an increase of 281 lb/sq.in. $(1937.5$ kPa) in the absolute value of the prestress at top and bottom. The accompanying increase in $f_{ts}$ is $0.85(281) = 239$ lb/sq.in. $(1647.9$ kPa).

### 3. Find the minimum prestressing force and the eccentricity $e_1$

Examination of Fig. 34 shows that $f_{cai}$ is not affected by the form of trajectory used. Therefore, as in the previous calculation procedure, $F_i = 85,920$ lb $(382,172.2$ N); $f_{tp} = 1074 - 85,920e_1/133 = -471$; $e_1 = 2.39$ in. $(60.706$ mm).

Although it is not required, the value of $f_{bp} = 1074 + 1074 - (-471) = +2619$ lb/sq.in. $(+18,058$kPa), or $f_{bp} = 2681 - 53/0.85 = +2619$ lb/sq.in. $(+18,058$kPa).

### 4. Establish the allowable range of values of $e_2$

At the supports, the tendons may be placed an equal distance above or below the center. Then $e_{2,max} = 1.96$ in. $(23.44$ mm); $e_{2,min} = -1.96$ in. $(-23.44$ mm).

## BEAM WITH CURVED TENDONS

The beam in the second previous calculation procedure is to be prestressed by tendons lying in a parabolic arc. Evaluate the allowable unit superimposed load, the magnitude of the prestressing force, the eccentricity of this force at midspan, and the increase in capacity accruing from the use of curved tendons.

## Calculation Procedure:

### 1. Tentatively set the initial and final stresses at midspan equal to their allowable values to secure the allowable unit superimposed load

Since the prestressing force has a parabolic trajectory, lines $EFG$ in Fig. 35b and c will be parabolic in the present case. Therefore, it is possible to achieve the full allowable initial stresses at midspan. Thus, $f_{bi} = f_{bp} - 374 = +2400; f_{ti} = f_{tp} + 374 = -190; f_{bp} = +2774$ lb/sq.in. (+19,126.7 kPa); $f_{tp} = -564$ lb/sq.in. ($-3888.8$ kPa); $f_{bf} = 0.85(2774) - 374 + f_{bs} = -425; f_{tf} = 0.85(-564) + 374 + f_{ts} = +2250; f_{bs} = -2409$ lb/sq.in. ($-16,610.1$ kPa); $f_{ts} = +2356$ lb/sq.in.(+16,244.6 kPa). The latter value controls.

Also, $w_s = 83(2356/374) = 523$ lb/lin ft (7632.6 N/m); 523/452 = 1.16. Thus the capacity is increased 16 percent.

When the foregoing calculations are compared with those in the earlier calculation procedure, the effect of using parabolic tendons is to permit an increase of 374 lb/sq.in. (2578.7 kPa) in the absolute value of the prestress at top and bottom. The accompanying increase in $f_{ts}$ is 0.85(374) = 318 lb/sq.in. (2192.6 kPa).

### 2. Find the minimum prestressing force and its eccentricity at midspan

As before, $F_i = 85,920$ lb (382,172.2 N); $f_{tp} = 1074 - 85,920e/133 = -564; e = 2.54$ in. (64.516 mm).

## DETERMINATION OF SECTION MODULI

A beam having a cross-sectional area of 500 sq.in. (3226 cm²) sustains a beam-weight moment equal to 3500 in.·kips (395.4 kN·m) at midspan and a superimposed moment that varies parabolically from 9000 in.·kips (1016.8 kN·m) at midspan to 0 at the supports. The allowable stresses are: *initial*, +2400 and −190 lb/sq.in. (+16,548 and −1310.1 kPa); *final*, + 2250 and −200 lb/sq.in. (+15,513.8 and −1379 kPa). The member will be prestressed by tendons deflected at the quarter points. Determine the section moduli corresponding to balanced design, the magnitude of the prestressing force, and its eccentricity in the center interval. Assume that the calculated eccentricity is attainable (i.e., that the centroid of the tendons will fall within the confines of the section while satisfying insulation requirements).

### Calculation Procedure:

### 1. Equate the critical initial stresses, and the critical final stresses, to their allowable values

Let $M_w$ and $M_s$ denote the indicated moments at midspan; the corresponding moments at the quarter point are three-fourths as large. The critical initial stresses occur at the quarter point, while the critical final stresses occur at midspan. After equating the stresses to their allowable values, solve the resulting simultaneous equations to find the section moduli and prestresses. Thus: *stresses in bottom fiber,* $f_{bi} = f_{bp} - 0.75M_w/S_b = +2400; f_{bf} = 0.85f_{bp} - M_w/S_b - M_s/S_b = -200$. Solving gives $S_b = (M_s + 0.3625M_w)/2240 = 4584$ in³ (75,131.7 cm³) and $f_{bp} = +2973$ lb/sq.in. (+20,498.8 kPa); *stresses in top fiber,* $f_{ti} = f_{tp} + 0.75(M_w/S_t) = -190; f_{tf} = 0.85f_{tp} + M_w/S_t + M_s/S_t = +2250$. Solving yields $S_t = (M_s + 0.3625M_w)/2412 = 4257$ in³ (69,772.2 cm³) and $f_{tp} = -807$ lb/sq.in. (−5564.2 kPa).

### 2. Evaluate $F_i$ and $e$

In this instance, $e$ denotes the eccentricity in the center interval. Thus $f_{bp} = F_i/A + F_ie/S_b = +2973; f_{tp} = F_i/A - F_ie/S_t = -807; F_i = (2973S_b - 807S_t)A/(S_b + S_t) = 576,500$ lb (2,564,272.0 N); $e = 2973S_b/F_i - S_b/A = 14.47$ in. (367.538 mm).

### 3. Alternatively, evaluate $F_i$ by assigning an arbitrary depth to the member

Thus, set $h = 10$ in. (254 mm); $y_b = S_t h/(S_b + S_t) = 4.815$ in. (122.301 mm); $f_{cai} = f_{bp} - (f_{bp} - f_{tp})y_b/h = 2973 - (2973 + 807)0.4815 = +1153$ lb/sq.in. (+7949.9 kPa); $F_i = 1153(500) = 576,500$ lb (2,564,272.0 N).

## EFFECT OF INCREASE IN BEAM SPAN

Consider that the span of the beam in the previous calculation procedure increases by 10 percent, thereby causing the midspan moment due to superimposed load to increase by 21 percent. Show that the member will be adequate with respect to flexure if all cross-sectional dimensions are increased by 7.2 percent. Compute the new eccentricity in the center interval, and compare this with the original value.

### Calculation Procedure:

### 1. Calculate the new section properties and bending moments

Thus $A = 500(1.072)^2 = 575$ sq.in. (3709.9 cm²); $S_b = 4584(1.072)^3 = 5647$ in³ (92,554.3 cm³); $S_t = 4257(1.072)^3 = 5244$ in³ (85,949.2 cm³); $M_s = 9000(1.21) = 10,890$ in.·kips (1230.4 kN·m); $M_w = 3500(1.072)^2(1.21) = 4867$ in.·kips (549.9 kN·m).

### 2. Compute the required section moduli, prestresses, prestressing force, and its eccentricity in the central interval, using the same sequence as in the previous calculation procedure

Thus $S_b = 5649$ in³ (92,587.1 cm³); $S_t = 5246$ in³ (85,981.9 cm³). Both these values are acceptable. Then $f_{bp} = +3046$ lb/sq.in. (+21,002.2 kPa); $f_{tp} = -886$ lb/sq.in. (-6108.9 kPa); $F_i = 662,800$ lb (2,948,134.4 N); $e = 16.13$ in. (409.7 mm). The eccentricity has increased by 11.5 percent.

In practice, it would be more efficient to increase the vertical dimensions more than the horizontal dimensions. Nevertheless, as the span increases, the eccentricity increases more rapidly than the depth.

## EFFECT OF BEAM OVERLOAD

The beam in the second previous calculation procedure is subjected to a 10 percent over-load. How does the final stress in the bottom fiber compare with that corresponding to the design load?

### Calculation Procedure:

### 1. Compute the value of $f_{bs}$ under design load

Thus, $f_{bs} = -M_s/S_b = -9,000,000/4584 = -1963$ lb/sq.in. (-13,534.8 kPa).

### 2. Compute the increment or $f_{bs}$ caused by overload and the revised value of $f_{bf}$

Thus, $\Delta f_{bs} = 0.10(-1963) = -196$ lb/sq.in. (-1351.4 kPa); $f_{bf} = -200 - 196 = -396$ lb/sq.in. (-2730.4 kPa). Therefore, a 10 percent overload virtually doubles the tensile stress in the member.

# PRESTRESSED-CONCRETE BEAM DESIGN GUIDES

On the basis of the previous calculation procedures, what conclusions may be drawn that will serve as guides in the design of prestressed-concrete beams?

### Calculation Procedure:

### 1. Evaluate the results obtained with different forms of tendons
The capacity of a given member is increased by using deflected rather than straight tendons, and the capacity is maximized by using parabolic tendons. (However, in the case of a pretensioned beam, an economy analysis must also take into account the expense incurred in deflecting the tendons.)

### 2. Evaluate the prestressing force
For a given ratio of $y_b/y_t$, the prestressing force that is required to maximize the capacity of a member is a function of the cross-sectional area and the allowable stresses. It is independent of the form of the trajectory.

### 3. Determine the effect of section moduli
If the section moduli are in excess of the minimum required, the prestressing force is minimized by setting the critical values of $f_{bf}$ and $f_{ti}$ equal to their respective allowable values. In this manner, points $A$ and $B$ in Fig. 34 are placed at their limiting positions to the left.

### 4. Determine the most economical short-span section
For a short-span member, an I section is most economical because it yields the required section moduli with the minimum area. Moreover, since the required values of $S_b$ and $S_t$ differ, the area should be disposed unsymmetrically about middepth to secure these values.

### 5. Consider the calculated value of e
Since an increase in span causes a greater increase in the theoretical eccentricity than in the depth, the calculated value of $e$ is not attainable in a long-span member because the centroid of the tendons would fall beyond the confines of the section. For this reason, long-span members are generally constructed as T sections. The extensive flange area elevates the centroidal axis, thus making it possible to secure a reasonably large eccentricity.

### 6. Evaluate the effect of overload
A relatively small overload induces a disproportionately large increase in the tensile stress in the beam and thus introduces the danger of cracking. Moreover, owing to the presence of many variable quantities, there is not a set relationship between the beam capacity at allowable final stress and the capacity at incipient cracking. It is therefore imperative that every prestressed-concrete beam be subjected to an ultimate-strength analysis to ensure that the beam provides an adequate factor of safety.

# KERN DISTANCES

The beam in Fig. 36 has the following properties: $A = 850$ sq.in. (5484.2 cm²); $S_b = 11,400$ in³ (186,846.0 cm³); $S_t = 14,400$ in³ (236,016.0 cm³). A prestressing force of 630 kips (2802.2 kN) is applied with an eccentricity of 24 in. (609.6 mm) at the section under

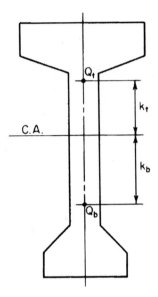

**FIGURE 36.** Kern points.

investigation. Calculate $f_{bp}$ and $f_{tp}$ by expressing these stresses as functions of the kern distances of the section.

### Calculation Procedure:

### 1. Consider the prestressing force to be applied at each kern point, and evaluate the kern distances

Let $Q_b$ and $Q_t$ denote the points at which a compressive force must be applied to induce a zero stress in the top and bottom fiber, respectively. These are referred to as the *kern points* of the section, and the distances $k_b$ and $k_t$, from the centroidal axis to these points are called the *kern distances*.

Consider the prestressing force to be applied at each kern point in turn. Set the stresses $f_{tp}$ and $f_{bp}$ equal to zero to evaluate the kern distances $k_b$ and $k_t$, respectively. Thus $f_{tp} = F_i/A - F_i k_b/S_t = 0$, Eq. $a$; $f_{bp} = F_i/A - F_i k_t/S_b = 0$, Eq. $b$. Then

$$k_b = \frac{S_t}{a} \quad \text{and} \quad k_t = \frac{S_b}{A} \tag{55}$$

And, $k_b = 14{,}400/850 = 16.9$ in. (429.26 mm); $k_t = 11{,}400/850 = 13.4$ in. (340.36 mm).

### 2. Express the stresses $f_{bp}$ and $f_{tp}$ associated with the actual eccentricity as functions of the kern distances

By combining the stress equations with Eqs. $a$ and $b$, the following equations are obtained:

$$f_{bp} = \frac{F_i(k_t + e)}{S_b} \quad \text{and} \quad f_{tp} = \frac{F_i(k_b + e)}{S_t} \tag{56}$$

Substituting numerical values gives $f_{bp} = 630{,}000(13.4 + 24)/11{,}400 = +2067$ lb/sq.in. ($+14{,}252.0$ kPa); $f_{tp} = 630{,}000(16.9 - 24)14{,}400 = -311$ lb/sq.in. ($-2144.3$ kPa).

### 3. Alternatively, derive Eq. 56 by considering the increase in prestress caused by an increase in eccentricity

Thus, $\Delta f_{bp} = F_i \Delta e/S_b$; therefore, $f_{bp} = F_i(k_t + e)/S_b$.

## MAGNEL DIAGRAM CONSTRUCTION

The data pertaining to a girder having curved tendons are $A = 500$ sq.in. (3226.0 cm²); $S_b = 5000$ in³ (81,950 cm³); $S_t = 5340$ in³ (87,522.6 cm³); $M_w = 3600$ in.·kips (406.7 kN·m); $M_s = 9500$ in.·kips (1073.3 kN·m). The allowable stresses are: *initial*, $+2400$ and $-190$ lb/sq.in. ($+16{,}548$ and $-1310.1$ kPa); *final*, $+2250$ and $-425$ lb/sq.in. ($+15{,}513.8$ and $-2930.4$ kPa). (*a*) Construct the Magnel diagram for this member. (*b*) Determine the minimum prestressing force and its eccentricity by referring to the diagram. (*c*) Determine the prestressing force if the eccentricity is restricted to 18 in. (457.2 mm).

**Calculation Procedure:**

**1. Set the initial stress in the bottom fiber at midspan equal to or less than its allowable value, and solve for the reciprocal of $F_i$**

In this situation, the superimposed load is given, and the sole objective is to minimize the prestressing force. The Magnel diagram is extremely useful for this purpose because it brings into sharp focus the relationship between $F_i$ and $e$. In this procedure, let $f_{bi}$ and $f_{bf}$ and so forth represent the allowable stresses.

Thus,

$$\frac{1}{F_i} \geq \frac{k_t + e}{M_w + f_{bi} S_b} \tag{57a}$$

**2. Set the final stress in the bottom fiber at midspan equal to or algebraically greater than its allowable value, and solve for the reciprocal of $F_i$**

Thus,

$$\frac{1}{F_i} \leq \frac{\eta(k_t + e)}{M_w + M_s + f_{bf} S_b} \tag{57b}$$

**3. Repeat the foregoing procedure with respect to the top fiber**

Thus,

$$\frac{1}{F_i} \geq \frac{e - k_b}{M_w + f_{ti} S} \tag{57c}$$

and

$$\frac{1}{F_i} \leq \frac{\eta(e - k_b)}{M_w + M_{bs} + f_{tf} S} \tag{57d}$$

**4. Substitute numerical values, expressing $F_i$ in thousands of kips**

Thus, $1/F_i \geq (10 + e)/15.60$, Eq. $a$; $1/F_i$ $(10 + e)/12.91$, Eq. $b$; $1/F_i \leq (e - 10.68)/4.61$, Eq. $c$; $1/F_i \leq (e - 10.68)/1.28$, Eq. $d$.

**5. Construct the Magnel diagram**

In Fig. 37, consider the foregoing relationships as equalities, and plot the straight lines that represent them. Each point on these lines represents a set of values of $1/F_i$ and $e$ at which the designated stress equals its allowable value.

When the section moduli are in excess of those corresponding to balanced design, as they are in the present instance, line $b$ makes a greater angle with the $e$ axis than does $a$, and line $d$ makes a greater angle than does $c$. From the sense of each inequality, it follows that $1/F_i$ and $e$ may have any set of values represented by a point within the quadrilateral $CDEF$ or on its circumference.

**6. To minimize $F_i$, determine the coordinates of point E at the intersection of lines b and c**

Thus, $1/F_i = (10 + e)/12.91 = (e - 10.68)/4.61$; so $e = 22.2$ in. (563.88 mm); $F_i = 401$ kips (1783.6 kN).

The Magnel diagram confirms the third design guide presented earlier in the section.

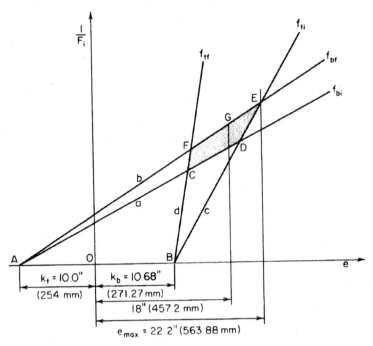

**FIGURE 37.** Magnel diagram.

## 7. For the case where e is restricted to 18 in. (457.2 mm), minimize $F_i$ by determining the ordinate of point G on line b

Thus, in Fig. 37, $1/F_i = (10 + 18)/12.91$; $F_i = 461$ kips (2050.5 kN).

The Magnel diagram may be applied to a beam having deflected tendons by substituting for $M_w$ in Eqs. 57a and 57c the beam-weight moment at the deflection point.

## CAMBER OF A BEAM AT TRANSFER

The following pertain to a simply supported prismatic beam: $L = 36$ ft (11.0 m); $I = 40,000$ in$^4$ (166.49 dm$^4$); $f'_{ci} = 4000$ lb/sq.in. (27,580.0 kPa); $w_w = 340$ lb/lin ft (4961.9 N/m); $F_i = 430$ kips (1912.6 kN); $e = 8.8$ in. (223.5 mm) at midspan. Calculate the camber of the member at transfer under each of these conditions: (a) the tendons are straight across the entire span; (b) the tendons are deflected at the third points, and the eccentricity at the supports is zero; (c) the tendons are curved parabolically, and the eccentricity at the supports is zero.

## Calculation Procedure:

### 1. Evaluate $E_c$ at transfer, using the ACI Code

Review the moment-area method of calculating beam deflections, which is summarized earlier. Consider an upward displacement (camber) as positive, and let the symbols $\Delta_p$, $\Delta_w$, and $\Delta_i$, defined earlier, refer to the camber at midspan.

Thus, using the ACI *Code*, $E_c = (145)^{1.5}(33)(4000)^{0.5} = 3,644,000$ lb/sq.in. (25,125.4 MPa).

### 2. *Construct the prestress-moment diagrams associated with the three cases described*

See Fig. 38. By symmetry, the elastic curve corresponding to $F_i$ is horizontal at midspan. Consequently, $\Delta_p$ equals the deviation of the elastic curve at the support from the tangent to this curve at midspan.

### 3. *Using the literal values shown in Fig. 38, develop an equation for $\Delta_p$ by evaluating the tangential deviation; substitute numerical values*

Thus, case *a*:

$$\Delta_p = \frac{ML^2}{8E_cI} \tag{58}$$

or $\Delta_p = 430,000(8.8)(36)^2(144)/[8(3,644,000)(40,000)] = 0.61$ in. (15.494 mm). For case *b*:

$$\Delta_p = \frac{M(2L^2 + 2La - a^2)}{24E_cI} \tag{59}$$

or $\Delta_p = 0.52$ in. (13.208 mm). For case *c*:

$$\Delta_p = \frac{5ML^2}{48E_cI} \tag{60}$$

or $\Delta_p = 0.51$ in. (12.954 mm).

### 4. *Compute $\Delta_w$*

Thus, $\Delta_w = -5w_wL^4/(384E_cI) = -0.09$ in. (−2.286 mm).

### 5. *Combine the foregoing results to obtain $\Delta_i$*

Thus: case *a*, $\Delta_i = 0.61 - 0.09 = 0.52$ in. (13.208 mm); case *b*, $\Delta_i = 0.52 - 0.09 = 0.43$ in. (10.922 mm); case *c*, $\Delta_i = 0.51 - 0.09 = 0.42$ in. (10.688 mm).

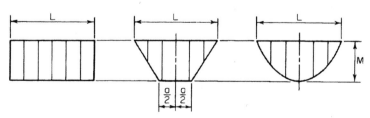

(a) Straight tendons     (b) Deflected tendons     (c) Parabolic tendons

**FIGURE 38.** Prestress-moment diagrams.

## DESIGN OF A DOUBLE-T ROOF BEAM

The beam in Fig. 39 was selected for use on a simple span of 40 ft (12.2 m) to carry the following loads: roofing, 12 lb/sq.ft.(574.5 N/m$^2$); snow, 40 lb/sq.ft.(1915.1 N/m$^2$); total, 52 lb/sq.ft.(2489.6 N/m$^2$). The member will be pretensioned with straight seven-wire strands, $7/16$ in. (11.11 mm) diameter, having an area of 0.1089 sq.in. (0.70262 cm$^2$) each and an ultimate strength of 248,000 lb/sq.in. (1,709,960.0 kPa). The concrete strengths are $f'_c$ = 5000 lb/sq.in. (34,475.0 kPa) and $f'_{ci}$ = 4000 lb/sq.in. (27,580.0 kPa). The allowable stresses are: *initial*, +2400 and −190 lb/sq.in. (+16,548.0 and −1310.1 kPa); *final*, +2250 and −425 lb/sq.in. (+15,513.8 and −2930.4 kPa). Investigate the adequacy of this section, and design the tendons. Compute the camber of the beam after the concrete has hardened and all dead loads are present. For this calculation, assume that the final value of $E_c$ is one-third of that at transfer.

### Calculation Procedure:

#### 1. *Compute the properties of the cross section*
Let $f_{bf}$ and $f_{tf}$ denote the respective stresses at *midspan* and $f_{bi}$ and $f_{ti}$ denote the respective stresses *at the support*. Previous calculation procedures demonstrated that where the section moduli are excessive, the minimum prestressing force is obtained by setting $f_{bf}$ and $f_{ti}$ equal to their allowable values.

Thus $A$ = 316 sq.in. (2038.8 cm$^2$); $I$ = 7240 in$^4$ (30.14 dm$^4$); $y_b$ = 10.98 in. (278.892 mm); $y_t$ = 5.02 in. (127.508 mm); $S_b$ = 659 in$^3$ (10,801.0 cm$^3$); $S_t$ = 1442 in$^3$ (23,614 cm$^3$); $w_w$ = (316/144)150 = 329 lb/lin ft (4801.4 N/m).

#### 2. *Calculate the total midspan moment due to gravity loads and the corresponding stresses*
Thus $w_s$ = 52(6) = 312 lb/lin ft (4553.3 N/m); $w_w$, = 329 lb/lin ft (4801.4 N/m); and $M_w$ + $M_s$ = ($1/8$)(641)(40$^2$)(12) = 1,538,000 in.·lb (173,763.2 N·m); $f_{bw}$ + $f_{bs}$ = −1,538,000/659 = −2334 lb/sq.in. (−16,092.9 kPa); $f_{tw}$ + $f_{ts}$ = +1,538,000/1442 = +1067 lb/sq.in. (+7357.0 kPa).

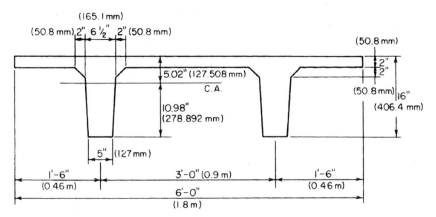

**FIGURE 39.** Double-T roof beam.

### 3. Determine whether the section moduli are excessive

Do this by setting $f_{bf}$ and $f_{ti}$ equal to their allowable values and computing the corresponding values of $f_{bi}$ and $f_{tf}$. Thus, $f_{bf} = 0.85 f_{bp} - 2334 = -425$; therefore, $f_{bp} = +2246$ lb/sq.in. (+15,486.2 kPa); $f_{ti} = f_{tp} = -190$ lb/sq.in. (−1310.1 kPa); $f_{bi} = f_{bp} = +2246 < 2400$ lb/sq.in.(+16,548.0 kPa). This is acceptable. Also, $f_{tf} = 0.85(-190) + 1067 = +905 < 2250$ lb/sq.in. (+15,513.8 kPa); this is acceptable. The section moduli are therefore excessive.

### 4. Find the minimum prestressing force and its eccentricity

Refer to Fig. 40. Thus, $f_{bp} = +2246$ lb/sq.in. (+15,486.2 kPa); $f_{tp} = -190$ lb/sq.in. (−1310.1 kPa); slope of $AB = 2246 - (-190)/16 = 152.3$ lb/(sq.in.·in.) (41.33 MPa/m); $F_i/A = CD = 2246 - 10.98 (152.3) = 574$ lb/sq.in. (3957.7 kPa); $F_i = 574(316) = 181,400$ lb (806,867.2 N); slope of $AB = F_i e/I = 152.3$; $e = 152.3(7240)/181,400 = 6.07$ in. (154.178 mm).

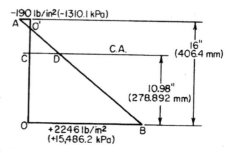

−190 lb/in²(−1310.1 kPa)

C.A.

16" (406.4 mm)

10.98" (278.892 mm)

+2246 lb/in² (+15,486.2 kPa)

**FIGURE 40.** Prestress diagram.

### 5. Determine the number of strands required, and establish their disposition

In accordance with the ACI *Code*, allowable initial force per strand = 0.1089 (0.70)(248,000) = 18,900 lb (84,067.2 N); number required = 181,400/18,900 = 9.6. Therefore, use 10 strands (5 in each web) stressed to 18,140 lb (80,686.7 N) each.

Referring to the ACI *Code* for the minimum clear distance between the strands, we find the allowable center-to-center spacing = $4(\frac{7}{16}) = 1\frac{3}{4}$ in. (44.45 mm). Use a 2-in. (50.8-mm) spacing. In Fig. 41, locate the centroid of the steel, or $y = (2 \times 2 + 1 \times 4)/5 = 1.60$ in. (40.64 mm); $v = 10.98 - 6.07 - 1.60 = 3.31$ in. (84.074 mm); set $v = 3\frac{5}{16}$ in. (84.138 mm).

### 6. Calculate the allowable ultimate moment of the member in accordance with the ACI Code

Thus, $A_s = 10(0.1089) = 1.089$ sq.in. (7.0262 cm²); $d = y_t + e = 5.02 + 6.07 = 11.09$ in. (281.686 mm); $p = A_s/(bd) = 1.089/[72(11.09)] = 0.00137$.

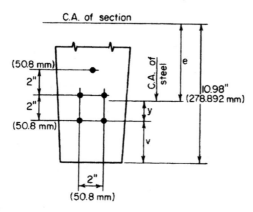

C.A. of section

(50.8 mm)

2"

2"

(50.8 mm)

C.A. of steel

e

10.98" (278.892 mm)

y

v

2"

(50.8 mm)

**FIGURE 41.** Location of tendons.

Compute the steel stress and resultant tensile force at ultimate load:

$$f_{su} = f_s' \left( 1 - \frac{0.5 \, p f_s'}{f_c'} \right) \tag{61}$$

Or, $f_{su} = 248{,}000(1 - 0.5 \times 0.00137 \times 248{,}000/5000) = 240{,}000$ lb/sq.in. (1,654,800 kPa); $T_u = A_s f_{su} = 1.089(240{,}000) = 261{,}400$ lb (1,162,707.2 N).

Compute the depth of the compression block. This depth, $a$, is found from $C_u = 0.85(5000)(72a) = 261{,}400$ lb (1,162,707.2 N); $a = 0.854$ in. (21.6916 mm); $jd = d - a/2 = 10.66$ in. (270.764 mm); $M_u = \phi T_u jd = 0.90(261{,}400)(10.66) = 2{,}500{,}000$ in.·lb (282,450.0 N·m).

Calculate the steel index to ascertain that it is below the limit imposed by the ACI Code, or $q = p f_{su}/f_c' = 0.00137 \, (240{,}000)/5000 = 0.0658 < 0.30$. This is acceptable.

## 7. Calculate the required ultimate-moment capacity as given by the ACI Code

Thus, $w_{DL} = 329 + 12(6) = 401$ lb/lin ft (5852.2 N/m); $w_{LL} = 40(6) = 240$ lb/lin ft (3502.5 N/m); $w_u = 1.5 w_{DL} + 1.8 w_{LL} = 1034$ lb/lin ft (15,090.1 N/m); $M_u$ required $= (\frac{1}{8})(1034)(40)^2(12) = 2{,}480{,}000 < 2{,}500{,}000$ in.·lb (282,450.0 N·m). The member is therefore adequate with respect to its ultimate-moment capacity.

## 8. Calculate the maximum and minimum area of web reinforcement in the manner prescribed in the ACI Code

Since the maximum shearing stress does not vary linearly with the applied load, the shear analysis is performed at ultimate-load conditions. Let $A_v$ = area of web reinforcement placed perpendicular to the longitudinal axis; $V_c'$ = ultimate-shear capacity of concrete; $V_p'$ = vertical component of $F_f$ at the given section; $V_u'$ = ultimate shear at given section; $s$ = center-to-center spacing of stirrups; $f_{pc}'$ = stress due to $F_f$, evaluated at the centroidal axis, or at the junction of the web and flange when the centroidal axis lies in the flange.

Calculate the ultimate shear at the critical section, which lies at a distance $d/2$ from the face of the support. Then distance from midspan to the critical section $= \frac{1}{2}(L - d) = 19.54$ ft (5.955 m); $V_u' = 1034(19.54) = 20{,}200$ lb (89,849.6 N).

Evaluate $V_c'$ by solving the following equations and selecting the smaller value:

$$V_{ci}' = 1.7b'd(f_c')^{0.5} \tag{62}$$

where $d$ = effective depth, in. (mm); $b'$ = width of web at centroidal axis, in. (mm); $b' = 2(5 + 1.5 \times 10.98/12) = 12.74$ in. (323.596 mm); $V_{ci}' = 1.7(12.74)(11.09)(5000)^{0.5} = 17{,}000$ lb (75,616.0 N). Also,

$$V_{cw}' = b'd(3.5 f_c'^{0.5} + 0.3 f_{pc}') + V_p' \tag{63}$$

where $d$ = effective depth or 80 percent of the overall depth, whichever is greater, in. (mm). Thus, $d = 0.80(16) = 12.8$ in. (325.12 mm); $V_p' = 0$. From step 4, $f_{pc}' = 0.85(574) = +488$ lb/sq.in. (3364.8 kPa); $V_{cw}' = 12.74(12.8)(3.5 \times 5000^{0.5} + 0.3 \times 488) = 64{,}300$ lb (286,006.4 N); therefore, $V_c' = 17{,}000$ lb (75,616.0 N).

Calculate the maximum web-reinforcement area by applying the following equation:

$$A_v = \frac{s(V_u' = \phi V_c')}{\phi d f_y} \tag{64}$$

where $d$ = effective depth at section of maximum moment, in. (mm). Use $f_y = 40{,}000$ lb/sq.in. (275,800.0 kPa), and set $s = 12$ in. (304.8 mm). Then $A_v = 12(20{,}200 - 0.85 \times$

17,000)/[0.85(11.09)(40,000)] = 0.184 sq.in./ft (3.8949 cm²/m). This is the area required at the ends.

Calculate the minimum web-reinforcement area by applying

$$A_v = \frac{A_s}{80} \frac{f_s'}{f_y} \frac{s}{(b'd)^{0.5}} \tag{65}$$

or $A_v = (1.089/80)(248,000/40,000)12/(12.74 \times 11.09)^{0.5} = 0.085$ sq.in./ft (1.7993 cm²/m).

### 9. Calculate the camber under full dead load

From the previous procedure, $E_c = (\frac{1}{3})(3.644)(10)^6 = 1.215 \times 10^6$ lb/sq.in. $(8.377 \times 10^6$ kPa); $E_c I = 1.215(10)^6(7240) = 8.8 \times 10^9$ lb·sq.in. $(25.25 \times 10^6$ N·m²); $\Delta_{ADL} = -5(401)$ $(40)^4(1728)/[384(8.8)(10)^9] = -2.62$ in. $(-66.548$ mm). By Eq. 58, $\Delta_p = 0.85(181,400)$ $(6.07)(40)^2(144)/[8(8.8)(10)^9] = 3.06$ in. $(77.724$ mm); $\Delta = 3.06 - 2.62 = 0.44$ in. $(11.176$ mm).


## DESIGN OF A POSTTENSIONED GIRDER

The girder in Fig. 42 has been selected for use on a 90-ft (27.4-m) simple span to carry the following superimposed loads: dead load, 1160 lb/lin ft (16,928.9 N/m); live load, 1000 lb/lin ft (14,593.9 N/m). The girder will be posttensioned with Freyssinet cables. The concrete strengths are $f_c' = 5000$ lb/sq.in. (34,475 kPa) and $f_{ci}' = 4000$ lb/sq.in. (27,580 kPa). The allowable stresses are: *initial*, +2400 and −190 lb/sq.in. (+16,548 and −1310.1 kPa); *final*, +2250 and −425 lb/sq.in. (+15,513.8 and −2930.4 kPa). Complete the design of this member, and calculate the camber at transfer.

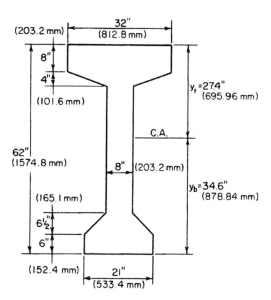

**FIGURE 42**

## Calculation Procedure:

### 1. Compute the properties of the cross section

Since the tendons will be curved, the initial stresses at midspan may be equated to the allowable values. The properties of the cross section are $A = 856$ sq.in. (5522.9 cm²); $I = 394,800$ in⁴ (1643 dm⁴); $y_b = 34.6$ in. (878.84 mm); $y_t = 27.4$ in. (695.96 mm); $S_b = 11,410$ in³ (187,010 cm³); $S_t = 14,410$ in³ (236,180 cm³); $w_w = 892$ lb/lin ft (13,017.8 N/m).

### 2. Calculate the stresses at midspan caused by gravity loads

Thus $f_{bw} = -950$ lb/sq.in. (−6550.3 kPa); $f_{bs} = -2300$ lb/sq.in. (−15,858.5 kPa); $f_{tw} = +752$ lb/sq.in. (+5185.0 kPa); $f_{ts} = +1820$ lb/sq.in. (+12,548.9 kPa).

### 3. Test the section adequacy

To do this, equate $f_{bf}$ and $f_{ti}$ to their allowable values and compute the corresponding values of $f_{bi}$ and $f_{tf}$. Thus $f_{bf} = 0.85 f_{bp} - 950 - 2300 = -425$; $f_{ti} = f_{tp} + 752 = -190$; therefore, $f_{bp} = +3324$ lb/sq.in. (+22,919.0 kPa) and $f_{tp} = -942$ lb/sq.in. (−6495.1 kPa); $f_{bi} = +3324 - 950 = +2374 < 2400$ lb/sq.in. (16,548.0 kPa). This is acceptable. And $f_{tf} = 0.85(-942) + 752 + 1820 = +1771 < 2250$ lb/sq.in. (15,513.8 kPa). This is acceptable. The section is therefore adequate.

### 4. Find the minimum prestressing force and its eccentricity at midspan

Do this by applying the prestresses found in step 3. Refer to Fig. 43. Slope of $AB = [3324 - (-942)]/62 = 68.8$ lb/(sq.in.·in) (18.68 kPa/mm); $F_i/A = CD = 3324 - 34.6(68.8) = 944$ lb/sq.in. (6508.9 kPa); $F_i = 944(856) = 808,100$ lb (3,594,428.8 N); slope of $AB = F_i e/I = 68.8$; $e = 68.8(394,800)/808,100 = 33.6$ in. (853.44 mm). Since $y_b = 34.6$ in. (878.84 mm), this eccentricity is excessive.

### 5. Select the maximum feasible eccentricity; determine the minimum prestressing force associated with this value

Try $e = 34.6 - 3.0 = 31.6$ in. (802.64 mm). To obtain the minimum value of $F_i$, equate $f_{bf}$ to its allowable value. Check the remaining stresses. As before, $f_{bp} = +3324$ lb/sq.in. (+22,919 kPa). But $f_{bp}, = F_i/856 + 31.6F_i/11,410 = +3324$; therefore $F_i = 844,000$ lb (3754.1 kN). Also, $f_{tp} = -865$ lb/sq.in. (−5964.2 kPa); $f_{bi} = +2374$ lb/sq.in. (+16,368.7 kPa); $f_{ti} = -113$ lb/sq.in. (−779.1 kPa); $f_{tf} = +1837$ lb/sq.in. (+12,666.1 kPa).

### 6. Design the tendons, and establish their pattern at midspan

Refer to a table of the properties of Freyssinet cables, and select 12/0.276 cables. The designation indicates that each cable consists of 12 wires of 0.276-in. (7.0104-mm) diameter.

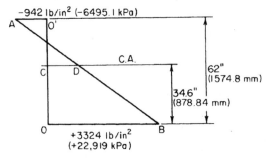

**FIGURE 43.** Prestress diagram.

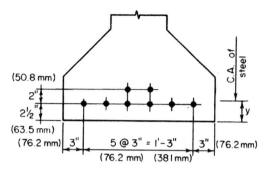

**FIGURE 44.** Location of tendons at midspan.

The ultimate strength is 236,000 lb/sq.in. (1,627,220 kPa). Then $A_s$ = 0.723 sq.in. (4.6648 cm²) per cable. Outside diameter of cable = 1⅝ in. (41.27 mm). Recommended final prestress = 93,000 lb (413,664 N) per cable; initial prestress = 93,000/0.85 = 109,400 lb (486,611.2 N) per cable. Therefore, use eight cables at an initial prestress of 105,500 lb (469,264.0 N) each.

A section of the ACI *Code* requires a minimum cover of 1½ in. (38.1 mm) and another section permits the ducts to be bundled at the center. Try the tendon pattern shown in Fig. 44. Thus, $y$ = [6(2.5) + 2(4.5)]/8 = 3.0 in. (76.2 mm). This is acceptable.

### 7. Establish the trajectory of the prestressing force

Construct stress diagrams to represent the initial and final stresses in the bottom and top fibers along the entire span.

For convenience, set $e$ = 0 at the supports. The prestress at the ends is therefore $f_{bp}$ = $f_{tp}$ = 844,000/856 = +986 lb/sq.in. (+6798.5 kPa). Since $e$ varies parabolically from maximum at midspan to zero at the supports, it follows that the prestresses also vary parabolically.

In Fig. 45a, draw the parabolic arc $AB$ with summit at $B$ to represent the absolute value of $f_{bp}$. Draw the parabolic arc $OC$ in the position shown to represent $f_{bw}$. The vertical distance between the arcs at a given section represents the value of $f_{bi}$; this value is maximum at midspan.

In Fig. 45b, draw $A'B'$ to represent the absolute value of the final prestress; draw $OC'$ to represent the absolute value of $f_{bw}$ + $f_{bs}$. The vertical distance between the arcs represents the value of $f_{bf}$. This stress is compressive in the interval $ON$ and tensile in the interval $NM$.

Construct Fig. 45c and d in an analogous manner. The stress $f_{ti}$ is compressive in the interval $OQ$.

### 8. Calculate the allowable ultimate moment of the member

The midspan section is critical in this respect. Thus, $d$ = 62 − 3 = 59.0 in. (1498.6 mm); $A_s$ = 8(0.723) = 5.784 sq.in. (37.3184 cm²); $p$ = $A_s/(bd)$ = 5.784/[32(59.0)] = 0.00306.

Apply Eq. 61, or $f_{su}$ = 236,000(1 − 0.5 × 0.00306 × 236,000/5000) = 219,000 lb/sq.in. (1,510,005.0 kPa). Also, $T_u$ = $A_s f_{su}$ = 5.784(219,000) = 1,267,000 lb (5,635,616.0 N). The concrete area under stress = 1,267,000/[0.85(5,000)] = 298 sq.in. (1922.7 cm²). This is the shaded area in Fig. 46, as the following calculation proves: 32(9.53) − 4.59(1.53) = 305 − 7 = 298 sq.in. (1922.7 cm²).

Locate the centroidal axis of the stressed area, or $m$ = [305(4.77) − 7(9.53 − 0.51)]/298 = 4.67 in. (118.618 mm); $M_u$ = $\theta T_u jd$ = 0.90(1,267,000)(59.0 − 4.67) = 61,950,000 in.·lb (6,999,111.0 N·m).

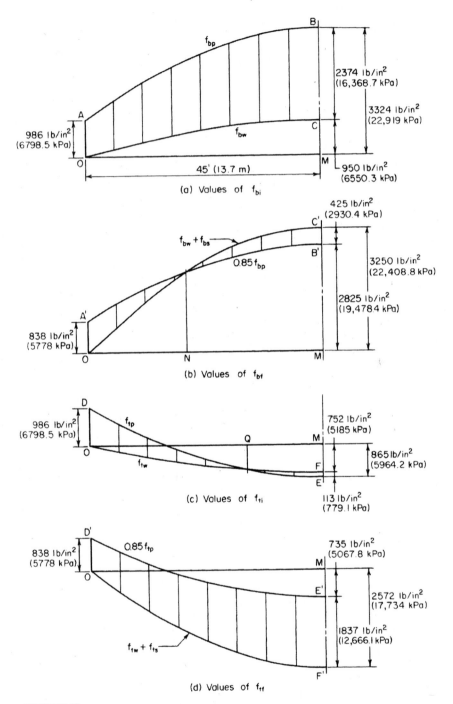

(a) Values of $f_{bi}$

(b) Values of $f_{bf}$

(c) Values of $f_{ti}$

(d) Values of $f_{tf}$

**FIGURE 45**

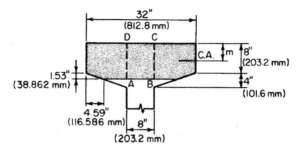

**FIGURE 46.** Concrete area under stress at ultimate load.

Calculate the steel index to ascertain that it is below the limit imposed by the ACI *Code*. Refer to Fig. 46. Or, area of $ABCD = 8(9.53) = 76.24$ sq.in. ($491.900$ cm$^2$). The steel area $A_{sr}$ that is required to balance the force on this web strip is $A_{sr} = 5.784(76.24)/298 = 1.48$ sq.in. ($9.549$ cm$^2$); $q = A_{sr}f_{su}(b'\ df_c') = 1.48(219,000)/[8(59.0)(5000)] = 0.137 < 0.30$. This is acceptable.

### 9. Calculate the required ultimate-moment capacity as given by the ACI Code

Thus, $w_u = 1.5(892 + 1160) + 1.8(1000) = 4878$ lb/lin ft ($71,189.0$ N/m); $M_u$ required $= (\frac{1}{8})(4878)(90)^2(12) = 59,270,000$ in.·lb ($6,696,324.6$ N·m). This is acceptable. The member is therefore adequate with respect to its ultimate-moment capacity.

### 10. Design the web reinforcement

Follow the procedure given in step 8 of the previous calculation procedure.

### 11. Design the end block

This is usually done by applying isobar charts to evaluate the tensile stresses caused by the concentrated prestressing forces. Refer to Winter et al.—*Design of Concrete Structures,* McGraw-Hill.

### 12. Compute the camber at transfer

Referring to earlier procedures in this section, we see that $E_cI = 3.644(10)^6(394,800) = 1.44 \times 10^{12}$ lb·in$^2$ ($4.132 \times 10^9$ N·m$^2$). Also, $\Delta_w = -5(892)(90)^4(1728)/[384(1.44)(10)^{12}] = -0.91$ in. ($-23.11$ mm). Apply Eq. 60, or $\Delta_p = 5(844,000)(31.6)(90)^2(144)/[48(1.44)(10)^{12}] = 2.25$ in. ($57.15$ mm); $\Delta_i = 2.25 - 0.91 = 1.34$ in. ($34.036$ mm).

## PROPERTIES OF A PARABOLIC ARC

Figure 47 shows the literal values of the coordinates at the ends and at the center of the parabolic arc $P_1P_2P_3$. Develop equations for $y$, $dy/dx$, and $d^2y/dx^2$ at an arbitrary point $P$. Find the slope of the arc at $P_1$ and $P_3$ and the coordinates of the summit $S$. (This information is required for the analysis of beams having parabolic trajectories.)

### Calculation Procedure:

### 1. Select a slope for the arc

Let $m$ denote the slope of the arc.

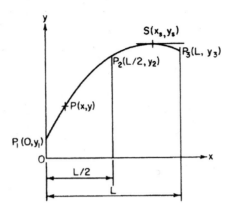

**FIGURE 47.** Parabolic arc.

## 2. Present the results
The equations are

$$y = 2(y_1 - 2y_2 + y_3)\left(\frac{x}{L}\right)^2 - (3y_1 - 4y_2 + y_3)\frac{x}{L} + y_1 \tag{66}$$

$$m = \frac{dy}{dx} = 4(y_1 - 2y_2 + y_3)\left(\frac{x}{L^2}\right) - \frac{3y_1 - 4y_2 + y_3}{L} \tag{67}$$

$$\frac{dm}{dx} = \frac{d^2y}{dx^2} = \frac{4}{L^2}(y_1 - 2y_2 + y_3) \tag{68}$$

$$m_1 = \frac{-(3y_1 - 4y_2 + y_3)}{L} \tag{69a}$$

$$m_3 = \frac{y_1 - 4y_2 + 3y_3}{L} \tag{69b}$$

$$x_s = \frac{(L/4)(3y_1 - 4y_2 + y_3)}{y_1 - 2y_2 + y_3} \tag{70a}$$

$$y_s = \frac{-(1/8)(3y_1 - 4y_2 + y_3)^2}{y_1 - 2y_2 + y_3} + y_1 \tag{70b}$$

## ALTERNATIVE METHODS OF ANALYZING A BEAM WITH PARABOLIC TRAJECTORY

The beam in Fig. 48 is subjected to an initial prestressing force of 860 kips (3825.3 kN) on a parabolic trajectory. The eccentricities at the left end, midspan, and right end,

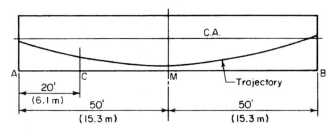

**FIGURE 48**

respectively, are $e_a = 1$ in. (25.4 mm); $e_m = 30$ in. (762.0 mm); $e_b = -3$ in. ($-76.2$ mm). Evaluate the prestress shear and prestress moment at section $C$ (a) by applying the properties of the trajectory at $C$; (b) by considering the prestressing action of the steel on the concrete in the interval $AC$.

### Calculation Procedure:

### 1. Compute the eccentricity and slope of the trajectory at C

Use Eqs. 66 and 67. Let $m$ denote the slope of the trajectory. This is positive if the trajectory slopes downward to the right. Thus $e_a - 2e_m + e_b = 1 - 60 - 3 = -62$ in. (1574.8 mm); $3e_a - 4e_m + e_b, = 3 - 120 - 3 = -120$ in. ($-3048$ mm); $e_m = 2(-62)(20/100)^2 + 120(20/100) + 1 = 20.04$ in. (509.016 mm); $m_c = 4(-62/12)(20/100^2) - (-120/12 \times 100) = 0.0587$.

### 2. Compute the prestress shear and moment at C

Thus $V_{pc} = -m_c F_i = -0.0587(860,000) = -50,480$ lb ($-224,535.0$ N); $M_{pc} = -F_i e = -860,000(20.04) = -17,230,000$ in.·lb ($-1,946,645.4$ N·m). This concludes the solution to part $a$.

### 3. Evaluate the vertical component w of the radial force on the concrete in a unit longitudinal distance

An alternative approach to this problem is to analyze the forces that the tendons exert on the concrete in the interval $AC$, namely, the prestressing force transmitted at the end and the radial forces resulting from curvature of the tendons.

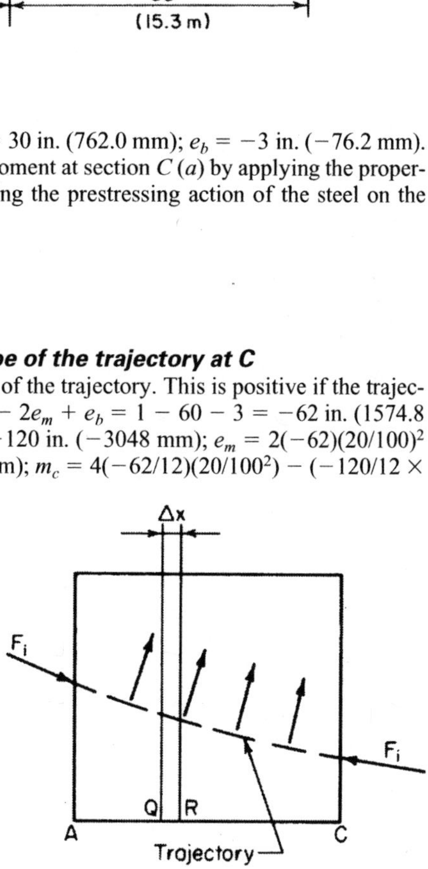

Consider the component $w$ to be positive if directed downward. In Fig. 49, $V_{pr} - V_{pq} = -F_i(m_r - m_q)$; therefore, $\Delta V_p/\Delta x = -F_i \Delta m/\Delta x$. Apply Eq. 68: $dV_p/dx = -F_i dm/dx = -(4F_i/L^2)(e_a - 2e_m + e_b)$; but $dV_p/dx = -w$. Therefore,

$$w = F_i \frac{dm}{dx} = \left( \frac{4F_i}{L^2} \right)(e_a - 2e_m + e_b) \tag{71}$$

**FIGURE 49.** Free-body diagram of concrete.

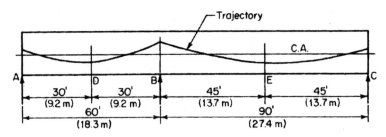

**FIGURE 50**

This result discloses that when the trajectory is parabolic, $w$ is uniform across the span. The radial forces are always directed toward the center of curvature, since the tensile forces applied at their ends tend to straighten the tendons. In the present instance, $w = (4F_i/100^2)(-62/12) = -0.002067F_i$ lb/lin ft ($-0.00678F_i$ N/m).

**4. Find the prestress shear at C**
By Eq. 69a, $m_a = -[-120/(100 \times 12)] = 0.1$; $V_{pa} = -0.1F_i$; $V_{pc} = V_{pa} - 20w = F_i(-0.1 + 20 \times 0.002067) = -0.0587F_i = -50,480$ lb ($-224,535.0$ N).

**5. Find the prestress moment at C**
Thus, $M_{pc} = M_{pa} + V_{pa}(240) - 20w(120) = F_i - 0.1 \times 240 + 20 \times 0.002067 \times 120) = -20.04F_i = -17,230,000$ in.·lb (1,946,645.4 N·m).

# PRESTRESS MOMENTS IN A CONTINUOUS BEAM

The continuous prismatic beam in Fig. 50 has a prestressing force of 96 kips (427.0 kN) on a parabolic trajectory. The eccentricities are $e_a = -0.40$ in. ($-10.16$ mm); $e_d = +0.60$ in. (15.24 mm); $e_b = -1.20$ in. ($-30.48$ mm); $e_e = +0.64$ in. (16.256 mm); $e_c = -0.60$ in. ($-15.24$ mm). Construct the prestress-moment diagram for this member, indicating all significant values.

## Calculation Procedure:

### 1. Find the value of $wL^2/4$ for each span by applying Eq. 71
Refer to Fig. 52. Since members $AB$ and $BC$ are constrained to undergo an identical rotation at B, there exists at this section a bending moment $M_{kb}$ in addition to that resulting from the eccentricity of $F_i$. The moment $M_{kb}$ induces reactions at the supports. Thus, at every section of the beam there is a moment caused by continuity of the member as well as the moment $-F_ie$. The moment $M_{kb}$ is termed the continuity moment; its numerical value is directly proportional to the distance from the given section to the end support. The continuity moment may be evaluated by adopting the second method of solution in the previous calculation

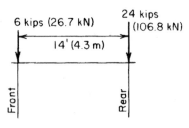

**FIGURE 51.** Free-body diagram of concrete.

procedure, since this renders the continuous member amenable to analysis by the theorem of three moments or moment distribution.

Determine $wL^2/4$ for each span: span $AB$, $w_1L_1^2/4 = F_i(-0.40 - 1.20 - 1.20) = -2.80F_i$ in.·lb $(-0.3163F_i$ N·m); span $BC$, $w_2L_2^2/4 = F_i(-1.20 - 1.28 - 0.60) = -3.08F_i$ in.·lb $(-0.3479F_i$ N·m).

### 2. Determine the true prestress moment at B in terms of $F_1$

Apply the theorem of three moments; by subtraction, find $M_{kb}$. Thus, $M_{pa}L_1 + 2M_{pb}(L_1 + L_2) + M_{pc}L_2 = -w_1L_1^3/4 - w_2L_2^3/4$. Substitute the value of $L_1$ and $L_2$, in feet (meters), and divide each term by $F_i$, or $0.40(60) + (2M_{pb} \times 150)/F_i + 0.60(90) = 2.80(60) + 3.08(90)$. Solving gives $M_{pb} = 1.224F_i$ in.·lb $(0.1383F_i$ N·m). Also, $M_{kb} = M_{pb} - (-F_ie_b) = F_i(1.224 - 1.20) = 0.024F_i$. Thus, the continuity moment at $B$ is positive.

### 3. Evaluate the prestress moment at the supports and at midspan

Using foot-pounds (newton-meters) in the moment evaluation yields $M_{pa} = 0.40(96,000)/12 = 3200$ ft·lb $(4339.2$ N·m); $M_{pb} = 1.224(96,000)/12 = 9792$ ft·lb $(13,278$ N·m); $M_{pc} = 0.60(96,000)/12 = 4800$ ft·lb $(6508.0$ N·m); $M_{pd} = -F_ie_d + M_{kd} = F_i(-0.60 + 1/2 \times 0.024)/12 = -4704$ ft·lb $(-6378$ N·m); $M_{pe} = F_i(-0.64 + 1/2 \times 0.024)/12 = -5024$ ft·lb $(-6812$ N·m).

### 4. Construct the prestress-moment diagram

Figure 52 shows this diagram. Apply Eq. 70 to locate and evaluate the maximum negative moments. Thus, $AF = 25.6$ ft $(7.80$ m); $BG = 49.6$ ft $(15.12$ m); $M_{pf} = -4947$ ft·lb $(-6708$ N·m); $M_{pg} = -5151$ ft·lb $(-6985$ N·m).

## PRINCIPLE OF LINEAR TRANSFORMATION

For the beam in Fig. 50, consider that the parabolic trajectory of the prestressing force is displaced thus: $e_a$ and $e_c$ are held constant as $e_b$ is changed to $-2.0$ in. $(-50.80$ mm), the eccentricity at any intermediate section being decreased algebraically by an amount directly proportional to the distance from that section to $A$ or $C$. Construct the prestress-moment diagram.

### Calculation Procedure:

#### 1. Compute the revised eccentricities

The modification described is termed a *linear transformation* of the trajectory. Two methods are presented. Steps 1 through 4 comprise method 1; the remaining steps comprise method 2.

The revised eccentricities are $e_a = -0.40$ in. $(-10.16$ mm); $e_d = +0.20$ in. $(5.08$ mm); $e_b = -2.00$ in. $(-50.8$ mm); $e_e = +0.24$ in. $(6.096$ mm); $e_c = -0.60$ in. $(-15.24$ mm).

#### 2. Find the value of $wL^2/4$ for each span

Apply Eq. 71: span $AB$, $w_1L_1^2/4 = F_i(-0.40 - 0.40 - 2.00) = -2.80F_i$; span $BC$, $w_2L_2^2/4 = F_i(-2.00 - 0.48 - 0.60) = -3.08F_i$.

These results are identical with those obtained in the previous calculation procedure. The change in $e_b$ is balanced by an equal change in $2e_d$ and $2e_e$.

#### 3. Determine the true prestress moment at B by applying the theorem of three moments; then find $M_{kb}$

Refer to step 2 in the previous calculation procedure. Since the linear transformation of the trajectory has not affected the value of $w_1$ and $w_2$, the value of $M_{pb}$ remains constant. Thus, $M_{kb} = M_{pb} - (-F_ie_b) = F_i(1.224 - 2.0) = -0.776F_i$.

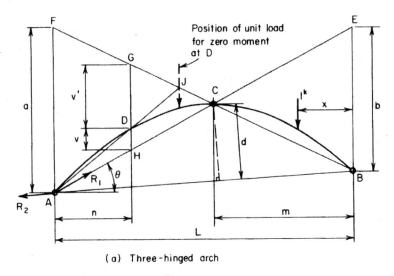

(a) Three-hinged arch

**FIGURE 52.** Prestress moment diagram.

#### 4. *Evaluate the prestress moment at midspan*

Thus, $M_{pd} = -F_i e_d + M_{kd} = F_i(-0.20 - \frac{1}{2} \times 0.776)/12 = -4704$ ft·lb ($-6378.6$ N·m);
$M_{pe} = F_i(-0.24 - \frac{1}{2} \times 0.776)/12 = -5024$ ft·lb ($-6812.5$ N·m).

These results are identical with those in the previous calculation procedure. The change in the eccentricity moment is balanced by an accompanying change in the continuity moment. Since three points determine a parabolic arc, the prestress moment diagram coincides with that in Fig. 52. This constitutes the solution by method 1.

#### 5. *Evaluate the prestress moments*

Do this by replacing the prestressing system with two hypothetical systems that jointly induce eccentricity moments identical with those of the true system.

Let $e$ denote the original eccentricity of the prestressing force at a given section and $\Delta e$ the change in eccentricity that results from the linear transformation. The final eccentricity moment is $-F_i(e + \Delta e) = -(F_i e + F_i \Delta e)$.

Consider the beam as subjected to two prestressing forces of 96 kips (427.0 kN) each. One has the parabolic trajectory described in the previous calculation procedure; the other has the linear trajectory shown in Fig. 53, where $e_a = 0$, $e_b = -0.80$ in. ($-20.32$ mm), and $e_c = 0$. Under the latter prestressing system, the tendons exert three forces on the concrete—

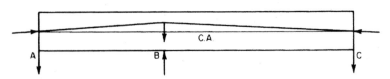

**FIGURE 53.** Hypothetical prestressing system and forces exerted on concrete.

one at each end and one at the deflection point above the interior support caused by the change in direction of the prestressing force.

The horizontal component of the prestressing force is considered equal to the force itself; it therefore follows that the force acting at the deflection point has no horizontal component.

Since the three forces that the tendons exert on the concrete are applied directly at the supports, their vertical components do not induce bending. Similarly, since the forces at $A$ and $C$ are applied at the centroidal axis, their horizontal components do not induce bending. Consequently, the prestressing system having the trajectory shown in Fig. 53 does not cause any prestress moments whatsoever. The prestress moments for the beam in the present instance are therefore identical with those for the beam in the previous calculation procedure.

The second method of analysis is preferable to the first because it is general. The first method demonstrates the equality of prestress moments before and after the linear transformation where the trajectory is parabolic; the second method demonstrates this equality without regard to the form of trajectory.

In this calculation procedure, the extremely important principle of linear transformation for a two-span continuous beam was developed. This principle states: The prestress moments remain constant when the trajectory of the prestressing force is transformed linearly. The principle is frequently applied in plotting a trial trajectory for a continuous beam.

Two points warrant emphasis. First, in a linear transformation, the eccentricities at the end supports remain constant. Second, the hypothetical prestressing systems introduced in step 5 are equivalent to the true system solely with respect to bending stresses; the axial stress $F_i/A$ under the hypothetical systems is double that under the true system.

## CONCORDANT TRAJECTORY OF A BEAM

Referring to the beam in the second previous calculation procedure, transform the trajectory linearly to obtain a concordant trajectory.

### Calculation Procedure:

#### 1. Calculate the eccentricities of the concordant trajectory

Two principles apply here. First, in a continuous beam, the prestress moment $M_p$ consists of two elements, a moment $-F_i e$ due to eccentricity and a moment $M_k$ due to continuity. The continuity moment varies linearly from zero at the ends to its maximum numerical value at the interior support. Second, in a linear transformation, the change in $-F_i e$ is offset by a compensatory change in $M_k$, with the result that $M_p$ remains constant.

It is possible to transform a given trajectory linearly to obtain a new trajectory having the characteristic that $M_k = 0$ along the entire span, and therefore $M_p = -F_i e$. The latter is termed a *concordant trajectory*. Since $M_p$ retains its original value, the concordant trajectory corresponding to a given trajectory is found simply by equating the final eccentricity to $-M_p/F_i$.

Refer to Fig. 50, and calculate the eccentricities of the concordant trajectory. As before, $e_a = -0.40$ in. $(-10.16$ mm$)$ and $e_c = -0.60$ in. $(-15.24$ mm$)$. Then $e_d = 4704(12)/96,000 = +0.588$ in. $(+14.9352$ mm$)$; $e_b = -9792(12)/96,000 = -1.224$ in. $(-31.0896$ mm$)$; $e_e = 5024(12)796,000 = +0.628$ in. $(15.9512$ mm$)$.

### 2. Analyze the eccentricities

All eccentricities have thus been altered by an amount directly proportional to the distance from the adjacent end support to the given section, and the trajectory has undergone a linear transformation. The advantage accruing from plotting a concordant trajectory is shown in the next calculation procedure.

## DESIGN OF TRAJECTORY TO OBTAIN ASSIGNED PRESTRESS MOMENTS

The prestress moments shown in Fig. 52 are to be obtained by applying an initial prestressing force of 72 kips (320.3 kN) with an eccentricity of $-2$ in. ($-50.8$ mm) at $B$. Design the trajectory.

### Calculation Procedure:

### 1. Plot a concordant trajectory

Set $e = M_p/F_i$, or $e_a = -3200(12)772,000 = -0.533$ in. ($-13.5382$ mm); $e_d = +0.784$ in. (19.9136 mm); $e_b = -1.632$ in. ($-41.4528$ mm); $e_e = +0.837$ in. (21.2598 mm); $e_c = -0.800$ in. ($-20.32$ mm).

### 2. Set $e_b$ = desired eccentricity, and transform the trajectory linearly

Thus, $e_a = -0.533$ in. ($-13.5382$ mm); $e_c = -0.800$ in. ($-20.32$ mm); $e_d = +0.784 - \frac{1}{2}(2.000 - 1.632) = +0.600$ in. ($+15.24$ mm); $e_e = +0.837 - 0.184 = +0.653$ in. ($+16.5862$ mm).

## EFFECT OF VARYING ECCENTRICITY AT END SUPPORT

For the beam in Fig. 50, consider that the parabolic trajectory in span $AB$ is displaced thus: $e_b$ is held constant as $e_a$ is changed to $-0.72$ in. ($-18.288$ mm), the eccentricity at every intermediate section being decreased algebraically by an amount directly proportional to the distance from that section to $B$. Compute the prestress moment at the supports and at midspan caused by a prestressing force of 96 kips (427.0 kN).

### Calculation Procedure:

### 1. Apply the revised value of $e_a$; repeat the calculations of the earlier procedure

Thus, $M_{pa} = 5760$ ft·lb (7810.6 N·m); $M_{pd} = -3680$ ft·lb ($-4990.1$ N·m); $M_{pb} = 9280$ ft·lb (12,583.7 N·m); $M_{pe} = -5280$ ft·lb ($-7159.7$ N·m); $M_{pc} = 4800$ ft·lb (6508.8 N·m).

The change in prestress moment caused by the displacement of the trajectory varies linearly across each span. Figure 54 compares the original and revised moments along $AB$. This constitutes method 1.

### 2. Replace the prestressing system with two hypothetical systems that jointly induce eccentricity moments identical with those of the true system

This constitutes method 2. For this purpose, consider the beam to be subjected to two prestressing forces of 96 kips (427.0 kN) each. One has the parabolic trajectory described in the earlier procedure; the other has a trajectory that is linear in each span, the eccentricities being $e_a = -0.72 - (-0.40) = -0.32$ in. ($-8.128$ mm), $e_b = 0$, and $e_c = 0$.

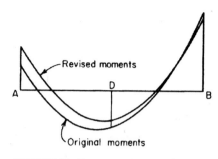

**FIGURE 54.** Prestress-moment diagrams.

### 3. Evaluate the prestress moments induced by the hypothetical system having the linear trajectory

The tendons exert a force on the concrete at $A$, $B$, and $C$, but only the force at $A$ causes bending moment.

Thus, $M_{pa} = -F_i e_a = -96,000(-0.32)/12 = 2560$ ft·lb (3471.4 N·m). Also, $M_{pa}L_1 + 2M_{pb}(L_1 + L_2) + M_{pc}L_2 = 0$. But $M_{pc} = 0$; therefore, $M_{pb} = -512$ ft·lb ($-694.3$ N·m); $M_{pd} = \frac{1}{2}(2560 - 512) = 1024$ ft·lb (1388.5 N·m); $M_{pe} = \frac{1}{2}(-512) = -256$ ft·lb ($-347.1$ N·m).

### 4. Find the true prestress moments by superposing the two hypothetical systems

Thus $M_{pa} = 3200 + 2560 = 5760$ ft·lb (7810.6 N·m); $M_{pd} = 4704 + 1024 = 3680$ ft·lb ($-4990.1$ N·m); $M_{pb} = 9792 - 512 = 9280$ ft·lb (12,583.7 N·m); $M_{pe} = 5024 - 256 = -5280$ ft·lb ($-7159.7$ N·m); $M_{pc} = 4800$ ft·lb (6508.8 N·m).


## DESIGN OF TRAJECTORY FOR A TWO-SPAN CONTINUOUS BEAM

A T beam that is continuous across two spans of 120 ft (36.6 m) each is to carry a uniformly distributed live load of 880 lb/lin ft (12,842.6 N/m). The cross section has these properties: $A = 1440$ sq.in. (9290.8 cm²); $I = 752,000$ in⁴ (3130.05 dm⁴); $y_b = 50.6$ in. (1285.24 mm); $y_t = 23.4$ in. (594.36 mm). The allowable stresses are: *initial*, $+2400$ and $-60$ lb/sq.in. ($+16,548.0$ and $-413.7$ kPa); *final*, $+2250$ and $-60$ lb/sq.in. ($+15,513.8$ and $-413.7$ kPa). Assume that the minimum possible distance from the extremity of the section to the centroidal axis of the prestressing steel is 9 in. (228.6 mm). Determine the magnitude of the prestressing force, and design the parabolic trajectory (*a*) using solely prestressed reinforcement; (*b*) using a combination of prestressed and non-prestressed reinforcement.


### Calculation Procedure:

### 1. Compute the section moduli, kern distances, and beam weight

For part *a*, an exact design method consists of these steps: First, write equations for the prestress moment, beam-weight moment, maximum and minimum potential superimposed-load moment, expressing each moment in terms of the distance from a given section to the adjacent exterior support. Second, apply these equations to identify the sections at which the initial and final stresses are critical. Third, design the prestressing system to restrict the critical stresses to their allowable range. Whereas the exact procedure is not laborious when applied to a prismatic beam carrying uniform loads, this procedure adopts the conventional, simplified method for illustrative purposes. This consists of dividing each span into a suitable number of intervals and analyzing the stresses at each boundary section.

For simplicity, set the eccentricity at the ends equal to zero. The trajectory will be symmetric about the interior support, and the vertical component $w$ of the force exerted by the tendons on the concrete in a unit longitudinal distance will be uniform across the entire length of member. Therefore, the prestress-moment diagram has the same form as the bending-moment diagram of a nonprestressed prismatic beam continuous over two equal spans and subjected to a uniform load across its entire length. It follows as a corollary that the prestress moments at the boundary sections previously referred to have specific *relative values* although their absolute values are functions of the prestressing force and its trajectory.

The following steps constitute a methodical procedure: Evaluate the relative prestress moments, and select a trajectory having ordinates directly proportional to these moments. The trajectory thus fashioned is concordant. Compute the prestressing force required to restrict the stresses to the allowable range. Then transform the concordant trajectory linearly to secure one that lies entirely within the confines of the section. Although the number of satisfactory concordant trajectories is infinite, the one to be selected is that which requires the minimum prestressing force. Therefore, the selection of the trajectory and the calculation of $F_i$ are blended into one operation.

Divide the left span into five intervals, as shown in Fig. 55. (The greater the number of intervals chosen, the more reliable are the results.)

Computing the moduli, kern distances, and beam weight gives $S_b = 14,860 \text{ in}^3$ (243,555.4 cm³); $S_t = 32,140 \text{ in}^3$ (526,774.6 cm³); $k_b = 22.32$ in. (566.928 mm); $k_t = 10.32$ in. (262,128 mm); $w_w = 1500$ lb/lin ft (21,890.9 N/m).

## 2. Record the bending-moment coefficients $C_1$, $C_2$, and $C_3$

Use Table 4 to record these coefficients at the boundary sections. The subscripts refer to these conditions of loading: 1, load on entire left span and none on right span; 2, load on entire right span and none on left span; 3, load on entire length of beam.

To obtain these coefficients, refer to the AISC *Manual*, case 29, which represents condition 1. Thus, $R_1 = (7/16)wL$; $R_3 = -(1/16)wL$. At section 3, for example, $M_1 = (7/16)wL(0.6L) - 1/2w(0.6L)^2 = [7(0.6) - 8(0.36)]wL^2/16 = 0.0825wL^2$; $C_1 = M_1/(wL^2) = +0.0825$.

To obtain condition 2, interchange $R_1$ and $R_3$. At section 3, $M_2 = -(1/16)wL(0.6L) = -0.0375wL^2$; $C_2 = -0.0375$; $C_3 = C_1 + C_2 = +0.0825 - 0.0375 = +0.0450$.

These moment coefficients may be applied without appreciable error to find the maximum and minimum potential live-load bending moments at the respective sections. The values of $C_3$ also represent the relative eccentricities of a concordant trajectory.

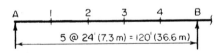

**FIGURE 55.** Division of span into intervals.

**TABLE 4.** Calculations for Two-Span Beam: Part $a$

| Section | 1 | 2 | 3 | 4 | B |
|---|---|---|---|---|---|
| 1 $C_1$ | +0.0675 | +0.0950 | +0.0825 | +0.0300 | −0.0625 |
| 2 $C_2$ | −0.0125 | −0.0250 | −0.0375 | −0.0500 | −0.0625 |
| 3 $C_3$ | +0.0550 | +0.0700 | +0.0450 | −0.0200 | −0.1250 |
| 4 $f_{bw}$, lb/sq.in. | −959 | −1,221 | −785 | +349 | +2,180 |
| (kPa) | (−6,611) | (−8,418) | (−5,412) | (+2406) | (+15,029) |
| 5 $f_{bs1}$, lb/ | −691 | −972 | −844 | −307 | +640 |
| sq.in. (kPa) | (−4,764) | (−6,701) | −5,819) | (−2,116) | (+4,412) |
| 6 $f_{bs2}$, lb/ | +128 | +256 | +384 | +512 | +640 |
| sq.in. (kPa) | (+882) | (+1,765) | (+2,647) | (+3,530) | (+4,412) |
| 7 $f_{tw}$, lb/sq.in. | +444 | +565 | +363 | −161 | −1,008 |
| (kPa) | (+3,060) | (+3895) | (+2,503) | (−1,110) | (−6,949) |
| 8 $f_{ts1}$, lb/sq.in. | +319 | +450 | +390 | +142 | −296 |
| (kPa) | (+2,199) | (+3,102) | (+2689) | (+979) | (−2,041) |
| 9 $f_{ts2}$, lb/sq.in. | −59 | −118 | −177 | −237 | −296 |
| (kPa) | (−407) | (−813) | (−1,220) | (−1,634) | (−2,041) |
| 10 $e_{con}$, in. | +17.19 | +21.87 | +14.06 | −6.25 | −39.05 |
| (mm) | (+436.6) | (+555.5) | (+357.1) | (−158.8) | (−991.9) |
| 11 $f_{bp}$, lb/sq.in. | +2,148 | +2,513 | + 1,903 | +318 | −2,243 |
| (kPa) | (+14,808) | (+17,325) | (+13,119) | (+2,192) | (−15,463) |
| 12 $f_{tp}$, lb/sq.in. | +185 | +16 | +298 | +1,031 | +2,215 |
| (kPa) | (+128) | (+110) | (+2,054) | (+7,108) | (+15,270) |
| $0.85f_{bp}$ | | | | | |
| 13 lb/sq.in. | +1,826 | +2,136 | +1,618 | +270 | −1,906 |
| (kPa) | (+12,588) | (+14,726) | (+11,154) | (+1,861) | (−13,140) |
| $0.85f_{tp}$ | | | | | |
| 14 lb/sq.in. | +157 | +14 | +253 | +876 | +1,883 |
| (kPa) | (+1,082) | (+97) | (+1,744) | (+6,039) | (+12,981) |

At midspan: $C_3 = +0.0625$ and $e_{con} = +19.53$ in. (496.1 mm)

Since the gravity loads induce the maximum positive moment at section 2 and the maximum negative moment at section $B$, the prestressing force and its trajectory will be designed to satisfy the stress requirements at these two sections. (However, the stresses at all boundary sections will be checked.) The Magnel diagram for section 2 is similar to that in Fig. 37, but that for section $B$ is much different.

### 3. Compute the value of $C_3$ at midspan
Thus, $C_3 = +0.0625$.

### 4. Apply the moment coefficients to find the gravity-load stresses
Record the results in Table 4. Thus $M_w = C_3(1500)(120)^2(12) = 259,200,000C_3$ in.·lb (29.3$C_3$ kN·m); $f_{bw} = -259,200,000C_3/14,860 = -17,440C_3$; $f_{bs1} = -10,230C_1$; $f_{bs2} = -10,230C_2$; $f_{tw} = 8065C_3$; $f_{ts1} = 4731C_1$; $f_{ts2} = 4731C_2$.

Since $S_t$ far exceeds $S_b$, it is manifest that the prestressing force must be designed to confine the bottom-fiber stresses to the allowable range.

**5. Consider that a concordant trajectory has been plotted; express the eccentricity at section B relative to that at section 2**

Thus, $e_b/e_2 = -0.1250/+0.0700 = -1.786$; therefore, $e_b = -1.786e_2$.

**6. Determine the allowable range of values of $f_{bp}$ at sections 2 and B**

Refer to Fig. 56. At section 2, $f_{bp} \leq +3621$ lb/sq.in. ($+24{,}966.8$ kPa), Eq. $a$; $0.85f_{bp} \geq 1221 + 972 - 60$; therefore, $f_{bp} \geq +2509$ lb/sq.in. ($+17{,}299.5$ kPa), Eq $b$. At section B, $f_{bp} \geq -2240$ lb/sq.in. ($-15{,}444.8$ kPa), Eq. $c$; $0.85f_{bp} \leq -(2180 + 1280) + 2250$; $f_{bp} \leq -1424$ lb/sq.in. ($-9818.5$ kPa), Eq. $d$.

**7. Substitute numerical values in Eq. 56, expressing $e_b$ in terms of $e_2$**

The values obtained are $1/F_i \leq (k_t + e_2)/(3621S_b)$, Eq $a'$; $1/F_i \leq (k_t + e_2)/(2509S_b)$, Eq. $b'$; $1/F_i \geq (1.786e_2 - k_t)/(2240S_b)$, Eq. $c'$; $1/F_i \leq (1.786e_2 - k_t)/(1424S_b)$, Eq. $d'$.

**8. Obtain the composite Magnel diagram**

Considering the relations in step 7 as equalities, plot the straight lines representing them to obtain the composite Magnel diagram in Fig. 57. The slopes of the lines have these relative values: $m_a = 1/3621$; $m_b = 1/2509$; $m_c = 1.786/2240 = 1/1254$; $m_d = 1.786/1424 = 1/797$. The shaded area bounded by these lines represents the region of permissible sets of values of $e_2$ and $1/F_i$.

**9. Calculate the minimum allowable value of $F_i$ and the corresponding value of $e_2$**

In the composite Magnel diagram, this set of values is represented by point $A$. Therefore, consider Eqs. $b'$ and $c'$ as equalities, and solve for the unknowns. Or, $(10.32 + e_2)/2509 = (1.786e_2 - 10.32)/2240$; solving gives $e_2 = 21.87$ in. ($555.5$ mm) and $F_i = 1{,}160{,}000$ lb ($5{,}159{,}680.0$ N).

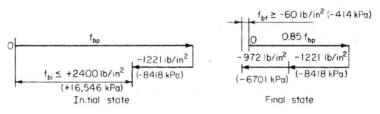

(a) Limiting values of $f_{bp}$ at section 2

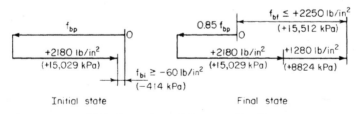

(b) Limiting values of $f_{bp}$ at section B

**FIGURE 56**

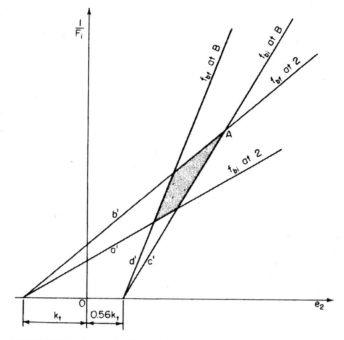

**FIGURE 57.** Composite Magnel diagram.

### 10. *Plot the concordant trajectory*

Do this by applying the values of $C_3$ appearing in Table 4; for example, $e_1 = +21.87$ (0.0550)/0.0700 = +17.19 in. (436.626 mm). At midspan, $e_m = +21.87(0.0625)/0.0700 = +19.53$ in. (496.062 mm).

Record the eccentricities on line 10 of the table. It is apparent that this concordant trajectory is satisfactory in the respect that it may be linearly transformed to one falling within the confines of the section; this is proved in step 14.

### 11. *Apply Eq. 56 to find $f_{bp}$ and $f_{tp}$*

Record the results in Table 4. For example, at section 1, $f_{bp} = 1,160,000(10.32 + 17.19)/14,860 = +2148$ lb/sq.in. (+14,810.5 kPa); $f_{tp} = 1,160,000(22.32 - 17.19)/32,140 = +185$ lb/sq.in. (+1275.6 kPa).

### 12. *Multiply the values of $f_{bp}$ and $f_{tp}$ by 0.85, and record the results*

These results appear in Table 4.

### 13. *Investigate the stresses at every boundary section*

In calculating the final stresses, apply the live-load stress that produces a more critical condition. Thus, at section 1, $f_{bi} = -959 + 2148 = +1189$ lb/sq.in. (+8198.2 kPa); $f_{bf} = -959 - 691 + 1826 = +176$ lb/sq.in. (+1213.6 kPa); $f_{ti} = +444 + 185 = +629$ lb/sq.in. (+4337.0 kPa); $f_{tf} = +444 + 319 + 157 = +920$ lb/sq.in. (+6343.4 kPa). At section 2: $f_{bi} = -1221 + 2513 = +1292$ lb/sq.in. (+8908.3 kPa); $f_{bf} = -1221 - 972 + 2136 = -57$ lb/sq.in. (−393.0 kPa); $f_{ti} = +565 + 16 = +581$ lb/sq.in. (+4006.0 kPa); $f_{tf} = +565 + 450 + 14 = +1029$ lb/sq.in. (+7095.0 kPa). At section 3: $f_{bi} = -785 + 1903 = +1118$ lb/sq.in. (+7706.8 kPa); $f_{bf} = -785 - 844 + 1618 = -11$ lb/sq.in. (−75.8 kPa); $f_{ti} = $

$+ 363 + 298 = +661$ lb/sq.in. ($+4558.0$ kPa); $= +363 + 390 + 253 = +1006$ lb/sq.in. ($+6936.4$ kPa). At section 4: $f_{bi} = +349 + 318 = +667$ lb/sq.in. ($+4599.0$ kPa); $f_{bf} = +349 - 307 + 270 = +312$ lb/sq.in. ($+2151.2$ kPa);or $f_{bf} = +349 + 512 + 270 = +1131$ lb/sq.in. ($7798.2$ kPa); $f_{ti} = -161 + 1031 = +870$ lb/sq.in. ($+5998.7$ kPa); $f_{tf} = -161 - 237 + 876 = +478$ lb/sq.in. ($+3295.8$ kPa), or $f_{tf} = -161 + 142 + 876 = +857$ lb/sq.in. ($+5909.0$ kPa). At section $B$: $f_{bi} = +2180 - 2243 = -63$ lb/sq.in. ($-434.4$ kPa); $f_{bf} = +2180 + 1280 - 1906 = +1554$ lb/sq.in. ($+10,714.8$ kPa); $f_{ti} = -1008 + 2215 = +1207$ lb/sq.in. ($+8322.3$ kPa); $f_{tf} = -1008 - 592 + 1883 = +283$ lb/sq.in. ($+1951.3$ kPa).

In all instances, the stresses lie within the allowable range.

### 14. Establish the true trajectory by means of a linear transformation

The imposed limits are $e_{max} = y_b - 9 = 41.6$ in. ($1056.6$ mm), $e_{min} = -(y_t - 9) = -14.4$ in. ($-365.76$ mm).

Any trajectory that falls between these limits and that is obtained by linearly transforming the concordant trajectory is satisfactory. Set $e_b = -14$ in. ($-355.6$ mm), and compute the eccentricity at midspan and the maximum eccentricity.

Thus, $e_m = +19.53 + \frac{1}{2}(39.05 - 14) = +32.06$ in. ($814.324$ mm). By Eq. 70b, $e_s = -(\frac{1}{8})(-4 \times 32.06 - 14)^2/(-2 \times 32.06 - 14) = +32.4$ in. ($+823.0$ mm) $< 41.6$ in. ($1056.6$ mm). This is acceptable. This constitutes the solution to part $a$ of the procedure. Steps 15 through 20 constitute the solution to part $b$.

### 15. Assign eccentricities to the true trajectory, and check the maximum eccentricity

The preceding calculation shows that the maximum eccentricity is considerably below the upper limit set by the beam dimensions. Refer to Fig. 57. If the restrictions imposed by line $c'$ are removed, $e_2$ may be increased to the value corresponding to a maximum eccentricity of $41.6$ in. ($1056.6$ mm), and the value of $F_i$ is thereby reduced. This revised set of values will cause an excessive initial tensile stress at $B$, but the condition can be remedied by supplying nonprestressed reinforcement over the interior support. Since the excess tension induced by $F_i$ extends across a comparatively short distance, the savings accruing from the reduction in prestressing force will more than offset the cost of the added reinforcement.

Assigning the following eccentricities to the true trajectory and checking the maximum eccentricity by applying Eq. 70b, we get $e_a = 0$; $e_m = +41$ in. ($1041.4$ mm); $e_b = -14$ in. ($-355.6$ mm); $e_s = -(\frac{1}{8})(-4 \times 41 - 14)^2/(-2 \times 41 - 14) = +41.3$ in. ($1049.02$ mm). This is acceptable.

### 16. To analyze the stresses, obtain a hypothetical concordant trajectory by linearly transforming the true trajectory

Let $y$ denote the upward displacement at $B$. Apply the coefficients $C_3$ to find the eccentricities of the hypothetical trajectory. Thus, $e_m/e_b = (41 - \frac{1}{2}y)/(-14 - y) = +0.0625/-0.1250$; $y = 34$ in. ($863.6$ mm); $e_a = 0$; $e_m = +24$ in. ($609.6$ mm); $e_b = -48$ in. ($-1219.2$ mm); $e_1 = -48$ ($+0.0550)/-0.1250 = +21.12$ in. ($536.448$ mm); $e_2 = +26.88$ in. ($682.752$ mm); $e_3 = +17.28$ in. ($438.912$ mm); $e_4 = -7.68$ in. ($-195.072$ mm).

### 17. Evaluate $F_i$ by substituting in relation (b') of step 7

Thus, $F_i = 2509(14,860)/(10.32 + 26.88) = 1,000,000$ lb ($4448$ kN). Hence, the introduction of nonprestressed reinforcement served to reduce the prestressing force by 14 percent.

### 18. Calculate the prestresses at every boundary section; then find the stresses at transfer and under design load

Record the results in Table 5. (At sections 1 through 4, the final stresses were determined by applying the values on lines 5 and 8 in Table 4. The slight discrepancy between the

**TABLE 5.** Calculations for Two-Span Continuous Beam: Part $b$

| Section | 1 | 2 | 3 | 4 | B |
|---|---|---|---|---|---|
| $e_{con}$, in. (mm) | +21.12 | +26.88 | +17.28 | −7.68 | −48.00 |
| | (536.4) | (+682.8) | (+438.9) | (−195.1) | (−1,219.2) |
| $f_{bp}$, lb/sq.in. (kPa) | +2,116 | +2,503 | +1,857 | +178 | −2,535 |
| | (+14,588) | (+17,256) | (+12,802) | (+1,227) | (−17,476) |
| $f_{tp}$, lb/sq.in. (kPa) | +37 | −142 | +157 | +933 | +2188 |
| | (+255) | (−979) | (+1,082) | (+6,660) | (+15,084) |
| $0.85f_{bp}$, lb/sq.in. (kPa) | +1,799 | +2,128 | +1,578 | +151 | −2,155 |
| | (+12,402) | (+14,670) | (+10,879) | (+1,041) | (−14,857) |
| $0.85f_{tp}$, lb/sq.in. (kPa) | +31 | −121 | +133 | +793 | +1,860 |
| | (+214) | (−834) | (+917) | (+5,467) | (+12,823) |
| $f_{bi}$, lb/sq.in. (kPa) | +1,157 | +1,282 | +1,072 | +527 | −355 |
| | (+7,976) | (+8,838) | (+7,390) | (+3,633) | (−2,447) |
| $f_{bf}$, lb/sq.in. (kPa) | +149 | −65 | −51 | +193 | +1,305 |
| | (+1,027) | (−448) | (−352) | (+1,331) | (+8,997) |
| $f_{ti}$, lb/sq.in. (kPa) | +481 | +423 | +520 | +772 | +1,180 |
| | (+3,316) | (+2,916) | (+3,585) | (+5,322) | (+8,135) |
| $f_{tf}$, lb/sq.in. (kPa) | +794 | +894 | +886 | +774 | +260 |
| | (+5,474) | (+6,163) | (+6108) | (+5,336) | (+1,792) |

final stress at 2 and the allowable value of −60 lb/sq.in. (−413.7 kPa) arises from the degree of precision in the calculations.)

With the exception of $f_{bi}$ at B, all stresses at the boundary sections lie within the allowable range.

### 19. Locate the section at which $f_{bi}$ = –60 lb/sq.in. (–413.7 kPa)

Since $f_{bp}$ and $f_{bw}$ vary parabolically across the span, their sum $f_{bi}$ also varies in this manner. Let $x$ denote the distance from the interior support to a given section. Apply Eq. 66 to find the equation for $f_{bi}$ using the initial-stress values at sections B, 3, and 1. Or, $-355 - 2 \times 1072 + 1157 = -1342$ (−9253.1 kPa); $3(-355) - 4(1072) + 1157 = -4196$ (−28,931.4 kPa); $f_{bi} = -2684(x/96)^2 + 4196x/96 - 355$. When $f_{bi} = -60$ (−413.7), $x = 7.08$ ft (2.15 m). The tensile stress at transfer is therefore excessive in an interval of only 14.16 ft (4.32 m).

### 20. Design the nonprestressed reinforcement over the interior support

As in the preceding procedures, the member must be investigated for ultimate-strength capacity. The calculation pertaining to any quantity that varies parabolically across the span may be readily checked by verifying that the values at uniformly spaced sections have equal "second differences." For example, with respect to the values of $f_{bi}$ recorded in Table 5, the verification is:

$$+1157 \qquad +1282 \qquad +1072 \qquad +527 \qquad -355$$
$$-125 \qquad +210 \qquad +545 \qquad +882$$
$$+335 \qquad +335 \qquad +337$$

The values on the second and third lines represent the differences between successive values on the preceding line.

## REACTIONS FOR A CONTINUOUS BEAM

With reference to the beam in the previous calculation procedure, compute the reactions at the supports caused by the initial prestressing force designed in part *a*.

### Calculation Procedure:

#### 1. Determine what causes the reactions at the supports
As shown in Fig. 51, the reactions at the supports result from the continuity at $B$, and $R_a = M_{kb}/L$.

#### 2. Compute the continuity moment at B; then find the reactions
Thus, $M_p = -F_i e + M_k = -F_i e_{con}$; $M_k = F_i(e - e_{con}) = 1160(-14 + 39.05) = 29{,}060$ in.·kips (3283 kN·m). $R_a = 29{,}060/[120(12)] = 20.2$ kips (89.8 kN); $R_B = -40.4$ kips $(-179.8$ kN).

## STEEL BEAM ENCASED IN CONCRETE

A concrete floor slab is to be supported by steel beams spaced 10 ft (3.05 m) on centers and having a span of 28 ft 6 in. (8.69 m). The beams will be encased in concrete with a minimum cover of 2 in. (50.8 mm) all around; they will remain unshored during construction. The slab has been designed as $4\frac{1}{2}$ in. (114.3 mm) thick, with $f_c' = 3000$ lb/sq.in. (20.7 MPa). The loading includes the following: live load, 120 lb/sq.ft.(5.75 kPa); finished floor and ceiling, 25 lb/sq.ft.(1.2 kPa). The steel beams have been tentatively designed as W16 × 40. Review the design.

### Calculation Procedure:

#### 1. Record the relevant properties of the section and the allowable flexural stresses
In accordance with the AISC *Specification*, the member may be designed as a composite steel-and-concrete beam, reliance being placed on the natural bond of the two materials to obtain composite action. Refer to Sec. 1 for the design of a composite bridge member. In the design of a composite building member, the effects of plastic flow are usually disregarded. Since the slab is poured monolithically, the composite member is considered continuous. Apply the following equations in computing bending moments in the composite beams: at midspan, $M = (\frac{1}{20})wL^2$; at support, $M = (\frac{1}{12})wL^2$.

The subscripts $c$, $ts$, and $bs$ refer to the extreme fiber of concrete, top of steel, and bottom of steel, respectively. The superscripts $c$ and $n$ refer to the composite and noncomposite sections, respectively.

Record the properties of the W16 × 40: $A = 11.77$ sq.in. (75.94 cm²); $d = 16.00$ in. (406.4 mm); $I = 515.5$ in⁴ (21.457 cm⁴); $S = 64.4$ in³ (1055.3 cm³); flange width $= 7$ in. (177.8 mm). By the AISC *Specification*, $f_s = 24{,}000$ lb/sq.in. (165.5 MPa). By the ACI Code, $n = 9$ and $f_c = 1350$ lb/sq.in. (9306.9 kPa).

#### 2. Transform the composite section in the region of positive moment to an equivalent section of steel; compute the section moduli
Refer to Fig. 58a and the AISC *Specification*. Use the gross concrete area. Then the effective flange width $= \frac{1}{4}L = \frac{1}{4}(28.5)12 = 85.5$ in. (2172 mm); spacing of beams $= 120$ in.

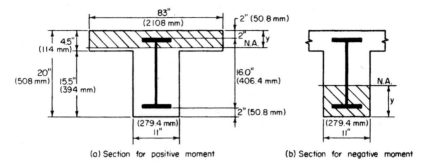

**FIGURE 58.** Steel beam encased in concrete. (*a*) Section for positive moment; (*b*) section for negative moment.

(3048 mm); $16t + 11 = 16(4.5) + 11 = 83$ in. (2108 mm); this governs. Transformed width $= 83/9 = 9.22$ in. (234.2 mm).

Assume that the neutral axis lies within the flange, and take static moments with respect to this axis; or $\frac{1}{2}(9.22y^2) - 11.77(10 - y) = 0$; $y = 3.93$ in. (99.8 mm).

Compute the moment of inertia. Slab: $(\frac{1}{3})9.22(3.93)^3 = 187$ in$^4$ (7783.5 cm$^4$). Beam: $515.5 + 11.77 \times (10 - 3.93)^2 = 949$ in$^4$ (39,500.4 cm$^4$); $I = 187 + 949 = 1136$ in$^4$ (47,283.9 cm$^4$); $S_c = 1136/3.93 = 289.1$ in$^3$ (4737.5 cm$^3$); $S_{bs} = 1136/14.07 = 80.7$ in$^3$ (1322.4 cm$^3$).

### 3. Transform the composite section in the region of negative moment to an equivalent section of steel; compute the section moduli

Referring to Fig. 58*b*, we see that the transformed width $= 11/9 = 1.22$ in. (31.0 mm). Take static moments with respect to the neutral axis. Or, $11.77(10 - y) - \frac{1}{2}(1.22y^2) = 0$; $y = 7.26$ in. (184.4 mm). Compute the moment of inertia. Thus, slab: $(\frac{1}{3})1.22(7.26)^3 = 155.6$ in$^4$ (6476.6 cm$^4$). Beam: $515.5 + 11.77(10 - 7.26)^2 = 603.9$ in$^4$ (25,136.2 cm$^4$); $I = 155.6 + 603.9 = 759.5$ in$^4$ (31,612.8 cm$^4$). Then $S_c = 759.5/7.26 = 104.6$ in$^3$ (1714.1 cm$^3$); $S_{ts} = 759.5/10.74 = 70.7$ in$^3$ (1158.6 cm$^3$).

### 4. Compute the bending stresses at midspan

The loads carried by the noncomposite member are: slab, $(4.5)150(10)/12 = 563$ lb/lin ft (8.22 kN/m); stem, $11(15.5)150/144 = 178$ lb/lin ft (2.6 kN/m); steel, 40 lb/lin ft (0.58 kN/m); total $= 563 + 178 + 40 = 781$ lb/lin ft (11.4 kN/m). The load carried by the composite member $= 145(10) = 1450$ lb/lin ft (21.2 kN/m). Then $M^n = (\frac{1}{8})781(28.5)^2 12 = 951,500$ in.·lb (107.5 kN·m); $M^c = (\frac{1}{20})1450(28.5)^2 12 = 706,600$ in.·lb (79.8 kN·m); $f_c = 706,600/[289.1(9)] = 272$ lb/sq.in. (1875 kPa), which is acceptable. Also, $f_{bs} = (951,500/64.4) + (706,600/80.7) = 23,530$ lb/sq.in. (162.2 MPa), which is acceptable.

### 5. Compute the bending stresses at the support

Thus, $M^c = 706,600(^{20}/_{12}) = 1,177,700$ in.·lb (132.9 kN·m); $f_c = 1,177,700/[104.6(9)] = 1251$ lb/sq.in. (8.62 MPa), which is satisfactory. Also, $f_{ts} = 1,177,700/70.7 = 16,600$ lb/sq.in. (114.9 MPa), which is acceptable. The design is therefore satisfactory with respect to flexure.

### 6. Investigate the composite member with respect to horizontal shear in the concrete at the section of contraflexure

Assume that this section lies at a distance of $0.2L$ from the support. The shear at this section is $V^c = 1450(0.3)(28.5) = 12,400$ lb (55.2 kN).

Refer to Sec. 1. Where the bending moment is positive, the critical plane for horizontal shear is considered to be the surface *abcd* in Fig. 59*a*. For simplicity, however, compute the shear flow at the neutral axis. Apply the relation $q = VQ/I$, where $Q = \frac{1}{2}(9.22)(3.93)^2 = 71.20$ in³ (1166.8 cm³) and $q = 12,400(71.20)/1136 = 777$ lb/lin in. (136 N/mm).

Resistance to shear flow is provided by the bond between the steel and concrete along *bc* and by the pure-shear strength of the concrete along *ab* and *cd*. (The term *pure shear* is used to distinguish this from shear that is used as a measure of diagonal tension.) The allowable stresses in bond and pure shear are usually taken as $0.03f_c'$ and $0.12f_c'$, respectively. Thus $bc = 7$ in. (177.8 mm); $ab = (2.52 + 2^2)^{0.5} = 3.2$ in. (81.3 mm); $q_{allow} = 7(90) + 2(3.2)360 = 2934$ lb/lin in. (419 N/mm), which is satisfactory.

### 7. *Investigate the composite member with respect to horizontal shear in the concrete at the support*

The critical plane for horizontal shear is *ef* in Fig. 59*b*. Thus $V^c = 1450(0.5)28.5 = 20,660$ lb (91.9 kN); $Q = 1.22(2)(7.26 - 1) = 15.27$ in³ (250.2 cm³); $q = 20,660(15.27)/759.5 = 415$ lb/lin in. (72.7 N/mm); $q_{allow} = 7(90) + 2(2)360 = 2070$ lb/lin in. (363 N/mm), which is satisfactory.

Mechanical shear connectors are not required to obtain composite action, but the beam is wrapped with wire mesh.

## COMPOSITE STEEL-AND-CONCRETE BEAM

A concrete floor slab is to be supported by steel beams spaced lift (3.35 m) on centers and having a span of 36 ft (10.97 m). The beams will be supplied with shear connectors to obtain composite action of the steel and concrete. The slab will be 5 in. (127 mm) thick and made of 3000-lb/sq.in. (20.7-MPa) concrete. Loading includes the following: live load, 200 lb/sq.ft.(9.58 kPa); finished floor, ceiling, and partition, 30 lb/sq.ft.(1.44 kPa). In addition, each girder will carry a dead load of 10 kips (44.5 kN) applied as a concentrated load at midspan prior to hardening of the concrete. Conditions at the job site preclude the use of temporary shoring. Design the interior girders, limiting the overall depth of steel to 20 in. (508 mm), if possible.

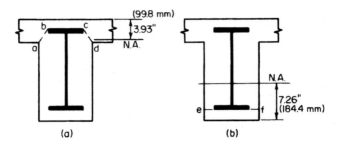

**FIGURE 59.** Critical planes for horizontal shear.

## Calculation Procedure:

### 1. Compute the unit loads $w_1$, $w_2$, and $w_3$

Refer to the AISC *Specification* and *Manual*. Although ostensibly we apply the elastic-stress method, the design of a composite steel-and-concrete beam in reality is based on the ultimate-strength behavior of the member. Loads that are present before the concrete has hardened are supported by the steel member alone; loads that are present after the concrete has hardened are considered to be supported by the composite member, regardless of whether these loads originated before or after hardening. The effects of plastic flow are disregarded.

The subscripts 1, 2, and 3 refer, respectively, to dead loads applied before hardening of the concrete, dead loads applied after hardening of the concrete, and live loads. The subscripts $b$, $ts$, and $tc$ refer to the bottom of the member, top of the steel, and top of the concrete, respectively. The superscripts $c$ and $n$ refer to the composite and noncomposite member, respectively.

We compute the unit loads for a slab weight of 63 lb/lin ft (0.92 kN/m) and an assumed steel weight of 80 lb/lin ft (1167.5 N/m): $w_1 = 63(11) + 80 = 773$ lb/lin ft (11.3 kN/m); $w_2 = 30(11) = 330$ lb/lin ft (4.8 kN/m); $w_3 = 200(11) = 2200$ lb/lin ft (32.1 kN/m).

### 2. Compute all bending moments required in the design

Thus, $M_1 = 12[(1/8)0.773(36)^2 + 1/4(10)36] = 2583$ in.·kips (291.8 kN·m); $M_2 = (1/8)0.330(36)^2 12 = 642$ in.·kips (72.5 kN·m). $M_3 = (1/8)2.200(36)^2 12 = 4277$ in.·kips (483.2 kN·m); $M^c = 2583 + 642 + 4277 = 7502$ in.·kips (847.6 kN·m); $M^n = 2583$ in.·kips (291.8 kN·m); $M_{DL} = 2583 + 642 = 3225$ in.·kips (364.4 kN·m); $M_{LL} = 4277$ in.·kips (483.2 kN·m).

### 3. Compute the required section moduli with respect to the steel, using an allowable bending stress of 24 kips/sq.in. (165.5 MPa)

In the composite member, the maximum steel stress occurs at the bottom; in the noncomposite member, it occurs at the top of the steel if a bottom-flange cover plate is used.

Thus, composite section, $S_b = 7502/24 = 312.6$ in³ (5122.6 cm³); noncomposite section, $S_{ts} = 2583/24 = 107.6$ in³ (1763.3 cm³).

### 4. Select a trial section by tentatively assuming that the composite-design tables in the AISC *Manual* are applicable

The *Manual* shows that a composite section consisting of a 5-in. (127-mm) concrete slab, a W18 × 55 steel beam, and a cover plate having an area of 9 sq.in. (58.1 cm²) provides $S_b = 317.5$ in³ (5202.9 cm³). The noncomposite section provides $S_{ts} = 113.7$ in³ (1863.2 cm³).

Since unshored construction is to be used, the section must conform with the *Manual* equation $1.35 + 0.35 M_{LL}/M_{DL} = 1.35 + 0.35(4277/3225) = 1.81$. And $S_b^c/S_b^n = 317.5/213.6 = 1.49$, which is satisfactory.

The flange width of the W18 × 55 is 7.53 in. (191.3 mm). The minimum allowable distance between the edge of the cover plate and the edge of the beam flange equals the size of the fillet weld plus 5/16 in. (7.9 mm). Use a 9 × 1 in. (229 × 25 mm) plate. The steel section therefore coincides with that presented in the AISC *Manual*, which has a cover plate thickness $t_p$ of 1 in. (25.4 mm). The trial section is therefore W18 × 55; cover plate is 9 × 1 in. (229 × 25 mm).

### 5. Check the trial section

The AISC composite-design tables are constructed by assuming that the effective flange width of the member equals 16 times the slab thickness plus the flange width of the steel. In the present instance, the effective flange width, as governed by the AISC, is $1/4L = 1/4(36)12 = 108$ in. (2743 mm); spacing of beams = 132 in. (3353 mm); $16t + 7.53 = 16(5) + 7.53 = 87.53$ in. (2223.3 mm), which governs.

The cross section properties in the AISC table may be applied. The moment of inertia refers to an equivalent section obtained by transforming the concrete to steel. Refer to Sec. 1. Thus $y_{tc} = 5 + 18.12 + 1 - 16.50 = 7.62$ in. (194 mm); $S_{tc} = I/y_{tc} = 5242/7.62 = 687.9$ in$^3$ (11,272.7 cm$^3$). From the ACI *Code*, $f_c = 1350$ lb/sq.in. (9.31 MPa) and $n = 9$. Then $f_c = M^c/(nS_{tc}) = 7,502,000/[9(687.9)] = 1210$ lb/sq.in. (8.34 MPa), which is satisfactory.

## 6.  *Record the relevant properties of the W18 × 55*
Thus, $A = 16.19$ sq.in. (104.5 cm$^2$); $d = 18.12$ in. (460 mm); $I = 890$ in$^4$ (37,044.6 cm$^4$); $S = 98.2$ in$^3$ (1609 cm$^3$); flange thickness $= 0.630$ in. (16.0 mm).

## 7.  *Compute the section moduli of the composite section where the cover plate is absent*
To locate the neutral axis, take static moments with respect to the center of the steel. Thus, transformed flange width $= 87.53/9 = 9.726$ in. (247.0 mm). Further,

| Element | A, sq.in. (cm$^2$) | y, in. (mm) | Ay, in$^3$ (cm$^3$) | Ay$^2$, in$^4$ (cm$^4$) | $I_o$, in$^4$ (cm$^4$) |
|---------|--------------------|-------------|---------------------|-------------------------|------------------------|
| W18 × 55 | 16.19 (104.5) | 0   (0) | 0   (0) | 0   (0) | 890 (37,044.6) |
| Slab | 48.63 (313.7) | 11.56 (294) | 562.2 (9,212.8) | 6,499 (270,509) | 101  (4,203,9) |
| Total | 64.82 (418.2) | ........ | 562.2 (9,212.8) | 6,499 (270,509) | 991 (41,248.5) |

Then $\bar{y} = 562.2/64.82 = 8.67$ in. (220 mm); $I = 6499 + 991 - 64.82(8.67)^2 = 2618$ in$^4$ (108,969.4 cm$^4$); $y_b = 9.06 + 8.67 = 17.73$ in. (450 mm); $y_{tc} = 9.06 + 5 - 8.67 = 5.39$ in. (136.9 mm); $S_b = 2618/17.73 = 147.7$ in$^3$ (2420 cm$^3$); $S_{tc} = 2618/5.39 = 485.7$ in$^3$ (7959 cm$^3$).

## 8.  *Verify the value of $S_b$*
Apply the value of the $K$ factor in the AISC table. This factor is defined by $K^2 = 1 - S_b$ without plate/$S_b$ with plate. The $S_b$ value without the plate $= 317.5(1 - 0.732) = 148$ in$^3$ (2425 cm$^3$), which is satisfactory.

## 9.  *Establish the theoretical length of the cover plate*
In Fig. 60, let $C$ denote the section at which the cover plate becomes superfluous with respect to flexure. Then, for the composite section, $w = 0.773 + 0.330 + 2.200 = 3.303$ kips/lin ft (48.2 kN/m); $P = 10$ kips (44.5 kN); $M_m = 7502$ in.·kips (847.6 kN·m); $R_a = 64.45$ kips (286.7 kN). The allowable values of $M_c$ are, for concrete, $M_c = 485.7(9)1.35/12 = 491.8$ ft·kips (666.9 kN·m) and, for steel, $M_c = 147.7(24)/12 = 295.4$ ft·kips (400.6 kN·m), which governs. Then $R_a x - \frac{1}{2}wx^2 = 295.4$; $x = 5.30$ ft (1.62 m). The theoretical length $= 36 - 2(5.30) = 25.40$ ft (7.74 m).

For the noncomposite section, investigate the stresses at the section $C$ previously located. Thus: $w = 0.773$ kips/lin ft (11.3 kN/m); $P = 10$ kips (44.5 kN); $R_a = 18.91$ kips (84.1 kN); $M_c = 18.91(5.30) - \frac{1}{2}(0.773) \times 5.30^2 = 89.4$ ft·kips (121.2 kN·m); $f_b = 89.4(12)/98.2 = 10.9$ kips/sq.in. (75.1 MPa), which is satisfactory.

## 10.  *Determine the axial force F in the cover plate at its end by computing the mean bending stress*
Thus $f_{mean} = My_{mean}/I = 295.4(12)916.50 - 0.50/5242 = 10.82$ kips/sq.in. (75.6 MPa); $F = Af_{mean} = 9(10.82) = 97.4$ kips (433.2 kN). Alternatively, calculate $F$ by applying the factor $12Q/I$ recorded in the AISC table. Thus, $F = 12QM/I = 0.33(295.4) = 97.5$ kips (433.7 kN).

## 11. Design the weld required to develop the cover plate at each end

Use fillet welds of E60 electrodes, placed along the sides but not along the end of the plate. The AISC *Specification* requires a minimum weld of $5/16$ in. (7.9 mm) for a 1-in. (25.4-mm) plate; the capacity of this weld is 3000 lb/lin in. (525 N/mm). Then, length = 97,400/3000 = 32.5 in. (826 mm). However, the AISC requires that the plate be extended 18 in. (457 mm) beyond the theoretical cutoff point, thus providing 36 in. (914 mm) of weld at each end.

## 12. Design the intermittent weld

The vertical shear at $C$ is $V_c = R_a - 5.30w = 64.45 - 5.30(3.303) = 46.94$ kips (208.8 kN); $q = VQ/I =$

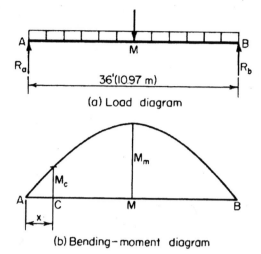

**FIGURE 60.** (*a*) Load diagram; (*b*) bending-moment diagram.

46,940(0.33)/12 = 1290 lb/lin in. (225.9 N/mm). The AISC calls for a minimum weld length of $1\frac{1}{2}$ in. (3.81 mm). Let $s$ denote the center-to-center spacing. Then $s = 2(1.5)3000/1290 = 7.0$ in. (177.8 mm). The AISC imposes an upper limit of 24 times the thickness of the thinner part joined, or 12 in. (304.8 mm). Thus, $s_{max} = 24(0.63) > 12$ in. (304.8 mm). Use a 7-in. (177.8-mm) spacing at the ends and increase the spacing as the shear diminishes.

## 13. Design the shear connectors

Use $3/4$-in. (19.1-mm) studs, 3 in. (76.2 mm) high. The design of the connectors is governed by the AISC *Specification*. The capacity of the stud = 11.5 kips (51.2 kN). From the AISC table, $V_h = 453.4$ kips (2016.7 kN). Total number of studs required = 2(453.4)/11.5 = 80. These are to be equally spaced.

# DESIGN OF A CONCRETE JOIST IN A RIBBED FLOOR

The concrete floor of a building will be constructed by using removable steel pans to form a one-way ribbed slab. The loads are: live load, 80 lb/sq.ft.(3.83 kPa); allowance for movable partitions, 20 lb/sq.ft.(0.96 kPa); plastered ceiling, 10 lb/sq.ft.(0.48 kPa); wood floor with sleepers in cinder-concrete fill, 15 lb/sq.ft.(0.72 kPa). The joists will have a clear span of 17 ft (5.2 m) and be continuous over several spans. Design the interior joist by the ultimate-strength method, using $f_c' = 3000$ lb/sq.in. (20.7 MPa) and $f_y = 40,000$ lb/sq.in. (275.8 MPa).

## Calculation Procedure:

## 1. Compute the ultimate load carried by the joist

A one-way ribbed floor consists of a concrete slab supported by closely spaced members called ribs, or joists. The joists in turn are supported by steel or concrete girders that

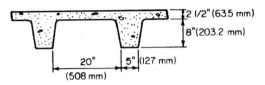

**FIGURE 61.** Ribbed floor.

frame to columns. Manufacturers' engineering data present the dimensions of steel-pan forms that are available and the average weight of floor corresponding to each form.

Try the cross section shown in Fig. 61, which has an average weight of 54 lb/sq.ft.(2.59 kPa). Although the forms are tapered to facilitate removal, assume for design purposes that the joist has a constant width of 5 in. (127 mm). The design of a ribbed floor is governed by the ACI *Code*. The ultimate-strength design of reinforced-concrete members is covered in Sec. 1.

Referring to the ACI *Code*, compute the ultimate load carried by the joist. Or, $w_u = 2.08[1.5(54 + 20 + 10 + 15) + 1.8(80)] = 608$ lb/lin ft (8.9 kN/m).

## 2. Determine whether the joist is adequate with respect to shear

Since the joist is too narrow to permit the use of stirrups, the shearing stress must be limited to the value given in the ACI *Code*. Or, $v_c = 1.1(2\phi)(f_c')(2\phi)^{0.5} = 1.1(2)(0.85)(3000)^{0.5} = 102$ lb/sq.in. (703.2 kPa).

Assume that the reinforcement will consist of no. 4 bars. With $3/4$ in. (19.1 mm) for fireproofing, as required by the ACI *Code*, $d = 8 + 2.5 - 1.0 = 9.5$ in. (241.3 mm). The vertical shear at a distance $d$ from the face of the support is $V_u = (8.5 - 0.79)608 = 4690$ lb (20.9 kN).

The critical shearing stress computed as required by the ACI *Code* is $v_u = V_u/(bd) = 4690/[5(9.5)] = 99$ lb/sq.in. (682.6 kPa) $< v_c$, which is satisfactory.

## 3. Compute the ultimate moments to be resisted by the joist

Do this by applying the moment equations given in the ACI *Code*. Or, $M_{u,pos} = (1/16)608(17)^2 12 = 132{,}000$ in.·lb (14.9 kN·m); $M_{u,neg} = (1/11)608(17)212 = 192{,}000$ in.·lb (21.7 kN·m).

Where the bending moment is positive, the fibers above the neutral axis are in compression, and the joist and tributary slab function in combination to form a T beam. Where the bending moment is negative, the joist functions alone.

## 4. Determine whether the joist is capable of resisting the negative moment

Use the equation $q_{max} = 0.6375k_1 87{,}000/(87{,}000 + f_y)$, or $q_{max} = 0.6375(0.85) 87{,}000/127{,}000 - 0.371$. By Eq. 6 of Sec. 1, $M_u = \phi bd^2 f_c' q(1 - 0.59q)$, or $M_u = 0.90(5)9.5^2 \times (3000)0.371(0.781) = 353{,}000$ in.·lb (39.9 kN·m), which is satisfactory.

## 5. Compute the area of negative reinforcement

Use Eq. 7 of Sec. 1. Or, $f_c = 0.85(3) = 2.55$ kips/sq.in. (17.6 MPa); $bdf_c = 5(9.5)2.55 = 121.1$; $2bf_c M_u/\phi = 2(5)2.55(192)/0.90 = 5440$; $A_s = [121.1 - (121.1^2 - 5440)^{0.5}]/40 = 0.63$ sq.in. (4.06 cm²).

## 6. Compute the area of positive reinforcement

Since the stress block lies wholly within the flange, apply Eq. 7 of Sec. 1, with $b = 25$ in. (635 mm). Or, $bdf_c = 605.6$; $2bf_c M_u/\phi = 18{,}700$; $A_s = [605.6 - (605.6^2 - 18{,}700)^{0.5}]/40 = 0.39$ sq.in. (2.52 cm²).

### 7. Select the reinforcing bars and locate the bend points

For positive reinforcement, use two no. 4 bars, one straight and one trussed, to obtain $A_s = 0.40$ sq.in. (2.58 cm²). For negative reinforcement, supplement the two trussed bars over the support with one straight no. 5 bar to obtain $A_s = 0.71$ sq.in. (4.58 cm²).

To locate the bend points of the trussed bars and to investigate the bond stress, follow the method given in Sec. 1.

## DESIGN OF A STAIR SLAB

The concrete stair shown in elevation in Fig. 62a, which has been proportioned in conformity with the requirements of the local building code, is to carry a live load of 100 lb/sq.ft. (4.79 kPa). The slab will be poured independently of the supporting members.

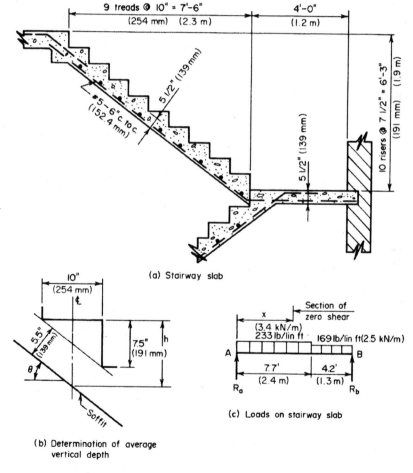

**FIGURE 62.** (a) Stairway slab; (b) determination of average vertical depth; (c) loads on stairway slab.

Design the slab by the working-stress method, using $f_c' = 3000$ lb/sq.in. (20.7 MPa) and $f_s = 20,000$ lb/sq.in. (137.9 MPa).

### Calculation Procedure:

### 1. *Compute the unit loads*
The working-stress method of designing reinforced-concrete members is presented in Sec. 1. The slab is designed as a simply supported beam having a span equal to the horizontal distance between the center of supports. For convenience, consider a strip of slab having a width of 1 ft (0.3 m).

Assume that the slab will be 5.5 in. (139 mm) thick, the thickness of the stairway slab being measured normal to the soffit. Compute the average vertical depth in Fig. 62b. Thus sec $\theta = 1.25$; $h = 5.5(1.25) + 3.75 = 10.63$ in. (270.0 mm). For the stairway, $w = 100 + 10.63(150)/12 = 233$ lb/lin ft (3.4 kN/m); for the landing, $w = 100 + 5.5(150)/12 = 169$ lb/lin ft (2.5 kN/m).

### 2. *Compute the maximum bending moment in the slab*
Construct the load diagram shown in Fig. 62c, adding about 5 in. (127 mm) to the clear span to obtain the effective span. Thus $R_a = [169(4.2)2.1 + 233(7.7)8.05]/11.9 = 1339$ lb (5.95 kN); $x = 1339/233 = 5.75$ ft (1.75 m); $M_{max} = \frac{1}{2}(1339)5.75(12) = 46,200$ in.·lb (5.2 kN·m).

### 3. *Design the reinforcement*
Refer to Table 1 to obtain the following values: $K_b = 223$ lb/sq.in. (1.5 MPa); $j = 0.874$. Assume an effective depth of 4.5 in. (114.3 mm). By Eq. 31, the moment capacity of the member at balanced design is $M_b = K_b b d^2 = 223(12)4.5^2 = 54,190$ in.·lb (6.1 kN·m). The steel is therefore stressed to capacity. (Upon investigation, a 5-in. (127-mm) slab is found to be inadequate.) By Eq. 25, $A_s = M/(f_s jd) = 46,200/[20,000(0.874)4.5] = 0.587$ sq.in. (3.79 cm²).

Use no. 5 bars, 6 in. (152.4 mm) on centers, to obtain $A_s = 0.62$ sq.in. (4.0 cm²). In addition, place one no. 5 bar transversely under each tread to assist in distributing the load and to serve as temperature reinforcement. Since the slab is poured independently of the supporting members, it is necessary to furnish dowels at the construction joints.

## *FREE VIBRATORY MOTION OF A RIGID BENT*

The bent in Fig. 63 is subjected to a horizontal load $P$ applied suddenly at the top. Using literal values, determine the frequency of vibration of the bent. Make these simplifying assumptions: The girder is infinitely rigid; the columns have negligible mass; damping forces are absent.

### Calculation Procedure:

### 1. *Compute the spring constant*
The amplitude (maximum horizontal displacement of the bent from its position of static equilibrium) is a function of the energy imparted to the bent by the applied load. The frequency of vibration is independent of this energy. To determine the frequency, it is necessary to find the spring constant of the vibrating system. This is the static force that is

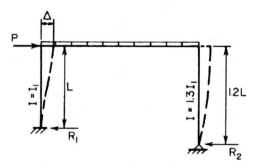

**FIGURE 63.** Vibrating bent.

required at the top to cause a horizontal displacement of one unit. Since the girder is considered to be infinitely rigid, the elastic curves of the columns are vertical at the top. Let $f$ = frequency; $k$ = spring constant; $M$ = total mass of girder and bodies supported by girder.

Using cases 22 and 23 in the AISC *Manual*, we see that when $\Delta = 1$, the horizontal reactions are $R_1 = 12EI_1/L^3$; $R_2 = 3E(1.3I_1)/(1.2L)^3 = 2.26EI_1/L^3$ $k = R_1 + R_2 = 14.26EI_1/L^3$.

## 2. *Compute the frequency of vibration*

Use the equation $f = (1/2\pi)(k/M)^{0.5} = (1/2\pi)(14.26EI_1/ML^3)^{0.5} = 0.601(EI_1/ML^3)^{0.5}$ Hz.

# SECTION 3
# TIMBER ENGINEERING

In designing timber members, the following references are often used: *Wood Handbook,* Forest Products Laboratory, U.S. Department of Agriculture, and *National Design Specification for Stress-Grade Lumber and Its Fastenings,* National Forest Products Association. The members are assumed to be continuously dry and subject to normal loading conditions.

For most species of lumber, the true or *dressed* dimensions are less than the nominal dimensions by the following amounts: $3/8$ in. (9.53 mm) for dimensions less than 6 in. (152.4 mm); $1/2$ in. (12.7 mm) for dimensions of 6 in. (152.4 mm) or more. The average weight of timber is 40 lb/ft$^3$ (6.28 kN/m$^3$). The width and depth of the transverse section are denoted by $b$ and $d$, respectively.

# BENDING STRESS AND DEFLECTION OF WOOD JOISTS

A floor is supported by $3 \times 8$ in. ($76.2 \times 203.2$ mm) wood joists spaced 16 in. (406.4 mm) on centers with an effective span of 10 ft (3.0 m). The total floor load transmitted to the joists is 107 lb/sq.in. (5.123 kN/m²). Compute the maximum bending stress and initial deflection, using $E = 1,760,000$ lb/sq.in. (12,135 kPa).

## Calculation Procedure:

### 1. Calculate the beam properties or extract them from a table
Thus, $A = 2^5/8(7^1/2) = 19.7$ sq.in. (127.10 cm²); beam weight $= (A/144)$ (lumber density, lb/ft³) $= (19.7/144)(40) = 5$ lb/lin ft (73.0 N/m); $I = (1/12)(2^5/8)(7^1/2)^3 = 92.3$ in⁴ (3841.81 cm⁴); $S = 92.3/3.75 = 24.6$ in³ (403.19 cm³).

### 2. Compute the unit load carried by the joists
Thus, the unit load $w = 107(1.33) + 5 = 148$ lb/lin ft (2159.9 N/m), where the factor 1.33 is the width, ft, of the floor load carried by each joist and $5 =$ the beam weight, lb/lin ft.

### 3. Compute the maximum bending stress in the joist
Thus, the bending moment in the joist is $M = (1/8)wL^2 12$, where $M =$ bending moment, in.·lb (N·m); $L =$ joist length, ft (m). Substituting gives $M = (1/8)(148)(10)^2(12) = 22,200$ in.·lb (2508.2 N·m). Then for the stress in the beam, $f = M/S$, where $f =$ stress, lb/sq.in. (kPa), and $S =$ beam section modulus, in³ (cm³); or $f = 22,200/24.6 = 902$ lb/sq.in. (6219.3 kPa).

### 4. Compute the initial deflection at midspan
Using the AISC *Manual* deflection equation, we see that the deflection $\Delta$ in. (mm) $= (5/384)wL^4/(EI)$, where $I =$ section moment of inertia, in⁴ (cm⁴) and other symbols are as before. Substituting yields $\Delta = 5(148)(10)^4(1728)/[384(1,760,000)(92.3)] = 0.205$ in. (5.2070 mm). In this relation, the factor 1728 converts cubic feet to cubic inches.

# SHEARING STRESS CAUSED BY STATIONARY CONCENTRATED LOAD

A $3 \times 10$ in. ($76.2 \times 254.0$ mm) beam on a span of 12 ft (3.7 m) carries a concentrated load of 2730 lb (12,143.0 N) located 2 ft (0.6 m) from the support. If the allowable shearing stress is 120 lb/sq.in. (827.4 kPa), determine whether this load is excessive. Neglect the beam weight.

## Calculation Procedure:

### 1. Calculate the reaction at the adjacent support
In a rectangular section, the shearing stress varies parabolically with the depth and has the maximum value of $v = 1.5V/A$, where $V =$ shear, lb (N).

The *Wood Handbook* notes that checks are sometimes present near the neutral axis of timber beams. The vitiating effect of these checks is recognized in establishing the allowable shearing stresses. However, these checks also have a beneficial effect, for they modify the shear distribution and thereby reduce the maximum stress. The amount of this reduction depends on the position of the load. The maximum shearing stress to be applied in design is given by $v = 10(a/d)^2v'/\{9[2 + (a/d)^2]\}$, where $v$ = true maximum shearing stress, lb/sq.in. (kPa); $v'$ = nominal maximum stress computed from 1.5V/A; $a$ = distance from load to adjacent support, in. (mm).

Computing the reaction $R$ at the adjacent support gives $R = V_{max} = 2730(12 - 2)712 = 2275$ lb (10,119.2 N). Then $v' = 1.5V/A = 1.5(2275)/24.9 = 137$ lb/sq.in. (944.6 kPa).

**2. Find the design stress**

Using the equation given in step 1, we get $(a/d)^2 = (24/9.5)^2 = 6.38$; $v = 10(6.38)(137)/[9(8.38)] = 116$ lb/sq.in. (799.8 kPa) < 120 lb/sq.in. (827.4 kPa). The load is therefore not excessive.


## SHEARING STRESS CAUSED BY MOVING CONCENTRATED LOAD

A 4 × 12 in. (101.6 × 304.8 mm) beam on a span of 10 ft (3.0 m) carries a total uniform load of 150 lb/lin ft (2189.1 N/m) and a moving concentrated load. If the allowable shearing stress is 130 lb/sq.in. (896.4 kPa), what is the allowable value of the moving load as governed by shear?


### Calculation Procedure:

**1. Calculate the reaction at the support**

The transient load induces the absolute maximum shearing stress when it lies at a certain critical distance from the support rather than directly above it. This condition results from the fact that as the load recedes from the support, the reaction decreases but the shear-redistribution effect becomes less pronounced. The approximate method of analysis recommended in the *Wood Handbook* affords an expedient means of finding the moving-load capacity.

Place the moving load $P$ at a distance of $3d$ or $1/4L$ from the support, whichever is less. Calculate the reaction at the support, disregarding the load within a distance of $d$ therefrom.

Thus, $3d = 2.9$ ft (0.884 m) and $1/4L = 2.5$ ft (0.762 m); then $R = V_{max} = 150(5 - 0.96) + 3/4P = 610 + 3/4P$.

**2. Calculate the allowable shear**

Thus, $V_{allow} = 2/3vA = 2/3(130)(41.7) = 3610$ lb (16,057.3 N). Then $610 + 3/4P = 3610$; $P = 4000$ lb (17,792.0 N).


## STRENGTH OF DEEP WOODEN BEAMS

If the allowable bending stress in a shallow beam is 1500 lb/sq.in. (10,342.5 kPa), what is the allowable bending moment in a 12 × 20 in. (304.8 × 508.0 mm) beam?


### Calculation Procedure:

**1. Calculate the depth factor F**

An increase in depth of a rectangular beam is accompanied by a decrease in the modulus of rupture. For beams more than 16 in. (406.4 mm) deep, it is necessary to allow for this reduction in strength by introducing a *depth factor F*.

Thus, $F = 0.81(d^2 + 143)/(d^2 + 88)$, where $d =$ dressed depth of beam, in. Substituting gives $F = 0.81(19.5^2 + 143)/(19.5^2 + 88) = 0.905$.

### 2. Apply the result of step 1 to obtain the moment capacity
Use the relation $M = FfS$, where the symbols are as given earlier. Thus, $M = 0.905 \times (1.5)(728.8)/12 = 82.4$ ft·kips (111.73 kN·m).

## DESIGN OF A WOOD-PLYWOOD BEAM

A girder having a 36-ft (11.0-m) span is to carry a uniform load of 550 lb/lin ft (8026.6 N/m), which includes its estimated weight. Design a box-type member of glued construction, using the allowable stresses given in the table. The modulus of elasticity of both materials is 1,760,000 lb/sq.in. (12,135.2 MPa), and the ratio of deflection to span cannot exceed 1/360. Architectural details limit the member depth to 40 in. (101.6 cm).

| | Lumber | Plywood |
|---|---|---|
| Tension, lb/sq.in. (kPa) | 1,500 (10,342.5) | 2,000 (13,790.0) |
| Compression parallel to grain, lb/sq.in. (kPa) | 1,350 (9,308.3) | 1,460 (10,066.7) |
| Compression normal to grain, lb/sq.in. (kPa) | 390 (2,689.1) | 405 (2,792.5) |
| Shear parallel to plane of plies, lb/sq.in. (kPa) | . . . . . | 72* (496.4) |
| Shear normal to plane of plies, lb/sq.in. (kPa) | . . . . . | 192 (1,323.8) |

*Use 36 lb/sq.in. (248.2 kPa) at contact surface of flange and web to allow for stress concentration.

### Calculation Procedure:

### 1. Compute the maximum shear and bending moment
Thus, $V = 1/2(550)(36) = 9900$ lb (44,035.2 N); $M = 1/8(wL^2)12 = 1/8(550)(36)^2 12 = 1,070,000$ in.·lb (120,888.6 N·m). To preclude the possibility of field error, make the tension and compression flanges alike.

### 2. Calculate the beam depth for a balanced condition
Assume that the member precisely satisfies the requirements for flexure and deflection, and calculate the depth associated with this balanced condition. To allow for the deflection caused by shear, which is substantial when a thin web is used, increase the deflection as computed in the conventional manner by one-half. Thus, $M = fI/c = 2fI/d = 2700I/d$, Eq. a. $\Delta = (7.5/48)L^2M/(EI) = L/360$, Eq. b.

Substitute in Eq. b the value of $M$ given by Eq. a; solve for $d$ to obtain $d = 37.3$ in. (947.42 mm). Use the permissible depth of 40 in. (1016.0 mm). As a result of this increase in depth, a section that satisfies the requirement for flexure will satisfy the requirement for deflection as well.

### 3. Design the flanges
Approximate the required area of the compression flange; design the flanges. For this purpose, assume that the flanges will be $5^1/2$ in. (139.7 mm) deep. The lever arm of the resultant forces in the flanges will be 34.8 in. (883.92 mm), and the average fiber stress will be 1165 lb/sq.in. (8032.7 kPa). Then $A = 1,070,000/[1165(34.8)] = 26.4$ sq.in. (170.33 cm²). Use three 2 × 6 in. (50.8 × 152.4 mm) sections with glued vertical laminations for both the

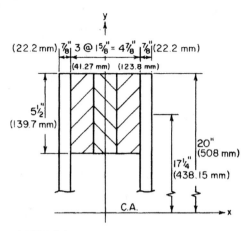

**FIGURE 1**

tension and compression flange. Then $A = 3(8.93) = 26.79$ sq.in. (170.268 cm²); $I_o = 3(22.5) = 67.5$ in⁴ (2809.56 cm⁴).

### 4. Design the webs
Use the approximation $t_w = 1.25V/dv_n = 1.25(9900)/[40(192)] = 1.61$ in. (40.894 mm). Try two ⁷/₈-in. (22.2-mm) thick plywood webs. A catalog of plywood properties reveals that the ⁷/₈-in. (22.2-mm) member consists of seven plies and that the parallel plies have an aggregate thickness of 0.5 in. (12.7 mm). Draw the trial section as shown in Fig. 1.

### 5. Check the bending stress in the member
For simplicity, disregard the webs in evaluating the moment of inertia. Thus, the moment of inertia of the flanges $I_f = 2(67.5 + 26.79 \times 17.25^2) = 16,080$ in⁴ (669,299.448 cm⁴); then the stress $f = Mc/I = 1,070,000(20)/16,080 = 1330 < 1350$ lb/sq.in. (9308.25 kPa). This is acceptable.

### 6. Check the shearing stress at the contact surface of the flange and web
Use the relation $Q_f = Ad = 26.79(17.25) = 462$ in³ (7572.2 cm²). The $q$ per surface $= VQ_f/(2I_f) = 9900(462)/[2(16,080)] = 142$ lb/lin in. (24.8 kN/m). Assume that the shearing stress is uniform across the surface, and apply 36 lb/sq.in. (248.2 kPa), as noted earlier, as the allowable stress. Then, $v = 142/5.5 = 26$ lb/sq.in. (179.3 kPa) $< 36$ lb/sq.in. (248.2 kPa). This is acceptable.

### 7. Check the shearing stress in the webs
For this purpose, include the webs in evaluating the moment of inertia but apply solely the area of the parallel plies. At the neutral axis $Q = Q_f + Q_w = 462 + 2(0.5)(20)(10) = 662$ in³ (10,850.2 cm³); $I = I_f + I_w = 16,080 + 2(1/12)(0.5)(40)^3 = 21,410$ in⁴ (89.115 dm⁴). Then $v = VQ/(It) = 9900(662)/[21,410(2)(0.875)] = 175$ lb/sq.in. (1206.6 kPa) $< 192$ lb/sq.in. (1323.8 kPa). This is acceptable.

### 8. Check the deflection, applying the moment of inertia of only the flanges
Thus, $\Delta = (7.5/384)wL^4/(EI_f) = 7.5(550)(36)^4(1728)/[384(1,760,000)(16,080)] = 1.10$ in. (27.94 mm); $\Delta/L = 1.10/[36(12)] < 1/360$. This is acceptable, and the trial section is therefore satisfactory in all respects.

**9. *Establish the allowable spacing of the bridging***
To do this, compare the moments of inertia with respect to the principal axes. Thus, $I_y = 2(1/12)(5.5)(4.875)^3 + 2(0.5)(40)(2.875)^2 = 433$ in$^4$ (18,022.8 cm$^4$); then $I_x/I_y = 16,080/433 = 37.1$.

For this ratio, the *Wood Handbook* specifies that "the beam should be restrained by bridging or other bracing at intervals of not more than 8 ft (2.4 m)."


# DETERMINING THE CAPACITY OF A SOLID COLUMN

An 8 × 10 in. (203.2 × 254 mm) column has an unbraced length of 10 ft 6 in. (3.20 m), the allowable compressive stress is 1500 lb/sq.in. (10,342.5 kPa), and $E = 1,760,000$ lb/sq.in. (12,135.2 MPa). Calculate the allowable load on this column (*a*) by applying the recommendations of the *Wood Handbook*; (*b*) by applying the provisions of the *National Design Specification.*


## Calculation Procedure:

### 1. *Record the properties of the member; evaluate k; classify the column*
Let $L$ = unbraced length of column, in. (mm); $d$ = smaller side of rectangular section, in. (mm); $f_c$ = allowable compressive stress parallel to the grain in short column of the same species, lb/sq.in. (kPa); $f$ = allowable compressive stress parallel to grain in column under investigation, lb/sq.in. (kPa).

The *Wood Handbook* divides columns into three categories: short, intermediate, and long. Let $K$ denote a parameter defined by the equation $K = 0.64(E/f_c)^{0.5}$.

The range of the slenderness ratio and the allowable stress for each category of column are as follows: *short column, $L/d \leq 11$ and $f = f_c$; intermediate column, $11 < L/d \leq K$ and $f = f_c[1 - 1/3(L/d/K)^4]$; long column, $L/d > K$ and $f = 0.274E/(L/d)^2$.*

For this column, the area $A = 71.3$ sq.in. (460.03 cm$^2$), using the dressed dimensions. Then $L/d = 126/7.5 = 16.8$. Also, $K = 0.64(1,760,000/1500)^{0.5} = 21.9$. Therefore, this is an intermediate column because $L/d$ lies between $K$ and 11.

### 2. *Compute the capacity of the member*
Use the relation capacity, lb (N) = $P = Af = 71.3(1500)[1 - 1/3(16.8/21.9)^4] = 94,600$ lb (420,780.8 N). This constitutes the solution to part *a*, using data from the *Wood Handbook*. For part *b*, data from the *National Design Specification* are used.

### 3. *Compute the capacity of the column*
Determine the stress from $f = 0.30E/(L/d)^2 = 0.30(1,760,000)/16.8^2 = 1870$ lb/sq.in. (12,893.6 kPa). Setting $f = 1500$ lb/sq.in. (10,342.5 kPa) gives $P = Af = 71.3(1500) = 107,000$ lb (475,936 N). Note that the smaller stress value is used when the column capacity is computed.


# DESIGN OF A SOLID WOODEN COLUMN

A 12-ft (3.7-m) long wooden column supports a load of 98 kips (435.9 kN). Design a solid section in the manner recommended in the *Wood Handbook*, using $f_c = 1400$ lb/sq.in. (9653 kPa) and $E = 1,760,000$ lb/sq.in. (12,135.2 MPa).

## Calculation Procedure:

### 1. Assume that d = 7.5 in. (190.5 mm), and classify the column

Thus, $L/d = 144/7.5 = 19.2$ and $K = 0.64(1,760,000/1400)^{0.5} = 22.7$. This is an intermediate column if the assumed dimension is correct.

### 2. Compute the required area and select a section

For an intermediate column, the stress $f = 1400(1 - \frac{1}{3}(19.2/22.7)4] = 1160$ lb/sq.in. (7998.2 kPa). Then $A = P/f = 98,000/1160 = 84.5$ sq.in. (545.19 cm$^2$).

Study of the required area shows that an $8 \times 12$ in. (203.2 $\times$ 304.8 mm) column having an area of 86.3 sq.in. (556.81 cm$^2$) should be used.

## INVESTIGATION OF A SPACED COLUMN

The wooden column in Fig. 2 is composed of three 3 $\times$ 8 in. (76.2 $\times$ 203.2 mm) sections. Determine the capacity of the member if $f_c = 1400$ lb/sq.in. (9653 kPa) and $E = 1,760,000$ lb/sq.in. (12,135.2 MPa).

## Calculation Procedure:

### 1. Record the properties of the elemental section

In analyzing a spaced column, it is necessary to assess both the aggregate strength of the elements and the strength of the built-up section. The end spacer blocks exert a restraining effect on the elements and thereby enhance their capacity. This effect is taken into account by multiplying the modulus of elasticity by a *fixity factor F*.

The area of the column $A = 19.7$ sq.in. (127.10 cm$^2$) when the dressed sizes are used. Also, $L/d = 114/2.625 = 43.4$; $F = 2.5$; $K = 0.64(2.5 \times 1,760,000/1400)^{0.5} = 35.9$. Therefore, this is a long column.

### 2. Calculate the aggregate strength of the elements

Thus, $f = 0.274E/(L/d)^2$ for a long column, or $f = 0.274(2.5)(1,760,000)/(43.4)^2 = 640$ lb/sq.in. (4412.8 kPa). $P = 3(19.7)(640) = 37,800$ lb (168,134.4 N).

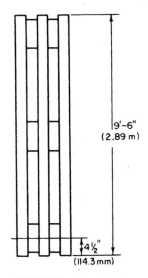

**FIGURE 2.** Spaced column.

### 3. Repeat the foregoing steps for the built-up member

Thus, $L/d = 114/7.5 \times 15.2$; $K = 22.7$; therefore, this is an intermediate column. Then $f = 1400(1 - \frac{1}{3}(15.2/22.7)^4] = 1306$ lb/sq.in. (9004.9 kPa) $> 640$ lb/sq.in. (4412.8 kPa).

The column capacity is therefore limited by the elements and $P = 37,800$ lb (168,134.4 N).

## COMPRESSION ON
## AN OBLIQUE PLANE

Determine whether the joint in Fig. 3 is satisfactory with respect to bearing if the allowable compressive stresses are 1400 and 400 lb/sq.in. (9653 and 2758 kPa) parallel and normal to the grain, respectively.

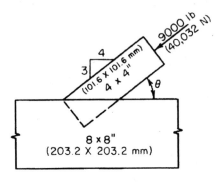

**FIGURE 3**

### Calculation Procedure:

**1. Compute the compressive stress**

Thus, $f = P/A = 9000/3.625^2 = 685$ lb/sq.in. (4723.1 kPa).

**2. Compute the allowable compression stress in the main member**

Apply Hankinson's equation: $N = PQ/(P \sin^2 \theta + Q \cos^2 \theta)$, where $P$ = allowable compressive stress parallel to grain, lb/sq.in. (kPa); $Q$ = allowable compressive stress normal to grain; lb/sq.in. (kPa); $N$ = allowable compressive stress inclined to the grain, lb/sq.in. (kPa); $\theta$ = angle between action line of $N$ and direction of grain. Thus, $\sin^2 \theta = 0.36$, $\cos^2 \theta = (4/5)^2 = 0.64$; then $N = 1400(400)/(1400 \times 0.36 + 400 \times 0.64) = 737$ lb/sq.in. (5081.6 kPa) > 685 lb/sq.in. (4723.1 kPa). Therefore, the joint is satisfactory.

**3. Alternatively, solve Hankinson's equation by using the nomogram in the Wood Handbook**

## DESIGN OF A NOTCHED JOINT

In Fig. 4, $M1$ is a 4 × 4, $F = 5500$ lb (24,464 N), and $\phi = 30°$. The allowable compressive stresses are $P = 1200$ lb/sq.in. (8274 kPa) and $Q = 390$ lb/sq.in. (2689.1 kPa). The projection of $M1$ into $M2$ is restricted to a vertical distance of 2.5 in. (63.5 mm). Design a suitable notch.

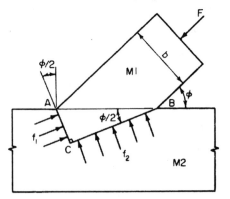

**FIGURE 4**

### Calculation Procedure:

**1. Record the values of the trigonometric functions of $\phi$ and $\phi/2$**

The most feasible type of notch is the one shown in Fig. 4, in which $AC$ and $BC$ bisect the angles between the intersecting edges. The allowable bearing pressures on these faces are therefore identical for the two members.

With $\phi = 30°$, $\sin 30° = 0.500$; $\sin 15° = 0.259$; $\cos 15° = 0.966$; $\tan 15° = 0.268$.

### 2. Find the lengths AC and BC

Express these two lengths as functions of $AB$. Or, $AB = b/\sin \phi)$; $AC = [b \sin (\phi/2)]/\sin \phi)$; $BC = [b \cos \phi/2)]/\sin \phi)$; $AC = 3.625(0.259/0.500) = 1.9$ in. (48.26 mm); $BC = 3.625(0.966/0.500) = 7.0$ in. (177.8 mm). The projection into $M2$ is therefore not excessive.

### 3. Evaluate the stresses $f_1$ and $f_2$

Resolve $F$ into components parallel to $AC$ and $BC$. Thus, $f_1 = (F \sin \phi)/(A \tan \phi/2)$; $f_2 = (F \sin \phi)[\tan (\phi/2)]/A$, where $A =$ crossectional area of $M1$. Substituting gives $f_1 = 783$ lb/sq.in. (5399 kPa); $f_2 = 56$ lb/sq.in. (386.1 kPa).

### 4. Calculate the allowable stresses

Compute the allowable stresses $N_1$ and $N_2$ on $AC$ and $BC$, respectively, and compare these with the actual stresses. Thus, by using Hankinson's equation from the previous calculation procedure, $N_1 = 1200(390)/(1200 \times 0.259^2 + 390 \times 0.966^2) = 1053$ lb/sq.in. (7260.4 kPa). This is acceptable because it is greater than the actual stress. Also, $N_2 = 1200(390)/(1200 \times 0.966^2 + 390 \times 0.259^2) = 408$ lb/sq.in. (2813.2 kPa). This is also acceptable, and the joint is therefore satisfactory.

---

## ALLOWABLE LATERAL LOAD ON NAILS

In Fig. 5, the Western hemlock members are connected with six 50d common nails. Calculate the lateral load $P$ that may be applied to this connection.

### Calculation Procedure:

### 1. Determine the member group

The capacity of this connection is calculated in conformity with Part VIII of the *National Design Specification*. Refer to the Specification to ascertain the classification of the species. Western hemlock is in group III.

### 2. Determine the properties of the nail

Refer to the *Specification* to determine the properties of the nail. Calculate the penetration-diameter ratio, and compare this value with that stipulated in the *Specification*. Thus, length $= 5.5$ in. (139.7 mm); diameter $= 0.244$ in. (6.1976 mm); penetration/diameter ratio $= (5.5 - 1.63)/0.244 = 15.9 > 13$. This is acceptable.

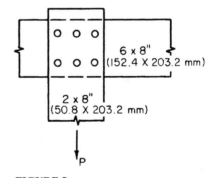

**FIGURE 5**

### 3. Find the capacity of the connection

Using the *Specification*, find the capacity of the nail. Then the capacity of the connection $= P = 6(165) = 990$ lb (4403.5 N).

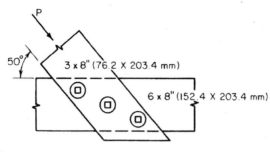

**FIGURE 6**

## CAPACITY OF LAG SCREWS

In Fig. 6, the cottonwood members are connected wtih three $5/8$-in. (15.88-mm) lag screws 8 in. (203.2 mm) long. Determine the load $P$ that may be applied to this connection.

### Calculation Procedure:

### 1. Determine the member group
The *National Design Specification* shows that cottonwood is classified in group IV.

### 2. Find the allowable screw loads
The *National Design Specification* gives the following values for each screw: allowable load parallel to grain = 550 lb (2446.4 N); allowable load normal to grain = 330 lb (1467.8 N).

### 3. Compute the allowable load on the connection
Use the Scholten nomogram, or $N = PQ/(P \sin^2 \theta + Q \cos^2 \theta)$, with $\theta = 50°$, and solve as given earlier. Either solution gives $P = 3(395) = 1185$ lb (5270.9 N).

## DESIGN OF A BOLTED SPLICE

A $6 \times 12$ in. (152.4 × 304.8 mm) southern pine member carrying a tensile force of 56 kips (249.1 kN) parallel to the grain is to be spliced with steel side plates, Fig. 7. Design the splice.

### Calculation Procedure:

### 1. Determine the number of bolts, and bolt size, required
Find the bolt capacity from the *National Design Specification*. The *Specification* allows a 25 percent increase in capacity of the parallel-to-grain loading when steel plates are used as side members.

Determine the number of bolts from $n = P/$capacity per bolt, lb (N), where $P = $ load, lb (N). By assuming $5/8$-in. (22.2-mm) diameter bolts, $n = 56,000/[3940(1.25)] = 11.4$; use 12 bolts. The value 1.25 in the denominator is the increase in bolt load mentioned above.

As a trial, use three rows of four bolts each, as shown in Fig. 7.

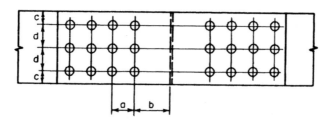

**FIGURE 7**

### 2. Determine whether the joint complies with the Specification

Assume $^{15}/_{16}$-in. (23.8-mm) diameter bolt holes. The gross area of the dressed lumber is 63.25 sq.in. (408.089 cm$^2$). The net area = gross area − area of the bolt holes = 63.25 − 3(0.94)(5.5) = 47.74 sq.in. (308.018 cm$^2$). The bearing area under the bolts = number of bolts [bolt diameter, in. (mm)] [width, in. (mm)] = 12(0.875)(5.5) = 57.75 sq.in. (372.603 cm$^2$). The ratio of the net to bearing area is 47.74/57.75 = 0.83 > 0.80. This is acceptable, according to the *Specification*. The joint is therefore satisfactory, and the assumptions are usable in the design.

### 3. Establish the longitudinal bolt spacing

Using the *Specification*, we find $a = 4(^7/_8) = 3.5$ in. (88.90 mm); $b_{min} = 7(^7/_8) = 6^1/_8$ in. (155.58 mm).

### 4. Establish the transverse bolt spacing

Using the *Specification* gives $L/D = 5.5(\%) = 6.3 > 6$. Make $c = 2$ in. (50.8 mm) and $d = 3^3/_4$ in. (95.25 mm).

# INVESTIGATION OF A TIMBER-CONNECTOR JOINT

The members in Fig. 8a have the following sizes: $A$, 4 × 8 in. (101.6 × 203.2 mm); $B$, 3 × 8 in. (76.2 × 203.2 mm). They are connected by six 4-in. (101.6-mm) split-ring connectors, in the manner shown. The lumber is dense structural redwood. Investigate the adequacy of this joint, and establish the spacing of the connectors.

### Calculation Procedure:

### 1. Determine the allowable stress

The *National Design Specification* shows that the allowable stress is 1700 lb/sq.in. (11,721.5 kPa).

### 2. Find the lumber group

The *Specification* shows this species is classified in group C.

### 3. Compute the capacity of the connectors

The *Specification* shows that the capacity of a connector in parallel-to-grain loading for group C lumber is 4380 lb (19,482.2 N). With six connectors, the total capacity is 6(4380) = 26,280 lb (116,890 N). This is acceptable.

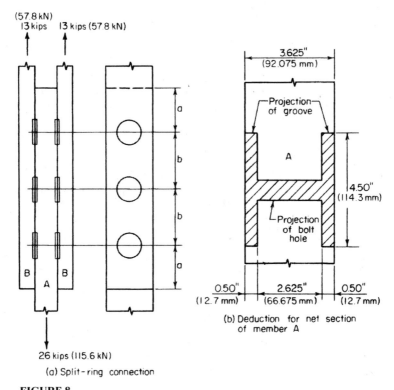

**FIGURE 8**

The *Specification* requires a minimum edge distance of $2^{3}/_4$ in. (69.85 mm). The edge distance in the present instance is $3^{3}/_4$ in. (95.25 mm).

### 4. Calculate the net area of member A

Apply the dimensions of the groove, which are recorded in the *Specification*. Referring to Fig. 8*b*, gross area = 27.19 sq.in. (175.430 cm²). The projected area of the groove and bolt hole = 4.5(1.00) + 0.813(2.625) = 6.63 sq.in. (42.777 cm²). The net area = 27.19 − 6.63 = 20.56 sq.in. (132.7 cm²).

### 5. Calculate the stress at the net section; compare with the allowable stress

The stress $f$ = load/net area = 26,000/20.56 = 1260 lb/sq.in. (8688 kPa). From the *Specification*, the allowable stress is $f_{\text{allow}}$ = $(^{7}/_8)(1700)$ = 1488 lb/sq.in. (10,260 kPa). Also from the *Specification*, $f_{\text{allow}}$ = 1650 lb/sq.in. (11,377 kPa). The joint is therefore satisfactory in all respects.

### 6. Establish the connector spacing

Using the *Specification*, apply the recorded values without reduction because the connectors are stressed almost to capacity. Thus, $a$ = 7 in. (177.8 mm) and $b$ = 9 in. (228.6 mm).

***Related Calculations.*** Today's timber engineering has evolved into engineered wood. As defined by Greenbuilding.org, "engineered wood is manufactured by bonding together wood strands, veneers, lumber, or other forms of wood fiber to produce a larger, integral composite unit that is stronger than the sum of its parts."

Today's mega homes are using large spans to create "great rooms" with unobstructed floor space. Some of these spans can be nearly 50 ft (15 m). Such spans are not possible with usual lumber. Instead, engineered wood is used. Typical engineered products available include I-joists that resemble a steel I-beam in shape, but are made solely of wood. Other products are rim board, oriented strand board, and plywood.

Most timber buildings today use a combination of regular lumber and engineered wood. Only the most expensive structures use solely engineered wood. According to *Building Products* magazine, engineered wood usually costs at least 10 percent more than traditional sawn lumber.

Among the popular building products offered in engineered wood are laminated veneer lumber (LVL), which can be used for long beams that are strong and do not warp over time. Oriented strand board (OSB), as described by Greenbuilding.org, "is manufactured from waterproof adhesives and wood strands arranged in cross-oriented layers. OSB is a solid-panel product of consistent quality. The production process utilizes a maximum of wood fiber from each tree that is harvested."

Engineered lumber is popular for floor and roof construction. When used in floors, engineered lumber produces a non-sag, non-bounce floor that has a long life. Such floors exhibit less shrinkage, crowning, warping, and other undesirable changes. For roof structures, engineered lumber shows the same desirable characteristics as in floors.

Georgia-Pacific states that engineered lumber outperforms sawn lumber because it is:

- *Stronger.* High-grade wood fiber, environmentally safe adhesives, and heat and pressure create virtually defect-free engineered lumber capable of supporting heavy loads over long spans.

- *Easier to work with.* Every piece is consistently true to size, lightweight and easy to cut on-site.

- *Environmentally sound.* GP engineered lumber uses 50 percent less timber and can be made from young, rapid-growth trees.

Thus, timber engineering is seeing rapid and highly beneficial changes in both the materials and design procedures engineers use. When designing any new timber structure, the engineer will be wise to see if engineered lumber can be included in those parts of the building where the engineered lumber will enhance the safety, strength, and usefulness of the design.

# SECTION 4
# SOIL MECHANICS

## Soil Mechanics

The basic notational system used is $c$ = unit cohesion; $s$ = specific gravity; $V$ = volume; $W$ = total weight; $w$ = specific weight; $\phi$ = angle of internal friction; $\tau$ = shearing stress; $\sigma$ = normal stress.

## COMPOSITION OF SOIL

A specimen of moist soil weighing 122 g has an apparent specific gravity of 1.82. The specific gravity of the solids is 2.53. After the specimen is oven-dried, the weight is 104 g. Compute the void ratio, porosity, moisture content, and degree of saturation of the original mass.

### Calculation Procedure:

### 1. Compute the weight of moisture, volume of mass, and volume of each ingredient

In a three-phase soil mass, the voids, or pores, between the solid particles are occupied by moisture and air. A mass that contains moisture but not air is termed *fully saturated*; this constitutes a two-phase system. The term *apparent specific gravity* denotes the specific gravity of the mass.

Let the subscripts $s$, $w$, and $a$ refer to the solids, moisture, and air, respectively. Where a subscript is omitted, the reference is to the entire mass. Also, let $e$ = void ratio = $(V_w + V_a)/V_s$; $n$ = porosity = $(V_w + V_a)/V$; MC = moisture content = $W_w/W_s$; $S$ = degree of saturation = $V_w/(V_w + V_a)$.

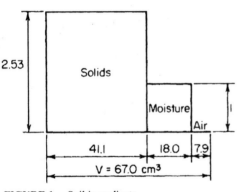

**FIGURE 1.**   Soil ingredients.

Refer to Fig. 1. A horizontal line represents volume, a vertical line represents specific gravity, and the area of a rectangle represents the weight of the respective ingredient in grams.

Computing weight and volume gives $W$ = 122 g; $W_s$ = 104 g; $W_w$ = 122 − 104 = 18 g; $V$ = 122/1.82 = 67.0 cm³; $V_s$ = 104/2.53 = 41.1 cm³; $V_w$ = 18.0 cm³; $V_a$ = 67.0 − (41.1 + 18.0) = 7.9 cm³.

### 2. Compute the properties of the original mass

Thus, $e$ = 100(18.0 + 7.9)/41.1 = 63.0 percent; $n$ = 100(18.0 + 7.9)/67.0 = 38.7 percent; MC = 100(18)/104 = 17.3 percent; $S$ = 100(18.0)1(18.0 + 7.9) + 69.5 percent. The factor of 100 is used to convert to percentage.

Soil composition is important from an environmental standpoint. Ever since the passage of the Environmental Protection Agency (EPA) Superfund Program by Congress, greater attention has been paid to soil composition by cities, states, and the federal government.

The major concern of regulators is with soil contaminated by industrial waste and trash. Liquid wastes can pollute soil and streams. Solid waste can produce noxious odors in the atmosphere. Some solid wastes are transported to "safe" sites for burning, where they may pollute the local atmosphere. Superfund money pays for the removal and burning of solid wastes.

A tax on chemicals provides the money for Superfund operations. Public and civic reaction to Superfund activities is most positive. Thus, quick removal of leaking drums of dangerous materials by federal agencies has done much to reduce soil contamination. Further, the Superfund Program has alerted industry to the dangers and effects of careless disposal of undesirable materials.

There are some 1200 dump sites on the Superfund Program agenda requiring cleanup. The work required at some sites ranges from excavation of buried waste to its eventual disposal by incineration. Portable and mobile incinerators are being used for wastes that do not pollute the air. Before any incineration can take place—either in fixed or mobile incinerators—careful analysis of the effluent from the incinerator must be made. For all these reasons, soil composition is extremely important in engineering studies.

## SPECIFIC WEIGHT OF SOIL MASS

A specimen of sand has a porosity of 35 percent, and the specific gravity of the solids is 2.70. Compute the specific weight of this soil in pounds per cubic foot (kilograms per cubic meter) in the saturated and in the submerged state.

### Calculation Procedure:

#### 1. Compute the weight of the mass in each state

Set $V = 1$ cm$^3$. The (apparent) weight of the mass when submerged equals the true weight less the buoyant force of the water. Thus, $V_w + V_a = nV = 0.35$ cm$^3$ $V_s = 0.65$ cm$^3$. In the saturated state, $W = 2.70(0.65) + 0.35 = 2.105$ g. In the submerged state, $W = 2.105 - 1 = 1.105$ g; or $W = (2.70 - 1)0.65 = 1.105$ g.

#### 2. Find the weight of the soil

Multiply the foregoing values by 62.4 to find the specific weight of the soil in pounds per cubic foot. Thus: saturated, $w = 131.4$ lb/ft$^3$ (2104.82 kg/m$^3$); submerged, $w = 69.0$ lb/ft$^3$ (1105.27 kg/m$^3$).

## ANALYSIS OF QUICKSAND CONDITIONS

Soil having a void ratio of 1.05 contains particles having a specific gravity of 2.72. Compute the hydraulic gradient that will produce a quicksand condition.

### Calculation Procedure:

#### Compute the minimum gradient causing quicksand

As water percolates through soil, the head that induces flow diminishes in the direction of flow as a result of friction and viscous drag. The drop in head in a unit distance is termed the *hydraulic gradient*. A quicksand condition exists when water that is flowing upward has a sufficient momentum to float the soil particles.

Let $i$ denote the hydraulic gradient in the vertical direction and $i_c$ the minimum gradient that causes quicksand. Equate the buoyant force on a soil mass to the submerged weight of the mass to find $i_c$. Or

$$i_c = \frac{s_s - 1}{1 + e} \tag{1}$$

For this situation, $i_c = (2.72 - 1)/(1 + 1.05) = 0.84$.

## MEASUREMENT OF PERMEABILITY
## BY FALLING-HEAD PERMEAMETER

A specimen of soil is placed in a falling-head permeameter. The specimen has a cross-sectional area of 66 cm$^2$ and a height of 8 cm; the standpipe has a cross-sectional area of 0.48 cm$^2$. The head on the specimen drops from 62 to 40 cm in 1 h 18 mm. Determine the coefficient of permeability of the soil, in centimeters per minute.

### Calculation Procedure:

### 1. Using literal values, equate the instantaneous discharge in the specimen to that in the standpipe
The velocity at which water flows through a soil is a function of the *coefficient of permeability*, or *hydraulic conductivity*, of the soil. By Darcy's law of laminar flow,

$$v = ki \tag{2}$$

where $i$ = hydraulic gradient, $k$ = coefficient of permeability, $v$ = velocity.
   In a falling-head permeameter, water is allowed to flow vertically from a standpipe through a soil specimen. Since the water is not replenished, the water level in the standpipe drops as flow continues, and the velocity is therefore variable. Let $A$ = cross-sectional area of soil specimen; $a$ = cross-sectional area of standpipe; $h$ = head on specimen at given instant; $h_1$ and $h_2$ = head at beginning and end, respectively, of time interval $T$; $L$ = height of soil specimen; $Q$ = discharge at a given instant.
   Using literal values, we have $Q = Aki = -a\, dh/dt$.

### 2. Evaluate k
Since the head $h$ is dissipated in flow through the soil, $i = h/L$. By substituting and rearranging, $(Ak/L)dT = -a\, dh/h$; integrating gives $AkT/L = a \ln (h_1/h_2)$, where ln denotes the natural logarithm. Then

$$k = \frac{aL}{AT} \ln \frac{h_1}{h_2} \tag{3}$$

Substituting gives $k = (0.48 \times 8/66 \times 78) \ln (62/40) = 0.000326$ cm/in.

## CONSTRUCTION OF FLOW NET

State the Laplace equation as applied to two-dimensional flow of moisture through a soil mass, and list three methods of constructing a flow net that are based on this equation.

### Calculation Procedure:

### 1. Plot flow lines and equipotential lines
The path traversed by a water particle flowing through a soil mass is termed a *flow line, stream-line,* or *path of percolation*. A line that connects points in the soil mass at which the head on the water has some assigned value is termed an *equipotential line*. A diagram consisting of flow lines and equipotential lines is called a *flow net*.

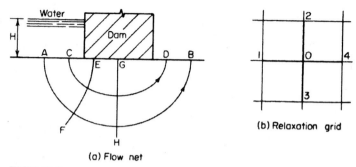

(a) Flow net

(b) Relaxation grid

**FIGURE 2**

In Fig. 2a, where water flows under a dam under a head $H$, lines $AB$ and $CD$ are flow lines and $EF$ and $GH$ are equipotential lines.

## 2. Discuss the relationship of flow and equipotential lines

Since a water particle flowing from one equipotential line to another of smaller head will traverse the shortest path, it follows that flow lines and equipotential lines intersect at right angles, thus forming a system of orthogonal curves. In a flow net, the equipotential lines should be so spaced that the difference in head between successive lines is a constant, and the flow lines should be so spaced that the discharge through the space between successive lines is a constant. A flow net constructed in compliance with these rules illustrates the basic characteristics of the flow. For example, a close spacing of equipotential lines signifies a rapid loss of head in that region.

## 3. Write the velocity equation

Let $h$ denote the head on the water at a given point. Equation 2 can be written as

$$v = -k\frac{dh}{dL} \tag{2a}$$

where $dL$ denotes an elemental distance along the flow line.

## 4. State the particular form of the general Laplace equation

Let $x$ and $z$ denote a horizontal and vertical coordinate axis, respectively. By investigating the two-dimensional flow through an elemental rectangular prism of homogeneous, isentropic soil, and combining Eq. 2a with the equation of continuity, the particular form of the general Laplace equation

$$\frac{\partial^2 h}{\partial x^2} + \frac{\partial^2 h}{\partial z^2} = 0 \tag{4}$$

is obtained.

This equation is analogous to the equation for the flow of an electric current through a conducting sheet of uniform thickness and the equation of the trajectory of principal stress. (This is a curve that is tangent to the direction of a principal stress at each point along the curve. Refer to earlier calculation procedures for a discussion of principal stresses.)

The seepage of moisture through soil may be investigated by analogy with either the flow of an electric current or the stresses in a body. In the latter method, it is merely necessary to load a body in a manner that produces identical boundary conditions and then to ascertain the directions of the principal stresses.

### 5. Apply the principal-stress analogy

Refer to Fig. 2a. Consider the surface directly below the dam to be subjected to a uniform pressure. Principal-stress trajectories may be readily constructed by applying the principles of elasticity. In the flow net, flow lines correspond to the minor-stress trajectories and equipotential lines correspond to the major-stress trajectories. In this case, the flow lines are ellipses having their foci at the edges of the base of the dam, and the equipotential lines are hyperbolas.

A flow net may also be constructed by an approximate, trial-and-error procedure based on the method of relaxation. Consider that the area through which discharge occurs is covered with a grid of squares, a part of which is shown in Fig. 2b. If it is assumed that the hydraulic gradient is constant within each square, Eq. 5 leads to

$$h_1 + h_2 + h_3 + h_4 - 4h_0 = 0 \qquad (5)$$

Trial values are assigned to each node in the grid, and the values are adjusted until a consistent set of values is obtained. With the approximate head at each node thus established, it becomes a simple matter to draw equipotential lines. The flow lines are then drawn normal thereto.

## SOIL PRESSURE CAUSED BY POINT LOAD

A concentrated vertical load of 6 kips (26.7 kN) is applied at the ground surface. Compute the vertical pressure caused by this load at a point 3.5 ft (1.07 m) below the surface and 4 ft (1.2 m) from the action line of the force.

### Calculation Procedure:

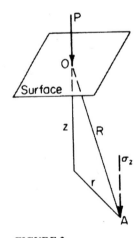

**FIGURE 3**

#### 1. Sketch the load conditions

Figure 3 shows the load conditions. In Fig. 3, $O$ denotes the point at which the load is applied, and $A$ denotes the point under consideration. Let $R$ denote the length of $OA$ and $r$ and $z$ denote the length of $OA$ as projected on a horizontal and vertical plane, respectively.

#### 2. Determine the vertical stress $\sigma_z$ at $A$

Apply the Boussinesq equation:

$$\sigma_z = \frac{3Pz^3}{2\pi R^5} \qquad (6)$$

Thus, with $P = 6000$ lb (26,688.0 N), $r = 4$ ft (1.2 m), $z = 3.5$ ft (1.07 m), $R = (4^2 + 3.5^2)^{0.5} = 5.32$ ft (1.621 m); then $\sigma_z = 3(6000)(3.5)^3/[2\pi(5.32)^5] = 28.8$ lb/sq.ft. (1.38 kPa).

Although the Boussinesq equation is derived by assuming an idealized homogeneous mass, its results agree reasonably well with those obtained experimentally.

## VERTICAL FORCE ON RECTANGULAR AREA CAUSED BY POINT LOAD

A concentrated vertical load of 20 kips (89.0 kN) is applied at the ground surface. Determine the resultant vertical force caused by this load on a rectangular area 3 × 5 ft (91.4 × 152.4 cm) that lies 2 ft (61.0 cm) below the surface and has one vertex on the action line of the applied force.

### Calculation Procedure:

#### 1. State the equation for the total force
Refer to Fig. 4a, where $A$ and $B$ denote the dimensions of the rectangle, $H$ its distance from the surface, and $F$ is the resultant vertical force. Establish rectangular coordinate axes along the sides of the rectangle, as shown. Let $C = A^2 + H^2$, $D = B^2 + H^2$, $E = A^2 + B^2 + H^2$, $\theta = \sin^{-1} H(E/CD)^{0.5}$ deg.

The force $dF$ on an elemental area $dA$ is given by the Boussinesq equation as $dF = [3Pz^3/(2\pi R^5)]\, dA$, where $z = H$ and $R = (H^2 + x^2 + y^2)^{0.5}$. Integrate this equation to obtain an equation for the total force $F$. Set $dA = dx\, dy$; then

$$\frac{F}{P} = 0.25 - \frac{\theta}{360°} + \frac{ABH}{2\pi E^{0.5}}\left(\frac{1}{C} + \frac{1}{D}\right) \tag{7}$$

#### 2. Substitute numerical values and solve for F
Thus, $A = 3$ ft (91.4 cm); $B = 5$ ft (152.4 cm); $H = 2$ ft (61.0 cm); $C = 13$; $D = 29$; $E = 38$; $\theta = \sin^{-1} 0.6350 = 39.4°$; $F/P = 0.25 - 0.109 + 0.086 = 0.227$; $F = 20(0.227) = 4.54$ kips (20.194 kN).

The resultant force on an area such as $abcd$ (Fig. 4b) may be found by expressing the area in this manner: $abcd = ebhf - eagf + fhcj - fgdj$. The forces on the areas on the right side of this equation are superimposed to find the force on $abcd$. Various diagrams and charts have been devised to expedite the calculation of vertical soil pressure.

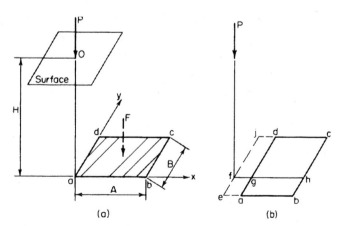

(a)          (b)

**FIGURE 4**

## VERTICAL PRESSURE CAUSED BY RECTANGULAR LOADING

A rectangular concrete footing 6 × 8 ft (182.9 × 243.8 cm) carries a total load of 180 kips (800.6 kN), which may be considered to be uniformly distributed. Determine the vertical pressure caused by this load at a point 7 ft (213.4 cm) below the center of the footing.

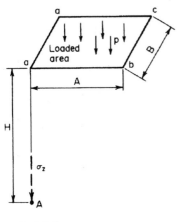

**FIGURE 5**

### Calculation Procedure:

**1. State the equation for $\sigma_z$**

Referring to Fig. 5, let $p$ denote the uniform pressure on the rectangle $abcd$ and $\sigma_z$ the resulting vertical pressure at a point $A$ directly below a vertex of the rectangle. Then

$$\frac{\sigma_z}{p} = 0.25 - \frac{\theta}{360} + \frac{ABH}{2\pi E^{0.5}}\left(\frac{1}{C} + \frac{1}{D}\right) \quad (8)$$

**2. Substitute given values and solve for $\sigma_z$**

Resolve the given rectangle into four rectangles having a vertex above the given point. Then $p = 180,000/[6(8)] = 3750$ lb/sq.ft. (179.6 kPa). With $A = 3$ ft (91.4 cm); $B = 4$ ft (121.9 cm); $H = 7$ ft (213.4 cm); $C = 58$; $D = 65$; $E = 74$; $\theta = $ sm$^{-1}$ $0.9807 = 78.7°$; $\sigma_z/p = 4(0.25 - 0.218 + 0.051) = 0.332$; $\sigma_z = 3750(0.332) = 1245$ lb/sq.ft. (59.6 kPa).

## APPRAISAL OF SHEARING CAPACITY OF SOIL BY UNCONFINED COMPRESSION TEST

In an unconfined compression test on a soil sample, it was found that when the axial stress reached 2040 lb/sq.ft. (97.7 kPa), the soil ruptured along a plane making an angle of 56° with the horizontal. Find the cohesion and angle of internal friction of this soil by constructing Mohr's circle.

### Calculation Procedure:

**1. Construct Mohr's circle in Fig. 6b**

Failure of a soil mass is characterized by the sliding of one part past the other; the failure is therefore one of shear. Resistance to sliding occurs from two sources: cohesion of the soil and friction.

Consider that the shearing stress at a given point exceeds the cohesive strength. It is usually assumed that the soil has mobilized its maximum potential cohesive resistance plus whatever frictional resistance is needed to prevent failure. The mass therefore remains in equilibrium if the ratio of the computed frictional stress to the normal stress is below the coefficient of internal friction of the soil.

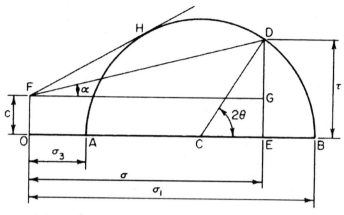

(a) Mohr's diagram for triaxial-stress condition

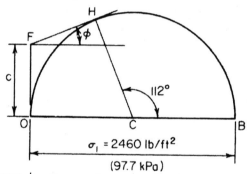

(b) Mohr's diagram for unconfined compression test

**FIGURE 6**

Consider a soil prism in a state of triaxial stress. Let $Q$ denote a point in this prism and $P$ a plane through $Q$. Let $c$ = unit cohesive strength of soil; $\sigma$ = normal stress at $Q$ on plane $P$; $\sigma_1$ and $\sigma_3$ = maximum and minimum normal stress at $Q$, respectively; $\tau$ = shearing stress at $Q$, on plane $P$; $\theta$ = angle between $P$ and the plane on which $\sigma_1$ occurs; $\phi$ = angle of internal friction of the soil.

For an explanation of Mohr's circle of stress, refer to an earlier calculation procedure; then refer to Fig. 6a. The shearing stress $ED$ on plane $P$ may be resolved into the cohesive stress $EG$ and the frictional stress $GD$. Therefore, $\tau = c + \sigma \tan \alpha$. The maximum value of $\alpha$ associated with point $Q$ is found by drawing the tangent $FH$.

Assume that failure impends at $Q$. Two conclusions may be drawn: The angle between $FH$ and the base line $OAB$ equals $\phi$, and the angle between the plane of impending rupture and the plane on which $\sigma_1$ occurs equals one-half angle $BCH$. (A soil mass that is on the verge of failure is said to be in *limit equilibrium*.)

In an unconfined compression test, the specimen is subjected to a vertical load without being restrained horizontally. Therefore, $\sigma_1$ occurs on a horizontal plane.

Constructing Mohr's circle in Fig. 6b, apply these values: $\sigma_1$ = 2040 lb/sq.ft. (97.7 kPa); $\sigma_3 = 0$; angle $BCH = 2(56°) = 112°$.

### 2. Construct a tangent to the circle

Draw a line through $H$ tangent to the circle. Let $F$ denote the point of intersection of the tangent and the vertical line through $O$.

### 3. Measure OF and the angle of inclination of the tangent

The results are $OF = c = 688$ lb/sq.ft. (32.9 kPa); $\phi = 22°$.

In general, in an unconfined compression test,

$$c = \frac{1}{2}\sigma_1 = \cot \theta' \qquad \phi = 2\theta' - 90° \qquad (9)$$

where $\theta'$ denotes the angle between the plane of failure and the plane on which $\sigma_1$ occurs. In the special case where frictional resistance is negligible, $\phi = 0$; $c = \frac{1}{2}\sigma_1$.

## APPRAISAL OF SHEARING CAPACITY OF SOIL BY TRIAXIAL COMPRESSION TEST

Two samples of a soil were subjected to triaxial compression tests, and it was found that failure occurred under the following principal stresses: sample 1, $\sigma_1 = 6960$ lb/sq.ft. (333.2 kPa) and $\sigma_3 = 2000$ lb/sq.ft. (95.7 kPa); sample 2, $\sigma_1 = 9320$ lb/sq.ft. (446.2 kPa) and $\sigma_3 = 3000$ lb/sq.ft. (143.6 kPa). Find the cohesion and angle of internal friction of this soil, both trigonometrically and graphically.

### Calculation Procedure:

### 1. State the equation for the angle $\phi$

*Trigonometric method:* Let $S$ and $D$ denote the sum and difference, respectively, of the stresses $\sigma_1$ and $\sigma_3$. By referring to Fig. 6a, develop this equation:

$$D - S \sin \phi = 2c \cos \phi \qquad (10)$$

Since the right-hand member represents a constant that is characteristic of the soil, $D_1 - S_1 \sin \phi = -S_2 \sin \phi$, or

$$\sin \phi = \frac{D_2 - D_1}{S_2 - S_1} \qquad (11)$$

where the subscripts correspond to the sample numbers.

### 2. Evaluate $\phi$ and $c$

By Eq. 11, $S_1 = 8960$ lb/sq.ft. (429.0 kPa); $D_1 = 4960$ lb/sq.ft. (237.5 kPa); $S_2 = 12,320$ lb/sq.ft. (589.9 kPa); $D_2 = 6320$ lb/sq.ft. (302.6 kPa); $\sin \phi = (6320 - 4960)/(12,320 - 8960)$; $\phi = 23°53'$. Evaluating $c$, using Eq. 10, gives $c = \frac{1}{2}(D \sec \phi - S \tan \phi) = 729$ lb/sq.ft. (34.9 kPa).

### 3. For the graphical solution, use the Mohr's circle

Draw the Mohr's circle associated with each set of principal stresses, as shown in Fig. 7.

### 4. Draw the envelope; measure its angle of inclination

Draw the envelope (common tangent) $FHH'$, and measure $OF$ and the angle of inclination of the envelope. In practice, three of four samples should be tested and the average value of $\phi$ and $c$ determined.

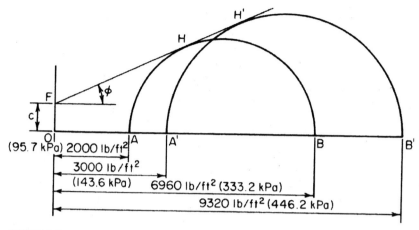

**FIGURE 7**

## EARTH THRUST ON RETAINING WALL CALCULATED BY RANKINE'S THEORY

A retaining wall supports sand weighing 100 lb/ft³ (15.71 kN/m³) and having an angle of internal friction of 34°. The back of the wall is vertical, and the surface of the backfill is inclined at an angle of 15° with the horizontal. Applying Rankine's theory, calculate the active earth pressure on the wall at a point 12 ft (3.7 m) below the top.

### Calculation Procedure:

#### 1. Construct the Mohr's circle associated with the soil prism

Rankine's theory of earth pressure applies to a uniform mass of dry cohesionless soil. This theory considers the state of stress at the instant of impending failure caused by a slight yielding of the wall. Let $h$ = vertical distance from soil surface to a given point, ft (m); $p$ = resultant pressure on a vertical plane at the given point, lb/sq.ft. (kPa); $\phi$ = ratio of shearing stress to normal stress on given plane; $\theta$ = angle of inclination of earth surface. The quantity $o$ may also be defined as the tangent of the angle between the resultant stress on a plane and a line normal to this plane; it is accordingly termed the *obliquity* of the resultant stress.

Consider the elemental soil prism *abcd* in Fig. 8a, where faces *ab* and *dc* are parallel to the surface of the backfill and faces *bc* and *ad* are vertical. The resultant pressure $p_v$ on *ab* is vertical, and $p$ is parallel to the surface. Thus, the resultant stresses on *ab* and *bc* have the same obliquity, namely, tan $\theta$. (Stresses having equal obliquities are called *conjugate* stresses.) Since failure impends, there is a particular plane for which the obliquity is tan $\phi$.

In Fig. 8b, construct Mohr's circle associated with this soil prism. Using a suitable scale, draw line *OD*, making an angle $\theta$ with the base line, where *OD* represents $p_v$. Draw line *OQ*, making an angle $\phi$ with the base line. Draw a circle that has its center $C$ on the base line, passes through $D$, and is tangent to *OQ*. Line *OD'* represents $p$. Draw *CM* perpendicular to *OD*.

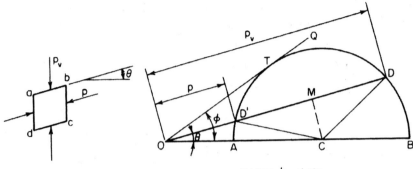

(a) Resultant pressures                    (b) Mohr's circle

**FIGURE 8**

## 2. Using the Mohr's circle, state the equation for p
Thus,

$$p = \frac{[\cos\theta - (\cos^2\theta\phi - \cos^2\phi)^{0.5}]wh}{\cos\theta + (\cos^2\theta - \cos^2\phi)^{0.5}} \quad (12)$$

By substituting, $w = 100$ lb/ft³ (15.71 kN/m³); $h = 12$ ft (3.7 m); $\theta = 15°$; $\phi = 34°$; $p = 0.321(100)(12) = 385$ lb/sq.ft. (18.4 kPa).

The lateral pressure that accompanies a slight displacement of the wall *away from* the retained soil is termed *active pressure*; that which accompanies a slight displacement of the wall *toward* the retained soil is termed *passive pressure*. By an analogous procedure, the passive pressure is

$$p = \frac{[\cos\theta + (\cos^2\theta - \cos^2\phi)^{0.5}]wh}{\cos\theta - (\cos^2\theta - \cos^2\phi)^{0.5}} \quad (13)$$

The equations of active and passive pressure are often written as

$$p_a = C_awh \qquad p_p = C_pwh \quad (14)$$

where the subscripts identify the type of pressure and $C_a$ and $C_p$ are the coefficients appearing in Eqs. 12 and 13, respectively.

In the special case where $\theta = 0$, these coefficients reduce to

$$C_a = \frac{1 - \sin\phi}{1 + \sin\phi} = \tan^2(45° - 1/2\phi) \quad (15)$$

$$C_p = \frac{1 + \sin\phi}{1 - \sin\phi} = \tan^2(45° - 1/2\phi) \quad (16)$$

The planes of failure make an angle of $45° + 1/2\phi$ with the principal planes.

# EARTH THRUST ON RETAINING WALL CALCULATED BY COULOMB'S THEORY

A retaining wall 20 ft (6.1 m) high supports sand weighing 100 lb/ft³ (15.71 kN/m³) and having an angle of internal friction of 34°. The back of the wall makes an angle of 8° with the vertical; the surface of the backfill makes an angle of 9° with the horizontal. The angle of friction between the sand and wall is 20°. Applying Coulomb's theory, calculate the total thrust of the earth on a 1-ft (30.5-cm) length of the wall.

### Calculation Procedure:

### 1. Determine the resultant pressure P of the wall

Refer to Fig. 9a. Coulomb's theory postulates that as the wall yields slightly, the soil tends to rupture along some plane BC through the heel.

Let $\delta$ denote the angle of friction between the soil and wall. As shown in Fig. 9b, the wedge ABC is held in equilibrium by three forces: the weight W of the wedge, the resultant pressure R of the soil beyond the plane of failure, and the resultant pressure P of the wall, which is equal and opposite to the thrust exerted by each on the wall. The forces R and P have the directions indicated in Fig. 9b. By selecting a trial wedge and computing its weight, the value of P may be found by drawing the force polygon. The problem is to identify the wedge that yields the maximum value of P.

In Fig. 9a, perform this construction: Draw a line through B at an angle $\phi$ with the horizontal, intersecting the surface at D. Draw line AE, making an angle $\delta + \phi$ with the back of the wall; this line makes an angle $\beta - \delta$ with BD. Through an arbitrary point C on the surface, draw CF parallel to AE. Triangle BCF is similar to the triangle of forces in Fig. 9b. Then $P = Wu/x$, where $W = w$(area ABC).

### 2. Set dP/dx = O and state Rebhann's theorem

This theorem states: The wedge that exerts the maximum thrust on the wall is that for which triangle ABC and BCF have equal areas.

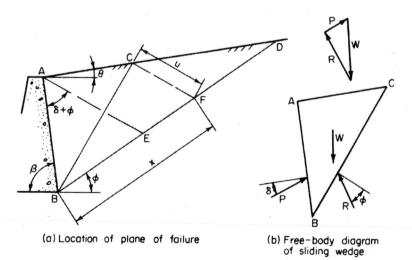

(a) Location of plane of failure        (b) Free–body diagram of sliding wedge

**FIGURE 9**

## 3. Considering BC as the true plane of failure, develop equations for $x^2$, u, and P

Thus,

$$x^2 = BE(BD) \tag{17}$$

$$u = \frac{AE(BD)}{x + BD} \tag{18}$$

$$P = \tfrac{1}{2}wu^2 \sin (\beta - \delta) \tag{19}$$

## 4. Evaluate P, using the foregoing equations

Thus, $\phi = 34°$; $\delta = 20°$; $\theta = 9°$; $\beta = 82°$; $\angle ABD = 64°$; $\angle BAE = 54°$; $\angle AEB = 62°$; $\angle BAD = 91°$; $\angle ADB = 25°$; $AB = 20 \csc 82° = 20.2$ ft (6.16 m). In triangle $ABD$: $BD = AB \sin 91°/\sin 25° = 47.8$ ft (14.57 m). In triangle $ABE$: $BE = AB \sin 54°/\sin 62° = 18.5$ ft (5.64 m); $AE = AB \sin 64°/\sin 62° = 20.6$ ft (6.28 m); $x^2 = 18.5(47.8)$; $x = 29.7$ ft (9.05 m); $u = 20.6(47.8)/(29.7 + 47.8) = 12.7$ ft (3.87 m); $P = \tfrac{1}{2}(100)(12.7)^2 \sin 62°$; $P = 7120$ lb per ft (103,909 N/m) of wall.

## 5. Alternatively, determine u graphically

Do this by drawing Fig. 9a to a suitable scale.

Many situations do not lend themselves to analysis by Rebhann's theorem. For instance, the backfill may be nonhomogeneous, the earth surface may not be a plane, a surcharge may be applied over part of the surface, etc. In these situations, graphical analysis gives the simplest solution. Select a trial wedge, compute its weight and the surcharge it carries, and find P by constructing the force polygon as shown in Fig. 9b. After several trial wedges have been investigated, the maximum value of P will become apparent.

If the backfill is cohesive, the active pressure on the retaining wall is reduced. However, in view of the difficulty of appraising the cohesive capacity of a disturbed soil, most designers prefer to disregard cohesion.

## EARTH THRUST ON TIMBERED TRENCH CALCULATED BY GENERAL WEDGE THEORY

A timbered trench of 12-ft (3.7-m) depth retains a cohesionless soil having a horizontal surface. The soil weighs 100 lb/ft³ (15.71 kN/m³), its angle of internal friction is 26°30', and the angle of friction between the soil and timber is 12°. Applying Terzaghi's general wedge theory, compute the total thrust of the soil on a 1-ft (30.5-cm) length of trench. Assume that the resultant acts at middepth.

### Calculation Procedure:

### 1. Start the graphical construction

Refer to Fig. 10. The soil behind a timbered trench and that behind a cantilever retaining wall tend to fail by dissimilar modes, for in the former case the soil is restrained against horizontal movement at the surface by bracing across the trench. Consequently, the soil behind a trench tends to fail along a curved surface that passes through the base and is vertical at its intersection with the ground surface. At impending failure, the resultant

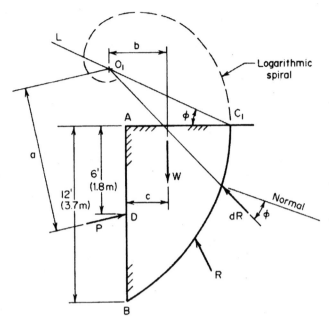

**FIGURE 10.** General wedge theory applied to timbered trench.

force $dR$ acting on any elemental area on the failure surface makes an angle $\phi$ with the normal to this surface.

The general wedge theory formulated by Terzaghi postulates that the arc of failure is a logarithmic spiral. Let $v_o$ denote a reference radius vector and $v$ denote the radius vector to a given point on the spiral. The equation of the curve is

$$r = r_o e^{\alpha \tan \phi} \tag{20}$$

where $r_o$ = length of $v_o$; $r$ = length of $v$; $\alpha$ = angle between $v_o$ and $v$; $e$ = base of natural logarithms = 2.718. . . .

The property of this curve that commends it for use in this analysis is that at every point the radius vector and the normal to the curve make an angle $\phi$ with each other. Therefore, if the failure line is defined by Eq. 20, the action line of the resultant force $dR$ at any point is a radius vector or, in other words, the action line passes through the center of the spiral. Consequently, the action line of the total resultant force $R$ also passes through the center.

The pressure distribution on the wall departs radically from a hydrostatic one, and the resultant thrust $P$ is applied at a point considerably above the lower third point of the wall. Terzaghi recommends setting the ratio $BD/AB$ at between 0.5 and 0.6.

Perform the following construction: Using a suitable scale, draw line $AB$ to represent the side of the trench, and draw a line to represent the ground surface. At middepth, draw the action line of $P$ at an angle of $12°$ with the horizontal.

On a sheet of transparent paper, draw the logarithmic spiral representing Eq. 20, setting $\phi$ = $26°30'$ and assigning any convenient value to $r_o$. Designate the center of the spiral as $O$.

Select a point $C_1$ on the ground surface, and draw a line $L$ through $C_1$ at an angle $\phi$ with the horizontal. Superimpose the drawing containing the spiral on the main drawing, orienting it in such a manner that $O$ lies on $L$ and the spiral passes through $B$ and $C_1$. On the main drawing, indicate the position of the center of the spiral, and designate this point as $O_1$. Line $AC_1$ is normal to the spiral at $C_1$ because it makes an angle $\phi$ with the radius vector, and the spiral is therefore vertical at $C_1$.

**2. Compute the total weight W of the soil above the failure line**

Draw the action line of $W$ by applying these approximations:

$$\text{Area of wedge} = \tfrac{2}{3}(AB)AC_1 \qquad c = 0.4AC_1 \qquad (21)$$

Scale the lever arms $a$ and $b$.

**3. Evaluate P by taking moments with respect to $O_1$**

Since $R$ passes through this point,

$$P = \frac{bW}{a} \qquad (22)$$

**4. Select a second point $C_2$ on the ground surface; repeat the foregoing procedure**

**5. Continue this process until the maximum value of P is obtained**

After investigating this problem intensively, Peckworth concluded that the distance $AC$ to the true failure line varies between $0.4h$ and $0.5h$, where $h$ is the depth of the trench. It is therefore advisable to select some point that lies within this range as the first trial position of $C$.

## THRUST ON A BULKHEAD

The retaining structure in Fig. 11a supports earth that weighs 114 lb/ft³ (17.91 kN/m³) in the dry state, is 42 percent porous, and has an angle of internal friction of 34° in both the

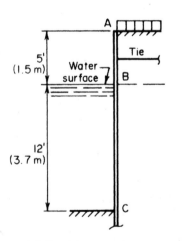

(a) Retaining structure          (b) Pressure diagram

**FIGURE 11**

dry and submerged state. The backfill carries a surcharge of 320 lb/sq.ft. (15.3 kPa). Applying Rankine's theory, compute the total pressure on this structure between $A$ and $C$.

### Calculation Procedure:

### 1. *Compute the specific weight of the soil in the submerged state*
The lateral pressure of the soil below the water level consists of two elements: the pressure exerted by the solids and that exerted by the water. The first element is evaluated by applying the appropriate equation with $w$ equal to the weight of the soil in the submerged state. The second element is assumed to be the full hydrostatic pressure, as though the solids were not present. Since there is water on both sides of the structure, the hydrostatic pressures balance one another and may therefore be disregarded.

In calculating the forces on a bulkhead, it is assumed that the pressure distribution is hydrostatic (i.e., that the pressure varies linearly with the depth), although this is not strictly true with regard to a flexible wall.

Computing the specific weight of the soil in the submerged state gives $w = 114 - (1 - 0.42)62.4 = 77.8$ lb/ft³ (12.22 kN/m³).

### 2. *Compute the vertical pressure at A, B, and C caused by the surcharge and weight of solids*
Thus, $p_A = 320$ lb/sq.ft. (15.3 kPa); $p_B = 320 + 5(114) = 890$ lb/sq.ft. (42.6 kPa); $p_C = 890 + 12(77.8) = 1824$ lb/sq.ft. (87.3 kPa).

### 3. *Compute the Rankine coefficient of active earth pressure*
Determine the lateral pressure at $A$, $B$, and $C$. Since the surface is horizontal, Eq. 171 applies, with $\phi = 34°$. Refer to Fig. 11$b$. Then $C_a = \tan^2 (450 - 170) = 0.283$; $p_A = 0.283(320) = 91$ lb/sq.ft. (4.3 kPa); $p_B = 252$ lb/sq.ft. (12.1 kPa); $p_C = 516$ lb/sq.ft. (24.7 kPa).

### 4. *Compute the total thrust between A and C*
Thus, $P = \frac{1}{2}(5)(91 + 252) + \frac{1}{2}(12)(252 + 516) = 5466$ lb (24,312.7 N).

## CANTILEVER BULKHEAD ANALYSIS

Sheet piling is to function as a cantilever retaining wall 5 ft (1.5 m) high. The soil weighs 110 lb/ft³ (17.28 kN/m³) and its angle of internal friction is 32°; the backfill has a horizontal surface. Determine the required depth of penetration of the bulkhead.

### Calculation Procedure:

### 1. *Take moments with respect to C to obtain an equation for the minimum value of d*
Refer to Fig. 12$a$, and consider a 1-ft (30.5-cm) length of wall. Assume that the pressure distribution is hydrostatic, and apply Rankine's theory.

The wall pivots about some point $Z$ near the bottom. Consequently, passive earth pressure is mobilized to the left of the wall betwen $B$ and $Z$ and to the right of the wall between $Z$ and $C$. Let

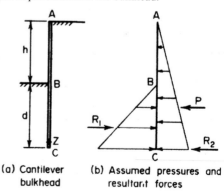

(a) Cantilever bulkhead

(b) Assumed pressures and resultant forces

**FIGURE 12**

$P$ = resultant active pressure on wall; $R_1$ and $R_2$ = resultant passive pressure above and below center of rotation, respectively.

The position of $Z$ may be found by applying statics. But to simplify the calculations, these assumptions are made: The active pressure extends from $A$ to $C$; the passive pressure to the left of the wall extends from $B$ to $C$; and $R_2$ acts at $C$. Figure 12$b$ illustrates these assumptions.

By taking moments with respect to $C$ and substituting values for $R_1$ and $R_2$,

$$d = \frac{h}{(C_p/C_a)^{1/3} -} \tag{23}$$

## 2. Substitute numerical values and solve for d
Thus, $45° + \frac{1}{2}\phi = 61°$; $45° - \frac{1}{2}\phi = 29°$. By Eqs. 15 and 16, $C_p/C_a = (\tan 61°/\tan 29°)^2$ $= 10.6$; $d = 5/[(10.6)^{1/3} - 1] = 4.2$ ft (1.3 m). Add 20 percent of the computed value to provide a factor of safety and to allow for the development of $R_2$. Thus, penetration $=$ $4.2(1.2) = 5.0$ ft (1.5 m).

# ANCHORED BULKHEAD ANALYSIS

Sheet piling is to function as a retaining wall 20 ft (6.1 m) high, anchored by tie rods placed 3 ft (0.9 m) from the top at an 8-ft (2.4-m) spacing. The soil weighs 110 lb/ft³ (17.28 kN/m³), and its angle of internal friction is 32°. The backfill has a horizontal surface and carries a surcharge of 200 lb/sq.ft. (9.58 kPa). Applying the equivalent-beam method, determine the depth of penetration to secure a fixed earth support, the tension in the tie rod, and the maximum bending moment in the piling.

## Calculation Procedure:

### 1. Locate C and construct the net-pressure diagram for AC
Refer to Fig. 13$a$. The depth of penetration is readily calculated if stability is the sole criterion. However, when the depth is increased beyond this minimum value, the tension in

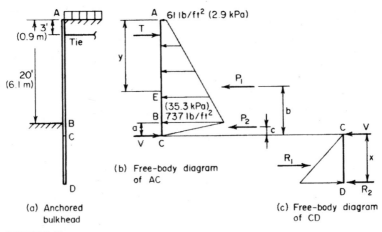

(a) Anchored bulkhead

(b) Free-body diagram of AC

(c) Free-body diagram of CD

**FIGURE 13**

the rod and the bending moment in the piling are reduced; the net result is a saving in material despite the increased length.

Investigation of this problem discloses that the most economical depth of penetration is that for which the tangent to the elastic curve at the lower end passes through the anchorage point. If this point is considered as remaining stationary, this condition can be described as one in which the elastic curve is vertical at $D$, the surrounding soil acting as a fixed support. Whereas an equation can be derived for the depth associated with this condition, such an equation is too cumbersome for rapid solution.

When the elastic curve is vertical at $D$, the lower point of contraflexure lies close to the point where the net pressure (the difference between active pressure to the right and passive pressure to the left of the wall) is zero. By assuming that the point of contraflexure and the point of zero pressure are in fact coincident, this problem is transformed to one that is statically determinate. The method of analysis based on this assumption is termed the *equivalent-beam* method.

When the piling is driven to a depth greater than the minimum needed for stability, it deflects in such a manner as to mobilize passive pressure to the right of the wall at its lower end. However, the same simplifying assumption concerning the pressure distribution as made in the previous calculation procedure is made here.

Let $C$ denote the point of zero pressure. Consider a 1-ft (30.5-cm) length of wall, and let $T$ = reaction at anchorage point and $V$ = shear at $C$.

Locate $C$ and construct the net-pressure diagram for $AC$ as shown in Fig. 13b. Thus, $w = 110$ lb/ft$^3$ (17.28 kN/m$^3$) and $\phi = 32°$. Then $C_a = \tan^2 (45° - 16°) = 0.307$; $C_p = \tan^2 (45° + 16°) = 3.26$; $C_p - C_a = 2.953$; $p_A = 0.307(200) = 61$ lb/sq.ft. (2.9 kPa); $p_B = 61 + 0.307(20)(110) = 737$ lb/sq.ft. (35.3 kPa); $a = 737/[2.953(110)] = 2.27$ ft (0.69 m).

## 2. Calculate the resultant forces $P_1$ and $P_2$

Thus, $P_1 = \frac{1}{2}(20)(61 + 737) = 7980$ lb (35,495.0 N); $P_2 = \frac{1}{2}(2.27)(737) = 836$ lb (3718.5 N); $P_1 + P_2 = 8816$ lb (39,213.6 N).

## 3. Equate the bending moment at $C$ to zero to find $T$, $V$, and the tension in the tie rod

Thus $b = 2.27 + (^{20}/_3)(737 + 2 \times 61)/(737 + 61) = 9.45$ ft (2.880 m); $c = ^2/_3(2.27) = 1.51$ ft (0.460 m); $\Sigma M_c = 19.27T - 9.45(7980) - 1.51(836) = 0$; $T = 3980$ lb (17,703.0 N); $V = 8816 - 3980 = 4836$ lb (21,510.5 N). The tension in the rod = $3980(8) = 31,840$ lb (141,624.3 N).

## 4. Construct the net-pressure diagram for $CD$

Refer to Fig. 13c and calculate the distance $x$. (For convenience, Fig. 13c is drawn to a different scale from that of Fig. 13b.) Thus $p_D = 2953(110x) = 324.8x$; $R_1 = \frac{1}{2}(324.8x^2) = 162.4x^2$; $\Sigma M_D = R_1x/3 - Vx = 0$; $R_1 = 3V$; $162.4x^2 = 3(4836)$; $x = 9.45$ ft (2.880 m).

## 5. Establish the depth of penetration

To provide a factor of safety and to compensate for the slight inaccuracies inherent in this method of analysis, increase the computed depth by about 20 percent. Thus, penetration = $1.20(a + x) = 14$ ft (4.3 m).

## 6. Locate the point of zero shear; calculate the piling maximum bending moment

Refer to Fig. 13b. Locate the point $E$ of zero shear. Thus $p_E = 61 + 0.307(110y) = 61 + 33.77y$; $\frac{1}{2}y(p_A + p_E) = T$; or $\frac{1}{2}y(122 + 33.77y) = 3980$; $y = 13.6$ ft (4.1 m), and $p_E = 520$ lb/sq.ft. (24.9 kPa); $M_{max} = M_E = 3980(10.6 - (13.6/3)(520 + 2 \times 61)/(520 + 61)] = 22,300$ ft·lb per ft (99.190 N·m/m) of piling. Since the tie rods provide intermittent rather than continuous support, the piling sustains biaxial bending stresses.

# STABILITY OF SLOPE BY METHOD OF SLICES

Investigate the stability of the slope in Fig. 14 by the method of slices (also known as the Swedish method). The properties of the upper and lower soil strata, designated as $A$ and $B$, respectively, are $A—w = 110$ lb/ft³ (17.28 kN/m³); $c = 0$; $\phi = 28°$; $B—w = 122$ lb/ft³ (19.16 kN/m³); $c = 650$ lb/sq.ft. (31.1 kPa); $\phi = 10°$. Stratum A is 36 ft (10.9 m) deep. A surcharge of 8000 lb/lin ft (116,751.2 N/m) is applied 20 ft (6.1 m) from the edge.

## Calculation Procedure:

### 1. Locate the center of the trial arc of failure passing through the toe

It is assumed that failure of an embankment occurs along a circular arc, the prism of soil above the failure line tending to rotate about an axis through the center of the arc. However, there is no direct method of identifying the arc along which failure is most likely to occur, and it is necessary to resort to a cut-and-try procedure.

Consider a soil mass having a thickness of 1 ft (30.5 cm) normal to the plane of the drawing; let $O$ denote the center of a trial arc of failure that passes through the toe. For a given inclination of embankment, Fellenius recommends certain values of $\alpha$ and $\beta$ in locating the first trial arc.

Locate $O$ by setting $\alpha = 25°$ and $\beta = 35°$.

### 2. Draw the arc AC and the boundary line ED of the two strata

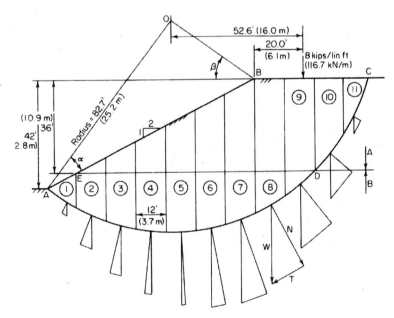

**FIGURE 14**

### 3. *Compute the length of arc AD*
Scale the radius of the arc and the central angle $AOD$, and compute the length of the arc $AD$. Thus, radius = 82.7 ft (25.2 m); arc $AD$ = 120 ft (36.6 m).

### 4. *Determine the distance horizontally from O to the applied load*
Scale the horizontal distance from $O$ to the applied load. This distance is 52.6 ft (16.0 m).

### 5. *Divide the soil mass into vertical strips*
Starting at the toe, divide the soil mass above $AC$ into vertical strips of 12-ft (3.7-m) width, and number the strips. For simplicity, consider that $D$ lies on the boundary line between strips 9 and 10, although this is not strictly true.

### 6. *Determine the volume and weight of soil in each strip*
By scaling the dimensions or using a planimeter, determine the volume of soil in each strip; then compute the weight of soil. For instance, for strip 5: volume of soil $A$ = 252 ft$^3$ (7.13 m$^3$); volume of soil $B$ = 278 ft$^3$ (7.87 m$^3$); weight of soil = 252(110) + 278(122) = 61,600 lb (273,996.8 N). Record the results in Table 1.

### 7. *Draw a vector below each strip*
This vector represents the weight of the soil in the strip. (Theoretically, this vector should lie on the vertical line through the center of gravity of the soil, but such refinement is not warranted in this analysis. For the interior strips, place each vector on the vertical centerline.)

### 8. *Resolve the soil weights vectorially into components normal and tangential to the circular arc*

### 9. *Scale the normal and tangential vectors; record the results in Table 1*

### 10. *Total the normal forces acting on soils A and B; total the tangential forces*
Failure of the embankment along arc $AC$ would be characterized by the clockwise rotation of the soil prism above this arc about an axis through $O$, this rotation being induced

**TABLE 1.**   Stability Analysis of Slope

| Strip | Weight, kips (kN) | Normal component, kips (kN) | Tangential component, kips (kN) |
|---|---|---|---|
| 1 | 10.3  (45.81) | 8.9    (39.59) | −5.2 (−23.13) |
| 2 | 28.1 (124.99) | 26.0  (115.65) | −10.7 (−47.59) |
| 3 | 41.9 (186.37) | 40.6  (180.59) | −10.4 (−46.26) |
| 4 | 53.0 (235.74) | 52.7  (234.41) | −5.5 (−24.46) |
| 5 | 61.6 (274.00) | 61.5  (273.55) | 2.6   (11.56) |
| 6 | 67.7 (301.13) | 66.5  (295.79) | 12.8   (56.93) |
| 7 | 71.0 (315.81) | 67.0  (298.02) | 23.4 (104.08) |
| 8 | 67.1 (298.46) | 58.8  (261.54) | 32.4 (144.12) |
| 9 | 54.8 (243.75) | 43.0  (191.26) | 34.0 (151.23) |
| 10 | 38.3 (170.36) | 24.9  (110.76) | 29.1 (129.44) |
| 11 | 14.3  (63.61) | 7.0    (31.14) | 12.5   (55.60) |
| Total, 1 to 9 | | 425.0 (1890.40) | |
| Total, 10 and 11 | | 31.9   (141.89) | |
| Grand total | | 456.9 (2032.29) | 115.0  (511.52) |

by the unbalanced tangential force along the arc and by the external load. Therefore, consider a tangential force as positive if its moment with respect to an axis through $O$ is clockwise and negative if this moment is counterclockwise. In the method of slices, it is assumed that the lateral forces on each soil strip approximately balance each other.

### 11. Evaluate the moment tending to cause rotation about 0

In the absence of external loads,

$$DM = r\Sigma T \tag{24}$$

where DM = disturbing moment; $r$ = radius of arc; $\Sigma T$ = algebraic sum of tangential forces.

In the present instance, DM = 82.7(115) + 52.6(8) = 9930 ft·kips (13,465.1 kN·m).

### 12. Sum the frictional and cohesive forces to find the maximum potential resistance to rotation; determine the stabilizing moment

In general,

$$F = \Sigma N \tan \phi \qquad C = cL \tag{25}$$

$$SM = r(F + C) \tag{26}$$

where $F$ = frictional force; $C$ = cohesive force; $\Sigma N$ = sum of normal forces; $L$ = length of arc along which cohesion exists; SM = stabilizing moment.

In the present instance, $F$ = 425 tan 10° + 31.9 tan 28° = 91.9 kips (408.77 kN); $C$ = 0.65(120) = 78.0; total of $F + C$ = 169.9 kips (755.72 kN); SM = 82.7(169.9) = 14,050 ft·kips (19,051.8 kN·m).

### 13. Compute the factor of safety against failure

The factor of safety is FS = SM/DM = 14,050/9930 = 1.41.

### 14. Select another trial arc of failure; repeat the foregoing procedure

### 15. Continue this process until the minimum value of FS is obtained

The minimum allowable factor of safety is generally regarded as 1.5.

## STABILITY OF SLOPE BY $\phi$-CIRCLE METHOD

Investigate the stability of the slope in Fig. 15 by the $\phi$-circle method. The properties of the soil are $w$ 120 lb/ft$^3$ (18.85 kN/m$^3$); $c$ = 550 lb/sq.ft. (26.3 kPa); $\phi$ = 4°.

### Calculation Procedure:

### 1. Locate the first trial position

The $\phi$-circle method of analysis formulated by Krey is useful where standard conditions are encountered. In contrast to the assumption concerning the stabilizing forces stated earlier, the $\phi$-circle method assumes that the soil has mobilized its maximum potential *frictional* resistance plus whatever cohesive resistance is needed to prevent failure. A comparison of the maximum available cohesion with the required cohesion serves as an index of the stability of the embankment.

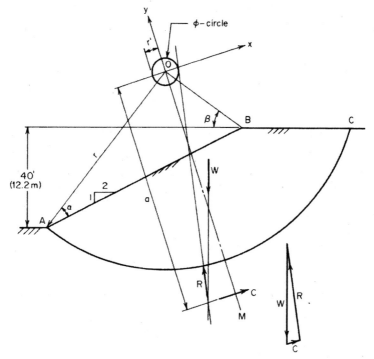

**FIGURE 15**

In Fig. 15, $O$ is the center of an assumed arc of failure $AC$. Let $W$ = weight of soil mass above arc $AC$; $R$ = resultant of all normal and frictional forces existing along arc $AC$; $C$ = resultant cohesive force developed; $L_a$ = length of arc $AC$; $L_c$ = length of chord $AC$. The soil above the arc is in equilibrium under the forces $W$, $R$, and $C$. Since $W$ is known in magnitude and direction, the magnitude of $C$ may be readily found if the directions of $H$ and $C$ are determined.

Locate the first trial position of $O$ by setting $\alpha = 25°$ and $\beta = 35°$.

## 2. Draw the arc AC and the radius OM bisecting this arc

## 3. Establlsh rectangular coordinate axes at 0, making OM the y axis

## 4. Obtain the needed basic data

Scale the drawing or make the necessary calculations. Thus, $r$ = 78.8 ft (24.02 m); $L_a$ = 154.6 ft (47.12 m); $L_c$ = 131.0 ft (39.93 m); area above arc = 4050 sq.ft. (376.2 m²); $W$ = 4050(120) = 486,000 lb (2,161,728 N); horizontal distance from $A$ to centroid of area = 66.7 ft (20.33 m).

## 5. Draw the vector representing W

Since the soil is homogeneous, this vector passes through the centroid of the area.

## 6. State the equation for C; locate its action line

Thus,

$$C = C_x = cL_c \tag{27}$$

The action line of $C$ is parallel to the $x$ axis. Determine the distance $a$ by taking moments about $O$. Thus $M = aC = acL_c$.

$$a = \left(\frac{L_a}{L_c}\right)r \tag{28}$$

Or $a = (154.6/131.0)78.8 = 93.0$ ft (28.35 m). Draw the action line of $C$.

### 7. Locate the action line of R

For this purpose, consider the resultant force $dR$ acting on an elemental area. Its action line is inclined at an angle $\phi$ with the radius at that point, and therefore the perpendicular distance $r'$ from $O$ to this action line is

$$r' = r \sin \phi \tag{29}$$

Thus, $r'$ is a constant for the arc $AC$. It follows that regardless of the position of $dR$ along this arc, its action line is tangent to a circle centered at $O$ and having a radius $r'$; this is called the $\phi$ circle, or friction circle. It is plausible to conclude that the action line of the total resultant is also tangent to this circle.

Draw a line tangent to the $\phi$ circle and passing through the point of intersection of the action lines of $W$ and $C$. This is the action line of $R$. (The moment of $H$ about $O$ is counterclockwise, since its frictional component opposes clockwise rotation of the soil mass.)

### 8. Using a suitable scale, determine the magnitude of C

Draw the triangle of forces; obtain the magnitude of $C$ by scaling. Thus, $C = 67,000$ lb (298,016 N).

### 9. Calculate the maximum potential cohesion

Apply Eq. 27, equating $c$ to the unit cohesive capacity of the soil. Thus, $C_{max} = 550(131)$ = 72,000 lb (320,256 N). This result indicates a relatively low factor of safety. Other arcs of failure should be investigated in the same manner.

## ANALYSIS OF FOOTING STABILITY BY TERZAGHI'S FORMULA

A wall footing carrying a load of 58 kips/lin ft (846.4 kN/m) rests on the surface of a soil having these properties: $w = 105$ lb/ft$^3$ (16.49 kN/m$^3$); $c = 1200$ lb/sq.ft. (57.46 kPa); $\phi = 15°$. Applying Terzaghi's formula, determine the minimum width of footing required to ensure stability, and compute the soil pressure associated with this width.

### Calculation Procedure:

### 1. Equate the total active and passive pressures and state the equation defining conditions at impending failure

While several methods of analyzing the soil conditions under a footing have been formulated, the one proposed by Terzaghi is gaining wide acceptance.

The soil underlying a footing tends to rupture along a curved surface, but the Terzaghi method postulates that this surface may be approximated by straight-line segments without introducing any significant error. Thus, in Fig. 16, the soil prism $OAB$ tends to heave by sliding downward along *OA* under active pressure and sliding upward along *ab* against passive pressure. As stated earlier, these planes of failure make an angle of $\alpha = 45° + \frac{1}{2}\phi$ with the principal planes.

Let $b$ = width of footing; $h$ = distance from ground surface to bottom of footing; $p$ = soil pressure directly below footing. By equating the total active and passive pressures, state the following equation defining the conditions at impending failure:

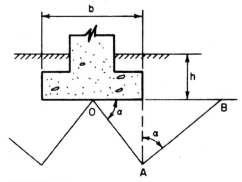

**FIGURE 16**

$$p = wh \tan^4 \alpha + \frac{wb(\tan^5 \alpha - \tan \alpha)}{4} + 2c (\tan \alpha + \tan^3 \alpha) \tag{30}$$

### 2. Substitute numerical values; solve for b; evaluate p

Thus, $h = 0$; $p = 58/b$; $\phi = 15°$; $\alpha = 45° + 7°30' = 52°30'$; $58/b = 0.105b(3.759 - 1.303)/4 + 2(1.2)(1.303 + 2.213)$; $b = 6.55$ ft (1.996 m); $p = 58,000/6.55 = 8850$ lb/sq.ft. (423.7 kPa).

## SOIL CONSOLIDATION AND CHANGE IN VOID RATIO

In a laboratory test, a load was applied to a soil specimen having a height of 30 in (762.0 mm) and a void ratio of 96.0 percent. What was the void ratio when the load settled 0.5 in. (12.7 mm)?

### Calculation Procedure:

### 1. Construct a diagram representing the volumetric composition of the soil in the original and final states

According to the Terzaghi theory of consolidation, the compression of a soil mass under an increase in pressure results primarily from the expulsion of water from the pores. At the instant the load is applied, it is supported entirely by the water, and the hydraulic gradient thus established induces flow. However, the flow in turn causes a continuous transfer of load from the water to the solids.

Equilibrium is ultimately attained when the load is carried entirely by the solids, and the expulsion of the water then ceases. The time rate of expulsion, and therefore of consolidation, is a function of the permeability of the soil, the number of drainage faces, etc. Let $H$ = original height of soil stratum; $s$ = settlement; $e_1$ = original void ratio; $e_2$ = final void ratio. Using the given data, construct the diagram in Fig. 17, representing the volumetric composition of the soil in the original and final states.

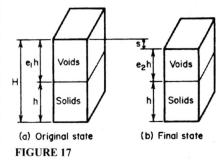

(a) Original state      (b) Final state

**FIGURE 17**

### 2. State the equation relating the four defined quantities
Thus,

$$s = \frac{H(e_1 - e_2)}{1 + e_1}$$ (31)

### 3. Solve for $e_2$
Thus: $H = 30$ in. (762.0 mm); $s = 0.50$ in. (12.7 mm); $e_1 = 0.960$; $e_2 = 92.7$ percent.


## COMPRESSION INDEX AND VOID RATIO OF A SOIL

A soil specimen under a pressure of 1200 lb/sq.ft. (57.46 kPa) is found to have a void ratio of 103 percent. If the compression index is 0.178, what will be the void ratio when the pressure is increased to 5000 lb/sq.ft. (239.40 kPa)?


### Calculation Procedure:

### 1. Define the compression index
By testing a soil specimen in a consolidometer, it is possible to determine the void ratio associated with a given compressive stress. When the sets of values thus obtained are plotted on semilogarithmic scales (void ratio vs. logarithm of stress), the resulting diagram is curved initially but becomes virtually a straight line beyond a specific point. The slope of this line is termed the *compression index*.

### 2. Compute the soil void ratio
Let $C_c$ = compression index; $e_1$ and $e_2$ = original and final void ratio, respectively; $\sigma_1$ and $\sigma_2$ = original and final normal stress, respectively.

Write the equation of the straight-line portion of the diagram:

$$e_1 - e_2 = C_c \log \frac{\sigma_1}{\sigma_2}$$ (32)

Substituting and solving give $1.03 - e_2 = 0.178 \log (5000/1200)$; $e_2 = 92.0$ percent. Note that the logarithm is taken to the base 10.

Landfills—where municipal and industrial wastes are discarded—are subject to soil consolidation because of gradual contraction of the components. To hasten this contraction and reduce the space needed for trash, some communities are mining established landfills.

When a trash landfill is mined, more than half of the contents may be combustible in an incinerator. Useful electric power can be produced by burning the recovered trash. In one landfill, some 54 percent of the trash is burned, 36 percent is recycled to cover new trash, and 10 percent is returned to the landfill as unrecoverable. The overall effect is to obtain useful power from the mined trash while reducing the volume of the trash by 75 percent. This allows more new trash to be stored at the landfill without increasing the area required.

Mining of landfills also saves closing costs, which can run into millions of dollars for even the smallest landfill. Current EPA regulations require a landfill to be monitored for environmental risks for 30 years after closing. Mining the landfill eliminates the need for closure while producing moneymaking power and reducing the storage volume needed for a specific amount of trash. So before soil consolidation tests are made for a landfill, plans for its possible mining should be reviewed.

## SETTLEMENT OF FOOTING

An 8-ft (2.4-m) square footing carries a load of 150 kips (667.2 kN) that may be considered uniformly distributed, and it is supported by the soil strata shown in Fig. 18. The silty clay has a compression index of 0.274; its void ratio prior to application of the load is 84 percent. Applying the unit weights indicated in Fig. 18, calculate the settlement of the footing caused by consolidation of the silty clay.

### Calculation Procedure:

### 1. *Compute the vertical stress at middepth before and after application of the load*

To simplify the calculations, assume that the load is transmitted through a truncated pyramid having side slopes of 2 to 1 and that the stress is uniform across a horizontal plane. Take the stress at middepth of the silty-clay stratum as the average for that stratum.

Compute the vertical stress $\sigma_1$ and $\sigma_2$ at middepth before and after application of the load, respectively. Thus: $\sigma_1 = 6(116) + 12(64) + 7(60) = 1884$ lb/sq.ft. (90.21 kPa); $\sigma_2 = 1884 + 150,000/33^2 = 2022$ lb/sq.ft. (96.81 kPa).

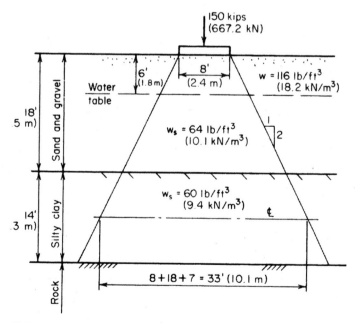

**FIGURE 18.** Settlement of footing.

## 2. Compute the footing settlement

Combine Eqs. 31 and 32 to obtain

$$s = \frac{HC_c \log (\sigma_2/\sigma_1)}{1 + e_1} \tag{33}$$

Solving gives $s = 14(0.274) \log (2022/1884)/(1 + 0.84) = 0.064$ ft $= 0.77$ in. (19.558 mm).

# DETERMINATION OF FOOTING SIZE BY HOUSEL'S METHOD

A square footing is to transmit a load of 80 kips (355.8 kN) to a cohesive soil, the settlement being restricted to $5/8$ in. (15.9 mm). Two test footings were loaded at the site until the settlement reached this value. The results were

| Footing size | Load, lb (N) |
|---|---|
| 1 ft 6 in. $\times$ 2 ft (45.72 $\times$ 60.96 cm) | 14,200 (63,161.6) |
| 3 ft $\times$ 3 ft (91.44 $\times$ 91.44 cm) | 34,500 (153,456.0) |

Applying Housel's method, determine the size of the footing in plan.

## Calculation Procedure:

### 1. Determine the values of p and s corresponding to the allowable settlement

Housel considers that the ability of a cohesive soil to support a footing stems from two sources: bearing strength and shearing strength. This concept is embodied in

$$W = Ap + Ps \tag{34}$$

where $W$ = total load; $A$ = area of contact surface; $P$ = perimeter of contact surface; $p$ = bearing stress directly below footing; $s$ = shearing stress along perimeter.

Applying the given data for the test footings gives: footing 1, $A = 3$ sq.ft. (2787 cm²), $P = 7$ ft (2.1 m); footing 2, $A = 9$ sq.ft. (8361 cm²), $P = 12$ ft (3.7 m). Then $3p + 7s = 14,200$; $9p + 12s = 34,500$; $p = 2630$ lb/sq.ft. (125.9 kPa); $s = 900$ lb/lin ft (13,134.5 N/m).

### 2. Compute the size of the footing to carry the specified load

Let $x$ denote the side of the footing. Then, $2630x^2 + 900(4x) = 80,000$; $x = 4.9$ ft (1.5 m). Make the footing 5 ft (1.524 m) square.

# APPLICATION OF PILE-DRIVING FORMULA

A 16 $\times$ 16 in. (406.4 $\times$ 406.4 mm) pile of 3000-lb/m² (20,685-kPa) concrete, 45 ft (13.7 m) long, is reinforced with eight no. 7 bars. The pile is driven by a double-acting steam hammer. The weight of the ram is 4600 lb (20,460.8 N), and the energy delivered is 17,000 ft·lb (23,052 J) per blow. The average penetration caused by the final blows is

0.42 in. (10.668 mm). Compute the bearing capacity of the pile by applying Redtenbacker's formula and using a factor of safety of 3.

## Calculation Procedure:

### 1. Find the weight of the pile and the area of the transformed section

The work performed in driving a pile into the soil is a function of the reaction of the soil on the pile and the properties of the pile. Therefore, the soil reaction may be evaluated if the work performed by the hammer is known. Let $A$ = cross-sectional area of pile; $E$ = modulus of elasticity; $h$ = height of fall of ram; $L$ = length of pile; $P$ = allowable load on pile; $R$ = reaction of soil on pile; $s$ = penetration per blow; $W$ = weight of falling ram; $w$ = weight of pile.

Redtenbacker developed the following equation by taking these quantities into consideration: the work performed by the soil in bringing the pile to rest; the work performed in compressing the pile; and the energy delivered to the pile:

$$Rs + \frac{R^2 L}{2AE} = \frac{W^2 h}{W + w} \tag{35}$$

Finding the weight of the pile and the area of the transformed section, we get $w$ = 16(16)(0.150)(45)/144 = 12 kips (53.4 kN). The area of a no. 7 bar = 0.60 m² (3.871 cm²); $n$ = 9; $A$ = 16(16) + 8(9 − 1)0.60 = 294 m² (1896.9 cm²).

### 2. Apply Eq. 191 to find R; evaluate P

Thus, $s$ = 0.42 in. (10.668 mm); $L$ = 540 in. (13,716 mm); $E_c$ = 3160 kips/m² (21,788.2 MPa.); $W$ = 4.6 kips (20.46 kN); $Wh$ = 17 ft·kips = 204 in·kips (23,052 J). Substituting gives 0.42$R$ + 540$R^2$/[2(294)(3160)] = 4.6(204)/(4.6 + 12); $R$ = 84.8 kips (377.19 kN); $P$ = $R$/3 = 28.3 kips (125.88 kN).

## CAPACITY OF A GROUP OF FRICTION PILES

A structure is to be supported by 12 friction piles of 10-in. (254-mm) diameter. These will be arranged in four rows of three piles each at a spacing of 3 ft (91.44 cm) in both directions. A test pile is found to have an allowable load of 32 kips (142.3 kN). Determine the load that may be carried by this pile group.

## Calculation Procedure:

### 1. State a suitable equation for the load

When friction piles are compactly spaced, the area of soil that is needed to support an individual pile overlaps that needed to support the adjacent ones. Consequently, the capacity of the group is less than the capacity obtained by aggregating the capacities of the individual piles. Let $P$ = capacity of group; $P_i$ = capacity of single pile; $m$ = number of rows; $n$ = number of piles per row; $d$ = pile diameter; $s$ = center-to-center spacing of piles; $\theta$ = $\tan^{-1} d/s$ deg. A suitable equation using these variables is the Converse-Labarre equation

$$\frac{P}{P_i} = mn - \left(\frac{\theta}{90°}\right)[m(n - 1) + n(m - 1)] \tag{36}$$

## 2. Compute the load

Thus $P_i = 32$ kips (142.3 kN); $m = 4$; $n = 3$; $d = 10$ in. (254 mm); $s = 36$ in. (914.4 mm); $\theta = \tan^{-1} 10/36 = 15.5°$. Then $P/32 = 12 - (15.5/90)(4 \times 2 + 3 \times 3)$; $P = 290$ kips (1289.9 kN).

# LOAD DISTRIBUTION AMONG HINGED BATTER PILES

Figure 19a shows the relative positions of four steel bearing piles that carry the indicated load. The piles, which may be considered as hinged at top and bottom, have identical cross sections and the following relative effective lengths: $A$, 1.0; $B$, 0.95; $C$, 0.93; $D$, 1.05. Outline a graphical procedure for determining the load transmitted to each pile.

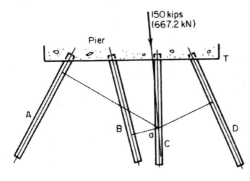

(a) Pile group and load

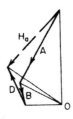

(b) Force polygon for $H_a$

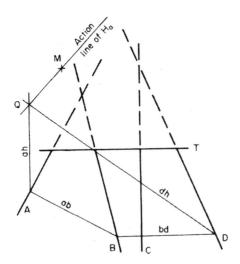

(c) Construction to locate action line of $H_a$

**FIGURE 19**

**Calculation Procedure:**

**1.  *Subject the structure to a load for purposes of analysis***
Steel and timber piles may be considered to be connected to the concrete pier by friction-less hinges, and bearing piles that extend a relatively short distance into compact soil may be considered to be hinge-supported by the soil.

Since four unknown quantities are present, the structure is statically indeterminate. A solution to this problem therefore requires an analysis of the deformation of the structure.

As the load is applied, the pier, assumed to be infinitely rigid, rotates to some new po-sition. This displacement causes each pile to rotate about its base and to undergo an axial strain. The contraction or elongation of each pile is directly proportional to the perpendi-cular distance $p$ from the axis of rotation to the longitudinal axis of that pile. Let $P$ denote the load induced in the pile. Then $P = \Delta L \, AE/L$. Since $\Delta L$ is proportional to $p$ and $AE$ is constant for the group, this equation may be transformed to

$$P = \frac{kp}{L} \qquad (37)$$

where $k$ is a constant of proportionality.

If the center of rotation is established, the pile loads may therefore be found by scaling the $p$ distances. Westergaard devised a simple graphical method of locating the center of rotation. This method entails the construction of string polygons, described in the first calculation procedure of this handbook.

In Fig. 19$a$ select any convenient point $a$ on the action line of the load. Consider the structure to be subjected to a load $H_a$ that causes the pier to rotate about $a$ as a center. The object is to locate the action line of this hypothetical load.

It is often desirable to visualize that a load is applied to a body at a point that in reality lies outside the body. This condition becomes possible if the designer annexes to the body an infinitely rigid arm containing the given point. Since this arm does not deform, the stresses and strains in the body proper are not modified.

**2.  *Scale the perpendicular distance from a to the longitudinal axis of each pile; divide this distance by the relative length of the pile***
In accordance with Eq. 37, the quotient represents the relative magnitude of the load in-duced in the pile by the load $H_a$. If rotation is assumed to be counterclockwise, piles $A$ and $B$ are in compression and $D$ is in tension.

**3.  *Using a suitable scale, construct the force polygon***
This polygon is shown in Fig. 19$b$. Construct this polygon by applying the results ob-tained in step 2. This force polygon yields the direction of the action line of $H_a$.

**4.  *In Fig. 19b, select a convenient pole O and draw rays to the force polygon***

**5.  *Construct the string polygon shown in Fig. 19c***
The action line of $H_a$ passes through the intersection point $Q$ of rays $ah$ and $dh$, and its di-rection appears in Fig. 19$b$. Draw this line.

**6.  *Select a second point on the action line of the load***
Choose point $b$ on the action line of the 150-kip (667.2-kN) load, and consider the struc-ture to be subjected to a load $H_b$ that causes the pier to rotate about $b$ as center.

**7.  *Locate the action line of $H_b$***
Repeat the foregoing procedure to locate the action line of $H_b$ in Fig. 19$c$. (The construc-tion has been omitted for clarity.) Study of the diagram shows that the action lines of $H_a$ and $H_b$ intersect at $M$.

### 8. Test the accuracy of the construction
Select a third point $c$ on the action line of the 150-kip (667.2-kN) load, and locate the action line of the hypothetical load $H_c$ causing rotation about $c$. It is found that $H_c$ also passes through $M$. In summary, these hypothetical loads causing rotation about specific points on the action line of the true load are all concurrent.

Thus, $M$ is the center of rotation of the pier under the 150-kip (667.2-kN) load. This conclusion stems from the following analysis: Load $H_a$ applied at $M$ causes zero deflection at $a$. Therefore, in accordance with Maxwell's theorem of reciprocal deflections, if the true load is applied at $a$, it will cause zero deflection at $M$ in the direction of $H_a$. Similarly, if the true load is applied at $b$, it will cause zero deflection at $M$ in the direction of $H_b$. Thus, $M$ remains stationary under the 150-kip (667.2-kN) load; that is, $M$ is the center of rotation of the pier.

### 9. Scale the perpendicular distance from M to the longitudinal axis of each pile
Divide this distance by the relative length of the pile. The quotient represents the relative magnitude of the load induced in the pile by the 150-kip (667.2-kN) load.

### 10. Using a suitable scale, construct the force polygon by applying the results from step 9
If the work is accurate, the resultant of these relative loads is parallel to the true load.

### 11. Scale the resultant; compute the factor needed to correct this value to 150 k/ps (667.2 kN)

### 12. Multiply each relative pile load by this correction factor to obtain the true load induced in the pile

## LOAD DISTRIBUTION AMONG PILES WITH FIXED BASES

Assume that the piles in Fig. 19a penetrate a considerable distance into a compact soil and may therefore be regarded as restrained against rotation at a certain level. Outline a procedure for determining the axial load and bending moment induced in each pile.

### Calculation Procedure:

### 1. State the equation for the length of a dummy pile
Since the Westergaard construction presented in the previous calculation procedure applies solely to hinged piles, the group of piles now being considered is not directly amenable to analysis by this method.

As shown in Fig. 20a, the pile $AB$ functions in the dual capacity of a column and cantilever beam. In Fig. 20b, let $A'$ denote the position of $A$ following application of the load. If secondary effects are disregarded, the axial force $P$ transmitted to this pile is a function of $\Delta_y$, and the transverse force $S$ is a function of $\Delta_x$.

Consider that the fixed support at $B$ is replaced with a hinged support and a pile $AC$ of identical cross section is added perpendicular to $AB$, as shown in Fig. 20b. If pile $AC$ deforms an amount $\Delta_x$ under an axial force $S$, the forces transmitted by the pier at each point of support are not affected by this modification of supports. The added pile is called a *dummy* pile. Thus, the given pile group may be replaced with an equivalent group consisting solely of hinged piles.

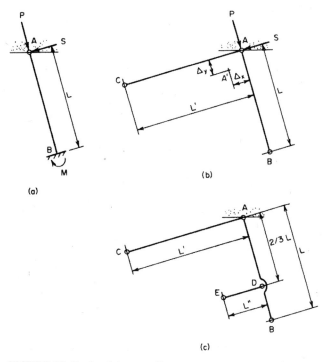

**FIGURE 20.** Real and dummy piles.

Stating the equation for the length $L'$ of the dummy pile, equate the displacement $\Delta_x$ in the equivalent pile group to that in the actual group. Or, $\Delta_x = SL'/AE = SL^3/8EI$.

$$L' = \frac{AL^3}{3I} \tag{38}$$

### 2. Replace all fixed supports in the given pile group with hinged supports

Add the dummy piles. Compute the lengths of these piles by applying Eq. 38.

### 3. Determine the axial forces induced in the equivalent pile group

Using the given load, apply Westergaard's construction, as described in the previous calculation procedure.

### 4. Remove the dummy piles; restore the fixed supports

Compute the bending moments at these supports by applying the equation $M = SL$.

## LOAD DISTRIBUTION AMONG PILES FIXED AT TOP AND BOTTOM

Assume that the piles in Fig. 19a may be regarded as having fixed supports both at the pier and at their bases. Outline a procedure for determining the axial load and bending moment induced in each pile.

## Calculation Procedure:

### 1. *Describe how dummy piles may be used*
A pile made of reinforced concrete and built integrally with the pier is restrained against rotation relative to the pier. As shown in Fig. 19c, the fixed supports of pile $AB$ may be replaced with hinges provided that dummy piles $AC$ and $DE$ are added, the latter being connected to the pier by means of a rigid arm through $D$.

### 2. *Compute the lengths of the dummy piles*
If $D$ is placed at the lower third point as indicated, the lengths to be assigned to the dummy piles are

$$L' = \frac{AL^3}{3I} \quad \text{and} \quad L'' = \frac{AL^3}{9I} \tag{39}$$

Replace the given group of piles with its equivalent group, and follow the method of solution in the previous calculation procedure.

# Economics of Cleanup Methods in Soil Mechanics

Many tasks in soil mechanics are hindered by polluted soil that must be cleaned before foundations, tunnels, sluiceways, or other structures can be built. Four procedures presented here give the economics and techniques currently used to clean contaminated soil sites. While there are numerous rules and regulations governing soil cleaning, these procedures will help the civil engineer understand the approaches being used today. With the information presented in these procedures the civil engineer should be able to make an intelligent choice of a feasible cleanup method. And the first procedure gives the economics of not polluting the soil—i.e., recycling polluting materials for profit. Such an approach may be the ultimate answer to soil redmediation—preventing pollution before it starts, using the profit potential as the motivating force for a "clean" planet.

## RECYCLE PROFIT POTENTIALS IN MUNICIPAL WASTES

Analyze the profit potential in typical municipal wastes listed in Table 2. Use data on price increases of suitable municipal waste to compute the profit potential for a typical city, town, or state.

## Calculation Procedure:

### 1. *Compute the percentage price increase for the waste shown*
Municipal waste may be classed in several categories: (1) newspapers, magazines, and other newsprint; (2) corrugated cardboard; (3) plastic jugs and bottles—clear or colored; (4) copper wire and pipe. Other wastes, such as steel pipe, discarded internal combustion engines, electric motors, refrigerators, air conditioners, etc., require specialized handling and are not generated in quantities as large as the four numbered categories. For

**TABLE 2.** Examples of Price Changes in Municipal Wastes*

|  | Price per ton, $ | |
| --- | --- | --- |
|  | Last year | Current year |
| Newspapers | 60 | 150 |
| Corrugated cardboard | 18 | 150 |
| Plastic jugs, bottles | 125 | 600 |
| Copper wire and pipe | 960 | 1200 |

*Based on typical city wastes.

this reason, they are not normally included in estimates of municipal wastes for a given locality.

For the four categories of wastes listed above, the percentage price increases in one year for an Eastern city in the United States were as follows: Category 1—newspaper: Percentage price increase = 100(current price, $ − last year's price, $)/last year's price, $. Or $100(150 − 60)/60 = 150$ percent. Category 2: Percentage price increase = $100(150 − 18)/18 = 733$ percent. Category 3: Percentage price increase = $100(600 − 125)/125 = 380$ percent. Category 4: Percentage price increase = $100(1200 − 960)/960 = 25$ percent.

## 2. Determine the profit potential of the wastes considered

Profit potential is a function of collection costs and landfill savings. When collection of several wastes can be combined to use a single truck or other transport means, the profit potential can be much higher than when more than one collection method must be used. Let's assume that a city can collect Category 1, newspapers, and Category 3, plastic, in one vehicle. The profit potential, $P$, will be: $P$ = (sales price of the materials to be recycled, $ per ton − cost per ton to collect the materials for recycling, $). With a cost of $80 per ton for collection, the profit for collecting 75 tons of Category 1 wastes would be $P$ = $75($150 − $80) = $5250$. For collecting 90 tons of Category 3 wastes, the profit would be $P$ = $90($600 − 80) = $46,800$.

Where landfill space is saved by recycling waste, the dollar saving can be added to the profit. Thus, assume that landfill space and handling costs are valued at $30 per ton. The profit on Category 1 waste would rise by $75($30) = $2250$, while the profit on Category 3 wastes would rise by $90($30) = $2700$. When collection is included in the price paid for municipal wastes, the savings can be larger because the city or town does not have to use its equipment or personnel to collect the wastes. Hence, if collection can be included in a waste recycling contract, the profits to the municipality can be significant. However, even when the municipality performs the collection chore, the profit from selling waste for recycling can still be high. In some cities the price of used newspapers is so high that gangs steal the bundles of papers from sidewalks before they are collected by the city trucks.

*Related Calculations.* Recyclers are working on ways to reuse almost all the ordinary waste generated by residents of urban areas. Thus, telephone books, magazines, color-printed advertisements, waxed milk jars, etc. are now being recycled and converted into useful products. The environmental impact of these activities is positive throughout. Thus, landfill space is saved because the recycled products do not enter landfill; instead they are remanufactured into other useful products. Indeed, in many cases, the energy required to reuse waste is less than the energy needed to produce another product for use in place of the waste.

Some products are better recycled in other ways. Thus, the United States discards, according to industry records, over 12 million computers a year. These computers, weighing an estimated 600 million pounds (272 million kg) contribute toxic waste to landfills. Better that these computers be contributed to schools, colleges, and universities where they can be put to use in student training. Such computers may be slower and less modern than today's models, but their value in training programs has little to do with their speed or software. Instead, they will enable students to learn, at minimal cost to the school, the fundamentals of computer use in their personal and business lives.

Recycling waste products has further benefits for municipalities. The U.S. Clean Air Act's Title V consolidates all existing air pollution regulations into one massive operating permit program. Landfills that burn, pollute the atmosphere. And most of the waste we're considering in this procedure burns when deposited in a landfill. By recycling this waste the hazardous air pollutants they may have produced while burning in a landfill are eliminated from the atmosphere. This results in one less worry and problem for the municipality and its officials. In a recent year, the U.S. Environmental Protection Agency took 2247 enforcement actions and levied some $165 million in civil penalties and criminal fines against violators.

Any recycling situation can be reduced to numbers because you basically have the cost of collection balanced against the revenue generated by sale of the waste. Beyond this are nonfinancial considerations related to landfill availability and expected life-span. If waste has to be carted to another location for disposal, the cost of carting can be factored into the economic study of recycling.

Municipalities using waste collection programs state that their streets and sidewalks are cleaner. They attribute the increased cleanliness to the organization of people's thinking by the waste collection program. While stiff fines may have to be imposed on noncomplying individuals, most cities report a high level of compliance from the first day of the program. The concept of the "green city" is catching on and people are willing to separate their trash and insert it in specific containers to comply with the law.

"Green" products, i.e., those that produce less pollution, are also strongly favored by the general population of the United States today. Manufacturing companies are finding a greater sales acceptance for their "green" products. Even automobile manufacturers are stating the percentage of each which is recyclable, appealing to the "green" thinking permeating the population.

Recent studies show that every ton of paper not landfilled saves 3 yd$^3$ (2.3 m$^3$) of landfill space. Further, it takes 95 percent less energy to manufacture new products from recycled materials. Both these findings are strong motivators for recycling of waste materials by all municipalities and industrial firms.

Decorative holiday trees are being recycled by many communities. The trees are chipped into mulch, which is given to residents and used by the community in parks, recreation areas, hiking trails, and landfill cover. Seaside communities sometimes plant discarded holiday trees on beaches to protect sand dunes from being carried away by the sea.

# CHOICE OF CLEANUP TECHNOLOGY
# FOR CONTAMINATED WASTE SITES

A contaminated waste site contains polluted water, solid wastes, dangerous metals, and organic contaminants. Evaluate the various treatment technologies available for such a site and the relative cost of each. Estimate the landfill volume required if the rate of solid-waste generation for the site is 1,500,000 lb (681,818 kg) per year. What land area will be required for this waste generation rate if the landfill is designed for the minimum recommended depth of fill? Determine the engineer's role in site cleanup and in the economic studies needed for evaluation of available alternatives.

## Calculation Procedure:

### 1. Analyze the available treatment technologies for cleaning contaminated waste sites

Table 3 lists 13 available treatment technologies for cleaning contaminated waste sites, along with the type of contamination for which each is applicable, and the relative cost of the technology. This tabulation gives a bird's eye view of technologies the engineer can consider for any waste site cleanup.

When approaching any cleanup task, the first step is to make a health-risk assessment to determine if any organisms are exposed to compounds on, or migrating from, a site. If there is such an exposure, determine whether the organisms could suffer any adverse health effects. The results of a health-risk assessment can be used to determine whether there is sufficient risk at a site to require remediation.

This same assessment of risks to human health and the environment can also be used to determine a target for the remediation effort that reduces health and environmental risks to acceptable levels. It is often possible to negotiate with regulatory agencies a remediation level for a site based on the risk of exposure to both a maximum concentration of materials and a weighted average. The data in Table 3 are useful for starting a site cleanup having the overall goals of protecting human health and the environment.

### 2. Make a health-risk assessment of the site to determine cleanup goals[1]

Divide the health-risk assessment into these four steps: (1) *Hazard Identification*—Asks "Does the facility or site pose sufficient risk to require further investigation?" If the answer is Yes, then: (*a*) Select compounds to include in the assessment; (*b*) Identify exposed populations; (*c*) Identify exposure pathways.

(2) *Exposure Assessment*—Asks "To how much of a compound are people and the environment exposed?" For exposure to occur, four events must happen: (*a*) release; (*b*) contact; (*c*) transport; (*d*) absorption. Taken together, these four events form an exposure pathway. There are many possible exposure pathways for a facility or site.

(3) *Toxicity Assessment*—Asks "What adverse health effects in humans are potentially caused by the compounds in question?" This assessment reviews the threshold and non-threshold effects potentially caused by the compounds at the environmental concentration levels.

(4) *Risk Characterization*—Asks "At the exposures estimated in the Exposure Assessment, is there potential for adverse health effects to occur; if so, what kind and to what extent?" The Risk Characterization develops a hazard index for threshold effects and estimates the excess lifetime cancer-risk for carcinogens.

### 3. Select suitable treatment methods and estimate the relative costs

The site contains polluted water, solid wastes, dangerous metals, and organic contaminants. Of these four components, the polluted water is the simplest to treat. Hence, we will look at the other contaminants to see how they might best be treated. As Table 3

---

[1]Hopper, David R., "Cleaning Up Contaminated Waste Sites," *Chemical Engineering,* Aug., 1989.

**TABLE 3.** Various Treatment Technologies Available to Clean Up a Contaminated Waste Site*

| Technology | Description | Applicable contamination | Relative cost |
|---|---|---|---|
| Soil vapor extraction | Air flow is induced through the soil by pulling a vacuum on holes drilled into the soil, and carries out volatilized contaminants | Volatile and some semivolatile organics | Low |
| Soil washing or soil flushing | Excavated soil is flushed with water or other solvent to leach out contaminants | Organic wastes and certain (soluble) inorganic wastes | Low |
| Stabilization and solidification | Waste is mixed with agents that physically immobilize or chemically precipitate constituents | Applies primarily to metals; mixed results when used to treat organics | Medium |
| Thermal desorption | Solid waste is heated to 200–800°F to drive off volatile contaminants, which are separated from the waste and further treated | Volatile and semivolatile organics; volatile metals such as elemental mercury | Medium to high |
| Incineration | Waste is burned at very high temperatures to destroy organics | Organic wastes; metals do not burn, but concentrate in ash | High |
| Thermal pyrolysis | Heat volatilizes contaminants into an oxygen-starved air system at temperatures sufficient to pyrolzye the organic contaminants; frequently, the heat is delivered by infrared radiation | Organic wastes | Medium to high |
| Chemical precipitation | Solubilized metals are separated from water by precipitating them as insoluble salts | Metals | Low |

| Aeration or air stripping | Contaminated water is pumped through a column where it is contacted with a countercurrent air flow, which strips out certain pollutants | Mostly volatile organics | Low |
| --- | --- | --- | --- |
| Steam stripping | Similar to air stripping except steam is used as the stripping fluid | Mostly volatile organics | Low |
| Carbon absorption | Organic contaminants are removed from a water or air stream by passing the stream through a bed of activated carbon that absorbs the organics | Most organics, though normally restricted to those with sufficient volatility to allow carbon regeneration | Low to medium when regeneration is possible |
| Bioremediation | Bacterial degradation of organic compounds is enhanced | Organic wastes | Low |
| Landfilling | Covering solid wastes with soil in a facility designed to minimize leachate formation | Solid, nonhazardous wastes | Low but rising fast |
| In situ vitrification | Electric current is passed through soil or waste, which increases the temperature and melts the waste or soil. The mass fuses upon cooling | Inorganic wastes, possibly organic wastes; not applicable to very large volumes | Medium |

*Chemical Engineering* magazine.

shows, thermal desorption treats volatile and semivolatile organics and volatile metals; cost is medium to high. Alternatively, incineration handles organic wastes and metals with an ash residue; cost is high. Nonhazardous solid wastes can be landfilled at low cost. But the future cost may be much higher because landfill costs are rising as available land becomes scarcer.

Polluted water can be treated with chemicals, aeration, or air stripping—all at low cost. None of these methods can be combined with the earlier tentative choices. Hence, the polluted water will have to be treated separately.

### 4. *Determine the landfill dimensions and other parameters*

Annual landfill space requirements can be determined from $V_A = W/1100$, where $V_A =$ landfill volume required, per year, $yd^3$ ($m^3$); $W =$ annual weight, lb (kg) of waste generated for the landfill; 1100 $lb/yd^3$ (650 $kg/m^3$) = solid waste compaction per $yd^3$ or $m^3$. Substituting for this site, $V_A = 1,500,000/1100 = 1363.6$ $yd^3$ (1043.2 $m^3$).

The minimum recommended depth for landfills is 20 ft (6 m); minimum recommended life is 10 years. If this landfill were designed for the minimum depth of 20 ft (6 m), it would have an annual required area of $1363.6 \times 27$ $ft^3/yd^3 = 36,817.2$ $ft^3/20$ ft high = 1840.8 sq.ft. (171.0 $m^2$), or 1840.9 sq.ft./43,560 sq.ft./acre = 0.042 acre (169.9 $m^2$ 0.017 ha) per year. With a 10-year life the landfill area required to handle solid wastes generated for this site would be $10 \times 0.042 = 0.42$ acre (1699.7 $m^2$, 0.17 ha); with a 20-year life the area required would be $20 \times 0.042 = 0.84$ acre (3399.3 $m^2$; 0.34 ha).

As these calculations show, the area required for this landfill is relatively modest—less than an acre with a 20-year life. However, in heavily populated areas the waste generation could be significantly larger. Thus, when planning a sanitary landfill, the usual assumption is that each person generates 5 lb (2.26 kg) per day of solid waste. This number is based on an assumption of half the waste (2.5 lb; 1.13 kg) being from residential sources and the other half being from commercial and industrial sources. Hence, in a city having a population of 1-million people, the annual solid-waste generation would be 1,000,000 people $\times$ 5 lb/day per person $\times$ 365 days per year = 1,825,000,000 lb (828,550,000 kg).

Following the same method of calculation as above, the annual landfill space requirement would be $V_A = 1,825,000,000/1100 = 1,659,091$ $yd^3$ (1,269,205 $m^3$). With a 20-ft (6-m) height for the landfill, the annual area required would be $1,659,091 \times 27/20 \times 43,560 = 51.4$ acres (208,002 $m^2$; 20.8 ha). Increasing the landfill height to 40 ft (12 m) would reduce the required area to 25.7 acres (104,037 $m^2$; 10.4 ha). A 60-ft high landfill would reduce the required area to 17.1 acres (69,334 $m^2$; 6.9 ha). In densely populated areas, landfills sometimes reach heights of 100 ft (30.5 m) to conserve horizontal space.

This example graphically shows why landfills are becoming so much more expensive. Further, with the possibility of air and stream pollution from a landfill, there is greater regulation of landfills every year. This example also shows why incineration of solid waste to reduce its volume while generating useful heat is so attractive to communities and industries. Further advantages of incineration include reduction of the possibility of groundwater pollution from the landfill and the chance to recover valuable minerals which can be sold or reused. Residue from incineration can be used in road and highway construction or for fill in areas needing it.

*Related Calculations.* Use this general procedure for tentative choices of treatment technologies for cleaning up contaminated waste sites. The greatest risks faced by industry are where human life is at stake. Penalties are severe where human health is endangered by contaminated wastes. Hence, any expenditures for treatment equipment can usually be justified by the savings obtained by eliminating lawsuits, judgments, and years of protracted legal wrangling. A good example is the asbestos lawsuits which have been in the courts for years.

To show what industry has done to reduce harmful wastes, here are results published in the *Wall Street Journal* for the years 1974 and 1993: Lead emissions declined from 223,686 tons in 1973 to 4885 tons in 1993 or to 2.2 percent of the original emissions; carbon monoxide emissions for the same period fell from 124.8 million tons to 97.2 million tons, or 77.9 percent of the original; rivers with fecal coliform above the federal standard were 31 percent in 1974 and 26 percent in 1994; municipal waste recovered for recycling was 7.9 percent in 1974 and 22.0 percent in 1994.

The simplest way to dispose of solid wastes is to put them in landfills. This practice was followed for years, but recent studies show that rain falling on landfilled wastes seeps through and into the wastes, and can become contaminated if the wastes are harmful. Eventually, unless geological conditions are ideal, the contaminated rainwater seeps into the groundwater under the landfill. Once in the groundwater, the contaminants must be treated before the water can be used for drinking or other household purposes.

Most landfills will have a leachate seepage area, Fig. 21. There may also be a contaminant plume, as shown, which reaches, and pollutes, the groundwater. This is why more and more communities are restricting, or prohibiting, landfills. Engineers are therefore more pressed than ever to find better, and safer, ways to dispose of contaminated wastes. And with greater environmental oversight by both Federal and State governments, the pressure on engineers to find safe, economical treatment methods is growing. The suggested treatments in Table 2 are a good starting point for choosing suitable and safe ways to handle contaminated wastes of all types.

Landfills must be covered daily. A 6-in (15-cm) thick cover of the compacted refuse is required by most regulatory agencies and local authorities. The volume of landfill cover, $ft^3$, required each day can be computed from: (Landfill working face length, ft)(landfill working width, ft)(0.5). Multiply by 0.0283 to convert to $m^3$. Since the daily cover, usually soil, must be moved by machinery operated by humans, the cost can be significant when the landfill becomes high-more than 30 ft (9.1 m). The greater the height of a landfill, the more optimal, in general, is the site and its utilization. For this reason, landfills have grown in height in recent years in many urban areas.

Table 3 is the work of David R. Hopper, Chemical Process Engineering Program Manager, ENSR Consulting and Engineering, as reported in Chemical Engineering magazine.

## CLEANING UP A CONTAMINATED WASTE SITE VIA BIOREMEDIATION

Evaluate the economics of cleaning up a 40-acre (161,872 m²) site contaminated with petroleum hydrocarbons, gasoline, and sludge. Estimates show that some 100,000 yd³ (76,500 m³) must be remediated to meet federal and local environmental requirements. The site has three impoundments containing weathered crude oils, tars, and drilling muds ranging in concentration from 3800 to 40,000 ppm, as measured by the Environmental Protection Agency (EPA) Method 8015M. While hydrocarbon concentrations in the soil are high, tests for flash point, pH, 96-h fish bioassay, show that the soil could be classified as nonhazardous. Total petroleum hydrocarbons are less than 500 ppm. Speed of treatment is not needed by the owner of the project. Show how to compute the net present value for the investment in alternative treatment methods for which the parameters are given in step 4 of this procedure.

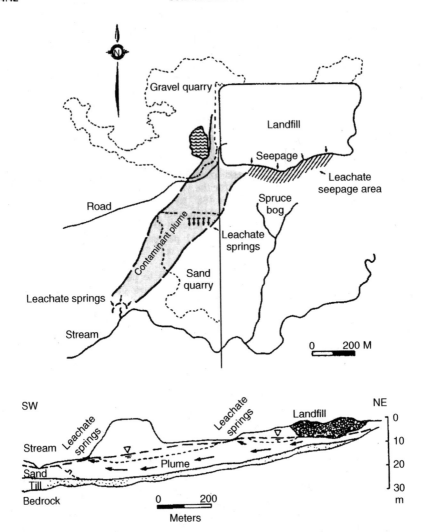

**FIGURE 21.** Leachate seepage in landfill. (*McGraw-Hill*).

## Calculation Procedure:

### 1. *Compare the treatment technologies available*

A number of treatment technologies are available to remediate such a site. Where total petroleum hydrocarbons are less than 500 ppm, as at this site, biological land treatment is
usually sufficient to meet regulatory and human safety needs. Further, hazardous and
nonhazardous waste cleanup via bioremediation is gaining popularity. One reason is the

**TABLE 4.** Comparison of Biological Treatment Technologies*

| Type/cost ($/yd³) | Advantages | Disadvantages |
|---|---|---|
| Land treatment $30−$90 | • Can be used for in situ or ex situ treatment depending upon contaminant and soil type<br>• Little or no residual waste streams generated<br>• Long history of effective treatment for many petroleum compounds (gasoline, diesel)<br>• Can be used as polishing treatment following soil washing or bioslurry treatment | • Moderate destruction efficiency depending upon contaminants<br>• Long treatment time relative to other methods<br>• In situ treatment only practical when contamination is within two feet of the surface<br>• Requires relatively large, dedicated area for treatment cell |
| Bioventing $50−$120 | • Excellent removal of volatile compounds from soil matrix<br>• Depending upon vapor treatment method, little or no residual waste streams to dispose<br>• Moderate treatment time<br>• Can be used for in situ or ex situ treatment depending upon contaminant and soil type | • Treatment of vapor using activated carbon can be expensive at high concentrations of contaminants<br>• System typically requires an air permit for operation |
| Bioreactor $150−$250 | • Enhanced separation of many contaminants from soil<br>• Excellent destruction efficiency of contaminants<br>• Fast treatment time | • High mobilization and demobilization costs for small projects<br>• Materials handling requirements increase costs<br>• Treated solids must be dewatered<br>• Fullscale application has only become common in recent years |

*Chemical Engineering* magazine.

high degree of public acceptance of bioremediation vs. alternatives such as incineration. The Resource Conservation and Recovery Act (RCRA) defines hazardous waste as specifically listed wastes or as wastes that are characteristically toxic, corrosive, flammable, or reactive. Wastes at this site fit certain of these categories.

Table 4 compares three biological treatment technologies currently in use. The type of treatment, and approximate cost, $/ft³ ($/m³), are also given. Since petroleum hydrocarbons are less than 500 ppm at this site, biological land treatment will be chosen as the treatment method.

Looking at the range of costs in Table 4 shows a minimum of $30/yd³ ($39/m³) for land treatment and a maximum of $250/yd³ ($327/m³) for bioreactor treatment. This is a ratio of $250/$30 = 8.3:1. Thus, where acceptable results will be obtained, the lowest cost treatment technology would probably be the most suitable choice.

## 2. Determine the cost ranges that might be encountered in this application

The cost ranges that might be encountered in this—or any other application—depend on the treatment technology which is applicable and chosen. Thus, with some 100,000 yd$^3$ (76,500 m$^3$) of soil to be treated, the cost ranges from Table 4 = 100,000 yd$^3$ × \$/yd$^3$. For *biological land treatment,* cost ranges = 100,000 × \$30 = \$3,000,000; 100,000 × \$90 = \$9,000,000. For *bioventing,* cost ranges = 100,000 × \$50 = \$5,000,000; 100,000 × \$120 = \$12,000,000. For *biorector treatment,* cost ranges = 100,000 × \$150 = \$15,000,000; 100,000 × \$250 = \$250,000,000. Thus, a significant overall cost range exists—from \$3,000,000 to \$25,000,000, depending on the treatment technology chosen.

The wide cost range computed above shows why it is so important that the engineer choose the most cost-effective system which accomplishes the desired cleanup in accordance with federal and state requirements. With an estimated 2000 hazardous waste sites currently known in the United States, and possibly several times that number in the rest of the world, the potential financial impact on companies and their insurers, is enormous. The actual waste site discussed in this procedure highlights the financial decisions engineers face when choosing a method of cleanup.

Once a cleanup (or remediation) method is tentatively chosen—after the site investigation and feasibility study by the engineer—the controlling regulatory agencies must be consulted for approval of the method selected. The planned method of remediation is usually negotiated with the regulatory agency before final approval is given. Once such approval is obtained, it is difficult to change the remediation method chosen. Hence, the engineer, and the organization involved, should find the chosen remediation method acceptable in every way possible.

## 3. Evaluate the time requirements of each biological treatment technology

Biological land treatment has been used for many years for treating petroleum residues. Also known as land-farming, this is the simplest and least expensive biological treatment technology. However, this method requires large amounts of land that can be dedicated to the treatment process for a period of several months to several years. Typically, land treatment involves the control of oxygen, nutrients, and moisture (to optimize microbial activity) while the soil is tilled or otherwise aerated.

Bioventing systems, Fig. 22, are somewhat more complex than land treatment, at a moderate increase in cost. They are used on soils with both volatile and nonvolatile hydrocarbons. Conventional vapor extraction technology (air stripping) of the volatile components is combined with soil conditioning (such as nutrient addition) to enhance microbial degradation. This treatment method can be used both in situ and ex situ. Relative to land treatment, space requirements are reduced. Treatment time is on the order of weeks to months.

Bioreactors are the most complex and expensive biological alternative. They can clean up contaminated water alone, or solids mixed with water (slurry bioreactors). The reactor can be configured from existing impoundments, aboveground tanks, or enclosed tanks (if emissions controls are required). Batch, semicontinuous, or continuous modes of operation can be maintained. The higher cost is often justified by the faster treatment time (on the order of hours to days) and the ability to degrade contaminants on difficult-to-treat soil matrices.

Since time is not a controlling factor in this application, biological land treatment, the least expensive method, will be chosen and applied.

## 4. Compute the net present value for alternative treatment methods

Where alternative treatment methods can be used for a hazardous waste site, the method chosen can be analyzed on the basis of the present net worth of the "cash flows" produced

**Bioventing system**

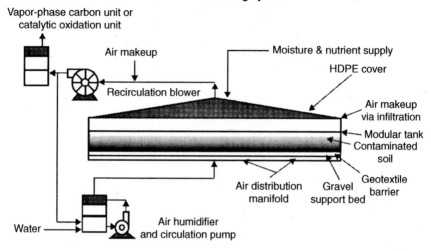

**FIGURE 22.** Pipes blowing air from the bottom of this enclosure separate contaminants from the soil. (*OHM Corp., Carla Magazino* and *Chemical Engineering.*)

by each method. Such "cash flows" can be estimated by converting savings in compliance, legal, labor, management, and other costs to "cash flows" for each treatment method. Determining the net present worth of each treatment method will then provide a comparative evaluation which will be an additional input in the final treatment choice decision.

The table below shows the estimated annual "cash flows" for two suitable treatment methods: Method A and Method B

| Year | Method A | Method B |
|------|----------|----------|
| 0 | −$180,000 | −$180,000 |
| 1 | 60,000 | 180,000 |
| 2 | 60,000 | 30,000 |
| 3 | 60,000 | 18,000 |
| 4 | 60,000 | 12,000 |

Interest rate charged on the investment is 12 percent.

Using the Net Present Value (NPV), or Discounted Cash Flow (DCF), equation for each treatment method gives, NPV, Treatment Method = Investment, first year + each year's cash flow × capital recovery factor for the interest rate on the investment. For the first treatment method, using a table of compound interest factors for an interest rate of 12 percent, NPV, treatment A = −$180,000 + $60,000/0.27741 = $36,286. In this relation, the cash flow for years 1, 2, and 3 repays the investment of $180,000 in the equipment. Hence, the cash flow for the fourth year is the only one used in the NPV calculation.

For the second treatment method, B, NPV = −$180,000 + $180,000/0.8929 + $30,000/0.7972 + $18,000/0.7118 + $12,000/0.6355 = $103,392. Since Treatment

Method B is so superior to Treatment Method A, B would be chosen. The ratio of NPV is 2.84 in favor of Method B over Method A.

Use the conventional methods of engineering economics to compare alternative treatment methods. The prime consideration is that the methods compared provide equivalent results for the remediation process.

## 5. Develop costs for combined remediation systems

Remediation of sites always involves evaluation of a diverse set of technologies. While biological treatment alone can be used for the treatment of many waste streams, combining bioremediation with other treatment technologies may provide a more cost-effective remedial alternative.

Figure 23 shows the costs of a full-scale groundwater treatment system treating 120 gal/min (7.6 L/s) developed for a site contaminated with pentachlorophenol (PCP), creosote, and other wood-treating chemicals at a forest-products manufacturing plant. The site contained contaminated groundwater, soil, and sludges. Capital cost, prorated for the life of the project, for the biological unit is twice that of an activated carbon system. However, the lower operating cost of the biological system results in a total treatment cost half the price of its nearest competitor. Carbon polishing adds 13 percent to the base cost.

For the systems discussed in the paragraph above, the choice of alternative treatment technologies was based on two factors: (1) Biological treatment followed by activated carbon polishing may be required to meet governmental discharge requirements. (2) Liquid-phase activated carbon, and UV-oxidation are well established treatment methods for contaminated groundwater.

Soils and sludges in the forest-products plant discussed above are treated using a bioslurry reactor. The contaminated material is slurried with water and placed into a mixed, aerated biotreatment unit where suspended bacteria degrade the contaminants.

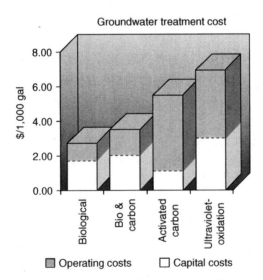

**FIGURE 23.** Under the right circumstances, biological treatment can be the lowest-cost option for groundwater cleanup. (*Carla Magazino* and *Chemical Engineering*.)

Observation of the short-term degradation of PCP in initial tests suggested that the majority of the degradation occurred in the first 10 to 30 days of treatment. These results suggested that treatment costs could be minimized by initial processing of soils in the slurry bioreactor followed by final treatment in an engineered land-farm.

Treatment costs for a bioslurry reactor system using a 30-day batch time, followed by land treatment, are shown in Fig. 24. The minimum cost, $62/ton, occurs with a 5-year remediation lifetime, Fig. 24. An equivalent system using only the bioreactor would require an 80+-day cycle time to reach the cleanup criteria. The treatment cost can be reduced by over $45/ton using the hybrid system.

Note that the costs given above are for a specific installation. While they are not applicable to all plants, the cost charts show how comparisons can be made and how treatment costs vary with various cleanup methods. You can assemble, and compare, costs for various treatment methods using this same approach.

**Related Calculations.** Bioremediation works because it uses naturally occurring microorganisms or consortia of microorganisms that degrade specific pollutants and, more importantly, classes of pollutants. Biological studies reveal degradation pathways essential to assure detoxification and mineralization. These studies also show how to enhance microbial activity, such as by the addition of supplementary oxygen and nutrients, and the adjustment of pH, temperature, and moisture.

Bioremediation can be effective as a pre- or post-treatment step for other cleanup techniques. Degradation of pollutants by microorganisms requires a carbon source, electron hydrocarbons (PAHs) found in coal tar, creosote, and some petroleum-compounds acceptor, nutrients, and appropriate pH, moisture, and temperature. The waste can be the carbon source or primary substrate for the organisms. Certain waste streams may also require use of a cosubstrate to trigger the production of enzymes necessary to degrade the primary substrate. Some wastes can be cometabolized directly along with the primary substrate.

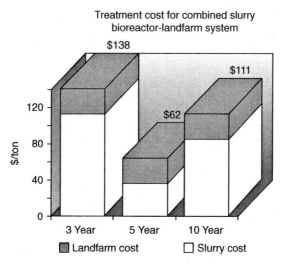

FIGURE 24. The treatment cost for this system reaches a minimum value after 5 years, then rises again. (*Carla Magazino* and *Chemical Engineering.*)

Regulatory constraints are perhaps the most important factor in selecting bioremediation as a treatment process. Regulations that define specific cleanup criteria, such as land disposal restrictions under the U.S. Resource Conservation and Recovery Act (RCRA), also restrict the types of treatment technologies to be used. Other technologies, such as incineration, have been used to define the "best demonstrated available technology" (BDAT) for hazardous waste treatment of listed wastes.

The schedule for a site cleanup can also be driven by regulatory issues. A consent decree may fix the timetable for a site remediation, which may eliminate the use of bioremediation, or limit the application to a specific biological treatment technology.

Specific cleanup tasks for which biological treatment is suitable include remediation of petroleum compounds (gasoline, diesel, bunker oil); polynuclear aromatic hydrocarbons (PAHs) found in coal tar, creosote, and some petroleum compounds; soils with volatile and nonvolatile hydrocarbons; contaminated water; drilling muds; polychlorinated biphenyls (PCBs). The general approach given here can be used for the named pollutants, plus others amenable to bioremediation.

Data in this procedure are the work of Chris Jespersen, P.E., Project Manager, OHM Remediation Services Corp., Douglas B. Jerger, Technical Director, Bioremediation, OHM Remediation Services Corp., and Jurgen H. Exner, Principal and President, JHE Technology Systems, Inc., as reported in *Chemical Engineering* magazine. The data in step 4 of this procedure were prepared by the *Handbook* editor.

David R. Hopper, Chemical Process Engineering Program Manager, ENSR Consulting and Engineering, writing in *Chemical Engineering* magazine, notes that:

> Many of today's contaminated sites are the result of accepted and lawful waste-disposal practices of years ago. While the methods of disposal have improved and the regulations preventing disposal techniques that might result in future contamination are in place, there is no guarantee that today's landfilled wastes will not end up being remediated in coming years. In addition, the new regulations and technologies have come at a time of increased disposal cost and ever-diminishing landfill capacity.
>
> Waste minimization, or pollution prevention, is one way of avoiding the whole disposal problem, and its associated long-term liability. By reducing the creation of waste by the manufacturing process, or recovering and recycling potential wastes between processes, the amount of waste to be disposed of is reduced. . . .
>
> Pollution prevention programs are gaining momentum at both the federal and state levels. Several states (e.g. Texas and New Jersey) have introduced legislation aimed at promoting waste reduction. Federal agencies (e.g. EPA, Department of Defense, Department of Energy, and Department of Interior) are actively supporting research and development of waste-minimization methods. However, the major driving force remains the economic benefits of reducing the amount of waste produced. Savings in raw materials and avoidance of the disposal costs result in attractive returns on investment for waste-minimizing process improvements. Between the potential savings and the future regulatory focus, waste minimization is likely to be an active, and beneficial, aspect of future waste-management programs.

## WORK REQUIRED TO CLEAN OIL-POLLUTED BEACHES

How much relative work is required to clean a 300-yd (274-m) long beach coated with heavy oil, if the width of the beach is 40 yd (36.6 m), the depth of oil penetration is 20 in (50.8 cm), the beach terrain is gravel and pebbles, the oil coverage is 60 percent of the beach, and the beach contains heavy debris?

## Calculation Procedure:

### 1. *Establish a work-measurement equation from a beach model*

After the *Exxon Valdez* ran aground on Bligh Reef in Prince William Sound, a study was made to develop a model and an equation that would give the relative amount of work needed to rid a beach of spilled oil. The relative amount of work remaining, expressed in clydes, is defined as the amount of work required to clean 100 yd (91.4 m) of lightly polluted beach. As the actual cleanup progressed, the actual work required was found to agree closely with the formula-predicted relative work indicated by the model and equation that were developed.

The work-measurement equation, developed by on-the-scene Commander Peter C. Olsen, U.S. Coast Guard Reserve, and Commander Wayne R. Hamilton, U.S. Coast Guard, is $S = (L/100)(EWPTCD)$, where $S$ = standardized equivalent beach work units, expressed in clydes; $L$ = beach-segment length in yards or meters (considered equivalent because of the rough precision of the model); $E$ = degree of contamination of the beach expressed as: light oil = 1; moderate oil = 1.5; heavy oil = 2; random tar balls and very light oil = 0.1; $W$ = width of beach expressed as: less than 30 m = 1; 30 to 45 m = 1.5; more than 45 m = 2; $P$ = depth of penetration of the oil expressed as: less than 10 cm = 1; 10 to 20 cm = 2; more than 30 cm = 3; $T$ = terrain of the beach expressed as: boulders, cobbles, sand, mud, solid rock without vertical faces = 1; gravel/pebbles = 2; solid rock faces = 0.1; $C$ = percent of oil coverage of the beach expressed as: more than 67 percent coverage = 1; 50 to 67 percent = 0.8; less than 50 percent = 0.5; $D$ = debris factor expressed as: heavy debris = 1.2; all others = 1.

### 2. *Determine the relative work required*

Using the given conditions, $S = (300/100)(2 \times 1.5 \times 1 \times 1 \times 0.8 \times 1.2) = 8.64$ clydes. This shows that the work required to clean this beach would be some 8.6 times that of cleaning 100 yd of lightly oiled beach. Knowing the required time input to clean the "standard" beach (100 yd, lightly oiled), the approximate time to clean the beach being considered can be obtained by simple multiplication. Thus, if the cleaning time for the standard lightly oiled beach is 50 h, the cleaning time for the beach considered here would be 50 (8.64) = 432 h.

**Related Calculations:** The model presented here outlines—in general—the procedure to follow to set up an equation for estimating the working time to clean any type of beach of oil pollution. The geographic location of the beach will not in general be a factor in the model unless the beach is in cold polar regions. In cold climates more time will be required to clean a beach because the oil will congeal and be difficult to remove.

A beach cleanup in Prince William Sound was defined as eliminating all gross amounts of oil, all migratory oil, and all oil-contaminated debris. This definition is valid for any other polluted beach be it in Europe, the Far East, the United States, etc.

Floating oil in the marine environment can be skimmed, boomed, absorbed, or otherwise removed. But oil on a beach must either be released by (1) scrubbing or (2) steaming and floated to the nearby water where it can be recovered using surface techniques mentioned above.

Where light oil—gasoline, naphtha, kerosene, etc.—is spilled in an accident on the water, it will usually evaporate with little damage to the environment. But heavy oil—No. 6, Bunker C, unrefined products, etc.—will often congeal and stick to rocks, cobbles, structures, and sand. Washing such oil products off a beach requires the use of steam and hot high-pressure water. Once the oil is freed from the surfaces to which it is adhering, it must be quickly washed away with seawater so that it flows to the nearby water where it can be recovered. Several washings may be required to thoroughly cleanse a badly polluted beach.

The most difficult beaches to clean are those comprised of gravel, pebbles, or small boulders. Two reasons for this are: (1) the surface areas to which the oil can adhere are much greater and (2) extensive washing of these surface areas is required. This washing action can carry away the sand and the underlying earth, destroying the beach. When setting up an equation for such a beach, this characteristic should be kept in mind.

Beaches with larger boulders having a moderate slope toward the water are easiest to clean. Next in ease of cleaning are sand and mud beaches because thick oil does not penetrate deeply in most instances.

Use this equation as is; and check its results against actual cleanup times. Then alter the equation to suit the actual conditions and personnel met in the cleanup.

The model and equation described here are the work of Commander Peter C. Olsen, U.S. Coast Guard Reserve and Commander Wayne B. Hamilton, U.S. Coast Guard, as reported in government publications.

*New Developments.*   Soil mechanics continues to be a subject of major interest to civil engineers worldwide. Every nation, it seems, has one or more technical or scientific organizations devoted to the study and advancement of soil mechanics. Why is there such an ongoing interest in soil mechanics? There are several reasons, including:

- Soil problems in critical transportation structures—tunnels, bridges, highways, embankment dams, retaining walls, etc.—continue to plague engineers worldwide.

- Natural disasters—hurricanes, earthquakes, tsunamis, tornadoes, cyclones, tidal waves, etc.—play havoc with soils, the structures they support, and with earthworks of many kinds.

- New construction projects face increasingly strict environmental regulations covering soils and previous pollution of earthworks. Unsaturated soils, expansive clay, seepage, soil compaction, landslides, foundations, rock fractures, and a variety of other factors must be considered by civil engineers in new designs. These factors are especially important in dam planning and construction.

As an example of the intense interest in soil mechanics, the American Society of Civil Engineers founded the Geo-Institute (G-I) in 1996. According to the published statement of the G-I, "the G-I represents more than 10,000 geotechnical engineers and over 35 Organizational Members who work to advance the geo-engineering community to help improve the built environment, mitigate natural hazards, and construct sound and reliable engineered facilities and structures. The G-I also serves as the United States of America member society of the International Society for Soil Mechanics and Geotechnical Engineering (ISSMGE)."

Another example is how the introduction of offshore wind turbines to generate renewable electrical energy challenges civil engineers specializing in foundations for these machines. Early installations used piling that took several days to install, provided good weather prevailed. Now shallow skirted foundations are being considered. Such foundations could be installed in hours using suction caissons. Suction foundations are already in use in offshore oil and gas installations. Research continues on these foundations at the University of Oxford, England.

Thus, civil engineers worldwide can continue to expect and see the ongoing research and development in the key areas of soil mechanics.

# SECTION 5

# SURVEYING, ROUTE DESIGN, AND HIGHWAY BRIDGES

# Surveying and Route Design

## *PLOTTING A CLOSED TRAVERSE*

Complete the following table for a closed traverse.

| Course | Bearing | Length, ft (m) |
|--------|---------|----------------|
| *a* | N32°27′E | 110.8 (33.77) |
| *b* |          | 83.6 (25.48) |
| *c* | S8°51′W | 126.9 (38.68) |
| *d* | S73°31′W |              |
| *e* | N18°44′W | 90.2 (27.49) |

**Calculation Procedure:**

### 1. *Draw the known courses; then form a closed traverse*

Refer to Fig. 1*a*. A line *PQ* is described by expressing its length *L* and its bearing *a* with respect to a reference meridian NS. For a closed traverse, such as *abcde* in Fig. 1*b*, the

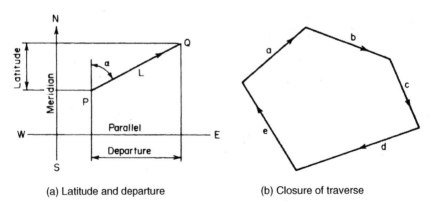

(a) Latitude and departure        (b) Closure of traverse

**FIGURE 1**

algebraic sum of the latitudes and the algebraic sum of the departures must equal zero. A positive latitude corresponds to a northerly bearing, and a positive departure corresponds to an easterly bearing.

In Fig. 2, draw the known courses $a$, $c$, and $e$. Then introduce the hypothetical course $f$ to form a closed traverse.

## 2. Calculate the latitude and departure of the courses

Use these relations:

$$\text{Latitude} = L \cos \alpha \tag{1}$$

$$\text{Departure} = L \sin \alpha \tag{2}$$

Computing the results for courses $a$, $c$, $e$, and $f$, we have the values shown in the following table.

| Course | Latitude, ft (m) | Departure, ft (m) |
|--------|------------------|-------------------|
| $a$ | +93.5 | +59.5 |
| $c$ | −125.4 | −19.5 |
| $e$ | +85.4 | −29.0 |
| Total | +53.5(+16.306) | +11.0(+3.35) |
| $f$ | −53.5(−16.306) | −11.0(−3.35) |

## 3. Find the length and bearing of f

Thus, tan $\alpha_f$ = 11.0/53.5; therefore, the bearing of $f$ = S11°37′W; length of $f$ = 53.5/cos $\alpha_f$ = 4.6 ft (16.64 m).

## 4. Complete the layout

Complete Fig. 2 by drawing line $d$ through the upper end of $f$ with the specified bearing and by drawing a circular arc centered at the lower end of $f$ having a radius equal to the length of $b$.

## 5. Find the length of d and the bearing of b

Solve the triangle $fdb$ to find the length of $d$ and the bearing of $b$. Thus, $B$ = 73°31′ − 11°37′ = 61°54′. By the law of sines, sin $F$ = $f$ sin $B$/$b$ = 54.6 sin 61°54′/83.6; $F$ = 35°11′; $D$ = 180° − (61°54′ + 35°11′) = 82°55′; $d$ = $b$ sin $D$/sin $B$ = 83.6 sin 82°55′/sin 61°54′ = 94.0 ft (28.65 m); $a_b$ = 180° − (73°31′ + 35°11′) = 71°18′. The bearing of $b$ = S71°18′E.

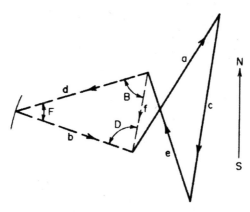

**FIGURE 2**

## AREA OF TRACT WITH RECTILINEAR BOUNDARIES

The balanced latitudes and departures of a closed transit-and-tape traverse are recorded in the table below. Compute the area of the tract by the DMD method.

| Course | Latitude, ft (m) | | Departure, ft (m) | |
|--------|------------------|--|-------------------|--|
| AB | −132.3 | (−40.33) | −135.6 | (−41.33) |
| BC | +9.6 | (2.93) | −77.5 | (−23.62) |
| CD | +97.9 | (29.84) | −198.5 | (−60.50) |
| DE | +161.9 | (49.35) | +143.6 | (43.77) |
| EF | −35.3 | (−10.76) | +246.7 | (75.19) |
| FA | −101.8 | (−31.03) | +21.3 | (6.49) |

### Calculation Procedure:

### 1. *Plot the tract*

Refer to Fig. 3. The sum of $m_1$ and $m_2$ is termed the *double meridian distance* (DMD) of course *AB*. Let *D* denote the departure of a course. Then

$$\text{DMD}_n = \text{DMD}_{n-1} + D_{n-1} + D_n \tag{3}$$

where the subscripts refer to two successive courses.

The area of trapezoid *ABba*, which will be termed the projection area of *AB*, equals half the product of the DMD and latitude of the course. A projection area may be either positive or negative.

Plot the tract in Fig. 4. Since *D* is the most westerly point, pass the reference meridian through *D*, thus causing all DMDs to be positive.

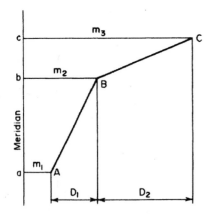

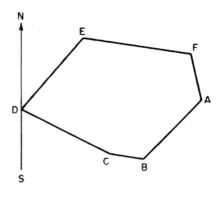

**FIGURE 3.** Double meridian distance.      **FIGURE 4**

## 2. Establish the DMD of each course by successive applications of Eq. 3

Thus, $DMD_{DE} = 143.6$ ft (43.77 m); $DMD_{EF} = 143.6 + 143.6 + 246.7 = 533.9$ ft (162.73 m); $DMD_{FA} = 533.9 + 246.7 + 21.3 = 801.9$ ft (244.42 m); $DMD_{AB} = 801.9 + 21.3 - 135.6 = 687.6$ ft (209.58 m); $DMD_{BC} = 687.6 - 135.6 - 77.5 = 474.5$ ft (144.62 m); $DMD_{CD} = 474.5 - 77.5 - 198.5 = 198.5$ ft (60.50 m). This is acceptable.

## 3. Calculate the area of the tract

Use the following theorem: The area of a tract is numerically equal to the aggregate of the projection areas of its courses. The results of this calculation are

| Course | Latitude | × | DMD | = 2 × Projection area |
|--------|----------|---|-----|----------------------|
| AB | −132.3 | | 687.6 | −90,970 |
| BC | +9.6 | | 474.5 | +4,555 |
| CD | +97.9 | | 198.5 | +19,433 |
| DE | +161.9 | | 143.6 | +23,249 |
| EF | −35.3 | | 533.9 | −18,847 |
| FA | −101.8 | | 801.9 | −81,634 |
| Total | | | | −144,214 |

$$\text{Area} = \frac{1}{2}(144,214) = 72,107 \text{ sq.ft. } (6698.74 \text{ m}^2)$$

# PARTITION OF A TRACT

The tract in the previous calculation procedure is to be divided into two parts by a line through $E$, the part to the west of this line having an area of 30,700 sq.ft. (2852.03 m²). Locate the dividing line.

## Calculation Procedure:

## 1. Ascertain the location of the dividing line EG

This procedure requires the solution of an oblique triangle. Refer to Fig. 5. It will be necessary to apply the following equations, which may be readily developed by drawing the altitude $BD$:

$$\text{Area} = \frac{1}{2}bc \sin \Delta \tag{4}$$

$$\tan C = \frac{c \sin A}{b - c \cos A} \tag{5}$$

In Fig. 6, let $EG$ represent the dividing line of this tract. By scaling the dimensions and making preliminary calculations or by using a planimeter, ascertain that $G$ lies between $B$ and $C$.

## 2. Establish the properties of the hypothetical course EC

By balancing the latitudes and departures of $DEC$, latitude of $EC = -(+161.9 + 97.9) = -259.8$ ft ($-79.18$ m); departure of $EC = -(+143.6 - 198.5) = +54.9$ ft ($+16.73$ m); length of $EC = (259.8^2 + 54.9^2)^{0.5} = 265.5$ ft (80.92 m). Then $DMD_{DE} = 143.6$ ft

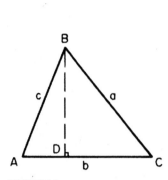

**FIGURE 5**

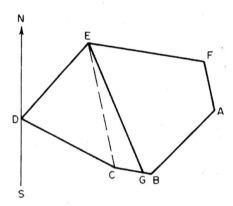

**FIGURE 6.** Partition of tract.

(43.77 m); $\text{DMD}_{EC} = 143.6 + 143.6 + 54.9 = 342.1$ ft (104.27 m); $\text{DMD}_{CD} = 342.1 + 54.9 - 198.5 = 198.5$ ft (60.50 m). This is acceptable.

### 3. Determine angle GCE by finding the bearings of courses EC and BC

Thus $\tan \alpha_{EC} = 54.9/259.8$; bearing of $EC = S11°55.9'E$; $\tan \alpha_{BC} = 77.5/9.6$; bearing of $BC = N82°56.3'W$; angle $GCE = 180° - (82°56.3' - 11°55.9') = 108°59.6'$.

### 4. Determine the area of triangle GCE

Calculate the area of triangle $DEC$; then find the area of triangle $GCE$ by subtraction. Thus

| Course | Latitude | × | DMD | = 2 × Projection area |
|--------|----------|---|-----|----------------------|
| CD | +97.9 | | 198.5 | +19,433 |
| DE | +161.9 | | 143.6 | +23,249 |
| EC | −259.8 | | 342.1 | −88,878 |
| Total | | | | −46,196 |

So the area of $DEC = \frac{1}{2}(46,196) = 23,098$ sq.ft. (2145.8 m²); area of $GCE = 30,700 - 23,098 = 7602$ sq.ft. (706.22 m²).

### 5. Solve triangle GCE completely

Apply Eqs. 4 and 5. To ensure correct substitution, identify the corresponding elements, making $A$ the known angle $GCE$ and $c$ the known side $EC$. Thus

| Fig. 5 | Fig. 6 | Known values | Calculated values |
|--------|--------|--------------|-------------------|
| A | GCE | 108°59.6' | |
| B | CEG | | 11°21.6' |
| C | EGG | | 59°38.8' |
| a | EG | | 291.0 ft (88.70 m) |
| b | GC | | 60.6 ft (18.47 m) |
| c | EC | 265.5 ft (80.92 m) | |

By Eq. 4, $7602 = \frac{1}{2}GC(265.5 \sin 108°59.6')$; solving gives $GC = 60.6$ ft (18.47 m). By Eq. 5, $\tan EGC = 265.5 \sin 108°59.6'/(60.6 - 265.5 \cos 108°59.6')$; $EGC = 59°38.8'$. By the law of sines, $EG/\sin GCE = EC/\sin EGC$; $EG = 291.0$ ft (88.70 m); $CEG = 180° - (108°59.6' + 59°38.8') = 11°21.6'$.

### 6. Find the bearing of course EG
Thus, $\alpha_{EG} = \alpha_{EC} + CEG = 11°55.9' + 11°21.6' = 23°17.5'$ bearing of $EG = S23°17.5'E$.

The surveyor requires the length and bearing of $EG$ to establish this line of demarcation. She or he is able to check the accuracy of both the fieldwork and the office calculations by ascertaining that the point $G$ established in the field falls on $BC$ and that the measured length of $GC$ agrees with the computed value.

## AREA OF TRACT WITH MEANDERING BOUNDARY: OFFSETS AT IRREGULAR INTERVALS

The offsets below were taken from stations on a traverse line to a meandering stream, all data being in feet. What is the encompassed area?

| Station | 0 + 00 | 0 + 25 | 0 + 60 | 0 + 75 | 1 + 010 |
|---------|--------|--------|--------|--------|---------|
| Offset  | 29.8   | 64.6   | 93.2   | 58.1   | 28.5    |

## Calculation Procedure:

### 1. Assume a rectilinear boundary between successive offsets; develop area equations
Refer to Fig. 7. When a tract has a meandering boundary, this boundary is approximated by measuring the perpendicular offsets of the boundary from a straight line $AB$. Let $d_r$ denote the distance along the traverse line between the first and the $r$th offset, and let $h_1, h_2, \ldots, h_n$ denote the offsets.

Developing the area equations yields

$$\text{Area} = \frac{1}{2}[d_2(h_1 - h_3) + d_3(h_2 - h_4) + \cdots + d_{n-1}(h_{n-2} - h_n) + d_n(h_{n-1} + h_n)] \quad (6)$$

Or,

$$\text{Area} = \frac{1}{2}[h_1 d_2 + h_2 d_3 + h_3(d_4 - d_2) + h_4(d_5 - d_3) + \cdots + h_n(d_n - d_{n-1})] \quad (7)$$

### 2. Determine the area, using Eq. 6
Thus, area $= \frac{1}{2}[25(29.8 - 93.2) + 60(64.6 - 58.1) + 75(93.2 - 28.5) + 110(58.1 + 28.5)] = 6590$ sq.ft. (612.2 m²).

### 3. Determine the area, using Eq. 7
Thus, area $= \frac{1}{2}[29.8 \times 25 + 64.6 \times 60 + 93.2(75 - 25) + 58.1(110 - 60) +$

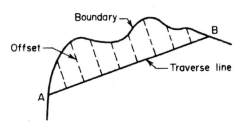

**FIGURE 7.** Tract with irregular boundary.

28.5(110 − 75)] = 6590 sq.ft. (612.2 m²). Hence, both equations yield the same result. The second equation has a distinct advantage over the first because it has only positive terms.

## DIFFERENTIAL LEVELING PROCEDURE

Complete the following level notes, and show an arithmetic check.

| Point | BS, ft (m) | HI | FS ft (m) | Elevation, ft (m) |
|-------|-----------|-----|-----------|-------------------|
| BM42  | 2.076 (0.63) | . . . | . . . . . | 180.482 (55.01) |
| TP1   | 3.408 (1.04) | . . . | 8.723 (2.66) | |
| TP2   | 1.987 (0.61) | . . . | 9.826 (2.99) | |
| TP3   | 2.538 (0.77) | . . . | 10.466 (3.19) | |
| TP4   | 2.754 (0.84) | . . . | 8.270 (2.52) | |
| BM43  | . . . | . . . | 11.070(3.37) | |

### Calculation Procedure:

### 1. Obtain the elevation for each point

Differential leveling is used to ascertain the difference in elevation between two successive benchmarks by finding the elevations of several convenient intermediate points, called turning points (TP). In Fig. 8, consider that the instrument is set up at $L1$ and $C$ is selected as a turning point. The rod reading $AB$ represents the backsight (BS) of $BM_1$, and the rod reading $CD$ represents the foresight (FS) of $TP_1$. The elevation of $BD$ represents the height of instrument (HI). The instrument is then set up at $L2$, and rod readings $CE$ and $FG$ are taken. Let $a$ and $b$ designate two successive turning points. Then

$$\text{Elevation}_a + BS_a = HI \qquad (8)$$

$$HI - FS_b = \text{elevation}_b \qquad (9)$$

Therefore,

$$\text{Elevation BM}_2 - \text{elevation BM}_1 = \Sigma BS - \Sigma FS \qquad (10)$$

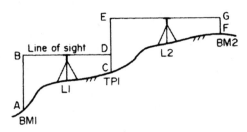

**FIGURE 8.** Differential leveling.

Apply Eqs. 8 and 9 successively to obtain the elevations recorded in the accompanying table.

| Point | BS, ft (m) | HI, ft (m) | FS, ft (m) | Elevation, ft (m) |
|---|---|---|---|---|
| BM42 | 2.076 (0.63) | 182.558 (55.64) | ..... | 180.482 (55.01) |
| TP1 | 3.408 (1.04) | 177.243 (54.02) | 8.723  (2.66) | 173.835 (52.98) |
| TP2 | 1.987 (0.61) | 169.404 (51.63) | 9.826  (2.99) | 167.417 (51.03) |
| TP3 | 2.538 (0.77) | 161.476 (49.22) | 10.466  (3.19) | 158.938 (48.44) |
| TP4 | 2.754 (0.84) | 155.960 (47.54) | 8.270  (2.52) | 153.206 (46.70) |
| BM43 | ..... | ..... | 11.070  (3.37) | 144.890 (44.16) |
| Total | 12.763 (3.89) | ..... | 48.355 (14.73) | |

## 2. Verify the result by summing the backsights and foresights

Substitute the results in Eq. 10: $144.890 - 180.482 = 12.763 - 48.355 = -35.592$.

## STADIA SURVEYING

The following stadia readings were taken with the instrument at a station of elevation 483.2 ft (147.28 m), the height of instrument being 5 ft (1.5 m). The stadia interval factor is 100, and the value of $C$ is negligible. Compute the horizontal distances and elevations.

| Point | Rod intercept, ft (m) | Vertical angle |
|---|---|---|
| 1 | 5.46(1.664) | $+2°40'$ on 8 ft (2.4 m) |
| 2 | 6.24 (1.902) | $+3°12'$ on 3 ft (0.9 m) |
| 3 | 4.83 (1.472) | $-1°52'$ on 4 ft (1.2 m) |

## Calculation Procedure:

### 1. State the equations used in stadia surveying

Refer to Fig. 9 for the notational system pertaining to stadia surveying. The transit is set up over a reference point $O$, the rod is held at a control point $N$, and the telescope is sighted at a point $Q$ on the rod; $P$ and $R$ represent the apparent locations of the stadia hairs on the rod.

The first column in these notes presents the rod intercept $s$, and the second column presents the vertical angle $a$ and the distance $NQ$. Then

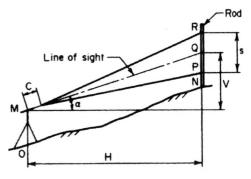

**FIGURE 9.** Stadia surveying.

$$H = Ks \cos^2\alpha + C \cos \alpha \tag{11}$$

$$V = \tfrac{1}{2} Ks \sin 2\alpha + C \sin \alpha \tag{12}$$

$$\text{Elevation of } N = \text{elevation of } O + OM + V - NQ \tag{13}$$

where $K$ = stadia interval factor; $C$ = distance from center of instrument to principal focus.

## 2. Substitute numerical values in the above equations

The results obtained are shown:

| Point | $H$, ft (m) | $V$, ft (m) | Elevation, ft (m) |
|-------|-------------|-------------|-------------------|
| 1 | 544.8 (166.06) | 25.4   (7.74) | 505.6 (154.11) |
| 2 | 622.0 (189.59) | 34.8   (10.61) | 520.0 (158.50) |
| 3 | 482.5 (147.07) | −15.7 (−4.79) | 468.5 (142.80) |

# VOLUME OF EARTHWORK

Figure 10*a* and *b* represent two highway cross sections 100 ft (30.5 m) apart. Compute the volume of earthwork to be excavated, in cubic yards (cubic meters). Apply both the average-end-area method and the prismoidal method.

## Calculation Procedure:

### 1. Resolve each section into an isosceles trapezoid and a triangle; record the relevant dimensions

Let $A_1$ and $A_2$ denote the areas of the end sections, $L$ the intervening distance, and $V$ the volume of earthwork to be excavated or filled.

*Method 1*: The average-end-area method equates the average area to the mean of the two end areas. Then

$$V = \frac{L(A_1 + A_2)}{2} \tag{14}$$

Figure 10*c* shows the first section resolved into an isosceles trapezoid and a triangle, along with the relevant dimensions.

### 2. Compute the end areas, and apply Eq. 14

Thus: $A_1 = [24(40 + 64) + (32 − 24)64]/2 = 1504$ sq.ft. (139.72 m²); $A_2 = [36(40 + 76) + (40 − 36)76]/2 = 2240$ sq.ft. (208.10 m²); $V = 100(1504 + 2240)/[2(27)] = 6933$ yd³ (5301.0 m³).

### 3. Apply the prismoidal method

*Method 2*: The prismoidal method postulates that the earthwork between the stations is a prismoid (a polyhedron having its vertices in two parallel planes). The volume of a prismoid is

$$V = \frac{L(A_1 + 4A_m + A_2)}{6} \tag{15}$$

where $A_m$ = area of center section.

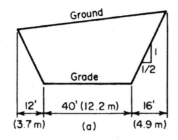

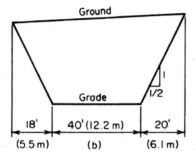

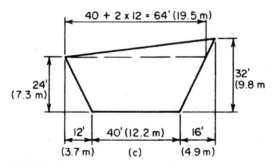

**FIGURE 10**

Compute $A_m$. Note that each coordinate of the center section of a prismoid is the arithmetic mean of the corresponding coordinates of the end sections. Thus, $A_m = [30(40 + 70) + (36 - 30)70]/2 = 1860$ sq.ft. (172.8 m²).

**4. Compute the volume of earthwork**

Using Eq. 15 gives $V = 100(1504 + 4 \times 1860 + 2240)/[6(27)] = 6904$ yd³ (5278.8 m³).

## DETERMINATION OF AZIMUTH OF A STAR BY FIELD ASTRONOMY

An observation of the sun was made at a latitude of 41°20′N. The altitude of the center of the sun, after correction for refraction and parallax, was 46°48′. By consulting a solar ephemeris, it was found that the declination of the sun at the instant of observation was 7°58′N. What was the azimuth of the sun?

### Calculation Procedures:

#### 1. *Calculate the azimuth of the body*

Refer to Fig. 11. The *celestial sphere* is an imaginary sphere on the surface of which the celestial bodies are assumed to be located; this sphere is of infinite radius and has the earth as its center. The *celestial equator,* or *equinoctial,* is the great circle along which the earth's equatorial plane intersects the celestial sphere. The *celestial axis* is the prolongation of the earth's axis of rotation. The *celestial poles* are the points at which the celestial axis pierces the celestial sphere. An *hour circle,* or a *meridian,* is a great circle that passes through the celestial poles.

The *zenith* and *nadir* of an observer are the points at which the vertical (plumb) line at the observer's site pierces the celestial sphere, the former being visible and the latter invisible to the observer. A *vertical circle* is a great circle that passes through the observer's zenith and nadir. The *observer's meridian* is the meridian that passes through the observer's zenith and nadir; it is both a meridian and a vertical circle.

In Fig. 11, $P$ is the celestial pole, $S$ is the apparent position of a star on the celestial sphere, and $Z$ is the observer's zenith.

The coordinates of a celestial body *relative to the observer* are the *azimuth,* which is the angular distance from the observer's meridian to the vertical circle through the body as measured along the observer's horizon in a clockwise direction; and the *altitude,* which is the angular distance of the body from the observer's horizon as measured along a vertical circle.

The *absolute* coordinates of a celestial body are the *right ascension,* which is the angular distance between the vernal equinox and the hour circle through the body as measured

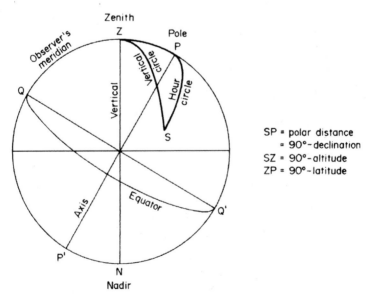

SP = polar distance
 = 90°−declination
SZ = 90°−altitude
ZP = 90°−latitude

**FIGURE 11.** The celestial sphere.

along the celestial equator; and the *declination*, which is the angular distance of the body from the celestial equator as measured along an hour circle.

The relative coordinates of a body at a given instant are obtained by observation; the absolute coordinates are obtained by consulting an almanac of astronomical data. The latitude of the observer's site equals the angular distance of the observer's zenith from the celestial equator as measured along the meridian. In the astronomical triangle *PZS* in Fig. 11, the arcs represent the indicated coordinates, and angle *Z* represents the azimuth of the body as measured from the north.

Calculating the azimuth of the body yields

$$\tan^2 \tfrac{1}{2} Z = \frac{\sin (S - L) \sin (S - h)}{\cos S \cos (S - p)} \tag{16}$$

where $L$ = latitude of site; $h$ = altitude of star; $p$ = polar distance = $90° -$ declination; $S$ = $\tfrac{1}{2}(L + h + p)$; $L$ = 41°20'; $h$ = 46°48'; $p$ = 90° − 7°58' = 82°02'; $S$ = $\tfrac{1}{2}(L + h + p)$ = 85°05'; $S - L$ = 43°45'; $S - h$ = 38°17'; $S - p$ = 3°03'.
Then

| | | | |
|---|---|---|---|
| log sin 43°45' | = | | 9.839800 |
| log sin 38°17' | = | | 9.792077 |
| | | | 9.631877 |
| log cos 85°05' | = | 8.933015 | |
| log cos 3°03' | = | 9.999384 | 8.932399 |
| 2 log tan $\tfrac{1}{2}Z$ | = | | 0.699478 |
| log tan $\tfrac{1}{2}Z$ | = | | 0.349739 |
| $\tfrac{1}{2}Z$ | = | 65°55'03.5" | $Z =$ |
| 131°50'07" | | | |

## 2. *Verify the solution by calculating Z in an alternative manner*

To do this, introduce an auxiliary angle $M$, defined by

$$\cos^2 M = \frac{\cos p}{\sin h \sin L} \tag{17}$$

Then
$$\cos (180° - Z) = \tan h \tan L \sin^2 M \tag{18}$$

Then

| | | |
|---|---|---|
| log cos 82°02' = | | 9.141754 |
| log sin 46°48' = | 9.862709 | |
| log sin 41°20' = | 9.819832 | 9.682541 |
| 2 log cos $M$ = | | 9.459213 |
| log cos $M$ = | | 9.729607 |
| log sin $M$ = | | 9.926276 |
| 2 log sin $M$ = | | 9.852552 |
| log tan 46°48' = | | 0.027305 |
| log tan 41°20' = | | 9.944262 |
| log cos (180° − $Z$) = | | 9.824119 |
| $Z$ = 131°50'07", as before | | |

## TIME OF CULMINATION OF A STAR

Determine the Eastern Standard Time (75th meridian time) of the upper culmination of Polaris at a site having a longitude 81°W of Greenwich. Reference to an almanac shows that the Greenwich Civil Time (GCT) of upper culmination for the date of observation is $3^h 20^m 05^s$.

### Calculation Procedure:

### 1. *Convert the longitudes to the hour-minute-second system*
The rotation of the earth causes a star to appear to describe a circle on the celestial sphere centered at the celestial axis. The star is said to be *at culmination* or transit when it appears to cross the observer's meridian.

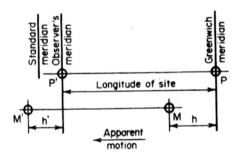

**FIGURE 12.** Culmination of Polaris.

In Fig. 12, $P$ and $M$ represent the position of Polaris and the mean sun, respectively, when Polaris is at the Greenwich meridian, and $P'$ and $M'$ represent the position of these bodies when Polaris is at the observer's meridian. The distances $h$ and $h'$ represent, respectively, the time of culmination of Polaris at Greenwich and at the observer's site, measured from local noon. Since the apparent velocity of the mean sun is less than that of the stars, $h'$ is less than $h$, the difference being approximately 10 s/h of longitude.

By converting the longitudes, 360° corresponds to 24 h; therefore, 15° corresponds to 1 h. Longitude of site = 81° = $5.4^h$ = $5^h 24^m 00^s$; standard longitude = 75° = $5^h$.

### 2. *Calculate the time of upper culmination at the site*
Correct this result to Eastern Standard Time. Since the standard meridian is east of the observer's meridian, the standard time is greater. Thus

| | |
|---|---|
| GCT of upper culmination at Greenwich | $3^h 20^m 05^s$ |
| Correction for longitude, 5.4 × 10 s | $54^s$ |
| Local civil time of upper culmination at site | $3^h 19^m 11^s$ |
| Correction to standard meridian | $24^m 00^s$ |
| EST of upper culmination at site | $3^h 43^m 11^s$ a.m. |

## PLOTTING A CIRCULAR CURVE

A horizontal circular curve having an intersection angle of 28° is to have a radius of 1200 ft (365.7 m). The point of curve is at station 82 + 30. (*a*) Determine the tangent distance, long chord, middle ordinate, and external distance. (*b*) Determine all the data necessary to stake the curve if the *chord* distance between successive stations is to be 100 ft (30.5 m). (*c*) Calculate all the data necessary to stake the curve if the *arc* distance between successive stations is to be 100 ft (30.5 m).

## Calculation Procedure:

### 1. *Determine the geometric properties of the curve*
*Part a.* Refer to Fig. 13: *A* is termed the *point of curve* (PC); *B* is the *point of tangent* (PT); and *V* the *point of intersection* (PI), or vertex. The notational system is $\Delta$ = intersection angle = angle between back and forward tangents = central angle *AOB*; *R* = radius of curve; *T* = tangent distance = *AV* = *VB*; *C* = long chord = *AB*; *M* = middle ordinate = *DC*; *E* = external distance = *CV*.

From the geometric relationships,

$$T = R \tan \tfrac{1}{2}\Delta \tag{19}$$

$$T = 1200(0.2493) = 299.2 \text{ ft } (91.20 \text{ m})$$

Also

$$C = 211 \sin \tfrac{1}{2}\Delta \tag{20}$$

$$C = 2(1200)(0.2419) = 580.6 \text{ ft } (176.97 \text{ m})$$

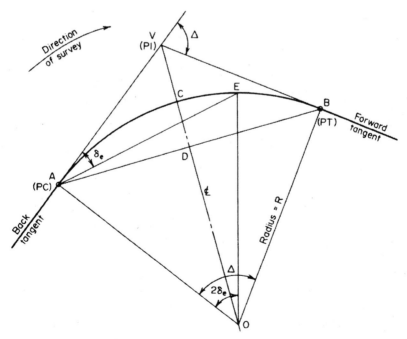

**FIGURE 13.** Circular curve.

And,

$$M = R(1 - \cos \tfrac{1}{2}\Delta) \tag{21}$$
$$M = 1200(1 - 0.9703) = 35.6 \text{ ft} (10.85 \text{ m})$$

Lastly,

$$E = R \tan \tfrac{1}{2}\Delta \tan \tfrac{1}{2}\Delta \tag{22}$$
$$E = 1200(0.2493)(0.1228) = 36.7 \text{ ft} (11.19 \text{ m})$$

### 2. Verify the results in step 1
Use the pythagorean theorem on triangle $ADV$. Or, $AD = \tfrac{1}{2}(580.6) = 290.3$ ft (88.48 m); $DV - 35.6 + 36.7 = 72.3$ ft (22.04 m); then $290.3^2 + 72.3^2 = 89,500$ sq.ft. (8314.6 m²), to the nearest hundred; $299.2^2 = 89,500$ sq.ft. (8314.6 m²); this is acceptable.

### 3. Calculate the degree of curve D
*Part b.* In Fig. 13, let $E$ represent a station along the curve. Angle $VAE$ is termed the *deflection angle* $\delta_e$ of this station; it is equal to one-half the central angle $AOE$. In the field, the curve is staked by setting up the transit at the $PC$ and then locating each station by means of its deflection angle and its chord distance from the preceding station.

Calculate the *degree of curve D*. This is the central angle formed by the radii to two successive stations or, what is the same in this instance, the central angle subtended by a *chord* of 100 ft (30.5 m). Then

$$\sin \tfrac{1}{2}D = \frac{50}{R} \tag{23}$$

So $\tfrac{1}{2}D = \arcsin 50/1200 = \arcsin 0.04167$; $\tfrac{1}{2}D = 2°23.3'$; $D = 4°46.6'$.

### 4. Determine the station at the PT
Number of stations on the curve $= 28°/4°46.6' = 5.862$; station of PT $= (82 + 30) + (5 + 86.2) = 88 + 16.2$.

### 5. Calculate the deflection angle of station 83 and the difference between the deflection angles of station 88 and the PT
For simplicity, assume that central angles are directly proportional to their corresponding chord lengths; the resulting error is negligible. Then $\delta_{83} = 0.70(2°23.3') = 1°40.3'$; $\delta_{PT} - \delta_{88} = 0.162(2°23.3') = 0°23.2'$.

### 6. Calculate the deflection angle of each station
Do this by adding $\tfrac{1}{2}D$ to that of the preceding station. Record the results thus:

| Station | Deflection angle |
| --- | --- |
| 82+30 | 0 |
| 83 | 1°40.3' |
| 84 | 4°03,6' |
| 85 | 6°26.9' |
| 86 | 8°50.2' |
| 87 | 11°13.5' |
| 88 | 13°36.8' |
| 88 + 16.2 | 14°00' |

## 7. Calculate the degree of curve in the present instance

*Part c.* Since the subtended central angle is directly proportional to its arc length, $D/100 = 360/(2\pi R)$; therefore,

$$D = 18,000/\pi R = 5729.58/R \text{ degrees} \qquad (24)$$

Then, $D = 5729.58/1200 = 4.7747° = 4°46.5'$.

## 8. Repeat the calculations in steps 4, 5, and 6

# INTERSECTION OF CIRCULAR CURVE AND STRAIGHT LINE

In Fig. 14, *MN* represents a straight railroad spur that intersects the curved highway route *AB*. Distances on the route are measured along the arc. Applying the recorded data, determine the station of the intersection point *P*.

## Calculation Procedure:

### 1. Apply trigonometric relationships to determine three elements in triangle ONP

Draw line *OP*. The problem resolves itself into the calculation of the central angle *AOP*, and this may be readily found by solving the oblique triangle *ONP*. Applying trigonometric relationships gives $AV = T = 800 \tan 54° = 1101.1$ ft (335.62 m); $AM = 1101.1 - 220 = 881.1$ ft (268.56 m); $AN = AM \tan 28° = 468.5$ ft (142.80 m); $ON = 800 - 468.5 = 331.5$ ft (101.04 m); $OP = 800$ ft (243.84 m); $ONP = 90° + 28° = 118°$.

### 2. Establish the station of P

*Solve triangle ONP* to find the central angle; then calculate arc *AP* and establish the station of *P*. By the law of sines, $\sin OPN = \sin ONP(ON)/OP$; therefore, $OPN = 21°27.7'$;

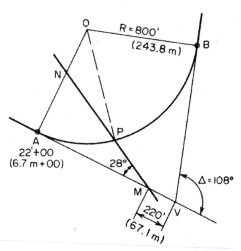

**FIGURE 14.** Intersection of curve and straight line.

$AOP = 180° - (118° + 21°27.7') = 40°32.3'$ arc $AP = 2\pi (800)(40°32.3')/360° =$ 566.0 ft (172.52 m); station of $P = (22 + 00) + (5 + 66) = 27 + 66$.

# REALIGNMENT OF CIRCULAR CURVE BY DISPLACEMENT OF FORWARD TANGENT

In Fig. 15, the horizontal circular curve $AB$ has a radius of 720 ft (219.5 m) and an intersection angle of 126°. The curve is to be realigned by rotating the forward tangent through an angle of 22° to the new position $V''B$ while maintaining the $PT$ at $B$. Compute the radius, and locate the PC of the new curve.

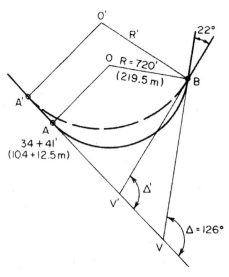

**FIGURE 15.** Displacement of forward tangent.

### Calculation Procedure:

**1. Find the tangent distance of the new curve**

Solve triangle $BV'V$ to find the tangent distance of the new curve and the location of $V'$. Thus, $\Delta' = 126° - 22° = 104°$; $VB = 720 \tan 63° = 1413.1$ ft (430.71 m). By the law of sines, $V'B = 14131 \sin 126°/\sin 104° = 1178.2$ ft (359.12 m); $V'V = 1413.1 \sin 22°/\sin 104° = 545.6$ ft (166.30 m).

**2. Compute the radius R'**

By Eq. 19, $R' = 1178.2 \cot 52° = 920.5$ ft (280.57 m).

**3. Determine the station of A'**

Thus, $AV = VB = 1413.1$ ft (403.71 m); $A'V' = V'B = 1178.2$ ft (359.12 m); $A'A = A'V' + V'V - AV = 310.7$ ft (94.70 m); station of new PC $= (34 + 41) - (3 + 10.7) = 31 + 30.3$.

**4. Verify the foregoing results**

Draw the long chords $AB$ and $A'B$. Then apply the computed value of $R'$ to solve triangle $BA'A$ and thereby find $A'A$. By Eq. 20, $A'B = 2R' \sin \frac{1}{2}\Delta' = 1450.7$ ft (442.17 m); $AA'B = \frac{1}{2}\Delta' = 52°$; $A'AB = 180° - \frac{1}{2}\Delta = 117°$; $ABA' = 180° - (52° + 117°) = 11°$. By the law of sines, $A'A = 1450.7 \sin 11°/\sin 117° = 310.7$ ft (94.70 m). This is acceptable.

# CHARACTERISTICS OF A COMPOUND CURVE

The tangents to a horizontal curve intersect at an angle of 68°22'. To fit the curve to the terrain, it is necessary to use a compound curve having tangent lengths of 955 ft (291.1 m)

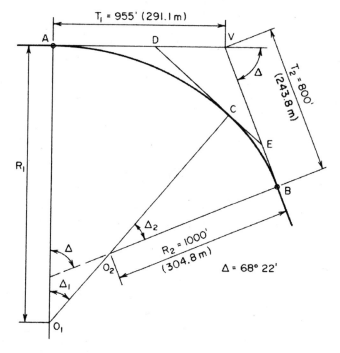

**FIGURE 16.** Compound curve.

and 800 ft (243.8 m), as shown in Fig. 16. The minimum allowable radius is 1000 ft (304.8 m). Compute the larger radius and the two central angles.

**Calculation Procedure:**

### 1. Calculate the latitudes and departures of the known sides

A *compound curve* is a curve that comprises two successive circular arcs of unequal radii that are tangent at their point of intersection, the centers of the arcs lying on the same side of their common tangent. (Where the centers lie on opposite sides of this tangent, the curve is termed a *reversed curve*.) In Fig. 16, $C$ is the point of intersection of the arcs, and $DE$ is the common tangent.

This situation is analyzed without applying any set equation to illustrate the general method of solution for compound and reversed curves. There are two unknown quantities: the radius $R_1$ and a central angle. (Since $\Delta_1 + \Delta_2 = \Delta$, either central angle may be considered the unknown.)

If the polygon $AVBO_2O_1$ is visualized as a closed traverse, the latitudes and departures of its sides are calculated, and the sum of the latitudes and sum of the departures are equated to zero, two simultaneous equations containing these two unknowns are obtained. For convenience, select $O_1A$ as the reference meridian. Then

| Side | Length, ft (m) | Bearing | Latitude | Departure |
|------|------|---------|----------|-----------|
| AV | 955 (291.1) | 90° | 0 | +955.00 |
| VB | 800 (243.8) | 21°38′ | −743.65 | +294.93 |
| $BO_2$ | 1000 (304.8) | 68°22′ | −368.67 | −929.56 |
| Total | . . . | . . . | −1112.32 | +320.37 |

## 2. Express the latitudes and departures of the unknown sides in terms of $R_1$ and $\Delta_1$

Thus, for side $O_2O_1$: length $= R_1 - 1000$; bearing $= \Delta_1$; latitude $= -(R_1 - 1000) \cos \Delta_1$; departure $= -(R_1 - 1000) \sin \Delta_1$.

Also, for side $O_1A$: length $= R_1$ bearing $= 0$; latitude $= R_1$ departure $= 0$.

## 3. Equate the sum of the latitudes and sum of the departures to zero; express $\Delta_1$ as a function of $R_1$

Thus, $\Sigma \text{lat} = R_1 - (R_1 - 1000) \cos \Delta_1 - 1112.32 = 0$; $\cos \Delta_1 = (R_1 - 1112.32)/(R_1 - 1000)$, or $1 - \cos \Delta_1 = 112.32/(R_1 - 1000)$, Eq. a. Also, $\Sigma \text{dep} = -(R_1 - 1000) \sin \Delta_1 + 320.37 = 0$; $\sin \Delta_1 = 320.37/(R_1 - 1000)$, Eq. b.

## 4. Divide Eq. a by Eq. b, and determine the central angles

Thus, $(1 - \cos \Delta_1)/\sin \Delta_1 = \tan \frac{1}{2}\Delta_1 = 112.32/320.37$; $\frac{1}{2}\Delta_1 = 19°19′13″$; $\Delta_1 = 38°38′26″$; $\Delta_2 = 68°22′ - \Delta_1 = 29°43′34″$.

## 5. Substitute the value of $\Delta_1$ in Eq. b to find $R_1$

Thus, $R_1 = 1513.06$ ft (461.181 m).

## 6. Verify the foregoing results by analyzing triangle DEV

Thus, $AD = R_1 \tan \frac{1}{2}\Delta_1 = 530.46$ ft (161.684 m); $DV = 955 - 530.46 = 424.54$ ft (129.400 m); $EB = R_2 \tan \frac{1}{2}\Delta_2 = 265.40$ ft (80.894 m); $VE = 800 - 265.40 = 534.60$ ft (162.946 m); $DE = 530.46 + 265.40 = 795.86$ ft (242.578 m). By the law of cosines, $\cos \Delta = -(DV^2 + VE^2 - DE^2)/[2(DV)(VE)]$; $\Delta = 68°22′$. This is correct.

# ANALYSIS OF A HIGHWAY TRANSITION SPIRAL

A horizontal circular curve for a highway is to be designed with transition spirals. The PI is at station 34 + 93.81, and the intersection angle is 52°48′. In accordance with the governing design criteria, the spirals are to be 350 ft (106.7 m) long and the degree of curve of the circular curve is to be 6° (arc definition). The approach spiral will be staked by setting the transit at the TS and locating 10 stations on the spiral by means of their deflection angles from the main tangent. Compute all data needed for staking the approach spiral. Also, compute the long tangent, short tangent, and external distance.

## Calculation Procedure:

### 1. Calculate the basic values

In the design of a road, a spiral is interposed between a straight-line segment and a circular curve to effect a gradual transition from rectilinear to circular motion, and vice versa. The type of spiral most frequently used is the clothoid, which has the property that the curvature at a given point is directly proportional to the distance from the start of the curve to the given point, measured along the curve.

Refer to Fig. 17. The key points are identified by the following notational system: PI = point of intersection of main tangents; TS = point of intersection of main tangent and approach spiral (tangent-to-spiral point); SC = point of intersection of approach spiral and circular curve (spiral-to-curve point); CS = point of intersection of circular curve and departure spiral (curve-to-spiral point); ST = point of intersection of departure spiral and main tangent (spiral-to-tangent point); PC and PT = point at which tangents to the circular curve prolonged are parallel to the main tangents (also referred to as the *offsets*). Distances are designated in the following manner: $L_s$ = length of spiral from TS to SC; $L$ = length of spiral from TS to given point on spiral; $R_c$ = radius of circular curve; $R$ = radius of curvature at given point on spiral; $T_s$ = length of main tangent from TS to PI; $E_s$ = external distance, i.e., distance from PI to midpoint of circular curve.

In addition, there is a long tangent (LT), short tangent (ST), and long chord (LC), as indicated with respect to the departure spiral.

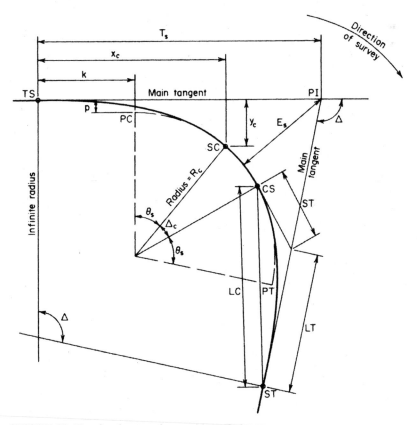

**FIGURE 17.** Notational system for transition spirals.

Place the origin of coordinates at the TS and the $x$ axis on the main tangent. Then $x_c$ and $y_c$ = coordinates of SC; $k$ and $p$ = abscissa and ordinate, respectively, of PC. The coordinates of the SC and PC are useful as parameters in the calculation of required distances. The distance $p$ is termed the *throw*, or *shift*, of the curve; it represents the displacement of the circular curve from the main tangent resulting from interposition of the spiral.

The basic angles are $\Delta$ = angle between main tangents, or intersection angle; $\Delta_c$ = angle between radii at SC and CS, or central angle of circular curve; $\theta_s$ = angle between radii of spiral at TS and SC, or central angle of entire spiral; $D_c$ = degree of curve of circular curve $D$ = degree of curve at given point on spiral; $\delta_s$ = deflection angle of SC from main tangent, with transit at TS; $\delta$ = deflection angle of given point on spiral from main tangent, with transit at TS.

Although extensive tables of spiral values have been compiled, this example is solved without recourse to these tables in order to illuminate the relatively simple mathematical relationships that inhere in the clothoid. Consider that a vehicle starts at the TS and traverses the approach spiral at constant speed. The degree of curve, which is zero at the TS, increases at a uniform rate to become $D_c$ at the SC. The basic equations are

$$\theta_s = \frac{L_s D_c}{200} = \frac{L_s}{2R_c} \tag{25}$$

$$x_c = L_s\left(1 - \frac{\theta_s^2}{10}\right) \tag{26}$$

$$y_c = L_s\left(\frac{\theta_s}{3} - \frac{\theta_s^3}{43}\right) \tag{27}$$

$$k = x_c - R_c \sin \theta_s \tag{28}$$

$$p = y_c - R_c(1 - \cos \theta_s) \tag{29}$$

$$\delta_s = \frac{L_s}{6R_c} = \frac{\theta_s}{3} \tag{30}$$

$$y = \left(\frac{L}{L_s}\right)^3 y_c \tag{31}$$

$$\delta = \left(\frac{L}{L_s}\right)^2 \delta_s \tag{32}$$

$$T_s = (R_c + p) \tan \tfrac{1}{2}\Delta + k \tag{33}$$

$$E_s = (R_c + p)(\sec \tfrac{1}{2}\Delta + 1) + p \tag{34}$$

$$LT = x_c - y_c \cot \theta_s \tag{35}$$

$$ST = y_c \csc \theta_s \tag{36}$$

Even though several of the foregoing equations are actually approximations, their use is valid when the value of $D_c$ is relatively small.

Calculating the basic values yields $\Delta = 52°48'$; $L_s = 350$ ft (106.7 m); $D_c = 6°$; $\theta_s = L_s D_c/200 = 350(6)/200 = 10.5° = 10°30'$, or $\theta_s = 10.5(0.017453) = 0.18326$ rad; $\Delta_c = 52°48' - 2(10°30') = 31°48'$; $D_c = 6(0.017453) = 0.10472$ rad; $R_c = 100/D_c = 954.93$ ft (291.063 m); $x_c = 350(1 - 0.18326^2/10) = 348.83$ ft (106.323 m); $y_c = 350(0.18326/3 - 0.18326^2/42) = 21.33$ ft (6.501 m); $k = 348.83 - 954.93 \sin 10°30' = 174.80$ ft (53.279 m); $p = 21.33 - 954.93(1 - \cos 10°30') = 5.34$ ft (1.628 m).

### 2. Locate the TS and SC
Thus, $T_s = (954.93 + 5.34) \tan 26°24' + 174.80 = 651.47$; station of TS $= (34 + 93.81) - (6 + 51.47) = 28 + 42.34$; station of SC $= (28 + 42.34) + (3 + 50.00) = 31 + 92.34$.

### 3. Calculate the deflection angles
Thus, $\delta_s = 10°30'/3 = 3°30' = 3.5°$. Apply Eq. 32 to find the deflection angles at the intermediate stations. For example, for point 7, $\delta = 0.7^2(3.5°) = 1.715° = 1°42.9'$.

Record the results in Table 1. The chord lengths between successive stations differ from the corresponding arc lengths by negligible amounts, and therefore each chord length may be taken as 35.00 ft (1066.8 cm).

### 4. Compute the LT, ST, and $E_s$
Thus, LT $= 348.83 - 21.33 \cot 10°30' = 233.75$ ft (7124.7 cm); ST $= 21.33 \csc 10°30' = 117.04$ ft (3567.4 cm); $E_s = (954.93 + 5.34)(\sec 26°24' - 1) + 5.34 = 117.14$ ft (3570.4 cm).

### 5. Verify the last three calculations by substituting in the following test equation
Thus

$$\frac{ST + R_c \tan \frac{1}{2}\Delta_c}{\cos \frac{1}{2}\Delta_c} = \frac{T_s - LT}{\cos \frac{1}{2}\Delta_c} = \frac{E_s - R_c (\sec \frac{1}{2}\Delta_c - 1)}{\sin \theta_s} \tag{37}$$

**TABLE 1.** Deflection Angles on Approach Spiral

| Point | Station | Deflection angle |
|---|---|---|
| TS | 28 + 42.34 | 0 |
| 1 | 77.34 | 0°02.1' |
| 2 | 29 + 12.34 | 0°08.4' |
| 3 | 47.34 | 0°18.9' |
| 4 | 82.34 | 0°33.6' |
| 5 | 30 + 17.34 | 0°52.5' |
| 6 | 52.34 | 1°15.6' |
| 7 | 87.34 | 1°42.9' |
| 8 | 31 + 22.34 | 2°14.4' |
| 9 | 57.34 | 2°50.1' |
| SC | 92.34 | 3°30.0' |

## TRANSITION SPIRAL: TRANSIT AT INTERMEDIATE STATION

Referring to the transition spiral in the previous calculation procedure, assume that lack of visibility from the TS makes these setups necessary: Points 4, 5, 6, and 7 will be located with the transit at point 3; points 8 and 9 and the SC will be located with the transit at point 7. Compute the orientation and deflection angles.

### Calculation Procedure:

### 1. Consider that the transit is set up at point 3 and a backsight is taken to the TS; find the orientation angle

In Fig. 18, assume that the spiral has been staked up to $P$ with the transit set up at the TS and that the remainder of the spiral is to be staked with the transit set up at $P$. Deflection angles are measured from the tangent through $P$ (the *local* tangent). The instrument is oriented by back-sighting to a preceding point $B$ and then turning the angle $\delta_b$. The orientation angle to $B$ and deflection angle to a subsequent point $F$ are

$$\delta_b = (2L_p + L_b)(L_p - L_b)\,\frac{\theta_s}{3L_s^2} \tag{38}$$

$$\delta_f = (2L_p + L_f)(L_f - L_p)\,\frac{\theta_s}{3L_s^2} \tag{39}$$

If $B$, $P$, and $F$ are points obtained by dividing the spiral into an integral number of arcs, these equations may be converted to these more suitable forms:

$$\delta_b = (2n_p + n_b)(n_p - n_b)\,\frac{\theta_s}{3n_s^2} \tag{38a}$$

$$\delta_f = (2n_p + n_f)(n_f - n_p)\,\frac{\theta_s}{3n_s^2} \tag{39b}$$

where $n$ denotes the number of arcs to the designated point.

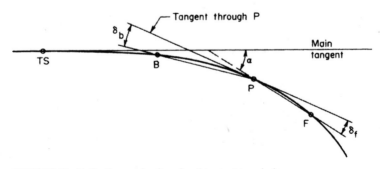

**FIGURE 18.** Deflection angles from local tangent to spiral.

Applying Eq. 38a to find the orientation angle and using data from the previous calculation procedure, we find $\theta_s = 10.5°$, $\theta_s/(3n_s^2) = 10.5°/[3(10^2)] = 0.035° = 2.1'$; $n_b = 0$; $n_p = 3$; $\delta_b = 6(3)(2.1') = 0°37.8'$.

## 2. Find the deflection angles from the tangent through point 3

Thus, by Eq. 39a: point 4, $\delta = (6 + 4)(2.1') = 0°21'$; point 5, $\delta = (6 + 5)(2)(2.1') = 0°46.2'$; point 6, $\delta = (6 + 6)(3)(2.1') = 1°15.6'$; point 7, $\delta = (6 + 7)(4)(2.1') = 1°49.2'$.

## 3. Consider that the transit is set up at point 7 and a backsight is taken to point 3; compute the orientation angle

Thus $n_b = 3$; $n_p = 7$; $\delta_b = (14 + 3)(4)(2.1') = 2°22.8'$.

## 4. Compute the deflection angles from the tangent through point 7

Thus point 8, $\delta = (14 + 8)(2.1') = 0°46.2'$; point 9, $\delta = (14 + 9)(2)(2.1') = 1°36.6'$ Sc, $\delta = (14 + 10)(3)(2.1') = 2°31.2'$.

## 5. Test the results obtained

In Fig. 18, extend chord $PF$ to its intersection with the main tangent, and let $\alpha$ denote the angle between these lines. Then

$$\alpha = (n_f^2 + n_f n_p + n_p^2)\,\frac{\theta_s}{3n_s^2} \tag{40}$$

This result should equal the sum of the angles applied in staking the curve from the TS to $F$. This procedure will be shown with respect to point 9.

For point 9, let $P$ and $F$ refer to points 7 and 9, respectively. Then $\alpha = (9^2 + 9 \times 7 + 7^2)(2.1') = 6°45.3'$. Summing the angles leading from the TS to point 9, we get

| | |
|---|---|
| Deflection angle from main tangent to point 3 | 0°18.9' |
| Orientation angle at point 3 | 0°37.8' |
| Deflection angle from local tangent to point 7 | 1°49.2' |
| Orientation angle at point 7 | 2°22.8' |
| Deflection angle from local tangent to point 9 | 1°36.6' |
| Total | 6°45.3' |

This test may be applied to each deflection angle beyond point 3.

# PLOTTING A PARABOLIC ARC

A grade of −4.6 percent is followed by a grade of +1.8 percent, the grades intersecting at station 54 + 20 of elevation 296.30 ft (90.312 m). The change in grade is restricted to 2 percent in 100 ft (30.5 m). Compute the elevation of every 50-ft (15.24-m) station on the parabolic curve, and locate the sag (lowest point of the curve). Apply both the average-grade method and the tangent-offset method.

## Calculation Procedure:

### 1. Compute the required length of curve

Using the notation in Figs. 19 and 20, we have $G_a = -4.6$ percent; $G_b = +1.8$ percent; $r$ = rate of change in grade = 0.02 percent per foot; $L = (G_b - G_a)/r = [1.8 - (-4.6)]/0.02 = 320$ ft (97.5 m).

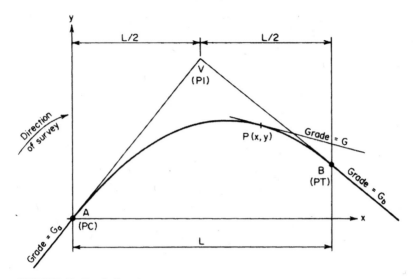

**FIGURE 19.** Parabolic arc.

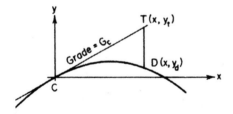

**FIGURE 20.** Tangent offset.

### 2. Locate the PC and PT

The station of the PC = station of the PI − L/2 = (54 + 20) − (1 + 60) = 52 + 60; station of PT = (54 + 20) + (1 + 60) = 55 + 80; elevation of PC = elevation of PI − $G_a L/2$ = 296.30 + 0.046(160) = 303.66 ft (92.556 m); elevation of PT − 296.30 + 0.018(160) = 299.18 ft (91.190 m).

### 3. Use the average-grade method to find the elevation of each station

Calculate the grade at the given station; calculate the average grade between the PI and that station, and multiply the average grade by the horizontal distance to find the ordinate. Equations used in analyzing a parabolic arc are

$$y = \frac{rx^2}{2} + G_a x \tag{41}$$

$$G = rx + G_a \tag{42}$$

$$y = (G_a + G)\frac{x}{2} \tag{43}$$

$$DT = -\frac{rx^2}{2} \tag{44a}$$

$$DT = (G_c - G_d) \frac{rx^2}{2} \tag{44b}$$

where DT = distance in Fig. 20.

Applying Eq. 42 with respect to station $53 + 00$ yields $x = 40$ ft (12.2 m); $G = 0.0002(40) - 0.046 = -0.038$; $G_{av} = (-0.046 - 0.038)/2 = -0.042$; $y = -0.042(40) = -1.68$ ft ($-51.206$ cm); elevation $= 303.66 - 1.68 = 301.98$ ft (9204.350 cm). Perform these calculations for each station, and record the results in tabular form as shown:

| Station | $x$, ft (m) | $G$ | $G_{av}$ | $y$, ft (m) | Elevation, ft (m) |
|---------|-------------|-----|----------|-------------|-------------------|
| 52 + 60 | 0 (0)      | −0.046 | −0.046 | 0 (0)        | 303.66 (92.56) |
| 53 + 00 | 40 (12.2)  | −0.038 | −0.042 | −1.68 (−0.51) | 301.98 (92.04) |
| 53 + 50 | 90 (27.4)  | −0.028 | −0.037 | −3.33 (−1.01) | 300.33 (91.54) |
| 54 + 00 | 140 (42.7) | −0.018 | −0.032 | −4.48 (−1.37) | 299.18 (91.19) |
| 54 + 50 | 190 (57.9) | −0.008 | −0.027 | −5.13 (−1.56) | 298.53 (90.99) |
| 55 + 00 | 240 (73.2) | +0.002 | −0.022 | −5.28 (−1.61) | 298.38 (90.95) |
| 55 + 50 | 290 (88.4) | +0.012 | −0.017 | −4.93 (−1.50) | 298.73 (91.05) |
| 55 + 80 | 320 (97.5) | +0.018 | −0.014 | −4.48 (−1.37) | 299.18 (91.19) |

### 4. *Verify the foregoing results*

Apply the principle that for a uniform horizontal spacing the "second differences" between the ordinate are equal. The results are shown:

### Calculation of Differences

| Elevations, ft (m) | First differences, ft (m) | Second differences, ft (m) |
|--------------------|---------------------------|----------------------------|
| 301.98 (92.04)     |                           |                            |
|                    | 1.65 (0.5029)             |                            |
| 300.33 (91.54)     |                           | 0.50 (0.1524)              |
|                    | 1.15 (0.3505)             |                            |
| 299.18 (91.19)     |                           | 0.50 (0.1525)              |
|                    | 0.65 (0.1981)             |                            |
| 298.53 (90.99)     |                           | 0.50 (0.1524)              |
|                    | 0.15 (0.0457)             |                            |
| 298.38 (90.95)     |                           | 0.50 (0.1524)              |
|                    | −0.35 (0.10668)           |                            |
| 298.73 (91.05)     |                           |                            |

### 5. *Apply the tangent-offset method to find the elevation of each station*

Since this method is based on Eq. 41, substitute directly in that equation. For the present case, the equation becomes $y = rx^2/2 + G_a x = 0.0001x^2 - 0.046x$. Record the calculations for $y$ in tabular form. The results, as shown, agree with those obtained by the average-grade method.

**Tangent-Offset Method**

| Station | $x$, ft (m) | $0.0001x^2$, ft (m) | $0.046x$, ft (m) | $y$, ft (m) |
|---|---|---|---|---|
| 52 + 60 | 0 (0) | 0 (0) | 0 (0) | 0 (0) |
| 53 + 00 | 40 (12.19) | 0.16 (0.05) | 1.84 (0.56) | −1.68 (−0.51) |
| 53 + 50 | 90 (27.43) | 0.81 (0.25) | 4.14 (1.26) | −3.33 (−1.01) |
| 54 + 00 | 140 (42.67) | 1.96 (0.60) | 6.44 (1.96) | −4.48 (−1.37) |
| 54 + 50 | 190 (57.91) | 3.61 (1.10) | 8.74 (2.66) | −5.13 (−1.56) |
| 55 + 00 | 240 (73.15) | 5.76 (1.76) | 11.04 (3.36) | −5.28 (−1.61) |
| 55 + 50 | 290 (88.39) | 8.41 (2.56) | 13.34 (4.07) | −4.93 (−1.50) |
| 55 + 80 | 320 (97.54) | 10.24 (3.12) | 14.72 (4.49) | −4.48 (−1.37) |

## 6. Locate the sag S

Since the grade is zero at this point, Eq. 42 yields $G_s = rx_s + G_a = 0$; therefore $x_s = -G_a/r = -(-0.046/0.0002) = 230$ ft (70.1 m); station of sag $= (52 + 60) + (2 + 30) = 54 + 90$; $G_{av} = \frac{1}{2}G_a = -0.023$; $y_s = -0.023(230) = -5.29$ ft (1.61 m); elevation of sag $= 303.66 - 5.29 = 298.37$ ft (90.943 m).

## 7. Verify the location of the sag

Do this by ascertaining that the offsets of the PC and PT from the tangent through $S$, which is horizontal, satisfy the tangent-offset principle. From the preceding results, tangent offset of PC $= 5.29$ ft (1.612 m); tangent offset of PT $= 5.29 - 4.48 = 0.81$ ft (0.247 m); distance to PC $= 230$ ft (70.1 m); distance to PT $= 320 - 230 = 90$ ft (27.4 m); $5.29/0.81 = 6.53$; $230^2/90^2 = 6.53$. Therefore, the results are verified.

## LOCATION OF A SINGLE STATION ON A PARABOLIC ARC

The PC of a vertical parabolic curve is at station $22 + 00$ of elevation 165.30, and the grade at the PC is $+3.2$ percent. The elevation of the station $24 + 00$ is 168.90 ft (51.481 m). What is the elevation of station $25 + 50$?

### Calculation Procedure:

## 1. Compute the offset of $P_1$ from the tangent through the PC

Refer to Fig. 21. The tangent-offset principle offers the simplest method of solution. Thus $x_1 = 200$ ft (61.0 m); $y_1 = 168.90 - 165.30 = 3.60$ ft (1.097 m); $Q_1T_1 = 200(0.032) = 6.40$ ft (1.951 m); $P_1T_1 = 6.40 - 3.60 = 2.80$ ft (0.853 m).

## 2. Compute the offset of $P_2$ from the tangent through the PC; find the elevation of $P_2$

Thus $x_2 = 350$ ft (106.7 m); $P_2T_2/(P_1T_1) = x_2^2/x_1^2$; $P_2T_2 = 2.80(350/200)^2 = 8.575$ ft (2.6137 m); $Q_2T_2 = 350(0.032) = 11.2$ ft (3.41 m); $Q_2P_2 = 11.2 - 8.575 = 2.625$ ft (0.8001 m); elevation of $P_2 = 165.30 + 2.625 = 167.925$ ft (51.184 m).

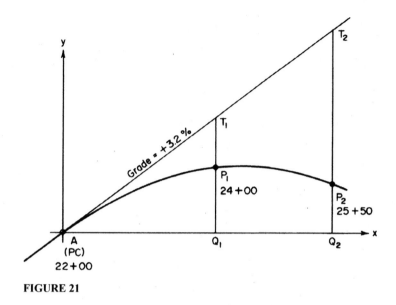

**FIGURE 21**

## LOCATION OF A SUMMIT

An approach grade of +1.5 percent intersects a grade of −2.5 percent at station 29 + 00 of elevation 226.30 ft (68.976 m). The connecting parabolic curve is to be 800 ft (243.8 m) long. Locate the summit.

### Calculation Procedure:

#### 1. Locate the PC

Draw a freehand sketch of the curve, and record all values in the sketch as they are obtained. Thus, station of PC = station of PI − $L/2$ = 25 + 00; elevation of PC = 226.30 − 400(0.015) = 220.30 ft (67.147 m).

#### 2. Calculate the rate of change in grade; locate the summit

Apply the average-grade method to locate the summit. Thus, $r = (-2.5 - 1.5)/800 = -0.005$ percent per foot.

Place the origin of coordinates at the PC. By Eq. 42, $x_s = -G_a/r = 1.5/0.005 = 300$ ft (91.44 m). From the PC to the summit, $G_{av} = \frac{1}{2}G_a = 0.75$ percent. Then $y_s = 300(0.0075) = 2.25$ ft (0.686 m); station of summit = (25 + 00) + (3 + 00) = 28 + 00; elevation of summit = 220.30 + 2.25 = 222.55 ft (67.833 m). The summit can also be located by the tangent-offset method.

## PARABOLIC CURVE TO CONTAIN
## A GIVEN POINT

A grade of −1.6 percent is followed by a grade of +3.8 percent, the grades intersecting at station 42 + 00 of elevation 210.00 ft (64.008 m). The parabolic curve connecting these grades is to pass through station 42 + 60 of elevation 213.70 ft (65.136 m). Compute the required length of curve.

**Calculation Procedure:**

**1. Compute the tangent offsets; establish the horizontal location of P in terms of L**

Refer to Fig. 22, where $P$ denotes the specified point. The given data enable computation of the tangent offsets $CP$ and $DP$, thus giving a relationship between the horizontal distances from $A$ to $P$ and from $P$ to $B$. Since the distance from the centerline of curve to $P$ is known, the length of curve may readily be found.

Computing the tangent offsets gives $CP = v - G_a h$ and $DP = v - G_b h$; but $CP/DP = (L/2 + h)^2/(L/2 - h)^2 = (L + 2h)^2/(L - 2h)^2$; therefore,

$$\frac{L + 2h}{L - 2h} = \left(\frac{v - G_a h}{v - G_b h}\right)^{1/2} \tag{45}$$

**2. Substitute numerical values and solve for L**

Thus, $G_a = -1.6$ percent; $G_b = +3.8$ percent; $h = 60$ ft (18.3 m); $v = 3.70$ ft (1.128 m); then $(L + 120)/(L - 120) = [(3.7 \times 0.016 \times 60)/(3.7 - 0.038 \times 60)]^{1/2} - 1.81$; so $L = 416$ ft (126.8 m).

**3. Verify the solution**

There are many ways of verifying the solution. The simplest way is to compare the offsets of $P$ and $B$ from a tangent through $A$. By Eq. 44b, offset of $B$ from tangent through $A = 208(0.016 + 0.038) = 11.232$ ft (3.4235 m). From the preceding calculations, offset of $P$

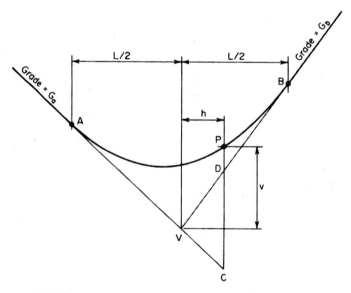

**FIGURE 22**

from tangent through $A = 4.66$ ft (1.4203 m); $4.66/11.232 = 0.415$; $(208 + 60)^2/(416)^2 = 0.415$. This is acceptable.

## SIGHT DISTANCE ON A VERTICAL CURVE

A vertical summit curve has tangent grades of $+2.6$ and $-1.5$ percent. Determine the minimum length of curve that is needed to provide a sight distance of 450 ft (137.2 m) to an object 4 in. (101.6 mm) in height. Assume that the eye of the motorist is 4.5 ft (1.37 m) above the roadway.

### Calculation Procedure:

### 1. State the equation for minimum length when S < L
The vertical curvature of a road must be limited to ensure adequate visibility across the summit. Consequently, the distance across which a given change in grade may be effected is subject to a lower limit imposed by the criterion of sight distance.

Let $S$ denote the required sight distance and $L$ the minimum length of curve. In Fig. 23, let $E$ denote the position of the motorist's eye and $P$ the top of an object. Assume that the curve has the maximum allowable curvature, so that the distance from $E$ to $P$ equals $S$.

Applying Eq. 44a gives

$$L = \frac{AS^2}{100[(2h_1)^{1/2} + (2h_2)^{1/2}]^2} \tag{46}$$

where $A = G_a - G_b$, in percent.

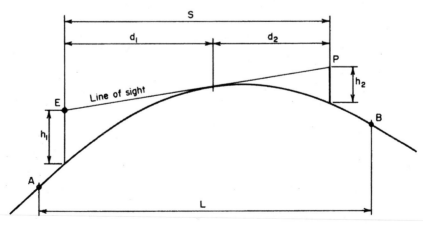

**FIGURE 23.** Visibility on vertical summit curve.

### 2. State the equation for L when S > L
Thus,

$$L = 2S - \frac{200(h_1^{1/2} + h_2^{1/2})^2}{A} \tag{47}$$

### 3. Assuming, tentatively, that S < L, compute L
Thus $h_1 = 4.5$ ft (1.37 m); $h_2 = 4$ in. $= 0.33$ ft (0.1 m); $A = 2.6 + 1.5 = 4.1$ percent; $L = 4.1(450)^2/[100(9^{1/2} + 0.67^{1/2})^2] = 570$ ft (173.7 m). Therefore, the assumption that $S < L$ is valid because $450 < 570$.

## MINE SURVEYING: GRADE OF DRIFT

A vein of ore has a strike of S38°20′E and a northeasterly dip of 33°14′. What is the grade of a drift having a bearing of S43°10′E?

### Calculation Procedure:

### 1. Express β as a function of α and θ
A vein of ore is generally assumed to have plane faces. The *strike*, or *trend*, of the vein is the bearing of any horizontal line in a face, and the *dip* is the angle of inclination of its face. A *drift* is a slightly sloping passage that follows the vein. Any line in a plane perpendicular to the horizontal is a *dip line*. The dip line is the steepest line in a plane, and the dip of the plane equals the angle of inclination of this line. With reference to the inclined plane *ABCD* in Fig. 24a, let α = dip of plane; β = angle of inclination of arbitrary line *AG*; θ = angle between horizontal projections of *AG* and dip line.

By expressing β as a function of α and θ: tan β = *AF/GF*; tan α = *AF/DF*; tan β/tan α = *DF/GF* = cos θ.

$$\tan \beta = \tan \alpha = \cos \theta \tag{48}$$

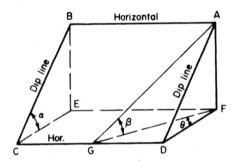

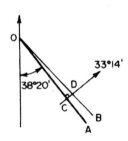

(a) Isometric view of inclined plane

(b) Strike-and-dip diagram (plan)

**FIGURE 24**

### 2. Find the grade of the drift

Apply Eq. 48. In Fig. 24$b$, $OA$ is a horizontal line in the vein, $OB$ is the horizontal projection of the drift, and the arrow indicates the direction of dip. Then angle $COD = 43°10' - 38°20' = 4°50'$; $\theta = $ angle $CDO = 90° - 4°50' = 85°10'$; $\tan \beta = \tan 33°14' \cos 85°10' = 0.0552$; grade of drift = 5.52 percent.

### 3. Alternatively, solve without the use of Eq. 48

In Fig. 24$b$, set $OD = 100$ ft (30.5 m); let $D'$ denote the point on the face of the vein vertically below $D$. Then $CD = 100 \sin 4°50' = 8.426$ ft (2.5682 m); drop in elevation from $O$ to $D' = $ drop in elevation from $C$ to $D' = 8.426 \tan 33°14' = 5.52$ ft (1.682 m). Therefore, grade = 5.52 percent.

## DETERMINING STRIKE AND DIP FROM TWO APPARENT DIPS

Three points on the hanging wall (upper face) of a vein of ore have been located by vertical boreholes. These points, designated $P$, $Q$, and $R$, have these relative positions: $P$ is 142 ft (43.3 m) above $Q$ and 130 ft (39.6 m) above $R$; horizontal projection of $PQ$, length = 180 ft (54.9 m) and bearing = S55°32'W; horizontal projection of $PR$, length = 220 ft (67.1 m) and bearing = N19°26'W. Determine the strike and dip of the vein by both graphical construction and trigonometric calculations.

### Calculation Procedure:

### 1. Plot the given data for the graphical procedure

In Fig. 25$a$, draw lines $PQ$ and $PR$ in plan in accordance with the given data for their horizontal projections. The angle of inclination of any line other than a dip line is an apparent dip of the vein.

### 2. Draw the elevations

In Fig. 25$b$ and $c$, draw elevations normal to $PQ$ and $PR$, respectively, locating the points in accordance with the given differences in elevation. Find the points $S$ and $T$ lying on $PQ$ and $PR$, respectively, at an arbitrary distance $v$ below $P$.

### 3. Draw the representation of the strike of the vein

Locate points $S$ and $T$ in Fig. 25$a$, and connect them with a straight line. This line is horizontal, and its bearing $\phi$, therefore, represents the strike of the vein.

### 4. Draw an edge view of the vein

In Fig. 25$d$, draw an elevation parallel to $ST$. Since this is an edge view of one line in the face, it is an edge view of the vein itself; it therefore represents the dip $\alpha$ of the vein in its true magnitude.

### 5. Determine the strike and dip

Scale angles $k$ and $\alpha$, respectively. In Fig. 25$a$, the direction of dip is represented by the arrow perpendicular to $ST$.

### 6. Draw the dip line for the trigonometric solution

In Fig. 26, draw an isometric view of triangle $PST$, and draw the dip line $PW$. Its angle of inclination $\alpha$ equals the dip of the vein. Let $O$ denote the point on a vertical line through $P$ at the same elevation as $S$ and $T$. Let $\beta_1$ and $\beta_2$ denote the angle of inclination of $PS$ and

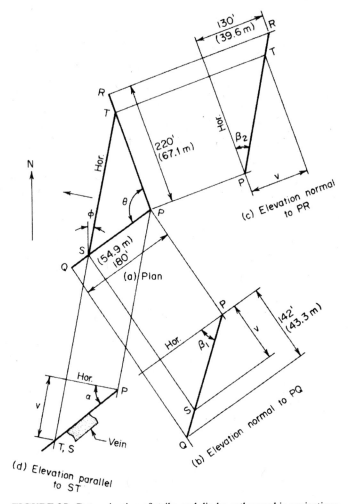

**FIGURE 25.**  Determination of strike and dip by orthographic projections.

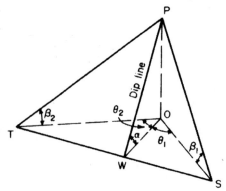

**FIGURE 26**

*PT*, respectively; and let $\theta$ = angle *SOT*, $\theta_1$ = angle *SOW*, $\theta_2$ = angle *TOW*, $m$ = tan $\beta_2$/ tan $\beta_1$.

### 7. Express $\theta_1$ in terms of the known angles $\beta_1$, $\beta_2$ and $\theta$

Then substitute numerical values to find the strike $\phi$ of the vein. Thus

$$\tan \theta_1 = \frac{m - \cos \theta}{\sin \theta} \tag{49}$$

For this vein, $m$ = tan $\beta_2$/tan $\beta_1$ = 130(180)/[220(142)] = 0.749040; $\theta$ = 180° − (55°32′ + 19°26′) = 105°02′. Substituting gives tan $\theta_1$ = (0.749040 + 0.259381)/0.965775; $\theta_1$ = 46°14′15″; $\phi$ = 55°32′ + 46°14′15″ − 90° − 11°46′15″; strike of vein = N11°46′15″E.

### 8. Compute the dip of the vein

Use Eq. 48, considering *PS* as the line of known inclination. Thus, tan $\alpha$ = tan $\beta_1$/cos $\theta_1$; $\alpha$ = 48°45′25″.

### 9. Verify these results

Apply Eq. 48, considering *PT* as the line of known inclination. Thus $\theta_2$ = $\theta$ − $\theta_1$ = 105°02′ − 46°14′15″ = 58°47′45″; tan $\alpha$ = tan $\beta_2$/cos $\theta_2$; $\alpha$ = 48°45′25″. This value agrees with the earlier computed value.

## DETERMINATION OF STRIKE, DIP, AND THICKNESS FROM TWO SKEW BOREHOLES

In Fig. 27*a*, *A* and *B* represent points on the earth's surface through which skew boreholes were sunk to penetrate a vein of ore. Point *B* is 110 ft (33.5 m) due south of *A*. The data for these boreholes are as follows. *Borehole through A*: surface elevation = 870 ft (265.2 m); inclination = 49°; bearing of horizontal projection = N58°30′E. The hanging wall and footwall (lower face of vein) were struck at distances of 55 ft (16.8 m) and 205 ft (62.5 m), respectively, measured along the borehole. *Borehole through B*: surface elevation = 842 ft (256.6 m); inclination = 73°; bearing of horizontal projection = S44°50′E. The hanging wall and footwall were struck at distances of 98 ft (29.9 m) and 182 ft (55.5 m), respectively, measured along the borehole. Determine the strike, dip, and thickness of the vein by both graphical construction and trigonometric calculations.

### Calculation Procedure:

### 1. Draw horizontal projections of the boreholes

Since the vein is assumed to have uniform thickness, the hanging wall and footwall are parallel. Two straight lines determine a plane. In the present instance, two points on the hanging wall and two points on the footwall are given, enabling one line to be drawn in each of two parallel planes. These planes may be located by using these principles:

a. Consider a plane *P* and line *L* parallel to each other. If through any point on *P* a line is drawn parallel to *L*, this line lies in plane *P*.

b. Lines that are parallel and equal in length appear to be parallel and equal in length in all orthographic views.

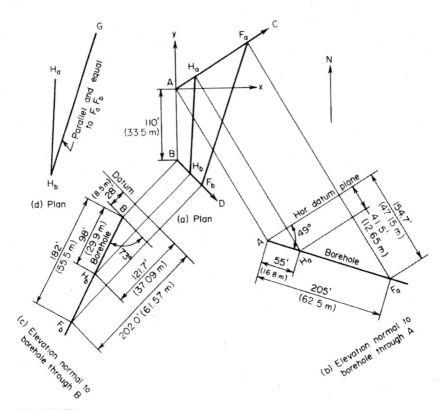

**FIGURE 27**

These principles afford a means of locating a second line in the hanging wall or footwall. Applying the specified bearings, draw the horizontal projections $AC$ and $BD$ of the boreholes in Fig. 27a.

## 2. Locate the points of intersection with the hanging wall and footwall in elevation

In Fig. 27b, draw an elevation normal to the borehole through $A$; locate the points of intersection $H_a$ and $F_a$ with the hanging wall and footwall, respectively. Select the horizontal plane through $A$ as datum.

## 3. Repeat the foregoing construction with respect to borehole through B

This construction is shown in Fig. 27c.

## 4. Locate the points of intersection in plan

In Fig. 27a, locate the points of intersection. Draw lines $H_aH_b$ and $F_aF_b$. The former lies in the hanging wall and the latter in the footwall. To avoid crowding, reproduce the plan of line $H_aH_b$ in Fig. 27d.

### 5. Draw the plan of a line $H_bG$ that is parallel and equal in length to $F_aF_b$

Do this by applying the second principle given above. In accordance with principle *a*, $H_bG$ lies in the hanging wall, and this plane is therefore determined. The ensuing construction parallels that in the previous calculation procedure.

### 6. Establish a system of rectangular coordinate axes

Use *A* as the origin (Fig. 27*a*). Make *x* the east-west axis, *y* the north-south axis, and *x* the vertical axis.

### 7. Apply the given data to obtain the coordinates of the intersection points and point G

For example, with respect to $F_a$, $y = 205 \cos 49° \cos 58°30'$. The coordinates of *G* are obtained by adding to the coordinates of $H_b$ the differences between the coordinates of $F_a$ and $F_b$. The results are shown:

| Point | x, ft (m) | y, ft (m) | z, ft (m) |
|-------|-----------|-----------|-----------|
| $H_a$ | 30.8 (9.39) | 18.9 (5.76) | −41.5 (−12.65) |
| $H_b$ | 20.2 (6.16) | −130.3 (−39.72) | −121.7 (−37.09) |
| $F_a$ | 114.7 (34.96) | 70.3 (21.43) | −154.7 (−47.15) |
| $F_b$ | 37.5 (11.43) | −147.7 (−45.02) | −202.0 (−61.57) |
| G | 97.4 (29.69) | 87.7 (26.73) | −74.4 (−22.68) |

### 8. For convenience, reproduce the plan of the intersection points, and G

This is shown in Fig. 28*a*.

### 9. Locate the point S at the same elevation as G

In Fig. 28*b*, draw an elevation normal to $H_aH_b$, and locate the point *S* on this line at the same elevation as *G*.

### 10. Establish the strike of the plane

Locate *S* in Fig. 28*a*, and draw the horizontal line *SG*. Since both *S* and *G* lie on the hanging wall, the strike of this plane is now established.

### 11. Complete the graphical solution

In Fig. 28*c*, draw an elevation parallel to *SG*. The line through $H_a$ and $H_b$ and that through $F_a$ and $F_b$ should be parallel to each other. This drawing is an edge view of the vein, and it presents the dip $\alpha$ and thickness *t* in their true magnitude. The graphical solution is now completed.

### 12. Reproduce the plan view

For convenience, reproduce the plan of $H_a$, $H_b$, and *G* in Fig. 28*d*. Draw the horizontal projection of the dip line, and label the angles as indicated.

### 13. Compute the lengths of lines $H_aH_b$ and $H_aG$

Compute these lengths as projected on each coordinate axis and as projected on a horizontal plane. Use absolute values. Thus, line $H_aH_b$: $L_x = 30.8 - 20.2 = 10.6$ ft (3.23 m); $L_y = 18.9 - (-130.3) = 149.2$ ft (45.48 m); $L_z = -41.5 - (-121.7) = 80.2$ ft (24.44 m); $L_{hor} = (10.6^2 + 149.2^2)^{0.5} = 149.6$ ft (45.60 m). Line $H_aG$: $L_x = 97.4 - 30.8 = 66.6$ ft (20.30 m); $L_y = 87.7 - 18.9 = 68.8$ ft (20.97 m); $L_z = -41.5 - (-74.4) = 32.9$ ft (10.03 m); $L_{hor} = (66.6^2 + 68.8^2)^{0.5} = 95.8$ ft (29.20 m).

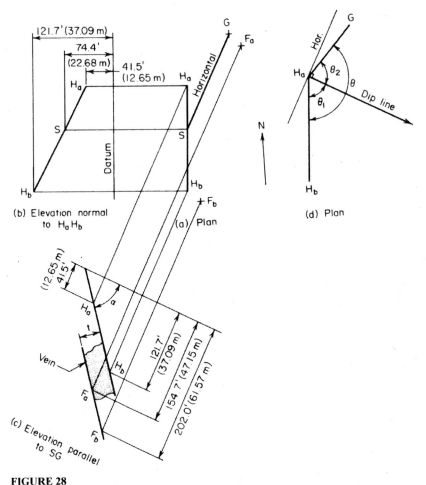

**FIGURE 28**

### 14. Compute the bearing and inclination of lines $H_aH_b$ and $H_aG$

Let $\phi_1$ = bearing of $H_aH_b$; $\phi_2$ = bearing of $H_aG$; $\beta_1$ = angle of inclination of $H_aH_b$; $\beta_2$ = angle of inclination of $H_aG$. Then tan $\phi_1$ = 10.6/149.2; $\phi_1$ = S4°04′W; tan $\phi_2$ = 66.6/68.8; $\phi_2$ = N44°04′E; tan $\beta_1$ = 80.2/149.6; tan $\beta_2$ = 32.9/95.8.

### 15. Compute angle $\theta$ shown in Fig. 28d; determine the strike of the vein, using Eq. 49

Thus, $\theta = 180° + \phi_1 - \phi_2 = 140°00′$; $m$ = tan $\beta_2$/tan $\beta_1$ = 0.6406; tan $\theta_1$ = ($m$ − cos 140°00′)/sin 140°00′; $\theta_1$ = 65°26′; $\theta_2$ = 74°34′ The bearing of the horizontal projection of the dip line = $\theta_1 - \phi_1$ = S61°22′E; therefore, the strike of the vein = N28°38′E.

### 16. Compute the dip $\alpha$ of the vein

By Eq. 48, tan $\alpha$ = tan $\beta_1$/cos $\theta_1$; $\alpha$ = 52°12′; or tan $\alpha$ = tan $\beta_2$/cos $\theta_2$; $\alpha$ = 52°14′. This slight discrepancy between the two computed values falls within the tolerance of these calculations. Use the average value $\alpha$ = 52°13′.

**17. Establish the relationship between the true thickness t of a vein and its apparent thickness t' as measured along a skew borehole**

Refer to Figs. 27 and 28. Let $\delta$ = angle of inclination of borehole; $\gamma$ = angle in plan between downward-sloping segments of borehole and dip line of vein. Then

$$t = t'(\cos \alpha \sin \delta - \sin \alpha \cos \delta \cos \gamma) \tag{50}$$

**18. Find the true thickness, using Eq. 50**

Thus, borehole through $A$: $\delta = 49°$; $\gamma = 180° - (58°30' + 61°22') = 60°08'$; $t' + 205 - 55 = 150$ ft (45.7 m); $t = 150(\cos 52°13' \sin 49° - \sin 52°13' \cos 49° \cos 60°08') = 30.6$ ft (9.3 m). For the borehole through $B$: $\delta = 73°$; $\gamma = 61°22' - 44°50' = 16°32'$; $t' = 182 - 98 = 84$ ft (25.6 m); $t = 84(\cos 52°13' \sin 73° - \sin 52°13' \cos 73° \cos 16°32') = 30.6$ ft (9.3 m). This agrees with the value previously computed.

# Aerial Photogrammetry

## FLYING HEIGHT REQUIRED TO YIELD A GIVEN SCALE

At what altitude above sea level must an aircraft fly to obtain vertical photography having an average scale of 1 cm = 120 m if the camera lens has a focal length of 152 mm and the average elevation of the terrain to be surveyed is 290 m?

### Calculation Procedure:

### 1. Write the equation for the scale of a vertical photograph

In aerial photogrammetry, the term *photograph* generally refers to the positive photograph, and the plane of this photograph is considered to lie on the object side of the lens. A photograph is said to be *vertical* if the optical axis of the lens is in a vertical position at the instant of exposure. Since the plane of the photograph is normal to the optical axis, this plane is horizontal.

In Fig. 29a, point $L$ is the *front nodal point* of the lens; a ray of light directed at this point leaves the lens without undergoing a change in direction. The point $o$ at which the optical axis intersects the plane of the photograph is called the *principal point*. The distance from the ground to the camera may be considered infinite in relation to the dimensions of the lens, and so the distance $Lo$ is equal to the focal length of the lens. The aircraft is assumed to be moving in a horizontal straight line, termed the *line of flight*, and the elevation of $L$ above the horizontal datum plane is called the *flying height*. The position of $L$ in space at the instant of exposure is called the *exposure station*. Where the area to be surveyed is relatively small, the curvature of the earth may be disregarded.

Since the plane of the photograph is horizontal, Fig. 29b is a view normal to this plane and so presents all distances in this plane in their true magnitude. In the photograph, the origin of coordinates is placed at $o$. The $x$ axis is placed parallel to the line of flight, with $x$ values increasing in the direction of flight, and the $y$ axis is placed normal to the $x$ axis.

In Fig. 29, $A$ is a point on the ground, $a$ is the image of $A$ on the photograph, and $O$ is a point at the same elevation as $A$ that lies on the prolongation of $Lo$. Thus, $o$ is the image of $O$.

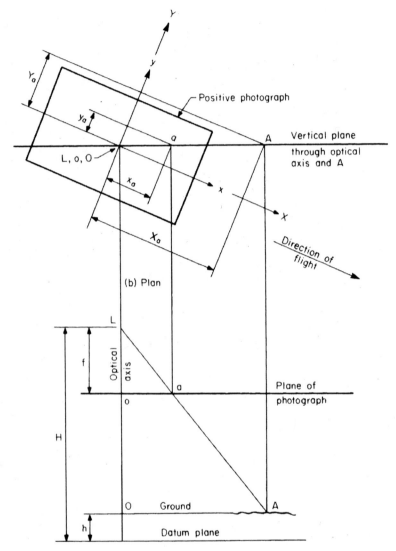

(b) Plan

(a) Elevation normal to vertical plane through optical axis and point A

**FIGURE 29**

The *scale* of a photograph, expressed as a fraction, is the ratio of a distance in the photograph to the corresponding distance along the ground. In this case, the ratio is 1 cm/120 m = 0.01 m/120 m = 1/12,000.

Let $H$ = flying height; $h$ = elevation of $A$ above datum; $f$ = focal length; $S$ = scale of photograph, expressed as a fraction. From Fig. 29, $S = oa/OA$, and by similar triangles $S = f/(H - h)$.

## 2. Solve this equation for the flying height

Take sea level as datum. From the foregoing equation, with the meter as the unit of length, $H = h + fS = 290 + 0.1527(1/12,000) = 290 + 0.152(12,000) = 2114$ m. This is the required elevation of $L$ above sea level.

# DETERMINING GROUND DISTANCE
# BY VERTICAL PHOTOGRAPH

Two points $A$ and $B$ are located on the ground at elevations of 250 and 190 m, respectively, above sea level. The images of $A$ and $B$ on a vertical aerial photograph are $a$ and $b$, respectively. After correction for film shrinkage and lens distortion, the coordinates of $a$ and $b$ in the photograph are $x_a = -73.91$ mm, $y_a = +44.78$ mm, $x_b = +84.30$ mm, and $y_b = -21.65$ mm, where the subscript identifies the point. The focal length is 209.6 mm, and the flying height is 2540 m above sea level. Determine the distance between $A$ and $B$ as measured along the ground.

## Calculation Procedure:

### 1. Determine the relationship between coordinates in the photograph and those in the datum plane

Refer to Fig. 29, and let $X$ and $Y$ denote coordinate axes that are vertically below the $x$ and $y$ axes, respectively, and in the datum plane. Omitting the subscript, we have $x/X = y/Y = oa/OA = S = f/(H - h)$, giving $X = x(H - h)/f$ and $Y = y(H - h)/f$.

### 2. Compute the coordinates of A and B in the datum plane

For $A$, $H - h = 2540 - 250 = 2290$ m. Substituting gives $X_A = (-0.07391)(2290)/0.2096 = -807.5$ m and $Y_A = (+0.04478)(2290)/0.2096 = +489.2$ m. For $B$, $H - h = 2540 - 190 = 2350$ m. Then $X_B = (+0.08430)(2350)/0.2096 = +945.2$ m, and $Y_B = (-0.02165)(2350)/0.2096 = -242.7$ m.

### 3. Compute the required distance

Let $\Delta X = X_A - X_B$, $\Delta Y = Y_A - Y_B$, and $AB =$ distance between $A$ and $B$ as measured along the ground. Disregarding the difference in elevation of the two points, we have $(AB)^2 = (\Delta X)^2 + (\Delta Y)^2$. Then $\Delta X = -1752.7$ m, $\Delta Y = 731.9$ m, and $(AB)^2 = (1752.7)^2 + (731.9)^2$, or $AB = 1899$ m.

# DETERMINING THE HEIGHT OF A
# STRUCTURE BY VERTICAL PHOTOGRAPH

In Fig. 30, points $A$ and $B$ are located at the top and bottom, respectively, and on the vertical centerline of a tower. These points have images $a$ and $b$, respectively, on a vertical aerial photograph having a scale of 1:10,800 with reference to the ground, which is approximately level. In the photograph, $oa = 76.61$ mm and $ob = 71.68$ mm. The focal length is 210.1 mm. Find the height of the tower.

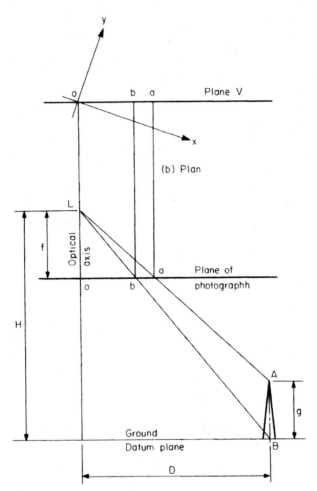

(b) Plan

(a) Elevation normal to vertical plane through
optical axis and center of tower (plane V)

**FIGURE 30**

**Calculation Procedure:**

**1. Compute the flying height with reference to the ground**
Take the ground as datum. Then scale $S = f/H$, or $H = f/S = 0.2101/(1/10,800) = 0.2101(10,800) = 2269$ m.

**2. Establish the relationship between height of tower and distances in the photograph**
Let $g$ = height of tower. In Fig. 30, $oa/D = f/(H - g)$ and $ob/D = f/H$. Thus, $oa/ob = (H - g)$. Solving gives $g = H(1 - ob/oa)$.

**3. Compute the height of tower**
Substituting in the foregoing equation yields $g = 2269(1 - 71.68/76.61) = 146$ m.

***Related Calculations.*** Let $A$ denote a point at an elevation $h$ above the datum, let $B$ denote a point that lies vertically below $A$ and in the datum plane, and let $a$ and $b$ denote the images of $A$ and $B$, respectively. As Fig. 30 shows, $a$ and $b$ lie on a straight line that passes through $o$, which is called a *radial line*. The distance $d = ba$ is the displacement of the image of $A$ resulting from its elevation above the datum, and it is termed the *relief displacement* of $A$. Thus, the relief displacement of a point is radially outward if that point lies above datum and radially inward if it lies below datum. From above, $ob/oa = (H - h)/H$, where $H$ = flying height above datum. Then $d = oa - ob = (oa)h/H$.

## DETERMINING GROUND DISTANCE BY TILTED PHOTOGRAPH

Two points $A$ and $B$ are located on the ground at elevations of 180 and 130 m, respectively, above sea level. Points $A$ and $B$ have images $a$ and $b$, respectively, on an aerial photograph, and the coordinates of the images are $x_a = +40.63$ mm, $y_a = -73.72$ mm, $x_b = -78.74$ mm, and $y_b = +20.32$ mm. The focal length is 153.6 mm, and the flying height is 2360 m above sea level. By use of ground control points, it was established that the photograph has a tilt of $2°54'$ and a swing of $162°$. Determine the distance between $A$ and $B$.

## Calculation Procedure:

### 1. Compute the transformed coordinates of the images
Refer to Fig. 31, where $L$ again denotes the front nodal point of the lens and $o$ denotes the principal point. A photograph is said to be *tilted*, or *near vertical*, if by inadvertence the optical axis of the lens is displaced slightly from the vertical at the time of exposure. The *tilt t* is the angle between the optical axis and the vertical. The *principal plane* is the vertical plane through the optical axis. Since the plane of the photograph is normal to the optical axis, it is normal to the principal plane. Therefore, Fig. 31*a* is an edge view of the plane of the photograph. Moreover, the angle between the plane of the photograph and the horizontal equals the tilt. In Fig. 31, $A$ is a point on the ground and $a$ is its image. Line $AQ$ is normal to the principal plane, $Q$ lies in that plane, and $q$ is the image of $Q$.

Consider the vertical line through $L$. The points $n$ and $N$ at which this line intersects the plane of the photograph and the ground are called the *nadir point* and *ground nadir point*, respectively. The line of intersection of the principal plane and the plane of the photograph, which is line *no* prolonged, is termed the *principal line*. Now consider the vertical plane through $o$ parallel to the line of flight. In the photograph, the $x$ axis is placed on the line at which this vertical plane intersects the plane of the photograph, with $x$ values increasing in the direction of flight. The $y$ axis is normal to the $x$ axis, and the origin lies at $o$. The *swing s* is the angle in the plane of the photograph, measured in a clockwise direction, between the positive side of the $y$ axis and the radial line extending from $o$ to $n$.

Transform the $x$ and $y$ axes in this manner: First, rotate the axes in a counterclockwise direction until the $y$ axis lies on the principal line with its positive side on the upward side of the photograph; then displace the origin from $o$ to $n$. Let $x'$ and $y'$ denote, respectively, the axes to which the $x$ and $y$ axes have been transformed. The $x'$ axis is horizontal. Let $\theta$ denote the angle through which the axes are rotated in the first step of the transformation. From Fig. 31*b*, $\theta = 180° - s$.

The transformed coordinates of a point in the plane of the photograph are $x' = x \cos \theta + y \sin \theta$; $y' = -x \sin \theta + y \cos \theta + f \tan t$. In this case, $t = 2°54'$ and $\theta = 180° - 162° = 18°$.

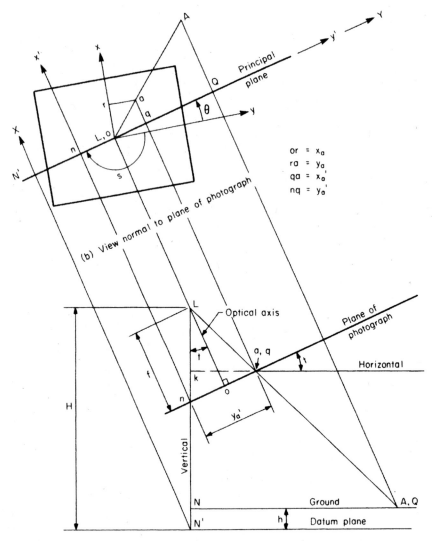

$$
\begin{aligned}
\text{or} &= x_a \\
\text{ra} &= y_a \\
\text{qa} &= x_a' \\
\text{nq} &= y_a'
\end{aligned}
$$

(b) View normal to plane of photograph

(a) Elevation normal to principal plane

**FIGURE 31**

Then $x_a' = +40.63 \cos 18° - 73.72 \sin 18° = +15.86$ mm; $y_a' = -(+40.63) \sin 18° + (-73.72) \cos 18° + 153.6 \tan 2°54' = -74.89$ mm. Similarly, $x_b' = -78.74 \cos 18° + 20.32 \sin 18° = -68.61$ mm; $y_b' = -(-78.74) \sin 18° + 20.32 \cos 18° + 153.6 \tan 2°54' = +51.44$ mm.

## 2. Write the equations of the datum-plane coordinates

Let $X$ and $Y$ denote coordinate axes that lie in the datum plane and in the same vertical planes as the $x'$ and $y'$ axes, respectively, as shown in Fig. 31. Draw the horizontal line $kq$

in the principal plane. Then $kq = \cos t$ and $Lk = f \sec t - y_1 \sin t$. From Fig. 31, $QA/qa = LQ/Lq$. From Fig. 31a, $LQ/Lq = LN/Lk = (H - h)/(f \sec t - y_1 \sin t)$. Setting $QA = X_A$, we have $qa = x_a{}'$, and omitting subscripts gives $X = x'(H - h)/(f \sec t - y' \sin t)$, Eq. a. From Fig. 31a, $NQ/kq = LN/Lk = (H - h)/(f \sec t - y_1 \sin t)$. Setting $NQ = Y_A$ and omitting subscripts, we get $Y = y'[(H - h)/(f \sec t - y_a{}' \sin t)] \cos t$, Eq. b.

### 3. Compute the datum-plane coordinates
First compute $f \sec t = 153.6 \sec 2°54' = 153.8$ mm. For $A$, $H - h = 2360 - 180 = 2180$ m, and $f \sec t - y' \sin t = 153.8 - (-74.89) \sin 2°54' = 157.6$ mm. Then $(H - h)/(f \sec t - y' \sin t) = 2180/0.1576 = 13,830$. By Eq. a, $X_A = (+0.01586)(13,830) = +219.3$ m. By Eq. b, $Y_A = (-0.07489)(13,830) \cos 2°54' = -1034.4$ m.

Similarly, for $B$, $H - h = 2360 - 130 = 2230$ m and $f \sec t - y' \sin t = 153.8 - 51.44 \sin 2°54' = 151.2$ mm. Then $(H - h)/(f \sec t - y' \sin t) = 2230/0.1512 = 14,750$. By Eq. a, $X_B = (-0.06861)(14,750) = -1012.0$ m. By Eq. b, $Y_B = (+0.05144)(14,750) \cos 2°54' = +757.8$ m.

### 4. Compute the required distance
Disregarding the difference in elevation of the two points and proceeding as in the second previous calculation procedure, we have $\Delta X = +219.3 - (-1012.0) = +1231.3$ m, and $\Delta Y = -1034.4 - 757.8 = -1792.2$ m. Then $(AB)^2 = (1231.3)^2 + (1792.2)^2$, or $AB = 2174$ m.

**Related Calculations.** The $X$ and $Y$ coordinates found in step 3 can be verified by assuming that these values are correct, calculating the corresponding $x'$ and $y'$ coordinates, and comparing the results with the values in step 2. The procedure is as follows. In Fig. 31a, let $v_A =$ angle $NLQ$. Then $\tan v_A = NQ/LN = Y_A/(H - h)$. Also, angle $oLq = v_A - t$. Now, $x_a'/X_A = Lq/LQ = f \sec (v_A - t)/[(H - h) \sec v_A]$. Rearranging and omitting subscripts, we get $x' = Xf \cos v_A/[(H - h) \cos (v_A - t)]$, Eq. c. Similarly, $y_a' = no + oq = f \tan t + f \tan (v_A - t)$. Omitting the subscript gives $y' = f[\tan t + f \tan (v_A - t)]$, Eq. d.

As an illustration, consider point $A$ in the present calculation procedure, which has the computed coordinates $X_A = +219.3$ m and $Y_A = -1034.4$ m. Then $\tan v_A = -1034.4/2180 = -0.4745$. Thus, $v_A = -25°23'$ and $v_A - t = -25°23' - 2°54' = -28°17'$. By Eq. c, $x' = (+219.3)(0.1536)(0.9035)/(2180)(0.8806) = +0.01585$ m $= +15.85$ mm. Applying Eq. d with $t = 2°54'$ gives $y' = 153.6(0.0507 - 0.5381) = -74.86$ mm. If we allow for round-off effects, these values agree with those in step 1.

The following equation, which contains the four coordinates $x'$, $y'$, $X$, and $Y$, can be applied to test these values for consistency:

$$\frac{f^2 + (y' - f \tan t)^2}{x'^2} = \frac{(H - h)^2 + Y^2}{X^2}$$

## DETERMINING ELEVATION OF A POINT BY OVERLAPPING VERTICAL PHOTOGRAPHS

Two overlapping vertical photographs contain point $P$ and a control point $C$ that lies 284 m above sea level. The air base is 768 m, and the focal length is 152.6 mm. The micrometer readings on a parallax bar are 15.41 mm for $P$ and 11.37 mm for $C$. By measuring the displacement of the initial principal point and obtaining its micrometer reading, it was established that the parallax of a point equals its micrometer reading plus 76.54 mm. Find the elevation of $P$.

## Calculation Procedure:

### 1. Establish the relationship between elevation and parallax

Two successive photographs are said to overlap if a certain amount of terrain appears in both. The ratio of the area that is common to the two photographs to the total area appearing in one photograph is called the *overlap*. (In practice, this value is usually about 60 percent.) The distance between two successive exposure stations is termed the *air base*. If a point on the ground appears in both photographs, its image undergoes a displacement from the first photograph to the second, and this displacement is known as the *parallax* of the point. This quantity is evaluated by using the micrometer of a *parallax bar* and then increasing or decreasing the micrometer reading by some constant.

Assume that there is no change in the direction of flight. As stated, the $x$ axis in the photograph is parallel to the line of flight, with $x$ values increasing in the direction of flight. Refer to Fig. 32, where photographs 1 and 2 are two successive photographs and the subscripts correspond to the photograph numbers. Let $A$ denote a point in the overlapping terrain, and let $a$ denote its image, with the proper subscript. Figure 32c discloses that $y_{1a} = y_{2a}$; thus, parallax occurs solely in the direction of flight. Let $p$ = parallax and $B$ = air base. Then $p = x_{1a} - x_{2a} = o_1m_1 - o_2m_2 = o_1m_1 + m_2o_2$. Thus, $m_1m_2 = B - p$. By proportion, $(B - p)/B = (H - h - f)/(H - h)$, giving $p/B = f/(H - h)$, or $p = Bf/(H - h)$, Eq. a. Thus, the parallax of a point is inversely proportional to the vertical projection of its distance from the front nodal point of the lens.

### 2. Determine the flying height

From the given data, $B$ = 768 m and $f$ = 152.6 mm. Take sea level as datum. For the control point, $h$ = 284 m and $p$ = 11.37 + 76.54 = 87.91 mm. From Eq. a, $H = h + Bf/p$, or $H = 284 + 768(0.1526)/0.08791 = 1617$ m.

### 3. Compute the elevation of P

For this point, $p$ = 15.41 + 76.54 = 91.95 mm. From Eq. a, $h = H - Bf/p$, or $h = 1617 - 768(0.1526)/0.09195 = 342$ m above sea level.

## DETERMINING AIR BASE OF OVERLAPPING VERTICAL PHOTOGRAPHS BY USE OF TWO CONTROL POINTS

The air base of two successive vertical photographs is to be found by using two control points, $R$ and $S$, that lie in the overlapping area. The images of $R$ and $S$ are $r$ and $s$, respectively. The following data were all obtained by measurement: The length of the straight line $RS$ is 2073 m. The parallax of $R$ is 92.03 mm, and that of $S$ is 91.85 mm. The coordinates of the images in the left photograph are $x_r = +86.46$ mm, $y_r = -54.32$ mm, $x_s = +29.41$ mm, and $y_s = +56.93$ mm. Compute the air base.

## Calculation Procedure:

### 1. Express the ground coordinates of the endpoints in terms of the air base

Refer to Fig. 32, and let $X$ and $Y$ denote coordinate axes that lie vertically below the $x_1$ and $y_1$ axes, respectively, and at the same elevation as $A$. Thus, $O_1$ is the origin of this system of coordinates. With reference to point $A$, by proportion, $X_A/x_{1a} = Y_A/y_{1a} = (H - h)/f$. From the previous calculation procedure, $(H - h)/f = B/p$. Omitting the subscript 1, we have

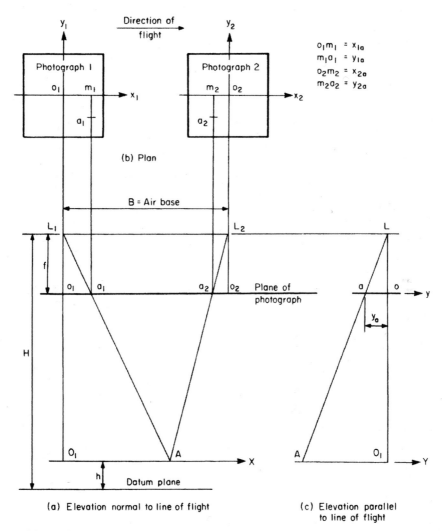

$$o_1m_1 = x_{1a}$$
$$m_1o_1 = y_{1a}$$
$$o_2m_2 = x_{2a}$$
$$m_2a_2 = y_{2a}$$

(b) Plan

B = Air base

Plane of photograph

(a) Elevation normal to line of flight

(c) Elevation parallel to line of flight

**FIGURE 32**

$X_A = (x_a/p)B$ and $Y_A = (y_a/p)B$. Then $X_R = (+86.46/92.03)B = +0.9395B$; $Y_R = (-54.32/92.03)B = -0.5902B$; $X_S = (+29.41/91.85)B = +0.3202B$; $Y_S = (+56.93/91.85)B = +0.6198B$.

## 2. Express the distance between the control points in terms of the air base; solve the resulting equation

Disregarding the difference in elevation of the two points, we have $(RS)^2 = (X_R - X_S)^2 + (Y_R - Y_S)^2$. Now, $X_R - X_S = +0.6193B$ and $Y_R - Y_S = -1.2100B$. Then $2073^2 = [(0.6193)^2 + (1.2100)^2]B^2$, or $B = 1525$ m.

## DETERMINING SCALE OF
## OBLIQUE PHOTOGRAPH

In a high-oblique aerial photograph, the distance between the apparent horizon and the principal point as measured along the principal line is 86.85 mm. The flying height is 2925 m above sea level, and the focal length is 152.7 mm. What is the scale of this photograph along a line that is normal to the principal line and at a distance of 20 mm above the principal point as measured along the principal line?

### Calculation Procedure:

### 1. Locate the true horizon in the photograph

Refer to Fig. 33. An *oblique* aerial photograph is one that is taken with the optical axis intentionally displaced from the vertical, and a *high-oblique* photograph is one in which this displacement is sufficiently large to bring the earth's surface into view. By definition, the principal plane is the vertical plane that contains the optical axis, and the principal line is the line of intersection of this vertical plane and the plane of the photograph.

Assume that the terrain is truly level. The *apparent horizon* is the slightly curved boundary line in the photograph between earth and sky. Consider a conical surface that has its vertex at the front nodal point $L$ and that is tangent to the spherical surface of the earth. If atmospheric refraction were absent, the apparent horizon would be the arc along which this conical surface intersected the plane of the photograph. The *true horizon* is the straight line along which the horizontal plane through $L$ intersects the plane of the photograph; it is normal to the principal line. In Fig. 33, $M_1$ and $M_2$ are lines in the principal plane that pass through $L$; line $M_1$ is horizontal, and $M_2$ is tangent to the earth's surface. Points $K_1$ and $K_2$ are the points at which $M_1$ and $M_2$, respectively, intersect the plane of the photograph; these points lie on the principal line. Point $K_1$ lies on the true horizon; if atmospheric refraction is tentatively disregarded, $K_2$ lies on the apparent horizon.

Refer to Fig. 34a. The principal plane contains the *angle of dip d*, which is angle $K_2LK_1$ the *apparent depression angle* $\alpha$, which is angle $oLK_2$ the (true) *depression angle* $\theta$,

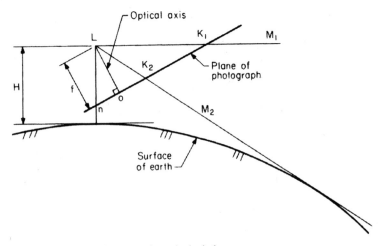

**FIGURE 33.** Elevation normal to principal plane.

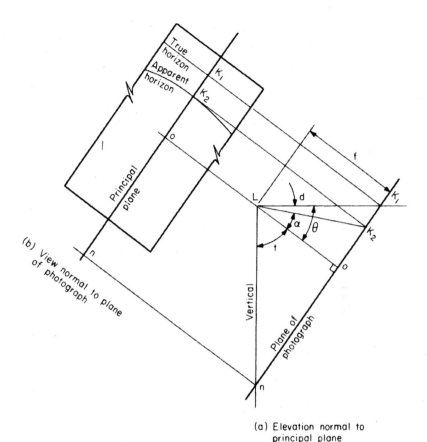

(a) Elevation normal to
principal plane

**FIGURE 34**

which is angle $oLK_1$. Then $\theta = d + a$. Let $H =$ flying height above sea level in meters, and $d' =$ angle of dip in minutes. Then $d' = 1.775\ 2\ H$, Eq. $a$. This relationship is based on the mean radius of the earth, and it includes allowance for atmospheric refraction. From Fig. 34a, $\tan \alpha = oK_2/f$, Eq. $b$. Then $d' = 1.775\ 2\ 2925 = 96.0'$, or $d = 1°36'$. Also, $\tan \alpha = 86.85/152.7 = 0.5688$, giving $\alpha = 29°38'$. Thus, $\theta = 1°36' + 29°38' = 31°14'$. From Fig. 34a, $oK_1 = f \tan \theta$, or $oK_1 = 152.7(0.6064) = 92.60$ mm. This dimension serves to establish the true horizon.

## 2. Write the equation for the scale of a constant-scale line

Since the optical axis is inclined, the scale $S$ of the photograph is constant only along a line that is normal to the principal line, and so such a line is called a constant-scale line. As we shall find, every constant-scale line has a unique value of $S$.

Refer to Fig. 35, where $A$ is a point on the ground and $a$ is its image. Line $AQ$ is normal to the principal plane, $Q$ lies in that plane, and $q$ is the image of $Q$. Line $Rq$ is a horizontal line in the principal plane. If the terrain is truly level and curvature of the earth may be disregarded, the vertical projection of the distance from $A$ to $L$ is $H$. Let $e =$ distance in photograph from true horizon to line $qa$. Along this line, $S = qa/QA = Lq/LQ = LR/LN$. But $LR = e \cos \theta$ and $LN = H$. Thus, $S = (e \cos \theta)/H$, Eq. $c$.

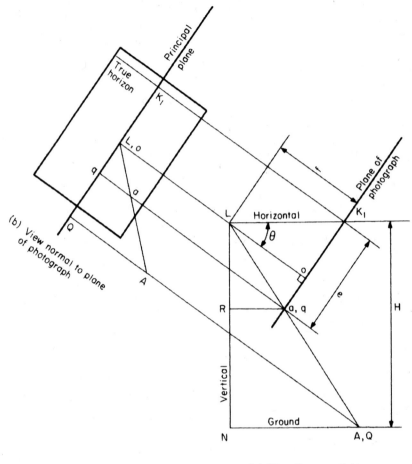

(a) Elevation normal to
principal plane

**FIGURE 35**

### 3. *Compute the scale along the specified constant-scale line*

From above, $\theta = 31°14'$ and $oK_1 = 92.60$ mm. Then $e = 92.60 - 20 = 72.60$ mm. By
Eq. *c*, $S = (0.07260)(0.8551)/2925 = 1/47,120$.

# Design of Highway Bridges

Where a bridge is supported by steel trusses, the stresses in the truss members are determined by applying the rules formulated in the truss calculation procedures given earlier in
this handbook.

The following procedures show the design of a highway bridge supported by concrete or steel girders. Except for the deviations indicated, the *Standard Specifications for Highway Bridges,* published by the American Association of State Highway and Transportation Officials (AASHTO), are applied.

The AASHTO *Specification* recognizes two forms of truck loading: the *H* loading, and the HS loading. Both are illustrated in the *Specification.* For a bridge of relatively long span, it is necessary to consider the possibility that several trucks will be present simultaneously. To approximate this condition, the AASHTO *Specification* offers various lane loadings, and it requires that the bridge be designed for the lane loading if this yields greater bending moments and shears than does the corresponding truck loading.

In designing the bridge members, it is necessary to modify the wheel loads to allow for the effects of dynamic loading and the lateral distribution of loads resulting from the rigidity of the floor slab.

The basic notational system is: DF = factor for lateral distribution of wheel loads; IF = impact factor; $P$ = resultant of group of concentrated loads.

The term *live load* as used in the following material refers to the wheel load after correction for distribution but before correction for impact.

## DESIGN OF A T-BEAM BRIDGE

A highway bridge consisting of a concrete slab and concrete girders is to be designed for these conditions: loading, HS20-44; clear width, 28 ft (8.5 m); effective span, 54 ft (16.5 m); concrete strength, 3000 lb/sq.in. (20,685 kPa); reinforcement, intermediate grade. The slab and girders will be poured monolithically, and the slab will include a $3/4$ in. (19.05 mm) wearing surface. In addition, the design is to make an allowance of 15 lb/sq.ft. (718 N/m²) for future paving. Design the slab and the cross section of the interior girders.

### Calculation Procedure:

#### 1. Record the allowable stresses and modular ratio given in the AASHTO Specification
Refer to Fig. 36, which shows the spacing of the girders and the dimensions of the members. The sizes were obtained by a trial-and-error method. Values from the *Specification* are: $n = 10$ in stress calculations; $f_c = 0.4f_c' = 1200$ lb/sq.in. (8274 kPa); for beams with web reinforcement, $v_{max} = 0.075f_c' = 225$ lb/sq.in. (1551.4 kPa); $f_s = 20,000$ lb/sq.in. (137.9 MPa); $u = 0.10f_c' = 300$ lb/sq.in. (2068.5 kPa).

#### 2. Compute the design coefficients associated with balanced design
Thus, $k = 1200/(1200 + 2000) = 0.375$, using Eq. 21, Section 2. Using Eq. 22, Section 2, $j = 1 - 0.125 = 0.875$. By Eq. 32, Section 2, $K = \frac{1}{2}(1200)(0.375)(0.875) = 197$ lb/sq.in. (1358.3 kPa).

#### 3. Establish the wheel loads and critical spacing associated with the designated vehicular loading
As shown in the AASHTO *Specification,* the wheel-load system comprises two loads of 16 kips (71.2 kN) each and one load of 4 kips (17.8 kN). Since the girders are simply supported, an axle spacing of 14 ft (4.3 m) will induce the maximum shear and bending moment in these members.

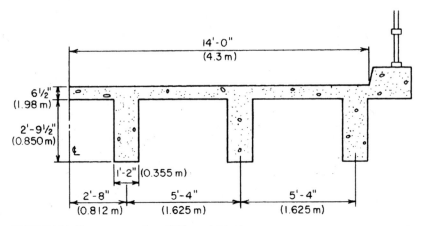

**FIGURE 36.**  Transverse section of T-beam bridge.


### 4.  Verify that the slab size is adequate and design the reinforcement

The AASHTO *Specification* does not present moment coefficients for the design of continuous members. The positive and negative reinforcement will be made identical, using straight bars for both. Apply a coefficient of $^1/_{10}$ in computing the dead-load moment. The *Specification* provides that the span length $S$ of a slab continuous over more than two supports be taken as the clear distance between supports.

In computing the effective depth, disregard the wearing surface, assume the use of No. 6 bars, and allow 1 in. (25.4 mm) for insulation, as required by AASHTO. Then, $d = 6.5 - 0.75 - 1.0 - 0.38 = 4.37$ in. (110.998 mm); $w_{DL} = (6.5/12)(150) + 15 = 96$ lb/lin ft (1401 N/m); $M_{DL} = (^1/_{10})w_{DL}S^2 = (^1/_{10})(96)(4.17)^2 = 167$ ft·lb (226 N·m); $M_{LL} = 0.8(S + 2)P_{20}/32$, by AASHTO, or $M_{LL} = 0.8(6.17)(16,000)/32 = 2467$ ft·lb (3345 N·m). Also by AASHTO, IF $= 0.30$; $M_{total} = 12(167 + 1.30 \times 2467) = 40,500$ in.·lb (4.6 kN·m). The moment corresponding to balanced design is $M_b = K_b bd^2 = 197(12)(4.37)^2 = 45,100$ in.·lb (5.1 kN·m). The concrete section is therefore excessive, but a 6-in. (152.4-mm) slab would be inadequate. The steel is stressed to capacity at design load. Or, $A_s = 40,500/(20,000 \times 0.875 \times 4.37) = 0.53$ sq.in. (3.4 cm²). Use No. 6 bars 10 in. (254 mm) on centers, top and bottom.

The transverse reinforcement resists the tension caused by thermal effects and by load distribution. By AASHTO, $A_t = 0.67(0.53) = 0.36$ sq.in. (2.3 cm²). Use five No. 5 bars in each panel, for which $A_t = 1.55/4.17 = 0.37$ sq.in. (2.4 cm²).

### 5.  Calculate the maximum live-load bending moment in the interior girder caused by the moving-load group

The method of positioning the loads to evaluate this moment is described in an earlier calculation procedure in this handbook. The resultant, Fig. 37, has this location: $d = [16(14) + 4(28)]/(16 + 16 + 4) = 9.33$ ft (2.85 m). Place the loads in the position shown in Fig. 38a. The maximum live-load bending moment occurs under the center load.

The AASHTO prescribes a distribution factor of $S/6$ in the present instance, where $S$ denotes the spacing of girders. However, a factor of $S/5$ will be applied here. Then DF $= 5.33/5 = 1.066$; $16 \times 1.066 = 17.06$ kips (75.9 kN); $4 \times 1.066 = 4.26$ kips (18.9 kN); $P = 2(17.06) + 4.26 = 38.38$ kips (170.7 kN); $R_L = 38.38(29.33)/54 = 20.85$ kips (92.7 kN). The maximum live-load moment is $M_{LL} = 20.85(29.34) - 17.06(14) = 372.8$ ft·kips (505 kN·m).

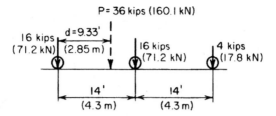

**FIGURE 37.** Load group and its resultant.

## 6. *Calculate the maximum live-load shear in the interior girder caused by the moving-load group*

Place the loads in the position shown in Fig. 38*b*. Do not apply lateral distribution to the load at the support. Then, $V_{LL} = 16 + 17.06(40/54) + 4.26(26/54) = 30.69$ kips (136.5 kN).

## 7. *Verify that the size of the girder is adequate and design the reinforcement*

Thus, $w_{DL} = 5.33(96) + 14(33.5/144)(150) = 1000$ lb/lin ft (14.6 kN/m); $V_{DL} = 27$ kips (120.1 kN); $M_{DL} = (^1/_8)(1)(54)^2 = 364.5$ ft·kips (494 kN·m). By AASHTO, IF $= 50/(54 + 125) = 0.28$; $V_{total} = 27 + 1.28(30.69) = 66.28$ kips (294.8 kN); $M_{total} = 12(364.5 + 1.28 \times 372.8) = 10,100$ in.·kips (1141 N·m).

In establishing the effective depth of the girder, assume that No. 4 stirrups will be supplied and that the main reinforcement will consist of three rows of No. 11 bars. AASHTO requires $1^1/_2$-in. (38.1-mm) insulation for the stirrups and a clear distance of 1 in. (25.4 mm) between rows of bars. However, 2 in. (50.8 mm) of insulation will be provided in this instance, and the center-to-center spacing of rows will be taken as 2.5 times the bar diameter. Then, $d = 5.75 + 33.5 - 2 - 0.5 - 1.375(0.5 + 2.5) = 32.62$ in. (828.548 mm);

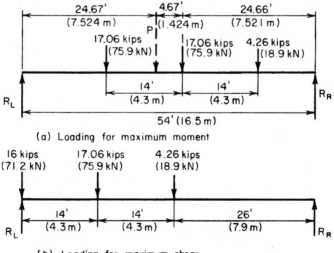

(a) Loading for maximum moment

(b) Loading for maximum shear

**FIGURE 38**

$v = V/b'jd = 66,280/(14 \times 0.875 \times 32.62) = 166 < 225$ lb/sq.in. (1144.6 < 1551.4 kPa). This is acceptable.

Compute the moment capacity of the girder at balanced design. Since the concrete is poured monolithically, the girder and slab function as a T beam. Refer to Fig. 16, Section 2 and its calculation procedure.

Thus, $k_b d = 0.375(32.62) = 12.23$ in. (310.642 mm); $12.23 - 5.75 = 6.48$ in. (164.592 mm). At balanced design, $f_{c1} = 1200(6.48/12.23) = 636$ lb/sq.in. (4835.2 kPa). The effective flange width of the T beam as governed by AASHTO is 64 in. (1625.6 mm); and $C_b = 5.75(64)(^1/_2)(1.200 + 0.636) = 338$ kips (1503 kN); $jd = 32.62 - (5.75/3)(1200 + 2 \times 636)/(1200 + 636) = 30.04$ in. (763.016 mm); $M_b = 338(30.04) = 10,150$ in.·kips (1146 kN·m). The concrete section is therefore slightly excessive, and the steel is stressed to capacity, or $A_s = 10,100/20(30.04) = 16.8$ sq.in. (108.4 cm²). Use 11 No. 11 bars, arranged in three rows.

AASHTO requires that the girders be tied together by diaphragms to obtain lateral rigidity of the structure.

## COMPOSITE STEEL-AND-CONCRETE BRIDGE

The bridge shown in cross section in Fig. 39 is to carry an HS20-44 loading on an effective span of 74 ft 6 in. (22.7 m). The structure will be unshored during construction. The concrete strength is 3000 lb/sq.in. (20,685 kPa), and the entire slab is considered structurally effective; the allowable bending stress in the steel is 18,000 lb/sq.in. (124.1 MPa). The dead load carried by the composite section is 250 lb/lin ft (3648 N/m). Preliminary design calculations indicate that the interior girder is to consist of W36 × 150 and a cover plate 10 × 1¹/₂ in. (254 × 38.1 mm) welded to the bottom flange. Determine whether the trial section is adequate and complete the design.

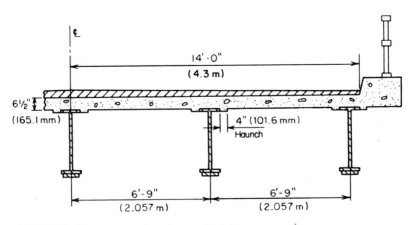

**FIGURE 39.** Transverse section of composite bridge.

## Calculation Procedure:

### 1. Record the relevant properties of the W36 × 150

The design of a composite bridge consisting of a concrete slab and steel girders is governed by specific articles in the AASHTO *Specification*.

Composite behavior of the steel and concrete is achieved by adequately bonding the materials to function as a flexural unit. Loads that are present before the concrete has hardened are supported by the steel member alone; loads that are applied after hardening are supported by the composite member. Thus, the steel alone supports the concrete slab, and the steel and concrete jointly support the wearing surface.

Plastic flow of the concrete under sustained load generates a transfer of compressive stress from the concrete to the steel. Consequently, the stresses in the composite member caused by dead load are analyzed by using a modular ratio three times the value that applies for transient loads.

If a wide-flange shape is used without a cover plate, the neutral axis of the composite section is substantially above the center of the steel, and the stress in the top steel fiber is therefore far below that in the bottom fiber. Use of a cover plate depresses the neutral axis, reduces the disparity between these stresses, and thereby results in a more economical section. Let $y'$ = distance from neutral axis of member to given point, in absolute value; $\bar{y}$ = distance from centroidal axis of WF shape to neutral axis of member. The subscripts $b$, $ts$, and $tc$ refer to the bottom of member, top of steel, and top of concrete, respectively. The superscripts $c$ and $n$ refer to the composite and noncomposite member, respectively.

The relevant properties of the W36 × 150 are $A$ = 44.16 sq.in. (284.920 cm$^2$); $I$ = 9012 in$^4$ (37.511 dm$^4$); $d$ = 35.84 in. (910.336 mm); $S$ = 503 in$^3$ (8244.2 cm$^3$); flange thickness = 1 in. (25.4 mm), approximately.

### 2. Compute the section moduli of the noncomposite section where the cover plate is present

To do this, compute the static moment and moment of inertia of the section with respect to the center of the W shape; record the results in Table 2. Refer to Fig. 40: $\bar{y}$ = − 280/59.16 = −4.73 in. (−120.142 mm); $y_b'$ = 19.42 − 4.73 = 14.69 in. (373.126 mm);

**TABLE 2.** Calculations for Girder with Cover Plate

|  | $A$ | $y$ | $Ay$ | $Ay^2$ | $I_o$ |
|---|---|---|---|---|---|
| Noncomposite: |  |  |  |  |  |
| W36 × 150 | 44.16 | 0 | 0 | 0 | 9,012 |
| Cover plate | 15.00 | −18.67 | −280 | 5,228 | 0 |
| Total | 59.16 | . . . | −280 | 5,228 | 9,012 |
| | | | | | |
| Composite, $n$ = 30: |  |  |  |  |  |
| Steel (total) | 59.16 |  | −280 | 5,228 | 9,012 |
| Slab | 16.90 | 21.17 | 358 | 7,574 | 60 |
| Total | 76.06 | . . . | 78 | 12,802 | 9,072 |
| | | | | | |
| Composite, $n$ = 10: |  |  |  |  |  |
| Steel (total) | 59.16 |  | −280 | 5,228 | 9,012 |
| Slab | 50.70 | 21.17 | 1,073 | 22,722 | 179 |
| Total | 109.86 | . . . | 793 | 27,950 | 9,191 |

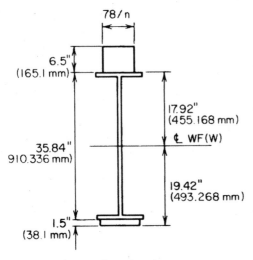

**FIGURE 40.** Transformed section.

$y'_{ts} = 17.92 + 4.73 = 22.65$ in. (575.31 mm). By the moment-of-inertia equation, $I = 5228 + 9012 - 59.16(4.73)^2 = 12,916$ in⁴ (53.76 dm⁴); $S_b = 879$ in³ (14,406.8 cm³); $S_{ts} = 570$ in³ (9342.3 cm³).

**3. Transform the composite section, with cover plate included, to an equivalent homogeneous section of steel; compute the section moduli**

In accordance with AASHTO, the effective flange width is $12(6.5) = 78$ in. (1981.2 mm). Using the method of an earlier calculation procedure, we see that when $n = 30$, $\bar{y} = 78/76.06 = 1.03$ in. (26.162 mm); $y'_b = 19.42 + 1.03 = 20.45$ in. (519.43 mm); $y'_{ts} = 17.92 - 1.03 = 16.89$ in. (429.006 mm); $y'_{tc} = 16.89 + 6.50 = 23.39$ in. (594.106 mm); $I = 12,802 + 9072 - 76.06(1.03)^2 = 21,793$ in⁴ (90.709 dm⁴); $S_b = 1066$ in³ (17,471.7 cm³); $S_{ts} = 1,290$ in³ (21,143.1 cm³); $S_{tc} = 932$ in³ (15,275.5 cm³).

When $n = 10$: $y = 7.22$ in. (183.388 mm); $y'_b = 26.64$ in. (676.66 mm); $y'_{ts} = 10.70$ in. (271.78 mm); $y'_{tc} = 17.20$ in. (436.88 mm); $I = 27,950 + 9191 - 109.86(7.22)^2 = 31,414$ in⁴ (130.7545 dm⁴); $S_b = 1179$ in³ (19,320.3 cm³); $S_{ts} = 2936$ in³ (48,121.0 cm³); $S_{tc} = 1826$ in³ (29,928.1 cm³).

**4. Transform the composite section, exclusive of the cover plate, to an equivalent homogeneous section of steel, and compute the values shown below**

Thus, when $n = 30$, $y'_b = 23.78$ in. (604.012 mm); $y'_{ts} = 12.06$ in. (306.324 mm); $I = 14,549$ in⁴ (60.557 dm⁴); $S_b = 612$ in³ (10,030.7 cm³). When $n = 10$, $y'_b = 29.23$ in. (742.442 mm); $y'_{ts} = 6.61$ in. (167.894 mm); $I = 19,779$ in⁴ (82.326 dm⁴); $S_b = 677$ in³ (11,096.0 cm³).

**5. Compute the dead load carried by the noncomposite member**

Thus,

|                                       | lb/lin ft      | N/m        |
|---------------------------------------|----------------|------------|
| Beam                                  | 150            | 2189.1     |
| Cover plate                           | 51             | 744.3      |
| Slab: 0.54(6.75)(150)                 | 547            | 7982.8     |
| Haunch: 0.67(0.083)(150)              | 8              | 116.8      |
| Diaphragms (approximate)              | 12             | 175.1      |
| Shear connectors (approximate)        | 6              | 87.6       |
| Total                                 | 774, say 780   | 11,383.2   |

### 6. Compute the maximum dead-load moments

Thus, $M_{DL}^c = (^1/8)(0.250)(74.5)^2(12) = 2080$ in.·kips (235.00 kN·m); $M_{DL}^n = (^1/8)$ $(0.780)(74.5)^2(12) = 6490$ in.·kips (733.24 kN·m).

### 7. Compute the maximum live-load moment, with impact included

In accordance with the AASHTO, the distribution factor is DF = 6.75/5.5 = 1.23; IF = 50/ (74.5 + 125) = 0.251, and 16(1.23)(1.251) = 24.62 kips (109.510 kN); 4(1.23)(1.251) = 6.15 kips (270.355 kN); $P_{LL+I}$ = 2(24.62) + 6.15 = 55.39 kips (246.375 kN). Refer to Fig. 38a as a guide. Then, $M_{LL+I}$ = 12[(55.39 × 39.58 × 39.58/74.5) − 24.62(14)] = 9840 in.·kips (1111.7 kN·m).

For convenience, the foregoing results are summarized here:

| | $M$, in·kips (kN·m) | $S_b$, in$^3$ (cm$^3$) | $S_{ts}$, in$^3$ (cm$^3$) | $S_{tc}$, in$^3$ (cm$^3$) |
|---|---|---|---|---|
| Noncomposite | 6,490 (733.2) | 879 (14,406.8) | 570 (9,342.3) | |
| Composite, dead loads | 2,080 (235.0) | 1,066 (17,471.7) | 1,290 (21,143.1) | 932 (15,275.5) |
| Composite, moving loads | 9,840 (1,111.7) | 1,179 (19,323.8) | 2,936 (48,121.0) | 1,826 (29,928.1) |

### 8. Compute the critical stresses in the member

To simplify the calculations, consider the sections of maximum live-load and dead-load stresses to be coincident. Then $f_b$ = 6490/879 + 2080/1066 + 9840/1179 = 17.68 kips/sq.in. (121.9 MPa); $f_{ts}$ = 6490/570 + 2080/1290 + 9840/2936 = 16.35 kips/sq.in. (112.7 MPa); $f_{tc}$ = 20807(30 × 932) + 98407(10 × 1826) = 0.61 kips/sq.in. (4.21 MPa). The section is therefore satisfactory.

### 9. Determine the theoretical length of cover plate

Let $K$ denote the theoretical cutoff point at the left end. Let $L_c$ = length of cover plate exclusive of the development length; $b$ = distance from left support to $K$; $m = L_c/L$; $d$ = distance from heavier exterior load to action line of resultant, as shown in Fig. 37; $r = 2d/L$.

From these definitions, $b (L − L_c)/2 = L(1 − m)/2$; $m = 1 − b/(0.5L)$. The maximum moment at $K$ due to live load and impact is

$$M_{LL+I} = \frac{(P_{LL+I}L)(1 − r + m − m^2)}{4} \tag{51}$$

The diagram of dead-load moment is a parabola having its summit at midspan.

To locate $K$, equate the bottom-fiber stress immediately to the left of $K$, where the cover plate is inoperative, to its allowable value. Or, $(P_{LL+I})/4 = 55.39(74.5)(12)/4 = 12,380$ in.·kips (1398.7 kN·m); $d$ = 9.33 ft (2.844 m); $r$ = 18.67/74.5 = 0.251; 6490(1 − $m^2$)/ 503 + 2080(1 − $m_2$)/612 + 12,380(0.749 + 0.251 in. − $m_2$)/677 = 18 kips/sq.in. (124.1 MPa); $m$ = 0.659; $L_c$ = 0.659(74.5) = 49.10 ft (14.97 m).

The plate must be extended toward each support and welded to the W shape to develop its strength.

### 10. Verify the result obtained in step 9

Thus, $b = ^1/2(74.5 − 49.10) = 12.70$ ft (3.871 m). At $K$: $M_{DL}^n = 12(^1/2 × 74.5 × 0.780 × 12.70 − ^1/2 × 0.780 × 12.70^2) = 3672$ in.·kips (414.86 kN·m); $M_{DL}^c$ = 3672(250/780) = 1177 in.·kips (132.98 kN·m). The maximum moment at $K$ due to the moving-load system occurs when the heavier exterior load lies directly at this section. Also $M_{LL+I} = 55.39(74.5 - 12.70 - 9.33)(12.70)(12)/74.5 = 5945$ in.·kips (671.7 kN·m); $f_b = 3672/503 + 1177/612 + 5945/677 = 18.0$ kips/sq.in. (124.11 MPa). This is acceptable.

## 11. Compute $V_{DL}$ and $V_{LL+I}$ at the support and at K

At the support $V_{DL}^c = \frac{1}{2}(0.250 \times 74.5) = 9.31$ kips (41.411 kN); IF = 0.251.

Consider that the load at the support is not subject to distribution. By applying the necessary correction, the following is obtained: $V_{LL+I} = 55.39(74.5 - 9.33)/74.5 - 16(1.251)(0.23) = 43.85$ kips (195.045 kN). At K: $V_{DL}^c = 9.31 - 12.70(0.250) = 6.13$ kips (27.266 kN); IF = 50/(61.8 + 125) = 0.268; $P_{LL+I} = 36(1.268)(1.23) = 56.15$ kips (249.755 kN); $V_{LL+I} = 56.15(74.5 - 12.70 - 9.33)/74.5 = 39.55$ kips (175.918 kN).

## 12. Select the shear connectors, and determine the allowable pitch p at the support and immediately to the right of K

Assume use of $3/4$-in. (19.1-mm) studs, 4 in. (101.6 mm) high, with four studs in each transverse row, as shown in Fig. 41. The capacity of a connector as established by AASHTO is

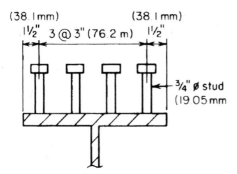

$110d^2(f_c')^{0.5} = 110 \times 0.75^2(3000)^{0.5} = 3390$ lb (15,078.7 N). The capacity of a row of connectors = 4(3390) = 13,560 lb (60,314.9 N).

The shear flow at the bottom of the slab is found by applying $q = VQ/I$, or $q_{DL}^c = 9310(16.90)(12.06 + 3.25)/14,549 = 166$ lb/lin in. (29,071.0 N/m); $q_{LL+I} = 43,850(50.70)(6.61 + 3.25)/19,779 = 1108$ lb/sq.in. (7639.7 kPa); $p = 13,560/(166 + 1108) = 10.6$ in. (269.24 mm).

Directly to the right of K: $q_{DL}^c = 6130(16.90)(16.89 + 3.25)/21,793 = 96$ lb/lin in. (16,812.2 N/m); $q_{LL+I} = 39,550(50.70)(10.70 + 3.25)/31,414 = 890$ lb/lin in. (155,862.9 N/m); $p = 13,560/(96 + 890) = 13.8$ in. (350.52 mm).

It is necessary to determine the allowable pitch at other sections and to devise a suitable spacing of connectors for the entire span.

**FIGURE 41.** Shear connectors.

## 13. Design the weld connecting the cover plate to the W shape

The calculations for shear flow are similar to those in step 12. The live-load deflection of an unshored girder is generally far below the limit imposed by AASHTO. However, where an investigation is warranted, the deflection at midspan may be calculated by assuming, for simplicity, that the position of loads for maximum deflection coincides with the position for maximum moment. The theorem of reciprocal deflections, presented in an earlier calculation procedure, may conveniently be applied in calculating this deflection. The girders are usually tied together by diaphragms at the ends and at third points to obtain lateral rigidity of the structure.

# Design Procedures for Complete Bridge Structures

## DESIGNING PRESTRESSED CONCRETE MEMBERS FOR A COMPLETE BRIDGE STRUCTURE

Show the steps to take in designing a prestressed concrete beam for a complete bridge structure. Give the equations to use, along with their nomenclature. Show the special steps to take for key steps in the design procedure for bridges.

### Calculation Procedure:

### 1. Compute the properties of the concrete cross section

Design of a prestressed concrete beam for an actual structure involves two steps: choice of the shape and dimensions of the concrete member and analysis of the member under the specified loading conditions to check unit stresses and determine the amount and details of the prestressing steel. Facility in the choice of a proper section will come with experience. In addition to having sufficient section modulus to carry the applied loads, the concrete cross section must be properly proportioned to provide room for the tensioning elements. Once the section has been chosen, the following method of analysis can be applied.

During the calculations it may become apparent that the concrete section chosen is not adequate or that it is larger than necessary. If it is not adequate, a new section must be designed and the calculations repeated. In some cases it will prove economical to use an oversize member even at low stresses because it can be fabricated in existing forms. When this is not the case, an effort should be made to select a section in which the working stresses are reasonably near those permitted by the specification.

If the cross section is not uniform for the full length of the beam it is usually best to analyze the section at the point of maximum moment and then check at any other points which might be critical because of the change in section. Properties to be computed are:

$A_c$ = area of entire concrete section (steel area not deducted)
$y_t$ = distance from top fiber to c.g.c. (center of gravity of entire concrete section)
$y_b$ = distance from bottom fiber to c.g.c.
$I_c$ = moment of inertia of entire concrete section about c.g.c.
$Z_t$ = section modulus of top fiber referred to c.g.c.
$Z_b$ = section modulus of bottom fiber referred to c.g.c.
$w_G$ = dead load of member per unit length

### 2. Compute the stresses in the member due to its own weight

$M_G$ = bending moment due to $w_G$
$f_G^t$ = stress in top fiber due to $M_G$
   $= M_G \div Z_t$
$f_G^b$ = stress in bottom fiber due to $M_G$
   $= M_G \div Z_b$

### 3. Compute stresses in the member due to applied loads

In most cases these will be made up of additional dead load such as roof deck or highway wearing surface and live load.

$w_S$ = additional dead load
$M_S$ = bending moment due to $w_S$
$f_S^t$ = stress in top fiber due to $M_S$
  $= M_S \div Z_t$
$f_S^b$ = stress in bottom fiber due to $M_S$
  $= M_S \div Z_b$
$w_L$ = distributed live load per unit length
$P_L$ = concentrated live load
$M_L$ = bending moment due to $w_L$ and/or $P_L$
$f_L^t$ = stress in top fiber due to $M_L$
  $= M_L \div Z_t$
$f_L^b$ = stress in bottom fiber due to $M_L$
  $= M_L \div Z_b$

### 4. Determine the magnitude and location of the prestressing force at the point of maximum moment

The prestressing force must meet two conditions:

1. It must provide sufficient compressive stress to offset the tensile stresses which will be caused by the bending moments.

2. It must not create stresses either tensile or compressive which are in excess of those permitted by the specification.

The stress in the concrete due to the prestressing force is a function of the magnitude of the force and also of its eccentricity $e$ with regard to the c.g.c.

Since we are considering a simple span beam, the moments due to the applied loads create compressive stresses in the top fiber and tensile stresses in the bottom fiber.

In order to meet the first condition, the prestressing force must create sufficient compressive stress in the bottom fiber to offset the tensile stresses from the bending moments. In other words $f_F^b$, stress in the bottom fiber due to the prestressing force $F$, must be equal in magnitude and of opposite sign to $f_G^b + f_S^b + f_L^b$. We can write

$$f_F^b = \frac{F}{A_c} + \frac{Fe}{Z_b}$$

Setting this value of $f_F^b$ equal in magnitude to and of opposite sign to the sum of the bending moment stresses, we get

$$\frac{F}{A_c} + \frac{Fe}{Z_b} = -f_G^b - f_S^b - f_L^b$$

Use of this equation will give zero stress in the bottom fiber under full design load. For some structures the specifications permit a small tensile stress $f_{tp}$ under design load conditions. In this case the magnitude of the compressive stress to be created by the prestressing force can be reduced by $f_{tp}$ as

$$\frac{F}{A_c} + \frac{Fe}{Z_b} = -f_G^b - f_S^b - f_L^b + f_{tp}$$

When no tensile stress is permitted, $f_{tp}$ equals zero.

In order to meet the second condition the prestressing force must not create excessive stresses in the top fiber. For most designs the prestressing force, because of its eccentricity, causes a tensile stress in the top fiber. Since the dead load is always acting and the compressive stress it causes helps to offset the tensile stress, the net stress in the top fiber is the stress caused by the prestressing force plus the stress caused by the dead-load bending moment. To keep the tensile stress in the top fiber within allowable limits we can write the following equation:

$$\frac{F}{A_c} - \frac{Fe}{Z_t} + f_G^t = f_{tp} \tag{52}$$

In this equation $F/A_c - Fe/Z_t$ represents the stress due to the prestressing force, $f_G^t$ is the stress due to dead-load bending moment, and $f_{tp}$ is the allowable tensile stress. This equation can be written

$$\frac{F}{A_c} - \frac{Fe}{Z_t} = -f_G^t + f_{tp} \tag{53}$$

In an actual design we would have numerical values from the calculations in Steps 1 to 3 for all factors in Eqs. (52) and (53) except $F$ and $e$. The solution of the two equations for the unknown quantities is quite simple. Multiply Eq. 53 by $Z_t/Z_b$ to get

$$\frac{Z_t}{Z_b}\frac{F}{A_c} - \frac{Fe}{Z_b} = \frac{Z_t}{Z_b}(f_G^t + f_{tp}) \tag{54}$$

Add Eq. 52 to Eq. 54. The terms $-Fe/Z_b$ and $Fe/Z_b$ cancel each other, giving

$$\left(1 + \frac{Z_t}{Z_b}\right)\frac{F}{A_c} = \frac{Z_t}{Z_b}(f_G^t + f_{tp}) - f_G^b - f_S^b - f_L^b + f_{tp} \tag{55}$$

In a specific design all the symbols in Eq. 55 except $F$ will have actual numerical values, so it can readily be solved for $F$.

The value of $e$ can be found by substituting the value of $F$ in Eq. 52 or (53). If $e$ is so large that the tendons would be below the bottom of the beam, see Step 5.

## 5. Select the tensioning elements to be used and their location in the member

Frequently $e$ will be so large that it refers to a point below the bottom of the member or so close to the bottom that the tendons cannot be satisfactorily located. There are two remedies for this situation.

If the member being considered is symmetrical (one in which the section modulus of the top equals the section modulus of the bottom) and has stresses near the maximum allowed, a new section should be chosen. The new section should have more concrete in the top than in the bottom, thus raising the c.g.c. above the middle of its height, but the section modulus of the bottom should not be less than that in the previous section.

For unsymmetrical sections in which the section modulus of the top is greater than that of the bottom or for symmetrical sections operating at low stresses, the value of $e$ can be arbitrarily reduced until the tendons are far enough above the bottom of the member to permit satisfactory details. Changing the value of $e$ will also change $F$. The new $F$ should be found by substituting all known values including $e$ in Eq. (52) and solving for $F$.

Decreasing $e$ and increasing $F$ will create a compressive stress in the top fiber. This can be computed by solving

$$f_F^t = \frac{F}{A_c} - \frac{Fe}{Z_t} \tag{56}$$

Check the maximum stress in the top fiber by adding

$$f_F^t + f_G^t + f_S^t + f_L^t$$

## 6. Establish the concrete strength at the time of prestressing and check the stresses under the initial prestress condition

The specifications permit higher unit stress in relation to $f'_{ci}$ under this condition than with relation to $f'_c$ under the final condition, so it is not always a governing factor but it must be checked.

## 7. Establish the path of the tendons; check critical points along the member under initial and final conditions

All the preceding calculations have been concerned with the point of maximum moment. In some members other points may also be critical. These can usually be located by inspection of the moment diagrams, member properties, and location of prestressing steel.

There are two combinations of conditions that should be checked for maximum stress.

1. Final prestress plus full design load

2. Initial prestress plus dead load only. (It is seldom necessary to check prestress alone without the benefit of dead load. As the prestressing force is applied, it creates a negative moment and the member develops a camber, which raises the center portion off the form. Since the member is resting on each end, its dead-weight bending moment is effective.)

## 8. Check the ultimate strength to make sure it meets the requirements of the design specifications

There is no constant ratio between the design strength and the ultimate strength of a prestressed concrete member as there is in structural steel. Two prestressed concrete members of different cross section can have exactly the same load-carrying capacity based on allowable design stresses yet have entirely different ultimate strengths.

If too much prestressing steel is used, failure of the member will occur by crushing of the concrete. This is not desirable because there is no warning of impending failure and the failure is of the explosive type.

## 9. Design the shear steel

Although an analysis of shear and diagonal tension by Mohr's circle method is sometimes used, experience indicates that the most satisfactory results are obtained by using an empirical formula based on test data.

## 10. Compute the camber

Use the standard formulas for deflection of elastic members such as would be applied to a structural steel member. Compute camber at time of prestressing and also for long-time loading. For normal designs, satisfactory accuracy is obtained by using the $I$ of the concrete cross section. Effect of holes for tendons and prestressing steel can be ignored.

## Notations Used in Design Procedures for Complete Structures

The following notations are used in the calculation procedures for the design of complete structures.

Cross-sectional constants:

$A_c$ = area of entire concrete section (steel area not deducted)
c.g.c. = center of gravity of entire concrete section
c.g.s. = center of gravity of steel area
$y_b$ = distance from bottom fiber to c.g.c.
$y_t$ = distance from top fiber to c.g.c.
$e$ = eccentricity of c.g.s. with respect to c.g.c.
$I_c$ = moment of inertia of entire concrete section about c.g.c.
$Z_b$ = section modulus of bottom fiber referred to c.g.c.
$Z_t$ = section modulus of top fiber referred to c.g.c.

Loads, moments, and forces:

$w_G$ = dead weight per unit length of prestressed member itself
$w_S$ = additional dead load per unit length
$w_D$ = total dead load per unit length = $w_G + w_S$
$w_T$ = uniform load per unit length due to parabolic path of tendons
$w_L$ = live load per unit length
$P_L$ = concentrated live load
$M_G$ = bending moment due to $w_G$
$M_S$ = bending moment due to $w_S$
$M_D$ = bending moment due to $w_D$
$M_L$ = bending moment due to $w_L$ and/or $P_L$
$M_e$ = bending moment due to eccentricity of prestress force
$M_u$ = bending moment under ultimate load condition
$V_L$ = live-load shear
$\quad V_u$ = ultimate load shear
$F$ = effective prestress force after deduction of all losses
$F_I$ = initial prestress force
$F_o$ = prestress force after release of tendons from external anchors (applicable to pretensioned members)
$F_A$ = arbitrarily assumed final tension

Concrete stresses:

$f_F^b, f_F^t$ = stress in bottom (top) fiber due to $F$

$f_{F_I}^b, f_{F_I}^t$ = stress in bottom (top) fiber due to $F_I$

$f_{F_o}^b, f_{F_o}^t$ = stress in bottom (top) fiber due to $F_o$

$f_G^b, f_G^t$ = stress in bottom (top) fiber due to $w_G$

$f_S^b, f_S^t$ = stress in bottom (top) fiber due to $w_S$

$f_D^b, f_D^t$ = stress in bottom (top) fiber due to $w_D$

$f_L^b, f_L^t$ = stress in bottom (top) fiber due to $w_L$ and/or $P_L$

$f_T^b, f_T^t$ = stress in bottom (top) fiber due to $w_T$

$f_{tp}$ = permissible tensile stress

$f^t$, $f^s$, $f^{ts}$ = Applicable to composite sections with different strengths of concrete

$f_{F_A}^b$, $f_{F_A}^t$ = stress in bottom (top) fiber due to $F_A$

Deflection or camber:

$\Delta_{F_I}$ = deflection due to $F_I$

$\Delta_{F_o}$ = deflection due to $F_o$

$\Delta_F$ = deflection due to $F$

$\Delta_G$ = deflection due to $w_G$

$\Delta_S$ = deflection due to $w_S$

$\Delta_D$ = deflection due to $w_D$

$\Delta_L$ = deflection due to $w_L$ and/or $P_L$

Summation of stress, camber, etc.:
The summation of two or more stresses can be written in two ways thus:

$f_F^b + f_G^b + f_L^b$ can also be written $f_{F+G+L}^b$.

$\Delta_F + \Delta_G + \Delta_L$ can also be written $\Delta_{F+G+L}$.

Steel stresses:

$f_{F_I}$ = stress in tendons due to $F_I$

$f_{F_o}$ = stress in tendons due to $F_O$

$f_F$ = stress in tendons due to $F$

This procedure is the work of H. Kent Preston, P.E., whose affiliations, at the time of its preparation, were: Engineer, Construction Materials, John A. Roebling's Sons Division; The Colorado Fuel and Iron Corporation; Fellow, American Society of Civil Engineers; Professional Member, Prestressed Concrete Institute. SI values were added by the handbook editor.

## DESIGN OF A PRESTRESSED CONCRETE BRIDGE GIRDER

Design a prestressed concrete bridge girder having an 80-ft (27.8-m) span; live load = AASHTO-H20-S16; girders spaced 3.5 ft (1.06 m) center-to-center. The girders are spaced to provide normal transverse distribution of load. Girder wearing surface = 2 in. (50.8 mm) of asphalt at 20 psf (97.6 kg/m²); initial tension on tendons = 175,000 psi. (1206 MPa); stress loss = 35,000 psi (241 MPa). As a start in the design, try the girder cross section shown in Fig. 42, with f'$_c$ = 5,000 psi. (34 MPa); f'$_{ci}$ = 4000 psi (27.5 MPa). The symbols used in this, and the following prestressed concrete calculation procedures, are shown in the generalized procedure that precedes this one.

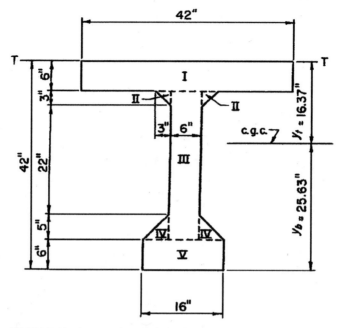

**FIGURE 42.** Cross section of girder.

## Calculation Procedure:

### 1. *Compute the properties of the concrete cross section in Fig. 42*

Find the moment of inertia $I_T$ about the top surface by taking moments about line *T-T*.

| Section | Area, $A$ | $y$ | $Ay$ | $Ay^2$ | $I_o$ |
|---|---|---|---|---|---|
| I $= 42 \times 6$ | $= 252$ | 3 | 756 | 2,268 | 756 |
| II $= 2 \times 3 \times 3 \times \frac{1}{2}$ | $= 9$ | 7 | 63 | 441 | 4 |
| III $= 6 \times 30$ | $= 180$ | 21 | 3,780 | 79,380 | 13,500 |
| IV $= 2 \times 5 \times 5 \times \frac{1}{2}$ | $= 25$ | 34.3 | 858 | 29,455 | 35 |
| V $= 16 \times 6$ | $= 96$ | 39 | 3,744 | 146,016 | 288 |
| Total | 562 | | 9,201 | 257,560 | 14,583 |
| | | | | 14,583 | |
| | | | | $I_T = 272,143$ | |

$y_t = 9201 \div 562 = 16.37$ in. (415.8 mm)
$y_b = 42.00 - 16.37 = 25.63$ in. (651 mm)
$I_c = 272,143 - 562(16.37^2) = 121,540$
$Z_t = 121,540 \div 16.37 = 7424$
$Z_b = 121,540 \div 25.63 = 4742$

Assume that the section is made of regular-weight concrete at 150 lb/ft³ (2400 kg/m³). Then

$$w_G = {}^{150}/_{144} \times 562 = 585 \text{ lb per ft (870.5 kg/m)}$$

## 2. Compute the stresses in girder at the center of the span due to its own dead weight

$$M_G = \frac{585(80^2) \times 12}{8} = 5{,}616{,}000 \text{ in·lb (634.0 kNm)}$$

$$f_G^t = 5{,}616{,}000 \div 7424 = +757 \text{ psi (compression) } (+5.22 \text{ MPa})$$

$$f_G^b = 5{,}616{,}000 \div 4742 = -1{,}184 \text{ psi (tension) } (-8.16 \text{ MPa})$$

## 3. Compute the stresses in the girder at center of the span due to applied loads

The only dead load besides the girder itself is the wearing surface at 20 psf (97.6 kg/m²) over the entire 3¹/₂-ft (1.07-m) width of the girder.

$$w_S = 20 \times 3.5 = 70 \text{ lb/lin ft (104.2 kg/m)}$$

$$M_S = \frac{70(80^2) \times 12}{8} = 672{,}000 \text{ in·lb (87.2 kNm)}$$

$$f_S^t = 672{,}000 \div 7424 = +91 \text{ psi } (+627 \text{ kPa})$$

$$f_S^b = 672{,}000 \div 4742 = -142 \text{ psi } (-978 \text{ kPa})$$

From AASHTO tables the live-load bending moment per lane is 1,164,900 ft·lb (1578.4 kNm). From AASHTO specification:

> Impact = 50/(80 + 125) = 24.4%
> Wheel load per stringer = 3.5 ÷ 5 = 0.70
> Wheel load = one-half lane load from which the net live-load moment per stringer is

$$M_L = 1{,}164{,}900 \times 1.244 \times .70 \times {}^{1}/_{2} \times 12 = 6{,}086{,}000 \text{ in·lb (687.6 kNm)}$$

$$f_L^t = 6{,}086{,}000 \div 7424 = +820 \text{ psi } (+5.65 \text{ MPa})$$

$$f_L^b = 6{,}086{,}000 \div 4742 = -1{,}283 \text{ psi } (-8.84 \text{ MPa})$$

## 4. Determine the magnitude and location of the prestressing force at the center of the span

This computation is based on final conditions, that is, after all stress losses have taken place.

For simplicity in this first example we shall assume the following limits on final stresses in the concrete:

Maximum compressive stress = $0.40 f_c' = 0.40 \times 5000 = 2000$ psi (13.8 MPa)
Maximum tensile stress = zero = $f_{tp}$

$$\frac{F}{A_c} + \frac{Fe}{Z_b} = -f_G^b - f_S^b - f_L^b + f_{tp} \tag{57}$$

Substitute in Eq. 57 all the known values from calculations in Steps 1, 2, and 3 to get

$$\frac{F}{562} + \frac{Fe}{4742} = 1184 + 142 + 1283 + 0$$

which reduces to

$$\frac{F}{562} + \frac{Fe}{4742} = +2609 \tag{58}$$

From this we see that the compressive stress created by prestressing will be 2609 psi (17.9 MPa) but the specification limits us to a maximum stress in the concrete of 2000 psi (13.8 MPa). At the center of the span the maximum stress will be the algebraic sum of the prestressing stress and the dead-load stress, or

$$2609 - 1184 = +1425 \text{ psi (9.8 MPa)}$$

which is within allowable limits. In Step 7 we shall find that the tendons must be curved up to keep the net stress within the required limits near the ends of the span where the dead-load stresses are small.

Equation (59)

$$\frac{F}{A_c} - \frac{Fe}{Z_t} = -f_G^t + f_{tp} \tag{59}$$

Substituting known values we get

$$\frac{F}{562} - \frac{Fe}{7424} = -757 + 0 \tag{60}$$

Multiplying Eq. 60 by $Z_t/Z_b = 7424/4742 = 1.56$, we get

$$\frac{1.56F}{562} - \frac{Fe}{4742} = -1180 \tag{61}$$

Adding,

$$\frac{2.56F}{562} = 1429$$

from which

$$F = 313{,}000 \text{ lb (141,977 kg)}$$

Substituting this value of $F$ in (58),

$$\frac{313,000}{562} + \frac{313,000e}{4742} = 2609$$

$$558 + 66.1e = 2609$$

$$e = 31.00 \text{ in. (787.4 mm)}$$

Since $y_b$ is only 25.63 in. (651 mm), this value of $e$ would put the tendons below the bottom of the girder.

## 5. Select the tensioning elements to be used and determine their location in the member

Choose a reasonable value for $e$ when the solution of the equations gives an $e$ too large to suit the dimensions of the girder. Try $e = 17.25$ in. (438.2 mm). Then the c.g.s. (center of gravity of the tendons) will be $25.63 - 17.25 = 8.38$ in. (218.9 mm) above the bottom of the girder, which should provide room for the tendons needed.

To find $F$ substitute in Eq. 58

$$\frac{F}{562} + \frac{17.25F}{4742} = 2609$$

Multiply by 562.

$$F + 2.04F = 1,466,000$$

$$F = 482,000 \text{ lb (218,828 kg)}$$

We shall assume that we have selected a group of tendons which have $F = 483,840$ lb (219,663 kg) and a c.g.s. that is 7.62 in. (193.5 mm) above the bottom of the girder. Then

$$e = 25.63 - 7.62 = 18.01 \text{ in. (457.5 mm)}$$

From

$$f_F^t = \frac{F}{A_c} - \frac{Fe}{Z_t} \tag{62}$$

Substituting known values,

$$f_F^t = \frac{483,840}{562} - \frac{483,840 \times 18.01}{7424}$$

$$f_F^t = 861 - 1174 = -313 \text{ psi } (-2.2 \text{ MPa})$$

Net stress in the top fiber under prestress plus dead load only is

$$f_F^t + f_G^t = -313 + 757 = +444 \text{ psi } (+3.06 \text{ MPa})$$

Net stress in the top fiber under all applied loads is

$$f_F^t + f_G^t + f_S^t + f_L^t = -313 + 757 + 91 + 820 = +1355$$

From this we see that the stress in the top fiber at the center of span will vary from +444 psi. (+3.06 MPa) under prestress plus dead load to +1,355 psi. (9.3 MPa) under prestress plus all applied loads. These stresses are within the specified limits of zero to + 2,000 psi. (13.8 MPa).

The stress in the bottom fiber due to prestress is

$$f_F^b = \frac{F}{A_c} + \frac{Fe}{Z_b} = \frac{483,840}{562} + \frac{483,840 \times 18.01}{4742} = +2699$$

Net stress in the bottom fiber under prestress plus dead load only is

$$f_F^b + f_G^b = +2699 - 1184 = +1515 \text{ psi } (+10.4 \text{ MPa})$$

Net stress in the bottom fiber under all applied loads is

$$f_F^b + f_G^b + f_S^b + f_L^b = +2699 - 1184 - 142 - 1283 = +90 \text{ psi } (+0.6 \text{ MPa})$$

From this we see that the stress in the bottom fiber at the center of span will vary from +1515 psi (10.4 MPa) under prestress plus dead load to +90 psi (0.6 MPa) under all applied loads. These stresses are within the specified limits of zero to +2000 psi (13.8 MPa).

Since both the top and bottom fiber stresses at the center of span are within the specified limits for all design bending moment conditions, the concrete cross section and tendons selected are satisfactory and it is probable that conditions at other points along the span can be met satisfactorily.

At this point we should review the results of our calculations and consider the economy of the member chosen. Under the extreme conditions of design load, the maximum stress in the top fiber is +1355 psi (9.3 MPa) and in the bottom fiber it is +1515 psi (10.4 MPa) yet the specification permits +2000 psi (13.8 MPa). Study Fig. 42 to see how we can save some concrete. The simplest method would be to leave the depth unchanged, making the top slab thinner and the bottom flange narrower. This would reduce the section modulus, increase the stresses to near the maximum allowed, and have little or no effect on the number of tendons, since the general shape and depth of the girder are not changed. The saving would be represented by the concrete saved and the smaller dead weight to be carried by the piers.

In this particular case we cannot follow the simplest method because of the details of the structure. The 6-in. (152.4-mm) top slab is needed to carry the concentrated loads of truck wheels, and the area of the bottom flange is needed for the placement of the tendons. The only remaining course is to reduce the depth of the girder. This is seldom economical because the only concrete saved is a small amount equal to the thickness of the web times the reduction in depth, and this is offset by the fact that a reduction in depth requires an increase in the prestressing force. Under the existing circumstances the only reason for changing the section chosen would be one external to the structure. For instance, it might pay to reduce the depth because clearance is a problem and a reduction in depth of girder would reduce the amount of fill in the approaches to the bridge.

For the purposes of this example we shall continue with the section shown in Fig. 42.

## 6. Establish the concrete strength, $f'_{ci}$, at the time of prestressing and check the stresses under the initial prestress condition

At the beginning of this example it was stated that $f'_{ci} = +4000$ psi (27.5 MPa). For a bridge the specification would set concrete stresses under initial tension at

Maximum compressive stress $= 0.60\ f'_{ci} = 0.60 \times 4000 = 2400$ psi (16.5 MPa)
Maximum tensile stress $= 3\sqrt{f'_{ci}} = 3\sqrt{4000} = -190$ psi (1,309.8 kPa)

The initial tension in the tendons was set at 175,000 psi (1206 MPa) and stress losses at 35,000 psi (241.3 MPa). From this the final tension will be $175,000 - 35,000 = 140,000$ psi. (965.2 MPa). The initial prestressing force $F_I$ can now be found in terms of the final prestressing force $F$.

$$F_I = F\,\frac{175,000}{140,000} = 1.25F \tag{63}$$

$$= 1.25 \times 483,840 = 604,800\ \text{lb (4169.5MPa)}$$

The stress in the top fiber due to the initial prestressing force $F_I$ can be found by using Eq. 62 and substituting $F_I$ for $F$.

$$f^t_{F_I} = \frac{F_I}{A_c} - \frac{F_I e}{Z_t}$$

Substituting,

$$f^t_{F_I} = \frac{604,800}{562} - \frac{604,800 \times 18.01}{7424}$$

$$= 1076 - 1467 = -391$$

Note that $F_I = 1.25F$ and $f^t_{F_I} = 1.25f^t_F$. The ratio between the stress due to $F$ and the stress in the same location due to $F_I$ is the same as the ratio between $F$ and $F_I$. This relationship can be applied to simplify the calculation of the stresses due to $F_I$ when the stresses due to $F$ are known. Thus in this example

$$f^t_{F_I} = 1.25f^t_F = 1.25(-313) = -391\ \text{psi} \ (-2695.6\ \text{kPa})$$

In the same manner

$$f^b_{F_I} = 1.25f^b_F = 1.25(+2699) = +3375\ \text{psi} \ (23.3\ \text{MPa})$$

Under initial prestress plus dead load

$$F^t_{F_I} = f^t_G = -391 + 757 = +366\ \text{psi} \ (2523\ \text{kPa})$$
$$f^b_{F_I} + f^b_G = +3375 - 1184 = +2191\ \text{psi} \ (15.1\ \text{MPa})$$

Under initial prestress plus all applied loads

$$f_{F_I}^t + f_G^t + f_S^t + f_L^t = -391 + 757 + 91 + 820 = +1277 \, \text{psi} \, (8.8 \, \text{MPa})$$
$$f_{F_I}^b + f_G^b + f_S^b + f_L^b = +3375 - 1184 - 142 - 1283 = +766 \, \text{psi} \, (5.28 \, \text{MPa})$$

From this we see that all the stresses under the condition of initial prestress are within the allowable stresses for that condition.

In a post-tensioned member, the tension in the tendons at the completion of the prestressing operation is $F_I$. There have been no stress losses.

In a pretensioned member the tension in the tendons after their load has been transferred from the anchorages to the concrete members is $F_o$. $F_o$ is less than $F_I$ by the amount of certain stress losses that take place as the load in the tendons is transferred.

## 7. Establish the path of the tendons and check any critical points along the member under initial and final conditions

The foregoing calculations show that the chosen prestressing force and its eccentricity will offset the tensile stresses at the point of maximum moment without creating excessive stresses under any condition. It is obvious, therefore, that this same force can be used to offset the tensile stresses at points of lesser moment. The problem is to locate the prestressing force at an elevation at each point along the girder such that the tensile forces are overcome without creating excessive stresses.

Since this is a simple span girder, there is no bending moment at the ends and the only stresses are those due to the prestressing force. If the prestressing force is left at the same eccentricity as at the center of the span, these stresses will be

$$f_{F_I}^t = -391 \, \text{psi} \, (-2.7 \, \text{MPa}) \qquad f_{F_I}^b = +3375 \, \text{psi} \, (23.3 \, \text{MPa})$$
$$f_F^t = -313 \, \text{psi} \, (-2.2 \, \text{MPa}) \qquad f_F^b = +2699 \, \text{psi} \, (18.6 \, \text{MPa})$$

All these stresses are greater than the allowable, but all can be brought within the allowable by decreasing the eccentricity $e$, i.e., raising the center of gravity of the prestressing force. How much should $e$ be decreased? At least enough to bring the stresses within those allowed by the specification.

Compute $e$ for this condition. A small reduction in $e$ will change the top fiber stress from tension to compression, so stress in the top fiber is not a governing condition. Under final prestress $e$ must be such that $f_F^b$ does not exceed 2000 psi (13.8 MPa). Then $f_{F_I}^b$ will be $2000 \times 1.25 = 2500$ psi (17.2 MPa). Since the allowable stress under initial prestress is only 2400 psi (16.5 MPa), $f_{F_I}^b$ is the governing condition.

$$f_{F_I}^b = \frac{F_I}{A_c} + \frac{F_I e}{Z_b}$$

$$f_{F_I}^b = 2400 = \frac{604{,}800}{562} + \frac{604{,}800e}{4742}$$

$$2400 = 1075 + 127.5e$$

$$e = (2400 - 1075) \div 127.5 = 10.40 \, \text{in.} \, (264.2 \, \text{mm})$$

Check the other three conditions:

$$f_{F_t}^t = \frac{F_t}{A_c} - \frac{F_t e}{Z_t}$$

$$= \frac{604{,}800}{562} - \frac{604{,}800 \times 10.40}{7424}$$

$$= 1075 - 845 = +230 \, \text{psi} \, (1585.6 \, \text{kPa})$$

As shown previously for this example $f_{F_t}^b = 1.25 f_F^b$; therefore we can write $f_F^b = f_{F_t}^b \div 1.25$. Then

$$f_F^b = 2400 \div 1.25 = +1920 \, \text{psi} \, (13.2 \, \text{MPa})$$

$$f_F^t = +230 \div 1.25 = +184 \, \text{psi} \, (1268.5 \, \text{kPa})$$

Since all these stresses are within allowable limits, we could set $e = 10.40$ in. (264.2 mm) at the ends of the girders. Then the c.g.s. would be $25.63 - 10.40 = 15.23$ in. (386.8 mm) above the bottom of the girder. As the girder is 42 in. (1,066.8 mm) deep, there is plenty of room to move the c.g.s. higher. Should it be raised and if so how much? Several factors enter into this decision.

1. The most important factor is the shape of the bending moment curve. The eccentricity of the tendons at any point along the girder must be large enough so that $f_F^b$ is equal to or greater than the tensile stress caused by the sum of the moments at that point. At the same time, at any point, $f_F^b + f_G^b$ must not be greater than the maximum allowable compressive stress.

2. In Step 10 we shall compute the camber, and the path of the tendons will have considerable effect on the result we get. Under prestress plus dead load the typical prestressed concrete girder will have an upward camber because the bottom fibers are shortened by a high compressive stress while the top fibers have only a small stress.

The magnitude of the camber is a function of the difference in stress between the top and bottom fibers. As the stress difference increases, the camber increases. The stress difference in each differential length of the girder contributes to the total camber, which is the sum of all these differential contributions. At the center of the span when the moment is large, the difference between the top and bottom fiber stresses must be large. As the bending moment decreases toward the supports, the difference is stress can remain the same or can decrease in proportion to the drop in moment. If the tendons are raised the minimum amount, to an $e$ of 10.40 in. (264.2 mm), the camber will be maximum. This camber can be decreased by raising the tendons.

By varying the elevation of the tendons the designer can adjust the magnitude of the camber as long as the requirements of other controlling factors are met.

3. In Step 9 we shall design web reinforcement as a function of the shear carried by the concrete section.

Since the tendons are on a slope, they have both a horizontal and a vertical component. The horizontal component creates the prestress in the girder, and the vertical component reduces the shear carried by the concrete section. That is, the tendons carry an amount of shear equal to their vertical component, thus reducing the shear the concrete must carry. As the tendons are raised at the ends, the shear they carry is increased.

The shear carried by the tendons is considered in the design of the web reinforcement, but changing the elevation of the tendons within the allowable limits seldom makes a significant change in the web reinforcement.

4. In Step 5 we chose what appeared to be the most economical tendons for this girder. We must now consider the characteristics of these tendons to make sure that they can be placed economically in the path chosen for them. In many instances the path is selected to suit the characteristics of the tendons being used.

For this example we shall assume that the details of the tendons limit the c.g.s. to 15.50 in. (393.7 mm) above the bottom of the girder. Then $e = 25.63 - 15.50 = 10.13$ in. (257.3 mm). With this $e$ the stresses at the end are

$$f_{F_i}^b = \frac{604,800}{562} + \frac{604,800 \times 10.13}{4742}$$
$$= 1076 + 1291 = +2367 \text{ psi (16.3 MPa)}$$
$$f_{F_i}^t = \frac{604,800}{562} - \frac{604,800 \times 10.13}{7424}$$
$$= 1076 - 825 = +251 \text{ psi (1.73 MPa)}$$
$$f_F^b = 2367 \div 1.25 = +1894 \text{ psi (13.1 MPa)}$$
$$f_F^t = 251 \div 125 = +200 \text{ psi (1.38 MPa)}$$

All these stresses are within the allowable.

Now that the position of the tendons has been established at the center of the span and at the ends of the girder, we must establish the path the tendons will follow between the two points. This can be done by plotting the curve of the tensile stress in the bottom fiber due to all applied loads and then establishing the path of the tendons so that the compressive stress they create is always greater than the tensile stress.

The moments due to the weight of the girder and the wearing surface are computed by conventional formulas. In computing live-load moment remember that Step 4 showed that this particular girder must be designed to carry 0.35 lane load and an impact factor of 24.4 percent.

| $X^*$ ft | $M_{G+S\dagger}$ | $M_L$ | $M_{G+S+L}$ | $f^t_{G+S+L}$ | $f^b_{G+S+L}$ |
|---|---|---|---|---|---|
| 8 | 189,000 | 195,000 | 384,000 | +620 | −972 |
| 16 | 336,000 | 339,000 | 675,000 | +1,090 | −1,710 |
| 24 | 440,000 | 438,000 | 878,000 | +1,420 | −2,220 |
| 32 | 504,000 | 492,000 | 996,000 | +1,610 | −2,520 |
| 40 | 524,000 | 507,000 | 1,031,000 | +1,668 | −2,609 |

\*$X$ is the distance from support to point being considered.
†Moments are in foot-pounds.

As shown in Fig. 43 we can now plot the stresses $f^b_{G+S+L}$ for the full length of the girder and the stresses $f^b_F$ at the center of span and at the end of the girder. We shall assume that the tendons being used are the type which follow straight lines rather than curved paths, that they remain at one elevation through the center portion of the girder's length and then change direction to move in straight lines to the already selected points at the ends of the girder. The problem is to choose the point at which the path of the tendons changes direction. In Fig. 43 this point has been located 11 ft 0 in. (3.35 m) from the center of the span. It could just as correctly have been located nearer to the center of the span as long as the curve of the compressive stress due to prestress remained above the curve

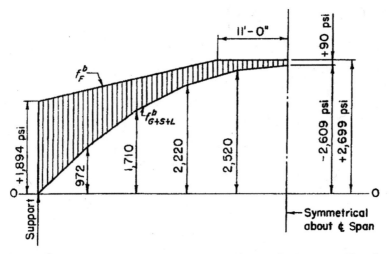

**FIGURE 43.** Diagram of stresses in bottom fiber under final prestress plus all applied loads.

of the tensile stress due to applied loads. Figure 44 shows the path chosen for the c.g.s. Since the tendons are at a constant elevation from the center of span to the point 11 ft 0 in. (3.35 m) away, the stress due to the tendons is constant in that portion of the girder. Since the tendons change elevation in a straight line from the 11-ft 0-in. (3.35-m) point to the end of the girder, the stress due to the tendons in that portion of the girder also changes in a straight line.

.Figure 43 is now completed. The stresses caused by the tendons are compressive and those caused by the applied loads are tensile, so the net stress, represented by the shaded area of Fig. 43, is the difference between the two.

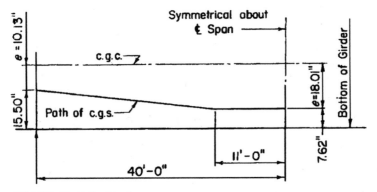

**FIGURE 44.** Path of tendons.

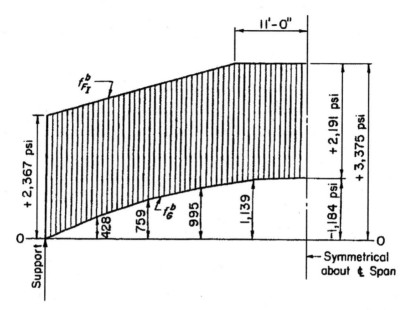

**FIGURE 45.** Diagram of stress in bottom fiber under initial prestress plus girder weight only.

The second part of Step 7 is to "check any critical points along the member under initial and final conditions."

Figure 43 provides a complete check on bottom fiber stresses under final prestress plus all applied loads. The other critical condition for bottom fiber stresses is initial prestress plus girder weight only. This is covered in Fig. 45. The net stress is shown by the shaded area.

Checking stresses already computed for the top fiber shows that no combination of loadings is critical. For reference as an example in cases where top fiber stress is critical Fig. 46 has been plotted for the condition of final prestress plus all applied loads. The net stress is shown by the shaded area.

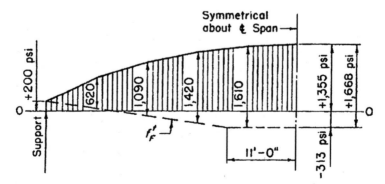

**FIGURE 46.** Diagram of stress in top fiber under final prestress plus all applied loads.

## 8. Check the ultimate strength to make sure it meets the requirements of the specification; check percentage of prestressing steel

First we must establish the location of the neutral axis under the ultimate condition. This is done by the formula

$$1.4\frac{dpf_{su}}{f'_c}$$

$$d = 18.01 + 16.37 = 34.38 \text{ in. (873.3 mm)}$$

The tendons selected give $A_s = 3.482$ and

$$f'_s = 248,000 \text{ psi (1709.7 Mpa)}$$
$$f'_c = 5000 \text{ psi (34.5 Mpa)}$$
$$P = \frac{A_S}{bd} = \frac{3.482}{42 \times 34.38} = 0.00241$$

From

$$f_{su} = f'_s\left(1 - \frac{0.5pf'_s}{f'_c}\right)$$

$$= 248,000\left(1 - \frac{0.5 \times 0.00241 \times 248,000}{5000}\right) = 233,000$$

Substituting these values we get

$$1.4\frac{34.38 \times 0.00241 \times 233,000}{5000} = 5.40 \text{ in. (137.2 mm)}$$

Since the flange thickness is greater than 5.40 in. (137.2 mm) the formula for rectangular sections applies. This is

$$M_u = A_s f_{su}d\left(1 - \frac{k_2}{k_1 k_3}\frac{pf_{su}}{f'_c}\right)$$

Given

$$\frac{k_2}{k_1 k_3} = 0.60$$

Substituting,

$$M_u = 3.482 \times 233,000 \times 34.38\left(1 - \frac{0.6 \times 0.00241 \times 233,000}{5000}\right)$$

$$= 26,020,000 \div 12 = 2,170,000 \text{ ft·lb (2940.4 kNm)}$$

This is the ultimate moment the girder can carry.

The specification will require that the minimum ultimate moment capacity of the girder be at least

$$1.5 \text{ dead-load moment} + 2.5 \text{ live-load moment}$$

From Step 2

$$M_G = 5,616,000 \div 12 = 468,000 \text{ ft·lb } (634.1 \text{ kNm})$$

From Step 3

$$M_S = 672,000 \div 12 = 56,000 \text{ ft·lb } (75.9 \text{ kNm})$$

and

$$M_L = 6,086,000 \div 12 = 507,167 (687.2 \text{ kNm})$$

Therefore the required ultimate moment is

$$1.5(468,000 + 56,000) + 2.5(507,167) = 786,000 + 1,267,918$$
$$= 2,053,918$$

Since this is less than $M_u$, the girder meets the ultimate strength requirement. Check the percentage of prestressing steel in accordance with

$$\frac{p f_{su}}{f'_c} = \frac{0.00241 \times 233,000}{5000} = 0.1123$$

Since this is less than 0.30, the girder is not over-reinforced. Web reinforcement is not needed when

$$\frac{p f'_s}{f'_c} \gtreqless 0.3 \frac{f_{sc}}{f'_s} \frac{b'}{b}$$

Substituting numerical values from calculations in preceding steps,

$$\frac{0.00241 \times 248,000}{5000} \gtreqless 0.3 \frac{140,000}{248,000} \times \frac{6}{42}$$
$$0.1195 \gtreqless 0.024$$

Therefore web reinforcement is definitely needed.

The total dead weight is 585 lb·ft (8.53 kN/m) of girder plus 70 lb per ft (1.02 kN/m) of wearing surface = 655 lb per ft (9.6 kN/m). This gives a shear at the quarter point of $655 \times 20 = 13,100$ lb (58.3 kN).

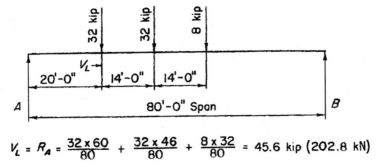

$$V_L = R_A = \frac{32 \times 60}{80} + \frac{32 \times 46}{80} + \frac{8 \times 32}{80} = 45.6 \text{ kip (202.8 kN)}$$

**FIGURE 47.** Truck loading which produces maximum shear at quarter point.

The live-load shear per lane at the quarter point is 45,600 lb (202.8 kN) as computed in Fig. 47. At the quarter point the shear and moment are distributed across the full width of the lane so that each girder carries only 35 percent of a lane load. As the truck approaches the end of the bridge, the amount of transverse distribution decreases. Since one line of wheels can be directly over one girder, the total shear per girder with no distribution approaches one-half of the lane-load shear. Until more complete data on transverse distribution of shear are available, the safe procedure is to design for one-half lane-load shear per girder. Then the live-load shear per girder is 0.50 × 45,600 = 22,800 lb (101.4 kN)

Ultimate shear factors are the same as ultimate moment factors, so

$$V_u = (1.5 \times 13,100) + (2.5 \times 22,800)$$
$$= 19,650 + 57,000 = 76,650 \text{ lb (340.9 kN)}$$

Compute the shear carried by the tendons under final prestress. From Fig. 44 the tangent of the tendons is $(15.50 - 7.62)/(29.0 \times 12) = 0.0226$, $F = 483,840$. Then the shear carried by the tendons is $483,840 \times 0.0226 = 10,935$ lb (48.6 kN).

Therefore the effective $V_u$ is 76,650 − 10,935 = 65,715 lb (292.3 kN).

Apply the formula

$$A_v = \frac{(V_u - V_c)s}{2f'_y - id}$$

For this example $V_c = 180b'jd$.

Since the tendons slope, $d$ at the quarter point is less than at mid-span. Refer to Fig. 44. The tendons slope 15.50 − 7.62 = 7.88 in. (200.2 mm) in 29 ft (8.4 m). Since the quarter point is 20 ft (6.1 m) from the end the drop of the tendons to this point is

$$\frac{20}{29} \times 7.88 = 5.44 \text{ in.} (138.2 \text{ mm})$$

$$10.13 = e \text{ at end from Fig. 44}$$

$$\underline{16.37} = \text{top fiber to c.g.c. from Fig. 42}$$

$$d = 31.94 \text{ in. (811.3 mm)}$$

Then     $p = \dfrac{3.482}{42 \times 31.94} = 0.00260$

$$f_{su} = 248{,}000 \left(1 - \frac{0.5 \times 0.00260 \times 248{,}000}{5000}\right) = 232{,}000$$

$j$ can be computed from the following portion of formula

$$\left(1 - \frac{k_2}{k_1 k_3} \frac{pf_{su}}{f'_c}\right)$$

Substituting numerical values,

$$j = \left(1 - 0.6 \frac{0.00260 \times 232{,}000}{5000}\right) = 0.928$$

Then $V_c = 180 \times 6 \times 0.928 \times 31.94 = 32{,}000$ lb (142.3 kN)
The maximum spacing of stirrups is three-fourths of the depth of the member.
Use $s = {}^3/_4 \times 42 = 31.5$ in. (800.1 mm)
Use intermediate-grade reinforcing bars for stirrups with $f'_V = 40{,}000$ psi (275.8 MPa).
Substituting known values,

$$A_v = \frac{(65{,}715 - 32{,}000)31.5}{2 \times 40.000 \times 0.928 \times 31.94} = 0.448 \,\text{sq.in.} \,(289 \text{ mm}^2)$$

The minimum amount of web reinforcement is

$$A_v = 0.0025 b' s$$

Substituting numerical values,

$$A_v = 0.0025 \times 6 \times 31.5 = 0.4725$$

Therefore this requirement governs, and the same stirrups can be used the full length of the girder.

Two $^1/_2$-in. (12.7-mm) diameter bars $= 2 \times 0.1963 = 0.3926$

$$31.5 \times \frac{0.3926}{0.4725} = 26.17$$

Use two $^1/_2$-in. (12.7-mm) diameter bars at 26-in. (660.4 mm) centers for the full length of the girder.

## 9. Compute camber

Although we use precise engineering formulas in computing the camber of prestressed concrete members, the results are accurate only within the accuracy with which we can determine the modulus of elasticity of the concrete.

A formula, $E_c = 1,800,000 + 500f'_c$, states that actual values can vary as much as 25 percent.

Compute instantaneous camber under prestress plus dead weight of girder only. At this time $f'_{ci} = 4000$ psi (27.6 MPa). Then

$$E_c = 1,800,000 + (500 \times 4000) = 3,800,000$$

Under this condition the camber will be the algebraic sum of the deflection due to dead load plus the deflection due to the prestress. Deflection due to dead load is computed by the standard formula

$$\Delta_G = \frac{5wl^4}{384EI}$$

$$= \frac{5 \times 585(80^4)\,12^3}{384 \times 3,800,000 \times 121,540} = -1.17\,\text{in. (29.7 mm)}$$

The minus sign indicates a downward deflection, which is a negative camber.

An eccentric prestressing force can be replaced by a force on the c.g.c. and a couple. We do the same thing in computing camber. The force on the c.g.c. can be ignored because it creates a uniform compressive stress over the entire cross section so that the entire section shortens the same amount and there is no change in camber. The couple produces a bending moment that does cause camber. The bending moment is equal to the prestressing force multiplied by its eccentricity with respect to the c.g.c. The initial prestressing force is 604,800 lb (2,690 kN). From Fig. 44 we can compute the bending moment due to the eccentricity of the prestressing force. At the ends of the girder

$$M_c = 604,800 \times 10.13 = 6,126,624\,\text{in·lb (691.7 kNm)}$$

At the center of span

$$M_c = 604,800 \times 18.01 = 10,892,448\,\text{in·lb (1229.8 kNm)}$$

The moment diagram for this condition is plotted in Fig. 48.

Deflection at the center of span due to the moments shown in Fig. 48 can be computed by the moment-area method. When applied to this particular problem, the moment-area method says that the deflection at the center of span is equal to the moment of the area of the $M/EI$ diagram about the support. The moment diagram in Fig. 48 has been divided into three simple sections, so the moment of the $M/EI$ diagram for each can be easily figured and the total deflection $\Delta_{F_1}$ can be obtained by adding the three results.

$$\Delta_I = \frac{6,126,624(40 \times 12)(20 \times 12)}{EI} = \frac{705,787(10^6)}{EI}$$

$$\Delta_{II} = \frac{4,765,824(29 \times 12)\tfrac{1}{2}(\tfrac{2}{3} \times 29 \times 12)}{EI} = \frac{192,387(10^6)}{EI}$$

$$\Delta_{III} = \frac{4,765,824(11 \times 12)(34.5 \times 12)}{EI} = \frac{260,443(10^6)}{EI}$$

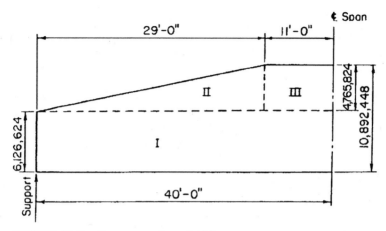

**FIGURE 48.** Bending moment due to initial prestress.

$$\Delta_{F_I} = \Delta_I + \Delta_{II} + \Delta_{III} = \frac{1,158,617(10^6)}{EI}$$

$$\Delta_{F_I} = 1,158,617(10^6) \div [3.8(10^6) \times 121,540] = +2.51 \text{ in. (63.8 mm)}$$

Net camber $= +2.51 - 1.17 = +1.34$ or an upward camber of 1.34 in. (34 mm).

Accurate computation of final camber in a member is even more difficult because of the variables involved.

The long-time increase in deflection under sustained loads can be 100 to 300 percent of the instantaneous deflection. Even the erection schedule can influence the final camber. If a bridge girder is erected and the wearing surface is applied as soon as the concrete in the girder reaches the required strength, the increase in camber will be a function of the camber under dead load plus wearing surface. If the girder alone is allowed to stand for some time before it is erected, a part of the increase in camber will be a function of the camber under dead load only and the final camber will be greater than if the wearing surface load had been applied sooner.

Choice of the percentage of increase in deflection must be based on experience in the locality of the structure and with the materials being used. We shall assume a 150 percent increase.

We shall also assume that the member is erected and the wearing surface placed shortly after the tensioning operation. This means that the major part of camber growth will take place with the wearing surface in place and will be a function of $\Delta_{F_I} + \Delta_G + \Delta_S$.

$$w_S = 70 \qquad w_G = 585$$

Thus

$$\Delta_S = \Delta \frac{w_S}{G w_G} = -1.17 \frac{70}{585} = -0.14 \text{ in. (3.6 mm)}$$

$$\Delta_{F_I} + \Delta_G + \Delta_S = +2.51 - 1.17 - 0.14 = +1.20 \text{ in. (30.5 mm)}$$

Total final camber is

$$1.20 + 150\% (1.20) = 3.00 \text{ in. (76.2 mm)}$$

This is a rather large camber for the average 80-ft 0-in. (24.4-m) span bridge girder especially in a multispan bridge on which an automobile would rise and fall 3 in. (76.2 mm) on every span.

This procedure is the work of H. Kent Preston, P.E., whose affiliations, at the time of its preparation, were: Engineer, Construction Materials, John A. Roebling's Sons Division; The Colorado Fuel and Iron Corporation; Fellow, American Society of Civil Engineers; Professional Member, Prestressed Concrete Institute. SI values were added by the handbook editor.

## DESIGN OF A PRESTRESSED CONCRETE BRIDGE

Design a prestressed concrete bridge with a span of 75 ft 0 in. (22.9 m), a roadway width of 28 ft 0 in. (8.5 m), a provision for future wearing surface of 20 psf (958 N/m²), and an AASHTO live load—H20-S16-44. The minimum strength of prestressed girders when the prestressing force is transferred from anchorages shall be 4000 psi (27.6 MPa). Minimum ultimate strength of girders at 28 days shall be 5000 psi (34.5 MPa). Minimum ultimate strength of the poured-in-place deck slab at 28 days shall be 4000 psi (27.6 MPa).

*Important Notice:* The design procedure given here follows the general AASHTO steps. However, the latest editions of AASHTO and Joint ACI-ASCE Recommendations should also be followed in actual design work. Whenever such AASHTO and ACI-ASCE steps are followed in this calculation procedure, this fact will be noted by the expression *design procedure* or *design guide.*

**Calculation Procedure:**

**1. Compute the properties of the concrete bridge cross section in Fig. 49**
Thus,

$$A_c = 560 \text{ sq.in. } (0.36 \text{ m}^2)$$
$$y_b = 20.27 \text{ in. } (514.9 \text{ mm})$$
$$I_c = 125,390 \text{ in. } (0.05 \text{ m}^4)$$

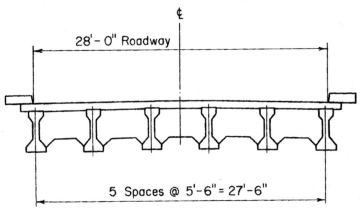

**FIGURE 49**

From these and Fig. 50 we can compute:

$$y_t = 45 - 20.27 = 24.73 \text{ in. (628 mm)}$$
$$Z_t = 125{,}390 \div 24.73 = 5070 \text{ in.}^3 \, (0.08 \text{ m}^3)$$
$$Z_b = 125{,}390 \div 20.27 = 6186 \text{ in.}^3 \, (0.10 \text{ m}^3)$$

Weight using regular-weight concrete $= 560 \times {}^{150}/_{144} = 583$ lb·ft (867.5 kg/m).

The above properties are for the beam alone. We also need the properties of the composite section. The design procedure requires that the difference in modulus of elasticity between beam and slab be considered in computing section properties of the composite section.

From the design guide

$$E_C = 1{,}800{,}000 + 500 f'_c$$

For the slab

$$E_C = 1{,}800{,}000 + (500 \times 4000) = 3{,}800{,}000$$

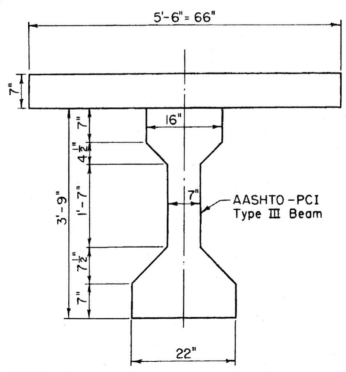

**FIGURE 50**

For the beam

$$E_C = 1,800,000 + (500 \times 5000) = 4,300,000$$

$$\text{Ratio} = 3,800,000 \div 4,300,000 = 0.88$$

Since the $E_C$ of the slab is less than the $E_C$ of the beam, its contribution to the stiffness, $EI$, of the composite section is less than if it were the same $E_C$ as the beam. In computing the section properties of the composite section, allowance for the difference in $E_C$ is made by multiplying the area of the slab by 0.88.

Find the section properties of the composite section taking moments about top of slab.

| Section | Area | $y$ | $Ay$ | $Ay^2$ | $I_0$ |
|---|---|---|---|---|---|
| 66 × 7 × 0.88 | 406 | 3.5 | 1,421 | 4,974 | 1,660 |
| Beam | 560 | 31.73 | 17,769 | 563,810 | 125,390 |
|  | 966 |  | 19,190 | 568,784 | 127,050 |
|  |  |  |  | 127,050 |  |
|  |  |  |  | 695,834 |  |

$$y_t = 19,190 \div 966 = 19.86 \text{ in. (504.4 mm)}$$
$$y_b = 52 - 19.86 = 32.14 \text{ in. (816.4 mm)}$$
$$I_c = 695,834 - 966(19.86^2) = 314,825$$
$$Z_t = 314,825 \div 19.86 = 15,852$$
$$Z_b = 314,825 \div 32.14 = 9795$$
$$\text{Weight of slab} = 66 \times 7 \times {}^{150}/_{144} = 480 \text{ lb/ft (714.2 kg/m)}$$

## 2. Compute the stresses in the beam at the center of the span due to the beam's own dead weight

$$M_G = \frac{583(75^2) \times 12}{8} = 4,915,000 \text{ in.·lb (555 kN/m)}$$
$$f_G^t = 4,915,000 \div 5070 = +969 \text{ psi } (+6.68 \text{ MPa})$$
$$f_G^b = 4,915,000 \div 6186 = -794 \text{ psi } (-5.47 \text{ MPa})$$

## 3. Find the stresses in the beam at the center of the span due to applied loads

The beam alone must support the dead weight of the slab and diaphragms. It does not act as a composite section with the slab until the slab has cured.

$$\text{Weight of slab} = w_{SS} = 480 \text{ lb/ft (714.2 kg/m)}$$
$$M_{SS} = \frac{480(75^2) \times 12}{8} = 4,055,000 \text{ in.·lb (457.8 kNm)}$$

The design procedure shows diaphragms at the one-third points of the span. The portion carried by one beam will be approximately 8 in. (203.2 mm) wide by 2 ft 6 in.

by 5 ft 6 in. (762 by 1676 mm) or a concentrated weight of $\frac{2}{3} \times 2.5 \times 5.5 \times 150 = 1375$ lb (6116 N). The moment $M_{SD}$ caused by this load at the one-third point will be

$$M_{SD} = 1375 \times 25 \text{ ft} \times 12 = 412,500 \text{ in·lb (46.5 kNm)}$$

The total moment carried by the beam only due to superimposed load is

$$\begin{aligned} M_S &= M_{SS} + M_{SD} \\ &= 4,055,000 + 412,500 = 4,467,500 \text{ in·lb (504.4 kNm)} \\ f_S^t &= 4,467,500 \div 5070 = +881 \text{ psi } (+6.1 \text{ MPa}) \\ f_S^b &= 4,467,500 \div 6186 = -722 \text{ psi } (-4.97 \text{ MPa}) \end{aligned}$$

The wearing surface and the live load are carried by the composite section. Analysis is based on the design procedure which says, "Strains vary linearly over the depth of the member throughout the entire load range." Figure 51b illustrates the elastic deformations developed when load is applied to the composite section.

Figure 51c shows the stresses developed in the composite section. When the applied bending moment is divided by the section modulus of the top fiber of the composite section, the resulting stress is that shown as $f^{ts}$ in Fig. 51c. Because of the difference in $E_C$ between the slab and the beam, the actual unit stress $f^s$ in the top fiber of the slab is less than $f^{ts}$ or

$$f^s = 0.88 f^{ts}$$

The stress in the top fiber of the beam is less than $f^{ts}$ because it is closer to the c.g.c. than the top of the slab.

$$f^t = \frac{12.86}{19.86} f^{ts} = 0.65 f^{ts}$$

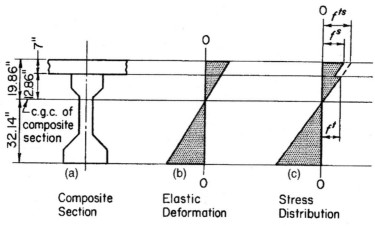

FIGURE 51

Wearing surface weight $w_{WS} = 20 \times 5.5 = 110$ lb/lin ft (1604.9 N/m)

$$M_{WS} = \frac{110(75^2) \times 12}{8} = 928,000 \text{ in·lb (104.8 kNm)}$$

$$f_{WS}^{ts} = 928,000 \div 15,852 = +59 \text{ psi } (+406.8 \text{ kPa})$$

$$f_{WS}^{b} = 928,000 \div 9795 = -95 \text{ psi } (-654.9 \text{ kPa})$$

$$f_{WS}^{t} = +59 \times 0.65 = +38 \text{ psi } (+261.9 \text{ kPa})$$

From design procedure tables the live-load bending moment per lane is 1,075,100 ft·lb (1456.8 kNm).

Impact = 50/(75 + 125) = 25%
Wheel load per stringer = 5.5 ÷ 5 = 1.1
Wheel load = one-half lane load
Net live-load moment $M_L$ per stringer is

$$M_L = 1,075,100 \times 1.25 \times 1.1 \times \tfrac{1}{2} \times 12 = 8,869,575 \text{ in·lb (1001.4 kNm)}$$

$$f_L^{ts} = 8,869,575 \div 15,852 = +560 \text{ psi } (+3.86 \text{ MPa})$$

$$f_L^{t} = +560 \times 0.65 = +364 \text{ psi } (+2.51 \text{ MPa})$$

$$f_L^{b} = 8,869,575 \div 9795 = -905 \text{ psi } (-6.24 \text{ MPa})$$

## 4. Determine the magnitude and location of the prestressing force at the center of the span

This computation is based on conditions after all stress losses. From the design procedure, maximum allowable compression = $0.40f_c' = 0.40 \times 5000 = 2000$ psi (13.8 MPa).

From the design procedure, the maximum permissible tensile stress $f_{tp}$ in the bottom fiber is zero.

We now have enough information to write the equation for stress in the bottom fiber in terms of $F$ and $e$.

$$\frac{F}{A_c} + \frac{Fe}{Z_b} = -f_G^b - f_S^b - f_L^b + f_{tp} \tag{64}$$

Substituting known values,

$$\frac{F}{560} + \frac{Fe}{6186} = +794 + 722 + 95 + 905 + 0$$

$$\frac{F}{560} + \frac{Fe}{6186} = +2516 \tag{65}$$

Under final conditions the maximum permissible tensile stress in the top fiber is zero. This, however, is not the governing factor because under final conditions the top fiber of the girder has a compressive stress caused by the dead-weight bending moment of the poured-in-place slab.

The governing factor is the stress in the top fiber under prestress plus the dead weight of the girder only. The most critical combination of prestress and girder weight exists when the strands are first released from their anchorages, at which time the tension in the strands is maximum, $F_o$, and the strength of the concrete is minimum, $f_{ci}'$. From the design procedure, the allowable tension at this point is

$$f_{tp} = 3\sqrt{f_{ci}'} = 3\sqrt{4000} = -190 \text{ psi } (-1.31 \text{ MPa})$$

From Eq. 65 the prestressing force will create a stress of $+2516$ psi (17.4 MPa) in the bottom fiber at the center of span. Since the maximum allowable stress is 2000 psi (13.8 MPa) some of the strands will slope up toward the end of the beam. Critical points for tension in the top fiber will be at the hold-down points, where stresses due to prestress are the same as at the center of span but where dead-load moment is less than that at the center of span. Assume that hold-down points are 10 ft 0 in. (3.1 m) each side of the center and find the stress in the top fiber due to the dead weight of the girder. Call the hold-down point "point $x$." See Fig. 56.

$$M_{Gx} = \frac{583 \times 27.5}{2}(75 - 27.5)12 = 4{,}570{,}000 \text{ in·lb (515. 9 kNm)}$$

$$f_{Gx}^t = 4{,}570{,}000 \div 5070 = +901 \text{ psi } (+6.2 \text{ MPa})$$
$$f_G^t - f_{Gx}^t = 969 - 901 = +68 \text{ psi } (+0.47 \text{MPa})$$

In order to stay within the allowable tensile stress at point $x$ the tensile stress at center of span must be 68 psi (0.47 MPa) less than the allowable or

$$f_{tp} = -190 + 68 = -122 \text{ psi } (-0.84 \text{ MPa})$$

Thus the allowable tensile stress in the top fiber under initial prestress plus the dead weight of the girder is 122 psi (0.84 MPa). The design procedure uses

$$\frac{F}{A_c} - \frac{Fe}{Z_t} = -f_G^t + f_{tp} \tag{53}$$

For the condition immediately after release of strands this is written as

$$\frac{F_o}{A_c} - \frac{F_o e}{Z_t} = -f_G^t + f_{tp} \tag{66}$$

For tensioning elements we shall probably use $7/16$-in. (11.1-mm) diameter strands at the initial tension of 18,900 lb (84.1 kN) recommended in the design guide. This is a unit stress of $18{,}900 \div 0.1089 = 173{,}600$ psi (1196.8 MPa). The design guide indicates a stress loss of 35,000 psi (241.3 MPa), which gives a final stress of $173{,}600 - 35{,}000 = 138{,}600$. The design guide states that the effective prestressing force $F_o$ in a pretensioned member immediately after transfer of load is less than the initial prestress $F_I$. In computing initial prestress plus dead-load stresses we can therefore use $F_o$. The value of $F_o$ is determined by subtracting the immediate losses from $F_I$. The value determined for $F_o$ will not be exact because it is based in part on factors which can vary from one pour to the next. In our computations we shall work toward minimum losses so that the actual $F_o$ be less than our computed value and the actual critical stresses will be less than those we compute.

*Elastic Shortening of Concrete.* Since the tendons in a pretensioned member are bonded to the concrete when their load is applied to the concrete, they will shorten as the concrete compresses and the amount of shortening will vary along the member as the net compressive stress in the concrete varies. Our first concern is the stress at the center of span.

Elastic shortening of concrete is partly a function of $F_o$, and $F_o$ is partly a function of the elastic shortening. An equation to give a direct value for $F_o$ would be involved and hardly justified by the lack of accuracy of some of the other available data. We know from experience that the immediate stress losses in a typical pretensioned member total 20,000 to 24,000 psi (137.9 to 165.5 MPa). We shall assume 20,000 psi (137.9 MPa) for our calculations and revise them if final calculations do not confirm this value.

We have shown that

$$f_{F_I} = 173{,}600 \text{ psi } (1196.8 \text{ MPa})$$
$$\text{Immediate losses} = 20{,}000 \text{ psi } (137.9 \text{ MPa})$$
$$f_{F_o} = 153{,}600 \text{ psi } (1058.9 \text{ MPa})$$

We have shown that

$$f_F = 138{,}600 \text{ psi } (955.5 \text{ MPa})$$

Therefore

$$f_{F_o} = \frac{153{,}600}{138{,}600} f_F = 1.108 f_F$$

From Eq. 10, $f_F^b$ will be set at $+2516$ psi ($+17.3$ MPa). Then

$$f_{F_o}^b = 2516 \times 1.108 = +2788 \text{ psi } (19.2 \text{ MPa})$$

From Step 2

$$f_G^b = -794 \text{ psi } (-5.47 \text{ MPa})$$
$$f_{F_o+G}^b = +2788 - 794 = +1994 \text{ psi } (13.7 \text{ MPa})$$

From the design guide

$$E_s = 27{,}000{,}000$$

and 

$$E_c = 1{,}800{,}000 + 500(4000) = 3{,}800{,}000$$

Thus the stress loss in the seven-wire strand resulting from a concrete compressive stress of 1994 psi (13.7 MPa) is $(27{,}000{,}000/3{,}800{,}000)\,(1994) = 14{,}200$ psi (97.9 MPa).

*Shrinkage of Concrete.* A conservative value for shrinkage at transfer of load is 0.0001 in./in. (0.003 mm/mm). This is equivalent to a stress loss in the strand of $0.0001 \times 27{,}000{,}000 = 2{,}700$ psi (18.6 MPa).

Since creep is a function of time and we are considering the moment at which the load is first transferred, the stress loss due to creep will be zero.

Tests on seven-wire strand tensioned to 70 percent of ultimate show that the initial rate of stress loss is high. At a normal transfer time, 18 to 20 hr after tensioning, it is about 3 percent of the initial tension. For this case therefore it would be $3\% \times 173{,}600 = 5200$ psi (35.9 Mpa).

In summary the immediate total stress loss is

$$14200 + 2700 + 5200 = 22{,}100 \text{ psi } (152.4 \text{ MPa})$$

We shall use 20,000 psi to remain on the conservative side. This gives

$$173{,}600 - 20{,}000 = 153{,}600$$

and

$$F_o = \frac{153{,}600}{138{,}600} (F) = 1.108F$$

Substituting this value in Eq. 11,

$$\frac{1.108F}{A_c} - \frac{1.108Fe}{Z_t} = -f_G^t + f_{tp} \tag{67}$$

Substituting known values in Eq. 67,

$$\frac{1.108F}{560} - \frac{1.108Fe}{5070} = -969 - 122$$

$$\frac{1.108F}{A_c} - \frac{1.108Fe}{5070} = -1091 \tag{68}$$

Multiplying 68 by

$$\frac{Z_t}{1.108Z_b} - \frac{5070}{1.108 \times 6186} = 0.74$$

we get

$$\frac{0.82F}{560} - \frac{Fe}{6186} = -807 \tag{69}$$

Adding 10 to 69,

$$\frac{1.82F}{560} = +1,709$$

$$F = 526,000 \text{ lb} \quad (2,339.6 \text{ kN})$$

Substituting this value of $F$ in 10,

$$\frac{526,000}{560} + \frac{526,000e}{6186} = +2516$$

$$940 + 85e = 2516$$

$$e = 18.54$$

$20.27 - 18.54 = 1.73$ in. (43.9 mm) from bottom of beam to c.g.s.

## 5. *Select the tensioning elements to be used and determine their location in the member*

Try $^7/_{16}$-in. (11.1-mm) diameter strands at a final tension of 138,600 psi as computed in Step 4. This is a tension of $138,600 \times 0.1089 = 15,120$ lb (6.7 kN) per strand.

In Step 4 we found that the c.g.s. of the 526,000-lb (2339.6-kN) force should be 1.73 in. $526,000 \div 15,120 = 34.8$ from the bottom. It is impossible to place 35 strands in a satisfactory pattern with the c.g.s. that close to the bottom. For a first trial we shall try 38 strands with $F = 574,560$ lb (2553.2 kN).

Substitute in the equation below to find $e$:

$$\frac{574,560}{560} + \frac{574,560e}{6186} = +2516$$

$$1,026 + 92.9e = 2516$$
$$e = 16.04 \text{ in. (407.4 mm)}$$
$$20.27 - 16.04 = 4.23 \text{ in (107.4 mm) bottom of beam to c.g.s.}$$

From the design guide, the minimum spacing center to center of strands is four times the strand diameter, or in this case $4 \times {}^{7}/_{16} = 1{}^{3}/_{4}$ in. (44.5 mm) center to center of strands. This gives a clear space between strands of $1{}^{3}/_{4} - {}^{7}/_{16} = 1{}^{5}/_{16}$ in. (33.3 mm). From the design guide, the maximum aggregate for this spacing is $1{}^{5}/_{16} \div 1.33 = 0.99$ in. (25.1 mm), or nominally 1 in. (25.4 mm) aggregate.

For easier pouring and for standardization many casting yards prefer to use a spacing of 2 in. (50.8 mm) center to center in both directions whenever possible. We shall establish the strand pattern shown in Fig. 52 and compute its center of gravity.

$$
\begin{array}{rcl}
30 \times 4 &=& 120 \\
4 \times 8 &=& 32 \\
\underline{4} \times 11 &=& \underline{44} \\
38 & & 196
\end{array}
$$

$196 \div 38 = 5.17$ in. (131.3 mm) bottom to c.g.s.

This is almost an inch (25.4 mm) too high.

The design guide requires a minimum cover of $1{}^{1}/_{2}$ in. (38.1 mm) for surfaces exposed to weather. This means the minimum distance from the bottom to the center of the bottom row of strands is $1{}^{1}/_{2}$ in. $+ {}^{7}/_{32}$ in. or nominally $1{}^{3}/_{4}$ in. (44.5 mm). If we maintain the same pattern but place the bottom row up $1{}^{3}/_{4}$ in. (44.5 mm) and use vertical spacing of five rows at $1{}^{3}/_{4}$ in. (44.5 mm), the center of gravity will be

$$
\begin{array}{rcl}
30 \times 3{}^{1}/_{2} &=& 105 \\
4 \times 7 &=& 28 \\
\underline{4} \times 9{}^{5}/_{8} &=& \underline{38.5} \\
38 & & 171.5
\end{array}
$$

$171.5 \div 38 = 4.50$ in. (114.3 mm) bottom to c.g.s.

This is still too high.

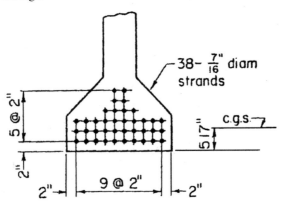

**FIGURE 52.**  Trial strand pattern at center of span.

By reducing the horizontal spacing to 1³/4 in. (44.5 mm) center to center we could get an additional row of strands which combined with 1³/4 in. (44.5 mm) vertical spacing would bring the c.g.s. down to the desired elevation. Such a pattern, however, puts three rows of strands in the web in those areas where the strands are sloping up. This makes it difficult to pour the bottom flange satisfactorily because the concrete must pass through the web with only 1⁵/16 in. (49.2 mm) clear space between the rows of strand and only 1¹/2 in. (38.1 mm) clear between the strands and the sides of the web.

We shall return to the much more desirable spacing of 2 in. (50.8 mm) center to center and add two strands as shown in Fig. 53. Compute the c.g.s.

$$
\begin{array}{rcrcr}
30 & \times & 4 & = & 120 \\
6 & \times & 8 & = & 48 \\
\underline{4} & \times & 11 & = & \underline{44} \\
40 & & & & 212
\end{array}
$$

$$212 \div 40 = 5.30 \text{ in. bottom to c.g.s.}$$
$$e = 20.27 - 5.30 = 14.97 \text{ in. (380.2 mm)}$$
$$F = 15,120 \times 40 = 604,800 \text{ lb (2,690.2 kN)}$$

Find the stress in the bottom fiber under the new $F$:

$$
f_F^b = \frac{604,800}{560} + \frac{604,800 \times 14.97}{6186}
$$

$$
= 1080 + 1464 = +2544 \text{ psi (17.5 MPa)}
$$

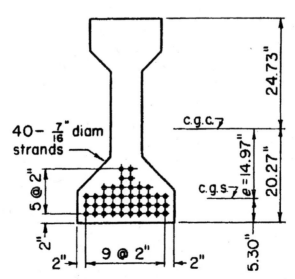

**FIGURE 53.** Final strand pattern at center of span.

The stress in the top fiber due to $F$ is

$$f_F^t = \frac{604,800}{560} - \frac{604,800 \times 14.97}{5070}$$

$$= 1080 - 1785 = -705 \text{ psi (4.86 MPa)}$$

From Step 4, $F_o = 1.108 \, F$. Therefore stresses due to $F_o$ are 1.108 times stresses due to $F$. Thus $f_{F_o}^t = 1.108 \times (-705) = -781$ psi (5.4 MPa).

The stress in the top fiber under the critical condition of $F_o$ plus the dead weight of the beam is

$$-781 + 969 = +188$$

The original equations were set up to give a stress of $-122$ psi (0.84 MPa) but the details made it necessary to use a higher prestressing force and smaller eccentricity than that indicated by the equations. This change in magnitude and location of the prestressing force is responsible for the resulting $+188$ psi (1.3 MPa).

Net stress in the top fiber of the beam under all applied loads is

$$f_F^t + f_G^t + f_S^t + f_{WS}^t + f_L^t = -705 + 969 + 881 + 38 + 364$$

$$= +1547 \text{ psi (10.7 MPa)}$$

From the foregoing calculations we see that the stress in the top fiber at the center of span will vary from $+188$ psi (1.3 MPa) under $F_o$ plus the dead weight of the girder to $+1547$ (10.7 MPa) psi under all applied loads. These stresses are within the specified limits of $-122$ to $+2000$ psi (13.8 MPa).

Net stress in the bottom fiber under prestress plus the weight of the beam only is

$$f_F^b + f_G^b = +2544 - 794 = +1750 \text{ psi (12.1 MPa)}$$

Net stress in the bottom fiber under all applied loads is

$$f_F^b + f_G^b + f_s^b + f_{ws}^b + f_L^b = +2544 - 794 - 722 - 95 - 905$$

$$= +28 \text{ psi (193 kPa)}$$

From this we see that stress in the bottom fiber will vary from $+1750$ (12.1 MPa) to $+28$ psi (193 kPa) which is within the limits of $+2000$ to zero.

Check net stress in the top of the poured-in-place slab under all applied loads.

$$f_{WS}^{ts} + f_L^{ts} = +59 + 560 = +619 \text{ psi (4.3 MPa)}$$

This would be the unit stress if the beam and slab had the same $E_c$. In Step 1 it was shown that the $E_c$ of the slab was 0.88 of the $E_c$ of the beam. Therefore the net stress in the top of the slab is

$$0.88 \times 619 = +545 \text{ psi (3.8 MPa)}$$

At this point we should review the economy of the section chosen. Maximum compressive stresses in the top and bottom fibers of the beam are less than the allowable, and there is no tensile stress in the top even under the conditions when it is allowable. The maximum stress in the poured-in-place slab is +545 psi (3.8 MPa).

We cannot take advantage of the tensile stress permitted in the top fiber. To do this we would use a smaller prestressing force with a greater eccentricity, which we found impossible when working out the strand pattern. The eccentricity could be increased by using one or more post-tensioned tendons, but the higher cost of these tendons would probably offset any other advantage.

Changing the cross section of the beam is not feasible. The section being used is an AASHTO-PCI standard, and the next smaller standard section is too small. The unused stress in the bottom fiber is not sufficient to take the additional load that would be created if the spacing center to center of beams were increased enough to eliminate one beam.

If the casting yards in the area can make the beams economically from 6000-psi (41.4-MPa) concrete, it might pay to investigate the economy of five beams at 6-ft 10 1/2-in. (2.1-m) centers in place of the six beams at 5-ft 6-in. (1.68-m) centers shown in Fig. 49. This would almost certainly involve the use of 1 3/4-in. (44.5-mm) center-to-center spacing in both directions for the strands.

A good place to effect an economy in this design may be in the poured-in-place slab, which has a maximum stress of only +545 psi (3.8 MPa). Within the limits of its requirements for carrying the loads to the beams, the slab can be made thinner or of lower strength concrete or both. For use in a composite section, the final strength of the concrete slab should not be less than 3000 psi (20.7 MPa).

If lower strength concrete is used in the slab, the section modulus of the composite section will be slightly reduced, which will cause higher stresses in the beam, and it may be necessary to use additional strands in each beam. Reducing the slab thickness will reduce the section modulus of the composite section, but it will also reduce the dead weight so that additional strands may not be necessary. In this case, however, the thinner slab will require more reinforcing steel to distribute the wheel loads to the beams.

In summary there are three changes in the design which might provide a more economical structure. Each change, however, involves additional costs of some sort which at least partially offset the savings. Approximate calculations incorporating the possible changes should be made, and the cost compared with the cost as already designed. If a change proves economical, it should be made and all the calculations in Steps 1 to 5 repeated for the new section.

For the purpose of this example, we shall assume that the section shown in Fig. 50 proved most economical, and we shall proceed with it.

## 6. Establish the concrete strength, $f'_{ci}$, at the time of prestressing and check stresses under the initial prestress condition

It has already been stated

$$f'_{ci} = +4000 \text{ psi (27.6 MPa)}$$

From the design guide

Allowable compression $= 0.60 f'_{ci} = 0.60 \times 4000 = +2400$ psi (16.6 MPa)

Allowable tension $= 3\sqrt{f'_{ci}} = 3\sqrt{4000} = -190$ psi (1.3 MPa)

From Step 4,

$$F_o = 1.108F$$
$$= 1.108 \times 604,800 = 670,000$$

From Step 5,

$$f^t_{F_o} = -781$$

and     $$f^t_{F_o} = f^t_G = -781 + 969 = +188$$

The stress in the top fiber under initial prestress plus all applied loads is

$$f^t_{F_o} + f^t_G + f^t_S + f^t_{WS} + f^t_L = -781 + 969 + 881 + 38 + 364$$
$$= +1471$$

$$f^b_{F_o} = \frac{F_o}{A_c} + \frac{F_o e}{Z_b}$$
$$= \frac{670,000}{560} + \frac{670,000 \times 14.97}{6,186}$$
$$= 1195 + 1621 = +2816$$

The stress in the bottom fiber under $F_o$ plus the girder only is

$$f^b_{F_o} + f^b_G = +2816 - 794 = +2022$$

The stress in the bottom fiber under $F_o$ plus all applied loads is

$$f^b_{F_o} + f^b_G + f^b_S + f^b_{WS} + f^b_L = +2816 - 794 - 722 - 95 - 905 = +300$$

From the foregoing calculations, all stresses at the center of span under $F_o$ are within the allowable limits of $-190$ to $+2400$ psi (16.5 MPa)

## 7. Establish the path of the tendons; check any critical points along the member under initial and final conditions

From previous calculations

$$f^t_{F_o} = -781 \text{ psi (5.4 MPa)} \quad f^b_{F_o} = +2816 \text{ psi (19.4 MPa)}$$
$$f^t_F = -705 \text{ psi (4.9 MPa)} \quad f^b_F = +2544 \text{ psi (17.5 MPa)}$$

Since these stresses, which are all in excess of the allowable, would exist at the ends of the beam if the strands were left in a straight line, it will be necessary to bend some of the strands up. We shall compute $e$ at the ends of the span to satisfy the requirement that $f^b_{F_o}$ shall not exceed $+2400$ psi (16.5 MPa).

$$f^b_{F_o} = +2400 = \frac{670,000}{560} + \frac{670,000e}{6186}$$
$$+2400 = +1196 + 108.3e$$
$$e = 11.12 \text{ in.}$$
$$f^b_F = 2400 \div 1.108 = +2166$$

Since this exceeds the allowable of 2000 psi (13.8 MPa) for final conditions, the final condition will govern.

$$f^b_F = 2000 = \frac{604,800}{560} + \frac{604,800e}{6186}$$

$$2000 = 1080 + 97.8e$$
$$e = 9.40 \text{ in. (238.8 mm)}$$
$$f^b_{F_o} = 2000 \times 1.108 = +2216$$

$$f^t_F = \frac{604{,}800}{560} - \frac{604{,}800 \times 9.40}{5070}$$
$$= 1080 - 1120 = -40$$

A tensile stress of $0.04 \times 5000 = 200$ psi (1.4 MPa) is permissible. In this case, however, we can choose the location of the c.g.s., so we shall make it at least high enough to eliminate tensile stress. Then

$$f^t_F = 0 = \frac{604{,}800}{560} - \frac{604{,}800e}{5070}$$
$$1080 = 119.3e$$
$$e = 9.05 \text{ in. (229.9 mm)}$$

For this value of $e$

$$f^t_{F_o} = 0 \times 1.108 = 0$$
$$f^b_F = \frac{604{,}800}{560} + \frac{604{,}800 \times 9.05}{6186}$$
$$= 1080 + 885 = +1965$$
$$f^b_{F_o} = 1.108 \times 1965 = +2177$$

As these stresses are all within the allowable, $e$ at the ends of the beam can be 9.05 in. (229.9 mm) or less.

$$20.27 - 9.05 = 11.22 \text{ in. (284.9 mm) from bottom to c.g.s.}$$

The strand pattern in Fig. 53 is arranged so that 12 center strands can be sloped up in the web. The required moment of the strand group about the bottom at the ends is $40 \times 11.22 = 449$. The moment of the 28 strands which will be left in a straight line is

$$
\begin{array}{rcl}
24 \times 4 &=& 96 \\
4 \times 8 &=& \underline{32} \\
&& 128 \\
449 - 128 &=& 321
\end{array}
$$

Thus the moment of the 12 raised strands must be 321, and the distance from the bottom to the center of gravity of the 12 strands is $321 \div 12 = 26.75$ in. (679.5 mm). This would be the lowest possible elevation of the raised strands to give stresses within the allowable.

Since higher elevations are permissible and in many cases desirable, we shall arbitrarily raise the 12 strands above the minimum to the position shown in Fig. 54 to illustrate the procedure. Find the c.g.s. for the pattern of strands in Fig. 54.

$$
\begin{array}{rcl}
24 \times 4 &=& 96 \\
4 \times 8 &=& 32 \\
\underline{12} \times 28^{1/4} &=& \underline{339} \\
40 && 467
\end{array}
$$

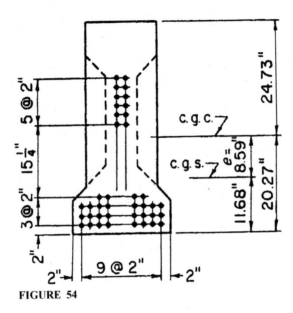

**FIGURE 54**

$$467 \div 40 = 11.68$$

$$e = 20.27 - 11.68 = 8.59 \text{ in. } (218.2 \text{ mm})$$

Stresses at ends for $e = 8.59$ in. are

$$f_F^t = \frac{604{,}800}{560} - \frac{604{,}800 \times 8.59}{5070}$$

$$= 1080 - 1025 = +55$$

$$f_{F_o}^t = +55 \times 1.108 = +61$$

$$f_F^b = \frac{604{,}800}{560} + \frac{604{,}800 \times 8.59}{6186}$$

$$= 1080 + 840 = +1920$$

$$f_{F_o}^b = +1920 \times 1.108 = +2127$$

The strand pattern is now established at the center of span, Fig. 53, and at the ends of the beam, Fig. 54. The next step is to establish the path of the strands along the member. In this particular case this means to establish the location of the hold-down points. The critical condition is usually the stress in the bottom fiber under full load. Stresses for this condition are plotted in Fig. 55, which is constructed as follows:

Stresses due to the prestressing force have already been computed at the center of span and at the ends. These are plotted.

The stress in the bottom fiber under all applied loads has already been computed at the center of span. It is zero at the ends. These are plotted.

Stresses under all applied loads are computed at various points along the span and then plotted (see Table 1 for values).

**TABLE 1.** Moments* and Stresses from Applied Loads

| $X$† | Precast section | | | | | | Composite section | | | | | | $f^t_{G+S+WS+L}$ | $f^b_{G+S+WS+L}$ |
|---|---|---|---|---|---|---|---|---|---|---|---|---|---|---|
| | $M_G$ | $f^t_G$ | $f^b_G$ | $M_S$ | $f^t_s$ | $f^b_s$ | $M_{WS}$ | $f^t_{WS}$ | $f^b_{WS}$ | $M_L$ | $f_L$ | $f^b_L$ | | |
| 7.5 | 147,500 | +340 | −286 | 132,000 | +312 | −256 | 27,800 | +14 | −34 | 288,000 | +142 | −353 | +817 | −929 |
| 15.0 | 262,500 | +620 | −508 | 237,000 | +561 | −460 | 49,500 | +24 | −61 | 500,000 | +246 | −612 | +1,451 | −1,641 |
| 22.5 | 344,500 | +814 | −667 | 314,000 | +744 | −610 | 65,000 | +32 | −80 | 638,000 | +314 | −781 | +1,904 | −2,138 |
| 30.0 | 393,800 | +930 | −762 | 358,000 | +848 | −695 | 74,400 | +36 | −91 | 718,000 | +354 | −880 | +2,168 | −2,428 |
| 37.5 | 410,000 | +969 | −794 | 372,000 | +881 | −722 | 77,400 | +38 | −95 | 739,000 | +364 | −905 | +2,252 | −2,516 |

*Moments are in foot-pounds.

† $X$ is the distance from support to point being considered.

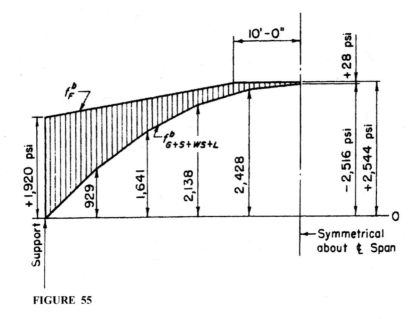

**FIGURE 55**

A horizontal line is drawn from the prestressing stress at the center of span to a point where a sloping straight line can be drawn to the prestressing stress at the end without cutting into the stress due to applied loads. The hold-downs will be located at the point where the line changes from horizontal to sloping.

The moments shown in Table 1 due to live loads at points other than center of span were computed by the simplified formula outlined in Appendix D. As shown in Step 3 the impact factor for this bridge is 25 percent and each beam carries 0.55 of a lane load.

In Fig. 55 the hold-down points are set at 10 ft 0 in. (3.1 m) each side of the center of span. We now have sufficient information to plot the path of the center of gravity of the strands in Fig. 56.

We must now check to make sure that stresses are within the allowable at all points along the beam under all conditions of loading and either initial or final prestress. A study of Table 1 indicates that maximum stresses will exist either under the dead load of the girder only or under all applied loads. There is no need to check the net stresses under the weight of the slab and wearing surface. The critical conditions then are:

I. Final prestress plus

    *A.* All applied loads

        1. Top fiber—Fig. 58

        2. Bottom fiber—Fig. 55

    *B.* Dead load of beam only

        1. Top fiber

        2. Bottom fiber

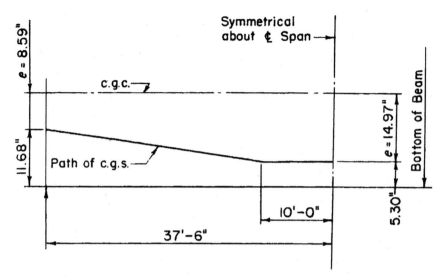

**FIGURE 56.** Path of center of gravity of tendons.

II. Initial prestress (after immediate losses) plus

    *A.* All applied loads

        1. Top fiber

        2. Bottom fiber

    *B.* Dead load of beam only

        1. Top fiber—Fig. 59

        2. Bottom Fiber—Fig. 57

Stress diagrams are plotted for conditions I*A*1, I*A*2, II*B*1, and II*B*2. The conditions not plotted are covered by the diagrams plotted as follows:

I*B*1 is less critical than II*B*1 because the critical stress in these cases is tension and the tension due to $F_o$ is greater than that due to $F$.

I*B*2 is less critical than II*B*2 because the critical stress in these cases is compression and the compression due to $F_o$ is greater than that due to $F$.

II*A*1 is less critical than I*A*1 because the critical stress in these cases is compression and the compression due to $F_o$ is less than that due to $F$.

II*A*2 is less critical than I*A*2 because the critical stress in these cases is tension and the compression due to $F$ is less than that due to $F_o$.

A study of the stress diagrams in Figs. 55 and 57 to 59 shows that all stresses are within the allowable.

**8. Check ultimate strength to make sure it meets the requirements of the specification; check percentage of prestressing steel**

Evaluate the formula

$$\frac{1.4 d p f_{su}}{f'_c}$$

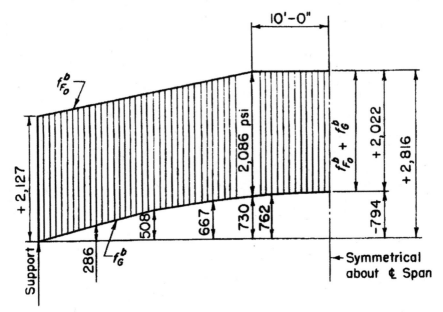

**FIGURE 57.** Diagram of stresses in bottom fiber under initial prestress plus dead weight of beam only. Shaded area represents net compressive stress.

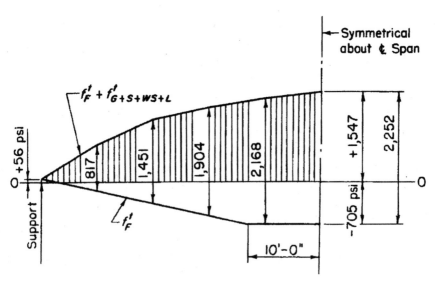

**FIGURE 58.** Diagram of stresses in top fiber under final prestress plus all applied loads. Shaded area represents net compressive stress.

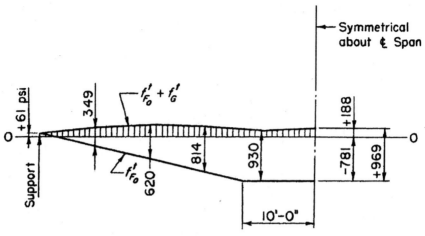

**FIGURE 59.** Diagram of stresses in top fiber under initial prestress plus dead weight of beam only. Shaded area represents net compressive stress.

In computing ultimate strength use the properties of the composite section. From Figs. 50 and 53

$$d = 52 \text{ in.} - 5.30 = 46.70 \text{ in.} \ (1186.2 \text{ mm})$$

From Fig. 53 and the design guide

$$A_s = 40 \times 0.1089 = 4.36 \text{ sq.in.} \ (2812.9 \text{ mm}^2)$$

$$p = \frac{A_s}{bd} = \frac{4.36}{(66 \times 0.88)46.70} = 0.00161$$

The ultimate bending moment is resisted by a couple composed of compression in the top fibers of the concrete section and tension in the tendons. In this example the top fibers involved are in the poured-in-place slab. In Step 1 it was shown that the $E_c$ of the slab was 0.88 of the $E_c$ of the beam. Since the width of 66 in. (1676 mm) used in computing $p$ is all the lower strength concrete, it must be multiplied by the factor of 0.88 in computing $p$.

$$f'_c = 5000 \text{ psi (34.5 MPa)}$$

$$M_u = A_s f_{su} d \left( 1 - \frac{k_2}{k_1 k_3} \frac{p f_{su}}{f'_c} \right)$$

From the design guide

$$f'_s = 27{,}000 \div 0.1089 = 248{,}000 \text{ psi (1709.7 MPa)}$$

From the design guide

$$f_{su} = f'_s\left(1 - 0.5\frac{pf'_s}{f'_c}\right)$$

or

$$f_{su} = 248,000\left(1 - 0.5\frac{0.00161 \times 248,000}{5000}\right)$$

$$= 248,000(1 - 0.040) = 238,000 \text{ psi}(1640.8 \text{ MPa})$$

Substituting numerical values in the formula below,

$$\frac{1.4 \times 46.70 \times 0.00161 \times 238,000}{5000} = 5.00$$

Since the flange thickness of the composite section is 7 in. (177.8 mm) which is greater than 5.00 in. (127 mm) the following formula for rectangular sections in the design guide applies:

$$M_u = A_s f_{su} d\left(1 - \frac{k_2}{k_1 k_3}\frac{pf_{su}}{f'_c}\right)$$

Given in the design guide

$$\frac{k_2}{k_1 k_3} = 0.6$$

Substituting

$$M_u = 4.36 \times 238,000 \times 46.70\left(1 - \frac{0.6 \times 0.00161 \times 238,000}{5,000}\right)$$

$$= 46,200,000 \div 12 = 3,850,000 \text{ ft·lb} (5219.8 \text{ kN/m})$$

This is the ultimate moment the member can carry.
From the design guide the minimum required ultimate is

$$1.5D + 2.5L$$

From Table 1 this is

$$1.5 (410,000 + 372,000 + 77,400) + 2.5 (739,000) = 3,136,600 \text{ ft·lb} (4251.8 \text{ kN/m})$$

Since this is less than $M_u$, the member has sufficient ultimate strength.
Check the percentage of prestressing steel

$$\frac{pf_{su}}{f'_c} = \frac{0.00161 \times 238,000}{5000} = 0.0766$$

Since this is less than 0.30, the member is not overreinforced.

## 9. *Design the shear steel*

Web reinforcement is not needed when

$$\frac{Pf'_s}{f'_c} \gtreqless 0.3\frac{f_{se}b'}{f'_s b}$$

Substituting numerical values from calculations in preceding steps,

$$\frac{0.00161 \times 248,000}{5000} \gtreqless 0.3\frac{140,000 \times 7}{248,000 \times 66}$$

$$0.0798 \gtreqless 0.018$$

Since that is not true, web reinforcement is required.

The critical section for shear in this member is described by the design guide.

| Dead weight is | |
| --- | --- |
| Beam only: | 583 lb/ft (8,505.9 N/m) |
| Poured-in-place slab: | 480 lb/ft (7,003.2 N/m) |
| Wearing surface: | 110 lb/ft (1,604.9 N/m) |
| Total: | 1173 lb/ft (17,114.1 N/m) |

Dead-load shear at the one-quarter point is

$$1173 \times \frac{75}{4} = 22,000$$

$$\frac{1,375}{23,375} \quad \begin{array}{l} \text{weight of diaphragm} \\ \text{lb (103,972 N)} \end{array}$$

The live-load shear at the quarter point is 45,100 lb (200,604 N) as computed in Fig. 60. From Step 3 one beam carries 0.55 lane load, so the live-load shear is $45,100 \times 0.55 = 24,800$ lb (110,310 N). The impact factor for loading in Fig. 60 is

$$I = \frac{50}{56.25 + 125} = 27.5\%$$

or total $V_L = 1.275 \times 24,800 = 31,600$ lb (140,557 N). For bridges where the distance center to center of beams is less than 5 ft 0 in. (1.52 m) each beam is designed to carry a shear equal to half the lane-load shear plus impact.

Ultimate shear factors are the same as ultimate moment factors, so

$$V_u = (1.5 \times 23,375) + (2.5 \times 31,600) = 114,000 \text{ lb } (507,072 \text{ N})$$

From Fig. 56 the slope of the c.g.s. of the strands is

$$\frac{11.68 - 5.30}{[(37'-6") - (10'-0")] \times 12} = 0.0193$$

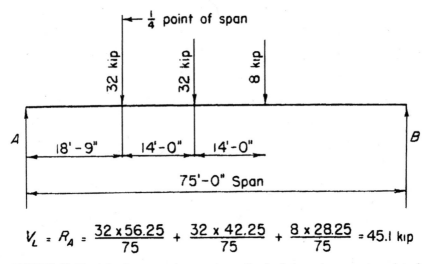

$$V_L = R_A = \frac{32 \times 56.25}{75} + \frac{32 \times 42.25}{75} + \frac{8 \times 28.25}{75} = 45.1 \text{ kip}$$

**FIGURE 60.** Truck loading to produce maximum live-load shear at one-quarter point of span.

The shear carried by the strands is

$$0.0193 \times 604,800 = 11,700 \text{ lb } (52,042 \text{ N})$$
$$\text{Effective } V_u = 114,000 - 11,700 = 102,300 \text{ lb } (450,030 \text{ N})$$

Apply the formula from the design guide

$$A_v = \frac{(V_u - V_c)s}{2f'_v \cdot jd}$$

In this example $V_c = 180b'jd$.

Since the tendons slope, $d$ at the quarter point is less than $d$ at midspan. Refer to Fig. 56. The tendons slope $11.68 - 5.30 = 6.38$ in. (162 mm) in 27.5 ft (8.38 m). Since the quarter point is 18.75 ft (5.72 m) from the end, the drop of the tendons to this point is

$$\frac{18.75}{27.5} (6.38) = 4.35 \text{ in. } (110.5 \text{ mm})$$

$$8.59 = e \text{ at end from Fig. 56}$$

$$24.73 = \text{c.g.c. to top fiber from Fig. 53}$$
$$\underline{7.00} = \text{poured-in-place slab}$$
$$d = 44.67$$

Then
$$p = \frac{4.36}{(66 \times 0.88) \, 44.67} = 0.00168$$

$$f_{su} = 248,000 \left( 1 - \frac{0.5 \times 0.00168 \times 248,000}{5000} \right) = 238,000$$

$j$ can be computed from the following portion of formula ($a$) in the design guide

$$j = 1 - \frac{k_2 p f_{su}}{k_1 k_3 f'_c}$$

Substituting numerical values,

$$j = 1 - 0.6 \frac{0.00168 \times 238,000}{5000} = 0.952$$

Then $V_c = 180 \times 7 \times 0.952 \times 44.67 = 53,600$ lb (238,413 N)

From the design guide the maximum spacing of stirrups is three-fourths of the depth of the member. Since this is a composite section, the provisions of the design guide should also be considered. From this the maximum spacing of ties between the precast and poured-in-place sections is 24 in. (609.6 mm). For the first trial we shall use $s = 24$ in. (609.6 mm) and intermediate-grade reinforcing steel bars which have a yield strength of $f'_a = 40,000$ psi (275.8 MPa).

Substituting numerical values in the equation for $A_v$,

$$A_v = \frac{(102,300 - 53,600)24}{2 \times 40,000 \times 0.952 \times 44.67} = 0.344 \text{ sq.in. (221.9 mm}^2)$$

From the design guide the minimum amount of web reinforcement is

$$A_v = 0.0025 b' s$$

Substituting numerical values,

$$A_v = 0.0025 \times 7 \times 24 = 0.420 \text{ sq.in. (270.9 mm}^2)$$

This requirement governs, and the same stirrups will be used the full length of the beam. Since the unit strength of the stirrups is not a factor in this requirement, we shall check the use of structural-grade bars having a yield strength of $f'_u = 33,000$ psi (227.5 MPa).

$$\frac{40,000}{33,000} (0.344) = 0.417 \text{ sq.in. (269 mm}^2)$$

This is less than 0.420, so we can furnish 0.420 sq.in. (270.9 mm²) of structural-grade bars every 24 in. (609.6 mm).

The area of two No. 4 bars is

$$2 \times 0.196 = 0.392 \text{ sq.in. (252.9 mm}^2)$$

$$\frac{0.392}{0.420} (24) = 22.4 \text{ in. (568.9 mm)}$$

Use two No. 4 bars at a maximum spacing of 22³/₈ in. (568.3 mm) center to center for the full length of the beam.

In a composite structure it is also necessary to check the shear between the precast section and the poured-in-place section. Use the formula

$$v = \frac{V_u Q}{I_c t'}$$

in which $t'$ is the width of the contact surface between the two sections. From the design guide "$Q$ = statical moment of cross section area, above or below the level being investigated for shear, about the centroid." Refer to Figs. 50 and 51 for dimensions used in computing $Q$.

$$Q = 7 \times 66 \times 0.88 (19.86 - 3.5) = 6650$$

The shear due to the dead weight of the beam, slab, and diaphragms is carried by the precast beam. The shear carried by the composite section is only that due to the wearing surface and the live load, which is

Wearing surface = 110 lb/ft × ⁷⁵/₄ × 1.5 = 3,100 lb (13.8 kN)
Live load = 31,600 lb × 2.5 = 79,000 lb (351.4 kN)
Applicable $V_u$ = 82,100 lb (365.2 kN)

(The 1.5 and 2.5 are ultimate load factors.) Substituting the numerical values in the formula,

$$v = \frac{82,100 \times 6650}{314,825 \times 16} = 109 \text{ psi (751 kPa)}$$

Since this is less than 150 psi (1032 kPa) the second item of the design guide applies. It requires the minimum steel tie requirements of the design guide and it also requires that the contact surface of the precast element be artificially roughened.

From the design guide the minimum requirement is two No. 3 bars at 12-in. (304.8-mm) centers or 2 × 0.11 = 0.22 sq.in. (142 mm²) in 12 in. (304.8 mm). For stirrups we are using two No. 4 bars which have an area of 0.392 sq.in. (0.392 mm²). The required spacing for these bars as ties is

$$\frac{0.392}{0.22} \times 12 = 21.4 \text{ in. (543.6 mm)}$$

Use two No. 4 bars at 21³/₈-in. (542.9-mm) centers for stirrups and ties. If the tie requirement were appreciably greater than the stirrup requirement, it might be more economical to use stirrups as required and intermediate dowels to complete the requirement for ties.

## 10. Compute camber

Precise computation of camber in a prestressed concrete member is difficult because $E_c$, determined by the formula given in the design guide can be in error by 25 percent. Other factors, some of them difficult to evaluate, also influence the accurate computation of camber. The following factors affect camber:

1. The actual prestressing force applied to the concrete member is less than the initial prestressing force by the stress losses in the steel due to

    a. Relaxation of stress in the strands while attached to the anchors in the casting bed
    b. Shrinkage of the concrete during curing
    c. Elastic shortening of the concrete when prestressed

2. Changes in conditions which occur as time passes

    a. Prestressing force decreases approaching $F$
    b. $E_c$ increases as concrete strength increases
    c. $E_c$ is less under a constant load than under a short-time load because of creep

3. Effect of erection procedure (applied here to the composite structure being designed)

    a. After the concrete member is prestressed, camber increases due to creep in the concrete. The rate of increase drops as tension in the strands drops, concrete strength increases, and rate of creep drops. The total increase is a function of the length of time that elapses between the prestressing operation and placement of the poured-in-place slab.
    b. When the slab and diaphragms are poured, their dead weight, which is carried by the beam, causes a deflection that reduces the camber in the beam.
    c. During its entire period of service the beam is under constant stress due to the prestressing force plus the dead-weight moment of beam, slab, and diaphragms. The camber tends to change.

There is no stress in the slab under this condition, but the cured slab forms a composite section with the beam, and this stiffer section acts to reduce the change in camber due to creep.

When computing camber the engineer should consider the degree of accuracy with which he/she knows the various properties of the structure and set up his/her analysis accordingly. For this structure we shall assume that the camber at the time the roadway slab is poured is equal to the instantaneous camber that would be caused by the application of the full initial prestressing force. In doing this we are assuming that the reduction in initial prestressing force due to relaxation, shrinkage, and elastic shortening is offset by the growth in camber due to creep in the concrete from the time of prestressing to the time the slab is poured.

At the time of prestressing $f'_c = 4000$ psi (27.6 MPa). From

$$E_c = 1,800,000 + 500 f'_c = 1,800,000 + (500 \times 4000) = 3,800,000$$

Deflection $\Delta_G$ due to the dead load of the beam is computed by the standard formula

$$\Delta_G = \frac{5wl^4}{384EI}$$

$$= \frac{5 \times 583(75^4)12^3}{384 \times 3,800,000 \times 125,390} = -0.87 \text{ in. } (-22.1\,\text{mm})$$

Deflection due to the eccentricity of the prestressing force is computed by the moment-area method.

At the ends of the girder

$$M_e = 8.59 \times 670,000 = 5,750,000 \text{ in·lb (649.2 kNm)}$$

At the center of span

$$M_e = 14.97 \times 670,000 = 10,030,000 \text{ in·lb (1132.4 kNm)}$$

The moment diagram for the bending moment due to prestress is plotted in Fig. 61. Taking moments about the support

$$\Delta_I = \frac{5,750,000(37.5 \times 12)(18.75 \times 12)}{EI} = \frac{582,000(10^6)}{EI}$$

$$\Delta_{II} = \frac{4,280,000(27.5 \times 12) \, {}^{1}\!/_{2}\,({}^{2}\!/_{3} \times 27.5 \times 12)}{EI} = \frac{155,000(10^6)}{EI}$$

$$\Delta_{III} = \frac{4,280,000(10 \times 12)(32.5 \times 12)}{EI} = \frac{200,000(10^6)}{EI}$$

$$\Delta_{F_o} = \Delta_I + \Delta_{II} + \Delta_{III} = \frac{937,000(10^6)}{EI}$$

$$\Delta_{F_o} = \frac{937,000(10^6)}{3,800,000 \times 125,390} = +1.97 \text{ in. (50 mm)}$$

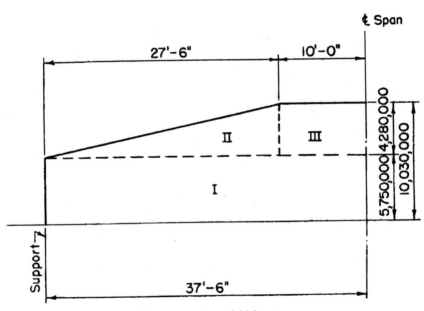

**FIGURE 61.** Diagram of bending moment due to initial prestress.

Net camber $= +1.97 - 0.87 = +1.10$ in. (27.9 mm)

When the slab and diaphragms are poured, the strength of the concrete in the beam will be 5,000 psi and

$$E_c = 1,800,000 + (500 \times 5000) = 4,300,000$$

We shall assume that the slab and diaphragm are poured in such a manner that their entire weight is carried by the beam before the slab concrete sets sufficiently to create a composite section. Deflection due to slab weight is

$$\Delta_{SS} = \frac{5 \times 480(75^4)12^3}{384 \times 4,300,000 \times 125,390} = -0.63 \text{ in. } (-16 \text{ mm})$$

Deflection at the center of span due to the diaphragms is

$$\Delta_{SD} = \frac{1375(25 \times 12)[3(75 \times 12)^2 - 4(25 \times 12)^2]}{24 \times 4,300,000 \times 125,390} = -0.07 \text{ in. } (-1.78 \text{ mm})$$

Total deflection from the slab and diaphragms is

$$-0.63 + (-0.07) = -0.70 \text{ in. } (-17.8 \text{ mm})$$

After the slab is poured, the net camber in the beam is $1.10 - 0.70 = +0.40$ in. (10.2 mm). Since all the stresses in the beam at this time will be sustained permanently, the camber will gradually increase owing to creep in the concrete. If the beam were acting independently, camber could be expected to increase 100 to 300 percent per the design guide. Actually the beam and slab now form a composite structure in which the stress in the slab is zero. The tendency of the beam to increase its camber is resisted by the composite section, so that the resultant increase is less than that would be expected if the beam were acting alone. We shall assume that the camber growth beyond this point would be 150 percent if the beam were acting independently. The resistance of the composite section will reduce this in the ratio of the moments of inertia of the two sections. Thus the camber growth will be

$$1.50(0.40)\frac{125,390}{314,825} = 0.25$$

Total final camber $= 0.25 + 0.40 = 0.65$ in. (16.5 mm)

Compute live-load deflection under the truck loading shown in Fig. 62a. Considering transverse load distribution and impact factor, the portion of a 32-kip (142.3 kN) axle load carried by one beam and slab unit is

$$32 \times 0.55 \times 1.25 = 22 \text{ kips (97.8 kN)}$$

and of an 8-kip (35.6 kN) axle load is

$$8 \times 0.55 \times 1.25 = 5.5 \text{ kips (24.5 kN)}$$

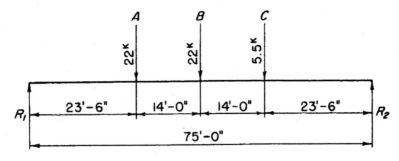

(*a*) Applied live load

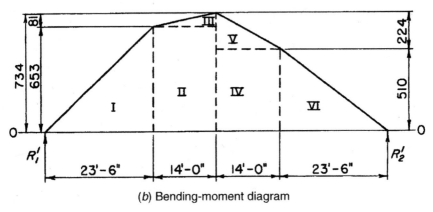

(*b*) Bending-moment diagram

**FIGURE 62**

We shall compute the deflection by the method of loading the beam with the $M/EI$ diagram. Deflection is equal to the moment caused by this load.

Compute the bending-moment diagram, referring to Fig. 62*a*.

$$R_1 = \frac{22 \times 51.5}{75.0} + \frac{22 \times 37.5}{75.0} + \frac{5.5 \times 23.5}{75.0} = 27.8 \text{ kips (123.7 kN)}$$

$$R_2 = 22 + 22 + 5.5 - 27.8 = 21.7 \text{ kips (96.5 kN)}$$

$$M_A = 23.5 \times 27.8 = 653 \text{ ft·kips (884.8 kNm)}$$

$$M_B = (37.5 \times 27.8) - (14.0 \times 22.0) = 734 \text{ ft·kips (994.6 kNm)}$$

$$M_C = 23.5 \times 21.7 = 510 \text{ ft·kips (691.1 kNm)}$$

Plot the bending-moment diagram (Fig. 62*b*).

Compute the moment at the center of span under the moment diagram applied to the beam in Fig. 62*b*. Take moments about $R_1'$.

I.   $23.5 \times 653 \times 0.5 = 7672 \times 15.7 = 120,500$

II.   $14.0 \times 653 \qquad = 9140 \times 30.5 = 278,500$

III.   $14.0 \times 81 \times 0.5 \ = 567 \times 32.83 = 18,600$

IV. $14.0 \times 510$ $= 7140 \times 44.5 = 317,600$
V. $14.0 \times 224 \times 0.5 = 1568 \times 42.17 = 66,100$
VI. $23.5 \times 510 \times 0.5 = \underline{5990} \times 59.3 = \underline{355,000}$
$\qquad\qquad\qquad\qquad\qquad 32,077 \qquad\qquad 1,156,300$

$R'_2 = 1,156,300 \div 75 = 15,430$ ft²·kips (6.38 kNm²)
$R'_1 = 32,077 - 15,430 = 16,647$ ft²·kips (6.83 kNm²)

Compute the moment at the center of span for Fig. 62*b*. Take moments of loads and reactions to the left of the center of span.

$$R'_1 = 37.5 \times 16,647 = +624,000$$
$$\text{I} = 21.8 \times \quad 7672 = -167,000$$
$$\text{II} = \quad 7.0 \times \quad 9140 = \quad -64,000$$
$$\text{III} = \quad 4.7 \times \quad 567 = \quad \underline{-2700}$$

$$M = +390,300 \text{ft}^3 \cdot \text{kips (50.7 kNm}^3\text{)}$$

$$\text{Deflection} = \frac{M}{EI}$$

or $\qquad \dfrac{390,300 \times 1000(12^3)}{4,300,000 \times 314,825} = 0.50$ in. (12.7 mm)

Final camber under live load = $0.65 - 0.50 = 0.15$ in. (3.8 mm)

This procedure is the work of H. Kent Preston, P.E., whose affiliations, at the time of its preparation, were: Engineer, Construction Materials, John A. Roebling's Sons Division; The Colorado Fuel and Iron Corporation; Fellow, American Society of Civil Engineers; Professional Member, Prestressed Concrete Institute. SI values were added by the handbook editor.

## DESIGN OF A DOUBLE-T ROOF IN LIGHTWEIGHT PRESTRESSED CONCRETE FOR A BRIDGE TOLL-STATION BUILDING

Design a double-T roof in lightweight concrete using prestressed members. Pertinent data on the design are given in the following paragraphs.

The majority of prestressed concrete members for buildings are made in standard shapes to suit the standard forms of the casting yards in the vicinity of the structure. Each producer has tables showing the details of its standard sections and their load-carrying capacity for various spans. Knowing the applied load and the span, the engineer can select the required section from the tables.

The following analysis determines the maximum span of a typical double-T section under specific conditions. Such an analysis would be used in setting up a table for standard sections. The conditions of design are:

1. Design in accordance with provisions of an accepted design guide for prestressed concrete.

2. Tendons to be seven-wire strands in a straight line. (Deflected strands almost always give better efficiency and more camber control, but straight strands are often used for simplicity of casting-bed operation. It is therefore desirable to present one analysis using straight strands.)

3. Lightweight concrete at 110 lb/ft³(1760 kg/m³) $f'_c$ = 5000 psi (34.5 MPa); $f'_{ci}$ = 4000 psi (27.6 MPa).

4. Roofing weight = 10 psf (48.8 kg/m²)

5. Live load = 30 psf (146.4 kg/m²)

6. We shall assume that actual tests on concrete made with the lightweight aggregate being used show that its $E_c$ is approximately 75 percent of that for standard concrete and that the stress loss in the strands is 7500 psi (51.7 MPa) greater than that in standard concrete.

## Calculation Procedure:

1. Compute properties of concrete section

See Fig. 63 for dimensions.
Take moments about the bottom of the section.

| Section | | | Area, $A$ | $y$ | $Ay$ | $Ay^2$ | $I_o$ |
|---|---|---|---|---|---|---|---|
| I = 72 × 2 | = | 144 | 15 | 2,160 | 32,400 | 48 |
| II = 6¹/₂ × 2 × 2 | = | 26 | 13 | 338 | 4,400 | 8 |
| III = 2 × 2 ×¹/₂ × 4 | = | 8 | 13.33 | 107 | 1,430 | 2 |
| IV = 5 × 12 × 2 | = | 120 | 6 | 720 | 4,320 | 1,440 |
| V = 1¹/₂ × 12 × ¹/₂ × 2 | = | 18 | 8 | 144 | 1,152 | 144 |
| | | 316 | | 3,469 | 43,702 | 1,642 |
| | | | | | 1,642 | |
| | | | | | 45,344 | |

$$y^b = 3469 \div 316 = 10.98$$
$$y^t = 16 - 10.98 = 5.02$$
$$I = 45,344 - 316(10.98^2) = 7250$$
$$Z_b = 7250 \div 10.98 = 660$$
$$Z_t = 7250 \div 5.02 = 1445$$

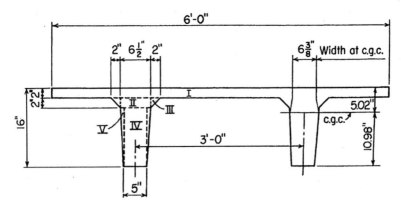

**FIGURE 63.**  Cross section of 16-in-deep double T.

Weight at 110 lb per cu ft

$$w_G = \frac{110 \times 316}{144} = 240 \text{ lb/ft (357.1 kg/m)}$$

The aim in this procedure is to determine the maximum span the member can support and this span is unknown at this stage of the computations. Our next step is to establish the details of the maximum permissible prestressing force for the member.

Since the strands are tensioned in a straight line rather than deflected, the maximum amount of prestress is limited by the stresses it produces at the end of the span where there is no counteracting dead-load moment.

Maximum allowable compressive stress in the bottom fiber is

$$0.45 \times 5000 = 2250 \text{ psi (15.5 MPa) under final prestress}$$

$$0.60 \times 4000 = 2400 \text{ psi (16.6 MPa) under initial prestress}$$

Maximum allowable tensile stress in the top fiber is

$$3\sqrt{4000} = 190 \text{ psi (1.3 MPa) under initial prestress}$$

$$0.04 \times 5000 = 200 \text{ psi (1.38 MPa) under final prestress}$$

Assume that the tendons will be $7/16$-in. (11.1-mm) diameter strands at an initial tension of 18,900 lb (84.1 kN) per strand. This is a stress of $18,900 \div 0.1089 = 173,600$ psi (1,196.8 MPa). The stress loss in standard concrete is 35,000 psi (241.3 MPa). Additional loss because of the lightweight aggregate being used is 7500 for a total of 42,500 psi (293 MPa). Final stress is $173,600 - 42,500 = 131,100$ psi (903.8 MPa). Find immediate stress losses between $F_I$ and $F_o$.

*Elastic Shortening of Concrete.* For this lightweight concrete a reasonable estimate of immediate losses is 25,000 psi (172.4 MPa). Then

$$f_{F_i} = 173,600 \text{ psi (1196 MPa)}$$
$$\text{Immediate losses} = \underline{25,000} \text{ psi(172.4 MPa)}$$
$$f_{F_o} = 148,600 \text{ psi (1024.5 MPa)}$$

Therefore

$$f_{F_o} = \frac{148,600}{131,100} f_F = 1.134 f_F$$

In this procedure our object is to compute the maximum capacity of the member, so we shall choose the magnitude and location of the prestressing force that will develop the maximum negative moment without exceeding allowable stresses. In pretensioned members these factors are usually governed by the stresses due to $F_o$. We can check this by assuming that the stresses due to $F_o$ are the maximum allowable, or

$$f_{F_o}^t = -190 \quad \text{and} \quad f_{F_o}^b = +2400$$

Then

$$f_F^t = -190 \div 1.134 = -167$$
$$f_F^b = +2400 \div 1.134 = +2120$$

Both of these are less than the maximum allowed, so $F_o$ is the governing factor. Using $F_o$ in place of $F$,

$$\frac{F_o}{A_c} - \frac{F_o e}{Z_t} = f_{F_o}^t$$

Substituting numerical values,

$$\frac{F_o}{316} - \frac{F_o e}{1445} = -190 \tag{70}$$

Using $F_o$ in place of $F$,

$$\frac{F_o}{A_c} + \frac{Fe}{Z_b} = f_{F_o}^b$$

Substituting numerical values,

$$\frac{F_o}{316} + \frac{F_o e}{660} = +2400 \tag{71}$$

Multiply (71) by $660/1445 = 0.457$ to get

$$\frac{0.457 F_o}{316} + \frac{F_o e}{1445} = +1097 \tag{72}$$

Add

$$\frac{\dfrac{F_o}{316} - \dfrac{F_o e}{1445} = -190}{\dfrac{1.457 F_o}{316} \qquad = +907}$$

$$F_o = 196,600$$
$$F = 196,600 \div 1.134 = 173,500 \text{ lb } (769.5 \text{ kN})$$

The area of one $7/16$-in (11.1-mm) strand is 0.1089 sq.in. (70.3 mm²). We have shown that the final stress in this lightweight concrete will be 131,100 psi (903.1 MPa) so the final load per strand will be

$$131,100 \div 0.1089 = 14,275 \text{ lb } (63.5 \text{ kN})$$
$$173,500 \div 14,275 = 12.15$$

We shall use the nearest even number of strands, which is 12. Then

$$F = 12 \times 14,275 = 171,300 \text{ lb } (761.9 \text{ kN})$$

and

$$F_o = 171,300 \times 1.134 = 194,200 \text{ lb } (863.8 \text{ kN})$$

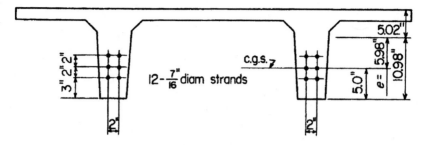

**FIGURE 64.** Trial strand pattern.

Since the force from 12 strands is slightly less than that computed for maximum prestress, the tensile stress in the top fiber will limit the eccentricity we can use. (If the calculations had required 11.6 strands, we would have used 12 strands but tensioned them only enough to give the required load instead of using their full allowable stress.) Substitute the numerical value of $F_o$ and solve for $e$.

$$\frac{194{,}200}{316} - \frac{194{,}200e}{1445} = -190$$

$$614 - 134.2e = -190$$

$$e = 5.98 \text{ in. (151.9 mm)}$$

$$10.98 - 5.98 = 5.00 \text{ in. (127 mm) from bottom to c.g.s.}$$

Use the strand pattern shown in Fig. 64. Compute the bottom fiber stress using

$$f_{F_o}^b = \frac{194{,}200}{316} + \frac{194{,}200 \times 5.98}{660} = +2376 \text{ psi (16.4 MPa)}$$

Stresses under final prestress are

$$f_F^t = -190 \div 1.134 = -167 \text{ psi } (-1.15 \text{ MPa})$$

$$f_F^b = +2376 \div 1.134 = +2090 \text{ psi } (+14.4 \text{ MPa})$$

From the design guide the allowable tension in a member of this type is

$$6\sqrt{f_c'} \quad \text{or} \quad 6\sqrt{5000} = -425 \text{ psi } (-2.93 \text{ MPa})$$

In going from its compressive stress of $+2090$ psi (14.4 MPa) under no load to its maximum allowable tensile stress of $-425$ psi ($-2.93$ MPa), the bottom fiber undergoes a stress change of $2090 - (-425) = 2515$ psi (36.2 MPa). This means that it can carry a total moment of $2515 \times 660 = 1{,}660{,}000$ in·lb (187.4 kNm) or 138,000 ft·lb (186.9 kNm).

Total applied load is 10 psf (48.8 kg/m²) for roofing plus 30 psf (146.4 kg/m²) live load = 40 psf (195.2 kg/m²) × 6-ft (1.8-m) width = 240 lb per lin ft (357.1 kg/m). Weight of double T = 240 lb per lin ft (357.1 kg/m). Total load = 240 + 240 = 480 lb per lin ft (714.2 kg/m). Substitute this load and the allowable moment in the standard formula for beams subjected to uniform loading.

$$M = \frac{wl^2}{8} \quad \text{or} \quad l^2 = \frac{8M}{w}$$

$$l^2 = \frac{8 \times 138{,}000}{480} = 2300 \qquad l = 48 \text{ ft (14.6 m)}$$

Since this particular lightweight concrete has a relatively low $E_c$, camber may be a problem, so we shall check it before we go into other calculations.

2. Compute camber

The design guide gives $E_c = 1,800,000 + 500f'_c$.

At the time of prestress release $E_c = 1,800,000 + (500 \times 4000) = 3,800,000$. This is for standard concrete, and our tests showed that the value for our concrete was about 75 percent of this, or $E_c = 75\% \times 3,800,000 = 2,850,000$.

Deflection: $\Delta_G$ due to dead load is

$$\Delta_G = \frac{5\,wl^4}{384\,EI} = \frac{5(240)\,48^4\,(12^3)}{384(2,850,000)7250} = -1.39 \text{ in. } (35.3 \text{ mm})$$

In our present procedure we shall assume that the camber at the time of erection is that which would be caused instantaneously by force $F_I$.

$$F_I = 18,900 \times 12 = 227,000 \text{ lb } (1009.7 \text{ kN})$$

Since the strands are straight, they create a constant negative moment for the full length of the member. This moment is $227,000 \times 5.98 = 1,360,000$ in·lb (153.5 kNm). From Fig. 65 the camber $\Delta F_I$ at the center of span due to $F_I$ is

$$\Delta F_I = \frac{1,360,000\,(48 \times 12)^2}{8 \times 2,850,000 \times 7250} = +2.73 \text{ in. } (69.3 \text{ mm})$$

Net camber $= 2.73 - 1.39 = +1.34$ in. (34 mm)

This is the approximate net camber when the members are erected if the time lapse between casting and erection is not too large.

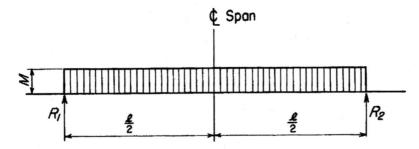

**FIGURE 65.** Deflection of beam to constant moment for full length of beam computed by moment-area method.

Deflection due to roofing at 60 lb per lin ft (89.3 kg/m) is

$$\Delta_s = \frac{5(60)48^4(12^3)}{384\,(2,850,000)7250} = -0.35 \text{ in. } (-8.89 \text{ mm})$$

Net camber under dead load at time of erection $= 1.34 - 0.35 = +0.99$ in. $(+25.2$ mm).
If camber growth is 150 percent, then final camber under dead load will be $0.99 + 150\%$ $(0.99) = +2.48$ in. $(62.9$ mm).

This might be considered a rather high camber for a 48-ft (14.6-m) span.

The design and details of a prestressed concrete member of this type can be altered by one or more of five methods to decrease the camber. They are:

1. Use a deeper double T which will have a higher moment of inertia and will be operating at lower unit stress. An 18-in. (457.2-mm) deep member would weigh. about 8 percent more than the 16-in. (406.4-mm) member.

2. Use standard concrete [150 lb/ft³ (2400 kg/m³)]. This will increase the dead weight about 36 percent [20 psf (97.6 kg/m³)], which adds considerably to the load on the supporting beams and columns. Stress loss will be less, but this advantage is offset by the additional dead weight of the member itself, which increases the total bending moment.

3. Use deflected strands. Computations for camber of members with deflected strands are carried out in the previous calculation procedure.

4. Use "partial prestress." For this particular section it would probably involve the same number of strands as shown in Fig. 64 but used at a lower initial tension. As a result the section would have the same ultimate strength as the fully prestressed section but it would develop higher tensile stresses under full live load.

5. Use a larger prestressing force. The magnitude of the camber is a function of the difference between the unit stress in the top fiber of the section and the unit stress in the bottom fiber. If the difference in stress is large, the camber is large. In the double-T section being considered, the stresses in the top fiber are always low. The difference between top and bottom fiber stress can be decreased by setting the magnitude and location of the prestressing force to put some compressive stress in the top fiber. Since we want to keep maximum stress in the bottom fiber, this means a larger prestressing force with a smaller $e$.

In this particular analysis our object is to establish the maximum capacity of the double T in Fig. 63 when made of lightweight aggregate with straight strands.

We shall determine the prestressing force that gives the maximum allowable compressive stress in the top fiber of the concrete and compute the camber. If this camber is too small, we can interpolate between the two conditions of prestress to get the desired camber.

The limiting condition for maximum prestress in the top fiber occurs under final prestress plus full live load. The dead- and live-load stresses are a function of the span chosen. The maximum span is dependent upon the compressive stress in the bottom fiber. From previous calculations the maximum $f_{F_o}^b = 2400$ psi (16.6 MPa) and $f_F^b = 2400 \div 1.134 = 2120$ psi (14.6 MPa). The resulting stress change in the bottom fiber is $2120 - (-425) = 2545$ psi (17.5 MPa) which gives a bending moment of $(2545 \times 660) \div 12 = 140,000$ ft·lb (189.7 kNm). Total load is 480 lb per ft (714.2 kg/m)

$$1^2 = \frac{8 \times 140,000}{480} = 2333 \qquad 1 = 48.2 \text{ ft } (14.7 \text{ m})$$

Use 48.0 ft (14.6 m). Compressive stress in the top fiber under full live-load moment $f_{G+S+L}^t$ is

$$f_{G+S+L}^t = \frac{140,000 \times 12}{1445} = +1161 \text{ psi } (+8.0 \text{ MPa})$$

From previous calculations the maximum allowable compressive stress is 2250 psi (15.5 MPa). Thus the maximum compressive stress in the top fiber due to final prestress is $2250 - 1161 = +1089$ psi (7.5 MPa). Using $f_F^t = +1089$ and $f_F^b = +2120$ psi (14.6 MPa) $F$ and $e$.

$$\frac{F}{316} - \frac{Fe}{1445} = +1089 \tag{73}$$

$$\frac{F}{316} + \frac{Fe}{660} = +2120 \tag{74}$$

Multiply Eq. 74 by $660/1445 = 0.457$ to get

$$\frac{0.457F}{316} + \frac{Fe}{1445} = +970$$

Add

$$\frac{F}{316} - \frac{Fe}{1445} = +1089$$
$$\overline{\frac{14.57F}{316} = 2059} \tag{75}$$

$$F = 446,000 \text{ lb } (1983.8 \text{ kN})$$

Substituting in 75,

$$\frac{446,000}{316} - \frac{446,000e}{1445} = +1089$$
$$1410 - 309e = +1089$$
$$e = 1.04 \text{ in. } (26.4 \text{ mm})$$

The ratio that $F_I$ has to $F$ will be the same as the ratio that the stress due to $F_I$ has to the stress due to $F$, or

$$F_I = \frac{446,000 \times 173,600}{131,100} = 590,000$$

$$M_{F_I} = F_I e = 590,000 \times 1.04 = 613,000 \text{ in·lb } (69.2 \text{ kNm})$$

$$\Delta_{F_I} = \frac{613,000(48 \times 12)^2}{8(2,850,000)7250} = +1.23 \text{ in. } (+31.2 \text{ mm})$$

$$\Delta_G = \frac{5(240)48^4(12^3)}{384(2,850,000)7250} = -1.39 \text{ in. } (-35.3 \text{ mm})$$

Under its own dead weight the section would have a negative camber of $1.23 - 1.39 = -.16$ in. $(-4.1$ mm$)$. Therefore the required prestress is somewhere between the first and second of the foregoing calculations. Its magnitude will depend upon the desired camber.

We shall arbitrarily try 14 strands $^7/_{16}$ in. $(11.1$ mm$)$ in diameter. Then

$$F_o = 14 \times 131{,}100 \times 0.1089 \times 1.134 = 227{,}000 \text{ lb } (1{,}009.7 \text{ kN})$$

Since we want to keep the maximum allowable prestress in the bottom fiber, we shall set $f^b_{F_o} = 2400$ psi. and solve for $e$.

$$\frac{227{,}000}{316} + \frac{227{,}000e}{660} = 2400$$
$$718 + 344e = 2400$$
$$e = 4.89 \text{ in. } (124.2 \text{ mm})$$
$$10.98 - 4.89 = 6.09 \text{ in. from bottom to c.g.s.}$$

Use the strand pattern shown in Fig. 66. Find its c.g.s.

$$
\begin{array}{llll}
4 & \times\ 2^3/_4 & = 11 \\
8 & \times\ 6^3/_4 & = 54 \\
\underline{2} & \times\ 10^3/_4 & = \underline{21.5} \\
14 & & 86.5
\end{array}
$$

$$86.5 \div 14 = 6.17 \text{ in. } (156.7 \text{ mm}) \text{ bottom to c.g.s.}$$
$$e = 10.98 - 6.17 = 4.81$$

Using the strand pattern in Fig. 66 as a final design, establish the maximum span of the member and check stresses, camber, and deflection.

$$F = F_o \div 1.134 = 227{,}000 \div 1.134 = 200{,}000 \text{ lb } (889.6 \text{ kN})$$
$$f^t_F = \frac{200{,}000}{316} - \frac{200{,}000 \times 4.81}{1445} = -33$$
$$f^b_F = \frac{200{,}000}{316} + \frac{200{,}000 \times 4.81}{660} = +2090$$

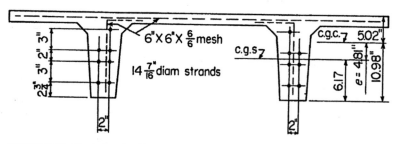

**FIGURE 66.** Final strand pattern.

Total stress change in the bottom under dead plus live load will be from $+2{,}090$ to $-425 = 2515$ psi (17.3 MPa). This is, entirely by coincidence, identical with the value computed using 10 strands with a larger $e$. From the previous computations this stress change is good for a span of 48 ft (14.6 m) and

$$\Delta_G = -1.39 \text{ in. } (-35.3 \text{ mm}) \quad \Delta_S = -0.35 \text{ in. } (-8.9 \text{ mm})$$

Check camber:

$$F_I = 14 \times 18{,}900 = 265{,}000 \text{ lb } (1178.7 \text{ kN})$$

$$M_{F_I} = 265{,}000 \times 4.81 = 1{,}275{,}000 \text{ in·lb } (143.9 \text{ kNm})$$

$$\Delta_{F_I} = \frac{1{,}275{,}000(48 \times 12)^2}{8(2{,}850{,}000)7250} = +2.56 \text{ in. } (65 \text{ mm})$$

$$\Delta_{F_I} - \Delta_G = 2.56 - 1.39 = +1.17 \text{ in. } (29.7 \text{ mm})$$

Net camber under dead load and weight of roofing is $1.17 - .35 = +.82$ in. (20.8 mm). If camber growth is 150 percent, then the final camber under dead load will be

$$0.82 + 150\%(0.82) = +2.05 \text{ in. } (52 \text{ mm})$$

When full live load is applied, concrete strength will be 5000 psi (34.5 MPa) and

$$E_c = 1{,}800{,}000 + 500(5000) = 4{,}300{,}000 \times 75\% = 3{,}225{,}000$$

$$\Delta_L = \frac{5(180)(48^4)(12^3)}{384(3{,}225{,}000)7250} = -0.92 \text{ in. } (-23.4 \text{ mm})$$

Under full live load the net camber will be $2.05 - 0.92 = +1.13$ in. (28.7 mm). This is a reasonable value, so we shall complete the design on this basis. The designer must remember that the camber calculations are only as accurate as the data on which they are based such as the value of $E_c$ at various stages, the time lapse before application of roofing, etc.
Check other critical stresses.

$$f^t_{F_0} = -33 \times 1.134 = -37$$
$$f^b_{F_0} = +2090 \times 1.134 = +2370$$

These are within the allowable limits. Since with straight strands the stresses from prestress are constant for the full length of the member, the only other critical stresses are those at mid-span under full load.

$$M_{G+S+L} = \frac{480(48^2)12}{8} = 1{,}658{,}000 \text{ in·lb}(186.3 \text{ kNm})$$

$$f^t_{G+S+L} = 1{,}658{,}000 \div 1445 = +1148$$
$$f^b_{G+S+L} = 1{,}658{,}000 \div 660 = -2512$$
$$f^t_{F+G+S+L} = -33 + 1148 = +1115$$
$$f^b_{F+G+S+L} = +2090 - 2512 = -422$$

Since these stresses are within the allowable limits and the camber was satisfactory, we can use the strand pattern shown in Fig. 66 for a 48-ft (14.6-m) span.

It should be noted that either the original design with greater camber or a partial pre-stress design is more economical where acceptable. The method we have chosen uses two extra strands for the purpose of reducing camber. Since the section is 6 ft (1.8 m) wide, we are using $1/3$ ft (0.1 m) of strand per square foot of roof. If 1 ft (0.3 m) of $7/16$-in. (11.1-mm) strand increases the selling price of the concrete member by 9 cents, then this method increases the selling price by 3 cents per square foot over the original design.

At this point it is suggested that the reader makes computations of his/her own using, sep-arately, Methods 1, 2, and 3 for decreasing camber as suggested near the beginning of this step. To give a true comparison each method should be designed to the roofing and live load used here and to a 48-ft (14.6-m) span. In comparing the results remember these factors:

*Method 1.* The deeper section uses more concrete and has more dead weight. It also makes the structure slightly higher and requires a higher wall to seal it off at the sides of the structure.

*Method 2.* The supporting structure must carry the additional dead weight. This may not be important if the double T's rest on a masonry wall, but it is important if they are supported by a girder.

*Method 3.* This method increases neither material cost nor dead weight. If the casting bed is equipped for efficiently deflecting strands, the additional cost will be small and this method will be more economical than 1 or 2.

3. Check ultimate strength to make sure it meets the requirements in the specification; check the percentage of prestressing steel

Evaluate the formula

$$\frac{1.4 d p f_{su}}{f_c'}$$

From Fig. 66

$$d = 16 - 6.17 = 9.83 \text{ in. (249.7 mm)}$$

From Fig. 66

$$A_S = 14 \times 0.1089 = 1.525 \text{ sq.in. (983.9 mm}^2)$$

$$P = \frac{A_S}{bd} = \frac{1.525}{72 \times 9.83} = 0.00215$$

From the design guide

$$f_S' = 27,000 \div 0.1089 = 248,000 \text{ psi}(1709.7 \text{ MPa})$$

From the design guide

$$
\begin{aligned}
f_{su} &= f_s'\left(1 - 0.5\frac{pf_s'}{f_c'}\right) \\
&= 248,000\left(1 - 0.5\frac{0.00215 \times 248,000}{5000}\right) \\
&= 248,000(1 - 0.053) = 235,000 \text{ psi (1620 MPa)} \\
f_c' &= 5000 \text{ psi (34.5 MPa)}
\end{aligned}
$$

Substituting in the formula,

$$\frac{1.4 \times 9.83 \times 0.00215 \times 235,000}{5000} = 1.39 \text{ in. } (35.3 \text{ mm})$$

Since this is less than the flange thickness of 2 in. (50.8 mm) the formula for rectangular sections in the design guide is applicable. This formula is

$$M_u = A_s f_{su} d \left( 1 - \frac{k_2}{k_1 k_3} \frac{p f_{su}}{f_c'} \right) \tag{a}$$

The statement in the design guide that $k_2/k_1 k_3 = 0.6$ is also correct for a lightweight concrete of the comparatively high strength being used here.

Substituting numerical values in (a),

$$M_u = 1525 \times 235,000 \times 9.83 \left( 1 - \frac{0.6 \times 0.00215 \times 235,000}{5000} \right)$$

$$= 3,312,000 \text{ in·lb} = 276,000 \text{ ft·lb } (373.9 \text{ kNm})$$

From the design guide the minimum ultimate required is

$$1.2D + 2.4L$$

or

$$1.8 \, (D + L)$$

Where values for $W$ are specified, the other expressions in the design guide should also be evaluated and checked.

The dead weight of the member plus the roofing is $240 + 60 = 300$ lb/lin ft. (446.4 kg/m). Then

$$M_D = \frac{300(48^2)}{8} = 86,400 \text{ ft·lb } (117 \text{ kNm})$$

$$M_L = \frac{180(48^2)}{8} = 51,800 \text{ ft·lb } (70.2 \text{ kNm})$$

$$1.2(86,400) + 2.4(51,800) = 228,000 \text{ ft·lb } (308.9 \text{ kNm})$$
$$1.8(86,400 + 51,800) = 249,000 \text{ ft·lb } (337.8 \text{ kNm})$$

Since both of these are less than $M_u$, the member has sufficient ultimate strength. Check the percentage of prestressing steel in accordance with the design guide.

$$\frac{p f_{su}}{f_c'} = \frac{0.00215 \times 235,000}{5000} = 0.1011$$

Since this is less than 0.30, the member is not overreinforced.

4. Design the shear steel

From the design guide web reinforcement is not needed when

$$\frac{p f_s'}{f_c'} \gtrapprox 0.3 \frac{f_{se} b'}{f_s' b}$$

Since shearing unit stress is normally greatest at the c.g.c., we shall use the web thickness at that point giving $b' = 2 \times 6^3/8 = 12^3/4$.

Substituting numerical values from calculations in preceding steps,

$$\frac{0.00215 \times 248,000}{5000} \gtrless 0.3\frac{131,100 \times 12.75}{248,000 \times 72}$$

$$0.1066 \gtrless 0.0281$$

Since this is not true, web reinforcement is required.

The web-reinforcement requirement for this member is described in the design guide. The maximum requirement occurs 16 in. (406 mm) from the support, at which point the loaded length producing shear is

$$24 \text{ ft } 0 \text{ in.} - 1 \text{ ft } 4 \text{ in.} = 22 \text{ ft } 8 \text{ in.} = 22.67 \text{ ft } (6.9 \text{ m})$$

$$\text{Dead-load shear} = 300 \text{ lb} \times 22.67 = 6800 \text{ lb } (30.2 \text{ kN})$$

$$\text{Live-load shear} = 180 \text{ lb} \times 22.67 = 4080 \text{ lb } (18.11 \text{ kN})$$

$$V_u = 1.2(6800) + 2.4(4080) = 17,950 \text{ lb } (79.8 \text{ kN})$$

$$V_u = 1.8(6800 + 4080) = 19,600 \text{ lb } (87.2 \text{ kN})$$

The $V_u$ to be used is 19,600 1b (87.2 kN). Since the strands are in a straight line, they do not carry any shear.

Compute web reinforcement using the formula in the design guide.

The maximum spacing of stirrups is three-quarters of the depth of the member. Use $s = 12$ in. (304.8 mm). Use stirrups of structural-grade steel, which has $f_y' = 33,000$ psi (227.5 MPa). For this example

$$V_c = 180b'jd$$

$j$ can be computed from the following portion of formula ($a$) in the design guide

$$j = \left(1 - \frac{k_2}{k_1 k_3} \frac{pf_{su}}{f_c'}\right)$$

Substituting previously computed values,

$$j = 1 - \frac{0.60 \times 0.00215 \times 235,000}{5000} = 0.939$$

$$V_c = 180 \times 12.75 \times 0.939 \times 9.83 = 21,200 \text{ 1b } (94.3 \text{ kN})$$

Substituting in the formula,

$$A_v = \frac{1}{2} \frac{(19,600 - 21,200)12}{33,000 \times 0.939 \times 9.83} = \text{a negative number}$$

which means that the concrete section will carry more than the existing shear at ultimate load. Under this condition the minimum requirement of the design guide will govern. It says

$$A_v = 0.0025b's = 0.0025 \times 12.75 \times 12 = 0.382 \text{ sq.in } (246.5 \text{ mm}^2)$$

It also says "This requirement may be excessive for members with unusually thick webs and the amount of web reinforcement may be reduced if tests demonstrate that the member can develop its required flexural capacity." This last statement applies to most double-T sections. It is common practice to use a 6 by 6 in. (152 by 152 mm) by 6/6 mesh in each leg of a double T for its full length. This provides $A_v = 4 \times 0.029 = 0.116$ sq.in (74 mm²) where $s = 12$ in. (304.8 mm).

This procedure is the work of H. Kent Preston, P.E., whose affiliations, at the time of its preparation, were: Engineer, Construction Materials, John A. Roebling's Sons Division; The Colorado Fuel and Iron Corporation; Fellow, American Society of Civil Engineers; Professional Member, Prestressed Concrete Institute. SI values were added by the handbook editor.

## DESIGN OF A POST-TENSIONED GIRDER FOR A BRIDGE TOLL-BOOTH

Design a post-tensioned girder for the following set of conditions:

Span: 100 ft 0 in. (30.5 m) center to center of bearings
Live load: 30 psf (146 kg/m²)
Roofing: 10 psf (48.8 kg/m²)
Double-T roof deck: 33 psf (161 kg/m²)
Girder spacing: 30 ft (9.1 m) center to center
Concrete: $f'_c$ = 5000 psi (34.5 MPa)
Concrete: $f'_{ct}$ = to be determined by calculations
Standard concrete at 150 1b per cu ft (256 kg/m³)
Tendons to be grouted after tensioning operation is complete.

### Calculation Procedure:

### 1. Compute the properties of the cross section in Fig. 67

Take moments about the bottom.

| Section | Area, A | y | Ay | Ay² | $I_o$ |
|---|---|---|---|---|---|
| I = 21 × 6 | = 126 | 3 | 378 | 1,134 | 378 |
| II = 8 × 52 | = 416 | 32 | 13,300 | 426,000 | 93,750 |
| III = 2 × 6.5 × 6 × ½ = | 39 | 8 | 312 | 2,496 | 78 |
| IV = 2 × 11 × 4 × ½ = | 44 | 56.7 | 2,500 | 141,500 | 40 |
| V = 30 × 8 | = 240 | 62 | 14,900 | 923,000 | 1,280 |
| | 865 | | 31,390 | 1,494,130 | 95,526 |
| | | | | 95,526 | |
| | | | | 1,589,656 | |

$$y_b = 31,390 \div 865 = 36.3$$
$$y_t = 66 - 36.3 = 29.7$$
$$I = 1,589,656 - 865(36.3^2) = 448,500$$
$$Z_t = 448,500 \div 29.7 = 15,100$$
$$Z_b = 448,500 \div 36.3 = 12,350$$
$$\text{Weight} = \frac{150 \times 865}{144} = 900 \text{ lb per ft (1341 kg/m)}$$

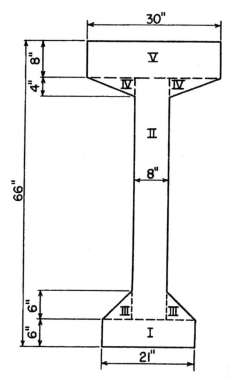

**FIGURE 67.** Cross section of girder.

## 2. Compute stresses in the member due to its own dead weight

$$M_G = \frac{900(100^2) \times 12}{8} = 13,500,000 \text{ in·lb } (1524 \text{ kNm})$$

$$f_G^t = 13,500,000 \div 15,100 = +894 \text{ psi } (+6.2 \text{ MPa})$$

$$f_G^b = 13,500,000 \div 12,350 = -1093 \text{ psi } (-7.54 \text{ MPa})$$

## 3. Compute stresses in the member due to applied loads

$$\text{Double T} = 33 \text{ psf} (161 \text{ kg/m}^2)$$

$$\text{Roofing} = \underline{10} \text{ psf} (48.8 \text{ kg/m}^2)$$
$$43 \text{ psf} (209.8 \text{ kg/m}^2)$$

$$w_s = 43 \times 30 \text{ ft} = 1290 \text{ lb/lin ft } (1920 \text{ kg/m})$$

$$M_s = \frac{1290(100^2) \times 12}{8} = 19,350,000 \text{ in·lb } (2,184.6 \text{ kNm})$$

$$f_s^t = 19,350,000 \div 15,100 = +1281$$

$$f_s^b = 19,350,000 \div 12,350 = -1567$$

Live load $= 30 \times 30 = 900$ lb/lin ft (1339 kg/m)

$$M_L = \frac{900(100^2) \times 12}{8} = 13{,}500{,}000 \text{ in·lb (1524 kNm)}$$

$$f_L^t = 13{,}500{,}000 \div 15{,}100 = +894 \text{ psi } (+6.2 \text{ MPa})$$

$$f_L^b = 13{,}500{,}000 \div 12{,}350 = -1093 \text{ psi } (-7.5 \text{ MPa})$$

## 4. Determine the magnitude and location of the prestressing force at the center of span

This computation is based on final conditions, that is, after all stress losses have taken place.
From

$$\text{Maximum compressive stress} = 0.45 \times 5000 = 2250 \text{ psi (15.5 MPa)}$$

$$\text{Maximum tensile stress in bottom} = 6\sqrt{5000} \,* = -425 \text{ psi} = f_{tp}$$

From

$$\frac{F}{A_c} + \frac{Fe}{Z_b} = -f_G^b - f_S^b - f_L^b + f_{tp}$$

Substituting numerical values,

$$\frac{F}{865} + \frac{Fe}{12{,}350} = +1093 + 1567 + 1093 - 425$$

$$\frac{F}{865} + \frac{Fe}{12{,}350} = +3328$$

From

$$\frac{F}{A_c} - \frac{Fe}{Z_t} = -f_G^t + f_{tp}$$

Since this member will constantly be under a large dead load, there will be no tensile stress in the top fiber under final conditions, so the tensile stress in the top fiber will be governed by the initial prestress condition. From the design guide this is $3\sqrt{f_{ci}'}$. Not knowing $f_{ci}'$ we shall assume it to be 4000 psi (27.6 MPa), which gives $3\sqrt{4000} = -190$ psi $(-1.3$ MPa). We shall also assume that the final prestress is 80 percent of the initial prestress giving

$$f_{tp} \text{ (for the top fiber)} = -190 \times 80 \text{ percent} = -150 \text{ psi } (-1.03 \text{ MPa})$$

Substituting

$$\frac{F}{865} - \frac{Fe}{15{,}100} = -894 - 150$$

$$= -1044$$

(78)

---

* This is not in strict accordance with the design guide. The author, accustomed to designing pretensioned structures, used an allowable tensile stress of $6\sqrt{f_c'}$. For post-tensioned bonded elements the design guide permits only $3\sqrt{f_c'}$. The discrepancy was not noted until the manuscript had been set in type. It does not change the design procedure but for an actual building the engineer should use $3\sqrt{f_c'}$ in accordance with the design guide.

Multiply (77) by 12,350/15,100 = 0.82 to get

$$\frac{0.82F}{865} + \frac{Fe}{15,100} = +2730$$

Add

$$\frac{F}{865} - \frac{Fe}{15,100} = -1044$$

$$\overline{\frac{1.82F}{865}} \quad = +1686$$

$$F = 801,000 \text{ lb (3563 kN)}$$

Substituting in Eq. 78

$$\frac{801,000}{865} - \frac{801,000e}{15,100} = -1044$$

$$926 - 53.0e = -1044$$

$$e = 37.17 \text{ in. (994 mm)}$$

Since $y_b$ is only 36.3 in. (922 mm) this value of $e$ would put the tendons below the bottom of the girder.

## 5. Select the tensioning elements to be used, and work out the details of their location in the member

Since the value of $e$ computed in Step 4 is too large for satisfactory details, we shall arbitrarily choose a smaller value. In a member of this type the c.g.s. for an $F$ of about 1,00,000 lb (4,448 kN) will be 4 to 5 in. (102 to 127 mm) above the bottom if the tendons are to be kept in an open pattern. If tendons are to be bunched as permitted, the distance can be reduced. We shall try 4.5 in. (114.3 mm) from the bottom to the c.g.s., which gives

$$e = 36.3 - 4.5 = 31.8 \text{ in. (808 mm)}$$

Substituting known values in Eq. (20),

$$\frac{F}{865} + \frac{31.8F}{12,350} = +3328$$

$$12,350F + (865 \times 31.8)F = 3328 \times 865 \times 12,350$$

$$F = 892,000 \text{ lb}$$

$$f_F^t = \frac{892,000}{865} - \frac{892,000 \times 31.8}{15,100} = -847 \text{ psi } (-5.8 \text{ MPa})$$

$$f_F^b = \frac{892,000}{865} + \frac{892,000 \times 31.8}{12,350} = +3328 \text{ psi } (+22.9 \text{ MPa})$$

Stresses under full load:

$$f_{F+G+S+L}^t = -847 + 894 + 1281 + 894 = +2222 \text{ psi (15.3 MPa)}$$

$$f_{F+G+S+L}^b = +3328 - 1093 - 1567 - 1093 = -425 \text{ psi } (-2.9 \text{ MPa})$$

Since these stresses are within the allowable, we can use the $F$ and $e$ computed to select the tendons and work out their pattern in the member.

In designing a pretensioned member it is standard procedure to select the size of seven-wire strand to be used and to work out a satisfactory pattern. This can be done because the properties of seven-wire strands have been standardized and they are available from a number of suppliers. Choosing the tendons for a post-tensioned member is another matter. There are several systems or methods of post-tensioning involving different types of tendons and anchor fittings, most of which are patented. The drawings and specifications must be so prepared that the proper magnitude and location of the prestressing force will be assured and also that each post-tensioning system can be used to the best advantage.

One common procedure is to specify the prestressing force and its location as shown in Fig. 68. (*A* would be given as a numerical value after calculations for Step 7 were completed.) The disadvantage to the method shown in Fig. 68 is that it is inflexible and therefore does not permit the most efficient use of the various systems. As an example let us assume that using the tendons of one system at full capacity, it takes 10.10 tendons to produce an *F* of 892,000 lb (3968 kN) but that 10 tendons of this system can be arranged so that their c.g.s. in less than $4\frac{1}{2}$ in. (114.3 mm) from the bottom, which gives a larger *e* than shown. The economical procedure would be to use 10 tendons and lower them enough to give the required compressive stress in the bottom fiber as long as this does not create excessive tensile stress in the top fiber. Working from the information given in Fig. 68 the bidder has no way of telling whether or not this method would work.

In order to obtain maximum efficiency in the choice of tendons the design drawings should give the properties of the concrete cross section and the permissible range of stresses due to the prestressing force.

The minimum value of $f_F^b$ must be large enough to keep the stress in the bottom fiber from exceeding $-425$ psi. ($-2.9$ MPa).

$$\text{Minimum } f_F^b = -f_G^b - f_S^b - f_L^b + f_{tp}$$

$$= 1093 + 1567 + 1093 - 425 = +3328$$

The maximum value of $f_F^b$ must keep the compressive stress under prestress plus dead load from exceeding $+2250$ psi (15.5 MPa).

$$\text{Maximum } f_F^b = 2{,}250 - f_G^b$$

$$= 2250 + 1093 = +3343 \text{ psi (23 MPa)}$$

The minimum tensile stress $f_F^t$ must be large enough so that the compressive stress under full load does not exceed the allowable $+2250$ psi (15.5 MPa).

$$\text{Minimum } f_F^t = 2250 - f_G^t - f_S^t - f_L^t$$

$$= 2250 - 894 - 1281 - 894 = -819$$

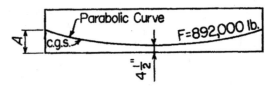

**FIGURE 68.** Computed magnitude and location of prestressing force.

The maximum tensile stress in the top fiber must not exceed the allowable $-150$ psi. ($-1,034$ kPa) under prestress plus dead load.

$$\text{Maximum } f_F^t = -150 - f_G^t$$
$$= -150 - 894 = -1044$$

In summary, at the center of span

$$f_F^b = +3328 \text{ to } +3343 \text{ psi } (+23 \text{ MPa})$$
$$f_F^t = -819 \text{ to } -1044 \text{ psi } (-7.2 \text{ MPa})$$

When the member is submitted to contractors for bids, these values as well as the properties of the cross section should be shown as illustrated in Fig. 69.

Another method of presentation is to list several different values for $B$ (Fig. 69) and to list the corresponding $F$ required for each value of $B$. With this method, all calculations are done by the designer and the bidder need only select the most economical combination of $B$ and $F$ which the details of his/her tendons can suit.

Any post-tensioning system whose properties meet the requirements of the specification can be used. For the purpose of this example we shall use the Freyssinet system. As a first trial we shall use the $A$ and $F$ shown in Fig. 69.

From Table 2, a 12/0.276 Freyssinet cable [a cable composed of 12 wires each 0.276-in. (7-mm) diameter and having a minimum ultimate strength of 236,000 psi (1627 MPa)] has a recommended final prestress of 93,000 lb (414 kN). The number of these cables required is

$$892,000 \div 93,000 = 9.6 \text{ cables}$$

We can use 10 cables or try to lower the c.g.s. enough to make 9 cables suffice.

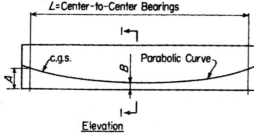

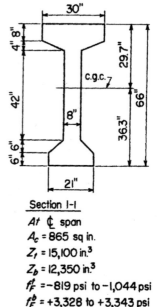

**Elevation**

One combination of values which gives satisfactory stresses is

$A = 36.3"$, $B = 4\frac{1}{2}"$, $F = 892,000$ lb

The values of $A$, $B$, and $F$ may be altered as long as $f_F^t$ and $f_F^b$ are kept within the limits shown hereon and the tendon spacing and cover coincide with "Tentative Recommendations for Prestressed Concrete."

Section I-I

At $\mathbb{C}$ span
$A_c = 865$ sq in.
$Z_t = 15,100$ in.$^3$
$Z_b = 12,350$ in.$^3$
$f_F^t = -819$ psi to $-1,044$ psi
$f_F^b = +3,328$ to $+3,343$ psi

**FIGURE 69.** Method recommended for showing prestressing requirements when submitting post-tensioned members for competitive bids.

**TABLE 2.** Properties of Freyssinet Cables

| Type of unit. . . . . . . . . . | $8 \times 0.196''$ | $10 \times 0.196''$ | $12 \times 0.196''$ | $18 \times 0.196''$ | $12 \times 0.276''$ |
|---|---|---|---|---|---|
| Minimum guaranteed ultimate tensile strength for uncoated cables, lb. . . | 60,000 | 75,000 | 90,000 | 135,000 | 168,500 |
| Recommended final prestress, lb. . . . . . . . . . | 34,000 | 43,000 | 51,000 | 77,000 | 93,000 |
| Steel area, sq.in. | 0.241 | 0.302 | 0.362 | 0.543 | 0.723 |
| Weight per lin ft, lb. . . . . . . | 0.82 | 1.03 | 1.23 | 1.85 | 2.45 |
| OD metal hose, in. . . . . . . | $1^{1}/8$ | $1^{1}/8$ | $1^{1}/4$ | $1^{5}/8$ | $1^{5}/8$ |
| ID metal hose, in. . . . . . . . | 1 | 1 | $1^{1}/8$ | $1^{1}/2$ | $1^{1}/2$ |
| Dimensions of anchorage: | | | | | |
|     A. . . . . . . . . . . . . . . . . | $3^{15}/16$ | $3^{15}/16$ | $3^{15}/16$ | $4^{23}/32$ | $4^{23}/32$ |
|     B. . . . . . . . . . . . . . . . | $3^{25}/32$ | $3^{25}/32$ | $3^{25}/32$ | $4^{13}/16$ | $4^{13}/16$ |
|     C. . . . . . . . . . . . . . . | $1^{7}/8$ | $1^{7}/8$ | $1^{7}/8$ | $2^{7}/16$ | $2^{7}/16$ |
|     D. . . . . . . . . . . . . . . | $1^{3}/32$ | $1^{3}/32$ | $1^{3}/32$ | $1^{15}/32$ | $1^{15}/32$ |

We shall try lowering the c.g.s. The $F$ for nine cables is $9 \times 93,000 = 837,000$ lb (3723 kN). From Fig. 69 the minimum value of $f_F^b = +3328$. Substitute known values and solve for $e$.

$$\frac{837,000}{865} + \frac{837,000e}{12,350} = +3328$$

$$968 + 67.8e = +3328$$

$$e = 34.8 \text{ in. (884 mm)}$$

$$36.3 - 34.8 = 1.5 \text{ in. (38 mm) bottom to c.g.s.}$$

We cannot arrange nine cables in a pattern that meets the specification requirements for cover and spacing when the c.g.s. is only 1.5 in. (38 mm) from the bottom.

An alternate would be to use Freyssinet cables 18/0.196, which have a recommended final prestress of 77,000 lb (343 kN) according to Table 2. The number of these cables required would be $892,000 \div 77,000 = 11.58$. The c.g.s. for 11 of these cables would be almost as low as for nine cables 12/0.276, so 12 cables would be required. Since the "in-place" cost of 12 of these cables would be higher than that of 10 of the larger cables, we shall use 10 cables 12/0.276. Since Fig. 69 gives the details for $F = 892,000$ lb (3968 kN), we shall use this value of

$$F = 892,000 \div 10 = 89,200 \text{ lb (397 kN) per cable}$$

See Fig. 70 for cable pattern. Check the c.g.s.

$$\begin{array}{r} 6 \times 2^{1}/2 = 15 \\ 2 \times 5^{7}/8 = 11.75 \\ \underline{2 \times 9^{1}/4 = 18.50} \\ 10 \qquad 45.25 \div 10 = 4.52 \end{array}$$

## 6. Establish the concrete strength $f'_{ci}$ at the time of prestressing and check stresses under the initial prestress condition

First we must compute the initial prestress $F_I$.

The area of the cable being used from Table 2 is 0.723 sq.in. (466 mm²). The final stress is $89,200 \div 0.723 = 123,400$ psi (848 MPa). From the design guide the stress loss is 25,000 psi (172 MPa), so the initial stress is $123,400 + 25,000 = 148,400$ psi (1023 MPa) and the initial tension is $148,400 \times 0.723 = 107,300$ lb (477 kN) per cable. Total $F_I = 107,300 \times 10 = 1,073,000$ lb (4773 kN).

Substituting, the stresses at center of span are

$$f_{F_I}^t = \frac{1,073,000}{865} - \frac{1,073,000 \times 31.8}{15,100} = -1020$$

$$f_{F_I}^b = \frac{1,073,000}{865} + \frac{1,073,000 \times 31.8}{12,350} = +3976$$

Adding dead-weight stresses,

$$f_{F_I+G}^t = -1020 + 894 = -126$$

$$f_{F_I+G}^b = +3976 - 1093 = +2883$$

From

$$\text{Maximum allowable tensile stress} = 3\sqrt{f_{ci}'}$$

$$\text{or } 126 = 3\sqrt{f_{ci}'} \qquad f_{ci}' = \left(\frac{126}{3}\right)^2$$

$$f_{ci}' = 1760 \text{ minimum}$$

$$\text{Maximum allowable compressive stress } 0.55 f_{ci}'$$

$$\text{or } f_{ci}' = 2883 \div 0.55 = 5242$$

Therefore the required $f_{ci}'$ is governed by the compressive stress and is slightly larger than the specified $f_c'$. This is a condition which often occurs in the design of post-tensioned members for buildings when the design guide is followed because the allowable stress at design loads is $0.45 f_{ci}'$ while the allowable stress under initial conditions is only $0.55 f_{ci}'$. Since the values are so close in this example, we shall simply specify $f_c' = f_{ci}' = 5300$ psi (36.5 MPa). This means that the concrete must have a minimum ultimate strength of 5300 psi (36.5 MPa) at the time of post-tensioning.

At the center of span the stress in the top fiber due to $F_I$ is

$$f_{F_I}^t = \frac{F_I}{A_c} - \frac{F_I e}{Z_t}$$

In this equation $F_I/A_c$ is a constant value of $+1240$ and is so listed in Table 2. $-F_I e/Z_t$ is made up of two constants $F_I$ and $Z_t$ and the variable $e$. In Fig. 71a, $e$ is equal to $y$, and at the center of span $e = y = B$. Thus at the center of span

$$-\frac{F_I e}{Z_t} = \frac{1,073,000 \times 31.8}{15,100} = -2260 = B$$

$$\frac{F_I e}{Z_b} = \frac{1,073,000 \times 31.8}{12,350} = +2763 = B$$

The values of $-F_I e/Z_t$ at the tenth points of the span can be computed using the formula or table of coefficients in Fig. 71.

We now have sufficient data and shall complete Table 3.

The figures in column 10 of Table 3 show that the compressive stress at points along the span is always less than that at the center of span, which is therefore the governing

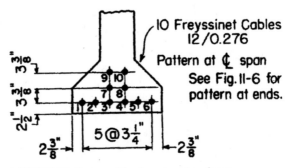

**FIGURE 70.** Pattern of tendons at center of span.

stress and which has already been provided for by making $f'_{ci}$ = 5300 psi (36.5 MPa). All the top fiber stresses in column 6 are well within the allowable.

Table 3 shows the critical condition under final prestress plus all applied loads. Stresses at the tenth points of the span are based on the parabolic curves in Fig. 71 in the same manner as those in Table 2.

$$\frac{F}{A_c} = \frac{892,000}{865} = +1031$$

At the center of span

$$-\frac{Fe}{Z_t} = \frac{892,000 \times 31.8}{15,100} = -1878$$

$$+\frac{Fe}{Z_b} = \frac{892,000 \times 31.8}{12,350} = +2297$$

Using these values we shall complete Table 3.

The figures in columns 6 and 10 of Table 3 show that the stresses are within the allowable for the full length of the member.

The elevation of the c.g.s. at the tenth points of the span is developed using the equation in Fig. 71.

In most cases of post-tensioned members such a requirement is not a serious drawback. The side forms can be removed for use elsewhere after the concrete has set, and the member can stand until completely cured. It is not holding up production as a pretensioned member on a casting bed would be.

### 7. Establish the path of the tendons and check any critical points along the member under initial and final conditions

Since all the loads on this member are uniform loads and the bending-moment curve of a uniform load is a parabola, the logical curve for the tendons is also a parabola. The lowest point of the parabola at the center of span is already established. If we can establish the highest points, at the ends of the member, and know the equation of the curve, the entire curve will be established. Within certain limits the location of the elevation of the ends of the curve is usually a matter of choice rather than design. It must be high enough

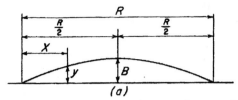

Curve of bending moment due to uniform load

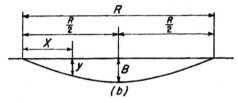

Curve of parabolic path of tendons

Equation for curves *(a)* and *(b)*

$$y = 4B \frac{X}{R}\left(1 - \frac{X}{R}\right)$$

Values of *y* for *X* at Tenth Points of Span as
Computed from Above Equation

| X | y |
|---|---|
| 0 | 0 |
| 0.1R or 0.9R | 0.36B |
| 0.2R or 0.8R | 0.64B |
| 0.3R or 0.7R | 0.84B |
| 0.4R or 0.6R | 0.96B |
| 0.5R | B |

$L = R\,(1 + 2.67\,n^2)$

$L$ = length along parabolic curve

$n = \dfrac{B}{R}$

**FIGURE 71.** Parabolic curves for uniform bending moment and path
of tendons.

so that the stresses it creates at the end of the member are within the allowable, and it
must permit suitable details for the tendon anchors. Unless some condition indicates
otherwise, a most convenient location is the c.g.c. For this example we shall locate the
end of the curve on the c.g.c.

The parabolic bending-moment curve due to a uniform load is shown in Fig. 71*a*. The
parabolic curve of the cables is shown in Fig. 71*b*. These curves have the same equation
except that in the bending-moment curve *B* and *y* are measured in foot-pounds while in
the cable curve *B* and *y* are measured in inches.

Now that the curve of the tendons is established, we can plot the stresses at points
along the span. Table 3 shows the critical condition under initial prestress plus the dead
load of the girder only. Since the section modulus of the girder is constant for its full
length, the stresses due to dead load will vary in accordance with the equation in Fig. 71,
and we already know the stresses at the center of span.

**TABLE 3.** Critical Conditions under Initial Prestress

| X | $\dfrac{F_t}{A_c}$ | $\dfrac{-F_t e}{Z_t}$ | $f_{F_t}^t = 2+3$ | $f_G^t$ | $f_{F_t+G}^t$ | $\dfrac{F_t e}{Z_b}$ | $f_{F_t}^b = 2+7$ | $f_G^b$ | $f_{F_t+G}^b$ |
|---|---|---|---|---|---|---|---|---|---|
| (1) | (2) | (3) | (4)* | (5) | (6) | (7) | (8)† | (9) | (10) |
| 0 | +1,240 | 0 | +1,240 | 0 | +1,240 | 0 | +1,240 | 0 | +1,240 |
| 0.1L or 0.9L | +1,240 | −814 | +426 | +322 | +748 | +985 | +2,225 | −393 | +1,832 |
| 0.2L or 0.8L | +1,240 | −1,446 | −206 | +572 | +366 | +1,751 | +2,991 | −700 | +2,291 |
| 0.3L or 0.7L | +1,240 | −1,898 | −658 | +750 | +92 | +2,298 | +3,538 | −918 | +2,620 |
| 0.4L or 0.6L | +1,240 | −2,170 | −930 | +858 | −72 | +2,626 | +3,866 | −1,050 | +2,816 |
| 0.5L | +1,240 | −2,260 | −1,020 | +894 | −126 | +2,736 | +3,976 | −1,093 | +2,883 |

*$f^t_{F_t}$ = column 2 plus column 3.
†$f^b_{F_t}$ = column 2 plus column 7.

**TABLE 3.** Critical Conditions under Final Prestress

| X | $\dfrac{F}{A_c}$ | $-\dfrac{Fe}{Z_t}$ | $f_F^t = 2+3$ | $f_{G+S+L}^t$ | $f_{F+G+S+L}^t$ | $\dfrac{Fe}{Z_b}$ | $f_F^b = 2+7$ | $f_{G+S+L}^b$ | $f_{F+G+S+L}^b$ |
|---|---|---|---|---|---|---|---|---|---|
| (1) | (2) | (3) | (4)* | (5) | (6) | (7) | (8)† | (9) | (10) |
| 0 | +1,031 | 0 | +1,031 | 0 | +1,031 | 0 | +1,031 | 0 | +1,031 |
| 0.1L or 0.9L | +1,031 | −676 | +355 | +1,105 | +1,460 | +827 | +1,858 | −1,351 | +507 |
| 0.2L or 0.8L | +1,031 | −1,202 | −171 | +1,964 | +1,793 | +1,470 | +2,501 | −2,402 | +99 |
| 0.3L or 0.7L | +1,031 | −1,578 | −547 | +2,578 | +2,031 | +1,930 | +2,961 | −3,153 | −192 |
| 0.4L or 0.6L | +1,031 | −1,803 | −772 | +2,946 | +2,174 | +2,205 | +3,236 | −3,603 | −367 |
| 0.5L | +1,031 | −1,878 | −847 | +3,069 | +2,222 | +2,297 | +3,328 | −3,753 | −425 |

*$f^t_F$ = column 2 plus column 3.
†$f^b_F$ = column 2 plus column 7.

5.134

We can use this equation to compute the stresses due to $F$:

$$f_{F_I} = \frac{F_I}{A_c} \pm \frac{Fe}{Z}$$

Substituting for the stresses due to $F_I$ at the ends of the span (where $e$ = zero because the cables are on the c.g.c.), we get

$$f_{F_I} = \frac{F_I}{A_c} \pm \frac{F(\text{zero})}{Z} = \frac{F_I}{A_c}$$

which means that the stress is uniform over the full depth of the member and equal to

$$\frac{F_I}{A_c} = \frac{1,073,000}{865} = +1240 \text{ psi } (8.55 \text{ MPa})$$

## 8. Check ultimate strength to make sure it meets the requirements of the specification

Check the percentage of prestressing steel.

Use the formula below to determine the location of the neutral axis under the ultimate condition.

$$1.4\frac{dpf_{su}}{f'_c}$$

$$d = 29.7 + 31.8 = 61.5$$

$$A_s = 0.723 \times 10 = 7.23 \text{ sq.in. } (4665 \text{ mm}^2)$$

$$f'_c = 5300$$

$$p = \frac{A_s}{bd} = \frac{7.23}{30 \times 61.5} = 0.00392$$

From

$$f_{su} = f'_s\left(1 - 0.5\frac{pf'_s}{f'_c}\right)$$

This formula is applicable because conditions 1 and 2 of the design guide are met by this member.

$$f_{su} = 236,000\left(1 - 0.5\frac{0.00392 \times 236,000}{5300}\right) = 215,000$$

Substituting these values in the equation,

$$1.4 \frac{61.5 \times 0.00392 \times 215,000}{5300} = 13.70$$

Since the flange thickness is less than this, the following formula applies:

$$M_u = A_{sr}f_{su}d\left(1 - 0.6\frac{A_{sr}f_{su}}{b'df'_c}\right) + 0.85f'_c(b - b')t(d - 0.5t)$$

$$b = 30$$
$$b' = 8$$
$$t = \text{average thickness of flange} = \text{area of flange} \div b$$

$$\text{Area of flange} = (30 \times 8) + (2 \times 11 \times 4 \times \tfrac{1}{2}) = 284$$

$$t = 284 \div 30 = 9.47$$
$$f'_c = 5300$$
$$A_{sf} = \frac{0.85f'_c(b - b')t}{f_{su}}$$

$$= \frac{0.85(5300)(30 - 8)9.47}{215,000} = 4.37$$

$$A_{sr} = A_s - A_{sf}$$
$$= 7.23 - 4.37 = 2.86$$

Substituting in formula (b),

$$M_u = 2.86 \times 215,000 \times 61.5\left(1 - 0.6\frac{2.86 \times 215,000}{8 \times 61.5 \times 5300}\right)$$

$$+ 0.85 \times 5300(30 - 8)9.47(61.5 - 0.5 \times 9.47)$$

$$= 32,450,000 + 53,250,000$$

$$= 85,700,000 \text{ in·lb} = 7,140,000 \text{ ft·lb} \ (9675 \text{ kNm})$$

Determine maximum required ultimate strength from

$$M_D = M_G + M_s = (13,500,000 + 19,350,000) \div 12 = 2,740,000 \text{ ft.lb} \ (3713 \text{ kNm})$$

$$M_L = 13,500,000 \div 12 = 1,125,000 \text{ ft·lb} \ (1,524.4 \text{ kNm})$$

$$1.2D + 2.4L = 1.2(2,740,000) + 2.4(1,125,000) = 5,990,000 \text{ ft·lb} \ (8116 \text{ kNm})$$

$$1.8(D + L) = 1.8(2,740,000 + 1,125,000) = 6,960,000 \text{ ft·lb} \ (9431 \text{ kNm})$$

The member has the required ultimate strength.
Check the percentage of steel in accordance with

$$\frac{A_{sr}f_{su}}{b'df'_c} = \frac{2.86 \times 215,000}{8 \times 61.5 \times 5300} = 0.236$$

Since this is less than 0.30, the member is not overreinforced.

### 9. Design of shear steel

From the design guide web reinforcement is not needed if

$$\frac{pf'_s}{f'_c} \gtrless 0.3 \frac{f_{se}b'}{f'_s b}$$

Substituting numerical values,

$$\frac{0.00392 \times 236,000}{5300} \gtrless 0.3 \frac{123,400 \times 8}{236,000 \times 30}$$

$$0.175 \gtrless 0.042$$

Since this is not true, web reinforcement is needed.

From the design guide maximum shear occurs 5 ft 6 in. (1.68 m) from the support. Determine ultimate shear in accordance with

$$W_D = w_G + w_S = 900 + 1290 = 2190 \text{ lb/ft (32 kN/m)}$$
$$W_L = 900 \text{ lb/ft (13.1 kN/m)}$$
$$1.2D + 2.4L = 1.2(2190) + 2.4(900) = 4790 \text{ lb/ft (69.8 kN/m)}$$
$$1.8(D + L) = 1.8(2190 + 900) = 5560 \text{ lb/ft (81.1 kN/m)}$$

Total ultimate shear 5 ft 6 in. (1.68 m) from the support is $5560(50 - 5.5) = 247,000$ lb (1099 kN). Part of this shear is carried by the tendons.

Using the symbols shown in Fig. 71b, the tangent of the angle of the curve with the horizontal at a point $X$ from the end of the curve is

$$\tan \phi = \frac{4B}{R}\left(1 - \frac{2X}{R}\right)$$

Substituting numerical values for the point on the curve of the tendons 5 ft 6 in. (1.68 m) from the support,

$$B = 31.8 \div 12 = 2.65 \text{ ft (0.81 m)}$$

$$\tan X = \frac{4 \times 2.65}{100}\left(1 - \frac{2 \times 5.5}{100}\right) = 0.0943$$

The shear carried by the cables at this point is equal to the vertical component of the final tension in the cables, which is

$$0.0943 \times 892,000 = 84,100 \text{ lb (373.4 kN)}$$
$$V_u = 247,000 - 84,100 = 162,900 \text{ lb (725 kN)}$$

Since the tendons are in a parabolic curve, $d$ at this point will be less than at mid-span. Compute $d$ using the formulas in Fig. 71 and the dimensions in Fig. 69. Using the symbols in Fig. 71,

$$R = 100 \text{ ft 0 in.} = 1200 \text{ in. (30.5 m)}$$
$$B = 36.3 - 4.5 = 31.8 \text{ in. (807.7 mm)}$$
$$X = 5 \text{ ft 6 in.} = 66 \text{ in. (1676 mm)}$$

Substituting in the formula,

$$y = 4(31.8)\frac{66}{1200}\left(1 - \frac{66}{1200}\right) = 6.6 \text{ in. (167.6 mm)}$$

Then

$$d = 6.6 + 29.7 = 36.3 \text{ in. (922 mm)}$$

$$p = \frac{7.23}{30 \times 36.3} = 0.00664$$

Since the bending moment at this point is small, failure will not occur by bending, so we are not concerned about the high percentage of steel.
From

$$f_{su} = 236,000\left(1 - \frac{0.5 \times 0.00664 \times 236,000}{5000}\right) = 199,000 \text{ psi (1372 MPa)}$$

Compute web reinforcing using the formula

$$A_v = \frac{1}{2}\frac{(V_u - V_c)s}{f_v'jd}$$

$j$ is computed using the following portion of formula $(a)$ in the design guide

$$j = 1 - \frac{k_2 p f_{su}}{k_1 k_3 f_c'}$$

$$j = 1 - \frac{0.6 \times 0.00664 \times 199,000}{5000} = 0.842$$

From

$$V_c = 180 \times 8 \times 0.842 \times 36.3 = 44,000 \text{ lb (196 kN)}$$

Using structural grade bars $f_v' = 33,000$

From the design guide maximum stirrup spacing $= 0.75 \times 66 = 49.5$
Use $s = 49.5$

Substituting numerical values in the formula,

$$A_v = \frac{1}{2} \times \frac{(162,900 - 44,000)49.5}{33,000 \times 0.842 \times 36.3} = 2.92 \text{ sq.in. (1884 mm}^2)$$

From the design guide the minimum web reinforcement is

$$A_v = 0.0025b's = 0.0025 \times 8 \times 49.5 = 0.99$$

Try two No. 5 bars for that portion of the beam where minimum reinforcement is required. The area of two No. 5 bars is $2 \times 0.307 = 0.614$ sq.in. (396 mm²)

$$s = \frac{0.614}{0.99} (49.5) = 30.7 \text{ in. (778.8 mm)}$$

Use two No. 5 bars at 30 in. (762 mm) on centers.

At the point 5 ft 6 in. (1.68 m) from the support where $A_v$ was computed as 2.92 sq.in. (1884 mm²), we shall try $s = 26$ in. (660 mm). Then the required stirrup area is

$$\frac{26}{49.5} (2.92) = 1.53 \text{ sq.in. (987 mm}^2)$$

Use two No. 8 bars $= 2 \times 0.78 = 1.56$ sq.in. (1006 mm²) at 26 in. (660 mm) centers. Go through a similar calculation for required web reinforcement at points 10 ft 0 in. (3.1 m) from the support, 15 ft 0 in. (4.6 m) from the support, etc., until a point is reached where the minimum of two #5 bars at 30-in. (762-mm) centers is sufficient. Use two No. 5 bars at 30-in. (762 mm) centers from this point to mid-span. The stirrup pattern will be symmetrical about mid-span. Note that the design guide requires that the web reinforcement in the middle third of the span be the same as that required at the third points. If this is greater than the minimum of $0.0025 \, b's$, then the third-point requirement will govern and the $0.0025b's$, will not apply to this design.

The foregoing calculations are based on the design guide. While this method is reasonable for prestressed concrete members at points where the tendons are near the bottom, the author feels that it is conservative at points of low bending moment where the tendons are at an appreciable distance above the bottom. All available test data show that the first sign of an impending shear failure is a diagonal tension crack. Thus it follows that there will be no shear failure if the diagonal tension stress is below the tensile strength of the concrete. Diagonal tension stress can be computed by Mohr's circle method. This stress is usually greatest at the neutral axis of the section. It is suggested that the maximum allowable diagonal tension stress under ultimate load be $6\sqrt{f'_c}$. Even if the diagonal tension proves low, the minimum web steel of $A_v = 0.0025b's$, should be used unless the "unusually thick webs" provision of the design guide is applicable.

## 10. *Compute camber*

In Step 7 we deliberately set the curve of the c.g.s. in a parabolic path with $e$ equal to zero at the ends of the member and 31.8 in. (807.7 mm) at the center of span. The bending moment due to $F_I$ is $F_Ie$. Since $e$ varies in a parabolic curve, the bending moment due to $F_I$ will also vary in a parabolic curve from zero at the ends of the member to $F_Ie$ at the center of span. Since a uniform load produces a parabolic bending-moment curve, it is apparent that the tendons exert a uniform vertical load $w_T$ against the member. Find $w_T$.

$$F_Ie = 1,073,000 \times 31.8 = 34,100,000 \text{ in·lb} = 2,841,000 \text{ ft·lb (3850 kNm)}$$

The formula for bending moment due to a uniform load is

$$M = \frac{wl^2}{8} \quad \text{or} \quad w = \frac{8M}{l^2}$$

Substituting,

$$w_T = \frac{8 \times 2,841,000}{100^2} = 2271 \text{ lb/ft (33 kN/m)}$$

The vertical uplift of 2271 lb/ft. (33 kN/m) exerted by the tendons is offset by the 900-lb/ft. (13.1 kN/m) dead weight of the member, so that the net uplift causing camber is $2271 - 900 = 1371$ lb/ft. (2.0 kN/m).

From

$$E_c = 1,800,000 + 500f'_c = 1,800,000 + 500(5300) = 4,400,000$$

The standard formula for deflection (or camber) due to a uniform load is

$$\Delta = \frac{5wl^4}{384EI} = \frac{5 \times 1371(100^4)12^3}{384 \times 4,400,000 \times 448,500} = 1.56 \text{ in. (39.6 mm)}$$

Since the concrete reached full strength before the tendons were tensioned, the member can be erected and subjected to the full dead load of the roof. If this is done, the growth in camber, before the roof load is applied, will be negligible.

Deflection due to roof load of $w_s = 1290$ lb/ft (18.8 kN/m) will be

$$\Delta_s = \frac{5 \times 290(100^4)12^3}{384 \times 4,400,000 \times 448,500} = 1.47 \text{ in. (37.3 mm)}$$

The net camber under dead load of the member plus double T's and roofing is $1.56 - 1.47 = 0.09$ in. (2.3 mm). If camber growth is 150 percent, the final camber will be

$$0.09 + 1.5 \ (0.09) = 0.22 \text{ in. (5.6 mm)}$$

Deflection under a live load of 900 lb per lin ft will be

$$\Delta_L = \frac{5 \times 900(100^4)12^3}{384 \times 4,400,000 \times 448,500} = 1.00 \text{ in. (25.4 mm)}$$

**End-block Details.** In Step 7 we chose 10 Freyssinet cables 12/0.276 for the tendons in this example and arranged them in the pattern shown in Fig. 70. As shown in Fig. 69 the c.g.s. is 36.3 in. (922 mm) above the bottom at the center of bearing. Using this information and the recommended spacing for Freyssinet cones, we can establish the pattern shown in Fig. 72.

Compare the details at the end of the member we are designing with the factors mentioned in the design guide. The prestressing force is concentrated in as small a space as details will permit, which means that the end block will have to distribute the force across the entire section. There is no eccentricity, so the end block has no stresses from this factor. Since this is a deep member and there are no conditions which require a particularly heavy end block, we shall follow the design guide and make the length of the end block about three-quarters of the beam depth, or 48 in. (1219 mm).

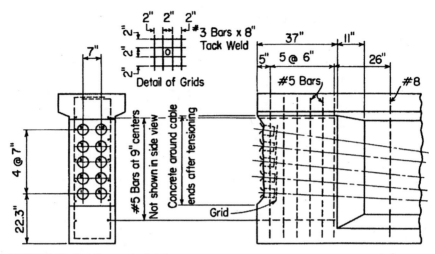

**FIGURE 72.** Details at end of girder.

The reinforcing used in end blocks is based on experience. Common practice for many designers of deep girders is to use two No. 5 bars at 6-in. (152-mm) centers for the length of the end block and two No. 5 bars at 9-in. (229-mm) centers for the height of the block. We have followed this practice as shown in Fig. 72.

The details of the end block of a post-tensioned member include provision for distributing the load from the anchor fittings to the concrete. The design guide calls for a reinforcing grid beneath the anchorage. The grid used with Freyssinet anchors is shown in Fig. 72. A similar grid can be used with other types of anchors and should be based on the recommendations of the supplier of the anchor fitting. No grid is needed when a bearing plate with welded steel tube attached is used in conjunction with a Roebling-type anchorage.

**Friction in Tendons.** When a tendon is post-tensioned, it elongates and therefore moves with respect to the tube or cored hole in which it is encased. The sliding of the tendon along the encasement creates friction, which reduces the tension in the tendon. The drop in tension due to friction increases with the distance from the jack and is a function of several factors as described in the design guide.

Calculations in Step 6 show that each Freyssinet cable in this girder should have an initial tension of 107,300 lb (477 kN). This is the tension required at the center of span. We shall use the method outlined in the design guide and compute the tension at the jack required to give 107,300 lb (477 kN) at the center of span. The applicable formula is

$$T_o = T_X e^{(KL + \mu\alpha)}$$

We shall consider cable 9, since it and cable 10 have the greatest curvature and therefore the most friction. See Fig. 69 for the cable curvature and Figs. 70 and 72 for the location of cable 9. For cable 9 the factors in the equation have the following values:

$$T_X = 107,300$$
$$e = 2.718$$
$$L = 50 \text{ ft } (15.2 \text{ m})$$
$$K = 0.0020$$
$$\mu = 0.30$$

The value of $\alpha$ is a function of the curvature of the cable. Since the cable is horizontal at the center of span, the angular change from the center of span to the end of the member is the angle of the cable at the end. This angle is computed by

$$\text{Elevation of cable above bottom at end of member} = 50.30$$
$$\text{Elevation of cable above bottom at center of span} = \underline{\hphantom{0}9.25}$$
$$\text{Rise} = B = \overline{41.05} \text{ in. (1043 mm)}$$
$$X = 0$$
$$R = 100 \times 12 = 1200$$

Substituting numerical values,

$$\tan \phi = \frac{4 \times 41.05}{1200}\left(1 - \frac{0}{1200}\right) = 0.1368$$

The angle whose tangent is 0.1368 is 7° 47' or 0.136 radian. Thus

$$\alpha = 0.136$$

Substituting numerical values,

$$T_o = 107,300(2.718)^{(0.0020 \times 50 + 0.30 \times 0.136)}$$
$$= 107,300(2.718)^{0.141}$$
$$= 107,300(1.154) = 123,800 \text{ lb (550.7 kN)}$$
$$\text{Unit stress} = 123,800 \div 0.723 = 171,200 \text{ psi (1180 MPa)}$$
$$171,200 \div 236,000 = 72.5\% \text{ of ultimate}$$

The design guide permits jack loads up to 80 percent of ultimate as long as the load is relaxed before the anchor fittings are set so that the load in the tendon after anchoring does not exceed 70 percent of ultimate. As the tension is partially relaxed at the jack, friction works in the opposite direction and there is no reduction in the tension at the center of span.

Similar computations should be made to determine the tension at the jacks for each of the other layers of cable. Since the other layers have less curvature, they will have less friction and therefore a lower tension at the jack.

**Transformed Section.** Throughout the calculations in this procedure we have used the properties computed for the section in Fig. 67 as a solid concrete member. Actually this member has 10 holes cored in it as shown in Fig. 70. Tendons are placed in these holes and tensioned, after which the holes are filled with grout. Obviously the actual stresses are not the same as those we have computed. We shall check the actual stresses at center of span.

Compute the properties of the section shown in Fig. 67 except with holes out for cables as shown in Fig. 70. The hole diameter is $1\frac{1}{2}$ in., and the area is 1.77 sq.in. (11.4 cm²). Take moments about the bottom. Begin with totals from calculations in Step 1.

|  | $A$ | $y$ | $Ay$ | $Ay^2$ | $I_0$ |
|---|---|---|---|---|---|
|  | 865 |  | 31,390 | 1,494,130 | 95,526 |
| $-6 \times 1.77 =$ | $-10.6$ | $2\frac{1}{2}$ | $-26$ | $-66$ |  |
| $-4 \times 1.77 =$ | $\underline{-7.1}$ | $7\frac{9}{16}$ | $\underline{-54}$ | $\underline{-408}$ | $\underline{\hphantom{95,526}}$ |
|  | 847.3 |  | 31,310 | 1,493,656 | 95,526 |
|  |  |  |  | 95,526 |  |
|  |  |  |  | 1,589,182 |  |

$$y_b = 31,310 \div 847.3 = 37.0$$
$$y_t = 66 - 37 = 29.0$$
$$I = 1,589,182 - 847.3(37^2) = 429,000$$
$$Z_t = 429,000 \div 29 = 14,800$$
$$Z_b = 429,000 \div 37 = 11,600$$

We shall assume that the tendons are to be tensioned and grouted before the double T's are erected. This means that the member will carry its own dead weight while the holes are out. Check dead-load stresses using the moment from Step 2.

$$f_G^t = 13,500,000 \div 14,800 = +912 \text{ psi } (+6.3 \text{ MPa})$$
$$f_G^b = 13,500,000 \div 11,600 = -1164 \text{ psi } (-8.0 \text{ MPa})$$

When the tendons have been grouted, they will work with the concrete section and their area should be added to its properties. Since the grout is not prestressed, its area will not be included.

$$E_c = 1,800,000 + 500(5300) = 4,400,000$$
$$E_S = 29,000,000$$
$$n = \frac{E_s}{E_c} = \frac{29,000,000}{4,400,000} = 6.6$$

The area of each cable = 0.723 sq.in. (4.66 cm$^2$), and it is equivalent to a concrete area of 6.6 × 0.723 = 4.77 sq.in. (30.8 cm$^2$). Compute the properties of sections with holes out and tendons added. Begin with totals for calculations of the section with holes out.

| | $A$ | $y$ | $Ay$ | $Ay^2$ | $I_0$ |
|---|---|---|---|---|---|
| | 847.3 | | 31,310 | 1,493,656 | 95,526 |
| 6 × 4.77 = | 28.6 | $2\,^1/_2$ | 71 | 178 | |
| 4 × 4.77 = | 19.1 | $7\,^9/_{16}$ | 145 | 1,095 | |
| | 895.0 | | 31,526 | 1,494,926 | 95,526 |
| | | | | 95,526 | |
| | | | | 1,590,455 | |

$$y_b = 31,526 \div 895 = 35.2$$
$$y_t = 66 - 35.2 = 30.8$$
$$I = 1,590,455 - 895(35.2)^2 = 480,500$$
$$Z_t = 480,500 \div 30.8 = 15,600$$
$$Z_b = 480,500 \div 35.2 = 13,650$$

Check stresses from applied loads using moments from Step 3.

$$f_s^t = 19,350,000 \div 15,600 = +1,240$$
$$f_s^b = 19,350,000 \div 13,650 = -1,417$$
$$f_L^t = 13,500,000 \div 15,600 = +865$$
$$f_L^b = 13,500,000 \div 13,650 = -989$$

Adding these stresses we get

$$f_{G+S+L}^t = +912 + 1240 + 865 = +3017$$
$$f_{G+S+L}^b = -1164 - 1417 - 989 = -3570$$

From Table 3 the values obtained for these stresses based on a solid concrete cross section were

$$f^t_{G+S+L} = +3069 \quad \text{and} \quad f^b_{G+S+L} = -3753$$

Check the stresses due to $F$ in the section with holes out.

$$e = 37.0 - 4.52 = 32.48$$

$$f^t_F = \frac{892,000}{847.3} - \frac{892,000 \times 32.48}{14,800} = -905$$

$$f^b_F = \frac{892,000}{847.3} + \frac{892,000 \times 32.48}{11,600} = +3550$$

Then

$$f^t_{F+G+S+L} = -905 + 3017 = +2112$$

$$f^b_{F+G+S+L} = +3350 - 3570 = -20$$

From Table 3 the values obtained for these stresses using a solid concrete cross section were

$$f^t_{F+G+S+L} = +2222 \quad \text{and} \quad f^b_{F+G+S+L} = -425$$

The foregoing calculations show that, in this case as in most cases, design based on a solid concrete cross section results in lower actual stresses than those found by computation. It is a common practice to base prestressed concrete computations on a solid cross section, but the effect of the holes should be given consideration in each design and should be checked if there is any doubt about their influence on actual stresses.

**Related Calculations.** The decision to use a post-tensioned member instead of a pretensioned one is influenced by so many different conditions that there are no rules that can be applied to determine the economical dividing line between the two. When the member is too large to be shipped from a casting yard to the job site, it is obvious that it must be cast at the job site and post-tensioned tendons will be required. When the size of the member is within shipping limitations, the following factors should be included in comparing the cost of the two methods:

1. Capacity of local casting beds. On long-span members the use of deflected tendons to offset dead weight is important. If facilities for deflecting enough strands for this purpose are not available, either a post-tensioned design or a pretensioned–post-tensioned combination is indicated.

2. Cross section of member. The cross section of a post-tensioned member is more efficient than that of a pretensioned member for the same loading if the web of the pretensioned member must be thickened appreciably to accommodate the deflected strands.

Post-tensioned members are used in bridges and buildings and for many special applications such as pile caps for piers. The girder designed in this procedure is a 100-ft (30.5-m)-span roof girder such as might be used over a school gym.

This procedure is the work of H. Kent Preston, P.E., whose affiliations, at the time of its preparation, were: Engineer, Construction Materials, John A. Roebling's Sons Division; The Colorado Fuel and Iron Corporation; Fellow, American Society of Civil Engineers; Professional Member, Prestressed Concrete Institute. SI values were added by the handbook editor.

# SECTION 6

# FLUID MECHANICS, PUMPS, PIPING, AND HYDRO POWER

---

## PART 1

# FLUID MECHANICS

---

## Hydrostatics

The notational system used in hydrostatics is as follows: $W$ = weight of floating body, lb (N); $V$ = volume of displaced liquid, ft$^3$ (m$^3$); $w$ = specific weight of liquid, lb/ft$^3$ (N/m$^3$); for water $w$ = 62.4 lb/ft$^3$ (9802 N/m$^3$), unless another value is specified.

### *BUOYANCY AND FLOTATION*

A timber member 12 ft (3.65 m) long with a cross-sectional area of 90 sq.in. (580.7 cm$^2$) will be used as a buoy in saltwater. What volume of concrete must be fastened to one end so that 2 ft (60.96 cm) of the member will be above the surface? Use these specific weights: timber = 38 lb/ft³ (5969 N/m³); saltwater = 64 lb/ft³ (10,053 N/m³); concrete = 145 lb/ft³ (22,777 N/m³).

## Calculation Procedure:

### 1. *Express the weight of the body and the volume of the displaced liquid in terms of the volume of concrete required*

Archimedes' principle states that a body immersed in a liquid is subjected to a vertical buoyant force equal to the weight of the displaced liquid. In accordance with the equations of equilibrium, the buoyant force on a floating body equals the weight of the body. Therefore,

$$W = Vw \tag{1}$$

Let $x$ denote the volume of concrete. Then $W = (90/144)(12)(38) + 145x = 285 + 145x$; $V = (90/144)(12 - 2) + x = 6.25 + x$.

### 2. *Substitute in Eq. 1 and solve for x*
Thus, $285 + 145x = (6.25 + x)64$; $x = 1.42$ ft³ (0.0402 m³).

## HYDROSTATIC FORCE ON A PLANE SURFACE

In Fig. 1, $AB$ is the side of a vessel containing water, and $CDE$ is a gate located in this plane. Find the magnitude and location of the resultant thrust of the water on the gate when the liquid surface is 2 ft (60.96 cm) above the apex.

## Calculation Procedure:

### 1. *State the equations for the resultant magnitude and position*
In Fig. 1, $FH$ denotes the centroidal axis of area $CDE$ that is parallel to the liquid surface, and $G$ denotes the point of application of the resultant force. Point $G$ is termed the *pressure center*.

Let $A$ = area of given surface, sq.ft. (cm²); $P$ = hydrostatic force on given surface, lb (N); $p_m$ = mean pressure on surface, lb/sq.ft. (kPa); $y_{CA}$ and $y_{PC}$ = vertical distance from centroidal axis and pressure center, respectively, to liquid surface, ft (m); $z_{CA}$ and $z_{PC}$ = distance along plane of given surface from the centroidal axis and pressure center, respectively, to line of intersection of this plane and the liquid surface, ft (m); $I_{CA}$ = moment of inertia of area with respect to its centroidal axis, ft⁴ (m⁴).

Consider an elemental surface of area $dA$ at a vertical distance $y$ below the liquid surface. The hydrostatic force $dP$ on this element is normal to the surface and has the magnitude

$$dP = wy\, dA \tag{2}$$

By applying Eq. 2 develop the following equations for the magnitude and position of the resultant force on the entire surface:

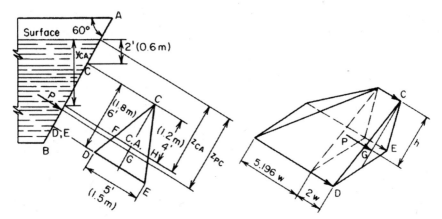

**FIGURE 1.** Hydrostatic thrust on plane surface.

**FIGURE 2.** Pressure prism.

$$P = wy_{CA}A \tag{3}$$

$$z_{PC} = \frac{I_{CA}}{Az_{CA}} + z_{CA} \tag{4}$$

### 2. Compute the required values, and solve the equations in step 1

Thus $A = \frac{1}{2}(5)(6) = 15$ sq.ft. (1.39 m²); $y_{CA} = 2 + 4 \sin 60° = 5.464$ ft (166.543 cm); $z_{CA} = 2 \csc 60° + 4 = 6.309$ ft (192.3 cm); $I_{CA}/A = (bd^3/36)/(bd/2) = d^2/18 = 2$ sq.ft. (0.186 m²); $P = 62.4(5.464)(15) = 5114$ lb (22.747 N); $z_{PC} = 2/6.309 + 6.309 = 6.626$ ft (201.960 cm); $y_{PC} = 6.626 \sin 60° = 5.738$ ft (174.894 cm). By symmetry, the pressure center lies on the centroidal axis through $C$.

An alternative equation for $P$ is

$$P = p_m A \tag{5}$$

Equation 3 shows that the mean pressure occurs at the centroid of the area. The above two steps constitute method 1 for solving this problem. The next three steps constitute method 2.

### 3. Now construct the pressure "prism" associated with the area

In Fig. 2, construct the pressure prism associated with area $CDE$. The pressures are as follows: at apex, $p = 2w$; at base, $p = (2 + 6 \sin 60°)w = 7.196w$.

The force $P$ equals the volume of this prism, and its action line lies on the centroidal plane parallel to the base. For convenience, resolve this prism into a triangular prism and rectangular pyramid, as shown.

### 4. Determine P by computing the volume of the pressure prism

Thus, $P = Aw[2 + \frac{2}{3}(5.196)] = Aw(2 + 3.464) = 15(62.4)(5.464) = 5114$ lb (22,747 N).

### 5. Find the location of the resultant thrust

Compute the distance $h$ from the top line to the centroidal plane. Then find $y_{PC}$. Or, $h = [2(\frac{2}{3})(6) + 3.464(\frac{3}{4})(6)]/5.464 = 4.317$ ft (131.582 cm); $y_{PC} = 2 + 4.317 \sin 60° = 5.738$ ft (174.894 cm).

# HYDROSTATIC FORCE
# ON A CURVED SURFACE

The cylinder in Fig. 3a rests on an inclined plane and is immersed in liquid up to its top, as shown. Find the hydrostatic force on a 1-ft (30.48-cm) length of cylinder in terms of $w$ and the radius $R$; locate the pressure center.

## Calculation Procedure:

### 1. Evaluate the horizontal and vertical component of the force dP on an elemental surface having a central angle dθ

Refer to Fig. 3b. Adopt this sign convention: A horizontal force is positive if directed to the right; a vertical force is positive if directed upward. The first three steps constitute method 1.

Evaluating $dP$ yields $dP_H = wR^2(\sin\theta - \sin\theta\cos\theta)\,d\theta$; $dP_V = wR^2(-\cos\theta + \cos^2\theta)\,d\theta$.

### 2. Integrate these equations to obtain the resultant forces $P_H$ and $P_V$; then find P

Here, $P_H = wR^2[(-\cos\theta + \frac{1}{2}\cos^2\theta)]_0^{7\pi/6} = wR^2[-(-0.866 - 1) = \frac{1}{2}(0.75 - 1)] = 1.742wR^2$, to right; $P_V = wR^2(-\sin\theta + \frac{1}{2}\theta + \frac{1}{4}\sin 2\theta)_0^{7\pi/6} = wR^2(0.5) + (1.833 + 0.217) = 2.550wR^2$, upward; $P = wR^2(1.742^2 + 2.550^2)^{0.5} = 3.087wR^2$.

### 3. Determine the value of θ at the pressure center

Since each elemental force $dP$ passes through the center of the cylinder, the resultant force $P$ also passes through the center. Thus, $\tan(180° - \theta_{PC}) = P_H/P_V = 1.741/2.550$; $\theta_{PC} = 145°41'$.

### 4. Evaluate $P_H$ and $P_V$

Apply these principles: $P_H$ = force on an imaginary surface obtained by projecting the wetted surface on a vertical plane; $P_V = \pm$ weight of real or imaginary liquid lying between the wetted surface and the liquid surface. Use the plus sign if the *real* liquid lies below the wetted surface and the minus sign if it lies above this surface.

Then $P_H$ = force, to right, on $AC$ + force, to left, on $EC$ = force, to right, on $AE$; $AE = 1.866R$; $p_m = 0.933\ wR$; $P_H = 0.933\ wR(1.866R) = 1.741\ wR^2$; $P_V$ = weight of imaginary

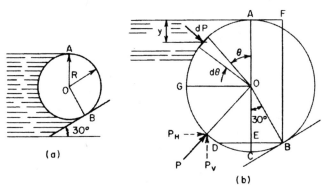

(a)

(b)

**FIGURE 3**

liquid above $GCB$ − weight of real liquid above $GA$ = weight of imaginary liquid in cylindrical sector $AOBG$ and in prismoid, $AOBF$. Volume of sector $AOBG$ = $[(7\pi/6)/(2\pi)](\pi R^2)$ = $1.833R^2$; volume of prismoid $AOBF$ = $\frac{1}{2}(0.5R)(R + 1.866R)$ = $0.717R^2$; $P_V = wR^2(1.833 + 0.717) = 2.550wR^2$.

## STABILITY OF A VESSEL

The boat in Fig. 4 is initially floating upright in freshwater. The total weight of the boat and cargo is 182 long tons (1813 kN); the center of gravity lies on the longitudinal (i.e., the fore-and-aft) axis of the boat and 8.6 ft (262.13 cm) above the bottom. A wind causes the boat to list through an angle of 6° while the cargo remains stationary relative to the boat. Compute the righting or upsetting moment (*a*) without applying any set equation; (*b*) by applying the equation for metacentric height.

**Calculation Procedure:**

### 1. Compute the displacement volume and draft when the boat is upright

The buoyant force passes through the center of gravity of the displaced liquid; this point is termed the *center of buoyancy.* Figure 5 shows the cross section of a boat rotated through an angle $\phi$. The center of buoyancy for the upright position is $B$; $B'$ is the center of buoyancy for the position shown, and $G$ is the center of gravity of the boat and cargo.

In the position indicated in Fig. 5, the weight $W$ and buoyant force $R$ constitute a couple that tends to restore the boat to its upright position when the disturbing force is removed; their moment is therefore termed *righting.* When these forces constitute a couple that increases the rotation, their moment is said to be *upsetting.* The wedges $OAC$ and $OA'C'$ are termed the *wedge of emersion* and *wedge of immersion,* respectively. Let $h$ = horizontal displacement of center of buoyancy caused by rotation; $h'$ = horizontal

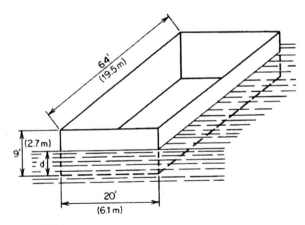

**FIGURE 4**

distance between centroids of wedge of emersion and wedge of immersion; $V'$ = volume of wedge of emersion (or immersion). Then

$$h = \frac{V'h'}{V} \qquad (6)$$

The displacement volume and the draft when the boat is upright are $W$ = 182 (2240) = 407.700 lb (1813 N); $V = W/w$ = 407.700/62.4 = 6530 ft$^3$ (184.93 m$^3$); $d$ = 6530/[64(20)] = 5.10 ft (155.448 cm).

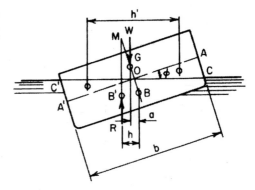

**FIGURE 5.** Location of resultant forces on inclined vessel.

### 2. Find h, using Eq. 6
Since $\phi$ is relatively small, apply this approximation: $h'$ = $2b/3$ = $2(20)/3$ = 13.33 ft (406.298 cm), $h$ = $^{1}/_{2}(10)(10 \tan 6°) \times (13.33)/[5.10(20)]$ = 0.687 ft (20.940 cm).

### 3. Compute the horizontal distance a (Fig. 5)
Thus, $BG$ = 8.6 − $^{1}/_{2}(5.10)$ = 6.05 ft (184.404 cm); $a$ = 6.05 sin 6° = 0.632 ft (19.263 cm).

### 4. Compute the moment of the vertical forces
Thus, $M$ = $W(h − a)$ = 407,700(0.055) = 22,400 ft·lb (30,374.4 N·m). Since $h > a$, the moment is righting. This constitutes the solution to part $a$. The remainder of this procedure is concerned with part $b$.

In Fig. 5, let $M$ denote the point of intersection of the vertical line through $B'$ and the line $BG$ prolonged. Then $M$ is termed the *metacenter* associated with this position, and the distance $GM$ is called the *metacentric height.* Also $BG$ is positive if $G$ is above $B$, and $GM$ is positive if $M$ is above $G$. Thus, the moment of vertical forces is righting or upsetting depending on whether the metacentric height is positive or negative, respectively.

### 5. Find the lever arm of the vertical forces
Use the relation for metacentric height:

$$GM = \frac{I_{WL}}{V \cos \phi} - BG \qquad (7)$$

where $I_{WL}$ = moment of inertia of original waterline section about axis through $O$. Or, $I_{WL}$ = $(^{1}/_{12})(64)(20)^3$ = 42,670 ft$^4$ (368.3 m$^4$); $GM$ = 42,670/6530 cos 6° − 6.05 = 0.52 ft (15.850 cm); $h − a$ = 0.52 sin 6° = 0.054 ft (1.646 cm), which agrees closely with the previous result.

# Mechanics of Incompressible Fluids

The notational system is $a$ = acceleration; $A$ = area of stream cross section; $C$ = discharge coefficient; $D$ = diameter of pipe or depth of liquid in open channel; $F$ = force; $g$ = gravitational acceleration; $H$ = total head, or total specific energy; $h_F$ = loss of head between two sections caused by friction; $h_L$ = total loss of head between two sections; $h_V$ = difference in velocity heads at two sections if no losses occur; $L$ = length of stream between two sections; $M$ = mass of body; $N_R$ = Reynolds number; $p$ = pressure;

$Q$ = volumetric rate of flow, or discharge; $s$ = hydraulic gradient = $-dH/dL$; $T$ = torque; $V$ = velocity; $w$ = specific weight; $z$ = elevation above datum plane; $\rho$ = density (mass per unit volume); $\mu$ = dynamic (or absolute) viscosity; $\nu$ = kinematic viscosity = $\mu/\rho$; $\tau$ = shearing stress. The units used for each symbol are given in the calculation procedure where the symbol is used.

If the discharge of a flowing stream of liquid remains constant, the flow is termed *steady*. Let subscripts 1 and 2 refer to cross sections of the stream, 1 being the upstream section. From the definition of steady flow,

$$Q = A_1V_1 = A_2V_2 = \text{constant} \qquad (8)$$

This is termed the *equation of continuity*. Where no statement is made to the contrary, it is understood that the flow is steady.

Conditions at two sections may be compared by applying the following equation, which is a mathematical statement of Bernoulli's theorem:

$$\frac{V_1^2}{2g} + \frac{p_1}{w} + z_1 = \frac{V_2^2}{2g} + \frac{p_2}{w} + z_2 + h_L \qquad (9)$$

The terms on each side of this equation represent, in their order of appearance, the *velocity head, pressure head,* and *potential head* of the liquid. Alternatively, they may be considered to represent forms of specific energy, namely, kinetic, pressure, and potential energy.

The force causing a change in velocity is evaluated by applying the basic equation

$$F = Ma \qquad (10)$$

Consider that liquid flows from section 1 to section 2 in a time interval $t$. At any instant, the volume of liquid bounded by these sections is $Qt$. The force required to change the velocity of this body of liquid from $V_1$ to $V_2$ is found from: $M = Qwt/g$; $a = (V_2 - V_1)/t$. Substituting in Eq. 10 gives $F = Qw(V_2 - V_1)/g$, or

$$F = \frac{A_1V_1w(V_2 - V_1)}{g} = \frac{A_2V_2w(V_2 - V_1)}{g} \qquad (11)$$

## VISCOSITY OF FLUID

Two horizontal circular plates 9 in. (228.6 mm) in diameter are separated by an oil film 0.08 in. (2.032 mm) thick. A torque of 0.25 ft·lb (0.339 N·m) applied to the upper plate causes that plate to rotate at a constant angular velocity of 4 revolutions per second (r/s) relative to the lower plate. Compute the dynamic viscosity of the oil.

### Calculation Procedure:

#### 1. Develop equations for the force and torque
Consider that the fluid film in Fig. 6a is in motion and that a fluid particle at boundary $A$ has a velocity $dV$ relative to a particle at $B$. The shearing stress in the fluid is

$$\tau = \mu \frac{dV}{dx} \qquad (12)$$

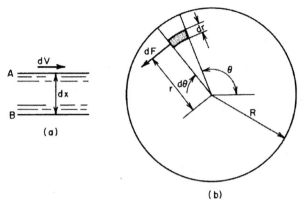

**FIGURE 6**

Figure 6b shows a cross section of the oil film, the shaded portion being an elemental surface. Let $m$ = thickness of film; $R$ = radius of plates; $\omega$ = angular velocity of one plate relative to the other; $dA$ = area of elemental surface; $dF$ = shearing force on elemental surface; $dT$ = torque of $dF$ with respect to the axis through the center of the plate.

Applying Eq. 12, develop these equations: $dF = 2\pi\omega\mu r^2\,dr\,d\theta/m$; $dT = r\,dF = 2\pi\omega\mu r^3\,dr\,d\theta/m$.

## 2. Integrate the foregoing equation to obtain the resulting torque; solve for $\mu$

Thus,

$$\mu = \frac{Tm}{\pi^2\omega R^4} \tag{13}$$

$T = 0.25$ ft·lb (0.339 N·m); $m = 0.08$ in. (2.032 mm); $\omega = 4$ r/s; $R = 4.5$ in. (114.3 mm); $\mu = 0.25(0.08)(12)^3/[\pi^2(4)(4.5)^4] = 0.00214$ lb·s/sq.ft. (0.1025 N·s/m²).

## APPLICATION OF BERNOULLI'S THEOREM

A steel pipe is discharging 10 ft³/s (283.1 L/s) of water. At section 1, the pipe diameter is 12 in. (304.8 mm), the pressure is 18 lb/sq.in. (124.11 kPa), and the elevation is 140 ft (42.67 m). At section 2, farther downstream, the pipe diameter is 8 in. (203.2 mm), and the elevation is 106 ft (32.31 m). If there is a head loss of 9 ft (2.74 m) between these sections due to pipe friction, what is the pressure at section 2?

## Calculation Procedure:

### 1. Tabulate the given data

Thus $D_1 = 12$ in. (304.8 mm); $D_2 = 8$ in. (203.2 mm); $p_1 = 18$ lb/sq.in. (124.11 kPa); $p_2 = ?$; $z_1 = 140$ ft (42.67 m); $z_2 = 106$ ft (32.31 m).

## 2. Compute the velocity at each section

Applying Eq. 8 gives $V_1$ = 10/0.785 = 12.7 ft/s (387.10 cm/s); $V_2$ = 10/0.349 = 28.7 ft/s (874.78 cm/s).

## 3. Compute $p_2$ by applying Eq. 9

Thus, $(p_2 - p_1)/w = (V_1^2 - V_2^2)/(2g) + z_1 - z_2 - h_F$ = $(12.7^2 - 28.7^2)/64.4 + 140 - 106 - 9$ = 14.7 ft (448.06 cm); $p_2$ = 14.7(62.4)/144 + 18 = 24.4 lb/sq.in. (168.24 kPa).

## FLOW THROUGH A VENTURI METER

A venturi meter of 3-in. (76.2-mm) throat diameter is inserted in a 6-in. (152.4-mm) diameter pipe conveying fuel oil having a specific gravity of 0.94. The pressure at the throat is 10 lb/sq.in. (68.95 kPa), and that at an upstream section 6 in. (152.4 mm) higher than the throat is 14.2 lb/sq.in. (97.91 kPa). If the discharge coefficient of the meter is 0.97, compute the flow rate in gallons per minute (liters per second).

## Calculation Procedure:

### 1. Record the given data, assigning the subscript 1 to the upstream section and 2 to the throat

The loss of head between two sections can be taken into account by introducing a *discharge coefficient* C. This coefficient represents the ratio between the actual discharge $Q$ and the discharge $Q_i$ that would occur in the absence of any losses. Then $Q = CQ_i$, or $(V_2^2 - V_1^2)/(2g) = C^2 h_V$.

Record the given data: $D_1$ = 6 in. (152.4 mm); $p_1$ = 14.2 lb/sq.in. (97.91 kPa); $z_1$ = 6 in. (152.4 mm); $D_2$ = 3 in. (76.2 mm); $p_2$ = 10 lb/sq.in. (68.95 kPa); $z_2$ = 0; $C$ = 0.97.

### 2. Express $V_1$ in terms of $V_2$ and develop velocity and flow relations

Thus,

$$V_2 = C\left[\frac{2gh_v}{(A_2/A_1)^2}\right]^{0.5} \tag{14a}$$

Also

$$Q = CA_2\left[\frac{2gh_v}{(A_2/A_1)^2}\right]^{0.5} \tag{14b}$$

If $V_1$ is negligible, these relations reduce to

$$V_2 = C(2gh_V)^{0.5} \tag{15a}$$

and

$$Q = CA_2(2gh_V)^{0.5} \tag{15b}$$

### 3. Compute $h_V$ by applying Eq. 9

Thus, $h_V = (p_1 - p_2)/w + z_1 - z_2$ = 4.2(144)/[0.94(62.4)] + 0.5 = 10.8 ft (3.29 m).

### 4. Compute Q by applying Eq. 14b

Thus, $(A_2/A_1)^2 = (D_2/D_1)^4 = {}^1/_{16}$; $A_2 = 0.0491$ sq.ft. (0.00456 m²); and $Q = 0.97(0.049)[64.4 \times 10.8/(1 - {}^1/_{16})]^{0.5} = 1.30$ ft³/s or, by using the conversion factor of 1 ft³/s = 449 gal/min (28.32 L/s), the flow rate is 1.30(449) = 584 gal/min (36.84 L/s).

## FLOW THROUGH AN ORIFICE

Compute the discharge through a 3-in. (76.2-mm) diameter square-edged orifice if the water on the upstream side stands 4 ft 8 in. (1.422 m) above the center of the orifice.

### Calculation Procedure:

### 1. Determine the discharge coefficient

For simplicity, the flow through a square-edged orifice discharging to the atmosphere is generally computed by equating the area of the stream to the area of the opening and then setting the discharge coefficient $C = 0.60$ to allow for contraction of the issuing stream. (The area of the issuing stream is about 0.62 times that of the opening.)

### 2. Compute the flow rate

Since the velocity of approach is negligible, use Eq. 15b. Or, $Q = 0.60(0.0491)(64.4 \times 4.67)^{0.5} = 0.511$ ft³/s (14.4675 L/s).

## FLOW THROUGH THE SUCTION PIPE OF A DRAINAGE PUMP

Water is being evacuated from a sump through the suction pipe shown in Fig. 7. The entrance-end diameter of the pipe is 3 ft (91.44 cm); the exit-end diameter, 1.75 ft (53.34 cm). The exit pressure is 12.9 in. (32.77 cm) of mercury vacuum. The head loss at the entry is one-fifteenth of the velocity head at that point, and the head loss in the pipe due to friction is one-tenth of the velocity head at the exit. Compute the discharge flow rate.

### Calculation Procedure:

### 1. Convert the pressure head to feet of water

The discharge may be found by comparing the conditions at an upstream point 1, where the velocity is negligible, with the conditions at point 3 (Fig. 7). Select the elevation of point 1 as the datum.

Converting the pressure head at point 3 to feet of water and using the specific gravity of mercury as 13.6, we have $p_3/w = -(12.9/12)13.6 = -14.6$ ft (−4.45 m).

### 2. Express the velocity head at 2 in terms of that at 3

By the equation of continuity, $V_2 = A_3V_3/A_2 = (1.75/3)^2 V_3 = 0.34V_3$.

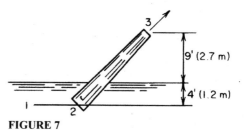

**FIGURE 7**

### 3. Evaluate $V_3$ by applying Eq. 9; then determine Q

Thus, $V_1^2/(2g) + p_1/w = V_3^2/(2g) + p_3/w + z_3 + (^1/_{15})V_2^2/(2g) + (^1/_{10})V_3^2/(2g)$, or $0 + 4 + 0 = V_3^2/(2g) - 14.6 + 13 + [V_3^2/(2g)](^1/_{15} \times 0.34^2 = ^1/_{10})$; $V_3 = 18.0$ ft/s (548.64 cm/s); then $Q_3 = A_3V_3 = 0.785(1.75)^2(18.0) = 43.3$ ft$^3$/s (1225.92 L/s).

## POWER OF A FLOWING LIQUID

A pump is discharging 8 ft$^3$/s (226.5 L/s) of water. Gages attached immediately upstream and downstream of the pump indicate a pressure differential of 36 lb/sq.in. (248.2 kPa). If the pump efficiency is 85 percent, what is the horsepower output and input?

### Calculation Procedure:

### 1. Evaluate the increase in head of the liquid

Power is the rate of performing work, or the amount of work performed in a unit time. If the fluid flows with a specific energy $H$, the total energy of the fluid discharged in a unit time is $QwH$. This expression thus represents the work that the flowing fluid can perform in a unit time and therefore the power associated with this discharge. Since 1 hp = 550 ft·lb/s,

$$1 \text{ hp} = \frac{QwH}{550} \tag{16}$$

In this situation, the power developed by the pump is desired. Therefore, $H$ must be equated to the specific energy added by the pump.

To evaluate the increase in head, consider the differences of the two sections being considered. Since both sections have the same velocity and elevation, only their pressure heads differ. Thus, $p_2/w - p_1/w = 36(144)/62.4 = 83.1$ ft (2532.89 cm).

### 2. Compute the horsepower output and input

Thus, $\text{hp}_{out} = 8(62.4)(83.1)/550 = 75.4$ hp; $\text{hp}_{in} = 75.4/0.85 = 88.7$ hp.

## DISCHARGE OVER A SHARP-EDGED WEIR

Compute the discharge over a sharp-edged rectangular weir 4 ft (121.9 cm) high and 10 ft (304.8 cm) long, with two end contractions, if the water in the canal behind the weir is 4 ft 9 in. (144.78 cm) high. Disregard the velocity of approach.

### Calculation Procedure:

### 1. Adopt a standard relation for this weir

The discharge over a sharp-edged rectangular weir without end contractions in which the velocity of approach is negligible is given by the Francis formula as

$$Q = 3.33bh^{1.5} \tag{17a}$$

where $b$ = length of crest and $h$ = head on weir (i.e., the difference between the elevation of the crest and that of the water surface upstream of the weir).

**2. Modify the Francis equation for end contractions**
With two end contractions, the discharge of the weir is

$$Q = 3.33(b - 0.2h)h^{1.5} \tag{17b}$$

Substituting the given values yields $Q = 3.33(10 - 0.2 \times 0.75)0.75^{1.5} = 21.3$ ft³/s (603.05 L/s).

## LAMINAR FLOW IN A PIPE

A tank containing crude oil discharges 340 gal/min (21.4 L/s) through a steel pipe 220 ft (67.1 m) long and 8 in. (203.2 mm) in diameter. The kinematic viscosity of the oil is 0.002 sq.ft./s (1.858 cm²/s). Compute the difference in elevation between the liquid surface in the tank and the pipe outlet.

## Calculation Procedure:

### 1. Identify the type of flow in the pipe
To investigate the discharge in a pipe, it is necessary to distinguish between two types of fluid flow—*laminar* and *turbulent*. Laminar (or *viscous*) flow is characterized by the telescopic sliding of one circular layer of fluid past the adjacent layer, each fluid particle traversing a straight line. The velocity of the fluid flow varies parabolically from zero at the pipe wall to its maximum value at the pipe center, where it equals twice the mean velocity.

Turbulent flow is characterized by the formation of eddy currents, with each fluid particle traversing a sinuous path.

In any pipe the type of flow is ascertained by applying a dimensionless index termed the *Reynolds number*, defined as

$$N_R = \frac{DV}{\nu} \tag{18}$$

Flow is considered laminar if $N_R < 2100$ and turbulent if $N_R > 3000$.

In laminar flow the head loss due to friction is

$$h_F = \frac{32L\nu V}{gD^2} \tag{19a}$$

or

$$h_F = \left(\frac{64}{N_R}\right)\left(\frac{L}{D}\right)\left(\frac{V^2}{2g}\right) \tag{19b}$$

Let 1 denote a point on the liquid surface and 2 a point at the pipe outlet. The elevation of 2 will be taken as datum.

To identify the type of flow, compute $N_R$. Thus, $D = 8$ in. (203.2 mm); $L = 220$ ft (6705.6 cm); $\nu = 0.002$ sq.ft./s (1.858 cm²/s); $Q = 340/449 = 0.757$, converting from gallons per minute to cubic feet per second. Then $V = Q/A = 0.757/0.349 = 2.17$ ft/s (66.142 cm/s). And $N_R = 0.667(2.17)/0.002 = 724$. Therefore, the flow is laminar because $N_R$ is less than 2100.

## 2. *Express all losses in terms of the velocity head*

By Eq. 19*b*, $h_F = (64/724)(220/0.667)V^2/(2g) = 29.2V^2/(2g)$. Where $L/D > 500$, the following may be regarded as negligible in comparison with the loss due to friction: loss at pipe entrance, losses at elbows, velocity head at the discharge, etc. In this instance, include the secondary items. The loss at the pipe entrance is $h_E = 0.5V^2/(2g)$. The total loss is $h_L = 29.7V^2/(2g)$.

## 3. *Find the elevation of 1 by applying Eq. 9*

Thus, $z_1 = V_2^2/(2g) + h_L = 30.7V_2^2/(2g) = 30.7(2.17)^2/64.4 = 2.24$ ft (68.275 cm).


# TURBULENT FLOW IN PIPE—APPLICATION OF DARCY-WEISBACH FORMULA

Water is pumped at the rate of 3 ft³/s (85.0 L/s) through an 8-in. (203.2-mm) fairly smooth pipe 2600 ft (792.48 m) long to a reservoir where the water surface is 180 ft (50.86 m) higher than the pump. Determine the gage pressure at the pump discharge.


## Calculation Procedure:

## 1. *Compute* $h_F$

Turbulent flow in a pipe flowing full may be investigated by applying the Darcy-Weisbach formula for friction head

$$h_F = \frac{fLV^2}{2gD} \tag{20}$$

where $f$ is a friction factor. However, since the friction head does not vary precisely in the manner implied by this equation, $f$ is dependent on $D$ and $V$, as well as the degree of roughness of the pipe. Values of $f$ associated with a given set of values of the independent quantities may be obtained from Fig. 8.

Accurate equations for $h_F$ are the following:
*Extremely smooth pipes:*

$$h_F = \frac{0.30LV^{1.75}}{1000D^{1.25}} \tag{21a}$$

*Fairly smooth pipes:*

$$h_F = \frac{0.38LV^{1.86}}{1000D^{1.25}} \tag{21b}$$

*Rough pipes:*

$$h_F = \frac{0.50LV^{1.95}}{1000D^{1.25}} \tag{21c}$$

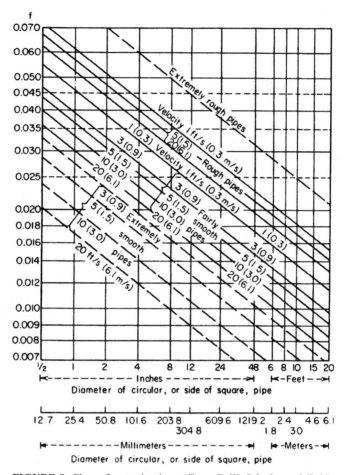

**FIGURE 8.** Flow of water in pipes. (*From E. W. Schoder and F. M. Dawson, Hydraulics, McGraw-Hill Book Company, New York, 1934. By permission of the publishers.*)

*Extremely rough pipes:*

$$h_F = \frac{0.69LV^2}{1000D^{1.25}}$$ (21d)

Using Eq. 21b gives $V = Q/A = 3/0.349 = 8.60$ ft/s (262.128 cm/s); $h_F = 0.38(2.6)(8.60)^{1.86}/0.667^{1.25} = 89.7$ ft (27.34 m).

## 2. Alternatively, determine $h_F$ using Eq. 20

First obtain the appropriate $f$ value from Fig. 8, or $f = 0.020$ for this pipe. Then $h_F = 0.020(2.600/0.667)(8.60^2/64.4) = 89.6$ ft (27.31 m).

## 3. Compute the pressure at the pump discharge

Use Eq. 9. Since $L/D > 500$, ignore the secondary items. Then $p_1/w = z_2 + h_F = 180 + 89.6 = 269.6$ ft (82.17 m), $p_1 = 269.6(62.4)/144 = 117$ lb/sq.in. (806.7 kPa).

## DETERMINATION OF FLOW IN A PIPE

Two reservoirs are connected by a 7000-ft (2133.6-m) fairly smooth cast-iron pipe 10 in. (254.0 mm) in diameter. The difference in elevation of the water surfaces is 90 ft (27.4 m). Compute the discharge to the lower reservoir.

### Calculation Procedure:

#### 1. Determine the fluid velocity and flow rate

Since the secondary items are negligible, the entire head loss of 90 ft (27.4 m) results from friction. Using Eq. 21b and solving for $V$, we have $90 = 0.38(7)V^{1.86}/0.833^{1.25}$; $V = 5.87$ ft/s (178.918 cm/s). Then $Q = VA = 5.87(0.545) = 3.20$ ft$^3$/s (90.599 L/s).

#### 2. Alternatively, assume a value of f and compute V

Referring to Fig. 8, select a value for $f$. Then compute $V$ by applying Eq. 20. Next, compare the value of $f$ corresponding to this result with the assumed value of $f$. If the two values differ appreciably, assume a new value of $f$ and repeat the computation. Continue this process until the assumed and actual values of $f$ agree closely.

## PIPE-SIZE SELECTION BY THE MANNING FORMULA

A cast-iron pipe is to convey water at 3.3 ft$^3$/s (93.430 L/s) on a grade of 0.001. Applying the Manning formula with $n = 0.013$, determine the required size of pipe.

### Calculation Procedure:

#### 1. Compute the pipe diameter

The Manning formula, which is suitable for both open and closed conduits, is

$$V = \frac{1.486R^{2/3}s^{1/2}}{n} \tag{22}$$

where $n$ = roughness coefficient; $R$ = hydraulic radius = ratio of cross-sectional area of pipe to the wetted perimeter of the pipe; $s$ = hydraulic gradient = $dH/dL$. If the flow is uniform, i.e., the area and therefore the velocity are constant along the stream, then the loss of head equals the drop in elevation, and the grade of the conduit is $s$.

For a circular pipe flowing full, Eq. 22 becomes

$$D = \left(\frac{2.159Qn}{s^{1/2}}\right)^{3/8} \tag{22a}$$

Substituting numerical values gives $D = (2.159 \times 3.3 \times 0.013/0.001^{1/2})^{3/8} = 1.50$ ft (45.72 cm). Therefore, use an 18-in. (457.2-mm) diameter pipe.

## LOSS OF HEAD CAUSED BY SUDDEN ENLARGEMENT OF PIPE

Water flows through a pipe at 4 ft³/s (113.249 L/s). Compute the loss of head resulting from a change in pipe size if (a) the pipe diameter increases abruptly from 6 to 10 in. (152.4 to 254.0 mm); (b) the pipe diameter increases abruptly from 6 to 8 in. (152.4 to 203.2 mm) at one section and then from 8 to 10 in. (203.2 to 254.0 mm) at a section farther downstream.

### Calculation Procedure:

### 1. Evaluate the pressure-head differential required to decelerate the liquid

Where there is an abrupt increase in pipe size, the liquid must be decelerated upon entering the larger pipe, since the fluid velocity varies inversely with area. Let subscript 1 refer to a section immediately downstream of the enlargement, where the higher velocity prevails, and let subscript 2 refer to a section farther downstream, where deceleration has been completed. Disregard the frictional loss.

Using Eq. 11 we see $p_2/w = p_1/w + (V_1 V_2 - V_2^2)/g$.

### 2. Combine the result of step 1 with Eq. 9

The result is Borda's formula for the head loss $h_E$ caused by sudden enlargement of the pipe cross section:

$$h_E = \frac{(V_1 - V_2)^2}{2g} \tag{23}$$

As this investigation shows, only part of the drop in velocity head is accounted for by a gain in pressure head. The remaining head $h_E$ is dissipated through the formation of eddy currents at the entrance to the larger pipe.

### 3. Compute the velocity in each pipe

Thus

| Pipe diam, in. (mm) | Pipe area, sq.ft. (m²) | Fluid velocity, ft/s (cm/s) |
|---|---|---|
| 6 (152.4) | 0.196 (0.0182) | 20.4 (621.79) |
| 8 (203.2) | 0.349 (0.0324) | 11.5 (350.52) |
| 10 (254.0) | 0.545 (0.0506) | 7.3 (222.50) |

### 4. Find the head loss for part a

Thus, $h_E = (20.4 - 7.3)^2/64.4 = 2.66$ ft (81.077 cm).

### 5. Find the head loss for part b

Thus, $h_E = [(20.4 - 11.5)^2 + (11.5 - 7.3)^2]/64.4 = 1.50$ ft (45.72 cm). Comparison of these results indicates that the eddy-current loss is attenuated if the increase in pipe size occurs in steps.

## DISCHARGE OF LOOPING PIPES

A pipe carrying 12.5 ft³/s (353.90 L/s) of water branches into three pipes of the following diameters and lengths; $D_1 = 6$ in. (152.4 mm); $L_1 = 1000$ ft (304.8 m); $D_2 = 8$ in. (203.2 mm); $L_2 = 1300$ ft (396.2 m); $D_3 = 10$ in. (254.0 mm); $L_3 = 1200$ ft (365.8 m). These pipes rejoin at their downstream ends. Compute the discharge in the three pipes, considering each as fairly smooth.

### Calculation Procedure:

### 1. Express Q as a function of D and L
Since all fluid particles have the same energy at the juncture point, irrespective of the loops they traversed, the head losses in the three loops are equal. The flow thus divides itself in a manner that produces equal values of $h_F$ in the loops.
   Transforming Eq. 21b,

$$Q = \frac{kD^{2.67}}{L^{0.538}} \tag{24}$$

where $k$ is a constant.

### 2. Establish the relative values of the discharges; then determine the actual values
Thus, $Q_2/Q_1 = (8/6)^{2.67}/1.3^{0.538} = 1.87$; $Q_3/Q_1 = (10/6)^{2.67}/1.2^{0.538} = 3.55$. Then $Q_1 + Q_2 + Q_3 = Q_1(1 + 1.87 + 3.55) = 12.5$ ft³/s (353.90 L/s). Solving gives $Q_1 = 1.95$ ft³/s (55.209 L/s); $Q_2 = 3.64$ ft³/s (103.056 L/s); $Q_3 = 6.91$ ft³/s (195.637 L/s).

## FLUID FLOW IN BRANCHING PIPES

The pipes *AM*, *MB*, and *MC* in Fig. 9 have the diameters and lengths indicated. Compute the water flow in each pipe if the pipes are considered rough.

### Calculation Procedure:

### 1. Write the basic equations governing the discharges
Let subscripts 1, 2, and 3 refer to *AM*, *MB*, and *MC*, respectively. Then $h_{F1} + h_{F2} = 110$; $h_{F1} + h_{F3} = 150$, Eq. *a*; $Q_1 = Q_2 + Q_3$, Eq. *b*.

### 2. Transform Eq. 21c
The transformed equation is

$$Q = 38.7D^{2.64}\left(\frac{h_F}{L}\right)^{0.513} \tag{25}$$

### 3. Assume a trial value for $h_{F1}$ and find the discharge; test the result
Use Eqs. *a* and 25 to find the discharges. Test the results for compliance with Eq. *b*. If we assume $h_{F1} = 70$ ft (21.3 m), then $h_{F2} = 40$ ft (12.2 m) and $h_{F3} = 80$ ft (24.4 m); $Q_1 =$

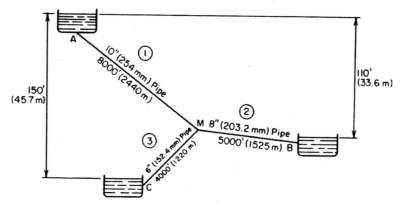

**FIGURE 9.** Branching pipes.

$38.7(0.833)^{2.64}(70/8000)^{0.513} = 2.10$ ft³/s (59.455 L/s). Similarly, $Q_2 = 1.12$ ft³/s (31.710 L/s) and $q_3 = 0.83$ ft³/s (23.499 L/s); $Q_2 + Q_3 = 1.95 < Q_1$. The assumed value of $h_{F1}$ is excessive.

**4. Make another assumption for $h_{F1}$ and the corresponding revisions**

Assume $h_{F1} = 66$ ft (20.1 m). Then $Q_1 = 2.10(66/70)^{0.513} = 2.04$ ft³/s (57.757 L/s). Similarly, $Q_2 = 1.18$ ft³/s (33.408 L/s); $Q_3 = 0.85$ ft³/s (24.065 L/s). $Q_2 + Q_3 = 2.03$ ft³/s (57.736 L/s). These results may be accepted as sufficiently precise.

## UNIFORM FLOW IN OPEN CHANNEL— DETERMINATION OF SLOPE

It is necessary to convey 1200 ft³/s (33,974.6 L/s) of water from a dam to a power plant in a canal of rectangular cross section, 24 ft (7.3 m) wide and 10 ft (3.0 m) deep, having a roughness coefficient of 0.016. The canal is to flow full. Compute the required slope of the canal in feet per mile (meters per kilometer).

### Calculation Procedure:

**1. Apply Eq. 22**

Thus, $A = 24(10) = 240$ sq.ft. (22.3 m²); wetted perimeter $=$ WP $= 24 + 2(10) = 44$ ft (13.4 m); $R = 240/44 = 5.45$ ft (1.661 m); $V = 1200/240 = 5$ ft/s (152.4 cm/s); $s = [nV/(1.486R^{2/3})]^2 = [0.016 \times 5/(1.486 \times 5.45^{2/3})]^2 = 0.000302$; slope $= 0.000302(5280$ ft/mi$) = 1.59$ ft/mi (0.302 m/km).

## REQUIRED DEPTH OF CANAL FOR SPECIFIED FLUID FLOW RATE

A trapezoidal canal is to carry water at 800 ft³/s (22,649.7 L/s). The grade of the canal is 0.0004; the bottom width is 25 ft (7.6 m); the slope of the sides is 1½ horizontal to

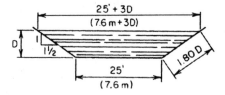

**FIGURE 10**

1 vertical; the roughness coefficient is 0.014. Compute the required depth of the canal, to the nearest tenth of a foot.

## Calculation Procedure:

### 1. Transform Eq. 22 and compute $AR^{2/3}$

Thus, $AR^{2/3} = nQ/(1.486s^{1/2})$, Eq. 22b. Or, $AR^{2/3} = 0.014(800)/[1.486(0.0004)^{1/2}] = 377$.

### 2. Express the area and wetted perimeter in terms of D (Fig. 10)

Side of canal $= D(1^2 + 1.5^2)^{0.5} = 1.80D$. $A = D(25 + 1.5D)$; WP $= 25 + 360D$.

### 3. Assume the trial values of D until Eq. 22b is satisfied

Thus, assume $D = 5$ ft (152.4 cm); $A = 162.5$ sq.ft. (15.10 m²); WP $= 43$ ft (1310.6 cm); $R = 3.78$ ft (115.2 cm); $AR^{2/3} = 394$. The assumed value of $D$ is therefore excessive because the computed $AR^{2/3}$ is greater than the value computed in step 1.

Next, assume a lower value for $D$, or $D = 4.9$ ft (149.35 cm); $A = 158.5$ sq.ft. (14.72 m²); WP $= 42.64$ ft (1299.7 cm); $R = 3.72$ ft (113.386 cm); $AR^{2/3} = 381$. This is acceptable. Therefore, $D = 4.9$ ft (149.35 cm).

## ALTERNATE STAGES OF FLOW; CRITICAL DEPTH

A rectangular channel 20 ft (609.6 cm) wide is to discharge 500 ft³/s (14,156.1 L/s) of water having a specific energy of 4.5 ft·lb/lb (1.37 J/N). (a) Using $n = 0.013$, compute the required slope of the channel. (b) Compute the maximum potential discharge associated with the specific energy of 4.5 ft·lb/lb (1.37 J/N). (c) Compute the minimum of specific energy required to maintain a flow of 500 ft³/s (14,156.1 L/s).

## Calculation Procedure:

### 1. Evaluate the specific energy of an elemental mass of liquid at a distance z above the channel bottom

To analyze the discharge conditions at a given section in a channel, it is advantageous to evaluate the specific energy (or head) by taking the elevation of the bottom of the channel *at the given section* as datum. Assume a uniform velocity across the section, and let $D = $ depth of flow, ft (cm); $H_e = $ specific energy as computed in the prescribed manner; $Q_u = $ discharge through a unit width of channel, ft³(s·ft) [L/(s·cm)].

Evaluating the specific energy of an elemental mass of liquid at a given distance $z$ above the channel bottom, we get

$$H_e = \frac{Q_u^2}{2gD^2} + D \tag{26}$$

Thus, $H_e$ is constant across the entire section. Moreover, if the flow is uniform, as it is here, $H_e$ is constant along the entire stream.

## 2. Apply the given values and solve for D

Thus, $H_e$ = 4.5 ft·lb/lb (1.37 J/N); $Q_u$ = 500/20 = 25 ft³/(s·ft) [2323 L/(s·m)]. Rearrange Eq. 26 to obtain

$$D^2(H_e - D) = \frac{Q_u^2}{2g} \tag{26a}$$

Or, $D^2(4.5 - D) = 25^2/64.4 = 9.705$. This cubic equation has two positive roots, $D$ = 1.95 ft (59.436 cm) and $D$ = 3.84 ft (117.043 cm). There are therefore two stages of flow that accommodate the required discharge with the given energy. [The third root of the equation is $D = -1.29$ ft ($-39.319$ cm), an impossible condition.]

## 3. Compute the slope associated with the computed depths

Using Eq. 22, at the lower stage we have $D$ = 1.95 ft (59.436 cm); $A$ = 20(1.95) = 39.0 sq.ft. (36,231.0 cm²); WP = 20 + 2(1.95) = 23.9 ft (728.47 cm); $R$ = 39.0/23.9 = 1.63 ft (49.682 cm); $V$ = 25/1.95 = 12.8 ft/s (390.14 cm/s); $s$ = $[nV/(1.486R^{2/3})]^2$ = (0.013 × 12.8/1.486 × 1.63^{2/3})^2 = 0.00654.

At the upper stage $D$ = 3.84 ft (117.043 cm); $A$ = 20(3.84) = 76.8 sq.ft. (71,347.2 cm²); WP = 20 + 2(3.84) = 27.68 ft (843.686 cm); $R$ = 76.8/27.68 = 2.77 ft (84.430 cm); $V$ = 25/3.84 = 6.51 ft/s (198.4 cm/s); $s$ = $[0.013 × 6.51/(1.486 × 2.77^{2/3})]^2$ = 0.000834. This constitutes the solution to part $a$.

## 4. Plot the D-$Q_u$ curve

For part $b$, consider $H_e$ as remaining constant at 4.5 ft·lb/lb (1.37 J/N) while $Q_u$ varies. Plot the D-$Q_u$ curve as shown in Fig. 11a. The depth that provides the maximum potential discharge is called the *critical depth* with respect to the given specific energy.

## 5. Differentiate Eq. 26 to find the critical depth; then evaluate $Q_{u,max}$

Differentiating Eq. 26 and setting $dQ_u/dD = 0$ yield

$$\text{Critical depth } D_c = \frac{2}{3}H_e \tag{27}$$

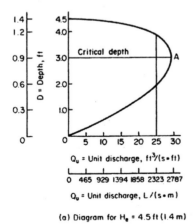

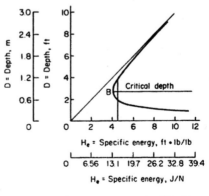

(a) Diagram for $H_e$ = 4.5 ft (1.4 m)

(b) Diagram for $Q_u$ = 25 ft³/(s·ft) [2323 L/(s·m)]

**FIGURE 11**

Or, $D_c = {}^2/_3(4.5) = 3.0$ ft (91.44 cm); $Q_{u,max} = [64.4(4.5 \times 3.0^2 - 3.0^2)]^{0.5} = 29.5$ ft³/(s·ft) (2741 L/(s·m)]; $Q_{max} = 29.5(20) = 590$ ft³/s (16,704.2 L/s). This constitutes the solution to part $b$.

### 6. Plot the D-$H_e$ curve
For part $c$, consider $Q_u$ as remaining constant at 25 ft³/(s·ft) [2323 L/(s·m)] while $H_c$ varies. Plot the D-$H_e$ curve as shown in Fig. 11$b$. (This curve is asymptotic with the straight lines $D = H_e$ and $D = 0$.) The depth at which the specific energy is minimum is called the *critical depth* with respect to the given unit discharge.

### 7. Differentiate Eq. 26 to find the critical depth; then evaluate $H_{e,min}$
Differentiating gives

$$D_c = \left( \frac{Q_u^2}{g} \right)^{1/3} \tag{28}$$

Then $D_c = (25^2/32.2)^{1/3} = 2.69$ ft (81.991 cm). Then $H_{e,min} = 25^2/[64.4(2.69)^2] + 2.69 = 4.03$ ft·lb/lb (1.229 J/N).

The values of $D$ as computed in part $a$ coincide with those obtained by referring to the two graphs in Fig. 11. The equations derived in this procedure are valid solely for rectangular channels, but analogous equations pertaining to other channel profiles may be derived in a similar manner.

## DETERMINATION OF HYDRAULIC JUMP

Water flows over a 100-ft (30.5-m) long dam at 7500 ft³/s (212,400 L/s). The depth of tailwater on the level apron is 9 ft (2.7 m). Determine the depth of flow immediately upstream of the hydraulic jump.

### Calculation Procedure:

### 1. Find the difference in hydrostatic forces per unit width of channel required to decelerate the liquid
Refer to Fig. 12. *Hydraulic jump* designates an abrupt transition from lower-stage to upper-stage flow caused by a sharp decrease in slope, sudden increase in roughness,

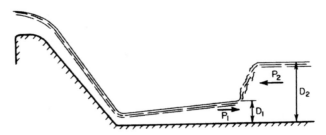

**FIGURE 12.** Hydraulic jump on apron of dam.

encroachment of backwater, or some other factor. The deceleration of liquid requires an increase in hydrostatic pressure, but only part of the drop in velocity head is accounted for by a gain in pressure head. The excess head is dissipated in the formation of a turbulent standing wave. Thus, the phenomenon of hydraulic jump resembles the behavior of liquid in a pipe at a sudden enlargement, as analyzed in an earlier calculation procedure.

Let $D_1$ and $D_2$ denote the depth of flow immediately upstream and downstream of the jump, respectively. Then $D_1 < D_c < D_2$. Refer to Fig. 11$b$. Since the hydraulic jump is accompanied by a considerable drop in energy, the point on the $D$-$H_e$ diagram that represents $D_2$ lies both above and to the left of that representing $D_1$. Therefore, the upstream depth is less than the depth that would exist in the absence of any loss.

Using literal values, apply Eq. 11 to find the difference in hydrostatic forces per unit width of channel that is required to decelerate the liquid. Solve the resulting equation for $D_1$:

$$D_1 = -\frac{D_2}{2} + \left( \frac{2V_2^2 D_2}{g} + \frac{D_2^2}{4} \right)^{0.5} \tag{29}$$

### 2. Substitute numerical values in Eq. 29

Thus, $Q_u = 7500/100 = 75$ ft³/(s·ft) [6969 L/(s·m)]; $V_2 = 75/9 = 8.33$ ft/s (2.538 m/s); $D_1 = -9/2 + (2 \times 8.33^2 \times 9/32.2 + 9^2/4)^{0.5} = 3.18$ ft (0.969 m).

# RATE OF CHANGE OF DEPTH IN NONUNIFORM FLOW

The unit discharge in a rectangular channel is 28 ft³/(s·ft) [2602 L/(s·m)]. The energy gradient is 0.0004, and the grade of the channel bed is 0.0010. Determine the rate at which the depth of flow is changing in the downstream direction (i.e., the grade of the liquid surface with respect to the channel bed) at a section where the depth is 3.2 ft (0.97 m).

## Calculation Procedure:

### 1. Express H as a function of D

Let $H$ = total specific energy at a given section as evaluated by selecting a fixed horizontal reference plane; $L$ = distance measured in downstream direction; $z$ = elevation of given section with respect to datum plane; $s_b$ = grade of channel bed = $-dz/dL$; $s_e$ = energy gradient = $-dH/dL$.

Express $H$ as a function of $D$ by annexing the potential-energy term to Eq. 26. Thus,

$$H = \frac{Q_u^2}{2gD^2} + D + z \tag{30}$$

## 2. Differentiate this equation with respect to L to obtain the rate of change of D; substitute numerical values

Differentiating gives

$$\frac{dD}{dL} = \frac{s_b - s_e}{1 - Q_u^2/(gD^3)} \tag{31a}$$

or in accordance with Eq. 28,

$$\frac{dD}{dL} = \frac{s_b - s_e}{1 - d_c^3/D^3} \tag{31b}$$

Substituting yields $Q_u^2/(gD^3) = 28^2/(32.2 \times 3.2^3) = 0.743$; $dD/dL = (0.0010 - 0.0004)/(1 - 0.743) = 0.00233$ ft/ft (0.00233 m/m). The depth is increasing in the downstream direction, and the water is therefore being decelerated.

As Eq. 31b reveals, the relationship between the actual depth at a given section and the critical depth serves as a criterion in ascertaining whether the depth is increasing or decreasing.

## DISCHARGE BETWEEN COMMUNICATING VESSELS

In Fig. 13, liquid is flowing from tank $A$ to tank $B$ through an orifice near the bottom. The area of the liquid surface is 200 sq.ft. (18.58 m²) in $A$ and 150 sq.ft. (13.93 m²) in $B$. Initially, the difference in water levels is 14 ft (4.3 m), and the discharge is 2 ft³/s (56.6 L/s). Assuming that the discharge coefficient remains constant, compute the time required for the water level in tank $A$ to drop 1.8 ft (0.54 m).

### Calculation Procedure:

## 1. By expressing the change in h during an elemental time interval, develop the time-interval equation

Let $A_a$ and $A_b$ denote the area of the liquid surface in tanks $A$ and $B$, respectively; let subscripts 1 and 2 refer to the beginning and end, respectively, of a time interval $t$. Then

$$t = \frac{2A_a A_b(h_1 - [h_1 h_2]^{0.5})}{Q_1(A_a + A_b)} \tag{32}$$

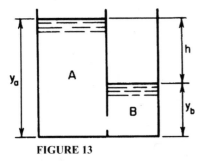

**FIGURE 13**

## 2. Find the value of h when $y_a$ diminishes by 1.8 ft (0.54 m)

Thus, $\Delta y_b = (-A_a/A_b)(\Delta y_a) = -(200/150)(-1.8) = 2.4$ ft (0.73 m); $\Delta h = \Delta y_a - \Delta y_b = -1.8 - 2.4 = -4.2$ ft (−1.28 m); $h_1 = 14$ ft (4.3 m); $h_2 = 14 - 4.2 = 9.8$ ft (2.99 m).

## 3. Substitute numerical values in Eq. 32 and solve for t

Thus, $t = 2(200)(150)[14 - (14 \times 9.8)^{0.5}]/[2(200 + 150)] = 196$ s = 3.27 min.

## VARIATION IN HEAD ON A WEIR WITHOUT INFLOW TO THE RESERVOIR

Water flows over a weir of 60-ft (18.3-m) length from a reservoir having a surface area of 50 acres (202,350 m²). If the inflow to the reservoir ceases when the head on the weir is 2 ft (0.6 m), what will the head be at the expiration of 1 h? Consider that the instantaneous discharge is given by Eq. 17a.

### Calculation Procedure:

### 1. Develop the time-interval equation
Let $A$ = surface area of reservoir and $C$ = numerical constant in discharge equation; and subscripts 1 and 2 refer to the beginning and end, respectively, of a time interval $t$. By expressing the change in head during an elemental time interval,

$$t = \frac{2A}{Cb(1/h_2^{0.5} - 1/h_1^{0.5})} \tag{33}$$

### 2. Substitute numerical values in Eq. 33; solve for $h_2$
Thus, $A = 50(43,560) = 2,178,000$ sq.ft. (202,336.2 m²); $t = 3600$ s; solving gives $h_2 = 1.32$ ft (0.402 m).

## VARIATION IN HEAD ON A WEIR WITH INFLOW TO THE RESERVOIR

Water flows over an 80-ft (24.4-m) long weir from a reservoir having a surface area of 6,000,000 sq.ft. (557,400.0 m²) while the rate of inflow to the reservoir remains constant at 2175 ft³/s (61,578.9 L/s). How long will it take for the head on the weir to increase from zero to 95 percent of its maximum value? Consider that the instantaneous rate of flow over the weir is $3.4bh^{1.5}$.

### Calculation Procedure:

### 1. Compute the maximum head on the weir by equating outflow to inflow
The water in the reservoir reaches its maximum height when equilibrium is achieved, i.e., when the rate of outflow equals the rate of inflow. Let $Q_i$ = rate of inflow; $Q_o$ = rate of outflow at a given instant; $t$ = time elapsed since the start of the outflow.
Equating outflow to inflow yields $3.4(80h_{max}^{1.5}) = 2175$; $h_{max} = 4.0$ ft (1.2 m); $0.95h_{max} = 3.8$ ft (1.16 m).

### 2. Using literal values, determine the time interval dt during which the water level rises a distance dh
Thus, with $C$ = numerical constant in the discharge equation,

$$dt = \frac{A}{Q_i - Cbh^{1.5}} \, dh \tag{34}$$

The right side of this equation is not amenable to direct integration. Consequently, the only feasible way of computing the time is to perform an approximate integration.

### 3. *Obtain the approximate value of the required time*
Select suitable increments of $h$, calculate the corresponding increments of $t$, and total the latter to obtain an approximate value of the required time. In calculating $Q_o$, apply the mean value of $h$ associated with each increment.

The precision inherent in the result thus obtained depends on the judgment used in selecting the increments of $h$, and a clear visualization of the relationship between $h$ and $t$ is essential. Let $m = dt/dh = A/(Q_i - Cbh^{1.5})$. The $m$-$h$ curve is shown in Fig. 14a. Then, $t = \int m \, dh$ = area between the $m$-$h$ curve and $h$ axis.

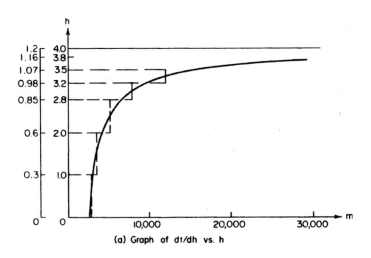

(a) Graph of dt/dh vs. h

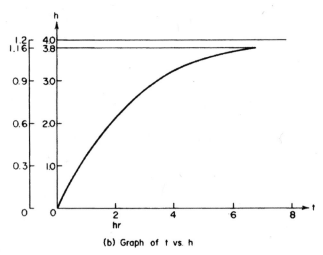

(b) Graph of t vs. h

**FIGURE 14**

**TABLE 1.** Approximate Integration of Eq. 34

| $\Delta h$, ft (m) | $h_b$, ft (m) | $h_m$, ft (m) | $m$, s/ft (s/m) | $\Delta t$, s |
|---|---|---|---|---|
| 1.0 (0.30) | 0   (0.00) | 0.5  (0.15) | 2,890 (9,633.3) | 2,890 |
| 1.0 (0.30) | 1.0 (0.30) | 1.5  (0.46) | 3,580 (11,933.3) | 3,580 |
| 0.8 (0.24) | 2.0 (0.61) | 2.4  (0.73) | 5,160 (17,308.3) | 4,130 |
| 0.4 (0.12) | 2.8 (0.85) | 3.0  (0.91) | 7,870 (26,250.0) | 3,150 |
| 0.3 (0.09) | 3.2 (0.98) | 3.35 (1.02) | 11,830 (39,444.4) | 3,550 |
| 0.2 (0.06) | 3.5 (1.07) | 3.6  (1.10) | 18,930 (63,166.7) | 3,790 |
| 0.1 (0.03) | 3.7 (1.13) | 3.75 (1.14) | 30,000 (100,000) | 3,000 |
| Total |  |  |  | 24,090 |

This area is approximated by summing the areas of the rectangles as indicated in Fig. 14, the length of each rectangle being equal to the value of $m$ at the center of the interval. Note that as $h$ increases, the increments $\Delta h$ should be made progressively smaller to minimize the error introduced in the procedure.

Select the increments shown in Table 1, and perform the indicated calculations. The symbols $h_b$ and $h_m$ denote the values of $h$ at the beginning and center, respectively, of an interval. The following calculations for the third interval illustrate the method: $h_m = \frac{1}{2}(2.0 + 2.8) = 2.4$ ft (0.73 m); $m = 6,000,000/(2175 - 3.4 \times 80 \times 2.4^{1.5}) = 5160$ s/ft (16,929.1 s/m); $\Delta t = m\,\Delta h = 5160(0.8) = 4130$ s. From Table 1 the required time is $t = 24,090$ s = 6 h 41.5 min.

The $t$-$h$ curve is shown in Fig. 14b. The time required for the water to reach its maximum height is difficult to evaluate with precision because $m$ becomes infinitely large as $h$ approaches $h_{max}$; that is, the water level rises at an imperceptible rate as it nears its limiting position.

## DIMENSIONAL ANALYSIS METHODS

The velocity of a raindrop in still air is known or assumed to be a function of these quantities: gravitational acceleration, drop diameter, dynamic viscosity of the air, and the density of both the water and the air. Develop the dimensionless parameters associated with this phenomenon.

### Calculation Procedure:

### 1. Using a generalized notational system, record the units in which the six quantities of this situation are expressed

Dimensional analysis is an important tool both in theoretical investigations and in experimental work because it clarifies the relationships intrinsic in a given situation.

A quantity that appears in every dimensionless parameter is termed *repeating*; a quantity that appears in only one parameter is termed *nonrepeating*. Since the engineer is usually more accustomed to dealing with units of force rather than of mass, the force-length-time system of units is applied here. Let $F$, $L$, and $T$ denote units of force, length, and time, respectively.

By using this generalized notational system, it is convenient to write the appropriate USCS units and then replace these with the general units. For example, with respect to acceleration: USCS units, ft/s$^2$; general units, $L/T^2$ or $LT^{-2}$. Similarly, with respect to density ($w/g$): USCS units, (lb/ft$^3$)/(ft/s$^2$); general units, $FL^{-3}/LT^{-2}$ or $FL^{-4}T^2$.

The results are shown in the following table.

| Quantity | Units |
|---|---|
| $V$ = velocity of raindrop | $LT^{-1}$ |
| $g$ = gravitational acceleration | $LT^{-2}$ |
| $D$ = diameter of drop | $L$ |
| $\mu_a$ = air viscosity | $FL^{-2}T$ |
| $\rho_w$ = water density | $FL^{-4}T^2$ |
| $\rho_a$ = air density | $FL^{-4}T^2$ |

### 2. Compute the number of dimensionless parameters present
This phenomenon contains six physical quantities and three units. Therefore, as a consequence of Buckingham's pi theorem, the number of dimensionless parameters is $6 - 3 = 3$.

### 3. Select the repeating quantities
The number of repeating quantities must equal the number of units (three here). These quantities should be independent, and they should collectively contain all the units present. The quantities $g$, $D$, and $\mu_a$ satisfy both requirements and therefore are selected as the repeating quantities.

### 4. Select the dependent variable V as the first nonrepeating quantity
Then write $\pi_1 = g^x D^y \mu_a^z V$, Eq. a, where $\pi_1$ is a dimensionless parameter and $x$, $y$, and $z$ are unknown exponents that may be evaluated by experiment.

### 5. Transform Eq. a to a dimensional equation
Do this by replacing each quantity with the units in which it is expressed. Then perform the necessary expansions and multiplications. Or, $F^0 L^0 T^0 = (LT^{-2})^x L^y \times (FL^{-2}T)^z LT^{-1}$, $F^0 L^0 T^0 = F^z L^{x+y-2z+1} T^{-2x+z-1}$, Eq. b.

Every equation must be dimensionally homogeneous; i.e., the units on one side of the equation must be consistent with those on the other side. Therefore, the exponent of a unit on one side of Eq. b must equal the exponent of that unit on the other side.

### 6. Evaluate the exponents x, y, and z
Do this by applying the principle of dimensional homogeneity to Eq. b. Thus, $0 = z$; $0 = x + y - 2z + 1$; $0 = -2x + z - 1$. Solving these simultaneous equations yields $x = -1/2$; $y = -1/2$; $z = 0$.

### 7. Substitute these values in Eq. a
Thus, $\pi_1 = g^{-1/2} D^{-1/2} V$, or $\pi_1 = V/(gD)^{1/2}$.

### 8. Follow the same procedure for the remaining nonrepeating quantities
Select $\rho_w$ and $\rho_a$ in turn as the nonrepeating quantities. Follow the same procedure as before to obtain the following dimensionless parameters: $\pi_2 = \rho_w(gD^3)^{1/2}/\mu_a$, and $\pi_3 = \rho_a(gD^3)^{1/2}/\mu_a = (gD^3)^{1/2}/v_a$, where $v_a$ = kinematic viscosity of air.

## HYDRAULIC SIMILARITY AND CONSTRUCTION OF MODELS

A dam discharges 36,000 ft³/s (1,019,236.7 L/s) of water, and a hydraulic pump occurs on the apron. The power loss resulting from this jump is to be determined by constructing a geometrically similar model having a scale of 1:12. (*a*) Determine the required discharge in the model. (*b*) Determine the power loss on the dam if the power loss on the model is found to be 0.18 hp (0.134 kW).

### Calculation Procedure:

### 1. Determine the value of $Q_m$

Two systems are termed similar if their corresponding variables have a constant ratio. A hydraulic model and its prototype must possess three forms of similarity: geometric, or similarity of shape; kinematic, or similarity of motion; and dynamic, or similarity of forces.

In the present instance, the ratio associated with the geometric similarity is given, i.e., the ratio of a linear dimension in the model to the corresponding linear dimension in the prototype. Let $r_g$ denote this ratio, and let subscripts $m$ and $p$ refer to the model and prototype, respectively.

Apply Eq. 17a to evaluate $Q_m$. Or $Q = C_1 b h^{1.5}$, where $C_1$ is a constant. Then $Q_m/Q_p = (b_m/h_p)(b_m/h_p)^{1.5}$. But $b_m/b_p = h_m/h_p = r_g$; therefore, $Q_m/Q_p = r_g^{2.5} = (1/12)^{2.5} = 1/499$; $Q_m = 36,000/499 = 72$ ft³/s (2038.5 L/s).

### 2. Evaluate the power loss on the dam

Apply Eq. 16 to evaluate the power loss on the dam. Thus, hp $= C_2 Q h$, where $C_2$ is a constant. Then $\text{hp}_p/\text{hp}_m = (Q_p/Q_m)(h_p/h_m)$. But $Q_p/Q_m = (1/r_g)^{2.5}$, and $h_p/h_m = 1/r_g$; therefore, $\text{hp}_p/\text{hp}_m = (1/r_g)^{3.5} = 12^{3.5} = 5990$. Hence, $\text{hp}_p = 5990(0.18) = 1078$ hp (803.86 kW).

---

## PART 2

# PUMP OPERATING MODES, AFFINITY LAWS, SPEED, AND HEAD

---

## SERIES PUMP INSTALLATION ANALYSIS

A new plant requires a system pumping capability of 45 gal/min (2.84 L/s) at a 26-ft (7.9-m) head. The pump characteristic curves for the tentatively selected floor-mounted units are shown in Fig. 15; one operating pump and one standby pump, each 0.75 hp (0.56 kW) are being considered. Can energy be conserved, and how much, with some other pumping arrangement?

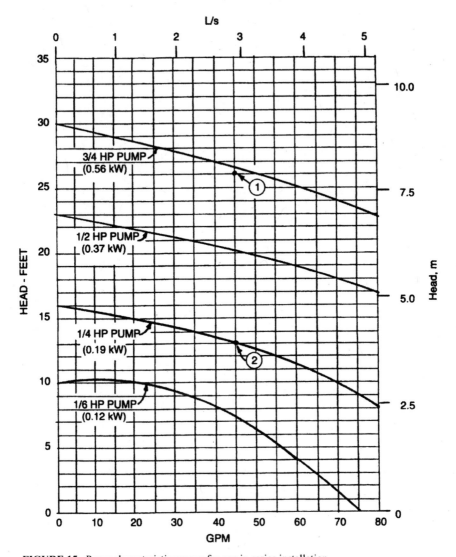

**FIGURE 15.** Pump characteristic curves for use in series installation.

## Calculation Procedure:

### 1. *Plot the characteristic curves for the pumps being considered*

Figure 15 shows the characteristic curves for the proposed pumps. Point 1 in Fig. 15 is the proposed operating head and flow rate. An alternative pump choice is shown at Point 2 in Fig. 15. If two of the smaller pumps requiring only 0.25 hp (0.19 kW) each are placed in series, they can generate the required 26-ft (7.9-m) head.

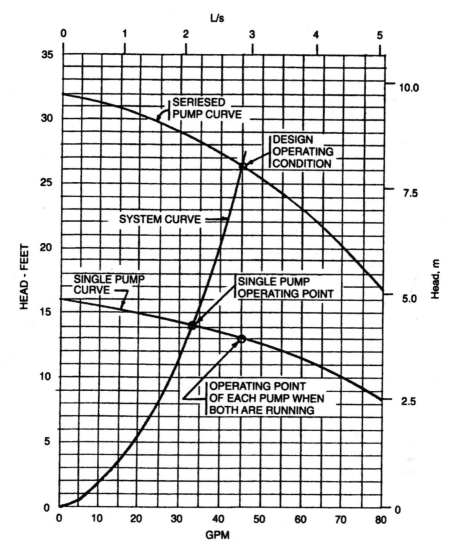

**FIGURE 16.** Seriesed-pump characteristic and system-head curves.

### 2. Analyze the proposed pumps

To analyze properly the proposal, a new set of curves, Fig. 16, is required. For the proposed series pumping application, it is necessary to establish a *seriesed pump curve*. This is a plot of the head and flow rate (capacity) which exists when both pumps are running in series. To construct this curve, double the single-pump head values at any given flow rate.

Next, to determine accurately the flow a single pump can deliver, plot the system-head curve using the same method fully described in the next calculation procedure. This curve is also plotted on Fig. 16.

Plot the point of operation for each pump on the seriesed curve, Fig. 16. The point of operation of each pump is on the single-pump curve when both pumps are operating. Each pump supplies half the total required head.

When a single pump is running, the point of operation will be at the intersection of the system-head curve and the single-pump characteristic curve, Fig. 16. At this point both the flow and the hp (kW) input of the single pump decrease. Series pumping, Fig. 16, requires the input motor hp (kW) for both pumps; this is the point of maximum power input.

### 3. Compute the possible savings

If the system requires a constant flow of 45 gal/min (2.84 L/s) at 26-ft (7.9-m) head the two-pump series installation saves (0.75 hp − 2 × 0.25 hp) = 0.25 hp (0.19 kW) for every hour the pumps run. For every 1000 hours of operation, the system saves 190 kWh. Since 2000 hours are generally equal to one shift of operation per year, the saving is 380 kWh per shift per year.

If the load is frequently less than peak, one-pump operation delivers 32.5 gal/min (2.1 L/s). This value, which is some 72 percent of full load, corresponds to doubling the saving.

**Related Calculations.** Series operation of pumps can be used in a variety of designs for industrial, commercial, residential, chemical, power, marine, and similar plants. A series connection of pumps is especially suitable when full-load demand is small; i.e., just a few hours a week, month, or year. With such a demand, one pump can serve the plant's needs most of the time, thereby reducing the power bill. When full-load operation is required, the second pump is started. If there is a need for maintenance of the first pump, the second unit is available for service.

This procedure is the work of Jerome F. Mueller, P.E., of Mueller Engineering Corp.


## PARALLEL PUMPING ECONOMICS

A system requires a flow of 80 gal/min (7.4 L/s) of 200°F (92.5°C) water at a 20°F (36°C) temperature drop and a 13-ft (3.96-m) system head. The required system flow can be handled by two pumps, one an operating unit and one a spare unit. Each pump will have an 0.5-hp (0.37-kW) drive motor. Could there be any appreciable energy saving using some other arrangement? The system requires 50 hours of constant pump operation and 40 hours of partial pump operation per week.


### Calculation Procedure:

### 1. Plot characteristic curves for the proposed system

Figure 17 shows the proposed pump selection. Looking at the values of the pump head and capacity in Fig. 17, it can be seen that if the peak load of 80 gal/min (7.4 L/s) were carried by two pumps, then each would have to pump only 40 gal/min (3.7 L/s) in a parallel arrangement.

### 2. Plot a characteristic curve for the pumps in parallel

Construct the paralleled-pump curve by doubling the flow of a single pump at any given head, using data from the pump manufacturer. At 13-ft head (3.96-m) one pump produces 40 gal/min (3.7 L/s); two pumps 80 gal/min (7.4 L/s). The resulting curve is shown in Fig. 18.

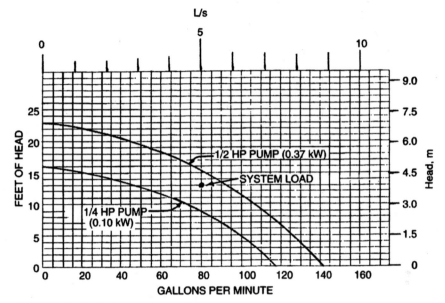

**FIGURE 17.** Typical pump characteristic curves.

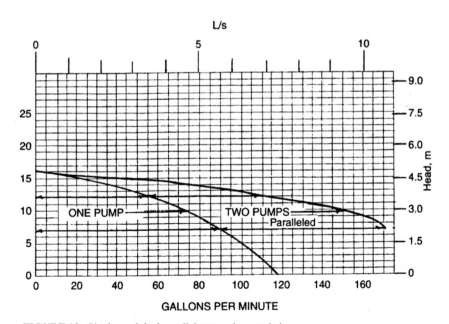

**FIGURE 18.** Single- and dual-parallel pump characteristic curves.

The load for this system could be divided among three, four, or more pumps, if desired. To achieve the best results, the number of pumps chosen should be based on achieving the proper head and capacity requirements in the system.

### 3. *Construct a system-head curve*

Based on the known flow rate, 80 gal/min (7.4 L/s) at 13-ft (3.96-m) head, a system-head curve can be constructed using the fact that pumping head varies as the square of the change in flow, or $Q_2/Q_1 = H_2/H_1$, where $Q_1$ = known design flow, gal/min (L/s); $Q_2$ = selected flow, gal/min (L/s); $H_1$ = known design head, ft (m); $H_2$ = resultant head related to selected flow rate, gal/min (L/s).

Figure 19 shows the plotted system-head curve. Once the system-head curve is plotted, draw the single-pump curve from Fig. 17 on Fig. 19, and the paralleled-pump curve from Fig. 18. Connect the different pertinent points of concern with dashed lines, Fig. 19.

The point of crossing of the two-pump curve and the system-head curve is at the required value of 80 gal/min (7.4 L/s) and 13-ft (3.96-m) head because it was so planned. But the point of crossing of the system-head curve and the single-pump curve is of particular interest.

The single pump, instead of delivering 40 gal/min (7.4 L/s) at 13-ft (3.96-m) head will deliver, as shown by the intersection of the curves in Fig. 19, 72 gal/min (6.67 L/s) at 10-ft (3.05-m) head. Thus, the single pump can effectively be a standby for 90 percent of the required capacity at a power input of 0.5 hp (0.37 kW). Much of the time in heating and air conditioning, and frequently in industrial processes, the system load is 90 percent, or less.

### 4. *Determine the single-pump horsepower input*

In the installation here, the pumps are the inline type with non-overload motors. For larger flow rates, the pumps chosen would be floor-mounted units providing a variety of

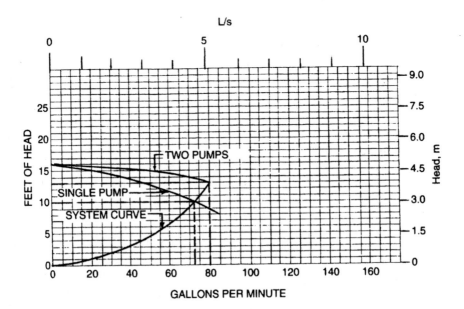

**FIGURE 19.** System-head curve for parallel pumping.

horsepower (kW) and flow curves. The horsepower (kW) for—say a 200-gal/min (18.6 L/s) flow rate would be about half of a 400-gal/min (37.2 L/s) flow rate.

If a pump were suddenly given a 300-gal/min (27.9 L/s) flow-rate demand at its crossing point on a larger system-head curve, the hp required might be excessive. Hence, the pump drive motor must be chosen carefully so that the power required does not exceed the motor's rating. The power input required by any pump can be obtained from the pump characteristic curve for the unit being considered. Such curves are available free of charge from the pump manufacturer.

The pump operating point is at the intersection of the pump characteristic curve and the system-head curve in conformance with the first law of thermodynamics, which states that the energy put into the system must exactly match the energy used by the system. The intersection of the pump characteristic curve and the system-head curve is the only point that fulfills this basic law.

There is no practical limit for pumps in parallel. Careful analysis of the system-head curve versus the pump characteristic curves provided by the pump manufacturer will frequently reveal cases where the system load point may be beyond the desired pump curve. The first cost of two or three smaller pumps is frequently no greater than for one large pump. Hence, smaller pumps in parallel may be more desirable than a single large pump, from both the economic and reliability standpoints.

One frequently overlooked design consideration in piping for pumps is shown in Fig. 20. This is the location of the check valve to prevent reverse-flow pumping. Figure 20 shows the proper location for this simple valve.

### 5. *Compute the energy saving possible*

Since one pump can carry the fluid flow load about 90 percent of the time, and this same percentage holds for the design conditions, the saving in energy is 0.9 × (0.5 kW − .25 kW) × 90 h per week = 20.25 kWh/week. (In this computation we used the assumption that 1 hp = 1 kW.) The annual savings would be 52 weeks × 20.25 kW/week = 1053 kWh/yr. If electricity costs 5 cents per kWh, the annual saving is $0.05 × 1053 = $52.65/yr.

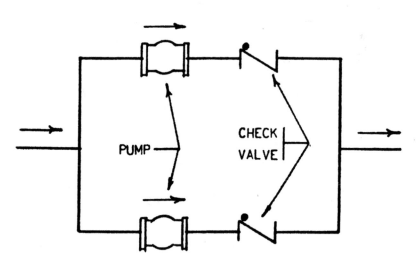

**FIGURE 20.** Check valve locations to prevent reverse flow.

While a saving of some \$52 per year may seem small, such a saving can become much more if: (1) larger pumps using higher horsepower (kW) motors are used; (2) several hundred pumps are used in the system; (3) the operating time is longer—168 hours per week in some systems. If any, or all, of these conditions prevail, the savings can be substantial.

**Related Calculations.** This procedure can be used for pumps in a variety of applications: industrial, commercial, residential, medical, recreational, and similar systems. When analyzing any system the designer should be careful to consider all the available options so the best one is found.

This procedure is the work of Jerome F. Mueller, P.E., of Mueller Engineering Corp.

## SIMILARITY OR AFFINITY LAWS FOR CENTRIFUGAL PUMPS

A centrifugal pump designed for an 1800-r/min operation and a head of 200 ft (60.9 m) has a capacity of 3000 gal/min (189.3 L/s) with a power input of 175 hp (130.6 kW). What effect will a speed reduction to 1200 r/min have on the head, capacity, and power input of the pump? What will be the change in these variables if the impeller diameter is reduced from 12 to 10 in. (304.8 to 254 mm) while the speed is held constant at 1800 r/min?

### Calculation Procedure:

### 1. Compute the effect of a change in pump speed

For any centrifugal pump in which the effects of fluid viscosity are negligible, or are neglected, the similarity or affinity laws can be used to determine the effect of a speed, power, or head change. For a *constant impeller diameter,* the laws are $Q_1/Q_2 = N_1/N_2$; $H_1/H_2 = (N_1/N_2)^2$; $P_1/P_2 = (N_1/N_2)^3$. For a *constant speed,* $Q_1/Q_2 = D_1/D_2$; $H_1/H_2 = (D_1/D_2)^2$; $P_1/P_2 = (D_1/D_2)^3$. In both sets of laws, $Q$ = capacity, gal/min; $N$ = impeller rpm; $D$ = impeller diameter, in.; $H$ = total head, ft of liquid; $P$ = bhp input. The subscripts 1 and 2 refer to the initial and changed conditions, respectively.

For this pump, with a constant impeller diameter, $Q_1/Q_2 = N_1/N_2$; $3000/Q_2 = 1800/1200$; $Q_2 = 2000$ gal/min (126.2 L/s). And, $H_1/H_2 = (N_1/N_2)^2 = 200/H_2 = (1800/1200)^2$; $H_2 = 88.9$ ft (27.1 m). Also, $P_1/P_2 = (N_1/N_2)^3 = 175/P_2 = (1800/1200)^3$; $P_2 = 51.8$ bhp (38.6 kW).

### 2. Compute the effect of a change in impeller diameter

With the speed constant, use the second set of laws. Or, for this pump, $Q_1/Q_2 = D_1/D_2$; $3000/Q_2 = {}^{12}/_{10}$; $Q_2 = 2500$ gal/min (157.7 L/s). And $H_1/H_2 = (D_1/D_2)^2$; $200/H_2 = ({}^{12}/_{10})^2$; $H_2 = 138.8$ ft (42.3 m). Also, $P_1/P_2 = (D_1/D_2)^3$; $175/P_2 = ({}^{12}/_{10})^3$; $P_2 = 101.2$ bhp (75.5 kW).

**Related Calculations.** Use the similarity laws to extend or change the data obtained from centrifugal pump characteristic curves. These laws are also useful in field calculations when the pump head, capacity, speed, or impeller diameter is changed.

The similarity laws are most accurate when the efficiency of the pump remains nearly constant. Results obtained when the laws are applied to a pump having a constant impeller diameter are somewhat more accurate than for a pump at constant speed with a changed impeller diameter. The latter laws are more accurate when applied to pumps having a low specific speed.

If the similarity laws are applied to a pump whose impeller diameter is increased, be certain to consider the effect of the higher velocity in the pump suction line. Use the similarity laws for any liquid whose viscosity remains constant during passage through the pump. However, the accuracy of the similarity laws decreases as the liquid viscosity increases.

## SIMILARITY OR AFFINITY LAWS IN CENTRIFUGAL PUMP SELECTION

A test-model pump delivers, at its best efficiency point, 500 gal/min (31.6 L/s) at a 350-ft (106.7-m) head with a required net positive suction head (NPSH) of 10 ft (3 m) and a power input of 55 hp (41 kW) at 3500 r/min, when a 10.5-in. (266.7-mm) diameter impeller is used. Determine the performance of the model at 1750 r/min. What is the performance of a full-scale prototype pump with a 20-in. (50.4-cm) impeller operating at 1170 r/min? What are the specific speeds and the suction specific speeds of the test-model and prototype pumps?

### Calculation Procedure:

### 1. Compute the pump performance at the new speed

The similarity or affinity laws can be stated in general terms, with subscripts $p$ and $m$ for prototype and model, respectively, as $Q_p = K_d^3 N_n Q_m$; $H_p = K_d^2 K_n^2 H_m$; $NPSH_p = K_d^2 K_n^2 NPSH_m$; $P_p = K_d^5 K_n^5 P_m$, where $K_d$ = size factor = prototype dimension/model dimension. The usual dimension used for the size factor is the impeller diameter. Both dimensions should be in the same units of measure. Also, $K_n$ = (prototype speed, r/min)/(model speed, r/min). Other symbols are the same as in the previous calculation procedure.

When the model speed is reduced from 3500 to 1750 r/min, the pump dimensions remain the same and $K_d = 1.0$; $K_n = 1750/3500 = 0.5$. Then $Q = (1.0)(0.5)(500) = 250$ r/min; $H = (1.0)^2(0.5)^2(350) = 87.5$ ft (26.7 m); NPSH = $(1.0)^2(0.5)^2(10) = 2.5$ ft (0.76 m); $P = (1.0)^5(0.5)^3(55) = 6.9$ hp (5.2 kW). In this computation, the subscripts were omitted from the equations because the same pump, the test model, was being considered.

### 2. Compute performance of the prototype pump

First, $K_d$ and $K_n$ must be found: $K_d = 20/10.5 = 1.905$; $K_n = 1170/3500 = 0.335$. Then $Q_p = (1.905)^3(0.335)(500) = 1158$ gal/min (73.1 L/s); $H_p = (1.905)^2(0.335)^2(350) = 142.5$ ft (43.4 m); $NPSH_p = (1.905)^2(0.335)^2(10) = 4.06$ ft (1.24 m); $P_p = (1.905)^5(0.335)^3(55) = 51.8$ hp (38.6 kW).

### 3. Compute the specific speed and suction specific speed

The specific speed or, as Horwitz[1] says, "more correctly, discharge specific speed," is $N_s = N(Q)^{0.5}/(H)^{0.75}$, while the suction specific speed $S = N(Q)^{0.5}/(NPSH)^{0.75}$, where all values are taken at the best efficiency point of the pump.

For the model, $N_s = 3500(500)^{0.5}/(350)^{0.75} = 965$; $S = 3500(500)^{0.5}/(10)^{0.75} = 13,900$. For the prototype, $N_s = 1170(1158)^{0.5}/(142.5)^{0.75} = 965$; $S = 1170(1156)^{0.5}/(4.06)^{0.75} = 13,900$. The specific speed and suction specific speed of the model and prototype are equal because these units are geometrically similar or homologous pumps and both speeds are mathematically derived from the similarity laws.

**Related Calculations.** Use the procedure given here for any type of centrifugal pump where the similarity laws apply. When the term *model* is used, it can apply to a production test pump or to a standard unit ready for installation. The procedure presented here is the work of R. P. Horwitz, as reported in *Power* magazine.[1]

---

[1]R. P. Horwitz, "Affinity Laws and Specific Speed Can Simplify Centrifugal Pump Selection," *Power*, November 1964.

## SPECIFIC SPEED CONSIDERATIONS
## IN CENTRIFUGAL PUMP SELECTION

What is the upper limit of specific speed and capacity of a 1750-r/min single-stage double-suction centrifugal pump having a shaft that passes through the impeller eye if it handles clear water at 85°F (29.4°C) at sea level at a total head of 280 ft (85.3 m) with a 10-ft (3-m) suction lift? What is the efficiency of the pump and its approximate impeller shape?

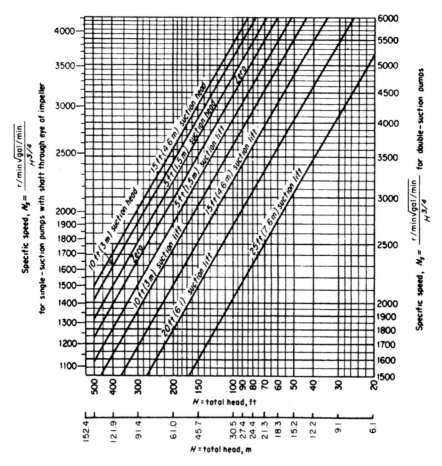

**FIGURE 21.** Upper limits of specific speeds of single-stage, single- and double-suction centrifugal pumps handling clear water at 85°F (29.4°C) at sea level. (*Hydraulic Institute.*)

### Calculation Procedure:

#### 1. *Determine the upper limit of specific speed*
Use the Hydraulic Institute upper specific-speed curve, Fig. 21, for centrifugal pumps or a similar curve, Fig. 22, for mixed- and axial-flow pumps. Enter Fig. 1 at the bottom at 280-ft (85.3-m) total head, and project vertically upward until the 10-ft (3-m) suction-lift curve is intersected. From here, project horizontally to the right to read the specific speed $N_s = 2000$. Figure 2 is used in a similar manner.

#### 2. *Compute the maximum pump capacity*
For any centrifugal, mixed- or axial-flow pump, $N_s = (gpm)^{0.5}(rpm)/H_t^{0.75}$, where $H_t =$ total head on the pump, ft of liquid. Solving for the maximum capacity, we get $gpm = (N_S H_t^{0.75}/rpm)^2 = (2000 \times 280^{0.75}/1750)^2 = 6040$ gal/min (381.1 L/s).

#### 3. *Determine the pump efficiency and impeller shape*
Figure 23 shows the general relation between impeller shape, specific speed, pump capacity, efficiency, and characteristic curves. At $N_S = 2000$, efficiency $= 87$ percent. The impeller, as shown in Fig. 23, is moderately short and has a relatively large discharge area. A cross section of the impeller appears directly under the $N_S = 2000$ ordinate.

**Related Calculations.** Use the method given here for any type of pump whose variables are included in the Hydraulic Institute curves, Figs. 21 and 22, and in similar curves available from the same source. *Operating specific speed,* computed as above, is sometimes plotted on the performance curve of a centrifugal pump so that the characteristics of the unit can be better understood. *Type specific speed* is the operating specific

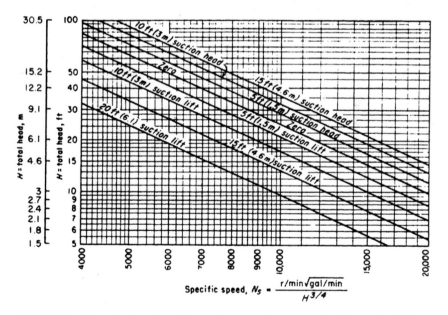

**FIGURE 22.** Upper limits of specific speeds of single-suction mixed-flow and axial-flow pumps. (*Hydraulic Institute.*)

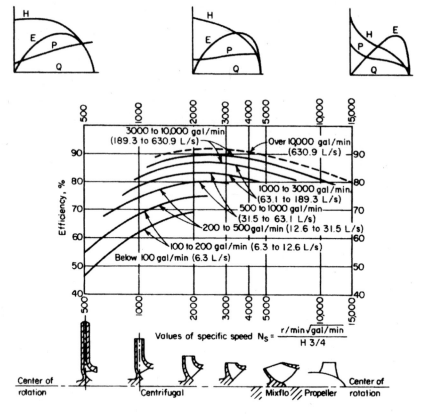

**FIGURE 23.** Approximate relative impeller shapes and efficiency variations for various specific speeds of centrifugal pumps. (*Worthington Corporation.*)

speed giving maximum efficiency for a given pump and is a number used to identify a pump. Specific speed is important in cavitation and suction-lift studies. The Hydraulic Institute curves, Figs. 21 and 22, give upper limits of speed, head, capacity and suction lift for cavitation-free operation. When making actual pump analyses, be certain to use the curves (Figs. 21 and 22) in the latest edition of the *Standards of the Hydraulic Institute.*

## SELECTING THE BEST OPERATING SPEED FOR A CENTRIFUGAL PUMP

A single-suction centrifugal pump is driven by a 60-Hz ac motor. The pump delivers 10,000 gal/min (630.9 L/s) of water at a 100-ft (30.5-m) head. The available net positive suction head = 32 ft (9.7 m) of water. What is the best operating speed for this pump if the pump operates at its best efficiency point?

**TABLE 1.** Pump Types Listed by Specific Speed*

| Specific speed range | Type of pump |
|---|---|
| Below 2,000 | Volute, diffuser |
| 2,000–5,000 | Turbine |
| 4,000–10,000 | Mixed-flow |
| 9,000–15,000 | Axial-flow |

*Peerless Pump Division, FMC Corporation.

## Calculation Procedure:

### 1. Determine the specific speed and suction specific speed

Ac motors can operate at a variety of speeds, depending on the number of poles. Assume that the motor driving this pump might operate at 870, 1160, 1750, or 3500 r/min. Compute the specific speed $N_S = N(Q)^{0.5}/(H)^{0.75} = N(10,000)^{0.5}/(100)^{0.75} = 3.14N$ and the suction specific speed $S = N(Q)^{0.5}/(NPSH)^{0.75} = N(10,000)^{0.5}/(32)^{0.75} = 7.43N$ for each of the assumed speeds. Tabulate the results as follows:

| Operating speed, r/min | Required specific speed | Required suction specific speed |
|---|---|---|
| 870 | 2,740 | 6,460 |
| 1,160 | 3,640 | 8,620 |
| 1,750 | 5,500 | 13,000 |
| 3,500 | 11,000 | 26,000 |

### 2. Choose the best speed for the pump

Analyze the specific speed and suction specific speed at each of the various operating speeds, using the data in Tables 1 and 2. These tables show that at 870 and 1160 r/min, the suction specific-speed rating is poor. At 1750 r/min, the suction specific-speed rating is excellent, and a turbine or mixed-flow type pump will be suitable. Operation at 3500 r/min is unfeasible because a suction specific speed of 26,000 is beyond the range of conventional pumps.

**Related Calculations.** Use this procedure for any type of centrifugal pump handling water for plant services, cooling, process, fire protection, and similar requirements.

**TABLE 2.** Suction Specific-Speed Ratings*

| Single-suction pump | Double-suction pump | Rating |
|---|---|---|
| Above 11,000 | Above 14,000 | Excellent |
| 9,000–11,000 | 11,000–14,000 | Good |
| 7,000–9,000 | 9,000–11,000 | Average |
| 5,000–7,000 | 7,000–9,000 | Poor |
| Below 5,000 | Below 7,000 | Very poor |

*Peerless Pump Division, FMC Corporation.

This procedure is the work of R. P. Horwitz, Hydrodynamics Division, Peerless Pump, FMC Corporation, as reported in *Power* magazine.

## TOTAL HEAD ON A PUMP HANDLING VAPOR-FREE LIQUID

Sketch three typical pump piping arrangements with static suction lift and submerged, free, and varying discharge head. Prepare similar sketches for the same pump with static suction head. Label the various heads. Compute the total head on each pump if the elevations are as shown in Fig. 24 and the pump discharges a maximum of 2000 gal/min (126.2 L/s) of water through 8-in. (203.2-mm) schedule 40 pipe. What hp is required to drive the

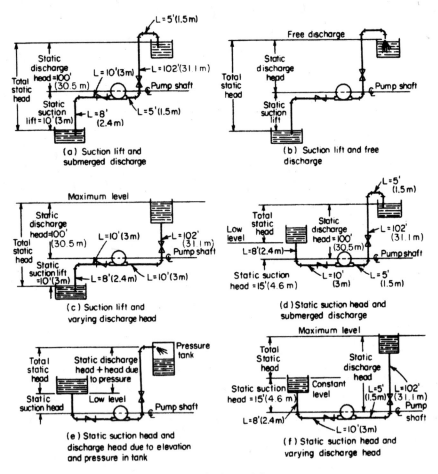

**FIGURE 24.** Typical pump suction and discharge piping arrangements.

pump? A swing check valve is used on the pump suction line and a gate valve on the discharge line.

### Calculation Procedure:

### 1. Sketch the possible piping arrangements
Figure 24 shows the six possible piping arrangements for the stated conditions of the installation. Label the total static head, i.e., the *vertical* distance from the surface of the source of the liquid supply to the free surface of the liquid in the discharge receiver, or to the point of free discharge from the discharge pipe. When both the suction and discharge surfaces are open to the atmosphere, the total static head equals the vertical difference in elevation. Use the free-surface elevations that cause the maximum suction lift and discharge head, i.e., the *lowest* possible level in the supply tank and the *highest* possible level in the discharge tank or pipe. When the supply source is *below* the pump centerline, the vertical distance is called the *static suction lift*; with the supply *above* the pump centerline, the vertical distance is called *static suction head*. With variable static suction head, use the lowest liquid level in the supply tank when computing total static head. Label the diagrams as shown in Fig. 24.

### 2. Compute the total static head on the pump
The total static head $H_{ts}$ ft = static suction lift, $h_{sl}$ ft + static discharge head $h_{sd}$ ft, where the pump has a suction lift, $s$ in Fig. 24$a$, $b$, and $c$. In these installations, $H_{ts} = 10 + 100 = 110$ ft (33.5 m). Note that the static discharge head is computed between the pump centerline and the water level with an underwater discharge, Fig. 24$a$; to the pipe outlet with a free discharge, Fig. 24$b$; and to the maximum water level in the discharge tank, Fig. 24$c$. When a pump is discharging into a closed compression tank, the total discharge head equals the static discharge head plus the head equivalent, ft of liquid, of the internal pressure in the tank, or $2.31 \times$ tank pressure, lb/sq.in.

Where the pump has a static suction head, as in Fig. 24$d$, $e$, and $f$, the total static head $H_{ts}$ ft $= h_{sd}$ − static suction head $h_{sh}$ ft. In these installations, $H_t = 100 - 15 = 85$ ft (25.9 m).

The total static head, as computed above, refers to the head on the pump without liquid flow. To determine the total head on the pump, the friction losses in the piping system during liquid flow must be also determined.

### 3. Compute the piping friction losses
Mark the length of each piece of straight pipe on the piping drawing. Thus, in Fig. 10$a$, the total length of straight pipe $L_t$ ft $= 8 + 10 + 5 + 102 + 5 = 130$ ft (39.6 m), if we start at the suction tank and add each length until the discharge tank is reached. To the total length of straight pipe must be added the *equivalent* length of the pipe fittings. In Fig. 10$a$ there are four long-radius elbows, one swing check valve, and one gate valve. In addition, there is a minor head loss at the pipe inlet and at the pipe outlet.

The equivalent length of one 8-in. (203.2-mm) long-radius elbow is 14 ft (4.3 m) of pipe, from Table 3. Since the pipe contains four elbows, the total equivalent length $= 4(14) = 56$ ft (17.1 m) of straight pipe. The open gate valve has an equivalent resistance of 4.5 ft (1.4 m); and the open swing check valve has an equivalent resistance of 53 ft (16.2 m).

The entrance loss $h_e$ ft, assuming a basket-type strainer is used at the suction-pipe inlet, is $h_e$ ft $= Kv^2/2g$, where $K =$ a constant from Fig. 5; $v =$ liquid velocity, ft/s; $g = 32.2$ ft/s$^2$ (980.67 cm/s$^2$). The exit loss occurs when the liquid passes through a sudden enlargement, as from a pipe to a tank. Where the area of the tank is large, causing a final velocity that is zero, $h_{ex} = v^2/2g$.

**TABLE 3.** Resistance of Fittings and Valves (length of straight pipe giving equivalent resistance)

| Pipe size | | Standard ell | | Medium-radius ell | | Long-radius ell | | 45° Ell | | Tee | | Gate valve, open | | Globe valve, open | | Swing check, open | |
|---|---|---|---|---|---|---|---|---|---|---|---|---|---|---|---|---|---|
| in. | mm | ft | m | ft | m | ft | m | ft | m | ft | m | ft | m | ft | m | ft | m |
| 6 | 152.4 | 16 | 4.9 | 14 | 4.3 | 11 | 3.4 | 7.7 | 2.3 | 33 | 10.1 | 3.5 | 1.1 | 160 | 48.8 | 40 | 12.2 |
| 8 | 203.2 | 21 | 6.4 | 18 | 5.5 | 14 | 4.3 | 10 | 3.0 | 43 | 13.1 | 4.5 | 1.4 | 220 | 67.0 | 53 | 16.2 |
| 10 | 254.0 | 26 | 7.9 | 22 | 6.7 | 17 | 5.2 | 13 | 3.9 | 56 | 17.1 | 5.7 | 1.7 | 290 | 88.4 | 67 | 20.4 |
| 12 | 304.8 | 32 | 9.8 | 26 | 7.9 | 20 | 6.1 | 15 | 4.6 | 66 | 20.1 | 6.7 | 2.0 | 340 | 103.6 | 80 | 24.4 |

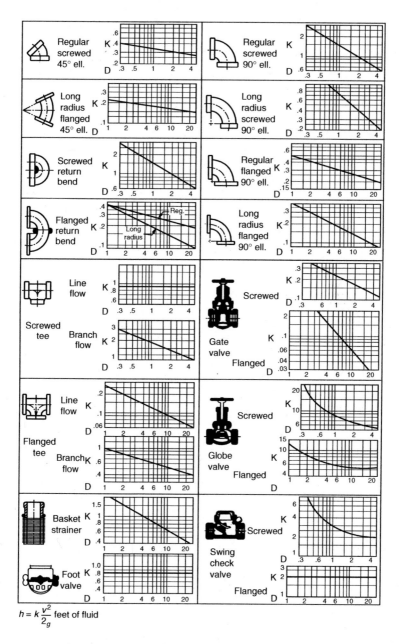

$$h = k \frac{v^2}{2_g} \text{ feet of fluid}$$

**FIGURE 25.** Resistance coefficients of pipe fittings. To convert to SI in the equation for $h$, $v^2$ would be measured in m/s and feet would be changed to meters. The following values would also be changed from inches to millimeters: 0.3 to 7.6, 0.5 to 12.7, 1 to 25.4, 2 to 50.8, 4 to 101.6, 6 to 152.4, 10 to 254, and 20 to 508. (*Hydraulic Institute.*)

The velocity $v$ ft/s in a pipe $= gpm/2.448d^2$. For this pipe, $v = 2000/[(2.448)(7.98)^2)] = 12.82$ ft/s (3.91 m/s). Then $h_e = 0.74(12.82)^2/[2(23.2)] = 1.89$ ft (0.58 m), and $h_{ex} = (12.82)^2/[(2)(32.2)] = 2.56$ ft (0.78 m). Hence, the total length of the piping system in Fig. 4$a$ is $130 + 56 + 4.5 + 53 + 1.89 + 2.56 = 247.95$ ft (75.6 m), say 248 ft (75.6 m).

Use a suitable head-loss equation, or Table 4, to compute the head loss for the pipe and fittings. Enter Table 4 at an 8-in. (203.2-mm) pipe size, and project horizontally across to 2000 gal/min (126.2 L/s) and read the head loss as 5.86 ft of water per 100 ft (1.8 m/30.5 m) of pipe.

The total length of pipe and fittings computed above is 248 ft (75.6 m). Then total friction-head loss with a 2000 gal/min (126.2-L/s) flow is $H_f$ ft $= (5.86)(248/100) = 14.53$ ft (4.5 m).

### 4. Compute the total head on the pump

The total head on the pump $H_t = H_{ts} + H_f$. For the pump in Fig. 24$a$, $H_t = 110 + 14.53 = 124.53$ ft (37.95 m), say 125 ft (38.1 m). The total head on the pump in Fig. 24$b$ and $c$ would be the same. Some engineers term the total head on a pump the *total dynamic head* to distinguish between static head (no-flow vertical head) and operating head (rated flow through the pump).

The total head on the pumps in Fig. 24$d$, $c$, and $f$ is computed in the same way as described above, except that the total static head is less because the pump has a static suction head. That is, the elevation of the liquid on the suction side reduces the total distance through which the pump must discharge liquid; thus the total static head is less. The static suction head is *subtracted* from the static discharge head to determine the total static head on the pump.

### 5. Compute the horsepower required to drive the pump

The brake hp input to a pump $bhp_i = (gpm)(H_t)(s)/3960e$, where $s =$ specific gravity of the liquid handled; $e =$ hydraulic efficiency of the pump, expressed as a decimal. The usual hydraulic efficiency of a centrifugal pump is 60 to 80 percent; reciprocating pumps, 55 to 90 percent; rotary pumps, 50 to 90 percent. For each class of pump, the hydraulic efficiency decreases as the liquid viscosity increases.

Assume that the hydraulic efficiency of the pump in this system is 70 percent and the specific gravity of the liquid handled is 1.0. Then $bhp_i = (2000)(127)(1.0)/(3960)(0.70) = 91.6$ hp (68.4 kW).

**TABLE 4.** Pipe Friction Loss for Water (wrought-iron or steel schedule 40 pipe in good condition)

| Diameter | | Flow | | Velocity | | Velocity head | | Friction loss per 100 ft (30.5 m) of pipe | |
|---|---|---|---|---|---|---|---|---|---|
| in. | mm | gal/min | L/s | ft/s | m/s | ft water | m water | ft water | m water |
| 6 | 152.4 | 1000 | 63.1 | 11.1 | 3.4 | 1.92 | 0.59 | 6.17 | 1.88 |
| 6 | 152.4 | 2000 | 126.2 | 22.2 | 6.8 | 7.67 | 2.3 | 23.8 | 7.25 |
| 6 | 152.4 | 4000 | 252.4 | 44.4 | 13.5 | 30.7 | 9.4 | 93.1 | 28.4 |
| 8 | 203.2 | 1000 | 63.1 | 6.41 | 1.9 | 0.639 | 0.195 | 1.56 | 0.475 |
| 8 | 203.2 | 2000 | 126.2 | 12.8 | 3.9 | 2.56 | 0.78 | 5.86 | 1.786 |
| 8 | 203.2 | 4000 | 252.4 | 25.7 | 7.8 | 10.2 | 3.1 | 22.6 | 6.888 |
| 10 | 254.0 | 1000 | 63.1 | 3.93 | 1.2 | 0.240 | 0.07 | 0.497 | 0.151 |
| 10 | 254.0 | 3000 | 189.3 | 11.8 | 3.6 | 2.16 | 0.658 | 4.00 | 1.219 |
| 10 | 254.0 | 5000 | 315.5 | 19.6 | 5.9 | 5.99 | 1.82 | 10.8 | 3.292 |

The theoretical or *hydraulic horsepower* $hp_h = (gpm)(H_t)(s)/3960$, or $hp_h = (2000) = (127)(1.0)/3900 = 64.1$ hp (47.8 kW).

**Related Calculations.** Use this procedure for any liquid—water, oil, chemical, sludge, etc.—whose specific gravity is known. When liquids other than water are being pumped, the specific gravity and viscosity of the liquid, as discussed in later calculation procedures, must be taken into consideration. The procedure given here can be used for any class of pump—centrifugal, rotary, or reciprocating.

Note that Fig. 25 can be used to determine the equivalent length of a variety of pipe fittings. To use Fig. 25, simply substitute the appropriate $K$ value in the relation $h = Kv^2/2g$, where $h$ = equivalent length of straight pipe; other symbols as before.

## PUMP SELECTION FOR ANY PUMPING SYSTEM

Give a step-by-step procedure for choosing the class, type, capacity, drive, and materials for a pump that will be used in an industrial pumping system.

### Calculation Procedure:

#### 1. Sketch the proposed piping layout

Use a single-line diagram, Fig. 26, of the piping system. Base the sketch on the actual job conditions. Show all the piping, fittings, valves, equipment, and other units in the system. Mark the *actual* and *equivalent* pipe length (see the previous calculation procedure) on the sketch. Be certain to include all vertical lifts, sharp bends, sudden enlargements, storage tanks, and similar equipment in the proposed system.

#### 2. Determine the required capacity of the pump

The required capacity is the flow rate that must be handled in gal/min, million gal/day, ft³/s, gal/h, bbl/day, lb/h, acre·ft/day, mil/h, or some similar measure. Obtain the required flow rate from the process conditions, for example, boiler feed rate, cooling-water flow rate, chemical feed rate, etc. The required flow rate for any process unit is usually given by the manufacturer or can be computed by using the calculation procedures given throughout this handbook.

Once the required flow rate is determined, apply a suitable factor of safety. The value of this factor of safety can vary from a low of 5 percent of the required flow to a high of 50 percent or more, depending on the application. Typical safety factors are in the 10 percent range. With flow rates up to 1000 gal/min (63.1 L/s), and in the selection of process pumps, it is common practice to round a computed required flow rate to the next highest round-number capacity. Thus, with a required flow rate of 450 gal/min (28.4 L/s) and a 10 percent safety factor, the flow of $450 + 0.10(450) = 495$ gal/min (31.2 L/s) would be rounded to 500 gal/min (31.6 L/s) *before* the pump was selected. A pump of 500-gal/min (31.6-L/s), or larger, capacity would be selected.

#### 3. Compute the total head on the pump

Use the steps given in the previous calculation procedure to compute the total head on the pump. Express the result in ft (m) of water—this is the most common way of expressing the head on a pump. Be certain to use the exact specific gravity of the liquid handled when expressing the head in ft (m) of water. A specific gravity less than 1.00 *reduces* the total head when expressed in ft (m) of water; whereas a specific gravity greater than 1.00

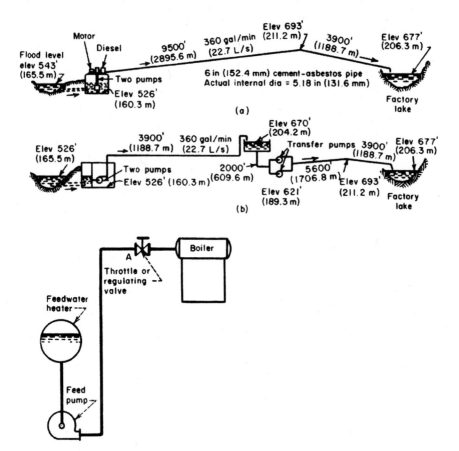

**FIGURE 26.** (*a*) Single-line diagrams for an industrial pipeline; (*b*) single-line diagram of a boiler-feed system. (*Worthington Corporation.*)

*increases* the total head when expressed in ft (m) of water. Note that variations in the suction and discharge conditions can affect the total head on the pump.

## 4. Analyze the liquid conditions

Obtain complete data on the liquid pumped. These data should include the name and chemical formula of the liquid, maximum and minimum pumping temperature, corresponding vapor pressure at these temperatures, specific gravity, viscosity at the pumping temperature, pH, flash point, ignition temperature, unusual characteristics (such as tendency to foam, curd, crystallize, become gelatinous or tacky), solids content, type of solids and their size, and variation in the chemical analysis of the liquid.

Enter the liquid conditions on a pump selection form like that in Fig. 27. Such forms are available from many pump manufacturers or can be prepared to meet special job conditions.

### Summary of Essential Data Required in Selection of Centrifugal Pumps

1. **Number of Units Required**

2. **Nature of the Liquid to Be Pumped**
   Is the liquid:
   *a.* Fresh or salt water, acid or alkali, oil, gasoline, slurry, or paper stock?
   *b.* Cold or hot and if hot, at what temperature? What is the vapor pressure of the liquid at the pumping temperature?
   *c.* What is its specific gravity?
   *d.* Is it viscous or nonviscous?
   *e.* Clear and free from suspended foreign matter or dirty and gritty? If the latter, what is the size and nature of the solids, and are they abrasive? If the liquid is of a pulpy nature, what is the consistency expressed either in percentage or in lb per cu ft of liquid? What is the suspended material?
   *f.* What is the chemical analysis, pH value, etc.? What are the expected variations of this analysis? If corrosive, what has been the past experience, both with successful materials and with unsatisfactory materials?

3. **Capacity**
   What is the required capacity as well as the minimum and maximum amount of liquid the pump will ever be called upon to deliver?

4. **Suction Conditions**
   Is there:
   *a.* A suction lift?
   *b.* Or a suction head?
   *c.* What are the length and diameter of the suction pipe?

5. **Discharge Conditions**
   *a.* What is the static head? Is it constant or variable?
   *b.* What is the friction head?
   *c.* What is the maximum discharge pressure against which the pump must deliver the liquid?

6. **Total Head**
   Variations in items 4 and 5 will cause variations in the total head.

7. Is the service continuous or intermittent?

8. Is the pump to be installed in a horizontal or vertical position? If the latter,
   *a.* In a wet pit?
   *b.* In a dry pit?

9. What type of power is available to drive the pump and what are the characteristics of this power?

10. What space, weight, or transportation limitations are involved?

11. **Location of installation**
    *a.* Geographical location
    *b.* Elevation above sea level
    *c.* Indoor or outdoor installation
    *d.* Range of ambient temperatures

12. Are there any special requirements or marked preferences with respect to the design, construction, or performance of the pump?

**FIGURE 27.** Typical selection chart for centrifugal pumps. (*Worthington Corporation.*)

## 5. *Select the class and type of pump*

Three *classes* of pumps are used today—centrifugal, rotary, and reciprocating, Fig. 28. Note that these terms apply only to the mechanics of moving the liquid—not to the service for which the pump was designed. Each class of pump is further subdivided into a number of *types*, Fig. 28.

Use Table 5 as a general guide to the class and type of pump to be used. For example, when a large capacity at moderate pressure is required, Table 5 shows that a centrifugal

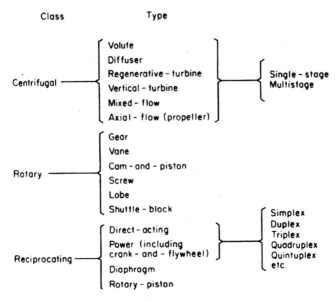

**FIGURE 28.** Modern pump classes and types.

pump would probably be best. Table 5 also shows the typical characteristics of various classes and types of pumps used in industrial process work.

Consider the liquid properties when choosing the class and type of pump, because exceptionally severe conditions may rule out one or another class of pump at the start. Thus, screw- and gear-type rotary pumps are suitable for handling viscous, nonabrasive liquid, Table 5. When an abrasive liquid must be handled, either another class of pump or another type of rotary pump must be used.

Also consider all the operating factors related to the particular pump. These factors include the type of service (continuous or intermittent), operating-speed preferences, future load expected and its effect on pump head and capacity, maintenance facilities available, possibility of parallel or series hookup, and other conditions peculiar to a given job.

Once the class and type of pump is selected, consult a rating table (Table 6) or rating chart, Fig. 29, to determine whether a suitable pump is available from the manufacturer whose unit will be used. When the hydraulic requirements fall between two standard pump models, it is usual practice to choose the next larger size of pump, unless there is some reason why an exact head and capacity are required for the unit. When one manufacturer does not have the desired unit, refer to the engineering data of other manufacturers. Also keep in mind that some pumps are custom-built for a given job when precise head and capacity requirements must be met.

Other pump data included in manufacturer's engineering information include characteristic curves for various diameter impellers in the same casing, Fig. 30, and variable-speed head-capacity curves for an impeller of given diameter, Fig. 31. Note that the required power input is given in Figs. 29 and 30 and may also be given in Fig. 31. Use of Table 6 is explained in the table.

Performance data for rotary pumps are given in several forms. Figure 32 shows a typical plot of the head and capacity ranges of different types of rotary pumps. Reciprocating-pump capacity data are often tabulated, as in Table 7.

**TABLE 5.** Characteristics of Modern Pumps

| | Centrifugal | | Rotary | Reciprocating | | |
|---|---|---|---|---|---|---|
| | Volute and diffuser | Axial flow | Screw and gear | Direct acting steam | Double acting power | Triplex |
| Discharge flow Usual maximum suction lift, ft (m) | Steady 15 (4.6) | Steady 15 (4.6) | Steady 22 (6.7) | Pulsating 22 (6.7) | Pulsating 22 (6.7) | Pulsating 22 (6.7) |
| Liquids handled | Clean, clear; dirty, abrasive; liquids with high solids content | | Viscous; non-abrasive | Clean and clear | | |
| Discharge pressure range | Low to high | | Medium | Low to highest produced | | |
| Usual capacity range | Small to largest available | | Small to medium | Relatively small | | |
| How increased head affects: Capacity Power input | Decrease Depends on specific speed | | None Increase | Decrease Increase | None Increase | None Increase |
| How decreased head affects: Capacity Power input | Increase Depends on specific speed | | None Decrease | Small increase Decrease | None Decrease | None Decrease |

**TABLE 6.** Typical Centrifugal-Pump Rating Table

| Size | | Total head | | | |
|---|---|---|---|---|---|
| gal/min | L/s | 20 ft, 4/min—hp | 6.1 m, r/min—kW | 25 ft, r/min—hp | 7.6 m, r/min—kW |
| 3 CL: | | | | | |
| 200 | 12.6 | 910—1.3 | 910—0.97 | 1010—1.6 | 1010—1.19 |
| 300 | 18.9 | 1000—1.9 | 1000—1.41 | 1100—2.4 | 1100—1.79 |
| 400 | 25.2 | 1200—3.1 | 1200—2.31 | 1230—3.7 | 1230—2.76 |
| 500 | 31.5 | — | — | — | — |
| 4 C: | | | | | |
| 400 | 25.2 | 940—2.4 | 940—1.79 | 1040—3 | 1040—2.24 |
| 600 | 37.9 | 1080—4 | 1080—2.98 | 1170—4.6 | 1170—3.43 |
| 800 | 50.5 | — | — | — | — |

*Example:* 1080—4 indicates pump speed is 1080 r/min; actual input required to operate the pump is 4 hp (2.98 kW).

*Source:* Condensed from data of Goulds Pumps, Inc.; SI values added by handbook editor.

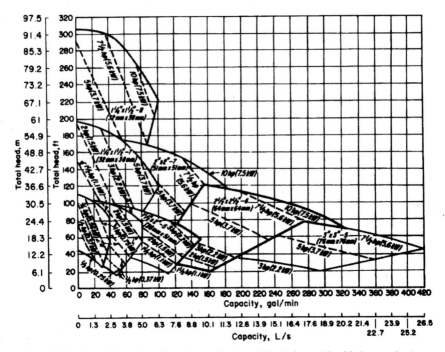

**FIGURE 29.** Composite rating chart for a typical centrifugal pump. (*Goulds Pumps, Inc.*)

### 6. Evaluate the pump chosen for the installation

Check the specific speed of a centrifugal pump, using the method given in an earlier calculation procedure. Once the specific speed is known, the impeller type and approximate operating efficiency can be found from Fig. 23.

Check the piping system, using the method of an earlier calculation procedure, to see whether the available net positive suction head equals, or is greater than, the required net positive suction head of the pump.

Determine whether a vertical or horizontal pump is more desirable. From the standpoint of floor space occupied, required NPSH, priming, and flexibility in changing the pump use, vertical pumps may be preferable to horizontal designs in some installations. But where headroom, corrosion, abrasion, and ease of maintenance are important factors, horizontal pumps may be preferable.

As a general guide, single-suction centrifugal pumps handle up to 50 gal/min (3.2 L/s) at total heads up to 50 ft (15.2 m); either single- or double-suction pumps are used for the flow rates to 1000 gal/min (63.1 L/s) and total heads to 300 ft (91.4 m); beyond these capacities and heads, double-suction or multistage pumps are generally used.

Mechanical seals are becoming more popular for all types of centrifugal pumps in a variety of services. Although they are more costly than packing, the mechanical seal reduces pump maintenance costs.

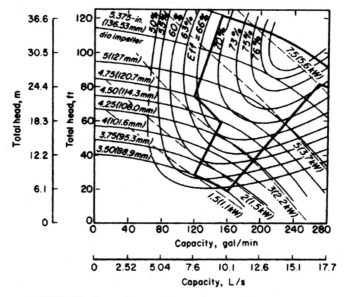

**FIGURE 30.** Pump characteristics when impeller diameter is varied within the same casing.

***Related Calculations.*** Use the procedure given here to select any class of pump—centrifugal, rotary, or reciprocating—for any type of service—power plant, atomic energy, petroleum processing, chemical manufacture, paper mills, textile mills, rubber factories, food processing, water supply, sewage and sump service, air conditioning and heating, irrigation and flood control, mining and construction, marine services, industrial hydraulics, iron and steel manufacture.

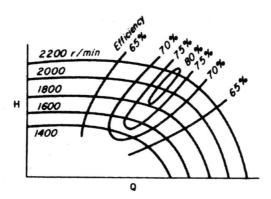

**FIGURE 31.** Variable-speed head-capacity curves for a centrifugal pump.

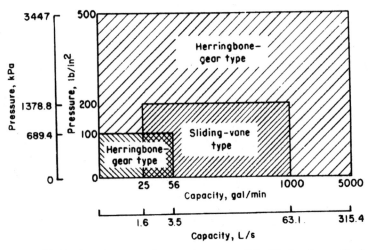

**FIGURE 32.** Capacity ranges of some rotary pumps. (*Worthington Corporation.*)

**TABLE 7.** Capacities of Typical Horizontal Duplex Plunger Pumps

| Size | | Cold-water pressure service | | | |
|---|---|---|---|---|---|
| | | | | Piston speed | |
| in. | cm | gal/min | L/s | ft/min | m/min |
| 6 × 3½ × 6 | 15.2 × 8.9 × 15.2 | 60 | 3.8 | 60 | 18.3 |
| 7½ × 4½ × 10 | 19.1 × 11.4 × 25.4 | 124 | 7.8 | 75 | 22.9 |
| 9 × 5 × 10 | 22.9 × 12.7 × 25.4 | 153 | 9.7 | 75 | 22.9 |
| 10 × 6 × 12 | 25.4 × 15.2 × 30.5 | 235 | 14.8 | 80 | 24.4 |
| 12 × 7 × 12 | 30.5 × 17.8 × 30.5 | 320 | 20.2 | 80 | 24.4 |

| Size | | Boiler-feed service | | | | | |
|---|---|---|---|---|---|---|---|
| | | | | Boiler | | Piston speed | |
| in. | cm | gal/min | L/s | hp | kW | ft/min | m/min |
| 6 × 3½ × 6 | 15.2 × 8.9 × 15.2 | 36 | 2.3 | 475 | 354.4 | 36 | 10.9 |
| 7½ × 4½ × 10 | 19.1 × 11.4 × 25.4 | 74 | 4.7 | 975 | 727.4 | 45 | 13.7 |
| 9 × 5 × 10 | 22.9 × 12.7 × 25.4 | 92 | 5.8 | 1210 | 902.7 | 45 | 13.7 |
| 10 × 6 × 12 | 25.4 × 15.2 × 30.5 | 141 | 8.9 | 1860 | 1387.6 | 48 | 14.6 |
| 12 × 7 × 12 | 30.5 × 17.8 × 30.5 | 192 | 12.1 | 2530 | 1887.4 | 48 | 14.6 |

*Source:* Courtesy of Worthington Corporation.

## ANALYSIS OF PUMP AND SYSTEM CHARACTERISTIC CURVES

Analyze a set of pump and system characteristic curves for the following conditions: friction losses without static head; friction losses with static head; pump without lift; system with little friction; much static head; system with gravity head; system with different pipe sizes; system with two discharge heads; system with diverted flow; and effect of pump wear on characteristic curve.

### Calculation Procedure:

#### 1. Plot the system-friction curve
Without static head, the system-friction curve passes through the origin (0,0), Fig. 33, because when no head is developed by the pump, flow through the piping is zero. For most piping systems, the friction-head loss varies as the square of the liquid flow rate in the system. Hence, a system-friction curve, also called a friction-head curve, is parabolic—the friction head increases as the flow rate or capacity of the system increases. Draw the curve as shown in Fig. 33.

#### 2. Plot the piping system and system-head curve
Figure 34$a$ shows a typical piping system with a pump operating against a static discharge head. Indicate the total static head, Fig. 34$b$, by a dashed line—in this installation $H_{ts}$ = 110 ft. Since static head is a physical dimension, it does not vary with flow rate and is a constant for all flow rates. Draw the dashed line parallel to the abscissa, Fig. 34$b$.

From the point of no flow—zero capacity—plot the friction-head loss at various flow rates—100, 200, 300 gal/min (6.3, 12.6, 18.9 L/s), etc. Determine the friction-head loss by computing it as shown in an earlier calculation procedure. Draw a curve through the points obtained. This is called the *system-head curve.*

Plot the pump head-capacity ($H$-$Q$) curve of the pump on Fig. 34$b$. The $H$-$Q$ curve can be obtained from the pump manufacturer or from a tabulation of $H$ and $Q$ values for the pump being considered. The point of intersection $A$ between the $H$-$Q$ and system-head curves is the operating point of the pump.

Changing the resistance of a given piping system by partially closing a valve or making some other change in the friction alters the position of the system-head curve and pump operating point. Compute the frictional resistance as before, and plot the artificial system-head curve as shown. Where this curve intersects the $H$-$Q$ curve is the new operating point of the pump. System-head curves are valuable for analyzing the suitability of a given pump for a particular application.

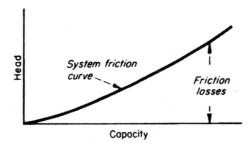

**FIGURE 33.** Typical system-friction curve.

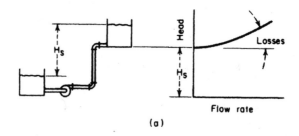

(a)

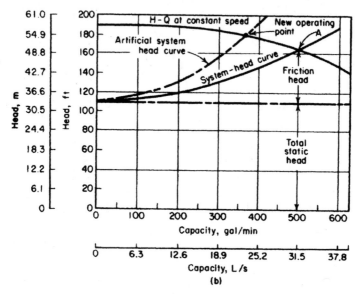

(b)

**FIGURE 34.** (a) Significant friction loss and lift; (b) system-head curve superimposed on pump head-capacity curve. (*Peerless Pumps.*)

### 3. Plot the no-lift system-head curve and compute the losses

With no static head or lift, the system-head curve passes through the origin (0,0), Fig. 35. For a flow of 900 gal/min (56.8 L/s) in this system, compute the friction loss as follows, using the Hydraulic Institute *Pipe Friction Manual* tables or the method of earlier calculation procedures:

|  | ft | m |
|---|---|---|
| Entrance loss from tank into 10-in. (254-mm) suction pipe, $0.5v^2/2g$ | 0.10 | 0.03 |
| Friction loss in 2 ft (0.61 m) of suction pipe | 0.02 | 0.01 |
| Loss in 10-in. (254-mm) 90° elbow at pump | 0.20 | 0.06 |
| Friction loss in 3000 ft (914.4 m) of 8-in. (203.2-mm) discharge pipe | 74.50 | 22.71 |
| Loss in fully open 8-in. (203.2-mm) gate valve | 0.12 | 0.04 |
| Exit loss from 8-in. (203.2-mm) pipe into tank, $v^2/2g$ | 0.52 | 0.16 |
| Total friction loss | 75.46 | 23.01 |

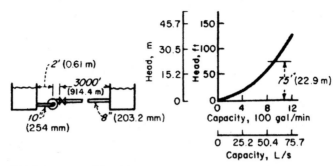

**FIGURE 35.** No lift; all friction head. (*Peerless Pumps.*)

Compute the friction loss at other flow rates in a similar manner, and plot the system-head curve, Fig. 35. Note that if all losses in this system except the friction in the discharge pipe were ignored, the total head would not change appreciably. However, for the purposes of accuracy, all losses should always be computed.

#### 4. Plot the low-friction, high-head system-head curve

The system-head curve for the vertical pump installation in Fig. 36 starts at the total static head, 15 ft (4.6 m), and zero flow. Compute the friction head for 15,000 gal/min as follows:

|  | ft | m |
|---|---|---|
| Friction in 20 ft (6.1 m) of 24-in. (609.6-mm) pipe | 0.40 | 0.12 |
| Exit loss from 24-in. (609.6-mm) pipe into tank, $v^2/2g$ | 1.60 | 0.49 |
| Total friction loss | 2.00 | 0.61 |

Hence, almost 90 percent of the total head of $15 + 2 = 17$ ft (5.2 m) at 15,000-gal/min (946.4-L/s) flow is static head. But neglect of the pipe friction and exit losses could cause appreciable error during selection of a pump for the job.

#### 5. Plot the gravity-head system-head curve

In a system with gravity head (also called negative lift), fluid flow will continue until the system friction loss equals the available gravity head. In Fig. 37 the available gravity head

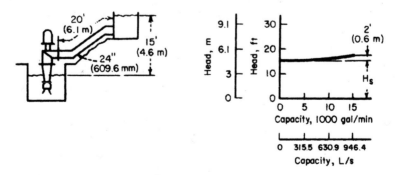

**FIGURE 36.** Mostly lift; little friction head. (*Peerless Pumps.*)

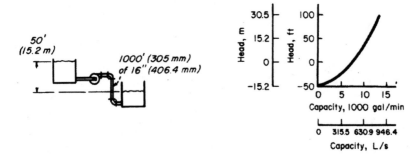

**FIGURE 37.** Negative lift (gravity head). (*Peerless Pumps.*)

is 50 ft (15.2 m). Flows up to 7200 gal/min (454.3 L/s) are obtained by gravity head alone. To obtain larger flow rates, a pump is needed to overcome the friction in the piping between the tanks. Compute the friction loss for several flow rates as follows:

|                                                                                           | ft  | m    |
| ----------------------------------------------------------------------------------------- | --- | ---- |
| At 5000 gal/min (315.5 L/s) friction loss in 1000 ft (305 m) of 16-in. (406.4-mm) pipe    | 25  | 7.6  |
| At 7200 gal/min (454.3 L/s), friction loss = available gravity head                       | 50  | 15.2 |
| At 13,000 gal/min (820.2 L/s), friction loss                                               | 150 | 45.7 |

Using these three flow rates, plot the system-head curve, Fig. 37.

### 6. Plot the system-head curves for different pipe sizes

When different diameter pipes are used, the friction loss vs. flow rate is plotted independently for the two pipe sizes. At a given flow rate, the total friction loss for the system is the sum of the loss for the two pipes. Thus, the combined system-head curve represents the sum of the static head and the friction losses for all portions of the pipe.

Figure 38 shows a system with two different pipe sizes. Compute the friction losses as follows:

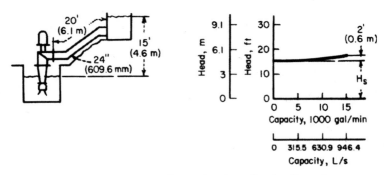

**FIGURE 38.** System with two different pipe sizes. (*Peerless Pumps.*)

|                                                                                          | ft  | m     |
|------------------------------------------------------------------------------------------|-----|-------|
| At 150 gal/min (9.5 L/s), friction loss in 200 ft (60.9 m) of 4-in. (102-mm) pipe        | 5   | 1.52  |
| At 150 gal/min (9.5 L/s), friction loss in 200 ft (60.9 m) of 3-in. (76.2-mm) pipe       | 19  | 5.79  |
| Total static head for 3- (76.2-) and 4-in. (102-mm) pipes                                | 10  | 3.05  |
| Total head at 150-gal/min (9.5-L/s) flow                                                 | 34  | 10.36 |

Compute the total head at other flow rates, and then plot the system-head curve as shown in Fig. 38.

### 7. Plot the system-head curve for two discharge heads

Figure 39 shows a typical pumping system having two different discharge heads. Plot separate system-head curves when the discharge heads are different. Add the flow rates for the two pipes at the same head to find points on the combined system-head curve, Fig. 39. Thus,

|                                                                              | ft  | m    |
|------------------------------------------------------------------------------|-----|------|
| At 550 gal/min (34.7 L/s), friction loss in 1000 ft (305 m) of 8-in. (203.2-mm) pipe | 10  | 3.05 |
| At 1150 gal/min (72.6 L/s) friction                                          | 38  | 11.6 |
| At 1150 gal/min (72.6 L/s), friction + lift in pipe 1                        | 88  | 26.8 |
| At 550 gal/min (34.7 L/s), friction + lift in pipe 2                         | 88  | 26.8 |

The flow rate for the combined system at a head of 88 ft (26.8 m) is 1150 + 550 = 1700 gal/min (107.3 L/s). To produce a flow of 1700 gal/min (107.3 L/s) through this system, a pump capable of developing an 88-ft (26.8-m) head is required.

### 8. Plot the system-head curve for diverted flow

To analyze a system with diverted flow, assume that a constant quantity of liquid is tapped off at the intermediate point. Plot the friction loss vs. flow rate in the normal manner for pipe 1, Fig. 40. Move the curve for pipe 3 to the right at zero head by an amount equal to $Q_2$, since this represents the quantity passing through pipes 1 and 2 but

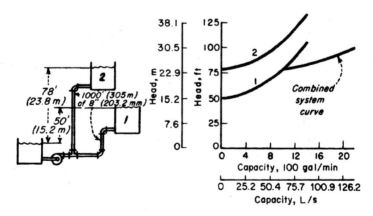

**FIGURE 39.** System with two different discharge heads. (*Peerless Pumps.*)

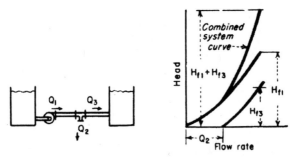

**FIGURE 40.** Part of the fluid flow is diverted from the main pipe. (*Peerless Pumps.*)

not through pipe 3. Plot the combined system-head curve by adding, at a given flow rate, the head losses for pipes 1 and 3. With $Q = 300$ gal/min (18.9 L/s), pipe 1 = 500 ft (152.4 m) of 10-in. (254-mm) pipe, and pipe 3 = 50 ft (15.2 m) of 6-in. (152.4-mm) pipe.

|  | ft | m |
|---|---|---|
| At 1500 gal/min (94.6 L/s) through pipe 1, friction loss | 11 | 3.35 |
| Friction loss for pipe 3 (1500 − 300 = 1200 gal/min) (75.7 L/s) | 8 | 2.44 |
| Total friction loss at 1500-gal/min (94.6-L/s) delivery | 19 | 5.79 |

## 9. Plot the effect of pump wear

When a pump wears, there is a loss in capacity and efficiency. The amount of loss depends, however, on the shape of the system-head curve. For a centrifugal pump, Fig. 41, the capacity loss is greater for a given amount of wear if the system-head curve is flat, as compared with a steep system-head curve.

Determine the capacity loss for a worn pump by plotting its $H$-$Q$ curve. Find this curve by testing the pump at different capacities and plotting the corresponding head. On the same chart, plot the $H$-$Q$ curve for a new pump of the same size, Fig. 41. Plot the system-head curve, and determine the capacity loss as shown in Fig. 41.

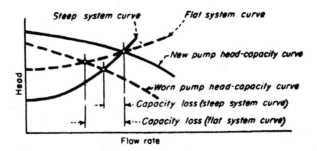

**FIGURE 41.** Effect of pump wear on pump capacity. (*Peerless Pumps.*)

**Related Calculations.**    Use the techniques given here for any type of pump—centrifugal, reciprocating, or rotary—handling any type of liquid—oil, water, chemicals, etc. The methods given here are the work of Melvin Mann, as reported in *Chemical Engineering*, and Peerless Pump Division of FMC Corp.

## NET POSITIVE SUCTION HEAD FOR HOT-LIQUID PUMPS

What is the maximum capacity of a double-suction pump operating at 1750 r/min if it handles 100°F (37.8°C) water from a hot well having an absolute pressure of 2.0 in. (50.8 mm) Hg if the pump centerline is 10 ft (30.5 m) below the hot-well liquid level and the friction-head loss in the suction piping and fitting is 5 ft (1.52 m) of water?

## Calculation Procedure:

### 1. Compute the net positive suction head on the pump

The net positive suction head $h_n$ on a pump when the liquid supply is *above* the pump inlet = pressure on liquid surface + static suction head − friction-head loss in suction piping and pump inlet − vapor pressure of the liquid, all expressed in ft absolute of liquid handled. When the liquid supply is *below* the pump centerline—i.e., there is a static suction lift—the vertical distance of the lift is *subtracted* from the pressure on the liquid surface instead of added as in the above relation.

The density of 100°F (37.8°C) water is 62.0 lb/ft³ (992.6 kg/m³), computed as shown in earlier calculation procedures in this handbook. The pressure on the liquid surface, in absolute ft of liquid = (2.0 in Hg)(1.133)(62.4/62.0) = 2.24 ft (0.68 m). In this calculation, 1.133 = ft of 39.2°F (4°C) water = 1 in Hg; 62.4 = lb/ft³ (999.0 kg/m³) of 39.2°F (4°C) water. The temperature of 39.2°F (4°C) is used because at this temperature water has its maximum density. Thus, to convert in Hg to ft absolute of water, find the product of (in Hg)(1.133)(water density at 39.2°F)/(water density at operating temperature). Express both density values in the same unit, usually lb/ft³.

The static suction head is a physical dimension that is measured in ft (m) of liquid at the operating temperature. In this installation, $h_{sh}$ = 10 ft (3 m) absolute.

The friction-head loss is 5 ft (1.52 m) of water. When it is computed by using the methods of earlier calculation procedures, this head loss is in ft (m) of water at maximum density. To convert to ft absolute, multiply by the ratio of water densities at 39.2°F (4°C) and the operating temperature, or (5)(62.4/62.0) = 5.03 ft (1.53 m).

The vapor pressure of water at 100°F (37.8°C) is 0.949 lb/sq.in. (abs) (6.5 kPa) from the steam tables. Convert any vapor pressure to ft absolute by finding the result of [vapor pressure, lb/sq.in. (abs)] (144 sq.in./sq.ft.)/liquid density at operating temperature, or (0.949)(144)/62.0 = 2.204 ft (0.67 m) absolute.

With all the heads known, the net positive suction head is $h_n$ = 2.24 + 10 − 5.03 − 2.204 = 5.01 ft (1.53 m) absolute.

### 2. Determine the capacity of the pump

Use the Hydraulic Institute curve, Fig. 42, to determine the maximum capacity of the pump. Enter at the left of Fig. 42 at a net positive suction head of 5.01 ft (1.53 m), and project horizontally to the right until the 3500-r/min curve is intersected. At the top, read the capacity as 278 gal/min (17.5 L/s).

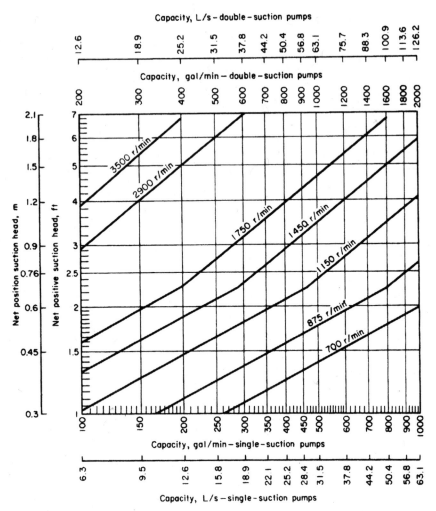

**FIGURE 42.** Capacity and speed limitations of pumps with the shaft through the impeller eye. (*Hydraulic Institute.*)

**_Related Calculations._** Use this procedure for any pump handling water at an elevated temperature. Consult the *Standards of the Hydraulic Institute* for capacity curves of pumps having different types of construction. In general, pump manufacturers who are members of the Hydraulic Institute rate their pumps in accordance with the *Standards*, and a pump chosen from a catalog capacity table or curve will deliver the stated capacity. A similar procedure is used for computing the capacity of pumps handling volatile petroleum liquids. When you use this procedure, be certain to refer to the latest edition of the *Standards*.

## PART 3

# CENTRIFUGAL PUMPS AND HYDRO POWER

## MINIMUM SAFE FLOW FOR A CENTRIFUGAL PUMP

A centrifugal pump handles 220°F (104.4°C) water and has a shutoff head (with closed discharge valve) of 3200 ft (975.4 m). At shutoff, the pump efficiency is 17 percent and the input brake horsepower is 210 (156.7 kW). What is the minimum safe flow through this pump to prevent overheating at shutoff? Determine the minimum safe flow if the NPSH is 18.8 ft (5.7 m) of water and the liquid specific gravity is 0.995. If the pump contains 500 lb (225 kg) of water, determine the rate of the temperature rise at shutoff.

### Calculation Procedure:

#### 1. *Compute the temperature rise in the pump*
With the discharge valve closed, the power input to the pump is converted to heat in the casing and causes the liquid temperature to rise. The temperature rise $t = (1 - e) \times H_s/778e$, where $t$ = temperature rise during shutoff, °F; $e$ = pump efficiency, expressed as a decimal; $H_s$ = shutoff head, ft. For this pump, $t = (1 - 0.17)(3200)/[7780(0.17)] = 20.4°F$ (36.7°C).

#### 2. *Compute the minimum safe liquid flow*
For general-service pumps, the minimum safe flow $M$ gal/min = 6.0(bhp input at shutoff)/$t$. Or, $M = 6.0(210)/20.4 = 62.7$ gal/min (3.96 L/s). This equation includes a 20 percent safety factor.

Centrifugal pumps usually have a maximum allowable temperature rise of 15°F (27°C). The minimum allowable flow through the pump to prevent the water temperature from rising more than 15°F (27°C) is 30 gal/min (1.89 L/s) for each 110-bhp (74.6-kW) input at shutoff.

#### 3. *Compute the temperature rise for the operating NPSH*
An NPSH of 18.8 ft (5.73 m) is equivalent to a pressure of 18.8(0.433)(0.995) = 7.78 lb/sq.in. (abs) (53.6 kPa) at 220°F (104.4°C), where the factor 0.433 converts ft of water to lb/sq.in. At 220°F (104.4°C), the vapor pressure of the water is 17.19 lb/sq.in. (abs) (118.5 kPa), from the steam tables. Thus, the total vapor pressure the water can develop before flashing occurs = NPSH pressure + vapor pressure at operating temperature = 7.78 + 17.19 = 24.97 lb/sq.in. (abs) (172.1 kPa). Enter the steam tables at this pressure, and read the corresponding temperature as 240°F (115.6°C). The allowable temperature rise of the water is then 240 − 220 = 20°F (36.0°C). Using the safe-flow relation of step 2, we find the minimum safe flow is 62.9 gal/min (3.97 L/s).

#### 4. *Compute the rate of temperature rise*
In any centrifugal pump, the rate of temperature rise $t_r$ °F/min = 42.4(bhp input at shutoff)/$wc$, where $w$ = weight of liquid in the pump, lb; $c$ = specific heat of the liquid in the pump, Btu/(lb·°F). For this pump containing 500 lb (225 kg) of water with a specific heat, $c = 1.0$, $t_r = 42.4(210)/[500(1.0)] = 17.8°F/min$ (32°C/min). This is a very rapid temperature rise and could lead to overheating in a few minutes.

***Related Calculations.*** Use this procedure for any centrifugal pump handling any liquid in any service—power, process, marine, industrial, or commercial. Pump manufacturers can supply a temperature-rise curve for a given model pump if it is requested. This curve is superimposed on the pump characteristic curve and shows the temperature rise accompanying a specific flow through the pump.

## SELECTING A CENTRIFUGAL PUMP TO HANDLE A VISCOUS LIQUID

Select a centrifugal pump to deliver 750 gal/min (47.3 L/s) of 1000-SSU oil at a total head of 100 ft (30.5 m). The oil has a specific gravity of 0.90 at the pumping temperature. Show how to plot the characteristic curves when the pump is handling the viscous liquid.

### Calculation Procedure:

#### 1. Determine the required correction factors

A centrifugal pump handling a viscous liquid usually must develop a greater capacity and head, and it requires a larger power input than the same pump handling water. With the water performance of the pump known—from either the pump characteristic curves or a tabulation of pump performance parameters—Fig. 43, prepared by the Hydraulic Institute, can be used to find suitable correction factors. Use this chart only within its scale limits; do not extrapolate. Do not use the chart for mixed-flow or axial-flow pumps or for pumps of special design. Use the chart only for pumps handling uniform liquids; slurries, gels, paper stock, etc., may cause incorrect results. In using the chart, the available net positive suction head is assumed adequate for the pump.

To use Fig. 43, enter at the bottom at the required capacity, 750 gal/min (47.3 L/s), and project vertically to intersect the 100-ft (30.5-m) head curve, the required head. From here project horizontally to the 1000-SSU viscosity curve, and then vertically upward to the correction-factor curves. Read $C_E = 0.635$; $C_Q = 0.95$; $C_H = 0.92$ for $1.0Q_{NW}$. The subscripts $E$, $Q$, and $H$ refer to correction factors for efficiency, capacity, and head, respectively; and $NW$ refers to the water capacity at a particular efficiency. At maximum efficiency, the water capacity is given as $1.0Q_{NW}$; other efficiencies, expressed by numbers equal to or less than unity, give different capacities.

#### 2. Compute the water characteristics required

The water capacity required for the pump $Q_w = Q_v/C_Q$ where $Q_v$ = viscous capacity, gal/min. For this pump, $Q_w = 750/0.95 = 790$ gal/min (49.8 L/s). Likewise, water head $H_w = H_v/C_H$, where $H_v$ = viscous head. Or, $H_w = 100/0.92 = 108.8$ (33.2 m), say 109 ft (33.2 m) of water.

Choose a pump to deliver 790 gal/min (49.8 L/s) of water at 109-ft (33.2-m) head of water, and the required viscous head and capacity will be obtained. Pick the pump so that it is operating at or near its maximum efficiency on water. If the water efficiency $E_w = 81$ percent at 790 gal/min (49.8 L/s) for this pump, the efficiency when handling the viscous liquid $E_v = E_w C_E$. Or, $E_v = 0.81(0.635) = 0.515$, or 51.5 percent.

The power input to the pump when handling viscous liquids is given by $P_v = Q_v H_v s/3960E_v$, where $s$ = specific gravity of the viscous liquid. For this pump, $P_v = (750) \times (100)(0.90)/[3960(0.515)] = 33.1$ hp (24.7 kW).

#### 3. Plot the characteristic curves for viscous-liquid pumping

Follow these eight steps to plot the complete characteristic curves of a centrifugal pump handling a viscous liquid when the water characteristics are known: (*a*) Secure a complete

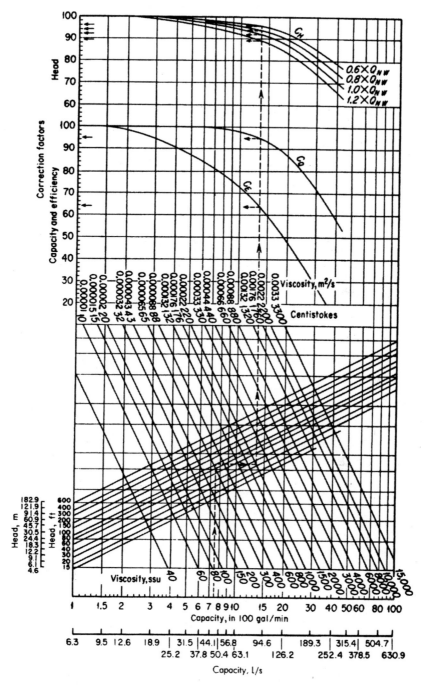

**FIGURE 43.** Correction factors for viscous liquids handled by centrifugal pumps. (*Hydraulic Institute.*)

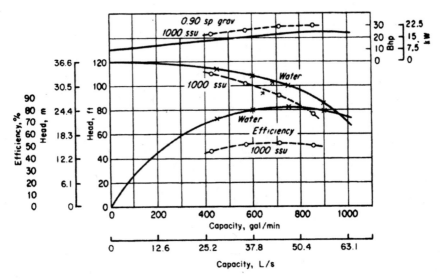

**FIGURE 44.** Characteristic curves for water (solid line) and oil (dashed line). (*Hydraulic Institute.*)

set of characteristic curves ($H$, $Q$, $P$, $E$) for the pump to be used. (*b*) Locate the point of maximum efficiency for the pump when handling water. (*c*) Read the pump capacity, $Q$ gal/min, at this point. (*d*) Compute the values of $0.6Q$, $0.8Q$, and $1.2Q$ at the maximum efficiency. (*e*) Using Fig. 43, determine the correction factors at the capacities in steps $c$ and $d$. Where a multistage pump is being considered, use the head per stage (= total pump head, ft/number of stages), when entering Fig. 43. (*f*). Correct the head, capacity, and efficiency for each of the flow rates in $c$ and $d$, using the correction factors from Fig. 43. (*g*) Plot the corrected head and efficiency against the corrected capacity, as in Fig. 43. (*h*) Compute the power input at each flow rate and plot. Draw smooth curves through the points obtained, Fig. 44.

   **Related Calculations.** Use the method given here for any uniform viscous liquid—oil, gasoline, kerosene, mercury, etc.—handled by a centrifugal pump. Be careful to use Fig. 1 only within its scale limits; *do not extrapolate*. The method presented here is that developed by the Hydraulic Institute. For new developments in the method, be certain to consult the latest edition of the Hydraulic Institute *Standards*.

## PUMP SHAFT DEFLECTION AND CRITICAL SPEED

What are the shaft deflection and approximate first critical speed of a centrifugal pump if the total combined weight of the pump impellers is 23 lb (10.4 kg) and the pump manufacturer supplies the engineering data in Fig. 45?

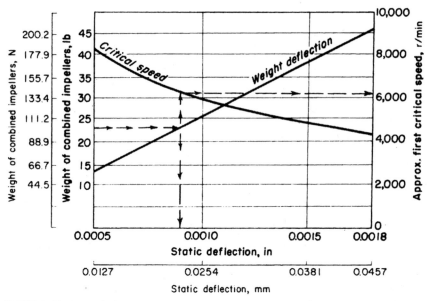

**FIGURE 45.** Pump shaft deflection and critical speed. (*Goulds Pumps, Inc.*)

## Calculation Procedure:

### 1. *Determine the deflection of the pump shaft*

Use Fig. 45 to determine the shaft deflection. Note that this chart is valid for only one pump or series of pumps and must be obtained from the pump builder. Such a chart is difficult to prepare from test data without extensive test facilities.

Enter Fig. 45 at the left at the total combined weight of the impellers, 23 lb (10.4 kg), and project horizontally to the right until the weight-deflection curve is intersected. From the intersection, project vertically downward to read the shaft deflection as 0.009 in. (0.23 mm) at full speed.

### 2. *Determine the critical speed of the pump*

From the intersection of the weight-deflection curve in Fig. 45 project vertically upward to the critical-speed curve. Project horizontally right from this intersection and read the first critical speed as 6200 r/min.

**Related Calculations.** Use this procedure for any class of pump—centrifugal, rotary, or reciprocating—for which the shaft-deflection and critical-speed curves are available. These pumps can be used for any purpose—process, power, marine, industrial, or commercial.

## *EFFECT OF LIQUID VISCOSITY ON REGENERATIVE-PUMP PERFORMANCE*

A regenerative (turbine) pump has the water head-capacity and power-input characteristics shown in Fig. 46. Determine the head-capacity and power-input characteristics for

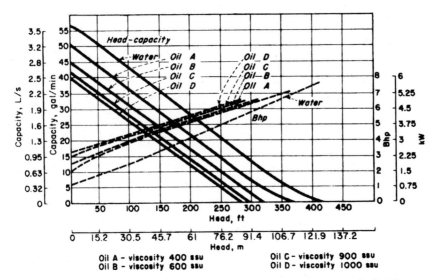

**FIGURE 46.** Regenerative pump performance when handling water and oil. (*Aurora Pump Division, The New York Air Brake Company.*)

four different viscosity oils to be handled by the pump—400, 600, 900, and 1000 SSU. What effect does increased viscosity have on the performance of the pump?

## Calculation Procedure:

### 1. Plot the water characteristics of the pump

Obtain a tabulation or plot of the water characteristics of the pump from the manufacturer or from their engineering data. With a tabulation of the characteristics, enter the various capacity and power points given, and draw a smooth curve through them, Fig. 46.

### 2. Plot the viscous-liquid characteristics of the pump

The viscous-liquid characteristics of regenerative-type pumps are obtained by test of the actual unit. Hence, the only source of this information is the pump manufacturer. Obtain these characteristics from the pump manufacturer or their test data, and plot them on Fig. 46, as shown, for each oil or other liquid handled.

### 3. Evaluate the effect of viscosity on pump performance

Study Fig. 46 to determine the effect of increased liquid viscosity on the performance of the pump. Thus at a given head, say 100 ft (30.5 m), the capacity of the pump decreases as the liquid viscosity increases. At 100-ft (30.5-m) head, this pump has a water capacity of 43.5 gal/min (2.74 L/s), Fig. 46. The pump capacity for the various oils at 100-ft (30.5-m) head is 36 gal/min (2.27 L/s) for 400 SSU; 32 gal/min (2.02 L/s) for 600 SSU; 28 gal/min (1.77 L/s) for 900 SSU; and 26 gal/min (1.64 L/s) for 1000 SSU, respectively. There is a similar reduction in capacity of the pump at the other heads plotted in Fig. 46. Thus, as a general rule, the capacity of a regenerative pump decreases with an increase in liquid viscosity at constant head. Or conversely, at constant capacity, the head developed decreases as the liquid viscosity increases.

Plots of the power input to this pump show that the input power increases as the liquid viscosity increases.

**Related Calculations.** Use this procedure for a regenerative-type pump handling any liquid—water, oil, kerosene, gasoline, etc. A decrease in the viscosity of a liquid, as compared with the viscosity of water, will produce the opposite effect from that of increased viscosity.

## EFFECT OF LIQUID VISCOSITY ON RECIPROCATING-PUMP PERFORMANCE

A direct-acting steam-driven reciprocating pump delivers 100 gal/min (6.31 L/s) of 70°F (21.1°C) water when operating at 50 strokes per minute. How much 2000-SSU crude oil will this pump deliver? How much 125°F (51.7°C) water will this pump deliver?

### Calculation Procedure:

#### 1. Determine the recommended change in pump performance

Reciprocating pumps of any type—direct-acting or power—having any number of liquid-handling cylinders—one to five or more—are usually rated for maximum delivery when handling 250-SSU liquids or 70°F (21.1°C) water. At higher liquid viscosities or water temperatures, the speed—strokes or rpm—is reduced. Table 1 shows typical recommended speed-correction factors for reciprocating pumps for various liquid viscosities and water temperatures. This table shows that with a liquid viscosity of 2000 SSU the pump speed should be reduced 20 percent. When 125°F (51.7°C) water is handled, the pump speed should be reduced 25 percent, as shown in Table 1.

#### 2. Compute the delivery of the pump

The delivery capacity of any reciprocating pump is directly proportional to the number of strokes per minute it makes or to its rpm.

When 2000-SSU oil is used, the pump strokes per minute must be reduced 20 percent, or (50)(0.20) = 10 strokes/min. Hence, the pump speed will be 50 − 10 = 40 strokes/min. Since the delivery is directly proportional to speed, the delivery of 2000-SSU oil = (40/50)(100) = 80 gal/min (5.1 L/s).

When handling 125°F (51.7°C) water, the pump strokes/min must be reduced 25 percent, or (50)(0.5) = 12.5 strokes/min. Hence, the pump speed will be 50.0 − 12.5 = 37.5

**TABLE 1.** Speed-Correction Factors

| Liquid viscosity, SSU | Speed reduction, % | Water temperature | | Speed reduction, % |
|---|---|---|---|---|
| | | °F | °C | |
| 250 | 0 | 70 | 21.1 | 0 |
| 500 | 4 | 80 | 26.7 | 9 |
| 1000 | 11 | 100 | 37.8 | 18 |
| 2000 | 20 | 125 | 51.7 | 25 |
| 3000 | 26 | 150 | 65.6 | 29 |
| 4000 | 30 | 200 | 93.3 | 34 |
| 5000 | 35 | 250 | 121.1 | 38 |

strokes/min. Since the delivery is directly proportional to speed, the delivery of 125°F (51.7°C) water = (37.5/50)(10) = 75 gal/min (4.7 L/s).

**Related Calculations.** Use this procedure for any type of reciprocating pump handling liquids falling within the range of Table 1. Such liquids include oil, kerosene, gasoline, brine, water, etc.

## EFFECT OF VISCOSITY AND DISSOLVED GAS ON ROTARY PUMPS

A rotary pump handles 8000-SSU liquid containing 5 percent entrained gas and 10 percent dissolved gas at a 20-in. (508-mm) Hg pump inlet vacuum. The pump is rated at 1000 gal/min (63.1 L/s) when handling gas-free liquids at viscosities less than 600 SSU. What is the output of this pump without slip? With 10 percent slip?

### Calculation Procedure:

### 1. Compute the required speed reduction of the pump
When the liquid viscosity exceeds 600 SSU, many pump manufacturers recommend that the speed of a rotary pump be reduced to permit operation without excessive noise or vibration. The speed reduction usually recommended is shown in Table 2.

With this pump handling 8000-SSU liquid, a speed reduction of 40 percent is necessary, as shown in Table 2. Since the capacity of a rotary pump varies directly with its speed, the output of this pump when handling 8000-SSU liquid = (1000 gal/min) × (1.0 − 0.40) = 600 gal/min (37.9 L/s).

### 2. Compute the effect of gas on the pump output
Entrained or dissolved gas reduces the output of a rotary pump, as shown in Table 3. The gas in the liquid expands when the inlet pressure of the pump is below atmospheric and the gas occupies part of the pump chamber, reducing the liquid capacity.

**TABLE 2.** Rotary Pump Speed Reduction for Various Liquid Viscosities

| Liquid viscosity, SSU | Speed reduction, percent of rated pump speed |
|---|---|
| 600 | 2 |
| 800 | 6 |
| 1,000 | 10 |
| 1,500 | 12 |
| 2,000 | 14 |
| 4,000 | 20 |
| 6,000 | 30 |
| 8,000 | 40 |
| 10,000 | 50 |
| 20,000 | 55 |
| 30,000 | 57 |
| 40,000 | 60 |

**TABLE 3.** Effect of Entrained or Dissolved Gas on the Liquid Displacement of Rotary Pumps (liquid displacement: percent of displacement)

| Vacuum at pump inlet, in Hg (mmHg) | Gas entrainment | | | | | Gas solubility | | | | | Gas entrainment and gas solubility combined | | | | |
|---|---|---|---|---|---|---|---|---|---|---|---|---|---|---|---|
| | 1% | 2% | 3% | 4% | 5% | 2% | 4% | 6% | 8% | 10% | 1% / 2% | 2% / 4% | 3% / 6% | 4% / 8% | 5% / 10% |
| 5 (127) | 99 | 97½ | 96½ | 95 | 93½ | 99½ | 99 | 98½ | 97 | 97½ | 98½ | 96½ | 96 | 92 | 91 |
| 10 (254) | 98½ | 97¼ | 95½ | 94 | 92 | 99 | 97½ | 97 | 95 | 95 | 97½ | 95 | 90 | 90 | 88¼ |
| 15 (381) | 98 | 96½ | 94½ | 92½ | 90½ | 97 | 96 | 94 | 92 | 90½ | 96 | 93 | 89½ | 86½ | 83¼ |
| 20 (508) | 97½ | 94½ | 92 | 89 | 86½ | 96 | 92 | 89 | 86 | 83 | 94 | 88 | 83 | 78 | 74 |
| 25 (635) | 94 | 89 | 84 | 79 | 75½ | 90 | 83 | 76½ | 71 | 66 | 85½ | 75½ | 68 | 61 | 55 |

For example, with 5 percent gas entrainment at 15 in Hg (381 mmHg) vacuum, the liquid displacement will be 90½ percent of the pump displacement, neglecting slip, or with 10 percent dissolved gas liquid displacement will be 90½ percent of the pump displacement; and with 5 percent entrained gas combined with 10 percent dissolved gas, the liquid displacement will be 83¼ percent of pump replacement.

*Source:* Courtesy of Kinney Mfg. Div., The New York Air Brake Co.

6.71

With a 20-in.(508-mm) Hg inlet vacuum, 5 percent entrained gas, and 10 percent dissolved gas, Table 3 shows that the liquid displacement is 74 percent of the rated displacement. Thus, the output of the pump when handling this viscous, gas-containing liquid will be (600 gal/min)(0.74) = 444 gal/min (28.0 L/s) without slip.

### 3. Compute the effect of slip on the pump output

Slip reduces rotary-pump output in direct proportion to the slip. Thus, with 10 percent slip, the output of this pump = (444 gal/min)(1.0 − 0.10) = 369.6 gal/min (23.3 L/s).

**Related Calculations.** Use this procedure for any type of rotary pump—gear, lobe, screw, swinging-vane, sliding-vane, or shuttle-block, handling any clear, viscous liquid. Where the liquid is gas-free, apply only the viscosity correction. Where the liquid viscosity is less than 600 SSU but the liquid contains gas or air, apply the entrained or dissolved gas correction, or both corrections.


## SELECTION OF MATERIALS
## FOR PUMP PARTS

Select suitable materials for the principal parts of a pump handling cold ethylene chloride. Use the Hydraulic Institute recommendation for materials of construction.


### Calculation Procedure:

### 1. Determine which materials are suitable for this pump

Refer to the data section of the Hydraulic Institute *Standards*. This section contains a tabulation of hundreds of liquids and the pump construction materials that have been successfully used to handle each liquid.

The table shows that for cold ethylene chloride having a specific gravity of 1.28, an all-bronze pump is satisfactory. In lieu of an all-bronze pump, the principal parts of the pump—casing, impeller, cylinder, and shaft—can be made of one of the following materials: austenitic steels (low-carbon 18-8; 18-8/Mo; highly alloyed stainless); nickel-base alloys containing chromium, molybdenum, and other elements, and usually less than 20 percent iron; or nickel-copper alloy (Monel metal). The order of listing in the *Standards* does not necessarily indicate relative superiority, since certain factors predominating in one instance may be sufficiently overshadowed in others to reverse the arrangement.

### 2. Choose the most economical pump

Use the methods of earlier calculation procedures to select the most economical pump for the installation. Where the corrosion resistance of two or more pumps is equal, the standard pump, in this instance an all-bronze unit, will be the most economical.

**Related Calculations.** Use this procedure to select the materials of construction for any class of pump—centrifugal, rotary, or reciprocating—in any type of service—power, process, marine, or commercial. Be certain to use the latest edition of the Hydraulic Institute *Standards*, because the recommended materials may change from one edition to the next.


## SIZING A HYDROPNEUMATIC
## STORAGE TANK

A 200-gal/min (12.6-L/s) water pump serves a pumping system. Determine the capacity required for a hydropneumatic tank to serve this system if the allowable high pressure in the tank and system is 60 lb/sq.in. (gage) (413.6 kPa) and the allowable low pressure is 30 lb/sq.in. (gage) (206.8 kPa). How many starts per hour will the pump make if the system draws 3000 gal/min (189.3 L/s) from the tank?

### Calculation Procedure:

#### 1. Compute the required tank capacity

In the usual hydropneumatic system, a storage-tank capacity in gal of 10 times the pump capacity in gal/min is used, if this capacity produces a moderate running time for the pump. Thus, this system would have a tank capacity of (10)(200) = 2000 gal (7570.8 L).

#### 2. Compute the quantity of liquid withdrawn per cycle

For any hydropneumatic tank the withdrawal, expressed as the number of gallons (liters) withdrawn per cycle, is given by $W = (v_L - v_H)/C$, where $v_L$ = air volume in tank at the lower pressure, ft$^3$ (m$^3$); $v_H$ = volume of air in tank at higher pressure, ft$^3$ (m$^3$); $C$ = conversion factor to convert ft$^3$ (m$^3$) to gallons (liters), as given below.

Compute $V_L$ and $V_H$ using the gas law for $v_H$ and either the gas law or the reserve percentage for $v_L$. Thus, for $v_H$, the gas law gives $v_H = p_L v_L / p_H$, where $p_L$ = lower air pressure in tank, lb/sq.in. (abs) (kPa); $p_H$ = higher air pressure in tank lb/sq.in. (abs) (kPa); other symbols as before.

In most hydropneumatic tanks a liquid reserve of 10 to 20 percent of the total tank volume is kept in the tank to prevent the tank from running dry and damaging the pump. Assuming a 10 percent reserve for this tank, $v_L = 0.1\ V$, where $V$ = tank volume in ft$^3$ (m$^3$). Since a 2000-gal (7570-L) tank is being used, the volume of the tank is 2000/7.481 ft$^3$/gal = 267.3 ft$^3$ (7.6 m$^3$). With the 10 percent reserve at the 44.7 lb/sq.in. (abs) (308.2-kPa) lower pressure, $v_L = 0.9\ (267.3) = 240.6$ ft$^3$ (6.3 m$^3$), where $0.9 = V - 0.1\ V$.

At the higher pressure in the tank, 74.7 lb/sq.in. (abs) (514.9 kPa), the volume of the air will be, from the gas law, $v_H = p_L v_L / p_H = 44.7\ (240.6)/74.7 = 143.9$ ft$^3$ (4.1 m$^3$). Hence, during withdrawal, the volume of liquid removed from the tank will be $W_g = (240.6 - 143.9)/0.1337 = 723.3$ gal (2738 L). In this relation the constant converts from cubic feet to gallons and is 0.1337. To convert from cubic meters to liters, use the constant 1000 in the denominator.

#### 3. Compute the pump running time

The pump has a capacity of 200 gal/min (12.6 L/s). Therefore, it will take 723/200 = 3.6 min to replace the withdrawn liquid. To supply 3000 gal/h (11,355 L/h) to the system, the pump must start 3000/723 = 4.1, or 5 times per hour. This is acceptable because a system in which the pump starts six or fewer times per hour is generally thought satisfactory.

Where the pump capacity is insufficient to supply the system demand for short periods, use a smaller reserve. Compute the running time using the equations in steps 2 and 3. Where a larger reserve is used—say 20 percent—use the value 0.8 in the equations in step 2. For a 30 percent reserve, the value would be 0.70, and so on.

**Related Calculations.** Use this procedure for any liquid system having a hydropneumatic tank—well drinking water, marine, industrial, or process.

## USING CENTRIFUGAL PUMPS AS HYDRAULIC TURBINES

Select a centrifugal pump to serve as a hydraulic turbine power source for a 1500-gal/min (5677.5-L/min) flow rate with 1290 ft (393.1 m) of head. The power application requires a 3600-r/min speed, the specific gravity of the liquid is 0.52, and the total available exhaust head is 20 ft (6.1 m). Analyze the cavitation potential and operating characteristics at an 80 percent flow rate.

## Calculation Procedure:

### 1. Choose the number of stages for the pump

Search of typical centrifugal-pump data shows that a head of 1290 ft (393.1 m) is too large for a single-stage pump of conventional design. Hence, a two-stage pump will be the preliminary choice for this application. The two-stage pump chosen will have a design head of 645 ft (196.6 m) per stage.

### 2. Compute the specific speed of the pump chosen

Use the relation $N_s = $ pump $rpm(Q)^{0.5}/H^{0.75}$, where $N_s = $ specific speed of the pump; $rpm$ = r/min of pump shaft; $Q = $ pump capacity or flow rate, gal/min; $H = $ pump head per stage, ft. Substituting, we get $N_s = 3600(1500)^{0.5}/(645)^{0.75} = 1090$. Note that the specific speed value is the same regardless of the system of units used—USCS or SI.

### 3. Convert turbine design conditions to pump design conditions

To convert from turbine design conditions to pump design conditions, use the pump manufacturer's conversion factors that relate turbine best efficiency point (bep) performance with pump bep performance. Typically, as specific speed $N_s$ varies from 500 to 2800, these bep factors generally vary as follows: the conversion factor for capacity (gal/min or L/min) $C_Q$, from 2.2 to 1.1; the conversion factor for head (ft or m) $C_H$, from 2.2 to 1.1; the conversion factor for efficiency $C_E$, from 0.92 to 0.99. Applying these conversion factors to the turbine design conditions yields the pump design conditions sought.

At the specific speed for this pump, the values of these conversion factors are determined from the manufacturer to be $C_Q = 1.24$; $C_H = 1.42$; $C_E = 0.967$.

Given these conversion factors, the turbine design conditions can be converted to the pump design conditions thus: $Q_p = Q_t/C_Q$, where $Q_p = $ pump capacity or flow rate, gal/min or L/min; $Q_t = $ turbine capacity or flow rate in the same units; other symbols are as given earlier. Substituting gives $Q_p = 1500/1.24 = 1210$ gal/min (4580 L/min).

Likewise, the pump discharge head, in feet of liquid handled, is $H_p = H_t/C_H$. So $H_p = 645/1.42 = 454$ ft (138.4 m).

### 4. Select a suitable pump for the operating conditions

Once the pump capacity, head, and rpm are known, a pump having its best bep at these conditions can be selected. Searching a set of pump characteristic curves and capacity tables shows that a two-stage 4-in. (10-cm) unit with an efficiency of 77 percent would be suitable.

### 5. Estimate the turbine horsepower developed

To predict the developed hp, convert the pump efficiency to turbine efficiency. Use the conversion factor developed above. Or, the turbine efficiency $E_t = E_p C_E = (0.77)(0.967) = 0.745$, or 74.5 percent.

With the turbine efficiency known, the output brake horsepower can be found from bhp $= Q_t H_t E_t s/3960$, where $s = $ fluid specific gravity; other symbols as before. Substituting, we get bhp $= 1500(1290)(0.745)(0.52)/3960 = 198$ hp (141 kW).

### 6. Determine the cavitation potential of this pump

Just as pumping requires a minimum net positive suction head, turbine duty requires a net positive exhaust head. The relation between the total required exhaust head (TREH) and turbine head per stage is the cavitation constant $\sigma_r = $ TREH/$H$. Figure 5 shows $\sigma_r$ vs. $N_s$

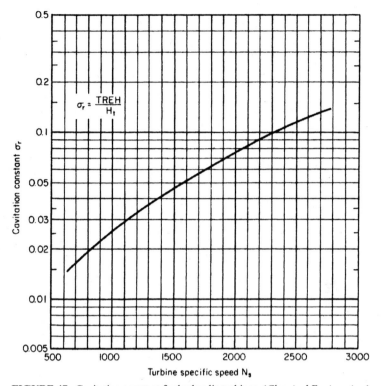

**FIGURE 47.** Cavitation constant for hydraulic turbines. (*Chemical Engineering.*)

for hydraulic turbines. Although a pump used as a turbine will not have exactly the same relationship, this curve provides a good estimate of $\sigma_r$ for turbine duty.

To prevent cavitation, the total available exhaust head (TAEH) must be greater than the TREH. In this installation, $N_s = 1090$ and TAEH $= 20$ ft (6.1 m). From Fig. 47, $\sigma_r = 0.028$ and TREH $= 0.028(645) = 18.1$ ft (5.5 m). Because TAEH $>$ TREH, there is enough exhaust head to prevent cavitation.

### 7. Determine the turbine performance at 80 percent flow rate

In many cases, pump manufacturers treat conversion factors as proprietary information. When this occurs, the performance of the turbine under different operating conditions can be predicted from the general curves in Figs. 48 and 49.

At the 80 percent flow rate for the turbine, or 1200 gal/min (4542 L/min), the operating point is 80 percent of bep capacity. For a specific speed of 1090, as before, the percentages of bep head and efficiency are shown in Figs. 48 and 49: 79.5 percent of bep head and percent of bep efficiency. To find the actual performance, multiply by the bep values, or, $H_t = 0.795(1290) = 1025$ ft (393.1 m); $E_t = 0.91(74.5) = 67.8$ percent.

The bhp at the new operating condition is then bhp $= 1200 (1025)(0.678)(0.52)/3960 = 110$ hp (82.1 kW).

In a similar way, the constant-head curves in Figs. 50 and 51 predict turbine performance at different speeds. For example, speed is 80 percent of bep speed at 2880 r/min. For a specific speed of 1090, the percentages of bep capacity, efficiency, and power are

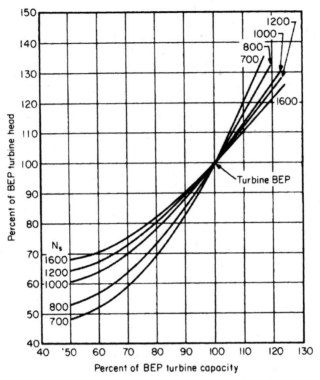

**FIGURE 48.** Constant-speed curves for turbine duty. (*Chemical Engineering.*)

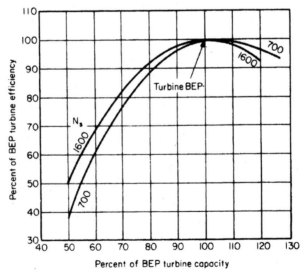

**FIGURE 49.** Constant-speed curves for turbine duty. (*Chemical Engineering.*)

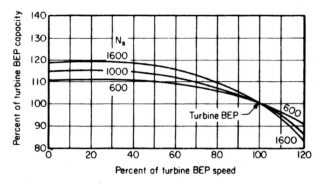

**FIGURE 50.** Constant-head curves for turbine duty. (*Chemical Engineering.*)

107 percent of the capacity, 94 percent of the efficiency, and 108 percent of the bhp. To get the actual performance, convert as before: $Q_t = 107(1500) = 1610$ gal/min (6094 L/min); $E_t = 0.94(74.5) = 70.0$ percent; bhp $= 1.08(189) = 206$ hp (153.7 kW).

Note that the bhp in this last instance is higher than the bhp at the best efficiency point. Thus more horsepower can be obtained from a given unit by reducing the speed and increasing the flow rate. When the speed is fixed, more bhp cannot be obtained from the unit, but it may be possible to select a smaller pump for the same application.

**Related Calculations.** Use this general procedure for choosing a centrifugal pump to drive—as a hydraulic turbine—another pump, a fan, a generator, or a compressor, where high-pressure liquid is available as a source of power. Because pumps are designed

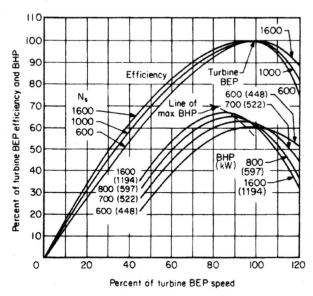

**FIGURE 51.** Constant-head curves for turbine duty. (*Chemical Engineering.*)

as fluid movers, they may be less efficient as hydraulic turbines than equipment designed for that purpose. Steam turbines and electric motors are more economical when steam or electricity is available.

But using a pump as a turbine can pay off in remote locations where steam or electric power would require additional wiring or piping, in hazardous locations that require non-sparking equipment, where energy may be recovered from a stream that otherwise would be throttled, and when a radial-flow centrifugal pump is immediately available but a hydraulic turbine is not.

In the most common situation, there is a liquid stream with fixed head and flow rate and an application requiring a fixed rpm; these are the turbine design conditions. The objective is to pick a pump with a turbine bep at these conditions. With performance curves such as Fig. 46, turbine design conditions can be converted to pump design conditions. Then you select from a manufacturer's catalog a model that has its pump bep at those values.

The most common error in pump selection is using the turbine design conditions in choosing a pump from a catalog. Because catalog performance curves describe pump duty, not turbine duty, the result is an oversized unit that fails to work properly.

This procedure is the work of Fred Buse, Chief Engineer, Standard Pump Aldrich Division of Ingersoll-Rand Co., as reported in *Chemical Engineering* magazine.

## SIZING CENTRIFUGAL-PUMP IMPELLERS FOR SAFETY SERVICE

Determine the impeller size of a centrifugal pump that will provide a safe continuous-recirculation flow to prevent the pump from overheating at shutoff. The pump delivers 320 gal/min (20.2 L/s) at an operating head of 450 ft (137.2 m). The inlet water temperature is 220°F (104.4°C), and the system has an NPSH of 5 ft (1.5 m). Pump performance curves and the system-head characteristic curve for the discharge flow (without recirculation) are shown in Fig. 53, and the piping layout is shown in Fig. 54. The brake horsepower (bhp) of an 11-in. (27.9-cm) and an 11.5-in. (29.2-cm) impeller at shutoff is 53 and 60, respectively. Determine the permissible water temperature rise for this pump.

### Calculation Procedure:

#### 1. Compute the actual temperature rise of the water in the pump

Use the relation $P_0 = P_v + P_{NPSH}$, where $P_0$ = pressure corresponding to the actual liquid temperature in the pump during operation, lb/sq.in. (abs) (kPa); $P_v$ = vapor pressure in the pump at the inlet water temperature, lb/sq.in. (abs) (kPa); $P_{NPSH}$ = pressure created by the net positive suction head on the pumps, lb/sq.in. (abs) (kPa). The head in feet (meters) must be converted to lb/sq.in. (abs) (kPa) by the relation lb/sq.in. (abs) = (NPSH, ft) (liquid density at the pumping temperature, lb/ft³)/(144 sq.in./sq.ft.). Substituting yields $P_0$ = 17.2 lb/sq.in. (abs) + 5(59.6)/144 = 19.3 lb/sq.in. (abs) (133.1 kPa).

Using the steam tables, find the saturation temperature $T_s$ corresponding to this absolute pressure as $T_s$ = 226.1°F (107.8°C). Then the permissible temperature rise is $T_p = T_s - T_{op}$, where $T_{op}$ = water temperature in the pump inlet. Or, $T_p$ = 226.1 − 220 = 6.1°F (3.4°C).

#### 2. Compute the recirculation flow rate at the shutoff head

From the pump characteristic curve with recirculation, Fig. 55, the continuous-recirculation flow $Q_B$ for an 11.5-in. (29.2-cm) impeller at an operating head of 450 ft (137.2 m) is

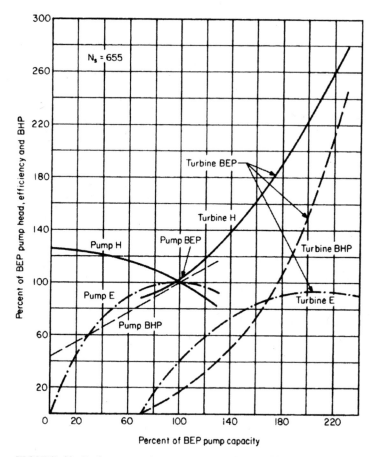

**FIGURE 52.** Performance of a pump at constant speed in pump duty and turbine duty. (*Chemical Engineering.*)

48.6 gal/min (177.1 L/min). Find the continuous-recirculation flow at shutoff head $H_s$ ft (m) of 540 ft (164.6 m) from $Q_s = Q_B(H_s/H_{op})^{0.5}$, where $H_{op}$ = operating head, ft (m). Or $Q_s = 48.6(540/450) = 53.2$ gal/min (201.4 L/min).

### 3. Find the minimum safe flow for this pump
The minimum safe flow, lb/h, is given by $w_{min} = 2545bhp/[C_pT_p + (1.285 \times 10^{-3})H_s]$, where $C_p$ = specific head of the water; other symbols as before. Substituting, we find $w_{min} = 2545(60)/[1.0(6.1) + (1.285 \times 10^{-3})(540)] = 22,476$ lb/h (2.83 kg/s). Converting to gal/min yields $Q_{min} = w_{min}/[(ft^3/h)(gal/min)(lb/ft^3)]$ for the water flowing through the pump. Or, $Q_{min} = 22,476/[(8.021)(59.6)] = 47.1$ gal/min (178.3 L/min).

### 4. Compare the shutoff recirculation flow with the safe recirculation flow
Since the shutoff recirculation flow $Q_s = 53.2$ gal/min (201.4 L/min) is greater than $Q_{min} = 47.1$ gal/min (178.3 L/min), the 11.5-in. (29.2-cm) impeller is adequate to provide safe continuous recirculation. An 11.25-in. (28.6-cm) impeller would not be adequate because $Q_{min} = 45$ gal/min (170.3 L/min) and $Q_s = 25.6$ gal/min (96.9 L/min).

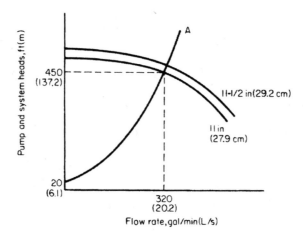

**FIGURE 53.** System-head curves without recirculation flow. (*Chemical Engineering.*)

**Related Calculations.**  Safety-service pumps are those used for standby service in a variety of industrial plants serving the chemical, petroleum, plastics, aircraft, auto, marine, manufacturing, and similar businesses. Such pumps may be used for water supply, fire protection, boiler feed, condenser cooling, and related tasks. In such systems the pump is usually oversized and has a recirculation loop piped in to prevent overheating by maintaining a minimum safe flow. Figure 54 shows a schematic of such a system. Recirculation is controlled by a properly sized orifice rather than by valves because an orifice is less expensive and highly reliable.

The general procedure for sizing centrifugal pumps for safety service, using the symbols given earlier, is this: (1) Select a pump that will deliver the desired flow $Q_A$, using

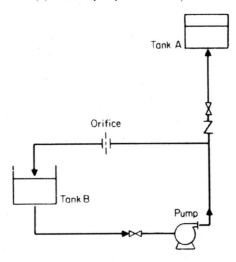

**FIGURE 54.** Pumping system with a continuous-recirculation line. (*Chemical Engineering.*)

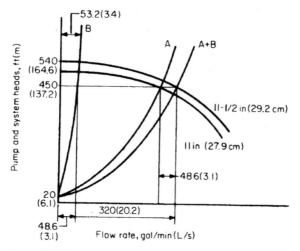

**FIGURE 55.** System-head curves with recirculation flow. (*Chemical Engineering.*)

the head-capacity characteristic curves of the pump and system. (2) Choose the next larger diameter pump impeller to maintain a discharge flow of $Q_A$ to tank $A$, Fig. 54, and a recirculation flow $Q_B$ to tank $B$, Fig. 54. (3) Compute the recirculation flow $Q_s$ at the pump shutoff point from $Q_s = Q_B(H_s/H_{op})^{0.5}$. (4) Calculate the minimum safe flow $Q_{min}$ for the pump with the larger impeller diameter. (5) Compare the recirculation flow $Q_s$ at the pump shutoff point with the minimum safe flow $Q_{min}$. If $Q_s \geq Q_{min}$, the selection process has been completed. If $Q_s < Q_{min}$, choose the next larger size impeller and repeat steps 3, 4, and 5 above until the impeller size that will provide the minimum safe recirculation flow is determined.

This procedure is the work of Mileta Mikasinovic and Patrick C. Tung, design engineers, Ontario Hydro, as reported in *Chemical Engineering* magazine.

## PUMP CHOICE TO REDUCE ENERGY CONSUMPTION AND LOSS

Choose an energy-efficient pump to handle 1000 gal/min (3800 L/min) of water at 60°F (15.6°C) at a total head of 150 ft (45.5 m). A readily commercially available pump is preferred for this application.

### Calculation Procedure:

#### 1. Compute the pump horsepower required

For any pump, $bhp_i = (gpm)(H_t)(s)/3960e$, where $bhp_i$ = input brake (motor) horsepower to the pump; $H_t$ = total head on the pump, ft; $s$ = specific gravity of the liquid handled; $e$ = hydraulic efficiency of the pump. For this application where $s = 1.0$ and a hydraulic efficiency of 70 percent can be safely assumed, $bhp_i = (1000)(150)(1)/(3960)(0.70) = 54.1$ bhp (40.3 kW).

## 2. Choose the most energy-efficient pump

Use Fig. 56, entering at the bottom at 1000 gal/min (3800 L/min) and projecting vertically upward to a total head of 150 ft (45.5 m). The resulting intersection is within area 1, showing from Table 4 that a single-stage 3500-r/min electric-motor-driven pump would be the most energy-efficient.

**Related Calculations.** The procedure given here can be used for pumps in a variety of applications—chemical, petroleum, commercial, industrial, marine, aeronautical, air-conditioning, cooling-water, etc., where the capacity varies from 10 to 1,000,000 gal/min (38 to 3,800,000 L/min) and the head varies from 10 to 10,000 ft (3 to 3300 m). Figure 14 is based primarily on the characteristic of pump specific speed $N_s = NQ^2/H^{3/4}$, where $N =$ pump rotating speed, r/min; $Q =$ capacity, gal/min (L/min); $H =$ total head, ft (m).

When $N_s$ is less than 1000, the operating efficiency of single-stage centrifugal pumps falls off dramatically; then either multistage or higher-speed pumps offer the best efficiency.

Area 1 of Fig. 56 is the densest, crowded both with pumps operating at 1750 and 3500 r/min, because years ago, 3500-r/min pumps were not thought to be as durable as 1750-r/min ones. Since the adoption of the AVS standard in 1960 (superseded by ANSI B73.1), pumps with stiffer shafts have been proved reliable.

Also responsible for many 1750-r/min pumps in area 1 has been the impression that the higher (3500-r/min) speed causes pumps to wear out faster. However, because impeller tip speed is the same at both 3500 and 1750 r/min [as, for example, a 6-in. (15-cm) impeller at 3500 r/min and a 12-in. (30-cm) one at 1740 r/min], so is the fluid velocity, and so should be the erosion of metal surface. Another reason for not limiting operating

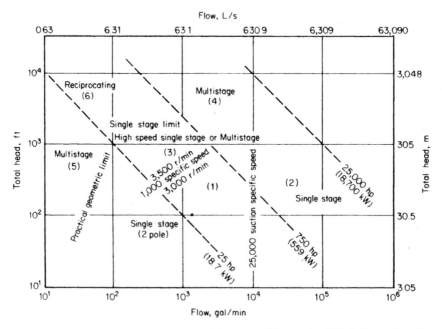

**FIGURE 56.** Selection guide is based mainly on specific speed, which indicates impeller geometry. (*Chemical Engineering.*)

**TABLE 4.** Type of Pump for Highest Energy Efficiency*

---

Area 1:  Single-stage, 3500 r/min
Area 2:  Single-stage, 1750 r/min or lower
Area 3:  Single-stage, above 3500 r/min, or multistage, 3500 r/min
Area 4:  Multistage
Area 5:  Multistage
Area 6:  Reciprocating

---

*Includes ANSI B73.1 standards, see area number in Fig. 56.

speed is that improved impeller inlet design allows operation at 3500 r/min to capacities of 5000 gal/min (19,000 L/min) and higher.

Choice of operating speed also may be indirectly limited by specifications pertaining to suction performance, such as that fixing the top suction specific speed $S$ directly or indirectly by choice of the sigma constant or by reliance on Hydraulic Institute charts.

Values of $S$ below 8000 to 10,000 have long been accepted for avoiding cavitation. However, since the development of the inducer, $S$ values in the range of 20,000 to 25,000 have become commonplace, and values as high as 50,000 have become practical.

The sigma constant, which relates NPSH to total head, is little used today, and Hydraulic Institute charts (which are being revised) are conservative.

In light of today's designs and materials, past restrictions resulting from suction performance limitations should be reevaluated or eliminated entirely.

Even if the most efficient pump has been selected, there are a number of circumstances in which it may not operate at peak efficiency. Today's cost of energy has made these considerations more important.

A centrifugal pump, being a hydrodynamic machine, is designed for a single peak operating-point capacity and total head. Operation at other than this best efficiency point (bep) reduces efficiency. Specifications now should account for such factors as these:

1. A need for a larger number of smaller pumps. When a process operates over a wide range of capacities, as many do, pumps will often work at less than full capacity, hence at lower efficiency. This can be avoided by installing two or three pumps in parallel, in place of a single large one, so that one of the smaller pumps can handle the flow when operations are at a low rate.

2. Allowance for present capacity. Pump systems are frequently designed for full flow at some time in the future. Before this time arrives, the pumps will operate far from their best efficiency points. Even if this interim period lasts only 2 or 3 years, it may be more economical to install a smaller pump initially and to replace it later with a full-capacity one.

3. Inefficient impeller size. Some specifications call for pump impeller diameter to be no larger than 90 or 95 percent of the size that a pump could take, so as to provide reserve head. If this reserve is used only 5 percent of the time, all such pumps will be operating at less than full efficiency most of the time.

4. Advantages of allowing operation to the right of the best efficiency point. Some specifications, the result of such thinking as that which provides reserve head, prohibit the selection of pumps that would operate to the right of the best efficiency point. This

eliminates half of the pumps that might be selected and results in oversized pumps operating at lower efficiency.

This procedure is the work of John H. Doolin, Director of Product Development, Worthington Pumps, Inc., as reported in *Chemical Engineering* magazine.

## SMALL HYDRO POWER CONSIDERATIONS AND ANALYSIS

A city is considering a small hydro power installation to save fossil fuel. To obtain the savings, the following steps will be taken: refurbish an existing dam, install new turbines, operate the generating plant. Outline the considerations a designer must weigh before undertaking the actual construction of such a plant.

### Calculation Procedure:

### 1. *Analyze the available head*
Most small hydro power sites today will have a head of less than 50 ft (15.2 m) between the high-water level and tail-water level, Fig. 57. The power-generating capacity will usually be 25 MW or less.

### 2. *Relate absolute head to water flow rate*
Because heads across the turbine in small hydro installations are often low in magnitude, the tail-water level is important in assessing the possibilities of a given site. At high-water flows, tail-water levels are often high enough to reduce turbine output, Fig. 58*a*. At some sites, the available head at high flow is extremely low, Fig. 58*b*.

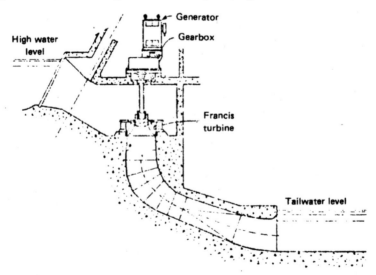

**FIGURE 57.** Vertical Francis turbine in open pit was adapted to 8-m head in an existing Norwegian dam. (*Power.*)

The actual power output from a hydro station is $P = HQwe/550$, where $P$ = horsepower output; $H$ = head across turbine, ft; $Q$ = water flow rate, ft$^3$/s; $w$ = weight of water, lb/ft$^3$; $e$ = turbine efficiency. Substituting in this equation for the plant shown in Fig. 58$b$, for flow rates of 500 and 1500 m$^3$/s, we see that a tripling of the water flow rate increases the power output by only 38.7 percent, while the absolute head drops 53.8 percent (from 3.9 to 1.8 m). This is why the tail-water level is so important in small hydro installations.

Figure 58$c$ shows how station costs can rise as head decreases. These costs were estimated by the Department of Energy (DOE) for a number of small hydro power installations. Figure 58 shows that station cost is more sensitive to head than to power capacity, according to DOE estimates. And the prohibitive costs for developing a completely new small hydro site mean that nearly all work will be at existing dams. Hence, any water exploitation for power must not encroach seriously on present customs, rights, and usages of the water. This holds for both upstream and downstream conditions.

### 3. Outline machinery choice considerations

Small-turbine manufacturers, heeding the new needs, are producing a good range of semi-standard designs that will match any site needs in regard to head, capacity, and excavation restrictions.

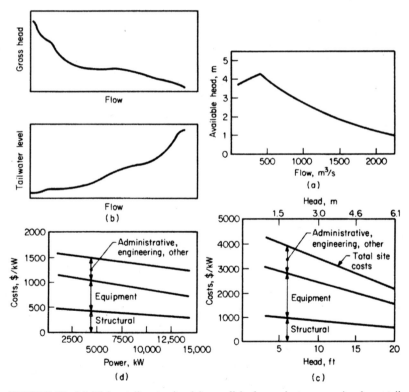

**FIGURE 58.** (*a*) Rising tail-water level in small hydro projects can seriously curtail potential. (*b*) Anderson-Cottonwood dam head dwindles after a peak at low flow. (*c*) Low heads drive DOE estimates up. (*d*) Linear regression curves represent DOE estimates of costs of small sites. (*Power.*)

The Francis turbine, Fig. 57, is a good example of such designs. A horizontal-shaft Francis turbine may be a better choice for some small projects because of lower civil-engineering costs and compatibility with standard generators.

Efficiency of small turbines is a big factor in station design. The problem of full-load versus part-load efficiency, Fig. 59, must be considered. If several turbines can fit the site needs, then good part-load efficiency is possible by load sharing.

Fitting new machinery to an existing site requires ingenuity. If enough of the old powerhouse is left, the same setup for number and type of turbines might be used. In other installations the powerhouse may be absent, badly deteriorated, or totally unsuitable. Then river-flow studies should be made to determine which of the new semistandard machines will best fit the conditions.

Personnel costs are extremely important in small hydro projects. Probably very few small hydro projects centered on redevelopment of old sites can carry the burden of workers in constant attendance. Hence, personnel costs should be given close attention.

Tube and bulb turbines, with horizontal or nearly horizontal shafts, are one way to solve the problem of fitting turbines into a site without heavy excavation or civil engineering works. Several standard and semistandard models are available.

In low head work, the turbine is usually low-speed, far below the speed of small generators. A speed-increasing gear box is therefore required. A simple helical-gear unit is satisfactory for vertical-shaft and horizontal-shaft turbines. Where a vertical turbine drives a horizontal generator, a right-angle box makes the turn in the power flow.

Governing and control equipment is not a serious problem for small hydro plants.

**Related Calculations.** Most small hydro projects are justified on the basis of continuing inflation, which will make the savings they produce more valuable as time passes. Although this practice is questioned by some people, the recent history of inflation seems to justify the approach.

As fossil-fuel prices increase, small hydro installations will become more feasible. However, the considerations mentioned in this procedure should be given full weight before proceeding with the final design of any plant. The data in this procedure were drawn from an ASME meeting on the subject with information from papers, panels, and discussion summarized by William O'Keefe, Senior Editor, *Power* magazine, in an article in that publication.

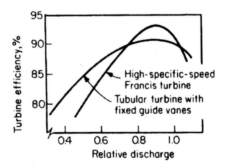

**FIGURE 59.** Steep Francis-turbine efficiency falloff frequently makes multiple units advisable.

## "CLEAN" ENERGY FROM SMALL-SCALE HYDRO SITES

A newly discovered hydro site provides a potential head of 65 ft (20 m). An output of 10,000 kW (10 MW) is required to justify use of the site. Select suitable equipment for this installation based on the available head and the required power output.

### Calculation Procedure:

#### 1. Determine the type of hydraulic turbine suitable for this site
Enter Fig. 60 on the left at the available head, 65 ft (20 m), and project to the right to intersect the vertical projection from the required turbine output of 10,000 kW (10 MW). These two lines intersect in the *standardized tubular unit* region. Hence, such a hydroturbine will be tentatively chosen for this site.

#### 2. Check the suitability of the chosen unit
Enter Table 5 at the top at the operating head range of 65 ft (20 m) and project across to the left to find that a tubular-type hydraulic turbine with fixed blades and adjustable gates will produce 0.25 to 15 MW of power at 55 to 150 percent of rated head. These ranges are within the requirements of this installation. Hence, the type of unit indicated by Fig. 60 is suitable for this hydro site.

   **Related Calculations.** Passage of legislation requiring utilities to buy electric power from qualified site developers is leading to strong growth of both site development and equipment suitable for small-scale hydro plants. Environmental concerns over fossil-fuel-fired and nuclear generating plants make hydro power more attractive. Hydro plants, in general, do not pollute the air, do not take part in the acid-rain cycle, are usually remote from populated areas, and run for up to 50 years with low maintenance and repair costs. Environmentalists rate hydro power as "clean" energy available with little, or no, pollution of the environment.

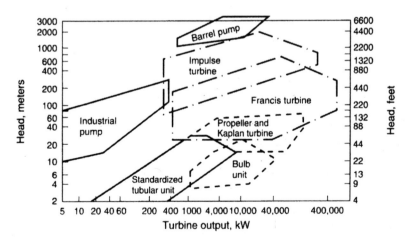

**FIGURE 60.** Traditional operating regimes of hydraulic turbines. New designs allow some turbines to cross traditional boundaries. (*Power.*)

**TABLE 5.** Performance Characteristics of Common Hydroturbines

| Type | Operating head range | | Capacity range | |
| --- | --- | --- | --- | --- |
| | Rated head, ft (m) | % of rated head | MW | % of design capacity |
| Vertical fixed-blade propeller | 7–120 (3–54) and over | 55–125 | 0.25–15 | 30–115 |
| Vertical Kaplan (adjustable blades and guide vanes) | 7–66 (3–30) and over | 45–150 | 1–15 | 10–115 |
| Vertical Francis | 25–300 (11–136) and over | 50–150 and over | 0.25–15 | 35–115 |
| Horizontal Francis | 25–500 (11–227) and over | 50–125 | 0.25–10 | 35–115 |
| Tubular (adjustable blades, fixed gates) | 7–59 (3–27) | 65–140 | 0.25–15 | 45–115 |
| Tubular (fixed blades, adjustable gates) | 7–120 (3–54) | 55–150 | 0.25–15 | 35–115 |
| Bulb | 7–66 (3–30) | 45–140 | 1–15 | 10–115 |
| Rim generator | 7–30 (3–14) | 45–140 | 1–8 | 10–115 |
| Right-angle-drive propeller | 7–59 (3–27) | 55–140 | 0.25–2 | 45–115 |
| Cross flow | 20–300 (9–136) and over | 80–120 | 0.25–2 | 10–115 |

*Source:* Power.

**6.88**

To reduce capital cost, most site developers choose standard-design hydroturbines. With essentially every high-head site developed, low-head sites become more attractive to developers. Table 5 shows the typical performance characteristics of hydroturbines being used today. Where there is a region of overlap in Table 5 or Fig. 60, site-specific parameters dictate choice and whether to install large units or a greater number of small units.

Delivery time and ease of maintenance are other factors important in unit choice. Further, the combination of power-generation and irrigation services in some installations make hydroturbines more attractive from an environmental view because two objectives are obtained: (1) "clean" power, and (2) crop watering.

Maintenance considerations are paramount with any selection; each day of downtime is lost revenue for the plant owner. For example, bulb-type units for heads between 10 and 60 ft (3 and 18 m) have performance characteristics similar to those of Francis and tubular units, and are often 1 to 2 percent more efficient. Also, their compact and, in some cases, standard design makes for smaller installations and reduced structural costs, but they suffer from poor accessibility. Sometimes the savings arising from the unit's compactness are offset by increased costs for the watertight requirements. Any leakage can cause severe damage to the machine.

To reduce the costs of hydroturbines, suppliers are using off-the-shelf equipment. One way this is done is to use centrifugal pumps operated in reverse and coupled to an induction motor. Although this is not a novel concept, pump manufacturers have documented the capability of many readily available commercial pumps to run as hydroturbines. The peak efficiency as a turbine is at least equivalent to the peak efficiency as a pump. These units can generate up to 1 MW of power. Pumps also benefit from a longer history of cost reductions in manufacturing, a wider range of commercial designs, faster delivery, and easier servicing—all of which add up to more rapid and inexpensive installations.

Though a reversed pump may begin generating power ahead of a turbine installation, it will not generate electricity more efficiently. Pumps operated in reverse are nominally 5 to 10 percent less efficient than a standard turbine for the same head and flow conditions. This is because pumps operate at fixed flow and head conditions; otherwise efficiency falls off rapidly. Thus, pumps do not follow the available water load as well unless multiple units are used.

With multiple units, the objective is to provide more than one operating point at sites with significant flow variations. Then the units can be sequenced to provide the maximum power output for any given flow rate. However, as the number of reverse pump units increases, equipment costs approach those for a standard turbine. Further, the complexity of the site increases with the number of reverse pump units, requiring more instrumentation and automation, especially if the site is isolated.

Energy-conversion-efficiency improvements are constantly being sought. In low-head applications, pumps may require specially designed draft tubes to minimize remaining energy after the water exits from the runner blades. Other improvements being sought for pumps are: (1) modifying the runner-blade profiles or using a turbine runner in a pump casing, (2) adding flow-control devices such as wicket gates to a standard pump design or stay vanes to adjust turbine output.

Many components of hydroturbines are being improved to reduce space requirements and civil costs, and to simplify design, operation, and maintenance. Cast parts used in older turbines have largely been replaced by fabricated components. Stainless steel is commonly recommended for guide vanes, runners, and draft-tube inlets because of better resistance to cavitation, erosion, and corrosion. In special cases, there are economic tradeoffs between using carbon steel with a suitable coating material and using stainless steel.

Some engineers are experimenting with plastics, but much more long-term experience is needed before most designers will feel comfortable with plastics. Further, stainless steel material costs are relatively low compared to labor costs. And stainless steel has proven most cost-effective for hydroturbine applications.

While hydro power does provide pollution-free energy, it can be subject to the vagaries of the weather and climatic conditions. Thus, at the time of this writing, some 30 hydroelectric stations in the northwestern part of the United States had to cut their electrical output because the combination of a severe drought and prolonged cold weather forced a reduction in water flow to the stations. Purchase of replacement power—usually from fossil-fuel-fired plants—may be necessary when such cutbacks occur. Thus, the choice of hydro power must be carefully considered before a final decision is made.

This procedure is based on the work of Jason Makansi, associate editor, *Power* magazine, and reported in that publication.

## USE OF SOLAR-POWERED PUMPS IN IRRIGATION AND OTHER SERVICES

Devise a solar-powered alternative energy source for driving pumps for use in irrigation to handle 10,000 gal/min (37.9 m³/min) at peak output with an input of 50 hp (37.3 kW). Show the elements of such a system and how they might be interconnected to provide useful output.

### Calculation Procedure:

#### 1. Develop a suitable cycle for this application
Figure 61 shows a typical design of a closed-cycle solar-energy powered system suitable for driving turbine-powered pumps. In this system a suitable refrigerant is chosen to provide the maximum heat absorption possible from the sun's rays. Water is pumped under pressure to the solar collector, where it is heated by the sun. The water then flows to a boiler where the heat in the water turns the liquid refrigerant into a gas. This gas is used to drive a Rankine-cycle turbine connected to an irrigation pump, Fig. 61.

The rate of gas release in such a closed system is a function of (a) the unit enthalpy of vaporization of the refrigerant chosen, (b) the temperature of the water leaving the solar collector, and (c) the efficiency of the boiler used to transfer heat from the water to the refrigerant. While there will be some heat loss in the piping and equipment in the system, this loss is generally considered negligible in a well-designed layout.

#### 2. Select, and size, the solar collector to use
The usual solar collector chosen for systems such as this is a parabolic tracking-type unit. The preliminary required area for the collector is found by using the rule of thumb which states: For parabolic tracking-type solar collectors the required sun-exposure area is 0.55 sq.ft. per gal/min pumped (0.093 m² per 0.00379 m³/min) at peak output of the pump and collector. Another way of stating this rule of thumb is: Required tracking parabolic solar collector area = 110 sq.ft. per hp delivered (13.7 m²/kW delivered).

Thus, for a solar collector designed to deliver 10,000 gal/min (37.9 m³/min) at peak output, the preliminary area chosen for this parabolic tracking solar collector will be, $A_p$ = (10,000 gal/min)(0.55 sq.ft./gal/min) = 550 sq.ft. (511 m²). Or, using the second rule of thumb, $A_p$ = (110)(50) = 5500 sq.ft. (511 m²).

Final choice of the collector area will be based on data supplied by the collector manufacturer, refrigerant choice, refrigerant properties, and the actual operating efficiency of the boiler chosen.

In this solar-powered pumping system, water is drawn from a sump basin and pumped to an irrigation canal where it is channeled to the fields. The 50-hp (37.3-kW) motor was

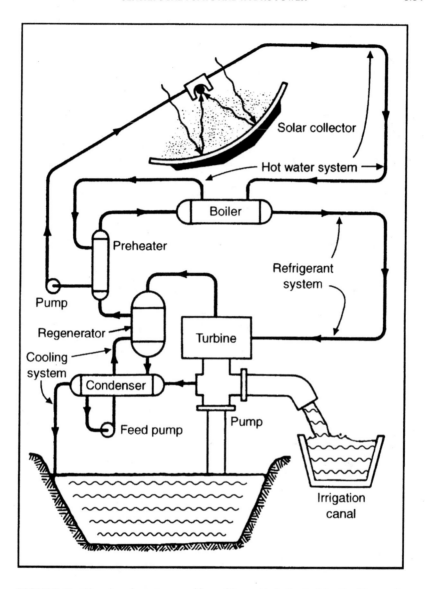

**FIGURE 61.** Closed-cycle system gassifies refrigerant in boiler to drive Rankine-cycle turbine for pumping water. (*Product Engineering,* Battelle Memorial Institute, and Northwestern Mutual Life Insurance Co.)

chosen because it is large enough to provide a meaningful demonstration of commercial size and it can be scaled up to 200 to 250 hp (149.2 to 186.5 kW) quickly and easily.

Sensors associated with the solar collector aim it at the sun in the morning, and, as the sun moves across the sky, track it throughout the day. These same sensing devices also rotate the collectors to a storage position at night and during storms. This is done to lessen the chance of damage to the reflective surfaces of the collectors. A backup control system is available for emergencies.

### 3. Predict the probable operating mode of this system

In June, during the longest day of the year, the system will deliver up to 5.6 million gallons (21,196 m³) over a 9.5-h period. Future provisions for energy storage can be made, if needed.

**Related Calculations.**    Solar-powered pumps can have numerous applications beyond irrigation. Such applications could include domestic water pumping and storage, ornamental fountain water pumping and recirculation, laundry wash water, etc. The whole key to successful solar power for pumps is selecting a suitable application. With the information presented in this procedure the designer can check the applicability and economic justification of proposed future designs.

In today's environmentally-conscious design world, the refrigerant must be carefully chosen so it is acceptable from both an ozone-depletion and from a thermodynamic standpoint. Banned refrigerants should not, of course, be used, even if attractive from a thermodynamic standpoint.

This procedure is the work of the editorial staff of *Product Engineering* magazine reporting on the work of Battelle Memorial Institute and the Northwestern Mutual Life Insurance Co. The installation described is located at MMLI's Gila River Ranch, southwest of Phoenix, Arizona. SI values were added by the handbook editor.

# SECTION 7

# WATER-SUPPLY AND STORM-WATER SYSTEM DESIGN

## Water-Well Analysis

### DETERMINING THE DRAWDOWN FOR GRAVITY WATER-SUPPLY WELL

Determine the depth of water in a 24-in. (61-cm) gravity well, 300 ft (91-m) deep, without stopping the pumps, while the well is discharging 400 gal/min (25.2 L/s). Tests show that the drawdown in a test borehole 80 ft (24.4 m) away is 4 ft (1.2 m), and in a test borehole 20 ft (6.1 m) away, it is 18 ft (5.5 m). The distance to the static groundwater table is 54 ft (16.5 m).

## Calculation Procedure:

### 1. Determine the key parameters of the well

Figure 1 shows a typical gravity well and the parameters associated with it. The Dupuit formula, given in step 2, below, is frequently used in analyzing gravity wells. Thus, from the given data, $Q = 400$ gal/min (25.2 L/s); $h_e = 300 - 54 = 246$ ft (74.9 m); $r_w = 1$ ft (0.3 m) for the well, and 20 and 80 ft (6.1 and 24.4 m), respectively, for the boreholes. For this well, $h_w$ is unknown; in the nearest borehole it is $246 - 18 = 228$ ft (69.5 m); for the farthest borehole it is $246 - 4 = 242$ ft (73.8 m). Thus, the parameters have been assembled.

### 2. Solve the Dupuit formula for the well

Substituting in the Dupuit formula

$$Q = K \frac{h_e^2 - h_w^2}{\log_{10}(r_e/r_w)} = K \frac{(h_e - h_w)(h_e + h_w)}{\log_{10}(r_e/r_w)}$$

we have,

$$300 = K \frac{(246 + 228)(246 - 228)}{\log_{10}(r_e/20)} = K \frac{(246 + 242)(246 - 242)}{\log_{10}(r_e/80)}$$

Solving, $r_e = 120$ and $K = 0.027$. Then, for the well,

$$300 = 0.027 \frac{(246 + h_w)(246 - h_w)}{\log_{10}(120/1)}$$

Solving $h_w$, = 195 ft (59.4 m). The drawdown in the well is $246 - 195 = 51$ ft (15.5 m).

**Related Calculations.** The graph resulting from plotting the Dupuit formula produces the "base-pressure curve," line ABCD in Fig. 1. It has been found in practice that the approximation in using the Dupuit formula gives results of practical value. The

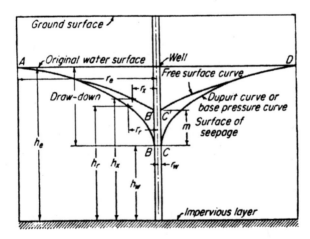

**FIGURE 1.** Hypothetical conditions of underground flow into a gravity well. (*Babbitt, Doland, and Cleasby.*)

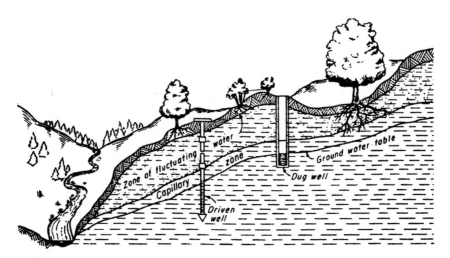

**FIGURE 2.** Relation between groundwater table and ground surface. (*Babbitt, Doland, and Cleasby.*)

results obtained are most nearly correct when the ratio of drawdown to the depth of water in the well, when not pumping, is low.

Figure 1 is valuable in analyzing both the main gravity well and its associated boreholes. Since gravity wells are, Fig. 2, popular sources of water supply throughout the world, an ability to analyze their flow is an important design skill. Thus, the effect of the percentage of total possible drawdown on the percentage of total possible flow from a well, Fig. 3, is an important design concept which finds wide use in industry today. Gravity wells are highly suitable for supplying typical weekly water demands, Fig. 4, of a moderate-size city. They are also suitable for most industrial plants having modest process-water demand.

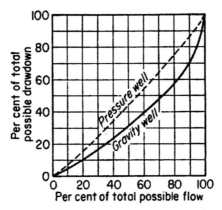

**FIGURE 3.** The effect of the percentage of total possible drawdown on the percentage of total possible flow from a well. (*Babbitt, Doland, and Cleasby.*)

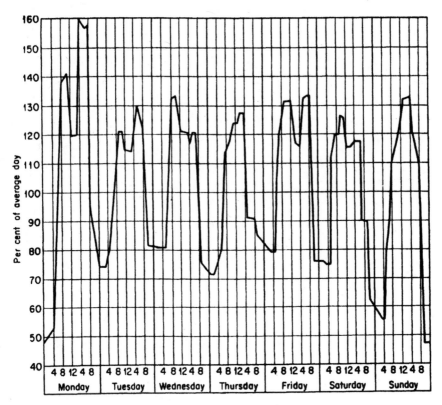

**FIGURE 4.** Demand curve for a typical week for a city of 100,000 population. (*Babbitt, Doland, and Cleasby.*)

This procedure is the work of Harold E. Babbitt, James J. Doland, and John L. Cleasby, as reported in their book, *Water Supply Engineering,* McGraw-Hill.

## FINDING THE DRAWDOWN OF A DISCHARGING GRAVITY WELL

A gravity well 12 in. (30.5 cm) in diameter is discharging 150 gal/min (9.5 L/s), with a drawdown of 10 ft (3 m). It discharges 500 gal/min (31.6 L/s) with a drawdown of 50 ft (15 m). The static depth of the water in the well is 150 ft (45.7 m). What will be the discharge from the well with a drawdown of 20 ft (6 m)?

### Calculation Procedure:

### 1. *Apply the Dupuit formula to this well*
Using the formula as given in the previous calculation procedure, we see that

$$150 = K\frac{(10)(290)}{\log_{10}(150C/0.5)} \quad \text{and} \quad 500 = K\frac{(50)(250)}{\log_{10}(500C/0.5)}$$

Solving for $C$ and $K$ we have

$$C = 0.21 \quad \text{and} \quad K = \frac{(500)(\log 210)}{12,500} = 0.093;$$

then

$$Q = 0.093\frac{(20)(280)}{\log_{10}(0.210Q/0.5)}$$

## 2. Solve for the water flow by trial

Solving by successive trial using the results in step 1, we find $Q = 257$ gal/min (16.2 L/s).

**Related Calculations.** If it is assumed, for purposes of convenience in computations, that the radius of the circle of influence, $r_e$, varies directly as $Q$ for equilibrium conditions, then $r_e = CQ$. Then the Dupuit equation can be rewritten as

$$Q = K\frac{(h_e + h_w)(h_e - h_w)}{\log_{10}(CQ/r_w)}$$

From this rewritten equation it can be seen that where the drawdown ($h_e - h_w$) is small compared with ($h_e + h_w$) the value of $Q$ varies approximately as ($h_e - h_w$). This straight-line relationship between the rate of flow and drawdown leads to the definition of the *specific capacity* of a well as the rate of flow per unit of drawdown, usually expressed in gallons per minute per foot of drawdown (liters per second per meter). Since the relationship is not the same for all drawdowns, it should be determined for one special foot (meter), often the first foot (meter) of drawdown. The relationship is shown graphically in Fig. 3 for both gravity, Fig. 1, and pressure wells, Fig. 5. Note also that since $K$ in

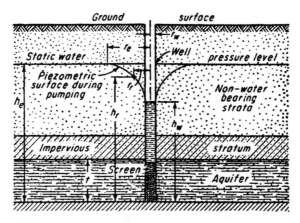

**FIGURE 5.** Hypothetical conditions for flow into a pressure well. (*Babbitt, Doland, and Cleasby.*)

different aquifers is not the same, the specific capacities of wells in different aquifers are not always comparable.

It is possible, with the use of the equation for $Q$ above, to solve some problems in gravity wells by measuring two or more rates of flow and corresponding drawdowns in the well to be studied. Observations in nearby test holes or boreholes are unnecessary. The steps are outlined in this procedure.

This procedure is the work of Harold E. Babbitt, James J. Doland, and John L. Cleasby, as reported in their book, *Water Supply Engineering*, McGraw-Hill. SI values were added by the handbook editor.

## ANALYZING DRAWDOWN AND RECOVERY FOR WELL PUMPED FOR EXTENDED PERIOD

Construct the drawdown-recovery curve for a gravity well pumped for two days at 450 gal/min (28.4 L/s). The following observations have been made during a test of the well under equilibrium conditions: diameter, 2 ft (0.61 m); $h_e = 50$ ft (15.2 m); when $Q = 450$ gal/min (28.4 L/s), drawdown $= 8.5$ ft (2.6 m); and when $r_x = 60$ ft (18.3 m), $(h_e - h_x) = 3$ ft (0.91 m). The specific yield of the well is 0.25.

### Calculation Procedure:

#### 1. Determine the value of the constant k
Use the equation

$$Q = \frac{k(h_e - h_x)h_e}{C_x \log_{10}(r_e/0.1h_e)} \quad \text{and} \quad k = \frac{QC_x \log_{10}(r_e/0.1h_e)}{(h_e - h_x)(h_e)}$$

Determine the value of $C_x$ when $r_w$, is equal to the radius of the well, in this case 1.0. The value of $k$ can be determined by trial. Further, the same value of $k$ must be given when $r_x = r_e$ as when $r_x = 60$ ft (18.3 m). In this procedure, only the correct assumed value of $r_e$ is shown—to save space.

Assume that $r_e = 350$ ft (106.7 m). Then, $1/350 = 0.00286$ and, from Fig. 6, $C_x = 0.60$. Then $k = (1)(0.60)(\log 350/5)/(8)(50) = (1)(0.6)(1.843)/400 = 0.00276$, $r_x/r_e = 60/350 = 0.172$, and $C_x = 0.225$. Hence, checking the computed value of $k$, we have $k = (1)(0.22)(1.843)/150 = 0.0027$, which checks with the earlier computed value.

#### 2. Compute the head values using k from step 1
Compute $h_e - (h_e^2 - 1.7 Q/k)^{0.5} = 50 - (2500 - 1.7/0.0027)^{0.5} = 6.8$.

#### 3. Find the values of T to develop the assumed values of $r_e$
For example, assume that $r_e = 100$. Then $T = (0.184)(100)^2(0.25)(6.8)/1 = 3230$ sec $= 0.9$ h, using the equation

$$T = \left(h_e - \sqrt{h_e^2 - 1.7\frac{Q}{k}}\right)\frac{0.184r_e^2 f}{Q}$$

#### 4. Calculate the radii ratio and $d_0$
These computations are: $r_e/r_w = 100/1 = 100$. Then, $d_0 = (6.8)(\log_{10} 100)/2.3 = 5.9$ ft (1.8 m), using the equation

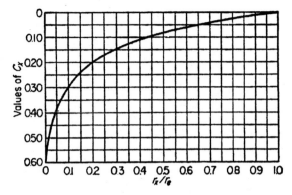

**FIGURE 6.** Values of $C_x$ for use in calculations of well performance. (*Babbitt, Doland, and Cleasby.*)

$$d_0 = \frac{1}{2.3} \left( h_e - \sqrt{h_e^2 - 1.7\frac{Q}{k}} \right) \log_{10} \frac{r_o}{r_w}$$

## 5. Compute other points on the drawdown curve

Plot the values found in step 4 on the drawdown-recovery curve, Fig. 7. Compute additional values of $d_0$ and $T$ and plot them on Fig. 7, as shown.

## 6. Make the recovery-curve computations

The recovery-curve, Fig. 7, computations are based the assumption that by imposing a negative discharge on the positive discharge from the well there will be in effect zero flow from the well, provided the negative discharge equals the positive discharge. Then, the sum of the drawdowns due to the two discharges at any time $T$ after adding the negative discharge will be the drawdown to the recovery curve, Fig. 7.

Assume some time after the pump has stopped, such as 6 h, and compute $r_e$, with $Q$, $f$, $k$, and $h_e$ as in step 3, above. Then $r_e = [(6 \times 3600 \times 1)/(0.184 \times 0.25 \times 6.8)]^{0.5} = 263$ ft (80.2 m). Then, $r_e/r_w = 263$; check.

## 7. Find the value of $d_0$ corresponding to $r_e$ in step 6

Computing, we have $d_0 = (6.8)(\log_{10})/2.3 = 7.15$ ft (2.2 m). Tabulate the computed values as shown in Table 1 where the value 7.15 is rounded off to 7.2.

Compute the value of $r_e$ using the total time since pumping started. In this case it is 48 + 6 = 54 h. Then $r_e = [(54 \times 3600 \times 1)/(0.184 \times 0.25 \times 6.8)]^{0.5} = 790$ ft (240.8 m). The $d_0$ corresponding to the preceding value of $r_e = 790$ ft (240.8 m) is $d_0 = (6.8)(\log_{10} 790)/2.3 = 8.55$ ft (2.6 m).

## 8. Find the recovery value

The recovery value, $d_r = 8.55 - 7.15 = 1.4$ ft (0.43 m). Coordinates of other points on the recovery curve are computed in a similar fashion. Note that the recovery curve does not attain the original groundwater table because water has been removed from the aquifer and it has not been restored.

***Related Calculations.*** If water is entering the area of a well at a rate $q$ and is being pumped out at the rate $Q'$ with $Q'$ greater than $q$, then the value of $Q$ to be used in computing the drawdown recovery is $Q' - q$. If this difference is of appreciable magnitude, a correction must be made because of the effect of the inflow from the aquifer into

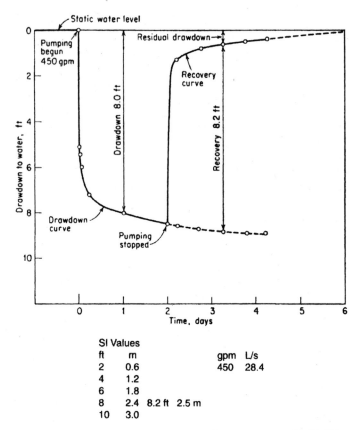

**FIGURE 7.** Drawdown-recovery curves for a gravity well. (*Babbitt, Doland, and Cleasby.*)

**TABLE 1.** Coordinates for the Drawdown-Recovery Curve of a Gravity Well

| (1) Time after pump starts, hr | (2) $\dfrac{r_e}{r_x} = r'_e$ | (3) $2.95 \times \log_{10} \dfrac{r_e}{r_w} = d_0$ | (4) Time after pump starts, hr | (5) $\dfrac{r_e}{r_x} = r'_e$ | (6) $2.95 \times \log_{10} \dfrac{r_e}{r_w} = d_0$ | (7) Time after pump stops, hr | (8) $\dfrac{r_e}{r_x} = r'_e$ | (9) $2.95 \times \log_{10} \dfrac{r_e}{r_w} = d_0$ | (10) Col 6 minus col 9 = $d_r$ |
|---|---|---|---|---|---|---|---|---|---|
| 0.25 | 54 | 5.10 | 54 | 784 | 8.5 | 6 | 263 | 7.2 | 1.3 |
| 0.50 | 76 | 5.45 | 66 | 872 | 8.7 | 18 | 455 | 7.9 | 0.8 |
| 1.00 | 107 | 6.0 | 78 | 950 | 8.8 | 30 | 587 | 8.2 | 0.6 |
| 6 | 263 | 7.2 | 90 | 1,020 | 8.9 | 42 | 694 | 8.4 | 0.5 |
| 24 | 526 | 8.0 | 102 | 1,085 | 8.9 | 54 | 784 | 8.5 | 0.4 |
| 48 | 745 | 8.5 | | | | | | | |

Conditions: $r_w = 1.0$ ft; $h_e = 50$ ft. When $Q = 1$ ft³/s and $r_x = 1.0$ ft $(h_e - h_x) = 8.0$ ft. When $Q = 1$ ft³/s and $r_x = 60$ ft, $(h_e - h_x) = 3.0$ ft. Specific yield $= 0.25$; $k$, as determined in step 1 of example, $= 0.0027$; and $h_e - (h_e^2 - 1.79Q/k)^{0.5} = 6.8$.

the cone of depression so the groundwater table will ultimately be restored, the recovery curve becoming asymptotic to the table.

This procedure is the work of Harold E. Babbitt, James J. Doland, and John L. Cleasby, as reported in their book, *Water Supply Engineering*, McGraw-Hill. SI values were added by the handbook editor.

## SELECTION OF AIR-LIFT PUMP FOR WATER WELL

Select the overall features of an air-lift pump, Fig. 8, to lift 350 gal/min (22.1 L/s) into a reservoir at the ground surface. The distance to groundwater surface is 50 ft (15.2 m). It is expected that the specific gravity of the well is 14 gal/min/ft (2.89 L/s/m).

### Calculation Procedure:

### 1. Find the well drawdown, static lift, and depth of this well
The drawdown at 350 gal/min is $d = 350/14 = 25$ ft (7.6 m). The static lift, $h$, is the sum of the distance from the groundwater surface plus the drawdown, or $h = 50 + 25 = 75$ ft (22.9 m).

Interpolating in Table 2 gives a submergence percentage of $s = 0.61$. Then, the depth of the well, $D$ ft is related to the submergence percentage thus: $s = D/(D + h)$. Or, $0.61 = D/(D + 75)$; $D = 117$ ft (35.8 m). The depth of the well is, therefore, $75 + 117 = 192$ ft (58.5 m).

### 2. Determine the required capacity of the air compressor
The rate of water flow in cubic feet per second, $Q_w$ is given by $Q_w = $ gal/min/(60 min/s)(7.5 ft³/gal) = $350/(60)(7.5) = 0.78$ ft³/s (0.022 m³/s). Then the volume of free air required by the air-lift pump is given by

$$Q_a = \frac{Q_w(h + h_1)}{75E \log r}$$

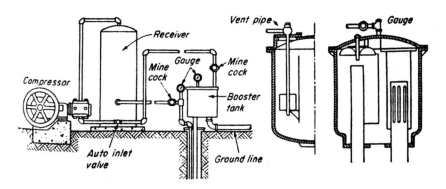

**FIGURE 8.** Sullivan air-lift booster. (*Babbitt, Doland, and Cleasby.*)

**TABLE 2.**  Some Recommended Submergence Percentages for Air Lifts

| Lift, ft | Up to 50 | 50–100 | 100–200 | 200–300 | 300–400 | 400–500 |
|---|---|---|---|---|---|---|
| Lift, m | Up to 15 | 15–30 | 30–61 | 61–91 | 91–122 | 122–152 |
| Submergence percentage | 70–66 | 66–55 | 55–50 | 50–43 | 43–40 | 40–33 |

where $Q_a$ = volume of free air required, ft³/min (m³/min); $h_1$ = velocity head at discharge, usually taken as 6 ft (1.8 m) for deep wells, down to 1 ft (0.3 m) for shallow wells; $E$ = efficiency of pump, approximated from Table 3; $r$ = ratio of compression = $(D + 34)/34$. Substituting, using 6 ft (1.8 m) since this is a deep well, we have, $Q_a = (0.779 \times 81)/(75 \times 0.35 \times 0.646) = 3.72$ ft³/s (0.11 m³/s).

### 3. Size the air pipe and determine the operating pressures

The cross-sectional area of the pipe = $Q'_a/V$. At the bottom of the well, $Q'_a = 3.72 (34/151) = 0.83$ ft³/s (0.023 m³/s). With a flow velocity of the air typically at 2000 ft/min (610 m/min), or 33.3 ft/s (10 m/s), the area of the air pipe is 0.83/33.3 = 0.025 sq.ft., and the diameter is $[(0.025 \times 4)/\pi]^{0.5} = 0.178$ ft or 2.1 in. (53.3 mm); use 2-in. (50.8 mm) pipe.

The pressure at the start is 142 ft (43 m); operating pressure is 117 ft (35.7 m).

### 4. Size the eductor pipe

At the well bottom, $A = Q/V$. $Q = Q_w + Q'_a = 0.78 + 0.83 = 1.612$ ft³/s (0.45 m³/s). The velocity at the entrance to the eductor pipe is 4.9 ft/s (1.9 m/s) from a table of eductor entrance velocities, available from air-lift pump manufacturers. Then, the pipe area, $A = Q/V = 1.61/4.9 = 0.33$. Hence, $d = [(4 \times 0.33)/\pi)]05 - 0.646$ ft, or 7.9 in. Use 8-in. (203 mm) pipe.

If the eductor pipe is the same size from top to bottom, then $V$ at top = $(Q_a + Q_w)/A = (3.72 + 0.78)(4)/(\pi \times 0.667^2) = 13$ ft/s (3.96 m/s). This is comfortably within the permissible maximum limit of 20 ft/s (6.1 m/s). Hence, 8-in. pipe is suitable for this eductor pipe.

**Related Calculations.**  In an air-lift pump serving a water well, compressed air is released through an air diffuser (also called a foot piece) at the bottom of the eductor pipe. Rising as small bubbles, a mixture of air and water is created that has a lower specific gravity than that of water alone. The rising air bubbles, if sufficiently large, create an upward water flow in the well, to deliver liquid at the ground level.

Air lifts have many unique features not possessed by other types of well pumps. They are the simplest and the most foolproof type of pump. In operation, the airlift pump gives the least trouble because there are no remote or submerged moving parts. Air lifts can be operated successfully in holes of any practicable size. They can be used in crooked holes

**TABLE 3.**  Effect of Submergence on Efficiencies of Air Lift*

| Ratio $D/h$ | 8.70 | 5.46 | 3.86 | 2.91 | 2.25 |
|---|---|---|---|---|---|
| Submergence ratio, $D/(D + h)$ | 0.896 | 0.845 | 0.795 | 0.745 | 0.693 |
| Percentage efficiency | 26.5 | 31.0 | 35.0 | 36.6 | 37.7 |

| Ratio $D/h$ | 1.86 | 1.45 | 1.19 | 0.96 |
|---|---|---|---|---|
| Submergence ratio, $D/(D + (h)$ | 0.650 | 0.592 | 0.544 | 0.490 |
| Percentage efficiency | 36.8 | 34.5 | 31.0 | 26.5 |

*At Hattiesburg MS.

not suited to any other type of pump. An air-lift pump can draw more water from a well, with sufficient capacity to deliver it, than any other type of pump that can be installed in a well. A number of wells in a group can be operated from a central control station where the air compressor is located.

The principal disadvantages of air lifts are the necessity for making the well deeper than is required for other types of well pumps, the intermittent nature of the flow from the well, and the relatively low efficiencies obtained. Little is known of the efficiency of the average air-lift installation in small waterworks. Tests show efficiencies in the neighborhood of 45 percent for depths of 50 ft (15 m) down to 20 percent for depths of 600 ft (183 m). Changes in efficiencies resulting from different submergence ratios are shown in Table 3. Some submergence percentages recommended for various lifts are shown in Table 2.

This procedure is the work of Harold E. Babbitt, James J. Doland, and John L. Cleasby, as reported in their book, *Water Supply Engineering,* McGraw-Hill. SI values were added by the handbook editor.

## Water-Supply and Storm-Water System Design

### WATER-SUPPLY SYSTEM FLOW-RATE AND PRESSURE-LOSS ANALYSIS

A water-supply system will serve a city of 100,000 population. Two water mains arranged in a parallel configuration (Fig. 9a) will supply this city. Determine the flow rate, size, and head loss of each pipe in this system. If the configuration in Fig. 9a were replaced by the single pipe shown in Fig. 9b, what would the total head loss be if

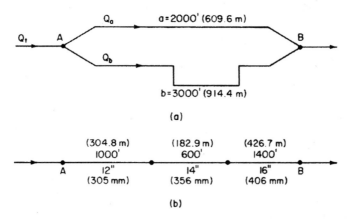

**FIGURE 9.** (*a*) Parallel water distribution system; (*b*) single-pipe distribution system.

$C = 100$ and the flow rate were reduced to 2000 gal/min (126.2 L/s)? Explain how the Hardy Cross method is applied to the water-supply piping system in Fig. 11.

### Calculation Procedure:

### 1. Compute the domestic water flow rate in the system
Use an average annual domestic water consumption of 150 gal/day (0.0066 L/s) per capita. Hence, domestic water consumption = (150 gal per capita per day)(100,000 persons) = 15,000,000 gal/day (657.1 L/s). To this domestic flow, the flow required for fire protection must be added to determine the total flow required.

### 2. Compute the required flow rate for fire protection
Use the relation $Q_f = 1020(P)^{0.5} [1 - 0.01(P)^{0.5}]$, where $Q_f$ = fire flow, gal/min; $P$ = population in thousands. Substituting gives $Q_f = 1020(100)^{0.5} [1 - 0.01(100)^{0.5}] = 9180$, say 9200 gal/min (580.3 L/s).

### 3. Apply a load factor to the domestic consumption
To provide for unusual water demands, many design engineers apply a 200 to 250 percent load factor to the average hourly consumption that is determined from the average annual consumption. Thus, the average daily total consumption determined in step 1 is based on an average annual daily demand. Convert the average daily total consumption in step 1 to an average hourly consumption by dividing by 24 h or 15,000,000/24 = 625,000 gal/h (657.1 L/s). Next, apply a 200 percent load factor. Or, design hourly demand = 2.00(625,000) = 1,250,000 gal/h (1314.1 L/s), or 1,250,000/60 min/h = 20,850, say 20,900 gal/min (1318.6 L/s).

### 4. Compute the total water flow required
The total water flow required = domestic flow, gal/min + fire flow, gal/min = 20,900 + 9200 = 30,100 gal/min (1899.0 L/s). If this system were required to supply water to one or more industrial plants in addition to the domestic and fire flows, the quantity needed by the industrial plants would be added to the total flow computed above.

### 5. Select the flow rate for each pipe
The flow rate is not known for either pipe in Fig. 9a. Assume that the shorter pipe a has a flow rate $Q_a$ of 12,100 gal/min (763.3 L/s), and the longer pipe b a flow rate $Q_b$ of 18,000 gal/min (1135.6 L/s). Thus, $Q_a + Q_b = Q_t = 12,100 + 18,000 = 30,100$ gal/min (1899.0 L/s), where $Q$ = flow, gal/min, in the pipe identified by the subscript a or b; $Q_t$ = total flow in the system, gal/min.

### 6. Select the sizes of the pipes in the system
Since neither pipe size is known, some assumptions must be made about the system. First, assume that a friction-head loss of 10 ft of water per 1000 ft (3.0 m per 304.8 m) of pipe is suitable for this system. This is a typical allowable friction-head loss for water-supply systems.

Second, assume that the pipe is sized by using the Hazen-Williams equation with the coefficient $C = 100$. Most water-supply systems are designed with this equation and this value of $C$.

Enter Fig. 10 with the assumed friction-head loss of 10 ft/1000 ft (3.0 m/304.8 m) of pipe on the right-hand scale, and project through the assumed Hazen-Williams coefficient $C = 100$. Extend this straight line until it intersects the pivot axis. Next, enter Fig. 10 on the left-hand scale at the flow rate in pipe a, 12,100 gal/min (763.3 L/s), and project to the previously found intersection on the pivot axis. At the intersection with the pipe-diameter scale, read the required pipe size as 27-in. (686-mm) diameter.

Note that if the required pipe size falls between two plotted sizes, the next *larger* size is used.

Now in any parallel piping system, the friction-head loss through any branch connecting two common points equals the friction-head loss in any other branch connecting the same two points. Using Fig. 10 for a 27-in. (686-mm) pipe, find the actual friction-head loss at 8 ft/1000 ft (2.4 m/304.8 m) of pipe. Hence, the total friction-head loss in pipe *a* is

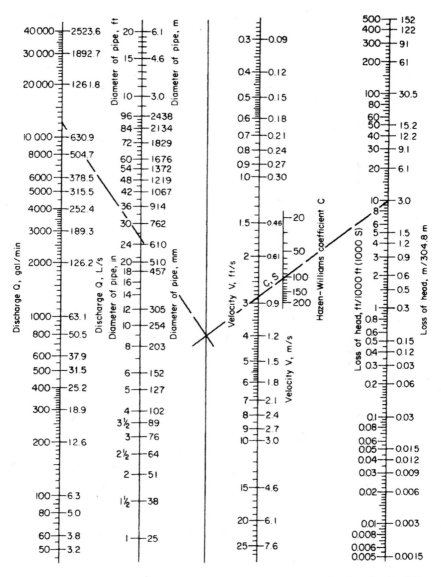

**FIGURE 10.** Nomogram for solution of the Hazen-Williams equation for pipes flowing full.

(2000 ft long)(8 ft/1000 ft) = 16 ft (4.9 m) of water. This is also the friction-head loss in pipe *b*.

Since pipe *b* is 3000 ft (914.4 m) long, the friction-head loss per 1000 ft (304.8 m) is total head loss, ft/length of pipe, thousands of ft = 16/3 = 5.33 ft/1000 ft (1.6 m/304.8 m). Enter Fig. 10 at this friction-head loss and *C* = 100. Project in the same manner as described for pipe *a*, and find the required size of pipe *b* as 33 in. (838.2 mm).

If the district being supplied by either pipe required a specific flow rate, this flow would be used instead of assuming a flow rate. Then the pipe would be sized in the same manner as described above.

### 7. Compute the single-pipe equivalent length

When we deal with several different sizes of pipe having the same flow rate, it is often convenient to convert each pipe to an *equivalent length* of a common-size pipe. Many design engineers use 8-in. (203-mm) pipe as the common size. Table 4 shows the equivalent length of 8-in. (203-mm) pipe for various other sizes of pipe with *C* = 90, 100, and 110 in the Hazen-Williams equation.

From Table 4, for 12-in. (305-mm) pipe, the equivalent length of 8-in. (203-mm) pipe is 0.14 ft/ft when *C* = 100. Thus, total equivalent length of 8-in. (203-mm) pipe = (1000 ft of 12-in. pipe)(0.14 ft/ft) = 140 ft (42.7 m) of 8-in. (203-mm) pipe. For the 14-in. (356-mm) pipe, total equivalent length = (600)(0.066) = 39.6 ft (12.1 m), using similar data from Table 4. For the 16-in. (406-mm) pipe, total equivalent length = (1400)(0.034) = 47.6 ft (14.5 m). Hence, total equivalent length of 8-in. (203-mm) pipe = 140 + 39.6 + 47.6 = 227.2 ft (69.3 m).

### 8. Determine the friction-head loss in the pipe

Enter Fig. 10 at the flow rate of 2000 gal/min (126.2 L/s), and project through 8-in. (203-mm) diameter to the pivot axis. From this intersection, project through *C* = 100 to read the friction-head loss as 100 ft/1000 ft (30.5 m/304.8 m), due to the friction of the water in the pipe. Since the equivalent length of the pipe is 227.2 ft (69.3 m), the friction-head loss in the compound pipe is (227.2/1000)(110) = 25 ft (7.6 m) of water.

**TABLE 4.**   Equivalent Length of 8-in. (203-mm) Pipe for *C* = 100

| Pipe diameter | | *C* = 90 | *C* = 100 | *C* = 110 |
|---|---|---|---|---|
| in. | mm | | | |
| 2 | 51 | 1012 | 851 | 712 |
| 4 | 102 | 34 | 29 | 24.3 |
| 6 | 152 | 4.8 | 4.06 | 3.4 |
| 8 | 203 | 1.19 | 1.00 | 0.84 |
| 10 | 254 | 0.40 | 0.34 | 0.285 |
| 12 | 305 | 0.17 | 0.14 | 0.117 |
| 14 | 356 | 0.078 | 0.066 | 0.055 |
| 16 | 406 | 0.040 | 0.034 | 0.029 |
| 18 | 457 | 0.023 | 0.019 | 0.016 |
| 20 | 508 | 0.0137 | 0.0115 | 0.0096 |
| 24 | 610 | 0.0056 | 0.0047 | 0.0039 |
| 30 | 762 | 0.0019 | 0.0016 | 0.0013 |
| 36 | 914 | 0.00078 | 0.00066 | 0.00055 |

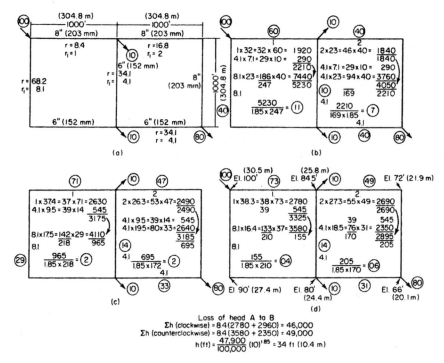

**FIGURE 11.** Application of the Hardy Cross method to a water distribution system.

***Related Calculations.*** Two pipes, two piping systems, or a single pipe and a system of pipes are said to be *equivalent* when the losses of head due to friction for equal rates of flow in the pipes are equal.

To determine the flow rates and friction-head losses in complex waterworks distribution systems, the Hardy Cross method of network analysis is often used. This method[1] uses trial and error to obtain successively more accurate approximations of the flow rate through a piping system. To apply the Hardy Cross method: (1) Sketch the piping system layout as in Fig. 11. (2) Assume a flow quantity, in terms of percentage of total flow, for each part of the piping system. In assuming a flow quantity note that (*a*) the loss of head due to friction between any two points of a closed circuit must be the same by any path by which the water may flow, and (*b*) the rate of inflow into any section of the piping system must equal the outflow. (3) Compute the loss of head due to friction between two points in each part of the system, based on the assumed flow in (*a*) the clockwise direction and (*b*) the counterclockwise direction. A difference in the calculated friction-head losses in the two directions indicates an error in the assumed direction of flow. (4) Compute a counterflow correction by dividing the difference in head, $\Delta h$ ft, by $n(Q)^{n-1}$, where $n = 1.85$ and $Q =$ flow, gal/min. Indicate the direction of this counterflow in the pipe by an arrow starting at the right side of the smaller value of $h$ and curving toward the larger value, Fig. 11. (5) Add or subtract the counterflow

[1]O'Rourke—*General Engineering Handbook,* McGraw-Hill.

**TABLE 5.**   Values of $r$ for 1000 ft (304.8 m) of Pipe Based on the Hazen-Williams Formula*

| $d$,in.(mm) | $C = 90$ | $C = 100$ | $C = 110$ | $C = 120$ | $C = 130$ | $C = 140$ |
|---|---|---|---|---|---|---|
| 4(102) | 340 | 246 | 206 | 176 | 151 | 135 |
| 6(152) | 47.1 | 34.1 | 28.6 | 24.3 | 21.0 | 18.7 |
| 8(203) | 11.1 | 8.4 | 7.0 | 6.0 | 5.2 | 4.6 |
| 10 (254) | 3.7 | 2.8 | 2.3 | 2.0 | 1.7 | 1.5 |
| 12 (305) | 1.6 | 1.2 | 1.0 | 0.85 | 0.74 | 0.65 |
| 14 (356) | 0.72 | 0.55 | 0.46 | 0.39 | 0.34 | 0.30 |
| 16 (406) | 0.38 | 0.29 | 0.24 | 0.21 | 0.18 | 0.15 |
| 18 (457) | 0.21 | 0.16 | 0.13 | 0.11 | 0.10 | 0.09 |
| 20 (508) | 0.13 | 0.10 | 0.08 | 0.07 | 0.06 | 0.05 |
| 24 (610) | 0.052 | 0.04 | 0.03 | 0.03 | 0.02 | 0.02 |
| 30 (762) | 0.017 | 0.013 | 0.011 | 0.009 | 0.008 | 0.007 |

Example: $r$ for 12-in. (305-mm) pipe 4000 ft (1219 m) long, with $C = 100$, is $1.2 \times 4.0 = 4.8$.
*Head loss in ft (m) $= r \times 10^{-5} \times Q^{1.85}$ per 1000 ft (304.8 m), $Q$ representing gal/min (L/s).

to or from the assumed flow, depending on whether its direction is the same or opposite. (6) Repeat this process on each circuit in the system until a satisfactory balance of flow is obtained.

To compute the loss of head due to friction, step 3 of the Hardy Cross method, use any standard formula, such as the Hazen-Williams, that can be reduced to the form $h = rQ^n L$, where $h =$ head loss due to friction, ft of water; $r =$ a coefficient depending on the diameter and roughness of the pipe; $Q =$ flow rate, gal/min; $n = 1.85$; $L =$ length of pipe, ft. Table 5 gives values of $r$ for 1000-ft (304.8-in.) lengths of various sizes of pipe and for different values of the Hazen-Williams coefficient $C$. When the percentage of total flow is used for computing $\Sigma h$ in Fig. 11, the loss of head due to friction in ft between any two points for any flow in gal/min is computed from $h = [\Sigma h$ (by percentage of flow)/ 100,000] (gal/min/ 100)^{0.85}. Figure 11 shows the details of the solution using the Hardy Cross method. The circled numbers represent the flow quantities. Table 6 lists values of numbers between 0 and 100 to the 0.85 power.

**TABLE 6.**   Value of the 0.85 Power of Numbers

| N | 0 | 1 | 2 | 3 | 4 | 5 | 6 | 7 | 8 | 9 |
|---|---|---|---|---|---|---|---|---|---|---|
| 0 | 0 | 1.0 | 1.8 | 2.5 | 3.2 | 3.9 | 4.6 | 5.2 | 5.9 | 6.5 |
| 10 | 7.1 | 7.7 | 8.3 | 8.9 | 9.5 | 10.0 | 10.6 | 11.1 | 11.6 | 12.2 |
| 20 | 12.8 | 13.3 | 13.8 | 14.4 | 14.9 | 15.4 | 15.9 | 16.4 | 16.9 | 17.5 |
| 30 | 18.0 | 18.5 | 19.0 | 19.5 | 20.0 | 20.5 | 21.0 | 21.5 | 22.0 | 22.5 |
| 40 | 23.0 | 23.4 | 23.9 | 24.3 | 24.8 | 25.3 | 25.8 | 26.3 | 26.8 | 27.3 |
| 50 | 27.8 | 28.2 | 28.7 | 29.1 | 29.6 | 30.0 | 30.5 | 31.0 | 31.4 | 31.9 |
| 60 | 32.4 | 32.9 | 33.3 | 33.8 | 34.2 | 34.7 | 35.1 | 35.6 | 36.0 | 36.5 |
| 70 | 37.0 | 37.4 | 37.9 | 38.3 | 38.7 | 39.1 | 39.6 | 40.0 | 40.5 | 41.0 |
| 80 | 41.5 | 42.0 | 42.4 | 42.8 | 43.3 | 43.7 | 44.1 | 44.5 | 45.0 | 45.4 |
| 90 | 45.8 | 46.3 | 46.7 | 47.1 | 47.6 | 48.0 | 48.4 | 48.8 | 49.2 | 49.6 |

## WATER-SUPPLY SYSTEM SELECTION

Choose the type of water-supply system for a city having a population of 100,000 persons. Indicate which type of system would be suitable for such a city today and 20 years hence. The city is located in an area of numerous lakes.

### Calculation Procedure:

### 1. Compute the domestic water flow rate in the system

Use an average annual domestic water consumption of 150 gal per capita day (gcd) (6.6 mL/s). Hence, domestic water consumption = (150 gal per capita day)(100,000 persons) = 15,000,000 gal/day (657.1 L/s). To this domestic flow, the flow required for fire protection must be added to determine the total flow required.

### 2. Compute the required flow rate for fire protection

Use the relation $Q_f = 1020(P)^{0.5} [1 - 0.01(P)^{0.5}]$, where $Q_f$ = fire flow, gal/min; $P$ = population in thousands. So $Q_f = 1020(100)^{0.5} [1 - 0.01 \times (100)^{0.5}] - 9180$, say 9200 gal/min (580.3 L/s).

### 3. Apply a load factor to the domestic consumption

To provide for unusual water demands, many design engineers apply a 200 to 250 percent load factor to the average hourly consumption that is determined from the average annual consumption. Thus, the average daily total consumption determined in step 1 is based on an average annual daily demand. Convert the average daily total consumption in step 1 to an average hourly consumption by dividing by 24 h, or 15,000,000/24 = 625,000 gal/h (657.1 L/s). Next, apply a 200 percent load factor. Or, design hourly demand = 2.00(625,000) = 1,250,000 gal/h (1314.1 L/s), or 1,250,000/(60 min/h) = 20,850, say 20,900 gal/min (1318.4 L/ s).

### 4. Compute the total water flow required

The total water flow required = domestic flow, gal/min + fire flow, gal/min = 20,900 + 9200 = 30,100 gal/min (1899.0 L/s). If this system were required to supply water to one or more industrial plants in addition to the domestic and fire flows, the quantity needed by the industrial plants would be added to the total flow computed above.

### 5. Study the water supplies available

Table 7 lists the principal sources of domestic water supplies. Wells that are fed by groundwater are popular in areas having sandy or porous soils. To determine whether a

**TABLE 7.** Typical Municipal Water Sources

| Source | Collection method | Remarks |
|---|---|---|
| Groundwater | Wells (artesian, ordinary, galleries) | 30 to 40 percent of an area's rainfall becomes groundwater |
| Surface freshwater (lakes, rivers, streams, impounding reservoirs) | Pumping or gravity flow from submerged intakes, tower intakes, or surface intakes | Surface supplies are important in many areas |
| Surface saltwater | Desalting | Wide-scale application under study at present |

well is suitable for supplying water in sufficient quantity, its specific capacity (i.e., the yield in gal/min per foot of drawdown) must be determined.

Wells for municipal water sources may be dug, driven, or drilled. Dug wells seldom exceed 60 ft (18.3 m) deep. Each such well should be protected from surface-water leakage by being lined with impervious concrete to a depth of 15 ft (4.6 m).

Driven wells seldom are more than 40 ft (12.2 m) deep or more than 2 in. (51 mm) in diameter when used for small water supplies. Bigger driven wells are constructed by driving large-diameter casings into the ground.

Drilled wells can be several thousand feet deep, if required. The yield of a driven well is usually greater than any other type of well because the well can be sunk to a depth where sufficient groundwater is available. Almost all wells require a pump of some kind to lift the water from its subsurface location and discharge it to the water-supply system.

Surface freshwater can be collected from lakes, rivers, streams, or reservoirs by submerged-, tower-, or crib-type intakes. The intake leads to one or more pumps that discharge the water to the distribution system or intermediate pumping stations. Locate intakes as far below the water surface as possible. Where an intake is placed less than 20 ft (6.1 m) below the surface of the water, it may become clogged by sand, mud, or ice.

Choose the source of water for this system after studying the local area to determine the most economical source today and 20 years hence. With a rapidly expanding population, the future water demand may dictate the type of water source chosen. Since this city is in an area of many lakes, a surface supply would probably be most economical, if the water table is not falling rapidly.

### 6. *Select the type of pipe to use*
Four types of pipes are popular for municipal water-supply systems: cast iron, asbestos cement, steel, and concrete. Wood-stave pipe was once popular, but it is now obsolete. Some communities also use copper or lead pipes. However, the use of both types is extremely small when compared with the other types. The same is true of plastic pipe, although this type is slowly gaining some acceptance.

In general, cast-iron pipe proves dependable and long-lasting in water-supply systems that are not subject to galvanic or acidic soil conditions.

Steel pipe is generally used for long, large-diameter lines. Thus, the typical steel pipe used in water-supply systems is 36 or 48 in. (914 or 1219 mm) in diameter. Use steel pipe for river crossings, on bridges, and for similar installations where light weight and high strength are required. Steel pipe may last 50 years or more under favorable soil conditions. Where unfavorable soil conditions exist, the lift of steel pipe may be about 20 years.

Concrete-pipe use is generally confined to large, long lines, such as aqueducts. Concrete pipe is suitable for conveying relatively pure water through neutral soil. However, corrosion may occur when the soil contains an alkali or an acid.

Asbestos-cement pipe has a number of important advantages over other types. However, it does not flex readily, it can be easily punctured, and it may corrode in acidic soils.

Select the pipe to use after a study of the local soil conditions, length of runs required, and the quantity of water that must be conveyed. Usual water velocities in municipal water systems are in the 5-ft/s (1.5-m/s) range. However, the velocities in aqueducts range from 10 to 20 ft/s (3.0 to 6.1 m/s). Earthen canals have much lower velocities—1 to 3 ft/s (0.3 to 0.9 m/s). Rock- and concrete-lined canals have velocities of 8 to 15 ft/s (2.4 to 4.6 m/s).

In cold northern areas, keep in mind the occasional need to thaw frozen pipes during the winter. Nonmetallic pipes—concrete, plastic, etc., as well as nonconducting metals—cannot be thawed by electrical means. Since electrical thawing is probably the most practical method available today, pipes that prevent its use may put the water system at a disadvantage if subfreezing temperatures are common in the area served.

### 7. Select the method for pressurizing the water system

Water-supply systems can be pressurized in three different ways: by gravity or natural elevation head, by pumps that produce a pressure head, and by a combination of the first two ways.

Gravity systems are suitable where the water storage reservoir or receiver is high enough above the distribution system to produce the needed pressure at the farthest outlet. The operating cost of a gravity system is lower than that of a pumped system, but the first cost of the former is usually higher. However, the reliability of the gravity system is usually higher because there are fewer parts that may fail.

Pumping systems generally use centrifugal pumps that discharge either directly to the water main or to an elevated tank, a reservoir, or a standpipe. The water then flows from the storage chamber to the distribution system. In general, most sanitary engineers prefer to use a reservoir or storage tank between the pumps and distribution mains because this arrangement provides greater reliability and fewer pressure surges.

Surface reservoirs should store at least a 1-day water supply. Most surface reservoirs are designed to store a supply for 30 days or longer. Elevated tanks should have a capacity of at least 25 gal (94.6 L) of water per person served, *plus* a reserve for fire protection. The capacity of typical elevated tanks ranges from a low of 40,000 gal (151 kL) for a 20-ft (6.1-m) diameter tank to a high of 2,000,000 gal (7.5 ML) for an 80-ft (24.4-m) diameter tank.

Choose the type of distribution system after studying the topography, water demand, and area served. In general, a pumped system is preferred today. To ensure continuity of service, duplicate pumps are generally used.

### 8. Choose the system operating pressure

In domestic water supply, the minimum pressure required at the highest fixture in a building is usually assumed to be 15 lb/sq.in. (103.4 kPa). The maximum pressure allowed at a fixture in a domestic water system is usually 65 lb/sq.in. (448.2 kPa). High-rise buildings (i.e., those above six stories) are generally required to furnish the pressure increase needed to supply water to the upper stories. A pump and overhead storage tank are usually installed in such buildings to provide the needed pressure.

Commercial and industrial buildings require a minimum water pressure of 75 lb/sq.in. (517.1 kPa) at the street level for fire hydrant service. This hydrant should deliver at least 250 gal/min (15.8 L/s) of water for fire-fighting purposes.

Most water-supply systems served by centrifugal pumps in a central pumping station operate in the 100-lb/sq.in. (689.5-kPa) pressure range. In areas of one- and two-story structures, a lower pressure, say 65 lb/sq.in. (448.2 kPa), is permissible. Where the pressure in a system falls too low, auxiliary or booster pumps may be used. These pumps increase the pressure in the main to the desired level.

Choose the system pressure based on the terrain served, quantity of water required, allowable pressure loss, and size of pipe used in the system. Usual pressures required will be in the ranges cited above, although small systems serving one-story residences may operate at pressures as low as 30 lb/sq.in. (206.8 kPa). Pressures over 100 lb/sq.in. (689.5 kPa) are seldom used because heavier piping is required. As a rule, distribution pressures of 50 to 75 lb/sq.in. (344.7 to 517.1 kPa) are acceptable.

### 9. Determine the number of hydrants for fire protection

Table 8 shows the required fire flow, number of standard hose streams of 250 gal/min (15.8 L/s) discharged through a 1 1/8-in. (28.6-mm) diameter smooth nozzle, and the average area served by a hydrant in a high-value district. A standard hydrant may have two or three outlets.

Table 8 indicates that a city of 100,000 persons requires 36 standard hose streams. This means that 36 single-outlet or 18 dual-outlet hydrants are required. More, of course,

**TABLE 8.**    Required Fire Flow and Hydrant Spacing*

| Population | Required fire flow, gal/min (L/s) | Number of standard hose streams | Average area served per hydrant, sq.ft. (m²)† | |
|---|---|---|---|---|
| | | | Direct streams | Engine streams |
| 22,000 | 4,500 (284) | 18 | 55,000 (5,110) | 90,000 (8,361) |
| 28,000 | 5,000 (315) | 20 | 40,000 (3,716) | 85,000 (7,897) |
| 40,000 | 6,000 (379) | 24 | 40,000 (3,716) | 80,000 (7,432) |
| 60,000 | 7,000 (442) | 28 | 40,000 (3,716) | 70,000 (6,503) |
| 80,000 | 8,000 (505) | 32 | 40,000 (3,716) | 60,000 (5,574) |
| 100,000 | 9,000 (568) | 36 | 40,000 (3,716) | 55,000 (5,110) |
| 125,000 | 10,000 (631) | 40 | 40,000 (3,716) | 48,000 (4,459) |
| 150,000 | 11,000 (694) | 44 | 40,000 (3,716) | 43,000 (3,995) |
| 200,000 | 12,000 (757) | 48 | 40,000 (3,716) | 40,000 (3,716) |

*National Board of Fire Underwriters.
†High-value districts.

could be used if better protection were desired in the area. Note that the required fire flow listed in Table 8 agrees closely with that computed in step 2 above.

**Related Calculations.** Use this general method for any water-supply system, municipal or industrial. Note, however, that the required fire-protection quantities vary from one type of municipal area to another and among different industrial exposures. Refer to *NFPA Handbook of Fire Protection*, available from NFPA, 60 Batterymarch Street, Boston, Massachusetts 02110, for specific fire-protection requirements for a variety of industries. In choosing a water-supply system, the wise designer looks ahead for at least 10 years when the water demand will usually exceed the present demand. Hence, the system may be designed so it is oversized for the present population but just adequate for the future population. The American Society for Testing and Materials (ASTM) publishes comprehensive data giving the usual water requirements for a variety of industries. Table 9 shows a few typical water needs for selected industries.

**TABLE 9.**    Selected Industrial Water and Steam Requirements*

| | Water | Steam |
|---|---|---|
| Air conditioning | 6000 to 15,000 gal (22,700 to 57,000 L) per person per season | . . . |
| Aluminum | 1,920,000 gal/ton (8.0 ML/t) | . . . |
| Cement, portland | 750 gal/ton cement (3129 L/t) | . . . |
| Coal, by-product coke | 1430 to 2800 gal/ton coke (5967 to 11,683 L/t) | 570 to 860 lb/ton (382 to 427 kg/t) |
| Rubber (automotive tire) | . . . | 120 lb (54 kg) per tire |
| Electricity | 80 gal/kW (302 L/kW) of electricity | . . . |

*Courtesy of American Society for Testing and Materials.

To determine the storage capacity required at present, proceed as follows: (1) Compute the flow needed to meet 50 percent of the present domestic daily (that is, 24-h) demand. (2) Compute the 4-h fire demand. (3) Find the sum of (1) and (2).

For this city, procedure (1) = (20,900 gal/min)(60 min/h)(24 h/day)(0.5) = 15,048,000 gal (57.2 ML) with the data computed in step 3. Also procedure (2) = (4 h)(60 min/h)(9200 gal/min) = 2,208,000 gal (8.4 ML), using the data computed in step 2, above. Then, total storage capacity required = 15,048,000 + 2,208,000 = 17,256,000 gal (65.3 ML). Where one or more reliable wells will produce a significant flow for 4 h or longer, the storage capacity can be reduced by the 4-h productive capacity of the wells.

## SELECTION OF TREATMENT METHOD FOR WATER-SUPPLY SYSTEM

Choose a treatment method for a water-supply system for a city having a population of 100,000 persons. The water must be filtered, disinfected, and softened to make it suitable for domestic use.

### Calculation Procedure:

### 1. Compute the domestic water flow rate in the system

When water is treated for domestic consumption, only the drinking water passes through the filtration plant. Fire-protection water is seldom treated unless it is so turbid that it will clog fire pumps or hoses. Assuming that the fire-protection water is acceptable for use without treatment, we consider only the drinking water here.

Use the same method as in steps 1 and 3 of the previous calculation procedure to determine the required domestic water flow of 20,900 gal/min (1318.6 L/s) for this city.

### 2. Select the type of water-treatment system to use

Water supplies are treated by a number of methods including sedimentation, coagulation, filtration, softening, and disinfection. Other treatments include disinfection, taste and odor control, and miscellaneous methods.

Since the water must be filtered, disinfected, and softened, each of these steps must be considered separately.

### 3. Choose the type of filtration to use

*Slow sand filters* operate at an average rate of 3 million gal/(acre·day) [2806.2 L/(m²·day)]. This type of filter removes about 99 percent of the bacterial content of the water and most tastes and odors.

*Rapid sand filters* operate at an average rate of 150 million gal/(acre·day) [1.6 L/(m²·s)]. But the raw water must be treated before it enters the rapid sand filter. This preliminary treatment often includes chemical coagulation and sedimentation. A high percentage of bacterial content—up to 99.98 percent—is removed by the preliminary treatment and the filtration. But color and turbidity removal is not as dependable as with slow sand filters. Table 10 lists the typical limits for certain impurities in water supplies.

The daily water flow rate for this city is, from step 1, (20,900 gal/min)(24 h/day) (60 min/h) = 30,096,000 gal/day (1318.6 L/s). If a slow sand filter were used, the required area would be (30.096 million gal/day)/[3 million gal/(acre·day)] = 10+ acres (40,460 m²).

**TABLE 10.**  Typical Limits for Impurities in Water Supplies

| Impurity | Limit, ppm | Impurity | Limit, ppm |
|---|---|---|---|
| Turbidity | 10 | Iron plus manganese | 0.3 |
| Color | 20 | Magnesium | 125 |
| Lead | 0.1 | Total solids | 500 |
| Fluoride | 1.0 | Total hardness | 100 |
| Copper | 3.0 | Ca + Mg salts | |

A rapid sand filter would require 30.096/150 = 0.2 acre (809.4 m$^2$). Hence, if space were scarce in this city—and it usually is—a rapid sand filter would be used. With this choice of filtration, chemical coagulation and sedimentation are almost a necessity. Hence, these two additional steps would be included in the treatment process.

Table 11 gives pertinent data on both slow and rapid sand filters. These data are useful in filter selection.

### 4. Select the softening process to use

The principal water-softening processes use: (*a*) lime and sodium carbonate followed by sedimentation or filtration, or both, to remove the precipitates and (*b*) zeolites of the sodium type in a pressure filter. Zeolite softening is popular and is widely used in municipal water-supply systems today. Based on its proven usefulness and economy, zeolite softening will be chosen for this installation.

**TABLE 11.**  Typical Sand-Filter Characteristics

| Slow sand filters | |
|---|---|
| Usual filtration rate | 2.5 to 6.0 × 10$^6$ gal/(acre·day) [2339 to 5613 L/(m$^2$·day)] |
| Sand depth | 30 to 36 in. (76 to 91 cm) |
| Sand size | 35 mm |
| Sand uniformity coefficient | 1.75 |
| Water depth | 3 to 5 ft (0.9 to 1.5 m) |
| Water velocity in underdrains | 2 ft/s (0.6 m/s) |
| Cleaning frequency required | 2 to 11 times per year |
| Units required | At least two to permit alternate cleaning |

| Fast sand filters | |
|---|---|
| Usual filtration rate | 100 to 200 × 10$^6$ gal/(acre·day) [24.7 to 49.4 kL/(m$^2$·day)] |
| Sand depth | 30 in. (76 cm) |
| Gravel depth | 18 in. (46 cm) |
| Sand size | 0.4 to 0.5 mm |
| Sand uniformity coefficient | 1.7 or less |
| Units required | At least three to permit cleaning one unit while the other two are operating |

## 5. Select the disinfection method to use

Chlorination by the addition of chlorine to the water is the principal method of disinfection used today. To reduce the unpleasant effects that may result from using chlorine alone, a mixture of chlorine and ammonia, known as chloramine, may be used. The ammonia dosage is generally 0.25 ppm or less. Assume that the chloramine method is chosen for this installation.

## 6. Select the method of taste and odor control

The methods used for taste and odor control are: (*a*) aeration, (*b*) activated carbon, (*c*) prechlorination, and (*d*) chloramine. Aeration is popular for groundwaters containing hydrogen sulfide and odors caused by microscopic organisms.

Activated carbon absorbs impurities that cause tastes, odors, or color, generally, 10 to 20 lb (4.5 to 9.1 kg) of activated carbon per million gallons of water is used, but larger quantities—from 50 to 60 lb (22.7 to 27.2 kg)—may be specified. In recent years, some 2000 municipal water systems have installed activated carbon devices for taste and odor control.

Prechlorination and chloramine are also used in some installations for taste and odor control. Of the two methods, chloramine appears more popular at present.

Based on the data given for this water-supply system, method *b, c,* or *d* would probably be suitable. Because method *b* has proven highly effective, it will be chosen tentatively, pending later investigation of the economic factors.

**Related Calculations.** Use this general procedure to choose the treatment method for all types of water-supply systems where the water will be used for human consumption. Thus, the procedure is suitable for municipal, commercial, and industrial systems.

Hazardous wastes of many types endanger groundwater supplies. One of the most common hazardous wastes is gasoline, which comes from the estimated 120,000 leaking underground gasoline-storage tanks. Major oil companies are replacing leaking tanks with new noncorrosive tanks. But the soil and groundwater must still be cleaned to prevent pollution of drinking-water supplies.

Other contaminants include oily sludges, organic (such as pesticides and dioxins), and nonvolatile organic materials. These present especially challenging removal and disposal problems for engineers, particularly in view of the stringent environmental requirements of almost every community.

A variety of treatment and disposal methods are in the process of development and application. For oily waste handling, one process combines water evaporation and solvent extraction to break down a wide variety of hazardous waste and sludge from industrial, petroleum-refinery, and municipal-sewage-treatment operations. This process typically produces dry solids with less than 0.5 percent residual hydrocarbon content. This meets EPA regulations for nonhazardous wastes with low heavy-metal contents.

Certain organics, such as pesticides and dioxins, are hydrophobic. Liquified propane and butane are effective at separating hydrophobic organics from solid particles in tainted sludges and soils. The second treatment method uses liquified propane to remove organics from contaminated soil. Removal efficiencies reported are: polychlorinated biphenyls (PCBs) 99.9 percent; polyaromatic hydrocarbons (PAHs) 99.5 percent; dioxins 97.4 percent; total petroleum hydrocarbons 99.9 percent. Such treated solids meet EPA land-ban regulations for solids disposal.

Nonvolatile organic materials at small sites can be removed by a mobile treatment system using up to 14 solvents. Both hydrophobic and hydrophilic solvents are used; all are nontoxic; several have Food and Drug Administration (FDA) approval as food additives. Used at three different sites (at this writing) the process reduced PCB concentration from 500 to 1500 ppm to less than 100 ppm; at another site PCB concentration was reduced from an average of 30 to 300 ppm to less than 5 ppm; at the third site PCBs were reduced from 40 ppm to less than 3 ppm.

## STORM-WATER RUNOFF RATE AND RAINFALL INTENSITY

What is the storm-water runoff rate from a 40-acre (1.6-km$^2$) industrial site having an imperviousness of 50 percent if the time of concentration is 15 min? What would be the effect of planting a lawn over 75 percent of the site?

### Calculation Procedure:

#### 1. Compute the hourly rate of rainfall

Two common relations, called the *Talbot formulas*, used to compute the hourly rate of rainfall $R$ in./h are $R = 360/(t + 30)$ for the heaviest storms and $R = 105/(t + 15)$ for ordinary storms, where $t$ = time of concentration, min. Using the equation for the heaviest storms because this relation gives a larger flow rate and produces a more conservative design, we see $R = 360/(15 + 30) = 8$ in./h (0.05 mm/s).

#### 2. Compute the storm-water runoff rate

Apply the *rational method* to compute the runoff rate. This method uses the relation $Q = AIR$, where $Q$ = storm-water runoff rate, ft$^3$/s; $A$ = area served by sewer, acres; $I$ = coefficient of runoff or percentage of imperviousness of the area; other symbols as before. So $Q = (40)(0.50)(8) = 160$ ft$^3$/s (4.5 m$^3$/s).

#### 3. Compute the effect of changed imperviousness

Planting a lawn on a large part of the site will increase the imperviousness of the soil. This means that less rainwater will reach the sewer because the coefficient of imperviousness of a lawn is lower. Table 12 lists typical coefficients of imperviousness for various surfaces. This tabulation shows that the coefficient for lawns varies from 0.05 to 0.25. Using a value of $I = 0.10$ for the $40(0.75) = 30$ acres of lawn, we have $Q = (30)(0.10)(8) = 24$ ft$^3$/s (0.68 m$^3$/s).

**TABLE 12.**   Coefficient of Runoff for Various Surfaces

| Surface | Coefficient |
|---|---|
| Parks, gardens, lawns, meadows | 0.05–0.25 |
| Gravel roads and walks | 0.15–0.30 |
| Macadamized roadways | 0.25–0.60 |
| Inferior block pavements with uncemented joints | 0.40–0.50 |
| Stone, brick, and wood-block pavements with tightly cemented joints | 0.75–0.85 |
| Same with uncemented joints | 0.50–0.70 |
| Asphaltic pavements in good condition | 0.85–0.90 |
| Watertight roof surfaces | 0.70–0.95 |

**TABLE 13.** Coefficient of Runoff for Various Areas

| Area | Coefficient |
|---|---|
| Business: | |
|   Downtown | 0.70−0.95 |
|   Neighborhood | 0.50−0.70 |
| Residential: | |
|   Single-family | 0.30−0.50 |
|   Multiunits, detached | 0.40−0.60 |
|   Multiunits, attached | 0.60−0.75 |
| Residential (suburban) | 0.25−0.40 |
| Apartment dwelling | 0.50−0.70 |
| Industrial: | |
|   Light industry | 0.50−0.80 |
|   Heavy industry | 0.60−0.90 |
| Playgrounds | 0.20−0.35 |
| Railroad yards | 0.20−0.40 |
| Unimproved | 0.10−0.30 |

The runoff for the remaining 10 acres (40,460 m$^2$) is, as in step 2, $Q = (10)(0.5)(8) = 40$ ft$^3$/s (1.1 m$^3$/s). Hence, the total runoff is $24 + 40 = 64$ ft$^3$/s (1.8 m$^3$/s). This is $160 − 64 = 96$ ft$^3$/s (2.7 m$^3$/s) less than when the lawn was not used.

**Related Calculations.** The time of concentration for any area being drained by a sewer is the time required for the maximum runoff rate to develop. It is also defined as the time for a drop of water to drain from the farthest point of the watershed to the sewer.

When rainfall continues for an extended period $T$ min, the coefficient of imperviousness changes. For impervious surfaces such as watertight roofs, $I = T/(8 + T)$. For improved pervious surfaces, $I = 0.3T/(20 + T)$. These relations can be used to compute the coefficient in areas of heavy rainfall.

Equations for $R$ for various areas of the United States are available in Steel—*Water Supply and Sewerage*, McGraw-Hill. The Talbot formulas, however, are widely used and have proved reliable.

The time of concentration for a given area can be approximated from $t = I(L/Si^2)^{1/3}$ where $L$ = distance of overland flow of the rainfall from the most remote part of the site, ft; $S$ = slope of the land, ft/ft; $i$ = rainfall intensity, in./h; other symbols as before. For portions of the flow carried in ditches, the time of flow to the inlet can be computed by using the Manning formula.

Table 13 lists the coefficient of runoff for specific types of built-up and industrial areas. Use these coefficients in the same way as shown above. Tables 12 and 13 present data developed by Kuichling and ASCE.

## SIZING SEWER PIPES FOR VARIOUS FLOW RATES

Determine the size, flow rate, and depth of flow from a 1000-ft (304.8-m) long sewer which slopes 5 ft (1.5 m) between inlet and outlet and which must carry a flow of 5 million gal/day (219.1 L/s). The sewer will flow about half full. Will this sewer provide the desired flow rate?

## Calculation Procedure:

### 1. Compute the flow rate in the half-full sewer
A flow of 1 million gal/day = 1.55 ft³/s (0.04 m³/s). Hence, a flow of 5 million gal/day = 5(1.55) = 7.75 ft³/s (219.1 L/s) in a *half-full* sewer.

### 2. Compute the full-sewer flow rate
In a *full sewer*, the flow rate is twice that in a half-full sewer, or 2(7.75) = 15.50 ft³/s (0.44 m³/s) for this sewer. This is equivalent to 15.50/1.55 = 10 million gal/day (438.1 L/s). Full-sewer flow rates are used because pipes are sized on the basis of being full of liquid.

### 3. Compute the sewer-pipe slope
The pipe slope $S$ ft/ft = $(E_i - E_0)/L$, where $E_i$ = inlet elevation, ft above the site datum; $E_o$ = outlet elevation, ft above site datum; $L$ = pipe length between inlet and outlet, ft. Substituting gives $S$ = 5/1000 = 0.005 ft/ft (0.005 in./in.).

### 4. Determine the pipe size to use
The Manning formula $v = (1.486/n)R^{2/3}S^{1/2}$ is often used for sizing sewer pipes. In this formula, $v$ = flow velocity, ft/s; $n$ = a factor that is a function of the pipe roughness; $R$ = pipe hydraulic radius = 0.25 pipe diameter, ft; $S$ = pipe slope, ft/ft. Table 14 lists values of $n$ for various types of sewer pipe. In sewer design, the value $n$ = 0.013 for pipes flowing full.

Since the Manning formula is complex, numerous charts have been designed to simplify its solution. Figure 12 is one such typical chart designed specifically for sewers.

Enter Fig. 12 at 15.5 ft³/s (0.44 m³/s) on the left, and project through the slope ratio of 0.005. On the central scale between the flow rate and slope scales, read the *next larger* standard sewer-pipe diameter as 24 in. (610 mm). When using this chart, always read the next larger pipe size.

### 5. Determine the fluid flow velocity
Continue the solution line of step 4 to read the fluid flow velocity as 5 ft/s (1.5 m/s) on the extreme right-hand scale of Fig. 12. This is for a sewer flowing *full*.

**TABLE 14.** Values of $n$ for the Manning Formula

| Type of surface of pipe | $n$ |
|---|---|
| Ditches and rivers, rough bottoms with much vegetation | 0.040 |
| Ditches and rivers in good condition with some stones and weeds | 0.030 |
| Smooth earth or firm gravel | 0.020 |
| Rough brick; tuberculated iron pipe | 0.017 |
| Vitrified tile and concrete pipe poorly jointed and unevenly settled; average brickwork | 0.015 |
| Good concrete; riveted steel pipe; well-laid vitrified tile or brickwork | 0.013* |
| Cast-iron pipe of ordinary roughness; unplaned timber | 0.012 |
| Smoothest pipes; neat cement | 0.010 |
| Well-planed timber evenly laid | 0.009 |

*Probably the most frequently used value.

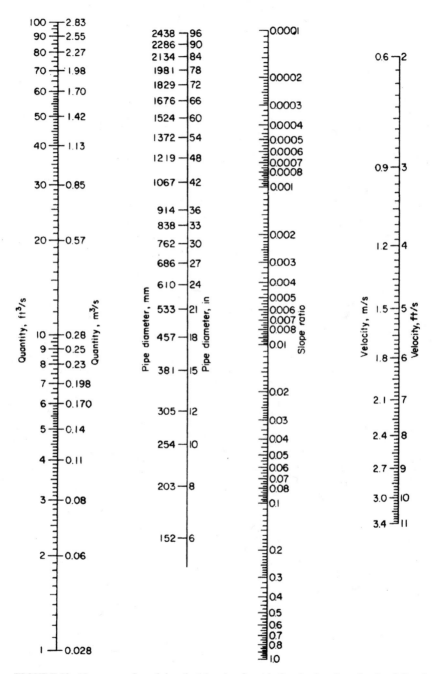

**FIGURE 12.** Nomogram for solving the Manning formula for circular pipes flowing full and $n = 0.013$.

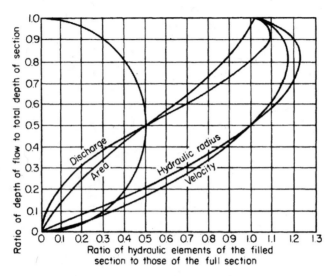

**FIGURE 13.** Hydraulic elements of a circular pipe.

### 6. *Compute the half-full flow depth*

Determine the full-flow capacity of this 24-in. (610-mm) sewer by entering Fig. 12 at the slope ratio, 0.005, and projecting through the pipe diameter, 24 in. (610 mm). At the left read the full-flow capacity as 16 ft³/s (0.45 m³/s).

The required half-flow capacity is 7.75 ft³/s (0.22 m³/s), from step 1. Determine the ratio of the required half-flow capacity to the full-flow capacity, both expressed in ft³/s. Or 7.75/16.0 = 0.484.

Enter Fig. 13 on the bottom at 0.484, and project vertically upward to the discharge curve. From the intersection, project horizontally to the left to read the depth-of-flow ratio as 0.49. This means that the depth of liquid in the sewer at a flow of 7.75 ft³/s (0.22 m³/s) is 0.49(24 in.) = 11.75 in. (29.8 cm). Hence, the sewer will be just slightly less than half full when handling the designed flow quantity.

### 7. *Compute the half-full flow velocity*

Project horizontally to the right along the previously found 0.49 depth-of-flow ratio until the velocity curve is intersected. From this intersection, project vertically downward to the bottom scale to read the ratio of hydraulic elements as 0.99. Hence, the fluid velocity when flowing half-full is 0.99(5.0 ft/s) = 4.95 ft/s (1.5 m/s).

**Related Calculations.** The minimum flow velocity required in sanitary sewers is 2 ft/s (0.6 m/s). At 2 ft/s (0.6 m/s), solids will not settle out of the fluid. Since the velocity in this sewer is 4.95 ft/s (1.5 m/s), as computed in step 7, the sewer meets, and exceeds, the minimum required flow velocity.

Certain localities have minimum slope requirements for sanitary sewers. The required slope produces a minimum flow velocity of 2 ft/s (0.6 m/s) with an *n* value of 0.013.

Storm sewers handling rainwater and other surface drainage require a higher flow velocity than sanitary sewers because sand and grit often enter a storm sewer. The usual minimum allowable velocity for a storm sewer is 2.5 ft/s (0.76 m/s); where possible, the sewer should be designed for 3.0 ft/s (0.9 m/s). If the sewer designed above were used for storm service, it would be acceptable because the fluid velocity is 4.95 ft/s (1.5 m/s). To prevent excessive wear of the sewer, the fluid velocity should not exceed 8 ft/s (2.4 m/s).

Note that Figs. 12 and 13 can be used whenever two variables are known. When a sewer flows at 0.8, or more, full, the partial-flow diagram, Fig. 13, may not give accurate results, especially at high flow velocities.

## SEWER-PIPE EARTH LOAD AND BEDDING REQUIREMENTS

A 36-in. (914-mm) diameter clay sewer pipe is placed in a 15-ft (4.5-m) deep trench in damp sand. What is the earth load on this sewer pipe? What bedding should be used for the pipe? If a 5-ft (1.5-m) wide drainage trench weighing 2000 lb/ft (2976.3 kg/m) of length crosses the sewer pipe at right angles to the pipe, what load is transmitted to the pipe? The bottom of the flume is 11 ft (3.4 m) above the top of the sewer pipe.

### Calculation Procedure:

### 1. Compute the width of the pipe trench
Compute the trench width from $w = 1.5d + 12$, where $w$ = trench width, in.; $d$ = sewer-pipe diameter, in. So $w = 1.5(36) + 12 = 66$ in. (167.6 cm), or 5 ft 6 in. (1.7 m).

### 2. Compute the trench depth-to-width ratio
To determine this ratio, subtract the pipe diameter from the depth and divide the result by the trench width. Or, $(15 - 3)/5.5 = 2.18$.

### 3. Compute the load on the pipe
Use the relation $L = kWw^2$, where $L$ = pipe load, lb/lin ft of trench; $k$ = a constant from Table 15; $W$ = weight of the fill material used in the trench, lb/ft$^3$ other symbol as before.

**TABLE 15.** Values of $k$ for Use in the Pipe Load Equation*

| Ratio of trench depth to width | Sand and damp topsoil | Saturated topsoil | Damp clay | Saturated clay |
|---|---|---|---|---|
| 0.5 | 0.46 | 0.46 | 0.47 | 0.47 |
| 1.0 | 0.85 | 0.86 | 0.88 | 0.90 |
| 1.5 | 1.18 | 1.21 | 1.24 | 1.28 |
| 2.0 | 1.46 | 1.50 | 1.56 | 1.62 |
| 2.5 | 1.70 | 1.76 | 1.84 | 1.92 |
| 3.0 | 1.90 | 1.98 | 2.08 | 2.20 |
| 3.5 | 2.08 | 2.17 | 2.30 | 2.44 |
| 4.0 | 2.22 | 2.33 | 2.49 | 2.66 |
| 4.5 | 2.34 | 2.47 | 2.65 | 2.87 |
| 5.0 | 2.45 | 2.59 | 2.80 | 3.03 |
| 5.5 | 2.54 | 2.69 | 2.93 | 3.19 |
| 6.0 | 2.61 | 2.78 | 3.04 | 3.33 |
| 6.5 | 2.68 | 2.86 | 3.14 | 3.46 |
| 7.0 | 2.73 | 2.93 | 3.22 | 3.57 |
| 7.5 | 2.78 | 2.98 | 3.30 | 3.67 |

*Iowa State Univ. Eng. Exp. Sta. Bull. 47.

**TABLE 16.**   Weight of Pipe-Trench Fill

| Fill | lb/ft³ | kg/m³ |
|---|---|---|
| Dry sand | 100 | 1601 |
| Damp sand | 115 | 1841 |
| Wet sand | 120 | 1921 |
| Damp clay | 120 | 1921 |
| Saturated clay | 130 | 2081 |
| Saturated topsoil | 115 | 1841 |
| Sand and damp topsoil | 100 | 1601 |

Enter Table 15 at the depth-to-width ratio of 2.18. Since this particular value is not tabulated, use the next higher value, 2.5. Opposite this, read $k = 1.70$ for a sand filling.

Enter Table 16 at damp sand, and read the weight as 115 lb/ft³ (1842.1 kg/m³). With these data the pipe load relation can be solved.

Substituting in $L = kWw^2$, we get $L = 1.70(115)(5.5)^2 = 5920$ lb/ft (86.4 N/mm). Study of the properties of clay pipe (Table 17) shows that 36-in. (914-mm) extra-strength clay pipe has a minimum average crushing strength of 6000 lb (26.7 kN) by the three-edge-bearing method.

### 4. Apply the loading safety factor

ASTM recommends a factor of safety of 1.5 for clay sewers. To apply this factor of safety, divide it into the tabulated three-edge-bearing strength found in step 3. Or, 6000/1.5 = 4000 lb (17.8 kN).

### 5. Compute the pipe load-to-strength ratio

Use the strength found in step 4. Or pipe load-to-strength ratio (also called the *load factor*) = 5920/4000 = 1.48.

**TABLE 17.**   Clay Pipe Strength

| Pipe size, in. (mm) | Minimum average strength, lb/lin ft (N/mm) | |
|---|---|---|
| | Three-edge-bearing | Sand-bearing |
| 4 (102) | 1000 (14.6) | 1500 (21.9) |
| 6 (152) | 1100 (16.1) | 1650 (24.1) |
| 8 (203) | 1300 (18.9) | 1950 (28.5) |
| 10 (254) | 1400 (20.4) | 2100 (30.7) |
| 12 (305) | 1500 (21.9) | 2250 (32.9) |
| 15 (381) | 1750 (25.6) | 2625 (38.3) |
| 18 (457) | 2000 (29.2) | 3000 (43.8) |
| 21 (533) | 2200 (32.1) | 3300 (48.2) |
| 24 (610) | 2400 (35.0) | 3600 (52.6) |
| 27 (686) | 2750 (40.2) | 4125 (60.2) |
| 30 (762) | 3200 (46.7) | 4800 (70.1) |
| 33 (838) | 3500 (51.1) | 5250 (76.7) |
| 36 (914) | 3900 (56.9) | 5850 (85.4) |

### 6. Select the bedding method for the pipe

Figure 14 shows methods for bedding sewer pipe and the strength developed. Thus, earth embedment, type 2 bedding, develops a load factor of 1.5. Since the computed load factor, step 5, is 1.48, this type of bedding is acceptable. (In choosing a type of bedding be certain that the load factor of the actual pipe is less than, or equals, the developed load factor for the three-edge-bearing strength.)

The type 2 earth embedment, Fig. 14, is a highly satisfactory method, except that the shaping of the lower part of the trench to fit the pipe may be expensive. Type 3 granular embedment may be less expensive, particularly if the crushed stone, gravel, or shell is placed by machine.

### 7. Compute the direct load transmitted to the sewer pipe

The weight of the drainage flume is carried by the soil over the sewer pipes. Hence, a portion of this weight may reach the sewer pipe. To determine how much of the flume weight

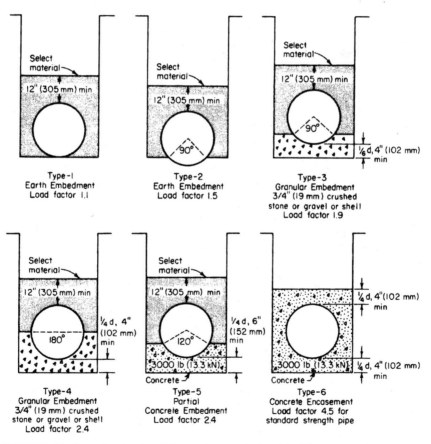

**FIGURE 14.** Strengths developed for various methods of bedding sewer pipes. (*W. S. Dickey Clay Manufacturing Co.*)

**TABLE 18.**  Proportion of Short Loads Reaching Pipe in Trenches

| Depth-to-width ratio | Sand and damp topsoil | Saturated topsoil | Damp clay | Saturated clay |
|---|---|---|---|---|
| 0.0 | 1.00 | 1.00 | 1.00 | 1.00 |
| 0.5 | 0.77 | 0.78 | 0.79 | 0.81 |
| 1.0 | 0.59 | 0.61 | 0.63 | 0.66 |
| 1.5 | 0.46 | 0.48 | 0.51 | 0.54 |
| 2.0 | 0.35 | 0.38 | 0.40 | 0.44 |
| 2.5 | 0.27 | 0.29 | 0.32 | 0.35 |
| 3.0 | 0.21 | 0.23 | 0.25 | 0.29 |
| 4.0 | 0.12 | 0.14 | 0.16 | 0.19 |
| 5.0 | 0.07 | 0.09 | 0.10 | 0.13 |
| 6.0 | 0.04 | 0.05 | 0.06 | 0.08 |
| 8.0 | 0.02 | 0.02 | 0.03 | 0.04 |
| 10.0 | 0.01 | 0.01 | 0.01 | 0.02 |

reaches the pipe, find the weight of the flume per foot of width, or 2000 lb/5 ft = 400 lb/ft (5.84 kN/mm) of width.

Since the pipe trench is 5.5 ft (1.7 m) wide, step 1, the 1-ft (0.3-m) wide section of the flume imposes a total load of 5.5(400) = 2200 lb (9.8 kN) on the soil beneath it.

To determine what portion of the flume load reaches the sewer pipe, compute the ratio of the depth of the flume bottom to the width of the sewer-pipe trench, or 11/5.5 = 2.0.

Enter Table 18 at a value of 2.0, and read the load proportion for sand and damp topsoil as 0.35. Hence, the load of the flume reaching each foot of sewer pipe is 0.35(2200) = 770 lb (3.4 kN).

**Related Calculations.**  A load such as that in step 7 is termed a *short load*; i.e., it is shorter than the pipe-trench width. Typical short loads result from automobile and truck traffic, road rollers, building foundations, etc. *Long loads* are imposed by weights that are longer than the trench is wide. Typical long loads are stacks of lumber, steel, and poles,

**TABLE 19.**  Proportion of Long Loads Reaching Pipe in Trenches

| Depth-to-width ratio | Sand and damp topsoil | Saturated topsoil | Damp yellow clay | Saturated yellow clay |
|---|---|---|---|---|
| 0.0 | 1.00 | 1.00 | 1.00 | 1.00 |
| 0.5 | 0.85 | 0.86 | 0.88 | 0.89 |
| 1.0 | 0.72 | 0.75 | 0.77 | 0.80 |
| 1.5 | 0.61 | 0.64 | 0.67 | 0.72 |
| 2.0 | 0.52 | 0.55 | 0.59 | 0.64 |
| 2.5 | 0.44 | 0.48 | 0.52 | 0.57 |
| 3.0 | 0.37 | 0.41 | 0.45 | 0.51 |
| 4.0 | 0.27 | 0.31 | 0.35 | 0.41 |
| 5.0 | 0.19 | 0.23 | 0.27 | 0.33 |
| 6.0 | 0.14 | 0.17 | 0.20 | 0.26 |
| 8.0 | 0.07 | 0.09 | 0.12 | 0.17 |
| 10.0 | 0.04 | 0.05 | 0.07 | 0.11 |

and piles of sand, coal, gravel, etc. Table 19 shows the proportion of long loads transmitted to buried pipes. Use the same procedure as in step 7 to compute the load reaching the buried pipe.

When a sewer pipe is placed on undisturbed ground and covered with fill, compute the load on the pipe from $L = kWd^2$, where $d$ = pipe diameter, ft; other symbols as in step 3. Tables 18 and 19 are the work of Prof. Anson Marston, Iowa State University.

To find the total load on trenched or surface-level buried pipes subjected to both fill and long or short loads, add the proportion of the long or short load reaching the pipe to the load produced by the fill.

Note that sewers may have several cross-sectional shapes—circular, egg, rectangular, square, etc. The circular sewer is the most common because it has a number of advantages, including economy. Egg-shaped sewers are not as popular as circular and are less often used today because of their higher costs.

Rectangular and square sewers are often used for storm service. However, their hydraulic characteristics are not as desirable as circular sewers.

## STORM-SEWER INLET SIZE AND FLOW RATE

What size storm-sewer inlet is required to handle a flow of 2 ft$^3$/s (0.057 m$^3$/s) if the gutter is sloped $^1/_4$ in./ft (2.1 cm/m) across the inlet and 0.05 in./ft (0.4 cm/m) along the length of the inlet? The maximum depth of flow in the gutter is estimated to be 0.2 ft (0.06 m), and the gutter is depressed 4 in. (102 mm) below the normal street level.

### Calculation Procedure:

#### 1. Compute the reciprocal of the gutter transverse slope
The *transverse slope* of the gutter across the inlet is $^1/_4$ in./ft (2.1 cm/m). Expressing the reciprocal of this slope as $r$, compute the value for this gutter as $r = 4 \times 12/1 = 48$.

#### 2. Determine the inlet capacity per foot of length
Enter Table 20 at the flow depth of 0.2 ft (0.06 m), and project to the depth of depression of the gutter of 4 in. (102 mm). Opposite this depth, read the inlet capacity per foot of length as 0.50 ft$^3$/s (0.014 m$^3$/s).

#### 3. Compute the required gutter inlet length
The gutter must handle a maximum flow of 2 ft$^3$/s (0.057 m$^3$/s). Since the inlet has a capacity of 0.50 ft$^3$/(s·ft) [0.047 m$^3$/(m·s)] of length, the required length, ft = maximum required capacity, ft$^3$/s/capacity per foot, ft$^3$/s = 2.0/0.50 = 4.0 ft (1.2 m). A length of 4.0 ft (1.2 m) will be satisfactory. Were a length of 4.2 or 4.4 ft (1.28 or 1.34 m) required, a 4.5-ft (1.37-m) long inlet would be chosen. The reasoning behind the choice of a longer length is that the extra initial investment for the longer length is small compared with the extra capacity obtained.

#### 4. Determine how far the water will extend from the curb
Use the relation $l = rd$, where $l$ = distance water will extend from the curb, ft; $d$ = depth of water in the gutter at the curb line, ft; other symbols as before. Substituting, we find $l = 48(0.2) = 9.6$ ft (2.9 m). This distance is acceptable because the water would extend out this far only during the heaviest storms.

**Related Calculations.** To compute the flow rate in a gutter, use the relation $F = 0.56(r/n)s^{0.5}d^{8/3}$, where $F$ = flow rate in gutter, ft$^3$/s; $n$ = roughness coefficient, usually

**TABLE 20.**  Storm-Sewer Inlet Capacity per Foot (Meter) of Length

| Flow depth in gutter, ft (mm) | Depression depth, in. (mm) | Capacity per foot length, ft³/s (m³/s) |
|---|---|---|
| 0.2 (0.06) | 0  (0) | 0.062  (5.76) |
| | 1  (25.4) | 0.141 (13.10) |
| | 2  (50.8) | 0.245 (22.76) |
| | 3  (76.2) | 0.358 (33.26) |
| | 4 (101.6) | 0.500 (46.46) |
| 0.3 (0.09) | 0  (0) | 0.115 (10.69) |
| | 1  (25.4) | 0.205 (19.05) |
| | 2  (50.8) | 0.320 (29.73) |
| | 3  (76.2) | 0.450 (41.81) |
| | 4 (101.6) | 0.590 (54.82) |

taken as 0.015; $s$ = gutter slope, in./ft; other symbols as before. Where the computed inlet length is 5 ft (1.5 m) or more, some engineers assume that a portion of the water will pass the first inlet and enter the next one along the street.

## STORM-SEWER DESIGN

Design a storm-sewer system for a 30-acre ($1.21 \times 10^5$-m²) residential area in which the storm-water runoff rate is computed to be 24 ft³/s (0.7 m³/s). The total area is divided into 10 plots of equal area having similar soil and runoff conditions.

### Calculation Procedure:

#### 1. Sketch a plan of the sewer system
Sketch the area and the 10 plots as in Fig. 15. A scale of 1 in. = 100 ft (1 cm = 12 m) is generally suitable. Indicate the terrain elevations by drawing the profile curves on the plot plan. Since the profiles (Fig. 15) show that the terrain slopes from north to south, the main sewer can probably be best run from north to south. The sewer would also slope downward from north to south, following the general slope of the terrain.

Indicate a storm-water inlet for each of the areas served by the sewer. With the terrain sloping from north to south, each inlet will probably give best service if it is located on the southern border of the plot.

Since the plots are equal in area, the main sewer can be run down the center of the plot with each inlet feeding into it. Use arrows to indicate the flow direction in the laterals and main sewer.

#### 2. Compute the lateral sewer size
Each lateral sewer handles 24 ft³/s/10 plots = 2.4 ft³/s (0.07 m³/s) of storm water. Size each lateral, using the Manning formula with $n$ = 0.013 and full flow in the pipe. Assume a slope ratio of 0.05 for each inlet pipe between the inlet and the main sewer. This means

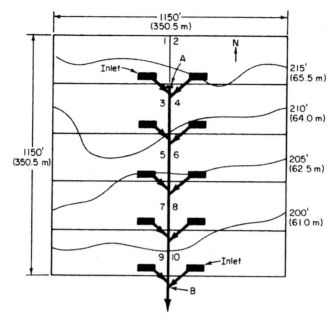

**FIGURE 15.** Typical storm-sewer plot plan and layout diagram.

that the inlet pipe will slope 1 ft in 20 ft (0.3 m in 6.1 m) of length. In an installation such as this, a slope ratio of 0.05 is adequate.

By using Fig. 12 for a flow of 2.4 ft³/s (0.0679 m³/s) and a slope of 0.05, an 8-in. (203-mm) pipe is required for each lateral. The fluid velocity is, from Fig. 12, 7.45 ft/s (2.27 m/s). This is a high enough velocity to prevent solids from settling out of the water. [The flow velocity should not be less than 2 ft/s (0.61 m/s).]

### 3. Compute the size of the main sewer

There are four sections of the main sewer (Fig. 15). The first section, section 3-4, serves the two northernmost plots. Since the flow from each plot is 2.4 ft³/s (0.0679 m³/s), the storm water that this portion of the main sewer must handle is 2(2.4) = 4.8 ft³/s (0.14 m³/s).

The main sewer begins at point $A$, which has an elevation of about 213 ft (64.9 m), as shown by the profile. At point $B$ the terrain elevation is about 190 ft (57.8 m). Hence, the slope between points $A$ and $B$ is about 213 − 190 = 23 ft (7.0 m), and the distance between the two points is about 920 ft (280.4 m).

Assume a slope of 1 ft/100 ft (0.3 m/30.5 m) of length, or 1/100 = 0.01 for the main sewer. This is a typical slope used for main sewers, and it is within the range permitted by a pipe run along the surface of this terrain. Table 21 shows the minimum slope required to produce a flow velocity of 2 ft/s (0.61 m/s).

Using Fig. 12 for a flow of 4.8 ft³/s (0.14 m³/s) and a slope of 0.01, we see the required size for section 3-4 of the main sewer is 15 in. (381 mm). The flow velocity in the pipe is 4.88 ft/s (1.49 m/s). The size of this sewer is in keeping with general design practice, which seldom uses a storm sewer less than 12 in. (304.8 mm) in diameter.

**TABLE 21.**   Minimum Slope of Sewers*

| Sewer diameter, in. (mm) | Minimum slope, ft/ 100 ft (m/30.5 m) of length |
|---|---|
| 4 (102) | 1.20 (0.366) |
| 6 (152) | 0.60 (0.183) |
| 8 (203) | 0.40 (0.122) |
| 10 (254) | 0.29 (0.088) |
| 12 (305) | 0.22 (0.067) |
| 15 (381) | 0.15 (0.046) |
| 18 (457) | 0.12 (0.037) |
| 20 (505) | 0.10 (0.030) |
| 24 (610) | 0.08 (0.024) |

*Based on the Manning formula with $n = 0.13$ and the sewer flowing either full or half full.

Section 5-6 conveys 9.6 ft³/s (0.27 m³/s). Using Fig. 12 again, we find the required pipe size is 18 in. (457.2 mm) and the flow velocity is 5.75 ft/s (1.75 m/s). Likewise, section 7-8 must handle 14.4 ft³/s (0.41 m³/s). The required pipe size is 21 in. (533 mm), and the flow velocity in the pipe is 6.35 ft/s (1.94 m/s). Section 9-10 of the main sewer handles 19.2 ft³/s (0.54 m³/s), and must be 24 in. (609.6 mm) in diameter. The velocity in this section of the sewer pipe will be 6.9 ft/s (2.1 m/s). The last section of the main sewer handles the total flow, or 24 ft³/s (0.7 m³/s). Its size must be 27 in. (686 mm), Fig. 12, although a 24-in. (610.0-mm) pipe would suffice if the slope at point B could be increased to 0.012.

**Related Calculations.** Most new sewers built today are the *separate* type, i.e., one sewer for sanitary service and another sewer for storm service. Sanitary sewers are usually installed first because they are generally smaller than storm sewers and cost less. *Combined sewers* handle both sanitary and storm flows and are used where expensive excavation for underground sewers is necessary. Many older cities have combined sewers.

To size a combined sewer, compute the sum of the maximum sanitary and stormwater flow for each section of the sewer. Then use the method given in this procedure after having assumed a value for n in the Manning formula and for the slope of the sewer main.

Where a continuous slope cannot be provided for a sewer main, a pumping station to lift the sewage must be installed. Most cities require one or more pumping stations because the terrain does not permit an unrestricted slope for the sewer mains. Motor-driven centrifugal pumps are generally used to handle sewage. For unscreened sewage, the suction inlet of the pump should not be less than 3 in. (76 mm) in diameter.

*New Developments.*   Water supply and storm-water system design are at the center of great technological and regulatory change. Engineering is being reinvented to meet changing demands, focusing on environmental impact and on securing water supplies and facilities against acts of terrorism or natural disasters.

There is greater emphasis today on advanced storm-water systems and risk assessment for water reuse. New productivity-enhancing water treatment methodologies include membrane filtration, heat drying, UV disinfection, zero discharge (ZD) design, and the application of Geographic Information Systems (GIS) to water supply and storm-water engineering.

To harden water facilities against potential terrorist acts, engineers are developing new, more secure water supply systems, as well as impact-resistant and fire-resistant materials as part of an overall safe design against impact and heat damage.

Engineers have developed a better understanding of existing operations and processes. New best practices have been developed for engineering, building, and running effective public water utilities. Particular attention is paid to upgrading storm-water system design and performance of existing, outdated systems. In addition, engineers today receive a better education in the vital fields of engineering economics and finance.

Further considerations emerging in recent years include storm-water system design for changing urban environments and the design of berms and levees to withstand worst-case events such as damaging hurricanes and severe flooding.

Engineers today have greater concern for the long-term health and environmental impacts of water systems. Most of these changes have come about out of necessity. Hence, there is increasing emphasis on the application of advanced tools such as GIS and ZD design, which makes this a challenging and rewarding field to be in.

# SECTION 8

# SANITARY WASTEWATER TREATMENT AND CONTROL

## KEVIN D. WILLS, M.S.E., P.E.
*Consulting Engineer*
*Stanley Consultants, Inc.*

## DESIGN OF A COMPLETE-MIX ACTIVATED SLUDGE REACTOR

Domestic wastewater with an average daily flow of 4.0 Mgd (15,140 m$^3$/d) has a five day Biochemical Oxygen Demand (BOD$_5$) of 240 mg/L after primary settling. The effluent is to have a BOD$_5$ of 10 mg/L or less. Design a complete-mix activated sludge reactor to treat the wastewater including reactor volume, hydraulic retention time, quantity of sludge wasted, oxygen requirements, food to microorganism ratio, volumetric loading, and WAS and RAS requirements.

**Calculation Procedure:**

## 1. *Compute the reactor volume*

The volume of the reactor can be determined using the following equation derived from Monod kinetics:

$$V_r = \frac{\theta_c QY(S_o - S)}{X_a (1 + k_d\theta_c)}$$

where $V_r$ = Reactor volume (Mgal) (m³)

$\theta_c$ = Mean cell residence time, or the average time that the sludge remains in the reactor (sludge age). For a complete-mix activated sludge process, $\theta_c$ ranges from 5 to 15 days. The design of the reactor is based on $\theta_c$ on the assumption that substantially all the substrate (BOD) conversion occurs in the reactor. A $\theta_c$ of 8 days will be assumed.

$Q$ = Average daily influent flow rate (Mgd) = 4.0 Mgd (15,140 m³/d)

$Y$ = Maximum yield coefficient (mg VSS/mg BOD₅). For the activated sludge process for domestic wastewater $Y$ ranges from 0.4 to 0.8. A $Y$ of 0.6 mg VSS/mg BOD₅ will be assumed. Essentially, $Y$ represents the maximum mg of cells produced per mg organic matter removed.

$S_O$ = Influent substrate (BOD₅) concentration (mg/L) = 240 mg/L

$S$ = Effluent substrate (BOD₅) concentration (mg/L) = 10 mg/L

$X_a$ = Concentration of microorganisms in reactor = Mixed Liquor Volatile Suspended Solids (MLVSS) in mg/L. It is generally accepted that the ratio MLVSS/MLSS ≈ 0.8, where MLSS is the Mixed Liquor Suspended Solids concentration in the reactor. MLSS represents the sum of volatile suspended solids (organics) and fixed suspended solids (inorganics). For a complete-mix activated sludge process, MLSS ranges from 1000 to 6500 mg/L. An MLSS of 4500 mg/L will be assumed. = > MLVSS = (0.8)(4500 mg/L) = 3600 mg/L.

$k_d$ = Endogenous decay coefficient ($d^{-1}$) which is a coefficient representing the decrease of cell mass in the MLVSS. The activated sludge process for domestic wastewater $k_d$ ranges from 0.025 to 0.075 $d^{-1}$. A value of 0.06 $d^{-1}$ will be assumed.

Therefore:

$$V_r = \frac{(8\ d)(4.0\ \text{Mgd})(0.6\ \text{mg VSS/mg BOD}_5)(240 - 10)\text{mg/L}}{(3600\ \text{mg/L})[1 + (0.06\ d^{-1})\ (8\ d)]}$$

$$= 0.83\ \text{Mgal} (110,955\ \text{ft}^3)\ (3140\ \text{m}^3)$$

## 2. *Compute the hydraulic retention time*

The hydraulic retention time ($\theta$) in the reactor is the reactor volume divided by the influent flow rate: $V_r/Q$. Therefore, $\theta = (0.83\ \text{Mgal})/(4.0\ \text{Mgd}) = 0.208$ days = 5.0 hours. For a complete-mix activated sludge process, $\theta$ is generally 3−5 hours. Therefore, the hydraulic retention time is acceptable.

## 3. *Compute the quantity of sludge wasted*

The observed cell yield, $Y_{obs} = Y/1 + k_d\theta_c = 0.6/[1 + (0.06\ d^{-1})(8\ d)] = 0.41$ mg/mg represents the actual cell yield that would be observed. The observed cell yield is always less than the maximum cell yield ($Y$).

The increase in MLVSS is computed using the following equation:

$$P_x = Y_{obs}Q(S_O - S)(8.34 \text{ lb/Mgal/mg/L})$$

where $P_x$ is the net waste activated sludge produced each day in (lb VSS/d).
Using values defined above:

$$P_x = \left(0.41 \frac{\text{mg VSS}}{\text{mg BOD}_5}\right)(4.0 \text{ Mgd})\left(240 \frac{\text{mg}}{\text{L}} - 10 \frac{\text{mg}}{\text{L}}\right)\left(8.34 \frac{\text{lb/Mgal}}{\text{mg/L}}\right)$$

$$= 3146 \text{ lb VSS/d} (1428.3 \text{ kg VSS/d})$$

This represents the increase of volatile suspended solids (organics) in the reactor. Of course the total increase in sludge mass will include fixed suspended solids (inorganics) as well. Therefore, the increase in the total mass of mixed liquor suspended solids (MLSS) $= P_{x(ss)} = (3146 \text{ lb VSS/d})/(0.8) = 3933 \text{ lb SS/d} (1785.6 \text{ kg SS/d})$. This represents the total mass of sludge that must be wasted from the system each day.

## 4. Compute the oxygen requirements based on ultimate carbonaceous oxygen demand ($BOD_L$)

The theoretical oxygen requirements are calculated using the $BOD_5$ of the wastewater and the amount of organisms ($P_x$) wasted from the system each day. If all $BOD_5$ were converted to end products, the total oxygen demand would be computed by converting $BOD_5$ to ultimate BOD ($BOD_L$), using an appropriate conversion factor. The "Quantity of Sludge Wasted" calculation illustrated that a portion of the incoming waste is converted to new cells which are subsequently wasted from the system. Therefore, if the $BOD_L$ of the wasted cells is subtracted from the total, the remaining amount represents the amount of oxygen that must be supplied to the system. From stoichiometry, it is known that the $BOD_L$ of one mole of cells is equal to 1.42 times the concentration of cells. Therefore, the theoretical oxygen requirements for the removal of the carbonaceous organic matter in wastewater for an activated-sludge system can be computed using the following equation:

$$\text{lb O}_2/\text{d} = (\text{total mass of BOD}_L \text{ utilized, lb/d})$$
$$- 1.42 (\text{mass of organisms wasted, lb/d})$$

Using terms that have been defined previously where $f$ = conversion factor for converting $BOD_5$ to $BOD_L$ (0.68 is commonly used):

$$\text{lb O}_2/\text{d} = \frac{Q(S_O - S)\left(8.34 \frac{\text{lb/Mgal}}{\text{mg/L}}\right)}{f} - (1.42)(P_x)$$

Using the above quantities:

$$\text{lb O}_2/\text{d} = \frac{(4.0 \text{ Mgd})(240 \text{ mg/L} - 10 \text{ mg/L})(8.34)}{0.68} - (1.42)(3146 \text{ lb/d})$$

$$= 6816 \text{ lb O}_2/\text{d} (3094.5 \text{ kg O}_2/\text{d})$$

This represents the theoretical oxygen requirement for removal of the influent $BOD_5$. However, to meet sustained peak organic loadings, it is recommended that aeration equipment be designed with a safety factor of at least 2. Therefore, in sizing aeration equipment a value of $(2)(6816 \text{ lb O}_2/\text{d}) = 13,632 \text{ lb O}_2/\text{d} \ (6188.9 \text{ kg O}_2/\text{d})$ is used.

### 5. Compute the food to microorganism ratio (F:M) and the volumetric loading ($V_L$)

In order to maintain control over the activated sludge process, two commonly used parameters are (1) the food to microorganism ratio (F:M) and, (2) the mean cell residence time ($\theta_c$). The mean cell residence time was assumed in Part 1 "Compute Reactor Volume" to be 8 days.

The food to microorganism ratio is defined as:

$$\text{F:M} = S_O \theta X_a$$

where F:M is the food to microorganism ratio in $d^{-1}$.

F:M is simply a ratio of the "food" or $BOD_5$ of the incoming waste, to the concentration of "microorganisms" in the aeration tank or MLVSS. Therefore, using values defined previously:

$$\text{F:M} = \frac{240 \text{ mg/L}}{(0.208 \text{ d})(3600 \text{ mg/L})} = 0.321 \ d^{-1}$$

Typical values for F:M reported in literature vary from $0.05 \ d^{-1}$ to $1.0 \ d^{-1}$ depending on the type of treatment process used.

A low value of F:M can result in the growth of filamentous organisms and is the most common operational problem in the activated sludge process. A proliferation of filamentous organisms in the mixed liquor results in a poorly settling sludge, commonly referred to as "bulking sludge."

One method of controlling the growth of filamentous organisms is through the use of a separate compartment as the initial contact zone of a biological reactor where primary effluent and return activated sludge are combined. This concept provides a high F:M at controlled oxygen levels, which provides selective growth of floc forming organisms at the initial stage of the biological process. An F:M ratio of at least $2.27 \ d^{-1}$ in this compartment is suggested in the literature. However, initial F:M ratios ranging from $20-25$ $d^{-1}$ have also been reported.

The volumetric (organic) loading ($V_L$) is defined as:

$$V_L = S_O Q/V_r = S_O/\theta$$

$V_L$ is a measure of the pounds of $BOD_5$ applied daily per thousand cubic feet of aeration tank volume. Using values defined previously:

$$V_L = (240 \text{ mg/L})/(0.208 \ d) = 1154 \text{ mg/L·d} = 72 \text{ lb/10}^3\text{ft}^3\text{·d} \ (1.15 \text{ kg/Mm}^3\text{·d})$$

Volumetric loading can vary from 20 to more than 200 $\text{lb/10}^3\text{ft}^3\text{·d}$ (0.32 to 3.2 $\text{kg/Mm}^3\text{·d}$), and may be used as an alternate (although crude) method of sizing aeration tanks.

### 6. Compute the waste activated sludge (WAS) and return activated sludge (RAS) requirements

Control of the activated sludge process is important to maintain high levels of treatment performance under a wide range of operating conditions. The principle factors used in process control are (1) maintaining dissolved-oxygen levels in the aeration tanks, (2) regulating the amount of Return Activated Sludge (RAS), and (3) controlling the Waste

Activated Sludge (WAS). As outlined previously in step 5 "Compute the Food to Microorganism Ratio and the Volumetric Loading," the most commonly used parameters for controlling the activated sludge process are the F:M ratio and the mean cell residence time ($\theta_c$). The Mixed Liquor Volatile Suspended Solids (MLVSS) concentration may also be used as a control parameter. Return Activated Sludge (RAS) is important in maintaining the MLVSS concentration and the Waste Activated Sludge (WAS) is important in controlling the mean cell residence time ($\theta_c$).

The excess waste activated sludge produced each day (see step 3 "Compute the Quantity of Sludge Wasted") is wasted from the system to maintain a given F:M or mean cell residence time. Generally, sludge is wasted from the return sludge line because it is more concentrated than the mixed liquor in the aeration tank, hence smaller waste sludge pumps are required. The waste sludge is generally discharged to sludge thickening and digestion facilities. The alternative method of sludge wasting is to withdraw mixed liquor directly from the aeration tank where the concentration of solids is uniform. Both methods of calculating the waste sludge flow rate are illustrated below.

Use Figs. 1 and 2 when performing mass balances for the determination of RAS and WAS.

$X =$ Mixed Liquor Suspended Solids (MLSS)—see step 1 "Compute the Reactor Volume."

$Q_r =$ Return Activated Sludge pumping rate (Mgd)

$X_r =$ Concentration of sludge in the return line (mg/L). When lacking site specific operational data, a value commonly assumed is 8000 mg/L.

$Q_e =$ Effluent flow rate (Mgd)

$X_e =$ Concentration of solids in effluent (mg/L). When lacking site specific operational data, this value is commonly assumed to be zero.

$Q_w =$ Waste Activated Sludge (WAS) pumping rate from the reactor (Mgd)

$Q_{w'} =$ Waste Activated Sludge (WAS) pumping rate from the return line (Mgd)

Other variables are as defined previously.

The actual amount of liquid that must be pumped to achieve process control depends on the method used and the location from which the wasting is to be accomplished. Also note that because the solids capture of the sludge processing facilities (i.e., thickeners,

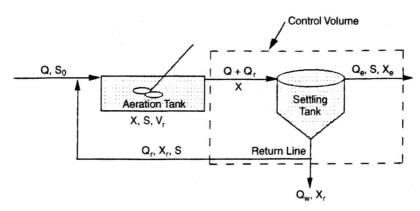

**FIGURE 1.** Settling tank mass balance.

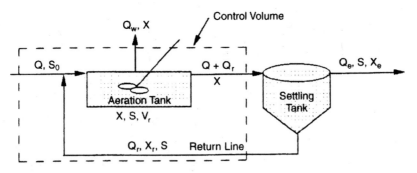

**FIGURE 2.** Aeration tank mass balance.

digesters, etc.) is not 100 percent and some solids are returned, the actual wasting rate will be higher than the theoretically determined value.

(a) *Waste Activated Sludge (WAS) pumping rate from the return line.* If the mean cell residence time is used for process control and the wasting is from the sludge return line (Fig. 1), the wasting rate is computed using the following:

$$\theta_c = \frac{V_r X}{(Q_{w'} X_r + Q_e X_e)}$$

Assuming that the concentration of solids in the effluent from the settling tank ($X_e$) is low, then the above equation reduces to:

$$\theta_c \approx \frac{V_r X}{Q_{w'} X_r} \qquad Q_{w'} = \frac{V_r X}{\theta_c X_r}$$

Using values defined previously:

$$Q_{w'} = \frac{(0.83 \text{ Mgal})(4500 \text{ mg/L})}{(8 \text{ d})(8000 \text{ mg/L})} = 0.0584 \text{ Mgd} = 58,400 \text{ gal/day } (221 \text{ m}^3/\text{d})$$

To determine the WAS pumping rate using this method, the solids concentration in both the aeration tank and the return line must be known.

If the food to microorganism ratio (F:M) method of control is used, the WAS pumping rate from the return line is determined using the following:

$$P_{x(ss)} = Q_{w'} X_r (8.34 \text{ lb/Mgal/mg/L})$$

Therefore:

$$Q_{w'} = \frac{3933 \text{ lb/d}}{(8000 \text{ mg/L})(8.34)} = 0.059 \text{ Mgd} = 59,000 \text{ gal/day } (223.3 \text{ m}^3/\text{d})$$

In this case, the concentration of solids in the sludge return line must be known. Note that regardless of the method used for calculation, if wasting occurs from the return line, the WAS pumping rate is approximately the same.

(b) *Waste Activated Sludge (WAS) pumping rate from the aeration tank.* If the mean cell residence time is used for process control, wasting is from the aeration tank (Fig. 2), and the solids in the plant effluent ($X_e$) are again neglected, then the WAS pumping rate is estimated using the following:

$$\theta_c \approx \frac{V_r}{Q_w} \quad Q_w \approx \frac{V_r}{\theta_c}$$

Using values defined previously:

$$Q_w = \frac{0.83 \text{ Mgal}}{8 \text{ d}} = 0.104 \text{ Mgd} = 104{,}000 \text{ gal/day } (393.6 \text{ m}^3/\text{d})$$

Note that in case (a) or (b) above, the weight of sludge wasted is the same (3933 lb SS/d) (1785.6 kg SS/d), and that either wasting method will achieve a $\theta_c$ of 8 days. As can be seen, wasting from the aeration tank produces a much higher waste flow rate. This is because the concentration of solids in the bottom of the settling tank (and hence the return line) is higher than in the aeration tank. Consequently, wasting a given mass of solids per day is going to require a larger WAS pumping rate (and larger WAS pumps) if done from the aeration tank as opposed to the return line. The Return Activated Sludge (RAS) pumping rate is determined by performing a mass balance analysis around either the settling tank or the aeration tank. The appropriate control volume for either mass balance analysis is illustrated in Figs. 1 and 2, respectively. Assuming that the sludge blanket level in the settling tank remains constant and that the solids in the effluent from the settling tank ($X_e$) are negligible, a mass balance around the settling tank (Fig. 1) yields the following equation for RAS pumping rate:

$$Q_r = \frac{XQ - X_r Q_{w'}}{X_r - X}$$

Using values defined previously, the RAS pumping rate is computed to be

$$Q_r = \frac{(4500 \text{ mg/L})(4.0 \text{ Mgd}) - (8000 \text{ mg/L})(0.0584 \text{ Mgd})}{8000 \text{ mg/L} - 4500 \text{ mg/L}}$$

$$= 5.0 \text{ Mgd } (18{,}925 \text{ m}^3/\text{d})$$

As outlined above, the required RAS pumping rate can also be estimated by performing a mass balance around the aeration tank (Fig. 2). If new cell growth is considered negligible, then the solids entering the tank will equal the solids leaving the tank. Under conditions such as high organic loadings, this assumption may be incorrect. Solids enter the aeration tank in the return sludge and in the influent flow to the secondary process. However, because the influent solids are negligible compared to the MLSS in the return sludge, the mass balance around the aeration tank yields the following equation for RAS pumping rate:

$$Q_r = \frac{X(Q - Q_w)}{X_r - X}$$

Using values defined previously, the RAS pumping rate is computed to be

$$Q_r = \frac{(4500 \text{ mg/L})(4.0 \text{ Mgd} - 0.104 \text{ Mgd})}{8000 \text{ mg/L} - 4500 \text{ mg/L}} = 5.0 \text{ Mgd } (18,925 \text{ m}^3/\text{d})$$

The ratio of RAS pumping rate to influent flow rate, or recirculation ratio ($\alpha$), may now be calculated:

$$\alpha = \frac{Q_r}{Q} = \frac{5.0 \text{ Mgd}}{4.0 \text{ Mgd}} = 1.25$$

Recirculation ratio can vary from 0.25 to 1.50 depending upon the type of activated sludge process used. Common design practice is to size the RAS pumps so that they are capable of providing a recirculation ratio ranging from 0.50 to 1.50.

It should be noted that if the control volume were placed around the aeration tank in Fig. 1 and a mass balance performed, or the control volume placed around the settling tank in Fig. 2 and a mass balance performed, that a slightly higher RAS pumping rate would result. However, the difference between these RAS pumping rates and the ones calculated above is negligible.

## DESIGN OF A CIRCULAR SETTLING TANK

Domestic wastewater with an average daily flow of 4.0 Mgd (15,140 m³/d) exits the aeration tank of a standard activated sludge treatment process. Design a circular settling tank to separate the sludge from the effluent. The settling tank will work in conjunction with the aeration tank. Assume a peaking factor of 2.5.

### Calculation Procedure:

#### 1. Determine the peak flow
Conventional examples of circular settling tank design utilize settling tests to size the tanks. However, it is more common that settling facilities must be designed without the benefit of settling tests. When this situation develops, published values of surface loading and solids loading rates are generally used. Because of the large amount of solids that may be lost in the effluent if design criteria are exceeded, surface loading rates should be based on peak flow conditions. Using a peaking factor of 2.5, the daily peak flow ($Q_p$) is:

$$Q_p = 2.5 \times 4.0 \text{ Mgd} = 10.0 \text{ Mgd } (37,850 \text{ m}^3/\text{d})$$

#### 2. Find the settling tank surface area using surface loading criteria
The recommended surface loading rates (settling tank effluent flow divided by settling tank area) vary depending upon the type of activated sludge process used. However, surface loading rates ranging from 200 to 800 gal/day/sq.ft. (8.09 to 32.4 L/m²·d) for average flow, and a maximum of 1000 gal/day/sq.ft. (40.7 L/m²·d) for peak flow are accepted design values.

The recommended solids loading rate on an activated sludge settling tank also varies depending upon the type of activated sludge process used and may be computed by dividing the total solids applied by the surface area of the tank. The preferred units are lb/sq.ft.·h (kg/m²·h). In effect, the solids loading rate represents a characteristic value for the suspension under consideration. In a settling tank of fixed area, the effluent quality will deteriorate if solids loading is increased beyond the characteristic value for the suspension. Without extensive experimental work covering all seasons and operating variables, higher rates should not be used for design. The recommended solids loading rates vary depending upon the type of activated sludge process selected. However, solids loading rates ranging from 0.8 to 1.2 lb/sq.ft.·h (3.9 to 5.86 kg/m²·h) for average flow, and 2.0 lb/sq.ft.·h (9.77 kg/m²·h) for peak flow are accepted design values.

For a $Q_p$ of 10.0 Mgd and a design surface loading rate of 1000 gal/day/sq.ft. at peak flow, the surface area (A) of a settling tank may be calculated:

$$1000 \text{ gal/day/sq.ft.} = \frac{10 \times 10^6 \text{ gal/day}}{A}$$

$$A = \frac{10 \times 10^6 \text{ gal/day}}{1000 \text{ gal/day/sq.ft.}} = 10,000 \text{ sq.ft. (929 m}^2)$$

### 3. Find the settling tank surface area using solids loading criteria

The total solids load on a clarifier consists of contributions from both the influent and the Return Activated Sludge (RAS). Assume the following (see "Design of A Complete-Mix Activated Sludge Reactor"):

$$Q_r = \text{RAS flow rate} = 1.25(Q) = 1.25(4.0 \text{ Mgd}) = 5.0 \text{ Mgd (18,925 m}^3/\text{d})$$

$$X = \text{MLSS in aeration tank} = 4500 \text{ mg/L}$$

Therefore, the maximum solids loading occurs at peak flow and maximum RAS flow rate. The maximum solids entering the clarifier is calculated using:

$$\text{Max. Solids (lb/d)} = (Q_p + Q_r)(X)(8.34 \text{ lb·L/mg·Mgal})$$

Using values given above,

$$\text{Max Solids (lb/d)} = (10 \text{ Mgd} + 5 \text{ Mgd})(4500 \text{ mg/L})(8.34 \text{ lb·L/mg·Mgal})$$

$$= 562,950 \text{ lb/d}$$

$$= 23,456 \text{ lb/h (10,649 kg/h) of Suspended Solids}$$

Therefore, using a solids loading rate of 2.0 lb/sq.ft.·h (9.77 kg/m²·h) at peak flow, the surface area of a settling tank may be calculated:

$$A = \frac{23,456 \text{ lb/h}}{2.0 \text{ lb/sq.ft.·h}} = 11,728 \text{ sq.ft. (1089.5 m}^2)$$

In this case, the solids loading dominates and dictates the required settling tank area.

### 4. Select the number of settling tanks

Generally, more than one settling tank would be constructed for operational flexibility. Two tanks will be sufficient for this example. Therefore, the surface area of each tank will be 11,728 sq.ft./2 = 5864 sq.ft. (544.8 m²). The diameter of each settling tank is then 86.41 ft. Use 87 ft (26.5 m). The total area of the two settling tanks is 11,889 sq.ft. (110.4.5 m²). For an average flow rate of 4.0 Mgd (15,140 m³/d) and an RAS flow rate of 5.0 Mgd (18,925 m³), the total solids entering the settling tanks at average daily flow is:

Solids (lb/d) = (4.0 Mgd + 5.0 Mgd)(4500 mg/L) (8.34 lb L/mg·Mgal)

= 337,770 lb/d = 14,074 lb/h (6389.6 kg/h)

Therefore, the solids loading on the settling tanks at design flow is:

$$\text{Solids Loading} = \frac{14,074 \text{ lb/h}}{11,889 \text{ sq.ft.}} \approx 1.18 \text{ lb/sq.ft.·h } (5.77 \text{ kg/m}^2\text{·h})$$

which is within the solids loading rate design criteria stated above.

**Related Calculations.** Liquid depth in a circular settling tank is normally measured at the sidewall. This is called the sidewater depth. The liquid depth is a factor in the effectiveness of suspended solids removal and in the concentration of the return sludge. Current design practice favors a minimum sidewater depth of 12 ft (3.66 m) for large circular settling tanks. However, depths of up to 20 ft (6.1 m) have been used. The advantages of deeper tanks include greater flexibility in operation and a larger margin of safety when changes in the activated sludge system occur.

# THICKENING OF A WASTE-ACTIVATED SLUDGE USING A GRAVITY BELT THICKENER

A wastewater treatment facility produces 58,000 gal/day (219.5 m³/d) of waste activated sludge containing 0.8 percent solids (8000 mg/L). Design a gravity belt thickener installation to thicken sludge to 5.0 percent solids based on a normal operation of 6 h/d and 5 d/wk. Use a gravity belt thickener loading rate of 1000 lb/h (454 kg/h) per meter of belt width. Calculate the number and size of gravity belt thickeners required, the volume of thickened sludge cake, and the solids capture in percent.

## Calculation Procedure:

### 1. Find the dry mass of sludge that must be processed

Gravity belt thickening consists of a gravity belt that moves over rollers driven by a variable speed drive unit. The waste activated sludge is usually pumped from the bottom of a secondary settling tank, conditioned with polymer and fed into a feed/distribution box at one end. The box is used to distribute the sludge evenly across the width of the moving belt. The water drains through the belt as the sludge is carried toward the discharge end of the thickener. The sludge is ridged and furrowed by a series of plow blades placed along the travel of the belt, allowing the water released from the sludge to pass through the belt. After the thickened sludge is removed, the belt travels through a wash cycle.

The 58,000 gal/day (219.5 m³/d) of waste activated sludge contains approximately 3933 lb/d (1785.6 kg/d) of dry solids: See *Design of a Complete-Mix Activated Sludge Reactor*, step 3—"Compute the Quantity of Sludge Wasted," and step 6—"Compute the WAS and RAS Requirements."

Based on an operating schedule of 5 days per week and 6 hours per day, the dry mass of sludge that must be processed is:

Weekly Rate: (3933 lb/d)(7 d/wk) = 27,531 lb/wk (12,499 kg/wk)

Daily Rate: (27,531 lb/wk)/(5 d/wk) = 5506 lb/d (2499.7 kg/d)

Hourly Rate: (5506 lb/d)/(6 h/d) = 918 lb/h (416.8 kg/h)

## 2. *Size the belt thickener*

Using the hourly rate of sludge calculated above, and a loading rate of 1000 lb/h per meter of belt width, the size of the belt thickener is:

$$\text{Belt Width} = \frac{918 \text{ lb/h}}{1000 \text{ lb/h·m}} = 0.918 \text{ m (3.01 ft)}$$

Use one belt thickener with a 1.0 m belt width. Note that one identical belt thickener should be provided as a spare.

The thickened sludge flow rate ($S$) in gal/day ($m^3/d$) and the filtrate flow rate ($F$) in gal/day ($m^3/d$) are computed by developing solids balance and flow balance equations:

(a) *Solids balance equation.* Solids in = solids out, which implies that: solids in sludge feed = solids in thickened sludge + solids in filtrate. Assume the following:

- Sludge feed specific gravity (s.g.) = 1.01
- Thickened sludge s.g. = 1.03
- Filtrate s.g. = 1.0
- Suspended solids in filtrate = 900 mg/L = 0.09%

Therefore, the solids balance equation on a daily basis becomes:

$$5506 \text{ lb} = (S, \text{gal/day})(8.34 \text{ lb/gal})(1.03)(0.05)$$
$$+ (F, \text{gal/day})(8.34 \text{ lb/gal})(1.0)(0.0009) \tag{1}$$
$$5506 \text{ lb/d} = 0.4295(S) + 0.0075(F)$$

(b) *Flow balance equation.* Flow in = flow out, which implies that: influent sludge flow rate + washwater flow rate = thickened sludge flow rate + filtrate flow rate. Daily influent sludge flow rate = (58,000 gal/day)(7/5) = 81,200 gal/day (307.3 $m^3/d$).

## 3. *Compute the thickened sludge and filtrate flow rates*

Washwater flow rate is assumed to be 16 gal/min (1.0 L/s). Washwater flow rate varies from 12 gal/min (0.757 L/s) to 30 gal/min (1.89 L/s) depending on belt thickener size. Therefore, with an operating schedule of 6 h/d (360 min/d) the flow balance equation on a daily basis becomes:

$$81,200 \text{ gal/day} + (16 \text{ gal/min})(360 \text{ min/d}) = S + F$$
$$86,960 \text{ gal/day} = S + F \tag{2}$$

Putting (Eq. 1) and (Eq. 2) in matrix format, and solving for thickened sludge flow rate ($S$) and filtrate flow rate ($F$):

$$\begin{bmatrix} 0.4295 & 0.0075 \\ 1 & 1 \end{bmatrix} \begin{bmatrix} S \\ F \end{bmatrix} = \begin{bmatrix} 5506 \\ 86,960 \end{bmatrix}$$

$S = 11,502$ gal/day (43.5 $m^3/d$) of thickened sludge at 5.0% solids

$F = 75,458$ gal/day (285.6 $m^3/d$) of filtrate

Therefore, the volume of thickened Waste Activated Sludge exiting the gravity belt thickener is 11,502 gal/day (43.5 m³/d) at 5.0 percent solids.

### 4. Determine the solids capture

The solids capture is determined using the following:

$$\text{Solids Capture (\%)} = \frac{\text{Solids in Feed} - \text{Solids in Filtrate}}{\text{Solids in Feed}} \times (100\%)$$

Using values defined previously:

$$\text{Solids Capture (\%)} = \frac{5506 \text{ lb/d} - [(75,458 \text{ gal/day})(8.34 \text{ lb/gal})(1.0)(0.009)]}{5506 \text{ lb/d}}$$

$$\times (100\%) = 89.7\%$$

Since only 89.7 percent of the solids entering the gravity belt thickener are captured, the thickener will actually be required to operate (360 min/d)/(0.897) = 400 min/d (6 hours 40 minutes per day) five days per week in order to waste the 3933 lb/d (1785.6 kg/d) of dry solids required. This implies that the actual volume of thickened sludge will be (11,502 gal/day)/(0.897) = 12,823 gal/day (48.5 m³/d). The actual filtrate flow rate will be (75,458 gal/day)/(0.897) = 84,123 gal/day (318.4 m³/d).

The thickened sludge is generally pumped immediately to sludge storage tanks or sludge digestion facilities. If the thickener is operated 6.67 h/d, the thickened sludge pumps (used to pump the thickened sludge to downstream processes) will be sized based on the following thickened sludge flow rate:

$$S = \frac{12,823 \text{ gal/day}}{(6.67 \text{ h/d})(60 \text{ min/h})} = 32 \text{ gal/min (2.02 L/s)}$$

Hydraulic (thickened sludge) throughput for a gravity belt thickener ranges from 25 (1.6 L/s) to 100 (6.3 L/s) gal/min per meter of belt width. The filtrate flow of 84,123 gal/day is generally returned to the head of the wastewater treatment facility for reprocessing.

## DESIGN OF AN AEROBIC DIGESTER

An aerobic digester is to be designed to treat the waste sludge produced by an activated sludge wastewater treatment facility. The input waste sludge will be 12,823 gal/day (48.5 L/d) (input 5 d/wk only) of thickened waste activated sludge at 5.0 percent solids—See *Thickening of a Waste-Activated Sludge Using a Gravity Belt Thickener*. Assume the following apply:

1. The minimum liquid temperature in the winter is 15°C (59°F), and the maximum liquid temperature in the summer is 30°C (86°F).

2. The system must achieve a 40 percent Volatile Suspended Solids (VSS) reduction in the winter.

3. Sludge concentration in the digester is 70 percent of the incoming thickened sludge concentration.

4. The volatile fraction of digester suspended solids is 0.8.

## Calculation Procedure:

### 1. *Find the daily volume of sludge for disposal*

Factors that must be considered in designing aerobic digesters include temperature, solids reduction, tank volume (hydraulic retention time), oxygen requirements, and energy requirements for mixing.

Because the majority of aerobic digesters are open tanks, digester liquid temperatures are dependent upon weather conditions and can fluctuate extensively. As with all biological systems, lower temperatures retard the process, whereas higher temperatures accelerate it. The design of the aerobic digester should provide the necessary degree of sludge stabilization at the lowest liquid operating temperature and should supply the maximum oxygen requirements at the maximum liquid operating temperature.

A major objective of aerobic digestion is to reduce the mass of the solids for disposal. This reduction is assumed to take place only with the biodegradable content (VSS) of the sludge, although there may be some destruction of the inorganics as well. Typical reduction in VSS ranges from 40 to 50 percent. Solids destruction is primarily a direct function of both basin liquid temperature and sludge age, as indicated in Fig. 3. The plot relates VSS reduction to degree-days (temperature × sludge age).

To ensure proper operation, the contents of the aerobic digester should be well mixed. In general, because of the large amount of air that must be supplied to meet the oxygen requirement, adequate mixing is usually achieved. However, mixing power requirements should always be checked.

The aerobic digester will operate 7 days per week, unlike the thickening facilities which operate intermittently due to larger operator attention requirements. The thickened sludge is input to the digester at 12,823 gal/day (48.5 L/d), 5 days per week. However, the volume of the sludge to be disposed of daily by the digester will be lower due to its operation 7 days per week (the "bugs" do not take the weekends off). Therefore the volume of sludge to be disposed of daily ($Q$) is:

$$Q_i = (12,823 \text{ gal/day})(5/7) = 9159 \text{ gal/day} = 1224 \text{ ft}^3/\text{d} \ (34.6 \text{ m}^3/\text{d})$$

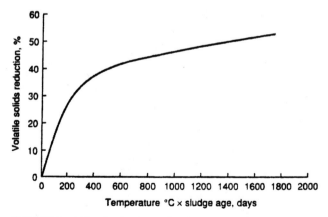

**FIGURE 3.** VSS reduction in aerobic digester vs. liquid temperature × sludge age. (Metcalf & Eddy, *Wastewater Engineering: Treatment, Disposal, and Reuse*, 3rd Ed., McGraw-Hill.)

## 2. *Determine the required VSS reduction*

The sludge age required for winter conditions is obtained from Fig. 3 using the minimum winter temperature and required VSS reduction.

To achieve a 40 percent VSS reduction in the winter, the degree-days required from Fig. 3 is 475°C·d. Therefore, the required sludge age is 475°C·d/15°C = 31.7 days. During the summer, when the liquid temperature is 30°C, the degree-days required is (30°C)(31.7 d) = 951°C·d. From Fig. 3, the VSS reduction will be 46 percent.

The total mass of solids processed by the digester will be 3933 lb/d (1785.6 kg/d) which is the total mass of solids wasted from the treatment facility—See *Design of a Complete-Mix Activated Sludge Reactor*, step 3. The total mass of VSS input to the digester is:

$$(0.8)(3933 \text{ lb/d}) = 3146 \text{ lb/d } (1428.3 \text{ kg/d}).$$

Therefore, during the winter:

- VSS reduction = (3146 lb/d)(0.40) = 1258 lb VSS reduced/d (571.1 kg/d)
- Digested (stabilized) sludge leaving the digester = 3933 lb/d − 1258 lb/d = 2675 lb/d (1214.5 kg/d).

## 3. *Compute the volume of digested sludge*

The volume of digested sludge is:

$$V = \frac{W_s}{(\rho)(\text{s.g.})(\% \text{ solids})}$$

where  $V$ = Sludge volume (ft³) (m³)
$W_s$ = Weight of sludge (lb) (kg)
$\rho$ = density of water (62.4 lb/ft³) (994.6 kg/m³)
s.g. = specific gravity of digested sludge (assume s.g. = 1.03)
% solids = percent solids expressed as a decimal (incoming sludge: 5.0%)

Therefore, the volume of the digested sludge is:

$$V = \frac{2675 \text{ lb/d}}{(62.4 \text{ lb/ft}^3)(1.03)(0.05)} = 832 \text{ ft}^3/\text{d} = 6223 \text{ gal/day } (23.6 \text{ L/d})$$

During the summer:

- VSS reduction = (3146 lb/d)(0.46) = 1447 lb VSS reduced/d (656.9 kg/d)
- Digested (stabilized) sludge leaving the digester = 3933 lb/d − 1447 lb/d = 2486 lb/d (1128.6 kg/d).
- Volume of digested sludge:

$$V = \frac{2486 \text{ lb/d}}{(62.4 \text{ lb/ft}^3)(1.03)(0.05)} = 774 \text{ ft}^3/\text{d} = 5790 \text{ gal/day } (21.9 \text{ L/d})$$

## 4. *Find the oxygen and air requirements*

The oxygen required to destroy the VSS is approximately 2.3 lb $O_2$/lb VSS (kg/kg) destroyed. Therefore, the oxygen requirements for winter conditions are:

$$(1258 \text{ lb VSS/d})(2.3 \text{ lb } O_2/\text{lb VSS}) = 2893 \text{ lb } O_2/\text{d } (1313.4 \text{ kg/d})$$

The volume of air required at standard conditions (14.7 lb/sq.in. and 68°F) (96.5 kPa and 20°C) assuming air contains 23.2 percent oxygen by weight and the density of air is 0.075 lb/ft³ is:

$$\text{Volume of Air} = \frac{2893 \text{ lb } O_2 d}{(0.075 \text{ lb/ft}^3)(0.232)} = 166{,}264 \text{ ft}^3/d \ (4705.3 \text{ m}^3/d)$$

For summer conditions:

- Oxygen required = (1447 lb/d)(2.3 lb $O_2$/d) = 3328 lb $O_2$/d (1510.9 kg/d)
- Volume of Air = 3328 lb $O_2$/d/(0.075 lb/ft³)(0.232) = 191,264 ft³/d (5412.8 m³/d)

Note that the oxygen transfer efficiency of the digester system must be taken into account to get the actual volume of air required. Assuming diffused aeration with an oxygen transfer efficiency of 10 percent, the actual air requirements at standard conditions are:

- Winter: volume of air = 166,264 ft³/d/(0.1)(1400 min/d) = 1155 ft³/min (32.7 m³/min)
- Summer: volume of air = 191,264 ft³/d/(0.1)(1440 min/d) = 1328 ft³/min (37.6 m³/min)

To summarize winter and summer conditions:

| Parameter | Winter | Summer |
|---|---|---|
| Total Solids In, lb/d (kg/d) | 3933 (1785.6) | 3933 (1785.6) |
| VSS In, lb/d (kg/d) | 3146 (1428.3) | 3146 (1428.3) |
| VSS Reduction, (%) | 40 | 46 |
| VSS Reduction, lb/d (kg/d) | 1258 (571.1) | 1447 (656.9) |
| Digested Sludge Out, gal/day (L/d) | 6223 (23.6) | 5790 (21.9) |
| Digested Sludge Out, lb/d (kg/d) | 2675 (1214.5) | 2486 (1128.6) |
| Air Requirements @ S.C., ft³/min (m³/min) | 1155 (32.7) | 1328 (37.6) |

## 5. *Determine the aerobic digester volume*

From the above analysis it is clear that the aerobic digester volume will be calculated using values obtained under the winter conditions analysis, while the aeration equipment will be sized using the 1328 ft³/min (37.6 m³/min) air requirement obtained under the summer conditions analysis.

The volume of the aerobic digester is computed using the following equation, assuming the digester is loaded with waste activated sludge only:

$$V = \frac{Q_i X_i}{X(K_d P_v + 1/\theta_c)}$$

where $V$ = Volume of aerobic digester, ft³ (m³)
$Q_i$ = Influent average flow rate to the digester, ft³/d (m³/d)
$X_i$ = Influent suspended solids, mg/L (50,000 mg/L for 5.0% solids)
$X$ = Digester total suspended solids, mg/L

$K_d$ = Reaction rate constant, $d^{-1}$. May range from 0.05 $d^{-1}$ at 15°C (59°F) to 0.14
   $d^{-1}$ at 25°C (77°F) (assume 0.06 $d^{-1}$ at 15°C)
$P_v$ = Volatile fraction of digester suspended solids (expressed as a decimal) = 0.8
   (80%) as stated in the initial assumptions.
$\theta_c$ = Solids retention time (sludge age), $d$

Using values obtained above with winter conditions governing, the aerobic digester
volume is:

$$V = \frac{(1224 \text{ ft}^3/\text{d})(50,000 \text{ mg/L})}{(50,000 \text{ mg/L})(0.7)[(0.06\ d^{-1})(0.8) + 1/31.7\ d]} = 21,982 \text{ ft}^3 \ (622.2 \text{ m}^3)$$

The air requirement per 1000 ft$^3$ (2.8 m$^3$) of digester volume with summer conditions
governing is:

$$\text{Volume of Air} = \frac{1328 \text{ ft}^3/\text{min}}{21.982 \text{ } 10^3\text{ft}^3} = 60.41 \text{ ft}^3/\text{min}/10^3\text{ft}^3 \ (0.97 \text{ m}^3/\text{min}/\text{Mm}^3)$$

The mixing requirements for diffused aeration range from 20 to 40 ft$^3$/min/10$^3$ft$^3$ (0.32 to
0.64 m$^3$/min/Mm$^3$). Therefore, adequate mixing will prevail.

## DESIGN OF AN AERATED GRIT CHAMBER

Domestic wastewater enters a wastewater treatment facility with an average daily flow
rate of 4.0 Mgd (15,140 L/d). Assuming a peaking factor of 2.5, size an aerated grit chamber for this facility including chamber volume, chamber dimensions, air requirement, and
grit quantity.

### Calculation Procedure:

#### 1. Determine the aerated grit chamber volume
Grit removal in a wastewater treatment facility prevents unnecessary abrasion and wear
of mechanical equipment such as pumps and scrappers, and grit deposition in pipelines
and channels. Grit chambers are designed to remove grit (generally characterized as nonputrescible solids) consisting of sand, gravel, or other heavy solid materials that have settling velocities greater than those of the organic putrescible solids in the wastewater.

In aerated grit chamber systems, air introduced along one side near the bottom causes
a spiral roll velocity pattern perpendicular to the flow through the tank. The heavier particles with their correspondingly higher settling velocities drop to the bottom, while the
rolling action suspends the lighter organic particles, which are carried out of the tank. The
rolling action induced by the air diffusers is independent of the flow through the tank.
Then non-flow-dependent rolling action allows the aerated grit chamber to operate effectively over a wide range of flows. The heavier particles that settle on the bottom of the tank
are moved by the spiral flow of the water across the tank bottom and into a grit hopper.
Screw augers or air lift pumps are generally utilized to remove the grit from the hopper.

The velocity of roll governs the size of the particles of a given specific gravity that
will be removed. If the velocity is too great, grit will be carried out of the chamber. If the

velocity is too small, organic material will be removed with the grit. The quantity of air is easily adjusted by throttling the air discharge or using adjustable speed drives on the blowers. With proper adjustment, almost 100 percent grit removal will be obtained, and the grit will be well washed. Grit that is not well washed will contain organic matter and become a nuisance through odor emission and the attraction of insects.

Wastewater will move through the aerated grit chamber in a spiral path as illustrated in Fig. 4. The rolling action will make two to three passes across the bottom of the tank at maximum flow and more at lesser flows. Wastewater is introduced in the direction of the roll.

At peak flow rate, the detention time in the aerated grit chamber should range from 2 to 5 minutes. A detention time of 3 minutes will be used for this example. Because it is necessary to drain the chamber periodically for routine maintenance, two redundant chambers will be required. Therefore, the volume of each chamber is:

$$V\ (\text{ft}^3) = \frac{(\text{peak flow rate, gal/day})(\text{detention time, min})}{(7.48\ \text{gal/ft}^3)(24\ \text{h/d})(60\ \text{min/h})}$$

Using values from above, the chamber volume is:

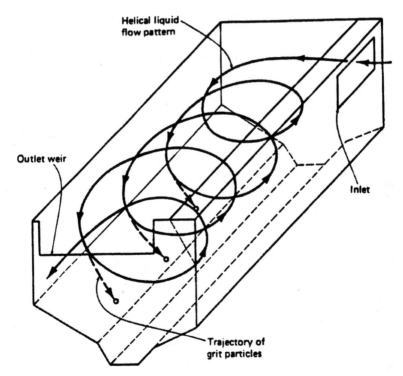

**FIGURE 4.** Aerated grit chamber. (Metcalf & Eddy, *Wastewater Engineering: Treatment, Disposal, and Reuse*, 3rd Ed., McGraw-Hill.)

$$V \text{ (ft}^3) = \frac{(2.5)(4 \times 10^6 \text{ gal/day})(3 \text{ min})}{(7.48 \text{ gal/ft}^3)(24 \text{ h/d})(60 \text{ min/h})} = 2785 \text{ ft}^3 \text{ (78.8 m}^3)$$

## 2. Determine the dimensions of the grit chamber

Width-depth ratio for aerated grit chambers range from 1:1 to 5:1. Depths range from 7 to 16 feet (2.1 to 4.87 m). Using a width-depth ratio of 1.2:1 and a depth of 8 feet (2.43 m), the dimensions of the aerated grit chamber are:

$$\text{Width} = (1.2)(8 \text{ ft}) = 9.6 \text{ ft (2.92 m)}$$

$$\text{Length} = (\text{volume})/[(\text{width})(\text{depth})] = \frac{2785 \text{ ft}^3}{(8 \text{ ft})(9.6 \text{ ft})} = 36.3 \text{ ft (11.1 m)}$$

Length-width ratios range from 3:1 to 5:1. As a check, length to width ratio for the aerated grit chamber sized above is: 36.3 ft/9.6 ft = 3.78:1, which is acceptable.

## 3. Determine the air supply required

The air supply requirement for an aerated grit chamber ranges from 2.0 to 5.0 ft$^3$/min/ft of chamber length (0.185 to 0.46 m$^3$/min·m). Using 5.0 ft$^3$/min/ft (0.46 m$^3$/min·m) for design, the amount of air required is:

$$\text{Air required (ft}^3/\text{min}) = (5.0 \text{ ft}^3/\text{min/ft})(36.3 \text{ ft}) = 182 \text{ ft}^3/\text{min (5.2 m}^3/\text{min})$$

## 4. Estimate the quantity of grit expected

Grit quantities must be estimated to allow sizing of grit handling equipment such as grit conveyors and grit dewatering equipment. Grit quantities from an aerated grit chamber vary from 0.5 to 27 ft$^3$/Mgal (3.74 to 201.9 m$^3$/L) of flow. Assume a value of 20 ft$^3$/Mgal (149.5 m$^3$/L). Therefore, the average quantity of grit expected is:

$$\text{Volume of grit (ft}^3/\text{d}) = (20 \text{ ft}^3/\text{Mgal})(4.0 \text{ Mgd}) = 80 \text{ ft}^3/\text{d (2.26 m}^3/\text{d})$$

Some advantages and disadvantages of the aerated grit chamber are listed below:

| Advantages | Disadvantages |
| --- | --- |
| The same efficiency of grit removal is possible over a wide flow range. | Power consumption is higher than other grit removal processes. |
| Head loss through the grit chamber is minimal. | Additional labor is required for maintenance and control of the aeration system. |
| By controlling the rate of aeration, a grit of relatively low putrescible organic content can be removed. | Significant quantities of potentially harmful volatile organics and odors may be released from wastewaters containing these constituents. |
| Preaeration may alleviate septic conditions in the incoming wastewater to improve performance of downstream treatment units. | Foaming problems may be created if influent wastewater has surfactants present. |
| Aerated grit chambers can also be used for chemical addition, mixing, preaeration, and flocculation ahead of primary treatment. | |

## DESIGN OF A SOLID-BOWL CENTRIFUGE FOR SLUDGE DEWATERING

A 4.0 Mgd (15,140 m³/d) municipal wastewater treatment facility produces 6230 gal/day (23.6 m³/d) of aerobically digested sludge at 5.0 percent solids. Determine design parameters for the specification of a solid-bowl centrifuge for dewatering the sludge including: number of centrifuges, solids feed rate, percent solids recovery, dewatered sludge (cake) discharge rate, centrifugal force, polymer dosage, and polymer feed rate. Assume the following apply:

- Feed sludge is aerobically digested at 5.0 percent solids.
- Dewatered sludge (cake) is to be 25 percent solids.
- Centrate assumed to be 0.3 percent solids.
- Polymer solution concentration is 25 percent.

### Calculation Procedure:

#### 1. Select the number of centrifuges
The separation of a liquid-solid sludge during centrifugal thickening is analogous to the separation process in a gravity thickener. In a centrifuge, however, the applied force is centrifugal rather than gravitational and usually exerts 1500 to 3500 times the force of gravity. Separation results from the centrifugal force-driven migration of the suspended solids through the suspending liquid, away from the axis of rotation. The increased settling velocity imparted by the centrifugal force as well as the short settling distance of the particles accounts for the comparatively high capacity of centrifugal equipment.

Centrifuges are commonly used for thickening or dewatering Waste Activated Sludge (WAS) and other biological sludges from secondary wastewater treatment. In the process, centrifuges reduce the volume of stabilized (digested) sludges to minimize the cost of ultimate disposal. Because centrifuge equipment is costly and sophisticated, centrifuges are most commonly found in medium to large wastewater treatment facilities.

The capacity of sludge dewatering to be installed at a given facility is a function of the size of a facility, capability to repair machinery on-site, and the availability of an alternative disposal means. Some general guidelines relating the minimal capacity requirements are listed in Table 1. This table is based on the assumption that there is no alternative mode of sludge disposal and that the capacity to store solids is limited.

**TABLE 1.**  Facility Capacity and Number of Centrifuges

| Facility size, Mgd (m³/d) | Dewatering operation, h/d | Centrifuges operating + spare @ gal/min (L/s) |
|---|---|---|
| 2 (7570) | 7 | 1 + 1 @ 25 (1.58) |
| 5 (18,930) | 7.5 | 1 + 1 @ 50 (3.16) |
| 20 (75,700) | 15 | 2 + 1 @ 50 (3.16) |
| 50 (189,250) | 22 | 2 + 1 @ 75 (4.73) |
| 100 (378,500) | 22 | 3 + 2 @ 100 (6.31) |
| 250 (946,250) | 22 | 4 + 2 @ 200 (12.62) |

(*Design Manual for Dewatering Municipal Wastewater Sludges,* U.S. EPA)

Using Table 1, the number of centrifuges recommended for a 4.0 Mgd (15,410 m³/d) wastewater treatment facility is one operational + one spare for a total of two centrifuges.

## 2. Find the sludge feed rate required

If the dewatering facility is operated 4 h/d, 7 d/wk, then the sludge feed rate is

$$\text{Sludge Feed Rate} = (6230 \text{ gal/day})/[(4 \text{ h/d})(60/\text{min/h})]$$

$$= 26 \text{ gal/min } (1.64 \text{ L/s})$$

Although a 4 h/d operation is below that recommended in Table 1, the sludge feed rate of 26 gal/min (1.64 L/s) is adequate for the size of centrifuge usually found at a treatment facility of this capacity. A longer operational day would be necessary if the dewatering facilities were operated only 5 days per week, or during extended periods of peak flow and solids loading.

Assume a feed sludge specific gravity of 1.03. The sludge feed in lb/h is calculated using the following equation:

$$W_s = \frac{(V)(\rho)(\text{s.g.})(\% \text{ solids})(60 \text{ min/h})}{7.48 \text{ gal/ft}^3}$$

$W_s$ = Weight flow rate of sludge feed, lb/h (kg/h)
$V$ = Volume flow rate of sludge feed, gal/min (L/s)
s.g. = specific gravity of sludge
% solids = percent solids expressed as a decimal
$\rho$ = density of water, 62.4 lb/ft³ (994.6 kg/m³)

Using values obtained above, the sludge feed in lb/h is:

$$W_s = \frac{(26 \text{ gal/min})(62.4 \text{ lb/ft}^3)(1.03)(0.05)(60 \text{ min/h})}{7.48 \text{ gal/ft}^3}$$

$$= 670 \text{ lb/h of dry solids } (304.2 \text{ kg/h})$$

## 3. Compute the solids capture

Since the solids exiting the centrifuge are split between the centrate and the cake, it is necessary to use a recovery formula to determine solids capture. Recovery is the mass of solids in the cake divided by the mass of solids in the feed. If the solids content of the feed, centrate, and cake are measured, it is possible to calculate percent recovery without determining total mass of any of the streams. The equation for percent solids recovery is

$$R = 100 \left( \frac{C_s}{F} \right) \left[ \frac{F - C_C}{C_S - C_C} \right]$$

where $R$ = Recovery, percent solids
$C_s$ = Cake solids, percent solids (25%)
$F$ = Feed solids, percent solids (5%)
$C_c$ = Centrate solids, percent solids (0.3%)

Therefore, using values defined previously:

$$R = 100(25/5)\left[\frac{(5-0.3)}{25-0.3}\right] = 95.14\%$$

### 4. Determine the Dewatered Sludge (Cake) Discharge Rate

The dewatered sludge (cake) discharge rate is calculated using the following:

Cake discharge rate (lb/h) dry solids = (sludge feed rate, lb/h)(solids recovery)

= (670 lb/h)(0.95 14) = 637.5 lb/h (289.4 kg/h) dry cake

The wet cake discharge in lb/h is calculated using the following:

$$\text{Wet cake discharge (lb/h)} = \frac{\text{Dry cake rate, lb/h}}{\text{Cake \% solids}}$$

$$\text{Wet cake discharge (lb/h)} = \frac{637.5 \text{ lb/h}}{0.25}$$

$$= 2550 \text{ lb/h wet cake (1157.7 kg/h)}$$

The volume of wet cake, assuming a cake density of 60 lb/ft$^3$ is calculated as follows:

$$\text{Volume of wet cake (ft}^3\text{/h)} = \frac{\text{Wet cake rate, lb/h}}{\text{Cake density, lb/ft}^3} = \frac{2550 \text{ lb/h}}{60 \text{ lb/ft}^3}$$

$$= 42.5 \text{ ft}^3\text{/h (1.2 m}^3\text{/h) wet cake}$$

For a dewatering facility operation of 4 h/d, the volume of dewatered sludge cake to be disposed of per day is:

$$(42.5 \text{ ft}^3\text{/h})(4 \text{ h/d}) = 170 \text{ ft}^3\text{/d} = 1272 \text{ gal/day (4.81 L/d)}$$

### 5. Find the percent reduction in sludge volume

The percent reduction in sludge volume is then calculated using the following:

$$\% \text{ Volume Reduction} = \frac{\text{Sludge volume in} - \text{Sludge volume out}}{\text{Sludge volume in}}$$

$$\times 100\%$$

$$= \frac{6230 \text{ gal/day} - 1272 \text{ gal/day}}{6,230 \text{ gal/day}}$$

$$\times 100\% = 79.6\%$$

Centrifuges operate at speed ranges that develop centrifugal forces from 1500 to 3500 times the force of gravity. In practice, it has been found that higher rotational speeds usually provide significant improvements in terms of performance, particularly on wastewater sludges.

In most cases, a compromise is made between the process requirement and O&M considerations. Operating at higher speeds helps achieve optimum performance, which is weighed against somewhat greater operating and maintenance costs. Increasing bowl speed usually increases solids recovery and cake dryness. Today most centrifuges used in wastewater applications can provide good clarity and solids concentration at $G$ levels between 1800 and 2500 times the force of gravity.

### 6. Compute the centrifugal force in the centrifuge

The centrifugal acceleration force ($G$), defined as multiples of gravity, is a function of the rotational speed of the bowl and the distance of the particle from the axis of rotation. In the centrifuge, the centrifugal force, $G$, is calculated as follows:

$$G = \frac{(2\pi N)^2 R}{32.2 \text{ ft/s}^2}$$

where $N$ = Rotational speed of centrifuge (rev/s)
$R$ = Bowl radius, ft (cm)

The rotational speed and bowl diameter of the centrifuge will vary depending upon the manufacturer. However, a rotational speed of 2450 r/min and a bowl diameter of 30 in. (72.6 cm) are common for this type of sludge dewatering operation.

Therefore, the centrifugal force is

$$G = \frac{[(2\pi)(2450 \text{ r/min}/60 \text{ s/min})]^2 (30 \text{ in.}/12 \text{ in./ft})(0.5)}{32.2 \text{ ft/s}^2} = 2555 \ Gs$$

### 7. Find the polymer feed rate for the centrifuge

The major difficulty encountered in the operation of centrifuges is the disposal of the centrate, which is relatively high in suspended, non-settling solids. The return of these solids to the influent of the wastewater treatment facility can result in the passage of fine solids through the treatment system, reducing effluent quality. Two methods are used to control the fine solids discharge and increase the capture. These are: (1) increased residence time in the centrifuge, and (2) polymer addition. Longer residence time of the liquid is accomplished by reducing the feed rate or by using a centrifuge with a larger bowl volume. Better clarification of the centrate is achieved by coagulating the sludge prior to centrifugation through polymer addition. Solids capture may be increased from a range of 50 to 80 percent to a range of 80 to 95 percent by longer residence time and chemical conditioning through polymer addition.

In order to obtain a cake solids concentration of 20 to 28 percent for an aerobically digested sludge, 5 to 20 pounds of dry polymer per ton of dry sludge feed (2.27 to 9.08 kg/ton) is required. For this example, 15 lb/ton (6.81 kg/ton) will be used. Usually this value is determined through pilot testing or plant operator trial and error.

The polymer feed rate in lb/h of dry polymer is calculated using the following:

$$\text{Polymer feed rate (lb/h)} = \frac{(\text{polymer dosage, lb/ton})(\text{dry sludge feed, lb/h})}{2000 \text{ lb/ton}}$$

Using values defined previously, the polymer feed rate is:

$$\text{Polymer feed rate (lb/h)} = \frac{(15 \text{ lb/ton})(670 \text{ lb/h})}{2000 \text{ lb/ton}}$$

$$= 5.0 \text{ lb/h of dry polymer (2.27 kg/h)}$$

Polymer feed rate in gal/h is calculated using the following:

$$\text{Polymer feed rate (gal/h)} = \frac{\text{polymer feed rate lb/h}}{(8.34 \text{ lb/gal})(\text{s.g.})(\% \text{ polymer concentration})}$$

where s.g. = specific gravity of the polymer solution
% polymer concentration expressed as a decimal

Using values defined previously:

$$\text{Polymer feed rate (gal/h)} = \frac{5.0 \text{ lb/h}}{(8.34 \text{ lb/gal})(1.0)(0.25)}$$

$$= 2.4 \text{ gal/h of } 25\% \text{ polymer solution } (0.009 \text{ L/h})$$

The polymer feed rate is used to size the polymer dilution/feed equipment required for the sludge dewatering operation.

**Related Calculations.** Selection of units for dewatering facility design is dependent upon manufacturer's rating and performance data. Several manufacturers have portable pilot plant units, which can be used for field testing if sludge is available. Wastewater sludges from supposedly similar treatment processes but different localities can differ markedly from each other. For this reason, pilot plant tests should be run, whenever possible, before final design decisions regarding centrifuge selection are made.

## SIZING OF A TRAVELING-BRIDGE FILTER

Secondary effluent from a municipal wastewater treatment facility is to receive tertiary treatment, including filtration, through the use of traveling bridge filters. The average daily flow rate is 4.0 Mgd (2778 gal/min) (15,140 m$^3$/d) and the peaking factor is 2.5. Determine the size and number of traveling bridge filters required.

### Calculation Procedure:

#### 1. Determine the peak flow rate for the filter system
The traveling bridge filter is a proprietary form of a rapid sand filter. This type of filter is used mainly for filtration of effluent from secondary and advanced wastewater treatment facilities. In the traveling bridge filter, the incoming wastewater floods the filter bed, flows through the filter medium (usually sand and/or anthracite), and exits to an effluent channel via an underdrain and effluent ports located under each filtration cell. During the backwash cycle, the carriage and the attached hood (see Fig. 5) move slowly over the filter bed, consecutively isolating and backwashing each cell. The washwater pump, located in the effluent channel, draws filtered wastewater from the effluent chamber and pumps it through the effluent port of each cell, forcing water to flow up through the cell thereby backwashing the filter medium of the cell. The backwash pump located above the hood draws water with suspended matter collected under the hood and transfers it to the backwash water trough. During the backwash cycle, wastewater is filtered continuously through the cells not being backwashed.

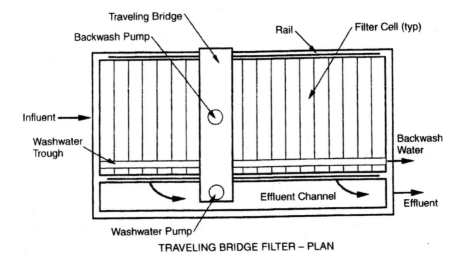

TRAVELING BRIDGE FILTER – PLAN

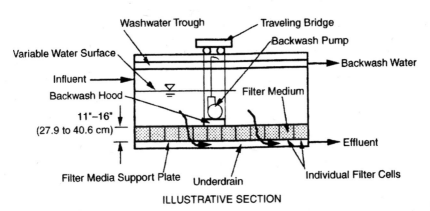

ILLUSTRATIVE SECTION

**FIGURE 5.** Traveling bridge filter.

Filtration in a traveling bridge filter is accomplished at a hydraulic loading typically in the range of 1.5 to 3.0 gal/min per square foot of filter surface (1.02 to 2.04 L/s·m²) at average daily flow. The maximum hydraulic loading used for design is typically 4.0 gal/min/sq.ft. (2.72 L/s·m²) at peak flow. The peak hydraulic loading is used to size the traveling bridge filter.

The peak flow for this treatment facility is calculated as follows:

$$\text{Peak flow} = (\text{peaking factor})(\text{average daily flow}) = (2.5)(4.0 \text{ Mgd})$$

$$= 10 \text{ Mdg} = 6944 \text{ gal/min} (438.2 \text{ L/s})$$

## 2. Find the required filter surface area

Filter surface area required is calculated using

$$\text{Filter surface area required (sq.ft.)} = \frac{\text{peak flow (gal/min)}}{\text{Hydraulic loading (gal/min·sq.ft.)}}$$

Using values from above:

$$\text{Filter surface area required (sq.ft.)} = \frac{6944 \text{ gal/min}}{4.0 \text{ gal/min·sq.ft.}} = 1736 \text{ sq.ft. (161.3 m}^2)$$

## 3. Determine the number of filters required

Standard filter widths available from various manufacturers are 8, 12, and 16 ft (2.44, 3.66, and 4.88 m). Using a width of 12 feet (3.66 m) and length of 50 feet (15.2 m) per filter, the area of each filter is

$$\text{Area of each filter} = (12 \text{ ft})(50 \text{ ft}) = 600 \text{ sq.ft. (55.7 m}^2)$$

The number of filters required is 1736 sq.ft./600 sq.ft. per filter = 2.89. Use 3 filters for a total filter area of 1800 sq.ft. (167.2 m²).

It must be kept in mind that most state and local regulations stipulate that "rapid sand filters shall be designed to provide a total filtration capacity for the maximum anticipated flow with at least one of the filters out of service." Therefore, 4 traveling bridge filters should be provided, each with filtration area dimensions of 12 ft wide × 50 ft long (3.66 m × 15.2 m).

The media depth for traveling bridge filters ranges from 11 in. to 16 in. (27.9 to 40.6 cm). Dual media may be used with 8 in. (20.3 cm) of sand underlying 8 in. (20.3 cm) of anthracite.

## 4. Find the hydraulic loading under various service conditions

The hydraulic loading with all filters in operation is

$$\text{Average flow:} \quad \frac{2778 \text{ gal/min}}{4(600 \text{ sq.ft.})} = 1.16 \text{ gal/min·sq.ft. (0.79 L/s·m}^2)$$

$$\text{Peak flow:} \quad \frac{6944 \text{ gal/min}}{4(600 \text{ sq.ft.})} = 2.89 \text{ gal/min·sq.ft. (1.96 L/s·m}^2)$$

Hydraulic loading with 1 filter out of service (3 active filters) is

$$\text{Average flow:} \quad \frac{2778 \text{ gal/min}}{3(600 \text{ sq.ft.})} = 1.54 \text{ gal/min·sq.ft. (1.05 L/s·m}^2)$$

$$\text{Peak flow:} \quad \frac{6944 \text{ gal/min}}{3(600 \text{ sq.ft.})} = 3.86 \text{ gal/min·sq.ft. (2.62 L/s·m}^2)$$

These hydraulic loadings are acceptable and may be used in specifying the traveling bridge filter.

The amount of backwash water produced depends upon the quantity and quality of influent to the filter. The backwash pumps are usually sized to deliver approximately 25 gal/min (1.58 L/s) during the backwash cycle. Backwash water is generally returned to the head of the treatment facility for reprocessing.

## DESIGN OF A RAPID-MIX BASIN
## AND FLOCCULATION BASIN

1.0 Mdg (3785 m³/d) of equalized secondary effluent from a municipal wastewater treatment facility is to receive tertiary treatment through a direct filtration process which includes rapid mix with a polymer coagulant, flocculation, and filtration. Size the rapid mix and flocculation basins necessary for direct filtration and determine the horsepower of the required rapid mixers and flocculators.


### Calculation Procedure:

### 1. Determine the required volume of the rapid mix basin
A process flow diagram for direct filtration of a secondary effluent is presented in Fig. 6. This form of tertiary wastewater treatment is used following secondary treatment when an essentially "virus-free" effluent is desired for wastewater reclamation and reuse.

The rapid mix basin is a continuous mixing process in which the principle objective is to maintain the contents of the tank in a completely mixed state. Although there are numerous ways to accomplish continuous mixing, mechanical mixing will be used here. In mechanical mixing, turbulence is induced through the input of energy by means of rotating impellers such as turbines, paddles, and propellers.

The hydraulic retention time of typical rapid mix operations in wastewater treatment range from 5 to 20 seconds. A value of 15 seconds will be used here. The required volume of the rapid mix basin is calculated as follows:

$$\text{Volume } (V) = (\text{hydraulic retention time})(\text{wastewater flow})$$

$$V = \frac{(15 \text{ s})(1 \times 10^6 \text{ gal/day})}{86,400 \text{ s/d}} = 174 \text{ gal} \cong 24 \text{ ft}^3 \text{ (0.68 m}^3\text{)}$$

### 2. Compute the power required for mixing
The power input per volume of liquid is generally used as a rough measure of mixing effectiveness, based on the reasoning that more input power creates greater turbulence, and greater turbulence leads to better mixing. The following equation is used to calculate the required power for mixing:

$$G = \sqrt{\frac{P}{\mu V}}$$

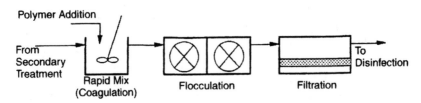

**FIGURE 6.** Process flow for direct filtration.

where $G$ = Mean velocity gradient $(s^{-1})$
$\quad P$ = Power requirement (ft·lb/s) (kW)
$\quad \mu$ = Dynamic viscosity (lb·s/sq.ft.) (Pa·s)
$\quad V$ = Volume of mixing tank $(ft^3)$ $(m^3)$

$G$ is a measure of the mean velocity gradient in the fluid. $G$ values for rapid mixing operations in wastewater treatment range from 250 to 1500 $s^{-1}$. A value of 1000 $s^{-1}$ will be used here. For water at 60°F (15.5°C), dynamic viscosity is $2.36 \times 10^{-5}$ lb·s/sq.ft. ($1.13 \times 10^{-3}$ Pa·s). Therefore, the required power for mixing is computed as follows:

$$P = G^2\mu V = (1000 \text{ s}^{-1})^2(2.36 \times 10^{-5} \text{ lb·s/sq.ft.})(24 \text{ ft}^3) = 566 \text{ ft·lb/s}$$

$$= 1.03 \text{ horsepower (0.77 kW)}$$

Use the next largest motor size available = 1.5 horsepower (1.12 kW). Therefore, a 1.5 horsepower (1.12 kW) mixer should be used.

### 3. Determine the required volume and power input for flocculation

The purpose of flocculation is to form aggregates, or flocs, from finely divided matter. The larger flocs allow a greater solids removal in the subsequent filtration process. In the direct filtration process, the wastewater is completely mixed with a polymer coagulant in the rapid mix basin. Following rapid mix, the flocculation tanks gently agitate the wastewater so that large "flocs" form with the help of the polymer coagulant. As in the rapid mix basins, mechanical flocculators will be utilized.

For flocculation in a direct filtration process, the hydraulic retention time will range from 2 to 10 minutes. A retention time of 8 minutes will be used here. Therefore, the required volume of the flocculation basin is

$$V = \frac{(8 \text{ min})(1 \times 10^6 \text{ gal/day})}{1440 \text{ min/d}} = 5556 \text{ gal } 743 \text{ ft}^3 \text{ (21 m}^3)$$

$G$ values for flocculation in a direct filtration process range from 20 to 100 $s^{-1}$. A value of 80 $s^{-1}$ will be used here. Therefore, the power required for flocculation is

$$P = G^2\mu V = (80 \text{ s}^{-1})^2(2.36 \times 10^{-5})(743 \text{ ft}^3)$$

$$= 112 \text{ ft·lb/s} = 0.2 \text{ horsepower (0.15 kW)}$$

Use the next largest motor size available = 0.5 horsepower (0.37 kW). Therefore, a 0.5 horsepower (0.37 kW) flocculator should be used.

It is common practice to taper the energy input to flocculation basins so that flocs initially formed will not be broken as they leave the flocculation facilities. In the above example, this may be accomplished by providing a second flocculation basin in series with the first. The power input to the second basin is calculated using a lower $G$ value (such as 50 $s^{-1}$) and hence provides a gentler agitation.

**Related Calculations.** If the flows to the rapid mix and flocculation basin vary significantly, or turn down capability is desired, a variable speed drive should be provided for each mixer and flocculator. The variable speed drive should be controlled via an output signal from a flow meter immediately upstream of each respective basin.

It should be noted that the above analysis provides only approximate values for mixer and flocculator sizes. Mixing is in general a "black art," and a mixing manufacturer is usually consulted regarding the best type and size of mixer or flocculator for a particular application.

## SIZING A POLYMER DILUTION/ FEED SYSTEM

1.0 Mgd (3,785 m³/d) of equalized secondary effluent from a municipal wastewater treatment facility is to undergo coagulation and flocculation in a direct filtration process. The coagulant used will be an emulsion polymer with 30 percent active ingredient. Size the polymer dilution/feed system including: the quantity of dilution water required and the amount of neat (as supplied) polymer required.

### Calculation Procedure:

#### 1. Determine the daily polymer requirements

Depending on the quality of settled secondary effluent, organic polymer addition is often used to enhance the performance of tertiary effluent filters in a direct filtration process: see *Design of a Rapid Mix Basin and Flocculation Basin*. Because the chemistry of the wastewater has a significant effect on the performance of a polymer, the selection of a type of polymer for use as a filter aid generally requires experimental testing. Common test procedures for polymers involve adding an initial polymer dosage to the wastewater (usually 1 part per million, ppm) of a given polymer and observing the effects. Depending upon the effects observed, the polymer dosage should be increased or decreased by 0.5 ppm increments to obtain an operating range. A polymer dosage of 2 ppm (2 parts polymer per $1 \times 10^6$ parts wastewater) will be used here.

In general, the neat polymer is supplied with approximately 25 to 35 percent active polymer, the rest being oil and water. As stated above, a 30 percent active polymer will be used for this example. The neat polymer is first diluted to an extremely low concentration using dilution water, which consists of either potable water or treated effluent from the wastewater facility. The diluted polymer solution usually ranges from 0.005 to 0.5 percent solution. The diluted solution is injected into either a rapid mix basin or directly into a pipe. A 0.5 percent solution will be used here.

The gallons per day (gal/day) (L/d) of active polymer required is calculated using the following:

$$\text{Active polymer (gal/day)} = (\text{wastewater flow, Mgd})$$
$$\times (\text{active polymer dosage, ppm})$$

Using the values outlined above:

Active polymer = (1.0 Mgd)(2 ppm) = 2 gal/day active polymer (pure polymer)

= 0.083 gal/hr (gal/h) (0.31 L/h)

#### 2. Find the quantity of dilution water required

The quantity of dilution water required is calculated using the following:

$$\text{Dilution water (gal/h)} = \frac{\text{active polymer, gal/h}}{\text{\% solution used (as a decimal)}}$$

Therefore, using values obtain above:

$$\text{Dilution water} = \frac{0.083 \text{ gal/h}}{0.005} = 16.6 \text{ gal/h (62.8 L/h)}$$

### 3. Find the quantity of neat polymer required

The quantity of neat polymer required is calculated as follows:

$$\text{Neat polymer (gal/h)} = \frac{\text{active polymer, gal/h}}{\text{\% active polymer in emulsion as supplied}}$$

Using values obtained above:

$$\text{Neat polymer} = \frac{0.083 \text{ gal/h}}{0.30} = 0.277 \text{ gal/h } (1.05 \text{ L/h})$$

This quantity of neat polymer represents the amount of polymer used in its "as supplied" form. Therefore, if polymer is supplied in a 55 gallon (208.2 L) drum, the time required to use one drum of polymer (assuming polymer is used 24 h/d, 7 d/wk) is:

$$\text{Time required to use one drum of polymer} = \frac{55 \text{ gal}}{0.277 \text{ gal/h}} \cong 200 \text{ h} = 8 \text{ days}$$

## DESIGN OF A TRICKLING FILTER USING THE NRC EQUATIONS

A municipal wastewater with a flow rate of 1.0 Mgd (3,785 m³/d) and a $BOD_5$ of 240 mg/L is to be treated by a two-stage trickling filter system. The effluent wastewater is to have a $BOD_5$ of 20 mg/L. Both filters are to have a depth of 7 feet (2.1 m) and a recirculation ratio of 2. Filter media will consist of rock. Size both stages of the trickling filter assuming the efficiency ($E$) of each stage is the same.

### Calculation Procedure:

### 1. Find the efficiency of the trickling filters

The modern trickling filter, shown in Fig. 7, consists of a bed of highly permeable medium to which microorganisms are attached and through which wastewater is percolated or trickled. The filter media usually consists of either rock or a variety of plastic packing materials. The depth of rock varies but usually ranges from 3 to 8 feet (0.91 to 244 m). Trickling filters are generally circular, and the wastewater is distributed over the top of the bed by a rotary distributor.

Filters are constructed with an underdrain system for collecting the treated wastewater and any biological solids that have become detached from the media. This underdrain system is important both as a collection unit and as a porous structure through which air can circulate. The collected liquid is passed to a settling tank where the solids are separated from the treated wastewater. In practice, a portion of the treated wastewater is recycled to dilute the strength of the incoming wastewater and to maintain the biological slime layer in a moist condition.

The organic material present in the wastewater is degraded by a population of microorganisms attached to the filter media. Organic material from the wastewater is absorbed onto the biological slime layer. As the slime layer increases in thickness, the microorganisms near the media face lose their ability to cling to the media surface. The

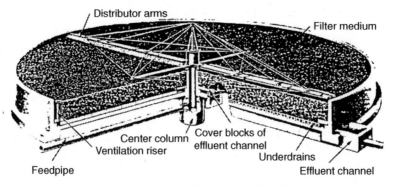

**FIGURE 7.** Cutaway view of a trickling filter. (Metcalf & Eddy, *Wastewater Engineering: Treatment, Disposal, and Reuse*, 3rd Ed., McGraw-Hill.)

liquid then washes the slime off the media, and a new slime layer starts to grow. The phenomenon of losing the slime layer is called "sloughing" and is primarily a function of the organic and hydraulic loading on the filter.

Two possible process flow schematics for a two-stage trickling filter system are shown in Fig. 8.

The NRC equations for trickling filter performance are empirical equations, which are primarily applicable to single and multistage rock systems with recirculation.

The overall efficiency of the two-stage trickling filter is calculated using:

$$\text{Overall efficiency} = \frac{\text{influent BOD}_5 - \text{effluent BOD}_5}{\text{influent BOD}_5} \times 100$$

Using the influent and effluent $BOD_5$ values presented in the problem statement, the overall efficiency is:

$$\text{Overall efficiency} = \frac{240 \text{ mg/L} - 20 \text{ mg/L}}{240 \text{ mg/L}} \times 100 = 91.7\%$$

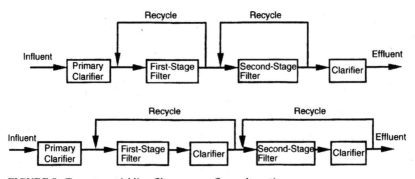

**FIGURE 8.** Two-stage trickling filter process flow schematics.

Also, overall efficiency $= E_1 + E_2(1 - E_1)$, and $E_1 = E_2$.

where $E_1 =$ The efficiency of the first filter stage, including recirculation and settling (%)
$E_2 =$ The efficiency of the second filter stage, including recirculation and settling (%)

Substituting $E_1$ for $E_2$, setting up as a quadratic equation, and solving for $E_1$:

$$E_1^2 - 2E_1 + 0.917 = 0 = \quad E_1 = 0.712 \text{ or } 71.2\%$$

Therefore, the efficiency of each trickling filter stage is 71.2 percent.

## 2. Analyze the first stage filter
For a single stage or first stage rock trickling filter, the NRC equation is

$$E_1 = \frac{100}{1 + 0.0561 \sqrt{\dfrac{W}{VF}}}$$

where $W =$ BOD$_5$ loading to the filter, lb/d (kg/d)
$V =$ Volume of the filter media, $10^3$ ft$^3$ (m$^3$)
$F =$ Recirculation factor

## 2a. Compute the recirculation factor of the filter
Recirculation factor represents the average number of passes of the influent organic matter through the trickling filter. The recirculation factor is calculated using

$$F = \frac{1 + R}{[1 + (R/10)]^2}$$

where $R =$ Recirculation ratio $= Q_r/Q$
$Q_r =$ Recirculation flow
$Q =$ Wastewater flow

Using values from above, the recirculation factor is

$$F = \frac{1 + 2}{[1 + (2/10)]^2} = 2.08$$

## 2b. Compute the BOD$_5$ loading for the first stage filter
The BOD$_5$ loading for the first stage filter is calculated using

$$W = (\text{Influent BOD}_5, \text{mg/L})(\text{Wastewater flow, Mgd})(8.34 \text{ lb/Mgal/mg/L})$$

Using values from above, the BOD$_5$ loading for the first stage filter is

$$W = (240 \text{ mg/L})(1.0 \text{ Mgd})(8.34) = 2002 \text{ lb BOD}_5/\text{d } (908.9 \text{ kg/d})$$

**2c.** *Compute the volume and diameter of the first stage filter*
Therefore, the volume of the first stage trickling filter is calculated as follows:

$$71.2 = \frac{100}{1 + 0.0561 \sqrt{\dfrac{2002\,\text{lb/d}}{V\,(2.08)}}} \qquad V = 18.51\ 10^3\ \text{ft}^3\ (523.8\ \text{m}^3)$$

Using the given depth of 7 feet (2.1 m), and a circular trickling filter, the area and diameter of the first stage filter are

$$\text{Area} = \frac{\text{volume}}{\text{depth}} \quad \frac{18.51 \times 10^3\ \text{ft}^3}{7\ \text{ft}} = 2{,}644\ \text{sq.ft.} \quad \text{diameter} = 58.02\ \text{ft}\ (17.7\ \text{m})$$

**3.** *Analyze the second stage filter*
The $BOD_5$ loading for the second stage trickling filter is calculated using

$$W' = (1 - E_1)W$$

where $W' =$          $BOD_5$ loading to the second stage filter
$W' = (1 - 0.712)(2002\ \text{lb/d}) = 577\ \text{lb}\ BOD_5/d\ (261.9\ \text{kg/d})$

The NRC equation for a second stage trickling filter is

$$E_2 = \frac{100}{1 + \dfrac{0.0561}{1 - E_1} \sqrt{\dfrac{W'}{VF}}}$$

Using terms defined previously and values calculated above, the volume of the second stage trickling filter is

$$E_2 = \frac{100}{1 + \dfrac{0.0561}{1 - 0.712} \sqrt{\dfrac{577\ \text{lb/d}}{V(2.08)}}} \qquad V = 64.33\ 10^3\ \text{ft}^3\ (1.82\ \text{m}^3)$$

The area and diameter of the second stage filter are

$$\text{Area} = \frac{64.33 \times 10^3\ \text{ft}^3}{7\ \text{ft}} = 9{,}190\ \text{sq.ft.} \quad \text{diameter} = 108.17\ \text{ft}\ (32.97\ \text{m})$$

**4.** *Compute the $BOD_5$ loading and hydraulic loading to each filter*
The $BOD_5$ (organic) loading to each filter is calculated by dividing the $BOD_5$ loading by the volume of the filter in $10^3\ \text{ft}^3\ (\text{m}^3)$:

$$\text{First stage filter:} \quad BOD_5\ \text{loading} = \frac{2002\ \text{lb/d}}{18.51\ 10^3\ \text{ft}^3} = 108.2\ \frac{\text{lb}}{10^3\ \text{ft}^3 \cdot \text{d}}$$

$$(1.74\ \text{kg/m}^3 \cdot \text{d})$$

Second stage filter: $\quad BOD_5$ loading $= \dfrac{577 \text{ lb/d}}{64.33 \; 10^3 \; ft^3} = 8.97 \; \dfrac{lb}{10^3 \; ft^3 \cdot d}$

$$(0.14 \text{ kg/m}^3\cdot d)$$

$BOD_5$ loading for a first stage filter in a two stage system typically ranges from 60 to 120 $lb/10^3 \; ft^3\cdot d$ (0.96 to 1.93 $kg/m^3\cdot d$). The second stage filter loading typically ranges from 5 to 20 $lb/10^3 \; ft^3\cdot d$ (0.08 to 0.32 $kg/m^3\cdot d$).

The hydraulic loading to each filter is calculated as follows:

$$\text{Hydraulic loading} = \dfrac{(1 + R)(Q)}{(\text{Area})(1440 \text{ min/d})}$$

First stage filter:

$$\text{Hydraulic loading} = \dfrac{(1 + 2)(1 \times 106 \text{ gal/day})}{(2644 \text{ sq.ft.})(1440 \text{ min/d})}$$

$$= 0.79 \text{ gal/min}\cdot\text{sq.ft.} \; (0.54 \text{ L/s}\cdot m^2)$$

Second stage filter:

$$\text{Hydraulic loading} = \dfrac{(1 + 2)(1 \times 10^6 \text{ gal/day})}{(9190 \text{ sq.ft.})(1440 \text{ min/d})}$$

$$= 0.23 \text{ gal/min}\cdot\text{sq.ft.} \; (0.156 \text{ L/s}\cdot m^2)$$

Hydraulic loading for two stage trickling filter systems typically ranges from 0.16 to 0.64 gal/min·sq.ft. (0.11 to 0.43 L/s·m²).

*Related Calculations.* In practice, the diameter of the two filters should be rounded to the nearest 5 ft (1.52 m) to accommodate standard rotary distributor mechanisms. To reduce construction costs, the two trickling filters are often made the same size. When both filters in a two-stage trickling filter system are the same size, the efficiencies will be unequal and the analysis will be an iterative one.

## DESIGN OF A PLASTIC MEDIA TRICKLING FILTER

A municipal wastewater with a flow of 1.0 Mgd (694 gal/min) (3,785 m³/d) and a $BOD_5$ of 240 mg/L is to be treated in a single-stage plastic media trickling filter without recycle. The effluent wastewater is to have a $BOD_5$ of 20 mg/L. Determine the diameter of the filter, the hydraulic loading, the organic loading, the dosing rate, and the required rotational speed of the distributor arm. Assume a filter depth of 25 feet (7.6 m). Also assume that a treatability constant ($k_{20/20}$) of 0.075 $(\text{gal/min})^{0.5}/\text{sq.ft.}$ was obtained in a 20 ft (6.1 m) high test filter at 20°C (68°F). The wastewater temperature is 30°C (86°F).

### Calculation Procedure:

### 1. Adjust the treatability constant for wastewater temperature and depth

Due to the predictable properties of plastic media, empirical relationships are available to predict performance of trickling filters packed with plastic media. However, the treatability constant must first be adjusted for both the temperature of the wastewater and the depth of the actual filter.

*Adjustment for temperature.* The treatability constant is first adjusted from the given standard at 20°C (68°F) to the actual wastewater temperature of 30°C (86°F) using the following equation:

$$k_{30/20} = k_{20/20}\theta^{T-20}$$

where $k_{30/20}$ = Treatability constant at 30°C (86°F) and 20 ft (6.1 m) filter depth
$k_{20/20}$ = Treatability constant at 20°C (68°F) and 20 ft (6.1 m) filter depth
$\theta$ = Temperature activity coefficient (assume 1.035)
$T$ = Wastewater temperature

Using above values:

$$k_{30/20} = [0.075 \text{ (gal/min)}^{0.5}/\text{sq.ft.}](1.035)^{30-20} = 0.106 \text{ (gal/min)}^{0.5}/\text{sq.ft.}$$

*Adjustment for depth.* The treatability constant is then adjusted from the standard depth of 20 feet (6.1 m) to the actual filter depth of 25 feet (7.6 m) using the following equation:

$$k_{30/25} = k_{30/20}(D_1/D_2)^x$$

where $k_{30/25}$ = Treatability constant at 30°C (86°F) and 25 ft (7.6 m) filter depth
$k_{30/20}$ = Treatability constant at 30°C (86°F) and 20 ft (6.1 m) filter depth
$D_1$ = Depth of reference filter (20 ft) (6.1 m)
$D_2$ = Depth of actual filter (25 ft) (7.6 m)
$x$ = Empirical constant (0.3 for plastic medium filters)

Using above values:

$$k_{30/25} = [0.106 \text{ (gal/min)}^{0.5}/\text{sq.ft.}](20/25)^{0.3}$$
$$= 0.099 \text{ (gal/min)}^{0.5}/\text{sq.ft. } [0.099 \text{ (L/s)}^{0.5}/\text{m}^2]$$

## 2. Size the plastic media trickling filter

The empirical formula used for sizing plastic media trickling filters is

$$\frac{S_e}{S_i} = \exp[-kD\,(Q_v)^{-n}]$$

where $S_e$ = BOD$_5$ of settled effluent from trickling filter (mg/L)
$S_i$ = BOD$_5$ of influent wastewater to trickling filter (mg/L)
$k_{20}$ = Treatability constant adjusted for wastewater temperature and filter depth = ($k_{30/25}$)
$D$ = Depth of filter (ft)
$Q_v$ = Volumetric flowrate applied per unit of filter area (gal/min·sq.ft.) (L/s·m$^2$) = $Q/A$
$Q$ = Flowrate applied to filter without recirculation (gal/min) (L/s)
$A$ = Area of filter (sq.ft.) (m$^2$)
$n$ = Empirical constant (usually 0.5)

Rearranging and solving for the trickling filter area ($A$):

$$A = Q\left(\frac{-\ln(S_e/S_i)}{(k_{30/25})D}\right)^{1/n}$$

Using values from above, the area and diameter of the trickling filter are

$$A = 694 \text{ gal/min} \left(\frac{-\ln(20/240)}{(0.099)25 \text{ ft}}\right)^{1/0.5} = 699.6 \text{ sq.ft.} \quad 29.9 \text{ ft } (9.1 \text{ m})$$

### 3. Calculate the hydraulic and organic loading on the filter

The hydraulic loading ($Q/A$) is then calculated:

Hydraulic loading $= 694$ gal/min/699.6 sq.ft. $= 0.99$ gal/min·sq.ft. ($0.672$ L/s·m$^2$)

For plastic media trickling filters, the hydraulic loading ranges from 0.2 to 1.20 gal/min·sq.ft. (0.14 to 0.82 L/s·m$^2$).

The organic loading to the trickling filter is calculated by dividing the BOD$_5$ load to the filter by the filter volume as follows:

$$\text{Organic loading} = \frac{(1.0 \text{ Mgd})(240 \text{ mg/L})(8.34 \text{ lb·L/mg·Mgal})}{(699.6 \text{ sq.ft.})(25 \text{ ft})(10^3 \text{ ft}^3/1000 \text{ ft}^3)}$$

$$= 114 \frac{\text{lb}}{10^3 \text{ ft}^3 \cdot \text{d}} \quad (557 \text{ kg/m}^2 \cdot \text{d})$$

For plastic media trickling filters, the organic loading ranges from 30 to 200 lb/10$^3$ ft$^3$·d (146.6 to 977.4 kg/m$^2$·d).

### 4. Determine the required dosing rate for the filter

To optimize the treatment performance of a trickling filter, there should be a continual and uniform growth of biomass and sloughing of excess biomass. To achieve uniform growth and sloughing, higher periodic dosing rates are required. The required dosing rate in inches per pass of distributor arm may be approximated using the following:

$$\text{Dosing rate} = (\text{organic loading, lb}/10^3 \text{ ft}^3 \cdot \text{d})(0.12)$$

Using the organic loading calculated above, the dosing rate is:

$$\text{Dosing rate} = (114 \text{ lb}/10^3 \text{ ft}^3 \cdot \text{d})(0.12) = 13.7 \text{ in./pass} (34.8 \text{ cm/pass})$$

Typical dosing rates for trickling filters are listed in Table 2. To achieve the typical dosing rates, the speed of the rotary distributor can be controlled by (1) reversing the location of some of the existing orifices to the front of the distributor arm, (2) adding reversed deflectors to the existing orifice discharges, and (3) by operating the rotary distributor with a variable speed drive.

### 5. Determine the required rotational speed of the distributor

The rotational speed of the distributor is a function of the instantaneous dosing rate and may be determined using the following:

$$n = \frac{1.6(Q_T)}{(A)(DR)}$$

**TABLE 2.**   Typical Dosing Rates for Trickling Filters

| Organic loading lb $BOD_5/10^3$ $ft^3 \cdot d$ $(kg/m^2 \cdot d)$ | Dosing rate, in./pass (cm/pass) |
|---|---|
| <25 (122.2) | 3 (7.6) |
| 50 (244.3) | 6 (15.2) |
| 75 (366.5) | 9 (22.9) |
| 100 (488.7) | 12 (30.5) |
| 150 (733.0) | 18 (45.7) |
| 200 (977.4) | 24 (60.9) |

(*Wastewater Engineering: Treatment, Disposal, and Reuse*, Metcalf & Eddy, 3rd Ed.)

where $n$ = Rotational speed of distributor (rpm)

$Q_T$ = Total applied hydraulic loading rate (gal/min·sq.ft.) (L/s·m²) = $Q + Q_R$

$Q$ = Influent wastewater hydraulic loading rate (gal/min·sq.ft.) (L/s·m²)

$Q_R$ = Recycle flow hydraulic loading rate (gal/min·sq.ft.) (L/s·m²) Note: recycle is assumed to be zero in this example

$A$ = Number of arms in rotary distributor assembly

$DR$ = Dosing rate (in./pass of distributor arm)

Assuming two distributor arms (two or four arms are standard), and using values from above, the required rotational speed is:

$$n = \frac{1.6(0.99 \text{ gal/min·sq.ft.})}{(2)(13.7 \text{ in./pass})} = 0.058 \text{ rpm}$$

This equates to one revolution every 17.2 minutes.

## SIZING OF A ROTARY-LOBE SLUDGE PUMP

A municipal wastewater treatment facility produces approximately 6,230 gal/day (23.6 m³/d) of aerobically digested sludge at 5 percent solids. The digested sludge is pumped to a sludge dewatering facility which is operated 4 h/d, 7 d/wk; 1000 ft (304.8 m) of 3 in. (76.3 mm) equivalent length pipe exists between the aerobic digester and the dewatering facility. The equivalent length of pipe includes all valves, fittings, discharge pipe, and suction pipe lengths in the sludge piping system. The static head on the sludge pump is 10 feet (3.0 m). Size a rotary-lobe pump transfer sludge from the digester to the dewatering facility, including pump discharge and head condition, rpm, and motor horsepower (kW).

### Calculation Procedure:

#### 1. *Find the flow rate required for the sludge pump*
A schematic of the sludge handling system is illustrated in Fig. 9. Rotary-lobe pumps are positive-displacement pumps in which two rotating synchronous lobes push the fluid through the pump. Although these types of pumps are advertised as self-priming, they are

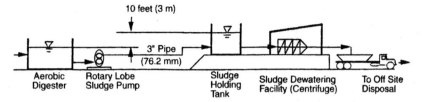

**FIGURE 9.** Sludge handling system.

generally located so as to have a suction head as shown in Fig. 9. A schematic of a rotary-lobe pump is shown in Fig. 10.

The required flow rate for the sludge pump using the 4 h/d, 7 d/wk operation scheme is:

$$\text{Flow rate (gal/min)} = \frac{6{,}230 \text{ gal/day}}{(4 \text{ h/d})(60 \text{ min/h})} = 26 \text{ gal/min (1.64 L/s)}$$

### 2. Compute the headloss in the piping system

The head loss through the piping system is calculated using the Hazen-Williams formula:

$$H = (0.2083)\left(\frac{100}{C}\right)^{1.85}\left(\frac{Q^{1.85}}{D^{4.8655}}\right)\left(\frac{L}{100}\right)$$

where $H$ = Dynamic head loss for clean water, ft (m)
$C$ = Hazen-Williams constant (use 100)
$Q$ = Flow rate in pipe, gal/min (L/s)
$D$ = Pipe diameter, in. (mm)
$L$ = Equivalent length of pipe, ft (m)

Note: There is an SI version of the Hazen-Williams formula; use it for SI calculations.

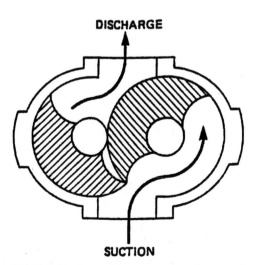

**FIGURE 10.** Rotary-lobe pump schematic.

Using values given above, the dynamic head loss in the piping system at the design flow rate of 26 gal/min (1.64 L/s) is:

$$H = (0.2083)\left(\frac{100}{100}\right)^{1.85}\left(\frac{(26\ \text{gal/min})^{1.85}}{(3\ \text{in.})^{4.8655}}\right)\left(\frac{1000\ \text{ft}}{100}\right) = 4.12\ \text{ft}\ (1.26\ \text{m})$$

This represents head loss in the sludge piping system for clean water only. To determine head loss when pumping sludge at 5 percent solids, a multiplication factor ($k$) is used. The value of $k$ is obtained from empirical curves (see Fig. 11) for a given solids content and pipeline velocity. The head loss when pumping sludge is obtained by multiplying the head loss of water by the multiplication factor.

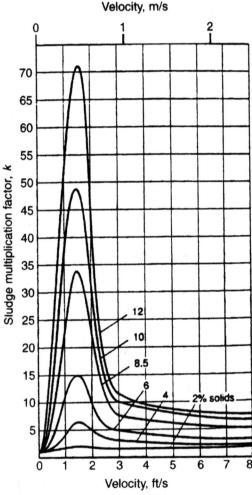

**FIGURE 11.** Head-loss multiplication factor for different pipe velocities vs. sludge concentration. (Metcalf & Eddy, *Wastewatwer Engineering: Treatment, Disposal, and Reuse*, 3rd Ed., McGraw-Hill.)

The velocity of 26 gal/min (1.64 L/s) in a 3 in. (76.3 mm) diameter pipe is

$$\text{Velocity} = \frac{26 \text{ gal/min}}{(7.48 \text{ gal/ft}^3)[(\pi/4)(3 \text{ in./12 in./ft})^2](60 \text{ s/min})} = 1.2 \text{ ft/s } (0.37 \text{ m/s})$$

Using Fig. 11 with a velocity of 1.2 ft/s (0.37 m/s) and a solids content of 5 percent, the multiplication factor $(k)$ is 12. Therefore, the dynamic head loss for this system when pumping 5 percent solids is:

$$\text{Dynamic Head Loss}_{5\%} = (\text{Dynamic Head Loss}_{water})(k)$$

$$\text{Dynamic Head Loss}_{5\%} = (4.12 \text{ ft})(12) = 49.44 \text{ ft } (15.1 \text{ m})$$

Use 50 ft of head loss (15.2 m)

The total head loss is the sum of the static head and the dynamic head loss$_{5\%}$. Therefore, the total head loss (Total Dynamic Head or TDH) for the system is

$$10 \text{ ft} + 50 \text{ ft} = 60 \text{ ft } (18.3 \text{ m})$$

This translates to a discharge pressure on the pump of

$$TDH = (60 \text{ ft})/(2.31 \text{ ft/psi.}) = 26 \text{ lb/sq.in. } (179.1 \text{ kPa})$$

Therefore, the design condition for the rotary-lobe pump is 26 gal/min (1.64 L/s) at 26 lb/sq.in. (179.1 kPa).

### 3. *Choose the correct pump for the application*
At this point, a rotary-lobe pump manufacturer's catalog is required in order to choose the correct pump curve for this application. This is accomplished by choosing a pump performance curve that meets the above design condition. An example of a manufacturer's curve that satisfies the design condition is shown in Fig. 12.

Plotting a horizontal line from 26 gal/min (1.64 L/s) on the left to the 26 lb/sq.in. (179.1 kPa) pressure line and reading down gives a pump speed of approximately 175 rpm. This means that for this pump to deliver 26 gal/min (1.64 L/s) against a pressure of 26 lb/sq.in. (179.1 kPa), it must operate at 175 rpm.

The motor horsepower required for the rotary-lobe pump is calculated using the following empirical formula (taken from the catalog of Alfa Laval Pumps, Inc. of Kenosha, Wisconsin):

$$\text{Hp} = \frac{N}{7124}\left[(0.043)(q)(P) + \frac{(N)(S_f)}{1000} + \frac{(q)(N_f)}{26.42}\right]$$

$\text{Hp} = $ Motor horsepower
$N = $ Pump speed (rpm)
$q = $ Pump displacement, gal/100 revolutions (L/100 revs)
$P = $ Differential pressure or TDH, psi., (kPa)
$S_f = $ Factor related to pump size which is calculated using: $S_f = (q)(0.757) + 3$
$N_f = $ Factor related to the viscosity of the pumped liquid which is calculated using
$\quad\quad N_f = 2.2 \sqrt[3]{\text{Viscosity (cp)}}$

The pump speed was found in Fig. 12 to be 175 rpm; the pump displacement is taken from the pump curve and is 25 gal/100 revs (94.6 L/100 revs); the differential pressure or

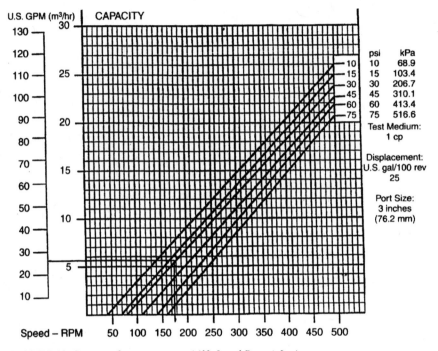

**FIGURE 12.** Pump performance curve. (*Alfa Laval Pumps, Inc.*)

TDH was calculated above to be 26 lb/sq.in. (179.1 kPa); $S_f = (25$ gal/100 revs)(0.757) + 3 = 21.925.

### 4. Determine the pump horsepower

The viscosity of a sewage sludge is dependent upon the percent solids and may be found using Table 3.

Using Table 3, a 5 percent solids sludge has a viscosity of 1,050 cp. Therefore:

$$N_f = 2.2\sqrt[3]{1050 \text{ cp}} = 22.36$$

Using the values outlined above, the motor horsepower is calculated:

$$HP = \frac{175 \text{ rpm}}{7124}\left[(0.043)(25 \text{ gal/100 revs})(26 \text{ psi.}) + \frac{(175 \text{ rpm})(21.925)}{1000} + \frac{(25)(22.36)}{26.42}\right]$$

$$= 1.3 \text{ hp } (0.97 \text{ kW})$$

The resulting horsepower of 1.3 hp (0.97 kW) is at best an informed estimate of the horse-power which will be absorbed at the pump shaft during pumping. It includes no service factor or margin for error, neither does it allow for inefficiency in power transmission systems.

**TABLE 3.** Viscosity of Sewage Sludge vs. Percent Solids

| Percent solids | Viscosity in centipoise (cp) |
|:---:|:---:|
| 1 | 10 |
| 2 | 80 |
| 3 | 250 |
| 4 | 560 |
| 5 | 1050 |
| 6 | 1760 |
| 7 | 2750 |
| 8 | 4000 |
| 9 | 5500 |
| 10 | 7500 |

*(Courtesy Alfa Laval Pumps, Inc.)*

## 5. Find the installed horsepower of the pump

Actual installed horsepower will need to be greater than this calculated horsepower to allow for the random torque increases due to large solids and to provide a prudent safety factor. Therefore, the minimum installed motor horsepower is calculated as follows:

$$\text{Installed Motor hp} = \frac{(1.2)(\text{Calculated hp})}{\text{Motor Drive Efficiency (\%)}} \times 100$$

Assuming a motor efficiency of 90 percent, the installed motor horsepower is

$$\text{Installed Motor hp} = \frac{(1.2)(1.3 \text{ hp})}{90\%} \times 100 = 1.73 \text{ hp } (1.29 \text{ kW})$$

Use the next largest motor size available, which is 2.0 hp (1.49 kW). Therefore, the rotary lobe sludge pump will have a 2.0 hp (1.49 kW) motor.

To summarize, the requirements for a rotary-lobe pump for this application are: design condition of 26 gal/min (1.64 L/s) at 26 lb/sq.in. (179.1 kPa), operating at 175 rpm with a 2.0 hp (1.49 kW) motor. Often a variable speed drive is provided so that the pump rpm (hence flow rate) may be adjusted to suit varying sludge flow rate demands at the downstream dewatering facility. Also, a second pump is generally provided as a spare.

## DESIGN OF AN ANAEROBIC DIGESTOR

A high rate anaerobic digestor is to be designed to treat a mixture of primary and Waste Activated Sludge produced by a wastewater treatment facility. The input sludge to the digester is 60,000 gal/day (227.1 m³/d) of primary and Waste Activated Sludge with an average loading of 25,000 lb/d (11,350 kg/d) of ultimate BOD ($BOD_L$). Assume the yield coefficient ($Y$) is 0.06 lb VSS/lb $BOD_L$ (kg/kg), and the endogenous coefficient ($k_d$) is 0.03 d$^{-1}$ at 35°C (95°F). Also assume that the efficiency of waste utilization in the digester is 60 percent. Compute the digester volume required, the volume of methane gas produced, the total volume of digester gas produced, and the percent stabilization of the sludge.

## Calculation Procedure:

### 1. *Determine the required digester volume and loading*

Anaerobic digestion is one of the oldest processes used for the stabilization of sludge. It involves the decomposition of organic and inorganic matter in the absence of molecular oxygen. The major applications of this process are in the stabilization of concentrated sludges produced from the treatment of wastewater.

In the anaerobic digestion process, the organic material is converted biologically, under anaerobic conditions, to a variety of end products including methane ($CH_4$) and carbon dioxide ($CO_2$). The process is carried out in an airtight reactor. Sludge, introduced continuously or intermittently, is retained in the reactor for varying periods of time. The stabilized sludge, withdrawn continuously or intermittently from the reactor, is reduced in organic and pathogen content and is nonputrescible.

In the high rate digestion process, as shown in Fig. 13, the contents of the digester are heated and completely mixed. For a complete-mix flow through digester, the mean cell residence time ($\theta_c$) is the same as the hydraulic retention time ($\theta$).

In the United States, the use and disposal of sewage sludge is regulated under 40 CFR Part 503 promulgated February 1993. The new regulation replaces 40 CFR Part 257—the original regulation governing the use and disposal of sewage sludge, in effect since 1979. The new regulations state that "for anaerobic digestion, the values for the mean-cell-residence time and temperature shall be between 15 days at 35°C to 55°C (95°F to 131°F) and 60 days at 20°C (68°F)."

Therefore, for an operating temperature of 35°C (95°F), a mean-cell-residence time of 15 days will be used. The influent sludge flow rate ($Q$) is 60,000 gal/day = 8,021 ft³/d (226.9 m³/d). The digester volume $V$ required is computed using

$$V = \theta_c Q \quad V = (15 \ d)(8,021 \ \text{ft}^3/\text{d}) = 120,315 \ \text{ft}^3 \ (3,404.9 \ \text{m}^3)$$

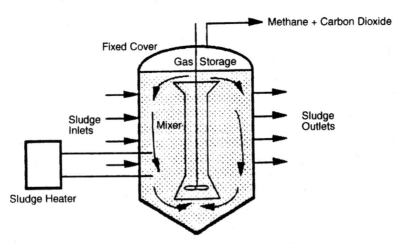

**FIGURE 13.** High-rate single-stage complete-mix anaerobic digester. (Adapted from Metcalf & Eddy, *Wastewater Engineering: Treatment, Disposal, and Reuse*, 3rd Ed., McGraw-Hill.)

The BOD entering the digester is 25,000 lb/d (11,350 kg/d). Therefore, the volumetric loading to the digester is

$$\text{Volumetric Loading} = \frac{25{,}000 \text{ lb BOD/d}}{120{,}315 \text{ ft}^3} = 0.21 \text{ lb/ft}^3\!\cdot\!\text{d } (3.37 \text{ kg/m}^3\!\cdot\!\text{d})$$

For high rate digesters, loadings range from 0.10 to 0.35 lb/ft$^3$·d (1.6 to 5.61 kg/m$^3$·d). Assuming 60 percent waste utilization, the BOD$_L$ exiting the digester is

$$(25{,}000 \text{ lb/d})(1 - 0.6) = 10{,}000 \text{ lb/d } (4540 \text{ kg/d})$$

## 2. *Compute the daily quantity of volatile solids produced*
The quantity of volatile solids produced each day is computed using

$$P_x = \frac{Y[(\text{BOD}_{\text{in}}, \text{ lb/d}) - (\text{BOD}_{\text{out}}, \text{ lb/d})]}{1 - k_d \theta_c}$$

where $P_x$ = Volatile solids produced, lb/d (kg/d)
$Y$ = Yield coefficient (lb VSS/lb BOD$_L$)
$k_d$ = Endogenous coefficient (d$^{-1}$)
$\theta_c$ = Mean cell residence time (d)

Using values obtained above, the volatile solids produced each day are

$$P_x = \frac{(0.06 \text{ lb VSS/lb BOD}_L)[(25{,}000 \text{ lb/d}) - (10{,}000 \text{ lb/d})]}{1 + (0.03 \text{ } d^{-1})(15 \text{ d})}$$

$$= 621 \text{ lb/d } (281.9 \text{ kg/d})$$

## 3. *Determine the volume of methane produced*
The volume of methane gas produced at standard conditions (32°F and 1 atm) (0°C and 101.3 kPa) is calculated using

$$V_{\text{CH}_4} = 5.62 \text{ ft}^3/\text{lb}[(\text{BOD}_{\text{in}}, \text{ lb/d}) - (\text{BOD}_{\text{out}}, \text{ lb/d}) - 1.42 \, P_x]$$

where $V_{\text{CH}_4}$ = Volume of methane gas produced at standard conditions (ft$^3$/d) (m$^3$/d)

Using values obtained above:

$$V_{\text{CH}_4} = 5.62 \text{ ft}^3/\text{lb}[(25{,}000 \text{ lb/d}) - (10{,}000 \text{ lb/d}) - 1.42(621 \text{ lb/d})]$$
$$= 79{,}344 \text{ ft}^3/\text{d } (2{,}245 \text{ m}^3/\text{d})$$

Since digester gas is approximately 2/3 methane, the volume of digester gas produced is

$$(79{,}344 \text{ ft}^3/\text{d})10.67 = 118{,}424 \text{ ft}^3/\text{d } (3351.4 \text{ m}^3/\text{d})$$

## 4. *Calculate the percent stabilization*
Percent stabilization is calculated using:

$$\% \text{ Stabilization} = \frac{[(\text{BOD}_{\text{in}}, \text{ lb/d}) - (\text{BOD}_{\text{out}}, \text{ lb/d}) - 1.42 \, P_x]}{\text{BOD}_{\text{in}}, \text{ lb/d}} \times 100$$

Using values obtained above:

$$\% \text{ Stabilization} = \frac{[(25,000 \text{ lb/d}) - (10,000 \text{ lb/d}) - 1.42(621 \text{ lb/d})]}{25,000 \text{ lb/d}}$$

$$\times 100 = 56.5\%$$

**Related Calculations.** The disadvantages and advantages of the anaerobic treatment of sludge, as compared to aerobic treatment, are related to the slow growth rate of the methanogenic (methane producing) bacteria. Slow growth rates require a relatively long retention time in the digester for adequate waste stabilization to occur. With methanogenic bacteria, most of the organic portion of the sludge is converted to methane gas, which is combustible and therefore a useful end product. If sufficient quantities of methane gas are produced, the methane gas can be used to operate duel-fuel engines to produce electricity and to provide building heat.

# DESIGN OF A CHLORINATION SYSTEM FOR WASTEWATER DISINFECTION

Chlorine is to be used for disinfection of a municipal wastewater. Estimate the chlorine residual that must be maintained to achieve a coliform count equal to or less than 200/100 ml in an effluent from an activated sludge facility assuming that the effluent requiring disinfection contains a coliform count of $10^7/100$ ml. The average wastewater flow requiring disinfection is 0.5 Mgd (1,892.5 m³/d) with a peaking factor of 2.8. Using the estimated residual, determine the capacity of the chlorinator. Per regulations, the chlorine contact time must not be less than 15 minutes at peak flow.

## Calculation Procedure:

### 1. Find the required residual for the allowed residence time
The reduction of coliform organisms in treated effluent is defined by the following equation:

$$\frac{N_t}{N_0} = (1 + 0.23C_t t)^{-3}$$

where $N_t$ = Number of coliform organisms at time $t$
$N_0$ = Number of coliform organisms at time $t_0$
$C_t$ = Total chlorine residual at time $t$ (mg/L)
$t$ = Residence time (min)

Using values for coliform count from above:

$$\frac{2 \times 10^2}{1 \times 10^7} = (1 + 0.23C_t t)^{-3}$$

$$2.0 \times 10^{-5} = (1 + 0.23C_t t)^{-3}$$

$$5.0 \times 10^4 = (1 + 0.23C_t t)^3$$

$$1 + 0.23 C_t t = 36.84$$

$$C_t t = 155.8 \text{ mg·min/L}$$

For a residence time of 15 minutes, the required residual is

$$C_t = (155.8 \text{ mg·min/L})/15 \text{ min} = 10.38 \text{ mg/L}$$

The chlorination system should be designed to provide chlorine residuals over a range of operating conditions and should include an adequate margin of safety. Therefore, the dosage required at peak flow will be set at 15 mg/L.

### 2. Determine the required capacity of the chlorinator

The capacity of the chlorinator at peak flow with a dosage of 15 mg/L is calculated using:

$$Cl_2 \text{ (lb/d)} = (\text{Dosage, mg/L})(\text{Avg flow, Mgd})(\text{P.F.})(8.34)$$

where
$Cl_2$ = Pounds of chlorine required per day (kg/d)
Dosage = Dosage used to obtain coliform reduction
Avg. Flow = Average flow
P.F. = Peaking factor for average flow
8.34 = 8.34 lb·L/Mgal·mg

Using values from above:

$$Cl_2 \text{ (lb/d)} = (15 \text{ mg/L})(0.5 \text{ Mgd})(2.8)(8.34) = 175 \text{ lb/d (79.5 kg/d)}$$

The next largest standard chlorinator size is 200 lb/d (90.8 kg/d). Therefore, two 200 lb/d (90.8 kg/d) chlorinators will be used with one serving as a spare. Although the peak capacity will not be required during most of the day, it must be available to meet chlorine requirements at peak flow.

### 3. Compute the daily consumption of chlorine

The average daily consumption of chlorine assuming an average dosage of 15 mg/L is

$$Cl_2 \text{ (lb/d)} = (15 \text{ mg/L})(0.5 \text{ Mgd})(8.34) = 62.5 \text{ lb/d (28.4 kg/d)}$$

A typical chlorination flow diagram is shown in Fig. 14. This is a compound loop system, which means the chlorine dosage is controlled through signals received from both effluent flow rate and chlorine residual.

## SANITARY SEWER SYSTEM DESIGN

What size main sanitary sewer is required for a midwestern city 30-acre ($1.21 \times 10^5$ m$^2$) residential area containing six-story apartment houses if the hydraulic gradient is 0.0035 and the pipe roughness factor $n = 0.013$? One-third of the area is served by a branch sewer. What should the size of this sewer be? If the branch and main sewers must also handle groundwater infiltration, determine the required sewer size. The sewer is below the normal groundwater level.

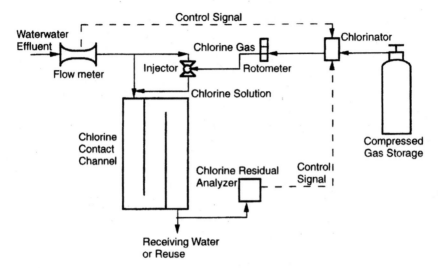

**FIGURE 14.** Compound-loop chlorination system flow diagram.

## Calculation Procedure:

### 1. *Compute the sanitary sewage flow rate*

Table 4 shows the typical population per acre for various residential areas and the flow rate used in sewer design. Using the typical population of 500 persons per acre (4046 m²) given in Table 4, we see the total population of the area served is (30 acres)(500 persons per acre) = 15,000 persons.

Since this is a midwestern city, the sewer design basis, per capita, used for Des Moines, Iowa, 200 gal/day (8.76 mL/s), Table 4, appears to be an appropriate value. Checking with the minimum flow recommended in Table 4, 100 gal/day (4.38 mL/s), we see the value of 200 gal/day (8.76 mL/s) seems to be well justified. Hence, the sanitary sewage flow rate that the main sewer must handle is (15,000 persons)(200 gal/day) = 3,000,000 gal/day.

### 2. *Convert the flow rate to cfs*

Use the relation $cfs = 1.55 \ (gpd/10^6)$, where $cfs$ = flow rate, ft³/s; $gpd$ = flow rate, gal/24 h. So $cfs = 1.55(3,000,000/1,000,000) = 465$ ft³/s (0.13 m³/s).

### 3. *Compute the required size of the main sewer*

Size the main sewer on the basis of its flowing full. This is the usual design procedure followed by experienced sanitary engineers.

(a) Use the chart in Fig. 12, Section 7, for the Manning formula, entering with the flow rate of 4.65 ft³/s (0.13 m³/s) and projecting to the slope ratio or hydraulic gradient of 0.0035. Read the required pipe diameter as 18 in. (457 mm).

(b) Use the Manning formula and the appropriate *conveyance factor* from Table 5. When the conveyance factor $C_f$ is used, the Manning formula becomes $Q = C_f S^{1/2}$, where $Q$ = flow rate through the pipe, ft³/s; $C_f$ = conveyance factor corresponding to a specific $n$ value listed in Table 5; $S$ = pipe slope or hydraulic gradient, ft/ft. Since $Q$ and $S$ are known, substitute and solve for $C_f$, or $C_f = Q/S^{1/2} = 4.65/(0.0035)^{1/2} = 78.5$. Enter Table 5

**TABLE 4.** Sanitary Sewer Design Factors

| Population data | | |
|---|---|---|
| | Typical population | |
| Type of area | Per acre | Per km$^2$ |
| Light residential | 15 | 3,707 |
| Closely built residential | 55 | 13,591 |
| Single-family residential | 100 | 24,711 |
| Six-story apartment district | 500 | 123,555 |

| Sewage-flow data | | |
|---|---|---|
| | Sewer design basis, per capita | |
| City | gal/day | mL/s |
| Berkeley, California | 92 | 4.03 |
| Cranston, Rhode Island | 167 | 7.32 |
| Des Moines, Iowa | 200 | 8.76 |
| Las Vegas, Nevada | 250 | 10.95 |
| Little Rock, Arkansas | 100 | 4.38 |
| Shreveport, Louisiana | 150 | 6.57 |

| Typical sewer design practice | | |
|---|---|---|
| | Design flow, per capita | |
| Sewer type | gal/day | mL/s |
| Laterals and submains | 400 | 17.5 |
| Main, trunks, and outfall | 250 | 10.95 |
| New sewers | Never 100 | Never 4.38 |

**TABLE 5.** Manning Formula Conveyance Factor

| Pipe diameter, in. (mm) | Pipe cross-sectional area, sq.ft. (m$^2$) | $n$ | | | |
|---|---|---|---|---|---|
| | | 0.011 | 0.013 | 0.015 | 0.017 |
| 6 (152) | 0.196 (0.02) | 6.62 | 5.60 | 4.85 | 4.28 |
| 8 (203) | 0.349 (0.03) | 14.32 | 12.12 | 10.50 | 9.27 |
| 10 (254) | 0.545 (0.05) | 25.80 | 21.83 | 18.92 | 16.70 |
| 12 (305) | 0.785 (0.07) | 42.15 | 35.66 | 30.91 | 27.27 |
| 15 (381) | 1.227 (0.11) | 76.46 | 64.70 | 56.07 | 49.48 |
| 18 (457) | 1.767 (0.16) | 124.2 | 105.1 | 91.04 | 80.33 |
| 21 (533) | 2.405 (0.22) | 187.1 | 158.3 | 137.2 | 121.1 |

at $n = 0.013$ and $C_f = 78.5$, and project to the exact or next higher value of $C_f$. Table 5 shows that $C_f$ is 64.70 for 15-in. (381-mm) pipe and 105.1 for 18-in. (457-mm) pipe. Since the actual value of $C_f$ is 78.5, a 15-in. (381-mm) pipe would be too small. Hence, an 18-in. (457-mm) pipe would be used. This size agrees with that found in procedure $a$.

### 4. Compute the size of the lateral sewer

The lateral sewer serves one-third of the total area. Since the total sanitary flow from the entire area is 4.65 ft³/s (0.13 m³/s), the flow from one-third of the area, given an even distribution of population and the same pipe slope, is $4.65/3 = 1.55$ ft³/s (0.044 m³/s). Using either procedure in step 3, we find the required pipe size = 12 in. (305 mm). Hence, three 12-in. (305-mm) laterals will discharge into the main sewer, assuming that each lateral serves an equal area and has the same slope.

### 5. Check the suitability of the main sewer size

Compute the value of $d^{2.5}$ for each of the lateral sewer pipes discharging into the main sewer pipe. Thus, for one 12-in. (305-mm) lateral line, where $d$ = smaller pipe diameter, in. $d^{2.5} = 12^{2.5} = 496$. For three pipes of equal diameter, $3d^{2.5} = 1488 = D^{2.5}$, where $D$ = larger pipe diameter, in. Solving gives $D^{2.5} = 1488$ and $D = 17.5$ in. (445 mm). Hence, the 18-in. (4570 mm) sewer main has sufficient capacity to handle the discharge of three 12-in. (305-mm) sewers. Note that Fig. 12, Section 7, shows that the flow velocity in both the lateral and main sewers exceeds the minimum required velocity of 2 ft/s (0.6 m/s).

### 6. Compute the sewer size with infiltration

Infiltration is the groundwater that enters a sewer. The quantity and rate of infiltration depend on the character of the soil in which the sewer is laid, the relative position of the groundwater level and the sewer, the diameter and length of the sewer, and the material and care with which the sewer is constructed. With tile and other jointed sewers, infiltration depends largely on the type of joint used in the pipes. In large concrete or brick sewers, the infiltration depends on the type of waterproofing applied.

Infiltration is usually expressed in gallons per day per mile of sewer. With very careful construction, infiltration can be kept down to 5000 gal/(day·mi) [0.14 L/(km·s)] of pipe even when the groundwater level is above the pipe. With poor construction, porous soil, and high groundwater level, infiltration may amount to 100,000 gal/(day·mi) [2.7 L/(km·s)] or more. Sewers laid in dense soil where the groundwater level is below the sewer do not experience infiltration except during and immediately after a rainfall. Even then, the infiltration will be in small amounts.

Assuming an infiltration rate of 20,000 gal/(day·mi) [0.54 L/(km·s)] of sewer and a sewer length of 1.2 mi (1.9 km) for this city, we see the daily infiltration is 1.2 (20,000) = 24,000 gal (90,850 L).

Checking the pipe size by either method in step 3 shows that both the 12-in. (305-mm) laterals and the 18-in. (457-mm) main are of sufficient size to handle both the sanitary and infiltration flow.

***Related Calculations.*** Where a sewer must also handle the runoff from firefighting apparatus, compute the quantity of fire-fighting water for cities of less than 200,000 population from $Q = 1020(P)^{0.5} [1 - 0.01(P)^{0.5}]$, where $Q$ = fire demand, gal/min; $P$ = city population in thousands. Add the fire demand to the sanitary sewage and infiltration flows to determine the maximum quantity of liquid the sewer must handle. For cities having a population of more than 200,000 persons, consult the fire department headquarters to determine the water flow quantities anticipated.

Some sanitary engineers apply a demand factor to the average daily water requirements per capita before computing the flow rate into the sewer. Thus, the maximum monthly water consumption is generally about 125 percent of the average annual demand but may range up to 200 percent of the average annual demand. Maximum daily demands of 150 percent of the average annual demand and maximum hourly demands of 200 to 250 percent of the annual average demand are commonly used for design by some sanitary engineers. To apply a demand factor, simply multiply the flow rate computed in step 2 by the appropriate factor. Current practice in the use of demand factors varies; sewers designed without demand factors are generally adequate. Applying a demand factor simply provides a margin of safety in the design, and the sewer is likely to give service for a longer period before becoming overloaded.

Most local laws and many sewer authorities recommend that no sewer be less than 8 in. (203 mm) in diameter. The sewer should be sloped sufficiently to give a flow velocity of 2 ft/s (0.6 m/s) or more when flowing full. This velocity prevents the deposit of solids in the pipe. Manholes serving sewers should not be more than 400 ft (121.9 m) apart.

Where industrial sewage is discharged into a sanitary sewer, the industrial flow quantity must be added to the domestic sewage flow quantity before the pipe size is chosen. Swimming pools may also be drained into sanitary sewers and may cause temporary overflowing because the sewer capacity is inadequate. The sanitary sewage flow rate from an industrial area may be less than from a residential area of the same size because the industrial population is smaller.

Many localities and cities restrict the quantity of commercial and industrial sewage that may be discharged into public sewers. Thus, one city restricts commercial sewage from stores, garages, beauty salons, etc., to 135 gal/day per capita. Another city restricts industrial sewage from factories and plants to 50,000 gal/(day·acre) [0.55 mL/(m·s)]. In other cities each proposed installation must be studied separately. Still other cities prohibit any discharge of commercial or industrial sewage into sanitary sewers. For these reasons, the local authorities and sanitary codes, if any, must be consulted before the design of any sewer is begun.

Before starting a sewer design, do the following: (*a*) Prepare a profile diagram of the area that will be served by the sewer. Indicate on the diagram the elevation above grade of each profile. (*b*) Compile data on the soil, groundwater level, type of paving, number and type of foundations, underground services (gas, electric, sewage, water supply, etc.), and other characteristics of the area that will be served by the sewer. (*c*) Sketch the main sewer and lateral sewers on the profile diagram. Indicate the proposed direction of sewage flow by arrows. With these steps finished, start the sewer design.

To design the sewers, proceed as follows: (*a*) Size the sewers using the procedure given in steps 1 through 6 above. (*b*) Check the sewage flow rate to see that it is 2 ft/s (0.56 m/s) or more. (*c*) Check the plot to see that the required slope for the pipes can be obtained without expensive blasting or rock removal.

Where the outlet of a building plumbing system is below the level of the sewer serving the building, a pump must be used to deliver the sewage to the sewer. Compute the pump capacity, using the discharge from the various plumbing fixtures in the building as the source of the liquid flow to the pump. The head on the pump is the difference between the level of the sewage in the pump intake and the centerline of the sewer into which the pump discharges, plus any friction losses in the piping.

## SELECTION OF SEWAGE-TREATMENT METHOD

A city of 100,000 population is considering installing a new sewage-treatment plant. Select a suitable treatment method. Local ordinances required that suspended matter in the sewage be reduced 80 percent, that bacteria be reduced 60 percent, and that the biochemical oxygen demand be reduced 90 percent. The plant will handle only domestic sanitary sewage. What are the daily oxygen demand and the daily suspended-solids content of the sewage? If an industrial plant discharges into this system sewage requiring 4500 lb (2041.2 kg) of oxygen per day, determine the population equivalent of the industrial sewage.

## Calculation Procedure:

### 1. Compute the daily sewage flow
With an average flow per capita of 200 gal/day (8.8 mL/s), this sewage treatment plant must handle per capita (200 gal/day)(100,000 population) = 20,000 gal/day (896.2 L/s).

### 2. Compute the sewage oxygen demand
Usual domestic sewage shows a 5-day oxygen demand of 0.12 to 0.17 lb/day (0.054 to 0.077 kg/day) per person. With an average of 0.15 lb (0.068 kg) per person per day, the daily oxygen demand of the sewage is (0.15)(100,000) = 15,000 lb/day (78/7 g/s).

### 3. Compute the suspended-solids content of the sewage
Usual domestic sewage contains about 0.25 lb (0.11 kg) of suspended solids per person per day. Using this average, we see the total quantity of suspended solids that must be handled is (0.25)(100,000) = 25,000 lb/day (0.13 kg/s).

### 4. Select the sewage-treatment method
Table 6 shows the efficiency of various sewage-treatment methods. Since the desired reduction in suspended matter, biochemical oxygen demand (BOD), and bacteria is known, this will serve as a guide to the initial choice of the equipment.

Study of Table 6 shows that a number of treatments are available that will reduce the suspended matter by 80 percent. Hence, any one of these methods might be used. The same is true for the desired reduction in bacteria and BOD. Thus, the system choice resolves to selection of the most economical group of treatment units.

For a city of this size, four steps of sewage treatment would be advisable. The first step, preliminary treatment, could include screening to remove large suspended solids, grit removal, and grease removal. The next step, primary treatment, could include sedimentation or chemical precipitation. Secondary treatment, the next step, might be of a biological type such as the activated-sludge process or the trickling filter. In the final step, the sewage might be treated by chlorination. Treated sewage can then be disposed of in fields, streams, or other suitable areas.

Choose the following units for this sewage treatment plant, using the data in Table 6 as a guide: rocks or screens to remove large suspended solids, grit chambers to remove grit, skimming tanks for grease removal, plain sedimentation, activated-sludge process, and chlorination.

Reference to Table 6 shows that screens and plain sedimentation will reduce the suspended solids by the desired amount. Likewise, the activated-sludge process reduces the BOD by up to 95 percent and the bacteria up to 95+ percent. Hence, the chosen system satisfies the design requirements.

### 5. Compute the population equivalent of the industrial sewage
Use the relation $Pe = R/D$, where $P_e$ = population equivalent of the industrial sewage, persons; $R$ = required oxygen of the sewage, lb/day; $D$ = daily oxygen demand, lb per person per day. So $P_e = 4500/0.15 = 30,000$ persons.

**Related Calculations.** Where sewage is combined (i.e., sanitary and storm sewage mixed), the 5-day per-capita oxygen demand is about 0.25 lb/day (0.11 kg/day). Where large quantities of industrial waste are part of combined sewage, the per-capita oxygen

**TABLE 6.** Typical Efficiencies of Sewage-Treatment Methods*

| Treatment | Percentage reduction | | |
| --- | --- | --- | --- |
| | Suspended matter | BOD | Bacteria |
| Fine screens | 5–20 | . . . | 10–20 |
| Plain sedimentation | 35–65 | 25–40 | 50–60 |
| Chemical precipitation | 75–90 | 60–85 | 70–90 |
| Low-rate trickling filter, with pre- and final sedimentation | 70–90+ | 75–90 | 90+ |
| High-rate trickling filter with pre- and final sedimentation | 70–90 | 65–95 | 70–95 |
| Conventional activated sludge with pre- and final sedimentation | 80–95 | 80–95 | 90–95+ |
| High-rate activated sludge with pre- and final sedimentation | 70–90 | 70–95 | 80–95 |
| Contact aeration with pre- and final sedimentation | 80–95 | 80–95 | 90–95+ |
| Intermittent sand filtration with presedimentation | 90–95 | 85–95 | 95+ |
| Chlorination: | | | |
|   Settled sewage | . . . | † | 90–95 |
|   Biologically treated sewage | . . . | † | 98–99 |

*Steel—*Water Supply and Sewerage,* McGraw-Hill.
†Reduction is dependent on dosage.

demand is usually about 0.5 lb/day (0.23 kg/day). To convert the strength of an industrial waste to the same base used for sanitary waste, apply the population equivalent relation in step 5. Some cities use the population equivalent as a means of evaluating the load placed on the sewage-treatment works by industrial plants.

Table 7 shows the products resulting from various sewage-treatment processes per million gallons of sewage treated. The tabulated data are useful for computing the volume of product each process produces.

Environmental considerations are leading to the adoption of biogas methods to handle the organic fraction of municipal solid waste (MSW). Burning methane-rich biogas can meet up to 60 percent of the operating cost of waste-to-energy plants. Further, generating biogas avoids the high cost of disposing of this odorous by-product. A further advantage is that biogas plants are exempt from energy or carbon taxes. Newer plants also handle industrial wastes, converting them to biogas.

Biogas plants are popular in Europe. The first anaerobic digestion plant capable of treating unsorted MSW handles 55,000 mt/yr. It treats wastestreams with solids contents of 30 to 35 percent. Automated sorting first removes metals, plastics, paperboard, glass, and inerts from the MSW stream. The remaining organic fraction is mixed with recycled water from a preceding compost-drying press to form a 30 to 35 percent solids sludge, which is pumped into one of the plant's three 2400-m$^3$ (84,720 ft$^3$) digesters.

Residence time in the digester is about 3 weeks with a biogas yield of 99 m$^3$/mt of MSW (3495 ft$^3$/t), or 146 m$^3$/mt (5154 ft$^3$/t) of sorted organic fraction. Overflow liquid from the digester is pressed, graded, and sold as compost. Mixtures of MSW, sewage

**TABLE 7.** Sludge and Other Products of Sewage-Treatment Processes per Million Gallons of Sewage Treated*

| Data | Treatment process | | | | | | | |
|---|---|---|---|---|---|---|---|---|
| | Racks | Fine screens | Grit chambers | Plain sedimentation | Septic tanks | Imhoff or separate tanks | Activated sludge | Trickling filter humus tanks |
| Character of product | Screenings | Screenings | Grit | Raw sludge | Digested sludge | Digested sludge | Raw sludge | Raw sludge |
| Average amount per million gallons | 4–8 ft³ (0.11–0.23 m³) | 10–30 ft³ (0.28–0.83 m³) | 2.5 ft³ (0.07 m³) | 2500 gal (9462.5 L) | 900 gal (3406.5 L) | 500 gal (1892.5 L) | 13,500 gal (51,098 L) | 500 gal (1892.5 L) |
| Average moisture content, percent | 80 | 80 | 15 | 95 | 90 | 85 | 99 | 92.5 |
| Specific gravity | | | | 1020 | 1040 | 1040 | 1005 | 1025 |
| Usual disposal methods | Burying, burning, or shredding and digestion with sludge | Burying, burning, or digesting with sludge | Filling land | Processing, digestion, or drying | Drying | Drying | Processing, digestion, or lagooning | Digestion and drying |

*O'Rourke—*General Engineering Handbook.* McGraw-Hill.

sludges, and animal slurries can also be digested in this process (Valorga) developed by Valorga SA (Vendargues, France). This is termed a dry process.

*Wet* processes handle wastestreams with only 10 to 15 percent solids content. Featuring more than one digestion stage, it is easier to control parameters such as pH and solids concentration than dry fermentation. The first plant to use wet digestion to process MSW is 20,000-mt/yr installation in Denmark. About two-thirds of the annual operating cost of $2 million is recovered through the sale of biogas. In a 14,000-mt/yr plant in Finland the biogas produced is used to fire a gas turbine. Multiple stages are said to make wet fermentation 65 percent faster than single-stage processes, with a 50 percent higher gas yield.

These developments show that sanitary engineers will be more concerned than ever with the environmental aspects of their designs. With the world population growing steadily every year and the longer lifespan of older individuals, biogas and similar recovery-conversion processes will become standard practice in every major country.

The data on biogas given above were reported in *Chemical Engineering.*

# SECTION 9
# ENGINEERING ECONOMICS

### MAX KURTZ, P.E.
*Consulting Engineer*

# Calculation of Interest, Principal, and Payments

## Symbols and Abbreviations

General: With discrete compounding, $i$ = interest rate per period, percent; $n$ = number of interest periods. With continuous compounding, $j$ = nominal annual interest rate, percent; interest period = 1 year.

Simple and compound interest—single payment: $P$ = value of payment at beginning of first interest period, also termed *present worth* of payment; $S$ = value of payment at end of $n$th interest period, also termed *future value* of payment.

Compound interest—uniform-payment series: $R$ = sum paid at end of each interest period for $n$ periods; $P$ = value of payments at beginning of first interest period, also termed *present worth* of payments; $S$ = value of payments at end of $n$th interest period, also termed *future value* of payments.

Compound interest—uniform-gradient series: $R_m$ = payment at end of $m$th interest period; $g$ = constant difference between given payment and preceding payment, also termed *gradient* of series. Then $R_m = R_1 + (m - 1)g$. Also, $P$ and $S$ have the same meaning as for uniform-payment series.

Compound interest—uniform-rate series: $R_m$ = payment at end of $m$th interest period; $r$ = constant ratio of given payment to preceding payment. Then $R_m = R_1 r^{m-1}$, and $P$ and $S$ have the same meaning as for uniform-payment series.

Compound-interest factors: *Single payment—S/P* = single-payment compound-amount (SPCA) factor; *P/S* = single-payment present-worth (SPPW) factor. *Uniform-payment series—S/R* = uniform-series compound-amount (USCA) factor; *R/S* = sinking-fund-payment (SFP) factor; *P/R* = uniform-series present-worth (USPW) factor; *R/P* = capital-recovery (CR) factor. *Uniform-rate series—S/R_1* = uniform-rate-series compound-amount (URSCA) factor; *P/R_1* = uniform-rate-series present-worth (URSPW) factor.

## Basic Equations

*Simple interest, single payment*

$$S = P(1 + ni) \tag{1}$$

*Compound interest with discrete compounding*

$$\text{SPCA} = (1 + i)^n \tag{2}$$

$$\text{SPPW} = (1 + i)^{-n} \tag{3}$$

$$\text{USCA} = \frac{(1 + i)^n - 1}{i} \tag{4}$$

$$\text{SFP} = \frac{i}{(1 + i)^n - 1} \tag{5}$$

$$\text{USPW} = \frac{(1 + i)^n - 1}{i(1 + I)^n} \tag{6}$$

$$CR = \frac{i(1 + i)^n}{(1 + i)^n - 1} \tag{7}$$

$$URSCA = \frac{r^n - (1 + i)^n}{r - i - 1} \tag{8}$$

$$URSPW = \frac{[r/(1 + i)]^n - 1}{r - i - 1} \tag{9}$$

A uniform-payment series that continues indefinitely is termed a *perpetuity*. For this case,

$$USPW = \frac{1}{i} \tag{6a}$$

$$CR = i \tag{7a}$$

*Compound interest with continuous compounding*

$$SPCA = e^{jn} \tag{10}$$

where $e$ = base of natural logarithms = 2.71828 . . .

$$SPPW = e^{-jn} \tag{11}$$

$$USCA = \frac{e^{jn} - 1}{e^j - 1} \tag{12}$$

$$USPW = \frac{1 - e^{-jn}}{e^j - 1} \tag{13}$$

The compound-interest factors for a single payment and for a uniform-payment series can be found by referring to compound-interest tables or by solving the relevant equations by calculator.

## DETERMINATION OF SIMPLE INTEREST

A company borrows $4000 at 6 percent per annum simple interest. What payment must be made to retire the debt at the end of 5 years?

### Calculation Procedure:

#### Apply the equation for simple interest
This equation is $S = P(1 + ni) = \$4000(1 + 5 \times 0.06) = \$5200$.
   *Note*: See the introduction to this section for the symbols used.

## COMPOUND INTEREST; FUTURE VALUE OF SINGLE PAYMENT

The sum of $2600 was deposited in a fund that earned interest at 8 percent per annum compounded quarterly. What was the principal in the fund at the end of 3 years?

## Calculation Procedure:

### 1. Compute the true interest rate and number of interest periods

Since there are four interest periods per year, the interest rate $i$ per period is $i = 8$ percent/4 = 2 percent per period. With a 3-year deposit period, the number $n$ of interest periods is $n = 3 \times 4 = 12$.

### 2. Apply the SPCA value given in a compound-interest table

Look up the SPCA value for the interest rate, 2 percent, and the number of interest periods, 12. Then substitute in $S = P(SPCA) = \$2600(1.268) = \$3296.80$.

## PRESENT WORTH OF SINGLE PAYMENT

On January 1 of a certain year, a deposit was made in a fund that earns interest at 6 percent per annum. On December 31, 7 years later, the principal resulting from this deposit was $1082. What sum was deposited?

## Calculation Procedure:

### Apply the SPPW relation

Obtain the SPPW factor for $i = 6$ percent, $n = 7$ years from the interest table. Thus $P = S(SPPW) = \$1082(0.6651) = \$719.64$.

## PRINCIPAL IN SINKING FUND

To accumulate capital for an expansion program, a corporation made a deposit of $200,000 at the end of each year for 5 years in a fund earning interest at 4 percent per annum. What was the principal in the fund immediately after the fifth deposit was made?

## Calculation Procedure:

### Apply the USCA factor

Obtain the USCA factor for $i = 4$ percent, $n = 5$ from the interest table. Substitute in the relation $S = R(USCA) = \$200,000(5.416) = \$1,083,200$.

## DETERMINATION OF SINKING-FUND DEPOSIT

The XYZ Corporation borrows $65,000, which it is required to repay at the end of 5 years at 8 percent interest. To accumulate this sum, XYZ will make five equal annual deposits in a fund that earns interest at 3 percent, the first deposit being made 1 year after negotiation of the loan. What is the amount of the annual deposit required?

## Calculation Procedure:

### 1. Compute the sum to be paid at the expiration of the loan

Obtain the SPCA factor from the interest table for $i = 8$ percent, $n = 5$. Then substitute in the relation $S = P(SPCA) = \$65,000(1.469) = \$95,485$.

**2. *Compute the annual deposit corresponding to this future value***

Obtain the SFP factor from the interest table for $i = 3$ percent, $n = 5$ and substitute in the relation $R = S(\text{SFP}) = \$95,485(0.18835) = \$17,985$.

## PRESENT WORTH OF A UNIFORM SERIES

An inventor is negotiating with two firms for assignment of rights to a patent. The ABC Corp. offers an annuity of 12 annual payments of \$15,000 each, the first payment to be made 1 year after sale of the patent. The DEF Corp. proposes to buy the patent by making an immediate lump-sum payment of \$120,000. If the inventor can invest the capital at 10 percent, which offer should be accepted?

### Calculation Procedure:

***Compute the present worth of the annuity, using an interest rate of 10 percent***

Obtain the USPW factor from an interest table for $i = 10$ percent, $n = 12$ and substitute in the relation $P = R(\text{USPW}) = \$15,000(6.814) = \$102,210$. Since the DEF Corp. offered an immediate payment of \$120,000, its offer is more attractive than the offer made by ABC Corp.

## CAPITAL-RECOVERY DETERMINATION

On January 1 of a certain year a company had a bank balance of \$58,000. The company decided to allot this money to an improvement program by making a series of equal payments 4 times a year for 5 years, beginning on April 1 of the same year. If the account earned interest at 4 percent compounded quarterly, what was the amount of the periodic payment?

### Calculation Procedure:

**1. *Compute the true interest rate and number of interest periods***

Since the annual rate = 4 percent and there are four interest periods per year, the rate per period is $i = 4$ percent/4 = 1 percent. And with a 5-year pay period, the number of interest periods = 5 years (4 periods per year) = 20 periods.

**2. *Compute the uniform payment, i.e., capital recovery***

The present worth of the sum is \$58,000. Obtain the CR factor from an interest table for $i = 1$ percent, $n = 20$ and substitute in the relation $R = P(\text{CR}) = \$58,000(0.05542) = \$3214.36$.

## EFFECTIVE INTEREST RATE

An account earns interest at the rate of 6 percent per annum, compounded quarterly. Compute the effective interest rate to four significant figures.

## Calculation Procedure:

### Compute the interest earned by $1 per year

With four interest periods per year, the interest rate per period $= i = 6$ percent/4 $= 1.5$ percent. In 1 year there are four interest periods for this account.

Find the compounded value of $1 at the end of 1 year from $S = (1 + i)^n = (1 + 0.015)^4 = \$1.06136$. Thus, the interest earned by $1 in 1 year $= \$1.06136 - 1.00000 = \$0.06136$. Hence, the effective interest rate $= 6.136$ percent.

## PERPETUITY DETERMINATION

What sum must be deposited to provide annual payments of $10,000 that are to continue indefinitely if the endowment fund earns interest of 4 percent compounded semiannually?

## Calculation Procedure:

### 1. Compute the effective interest rate

Using the same procedure as in the previous calculation procedure for $1, we find the effective interest rate $i_e = (1.02)^2 - 1 = 0.04040$, or 4.04 percent.

### 2. Apply the USPW relation

The endowment or principal required $= P =$ payment/$i_e$, or $P = \$10,000/0.0404 = \$247,525$.

## DETERMINATION OF EQUIVALENT SUMS

Jones Corp. borrowed $900 from Brown Corp. on January 1 of year 1 and $1200 on January 1 of year 3. Jones Corp. made a partial payment of $700 on January 1 of year 4. It was agreed that the balance of the loan would be discharged by two payments, one on January 1 of year 5 and the other on January 1 of year 6, with the second payment being 50 percent larger than the first. If the interest rate is 6 percent, what is the amount of each payment?

## Calculation Procedure:

### 1. Construct a line diagram indicating the loan data

Figure 1 shows the line diagram for these loans and is typical of the diagrams that can be prepared for any similar set of loans.

### 2. Select a convenient date for evaluating all the sums

For this situation, select January 1 of year 6. Mark the valuation date on Fig. 1, as shown.

### 3. Evaluate each sum at the date selected

Use the applicable interest rate, 6 percent, and the equivalence equation, value of money borrowed = value of money paid. Substituting the applicable SPCA factor from the interest table for each of the interest periods involved, or $n = 5$, $n = 3$, $n = 2$, and $n = 1$, respectively, gives $\$900(\text{SPCA}) + \$1200(\text{SPCA}) = \$700(\text{SPCA}) + x(\text{SPCA}) + 1.5x$, where

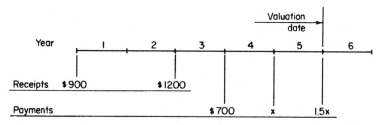

**FIGURE 1.** Time, receipt, and payment diagram.

$x$ = payment made on January 1 of year 5 and $1.5x$ = payment made on January 1 of year 6. Substituting, we get $900(1.338) + 1200(1.191) = 700(1.124) + 1.06x + 1.5x$; $x = 721.30$. Hence, $1.5x = 1081.95$.

**Related Calculations.** Note that this procedure can be used for more than two loans and for payments of any type that retire a debt.

## ANALYSIS OF A NONUNIFORM SERIES

On January 1 of a certain year, ABC Corp. borrowed $1,450,000 for 12 years at 6 percent interest. The terms of the loan obliged the firm to establish a sinking fund in which the following deposits were to be made: $200,000 at the end of the second to the sixth years; $250,000 at the end of the seventh to the eleventh years; and one for the balance of the loan at the end of the twelfth year. The interest rate earned by the sinking fund was 3 percent. Adverse financial conditions prevented the firm from making the deposit of $200,000 at the end of the fifth year. What was the amount of the final deposit?

### Calculation Procedure:

### 1. *Prepare a money-time diagram*
Figure 2 shows a money-time diagram for this situation, where $x$ = deposit made at end of twelfth year.

### 2. *Compute the principal of the loan at the end of the twelfth year*
Use the relation $S = P(\text{SPCA})$ for $i$ = 6 percent, $n$ = 12. Obtain the SPCA value from an interest table, and substitute in the above relation, or $S = 1,450,000(2.012) = 2,917,400$.

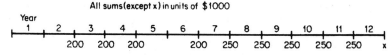

**FIGURE 2.** Money-time diagram.

### 3. Set up an expression for the principal in the sinking fund at the end of the twelfth year

From Fig. 2, principal = $200,000(USCA, $n$ = 3)(SPCA, $n$ = 8) + $200,000(SPCA, $n$ = 6) + $250,000(USCA, $n$ = 5)(SPCA, $n$ = 1) + $x$. With an interest rate of 3 percent, principal = $200,000(3.091)(1.267) + $200,000(1.194) + $250,000(5.309)(1.030) + $x$, or principal = $2,389,100 + $x$.

### 4. Compute the final deposit

Equate the principal in the sinking fund to the principal of the loan: $2,389,100 + $x$ = $2,917,400. Thus, $x$ = $528,300.

## UNIFORM SERIES WITH PAYMENT PERIOD DIFFERENT FROM INTEREST PERIOD

Deposits of $2000 each were made in a fund earning interest at 4 percent per annum compounded quarterly. The interval between deposits was 18 months. What was the balance in the account immediately after the fifth deposit was made?

### Calculation Procedure:

### 1. Compute the actual interest rate

Replace the interest rate $i_3$ for the quarterly period with an equivalent rate $i_{18}$ for the 18-month period. Or, $i_{18} = (1 + i_3)^n - 1 = (1.01)^6 - 1 = 6.15$ percent.

### 2. Compute the USCA value

Apply the equation USCA = $[(1 + i)^n - 1]/i$, or USCA = $[(1.0615)^5 - 1]/0.0615 = 5.654$.

### 3. Compute the principal in the fund

Use the relation $S = R$(USCA) = $2000(5.654) = $11,308.

## UNIFORM-GRADIENT SERIES: CONVERSION TO UNIFORM SERIES

A loan was to be amortized by a group of six end-of-year payments forming an ascending arithmetic progression. The initial payment was to be $5000, and the difference between successive payments was to be $400, as shown in Fig. 3. But the loan was renegotiated to

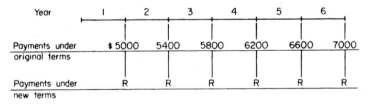

**FIGURE 3.** Diagram showing changed payment plan.

provide for the payment of equal rather than uniformly varying sums. If the interest rate of the loan was 8 percent, what was the annual payment?

## Calculation Procedure:

### 1. Apply the equivalent-uniform-series equation

Let $R_1$ = initial payment in a uniform-gradient series; $g$ = difference between successive payments; $n$ = number of payments; $R_e$ = periodic payment in an equivalent uniform series. Then $R_e = R_1 + (g/i)(1 - n\text{SFP})$. Substituting with $R_1 = \$5000$, $g = \$400$, $n = 6$, and $i = 8$ percent, we find $R_e = \$5000 + (\$400/0.08)(1 - 6 \times 0.13632) = \$5911$.

### 2. As an alternative, use the uniform-gradient conversion (UGC) factor

With $n = 6$ and $i = 8$ percent, UGC = 2.28. Then, $R_e = \$5000 + \$400(2.28) = \$5912$.

## PRESENT WORTH OF UNIFORM-GRADIENT SERIES

Under the terms of a contract, Brown Corp. was to receive a payment at the end of each year from year 1 to year 7, with the payments varying uniformly from $8000 in year 1 to $5000 in year 7. At the beginning of year 1, Brown Corp. assigned its annuity to Edwards Corp. at a price that yielded Edwards Corp. a 6 percent investment rate. What did Edwards Corp. pay for the annuity?

## Calculation Procedure:

### 1. Apply the relation of step 1 of the previous calculation procedure

The relation referred to converts a uniform-gradient series to an equivalent uniform series. Thus, with $g = -\$500$, $n = 7$, and $i = 6$ percent, we get $R_e = \$8000 + (-\$500/0.06) \times (1 - 7 \times 0.11914) = \$6617$.

### 2. Compute the present worth of the equivalent annuity

Use the relation $P = R_e(\text{USPW}) = \$6617(5.582) = \$36,936$.

## FUTURE VALUE OF UNIFORM-RATE SERIES

A deposit was made in a fund at the end of each year for 8 consecutive years. The first deposit was $1000, and each deposit thereafter was 25 percent more than the preceding deposit. If the interest rate of the fund was 7 percent per annum, what was the principal in the fund immediately after the eighth deposit was made?

## Calculation Procedure:

### 1. Compute the URSCA value

A uniform-rate series is a set of payments made at equal intervals in which the payments form a geometric progression (i.e., the ratio of a given payment to the preceding payment is constant). In this instance, the deposits form a uniform-rate series because each deposit is 1.25 times the preceding deposit. Apply Eq. 8: $\text{URSCA} = [r^n - (1 + i)^n]/(r - i - 1)$, = interest rate for the payment period. With $r = 1.25$, $n = 8$, and $i = 7$ percent, $\text{URSCA} = [(1.25)^8 - (1.07)^8]/(1.25 - 0.07 - 1) = 23.568$.

### 2. Compute the future value of the set of deposits
Use the relation $S = R_1(\text{URSCA})$, where $R_1$ = first payment. Then $S = \$1000(23.568) = \$23,568$.

## DETERMINATION OF PAYMENTS UNDER UNIFORM-RATE SERIES

At the beginning of year 1, the sum of \$30,000 was borrowed with interest at 9 percent per annum. The loan will be discharged by payments made at the end of years 1 to 6, inclusive, and each payment will be 95 percent of the preceding payment. Find the amount of the first and sixth payments.

### Calculation Procedure:

### 1. Compute the URSPW value of the uniform-rate series
Apply Eq. 9: $\text{URSPW} = \{[r/(1 + i)]^n - 1\}/(r - i - 1)$, where the symbols are as defined in the previous calculation procedure. With $r = 0.95$, $n = 6$, and $i = 9$ percent, $\text{URSPW} = [(0.95/1.09)^6 - 1]/(0.95 - 0.09 - 1) = 4.012$.

### 2. Find the amount of the first payment
Use the relation $P = R_1(\text{URSPW})$, where $R_1$ = first payment. Then $\$30,000 = R_1(4.012)$, or $R_1 = \$7477.60$.

### 3. Find the amount of the sixth payment
Use the relation $R_m = R_1 r^{m-1}$, where $R_m$ = $m$th payment. Then $R_6 = \$7477.60(0.95)^5 = \$5786.00$.

## CONTINUOUS COMPOUNDING

If \$1000 is invested at 6 percent per annum compounded continuously, what will it amount to in 5 years?

### Calculation Procedure:

### Apply the continuous compounding equation
Use the relation $\text{SPCA} - e^{jn}$, where $e$ = base of the natural logarithm system = 2.71828 ..., $j$ = nominal interest rate, $n$ = number of years. Substituting gives $\text{SPCA} = (2.718)^{0.30} = 1.350$. Then $S = P(\text{SPCA}) = \$1000(1.350) = \$1350$.

## FUTURE VALUE OF UNIFORM SERIES
## WITH CONTINUOUS COMPOUNDING

An inventor received a royalty payment of $25,000 at the end of each year for 7 years. The royalties were invested at 12 percent per annum compounded continuously. What was the inventor's capital at the expiration of the 7-year period?

### Calculation Procedure:

### 1. Compute the USCA value

Apply Eq. 12: USCA $- (e^{jn} - 1)/(e^{f} - 1)$, where $n$ = number of annual payments in uniform-payment series and $e$ and $j$ are as defined in the previous calculation procedure. Thus, with $n = 7$ and $j = 12$ percent, USCA $= (e^{0.84} - 1)/(e^{0.12} - 1) = 10.325$.

### 2. Compute the future value of the series

Set $S = R(\text{USCA}) = \$25,000(10.325) = \$258,100$.

**Related Calculations.** Note that if interest were compounded annually at 12 percent, the USCA value would be 10.089.

## PRESENT WORTH OF CONTINUOUS CASH
## FLOW OF UNIFORM RATE

An investment syndicate is contemplating purchase of a business that is expected to yield an income of $200,000 per year continuously and at a constant rate for the next 5 years. If the syndicate wishes to earn 18 percent on its investment, what is the maximum price it should offer for the business?

### Calculation Procedure:

### 1. Compute the present-worth factor

Apply the equation CFPW $= (1 - e^{-jn})/j$, where CFPW = present-worth factor for a continuous cash flow of uniform rate and $n$ = number of years of the flow. Where the cash flow is continuous, it is understood that the given interest or investment rate is based on continuous compounding. Thus, with $n = 5$ and $j = 18$ percent, CFPW $= (1 - e^{-0.90})/0.18 = 3.297$.

### 2. Compute the present worth of the income

Set $P = R(\text{CFPW})$, where $R$ = annual cash-flow rate. Then $P = \$200,000(3.297) = \$659,400$.

## FUTURE VALUE OF CONTINUOUS CASH
## FLOW OF UNIFORM RATE

The sum of $30 will be invested daily in a venture that yields 14 percent per annum. What will be the accumulated capital at the expiration of 18 months?

## Calculation Procedure:

### 1. *Compute the cash-flow rate*

Where money is invested daily, the cash flow may be considered to be continuous for all practical purposes. Assume that deposits are made every day of the year. The cash-flow rate $R = \$30(365) = \$10,950$ per year.

### 2. *Compute the future-value factor*

Apply the equation CFFV $- (e^{jn} - 1)/j$, where CFFV = future-value factor for a continuous cash flow of uniform rate. Thus, with $n = 1.5$ and $j = 14$ percent, CFFV $= (e^{0.21} - 1)/0.14 = 1.669$.

### 3. *Compute the future value of the money invested*

Set $S = R(\text{CFFV}) = \$10,950(1.669) = \$18,280$.

# Depreciation and Depletion

## Notational System

Here $D_U$ = depreciation charge for $U$th year; $D$ = annual depreciation; $\Sigma D_U$ = cumulative depreciation at end of $U$th year $= D_1 + D_2 + D_3 + \cdots + D_U$, where the subscript numbers refer to the year numbers; $P_0$ = original cost of asset; $P_U$ = book value of asset at end of $U$th year $= P_0 - \Sigma D_U$; IRS = Internal Revenue Service; $L$ = salvage value; $W$ = wearing value, or total depreciation $= P_0 - L$; $N$ = longevity or life of asset, years.

## *STRAIGHT-LINE DEPRECIATION*

The initial cost of a machine, including its installation, is $15,000. The IRS life of this machine is 10 years. The estimated salvage value of the machine is $1000, and the cost of dismantling the machine is estimated to be $200. Using straight-line depreciation, what is the annual depreciation charge? What is the book value of the machine at the end of the seventh year?

## Calculation Procedure:

### 1. *Compute the annual depreciation charge*

When straight-line depreciation is used, the annual depreciation charge is constant, $D = W/N$. Since $P_0 = \$15,000$, $L = \$1000 - \$200 = \$800$, $W = \$15,000 - \$800 = \$14,200$, $N = 10$. Then $D = \$14,200/10 = \$1420$.

### 2. *Compute the book value of the machine at the end of the seventh year*

$\Sigma D_7 = 7D = 7(\$1420) = \$9940$. Then $P_7 = \$15,000 - \$9940 = \$5060$.

## STRAIGHT-LINE DEPRECIATION WITH TWO RATES

An asset having an initial cost of $30,000 has a life expectancy of 15 years and an estimated salvage value of $5000. What are the depreciation charges under a modified straight-line method in which 60 percent of the total depreciation is considered to occur during the first 5 years of the life of the asset?

### Calculation Procedure:

#### 1. Proportion the total wearing value of the asset

Divide the asset's life span into the two specified intervals, and proportion the total wearing value between them. Thus, $W = \$30,000 - \$5000 = \$25,000$; $N = 15$; $W_1 =$ first-period wearing value $= 0.60(\$25,000) = \$15,000$; $W_2 =$ second-period wearing value $= 0.40(\$25,000) = \$10,000$.

#### 2. Compute the annual depreciation charge

For the first 5 years, $D = \$15,000/5 = \$3000$. For the next 10 years, $D = \$10,000/10 = \$1000$.

## DEPRECIATION BY ACCELERATED COST RECOVERY SYSTEM

An asset having a first cost of $120,000 is to be depreciated by the Accelerated Cost Recovery System (ACRS). This asset is assigned a 5-year cost-recovery period, and the following depreciation factors are to be applied: year 1, 20.0 percent; year 2, 32.0 percent; year 3, 19.2 percent; years 4 and 5, 11.5 percent; year 6, 5.8 percent. Compute the depreciation charges and the book value of the asset during the cost-recovery period.

### Calculation Procedure:

#### 1. Compute the depreciation charges

The ACRS for allocating depreciation was adopted by the federal government in 1981, but it subsequently underwent several modifications. ACRS was designed to allow a firm to write off an asset rapidly, the expectation being that industry would thus be encouraged to modernize its plants and facilities.

The salient features of ACRS are as follows: Each asset is assigned a cost-recovery period during which depreciation is to be charged, and this period is independent of its estimated longevity; the estimated salvage value is ignored; the depreciation for a given year is computed by multiplying the first cost of the asset by a specified depreciation factor; the initial depreciation charge occurs in the year the asset is placed in service, and the depreciation charge for that year is independent of the specific date at which this placement occurs. Since many assets are placed in service relatively late in the year, the allowable depreciation charge for the first year is low compared with that for the second year, and depreciation is charged for one year beyond the cost-recovery period. If the salvage value that accrues from disposal of the asset exceeds the book value of the asset at that date, the excess is subject to taxation.

The depreciation charges are recorded in the accompanying table.

## 2. *Compute the end-of-year book values*

The results are recorded in the accompanying table. Currently, the federal government recognizes only the straight-line method and ACRS for allocating depreciation. However, many state governments still recognize other methods. Moreover, a firm may wish to compute depreciation by some other method for its private records as a means of obtaining a more accurate appraisal of its annual profit.

| Year | Depreciation charge, $ | Book value at year end, $ |
|------|------------------------|---------------------------|
| 1 | 120,000(0.200) = 24,000 | 120,000 − 24,000 = 96,000 |
| 2 | 120,000(0.320) = 38,400 | 96,000 − 38,400 = 57,600 |
| 3 | 120,000(0.192) = 23,040 | 57,600 − 23,040 = 34,560 |
| 4 | 120,000(0.115) = 13,800 | 34,560 − 13,800 = 20,760 |
| 5 | 120,000(0.115) = 13,800 | 20,760 − 13,800 =  6,960 |
| 6 | 120,000(0.058) =  6,960 | 6,960 −  6,960 =     0 |

# SINKING-FUND METHOD: ASSET BOOK VALUE

A factory constructed at a cost of $9,000,000 has an anticipated salvage value of $400,000 at the end of 30 years. What is the book value of this factory at the end of the tenth year if depreciation is charged by the sinking-fund method with an interest rate of 5 percent?

## Calculation Procedure:

### 1. *Compute the cumulative depreciation*

This method of depreciation accounting assumes that when the asset is retired, it is replaced by an exact duplicate and that replacement capital is accumulated by making uniform end-of-year deposits in a reserve fund. The cumulative depreciation $\Sigma D_U$ is therefore equated to the principal in the fund at the end of the $U$th year. Or, $\Sigma D_U = W(\text{SFP})(\text{USCA})$. So $W = \$9,000,000 - \$400,000 = \$8,600,000$, SFP $= 0.01505$ for 30 years, $U = 10$ years, and $i = 5$ percent, $\Sigma D_{10} = \$8,600,000(0.01505)(12.578) = \$1,628,000$.

### 2. *Compute the book value*

At the end of 10 years, the book value $P_{10} = P_0 - \Sigma D_{10} = \$9,000,000 - \$1,628,000 = \$7,372,000$.

## SINKING-FUND METHOD: DEPRECIATION CHARGES

An asset costing $20,000 is expected to remain serviceable for 5 years and to have a salvage value of $3000. Compute the depreciation charges, using the sinking-fund method and an interest rate of 4 percent.

### Calculation Procedure:

#### 1. Compute the annual sinking-fund payment

Use the relation $R = W(\text{SFP})$. With $W = \$20,000 - \$3000 = \$17,000$, $N = 5$ years, and $i = 4$ percent, SFP = 0.18463. Then $R = \$17,000(0.18463) = \$3139$.

#### 2. Compute the annual depreciation charges

Use the relation $D_U = R(\text{SPCA})$, or $D_1 = \$3139(1.000) = \$3139$; $D_2 = \$3139(1.040) = \$3265$; $D_3 = \$3139(1.082) = \$3396$; $D_4 = \$3139(1.125) = \$3531$; $D_5 = \$3139(1.170) = \$3673$. Then $\Sigma D_5 = \$17,004$.

## FIXED-PERCENTAGE (DECLINING-BALANCE) METHOD

An asset cost $5000 and has a life expectancy of 6 years and an estimated salvage value of $800. Construct a depreciation schedule for this asset, using the fixed-percentage method.

### Calculation Procedure:

#### 1. Compute the rate of depreciation

Use the relation $h = 1 - (L/P_0)^{1/N}$, where $h$ = rate of depreciation. Substituting gives $h = 1 - (800/5000)1/6 = 0.2632$, or 26.32 percent.

#### 2. Compute the end-of-year book value

Use the relation $D_1 = hP_0 = 0.2632(\$5000) = \$1316$. Then $P_1 = P_0 - D_1 = \$5000 - \$1316 = \$3684$. Likewise, $D_2 = 0.2632(\$3684) = \$969.63$; $P_2 = \$3684 - \$969.63 = \$2714.37$. In a similar manner, $D_3 = \$714.42$; $P_3 = \$1999.95$; $D_4 = \$526.39$; $P_4 = \$1473.56$; $D_5 = \$387.84$; $P_5 = \$1085.72$; $D_6 = \$285.76$; $P_6 = \$799.96$.

## COMBINATION OF FIXED-PERCENTAGE AND STRAIGHT-LINE METHODS

An asset cost $20,000 and has a life of 8 years and a salvage value of $1000. The IRS permits use of the double-declining-balance method to charge depreciation. Compute the depreciation charges.

**TABLE 1.**   Depreciation by the Double-Declining-Balance Method

| Year | Depreciation charge, $ | Book value at year end, $ | $D'$, $ |
|------|------------------------|---------------------------|---------|
| 0 | . . . | 20,000 | |
| 1 | 5,000 | 15,000 | 2,000 |
| 2 | 3,750 | 11,250 | 1,708 |
| 3 | 2,813 | 8,437 | 1,487 |
| 4 | 2,109 | 6,328 | 1,332 |
| 5 | 1,582 | 4,746 | 1,249 |
| 6 | 1,187 | 3,559 | 1,280 |
| 7 | 890 | 2,669 | 1,669 |
| 8 | 667 | 2,002 | |

## Calculation Procedure:

### 1. Compute the rate of depreciation
Under the double-declining-balance method, depreciation is initially charged on a fixed-percentage basis, with $2/N$ as the rate of depreciation. Thus, rate of depreciation = $2/8$ = 0.25, or 25 percent.

### 2. Compute the depreciation charge for each year by the fixed-percentage method
For the first year, depreciation charge = 0.25($20,000) = $5000. Then the book value at the end of the first year = $20,000 − $5000 = $15,000. Following this procedure, construct Table 1.

### 3. Compute the depreciation for the transfer study
Assume that the transfer in depreciation accounting from the fixed-percentage to the straight-line method is made at the end of a particular year. Calculate the annual depreciation charge $D'$ that applies for the remaining life of the asset.

For example, at the end of the third year the book value is $8437, and the depreciation that remains to be charged during the last 5 years is $7437. Then $D'$ = $7437/5 = $1487. Record the values found in this manner in Table 1.

### 4. Determine the transfer date
To establish the transfer date, compare each value of $D'$ with the depreciation charge that will occur in the following year if the fixed-percentage method is used. This comparison shows that the method should be revised at the end of the fifth year because after that time the fixed-percentage method results in a smaller depreciation charge. The depreciation charges (Table 1) are thus $D_1$ = $5000; $D_2$ = $3750; $D_3$ = $2813; $D_4$ = $2109; $D_5$ = $1582; $D_6 = D_7 = D_8$ = $1249.

## CONSTANT-UNIT-USE METHOD OF DEPRECIATION

A machine cost $38,000 and has a life of 5 years and a salvage value of $800. The production output of this machine in units per year is: first year, 2000; second year, 2500;

third year, 2250; fourth year, 1750; fifth year, 1500 units. If the depreciation is ascribable to use rather than the effects of time, and the units produced are of uniform quality, what are the annual depreciation charges?

### Calculation Procedure:

### 1. *Determine the depreciation charge per production unit*
Proportion the wearing value on the basis of annual production. Since $W = \$38,000 - \$800 = \$37,200$ and 10,000 units are produced in 5 years, the depreciation charge per production unit $= \$37,200/10,000 = \$3.72$.

### 2. *Compute the annual depreciation charge*
Since the annual depreciation charge is a function of the production rate, take the product of the depreciation charge per production unit and the annual production. Or, $D_1 = \$3.72(2000) = \$7440$; $D_2 = \$9300$; $D_3 = \$8370$; $D_4 = \$6510$; $D_5 = \$5580$.

## DECLINING-UNIT-USE METHOD OF DEPRECIATION

Using the same data as in the previous calculation procedure, assume that depreciation will be charged by weighting the units produced according to their relative quality. This method reflects the quality loss resulting from increased use of the machine. The quality weights assigned this machine are: first 4000 units produced, 2.0; next 3000 units, 1.5; remainder, 1.0. Compute the depreciation charges for this machine.

### Calculation Procedure:

### 1. *Compute the number of depreciation units*
The depreciation units are related to the annual production by applying the assigned quality rates. Thus

| Year | Depreciation units | | |
|---|---|---|---|
| 1 | 2,000 × 2 | = | 4,000 |
| 2 | ⎰ 2,000 × 2 | = | 4,000 |
|   | ⎱ 500 × 1.5 | = | 750 |
| 3 | 2,250 × 1.5 | = | 3,375 |
| 4 | ⎰ 250 × 1.5 | = | 375 |
|   | ⎱ 1,500 × 1 | = | 1,500 |
| 5 | 1,500 × 1 | = | 1,500 |
|   | Total | | 15,500 |

### 2. *Proportion the wearing value*
Consider the number of depreciation units as the criterion. Or, depreciation charge per depreciation unit $= \$37,200/15,500 = \$2.40$.

### 3. Compute the annual depreciation

Take the product of the depreciation charge per depreciation unit and the annual depreciation units. Or, $D_1 = \$2.40(4000) = \$9600$; likewise, $D_2 = \$11,400$; $D_3 = \$8100$; $D_4 = \$4500$; $D_5 = \$3600$. Taking the sum of these charges, we see that the total depreciation $= \$37,200$.

## SUM-OF-THE-DIGITS METHOD OF DEPRECIATION

A machine costing $15,000 is expected to remain serviceable for 7 years. The machine will have a salvage value of $1000. What are the annual depreciation charges based on the sum-of-the-digits method?

### Calculation Procedure:

### 1. Compute the machine wearing value

The wearing value $W$, or total depreciation $= \$15,000 - \$1000 = \$14,000$.

### 2. Compute the annual depreciation

Use the relation $D_U = W(N - U + 1)/0.5[N(N + 1)]$, where $U =$ year number. Thus, for $U = 1, D_1 = \$3500$. Likewise, for $U = 2, D_2 = \$3000$; for $U = 3, D_3 = \$2500$; for $U = 4, D_4 = \$2000$; for $U = 5, D_5 = \$1500$; for $U = 6, D_6 = \$1000$; for $U = 7, D_7 = \$500$.

## COMBINATION OF TIME- AND USE-DEPRECIATION METHODS

A machine cost $38,000 and has a life of 5 years and a salvage value of $800. Studies show that one-third of the total depreciation stems from the effects of time and two-thirds stems from use. Compute the annual depreciation charges if time depreciation is based on sum of the digits and use depreciation on a production basis with all units of equal quality. Use the same production as in the third previous procedure.

### Calculation Procedure:

### 1. Divide the wearing value into its two elements

Knowing the respective depreciation proportions, let the subscripts $t$ and $u$ refer to time and use, respectively. Also, $W = \$38,000 - \$800 = \$37,200$, and $W_t = \frac{1}{3}(\$37,200) = \$12,400$; $W_u = \frac{2}{3}(\$37,200) = \$24,800$.

### 2. Compute the annual depreciation charge

For the first year, $D_{t1} = W_t N/[N(N + 1/2)] = \$12,400(5)/[5(6/2)] = \$4133$. Also, $D_{u1} = (\$24,800/10,000 \text{ units})(2000 \text{ units the first year}) = \$4960$. Thus, the total depreciation for the first year is $D_1 = \$4133 + \$4960 = \$9093$.

## EFFECTS OF DEPRECIATION ACCOUNTING ON TAXES AND EARNINGS

The QRS Corp. purchased capital equipment for use in a 5-year venture. The equipment cost $240,000 and had zero salvage value. If the income tax rate was 52 percent and the annual income from the investment was $83,000 before taxes and depreciation, what was the average rate of earnings if the profits after taxes were invested in tax-free bonds yielding 3 percent? Compare the results obtained when depreciation is computed by the straight-line and sum-of-the-digits methods.

### Calculation Procedure:

#### 1. Compute the taxable income
With straight-line depreciation, the depreciation charge is $240,000/5 = $48,000 per year. Then the taxable income = $83,000 − $48,000 = $35,000, because depreciation is fully deductible from gross income.

#### 2. Compute the annual tax payment
With a tax rate of 52 percent, the annual tax payment, excluding other deductions, is 0.52($35,000) = $18,200.

#### 3. Compute the net income
The net cash income = gross income − tax payment, if there are no other expenses. Or, net income = $83,000 − $18,200 = $64,800.

#### 4. Determine the capital accumulated by investing the net income in bonds
Use the USCA factor for $i = 3$ percent, $n = 5$ years. Or, $S = R$(USCA) = $64,800(5.309) = $344,000.

#### 5. Compute the average earnings rate on the venture
Use the relation SPCA = $(1 + i)^n$, where SPCA = $344,000/$240,000 = $(1 + i)^5$ $i$ = 7.47 percent.

#### 6. Compute the sum-of-the-digits annual depreciation
Using the previously developed procedure for sum-of-the-digits depreciation charges gives $D_1 = $80,000; $D_2 = $64,000; $D_3 = $48,000; $D_4 = $32,000; $D_5 = $16,000.

#### 7. Compute the annual tax and net income
Using the same method as in steps 2 and 3, we find the annual net income $R$ is $R_1 = $81,440; $R_2 = $73,120; $R_3 = $64,800; $R_4 = $56,480; $R_5 = $48,160.

#### 8. Determine the capital accumulated
Use the respective SPCA values for $i = 3$ percent and years 1 through 5 for the income earned in each year. Or, $S = $81,440(1.126) + $73,120(1.093) + $64,800(1.061) + $56,480(1.030) + $48,160 = $346,700.

#### 9. Compare the average earnings rate on the venture
By the method of step 5, $346,700/$240,000 = $(1 + i)^5$; $i$ = 7.63 percent.

The computed interest rates apply to a composite investment—the purchase and operation of the capital equipment and the purchase of bonds. The total income accruing from the first element is $324,000, regardless of the depreciation method used. However, the timing as well as the amount of this income is important.

The straight-line method produces a uniform annual depreciation charge, tax payment, and net income. Under the sum-of-digits method, these amounts are nonuniform; the net income is highest in the first year and then gradually declines. Therefore, the interest earned through the purchase of bonds is higher if the firm adopts the sum-of-the-digits method.

If the interest rate associated with the second element of this composite investment had been higher, say 4 or 5 percent, the disparity between the two average returns would have been correspondingly higher.


## DEPLETION ACCOUNTING BY THE SINKING-FUND METHOD

An oil field is anticipated to yield an annual income, before depletion allowances, of $120,000. The field will be dry after 5 years, at which time the land will have a residual value of $60,000. If a firm desires a return of 10 percent on its investment, what is the maximum amount it should invest in this oil field? Use a 4 percent interest rate for the sinking fund.

### Calculation Procedure:

#### 1. Determine the replacement cost of the asset
In this method of depletion accounting, it is assumed that the firm deposits a portion of the annual income in a reserve fund to accumulate the capital needed to replace the asset. Let $C$ denote the investment required. Then the replacement cost $r = C - \$60,000$ for this venture.

#### 2. Compute the annual deposit required
Let $d =$ annual deposit required. Then $d = r(\text{SFP})$ for this venture, or any similar situation. With $i = 4$ percent, $n = 5$, $d = (C - \$60,000)(0.18463) = 0.18463C - 11,077.80$.

#### 3. Compute the investment required
Set the residual income equal to 10 percent of the investment and solve for $C$. Or, $120,000 - (0.18463C - 11,077.80) = 0.10C$; $C = \$460,520$.

**Related Calculations.** Note that this method can be applied to any situation where there is a gradual depletion of a valuable, profit-generating asset. Further, the method given here is homologous to the sinking-fund method of depreciation accounting.


## INCOME FROM A DEPLETING ASSET

An oil field purchased for $800,000 is expected to be dry at the end of 4 years. If the resale value of the land is $20,000, what annual income is required to yield an investment rate of 8 percent? Use a sinking-fund rate of 3 percent.

### Calculation Procedure:

#### 1. Compute the annual deposit required to accumulate the replacement capital
The replacement cost $= \$800,000 - \$20,000 = \$780,000 = r$. Use the relation annual deposit $d = r(\text{SFP})$. With $i = 3$ percent, $n = 4$, $d = \$780,000(0.23903) = \$186,440$.

## 2. *Compute the annual income required*

Combine the annual return on the invested capital with the reserve-fund deposit to obtain the required annual income from the asset. Or, annual return on investment = 0.08($800,000) = $64,000. Then the required annual income = $64,000 + $186,440 = $250,440.

## DEPLETION ACCOUNTING
## BY THE UNIT METHOD

The sum of $500,000 was expended in purchasing and developing a mine. During the first 2 years, ore was extracted at these rates: first year, 20,000 tons; second year, 18,000 tons. Originally, the mine was estimated to have a capacity of 230,000 tons, but at the beginning of the second year the remaining capacity was estimated to be only 170,000 tons. Compute the depletion allowance for the first 2 years by the unit method.

### Calculation Procedure:

### 1. *Compute the depletion allowance for the first year*

Under the unit method, it is assumed that the entire capital invested in a depleting asset is consumed in the venture, and the loss of capital is prorated over the life of the venture on the basis of the amount of mineral extracted each year. Thus, for the first year, depletion = $500,000(20,000/230,000) = $43,480.

### 2. *Compute the depletion allowance for the second year*

At the beginning of the second year, the unrecovered capital is $500,000 − $43,480 = $456,520, and the estimated amount of ore remaining is 170,000 tons. Thus, for the second year, depletion = $456,520(18,000/170,000) = $48,340.

## Cost Comparisons of Alternative Proposals

### Annual Cost

For analytical purposes, it is desirable to convert the estimated costs associated with a proposed scheme to an equivalent series of uniform annual payments. The annual payment thus obtained is termed the annual cost of the scheme. The interest rate applied in making this conversion is the minimum investment rate that is considered acceptable by the organization making the investment or incurring the costs.

Where alternative schemes are being evaluated on the basis of their annual cost, the usual procedure is to exclude those expenses that are identical for all schemes, because they do not affect the comparison.

## Notational System

Here $P$ = initial cost of asset acquired in the proposed scheme; $L$ = salvage value of the asset; $N$ = life of asset, years; $i_1$ = interest rate; $c$ = sum of annual costs of operation, maintenance, etc., that are assumed to remain constant for the asset life; $A$ = annual cost = $(P - L)(CR) + Li_1 + c$, where CR is the capital-recovery factor from the compound-interest tables for $i = i_1$, $n = N$; other symbols are as defined earlier. Also, $A$ = $(P - L)(SFP) + Pi_1 + c$, for the same interest and life as the above annual-cost relation.

## DETERMINATION OF ANNUAL COST OF AN ASSET

A firm contemplates building a new warehouse. A choice is to be made between a brick and a galvanized-iron structure. The cost data associated with each structure are as follows:

|  | Brick | Galvanized iron |
|---|---|---|
| First cost, $ | 80,000 | 36,000 |
| Salvage value, $ | 15,000 | 4,000 |
| Life, years | 40 | 15 |
| Annual maintenance cost, $ | 1,000 | 2,300 |
| Annual taxes, $/$100 | 1.30 | 1.30 |
| Annual insurance, $/$1000 | 2 | 5 |

If this firm earns 6 percent on its invested capital, which type of structure is the more economical one?

## Calculation Procedure:

### 1. Compute the operating and maintenance costs

For the brick building, the annual operating and maintenance cost = $c$ = maintenance cost per year, $ + annual taxes, $ + annual insurance cost, $, or $1000 + 0.013($80,000) + 0.002($80,000) = $2200.

For the galvanized-iron building, $c$ = $2300 + 0.013($36,000) + 0.005($36,000) = $2948.

### 2. Compute the annual cost of each building

Use the capital-recovery equation. Thus, for the brick building, $A$ = ($80,000 − $15,000)(0.06646) + $15,000(0.06) + $2200 = $7420.

For the galvanized-iron building, $A$ = ($36,000 − $4000)(0.10296) + $4000(0.06) + $2948 = $6483.

Since the galvanized-iron building has a lower annual cost, it is the more economical structure.

**Related Calculations.** This general method of computing annual costs can be used for any number of industrial or commercial assets regardless of whether they are stationary, moving, or water- or air-borne. The key fact is that accurate costs are required if the annual cost comparison is to have validity.

## MINIMUM ASSET LIFE TO JUSTIFY A HIGHER INVESTMENT

The timber floor of a bridge is to be replaced, and consideration is being given to treating the timber to prolong its life and reduce maintenance costs. An untreated timber floor costs $5000 and has an annual maintenance cost of $500 and a life of 10 years. A treated timber floor costs $8500 and has an annual maintenance cost of $300. How long should the treated timber last to make it more economical than the untreated timber? Use an interest rate of 5 percent.

### Calculation Procedure:

### 1. Compute the annual cost of the untreated timber floor
Using the capital-recovery factor, we see the annual cost is $5000(0.12950) + $500 = $1147.50.

### 2. Set up an expression for the annual cost of the treated timber floor
The annual cost is $8500(CR) + $300.

### 3. Compute the minimum life required to justify treating the timber
Equate the annual costs, giving $8500(CR) + $300 = $1147.50, or CR = 0.09971. Interpolating in the compound-interest table for 5 percent, we find $N = 14.3$ years. The life of the treated timber floor must exceed 14.3 years to make it more economical.

## COMPARISON OF EQUIPMENT COST AND INCOME GENERATED

A firm is considering purchasing equipment that will reduce annual labor costs by $4000. The equipment costs $30,000 and has a salvage value of $5000 and a life of 7 years. The annual maintenance cost is $600. While not in use by the firm, the equipment can be rented to others to generate an income of $1000 per year. If money can be invested for an 8 percent return, is the firm justified in buying the equipment?

### Calculation Procedure:

### 1. Compute the annual cost of using the equipment
Using the capital-recovery-factor annual cost, we get $A = ($30,000 - $5000)(0.19207) + $5000(0.08) + $600 = $5802$.

### 2. Compute the annual cost of not purchasing the equipment
If the equipment is not purchased, the firm will incur an extra labor cost of $4000 over that with the equipment. Also, the rental income that would be obtained from the equipment will be lost. Hence, the total annual cost without the equipment would be $A = $4000 + $1000 = $5000$.

Since the annual cost with the equipment would be $5802, the firm should not purchase the equipment because without it the annual cost is only $5000.

## SELECTION OF RELEVANT DATA
## IN ANNUAL-COST STUDIES

An existing factory must be enlarged or replaced to accommodate new production machinery. The structure was built at a cost of $130,000. Its present book value, based on straight-line depreciation, is $35,000, but it has been appraised at $40,000. If the structure is altered, the cost will be $80,000 and its service life will be extended 8 years, with a salvage value of $30,000. A new factory could be purchased for $250,000. It would have a life of 20 years and a salvage value of $35,000. Annual maintenance costs of the new building would be $8000, compared with $5000 in the enlarged structure. However, the improved layout in the new building would reduce annual production costs by $12,000. All other expenses for the two structures are estimated as being equal. Using an investment rate of 8 percent, determine which is the more attractive investment for this firm.

### Calculation Procedure:

### 1. Segregate the relevant data for the existing structure
Relevant data—present resale value. Irrelevant data—cost of construction and present book value.

### 2. Record the pertinent cost data for each scheme
Classify the income that would accrue from one scheme as a "cost" of its alternative. Thus

|  | Enlarged building | New building |
|---|---|---|
| Initial cost or payment, $ | 80,000 | 250,000 |
| Resale value existing building, $ | 40,000 | |
| Total first cost, $ | 120,000 | 250,000 |
| Salvage value, $ | 30,000 | 35,000 |
| Life, years | 8 | 20 |
| Operating cost, $ | 5,000 | 8,000 |
| Production "cost," $ | 12,000 | |

### 3. Compute the annual cost of the enlarged building
Using the capital-recovery factor for $i_1 = 8$ percent, $n = 8$ years, we have $A = (\$120,000 - \$30,000)(0.17401) + \$30,000(0.08) + \$5000 + \$12,000 = \$35,061$.

### 4. Compute the annual cost of the new building
Using the capital-recovery factor for $i = 8$ percent, $n = 20$ years gives $A = (\$250,000 - \$35,000)(0.10185) + \$35,000(0.08) + \$8000 = \$32,698$.

Since the new building has an annual cost almost $2400 less than the enlarged existing structure, the new building is the more economical choice.

**Related Calculations.** This general procedure can be used to compare any two or more alternatives having characteristics similar to those described above.

## DETERMINATION OF MANUFACTURING BREAK-EVEN POINT

A manufacturing firm has a choice between two machines to produce a product. The relevant data are as follows:

|  | Machine A | Machine B |
|---|---|---|
| First cost, $ | 20,000 | 28,000 |
| Salvage value, $ | 2,000 | 0 |
| Life, years | 10 | 6 |
| Annual operating cost, $ | 3,000 + 5.00 per unit | 2,500 + 1.50 per unit |

If money is worth 7 percent, what annual production is required to justify purchase of machine B?

### Calculation Procedure:

### 1. Compute the annual cost of the first machine

Let $x$ denote the number of units produced annually. Then, by using the capital-recovery factor, $A = (\$20,000 - \$2000)(0.14238) + \$2000(0.07) + \$3000 + 5x = \$5703 + 5x$ for machine A.

### 2. Compute the annual cost of the second machine

Using the same procedure for machine B gives $A = (\$28,000)(0.20980) + \$2500 + 1.5x = \$8374 + 1.5x$.

### 3. Equate the annual costs, and solve for the unknown

Substituting the annual costs from steps 1 and 2 yields $\$5703 + 5x = \$8374 + 1.5x$; $x = 763$ units.

This is the break-even point at which the costs of each machine are equal. If production is expected to exceed this volume, machine B is the economical choice.

## COST COMPARISON WITH NONUNIFORM OPERATING COSTS

Two alternative machines have the following data:

|  | Machine A | Machine B |
|---|---|---|
| First cost, $ | 6,800 | 12,000 |
| Salvage value, $ | . . . | 1,000 |
| Life, years | 6 | 10 |

For machine A, the estimated annual operating cost is $1240. For machine B, it is $800 for the first 4 years, $1200 for the next 3 years, and $1500 for the remaining 3 years. Determine which machine is more economical, using an 8 percent interest rate.

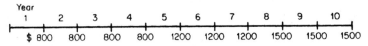

**FIGURE 4.** Annual operating costs for machine B.

## Calculation Procedure:

### 1. Compute the annual cost of machine A

By using the capital-recovery factor, $A = \$6800(0.21632) + \$1240 = \$2711$.

### 2. Construct a money-time diagram for machine B

Figure 4 shows the annual operating costs for machine B.

### 3. Convert the operating costs for machine B to an equivalent uniform series

The value $S$ of these costs as of the end of the tenth year is $S = \$800(USCA, n = 4)(SPCA, n = 6) + \$1200(USCA, n = 3)(SPCA, n = 3) + \$1500(USCA, n = 3)$, or $S = \$800(4.506)(1.587) + \$1200(3.246)(1.260) + \$1500(3.246) = \$15,498$. Now apply the relationship $R = S(SFP, n = 10)$, where $R$ = annual payment of a uniform series that is equivalent to the actual operating costs. Then $R = \$15,498(0.06903) = \$1070$. This is the equivalent uniform annual operating cost for machine B.

### 4. Compute the annual cost of machine B, and compare the two machines

Using the capital-recovery factor, we find $A = (\$12,000 - \$1000)(0.14903) + \$1000(0.08) + \$1070 = \$2789$. Machine A has a lower annual cost, and so it is more economical.

   **Related Calculations.** As an alternative method in step 3, compute the value $P'$ of the operating costs as of the purchase date. Then $P' = \$800(USPW, n = 4) + \$1200(USPW, n = 3)(SPPW, n = 4) + \$1500(USPW, n = 3)(SPPW, n = 7)$, or $P' = \$800(3.312) + \$1200(2.577)(0.7350) + \$1500(2.577)(0.583) = \$7176$. Now apply the relationship $R = P'(CR, n = 10)$, or $R = \$7176(0.14903) = \$1069$. Note that the *arithmetic mean* of the annual operating costs for machine B is $\$1130$. However, since the costs increase with time and the earlier payments in a series have a more pronounced effect than the later payments, the equivalent annual operating cost is less than $\$1130$.

## ECONOMICS OF EQUIPMENT REPLACEMENT

A machine having an installed cost of $\$10,000$ was used for 5 years. During that time its trade-in value and operating costs changed as follows:

| End of year | Salvage value, $ | Operating cost, $/year |
|:---:|:---:|:---:|
| 1 | 6000 | 2300 |
| 2 | 4000 | 2500 |
| 3 | 3200 | 3300 |
| 4 | 2500 | 4800 |
| 5 | 2000 | 6800 |

If the cost of a new machine remained constant during this time, at what date would it be most economical to replace the machine with a duplicate? Use a 7 percent interest rate.

## Calculation Procedure:

### 1. *Compute the present worth of all payments on the asset*

Let $P'$ denote the present worth (i.e., the value at the date of purchase) of all expenditures ascribable to an asset. In the capital-recovery annual-cost equation, substitute $P'$ for $P$ and set $c = 0$ to obtain the following alternative equation: $A = (P' - L)(CR) + Li_1$. Using $i_1 = 7$ percent, compute the present worth of the operating costs. Or,

| Year | |
|---|---|
| 1 | PW = ($2300)(0.9346) = $2150 |
| 2 | PW = ($2500)(0.8734) = $2184 |
| 3 | PW = ($3300)(0.8163) = $2694 |
| 4 | PW = ($4800)(0.7629) = $3662 |
| 5 | PW = ($6800)(0.7130) = $4848 |

### 2. *Determine the present worth for each life span*

Take the sum of the installed cost, $10,000, and the present worth of the operating cost found in step 1. Or,

| Life, years | |
|---|---|
| 0 | $P' = \$10,000 +\quad \$0 = \$10,000$ |
| 1 | $P' = \$10,000 +\$2,150 = \$12,150$ |
| 2 | $P' = \$12,150 +\$2,184 = \$14,334$ |
| 3 | $P' = \$14,334 \pm\$2,694 = \$17,028$ |
| 4 | $P' = \$17,028 +\$3,662 = \$20,690$ |
| 5 | $P' = \$20,690 +\$4,848 = \$25,538$ |

### 3. *Apply the annual-cost equation developed in step 1*

| Life, years | |
|---|---|
| 1 | $A = \$6,150(1.07000) + \$6,000(0.07) = \$7,001$ |
| 2 | $A = \$10,334(0.55309) + \$4,000(0.07) = \$5,996$ |
| 3 | $A = \$13,828(0.38105) + \$3,200(0.07) = \$5,493$ |
| 4 | $A = \$18,190(0.29523) + \$2,500(0.07) = \$5,545$ |
| 5 | $A = \$23,538(0.24389) + \$2,000(0.07) = \$5,881$ |

Inspect these annual costs to determine when the minimum annual cost occurs. Since the annual cost is a minimum when $N = 3$, the asset should be retired at the end of the third year.

## ANNUAL COST BY THE AMORTIZATION (SINKING-FUND-DEPRECIATION) METHOD

A machine costs $30,000 and will be retired at the end of 8 years with a salvage value of $5000. The annual operating cost is $3200. Determine the annual cost by the amortization method if the interest rate on the loan is 6 percent and that of the sinking fund is 3 percent.

### Calculation Procedure:

#### Compute the annual cost of the asset

The amortization method is based on the following assumptions: The asset is purchased with borrowed funds; interest on the loan is paid annually; the loan principal is paid as a lump sum at the retirement of the asset; the funds required to retire the debt are accumulated by uniform annual deposits in a reserve fund. This assumed method of financing is unrealistic; the amortization method is therefore approximate.

Let $i_1$ = interest rate on loan; $i_2$ = interest rate on sinking fund. Then $A = (P - L)(\text{SFP}) + Pi_1 + c$. In this equation the SFP factor is based on $I_2$. Apply this equation, using $P = \$30,000$, $L = \$5000$, $N = 8$, $c = \$3200$, $i_1 = 6$ percent, $i_2 = 3$ percent. Thus, $A = \$7812$.

## ANNUAL COST BY THE STRAIGHT-LINE-DEPRECIATION METHOD

The director of a corporation recommends that a firm buy a computer instead of renting at the rate of $50 per hour. A new computer costs $120,000; annual operating, maintenance, and insurance costs total $8500. The computer will be traded at the end of 10 years for $30,000. The director forecasts computer usage for 480 h/year. He bases his calculation of annual cost on the straight-line-depreciation method with an interest rate of 6 percent. Is his recommendation sound?

### Calculation Procedure:

#### 1. Compute the annual cost of owning the asset

The straight-line method is an approximate one which assumes that the asset is purchased with borrowed funds. However, the method disregards the timing of payments and considers only their arithmetic average. Thus, the annual cost $A = (P - L)/N + (P - L)i_1(N + 1)/2N + Li_1 + c$. So $A = \$90,000/10 + \$90,000(0.06)(11/20) + \$30,000(0.06) + \$8500 = \$22,270$.

#### 2. Compute the annual cost of renting the asset

The annual cost of renting the asset = (hourly rate, $)(annual use, hr) = ($50)(480) = $24,000.

Since the annual cost of owning the asset is less than the annual cost of renting it, the firm would save money by owning the asset. Note that this is an approximate method.

### Present Worth of Future Costs

A cost analysis of alternative schemes may be performed by computing the present worth of all expenses incurred in each scheme during a stipulated period called the analysis period. This period should encompass an integral number of lives of each asset required under the alternative schemes.

## *PRESENT WORTH OF FUTURE COSTS OF AN INSTALLATION*

A city contemplates increasing the capacity of existing water-transmission lines. Two plans are under consideration: Plan A requires construction of a parallel pipeline, flow being maintained by gravity. The initial cost is $800,000, and the life is 60 years with an annual operating cost of $1000. Plan B requires construction of a booster pumping station costing $210,000 with a life of 30 years. The pumping equipment costs an additional $50,000; it has a life of 15 years and a salvage value of $10,000. The annual operating cost is $35,000. Which is the more economical plan if the interest rate is 6 percent?

### Calculation Procedure:

### 1. *Construct a money-time diagram of Method A*
Figure 5 shows the money-time diagram. Note that this diagram uses 60 years as the analysis period. Record on the money-time diagram the capital expenditures during this 60-year period.

### 2. *Compute the total present worth of Method B*
For plan A, using the USPW factor for $n = 60$ years, we get PW = $800,000 + $1000(16.161) = $816,160. For plan B, by using the SPPW factor for the payments shown in Fig. 5, and the uniform series present-worth factor for the operating cost, PW = $260,000 + $40,000(SPPW) + $250,000(SPPW) + $40,000(SPPW) + $35,000(USPW) − $10,000(SPPW) = $260,000 + $40,000(0.4173) + $250,000(0.1741) + $40,000(0.0727) + $35,000(16.161) − $10,000(0.0303) = $888,460.

Since the present worth of plan A is less than that of plan B, the scheme for plan A should be adopted because it is more economical.

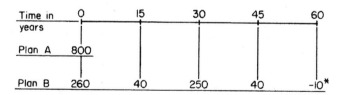

*Income from disposal of equipment.
All sums in units of $1000

**FIGURE 5.** Money-time diagram.

## Capitalized Cost

In computing the present worth of the costs associated with a proposed scheme, it is often advantageous to select an analysis period of infinite duration. The present worth of the future costs is then referred to as the capitalized cost of the scheme.

Since each expenditure recurs indefinitely during the analysis period, the various costs constitute a group of perpetuities. Thus, the capitalized cost $C_c$ is $C_c = [(P - L)/i_1](CR) + L + c/i_1$, or $C_c = [(P - L)/i_1](SFP) + P + c/i_1$.

If an asset is considered to have an infinite life span, these equations reduce to $C_c = P + c/i_1$. In these equations, $i = i_1$, $n = N$.

## DETERMINATION OF CAPITALIZED COST

Two methods of conveying water for an industrial plant are being analyzed. Method A uses a tunnel, and method B a ditch and flume. The costs are as follows:

|                        | Method A | Method B |        |
|                        | Tunnel   | Ditch    | Flume  |
|------------------------|----------|----------|--------|
| First cost, $         | 180,000  | 50,000   | 40,000 |
| Salvage value, $      | ...      | ...      | 5,000  |
| Life, years            | Infinite | 50       | 15     |
| Operating cost, $/year | 2,300    | 2,000    | 3,600  |

Evaluate these two alternatives on the basis of capitalized cost, using a 5 percent interest rate.

## Calculation Procedure:

### 1. Compute the capitalized cost of method A
Since the tunnel has an infinite life, $C_c = P + c/i_1 = \$180,000 + \$2300/0.05 = \$226,000$.

### 2. Compute the capitalized cost of method B
Using the capital-recovery factor for $n = 50$ years, $i = 5$ percent, we find for the ditch $C_c = (\$50,000/0.05)(0.05478) + \$2000/0.05 = \$94,780$.

Using a similar procedure for the flume, which has a 15-year life, gives $C_c = (\$35,000/0.05)(0.09634) + \$5000 + \$3600/0.05 = \$144,440$. The total capitalized cost for method B = the sum of the flume and ditch costs, or $\$239,220$. Since method A costs less, it is more economical.

## CAPITALIZED COST OF ASSET WITH UNIFORM INTERMITTENT PAYMENTS

What is the capitalized cost of a bridge costing $85,000 and having a 25-year life, a $10,000 salvage value, $400 annual maintenance cost, and repairs at 5-year intervals of $2000, if the interest rate is 5 percent?

## Calculation Procedure:

### 1. Convert the assumed repair costs to an equivalent series of uniform annual payments

Assume that the repairs are made at the end of every 5-year interval, including the replacement date. Using the SFP factor, we see the equivalent series of uniform annual payments $R_1 = \$2000(\text{SFP})$ for $i = 5$ percent, $n = 5$ years, or $R_1 = \$2000(0.18097) = \$362$.

### 2. Convert the true repair costs to an equivalent series of uniform annual payments

Repairs are omitted when the bridge is scrapped at the end of 25 years, thereby saving $2000 in the final 5-year period. Convert this amount to an equivalent series of uniform annual payments (i.e., savings) and subtract from the result in step 1. Or, $R_2 = \$2000(\text{SFP})$ for $i = 5$ percent, $n = 25$ years. Or, $R_2 = \$2000(0.02095) = \$42$. Thus the annual cost of the repairs $= \$362 - \$42 = \$320$.

### 3. Compute the capitalized cost

Using the capital-recovery factor for $i = 5$ percent, $n = 25$ years, we get $C_c = (\$75,000/0.05)(0.07095) + \$10,000 + \$400/0.05 + \$320/0.05 = \$130,830$.

**Related Calculations.** An alternative solution could be worked as follows: Since the $2000 saving at the end of every 25-year interval coincides in timing with the income of $10,000 from the sale of the old bridge as scrap, this saving can be combined with the salvage value to obtain an effective value of $12,000 for salvage. The annual cost of repairs is therefore taken as $362, the value of $R_1$, step 1. Applying the capital-recovery factor gives $C_c = [(\$85,000 - \$12,000)/0.05](0.07095) + \$12,000 + \$400/0.05 + \$362/0.05 = \$130,830$. This agrees with the previously determined value.

## CAPITALIZED COST OF ASSET WITH NONUNIFORM INTERMITTENT PAYMENTS

A bridge has the same cost data as in the previous calculation procedure except for the repairs, which are as follows:

| End of year | Repair cost, $ |
|---|---|
| 10 | 2000 |
| 15 | 3500 |
| 20 | 1500 |

What is the capitalized cost of the bridge if the interest rate is 5 percent?

## Calculation Procedure:

### 1. Compute the present worth of the repairs for one life span

Use the single-payment present-worth factor for each of the repair periods. Or, $PW = \$2000(0.6139) + \$3500(0.4810) + \$1500(0.3769) = \$3477$.

### 2. *Convert the result of step 1 to an equivalent series of uniform annual payments*

Using the capital-recovery factor, we find the annual cost of repairs = $3477(CR)$, where $i = 5$ percent, $n = 25$ years. Or, $c_a = \$3477(0.07095) = \$247$.

### 3. *Compute the capitalized cost*

Using the same method as in step 3 of the previous calculation procedure gives $C_c = \$106,430 + \$10,000 + \$8000 + \$247/0.05 = \$129,370$.

*Related Calculations.* An alternative way of solving this problem is to combine the present worth of the payments for repairs ($3477) with the initial cost ($85,000) to obtain an equivalent initial cost $P'$. Then, $P' = \$88,477$, and $P' - L = \$88,477 - \$10,000 = \$78,477$. By applying the capital-recovery factor, $C_c = \$129,370$ as before.


## STEPPED-PROGRAM CAPITALIZED COST

A firm plans to build a new warehouse with provision for anticipated growth. Two alternative plans are available.

|  | Plan A | Plan B |
|---|---|---|
| First cost, $ | 100,000 | 80,000 |
| Salvage value, $ | 10,000 | 15,000 |
| Life, years | 25 | 30 |
| Annual maintenance, $ | 1,400 | 1,200  first 10 years, |
|  |  | 1,800  thereafter |
| Cost of enlarging structure | | |
| 10 years hence, $ | . . . | 40,000 |

If money is worth 10 percent, which is the more economical plan?


## Calculation Procedure:

### 1. *Compute the total present worth of the second plan costs*

Let $P'$ represent the total present worth of the costs associated with plan B for one life span. Using the SPPW for $i = 10$ percent, $n = 10$ years, for the cost of enlarging the structure, and the USPW for the annual maintenance *after* expansion, and the *difference* between the annual maintenance costs of this structure and the original structure, we get $P' = \$80,000 + \$40,000(0.3855) + \$1800(9.427) - \$600(6.144) = \$108,700$.

### 2. *Compute the capitalized cost of each alternative*

Using the capital-recovery factor for plan A with $i = 10$ percent, $n = 25$ years yields $C_c = [(\$100,000 - \$10,000)/0.10](0.11017) + \$10,000 + \$1400/0.10 = \$123,150$.

For plan B, by using the present worth from step 1, $C_c = [(\$108,700 - \$15,000)/0.10](0.10608) + \$15,000 = \$114,400$. Note that the capital-recovery factor for plan B is for 30 years.

Since plan B has the lower capitalized cost, it is more economical.

### Cost Comparisons with Taxation and Technological Advances

In the preceding material, the costs of alternative proposals were compared by disregarding taxation and assuming that financial and technological conditions remain static. The cost analysis is now made more realistic by including the effects of taxation and technological advances. Later the effects of inflation also are included.

## CALCULATION OF ANNUAL COST ON AFTER-TAX BASIS

An asset has the following cost data: First cost, $80,000; life, 10 years; salvage value, $5000; annual operating cost, $3600. The firm that owns the asset is subject to a tax rate of 47 percent, and its investment rate is 8 percent after payment of taxes. Compute the after-tax annual cost of this asset if depreciation is allocated by (a) the straight-line method and (b) the sum-of-digits method.

### Calculation Procedure:

### 1. Compute the annual depreciation charge under the straight-line method

The charge is $D = (\$80{,}000 - \$5000)/10 = \$7500$.

### 2. Compute the annual cost under straight-line depreciation

Most income earned by a corporation is subject to the payment of corporate income tax. The *effective* (or *after-tax*) income is the difference between the original income and the tax payment pertaining to that income. The before-tax investment rate $i_b$ = rate of return on an investment as calculated on the basis of original income; the after-tax investment rate $i_a$ = rate of return as calculated on the basis of effective income. Every cost incurred in operating an asset serves to reduce taxable income and thus the tax payment. The *effective* cost is the difference between the actual expenditure and the tax savings that results from the expenditure. The cost of an asset is said to be computed on an after-tax basis if all calculations are based on effective costs and the after-tax investment rate.

Let $t$ = tax rate and $D$ = annual depreciation charge. Where annual operating costs and depreciation charges are uniform, the annual cost $A = (P - L)(\text{CR}, n = N, i = i_a) + Li_a + c(1 - t) - Dt$. The last term represents the tax savings that accrues from the depreciation charge. With $n = 10$, $i_a = 8$ percent, and $t = 47$ percent, $A = (\$80{,}000 - \$5000)(0.14903) + \$5000(0.08) + \$3600(0.53) - \$7500(0.47) = \$9960$.

### 3. Compute the annual depreciation charges under the sum-of-digits method

As given in an earlier calculation procedure, $D_U = W(N - U + 1)/0.5[N(N + 1)]$, where $D_U$ = depreciation charge for $U$th year and $W$ = total depreciation. With $W = \$75{,}000$ and $N = 10$, $D_1 = \$13{,}636$, and every depreciation charge thereafter is $1363.64 less than the preceding charge.

### 4. Convert the depreciation charges under the sum-of-digits method to an equivalent uniform depreciation charge, using an 8 percent interest rate

Refer to an earlier calculation procedure for converting a uniform-gradient series to an equivalent uniform series. The equivalent uniform depreciation charge $D = D_1 +$

$(g/i)(1 - n\text{SFP})$. With $D_1 = \$13,636$, $g = -\$1363.64$, $i = 8$ percent, and $n = 10$, $D = \$13,636 + (-\$1363.64/0.08)[1 - 10(0.06903)] = \$8357$.

### 5. Compute the annual cost under sum-of-digits depreciation

Referring to step 2 and taking the difference between the equivalent depreciation charge in the present case and the depreciation charge under the straight-line method, we determine the annual cost $A = \$9960 - (\$8357 - \$7500)(0.47) = \$9557$.

**Related Calculations.** A comparison of the two values of annual cost—$9960 when straight-line depreciation is used and $9557 when sum-of-digits depreciation is used—confirms the statement made in an earlier calculation procedure. Since tax savings accrue more quickly under sum-of-digits depreciation than under straight-line depreciation, the former method is more advantageous to the firm. In general, a firm seeks to write off an asset rapidly in order to secure tax savings as quickly as possible, thus allowing it to retain more capital for investment. For this reason depreciation accounting is subject to stringent regulation by the IRS.

## COST COMPARISON WITH ANTICIPATED DECREASING COSTS

Two alternative machines, A and B, are available for a manufacturing operation. The life span is 4 years for machine A and 6 years for machine B. The equivalent uniform annual cost is estimated to be $16,000 for machine A and $15,000 for machine B. However, as a result of advances in technology, the annual cost is expected to decline at a constant rate from one life to the next, the rate of decline being 10 percent for machine A and 6 percent for machine B. Applying an investment rate of 12 percent, determine which machine is preferable.

### Calculation Procedure:

### 1. Select the analysis period, and compute annual costs for this period

The cost comparison will be made by the present-worth method. The analysis period is 12 years, since this is the lowest common multiple of 4 and 6. The annual costs are as follows: Machine A: first life, $16,000; second life, $16,000(0.90) = \$14,400$; third life, $\$14,400(0.90) = \$12,960$. Machine B: first life, $15,000; second life, $\$15,000(0.94) = \$14,100$.

### 2. Construct a money-time diagram

The equivalent uniform annual payments are shown in Fig. 6.

### 3. Compute the present worth of costs for the first analysis period, and identify the more economical machine

For machine A, PW $= \$16,000(\text{USPW}, n = 4) + \$14,400(\text{USPW}, n = 4)(\text{SPPW}, n = 4) + \$12,960(\text{USPW}, n = 4)(\text{SPPW}, n = 8)$. With $i = 12$ percent, PW $= \$16,000(3.037) + \$14,400(3.037)(0.6355) + \$12,960(3.037)(0.4039) = \$92,280$. For machine B, PW $= \$15,000(\text{USPW}, n = 6) + \$14,100(\text{USPW}, n = 6)(\text{SPPW}, n = 6)$, or PW $= \$15,000(4.111) + \$14,100(4.111)(0.5066) = \$91,030$. Machine B should be used for the first 12 years because it costs less.

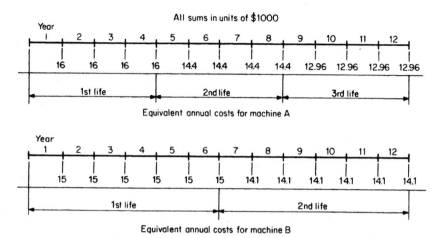

**FIGURE 6.** Equivalent payments for 12-year analysis period.

### 4. Compute the present worth of costs for the second analysis period

The second 12-year period encompasses the fourth, fifth, and sixth lives of machine A and the third and fourth lives of machine B. The "present" is the beginning of the second 12-year period. The annual cost of machine A during its fourth life is $(0.90)^3$ times the annual cost during its first life. Therefore, the results of step 3 can be applied. For machine A, PW = $92,280(0.90)^3$ = \$67,270. For machine B, PW = $91,030(0.94)^2$ = \$80,430. Thus, machine A should be used after the first 12 years. Realistically, since the transfer from machine B to machine A can be made at the end of the first 6-year period, the decision should be reviewed at that time in the light of currently available forecasts.

## ECONOMY OF REPLACING AN ASSET WITH AN IMPROVED MODEL

A machine has been in use for 3 years, and its cost data for the next 8 years are shown in Table 2, where the years are counted from the present. An improved model of this machine has just appeared on the market, and according to estimates it has an optimal life of 6 years with an equivalent uniform annual cost of \$9400. No additional improvements are anticipated in the near future. If money is worth 10 percent, when will it be most economical to retire the existing machine?

### Calculation Procedure:

### 1. Compute an equivalent single end-of-life payment for each prospective remaining life

Let $R$ = remaining life of machine, years. The annual cost corresponding to every possible value of $R$ will be found by a method that is a variation of that used in an earlier calculation procedure. Let $c_R$ = operating cost at end of $R$th year and $F_R$ = equivalent single payment

**TABLE 2**

| Year | Salvage value at end, $ | Annual operating cost, $ |
|------|-------------------------|--------------------------|
| 0 | 12,000 | |
| 1 | 8,000 | 4,700 |
| 2 | 5,000 | 5,200 |
| 3 | 4,000 | 5,800 |
| 4 | 3,500 | 6,600 |
| 5 | 3,000 | 7,500 |
| 6 | 2,700 | 8,500 |
| 7 | 2,600 | 9,700 |
| 8 | 2,500 | 10,900 |

at end of $R$th year. Then $F_R = F_{R-1}(1 + i) + c_R$. By retaining the existing machine, the firm forfeits an income of $12,000, and this is equivalent to making a payment of that amount now. Then $F_0 = \$12,000$; $F_1 = \$12,000(1.10) + \$4700 = \$17,900$; $F_2 = \$17,900(1.10) + \$5200 = \$24,890$; $F_3 = \$24,890(1.10) + \$5800 = \$33,179$; etc. The results are shown in Table 3.

## 2. Compute the annual cost for every prospective remaining life

Let $A_R$ = annual cost for a remaining life of $R$ years, and $L_R$ = salvage value at end of $R$th year. Then $A_R = (F_R - L_R)(\text{SFP}, n = R)$. Thus, with $i = 10$ percent, $A_1 = (\$17,900 - \$8000)1 = \$9900$; $A_2 = (\$24,890 - \$5000)(0.47619) = \$9471$; $A_3 = (\$33,179 - \$4000)(0.30211) = \$8815$; etc. The results are shown in Table 3.

## 3. Determine whether the existing machine should be retired now

When an asset is purchased and installed, its resale value drops sharply during the early years of its life, and thus the firm incurs a rapid loss of capital during those years. The result is that the annual cost for the remaining life of an existing asset is considerably less than the annual cost when the asset was first purchased.

**TABLE 3.**    Calculation of Annual Cost

| Remaining life, years | $F$, $ | $L$, $ | SFP | Annual cost, $ |
|-----------------------|--------|--------|------|----------------|
| 0 | 12,000 | | | |
| 1 | 17,900 | 8,000 | 1.00000 | 9,900 |
| 2 | 24,890 | 5,000 | 0.47619 | 9,471 |
| 3 | 33,179 | 4,000 | 0.30211 | 8,815 |
| 4 | 43,097 | 3,500 | 0.21547 | 8,532 |
| 5 | 54,907 | 3,000 | 0.16380 | 8,502 |
| 6 | 68,897 | 2,700 | 0.12961 | 8,580 |
| 7 | 85,487 | 2,600 | 0.10541 | 8,737 |
| 8 | 104,936 | 2,500 | 0.08744 | 8,957 |

Table 3 shows that the optimal remaining life of the existing machine is 5 years and the corresponding annual cost is $8502. Since this is less than the annual cost of the new machine ($9400), the existing machine should be retained for at least 5 years.

## 4. Determine precisely when the existing machine should be replaced

Since costs increase beyond the fifth year, the existing machine and the improved model will be compared on a year-by-year basis. Let $B_R$ = cost of retaining existing machine 1 year beyond the $R$th year. Then $B_R = L_R(1 + i) - L_{R+1} + c_{R+1}$. Thus, $B_5$ = $3000(1.10) - $2700 + $8500 = $9100. Since this is less than the annual cost of the new model, the existing machine should not be retired 5 years hence. Continuing, we find $B_6$ = $2700(1.10) - $2600 + $9700 = $10,070, which exceeds $9400. Therefore, the existing machine should be retired 6 years hence.

## ECONOMY OF REPLACEMENT UNDER CONTINUING IMPROVEMENTS

A newly acquired machine costs $40,000, and it has the salvage values and annual operating costs shown in Table 4. It is anticipated that a new model will become available at the end of each year. All future models will have first costs and salvage values identical with those of the present model, but the annual operating cost for a given model will be $600 lower than the corresponding annual operating cost of the preceding model. For example, the model that becomes available 1 year hence will have an operating cost of $11,400 for the first year, $12,400 for the second year, etc. Applying an interest rate of 10 percent, determine how long this machine should be held.

### Calculation Procedure:

### 1. Establish the excess operating costs in relation to a 1-year life

When the machine is retired, it will be replaced with the model that becomes available at that date. First assume that the machine is retired at the end of each year. The operating costs for the next 8 years are shown in Table 5. Now assume that the machine is held for 8 years. Subtracting the values just found from the values in Table 4 gives the excess operating costs for an 8-year life; these are shown in Table 5. This table also gives the excess

## TABLE 4

| Year | Salvage value at end, $ | Annual operating cost, $ |
|---|---|---|
| 1 | 25,000 | 12,000 |
| 2 | 20,000 | 13,000 |
| 3 | 17,000 | 14,600 |
| 4 | 15,000 | 16,500 |
| 5 | 13,500 | 18,800 |
| 6 | 12,000 | 21,500 |
| 7 | 11,000 | 24,500 |
| 8 | 10,000 | 28,000 |

**TABLE 5**

| Year | Operating cost for 1-year life, $ | Excess operating cost for 8-year life, $ |
|------|-----------------------------------|------------------------------------------|
| 1 | 12,000 | 0 |
| 2 | 11,400 | 1,600 |
| 3 | 10,800 | 3,800 |
| 4 | 10,200 | 6,300 |
| 5 | 9,600 | 9,200 |
| 6 | 9,000 | 12,500 |
| 7 | 8,400 | 16,100 |
| 8 | 7,800 | 20,200 |

operating costs for every prospective life of the machine. For example, if the machine is held 3 years, the excess operating cost is $1600 for the second year and $3800 for the third year, and these values apply to each subsequent life. Since only differences in cost are significant, the prospective lives of the machine will be compared by applying the excess rather than the actual operating costs.

### 2. Compute an equivalent single end-of-life payment for every prospective life

Annual costs will be computed by using the same method as in the previous calculation procedure, but applying excess operating costs. Thus, with $i = 10$ percent, $F_1 = \$40,000(1.10) = \$44,000$; $F_2 = \$44,000(1.10) + \$1600 = \$50,000$; $F_3 = \$50,000(1.10) + \$3800 = \$58,800$; etc. The results are shown in Table 6.

### 3. Compute the annual cost for every prospective life

Proceeding as in the previous calculation procedure gives $A_1 = (\$44,000 - \$25,000)1 = \$19,000$; $A_2 = (\$50,000 - \$20,000)(0.47619) = \$14,286$; $A_3 = (\$58,800 - \$17,000)(0.30211) = \$12,628$; etc. The results are shown in Table 6.

### 4. Identify the most economical life of the machine

Table 6 reveals that a 4-year life has the minimum annual cost.

**Related Calculations.** Each excess annual operating cost shown in Table 5 consists of two parts: a *deterioration cost*, which is the increase in operating cost due to aging

**TABLE 6.**   Calculation of Annual Cost

| Life, years | F, $ | L, $ | SFP | Annual cost, $ |
|-------------|--------|--------|---------|----------------|
| 1 | 44,000 | 25,000 | 1.00000 | 19,000 |
| 2 | 50,000 | 20,000 | 0.47619 | 14,286 |
| 3 | 58,800 | 17,000 | 0.30211 | 12,628 |
| 4 | 70,980 | 15,000 | 0.21547 | 12,062 |
| 5 | 87,278 | 13,500 | 0.16380 | 12,085 |
| 6 | 108,506 | 12,000 | 0.12961 | 12,508 |
| 7 | 135,456 | 11,000 | 0.10541 | 13,119 |
| 8 | 169,203 | 10,000 | 0.08744 | 13,921 |

of the machine, and an *obsolescence cost*, which results from the development of an improved model. For example, at the end of the fourth year the deterioration cost is $16,500 − $12,000 = $4500, and the obsolescence cost is $600 × 3 = $1800. If the quality of the product declines as the machine ages, the resulting loss of income can be added to the deterioration cost.

## ECONOMY OF REPLACEMENT ON AFTER-TAX BASIS

A machine was purchased 3 years ago at a cost of $45,000. It had a life expectancy of 7 years and anticipated salvage value of $3000. It has been depreciated by the sum-of-digits method. The net resale value of the machine is $13,000 at present and is expected to be $9000 a year hence. The operating cost during the coming year will be $2600. A newly developed machine can be substituted for the existing one. According to estimates, this machine will have an optimal life of 5 years with an annual cost of $4800 on an after-tax basis. The tax rate is 45 percent for ordinary income and 30 percent for long-term capital gains. The desired investment rate on an after-tax basis is 8 percent. Determine whether the existing machine should be replaced at present.

### Calculation Procedure:

### 1. Compute the depreciation charges for the first 4 years
Refer to an earlier calculation procedure for sum-of-digits depreciation. The charges are $D_1 = \$10,500$; $D_2 = \$9000$; $D_3 = \$7500$; $D_4 = \$6000$.

### 2. Compute the book value at the end of the third and fourth years
Let $B_R$ = book value at end of $R$th year. Then $B_3 = \$45,000 − (\$10,500 + \$9,000 + \$7,500) − \$18,000$ and $B_4 = \$18,000 − \$6000 = \$12,000$.

### 3. Compute the cost of retaining the machine through the fourth year
Income that accrues from normal business operations is called *ordinary income*; other forms of income are called *capital gains*. The difference between the net income that accrues from selling an asset and its book value at the date of sale is a capital gain (or loss). If the asset was held for a certain minimum amount of time, this capital gain (or loss) is subject to a tax rate different from that for ordinary income.

Let $R$ = age of asset, years. The after-tax cost of retaining the asset through the $(R + 1)$st year, as evaluated at the end of that year, is $[L_R(1 − t_c) + B_R t_c](1 + i_a) + c_{R+1}(1 − t_o) − L_{R+1}(1 − t_c) − B_{R+1}t_c − D_{R+1}t_o$, where $i_a$ = after-tax investment rate; $t_o$ and $t_c$ = tax rate on ordinary income and long-term capital gains, respectively; $L$ = true salvage value; $c$ = annual operating cost; and the subscript refers to the age of the asset. The expression in brackets is the income that would be earned if the asset were sold at the end of the $R$th year; if the asset is retained, this income is forfeited and becomes part of the cost of retention. With $i_a$ = 8 percent, $t_o$ = 45 percent, $t_c$ = 30 percent, $L_3 = \$13,000$, $L_4 = \$9000$, and $c_4 = \$2600$, the cost of retaining the machine through the fourth year is $[\$13,000(0.70) + \$18,000(0.30)](1.08) + \$2600(0.55) − \$9000(0.70) − \$12,000(0.30) − \$6000(0.45) = \$4490$.

### 4. Determine whether the existing machine should be retired now

Since the cost of retaining the machine for 1 additional year ($4490) is less than the annual cost of the new machine ($4800), the existing machine should not be retired at present.

# Effects of Inflation

## Notational System

Here $C_0$ and $C_1$ are the costs of a commodity now and 1 year hence, respectively, and $f =$ annual rate of inflation during the coming year with respect to this commodity. Then $f = (C_1 - C_0)$, or $C_1 = C_0(1 + f)$. Also, $C_n =$ cost of the commodity $n$ years hence. If the annual rate of inflation remains constant at $f$, then $C_n = C_0(1 + f)^n = C_0(\text{SPCA}, i = f)$. In the subsequent material, it is understood that the given inflation rate applies to the asset under consideration.

## DETERMINATION OF REPLACEMENT COST WITH CONSTANT INFLATION RATE

A machine has just been purchased for $60,000. It is anticipated that the machine will be held 5 years, that it will have a salvage value of $4000 as based on current prices, and that the annual rate of inflation during the next 5 years will be 7 percent. The machine will be replaced with a duplicate, and the firm will accumulate the necessary capital by making equal end-of-year deposits in a reserve fund that earns 6 percent per annum. Determine the amount of the annual deposit.

## Calculation Procedure:

### 1. Compute the required replacement capital

Both the cost of a new machine and the salvage value of the existing machine increase at the given rate. Thus, the amount of money the firm must accumulate to buy a new machine is $(\$60,000 - \$4000)(1.07)^5 = \$56,000(1.403) = \$78,568$.

### 2. Compute the annual deposit

Use this relation: Annual deposit $R = S(\text{SFP})$. With $i = 6$ percent and $n = 5$, $R = \$78,568(0.17740) = \$13,938$.

## DETERMINATION OF REPLACEMENT COST WITH VARIABLE INFLATION RATE

In the preceding calculation procedure, determine the amount of the annual deposit if the annual rate of inflation is expected to be 7 percent for the next 3 years and 9 percent thereafter.

## Calculation Procedure:

### 1. Compute the required replacement capital
Replacement capital $= \$56,000(1.07)^3(1.09)^2 = \$56,000(1.225)(1.188) = \$81,497$.

### 2. Compute the annual deposit
From the preceding calculation procedure, annual deposit $= \$81,497(0.17740) = \$14,458$.


# PRESENT WORTH OF COSTS IN INFLATIONARY PERIOD

An asset with a first cost of $70,000 is expected to last 6 years and to have the following additional cost data as based on present costs: salvage value, $5000; annual maintenance, $8400; major repairs at the end of the fourth year, $9000. The asset will be replaced with a duplicate when it is retired. Using an interest rate of 12 percent and an inflation rate of 8 percent per year, find the present worth of costs of this asset for the first two lives (i.e., for 12 years).


## Calculation Procedure:

### 1. Compute the present worth of the capital expenditures for the first life
The "present" refers to the beginning of the first life. The payment for repairs will be $9000(1.08)^4$, and the present worth of this payment is $\$9000(1.08)^4$(SPPW, $n = 4$, $i = 12$ percent) $= \$9000(1.08)^4/(1.12)^4 = \$7780$. Similarly, the present worth of the salvage value is $\$5000(1.08)^6/(1.12)^6 = \$4020$. Thus, the present worth of capital expenditures for the first life is $\$70,000 + \$7780 - \$4020 = \$73,760$.

### 2. Compute the present worth of maintenance for the first life
The annual payments for maintenance constitute a uniform-rate series in which the first payment $R_1 = \$8400(1.08) = \$9072$ and the ratio of one payment to the preceding payment is $r = 1.08$. By Eq. 9, the present-worth factor of the series is URSPW $= [(1.08/1.12)^6 - 1]/(1.08 - 1.12) = 4.901$. Then present worth of series $= R_1$(URSPW) $= \$9072(4.901) = \$44,460$.

### 3. Compute the present worth of costs for the first life
Summing the results, we see that present worth $= \$73,760 + \$44,460 = \$118,220$.

### 4. Compute the present worth of costs for the second life
Since each payment in the second life is $(1.08)^6$ times the corresponding payment in the first life, the value of all payments in the second life, evaluated at the beginning of that life, is $(1.08)^6$ times that for the first life, or $\$118,220(1.08)^6$. The present worth of this amount is $\$118,220(1.08)^6/(1.12)^6 = \$95,040$.

### 5. Compute the present worth of costs for the first two lives
Summing the results yields PW $= \$118,220 + \$95,040 = \$213,260$.
    **Related Calculations.** Let $h = [(1 + f)/(1 + i)]^N$, where $N =$ life of asset, years. In the standard case, where all annual payments as based on present costs are equal and no extraordinary intermediate payments occur, the present worth of costs for the first life is $P - Lh + c(1 + f)(h - 1)/(f - i)$, where $P =$ initial cost; $L =$ salvage value as based on present costs; $c =$ annual payment for operation, maintenance, etc., as based

on present costs. Where extraordinary payments occur, simply add the present worth of these payments, as was done in the present case with respect to repairs at the end of the fourth year. In the special case where $f = i$, the present worth of costs for the first life is $P - L + Nc$.

## COST COMPARISON WITH ANTICIPATED INFLATION

Two alternative machines have the following cost data as based on present costs:

|  | Machine A | Machine B |
|---|---|---|
| First cost, $ | 45,000 | 80,000 |
| Salvage value, $ | 3,000 | 2,000 |
| Life, years | 4 | 6 |
| Annual maintenance, $ | 8,000 | 6,000 |

Determine which machine is more economical, using an interest rate of 10 percent and annual inflation rate of 7 percent.

### Calculation Procedure:

#### 1. Establish the method of cost comparison
The present-worth method is suitable here. Select an analysis period of 12 years, which encompasses three lives of machine A and two lives of machine B.

#### 2. Compute the present worth of costs of machine A for the first life
Refer to the equation given at the conclusion of the preceding calculation procedure. Set $h = (1.07/1.10)^4 = 0.89529$. By reversing the sequence in the last two terms of the equation, present worth = $45,000 - \$3000(0.89529) + \$8000(1.07)(1 - 0.89529)/(0.10 - 0.07) = \$72,190$.

#### 3. Compute the present worth of costs of machine A for the first three lives
Refer to step 4 of the preceding calculation procedure. Thus, PW = $72,190[1 + (1.07/1.10)^4 + (1.07/1.10)^8] = \$72,190(2.69684) = \$194,680$.

#### 4. Compute the present worth of costs of machine B for the first life
Set $h = (1.07/1.10)^6 = 0.84712$. The present worth of costs for the first life = $80,000 - \$2000(0.84712) + \$6000(1.07)(1 - 0.84712)/(0.10 - 0.07) = \$111,020$.

#### 5. Compute the present worth of costs of machine B for the first two lives
PW = $111,020(1 + 0.84712) = \$205,070$.

#### 6. Determine which machine is preferable
Machine A has the lower cost and so is preferable.

## ENDOWMENT WITH ALLOWANCE
## FOR INFLATION

An endowment fund is to provide perpetual annual payments to a research institute. The first payment, to be made 1 year hence, will be $10,000. Each subsequent payment will be 2 percent more than the preceding payment, to allow for inflation. If the interest rate of the fund is 7 percent per annum, what amount must be deposited in the fund now? Verify the result.

### Calculation Procedure:

### 1. Compute the amount to be deposited

The payments form a uniform-rate series, and the amount to be deposited $= P =$ present worth of series. Refer to Eq. 9 for the present-worth factor. When $r < 1 + i$ and $n$ is infinite, URSPW $= 1/(1 + i - r)$. With $i = 7$ percent and $r = 1.02$, URSPW $= 1/(1.07 - 1.02) = 20$. Then $P = R_1(\text{URSPW}) = \$10,000(20) = \$200,000$.

### 2. Prove that this deposit will provide an endless
### stream of payments

The proof consists in finding the rate at which the principal in the fund is growing. At the end of the first year, principal $= \$200,000(1.07) - \$10,000 = \$204,000$. The rate of increase in principal $= (\$204,000 - \$200,000)/\$200,000 = 2$ percent per year. Similarly, at the end of the second year, principal $= \$204,000(1.07) - \$10,000(1.02) = \$208,080$. The rate of increase in principal $= (\$208,080 - \$204,000)/\$204,000 = 2$ percent per year. Thus, the end-of-year principal expands at the same rate as the payments, and so the payments can continue indefinitely.

*Related Calculations.* If the interest period of the fund differs from the payment period, it is necessary to use the interest rate corresponding to the payment period. For example, assume that the interest rate is 7 percent per annum compounded quarterly. The corresponding annual (or effective) rate is $i = (1.0175)^4 - 1 = 7.186$ percent, and URSPW $= 1/(1.07186 - 1.02) = 19.283$. The amount to be deposited $= \$192,830$. Note that if $r \geq 1 + i$, URSPW becomes infinite as $n$ becomes infinite. Thus, if the interest rate of the fund is 7 percent per annum, it is impossible to allow the payments to increase by 7 percent or more.

# Evaluation of Investments

## PREMIUM-WORTH METHOD OF
## INVESTMENT EVALUATION

A firm contemplates investing in a depleting asset and has a choice between two enterprises. Project A requires the investment of $57,500; project B requires the investment of $63,000. The forecast end-of-year dividends are as follows:

| Year | Project A, $ | Project B, $ |
|------|------|------|
| 1 | 10,000 | 15,000 |
| 2 | 15,000 | 25,000 |
| 3 | 25,000 | 30,000 |
| 4 | 20,000 | 20,000 |
| 5 | 10,000 | |

After weighing the risks involved, the firm decides that the minimum acceptable rate of return on project A is 10 percent; on project B, 12 percent. Evaluate these investments by the premium-worth method. If both investments are satisfactory, determine which is more satisfactory.

## Calculation Procedure:

### 1. Compute the present worth of the dividends from both investments

The *present* generally refers to the date on which the investment is made. Where the present worth is greater than the sum invested, the excess is termed the *premium worth*. Such a result signifies that the true investment rate exceeds the minimum acceptable rate.

For any year, PW = (dividend, $)(PW factor for 10 percent and the number of years involved). Thus, for project A:

| Year | PW |
|------|------|
| 1 | $10,000(0.9091) = $9,091 |
| 2 | 15,000(0.8264) = 12,396 |
| 3 | 25,000(0.7513) = 18,783 |
| 4 | 20,000(0.6830) = 13,660 |
| 5 | 10,000(0.6209) = 6,209 |
| Total | $60,139 |

Then the premium worth = $60,139 − 57,500 = $2639.

By using a similar procedure, the present worth of project B at 12 percent is as follows:

| Year | PW |
|------|------|
| 1 | $15,000(0.8929) = $13,394 |
| 2 | 25,000(0.7972) = 19,930 |
| 3 | 30,000(0.7118) = 21,354 |
| 4 | 20,000(0.6355) = 12,710 |
| Total | $67,388 |

Then the premium worth = $67,388 − $63,000 = $4388.

### 2. Determine the relative values of the investments

Since both investments satisfy the minimum requirements, determine their relative values by computing the premium-worth percentage (i.e., the ratio of the premium worth to the capital invested). Thus, for project A the premium-worth percentage is $2639(100)/$57,500 = 04.6 percent. For project B the premium-worth percentage is $4388(100)/$63,000 = 7.0 percent. Thus, project B is the more attractive because it has a higher premium-worth percentage.

## *VALUATION OF CORPORATE BONDS*

A \$10,000, 4 percent corporation bond paying semiannual dividends is redeemable at 102 at the end of 15 years. What is the maximum price an investor should pay for this bond if she desires a return of 6 percent compounded semiannually?

### Calculation Procedure:

### 1. *Determine the semiannual dividend and redemption payment*
The dividend = (principal, \$)$i/2$ = \$10,000(0.04/2) = \$200. Also, the redemption payment = (redemption price/100)(principal) = (102/100)(\$10,000) = \$10,200.

### 2. *Compute the purchase price*
Using an interest rate of 6/2 = 3 percent per semiannual period, compute the present worth of the dividends and the redemption payment. Equate the present worth to the purchase price of the bond. Or, purchase price = (dividend, \$)(USPW) + (redemption payment, \$)(SPPW), for $i$ = 3 percent, $n$ = 30. Hence, purchase price = (\$200)(19.60) + (\$10,200)(0.4120) = \$8122.

## *RATE OF RETURN ON BOND INVESTMENT*

A \$10,000, 6 percent, 20-year bond paid dividends semiannually and was redeemed at par. An investor bought the bond for \$11,500 at its date of issue and held it to maturity. What interest rate did the holder earn?

### Calculation Procedure:

### 1. *Record the payment and receipts associated with the investment*
The payment was \$11,500 at the date of issue. The receipt for each semiannual interest period was (6 percent/2)(\$10,000) = \$300 for 40 periods. Also, \$10,000 was received at the end of the 40 periods. The correct interest rate is that which will make the payment equal the receipts.

### 2. *Select a trial interest rate and compute the results*
Selecting an interest rate of 2.5 percent as a trial, compute the value of the receipts at the date of issue, using the USPW factor for the dividends and the SPPW factor for the principal repayment. Or, (\$300)(25.103) + \$10,000(0.3724) = \$11,255. Since the purchase price exceeded this value, the true interest rate was less than 2.5 percent.

### 3. *Select another trial interest rate*
Repeat the previous calculation, using a 2 percent rate. Or, \$300(27.355) + \$10,000 (0.4529) = \$12,736.

### 4. *Interpolate linearly between the trial values*

| Interest rate, % | Purchase price, \$ |
|:---:|:---:|
| 2.5 | 11,255 |
| $i$ | 11,500 |
| 2 | 12,736 |

This interpolation gives $i = 2.42$ percent per semiannual period, or 4.84 percent per annum compounded semiannually.

## INVESTMENT-RATE CALCULATION AS ALTERNATIVE TO ANNUAL-COST CALCULATION

In the Comparison of Equipment Cost and Income Generated procedure in this section, it was concluded that the proposed investment in labor-saving equipment could not be justified because it failed to yield the minimum acceptable rate of 8 percent. Determine the actual rate of return for this investment.

### Calculation Procedure:

### 1. *Compute the net annual dividend*

| | |
|---|---|
| Labor saving | $4000 |
| Rental income | 1000 |
| Total | $5000 |
| Less maintenance | 600 |
| Net dividend | $4400 |

### 2. *Select a trial interest rate*
Using an interest rate of 5 percent, determine the present worth of the dividends and the equipment salvage value. Thus, (net dividend, $)(USPW) + (salvage value, $)(SPPW), for $i = 5$ percent, $n = 7$ years. Or, $4400(5.786) + $5000(0.7107) = $29,012$. Since the investment was $30,000, the actual interest rate is smaller.

### 3. *Test another trial interest rate*
Using a 4 percent interest rate and repeating the calculation in step 2, we get $4400 (6.002) + $5000(0.7599) = $30,208$.

### 4. *Interpolate linearly to obtain the actual interest rate*
Linear interpolation yields a rate of $i = 4.2$ percent. This verifies that the earlier results were valid.

## ALLOCATION OF INVESTMENT CAPITAL

In devising a program for investment of $8000 in surplus funds, a firm has a choice between two plans. Each plan pays an annual dividend and repayment of the invested capital when the venture terminates. Under plan A the dividend varies with the sum invested in the manner shown below. Under plan B the dividend rate is 10 percent, irrespective of the sum invested. In what manner should this firm divide its investment capital to secure the maximum return?

## Calculation Procedure:

### 1. *List the annual dividends obtainable*
The table below shows the dividend that can be expected under plan A.

| Investment, $ | Annual dividend, $ | Dividend rate, % |
|---|---|---|
| 1000 | 300 | 30.0 |
| 2000 | 540 | 27.0 |
| 3000 | 720 | 24.0 |
| 4000 | 900 | 22.5 |
| 5000 | 950 | 19.0 |
| 6000 | 1020 | 17.0 |
| 7000 | 1220 | 17.4 |
| 8000 | 1300 | 16.3 |

### 2. *Construct a dividend-investment diagram*
Figure 7 shows the dividend-investment diagram for this situation. Points $A$ to $H$ represent the sets of values under plan $A$. The slope of a line connecting any two points represents the rate of return on the incremental investment. For example, the slope of line $EG = \$270/\$2000 = 0.135$, or 13.5 percent represents the rate obtained on the $2000 investment added in going from $E$ to $G$, Fig. 7.

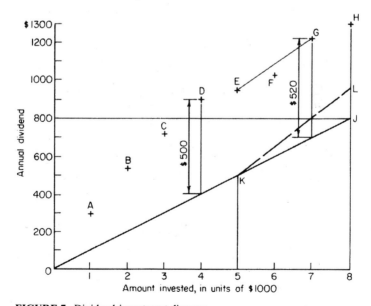

**FIGURE 7.** Dividend-investment diagram.

### 3. Determine the investments to make

Draw line *OJ*, Fig. 7, having a slope of 10 percent, the dividend rate under plan B. Next, determine which of the points, *A* to *H*, is most distant from line *OJ*. Do this by scaling the vertical offsets or by drawing lines through these points parallel to *OJ*.

Point *G*, which has a vertical offset of $520, is the most distant one. Therefore, $7000 is the appropriate sum to invest in plan A because of the following: (*a*) When the investment is extended from some lower level, such as $5000, to the stipulated level, the rate of return on this incremental investment, which is represented by the slope of line *EG*, exceeds 10 percent. (*b*) If the investment is carried beyond *G*, the rate of return on this incremental investment, represented by the slope of line *GH*, is less than 10 percent. Hence, this firm should allocate $7000 to plan A and $1000 to plan B.

**Related Calculations.** As an alternative, construct the following tabulation to determine the total annual dividend corresponding to every possible division of the capital. Study of this table shows that the maximum dividend of $1320 accrues when $7000 is allocated to plan A and $1000 to plan B.

| Investment, $ | | Dividend, $ | | |
|---|---|---|---|---|
| Plan A | Plan B | Plan A | Plan B | Total dividend, $ |
| | 8000 | . . . | 800 | 800 |
| 1000 | 7000 | 300 | 700 | 1000 |
| 2000 | 6000 | 540 | 600 | 1140 |
| 3000 | 5000 | 720 | 500 | 1220 |
| 4000 | 4000 | 900 | 400 | 1300 |
| 5000 | 3000 | 950 | 300 | 1250 |
| 6000 | 2000 | 1020 | 200 | 1220 |
| 7000 | 1000 | 1220 | 100 | 1320 |
| 8000 | . . . | 1300 | . . . | 1300 |

## ALLOCATION OF CAPITAL TO TWO INVESTMENTS WITH VARIABLE RATES OF RETURN

Suppose that the dividend under plan B in the previous procedure is 15 percent of the first $3000 invested and 10 percent of the excess. Determine the optimal division of the $8000 investment between the two plans.

### Calculation Procedure:

### 1. Construct a dividend-investment diagram

Use Fig. 7 and draw line *OK* having a slope of 10 percent and line *KL* having a slope of 15 percent, where *K* has an abscissa of $5000. The ordinate of each point on the line *OKL* represents the prospective plan B dividend that is forfeited by allocating part of the investment capital to plan A. The optimal division of the investment capital is that for which the excess of plan A dividends over forfeited plan B dividends is the maximum.

## 2. *Determine the investment allocation*

Find which of the points from *A* to *H* is most distant from the line *OKL*. This is point *D*, which has a vertical offset of $500. Therefore, the firm should allocate $4000 to plan A and $4000 to plan B.

**Related Calculations.** Alternatively, calculate the total dividend corresponding to every possible division of the available capital. For example, if $1000 is allocated to plan A and $7000 to plan B: Dividend under plan A = $300; dividend under plan B = $3000(0.15) + $4000(0.10) = $850; total dividend = $1150. Using this technique, we find the maximum total dividend to be $1450; this occurs when the capital is divided equally between two plans. Thus, the previous findings are verified.

This procedure and the previous one show two methods of establishing the optimal division of available capital, i.e., computing the rate of return on an incremental investment and computing the total dividend. The latter represents a more straightforward approach, particularly where both alternative investments yield a variable rate of return.

# ALLOCATION OF CAPITAL TO THREE INVESTMENTS BY DYNAMIC PROGRAMMING

A syndicate has $600,000 available for investment; and three investment plans, A, B, and C, are under consideration. Under each plan, the amount that can be invested is a multiple of $100,000 and the investors receive annual dividends and recover their capital when the venture terminates at the expiration of 5 years. The annual dividends corresponding to the various levels of investment are shown in Table 7. The investments can be combined in any manner whatever. Devise the most profitable composite investment.

## Calculation Procedure:

## 1. *Identify the most profitable combination of plans A and B and determine the corresponding annual dividend if $600,000 is placed in this combination*

The problem of identifying the most profitable combination of all three plans can be solved by dynamic programming. By this technique, the most profitable combination will be formed in stages, starting with combinations of A and B, identifying the most profitable ones, and then expanding these to include C.

## TABLE 7

| Amount invested, $ | Annual dividend, $ | | |
|---|---|---|---|
| | Plan A | Plan B | Plan C |
| 100,000 | 25,000 | 10,000 | 15,000 |
| 200,000 | 44,000 | 32,000 | 31,000 |
| 300,000 | 63,000 | 60,000 | 48,000 |
| 400,000 | 80,000 | 91,000 | 56,000 |
| 500,000 | 89,000 | 93,000 | 79,000 |
| 600,000 | 95,000 | 94,000 | 102,000 |

**TABLE 8.**   Combinations of Plans A and B with Total
Investment of $600,000 (multiply all values in table by 1000)

| Individual investment, $ | | Annual dividend, $ |
| Plan A | Plan B | Annual dividend, $ |
|--------|--------|--------------------|
| 600 | 0   | 95 + 0 =  95 |
| 500 | 100 | 89 + 10 =  99 |
| 400 | 200 | 80 + 32 = 112 |
| 300 | 300 | 63 + 60 = 123 |
| 200 | 400 | 44 + 91 = 135 |
| 100 | 500 | 25 + 93 = 118 |
| 0   | 600 | 0 + 94 =  94 |

The possible combinations of plans A and B corresponding to a total investment of
$600,000 are shown in Table 8, and their corresponding annual dividends are computed
by applying the values given in Table 7. The most profitable combination for the stipulated total investment is one in which $200,000 is placed in plan A and $400,000 is placed in
plan B. The corresponding annual dividend is $135,000.

### 2. Identify the most profitable combination of plans A and B and determine the corresponding annual dividend if any amount is placed in this combination

The amount that can be placed in this combination is a multiple of $100,000 with an up-
per limit of $600,000. Repeat the procedure in step 1 to obtain the results shown in
Table 9. The combinations listed in this table are candidates for the most profitable combination of all three plans, and the other combinations of A and B are now discarded.

### 3. Compute the maximum dividend that can be obtained from a combination of all three plans

The calculations are shown in Table 10. As an illustration, assume that $400,000 will be
placed in the A-B combination, leaving $600,000 − $400,000 = $200,000 for plan C.
From Table 9, the annual dividend from the A-B combination is $91,000; from Table 7,

**TABLE 9.**   Optimal Combinations of Plans A and B (multiply all
values in table by 1000)

| Total investment, $ | Individual investment, $ | | Annual dividend, $ |
| | Plan A | Plan B | |
|---------------------|--------|--------|--------------------|
| 600 | 200 | 400 | 44 + 91 = 135 |
| 500 | 100 | 400 | 25 + 91 = 116 |
| 400 | 0   | 400 | 0 + 91 =  91 |
| 300 | 300 | 0   | 63 + 0 =  63 |
| 200 | 200 | 0   | 44 + 0 =  44 |
| 100 | 100 | 0   | 25 + 0 =  25 |

**TABLE 10.**  Combinations of Plans A, B, and C (multiply all values in table by 1000)

| Combination of plans A and B | Plan C | Annual dividend, $ |
|---|---|---|
| | Individual investment, $ | |
| 600 | 0 | 135 + 0 = 135 |
| 500 | 100 | 116 + 15 = 131 |
| 400 | 200 | 91 + 31 = 122 |
| 300 | 300 | 63 + 48 = 111 |
| 200 | 400 | 44 + 56 = 100 |
| 100 | 500 | 25 + 79 = 104 |
| 0 | 600 | 0 + 102 = 102 |

the dividend from plan C is $31,000. Thus, the total dividend is $91,000 + $31,000 = $122,000. Table 10 shows that the maximum possible dividend is $135,000.

**4. Identify the most profitable combination of all three plans**

From Table 10, the most profitable combination results from placing $600,000 in the A-B combination and nothing in plan C. From Table 9, the A-B combination consists of placing $200,000 in A and $400,000 in B. Thus, the most profitable way of dividing the capital is $200,000 in plan A, $400,000 in plan B, and nothing in plan C.

**Related Calculations.** This problem can be solved directly by forming all possible combinations of plans A, B, and C and computing their annual dividends; the number of combinations is 28. However, where the number of combinations is very large, the direct method becomes unwieldy. Dynamic programming provides a systematic way of solving the problem, and it reduces the number of calculations. It will be applied again in a later calculation procedure.

## ECONOMIC LEVEL OF INVESTMENT

A firm planned to purchase and improve property in the expectation that land values in the area would appreciate in the near future. The question arose as to how large an investment should be made. The following data were compiled for five alternative plans, each representing a different level of investment.

| | Plan | | | | |
|---|---|---|---|---|---|
| | A | B | C | D | E |
| Investment, $ | 200,000 | 270,000 | 340,000 | 410,000 | 460,000 |
| Rate of return, % | 14.1 | 13.8 | 12.5 | 11.6 | 12.3 |

If 12 percent is considered the minimum acceptable rate of return, determine the most attractive plan.

## Calculation Procedure:

### 1. *Establish a basis of comparison for the investments*
To establish a basis of comparison, assume that each investment pays an annual dividend and that the invested capital remains intact until the venture terminates. (Although these assumptions are not realistic, they are entirely valid for comparative purposes.)

### 2. *Calculate the annual dividend under each plan*
Thus, for plan A, the annual dividend = $200,000(0.141) = $28,200. Compute the dividends for the other plans in the same manner.

### 3. *Construct a dividend-investment diagram*
Use the same procedure as for Fig. 7. Plot the points representing the sets of values associated with the five plans.

Draw a line through the origin of the dividend-investment diagram with a slope of 12 percent. Determine which point is most distant from this line. This point corresponds to the most profitable rate of return. Study of the plot shows that plan B should be adopted.

**Related Calculations.** To compare these five plans algebraically, assume that the firm has a total available capital of $460,000 (the investment required under plan E) and that the amount remaining after investment in one of the five plans will be allocated to another investment yielding an annual dividend of 12 percent.

Next, calculate the total annual dividend corresponding to each plan.

| Plan | Dividend, $ |
|------|-------------|
| A | 200,000(0.141) + 260,000(0.12) = 59,400 |
| B | 270,000(0.138) + 190,000(0.12) = 60,060 |
| C | 340,000(0.125) + 120,000(0.12) = 56,900 |
| D | 410,000(0.116) + 50,000(0.12) = 53,560 |
| E | 460,000(0.123)              = 56,580 |

Since plan B yields the highest total dividend, it is the best choice.

## RELATIONSHIP BETWEEN BEFORE-TAX AND AFTER-TAX INVESTMENT RATES

A corporation is investigating a proposed investment under which it will receive annual dividends and recover its capital when the venture terminates in 12 years. Since the venture is highly speculative, the firm wishes to earn a minimum of 15 percent on its capital as calculated after the payment of taxes. If income from the investment will be taxed at 56 percent, what must be the minimum rate of return as calculated before the payment of taxes?

## Calculation Procedure:

### *Compute the minimum acceptable before-tax investment rate*
Use the relation $i_b = i_a/(1 - t)$, where $i_b$ and $i_a$ = before-tax and after-tax investment rates, respectively; $t$ = tax rate. Thus, $i_b = 0.15/0.44 = 34.1$ percent.

## APPARENT RATES OF RETURN
## ON A CONTINUING INVESTMENT

A firm leasing construction equipment purchased an asset for $24,000, charging depreciation on a straight-line basis. The life used was 4 years; salvage value, zero. The asset was used for 6 years and scrapped for $800. Net revenues obtained from this asset are listed in Table 11. The firm's normal income was taxed at 50 percent, but the proceeds from the salvage sale were taxed at 25 percent. What were the apparent rates of return on this asset investment, after taxes, computed during the life of the asset?

### Calculation Procedure:

### 1. Compute the annual depreciation charge
Using the straight-line method and a 4-year life, we get the annual depreciation = $24,000/4 = $6000, assuming zero salvage. Record the depreciation charge in the third column of Table 11.

### 2. Compute the net profit before taxes
Deduct from the annual net revenue the annual depreciation charge, Table 11, and enter the result in column 4. Thus, for the first year with a revenue of $10,000, the net income before taxes = $10,000 − $6000 = $4000.

### 3. Compute the after-tax profit
With a tax of 50 percent of the profit before taxes, multiply the value in Table 11, column 4, by 0.50 to determine the after-tax profit. Thus, for year 1, the after-tax profit = $4000(0.50) = $2000.

### 4. Record the asset book value at the beginning of the year
In this type of calculation, the book value = the unrecovered capital investment for that year. Or, for year 1, the book value = $24,000. For year 2, the book value = $24,000 − $6000 = $18,000. In this relation, $6000 is the depreciation during year 1.

### 5. Compute the apparent rate of return
Divide the after-tax profit for any year by the book value of the asset at the beginning of the year to determine the apparent rate of return. Or, for year 2, apparent rate of return = $1800/$18,000 = 0.10, or 10.0 percent.

**TABLE 11.** Determination of Apparent Rates of Return

| Year | Net revenue, $ | Depreciation charge, $ | Net profit before tax, $ | Net profit after tax, $ | Book value beginning of year, $ | Apparent rate of return, % |
|------|------|------|------|------|------|------|
| 1 | 10,000 | 6,000 | 4,000 | 2,000 | 24,000 | 8.3 |
| 2 | 9,600 | 6,000 | 3,600 | 1,800 | 18,000 | 10.0 |
| 3 | 8,000 | 6,000 | 2,000 | 1,000 | 12,000 | 8.3 |
| 4 | 6,400 | 6,000 | 400 | 200 | 6,000 | 3.3 |
| 5 | 4,400 | . . . | 4,400 | 2,200 | . . . | Infinite |
| 6 | 2,400 | . . . | 2,400 | 1,200 | . . . | Infinite |
|  | 800* | . . . | 800 | 600 |  |  |

*Income from sale of asset.

## *TRUE RATE OF RETURN ON A COMPLETED INVESTMENT*

Refer to the previous calculation procedure. What was the actual after-tax rate of return yielded by this investment, computed at the conclusion of the venture?

### Calculation Procedure:

### 1. *Determine the after-tax income*
In this situation, only the actual disbursements and receipts, as well as their timing, are pertinent. The depreciation charges, which arise from bookkeeping entries, are irrelevant.

To determine the after-tax income, deduct the tax payment from the net revenue listed in Table 11 to obtain the after-tax income. List this income in Table 12.

### 2. *Determine the present worth of the annual receipts*
Compute the present worth of each year's after-tax income for years 1 through 6, and take the sum. To perform this computation, assume an interest rate that is believed to approximate the actual rate of return on the $24,000 investment.

At 12 percent, present worth of the after-tax income = $24,444. At 15 percent, present worth of the after-tax income = $22,874. By linear interpolation for a present worth of $24,000, $i$ = rate of return = 12.8 percent.

## *AVERAGE RATE OF RETURN ON COMPOSITE INVESTMENT*

Suppose that the income in the previous calculation procedure were reinvested at 8 percent after taxes, until the end of the fourth year. Thereafter, the income received was reinvested at 10 percent. What was the average rate of return on the $24,000 capital during the 6-year period?

### Calculation Procedure:

### 1. *Compute the value of the original capital at the end of the sixth year*
Thus, by using the SPCA factor for the after-tax income listed for each year in Table 12 for $i$ = 8 or 10 percent, the value of the original capital at the end of the sixth year =

**TABLE 12.**   Determination of True Rate of Return

| Year | Net revenue, $ | Tax payment, $ | After-tax income, $ |
|------|----------------|----------------|---------------------|
| 1 | 10,000 | 2,000 | 8,000 |
| 2 | 9,600 | 1,800 | 7,800 |
| 3 | 8,000 | 1,000 | 7,000 |
| 4 | 6,400 | 200 | 6,200 |
| 5 | 4,400 | 2,200 | 2,200 |
| 6 | 3,200 | 1,400 | 1,800 |

$8000(1.469) + $7800(1.360) + $7000(1.260) + $6200(1.166) + $2200(1.100) + $1800 = $42,629.

## 2. Compute the average investment rate

Let $i'$ = average investment rate. Equate the original investment to $42,629 at a date 6 years in the future, and solve for $i'$. Thus, $24,000(SPCA for $i'$) = $42,629; $i'$ = 10.1 percent.

# RATE OF RETURN ON A SPECULATIVE INVESTMENT

A firm purchased a parcel of land for $25,000 and spent $600 during the first year to improve the property. (This investment for improvements should be considered a lump-sum end-of-year payment.) The expenses for real estate tax, insurance, and maintenance totaled $1200 per year. At the end of 5 years, the firm sold the property at a price that yielded $48,700 after payment of legal fees and commissions. In computing the federal income tax, the firm deducted the ordinary expenses of holding this property from the income derived from other sources. This income was subject to a 53 percent tax rate. The profit on the sale of the land was taxed at the 25 percent capital-gains rate. What was the rate of return on the investment?

## Calculation Procedure:

### 1. Determine the effective annual payment

The expenses related to possession of the land served to reduce the income tax payments. Therefore, the *effective* cost of holding the property (or any similar asset) was less than the actual expenses. To obtain the effective annual payment, deduct the annual income tax saving from the annual payment related to the asset. Thus, effective annual payment = $1200(1.00 − 0.53) = $564.

### 2. Compute the net proceeds from the sale of the asset

Deduct the capital-gains tax from the selling price of the asset to obtain the net proceeds. This is often called the *effective selling price*. Thus, capital gains = $48,700 − ($25,000 + $600) = $23,100. The capital-gains tax = $23,100(0.25) = $5775. Hence, net proceeds = $48,700 − $5775 = $42,925.

### 3. Set up an equation for the rate of return

Selecting the date at which the asset was sold as the reference date, express the value of every sum of money, and equate the total effective payments to the income. Thus, $25,000(SPCA for $n$ = 5 years, $i$ = ?) + $600(SPCA for $n$ = 4 years, $i$ = ?) + $564(USCA for $n$ = 5 years, $i$ = ?) = $42,925.

### 4. Solve the rate-of-return equation, using trial values

As a trial, set $i$ = 10 percent, and evaluate the left-hand side of the relation in step 3. Thus, $25,000(1.611) + $600(1.464) + $564(6.105) = $44,597.

Since the actual income, $42,925, was less than $44,597, the assumed rate of return is too high. Try 8 percent. Then $25,000(1.469) + $600(1.360) + $564(5.867) = $40,850. This is less than the actual income. Interpolating linearly between the two trial values yields $i$ = 9.1 percent.

***Related Calculations.*** As a general guide for selecting trial rate-of-return values, choose a higher value and a lower value around the estimated true rate of return. Check the result by computing the dollar return. Interpolate linearly when higher and lower dollar returns are obtained.

## INVESTMENT AT AN INTERMEDIATE DATE (AMBIGUOUS CASE)

A firm purchased an oil-producing property under terms which did not require an immediate payment to the seller but which did require payment of royalties on income from sale of the oil.

By the end of the third year, the primary reserves were nearly exhausted, and the firm spent $2,830,000 on a water-injection program to extend the oil yield. Operations were continued until the end of the sixth year. The income from the venture is listed in Table 13. Compute the rate of return on this investment. Is more than one solution obtained? How may the ambiguity inherent in this type of investment be resolved?

### Calculation Procedure:

#### 1. *Set up an equation for the rate of return*
Selecting the end of the third year as the reference date, express the value of every sum of money. Consider receipts to be positive and expenditures to be negative. Then $600,000(SPCA for $n = 2$, $i = ?$) + $300,000(SPCA for $n = 1$, $i = ?$) + $100,000 + $1,220,000(SPPW for $n = 1$, $i = ?$) + $500,000(SPPW for $n = 2$, $i = ?$) + $200,000(SPPW for $n = 3$, $i = ?$) − $2,830,000 = 0.

#### 2. *Solve the rate-of-return equation, using trial values*
Assign a series of trial values for $i$ in the equation in step 1. Record the results in Table 14. Then, by linear interpolation, $i = 9.8$ percent, or $i = 30.1$ percent.

#### 3. *Evaluate the rates of return obtained*
The polynomial in step 1 resembles a quadratic polynomial since it contains either two real roots or none. That there are two values of $i$ which satisfy this equation is explained as follows.

**TABLE 13.** Income from an Asset

| Year | Net income, $ |
|---|---|
| 1 | 600,000 |
| 2 | 300,000 |
| 3 | 100,000 |
| 4 | 1,220,000 |
| 5 | 500,000 |
| 6 | 200,000 |

**TABLE 14.** Trial Calculations for Rate-of-Return Equation

| Interest rate, % | Value of polynomial, $ |
|---|---|
| 8 | 10,600 |
| 10 | −1,400 |
| 15 | −21,300 |
| 20 | −26,400 |
| 25 | −19,400 |
| 30 | −700 |
| 40 | 65,400 |

First, consider that $i = 9.8$ percent, causing the polynomial to assume the value of zero. Then replace 9.8 percent with the higher rate of 30.1 percent. Second, when this substitution is made, the value of the income received prior to the end of the third year is increased by a certain amount. The value of the income received after that date is decreased by the same amount. Hence, the value of the polynomial remains zero.

### 4. Make a realistic appraisal of the investment

A realistic appraisal of an investment of this type requires consideration of the reinvestment rate earned by either the entire income or that part of the income received prior to the expenditure. In the present instance, assume that the income received up to the end of the third year was reinvested at 8 percent. Its value at the date of the expenditure for water injection is, by the equation from step 1, $600,000(1.166) + $300,000(1.080) + $100,000 = $1,123,600.

Then the effective investment = $2,830,000 − $1,123,600 = $1,706,400. To determine the rate of return, set the effective investment $1,706,400 = $1,220,000(SPPW for $n = 1$) + $500,000(SPPW for $n = 2$) + $200,000(SPPW for $n = 3$) and solve for $i$. The result of this solution is $i = 8.5$ percent.

**Related Calculations.** This procedure illustrates the fact that in financial analyses it is not possible to place exclusive reliance on mathematical results. However rigorous the mathematical solution may appear to be, the results must be interpreted in a practical manner. Note that this procedure may be used for any type of asset.

## PAYBACK PERIOD OF AN INVESTMENT

A firm has a choice of two alternative investment plans, A and B. Each plan requires an immediate expenditure of $2,000,000, lasts 10 years, and yields an income at the end of each year. Under plan A, the annual income is expected to be $450,000 for the first 5 years and $33,000 for the remaining 5 years. Under plan B, the annual income is expected to be $150,000 for the first 3 years, $250,000 for the next 3 years, and $650,000 for the last 4 years. If the decision is to be based on a short payback period, which investment plan should the firm adopt?

### Calculation Procedure:

### 1. Compute the payback period under plan A

For various reasons, a firm often prefers an investment that allows it to recover its capital quickly. The speed with which capital is recovered is measured by the *payback period*, defined thus: Assume that all income accruing from the investment initially represents recovered capital, and all income accruing after capital has been fully recovered represents interest. The time required for completion of capital recovery is called the payback period.

Under plan A, the first four payments total $1,800,000, and the first five payments total $2,250,000. Thus, the fifth payment completes capital recovery, and the payback period is 5 years.

### 2. Compute the payback period under plan B

The first seven payments total $1,850,000, and the first eight payments total $2,500,000. Thus, the payback period is 8 years.

**3.  Select the investment plan**
The firm should adopt plan A because it has the lower payback period.
   **Related Calculations.** The investment rate is 6.0 percent for plan A and 10.0 percent for plan B. However, since the income under plan B is largely deferred, use of the payback period as a criterion in investment appraisal places plan B at a disadvantage.

## PAYBACK PERIOD TO YIELD A GIVEN INVESTMENT RATE

An asset has a first cost of $40,000 and maximum life of 10 years. Its resale value will be $3500 at the end of the first year, and then it will diminish by $500 per year, becoming zero at the end of the eighth year. The end-of-year income that accrues from use of this asset will be $12,000 for the first 2 years, $8000 for the next 3 years, $6000 for the next 3 years, and $2000 for the last 2 years. Determine how long this asset must be held to secure a 10 percent return on the investment.

### Calculation Procedure:

#### 1.  Establish the criterion for finding the life of the asset
As the preceding calculation procedure showed, a firm that considers solely how long it takes an investment to restore the sum invested is apt to undertake investments of relatively low yield. A more logical approach is to consider how long it takes an investment to restore the sum invested and yield a certain minimum rate of return.
   Let $N$ = life of asset, years; $i$ and $i'$ = required investment rate and true investment rate, respectively; $V_{exp}$, and $V_{inc}$ = value of expenditures and value of income, respectively, where all sums of money are evaluated at a specific date and by using $i$ as the interest rate. If $V_{exp} = V_{inc}$, then $i' = i$. Thus, the problem is to find the value of $N$ at which this equality of expenditures and income becomes a fact.

#### 2.  Perform the calculations
Evaluate all sums of money at the date of purchase, using an interest rate of 10 percent. Set $N = 1$. Then $V_{exp}$, = $40,000 - $3500(SPPW, $n = 1$) = $40,000 - $3500(0.90909) = $36,818. Also, = $12,000(0.90909) = $10,909. Since $V_{exp} > V_{inc}$, $i' < 10$ percent.
   Now set $N = 2$. Then $V_{exp}$ = $40,000 - $3000(SPPW, $n = 2$) = $40,000 - $3000(0.82645) = $37,521. Applying the previous result and adding the income at the end of the second year, we find $V_{inc}$ = $10,909 + $12,000(0.82645) = $20,826. Thus, $i' < 10$ percent.
   Set $N = 3$. Then $V_{exp}$ = $40,000 - $2500(0.75131) = $38,122. Also, $V_{inc}$ = $20,826 + $8000(0.75131) = $26,836.
   Continue these calculations to obtain the results in Table 15. This table shows that $i' < 10$ percent when $N = 5$ and $i' > 10$ percent when $N = 6$. Thus, the asset must be held 6 years to secure a 10 percent rate of return.

## BENEFIT-COST ANALYSIS

A proposed flood-control dam is expected to have an initial cost of $5,000,000 and to require annual maintenance of $24,000. It will also require major repairs and reconstruction

**TABLE 15.** Value of Expenditures and Income

| Life of asset, years | Value of expenditures, $ | Value of income, $ |
|---|---|---|
| 1 | 36,818 | 10,909 |
| 2 | 37,521 | 20,826 |
| 3 | 38,122 | 26,836 |
| 4 | 38,634 | 32,300 |
| 5 | 39,069 | 37,267 |
| 6 | 39,435 | 40,654 |

costing $120,000 at the end of every 10-year period. The life of the dam may be assumed to be infinite. The reduction in losses due to flood damage is estimated to be $300,000 per year. However, there will be an immediate loss of $100,000 in the value of the property surrounding the dam, and this loss will be borne by the public. Applying an interest rate of 6 percent, determine whether the proposed dam is feasible.

**Calculation Procedure:**

**1. Compute the present worth of costs**
With reference to a federal project, any income or reduction in loss that accrues to the public is called a *benefit*, any loss that accrues to the public is called a *disbenefit*, and the difference between the benefits and disbenefits is called the *net benefit*. The ratio of net benefit to costs is called the *benefit-cost (B/C) ratio*. If this ratio exceeds 1, the project is considered desirable.

A uniform-payment series that continues indefinitely is called a *perpetuity*. The value of a perpetuity at its origin date (i.e., one payment period before the first payment) is $R/[(1 + i)^m - 1]$, where $R =$ periodic payment, $i =$ interest rate, and $m =$ number of interest periods in one payment period.

The present worths are: First cost, PW $= \$5,000,000$; annual maintenance, PW $=$ $\$24,000/0.06 = \$400,000$; repairs and reconstruction, PW $= \$120,000/[(1.06)^{10} - 1] =$ $\$151,700$. Then PW of costs $= \$5,000,000 + \$400,000 + \$151,700 = \$5,551,700$.

**2. Compute the present worth of net benefit**
The present worths are: Savings, PW $= \$300,000/0.06 = \$5,000,000$; devaluation of property, PW $= \$100,000$. Then PW of net benefit $= \$5,000,000 - \$100,000 =$ $\$4,900,000$.

**3. Determine whether the dam is feasible**
Since $B/C$ ratio $= \$4,900,000/\$5,551,700 < 1$, the dam is not feasible.

# Analysis of Business Operations

## LINEAR PROGRAMMING TO MAXIMIZE INCOME FROM JOINT PRODUCTS

A firm manufactures two articles, A and B. The unit cost of production, exclusive of fixed costs, is $10 for A and $7 for B. The unit selling price is $16 for A and $13.50 for B. The estimated maximum monthly sales potential of A is 9000 units; of B, 7000 units. It is the policy of the firm to produce only as many units as can readily be sold. If production is restricted to one article, the factory can turn out 13,000 units of A or 8500 units of B per month. The capital allotted to monthly production after payment of fixed costs is $100,000. What monthly production of each article will yield the maximum profit?

### Calculation Procedure:

#### 1. *Express the production constraints imposed by sales and capital*
Let $N_A$ and $N_B$ denote the number of articles A and B, respectively, produced monthly. Then potential sales: $N_A \leq 9000$, Eq. *a*; $N_B \leq 7000$, Eq. *b*. Available capital: $10N_A + 7N_B \leq \$100,000$, Eq. *c*.

#### 2. *Determine the production constraint imposed by the plant capacity*
The number of months required to produce $N_A$ units of A is $N_A/13,000$. Likewise, to produce $N_B$ units of B would be $N_B/8500$. Then, $N_A/13,000 + N_B/8500 \leq 1$, or $8.5N_A + 13N_B \leq 110,500$, Eq. *d*.

#### 3. *Express the monthly profit in equation form*
Before fixed costs are deducted, the profit $P = (16 - 10)N_A + (13.5 - 7)N_B$, or $P = 6N_A + 6.5N_B$, Eq. *e*.

#### 4. *Construct a monthly production chart*
Considering the expressions *a* to *d* above to be equalities, plot the straight lines representing them (Fig. 8).

Since these expressions actually establish upper limits to the values of $N_A$ and $N_B$, the point representing the joint production of articles A and B must lie either within the shaded area, which is termed the *feasible region*, or on one of its boundary lines.

#### 5. *Plot an equal-profit line*
Assign the arbitrary value of $30,000 to $P$, and plot the straight line corresponding to Eq. *e* above. Every point on this line (Fig. 8) represents a set of values for $N_A$ and $N_B$ for which the profit is $30,000. This line is therefore termed an equal-profit line.

Next, consider that $P$ assumes successively greater values. As $P$ does so, the equal-profit line moves away from the origin while remaining parallel to its initial position.

#### 6. *Maximize the profit potential*
To maximize the profit, locate the point in Fig. 8 at which the equal-profit line, in its outward displacement, is on the verge of leaving the feasible region. This is point $Q$, which lies at the intersection of the lines representing the equalities *c* and *d*.

#### 7. *Determine the number of units for maximum profit*
Establish the coordinates of the maximum-profit point $Q$ either by reading them from the chart, Fig. 8, or by solving the equalities *c* and *d* simultaneously. The results are $N_A = 7468$ units; $N_B = 3617$ units.

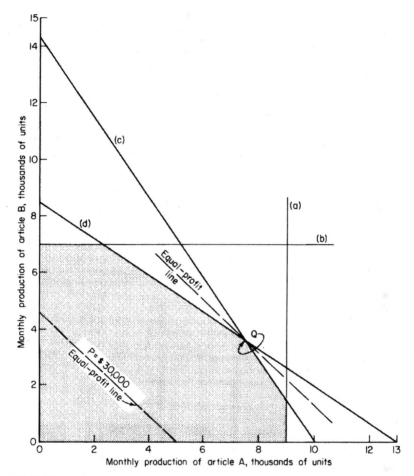

**FIGURE 8.** Linear programming solution.

***Related Calculations.*** Note that this method can be used for any type of product manufactured by any means.

## ALLOCATION OF PRODUCTION AMONG MULTIPLE FACILITIES WITH NONLINEAR COSTS

A firm must produce 700 units per month of a commodity, and three machines, A, B, and C, are available for this purpose. Production costs are $C_A = 0.28N_A^{1.42} + 400$; $C_B = 0.36N_B^{1.47} + 500$; $C_C = 0.30N_B^{1.53} + 420$, where $N$ = number of units produced monthly;

$C$ = monthly cost of production, \$; and the subscript refers to the machine. Find the most economical manner of allocating production among the three machines.

## Calculation Procedure:

### 1. Write the equations of incremental costs
The objective is to minimize the total cost of production. Since costs vary nonlinearly, this situation does not lend itself to linear programming.

Assume that $N$ units have been produced on a given machine. The incremental (or marginal) *cost* at that point is the cost of producing the $(N + i)$th unit. Let $I$ = incremental cost, \$. If $N$ is large, $I \approx dC/dN$. By differentiating the foregoing expressions, this approximation gives $I_A = 0.3976N_A^{0.42}$, $I_B = 0.5292N_B^{0.47}$, $I_C = 0.4590N_C^{0.53}$, where the subscript refers to the machine. Also, if $N$ is large, cost of producing $N$th unit $\approx$ cost of producing $(N + 1)$th unit.

### 2. Establish the condition at which the total cost of production is minimum
Arbitrarily set $N_A = 150$, $N_B = 250$, $N_C = 300$, which gives a total of 700 units. The incremental costs are $I_A = \$3,2614$, $I_B = \$7.0901$, and $I_C = \$9.4338$. Also, when $N_A = 151$, then $I_A = \$3.2705$. The total cost of production can be reduced by shifting 1 unit from machine B to machine A and 1 unit from machine C to machine A, with the reduction being approximately $\$7.0901 + \$9.4338 - (\$3.2614 + 3.2705) = \$9.9920$. Thus, the arbitrary set of $N$ values given above does not yield the minimum total cost.

Clearly the total cost of production is minimum when all three incremental costs are equal (or as equal as possible, since $N$ is restricted to integral values).

### 3. Find the most economical allocation of production
At minimum total cost, $I_A = I_B = I_C$ or $0.3976N_A^{0.42} = 0.5292N_B^{0.47} = 0.4590N_C^{0.53}$, Eq. $a$; and $N_A + N_B + N_C = 700$, Eq. $b$. By a trial-and-error solution, $N_A = 468$, $N_B = 132$, and $N_C = 100$.

Alternatively, proceed as follows: From Eq. $a$, $N_B = 0.5442N_A^{0.8936}$ and $N_C = 0.7627N_A^{0.7925}$. Substituting in Eq. $b$ gives $N_A + 0.5442N_A^{0.8936} + 0.7627N_A^{0.7925} = 700$. Assign trial values to $N_A$ until this equation is satisfied. The solution is $N_A = 468$, and the remaining values follow.

### 4. Devise a semigraphical method of solution
In Fig. 9, plot the incremental-cost curves. Pass an arbitrary horizontal line $L$ through these curves to obtain a set of $N$ values at which $I_A = I_B = I_C$. Scale the $N$ values, and find their sum. Now displace the horizontal line until the sum of the $N$ values is 700.

**Related Calculations.** Allocation problems of this type usually are solved by applying *Lagrange multipliers*. However, as the previous solution demonstrates, the use of simple economic logic can circumvent the need for abstract mathematical concepts.

## OPTIMAL PRODUCT MIX WITH NONLINEAR PROFITS

A firm manufactures three articles, A, B, and C, and it can sell as many units as it can produce. The monthly profits, exclusive of fixed costs, are $P_A - 4.75N_A - 0.0050N_A^2$, $P_B = 2.60N_A - 0.0014N_B^2$, and $P_C = 2.25N_C - 0.0010N_C^2$, where $N$ = number of units produced

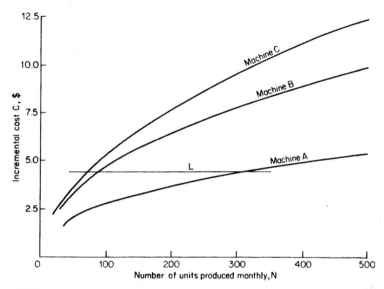

**FIGURE 9.** Incremental-cost curves.

monthly, $P$ = monthly profit, and the subscript refers to the article. If production is restricted to one article, the firm can produce 1000 units of A, 1500 units of B, and 1800 units of C per month. What monthly production of each article will yield the maximum profit?

### Calculation Procedure:

### 1. *Express the constraint imposed on production*
Let $T$ = number of months required to produce $N$ units of an article, with a subscript to identify the article. Then $T_A = N_A/1000$; $T_B = N_B/1500$; and $T_C = N_C/1800$. Since 1 month is available, $N_A/1000 + N_B/1500 + N_C/1800 = 1$, or $1.8N_A + 1.2N_B + N_C = 1800$, Eq. *a*.

### 2. *Determine how the values of N can vary*
Assume for simplicity that $N_A$ is restricted to integral values but $N_C$ and $N_C$ can assume non-integral values. Equation *a* reveals that if $N_A$ increases by 1 unit, $N_B$ must decrease by 1.8/1.2 = 1.5 units, or $N_C$ must decrease by 1.8 units. Expressed formally, the partial derivatives are $\partial N_B/\partial N_A = -1.5$ and $\partial N_C/\partial N_A = -1.8$.

### 3. *Write the equations of incremental profits*
If $N$ units of an article have been produced, the incremental profit at that point is the profit that accrues from producing the $(N + 1)$th unit. Let $I$ = incremental profit. If $N$ is large, $I \approx dP/dN$. By differentiating the foregoing expressions, the incremental profits are $I_A = 475 - 0.0100N_A$, $I_B = 2.60 - 0.0028N_B$, and $I_C = 2.25 - 0.0020N_C$, where the subscript refers to the article. Also, if $N$ is large, the profit from the $N$th unit $\approx$ profit from the $(N + 1)$th unit.

### 4. *Establish the condition at which the total profit is maximum*
Arbitrarily set $N_A = 300$, $N_B = 400$, $N_C = 780$, satisfying Eq. *a*. The incremental profits are $I_A = \$1750$; $I_B = \$1480$ and $1.5I_B = \$2220$; $I_C = \$0690$ and $18I_C = \$1.242$. Also, when $N_B =$

401.5, then $1.5I_B$ = \$2.214. The total profit can be increased by reducing $N_A$ by 1 unit, reducing $N_C$ by 1.8 units, and increasing $N_B$ by 2(1.5) = 3 units, with the increase in profit being approximately \$2.220 + \$2.214 − (\$1.750 + \$1.242) = \$1.442. Thus, the arbitrary set of $N$ values given above does not yield the maximum profit.

So the total profit is maximum when $I_A$ = $1.5I_B$ = $1.8I_C$, or $4.75 − 0.0100N_A$ = $3.90 − 0.0042N_B$ = $4.05 − 0.0036N_C$, Eq. *b*.

### 5.  *Find the production that will maximize profit*
Applying Eq. *b*, express $N_B$ and $N_C$ in terms of $N_A$. Substitute these expressions in Eq. *a*, and solve the resulting equation for $N_A$. Then calculate $N_B$ and $N_C$. The results are $N_A$ = 301, $N_B$ = 514, and $N_C$ = 641.

### 6.  *Devise a semigraphical method of solution*
In Fig. 10, plot the straight lines that represent $I_A$, $1.5I_B$, and $1.8I_C$. Pass an arbitrary horizontal line $L$ through these lines to obtain a set of $N$ values at which $I_A$ = $1.5I_B$ = $1.8I_C$. Scale the $N$ values, and determine whether they satisfy Eq. *a*. Now displace the horizontal line until the $N$ values do satisfy this equation.


## DYNAMIC PROGRAMMING TO MINIMIZE COST OF TRANSPORTATION

A firm must ship merchandise by truck from town A to town E, and the trip will last 4 days. The driver will stop in district B the first night, district C the second night, and district D the third night. The number of towns in each district is: district B, three; district C, two; district D, three. The driver can stay overnight in any of these towns, and the cost of

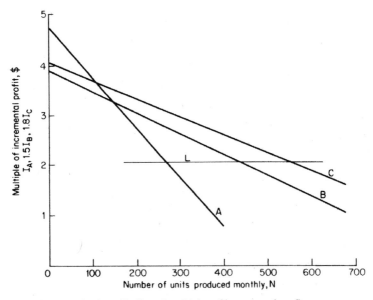

**FIGURE 10.** Plotting of indicated multiples of incremental profit.

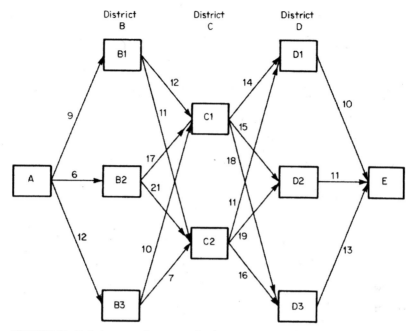

**FIGURE 11.** Relative cost of transportation between successive stops.

lodging is the same in all. The relative cost of traveling from one town to another is recorded in Fig. 11. Design the most economical route.

## Calculation Procedure:

### 1. Determine the minimum cost of transportation from towns C1 and C2 to town E

The design will be executed by dynamic programming, which was applied in an earlier calculation procedure to identify the most lucrative combination of investments. The most economical route from A to E will be constructed in stages, in reverse order.

The cost of transportation from Cl to E is as follows: for C1-D1-E, 14 + 10 = 24; for C1-D2-E, 15 + 11 = 26; for C1-D3-E, 18 + 13 = 31. Thus, the minimum cost is 24. The cost of transportation from C2 to E is: for C2-D1-E, 11 + 10 = 21; for C2-D2-E, 19 + 11 = 30; for C2-D3-E, 16 + 13 = 29. Thus, the minimum cost is 21. Record these minimum costs and their corresponding towns in district D in Fig. 12; they are the only costs that are relevant from now on.

### 2. Determine the minimum cost of transportation from towns B1, B2, and B3 to town E

Refer to Fig. 12. The cost of transportation from B1 to E is: for B1-C1-E, 12 + 24 = 36; for B1-C2-E, 11 + 21 = 32. Thus, the minimum cost is 32. The cost of transportation from B2 to E is: for B2-C1-E, 17 + 24 = 41; for B2-C2-E, 21 + 21 = 42. Thus, the minimum cost is 41. The cost of transportation from B3 to E is: for B3-C1-E, 10 + 24 = 34; for B3-C2-E, 7 + 21 = 28. Thus, the minimum cost is 28. Record these minimum costs and their corresponding towns in district C in Fig. 13.

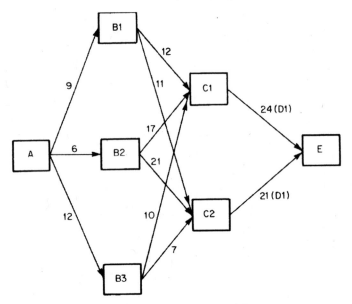

**FIGURE 12.** First stage in finding most economical route.

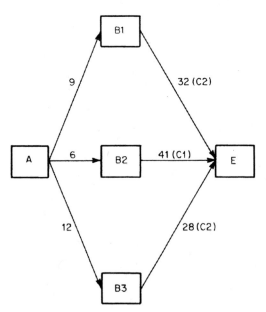

**FIGURE 13.** Second stage in finding most economical route.

### 3. *Determine the minimum cost of transportation from town A to town E*

Refer to Fig. 13. The cost of transportation from A to E is: for A-B1-E, 9 + 32 = 41; for A-B2-E, 6 + 41 = 47; for A-B3-E, 12 + 28 = 40. Thus, the minimum cost is 40, and the corresponding town in district B is B3.

### 4. *Identify the most economical route*

Refer to step 3 and Figs. 13 and 12, in that order. The most economical route is A-B3-C2-D1-E. From Fig. 11, the cost of transportation corresponding to this route is 12 + 7 + 11 + 10 = 40, which agrees with the result in step 3.

  **Related Calculations.** The number of alternative routes from town A to town E is 3 × 2 × 3 = 18. Therefore, the most economical route can be found by listing all 18 routes and computing their respective costs. However, the solution by dynamic programming given above simplifies the work.

## OPTIMAL INVENTORY LEVEL

A firm is under contract to supply 41,600 parts per year and plans to produce them in equal lots spaced at equal intervals. The production capacity is 800 parts per day. Setup and teardown cost for the production machines is $550 for each run. The cost of storage, insurance, and interest on the investment is $1.40 per part for each year the part is carried in inventory. The regular production cost, exclusive of setup and teardown, is $5 per part. A reserve stock of parts is not needed. Determine the most economical lot size and the corresponding cost of production.

### Calculation Procedure:

### 1. *Compute the parts delivery rate*

Assume that the parts are delivered to the buyer at a uniform rate, and compute the daily delivery rate. Since there are approximately 260 working days per year, the rate of delivery = 41,600 parts/260 days = 160 parts per day.

### 2. *Construct an inventory-time diagram*

Figure 14 shows such a diagram, starting with zero inventory.

### 3. *Compute the peak inventory for a lot size of N*

The time $OA$ required to produce 1 lot, Fig. 14, = lot size/maximum production rate = $N/800$, days. The slope of $OB$ = rate of production − rate of delivery = 800 − 160 = 640 parts per day. Then $AB = (N/800)(640) = 0.8N$ parts.

### 4. *Compute the total annual cost in terms of N*

The number of runs per year = 41,600/N. Also, the annual cost of setup and teardown = $550(41,600/N) = 22,880,000/N$. Further, the average

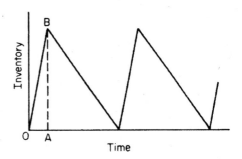

**FIGURE 14.** Variation in inventory level.

inventory $= 0.5AB = 0.4N$ parts. By taking the product of the carrying cost and the average inventory, the annual cost of carrying the inventory $= \$1.40(0.4N) = 0.56N$. With a \$5 per unit regular cost, the annual regular cost $= \$5(41,600$ units$) = \$208,000$. Then the annual total cost $C = (22,880,000/N) + 0.56N + 208,000$.

### 5.  Find the economical lot size

To minimize $C$, set the derivative of $C$ with respect to $N$ equal to zero; solve for $N$ to find the economical lot size. Thus, $dC/dN = -(22,880,000/N^2) + 0.56 = 0$; $N = 6392$ parts per lot.

### 6.  Compute the total annual cost

Substitute the number of parts from step 5 in the total annual-cost equation in step 4. Or, $C = 3580 + 3580 + 208,000 = \$215,160$.


## EFFECT OF QUANTITY DISCOUNT ON OPTIMAL INVENTORY LEVEL

Given the data from the previous calculation procedure, the firm finds that it can obtain quantity discounts if the parts are produced in lots of 7500 or more. These discounts reduce the regular production cost from \$5 to \$4.80 per part; this saving reduces the interest cost on inventory by \$0.02 per part. Determine the most economical lot size under these conditions.


**Calculation Procedure:**

### 1.  Determine the number of parts for minimum cost

Assume that $N \geq 7500$. Proceeding as before, express $C$ in terms of $N$, and set $dC/dN = 0$.

The annual cost of carrying the inventory $= \$1.38(0.4N) = 0.552N$. Also, the annual regular cost $= 41,600(\$4.80) = \$199,680$. Also, $C = (22,880,000/N) + 0.552N + 199,680$. And $dC/dN = -(22,880,000/N2) + 0.552 = 0$. For minimum cost, $N = 6438$ parts. However, since discounts are not obtained until $N$ reaches 7500, the last calculation lacks significance for this situation.

### 2.  Compute the economical lot size

Set $N = 7500$ and substitute in the cost equation above. Then $C = 3051 + 4140 + 199,680 = \$206,871$. Since this result is less than the value of \$215,160 computed in the previous calculation procedure corresponding to 6392 parts, the economical lot size is 7500 parts.


## PROJECT PLANNING BY THE CRITICAL-PATH METHOD

Table 16 lists the activities performed in preparing a building site and installing the utilities. Assuming that the estimated durations are precise, determine the minimum time needed to complete the project. Identify the critical path. Upon completion of the project, it was found that each activity was undertaken at the earliest possible date and that its duration coincided with the estimate, except for the following: activity D was started 3 days late; activity H required 9 days instead of 6; activity I required 5 days instead of 4. Determine the duration of the project.

## Calculation Procedure:

### 1. Identify the predecessor(s) of each activity; tabulate results

The critical-path method (CPM) offers a systematic means of scheduling activities in a project and analyzing the consequences of departures from the schedule. The procedure consists of devising a logical concatenation of activities after ascertaining the relationships that exist among them. For example, activities D and E, Table 16, are independent of each other and therefore may be performed concurrently. But activities D and F are sequentially related—F cannot commence until D is finished. Thus, D is the immediate predecessor of F. Using these principles, list the related activities as shown in Table 17.

**TABLE 16.** Project Activities

| Mark | Activity | Estimated duration, days |
|------|----------|:---:|
| A | Clear site | 4 |
| B | Survey and lay out site | 3 |
| C | Rough grade | 3 |
| D | Excavate for sewer | 8 |
| E | Excavate for electrical manholes | 1 |
| F | Install sewer and backfill | 4 |
| G | Install electrical manholes | 6 |
| H | Install overhead pole line | 6 |
| I | Install electrical duct bank | 4 |
| J | Pull in power feeder | 5 |
| K | Construct foundations for water tank | 3 |
| L | Erect water tank | 8 |
| M | Install piping and valves for water tank | 12 |
| N | Drill well | 14 |
| O | Install well pump | 2 |
| P | Install underground water piping | 9 |
| Q | Connect all piping | 2 |

**TABLE 17.** Related CPM Activities

| Activity | Predecessor | Activity | Predecessor |
|:---:|:---:|:---:|:---:|
| B | A | J | H and I |
| C | B | K | C |
| D | C | L | K |
| E | C | M | L |
| F | D | N | C |
| G | E | O | N |
| H | C | P | O |
| I | F and G | Q | M and P |

## 2. Construct the network for the project, Fig. 15

The network is a delineation of the sequence in which the activities are to be performed. Each activity is represented by a horizontal arrow, which may or may not be to scale. The arrow representing a given activity is placed to the right of its immediate predecessor activity. Where there are multiple predecessors or successors, broken arrows are used to transfer from one activity to another. The duration of each activity is recorded under its corresponding arrow.

Completion of an activity and the start of its successor constitute an event. Commencement of a given activity is termed its *i event*; completion of an activity is termed its *j event*. A number is assigned to each event and is recorded in the network in a circle between consecutive arrows. Each activity is identified by the events it separates. For instance, 6-7 designates *erect water tank.* A chain of activities extending from inception to completion of the project is termed a path. In this project there are the following five paths:

0-1-2-3-4-5-8-13

0-1-2-3-6-7-8-13

0-1-2-3-9-11-12-13

0-1-2-3-10-11-12-13

0-1-2-3-12-13

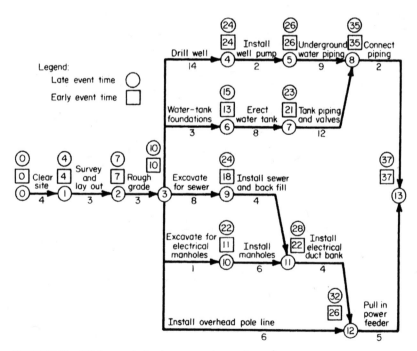

**FIGURE 15.** CPM network for site-preparation project.

### 3. Compute the early event time $T_E$ of each event

The early event time is the earliest possible date at which the event may occur. Compute the early event time from $T_{E(n)} = T_{E(n-1)} + D$, where $T_{E(n)}$ = early event time of a given event; $= T_{E(n-1)}$ = early event time of preceding event; $D$ = duration of intervening activity. Where an event has multiple immediate predecessors, this equation yields multiple values of $T_E$; the correct value is the maximum value.

Table 18 shows the calculations for the early event times. In the calculations, the starting date of the project was used as the datum. Record the early event times on the network by entering the time (usually in days) in a square above each event. From Table 18, the minimum duration of this project is 37 days.

### 4. Compute the late event time $T_L$ of each event

The late event time of each event is the latest date at which the event may occur without extending the duration of the project beyond the minimum time. Use the relation $= T_{L(n)} = T_{L(n-1)} - D$, where $= T_{L(n)}$ = late event time of a given event; $T_{L(n-1)}$ = late event time of succeeding event; $D$ = duration of intervening activity. Both early and late event times are usually measured in days, but on unusually long projects they may be measured in months. Where an event has multiple immediate successors, the equation above yields multiple values of $T_L$; the correct result is the minimum value.

Table 19 shows the calculations of the late event times. Enter the late event time on the network in a circle above each event.

### 5. Compute the float of each activity

*Float* is the time, usually in days, that the completion of each activity may be delayed without extending the duration of the project, with the understanding that no other delays will occur. Compute the float from $F = T_{L(j)} - (T_{E(i)} + D)$, where $F$ = float, usually in days; $T_{L(j)}$ = late event time of completion in the same time as $F$; $T_{E(i)}$ = early event starting time, in the same time units as $F$. The expression in parentheses represents the

**TABLE 18.** Calculation of Early Event Times

| Event | | $T_E$, days |
|---|---|---|
| 0 | | 0 |
| 1 | | 4 |
| 2 | | $4 + 3$   $= 7$ |
| 3 | | $7 + 3$   $= 10$ |
| 4 | | $10 + 14 = 24$ |
| 5 | | $24 + 2$  $= 26$ |
| 6 | | $10 + 3$  $= 13$ |
| 7 | | $13 + 8$  $= 21$ |
| 8 | | $26 + 9$  $= 35$ |
| | or | $21 + 12 = 33$ (disregard) |
| 9 | | $10 + 8$  $= 18$ |
| 10 | | $10 + 1$  $= 11$ |
| 11 | | $18 + 4$  $= 22$ |
| | or | $11 + 6$  $= 17$ (disregard) |
| 12 | | $22 + 4$  $= 26$ |
| | or | $10 + 6$  $= 16$ (disregard) |
| 13 | | $35 + 2$  $= 37$ |
| | or | $26 + 5$  $= 31$ (disregard) |

**TABLE 19.** Calculation of Late Event Times

| Event | $T_L$, days |
|---|---|
| 13 | 37 |
| 12 | $37 - 5 = 32$ |
| 11 | $32 - 4 = 28$ |
| 10 | $28 - 6 = 22$ |
| 9 | $28 - 4 = 24$ |
| 8 | $37 - 2 = 35$ |
| 7 | $35 - 12 = 23$ |
| 6 | $23 - 8 = 15$ |
| 5' | $35 - 9 = 26$ |
| 4 | $26 - 2 = 24$ |
| 3 | $24 - 14 = 10$ |
| or | $15 - 3 = 12$ (disregard) |
| or | $24 - 8 = 16$ (disregard) |
| or | $22 - 1 = 21$ (disregard) |
| or | $32 - 6 = 26$ (disregard) |
| 2 | $10 - 3 = 7$ |
| 1 | $7 - 3 = 4$ |
| 0 | $4 - 4 = 0$ |

earliest possible date at which the activity may be completed. Table 20 shows the float calculations.

### 6. *Identify the critical path*

An activity is *critical* if any delay in its completion will extend the duration of the project. The path on which the critical activities are located is termed the critical path. (There may be several critical paths associated with a project.) In the terminology of CPM, a critical activity is one having zero float. The critical path for this project is therefore 0-1-2-3-4-5-8-13.

### 7. *Verify the results of step 6*

Plot the project activities on a time scale, Fig. 16. This diagram was constructed under the assumption that each activity commences at the earliest possible date.

Note in Fig. 16 that the float of a given activity equals the total gap in the chain extending from the completion of that activity to the completion of the project. For instance, 6-7 has a float of 2 days, and 10-11 has a float of $5 + 6 = 11$ days.

### 8. *Indicate where the actual schedule departed from the forecast*

List the data as follows:

| Old mark | New mark | Delay in completion, days |
|---|---|---|
| D | 3-9 | 3 |
| H | 3-12 | 3 |
| I | 11-12 | 1 |

**TABLE 20.**   Calculation of Project Float*

| Activity | $T_{L(j)}$ | $T_{E(i)}$ | D | F |
|---|---|---|---|---|
| 0-1 | 4 | 0 | 4 | 0 |
| 1-2 | 7 | 4 | 3 | 0 |
| 2-3 | 10 | 7 | 3 | 0 |
| 3-4 | 24 | 10 | 14 | 0 |
| 4-5 | 26 | 24 | 2 | 0 |
| 5-8 | 35 | 26 | 9 | 0 |
| 3-6 | 15 | 10 | 3 | 2 |
| 6-7 | 23 | 13 | 8 | 2 |
| 7-8 | 35 | 21 | 12 | 2 |
| 8-13 | 37 | 35 | 2 | 0 |
| 3-9 | 24 | 10 | 8 | 6 |
| 9-11 | 28 | 18 | 4 | 6 |
| 3-10 | 22 | 10 | 1 | 11 |
| 10-11 | 28 | 11 | 6 | 11 |
| 11-12 | 32 | 22 | 4 | 6 |
| 3-12 | 32 | 10 | 6 | 16 |
| 12-13 | 37 | 26 | 5 | 6 |

*Measured in days.

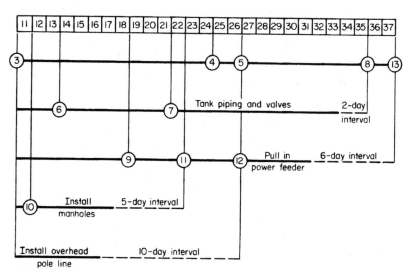

**FIGURE 16.**   Activity-time diagram.

### 9. Determine the true duration of the project

Treating each departure individually, deduce the effects of that departure by referring to Fig. 16. Combine these effects where they are cumulative. On the basis of these results, establish the true duration of the project. Thus activity 3-9: events 11 and 12 would be delayed 3 days; activity 3-12: event 12 would not be delayed, since there is a latitude of 10 days along this path; activity 11-12: event 12 would be delayed 1 day. *Summary*: Event 12 is delayed 4 days; event 13 is not delayed, since there is a latitude of 6 days along this path. Therefore, the true duration of the project = 37 days, as forecast.

## PROJECT PLANNING BASED ON AVAILABLE WORKFORCE

A manufacturing firm has a contract to build a pilot model of a newly invented machine. To plan the work, the firm constructed the CPM network in Fig. 17 and compiled the data in Table 21. The following activities must be performed as a unit, without loss of continuity: 0-1-2-4; 2-3-4; 5-7-8. Activities 4-8 and 6-8 may be performed piecemeal, if this proves convenient. The workforce available for assignment to this project is 15 workers for the first 8 days, 25 for the remaining time. Each employee is capable of performing all 11 activities. But the constraints imposed by the available facilities limit the number of workers for each activity to that shown in Table 21. Overtime is not permissible. Devise a schedule that will allow completion of this project at the earliest possible date.

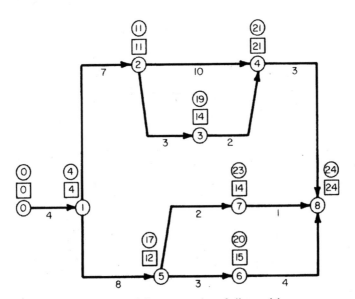

**FIGURE 17.** CPM network for construction of pilot model.

**TABLE 21.** Time and Workforce Requirements for a Technical Project

| Activity, Fig. 17 | Duration, days | Workers required |
|---|---|---|
| 0-1 | 4 | 3 |
| 1-2 | 7 | 5 |
| 2-4 | 10 | 9 |
| 2-3 | 3 | 9 |
| 3-4 | 2 | 12 |
| 4-8 | 3 | 4 |
| 1-5 | 8 | 6 |
| 5-6 | 3 | 10 |
| 6-8 | 4 | 8 |
| 5-7 | 2 | 6 |
| 7-8 | 1 | 7 |

## Calculation Procedure:

### 1. Compute the early and late event times
The results of these calculations, made in accordance with the previous calculation procedure, are shown in Fig. 17.

### 2. Identify the critical path
Since the critical path is the longest path through the network, Fig. 17 shows that this is 0-1-2-4-8. Note that the critical path sets a lower limit of 24 days on the duration of the project. But the workforce limitations may lengthen the project beyond 24 days. Thus, the objective will be to devise a schedule that fits noncritical activities into the 24-day period while satisfying the workforce availability.

### 3. Schedule the project, assuming unlimited workforce
As a first trial, assume that unlimited workforce is available, and schedule each activity to start at the *earliest* possible date. Construct the workforce-time diagram for this condition, as shown in Fig. 18a. Study of the diagram shows that this schedule is unsatisfactory because the workforce requirements exceed the available workers on days 12 to 15, inclusive.

### 4. Schedule the project with the latest possible start
Assume unlimited workforce again, and schedule each activity to start at the *latest* possible date. Construct the corresponding workforce-time diagram, Fig. 18b. Study of the diagram shows that this schedule is also unsatisfactory, but it is an improvement over the schedule in step 3.

Although both these schedules are unsatisfactory, they are useful because their workforce-time diagrams reveal the boundaries of each activity or chain of activities based on a project duration of 24 days. For example, the chain 5-7-8 may start at any time between days 12 and 21, Fig. 18. This information is not explicitly supplied by the network, since the late event time for event 5 is determined by the chain 5-6-8.

### 5. Shift noncritical activities to obtain a suitable schedule
Using the allowable workforce limits, shift noncritical activities such that the project can be completed in 24 days using the available workers.

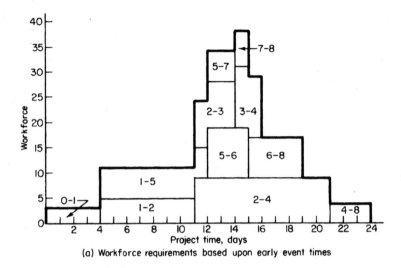

(a) Workforce requirements based upon early event times

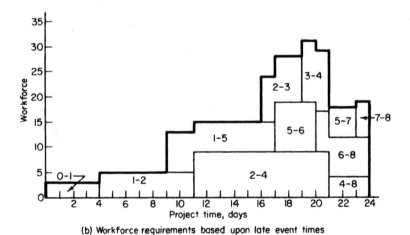

(b) Workforce requirements based upon late event times

**FIGURE 18**

Construct the schedule shown in Fig. 19. Note that the workforce requirements are less than the available personnel. Further, the schedule preserves the integrity of the three chains of activities mentioned earlier. Although fragmentation of activity 6-8 is permissible, it proved unnecessary. With the schedule shown, the project will be finished in 24 days.

***Related Calculations.*** Note that this procedure can be used for any type of project requiring allocation of workforce or other resources.

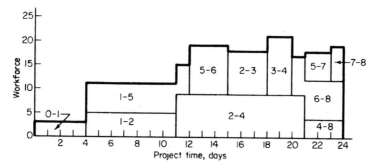

**FIGURE 19.** Workforce requirements based on project schedule.

# Statistics, Probability, and Their Applications

## Basic Statistics

If the value assumed by a variable on a given occasion cannot be predicted because it is influenced by chance, the variable is known as a *random*, or *stochastic*, variable. The number of times the variable assumes a given value is called the *frequency* of that value. A number that may be considered representative of all values of the variable is called an average. There are several types of averages, such as arithmetic mean, geometric mean, harmonic mean, median, mode, etc. Each is used for a specific purpose. The *standard deviation* is a measure of the dispersion, or scatter, of the values of the random variable; it is approximately equal to the amount by which a given value of the variable may be expected to differ from the arithmetic mean, in either direction. The variance is the square of the standard deviation. Where no mention of frequency appears, it is understood that all frequencies are 1.

## Notational System

Here $X$ = random variable; $X_i$ = $i$th value assumed by $X$; $f_i$ = frequency of $X_i$; $n$ = sum of frequencies; $\bar{X}$ = arithmetic mean of values of $X$; $X_{med}$ = median of these values; $d_i$ = deviation of $X_i$, from $\bar{X} = X_i - \bar{X}$; $A$ = an assumed arithmetic mean; $d_{A,i}$ = deviation of $X_i$ from $A = X_i - A$; $s$ = standard deviation; $s^2$ = variance. In the following material, the subscript $i$ will be omitted.

## DETERMINATION OF ARITHMETIC MEAN, MEDIAN, AND STANDARD DEVIATION

Column 2 of Table 22 presents the number of units of a commodity that were sold monthly by a firm for 7 consecutive months. Find the arithmetic mean, median, and standard deviation of the number of units sold monthly.

## TABLE 22

| (1) Month | (2) Number of units sold $X$ | (3) $d = X - 43$ | (4) $d^2$ | (5) $d_A = X - 40$ | (6) $d_A^2$ |
|---|---|---|---|---|---|
| 1 | 32 | −11 | 121 | −8 | 64 |
| 2 | 49 | 6 | 36 | 9 | 81 |
| 3 | 51 | 8 | 64 | 11 | 121 |
| 4 | 44 | 1 | 1 | 4 | 16 |
| 5 | 37 | −6 | 36 | −3 | 9 |
| 6 | 41 | −2 | 4 | 1 | 1 |
| 7 | 47 | 4 | 16 | 7 | 49 |
| Total | 301 | 0 | 278 | 21 | 341 |

## Calculation Procedure:

### 1. Compute the arithmetic mean
Let $X$ = number of units sold monthly. Find the sum of the values of $X$, which is 301. Then set $\bar{X} = (\Sigma X)/n$, or $\bar{X} = 301/7 = 43$.

### 2. Find the median
Consider that all values of $X$ are arranged in ascending order of magnitude. If $n$ is odd, the value that occupies the central position in this array is called the *median*. If $n$ is even, the median is taken as the arithmetic mean of the two values that occupy the central positions. In either case, the total frequency of values below the median equals the total frequency of values above the median. The median is useful as an average because the arithmetic mean can be strongly influenced by an extreme value at one end of the array and thereby offer a misleading view of the data.

In the present instance, the array is 32, 37, 41, 44, 47, 49, 51. The fourth value in the array is 44; then $X_{med} = 44$.

### 3. Compute the standard deviation
Compute the deviations of the $X$ values from $\bar{X}$, and record the results in column 3 of Table 22. The sum of the deviations must be 0. Now square the deviations, and record the results in column 4. Find the sum of the squared deviations, which is 278. Set the variance $s^2 = (\Sigma d^2)/n = 278/7$. Then set the standard deviation $s = \sqrt{278/7} = 6.30$.

### 4. Compute the arithmetic mean by using an assumed arithmetic mean
Set $A = 40$. Compute the deviations of the $X$ values from $A$, record the results in column 5 of Table 22, and find the sum of the deviations, which is 21. Set $\bar{X} = A + (\Sigma d_A)/n$, or $\bar{X} = 40 + 21/7 = 43$.

### 5. Compute the standard deviation by using the arithmetic mean assumed in step 3
Square the deviations from $A$, record the results in column 6 of Table 22, and find their sum, which is 341. Set $s^2 = (\Sigma d_A^2)/n - [(\Sigma d_A)/n]^2 = 341/7 - (21/7)^2 = 341/7 - 9 = 278/7$. Then $s = \sqrt{278/7} = 6.30$.

**Related Calculations.** Note that the equation applied in step 5 does not contain the true mean $\bar{X}$. This equation serves to emphasize that the standard deviation is purely a measure of dispersion and thus is independent of the arithmetic mean. For example, if all values of $X$ increase by a constant $h$, then $\bar{X}$ increases by $h$, but $s$ remains constant. Where $\bar{X}$ has a nonintegral value, the use of an assumed arithmetic mean $A$ of integral value can result in a faster and more accurate calculation of $s$.

## DETERMINATION OF ARITHMETIC MEAN AND STANDARD DEVIATION OF GROUPED DATA

In testing a new industrial process, a firm assigned a standard operation to 24 employees in its factory and recorded the time required by each employee to complete the operation. The results are presented in columns 1 and 2 of Table 23. Find the arithmetic mean and standard deviation of the time of completion.

### Calculation Procedure:

### 1. *Record the class midpoints*
Where the number of values assumed by a variable is very large, a comprehensive listing of these values becomes too cumbersome. Therefore, the data are presented by grouping the values in *classes* and showing the frequency of each class. The range of values of a given class is its class interval, and the end values of the interval are the class limits. The difference between the upper and lower limits is the class width, or class size. Thus, in Table 23, all classes have a width of 4 min. The arithmetic mean of the class limits is the midpoint, or mark. In analyzing grouped data, all values that fall within a given class are replaced with the class midpont. The midpoints are recorded in column 3 of Table 23, and they are denoted by $X$.

### 2. *Compute the arithmetic mean*
Set $\bar{X} = (\Sigma fX)/n$, or $\bar{X} = (3 \times 22 + 9 \times 26 + 7 \times 30 + 5 \times 34)/24 = 680/24 = 28.33$ min.

### 3. *Compute the standard deviation*
Set $s^2 = (\Sigma fd^2)/n$, or $s^2 = [3(-6.33)^2 + 9(-2.33)^2 + 7(1.67)^2 + 5(5.67)^2]/24 = 14.5556$. Then $s = \sqrt{14.5556} = 3.82$ min.

### 4. *Compute the arithmetic mean by the coding method*
This method simplifies the analysis of grouped data where all classes are of uniform width, as in the present case. Arbitrarily selecting the third class, assign the integer 0 to

## TABLE 23

| (1)<br>Time of<br>completion, min<br>(class interval) | (2)<br>Number of<br>employees<br>(frequency $f$) | (3)<br>Midpoint<br>$X$ | (4)<br>Code<br>$c$ |
|---|---|---|---|
| 20 to less than 24 | 3 | 22 | $-2$ |
| 24 to less than 28 | 9 | 26 | $-1$ |
| 28 to less than 32 | 7 | 30 | 0 |
| 32 to less than 36 | 5 | 34 | 1 |
| Total | 24 | | |

this class, and then assign integers to the remaining classes in consecutive and ascending order, as shown in column 4 of Table 23. These integers are the *class codes*. Let $c$ = class code, $w$ = class width, and $A$ = midpoint of class having the code 0. Compute $\Sigma fc$, or $\Sigma fc$ = $3(-2) + 9(-1) + 7(0) + 5(1) = -10$. Now set $\bar{X} = A + w(\Sigma fc)/n$, or $\bar{X} = 30 + 4(-10)/24 = 28.33$ min.

**5. Compute the standard deviation by the coding method**

Using the codes previously assigned, compute $\Sigma fc^2$, or $\Sigma fc^2 = 3(-2)^2 + 9(-1)^2 + 7(0)^2 + 5(1)^2 = 26$. Now set $s^2 = w^2\{(\Sigma fc^2)/n - [(\Sigma fc)/n]^2\}$. Then $s^2 = 16[26/24 - (-10/24)^2] = 14.5556$, and $s = \sqrt{14.5556} = 3.82$ min.

## Permutations and Combinations

An arrangement of objects or individuals in which the order or rank is significant is called a *permutation*. A grouping of objects or individuals in which the order or rank is not significant, or in which it is predetermined, is called a *combination*. Assume that $n$ objects are available and that $r$ of these objects are selected to form a permutation or combination. If interest centers on only the identity of the $r$ objects selected, a combination is formed; if interest centers on both the identity and the order or rank of the $r$ objects, a permutation is formed. In the following material, the $r$ objects all differ from one another.

Where necessary, the number of permutations or combinations that can be formed is computed by applying the following law, known as the multiplication law: If one task can be performed in $m_1$ different ways and another task can be performed in $m_2$ different ways, the set of tasks can be performed in $m_1 m_2$ different ways.

## Notational System

Here $n!$ (read "$n$ factorial" or "factorial $n$") = product of first $n$ integers, and the integers are usually written in reverse order. Thus, $5! = 5 \times 4 \times 3 \times 2 \times 1 = 120$. For mathematical consistency, $0!$ is taken as 1.

Also, $P_{n,r}$ = number of permutations that can be formed of $n$ objects taken $r$ at a time; and $C_{n,r}$ = number of combinations that can be formed of $n$ objects taken $r$ at a time.

# NUMBER OF WAYS OF ASSIGNING WORK

A firm has three machines, A, B, and C, and each machine can be operated by only one individual at a time. The number of employees who are qualified to operate a machine is: machine A, five; machine B, three; machine C, seven. In addition to these 15 employees, Smith is qualified to operate all three machines. In how many ways can operators be assigned to the machines?

## Calculation Procedure:

### 1. Compute the number of possible assignments if Smith is excluded

Apply the multiplication law. The number of possible assignments = $5 \times 3 \times 7 = 105$.

### 2. Compute the number of possible assignments if Smith is selected

If Smith is assigned to machine A, the number of possible assignments to B and C = $3 \times 7 = 21$. If Smith is assigned to machine B, the number of possible assignments to A and C = $5 \times 7 = 35$. If Smith is assigned to machine C, the number of possible assignments to A and B = $5 \times 3 = 15$. Thus, the number of possible assignments with Smith selected = $21 + 35 + 15 = 71$.

### 3. Compute the total number of possible assignments

By summation, the number of ways in which operators can be assigned to the three machines = $105 + 71 = 176$.

## FORMATION OF PERMUTATIONS SUBJECT TO A RESTRICTION

Permutations are to be formed of the first seven letters of the alphabet, taken four at a time, with the restriction that d cannot be placed anywhere to the left of c. For example, the permutation edgc is unacceptable. How many permutations can be formed?

### Calculation Procedure:

### 1. Compute the number of permutations in the absence of any restriction

Use the relation $P_{n,r} = n!/(n-r)!$, or $P_{7,4} = 7!/3! = 7 \times 6 \times 5 \times 4 = 840$.

### 2. Compute the number of permutations that violate the imposed restriction

Form permutations that violate the restriction. Start by placing d in the first position. Letter c can be placed in any of the three subsequent positions. Two positions now remain unoccupied, and five letters are available; these positions can be filled in $5 \times 4 = 20$ ways. Thus, the number of permutations in which d occupies the first position and c some subsequent position is $3 \times 20 = 60$. Similarly, the number of permutations in which d occupies the second position and c occupies the third or fourth position is $2 \times 20 = 40$, and the number of permutations in which d occupies the third position and c occupies the fourth position is $1 \times 20 = 20$.

By summation, the number of unacceptable permutations = $60 + 40 + 20 = 120$.

### 3. Compute the number of permutations that satisfy the requirement

By subtraction, the number of acceptable permutations = $840 - 120 = 720$.

## FORMATION OF COMBINATIONS SUBJECT TO A RESTRICTION

A committee is to consist of 6 individuals of equal rank, and 15 individuals are available for assignment. However, McCarthy will serve only if Polanski is also on the committee. In how many ways can the committee be formed?

## Calculation Procedure:

### 1. *Compute the number of possible committees in the absence of any restriction*

Since the members will be of equal rank, each committee represents a combination. Use the relation $C_{n,r} = n!/[r!(n - r)!]$, or $C_{15,6} = 15!/(6!9!) = (15 \times 14 \times 13 \times 12 \times 11 \times 10)/(6 \times 5 \times 4 \times 3 \times 2) = 5005$.

### 2. *Compute the number of possible committees that violate the imposed restriction*

Assign McCarthy to the committee, but exclude Polanski. Five members remain to be selected, and 13 individuals are available. The number of such committees $= C_{13,5} = 13!/(5!8!) = (13 \times 12 \times 11 \times 10 \times 9)/(5 \times 4 \times 3 \times 2) = 1287$.

### 3. *Compute the number of possible committees that satisfy the requirement*

By subtraction, the number of ways in which the committee can be formed $= 5005 - 1287 = 3718$.

## Probability

If the outcome of a process cannot be predicted because it is influenced by chance, the process is called a *trial*, or *experiment*. The outcome of a trial or set of trials is an *event*. Two events are *mutually exclusive* if the occurrence of one excludes the occurrence of the other. Two events are *independent* of each other if the occurrence of one has no effect on the likelihood that the other will occur.

Assume that a box contains 17 objects, 12 of which are spheres. If an object is to be drawn at random and all objects have equal likelihood of being drawn, then the probability that a sphere will be drawn is 12/17. Thus, the probability of a given event can range from 0 to 1. The lower limit corresponds to an impossible event, and the upper limit corresponds to an event that is certain to occur. If two events are mutually exclusive, the probability that either will occur is the sum of their respective probabilities. If two events are independent of each other, the probability that *both* will occur is the product of their respective probabilities.

Assume that a random variable is discrete and the number of values it can assume is finite. A listing of these values and their respective probabilities is called the *probability distribution* of the variable. Where the number of possible values is infinite, the probability distribution is expressed by stating the functional relationship between a value of the variable and the corresponding probability. Where the random variable is continuous, the method of expressing its probability distribution is illustrated in the calculation procedure below pertaining to the normal distribution.

## Notational System

Here $E$ = given event; $X$ = random variable; $P(E)$ = probability that event $E$ will occur; $P(X_i)$ = probability that $X$ will assume the value $X_i$; $\mu$ and $\sigma$ = arithmetic mean and standard deviation, respectively, of a probability distribution.

## PROBABILITY OF A SEQUENCE OF EVENTS

A box contains 12 bolts. Of these, 8 have square heads and 4 have hexagonal heads. Seven bolts will be removed from the box, individually and at random. What is the probability that the second and third bolts drawn will have square heads and the sixth bolt will have a hexagonal head?

### Calculation Procedure:

### 1. Compute the total number of ways in which the bolts can be drawn

The sequence in which the bolts are drawn represents a permutation of 12 bolts taken 7 at a time, and each bolt is unique. The total number of permutations $= P_{12,7} = 12!/5!$.

### 2. Compute the number of ways in which the bolts can be drawn in the manner specified

If the bolts are drawn in the manner specified, the second and third positions in the permutation are occupied by square-head bolts and the sixth position is occupied by a hexagonal-head bolt. Construct such a permutation, in these steps: Place a square-head bolt in the second position; the number of bolts available is 8. Now place a square-head bolt in the third position; the number of bolts available is 7. Now place a hexagonal-head bolt in the sixth position; the number of bolts available is 4. Finally, fill the four remaining positions in any manner whatever; the number of bolts available is 9.

The second position can be filled in 8 ways, the third position in 7 ways, the sixth position in 4 ways, and the remaining positions in $P_{9,4}$ ways. By the multiplication law, the number of acceptable permutations is $8 \times 7 \times 4 \times P_{9,4} = 224(9!/5!)$.

### 3. Compute the probability of drawing the bolts in the manner specified

Since all permutations have an equal likelihood of becoming the true permutation, the probability equals the ratio of the number of acceptable permutations to the total number of permutations. Thus, probability $= 224(9!/5!)/(12!/5!) = 224(9!)/12! = 224(12 \times 11 \times 10) = 224/1320 = 0.1697$.

### 4. Compute the probability by an alternative approach

As the preceding calculations show, the exact positions specified (second, third, and sixth) do not affect the result. For simplicity, assume that the first and second bolts are to be square-headed and the third bolt hexagonal-headed. The probabilities are: first bolt square-headed, 8/12; second bolt square-headed, 7/11; third bolt hexagonal-headed, 4/10. The probability that all three events will occur is the product of their respective probabilities. Thus, the probability that bolts will be drawn in the manner specified $= (8/12)(7/11)(4/10) = 224/1320 = 0.1697$. Note also that the precise number of bolts drawn from the box (7) does not affect the result.

## PROBABILITY ASSOCIATED WITH A SERIES OF TRIALS

During its manufacture, a product passes through five departments, A, B, C, D, and E. The probability that the product will be delayed in a department is: A, 0.06; B, 0.15; C, 0.03; D. 0.07; E, 0.13. These values are independent of one another in the sense that the time for which the product is held in one department has no effect on the time it spends in any sub-sequent department. What is the probability that there will be a delay in the manufacture of this product?

### Calculation Procedure:

### 1. Compute the probability that the product will be manufactured without any delay

Since it is certain that the product either will or will not be delayed in a department and the probability of certainty is 1, probability of no delay = 1 − probability of delay. Thus, the probability that the product will pass through department B without delay = 1 − 0.15 = 0.85. The probability that the product will pass through every department without delay is the product of the probabilities of these individual events. Thus, probability of no delay in manufacture = (0.94)(0.85)(0.97)(0.93)(0.87) = 0.6271.

### 2. Compute the probability of a delay in manufacture

Probability of delay in manufacture = 1 − probability of no delay in manufacture = 1 − 0.6271 = 0.3729.

**Related Calculations.** This method of calculation can be applied to any situation where a series of trials occurs, either simultaneously or in sequence, and any trial can cause the given event. Thus, assume that several projectiles are fired simultaneously and the probability of landing in a target area is known for each projectile. The above method can be used to find the probability that at least one projectile will land in the target area.

## BINOMIAL PROBABILITY DISTRIBUTION

A case contains 14 units, 9 of which are of type A. Five units will be drawn at random from the case; and as a unit is drawn, it will be replaced with one of identical type. If $X$ denotes the number of type A units drawn, find the probability distribution of $X$ and the average value of $X$ in the long run.

### Calculation Procedure:

### 1. Compute the probability corresponding to a particular value of X

Consider that $n$ independent trials are performed, and let $X$ denote the number of times an event $E$ occurs in these $n$ trials. The probability distribution of $X$ is called *binomial*. In this case, since each unit drawn is replaced with one of identical type, each drawing is inde-pendent of all preceding drawings; therefore, $X$ has a binomial probability distribution. The event $E$ consists of drawing a type A unit.

With respect to every drawing, probability of drawing a type A unit = 9/14, and prob-ability of drawing a unit of some other type = 5/14. Arbitrarily set $X = 3$, and assume that the units are drawn thus: A-A-A-N-N, where N denotes a type other than A. The proba-bility of drawing the units in this sequence = (9/14)(9/14)(9/14)(5/14)(5/14) = $(9/14)^3(5/14)^2$. Clearly this is also the probability of drawing 3 type A units in any other sequence. Since the type A units can occupy any 3 of the 5 positions in the set of draw-ings and the exact positions do not matter, the number of sets of drawings that contain

3 type A units $= C_{5,3}$. Summing the probabilities, we find $P(3) = C_{5,3}(9/14)^3(5/14)^2 = [5!/(3!2!)](9/14)^3(5/14)^2 = 0.3389$.

### 2. Write the equation of binomial probability distribution

Generalize from step 1 to obtain $P(X) = C_{n,X}P^X(1 - P)^{n-X}$ where $P$ = probability event $E$ will occur on a single trial. Here $P = 9/14$.

### 3. Apply the foregoing equation to find the probability distribution of X

The results are $P(0) = 1(9/14)^0(5/14)^5 = 0.0058$. Similarly, $P(1) = 0.0523$; $P(2) = 0.1883$; $P(3) = 0.3389$ from step 1; $P(4) = 0.3050$; $P(5) = 0.1098$.

### 4. Verify the values of probability

Since it is certain that $X$ will assume some value from 0 to 5, inclusive, the foregoing probabilities must total 1. There sum is found to be 1.0001, and the results are thus confirmed.

### 5. Compute the average value of X in the long run

Consider that there are an infinite number of cases of the type described and that 5 units will be drawn from each case in the manner described, thereby generating an infinite set of values of $X$. Since the chance of obtaining a type A unit on a single drawing is 9/14, the average number of type A units that will be obtained in 5 drawings is $5(9/14) = 45/14 = 3.21$. Thus, the arithmetic mean of this infinite set of values of $X$ is 3.21.

Alternatively, find the average value of $X$ by multiplying all $X$ values by their respective probabilities, to get $0.0523 + 2(0.1883) + 3(0.3389) + 4(0.3050) + 5(0.1098) = 3.21$. The arithmetic mean of an infinite set of $X$ values is also called the *expected value* of $X$.

## PASCAL PROBABILITY DISTRIBUTION

Objects are ejected randomly from a rotating mechanism, and the probability that an object will enter a stationary receptacle after leaving the mechanism is 0.35. The process of ejecting objects will continue until four objects have entered the receptacle. Let $X$ denote the number of objects that must be ejected. Find (*a*) the probability corresponding to every $X$ value from 4 to 10, inclusive; (*b*) the probability that more than 10 objects must be ejected; (*c*) the average value of $X$ in the long run.

### Calculation Procedure:

### 1. Compute the probability corresponding to a particular value of X

Consider that a trial is performed repeatedly, each trial being independent of all preceding trials, until a given event $E$ has occurred for the $k$th time. Let $X$ denote the number of trials required. The variable $X$ is said to have a *Pascal* probability distribution. (In the special case where $k = 1$, the probability distribution is called *geometric*.) In the present situation, the given event is entrance of the object into the receptacle, and $k = 4$.

Use this code: A signifies the object has entered; B signifies it has not. Arbitrarily set $X = 9$, and consider this sequence of events: A-B-B-A-B-B-B-A-A, which contains four A's and five B's. The probability of this sequence, and of every sequence containing four A's and five B's, is $(0.35)^4(0.65)^5$. Other arrangements corresponding to $X = 9$ can be obtained by holding the fourth A in the ninth position and rearranging the preceding letters, which consist of three A's and five B's. Since the A's can be assigned to any 3 of the 8 positions, the number of arrangements that can be formed is $C_{8,3}$. Thus, $P(9) = C_{8,3}(0.35)^4(0.65)^5 = 56(0.35)^4(0.65)^5 = 0.0975$.

### 2. Write the equation of Pascal probability distribution

Generalize from step 1 to obtain $P(X) = C_{X-1,k-1}P^k(1 - P)^{X-k}$, where $P = $ probability that event $E$ will occur on a single trial. Here $P = 0.35$.

### 3. Apply the foregoing equation to find the probabilities corresponding to the given X values

The results are $P(4) = 1(0.35)^4(0.65)^0 = 0.0150$; $P(5) = 4(0.35)^4(0.65)^1 = 0.0390$; $P(6) = 10(0.35)^4(0.65)^2 = 0.0634$. Similarly, $P(7) = 0.0824$; $P(8) = 0.0938$; $P(9) = 0.0975$ from step 1; $P(10) = 0.0951$.

Thus, as $X$ increases, $P(X)$ increases until $X = 9$, and then it decreases. The variable $X$ can assume an infinite number of values in theory, and the corresponding probabilities form a converging series having a sum of 1.

### 4. Compute the probability that 10 or fewer ejections will be required

Sum the values in step 3; $P(X \le 10) = 0.4862$.

### 5. Compute the probability that more than 10 ejections will be required

Since it is certain that $X$ will assume a value of 10 or less or a value of more than 10, $P(X > 10) = 1 - 0.4862 = 0.5138$.

### 6. Compute the average number of ejections required in the long run

Consider that the process of placing a set of four objects in the receptacle is continued indefinitely, thereby generating an infinite set of values of $X$. Since there is a 35 percent chance that a specific object will enter the receptacle after being ejected from the mechanism, it will require an average of $1/0.35 = 2.86$ ejections to place one object in the receptacle and an average of $4(1/0.35) = 11.43$ ejections to place four objects in the receptacle. Thus, the infinite set of values of $X$ has an arithmetic mean of 11.43.

## POISSON PROBABILITY DISTRIBUTION

A radioactive substance emits particles at an average rate of 0.08 particles per second. Assuming that the number of particles emitted during a given time interval has a Poisson distribution, find the probability that the substance will emit more than three particles in a 20-s interval.

### Calculation Procedure:

### 1. Compute the average number of particles emitted in 20 s

Let $T$ denote an interval of time, in suitable units. Consider that an event $E$ occurs randomly in time but the average number of occurrences of $E$ in time $T$, as measured over a relatively long period, remains constant. Let $m = $ average (or expected) number of occurrences of $E$ in $T$, and $X = $ true number of occurrences of $E$ in $T$. The variable $X$ is said to have a Poisson probability distribution.

In the present case, $X = $ number of particles emitted in 20 $s$, and $m = 20(0.08) = 1.6$.

## 2. Compute the probability that X ≤ 3
Use the relation $P(X) = m^X/[e^m(X!)]$, where $e$ = base of natural logarithms = 2.71828. . . . Thus, $e^m = e^{1.6} = 4.95303$. Then $P(0) = (1.6)^0/(4.95303 \times 1) = 0.2019$; $P(1) = (1.6)^3/(4.95303 \times 1) = 0.3230$; $P(2) = (1.6)^2/(4.95303 \times 2) = 0.2584$; $P(3) = (1.6)^3/(4.95303 \times 6) = 0.1378$. Sum these results to obtain $P(X \le 3) = 0.9211$.

## 3. Compute the probability that X > 3
$P(X > 3) = 1 - 0.9211 = 0.0789$.

*Related Calculations.* The probabilities in step 2 also can be found by referring to a table of Poisson probability. The foregoing discussion pertains to an event that occurs in *time*, but analogous comments apply to an event that occurs in *space*. For example, assume that a firm manufactures long rolls of tape. Defects in the tape occur randomly, but the average number of defects in a 300-m length, as measured across long distances, is constant. The number of defects in a given length of tape has a Poisson distribution. The Poisson distribution is an extreme case of the binomial distribution. As the probability that event $E$ will occur on a single trial becomes infinitesimally small and the number of trials becomes infinitely large, the binomial distribution approaches the Poisson distribution as a limit.

## COMPOSITE EVENT WITH POISSON DISTRIBUTION

With reference to the preceding calculation procedure, a counting device is installed to determine the number of particles emitted. The probability that the device will actually count an emission is 0.90. Find the probability that the number of emissions counted in a 20-s interval will be 3.

### Calculation Procedure:

### 1. Compute the average number of emissions counted in 20 s
In the present case, event $E$ is that an emission is counted. This event is a composite of two basic events: a particle is emitted, and the device functions properly. Thus, $m = 20(0.08)(0.90) = 1.44$.

### 2. Compute the probability that X = 3
Use the equation given in the preceding calculation procedure, or $P(3) = (1.44)3/[e^{1.44}(3!)] = 0.1179$.

## NORMAL DISTRIBUTION

A continuous random variable $X$ has a normal probability distribution with an arithmetic mean of 14 and a standard deviation of 2.5. Find the probability that on a given occasion $X$ will assume a value that (*a*) lies between 14 and 17; (*b*) lies between 12 and 16.2; (*c*) is less than 10.

## Calculation Procedure:

### 1. Compute the values of z corresponding to the specified boundary values of X

If a random variable $X$ is continuous, the probability that $X$ will assume a value between $X_j$ and $X_k$ is represented graphically by constructing a probability diagram in this manner: Plot values of $X$ on the horizontal axis; then construct a curve such that $P(X_j < X < X_k) =$ area bounded by the curve, the horizontal axis, and vertical lines at $X_j$ and $X_k$. The ordinate of this curve is denoted by $f(X)$ and is called the *probability density function*. The total area under the curve is 1, the probability of certainty.

A continuous random variable has a *normal* or *gaussian* probability distribution if the range of its possible values is infinite and its probability curve has an equation of this form: $f(X) = (1/b\sqrt{2\pi})_e^{-(X-a)2/2b^2}$ where $a$ and $b$ are constants and $e =$ base of natural logarithms. Figure 20 is the probability diagram; the curve is bell-shaped and symmetric about a vertical line through the summit.

Consider that the trial that yields a value of $X$ is repeated indefinitely, generating an infinite set of values of $X$. Let $\mu$ and $\sigma =$ arithmetic mean and standard deviation, respectively, of this set of values. The summit of the probability curve lies at $X = \mu$. By symmetry, the area under the curve to the left and to the right of $X = \mu$ is 0.5.

The deviation of $X$, from $\mu$ is expressed in *standard units* in this form: $z_i = (X_i - \mu)/\sigma$. Thus, for $X = 14$, $z = 0$; for $X = 17$, $z = (17 - 14)/2.5 = 1.20$; for $X = 12$, $z = (12 - 14)/2.5 = -0.80$; etc. Record the $z$ values in Table 24.

**TABLE 24**

| X | z | A(z) |
|------|-------|---------|
| 14 | 0 | 0 |
| 17 | 1.20 | 0.38493 |
| 12 | -0.80 | 0.28814 |
| 16.2 | 0.88 | 0.31057 |
| 10 | -1.60 | 0.44520 |

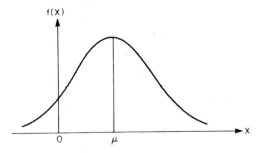

**FIGURE 20.** Curve of normal probability distribution.

## 2. *Find the values of A(z)*

Let $A(z_i)$ = area under probability curve from centerline (where $X = \mu$) to $X = X_i$; this area = $P(\mu < X < X_i)$. Obtain the values of $A(z)$ from the table of areas under the normal probability curve. Refer to Table 25, which is an excerpt from this table. Thus, if $z = 1.60$, $A(z) = 0.44520$; if $z = 1.78$, $A(z) = 0.46246$. Note that $A(-z_i) = A(z)$ by symmetry. Record the values of $A(z)$ in Table 24.

## 3. *Compute the required probabilities*

Refer to Fig. 21. Apply the areas in Table 24 to obtain these results: $P(14 < X < 17) = 0.38493$; $P(12 < X < 16.2) = 0.28814 + 0.31057 = 0.59871$; $P(X < 10) = 0.5 - 0.44520 = 0.05480$.

**Related Calculations.** Many random variables that occur in nature have a normal probability distribution. For example, the height, weight, and intelligence of members of a species have normal distributions. Although in theory this distribution applies solely where the range of $X$ values is infinite, in practice the distribution is applied as a valid approximation where the range of $X$ values is finite.

## APPLICATION OF NORMAL DISTRIBUTION

The time required to perform a manual operation is assumed to have a normal distribution. Studies of past performance disclose that the average time required is 5.80 h and the standard deviation is 0.50 h. Find the probability (to three decimal places) that the operation will be performed within 5.25 h.

### Calculation Procedure:

## 1. *Compute the value of z corresponding to the boundary value of X*

Let $X$ = time required to perform the operation, and refer to the preceding calculation procedure for the definition of $z$. For $X = 5.25$, $z = (5.25 - 5.80)/050 = -1.10$.

**TABLE 25.**   Area under the Normal Curve

| z | .00 | .01 | .02 | .03 | .04 |
|---|-----|-----|-----|-----|-----|
| 1.5 | .43319 | .43448 | .43574 | .43699 | .43822 |
| 1.6 | .44520 | .44630 | .44738 | .44845 | .44950 |
| 1.7 | .45543 | .45637 | .45728 | .45818 | .45907 |

| z | .05 | .06 | .07 | .08 | .09 |
|---|-----|-----|-----|-----|-----|
| 1.5 | .43943 | .44062 | .44179 | .44295 | .44408 |
| 1.6 | .45053 | .45154 | .45254 | .45352 | .45449 |
| 1.7 | .45994 | .46080 | .46164 | .46246 | .46327 |

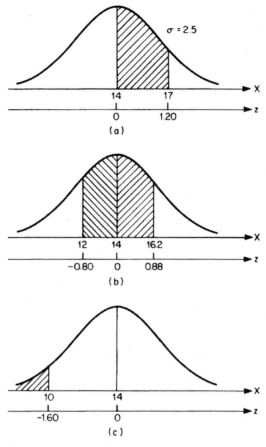

**FIGURE 21**

### 2. Find the value of A(z)
Refer to the table of areas under the normal probability curve, and take the absolute value of $z$. If $z = 1.10$, $A(z) = 0.364$.

### 3. Compute the required probability
The area under consideration lies to the left of a vertical line at $X = 5.25$, and the area found in step 2 lies between this line and the centerline. Then $P(X < 5.25) = 0.5 - 0.364 = 0.136$.

## NEGATIVE-EXPONENTIAL DISTRIBUTION

The mean life span of an electronic device that operates continuously is 2 months. If the life span of the device has a negative-exponential distribution, what is the probability that the life span will exceed 3 months?

## Calculation Procedure:

### 1. *Write the equation of cumulative probability*

Refer to the calculation procedure on the normal distribution for definitions pertaining to a continuous random variable. A variable $X$ is said to have a *negative-exponential* (or simply *exponential*) probability distribution if its probability density function is of this form: $f(X) = 0$ if $X < 0$ and $f(X) = ae^{-aX}$ if $X \geq 0$ Eq. *a*, where $a =$ positive constant and $e =$ base of natural logarithms. Figure 22 shows the probability diagram. The arithmetic mean of $X$ is $\mu = 1/a$, Eq. *b*.

Let $X =$ life span of device, months, and let $K$ denote any positive number. Integrate Eq. *a* between the limits of 0 and $K$, giving $P(X \leq K) = 1 - e^{-aK}$, Eq. *c*. Then $P(X > K) = e^{-aK}$, Eq. *d*.

### 2. *Compute the required probability*

Compute $a$ by Eq. *b*, giving $a = 1/\mu = 1/2 = 0.5$. Set $K = 3$ months. By Eq. *d*, $P(X > 3) = e^{-1.5} = 1/e^{1.5} = 0.2231$.

## Statistical Inference

Consider that there exists a set of objects, which is called the *population*, or *universe*. Also consider that interest centers on some property of these objects, such as length, molecular weight, etc., and that this property assumes many values. Thus, associated with the population is a set of *numbers*. This set of numbers has various characteristics, such as arithmetic mean and standard deviation. A characteristic of this set of numbers is called a *parameter*. For example, assume that the population consists of five spheres and that they have the following diameters: 10, 13, 14, 19, and 21 cm. The diameters have an arithmetic mean of 15.4 cm and standard deviation of 4.03 cm, and these values are parameters of the given population.

Now consider that a subset of these objects is drawn. This subset is called a *sample*, and a characteristic of the sample is called a *statistic*. Thus, using the previous illustration, assume that the sample consists of the spheres having diameters of 14, 19, and 21 cm. These diameters have an arithmetic mean of 18 cm and standard deviation of 2.94 cm, and these values are statistics of the sample drawn. The number of objects in the sample is the sample *size*.

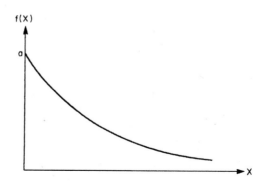

**FIGURE 22.** Negative-exponential probability distribution.

In many instances, it is impossible to evaluate a parameter precisely, for two reasons: The population may be so large as to preclude measurement of every object, and measurement may entail destruction of the object, as in finding the breaking strength of a cable. In these cases it is necessary to estimate the parameter by drawing a representative sample and evaluating the corresponding statistic. The process of estimating a parameter by means of a statistic is known as *statistical inference*.

Since a statistic is a function of the manner in which the sample is drawn and thus is influenced by chance, the statistic is a random variable. The probability distribution of a statistic is called the *sampling distribution* of that statistic. Consider that all possible samples of a given size have been drawn and the statistic $S$ corresponding to each sample has been calculated. A characteristic of this set of values of $S$, such as the arithmetic mean, is referred to as a characteristic of the sampling distribution of $S$. In the subsequent material, the term *mean* refers exclusively to the arithmetic mean.

## Notational System

Table 26 is presented for ease of reference. Here $N$ = number of objects in the population; $\mu$ and $\sigma$ = arithmetic mean and standard deviation, respectively, of the population; $n$ = number of objects in the sample; $\bar{X}$ and $s$ = arithmetic mean and standard deviation, respectively, of the sample; $\mu_S$ and $\sigma_S$ = arithmetic mean and standard deviation, respectively, of the sampling distribution of the statistic $S$.

## Basic Equations

The mean and standard deviation of the sampling distribution of the mean are

$$\mu_{\bar{X}} = \mu \tag{14}$$

$$\sigma_{\bar{X}} = \sigma \sqrt{\frac{N - n}{n(N - 1)}} \tag{15}$$

If the population is infinite, Eq. 15 reduces to

$$\sigma_{\bar{X}} = \frac{\sigma}{\sqrt{n}} \tag{15a}$$

**TABLE 26.**   Notation

| Characteristic | Sample | Population | Sampling distribution of a statistic $S$ |
|---|---|---|---|
| Mean | $\bar{X}$ | $\mu$ | $\mu_S$ |
| Standard deviation | $s$ | $\sigma$ | $\sigma_S$ |
| Number of items | $n$ | $N$ | |

The quantity $\mu_{\bar{X}}$ is an index of the diversity of the sample means. As the sample size increases, the samples become less diverse.

Since a sample represents a combination of $N$ objects taken $n$ at a time, the number of samples that may be drawn is $C_{N,n} = N!/[n!(N - n)!]$.

## SAMPLING DISTRIBUTION OF THE MEAN

The population consists of 5 objects having the numerical values 15, 18, 27, 36, and 54; the sample size is 3. Find the mean and standard deviation of the sampling distribution of the mean.

### Calculation Procedure:

**1. Compute the mean and variance of the population**
Mean $\mu = (15 + 18 + 27 + 36 + 54)/5 = 30$; variance $\sigma^2 = [(15 - 30)^2 + (18 - 30)^2 + (27 - 30)^2 + (36 - 30)^2 + (54 - 30)^2]/5 = 198$.

**2. Compute the properties of the sampling distribution**
Apply Eq. 14 to find the mean of the sampling distribution of the mean, or $\mu_{\bar{X}} = 30$. Apply Eq. 15 to find the variance of the sampling distribution, or $\sigma_{\bar{X}}^2 = 198(5 - 3)/(3 \times 4) = 33$. Then $\sigma_{\bar{X}} \sqrt{33} = 5.74$.

**3. Compute the required properties without recourse to any set equations**
If the population is finite, the number of possible samples is finite. Since all samples have an equal likelihood of becoming the true sample, the sampling distribution of a statistic can be found by forming all possible samples and computing the statistic under consideration for each.

Record all possible samples in the first column of Table 27; the number of these samples is $C_{5,3} = 10$. Now compute the mean $\bar{X}$ of each sample, record the results in the second

**TABLE 27.** Properties of Sampling Distribution of the Mean

| Sample | Sample mean $\bar{X}$ | Deviation $d$ $= \bar{X} - 30$ | $d^2$ |
|--------|--------|--------|--------|
| 15, 18, 27 | 20 | −10 | 100 |
| 15, 18, 36 | 23 | −7 | 49 |
| 15, 18, 54 | 29 | −1 | 1 |
| 15, 27, 36 | 26 | −4 | 16 |
| 15, 27, 54 | 32 | 2 | 4 |
| 15, 36, 54 | 35 | 5 | 25 |
| 18, 27, 36 | 27 | −3 | 9 |
| 18, 27, 54 | 33 | 3 | 9 |
| 18, 36, 54 | 36 | 6 | 36 |
| 27, 36, 54 | 39 | 9 | 81 |
| Total | 300 | 0 | 330 |

column, and total them. This column contains full information concerning the sampling distribution of the mean. Thus, since no duplications occur, $P(\bar{X} = 20) = 1/10$; $P(\bar{X} = 23) = 1/10$; etc. Compute the mean of the possible values of $\bar{X}$, or $\mu_{\bar{X}} = 300/10 = 30$. Record the deviations from 30 in Table 27, square the deviations, and total the results. Compute the variance of the possible values of $\bar{X}$, or $\sigma_{\bar{X}}^2 = 330/10 = 33$. Then $\sigma_{\bar{X}} \sqrt{33} = 5.74$. These results are consistent with those in step 2.

## ESTIMATION OF POPULATION MEAN ON BASIS OF SAMPLE MEAN

A firm produces rods, and their lengths vary slightly because of unavoidable differences in manufacture. Assume that the lengths are normally distributed. One hundred rods were selected at random, and they were found to have a mean length of 1.856 m and a standard deviation of 0.074 m. Estimate the mean length of all rods manufactured by this firm, using a 95 percent confidence level.

### Calculation Procedure:

#### 1. Compute the z value corresponding to the given confidence level

Let $X$ = length of a rod. The population consists of all rods manufactured by the firm, and it may be considered infinite. There are two types of estimates: a point estimate, which assigns a specific value to $X$, and an interval estimate, which states that $X$ lies within a given interval. This interval is called a confidence interval, its boundaries are called the confidence limits, and the probability that the estimate is correct is called the confidence level, or confidence coefficient. Statistical inference can supply only interval estimates.

The *central-limit theorem* states: (*a*) If the population is extremely large and the probability distribution of $X$ is normal, then the sampling distribution of the sample mean $\bar{X}$ is also normal; (*b*) if the population is extremely large but the probability distribution of $X$ is not normal, the sampling distribution of $\bar{X}$ is approximately normal if the sample size is 30 or more. Thus, in the present case, the sampling distribution of $\bar{X}$ is considered to be normal.

Figure 23 is the sampling distribution diagram of the sample mean $\bar{X}$. Let $M$ = area under curve from $B$ to $C$. If a sample is drawn at random, there is a probability $M$ that the true sample mean $\bar{X}_j$ lies within the interval $BC$, or $P(\mu_{\bar{X}} - z_i\sigma_{\bar{X}} < \bar{X}_j < \mu_{\bar{X}} + z_i\sigma_{\bar{X}}) = M$. This equation can be transformed to $P(\bar{X}_j - z_i\mu_{\bar{X}} < \mu_{\bar{X}} < \bar{X}_j + z_i\sigma_{\bar{X}}) = M$, Eq. *a*.

In the present case, $\bar{X}_j = 1.856$ m, $s = 0.074$ m, $n = 100$, and $M = 0.95$. Then area under curve from $A$ to $C = (0.50)(0.95) = 0.475$. From the table of areas under the normal curve, if $A(z_i) = 0.475$, $z_i = 1.96$.

#### 2. Set up expressions for the mean and standard deviation of the sampling distribution of the mean

By Eq. 14, $\mu_{\bar{X}} = \mu$, where $\mu$ is the population mean to be estimated. Use the standard deviation $s$ of the sample as an estimate of the standard deviation $\sigma$ of the population. Then $\sigma = 0.074$ m, and by Eq. 15*a*, $\sigma_{\bar{X}} = 0.074/\sqrt{100} = 0.0074$ m.

#### 3. Estimate the mean length of the rods

Refer to Eq. *a*, and compute $z_i\sigma_{\bar{X}} = (1.96)(0.0074) = 0.015$ m. Compute the confidence limits in Eq. *a*, or $1.856 - 0.015 = 1.841$ m and $1.856 + 0.015 = 1.871$ m. Equation *a*

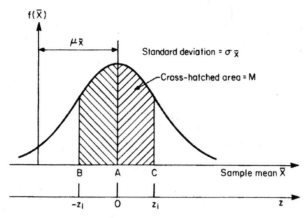

**FIGURE 23.** Sampling distribution of the mean.

becomes $P(1.841 < \mu < 1.871) = 0.95$. Thus, there is a 95 percent probability that the mean length of all rods lies between 1.841 and 1.871 m.

**Related Calculations.** Note that the confidence interval is a function of the degree of probability that is demanded, and the two quantities vary in the same direction. For example, if the confidence level were 90 percent, the confidence interval would be 1.844 to 1.868 m.

## DECISION MAKING ON STATISTICAL BASIS

Units of a commodity are produced individually, and studies have shown that the time required to produce a unit has a mean value of 3.50 h and a standard deviation of 0.64 h. An industrial engineer claims that a modification of the production process will substantially reduce production time. The proposed method was tested on 40 units, and it was found that the mean production time was 3.37 h per unit. Management has decided that it will make the proposed modification only if there is a probability of 95 percent or more that the engineer's claim is valid. What is your recommendation?

### Calculation Procedure:

#### 1. Formulate the null and alternative hypotheses
The population consists of all units that will be produced under the modified method if it is adopted, and the sample consists of the 40 units actually produced under this method. An assumption based on conjecture is termed a *hypothesis*. A hypothesis that is formulated merely to provide a basis for investigation is a *null* hypothesis, and any hypothesis that contradicts the null hypothesis is an *alternative* hypothesis. However, interest centers on the particular alternative hypothesis that is significant in the given case. The null and alternative hypotheses are denoted by $H_0$ and $H_1$, respectively.

Let $X$ = time required to produce 1 unit, h. Place the burden of proof on the industrial engineer by assuming that production time under the modified method is identical with that under the present method. Thus, the hypotheses are $H_0$: $\mu = 3.50$ h and $\sigma = 0.64$ h; $H_1$: $\mu < 3.50$ h.

## 2. Compute the properties of the sampling distribution of the mean as based on the null hypothesis

Apply Eqs. 14 and 15a, giving $\mu_{\bar{X}} = 3.50$ h and $\sigma_{\bar{X}} = 0.64/40 = 0.101$ h.

## 3. Compute the critical value of $\bar{X}$

By the central-limit theorem given in the preceding calculation procedure, the sampling distribution of the sample mean $\bar{X}$ may be considered normal, and the sampling distribution diagram is shown in Fig. 24a. Management has imposed a requirement of 95 percent probability. Therefore, the null hypothesis is disproved and the alternative hypothesis validated if the true sample mean has a value less than that corresponding to 95 percent of all possible samples. In Fig. 24a, locate $B$ such that the area to the right of $B = 0.95$; then area from $A$ to $B = 0.95 - 0.50 = 0.45$. The null hypothesis is to be accepted or rejected

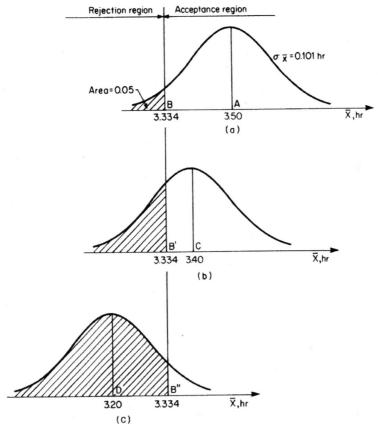

**FIGURE 24.** Sampling distribution of mean production time corresponding to three distinct values of the population mean.

according to whether the true value of $\bar{X}$ lies to the right or left of $B$, respectively, and the regions are labeled as shown. The values of $\bar{X}$ and $z$ at the boundary of the acceptance and rejection regions are called the *critical* values.

At $B$, $A(z) = 0.45$. From the table of areas under the normal curve, $z = -1.645$. Thus, at $B$, $\bar{X} = 3.50 + (-1.645)(0.101) = 3.334$ h.

### 4. Make a recommendation

Since the true sample mean of 3.37 h falls to the right of $B$, the null hypothesis stands. Therefore, we must recommend that the modified method of production be disapproved and the present method retained.

This recommendation does not necessarily imply that the industrial engineer's claim is invalid. The decision must be based on probability rather than certainty, and the test results have failed to demonstrate a 95 percent probability that the modified method is superior to the present method. The difference between the assumed population mean of 3.50 h and the sample mean of 3.37 h can be ascribed to chance.

**Related Calculations.** If the null hypothesis is rejected when, in fact, it is true, a *Type I* error has been committed. The probability of committing this error is denoted by $\alpha$, and the acceptable value of $\alpha$ is termed the *level of significance*. In this case, if the null hypothesis is correct, the sampling distribution of $\bar{X}$ is as shown in Fig. 24a. The hypothesis will be rejected if $\bar{X}$ assumes a value to the left of $B$, and the probability of this event is $1 - 0.95 = 0.05$. Thus, the level of significance is 0.05.

Whether a null hypothesis is accepted or rejected depends largely on the level of significance imposed. Therefore, selecting an appropriate level of significance is one of the crucial problems that arise in statistical decision making. The selection must be based on the amount of the loss that would result from a false decision.

## PROBABILITY OF ACCEPTING A FALSE NULL HYPOTHESIS

With reference to the preceding calculation procedure, the time required to produce 1 unit under the modified method has these characteristics: The standard deviation remains 0.64 h, but the arithmetic mean is (a) 3.40 h; (b) 3.20 h. Determine the probability that the industrial engineer's proposal will be vetoed despite its merit.

### Calculation Procedure:

### 1. Compute the critical value of z in each case

Since $\sigma$ remains 0.64 h and the sample size is still 40, $\sigma_{\bar{X}}$ remains 0.101 h. Refer to Fig. 24b and c, which gives the sampling distributions of $\bar{X}$ when $\mu = 3.40$ h and $\mu = 3.20$ h, respectively. The null hypothesis will be accepted if $\bar{X} > 3.334$, and it is necessary to calculate the probability of this event.

In Fig. 24b, at $B'$, $z = (3.334 - 3.40)/0.101 = -0.653$. In Fig. 24c, at $B''$, $z = (3.334 - 3.20)/0.101 = 1.327$.

### 2. Compute the required probabilities

Refer to the table of areas under the normal curve. When $z = -0.653$, $A(z) = 0.243$. In Fig. 24b, area to right of $B' = 0.243 + 0.5 = 0.743$. Thus, when $\mu = 3.40$ h, there is a probability of 74.3 percent that the proposal will be vetoed. Similarly, when $z = 1.327$, $A(z) = 0.408$. In Fig. 24c, area to right of $B'' = 0.5 - 0.408 = 0.092$. Thus, when $\mu = 3.20$ h, there is a probability of 9.2 percent that the proposal will be vetoed.

**Related Calculations.** If the null hypothesis is accepted when, in fact, it is false, a *Type II error* has been committed, and the probability of committing this error is denoted by $\beta$. Thus, this calculation procedure involves the determination of $\beta$. It follows that $1 - \beta$ is the probability that a false null hypothesis will be rejected. The process of drawing and analyzing a sample represents a test of the null hypothesis, and the quantities $\beta$ and $1 - \beta$ are called the *operating characteristic* and power, respectively, of the test. Thus, the power of a test is its ability to detect that the null hypothesis is false if such is truly the case.

Consider that a diagram is constructed in which assumed values of the parameter are plotted on the horizontal axis and the corresponding values of $\beta$ resulting from the null hypothesis are plotted on the vertical axis. The curve thus obtained is called an *operating-characteristic curve*. Similarly, the curve obtained by plotting values of $1 - \beta$ against assumed values of the parameter is called a *power curve*.


# DECISION BASED ON PROPORTION OF SAMPLE

A firm receives a large shipment of small machine parts, and it must determine whether the number of defectives in a shipment is tolerable. Its policy is as follows: A shipment is accepted only if the estimated incidence of defectives is 3 percent or less, the decision is based on an inspection of 250 parts selected at random, and a shipment is rejected only if there is a probability of 90 percent or more that the incidence of defectives exceeds 3 percent. What is the highest incidence of defectives in the sample if the shipment is to be considered acceptable?


## Calculation Procedure:

### 1. Formulate the null hypothesis
Consider that a set of objects consists of type A and type B objects. The ratio of the number of type A objects to the total number of objects is called the *proportion* of type A objects. Let $P$ and $p$ = proportion of type A objects in the population and sample, respectively.

In this case, the population consists of all machine parts in the shipment, the sample consists of the 250 parts that are inspected, and interest centers on the proportion of defective parts. To provide a basis for investigation, assume that the proportion of defectives in the shipment is precisely 3 percent. Thus, the null hypothesis is $H_0: P = 0.03$.

### 2. Compute the properties of the sampling distribution of the proportion as based on the null hypothesis
Consider that all possible samples of a given size are drawn and their respective values of $p$ determined, thus obtaining the sampling distribution of $p$. As before, let $N$ and $n$ = number of objects in the population and sample, respectively. The sampling distribution of $p$ has these values: the mean $\mu_p = P$, Eq. $a$; the variance $\sigma_p^2 = P(1 - P)(N - n)/[n(N - 1)]$, Eq. $b$. Where the population is infinite, $\sigma_p^2 = P(1 - P)/n$, Eq. $c$. In the present case, $P = 0.03$, $N$ may be considered infinite, and $n = 250$. By Eq. $a$, $\mu_p = 0.03$; by Eq. $c$, $\sigma_p^2 = (0.03)(0.97)/250 = 0.0001164$. Then standard deviation $\sigma_p = 0.0108$.

### 3. Compute the critical value of p
For simplicity, treat the number of defective parts as a continuous rather than a discrete variable; then $P$ and $p$ are also continuous. Since the sample is very large, the sampling

distribution of $p$ is approximately normal, and it is shown in Fig. 25a. The null hypothesis is to be rejected if $p$ assumes a value greater than that corresponding to 90 percent of all possible samples. In Fig. 25a, locate $B$ such that area to the left of $B = 0.90$; then area from $A$ to $B = 0.90 - 0.50 = 0.40$. At $B$, $A(z) = 0.40$. From the table of areas under the normal curve, $z = 1.282$. Thus, at $B$, $p = 0.03 + (1.282)(0.0108) = 0.044$.

#### 4. State the decision rule

If the proportion of defectives in the sample is 4.4 percent or less, accept the shipment; if the proportion is greater, reject the shipment.

By setting the limiting proportion of defectives in the sample at 4.4 percent as compared with the limiting proportion of 3 percent in the population, allowance is being made for the random variability of sample results.

## PROBABILITY OF ACCEPTING AN UNSATISFACTORY SHIPMENT

With reference to the preceding calculation procedure, what is the probability that a shipment in which the incidence of defectives is 5 percent will nevertheless be accepted?

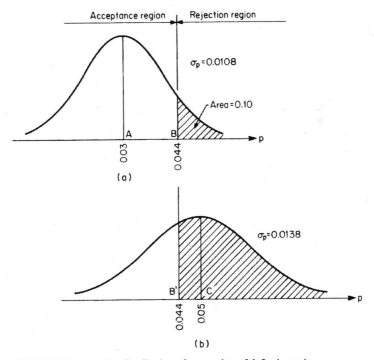

**FIGURE 25.** Sampling distribution of proportion of defective units.

**Calculation Procedure:**

## 1. *Compute the true properties of the sampling distribution of the proportion*

Apply Eqs. $a$ and $c$ of the previous calculation procedure, giving $\mu_p = 0.05$ and $\sigma_p^2 = (0.05)(0.95)/250 = 0.0001900$. Then $\sigma_p = 0.0138$. The sampling distribution diagram appears in Fig. 25$b$.

## 2. *Compute the probability that the shipment will be accepted*

The shipment will be accepted if $p < 0.044$, and it is necessary to calculate the probability of this event. In Fig. 25$b$, at $B'$, $z = (0.044 - 0.05)/0.0138 = -0.435$. From the table of areas under the normal curve, $A(z) = 0.168$. Then the area to the left of $B' = 0.5 - 0.168 = 0.332$. Thus, there is a probability of 33.2 percent that the shipment will be accepted.

## Reliability

Consider that a device operates continuously and fails abruptly. The life span of the device is a continuous random variable. The reliability of the device corresponding to a given length of time $t$, denoted by $R(t)$, is the probability that its life span will exceed $t$. Let $T$ = life span. Then $R(t) = P(T > t)$.

Refer to Fig. 26, which is the assumed *life-span curve* of a device. The diagram is constructed so that $P(t_1 < T \le t_2)$ = area under curve from $t_1$ to $t_2$. Thus, a life-span curve is the probability curve of the continuous variable $T$. Left $f(t)$ = ordinate of life-span curve = probability-density function. From the definition of reliability, it follows that $R(t)$ = area under curve to right of $t$, or

$$R(t) = \int_t^\infty f(t)\, dt \tag{16a}$$

and

$$f(t) = \frac{dR(t)}{dt} \tag{16b}$$

A mechanism formed by the assemblage of devices is called a *system*, and the individual device is called a *component* of the system. Assume that a system consists of

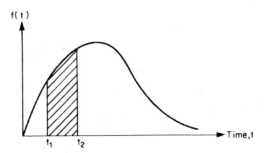

**FIGURE 26.** Life-span curve.

**FIGURE 27.** System with components in series.

two components, $C_1$ and $C_2$, and let the subscripts 1, 2, and $S$ refer to $C_1$, $C_2$, and the system, respectively. If the components are arranged in series, as shown in Fig. 27, the system is operating only if *both* components are operating. Thus, the reliability of the system is

$$R_S(t) = R_1(t)R_2(t) \tag{17}$$

If the components are arranged in parallel, as shown in Fig. 28, the system is operating if *either* component is operating. To express it another way, the system fails if both components fail, and

$$1 - R_S(t) = [1 - R_1(t)][1 - R_2(t)]$$

or

$$R_S(t) = 1 - [1 - R_1(t)][1 - R_2(t)] \tag{18}$$

Equations 17 and 18 can be generalized to include any number of components. A system having components in series has a reliability less than that of any component; a system having components in parallel has a reliability greater than that of any component.

## *DEVICE WITH NEGATIVE-EXPONENTIAL LIFE SPAN*

A certain type of earth satellite has a negative-exponential life span with a mean value of 15 months. Four satellites of this type are launched simultaneously. If $X$ denotes the number of satellites that remain in orbit at the expiration of 1 year, establish the probability distribution of $X$.

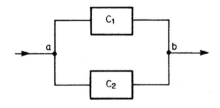

**FIGURE 28.** System with components in parallel.

**Calculation Procedure:**

### 1. *Compute the probability that a particular satellite will survive the first year*

Refer to the earlier calculation procedure pertaining to the negative-exponential probability distribution. A device has a negative-exponential life span if its life-span curve has an equation of this form: $f(t) = ae^{-at}$, Eq. $a$, where $a$ = positive constant and $e$ = base of natural logarithms. From Eq. 16$a$, $R(t) = e^{-at}$, Eq. $b$. Figure 29 presents the life-span and reliability diagrams. The mean life span $\mu = 1/a$, Eq. $c$.

Take 1 month as the unit of time. In this case, $\mu = 15$; then $a = 1/15$. By Eq. $b$, $R(t) = e^{-t/15}$, or $R(12) = e^{12/15} = e^{-0.8} = 1/e^{0.8} = 0.4493$. Thus, there is a probability of 0.4493 that a particular satellite will survive the first year.

### 2. *Establish the probability distribution of X*

Refer to the earlier calculation procedure pertaining to the binomial probability distribution. Launching a satellite may be viewed as a trial to determine whether the satellite will survive the first year. Since all satellites operate independently, the trials are independent of one another, and therefore $X$ has a binomial probability distribution.

Apply the equation in step 2 of the procedure for the binomial distribution, with $n = 4$, $P = 0.4493$, and $1 - P = 0.5507$. Now, $C_{4,0} = C_{4,4} = 1$; $C_{4,1} = C_{4,3} = 4$; $C_{4,2} = 6$. Then $P(0) = 1(0.5507)^4 = 0.092$; $P(1) = 4(0.4493)(0.5507)^3 = 0.300$; $P(2) = 6(0.4493)^2(0.5507)^2 = 0.367$; $P(3) = 4(0.4493)^3(0.5507) = 0.200$; $P(4) = 1(0.4493)^4 = 0.041$. These probabilities total 1, as they must.

***Related Calculations.*** It can readily be shown that a device that has a negative-exponential life span and has been operating for some time has the same probability of surviving the next unit of time as one that was just activated. Thus, the age of the device is completely irrelevant in predicting its remaining life. Thus failure is caused not by cumulative damage resulting from use but by a sudden accidental occurrence, and the probability of this occurrence during the next unit of time is independent of the age of the device. To apply an analogy, the probability that an individual who travels extensively by plane will become the victim of a plane crash during the next year has no relation to the amount of air travel that person has done in the past.

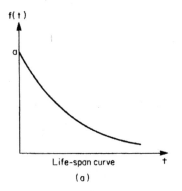

Life-span curve

(a)

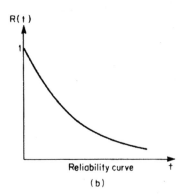

Reliability curve

(b)

**FIGURE 29**

## CORRESPONDENCE BETWEEN POISSON FAILURE AND NEGATIVE-EXPONENTIAL LIFE SPAN

The failure of a certain type of device has a Poisson probability, and the mean number of failures in 1500 h of operation is 6. What is the reliability of the device for 270 h of operation?

### Calculation Procedure:

### 1. Compute the mean life span

Refer to the previous calculation procedure pertaining to the Poisson probability distribution. Consider the following: A device is set in operation. When this device fails, a device of identical type is set in operation, and this replacement process continues indefinitely. Let $X$ denote the number of failures in time $t$, and assume that $X$ has a Poisson probability distribution. Thus the probability that exactly 1 failure will occur in 1 h remains constant as time elapses. It can readily be shown that the life span of the device, which is the time interval between successive failures, has a negative-exponential probability distribution.

   Select 1 h as the unit of time. Then mean life span $\mu = 1500/6 = 250$ h.

### 2. Compute the reliability

Apply Eq. $c$ of the preceding calculation procedure, giving $a = 1/\mu = 1/250$. Now apply Eq. $b$, giving $R(270) = e^{-270/250} = e^{-1.08} = 0.340$.

## PROBABILITY OF FAILURE DURING A SPECIFIC PERIOD

The life span of a device is negative-exponential, and its mean value is 8 days. What is the probability that the device will fail on the fifth day?

### Calculation Procedure:

### 1. Set up the probability equation

Set $T$ = life span, and refer to Fig. 26. As previously stated, $P(t_1 < T \le t_2)$ = area under curve from $t_1$ to $t_2$. It follows that $P(t_1 < T \le t_2) = R(t_1) - R(t_2)$. Take 1 day as the unit of time. So $P(4 < T \le 5) = R(4) - R(5)$.

### 2. Compute the probability

Set $a = 1/\mu = 1/8$. Then $R(t) = e^{-at} = e^{-t/8}$, or $R(4) - e^{-4/8} = 0.607$ and $R(5) - e^{-5/8} = 0.535$. Thus, $P(4 < T \le 5) = 0.607 - 0.535 = 0.072$.

   **Related Calculations.** Assume that the device has been operating for some time. In accordance with the statement previously made, the probability that this device will fail on the fifth day from the present is 0.072, regardless of the present age of the device.

## SYSTEM WITH COMPONENTS IN SERIES

A system consists of three type A components and two type B components, all arranged in series. These components have negative-exponential life spans, and the mean life span is 30 h for type A and 36 h for type B. Find the reliability of the system for 9 h of operation.

### Calculation Procedure:

### 1. Compute the reliability of each component for 9 h
Let the subscripts $A$ and $B$ refer to the type of component, and take 1 h as the unit of time. Then $a_A = 1/\mu_A = 1/30$, and $R_A(t) = e^{-t/30}$, or $R_A(9) = e^{-9/30} = 0.7408$. Similarly, $R_B(9) = e^{-9/36} = 0.7788$.

### 2. Compute the reliability of the system for 9 h
Apply Eq. 17: $R_S(9) = (0.7408)^3(0.7788)^2 = 0.247$.

### 3. Compute the reliability of the system by an alternative method
Apply Eq. 17 to prove that the system also has a negative-exponential life span. Now assume that when a component fails, it is instantly replaced with one of identical type, thus maintaining continuous operation. In 180 h of operation, the mean number of failures of an individual component is 180/30 = 6 for type A and 180/36 = 5 for type B. Since failure of any component causes failure of the system, the mean number of failures of the system in 180 h is $3 \times 6 + 2 \times 5 = 28$. Thus, the mean life span of the system is $\mu_S = 180/28$, and $a_S = 28/180$. Then $a_S t = (28/180)9 = 1.4$, and $R_S(9) = e^{-1.4} = 0.247$.

In the foregoing calculations, 180 h was selected for convenience, since 180 is the lowest common multiple of 30 and 36. However, a period of any length whatever can be selected.

## SYSTEM WITH COMPONENTS IN PARALLEL

With reference to the system in Fig. 30, the reliability of each component for a 60-day period is as indicated. For example, the reliability of $C_1$ is 0.18. Determine the probability

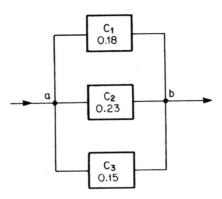

**FIGURE 30**

that the system will be operating at the expiration of 60 days as a result of each of the following causes: (a) only one component survives; (b) only two components survive; (c) all three components survive.

## Calculation Procedure:

### 1. Compute the probability that a component fails during the 60-day period
The probability of failure is: for $C_1$, $1 - 0.18 = 0.82$; for $C_2$, $1 - 0.23 = 0.77$; for $C_3$, $1 - 0.15 = 0.85$.

### 2. Compute the probability that the system survives because one and only one component survives
Multiply the probabilities of the individual events. Thus, $P(\text{only } C_1 \text{ survives}) = (0.18)(0.77)(0.85) = 0.11781$; $P(\text{only } C_2 \text{ survives}) = (0.82)(0.23)(0.85) = 0.16031$; $P(\text{only } C_3 \text{ survives}) = (0.82)(0.77)(0.15) = 0.09471$. Sum the results: $0.11781 + 0.16031 + 0.09471 = 0.37283$. This is the probability that only one component survives.

### 3. Compute the probability that the system survives because two and only two components survive
Proceed as in step 2. Thus, $P(\text{only } C_1 \text{ and } C_2 \text{ survive}) = (0.18)(0.23)(0.85) = 0.03519$; $P(\text{only } C_1 \text{ and } C_3 \text{ survive}) = (0.18)(0.77)(0.15) = 0.02079$; $P(\text{only } C_2 \text{ and } C_3 \text{ survive}) = (0.82)(0.23)(0.15) - 0.02829$. Sum the results: $0.03519 + 0.02079 + 0.02829 = 0.08427 = $ the probability that only two components survive.

### 4. Compute the probability that the system survives because all three components survive
$P(\text{all survive}) = (0.18)(0.23)(0.15) = 0.00621$.

### 5. Verify the foregoing results
Sum the results in steps 2, 3, and 4: $R_S(60) = 0.37283 + 0.08427 + 0.00621 = 0.46331$. Now apply Eq. 18, giving $R_S(60) = 1 - (0.82)(0.77)(0.85) = 0.46331$. The equality of the two values confirms the results obtained in the previous steps.

## SYSTEM WITH IDENTICAL COMPONENTS IN PARALLEL

A certain type of component has a reliability of 0.12 for 20 days. How many such components must be connected in parallel if the reliability of the system is to be at least 0.49 for 20 days?

## Calculation Procedure:

### 1. Write the equation for the reliability of the system
Let $n = $ number of components required. Apply Eq. 18, giving $R_S(20) = 1 - (1 - 0.12)^n = 1 - (0.88)^n$, Eq. a.

### 2. Determine the number of components
Set $R_S(20) = 0.49$ and solve Eq. a for $n$, giving $n = (\log 0.51)/(\log 0.88) = 5.3$. Use six components.

## ANALYSIS OF COMPOSITE SYSTEM
## BY CONVENTIONAL METHOD

A system is constructed by arranging the components in the manner shown in Fig. 31a, and the reliability of each component for a given time $t$ is recorded in the drawing. For example, the reliability of $C_1$ is 0.58. Find the reliability of the system for time $t$.

### Calculation Procedure:

### 1. Perform the first cycle in transforming the system to a simpler one

A system in which the components are arranged solely in series or in parallel is a *simple* system, and one that combines series and parallel arrangements is a composite system.

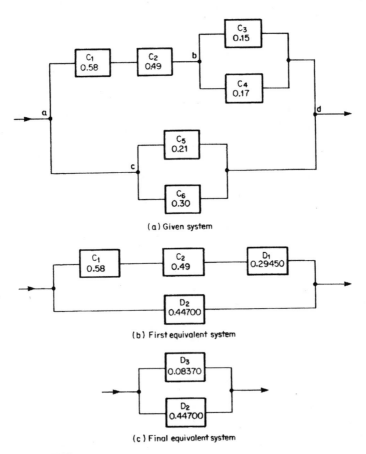

(a) Given system

(b) First equivalent system

(c) Final equivalent system

**FIGURE 31**

A composite system may be regarded as composed of subsystems, with a subsystem being a set of components arranged solely in series or parallel formation. A subsystem can be replaced with its resultant, which is a single component that has a reliability equal to that of the subsystem. Therefore, the conventional method of analyzing a composite system consists of resolving the system into sub-systems and replacing the subsystems with their resultants, continuing the process until the given system has been transformed to an equivalent simple system.

Let $D_1$ and $D_2$ denote the resultants of $C_3$ and $C_4$ and of $C_5$ and $C_6$, respectively. Apply Eq. 18 to obtain these reliabilities: for $D_1$, $1 - (0.85)(0.83) = 0.29450$; for $D_2$, $1 - (0.79)(0.70) = 0.44700$. Replace these components with their resultants, producing the equivalent composite system shown in Fig. 31b.

### 2. Perform the second cycle
Let $D_3$ denote the resultant of $C_1$, $C_2$, and $D_1$. Apply Eq. 17: reliability of $D_3 = (0.58)(0.49)(0.29450) = 0.08370$. Replace these components with $D_3$, producing the equivalent simple system shown in Fig. 31c.

### 3. Compute the reliability of the system
Apply Eq. 18. The reliability of the system in Fig. 31c is $R_S(t) = 1 - (0.91630)(0.55300) = 0.49329$. This is also the reliability of the original system.

## ANALYSIS OF COMPOSITE SYSTEM BY ALTERNATIVE METHOD

With reference to the preceding calculation procedure, find the reliability of the system by the moving-particle method.

### Calculation Procedure:

### 1. Compute the number of particles that traverse the system by way of $C_1$, $C_2$, and either $C_3$ or $C_4$
The alternative method of analyzing a composite system is based on this conception: During a given interval, a certain number of particles enter the system at one terminal and seek to move through the system to the other terminal. Each component offers resistance to the movement of these particles, and the proportion of particles that penetrate a component is equal to the reliability of that component. If a particle is obstructed at any point along its path, it returns to an earlier point and then proceeds along an alternative path if one is available. However, a particle can enter a component in a given direction only once. The reliability of the system is equal to the proportion of particles that traverse the system.

Consider that during a given interval 1,000,000 particles arrive at point $a$ in Fig. 31a, seeking a path to $d$. They can reach $d$ by passing through $C_1$, $C_2$, and either $C_3$ or $C_4$, or by passing through $C_5$ or $C_6$. Assume that the particles attempt passage by the first route, and refer to the schematic drawing in Fig. 32. The number of particles that penetrate $C_1 = 1,000,000(0.58) = 580,000$, and the number that then penetrate $C_2 = 580,000(0.49) = 284,200$. Assume that these particles now enter $C_3$. The number of particles that penetrate $C_3 = 284,200(0.15) = 42,630$. The number that fail to penetrate $C_3 = 284,200 - 42,630 = 241,570$; these particles return to $b$ in Fig. 31a and enter $C_4$. The number that penetrate

$C_4 = 241,570(0.17) = 41,067$. Thus, the number of particles that reach $d$ by way of $C_1$, $C_2$, and either $C_3$ or $C_4 = 42,630 + 41,067 = 83,697$.

As an alternative calculation, the number of particles that fail to penetrate $C_3 = 284,200(0.85) - 241,570$.

Note that the *proportion* of particles that traverse the system by the indicated route is $83,697/1,000,000 = 0.08370$ (to five decimal places), and this is the reliability of $D_3$ in Fig. 31$c$.

### 2. Compute the number of particles that traverse the system by way of either $C_5$ or $C_6$

Refer to Fig. 32. The number of particles that fail to penetrate a component is: for $C_1$, $1,000,000 - 580,000 = 420,000$; for $C_2$, $580,000 - 284,200 = 295,800$; for $C_4$, $241,570 - 41,067 = 200,503$. The total is $420,000 + 295,800 + 200,503 = 916,303$. These particles return to $a$ in Fig. 31$a$ and then proceed to $c$. Assume that they now enter $C_5$. The number of particles that penetrate $C_5 = 916,303(0.21) = 192,424$, and the number that fail to penetrate $C_5 = 916,303 - 192,424 - 723,879$. The latter enter $C_6$, and the number that penetrate $C_6 = 723,879(0.30) = 217,164$. Thus, the number of particles that reach $d$ by way of either $C_5$ or $C_6 = 192,424 + 217,164 = 409,588$.

Note that the *proportion* of particles that traverse this route is $409,588/916,303 = 0.44700$, and this is the reliability of $D_2$ in Fig. 31$c$.

### 3. Compute the reliability of the system

From steps 1 and 2 (or from Fig. 32), the number of particles that traverse the system from $a$ to $d = 83,697 + 409,588 = 493,285$. The proportion of particles that traverse the system $= 493,285/1,000,000 = 0.49329$, and this is the reliability of the system. This result is consistent with that in the preceding calculation procedure.

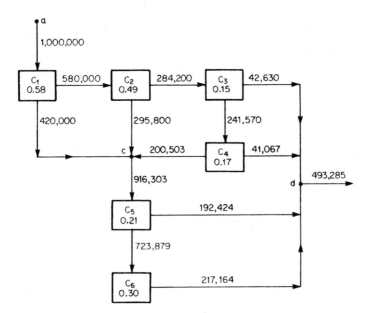

**FIGURE 32**

Alternatively, find the number of particles that traverse the system thus: A particle fails to traverse the system if it fails to penetrate $C_6$. From Fig. 32, the number of such particles is $723,879 - 217,164 = 506,715$. Thus, the number of particles that traverse the system $= 1,000,000 - 506,715 = 493,285$.

**Related Calculations.** The moving-particle method discloses certain principles very clearly. For example, assume that a simple composite system has components in series. To traverse the system, a particle must penetrate *all* components, and therefore the resistance of each component contributes to the resistance of the system. Thus, the resistance of the system exceeds that of any component, and the *reliability* of the system is less than that of any component. Now assume that a simple composite system has components in parallel. These components offer alternative paths for the moving particles, and therefore the reliability of the system exceeds that of any component.

## ANALYSIS OF SYSTEM WITH SAFEGUARD BY CONVENTIONAL METHOD

A system is constructed by arranging the components in the manner shown in Fig. 33, and the reliability of each component for a given time $t$ is recorded in the drawing. Find the reliability of the system for time $t$.

### Calculation Procedure:

#### 1. Identify the types of failure

The system operates if any of the following pairs of components operate: $C_1$ and $C_4$; $C_2$ and $C_4$; $C_2$ and $C_5$; $C_3$ and $C_5$. Thus, if $C_1$ and $C_3$ both fail, the system continues to operate through $C_2$, and therefore $C_2$ is a safeguard. The reliability of the system can be found most simply by determining the probability that the system will fail.

There are several modes of potential failure, but they can all be encompassed within two broad types. A *type 1 failure* occurs if each of the following events occurs: (*a*) $C_2$ fails; (*b*) either $C_1$ or $C_4$ fails, or both fail; (*c*) either $C_3$ or $C_5$ fails, or both fail. A *type 2 failure* occurs if each of the following events occurs: (*a*) $C_5$ operates; (*b*) $C_4$ fails; (*c*) $C_5$ fails.

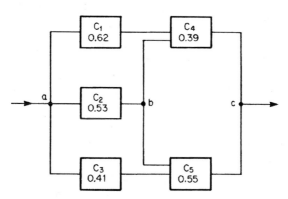

**FIGURE 33**

### 2. Compute the probability of a type 1 failure

To simplify the notation, let $R$ = reliability of a component, with a subscript identical with that of the component, and $R_S$ = reliability of the system.

As previously stated, if two events are independent of each other, the probability that both will occur is the product of their respective probabilities. Consider a type 1 failure. The probability that $C_2$ fails is $1 - R_2$. The probability that both $C_1$ and $C_4$ operate is $R_1$, $R_4$ thus, the probability that either or both components fail is $1 - R_1$, $R_4$. Similarly, the probability that $C_3$ or $C_5$ fails or both fail is $1 - R_3R_5$. Thus, the probability of a type 1 failure is $P(\text{type } 1) = (1 - R_2)(1 - R_1R_4)(1 - R_3R_5)$, or $P(\text{type } 1) = (0.47)[1 - (0.62)(0.39)][1 - (0.41)(0.55)] = 0.27600$.

### 3. Compute the probability of a type 2 failure

Multiply the probabilities of the three specified events, giving $P(\text{type } 2) = R_2(1 - R_4) \times (1 - R_3)$ or $P(\text{type } 2) = (0.53)(0.61)(0.45) = 0.14549$.

### 4. Compute the reliability of the system

The probability that either of two mutually exclusive events will occur is the sum of their respective probabilities. From steps 2 and 3, the probability that the system will fail is $0.27600 + 0.14549 = 0.42149$. Then $R_S = 1 - 0.42149 = 0.57851$.


## ANALYSIS OF SYSTEM WITH SAFEGUARD BY ALTERNATIVE METHOD

With reference to the preceding calculation procedure, find the reliability of the system by the moving-particle method.


### Calculation Procedure:

### 1. Compute the number of particles that traverse the system by way of $C_2$

Consider that during a given interval 1,000,000 particles arrive at point $a$ in Fig. 33, seeking a path to $c$. They can reach $c$ by any of three routes: $C_2$ and either $C_4$ or $C_5$; $C_1$ and $C_4$; $C_3$ and $C_5$. Assume that the particles attempt passage by the first route, and refer to Fig. 34. The number of particles that penetrate $C_2 = 1,000,000(0.53) = 530,000$. Assume that these particles now enter $C_4$. The number of particles that penetrate $C_4 = 530,000(0.39) = 206,700$, and the number that fail to penetrate $C_4 = 530,000 - 206,700 = 323,300$. The latter return to $b$ in Fig. 33 and then enter $C_5$. The number that penetrate $C_5 = 323,300(0.55) = 177,815$. Thus, the number of particles that reach $c$ by way of $C_2$ and either $C_4$ or $C_5 = 206,700 + 177,815 = 384,515$.

### 2. Compute the number of particles that traverse the system by way of $C_1$ and $C_4$

Refer to Fig. 34. The number of particles that fail to penetrate $C_2 = 1,000,000 - 530,000 = 470,000$. These particles return to $a$ in Fig. 33; assume that they then enter $C_1$. The number of particles that penetrate $C_1 = 470,000(0.62) = 291,400$, and the number that then penetrate $C_4 = 291,400(0.39) = 113,646$. Thus, 113,646 particles reach $c$ by way of $C_1$ and $C_4$.

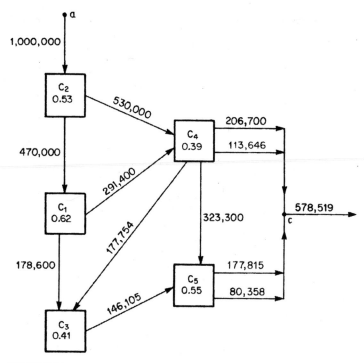

**FIGURE 34**

### 3. Compute the number of particles that traverse the system by way of $C_3$ and $C_5$

From step 2, the number of particles that fail to penetrate $C_1 = 470,000 - 291,400 = 178,600$, and the number that fail to penetrate $C_4 = 291,400 - 113,646 = 177,754$. These particles return to $a$ in Fig. 33 and then enter $C_3$. Refer to Fig. 34. The number of particles that penetrate $C_3 = (178,600 + 177,754)(0.41) = 146,105$, and the number that then penetrate $C_5 = 146,105(0.55) = 80,358$. Thus, 80,358 particles reach $c$ by way of $C_3$ and $C_5$.

### 4. Compute the reliability of the system

From steps 1, 2, and 3 (or from Fig. 34), the number of particles that traverse the system from $a$ to $c = 384,515 + 113,646 + 80,358 = 578,519$. The *proportion* of particles that traverse the system $= 578,519/1,000,000 = 0.57852$, and this is the reliability of the system. This result is consistent with that in the preceding calculation procedure.

## Making Business Decisions under Uncertainty

The industrial world is characterized by uncertainty, and so many business decisions must be based on considerations of probability. The calculation procedures that follow illustrate several techniques that have been developed for making decisions of this type.

## *OPTIMAL INVENTORY TO MEET*
## *FLUCTUATING DEMAND*

A firm sells a commodity that is used only during the winter. Because the commodity deteriorates with age, units of the commodity that remain unsold by the end of the season cannot be carried over to the following winter. To allow time for manufacture, the firm must place its order for the commodity before July 1. Thus, the firm must decide how many units to stock. For simplicity, the firm orders only in multiples of 10, and it assumes that the number of units demanded by its customers is also a multiple of 10.

A study of past records reveals that the number of units demanded per season ranges from 150 to 200, and the probabilities are as shown in Table 28. The cost of the commodity, including purchase price and allowance for handling, storage, and insurance, is $50 per unit; the selling price is $75 per unit. Units that are not sold can be disposed of as scrap for $6 each. If the firm is unable to satisfy the demand, it suffers a loss of goodwill because there is some possibility of permanently losing customers to a competitor; this loss of goodwill is assigned the value of $4 per unsold unit. How many units of this commodity should the firm order?

### Calculation Procedure:

### 1. *Set up the equations for profit*
A firm that sells a perishable commodity with a widely fluctuating demand runs a risk at each end of the spectrum. If its stock is excessive, it suffers a loss on the unsold units; if its stock is inadequate, it forfeits potential profits and suffers a loss of goodwill. So it must determine how large a stock to maintain to maximize profits in the long run, applying past demand as a guide.

Let $X$ = number of units ordered; $Y$ = number of units demanded; $P$ = profit (exclusive of fixed costs), $. If $X = Y$, then $P = (75 - 50)X$, or $P = 25X$, Eq. *a*. If $X > Y$, then $P = 75Y - 50X + 6(X - Y)$, or $P = -44X + 69Y$, Eq. *b*. If $X < Y$, then $P = (75 - 50)X - 4(Y - X)$, or $P = 29X - 4Y$, Eq. *c*.

### 2. *Construct the profit matrix*
In Table 29, list all possible values of $X$ in the column at the left and all possible values of $Y$ in the row across the top. Compute the value of $P$ for every possible combination of $X$ and $Y$, and record the value in the table. Thus, assume $X = Y = 160$; by Eq. *a*, $P = 25 \times 160 = $4000$. Now assume $X = 180$ and $Y = 160$; by Eq. *b*, $P = -44X 180 + 69 \times 160 = $3120$. Finally, assume $X = 160$ and $Y = 200$; by Eq. *c*, $P = 29 \times 160 - 4 \times 200 = $3840$. Table 29 shows that $P$ can range from $1550 (when the stock is highest and the demand is lowest) to $5000 (when the demand is highest and the stock is adequate for the demand).

**TABLE 28.** Demand Probabilities

| Number of units demanded | 150 | 160 | 170 | 180 | 190 | 200 |
|---|---|---|---|---|---|---|
| Probability, percent | 8 | 13 | 20 | 32 | 18 | 9 |

**TABLE 29.** Values of $P$

| Number of units ordered $X$ | Number of units demanded $Y$ | | | | | |
|---|---|---|---|---|---|---|
| | 150 | 160 | 170 | 180 | 190 | 200 |
| 150 | 3750 | 3710 | 3670 | 3630 | 3590 | 3550 |
| 160 | 3310 | 4000 | 3960 | 3920 | 3880 | 3840 |
| 170 | 2870 | 3560 | 4250 | 4210 | 4170 | 4130 |
| 180 | 2430 | 3120 | 3810 | 4500 | 4460 | 4420 |
| 190 | 1990 | 2680 | 3370 | 4060 | 4750 | 4710 |
| 200 | 1550 | 2240 | 2930 | 3620 | 4310 | 5000 |
| Probability of $Y$ | 0.08 | 0.13 | 0.20 | 0.32 | 0.18 | 0.09 |

Alternatively, find the values of $P$ thus: In Table 29, insert all values lying on the diagonal from the upper left-hand corner to the lower right-hand corner by applying Eq. $a$. In each column, proceed upward from this diagonal by successively deducting $290, in accordance with Eq. $c$. Then proceed downward from the diagonal by successively deducting $440, in accordance with Eq. $b$.

**3. Compute the expected profit corresponding to each value of X**

As stated earlier, if all possible values of a random variable are multiplied by their respective probabilities and the products are added, the result equals the arithmetic mean of the variable in the long run, and it is also called the expected value of the variable. For convenience, repeat the probability corresponding to every possible value of $Y$ at the bottom of Table 29. Let $E(P)$ = expected value of $P$. When $X$ = 150, $E(P)$ = $3750(0.08) + $3710(0.13) + $3670(0.20) + $3630(0.32) + $3590(0.18) + $3550(0.09) = $3643.60. When $X$ = 160, $E(P)$ = $3310(0.08) + $4000(0.13) + $3960(0.20) + $3920(0.32) + $3880(0.18) + $3840(0.09) = $3875.20. Continue these calculations to obtain: when $X$ = 170, $E(P)$ = $4011.90; when $X$ = 180, $E(P)$ = $4002.60; when $X$ = 190, $E(P)$ = $3759.70; when $X$ = 200, $E(P)$ = $3385.40.

**4. Determine how many units the firm should order**

The results in step 3 show that the expected profit is maximum when $X$ = 170. Therefore, the firm should order 170 units. If the fluctuation in demand follows the same pattern as in the past, the firm will maximize its profits in the long run by maintaining a stock of this size.

## FINDING OPTIMAL INVENTORY BY INCREMENTAL-PROFIT METHOD

With reference to the preceding calculation procedure, determine how many units the firm should order by applying incremental analysis.

**Calculation Procedure:**

**1. Set up the equation for expected incremental profit**

Consider that the firm increases the number of units ordered by 10. In doing this, the firm has undertaken an *incremental investment*, and the profit that accrues from this incremental investment is called the *incremental profit*. Since the objective is to maximize profits from the sale of this commodity without reference to the rate of return that the firm earns on invested capital, the incremental investment is justified if the incremental profit has a positive value.

If a demand for these 10 additional units exists, the firm earns a direct profit of 10($75 − $50) = $250, and it reduces its loss of goodwill by 10($4) = $40. Thus, the *effective* profit = $250 + $40 = $290. If a demand for the 10 additional units does not exist, the firm incurs a loss of 10($50 − $6) = $440. Let $P$(sold) and $P$(not sold) = probability the 10 additional units will be sold and will not be sold, respectively, and $E(\Delta P)$ = expected incremental profit, $. Then $E(\Delta P) = 290\,[P(\text{sold})] - 440\,[P(\text{not sold})]$. Set $P$(not sold) = 1 − $P$(sold), giving $E(\Delta P) = 730\,[P(\text{sold})] - 440$, Eq. *a*.

### 2. *Apply this equation to find the optimal inventory*

From the preceding calculation procedure, $E(P)$ is positive if $X = 150$; thus, the firm should order at least 150 units. Assume $X$ increases from 150 to 160. From Table 28, $P$(sold) = 1 − 0.08 = 0.92. By Eq. *a*, $E(\Delta P) = 730(0.92) - 440 = \$231.60 > 0$, and the incremental investment is justified. Assume $X$ increases from 160 to 170. Then $P$(sold) = 1 − (0.08 + 0.13) = 0.79. By Eq. *a*, $E(\Delta P) = 730(0.79) - 440 = \$136.70 > 0$, and the incremental investment is justified. Assume $X$ increases from 170 to 180. Then $P$(sold) = 1 − (0.08 + 0.13 + 0.20) = 0.59. By Eq. *a*, $E(\Delta P) = 730(0.59) - 440 = -\$9.30 < 0$, and the incremental investment is not justified. Thus, the firm should order 170 units.

### 3. *Devise a direct method of solution*

Determine when $E(\Delta P)$ changes sign by setting $E(\Delta P) = 730\,[P(\text{sold})] - 440 = 0$, giving $P$(sold) = 440/730 = 0.603. This is the lower limit of $P$(sold) if the incremental investment is to be justified. Now, $P$(sold) first goes below this value when $X = 180$; thus, the expected profit is maximum when $X = 170$.

**Related Calculations.** From the preceding calculation procedure, when $X = 150$, $E(P) = \$3643.60$; when $X = 160$, $E(P) = \$3875.20$. Thus, when $X$ increases from 150 to 160, $E(\Delta P) = \$3875.20 - \$3643.60 = \$231.60$, and this is the result obtained in step 2. Similarly, from the preceding calculation procedure, when $X$ increases from 160 to 170, $E(\Delta P) = \$4011.90 - \$3875.20 = \$136.70$, and this is the result obtained above. The two methods of solution yield consistent results.

The incremental-profit method is less time-consuming than the method followed in the preceding calculation procedure, and it is particularly appropriate when the firm sets a minimum acceptable rate of return. Thus, assume that the firm will undertake an investment only if the expected rate of return is 15 percent or more. When the firm orders 10 additional units, it undertakes an incremental investment of $440. This incremental investment is justified only if the expected incremental profit is at least $440(0.15), or $66.

## SIMULATION OF COMMERCIAL ACTIVITY BY THE MONTE CARLO TECHNIQUE

A firm sells and delivers a standard commodity. The terms of sale require that the firm deliver the product within 1 day after an order is placed. In the past, the volume of orders received averaged 3315 units per week, with the variation in volume shown in Table 30.

The firm currently employs a trucking company. But the firm contemplates purchasing its own fleet of trucks to make deliveries. It is therefore necessary to decide how many trucks are to be purchased. Several plans are under consideration. The shipping facilities under plan A have an estimated average capacity of 3405 units per week.

**TABLE 30.**  Frequency Distribution

| Orders received per week | | | Weekly shipping capacity | | |
|---|---|---|---|---|---|
| Number of units | Relative frequency | Median value | Number of units | Relative frequency | Median value |
| 3000–3099 | 0.05 | 3050 | 3300–3349 | 0.15 | 3325 |
| 3100–3199 | 0.10 | 3150 | 3350–3399 | 0.30 | 3375 |
| 3200–3299 | 0.35 | 3250 | 3400–3449 | 0.35 | 3425 |
| 3300–3399 | 0.25 | 3350 | 3450–3499 | 0.20 | 3475 |
| 3400–3499 | 0.15 | 3450 | Total | 1.00 | |
| 3500–3599 | 0.10 | 3550 | | | |
| Total | 1.00 | | | | |

Experience indicates that this capacity may be expected to vary in the manner shown in Table 30.

When the volume of daily orders exceeds the shipping capacity, sales will be lost; when the reverse condition occurs, trucks will be idle. Lost sales are valued at $2.40 per unit, which includes an allowance for partial loss of goodwill. Unused shipping capacity is valued at $1.10 per unit. Applying the Monte Carlo technique, estimate the amount of these losses if plan A is adopted.

## Calculation Procedure:

### 1. Determine the average weekly losses

In Table 30, record the median value for each range, as shown in the third and sixth columns. For convenience, apply only these median values in the calculations. This procedure is equivalent to assuming, for example, that the volume of prospective sales varies discretely from 3050 to 3550 units with an interval of 100 units between consecutive values.

Analysis of Table 30 reveals that the excess of weekly shipping capacity over delivery requirements may range between 425 units (3475 − 3050) and −225 units (3325 − 3550), and that it may assume any of the following values:

| | | | | |
|---|---|---|---|---|
| 425 | 375 | 325 | 275 | 225 |
| 175 | 125 | 75 | 25 | −25 |
| −75 | −125 | −175 | −225 | |

To evaluate the average weekly losses, it is necessary to evaluate the frequency with which these values are likely to exist. The Monte Carlo technique is a probabilistic device that circumvents the mathematical complexity inherent in a rigorous solution by resorting to a set of numbers generated in a purely random manner. Tables of random numbers are published in books listed in the references for this section.

### 2. Compute the cumulative frequency of the prospective sales

The cumulative frequency of each value of prospective sales is the relative frequency with which orders of the designated magnitude, or less, are received. The results of this calculation appear in Table 31.

**TABLE 31.**   Cumulative Frequency of
Prospective Sales

| Number of units demanded | Cumulative frequency |
|---|---|
| 3050 | 0.05 |
| 3150 | 0.15 |
| 3250 | 0.50 |
| 3350 | 0.75 |
| 3450 | 0.90 |
| 3550 | 1.00 |

### 3. *Prepare a histogram of the frequency distributions*
Plot the cumulative-frequency values in Fig. 35. Draw horizontal and vertical lines as shown. The relative frequency of a given value of the prospective sales is represented by the length of the vertical line directly above the value.

### 4. *Select random numbers for the solution*
Refer to a table of random numbers. Select the first 10 numbers found in the table. Enter these numbers in the second column of Table 32. (In actual practice, a larger quantity of random numbers would be selected.)

### 5. *Use the random numbers in the solution*
Consider each random number as a cumulative frequency. Refer to the histogram, Fig. 35, to find the volume of orders corresponding to this value of the random number. Then, draw a horizontal through the random-number value of 0.488 on the vertical axis of Fig. 35. This line intersects the vertical that lies above the value of 3250 on the horizontal axis. Therefore, enter in Table 32 the value of 3250 opposite the random number 0.488.

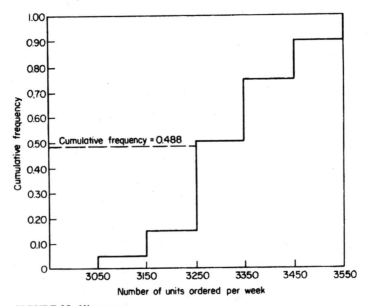

**FIGURE 35.** Histogram.

**TABLE 32.**   Simulated Values of Prospective Sales and Shipping Capacity

| Week | Random number | Number of units demanded | Random number | Shipping capacity |
|------|------|------|------|------|
| 1 | 0.488 | 3250 | 0.339 | 3375 |
| 2 | 0.322 | 3250 | 0.697 | 3425 |
| 3 | 0.274 | 3250 | 0.031 | 3325 |
| 4 | 0.557 | 3350 | 0.052 | 3325 |
| 5 | 0.931 | 3550 | 0.506 | 3425 |
| 6 | 0.986 | 3550 | 0.865 | 3475 |
| 7 | 0.682 | 3350 | 0.948 | 3475 |
| 8 | 0.179 | 3250 | 0.308 | 3375 |
| 9 | 0.881 | 3450 | 0.218 | 3375 |
| 10 | 0.834 | 3450 | 0.367 | 3375 |

**6.  Repeat steps 3 to 5 for the shipping capacity**

Enter the results in Table 32 in the same manner as for the units demanded, step 5.

**7.  Evaluate the loss on sales and unused capacity**

Compare the simulated prospective sales with the simulated capacity. For example, during week 1, the loss on unused capacity = $1.10(3375 - 3250) = \$137.50$, given the data from Table 32. Likewise, during week 4, loss on lost sales = $2.40(3350 - 3325) = \$60.00$.

**8.  Determine the average weekly losses**

Total the computed losses obtained in step 7, and divide by 10 to obtain the following average weekly values:

| | |
|---|---|
| Loss on unused capacity | $68.75 |
| Loss on forfeited sales | 90.00 |
| Total | $158.75 |

If more trucking facilities are procured, the forfeited sales will be reduced, but the unused capacity will be increased. The optimal number of trucks to be purchased is that for which the total loss is a minimum.

## LINEAR REGRESSION APPLIED TO SALES FORECASTING

A firm had the following sales for 5 consecutive years:

| Year | Sales, $000 |
|------|------|
| 19AA | 348 |
| 19BB | 377 |
| 19CC | 418 |
| 19DD | 475 |
| 19EE | 500 |

In 19FF, the firm decided to expand its production facilities in anticipation of future growth, and therefore it required a forecast of future sales. Apply linear regression to discern the sales trend. What is the projected sales volume for 19JJ?

## Calculation Procedure:

### 1. Plot a scatter diagram for the given data

Regression analysis is applied where a causal relationship exists between two variables, although the relationship is obscured by the influence of random factors. The problem is to establish the relationship on the basis of observed data. Here we assume that the sales volume is a linear function of time.

Consider the annual sales income to be a lump sum received at the end of the given year, and plot the sales data as shown in Fig. 36. The aggregate of points is termed a scatter diagram. This diagram will be replaced by a straight line that most closely approaches the plotted points; this straight line is called the *regression line*, or *line of best fit*.

### 2. Set up the criterion for the regression line

Draw the arbitrary straight line in Fig. 36, and consider the vertical deviation e of a point in the scatter diagram from this arbitrary line. The regression line is taken as the line for which the sum of the squares of the deviations is minimum.

Let $Y$ denote the ordinate of a point in the scatter diagram and $Y_R$ the corresponding ordinate on the regression line. By definition, $\Sigma e^2 = \Sigma(Y - Y_R)^2 = $ minimum.

### 3. Write the equation of the regression line

Let $n$ denote the number of points in the scatter diagram, and let $Y_R = a + bX$ be the equation of the regression line, where $X$ denotes the year number as measured from some convenient datum. To find the regression line, parameters $a$ and $b$ must be evaluated.

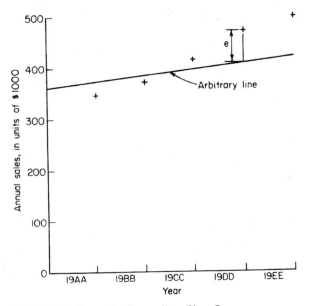

**FIGURE 36.** Regression line, or line of best fit.

**TABLE 33.**   Locating a Regression Line

| Year | $X$ | $Y$ | $X^2$ | $XY$ | $Y_R$ |
|------|-----|-----|-------|------|-------|
| 19AA | −2 | 348 | 4 | −696 | 343.2 |
| 19BB | −1 | 377 | 1 | −377 | 383.4 |
| 19CC | 0 | 418 | 0 | 0 | 423.6 |
| 19DD | 1 | 475 | 1 | 475 | 463.8 |
| 19EE | 2 | 500 | 4 | 1000 | 504.0 |
| Total | 0 | 2118 | 10 | 402 | |

Since $\Sigma e^2$ is to have a minimum value, express the partial derivatives of $\Sigma e^2$ with respect to $a$ and $b$, and set these both equal to zero. Then derive the following simultaneous equations containing the unknown quantities a and b:

$$\Sigma Y = an + b\Sigma X$$

$$\Sigma XY = a\Sigma X + b\Sigma X^2$$

**4. Simplify the calculations**
Select the median date (the end of 19CC) as a datum. This selection causes the term $\Sigma X$ to vanish.

**5. Determine the values of $\Sigma X^2$ and $\Sigma XY$**
Prepare a tabulation such as Table 33. Use the data for each year in question.

**6. Solve for parameters a and b**
Substitute in the equations in step 3, and solve for $a$ and $b$. Thus $2118 = 5a$; $402 = 10b$; $a = 423.6$; $b = 40.2$.

**7. Write the regression equation; extrapolate for the year in question**
Here $Y_R = 423.6 + 40.2X$. For 19JJ: $X = 7$; $Y_R = 423.6 + 40.2 (7) = 705$. Hence, the forecast sales for 19JJ = \$705,000. For comparative purposes, the past sales volumes as determined by the regression line are listed in Table 33.

## STANDARD DEVIATION FROM REGRESSION LINE

Using the data in the previous calculation procedure, appraise the reliability of the regression line in forecasting future sales by computing the standard deviation of the points in the scatter diagram, using the regression line as the datum from which the deviation is measured.

**Calculation Procedure:**

**1. Calculate the deviation of each point; square the result**
The standard deviation serves as an index of the dispersion of the points in the scatter diagram. The standard deviation $\sigma = \sqrt{\Sigma e^2 / n}$.

**TABLE 34.** Determining the Standard Deviation

| Year | $Y - Y_R = e$ | $e^2$ |
|------|---------------|-------|
| 19AA | $348 - 343.2 = \phantom{-}4.8$ | 23.0 |
| 19BB | $377 - 383.4 = -6.4$ | 41.0 |
| 19CC | $418 - 423.6 = -5.6$ | 31.4 |
| 19DD | $475 - 463.8 = \phantom{-}11.2$ | 125.4 |
| 19EE | $500 - 504.0 = -4.0$ | 16.0 |
| Total | | 236.8 |

Calculate the value of $e$ for each point, Fig. 36. Enter the results for each year in a tabulation such as Table 34. Then, $\sigma = \sqrt{236.8/5} = 6.9$.

**2. Determine the monetary value represented by the standard deviation**

Since the given monetary values are expressed in thousands of dollars, the value of the standard deviation $= 6.9 (\$1000) = \$6900$.

## SHORT-TERM FORECASTING WITH A MARKOV PROCESS

The XYZ Company manufactures a machine that is available in three models, A, B, and C. There are currently 1200 such machines in use, divided as follows: model A, 460; model B, 400; model C, 340. On the basis of a survey, the XYZ Company has established probabilities corresponding to two successive purchases, and they are recorded in Table 35. Thus, if a firm currently owns model B, there is a probability of 0.5000 that its next model will be A; if a firm currently owns model C, there is a probability of 0.6154 that its next model will also be C. Assume that each machine will remain in service for precisely 1 year, after which it will be replaced with another machine manufactured by the XYZ Company. Also assume that the XYZ Company will not acquire any new customers in the foreseeable future. Estimate the number of units of each model that will be in use 1 year, 2 years, and 3 years hence.

**TABLE 35.** Probabilities for Two Successive Purchases

| Present model | Next model | | |
|---------------|------|------|------|
| | A | B | C |
| A | .4167 | .3333 | .2500 |
| B | .5000 | .3000 | .2000 |
| C | .1538 | .2308 | .6154 |

## Calculation Procedure:

### 1. Set up the basic equations that link two successive years

Assume that a trial will be performed repeatedly and that the outcome of one trial directly influences the outcome of the succeeding trial. A trial of this type is called a *Markov process*. In this situation, the purchase of a machine is a Markov process because the model that a firm selects on one occasion has a direct bearing on the model it selects on the following occasion. The probabilities in Table 35 are termed *transition probabilities*, and the table itself is called a *transition matrix*.

Let $X_{A,n}$ = expected number of units of model A that will be in use $n$ years hence. Multiply the expected values for $n$ years hence by their respective probabilities to obtain the expected values for $n + 1$ years hence, giving

$$X_{A,n+1} = 0.4167X_{A,n} + 0.5000X_{B,n} + 0.1538X_{C,n} \qquad (a)$$

$$X_{B,n+1} = 0.3333X_{A,n} + 0.3000X_{B,n} + 0.2308X_{C,n} \qquad (b)$$

$$X_{C,n+1} = 0.2500X_{A,n} + 0.2000X_{B,n} + 0.6154X_{C,n} \qquad (c)$$

### 2. Calculate the expected values for 1 year hence

Apply Eqs. *a*, *b*, and *c* with $n = 0$ and $X_{A,0} = 460$, $X_{B,0} = 400$, $X_{C,0} = 340$. Then $X_{A,1} = (0.4167)460 + (0.5000)400 + (0.1538)340 = 444$; $X_{B,1} = (0.3333)460 + (0.3000)400 + (0.2308)340 = 352$; $X_{C,1} = (0.2500)460 + (0.2000)400 + (0.6154)340 = 404$. Record the results in Table 36.

### 3. Calculate the expected values for 2 years hence

Apply Eqs. *a*, *b*, and *c* with $n = 1$ and the values of $X_{A,1}$, $X_{B,1}$, and $X_{C,1}$, shown in Table 36. Then $X_{A,2} = (0.4167)444 + (0.5000)352 + (0.1538)404 = 423$; $X_{B,2} = (0.3333)444 + (0.3000)352 + (0.2308)404 = 347$; $X_{C,2} = (0.2500)444 + (0.2000)352 + (0.6154)404 = 430$. Record the results in Table 36.

### 4. Calculate the expected values for 3 years hence

Apply Eqs. *a*, *b*, and *c* for the third cycle. Then $X_{A,3} = (0.4167)423 + (0.5000)347 + (0.1538)430 = 416$; $X_{B,3} = (0.3333)423 + (0.3000)347 + (0.2308)430 = 344$; $X_{C,3} = (0.2500)423 + (0.2000)347 + (0.6154)430 = 440$. Record the results in Table 36.

### 5. Determine the expected values with the aid of a diagram

Refer to Fig. 37, which shows the expected manner in which units of a given model will be replaced. Each value of $X$ is recorded in the appropriate box. Multiply the values of $X_{A,0}$, $X_{B,0}$, and $X_{C,0}$ by the corresponding probabilities to find the expected replacements during the first year. Thus, with reference to the 460 units of model A, the expected replacements are as follows: model A, $460(0.4167) = 192$; model B, $460(0.3333) = 153$; model C, $460(0.2500) = 115$. Record all values in Fig. 37. Then $X_{A,1} = 192 + 200 + 52 = 444$; $X_{B,1} = 153 + 120 + 79 = 352$; $X_{C,1} = 115 + 80 + 209 = 404$. Repeat the cycle of calculations for the second and third years. The values in Fig. 37 agree with those in Table 36.

**TABLE 36.**   Expected Number of Units in Use

| Elapsed time, years | $X_A$ | $X_B$ | $X_C$ |
|---|---|---|---|
| 0 | 460 | 400 | 340 |
| 1 | 444 | 352 | 404 |
| 2 | 423 | 347 | 430 |
| 3 | 416 | 344 | 440 |

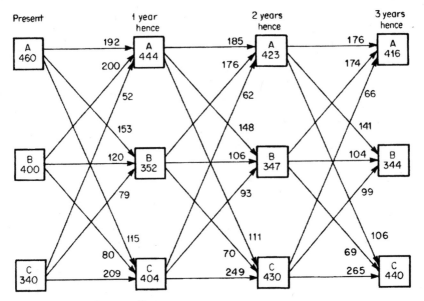

**FIGURE 37.**  Replacement diagram

**Related Calculations.** Matrix multiplication provides a compact procedure for solving problems pertaining to a Markov process. Let **P** denote the matrix in Table 35 and $R_n$ denote a row vector consisting of $X_{A,n}$, $X_{B,n}$, and $X_{C,n}$. The values of these variables appear in Table 36. Then

$$\mathbf{R_1} = \mathbf{R_0 P} = [460 \quad 400 \quad 340] \begin{bmatrix} 0.4167 & 0.3333 & 0.2500 \\ 0.5000 & 0.3000 & 0.2000 \\ 0.1538 & 0.2308 & 0.6154 \end{bmatrix} = [444 \quad 352 \quad 404]$$

Similarly, $\mathbf{R_2} = \mathbf{R_1 P} = \mathbf{R_0 P^2}$, and $\mathbf{R_3} = \mathbf{R_2 P} = \mathbf{R_0 P^3}$. In general, $\mathbf{R_n} = \mathbf{R_0 P^n}$.

## LONG-TERM FORECASTING WITH A MARKOV PROCESS

With reference to the preceding calculation procedure, estimate the number of units of each model that will ultimately be in use simultaneously.

### Calculation Procedure:

### 1. Form a system of simultaneous equations containing the limits of the expected values

In the long run, the probability that a firm will buy a given model is solely a function of the specific needs of that firm and the characteristics of each model; it is independent of the particular model that the firm happens to own at present. Therefore, $X_{A,n}$, $X_{B,n}$, and $X_{C,n}$ approach definite limits as $n$ increases beyond bound. The values of these variables when $n$ has a finite value constitute *transient conditions*, and the values when $n$ is infinite constitute the *steady-state conditions*. In practice, however, the steady-state conditions may be considered to exist when all differences between transient and steady-state values become less than some specified small number.

Let $X_{A,n} = \lim X_{A,n}$. In Eqs. *a* and *b* of the preceding calculation procedure, replace the transient values with their respective limits and rearrange:

$$-0.5833X_{A,u} + 0.5000X_{B,u} + 0.1538X_{C,u} = 0 \qquad (a')$$

$$0.3333X_{A,u} - 0.7000X_{B,u} + 0.2308X_{C,u} = 0 \qquad (b')$$

Also,

$$X_{A,u} + X_{B,u} + X_{C,u} = 1200 \qquad (d)$$

### 2. Solve the system of equations

The results are $X_{A,u} = 411$; $X_{B,u} = 343$; $X_{C,u} = 446$. Thus, it is expected that there will ultimately be 411 units of model A, 343 units of model B, and 446 units of model C in use simultaneously. Note that the values of $X_{A,3}$, $X_{B,3}$, and $X_{C,3}$ in Table 36 are very close to the limiting values. Thus, the expected values approach their respective limits rapidly.

**Related Calculations.** Many problems in engineering, economics, and other areas lend themselves to solution as Markov processes. The computational techniques applied in this calculation procedure and the preceding one are entirely general, and they may be applied to any problem where a Markov process exists.

## VERIFICATION OF STEADY-STATE CONDITIONS FOR A MARKOV PROCESS

Verify the accuracy of the results obtained in the preceding calculation procedure by devising an alternative method of solution.

### Calculation Procedure:

### 1. Construct a recurring series of outcomes that conforms with the given process

Assume that a Markov process has three possible outcomes, A, B, and C, and that the first 35 outcomes were these:

B-A-A-B-B-A-C-C-C-B-A-A-A-C-A-A-A-C-C-B-A-B-A-B-C-C-C-A-B-C-B-B

This series consists of 12 A's, 10 B's, and 13 C's. Also assume that this series of outcomes will recur indefinitely. Thus, the last outcome in the series will be followed by B. It will be demonstrated that this series is relevant to the preceding calculation procedure.

### 2. Compute the transition probabilities as established by the recurring series

Count the successors of the outcomes in this series, and then compute the relative frequencies of the various successions. Refer to Table 37 for the calculations. Since the given series of outcomes will recur indefinitely, the relative frequencies in Table 37 equal the *transition probabilities* corresponding to the present Markov process. Thus, the probability that A will be followed by B is 0.3333, and the probability that C will be followed by A is 0.1538. Since these transition probabilities coincide with those in Table 35, it follows that

**TABLE 37**

| Given outcome | Successor | Frequency of successor | Relative frequency of successor |
|---------------|-----------|------------------------|---------------------------------|
| A | A | 5 | 5/12 = 0.4167 |
|   | B | 4 | 4/12 = 0.3333 |
|   | C | 3 | 3/12 = 0.2500 |
|   |   | Total  12 | |
| B | A | 5 | 5/10 = 0.5000 |
|   | B | 3 | 3/10 = 0.3000 |
|   | C | 2 | 2/10 = 0.2000 |
|   |   | Total  10 | |
| C | A | 2 | 2/13 = 0.1538 |
|   | B | 3 | 3/13 = 0.2308 |
|   | C | 8 | 8/13 = 0.6154 |
|   |   | Total  13 | |

the present recurring series provides a basis for investigating the Markov process in the preceding calculation procedure.

**3. Compute the steady-state probabilities**

In the long run, the probability that a given outcome will occur is independent of some outcome in the distant past. In the recurring series, the relative frequencies of the outcomes are: outcome A, 12/35; outcome B, 10/35; outcome C, 13/35. These relative frequencies are the steady-state probabilities corresponding to the Markov process.

**4. Compute the expected number of units in use at steady-state conditions**

In the preceding calculation procedure, the total number of machines that will be in use simultaneously is 1200. Multiply the steady-state probabilities found in step 3 by 1200 to obtain the expected number of units of each model that ultimately will be in use simultaneously. The results are: model A, 1200(12/35) = 411; model B, 1200(10/35) = 343; model C, 1200(13/35) = 446. These results coincide with those obtained in the preceding calculation procedure, and so the latter are confirmed.

**Related Calculations.** In constructing the recurring series of outcomes, it is necessary to apply the *principle of succession*. Assume that a Markov process has three possible outcomes, A, B, and C; and let $N(A\text{-}B)$ = number of times that A is followed by B. The principle is $N(A\text{-}B) + N(A\text{-}C) = N(B\text{-}A) + N(C\text{-}A)$. As an illustration, consider the following skeletal series, where each outcome is followed by a different outcome:

$$A\text{-}C\text{-}A\text{-}C\text{-}B\text{-}A\text{-}B\text{-}A\text{-}C\text{-}B\text{-}A\text{-}C\text{-}B\text{-}C\text{-}A\text{-}C$$

The last outcome will be followed by A. Then $N(A\text{-}B) + N(A\text{-}C) = N(B\text{-}A) + N(C\text{-}A) = 6$; $N(B\text{-}A) + N(B\text{-}C) = N(A\text{-}B) + N(C\text{-}B) = 4$; $N(C\text{-}A) + N(C\text{-}B) = N(A\text{-}C) + N(B\text{-}C) = 6$. Now this skeletal series can be expanded to the true series by allowing one outcome to be followed by the same outcome. For example, assume the requirements are $N(A\text{-}A) = 3$, $N(B\text{-}B) = 5$, and $N(C\text{-}C) = 6$. A true recurring series is

$$A\text{-}A\text{-}C\text{-}C\text{-}C\text{-}C\text{-}A\text{-}C\text{-}C\text{-}C\text{-}B\text{-}B\text{-}B\text{-}A\text{-}B\text{-}B\text{-}A\text{-}C\text{-}C\text{-}B\text{-}B\text{-}B\text{-}A\text{-}A\text{-}C\text{-}B\text{-}C\text{-}A\text{-}A\text{-}C$$

# BIBLIOGRAPHY*

## SECTION 1—STUCTURAL STEEL ENGINEERING AND DESIGN

**REFERENCES:** Abbett—*American Civil Engineering Practice*, Wiley; Ambrose—*Simplified Design of Steel Structures*, Wiley; American Institute of Steel Construction—*Manual of Steel Construction*, American Society of Civil Engineers; Beedle, et al.—*Structural Steel Design*, Ronald; Beedle—*Plastic Design of Steel Frames*, Wiley; Borg and Gennaro—*Advanced Structural Analysis*, Van Nostrand; Bowles—*Structural Steel Design*, McGraw-Hill; Brockenbrough and Merritt—*Structural Steel Designer's Handbook*, McGraw-Hill; Bungale—*Steel, Concrete, and Composite Design of Tall Buildings*, McGraw-Hill; Crawley and Dillion—*Steel Buildings: Analysis and Design*, Wiley; Gaylord and Gaylord—*Structural Engineering Handbook*, McGraw-Hill; Gerstle—*Basic Structural Design*, McGraw-Hill; Ginzburg—*Metallurgical Design of Flat Rolled Steels (Manufacturing Engineering and Materials Processing)*, CRC; Gizejowski, Kozlowski, Sleczka, and Ziolko—*Progress in Steel, Composite and Aluminium Structures*, Taylor & Francis; Grinter—*Design of Modern Steel Structures*, Macmillan; Gupta—*Response Spectrum Method in Seismic Analysis and Design of Structures*, CRC; Jensen—*Applied Strength of Materials*, McGraw-Hill; Kurtz—*Comprehensive Structural Design Guide*, McGraw-Hill; Lathers—*Advanced Design in Structural Steel*, Prentice Hall; Macginley, Hassan, and Al-Nageim—*Steel Structures: Practical Design Studies*, Spon; Mazzolani—*Behaviour of Steel Structures in Seismic Areas*, Taylor & Francis; Mazzolani—*Ductility of Seismic-Resistant Steel Structures*, Taylor & Francis; Merritt—*Standard Handbook for Civil Engineers*, McGraw-Hill; Roark—*Formulas for Stress and Strain*, McGraw-Hill; Salmon and Johnson—*Steel Structures: Design and Behavior*, Prentice Hall; Scharff—*Residential Steel Framing Handbook*, McGraw-Hill; Seely—*Resistance of Materials*, Wiley; Urquhart—*Civil Engineering Handbook*, McGraw-Hill; Vinnakota—*Steel Structures*, McGraw-Hill.

## SECTION 2—REINFORCED AND PRESTRESSED CONCRETE ENGINEERING AND DESIGN

**REFERENCES:** Nawy—*Prestressed Concrete: A Fundamental Approach*, Prentice Hall; Nilson, Darwin, and Dolan—*Design of Concrete Structures*, McGraw-Hill; Peurifoy and Oberlender—*Formwork for Concrete Structures*, Techno Press; *Prestressed Concrete Analysis and Design: Fundamentals*, Techno Press; Raina—*Concrete Bridges*, McGraw-Hill; Gaventa—*Concrete Design*, Mitchell Beazley; Goodman and Karol—*Theory and Prac-*

---

*Where a code, book, or manual listed here is published by an engineering society (American Society of Civil Engineers), an association (American Water Works Association [AWWA]), and so on, the publisher is the organization listed as its author.

**B.1**

*tice of Foundation Engineering*, Macmillan; American Association of State Highways Officials—*A Policy on Geometric Design of Rural Highways*; American Concrete Institute—*Building Code Requirements for Reinforced Concrete*; Beele and Jaffe—*Concrete and Masonry Databook*, McGraw-Hill; Chellis—*Pile Foundations*, McGraw-Hill; Chi and Connolly—*Design of Prestressed Concrete Beams*, McGraw-Hill; Davis, Foote, and Kelly—*Surveying: Theory and Practice*, McGraw-Hill; Dunham—*Theory and Practice of Reinforced Concrete*, McGraw-Hill; Evans and Bennett—*Prestressed Concrete*, Wiley; Hickerson—*Route Surveys and Design*, McGraw-Hill; Huntington—*Earth Pressures and Retaining Walls*, Wiley; Jones—*Geometric Design of Modern Highways*, Wiley; Brockenbrough—*Highway Engineering Handbook*, McGraw-Hill; Kitter and Paquette—*Highway Engineering*, Ronald; LaLonde and James—*Concrete Engineering Handbook*, McGraw-Hill; Laursen—*Matrix Analysis of Structures*, McGraw-Hill; Leet and Bernal—*Reinforced Concrete Design*, McGraw-Hill; Magnel—*Prestressed Concrete*, McGraw-Hill; Meyer—*Route Survey: International Textbook*, McGraw-Hill; Weaver—*Computer Programs for Structural Analysis*, Van Nostrand; Winter, et al.—*Design of Concrete Structures*, McGraw-Hill.

## SECTION 3—TIMBER ENGINEERING

**REFERENCES:** Forest Products Laboratory—*Wood and Wood Based Materials: A Handbook For Engineers, Architects and Builders*; American Institute of Timber Construction—*Timber Construction Manual*, Wiley; Canadian Institute of Timber Construction—*Timber Construction*; Avery and Burkhart—*Forest Measurements*, McGraw-Hill; Breyer, Fridley, Cobeen, et al.—*Design of Wood Structures*, McGraw-Hill; Canadian Wood Council—*Wood Reference Handbook: A Guide to the Architectural Use of Wood in Building Construction*; Faherty—*Wood Engineering and Construction Handbook*; Breyer, et al.—*Design of Wood Structures*, McGraw-Hill; Jensen—*Applied Strength of Materials*, McGraw-Hill; Kurtz—*Comprehensive Structural Design Guide*, McGraw-Hill; P. Morlier—*Creep in Timber Structures*, Spon; Roark—*Formulas for Stress and Strain*, McGraw-Hill; Scofield and O'Brien—*Modern Timber Engineering*, Southern Pine Association; Seely—*Resistance of Materials*, Wiley; Shanley—*Mechanics of Materials*, McGraw-Hill; Thelandersson and Larsen—*Timber Engineering*, Wiley; Timber Engineering Company—*Timber Design and Construction Handbook*, McGraw-Hill; Timoshenko and Young—*Theory of Structures*, McGraw-Hill; Urquhart—*Civil Engineering Handbook*, McGraw-Hill; Williamson—*APA Engineered Wood Handbook*, McGraw-Hill.

## SECTION 4—SOIL MECHANICS

**REFERENCES:** Summer—*Handbook of Soil Science*, CRC; Warrick—*Soil Physics Companion*, CRC; Day—*Foundation Engineering Handbook*, McGraw-Hill; Day—*Geotechnical and Foundation Engineering*, McGraw-Hill; Steinberg—*Geomembranes and the Control of Expansive Soils*, McGraw-Hill; Thien and Graveel—*Laboratory Manual for Soil Science*, McGraw-Hill; Budhu—*Soil Mechanics and Foundations*, Wiley; Smith—*Smith's Elements of Soil Mechanics*, Blackwell; Craig—*Craig's Soil Mechanics*, Spon; Bardet—*Experimental Soil Mechanics*, Prentice Hall; McCarthy—*Essentials of Soil Mechanics and Foundations: Basic Geotechnics*, Prentice Hall; Aysen—*Soil Mechanics Basic Concepts and Engineering Applications*, Taylor & Francis; Shanley—*Mechanics of*

Materials, McGraw-Hill; Scott and Schoustra—*Soil: Mechanics and Engineering*, McGraw-Hill; Spangler—*Soil Engineering*, International Textbook; Streeter—*Fluid Mechanics*, McGraw-Hill; Teng—*Foundation Design*, Prentice Hall; Terzaghi and Peck—*Soil Mechanics in Engineering Practice*, Wiley; U.S. Department of the Interior, Bureau of Reclamation—*Earth Manual*, GPO.

## SECTION 5—SURVEYING, ROUTE DESIGN, AND HIGHWAY BRIDGES

**REFERENCES:** Raina—*Concrete Bridges: Structural Engineering Handbook*, McGraw-Hill; Cuomo—*Surveying Principles for Civil Engineers: Review for the Engineering Surveying Section of the California Special Civil Engineer Examination*, Professional Publications; Schofield—*Engineering Surveying*, Butterworth-Heinemann; Anderson and Mikhail—*Surveying*, McGraw-Hill; Barker and Puckett—*Design of Highway Bridges: Based on AASHTO LRFD, Bridge Design Specifications*, Wiley; Tonias—*Bridge Engineering: Design, Rehabilitation, and Maintenance of Modern Highway Bridges*, McGraw-Hill; Davis, Foote, and Kelly—*Surveying: Theory and Practice*, McGraw-Hill; Hickerson—*Route Surveys and Design*, McGraw-Hill; Meyer—*Route Survey*, International Textbook, McGraw-Hill; Brockenbrough and Frederick—*Structural Steel Designer's Handbook*, McGraw-Hill; Wolf and Dewitt—*Elements of Photogrammetry with Applications in GIS*, McGraw-Hill.

## SECTION 6—FLUID MECHANICS, PUMPS, PIPING, AND HYDRO POWER

**REFERENCES:** Miller and Malinowski—*Power System Operation*, McGraw-Hill; Pressman—*Switching Power Supply Design*, McGraw-Hill; Gevorkian—*Sustainable Energy Systems in Architectural Design*, McGraw-Hill; Cimbala and Cengel—*Essentials of Fluid Mechanics*, McGraw-Hill; Liou and Fang—*Microfluid Mechanics*, McGraw-Hill; American Water Works Association—*American National Standard for Vertical Turbine Pumps;* Anderson—*Computational Fluid Dynamics*, McGraw-Hill; Antaki—*Piping and Pipeline Engineering*, Marcel Dekker; Bausbacher and Hunt—*Process Plant Layout and Piping Design*, Prentice Hall; Bradley—*Petroleum Engineering Handbook*, Society of Petroleum Engineers; Brenkert—*Elementary Theoretical Fluid Mechanics*, Wiley; Carscallen and Oosthuizen—*Compressible Fluid Flow*, McGraw-Hill; CASTI Publishing—*Casti Guidebook to ASME B31.3—Process Piping*, McGraw-Hill; Cooper, Heald, Karassik, and Messina—*Pump Handbook*, McGraw-Hill; European Association for Pump Manufacture—*Net Positive Suction Head for Rotodynamic Pumps: A Reference Guide*, Elsevier; European Committee Pump Manufacturers Staff—*Europump Terminology*, French & European Publications; Evett, Giles and Liu—*Fluid Mechanics and Hydraulics*, McGraw-Hill; Finnemore and Franzini—*Fluid Mechanics With Engineering Applications*, McGraw-Hill; Frankel—*Facility Piping Systems Handbook*, McGraw-Hill; Hehn—*Plant Engineering's Fluid Power Handbook*, Gulf Professional Publishing; Hicks—*Pump Application Engineering*, McGraw-Hill; Hicks—*Pump Operation and Maintenance*, McGraw-Hill; Japikse—*Centrifugal Pump Design and Performance*, Concepts ETI; Larock, Jeppson, and Watters—*Hydraulics of Pipeline Systems*, CRC; Lobanoff and Ross—*Centrifugal Pumps: Design and Application*, Gulf Professional Publishing; McKetta—*Piping Design Handbook*, Marcel Dekker; Menon—*Piping Calculations Manual*, McGraw-Hill; Mohitpour, Golshan, and Murray—*Pipeline Design & Construction*, ASME; Nayyar—*Piping Handbook*, McGraw-Hill; Paidoussis—*Fluid Structure Interactions*, Academic Press; Parisher and Rhea—*Pipe Drafting and Design*, Gulf Professional Publishing; Pennock—*Piping Engineering Leadership for Process Plant Projects*, Gulf Professional Publishing; Rishel—*HVAC Pump Handbook*, McGraw-Hill; Rishel—*Water Pumps and Pumping Systems*, McGraw-Hill; Saleh—*Fluid Flow Handbook*, McGraw-Hill; Sanks—*Pumping Station Design*, Butterworth-Heinemann; Shames—*Mechanics of Fluids*, McGraw-Hill; Stepanoff—*Centrifugal and Axial Flow Pumps: Theory, Design, and Application*, Krieger; Sturtevant—*Introduction to Fire Pump Operations*, Delmar; Swindin—*Pumps in Chemical Engineering*, Wexford College Press; Tannehill, Anderson, and Pletcher—*Computational Fluid Mechanics and Heat Transfer*, Taylor & Francis; Woodson—*National Plumbing Codes Handbook*, McGraw-Hill; Woodson—*International Plumbing Codes Handbook*, McGraw-Hill.

## SECTION 7—WATER-SUPPLY AND STORM-WATER SYSTEM DESIGN

Gribbin—*Introduction to Hydraulics & Hydrology: With Applications for Stormwater Management*, Delmar; Thornton—*Water Loss Control Manual*, McGraw-Hill; Gribbin—*Hydraulics and Hydrology for Stormwater Management*, Delmar; Mays—*Water Supply Systems Security*, McGraw-Hill; Mays—*Urban Water Supply Management Tools*, McGraw-Hill; Mays—*Water Resources Handbook*, McGraw-Hill; Woodson—*Plumber's and Pipe Fitter's Calculations Manual*, McGraw-Hill; Woodson—*International and Uniform Plumbing Codes Handbook*, McGraw-Hill; Lin and Lee—*Water and Wastewater Calculations Manual*, McGraw-Hill; Uzair—*GIS Tools for Water, Wastewater, and Stormwater Systems*, American Society of Civil Engineers; Nathanson—*Basic Environmental Technology: Water Supply, Waste Management, and Pollution Control*, Prentice Hall; Dodson—*Storm Water Pollution Control: Municipal, Industrial and Construction NPDES Compliance*, McGraw-Hill; Roberts—*Water Quality Control Handbook*, McGraw-Hill; Lee and Lin—*Handbook of Environmental Engineering Calculations*, McGraw-Hill; Mays—*Stormwater Collection Systems Design Handbook*, McGraw-Hill; Mays—*Urban Stormwater Management Tools*, McGraw-Hill; Davis and McCuen—*Stormwater Management for Smart Growth*, Springer; Pitt—*Groundwater Contamination from Stormwater Infiltration*, CRC.

## SECTION 8—SANITARY WASTEWATER TREATMENT AND CONTROL

**REFERENCES:** Crites—*Small & Decentralized Wastewater Management Systems*, McGraw-Hill; Tchobanoglous, et al.—*Wastewater Engineering*, McGraw-Hill; Lin and Lee—*Water and Wastewater Calculations Manual*, McGraw-Hill; Water Environment Federation—*Upgrading and Retrofitting Water and Wastewater Treatment Plants*, McGraw-Hill; Boss, Day, and Jones—*Biological Risk Engineering Handbook: Infection Control and Decontamination*; Cornell—*Chlorination/Chloramination Handbook*, American Water Works Association; Crites and Tchobanoglous—*Small & Decentralized Wastewater Management Systems*, McGraw-Hill; Dodson—*Storm Water Pollution Control: Municipal, Industrial and Construction NPDES Compliance*, McGraw-Hill; Droste—*Theory and Practice of Water and Wastewater Treatment*, Wiley; Gribbin—*Hydraulics and Hydrol-*

*ogy for Stormwater Management*, Delmar; Hammer—*Water and Wastewater Technology*, Prentice Hall; Judd and Jefferson—*Membranes for Industrial Wastewater Recovery and Re-use*; Lin and Lee—*Water and Wastewater Calculations Manual*, McGraw-Hill; Crites et al.—*Land Treatment Systems for Municipal and Industrial Wastes*, McGraw-Hill; Parcher—*Wastewater Collection System Maintenance*, Technomic; Qasim—*Wastewater Treatment Plants: Planning, Design, and Operation*, CRC; Salvato and Sanks—*Pumping Station Design*, Butterworth-Heinemann; Sharma and Lewis—*Waste Containment Systems, Waste Stabilization, and Landfills: Design and Evaluation*, Wiley; Tchobanoglous, Burton, and Stensel—*Wastewater Engineering: Treatment and Reuse*, McGraw-Hill; Vesilind—*Wastewater Treatment Plant Design*, Water Environment Federation; Asano—*Wastewater Reclamation and Reuse*, CRC; Water Environment Federation—*Operation of Municipal Wastewater Treatment Plants*; Water Works Association, American Society of Civil Engineers—*Water Treatment Plant Design*, McGraw-Hill; White—*Handbook of Chlorination and Alternative Disinfectants*, Wiley; AWWA—*Water Chlorination/Chloramination Practices and Principles (AWWA Manual)*.

## SECTION 9—ENGINEERING ECONOMICS

**REFERENCES:** Newnan, Eschenbach, and Lavelle—*Engineering Economic Analysis* (CD-ROM), Oxford University Press; Sullivan, Wicks, and Luxhoj—*Engineering Economy*, Prentice Hall; Park—*Contemporary Engineering Economics*, Prentice Hall; White, et al.—*Principles of Engineering Economic Analysis*, Wiley; Park—*Fundamentals of Engineering Economics*, Prentice Hall; Newnan and Lavelle—*Essentials of Engineering Economic Analysis*, Oxford University Press; Eide—*Engineering Fundamentals and Problem Solving*, McGraw-Hill; Newnan, Eschenbach, and Lavelle—*Engineering Economic Analysis*; Peters, et al.—*Plant Design and Economics for Chemical Engineers*, McGraw-Hill; Kurtz—*Handbook of Engineering Economics*, McGraw-Hill; Barish and Kaplan—*Economic Analysis for Engineering and Managerial Decision Making*, McGraw-Hill; DeGarmo, et al.—*Engineering Economy*, Macmillan; Grant and Leavenworth—*Principles of Engineering Economy*, Ronalds; Kasmer—*Essentials of Engineering Economics*, McGraw-Hill; Cissell—*Mathematics of Finance*, Houghton Mifflin; Clifton and Fyffe—*Project Feasibilty Analysis*, Wiley; Sullivan and Claycombe—*Fundamentals of Forecasting*, Reston; Weston and Brigham—*Essentials of Managerial Finance*, Dryden Press; Lock—*Engineer's Handbook of Management Techniques*, Grove Press (London, England); Jelen—*Project and Cost Engineers' Handbook*, American Association of Cost Engineers; Kharbanda—*Process Plant and Equipment Cost Estimation*, Vivek Enterprises (Bombay, India); Ostwald—*Cost Estimation for Engineering and Management*, Prentice Hall; American Association of Cost Engineers—*Cost Engineers' Notebook*; Gass—*Linear Programming: Methods and Applications*, McGraw-Hill, Wesley; Allen—*Probability and Statistics, and Queuing Theory*, Academic Press; Beightler—*Foundations of Optimization*, Prentice Hall; Brownlee—*Statistical Theory and Methodology in Science and Engineering*, Wiley; Quinn—*Probability and Statistics*, Harper & Row; Park—*Cost Engineering*, Wiley; Taylor—*Managerial and Engineering Economy*, Praeger; Jelen and Black—*Cost and Optimization Engineering*, McGraw-Hill; Riggs—*Engineering Economics*, McGraw-Hill; Meyer—*Introductory Probability and Statistical Applications*, Addison-Wesley; Renwick—*Introduction to Investments and Finance*, Macmillan; O'Brien—*CPM in Construction Management*, McGraw-Hill; Gupta and Cozzolino—*Fundamentals of Operations Research for Management*, Holden-Day.

# INDEX